MW00800710

Mustaches and Mayhem

Charlie O's Three-Time Champions

THE OAKLAND ATHLETICS: 1972-74

Edited by Chip Greene

Associate Editors Greg Erion, Len Levin, and Bill Nowlin

Society for American Baseball Research, Inc.
Phoenix, AZ

Vic Harris for Don minaler 72
Clet Lemon for Stan Bahnson 75
Dan Ford for Pat Bourque 75

Mustaches and Mayhem: Charlie O's Three-Time Champions
The Oakland Athletics: 1972-74

Edited by Chip Greene
Associate Editors Greg Erion, Len Levin, and Bill Nowlin

ISBN 978-1-943816-07-1
(Ebook ISBN 978-1-943816-06-4)

Cover and book design: Gilly Rosenthol

Front cover photograph by Ron Riesterer/Photoshelter.
Rear cover photograph courtesy of the Oakland A's.

All photography courtesy of Dwayne Labakas, except as noted below.

Photographs courtesy of the National Baseball Hall of Fame Library, by Doug McWilliams appear on pages 22, 114, 130, 155, 210, 217, 222, 269, 281, 285, 291, 307, 315, 322, 372, 384, 392, 419, 424, 437, 449, 455, 470, 478, 481, 510, 511, 517, 521, 527, and 559.

Also courtesy of the National Baseball Hall of Fame Library are the photographs on pages 14, 17, 126, 140, 297, 365, 380, 392, and 406.

Photographs courtesy of the Oakland A's appear on pages 13, 204, and 235. Thanks to Debbie Gallas of the A's for assistance throughout.

Photograph of Charlie O. on page 25 courtesy of Ron Riesterer/Photoshelter.

Society for American Baseball Research
Cronkite School at ASU
555 N. Central Ave. #416
Phoenix, AZ 85004
Phone: (602) 496-1460
Web: www.sabr.org
Facebook: Society for American Baseball Research
Twitter: @SABR

Table of Contents

Foreword

I was deeply honored when approached to write this foreword about my team, the Oakland A's. The "colorful" and disparate make-up of this talented bunch has always begged the question: What made this group *"tick"*?

Every team brings contrasting personalities together. This is an inescapable fact, for winning is the number one consideration. Otherwise, why even keep score? As Hall of Fame football coach Vince Lombardi was fond of saying, "Winning isn't everything. It's the only thing."

Over the course of a grueling 162-game championship season (not counting playoff and series games) tempers can flare—and often do. Every good team has big egos, low boiling points, and high testosterone levels. If you win, the journalists will call it "chemistry:" the harmonious composition of players and management. Of course, if you should lose, the same journalists still call it "chemistry," alluding to team disharmony, disorganization, and turmoil. If the latter be the case, the problems inevitably continue simmering, ultimately worsen, and the cast of personnel and/or culture inevitably changes.

Separating fact from fiction is often dependent on the personal biases of the journalists themselves. But, the inescapable reality is teams win with talent, perseverance, and grit. Teams are not put together for chemistry; they are formed around talent. Make no mistake about this. As our Hall of Fame manager, Dick Williams, told the team after winning the 1972 World Series against the Cincinnati Reds: "The writers think I'm a genius. That's a bunch of crap. If I'm a genius, you guys made me one. No one wins without the horses."

Chemistry is not a product of putting together "nice" or "compatible" players. Chemistry is a product of winning. The more you win, the better the chemistry. Chemistry is therefore a group dynamic that transcends individual personalities and, as previously stated, often changes during the course of a long season.

The Kansas City A's organization of the mid 1960s were very aggressive signing amateur talent. There was no amateur draft in those days; teams could go after and sign anyone. The A's signed and stockpiled better talent than other organizations during those years. When the team subsequently moved to Oakland in 1968, they had cornered the best young amateur talent out there. They were loaded and ready to dominate.

In 1971, while playing for the Washington Senators, I was called into manager Ted Williams' office after a night game in Minnesota. "We've traded you to Oakland. You've hit 50 home runs over the past two seasons for me and they need a power-hitting first baseman. This is a helluva break for you." So myself and Darold Knowles, a top-drawer middle-inning LH reliever, were shipped to Oakland.

Going from a perennial last-place team to a powerhouse with World Series potential re-energized me, as it would any other player. My new A's teammates and I were all close to the same age: young, talented, uninhibited, and confident. They were good and they knew it. I realized this the minute I walked into their clubhouse when first joining the team in Baltimore to play the Orioles.

Manager Dick Williams quickly called me into his office. "These guys are ultra-competitive, Mike. You'll fit right in. We think you're the missing link we've needed to take us to the postseason." I was flattered, but knew I had to cut it or I was out. I wasn't one of "Mr. Finley's Boys;" he was definitely partial to those he signed as amateurs. Mr. Finley always let the players he didn't originally sign know that you either got the job done—or you were history. As fate would have it, I got it done, and played an integral part in the A's inexorable journey to competitive greatness.

The team immediately went on a tear and started to get some serious national attention. The better we did, the cockier we got, the better the late-night stories, and the closer we all became. A veritable "Band of Brothers." Everyone had the other's back—and to add to our camaraderie— a common "enemy:" the owner himself.

This was the most awesome group of athletes I had ever been around. We had fun. Lots of fun. The more we won, the more fun we had. It was always something special walking into the clubhouse the next after a game and hearing the shenanigans and mischief that transpired. I sometimes wondered how we could go out "the night after the night before" and play as hard as we did.

I think it was in 1972, we were playing a night game against the California Angels in Anaheim. The game went into extra innings and we finally got on a plane around 3:00am for a flight to New York City to play the Yankees: a day-doubleheader, no less, which was scheduled at 1:00pm. We didn't arrive in New York until 10:00am, so the team bus went directly to Yankee Stadium from the airport.

We shut out the Yankees in both games. Afterward, the New York press surrounded manager Dick Williams in his office and asked him if he was surprised at how well his team played with such little rest. "Hell, no. This was just another routine day for most of 'em."

This anecdote played an intangible part in the enduring chemistry that helped unite us.

Rod Dedeaux, the legendary and renowned baseball coach at the University of Southern California, coached the first United States Olympic baseball team in Tokyo in 1964. I was fortunate to be selected to that elite team. If one of us made a mental mistake during a game, when you got back in the dugout, Coach Dedeaux would make a gala presentation by placing a female's blond wig on your head, which you had to wear in the dugout for an inning. Talk about looking stupid! But it was all done in jest, solidified the team's chemistry, and turned a potentially embarrassing situation for the player into one of levity. Rod Dedeaux was a great coach for a reason.

The A's, as a team, basically did the same thing. We were never afraid to let our teammates know if they messed up during a game, though it seemed like the message was always said in a joking way and everyone on the team bus got a good laugh out of it. We would "serenade" the player with one of our famous "hymns" (which would be difficult to fit into a "Mature Audience"-rated program). It was cool to be able to laugh at mistakes and move on. However, with a team of personalities like we had, on rare occasions tempers *would* flare and players had to be physically separated. But, this was all part of the A's DNA and what made us tick.

I remember the great Oakland Raiders football team at that time was known as a hostile, rebel-rousing bunch of "social deviants." Of course, this made for good copy and "branded" the team. Knowing some of them personally at that time helped me understand the importance of a banner for the team to rally around. We've seen this over the years with good teams in all sports. I wouldn't call us "social deviants" by any stretch of the imagination, but we were a team sorely needing *something* to rally around.

Mr. Finley probably didn't realize it at the time, but he did something to help our sought-after team identity. During the 1972 season, future Hall of Famer Reggie Jackson started growing a beard. The team "rule" at that time was no facial hair would be tolerated. Reggie always had a penchant for the limelight and often did things to individualize his self-importance, often at the expense of the team. Dick Williams talked to him about shaving off his beard. He was told that it was really painful to shave because of the ethnic nature of his skin, characteristic of many bumps and ingrown hair follicles. In short, Reggie did nothing about it.

Mr. Finley recognized he had a potential team morale problem at this point and personally got into the act. He couldn't let one player defy his team rules and not allow everyone to do the same. He talked with Reggie and Reggie tested his star power by simply telling him that he was "the straw that stirred the drink." Well, everyone on the team knew it was "Reggie being Reggie" and that he was "Mr. Finley's Boy"—so the club did nothing about it. He would be the *only* one allowed to grow facial hair. Characteristic of our team, we got pissed off, and we decided we had had enough of Reggie's attitude. Everyone decided to grow some type of facial hair.

Having lost control of the situation, Mr. Finley decided that he would make "lemonade out of lemons." He staged a "Mustache Day" at the Oakland-Alameda Coliseum: anyone who attended the game with facial hair would be admitted free of charge. In addition, he commemorated the event by presenting each of us with a gold-plated mustache spoon as a remembrance.

The result? Mr. Finley looked like a hero instead of a pushover, we got the identity we craved with our facial hair, and Reggie (temporarily) lost his individuality. In short, it made us a tighter group, Reggie notwithstanding.

Dick Williams knew there was no love lost for the ornery Mr. Finley by his team and would go out of his way to make it clear that we weren't alone. Dick tired endlessly of Mr. Finley meddling with his on-the-field running of the team. Especially when it came to making out the game's starting lineup. Dick was not a "yes-man" and was one of the reasons he was revered by us.

On a "whim," Mr. Finley would instruct Dick to play a bench player *he* thought would make an impact on that day's game. Often times, this meant taking one of his core eight players and sitting him down. This could happen to any one of us—even if the player was on a batting tear. This would infuriate the manager, who was left with the tough task of changing his already posted lineup and smoothing out the affected player's ego. His meddling finally became so bad that Dick resigned after consecutive World Series championships in 1972 and 1973. I liked Dick. He was a "man's man" and I thought he ran a ball game better than any other manager at that time. He got the best

out of everyone, despite the owner's incessant interference.

Dick was a risk-taker, which further endeared him to us. We were talented but had never been on the "Big Stage," in contrast to the powerful Cincinnati team already branded "Big Red Machine." The 1972 World Series opened in their home park. We were huge underdogs—but that seemed to help our motivation.

The Reds featured Pete Rose, Johnny Bench, and Joe Morgan. We had lost Reggie Jackson for the World Series due to a leg injury he suffered in a home plate collision in the playoffs with Detroit Tigers catcher Bill Freehan (on the back-end of a successful double steal with me on first and Reggie on third).

But, we did have Campy Campaneris, Matty Alou, Joe Rudi, Sal Bando, Dave Duncan, Gene Tenace, George Hendrick, and Dick Green ready to go. Oh, and lest I forget: Catfish Hunter, Vida Blue, Ken Holtzman, Blue Moon Odom, and Rollie Fingers.

Speaking of Rollie, he was part of one of the biggest baseball "hoodwinks" I can ever remember. Johnny Bench was the unfortunate fall-guy. I'm not sure which game it was in Oakland, but Bench was the hitter in a very close game. I believe two men were on, first base was open, with two outs. The count went to three balls and two strikes. Dick Williams jogged out to the mound to talk to Rollie. A bad pitch here to a great hitter like Johnny could mean three runs and losing the game. I trotted in to the mound.

Dick told Rollie to fake an intentional pass to Bench, but throw a strike. But he didn't want Rollie to throw a fastball because Bench was a fastball hitter. In typical Rollie fashion, he blurted out, "Are you kidding? Is this Little League or what?"

With Johnny standing in the box expecting a wide pitchout, Rollie broke off one of his patented sliders for called strike three. Gotta love him. We still laugh about it to this day.

Gene Tenace had been a backup catcher for us, but Dick (or more likely a Finley whim!) decided to start him in the 1972 World Series. He responded with one of the finest World Series performances the Fall Classic has ever seen. He batted .348 with four homers and nine RBIs, including two hits and two RBIs in a deciding Game Seven. Without Geno's home runs, there's no Game Seven and no Ring. He made it possible.

We had some characters. Real "beauties" you might say. Holtzman was a *professional* instigator and "needler," always getting under somebody's skin. Vida was Vida, a wide-eyed young kid from Louisiana with an infectious personality and immeasurable talent; you couldn't help liking him. Campy was, in my opinion, the catalyst of the team; our "table-setter." Low-key, a consummate professional and gentleman. One of Campy's favorite diversions was attaching a wallet (with a one-dollar bill half-way sticking out) to some very thin fishing line and suspending it from his hotel window. When some pedestrian would try to pick it up he'd jerk on it. If the pedestrian would run after it that was frosting on the cake for him. Like I said, it's a long season.

Campy was also a fierce competitor despite his seemingly outward appearance to the contrary. During the 1972 playoffs, Billy Martin, the Detroit Tigers' fiery manager, ordered his pitcher Lerrin LaGrow to throw at Campy's feet, trying to sideline our base-stealing star. Campy had already singled, stole second and third, and then scored the first run of the game. He would also get two more hits and score yet another run before facing LaGrow. He hit Campy in the ankle; Campy threw his bat at LaGrow precipitating a dugout-clearing brawl. Ever the competitor, Campy felt he did what he had to. You've got to respect a teammate like that. It fired us up.

Captain Sal Bando did a nice job trying to keep Reggie happy and the team from killing him. Believe me, this was no easy task, but Sal was up to it. I thought Dick Green was, by far, the best damn defensive second baseman I had ever seen. A real acrobat in the field. Nothing bothered "Greenie," who always had a big smile on his face and the loudest, most contagious laugh on the club.

Joe Rudi just went about his business in a low-key style. You'd hardly know he was there until after the game when you looked up and realized he had three hits, two RBIs, and a great catch in the outfield. His leaping catch against the left-field wall saved Game Seven for us. Dave Duncan, also low-key but a fierce competitor, was a power-hitting catcher that everyone respected and liked. Gene Tenace was a fun-loving Italian kid that brought a lot of life to the clubhouse. "Blue Moon" Odom was also someone who everyone liked and let his feelings be known of his personal dislike of Reggie. This led to an altercation on the team bus when Reggie went off verbally on Moon. Ah, the good old days....

I could probably write a book about Hall of Famer Rollie Fingers. He just made everyone laugh, always playing a "naïve" role and the perfect foil for Holtzman's needling. It was hard to believe that a happy-go-lucky guy like him off the field could transform into such a "lights out" reliever when he crossed the white lines. Nothing fazed him. Kenny always said he was "too damn dumb to know what was really going on." Maybe that was what made him so unflappable in tight situations. And endearing to all of us.

Hall of Famer "Catfish" Hunter was, well, maybe the best teammate anyone could ask for and a great guy. He was another of our many team agitators, someone you just couldn't get mad at. He was always on Reggie's case. Happy-go-lucky off the field, but I can't think of anyone I played with that I would rather see start a *big* game. As they say, he had "ice cubes in his veins."

And, the supporting cast was just as great. Mike Hegan and Don Mincher kept everyone loose. They and I had a word routine that everyone on the team contributed to. Things like, "Hey Minch! You know what ostentatious means, don't you?" He'd think a bit and come back with, "Yeah, I know. It's a town in Texas." And it would go on from there. In fact, before Game Three in Oakland, me, "Mo" (of course, he was known as "Mo" Hegan), and Minch did a pregame interview demonstrating our word game on national TV.

Smooth-fielding Ted Kubiak was always ready to fill-in when he was needed. He didn't get the nickname "Smooth" for nothing. He could really "pick it." Dal Maxvill was a veteran infielder you could always count on to come through. I could go on and on. Everyone contributed in their own way.

Then, of course, there was Hall of Famer Reggie Jackson. Our "lightning rod" for all things good and bad. A great talent. I actually liked him despite his eccentricities. He'd "go off the reservation" once in a while and have to be brought down to earth by the guys, but overall, he played hard for us. It was unfor-tunate that he was sidelined and didn't play in the '72 Series. He deserved to be there to show his ample talents to the entire country. But, he got his opportuni-ties in later years and certainly made the most of them.

To this day I am proud to have "walked the walk" with these men. A lot can be said of my team. Disparate? No doubt. Winners? You bet. I consider them all great friends. A terrific bunch, for sure!

—Mike Epstein, December 5, 2014

Introduction

Champions Three Times Over

By Chip Greene

In 1976, Reggie Jackson, then arguably baseball's biggest superstar, joined my favorite team, the Baltimore Orioles, in a trade from the Oakland A's. Accompanying him was gritty left-handed pitcher Ken Holtzman. Coming a year after the shocking change of teams from the A's to the Yankees by free-agent pitcher Catfish Hunter, the trade brought excitement to Baltimore in equal measure with what was assuredly disgust on the part of A's fans. For Hunter, Jackson, and Holtzman had been integral pieces of Oakland's three consecutive championships, and now each was gone. It was just the beginning of the dismantling of one of the premier teams in baseball history.

With the advent of free agency looming, other stars soon found themselves headed out of Oakland. In June 1976 Commissioner Bowie Kuhn tried to stem the tide of an Oakland housecleaning when he blocked the proposed sale of former Cy Young award winner Vida Blue to the Yankees for $1.5 million as well as that of star left fielder Joe Rudi and relief ace Rollie Fingers to the Red Sox for $2 million. As it turned out, Kuhn was only delaying the inevitable. The breakup of the three-time champions occurred with lightning speed.

For five years the Oakland A's had been a glorious franchise. Built from the inside out, with a stable of young homegrown talent who had matured together in the minor leagues, from 1971 through 1975, Oakland won five consecutive American League West titles, winning it all in the middle three of those seasons. In the process, the core starting lineup of Bando at third; Campaneris at short; Green at second; Rudi in left; Jackson in right; Tenace catching or playing first; and Hunter, Odom, and Fingers on the mound, together with such imports as Holtzman and Bill North, took

the field and withstood both their own internal squabbling and one of the most notorious owners the game has ever known to defeat all comers and permanently etch their names as one of the greatest teams ever assembled.

Their common foe was always Charles Oscar Finley. If the A's players sometimes fought with one another as well as their opponents, the bond most of them shared was a loathing of the A's irascible, overbearing, pompous, manipulative, scheming, cantankerous, bombastic, often prevaricating, but flamboyant, creative, forward-thinking, and inventive owner. Indeed, so frequently did Finley meddle in the affairs of his team, so often did he commit some seemingly egregious offense against one or another player, that the result became a shared commitment among the A's personnel to band together against Finley's dictates and misbehavior and denounce him as an abhorrent and often juvenile cheapskate and a louse. Finley became the unifying negative force in the locker room (not that he ever really minded, if it meant his team would win) and the players took that camaraderie to the field and won in spite of his churlish behavior.

This book chronicles the lives and times of those men and those teams. Included is a biography of each player who appeared in an Oakland uniform in each of the three championship years, together with the managers, coaches, Finley himself, and Monte Moore, who broadcast the games. As baseball seasons begin with spring training and end with the World Series, so too is each season here similarly recapped, in chronological order, with the men who joined the team in a particular season included in that year's account. Documenting multiple seasons was, of course, a major undertaking, and would not have been accomplished without the dedication and able writing of a number of SABR volunteers, each of whom I sincerely thank and whose excellent work speaks for itself in the pages that follow.

Beyond the outstanding writing, however, I extend my heartfelt appreciation to an editorial team which for the better part of two years read every word and checked every fact to ensure that we got it right. In particular, this book would not have been produced without the commitment of Bill Nowlin, Len Levin, and Greg Erion. For their assistance, I am eternally indebted.

Chip Greene
Waynesboro, Pennsylvania
November 29, 2014

The A's:
Westward-Ho, In Stages

By Curt Smith

Rock and roll is the *métier* of choice at the Oakland-Alameda County Coliseum (a.k.a. O.co Coliseum since 2011). For example, the Allman Brothers Band's hit "Ramblin' Man" can often be heard at the baseball Athletics' 35,067-capacity home. It is fitting, given the franchise's peregrination from Philadelphia to Kansas City in 1955 and then to Oakland in 1968. In particular, the Coliseum's ups and downs deserve reliving — especially the Summitry of 1972-74. As Oscar Wilde once said: "Grief has turned her fair."

The Athletics' trek began with original owner, manager, and president Cornelius McGillicuddy — Connie Mack. In 1909 he opened Shibe Park at Philadelphia's 21st Street and West Lehigh Avenue. Shibe touted baseball's first ramps, umpire and visiting team rooms, terra-cotta trim above each archway and windows, and the cupola — the age's skybox. The first double-decked arena was built by modern material and design — cutting off, lifting, and pushing forward the top half of a deep single deck.

After Shibe, supports linked most parks' upper and lower levels, putting fans nearer the diamond than in the past wooden-seat age. For the first time, concrete and steel let you round façade angles behind the plate, extend stands down each foul line, and form the double deck. Shibe flaunted a Beaux Arts tower and churchlike dome behind the plate, miming the French Renaissance, and also a green wall and seamless web of angled blocks, planes, and triangles. Presiding was McGillicuddy, tall and gaunt, in suit and tie, a scorecard in one hand, signaling to fielders from the dugout, his name trimmed to Mack to fit a box score.

In 1910-14 Mack's Athletics won four pennants, three World Series, and more games than any other club.

Mack then sold or traded players, partly to pay for Shibe. Living on thin profit's edge, he added left-field seats, then covered the pavilion. By 1925 a second tier tied third and first base, respectively, to center field and right field's corner. "Seventy percent of the park was now double-decked," sportswriter Allen Lewis noted. "Shibe stayed that way the rest of its life." The park's last big-league match was played there on October 1, 1970.

Like a bobbed cork, Shibe Park again rose in 1929-31, hosting each American League titlist, then resurfaced in the public eye in 1941 as Ted Williams went 6-for-8 there in a last-day doubleheader to finish with a .406 average. A decade later, A's pitcher Bobby Shantz won the 1952 AL MVP award. It wasn't enough to overcome 1954's wretched 51-103 record and 304,666 attendance. That winter Mack, for whom Shibe had been renamed in 1953, sold the A's to Kansas City tycoon Arnold Johnson. "We just couldn't make a go of it," said Connie, who retired in 1950 and died, at 93, in 1956. Instead, the franchise chose to go about 1,125 miles west, to a city that soon deserved better than it got.

"For years Kansas City had been a great Yankees farm club," recalled *Kansas City Star* sports editor Ernie Mehl. "Mantle, Rizzuto, they all played here with the American Association Blues." In 1938 Muehlebach Field was renamed Ruppert Stadium after Yankees owner Jacob Ruppert. When Arnold Johnson bought the Athletics in 1954, he renamed the stadium after the Triple-A Blues. In 1945 Johnson's pals Del Webb and Dan Topping had bought the Yankees. After Mehl convinced him that Kansas City deserved a club, Johnson used Webb and Topping to run interference, get the AL to OK the A's sale, and move them from Philadelphia. Kansas City straightaway gave Johnson $500,000 for Blues Stadium, renaming it Municipal.

Johnson bought the Braves Field scoreboard for $100,000, put it in right-center field, and moved the plate 25 feet toward the outfield. Dimensions fell, rose, then fell again. At Shibe Park center field had been as much as 468 feet from home plate. At Municipal, center veered from 410 to 430; left, 312, 369; left-center, 375, 408. The bottom of the light tower was in play. Right-center followed the bouncing ball from 382 to 360; right, 347, 325. Wall heights wavered: left, 10 to 38; center, 10 to 40; right, 4 to 40. In 1955 the city rebuilt and double-decked Municipal Stadium in 22 weeks: capacity 30,296. Over time, the Athletics, like the park's lengths, shrank.

On April 12, 1955, former President Harry Truman, flanked by Connie Mack, threw out the first ball at Kansas City's big-league opener. "The Boss is the real fan," Harry said of his wife, Bess. Her rookie Athletics finished sixth (in 13 years, Missouri's A's never made the first division) and drew 1,393,054 (quadrupling Philadelphia's last year). The following season the club won just 52 games and attendance fell to 1,015,154, a mark the franchise wouldn't hit again until 1973. Midway through the 1957 season, skipper Lou Boudreau was fired: over the club's remaining nine years in Kansas City, nine other managers succeeded him. Bob Cerv bashed 38 homers in 1958. In 1960 Municipal hosted an All-Star Game, Nationals winning, 5-3. Seven Yankees made the AL All-Star team—a common trend.

"The Yankees! They called us their cousins!" cried 1955-61 A's broadcaster Merle Harmon. "Johnson kept trading our fine players—Art Ditmar, Bobby Shantz, Ralph Terry, Hector Lopez—the Yankees got every one." The New York Central Railroad shipped Vic Power, Irv Noren, Enos Slaughter, and Jerry Lumpe west. In late 1959, KC dealt Roger Maris to the Big Apple for Norm Siebern, Don Larsen, Hank Bauer, and Marv Throneberry. "Oh," said Merle, "and how the trades goaded our fans." One July night the A's ripped New York for 27 hits. "For one night *we* felt like the powerhouse." Self-effacement lit the air. "'Course, that feeling didn't last for long."

What did last was disarray. Through 1960 the A's never settled above sixth place. That December, Chicago insurance broker Charles O. Finley bought 52 percent of the club from the Johnson estate, Arnold having died in March. Finley tried to bully a rental reduction. He also showed a fine baseball sense and showman's yen to please. In 1961 Lew Krausse got $125,000 to sign. "The first great bonus baby," said Mehl, and "the first pitcher to start without any minor-league experience." Blue Moon Odom and Catfish Hunter signed for $64,000 and $75,000, respectively. Bert Campaneris arrived from Venezuela. Sal Bando jumped from Arizona State. Alumni Rick Monday and Reggie Jackson led baseball's 1965-66 free-agent draft. "Finley was his own scouting system," said Harmon, "signing them all." He seemed less adept at winning and drawing. The style was mom 'n' pop, not U.S. Steel.

"We've got nowhere to go but up," eighth-placers once cried in an eight-team league. The 1961 A's differed: tied for last in expansion's new 10-team AL. Only 683,817 found the park, two miles east of downtown. By 1964 Finley wanted to move to Louisville. The AL told him to sign a KC lease or lose the team. Campaneris, who went on to star at shortstop for the 1972-74 Oakland world champions, pitched ambidextrously for 1962 Class A Daytona Beach. At 22, Campy debuted in the big leagues with two homers in a game, his aid not enough: The 1964 club went 57-105. One day in 1965 he played each position versus California. That September Satchel Paige, 59, pitched for the first time in the majors since 1953: one hit in three innings. "If you think I'm gonna throw anyplace but your letters, shame on ya!" he growled. Finley's shame was the Yankees: He envied, but hated, them.

On August 18, 1962, New York drew Municipal's best crowd—an overflow 35,147. "What a social occasion," said Mehl. "People from all over Mid-America arrived by car, bus, and train." Many sat on a grass slope between the right-field fence and Brooklyn Avenue behind it. It was too steep to be mowed. Finley imported sheep and dyed them A's green and gold. An employee with a shepherd's cap, cloak, and stick managed the animals. "When the Yankees played [invariably, selling out]," laughed Bando, Finley put the sheep behind the fence. One day a man accosted him and said he had sat on sheep manure. "My pants are ruined. What you gonna do about it?" Finley had them cleaned and pressed.

By 1965 Finley, increasingly at sea, became convinced that the Yankees' dynasty stemmed from the 296-foot right-field line at The Big Ballpark in the Bronx. His riposte: the Pennant Porch, a four-foot-high fence 296 feet from the plate. "Baseball regulations said it had to be at least 325," said Harmon. Defiant, Finley ad-libbed a 325 line, indenting it to 296 five feet from the pole. The AL cried foul. Charlie finally painted "K.C. One-Half Pennant Porch" at the 325-foot pole. Stymied *on* the field, Finley again looked *beyond* it. Recalling Shibe's opulence, you mused what Philly's high society might have thought of *this*.

Finley built a children's zoo on an incline beyond right field. Its cast included his mule mascot Charlie O., a Chinese golden pheasant, German checker rabbits, peafowl, a German shorthaired pointer dog named Old Drum, and Capuchin monkeys. The Kansas City Farmers Market kept them happy, Tigers pitchers once feeding the monkeys vodka-soaked oranges. Another time Finley led a young Nebraskan on a tour. "He thinks they're going to the zoo," said Campy. "Instead, they wandered by mistake on the field [near outfielder Jim Landis] as the pitch was being thrown." The style was home style: A "Sam's Baseball Parking" sign still spruces a nearby bridge. Finley listened by radio from his Indiana home. He had a soft spot for Paige, ensuring his pension. Groundskeeper Smokey Olson used Charlie O.'s blanket to warm Satch's legs in a bullpen rocking chair.

Some thought Finley *off* his rocker. "Charlie didn't want umpires to have to stash baseballs in their pocket," said longtime A's Voice Monte Moore, "so he built Harvey the Mechanical Rabbit," rigged a basket, and buried him behind the plate. "The ump would point to a ballboy, who pushed a button," making the rabbit rise, unload stock, and return to terra firma. Finley felt umpires demeaned by cleaning home plate—thus, "Little Blowhard," a compressed-air jet. Not everyone

was aware of Finley's brainchild. In sequence, one batter readied for a pitch, the ump pressed the button, the airjet hissed, and the hitter, stunned, leapt straight up and fell backward in the box. Little worked. The 1967 A's finished last, drew a next-to-AL-last 726,639, and in 1968 vamoosed to Oakland. A year later the league expanded to Seattle and back to Kansas City. The A's were succeeded by the Royals, more quickly at the box office than on the field.

Finley arrived in Oakland already with the reputation for making Jack Benny seem generous. In August 1967 the A's flew a regularly scheduled plane from Boston to Kansas City, "Finley so cheap he spread us three across in coach," said first baseman Ken Harrelson. Priorities: Charlie O. went first class. En route, Lew Krausse had too much to drink. Finley wanted to suspend him. Manager Alvin Dark refused, leading Finley to fire him, at which point Harrelson called Charlie "detrimental to baseball." Next day Finley called, swearing, asking if Harrelson wanted his unconditional release. Hawk said no, wanting and needing his $12,500 annual salary. Charlie said he would call back. Instead, he had Harrelson's roommate, Mike Hershberger, phone: "As of this moment, you're no longer a member of the green and gold." Released, Hawk became baseball's first free agent, signing with Boston. Harrelson's take: "Charlie built a lot of things—a prime-time World Series, a great A's team, free agency—by mistake."

Oakland's reputation had been forged by Gertrude Stein, who said famously, "There's no there there"—although the city had hosted minor-league baseball continuously since the Oakland Pioneers of 1879. It had never had a major-league club, however, until Finley relocated the A's. Starting in 1911, the Oakland Oaks of the Pacific Coast League played in homespun Oaks Park, near Emeryville. The bleachers began ten feet off the ground. "That way," said owner J. Cal Ewing, "we can avoid a white hitter's backdrop." The clubhouse also had a washing machine. "If you want to look neat on the field," said trainer Red Adams, "you have to start from inside out." Casey Stengel won the 1948 pennant with "Nine Old Men," the team averaging 34 years old. The park was older. "Every time a ball hit the left-field fence," said ex-NL batting champion Ernie Lombardi, "the boards fell down." The Oaks moved to Vancouver in 1958 when the National League Giants arrived across San Francisco Bay. In late 1967 Finley moved into a park at Oakland's C.W. Nimitz Freeway and Hegenberger Road. Divide and conquer may work in politics. It nearly killed baseball in the Bay.

Public funds built the Oakland-Alameda County Coliseum for the American Football League Raiders. It was symmetrical, like most new 1960s multisport facilities. Lines were 330 feet long. Alleys were 378 (later, 375, 372, and 367), center field was 410 (400 in 1969, 396, 397, and 400 again in 1990), and foul ground reached to Berkeley. ("Balls kept getting caught," said 1968 skipper Bob Kennedy. "Cost you 10 points a year.") Tall grass stemmed triples. Heavy night air killed would-be dingers. The backstop—a notch in the stands—lay a league-high 90 feet from the plate. The Coliseum lay hard by parking lots nowhere near downtown Oakland. It was easy to reach by highway and train, but had little buzz, less community shopping and dining, and outside concrete walls made increasingly dull by the brick and sandstone exterior of the 1990s and beyond "old new" parks: a Camden Yards, a Target Field, the phantasmagoric PNC Park.

Set in the ground like a D-Day concrete pillbox, barely visible from the Freeway, the Coliseum's appearance fit the neighborhood, plain and rough and spartan. "No cable cars or great skyline," said Half Moon Bay native and future A's and Giants voice Jon Miller, "just train tracks and warehouses." A visitor descended to the ticket window, sighting a next door complex housing skating and hockey and hoops. The Coliseum—almost from the start, wags dubbed it the *Mausoleum*—was stark, outside and in: no arch, roof, or sculpture. Official baseball capacity was 50,000. Three tiers reached beyond each line. A single 7,000-seat bleacher deck trimmed the 8- foot (10 in 1981) outfield wall. A green hill lay beyond it. "Given the park's sterility," read the *Oakland Tribune*, "you focus on the hill, not field."

The Coliseum premiered on April 17, 1968. First pitcher: Lew Krausse. Batter: Baltimore's Curt Blefary. Homer: Oriole Boog Powell. Score: Orioles, 4-1. First ball: thrown out by California Governor Ronald Reagan. "One thing I'm sure of," he said of Income Tax Day, "is that a lot of you paid your taxes." Boos rained from 50,164. Reagan smiled. "Up to a few moments ago, I was glad to be here." Straight off, the A's practiced hand-to-mouth artwork. Charlie O. stepped from a luxury van, stopped at each base, and bowed. Tennessee Ernie Ford and a marching band readied for the National Anthem. "But Finley couldn't negotiate an agreement on live music from the union," said Monte Moore. "We played a recording."

Finley's $1 million right-field scoreboard flopped for several months. The pitcher's mound lay on a steel shell for Oakland's soccer team. The exposed shell was covered between innings. "Opening Night had sort of a wing-it feel," confessed Charlie. A worse feel was empty seats. On May 8, 1968, Catfish Hunter threw a perfect game against Minnesota at the Coliseum—the AL's first since 1922. The game wasn't televised. No TV outlet even covered it. Improbably, given today's media landscape, all that remains is the last radio out. In the ninth inning Hunter faced Rich Reese: A's ahead, 6-0, two out, and full count. Reese fouled off a panoply of pitches, then fanned. Moore and Al Helfer divided 1968 A's radio, Al doing the night's last 4½ innings. From the old school, Helfer never noted the no-hitter till it happened, afraid that he might jinx it.

Al said only, "My goodness, the boy has pitched a no-hitter" at the end—a hard drinker, he may not have noticed that "the boy" had also pitched a *perfect game*. Either way, a tiny announced crowd of 6,298 watched. "Baseball hadn't caught on yet in the Bay," Moore said. "What those of little faith missed." Bay baseball beat writer Bob Stevens believed that "Finley thought you could create new fans in the Bay Area." Instead, he stole the Giants', dividing a finite market. In 1968 both clubs drew a combined attendance of 1,711,069 versus the 1966 Giants' 1,657,191. Oakland's 837,466 placed eighth in league attendance. Those missing in action for the no-hitter could have seen the Athletics' first .500 year since 1952.

The following year the A's installed the 24-foot-high and 126-foot-wide "Finley Fun [computer score] Board" with cartoons and other graphics. They had much to hail in 1969-70—in one year or the other, Reggie Jackson's 47 homers, Sal Bando's 113 RBIs, and Vida Blue's no-hitter—but even fewer showed up to celebrate. "Youngest [21] to no-hit anyone since Daffy Dean," Finley said of Blue. On the other hand, the '69 and '70 A's each drew less than 800,000, Vida's gem luring 4,284. "Charlie was hung up on his color scheme—white, gold, and Kelly green," added Hunter. "I remember one home opener had gold-covered bases." Ironically, more marketing gold would have reaped more green.

From the start Oakland was unsure how to view the enigmatic Finley. After high school, the son of a steelworker entered the mills, sold insurance at night, formed a company, and was a millionaire by 35. Buying the A's, Finley badgered grounds help, phoned the dugout, hatched trades, and had a reverence for talent developed there. In 1970 he hired baseball's Jackie Gleason to do radio and TV. Holy Cow! It might be! It could be! It was! Harry Caray became the A's Voice for a season, selling beer, sacking pomp, and on his arrival in Oakland predicting that "here was a club that'll soon be a world champion," youth not wasted on the young. "Sal Bando, Bert Campaneris, and Dick Green, left to right in the infield and all in their early 20s," he said. "Don Mincher and Mike Epstein at first base. Gene Tenace behind the plate. Joe Rudi, Rick Monday, and Reggie Jackson in the outfield." Pitching wed "Vida Blue and Catfish Hunter and Blue Moon Odom and Kenny Holtzman. On and on."

Quoting Ring Lardner, to some Finley seemed to treat employees like a side dish he declined to order. Caray said Finley treated him like a friend. He let Harry use Charlie's penthouse on a lake and his Cadillac—"gave me the keys. I only wish his team had been in the Midwest where my roots were"—Caray left after 1970 to join the White Sox—"but you didn't have to be a scientist to know they were going to be

great." Finley had one scout, carried a briefcase, lived two time zones away, yet "wound up with this world of talent." Without free agency forcing Finley to break up the A's, "he'd have won a ton of titles more."

There was a lot to follow, if only Charlie could arrange it. One year he didn't sign a commercial station to carry games in English, giving A's rights to the UCLA-Berkeley radio outlet, its peewee signal limited to the campus and a few downtown blocks. Meanwhile, his 1,000-watt Spanish AM flagship station reached most of the area, an engineer explaining that because its tower/transmitter was installed on top of cement pillars in the bay, water as a conduit increased power. This didn't help Oakland English-speaking listeners even as, ironically, the A's English radio network stretched to Honolulu. A protester phoned Finley: "It's nice they can hear you in Hawaii. Why can't we hear you *here*?"

Those who heard, rejoiced. In 1971 Blue burst like Vesuvius: 24-8, 8 shutouts, and a 1.82 earned-run average, receiving the MVP Award. Oakland won the West, still drew only 914,993, and lost the League Championship Series to Baltimore. One night league executives had dinner in Oakland's Jack London Square. Casey Stengel, 81, began giving tales the "Stengel treatment." Suddenly the mule Charlie O. entered, wandered to Casey's table, and nudged the Ol' Perfessor, by now slightly wasted. "A very remarkable horse," Stengel mused. "He hasn't seen me for a year, and still remembers." There was much to remember about the next three years—Oakland's 1972-74 dynasty—baseball's first threepeat since the 1949-53 Yankees. The minor stars changed, but the firmament's brilliance remained.

SOURCES

Virtually all material, including quotes, is derived from Curt Smith's books *Voices of The Game, Storied Stadiums, Voices of Summer, The Voice, Pull Up a Chair, A Talk in the Park,* and *Mercy! A Celebration of Fenway Park's Centennial Told Through Red Sox Radio and TV* (published, in order: Simon & Schuster 1992; Carroll & Graf 2001 and 2005, respectively; the Lyons Press, 2007: and Potomac Books 2009, 2010, and 2012, respectively.)

Books

The Oakland Athletics: 1972-74

Lowry, Philip, *Green Cathedrals: The Ultimate Celebration of All Major League Ballparks* (New York: Walker & Company, 2006).

Silverman, Matthew, *Swinging '73: Baseball's Wildest Season* (Guilford, Connecticut: The Lyons Press, 2013).

Websites

Baseball-reference.com

Charlie Finley

By Mark Armour

He owned and operated the Kansas City and Oakland Athletics for 20 years. Nearly everyone, including fellow owners, players, the fans of his teams, the media, and the baseball commissioner, disliked or even despised him. When his team lost, he blamed everyone but himself. When they won, he was apt to call the radio booth during the game if his name was not mentioned often enough. He was a self-made millionaire who, in the words of sportswriter Jim Murray, "worshipped his creator."[1]

Working at a time when baseball abhorred change of any stripe, Charlie Finley had more ideas and imagination than all his fellow owners put together. Tactless, rude, and vulgar, he could outwork everyone, running his insurance company in Chicago while badgering his baseball employees at long distance. Working in an age before cellular telephones, Finley spent hours on the phone, usually with someone who would rather have been doing anything other than talking to Charlie. He was a professional salesman, and worked his fellow owners by browbeating them until they might finally give in. Most of the crazy ideas he advanced—orange baseballs and bases—never caught on, but a few that did—World Series night games, the designated hitter—changed the game forever.

It is impossible to write about the great 1970s Athletics, a team that won three consecutive World Series titles, without presenting Finley as the star of the show; the baseball team, even the games themselves, often seemed a sidelight to some other story. This is exactly how Finley wanted it. Ron Bergman, who covered the Oakland Athletics for the *Oakland Tribune*, once wrote, "Finley makes the games incidental. After the 1973 Series was over … I had to go back and read about the games to see what happened."[2] Several books were written about the A's during their glory years, and every one of them placed Finley front and center.

Finley ran the entire operation to an extent that was startling. He not only made all the baseball decisions in Oakland—deciding whom to draft or sign, making trades, suggesting the lineup, advising in-game strategy—he often wrote the copy for the yearbook, made out the song lists for the organist, decided the menu for the press room during the World Series, and designed the uniforms. Finley had to approve all injuries before a player could be put on the disabled list. Not surprisingly, he went through office staffers at an alarming rate. People soon tire of being screamed at, humiliated, and treated, as one former employee put it, "worse than animals."

And yet he won. And what's more, Finley won almost entirely with players that his organization had signed and developed. The Athletics were built precisely the way we imagine a great team ought to be built: They

signed or drafted dozens of quality players, sifted through them for a few years until several developed, made a couple of key trades to redistribute the talent, and provided depth with veteran role players. It worked splendidly, and likely would have continued to work splendidly had the game's labor system not changed. Once the players had to be treated on nearly equal ground, Finley's techniques were no longer successful. For this, Finley had himself to blame, for no one did more to incite the player revolution than Charlie.

If the architect of the great Athletics had been anyone other than Finley, he might have received a book contract, and spent his retirement years giving speeches on college campuses. Since it *was* Finley, everyone could hardly wait until he got out of baseball so that they could unplug their noses. It is amusing to imagine what the other owners must have felt watching this man hoist the World Series trophy every year on national television.

Charles Oscar Finley was born on February 22, 1918, just outside Birmingham, in an area that is now incorporated as Ensley, Alabama. Randolph Finley, Charles's grandfather had come to the area from Ireland and worked in the steel mills. He and Emma Caroline Finley raised 11 children, one of whom, Oscar, was Charles's father. Emma Fields, Charles's mother, came from Georgia originally, but her family made it to Birmingham when she was a child. Oscar met Emma when he was working as an apprentice at the steel mill. They soon married, settled in a residential neighborhood, and were very active in the Baptist Church.

Oscar and Emma had three children: Thelma, Charles, and Fred. Charles, the middle child, was an extraordinary businessman even as a youngster. By the age of 12 he mowed lawns six days a week, eventually hiring and organizing a crew of people. He sold newspapers and magazines all over Birmingham, with his mother driving the car. He sold eggs. He made and sold cheap wine during the Prohibition era. He was also the batboy for the Birmingham Barons, and he loved the game, playing it whenever he could.

In 1933 the steel mills began laying people off, so Oscar moved his family to Gary, Indiana. In his new city Charlie quickly found ways to make money, working, always working. He didn't just play baseball—he organized his own team and found a sponsor. After graduating from Mann High School in 1936, he worked in a steel mill for five years. Laid off in 1941, and classified as 4-F for induction into the service, he went to work in an ordnance plant east of Gary in LaPorte, Indiana. That same year he married Shirley McCartney, a local woman from a well-respected and well-to-do family. He remained employed at the plant until 1946.

In the meantime Finley began selling insurance on the side, and he was so good at it that he left his job and began working for a Travelers agent in Gary. He set sales records for the company that held until the 1960s. Ironically, the one person he forgot to insure was himself, and this mistake nearly ruined everything. A severe bout of tuberculosis hospitalized him for 2½ years and nearly cost him his life. Typically, he spent all of this idle time planning his next move. He developed a plan to sell life insurance to doctors and surgeons. When he left the hospital, he started his own company, and it quickly became one of the largest insurance carriers in the country. Within a few years he was a multimillionaire.

Finley was also a lifelong baseball nut, playing on lots of local organized teams before his illness. Once he became rich, he spent several years attempting to buy a major-league team. He first tried to purchase the Philadelphia Athletics from the Mack family in 1953, and was later a spurned bidder for the Tigers, the White Sox, and the expansion Los Angeles Angels. Finally, in December 1960 he bought a controlling interest in the Kansas City Athletics from the estate of Arnold Johnson, and within a few months he had bought out all of the other investors. The club he bought had been terrible for many years, and had finished in last place, 39 games behind the Yankees, in 1960.

Finley's first baseball move was to hire "Trader" Frank Lane to run the team, a sure sign that he wanted a quick fix. Early in the season, Finley overruled a few of Lane's moves, and it was soon apparent who was running the show. Though working under an eight-year contract, Lane did not make it through his first season. Calling Finley a liar and "an egotist," he later went to court to get some of the money Finley owed him. The man who "replaced" Lane was Pat Friday, who also worked for Finley in his insurance company. Within a few years, Finley's front office consisted mainly of his wife, Shirley, his cousin Carl Finley, and his son, Charles Jr. The traveling secretary was apt to be a college intern.

Finley's first manager was Joe Gordon, who once reportedly handed the home-plate umpire a lineup card that was inscribed: "Approved by C.O.F."[3] Gordon lasted 60 games. When Finley decided to hire his right fielder as the new manager, he instructed the P.A. announcer to call out: "Hank Bauer, your playing days are over. You have been named manager of the Kansas City A's." Bauer trotted in to the dugout.

Finley quickly concluded that he understood the game better than anyone else. One classic example involved promising outfielder Manny Jiminez. In July 1962, Manny, a 22-year-old rookie, was hitting .337 with 10 home runs. When asked about his rising star, Finley snapped, "I don't pay Jiminez to hit singles." He ordered Bauer to get him to swing for the fences: "Get that smart Cuban in your office, and get another Cuban to interpret and bang your fist on the desk. We'll see what happens."[4] What happened was that Jiminez, who was not Cuban at all but Dominican, hit .301, but with only one home run for the rest of year, and showed up in 1963 without a starting job.

Finley spent a lot of time complaining about the city and the ballpark and trying to move the team. In his first few years in Kansas City he publicly courted the communities of Atlanta, Dallas-Fort Worth, and Oakland, and several times sought league permission to move. In January 1964 Finley signed a lease with the state of Kentucky to use Fairgrounds Stadium in Louisville. Unfortunately, he failed to notify the American League. Ten days later, the league voted 9 to 1 against the shift, and gave Finley until February 1 to conclude a lease in Kansas City.

Finley remained undeterred. He flew to Oakland, signed a letter of intent to move his team there, and told the league he would sign no more than a two-year lease in Kansas City. In an emergency league meeting, the owners voted 9 to 1 that the lease being offered by Kansas City was fair and reasonable and called another meeting to consider expelling Finley from the league. He finally gave in and signed an ironclad four-year lease to keep the Athletics in Kansas City through 1967.

When he first acquired the team, Finley tried anything and everything to interest people in his team: cow-milking contests, greased-pig contests, a sheep pasture (with a shepherd) beyond right field, a zoo beyond left. He installed a mechanical rabbit named Harvey behind home plate to pop up and hand the umpire new baseballs. He had "Little Blowhard," a compressed-air device inside of home plate that blew dirt away. He hired Miss U.S.A to be the batgirl. He installed a yellow cab to bring in pitchers from the bullpen. He released helium balloons with A's tickets throughout the countryside. He installed lights in the dugout so that the fans could see the manager and players discussing strategy. He shot off fireworks in the park, but the neighbors complained and the city made him desist. Finley sued the city.

During Finley's early tenure in Kansas City, the team received a lot of attention for its uniforms, for which the owner himself, of course, selected the design. Finley first introduced the sleeveless top to the American League in 1962, and the following year he shocked baseball traditionalists by dressing his team head-to-toe in yellow with green trim. The Athletics' lone All-Star Game representative in 1963, Norm Seibern, did not play in the game, reportedly because manager Ralph Houk thought that the Athletics uniform was a disgrace to the American League. In 1966 the team added "kangaroo white" shoes to its ensemble.

The one thing Finley promised the good people of Kansas City that he actually delivered on might have been the biggest long shot: He got the Beatles to play at Municipal Stadium. The 1964 tour, their first in North America, was already ongoing when (after several attempts) he lured the biggest sensation in pop music history for $150,000 — at the time the largest fee ever paid for a music concert.

In 1965 Finley introduced the baseball world to his new mascot, a Missouri mule, predictably named Charlie O. Not only did the mule have its own pen just outside the park, it also went on a few road trips and stayed in the team's hotel. In Yankee Stadium, Finley got Ken Harrelson to ride Charlie O., and the frightened mule ran around trying to buck him off. Only the Chicago White Sox did not let Charlie O. on the field, so Finley arranged a protest rally across the street from Comiskey Park with pretty models and a six-piece band, which played appropriate tunes, like "Mule Train." One afternoon in Kansas City, he led the mule onto the field through the center-field fence before realizing that the game had already started.

In late 1965 he signed the 59-year-old Satchel Paige to start a game against the Red Sox in Kansas City. Allowing only a single to Carl Yastrzemski, Paige threw three shutout innings. Soon thereafter, Bert Campaneris played all nine positions in a game, before finally leaving in the ninth inning when, while playing catcher, he was involved in a collision at home plate. After the season, coach Whitey Herzog had seen enough: "This is nothing more than a damned sideshow. Winning over here is a joke."[5]

Despite all of these early efforts at promotion, the Athletics had miserable attendance throughout Finley's years in Kansas City. In 1960, the year before Finley bought the team, the Athletics drew only 774,944 fans. This was a modest total, even for the time, but it was more than Finley ever attracted in any of his seven years in Kansas City. In 1965 the team attracted only 528,344 admissions. In their first season in 1969, the Kansas City Royals easily surpassed Finley's highest attendance figure.

Finley was also full of bright ideas to improve the game. He wanted interleague play and realignment to promote geographic rivalries. He pushed for World Series and All-Star Games at night. He wanted the season shortened. He cajoled for the adoption of a

designated hitter for the pitcher. He proposed a designated runner, who could freely pinch-run for a player any time he got on without replacing him in the lineup. He tried to get the owners to adopt a three-ball walk and actually used the rule in one preseason game in 1971. (There were 19 walks in the game, and it was not tried again.) He pushed to have active players made eligible for the Hall of Fame. He installed a clock in the scoreboard to enforce a long ignored rule that mandated no more than twenty seconds between pitches.

Finley continually tried to add elements of color to the game. His first year in Kansas City, he painted the box seats and the outfield fences citrus yellow and the foul poles fluorescent pink. At the league meetings in 1970, Finley proposed colored bases and colored foul lines, and the A's received permission to use gold bases for their home opener. A few years later, he pushed for orange baseballs, which he carried with him everywhere he went. He even received permission to use the balls in a spring-training game. About this time most tennis organizations began using a yellow ball, and one cannot help but think that the orange baseball might have caught on if Finley had not been the author of the idea.

Finley once offered the following advice to a hypothetical man thinking of becoming a baseball owner: "Do not go into any league meeting looking alert and awake; slump down like you've been out all night and keep your eyes half closed, and when it is your turn to vote you ask to pass. Then you wait and see how the others vote, and you vote the same way. Suggest no innovations. Make no efforts at change. That way you will be very popular with your fellow owners."[6]

After being forced to sign his lease in early 1964, Finley essentially stopped trying to promote the team. Ernie Mehl wrote in the *Kansas City Star,* "Had the ownership made a deliberate attempt to sabotage a baseball organization, it could not have succeeded as well. … It is somewhat the sensation one has in walking through a hall of mirrors designed to distort, where nothing is normal, where everything appears out of focus."[7] Finley responded by staging "Ernie Mehl Appreciation Day" and planned to present Mehl with a "poison pen." When Mehl did not attend, Finley arranged to have a truck circle the park with a caricature of Mehl dipping his pen in "poison ink."

Star reporter Joe McGuff wrote a letter to the American League offices claiming: "Finley has done nothing to promote the season ticket sale. He has never had one salesman on the street. The A's do not have a ticket outlet outside of Greater Kansas City."[8] Finley ignored booster clubs. He gave no support to local groups that organized ticket-buying programs. He made only cursory attempts at selling radio and TV rights. He decided that the city did not care about him so, by God, he was not going to care about the city.

Finley constantly fiddled with the dimensions of his ballpark, until it reached the point of absurdity. His first year he thought the Kansas City pitchers needed help, so he moved the left field fence back 40 feet. By 1964 he had determined that the Yankees won every year not because of their great talent, but because of the dimensions of their ballpark: deep in most of left and center fields with a short distance in right. Finley decided to make his right-field configuration identical to that in Yankee Stadium.

Unfortunately for Finley, as of 1958 the rules decreed a minimum distance of 325 feet down the foul lines with the exception of those parks already with shorter dimensions. Never one to be put off by something as silly as the rules of the game, Finley ordered that his fence conform to the Yankee Stadium dimensions from center field to right field until it reached a point five feet from the foul line and 296 feet from home plate (the Yankee Stadium distance). From there, the fence angled sharply back out so that it was exactly 325 feet away when it reached the foul line. He thus neatly skirted the rule, which stipulated the distances only on the foul line, not the distance five feet from the line. He painted "KC pennant porch" on the new fence (which was exactly 44 inches high, as it was in Yankee Stadium).

After two exhibition games, American League President Joe Cronin told Finley that *all* of the fence must be at least 325 feet from the plate. Finley moved the fence back to 325, changed the sign to say "One-Half Pennant Porch" and painted a line on the field that represented the Yankee Stadium dimensions. He then ordered the public address announcer to call out, "That would have been a home run at Yankee Stadium" for every fly ball that went past this line.[9]

This was no joke to Finley. He was apoplectic about the Yankees, and believed the rules were deliberately stacked so that they won the pennant every year. Before its reconstruction in 1974-75, Yankee Stadium had monuments for Miller Huggins, Lou Gehrig, and Babe Ruth in deep left-center field. Finley threatened to put a statue of Connie Mack right in the middle of center field, saying: "They let the Yankees have their monuments out in the playing area, but if I put one up they'll probably try to run me out of baseball."[10]

In the meantime, Finley traded for Rocky Colavito and Jim Gentile to hit home runs over his new fences. This strategy sort of worked in that the team finished third in the league with 166 home runs, including 34 by Colavito and 28 by Gentile. But Kansas City pitchers allowed 220 home runs, a major-league record that lasted until 1987. The 1964 Athletics finished last with a record of 57-105.

The next year, Finley moved the fence back, put a 40-foot screen above it and got rid of Colavito and Gentile. These actions suggest a management that does not have any idea what it is doing. Just as the pitchers and hitters begin to figure out how best to deal with the dimensions of the park, the next year they come back and have to learn all over again. In 1965 the Athletics remained in last place, with a record of 59-103. The screen stayed, and Municipal Stadium remained a pitcher's park as long as the A's stayed there.

Although Finley likely never relinquished the idea of leaving Kansas City once his four-year lease expired, there was nothing much for him to do about it in the meantime. He could now concentrate all of his considerable energies on a different task—signing players for his team. From 1964 to 1966, Finley invested perhaps $2 million in 200 players. This group included three future members of the Baseball Hall of Fame (Jim "Catfish" Hunter, Rollie Fingers, and Reggie Jackson) and several other future All-Stars (Rick Monday, Joe Rudi, Gene Tenace, John "Blue Moon" Odom, and Sal Bando). With all these players in place, the team began to get better.

The 1966 team won 74 games, their best showing in Kansas City. Their rise was highlighted in a spring 1967 cover story in *Sports Illustrated* predicting great things ahead, perhaps as soon as that season. It did not happen that quickly, and the 1967 season was marred by a bizarre player revolt.

On August 3, 1967, the Athletics returned home from Boston on a commercial flight, and a few players got a little rowdy. A couple of weeks later Finley, who had not been present, investigated briefly and fined and suspended pitcher Lew Krausse. Krausse was known as something of a drinker and was certainly in the middle of whatever happened, but according to his teammates there was no particular reason for singling him out. The players backed Krausse and issued a joint statement suggesting that the event had been blown out of proportion and blaming the whole episode on Finley's "go betweens."

Finley did not like back talk, especially from the hired help, and things deteriorated quickly from there. He first demanded that the players publicly retract their statement, which they refused to do. Inevitably, Finley fired manager Alvin Dark, who knew about the players' statement and had failed to forewarn his boss about it. Ken Harrelson was quoted referring to Finley as a "menace to baseball."[11] Finley responded by giving Harrelson, one of the better players on the team, his unconditional release. The Hawk turned his freedom into a $75,000 contract with the pennant-bound Boston Red Sox. The ramifications of Harrelson's free agency so disturbed major-league owners that they amended the rules so that, in the future, a released player had to pass through waivers before becoming a free agent.

The surviving players sought and received a hearing with Commissioner William Eckert, causing Finley to threaten retribution against those who planned to participate. The players contacted Marvin Miller, the new head of the Major League Players Association, who subsequently filed an unfair labor practice charge with the National Labor Relations Board. On September 11 there was a 14-hour meeting with the commissioner, and Finley agreed to back down in exchange for the players dropping the charge. It eventually all blew over, but this proved a watershed event. From this point forward, whenever the players union needed a symbolic bogeyman, Charlie Finley was generally around to stand in.

Finley's four-year lease at Municipal Stadium ended in 1967. This time Finley had laid the groundwork for his escape by quietly gathering the votes of his fellow American League owners. On October 18 the league formally approved his move to Oakland as part of a package deal that included the league expanding to two cities, including Kansas City. Finley likely chose Oakland over other possibilities because it had a brand new ballpark ready to go. The city of Oakland, cognizant of whom they were dealing with, drew up a strict 20-year lease with no option for moving. Finley signed, but was talking with Toronto by 1970.

Once he was settled in Oakland, Finley branched out to buy two other sports teams: the Oakland Seals of the National Hockey League (renamed the California Seals), and the Memphis Stars of the American Basketball Association (renamed the Tams). Both teams changed colors to Finley's favored green and gold, but neither could draw fans or win games. In 1974 both teams were taken over by their respective leagues.

Meanwhile, with his baseball club gradually improving, Finley worked equally hard to keep them from getting his money. He went through very public and openly hostile holdouts with Reggie Jackson (in 1970) and Vida Blue (1972), both times using humiliation and degradation to get his stars to come to terms. Both men were popular and well-liked players who never again seemed to play with the carefree joy they had before Charlie put them in their place. In both cases, Commissioner Bowie Kuhn, rarely considered friendly to the interests of players, intervened to get things settled.

A funny thing about Finley was that he could be very generous on his own terms. He was reprimanded or fined several times for giving impromptu performance bonuses (which were and continue to be forbidden) to players for pitching a no-hitter, hitting a game-winning home run, or some other such thing. For many years he offered to invest the money of players in the stock market risk-free—Finley gave the player all gains and assumed all losses. At contract time, on the other hand, he considered it a personal insult if a player was not satisfied with his offer. As he told writer Bill Libby, "We have not won a pennant, but we will win one, we will win more than one with these players who are like my own sons, and I am only sad when they will not accept my counsel, the counsel of a man who is older and wiser than they."[12]

Led by Blue, the A's won 101 games in 1971 and the division by 16 games. The team fell short in the playoffs, but the core of this team remained nearly intact for five straight division titles. Bando, Campaneris, Green, Jackson, and Rudi held down five of the eight regular lineup spots. Hunter, Blue, and Fingers starred on the pitcher's mound.

Finley made two great trades that solidified the dynasty. After the 1971 season he traded Rick Monday to the Cubs for left-handed pitcher Ken Holtzman. A year later, now realizing that he needed a center fielder, Finley traded Bob Locker to the Cubs for Billy North. North anchored center field for the A's for the next several seasons.

With his great young team in place, Finley constantly tinkered with the depth of his club, making trade after trade, either to fill in the gaps or because he liked making deals. Finley acquired a huge number of veterans to play a role during the five-year string of division titles. He outworked the other general managers during most of his 20-year career as owner, but he pushed himself even harder once he realized how good his team had become. In 1972 alone he made 19 trades, many of them during the season. Dick Williams later claimed that he found out about trades by seeing who was in the dugout when he showed up for work.

For spring training of 1972, Reggie Jackson showed up with a mustache. After privately trying to get Jackson to shave it off, Finley instead decided to capitalize on the act of rebellion. He staged a "Mustache Night," let mustached patrons in for a reduced price, and gave each player a small bonus if they wore mustaches for that night's game. All players and coaches obliged, and most kept their mustaches all season. A few even sported beards. The team, dubbed "The Mustache Gang" in the press, went on to beat the clean-cut Cincinnati Reds in the World Series.

The Sporting News named Finley its "Man of the Year." Jackson and Blue, each once the biggest star in all of baseball, were now back in their rightful place as mere players. The only star on the team was Finley. In case anyone had missed it, he reprinted the *Sporting News* cover photo in the 1973 A's yearbook.

After another pennant the next season, the 1973 World Series finally turned Finley into a national pariah, an identity he would never overcome. After Mike

Andrews made two errors in the 12th inning of Game Two, helping the Mets beat the A's 10-7, Finley forced Andrews to sign a statement claiming that his shoulder was injured and that he could no longer play. Finley added Manny Trillo to the roster to replace Andrews, who left the team and flew home. The players, in the middle of a deadlocked series, rallied to their teammate. Sal Bando: "That's a joke. I've seen some bush things on this club, but this is going too far."[13] Reggie Jackson added, "All that nonbaseball stuff takes the little boy out of you."[14] The whole team seemed defeated and uninterested in playing. The A's players showed up for Game Three in New York with Andrews' number on their sleeves.

Commissioner Kuhn ordered Finley to reinstate Andrews, who reached New York in time for the fourth game the next night and pinch-hit in the eighth inning. He received a prolonged standing ovation from the New York crowd — Finley did not stand — before grounding out off Jon Matlack. One A's employee expressed the general feeling: "Although it hurt Andrews, a lot of people were glad it happened because for the first time it directed attention at the way Finley treated people, even if it was far from the first time he'd treated them that way. All of a sudden he was not just a quaint old guy, a fellow who did funny things, but a man who could hurt people and did."[15] The A's released Andrews at the end of the season, and he never again played in the major leagues.

The aftermath of the seventh-game victory was eerie. The Oakland locker room was subdued, as if everyone just wanted to get out and go home. Yogi Berra, the manager of the Mets, walked in and commented, "This doesn't look like a winning dressing room to me." Manager Dick Williams announced that he was quitting, and Jackson said, "I wish I could get out with him." When a writer suggested to Jackson that Finley deserved credit for getting the team riled up, the star responded, "Please don't give that man credit. ... It would have been the easiest thing in the world for this team to lie down because of what that man did. He spoiled what should have been a beautiful thing."[16]

At this point in the story, Reggie Jackson's star finally rose and replaced Finley's at the top of his team. He was voted the World Series MVP, not only for his play on the field, but for the way he conducted himself as a sincere, intelligent man in the face of what was finally recognized as nearly intolerable working conditions. Finley had spent years trying to be the center of the team, and he had succeeded even after his team had so many star players. Finley's childish behavior in 1973 challenged his players to step forward, and Jackson did.

The departure of Williams resulted in yet another long circus, as Finley first publicly supported Williams's decision but later refused to let him out of his contract. No one quit on Finley. Williams signed to manage the Yankees, a move the American League blocked. Finley demanded compensation, which the Yankees refused to give, precluding Williams from getting the job. Williams remained out of work until midsummer, when he signed to manage the lowly California Angels. The A's lingered without a manager until late February, when Finley finally hired old friend Alvin Dark for 1974.

By 1974 much of the fun was gone. While Finley had flown in to get retractions from players for the occasional criticism in years past, by now the pretense of kissing up to the boss was ancient history. Captain Sal Bando claimed, "I would say all but a few of our players hate him. It binds us together."[17]

The 1974 team struggled to hold off the surprising Texas Rangers and won only 90 games. Once the postseason bell rang, they rallied to capture their third straight world championship. Unbelievably, yet another player-relations nightmare dominated the 1974 postseason. This time it involved not a backup infielder but the contract of a 25-game winner, Jim "Catfish" Hunter.

In January 1974 Hunter had signed a two-year contract for a salary of $100,000 per year. The arrangement included a wrinkle: Half his salary was to be paid into a life-insurance fund as a form of deferred payment. On the day before the World Series began in Los Angeles, the story broke that Finley had not paid the

mandated $50,000 to the insurance company, even after receiving written notice in mid-September. Hunter reportedly planned to ask for his release from his contract as soon as the World Series was over. Finley, obviously more worried than he admitted, went into the clubhouse with American League President Lee McPhail to present Hunter with a check for the amount due. Hunter refused to accept the check and told Finley that they would discuss it after the Series was over.

After a month of rumors in the press, a hearing was held on November 26 in New York City in front of arbitrator Peter Seitz. On December 13 Seitz found for Hunter and declared him a free agent. The baseball world went berserk—never before had a player of Hunter's caliber been available to the highest bidder at the height of his career. A three-week bidding war ensued among nearly every team in baseball. The Yankees landed Hunter with a five-year deal totaling $3.75 million, more than three times the annual rate for the top stars in the game. The players could not

help but notice what they could make on the free market.

After one last division title, but no World Series, the Athletic dynasty effectively died on December 12, 1975, when arbitrator Seitz dropped another bombshell. This time he declared Dodgers pitcher Andy Messersmith and Expos pitcher Dave McNally free agents after they had played out the season without signing contracts. This decision ultimately put an end to the effects of baseball's reserve clause, which bound a player to his team in perpetuity.

Finley's team was finished. Once Charlie had to bargain with players as equals, once he had to look an agent in the eye and come to terms, well, he just was not capable of competing. Charlie Finley did not, and could not, operate in this manner. The whole team hated him and had seen their teammate Hunter go on to happiness and wealth in another city, leaving little doubt what they were going to do with their freedom. Finley traded Jackson and Ken Holtzman during spring training in 1976. Sal Bando, Gene Tenace, Bert Campaneris, Rollie Fingers, and Joe Rudi (along with Jackson, now an Oriole) became free agents that fall. By 1977 the Athletics were in last place, behind even the first-year Seattle Mariners.

In June 1976 Finley attempted to make the best of a bad situation by selling Blue to the Yankees and Fingers and Rudi to the Red Sox for a total of $3.5 million. Because he was about to lose all three at the end of the year anyway, it seemed like a wise idea. Bowie Kuhn voided the sales, claiming they were not "in the best interests of baseball." Finley sued Kuhn for restraint of trade, but lost his case a few years later. Even with the passage of time, it is hard to find justification for Kuhn's action, other than trying to destroy Finley.

After three losing seasons, in 1980 Charlie hired Billy Martin to run the team, and there were signs that the team was going to rise again, behind new stars like Rickey Henderson and Mike Norris. But Finley's time was over. Shirley Finley filed for divorce that summer, and when she refused to accept a share of the baseball team, he was forced to sell. He eventually sold to Walter A. Haas, Jr., before the next season.

Finley lived out his remaining days in Chicago running his insurance company. He died in 1996, leaving seven children. For a man who spent 20 years in the game and won three championships, he left very few friends in the game.

NOTES

1   Mark L. Armour and Daniel R. Levitt, *Paths to Glory* (Dulles, Virginia: Brassey's Inc., 2003), 234.

2   Herbert Michelson, *Charlie O* (New York: Bobbs Merrill, 1975), 294.

3   Michelson, *Charlie O*, 94.

4   Bill Wise, ed., *The 1963 Official Baseball Almanac* (Greenwich, Connecticut: Fawcett, 1963), 58.

5   "Finley's Follies," *Sport Annual*, 1966.

6   Edwin Shrake, "A Man and a Mule in Missouri," *Sports Illustrated*, July 27, 1965, 43.

7   Bill Libby, *Charlie O. & The Angry A's* (Garden City New York: Doubleday, 1975), 275.

8   John Peterson, *The Kansas City Athletics* (Jefferson, North Carolina: McFarland, 2003), 210.

9   Bill James, *The 1986 Baseball Abstract*, (New York: Ballantine Books, 1985).

10 John Peterson, *The Kansas City Athletics* (Jefferson, North Carolina: McFarland, 2003), 210.

11 Brent Musberger, "The Charlie O. Finley Follies, *Sports Illustrated*, September 4, 1967.

12 Libby, *Charlie O. & The Angry A's*, 10.

13 Michelson, *Charlie O*, 251.

14 Michelson, *Charlie O*, 251.

15 Libby, *Charlie O. & The Angry A's*, 20.

16 Libby, *Charlie O. & The Angry A's*, 279-280.

17 Armour and Levitt, *Paths to Glory*, 256.

Charlie O.

By Norm King

There was actually method to the madness behind Charlie Finley's idea that people would want to see his ass.

Finley had some bizarre ideas when he owned the Kansas City-Oakland A's, such as orange baseballs and designated runners, but even he didn't go so far as to moon the fans. In 1965, however, he bought a new mascot for the Kansas City team as a gimmick to bring people to the ballpark — a mule named, appropriately, Charlie O. It seemed that everything was up to date in Kansas City except fans' interest in watching an inept baseball team, and Finley needed to find ways of attracting people to Municipal Stadium.

Finley and his promotions director, Jim Schaaf, staged all kinds of shenanigans. In addition to standard bat days and ball nights, they concocted events like "Automobile Industry Night," where they would dress cars up and give them away to fans as is. This meant that the winning fans could drive the car off the lot, but there was no guarantee the car would get much beyond the lot without breaking down. Part of the fun included having the players arrive on the field in limousines.

This whole business with Charlie O. started the winter before the 1965 season. The A's had finished 10th in the American League in 1964 with a 57-105 record and had attracted only 642,478 fans (ninth in the league). Finley, always on the lookout for new ideas, called Schaaf at 4 o'clock one wintry morning after reading an article in the *Chicago Tribune* about how Missouri mules helped the Allies win World War I by lugging ammunition and supplies through the mud and snow of France faster than the Germans could. Finley ordered Schaaf to get the finest mule in the state of Missouri.

How one determines which mule is the finest in the state is a daunting task. Schaaf nonetheless persevered.

He called up Howard Benjamin, the owner of Benjamin Stables, which housed War Paint, the horse that ran around Municipal Stadium every time the American Football League's Kansas City Chiefs scored a touchdown. Through his connections, Benjamin found Charlie O. Schaaf and Finley went to see the animal, whose parentage is unknown except for the fact that his mother was a horse and his father a donkey (them's not fightin' words; that's the way it is with all mules). Finley was smitten.

On Opening Night 1965, Warren Hearnes, the governor of Missouri (and a Democrat) presented Charlie O. to Finley, who rode his namesake around the field to the fans' amusement.

Charlie O. was a big hit. He stood 16.2 hands high and weighed 1,400 pounds according to the 1971 Oakland A's yearbook.[1] He wore a uniform that consisted of a blanket, a bridle, and an A's cap, all in the team's green and gold colors. He was driven to the stadium in a trailer equipped with air conditioning and a stereo system, which caused players to gripe that he was getting more perks than they were. He spent the games in the stadium's picnic area zoo so that fans could pet him. He was also a community ambassador for the team. When a high school in Lawson, Kansas, unveiled a new scoreboard for its athletic field that it had purchased through a fundraising drive, Charlie O. was there for the dedication. A Kansas City country singer, Gene McKown, even recorded a song called "Charlie O. The Mule."

Finley also took Charlie O. to all the other cities in the American League in 1965 and 1966 to much media fanfare. Even Howard Cosell attended the press conference in New York in '65.

Charlie O. was not allowed on the field when he visited Chicago's Comiskey Park. Ever the operator, Finley quickly organized a protest across the street from the stadium with pretty girls acting as protesters and a six-piece band playing songs like "Mule Train."

Alas, for the all the hubbub, Charlie O. wasn't the fan magnet that Finley hoped he would be. The A's attendance in 1965 (a league-worst 528,344) was even lower than it had been the previous year.

When the A's moved to Oakland after the 1967 season, Charlie O. went with them and was along for the ride during he A's glory years of the early 1970s. He once even startled Boston Red Sox catcher Carlton Fisk during the 1975 American League Championship Series when he (the mule, not Fisk) was led into an Oakland hotel coffee shop. He died of deterioration of the liver on December 15, 1976, at the age of 20 (80 in human years).

"He symbolized the stubbornness of his owner, Charles O. Finley, the never-say-die proprietor of the A's," wrote Ron Bergman in *The Sporting News*. "And Charlie O. represented what was good about the franchise and the wonder world of the young on Sunday afternoons at the ballpark."[2]

SOURCES

Armour, Mark, SABR biography of Charlie Finley.

Green, G. Michael, and Roger D. Launius, *Charlie Finley: The Outrageous Story of Baseball's Super Showman* (New York: Walker and Company, 2010).

Independent Press Telegram (Long Beach, California).

Kansas City Star.

Spartanburg (North Carolina) *Herald*

The Sporting News

1971 Oakland A's Yearbook

NOTES

1   A hand is 4 inches and each number after the decimal represents an inch, so Charlie O. measured 5-feet-6 from the ground to his withers.

2   Ron Bergman, "A's Fans Mourn Charlie O., the Mule," *The Sporting News*, January 1, 1977.

Charles O. Finley with former Yankee and Mets manager Casey Stengel...and "Charlie "O" the mule. (1968 photo at the Oakland-Alameda County Coliseum)

Building a Champion

Charlie Finley and the core of the Oakland A's 1972-74 championship teams

By Chip Greene

"Equal parts carnival barker, professional bully, world-class tightwad, and uncanny builder of championship baseball teams, Oakland A's owner Charlie Finley left a stamp on baseball that can still be seen more than 30 years after his departure from the game."[1] So wrote reviewer Alan Moores for the magazine *Booklist* in his 2010 review of G. Michael Green and Roger D. Launius's excellent book, *Charlie Finley, The Outrageous Story of Baseball's Super Showman*.[2]

Indeed, Finley was a man of great complexity. If he was "a skinflint who alienated players and fans"[3] alike, so too was he a brilliant showman who introduced to the game such concepts as designated hitters and designated runners, orange baseballs, and night games in the World Series. Likewise, if Finley was "a loudmouth, a tyrant and a miser,"[4] he was also, in the words of author Launius, a man of "ingenious mind" who "often demonstrated innovation and vision between his bullshit."[5]

Of such cantankerous and creative personalities are legends often made.

Yet, if Finley's legacy is largely that of an ornery cuss who feuded alike with baseball's powers that be and his own players, and a man who "professed indifference to the often savage bickering among his players and to their contempt for him,"[6] it's easy to overlook his most brilliant and lasting accomplishment: For when the ranting, the raving, and the vitriol from both sides subsided, Finley could "point to three straight world championships as an acceptable trade-off"[7] for his boorish behavior. Despite the contentious nature of the relationship between Finley and the A's players, they achieved heights that few other teams in any sport have equaled—three consecutive championships.

Finley the baseball executive built those teams; in their construction, he knew what he was doing. More than simply the A's owner, Finley was also a shrewd evaluator of baseball talent, and wore a lot of front-office hats. Referring to another legendary dysfunctional championship organization, the marketing introduction to Finley's biography suggested that, "Before the 'Bronx Zoo' of George Steinbrenner and Billy Martin were the Oakland Athletics of the early 1970s, one of the most successful, most colorful—and most chaotic—baseball teams of all time. They were all of those things because of Charlie Finley. Not only the A's owner, he was also the general manager, personally assembling his team, deciding his players' salaries, and making player moves during the season—a level of involvement no other owner, not even Steinbrenner, engaged in."[8]

That eye for talent developed from a lifelong obsession with baseball, which gave Finley an appreciation for what was needed to win ballgames. Because of this, according to Launius, "Finley had an innate understanding of how to build a championship club. He could find talent, sign it, and develop it. For instance, he could call up other teams' scouts and get them to tell him who their hot properties were and then go sign these players out from underneath them. Finley was the master manipulator and super salesman."[9]

Finley's talent was no less acknowledged by those who played for him. Reminiscing to sportswriter Leonard Koppett of the *New York Times* upon Finley's death in 1996, Catfish Hunter, whose own stormy relationship with Finley is well-documented, stated that Finley "was the type of owner who knew a lot about baseball and knew how to get great players and win; he was 10 to 20 years ahead of his time."[10]

The testament to Finley's talents as an evaluator lay in the core of Oakland's championship teams, which was assembled and developed primarily while the A's were in Kansas City. Under his auspices, A's scouts including Marv Olson, Ray Sanders, Don Pries, Felix Delgado, Clyde Kluttz, and Jack Sanford fanned out across the country and Latin America and unearthed the athletes who developed together in Finley's farm system and later came of age in Oakland. As a result of this scouting network, we can envision the sight of

Home Grown A's Who Played On All Three Championship Teams

Player	Year joined the A's	How selected	School
Dick Green	1960	Signed by the KC A's as amateur free agent	Mitchell HS, Mitchell, SD
Bert Campaneris	1961	Signed by the KC A's as amateur free agent	Cuba
Ted Kubiak*	1961	Signed by the KC A's as amateur free agent	Highland Park (NJ) High School
Joe Rudi	1964	Signed by the KC A's as amateur free agent	Downey High School, Modesto, CA
Jim "Catfish" Hunter	1964	Signed by the KC A's as amateur free agent	Perquimans High School, Hertford, NC
John "Blue Moon" Odom	1964	Signed by the KC A's as amateur free agent	Ballard Hudson High School, Macon, GA
Rollie Fingers	1964	Signed by the KC A's as amateur free agent	Upland High School, Upland, CA
Gene Tenace	1965	Drafted by the KC A's, 20th round MLB amateur draft	Valley Local high School, Lucasville, OH
Sal Bando	1965	Drafted by the KC A's, 6th round, inaugural MLB amateur draft	Arizona State University
Reggie Jackson	1966	Drafted by the KC A's, 1st round, second overall pick, MLB amateur draft	Arizona State University
Dave Hamilton	1966	Drafted by the KC A's, 5th round, MLB amateur draft	Edmonds High School, Edmonds, WA
Vida Blue	1967	Drafted by the KC A's, 2nd round, 27th overall pick, MLB amateur draft	DeSoto High School, Mansfield, LA

*Kubiak was signed as a free agent by Kansas City in 1961. After six seasons in the A's farm system, he joined Kansas City in 1967 and moved with the team to Oakland, playing through the 1969 season. However, in 1970 Kubiak was traded to Milwaukee and subsequently played for two more teams before Finley reacquired him in a trade midway through the 1972 season.

Finley sitting in a family kitchen in Hertford, North Carolina, or Macon, Georgia, sharing pork chops, grits, or corn on the cob and discussing with wide-eyed yet perhaps skeptical parents what he would do for their sons, then writing sometimes substantial checks to ensure that he obtained the services of the young men he was sure would bring his team success.

Over the course of the A's three consecutive world championships, 75 players appeared in at least one regular-season game for Oakland. Of those, only 17 played all three seasons; and of those, 12 players were signed or drafted by Kansas City and developed within the organization. That core group is represented in the table above.

NOTES

1   amazon.com/Charlie-Finley-Outrageous-Baseballs-Showman/dp/B0057DCJL8.

2   G. Michael Green and Roger D. Launius, *Charlie Finley, The Outrageous Story of Baseball's Super Showman* (New York: Walker and Company, 2010).

3   nwitimes.com/niche/shore/profiles/new-biography-reveals-the-good-and-bad-of-laporte-s/article_700350a3-6de2-53ce-8ddb-58f644efb69f.html.

4   espn.go.com/classic/biography/s/Finley_Charles.html.

5   launiusr.wordpress.com/2012/02/24/bill-veeck-and-charlie-finley-what-about-mlb-hall-of-fame-enshrinement/.

6   espn.go.com/classic/biography/s/Finley_Charles.html.

7   Ibid.

8   amazon.com/Charlie-Finley-Outrageous-Baseballs-Showman/dp/B0057DCJL8..

9   content.usatoday.com/communities/dailypitch/post/2010/06/as-former-owner-charlie-o-finley-revolutionized-game-died-broken-man/1#.VGYaXKg05Ms.

10   nytimes.com/1996/02/20/sports/charles-o-finley-baseball-team-owner-who-challenged-traditions-diesat-77.html.

Sal Bando

By Gregory H. Wolf

Team captain Sal Bando was the glue that held the volatile Oakland A's together during their three-year run as World Series champions (1972-1974). Respected by teammates, peers, and his managers, Bando was Oakland's unequivocal leader, a durable, rough-and-tumble third baseman who averaged 23 home runs and 90 runs batted in over an eight-year span in an offensively depressed era (1969-1976). Often overlooked while playing in the shadows of teammate Reggie Jackson and arguably the best third baseman in big-league history, Brooks Robinson, the four-time All-Star Bando finished second, third, and fourth in the AL Most Valuable Player voting from 1971 to 1974, and clouted 242 home runs in his 16-year big-league career (1966-1981)

Salvatore Leonard Bando was born on February 13, 1944, in Cleveland. His parents were both athletic; Ben Bando, a self-employed carpenter, was an accomplished infielder in slow- and fast-pitch softball leagues. Mother Angela Bando, a homemaker and admitted tomboy, played softball and basketball. Sal and his younger siblings, Victoria and future big-league catcher Chris, grew up in middle-class Warrensville Heights, located about 16 miles southeast of Cleveland. Sal was an athletic youngster whose parents encouraged him to pursue his passions. "As soon as Sal was old enough to throw a ball," said father Ben. "He'd say, 'C'mon, dad, let's play catch.' I didn't teach him. I just played with him and let him do what came naturally."[1] Sal was a star athlete at Warrensville Heights High School, where he was an All-City quarterback with aspirations of playing in the Big Ten Conference; he also played shortstop in baseball and forward in basketball, and ran track. During the summer Sal played baseball in the Connie Mack League, where he came under the tutelage of Rick Leskovec, a math instructor at Arizona State University and coach of the Go team. Lescovec moved Bando

to third base and later recommended him to ASU head baseball coach Bobby Winkles who offered Bando a scholarship upon graduation in 1962.

Bando's two-year baseball career at Arizona State signaled even greater things to come. As a sophomore in 1964 the strong-armed third baseman batted .347 and led the Sun Devils to the Western Athletic Conference Championship and the institution's first berth in the College World Series. In 1965 the right-hander hit at a .317 clip, was named all-conference, and helped lead a talent-heavy team (nine players were drafted by the big leagues) to the WAC title and College World Series Championship. He batted .480 (12-for-25) with nine runs batted in the CWS and was named the tournament's most outstanding player. (Bando was inducted into the College Baseball Hall of Fame in 2013.) The Kansas City Athletics drafted

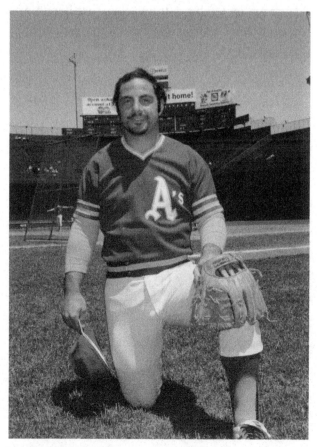

Bando in the sixth round in the inaugural major-league draft. He was signed by Athletics scout Henry Peters and received a reported $35,000 bonus.[2]

Bando progressed quickly through the Athletics farm system. In 1965 he was assigned to the Burlington (Iowa) Bees in the Class A Midwest League. In a half-season with the team, he was named to the league's all-star team and batted .262. Bando was a nonroster invitee at the A's spring training in 1966, but was among those cut early, and assigned to Mobile of the Double-A Southern League. The A's praised Bando for his "truly spectacular arm" at third base, but were also concerned about his hitting.[3] A spray hitter in college with little power, Bando improved his average to .277 at Mobile and showed some pop in his bat with 12 home runs. With the A's en route to their 14th consecutive losing season, Bando was a September call-up, and went 0-for-3 against Jim Lonborg in a 7-0 loss to the Boston Red Sox in his major-league debut on September 3 at Kansas City's Municipal Stadium. As a pinch-hitter, Bando collected his first hit (a single) off Clyde Wright of the California Angels on September 7. It was clear that Bando was the club's third baseman of the future; the question was when the future began.

After another abbreviated spring training, Bando was assigned to the Vancouver Mounties of the Triple-A Pacific Coast League. On May 10 the A's traded third baseman Ed Charles (who had occupied the hot corner since 1962), paving the way for Bando. Sal impressed with his defense, but struggled at the plate, hitting only .143 (9-for-63) in four weeks, and was sent back to Vancouver to iron out his hitting woes. "That was the first blow I'd ever had in baseball," recalled Bando. "I was hurt that they thought I couldn't play in the majors."[4] A's manager Al Dark had instructed Bando to crouch in his batting stance, but Mounties manager Mickey Vernon suggested that the 24-year-old take a more natural approach and stand straighter to help extend his arms and open up his swing.[5] Responding to Vernon's mentorship, Bando batted .291 and showed a discerning eye at the plate (.392 on-base percentage). He was named to the PCL All-Star second team and

voted best defensive third baseman in a poll of league managers. Bando earned another September call-up and batted a more respectable .239 (16-for-67), and finished with a .192 average and only five extra-base hits (no home runs) in 130 at-bats for both his stints in the majors. In preparation of a full season at third base, Bando was sent to Arecibo in the Puerto Rican winter league, where he was among the league's hottest hitters, batting well over .300.

The A's 13-year experiment in Kansas City came to a conclusion with the club's move to Oakland in 1968. Excitement was palpable during spring training when "slugging sensation" Bando surprisingly walloped ten home runs.[6] "Tabbed for greatness" (in the words of *The Sporting News*), Bando launched his first big-league home run in the second game of the season (a two-run shot off Phil Ortega in a 9-6 win over the Washington Senators), but didn't hit another one until the 30th game. In the "Year of the Pitcher," when AL batters hit a composite .230, Bando finished the season with a solid .251 batting average and nine home runs, and was second on the team with 67 runs batted in. More importantly, the A's notched their first winning season since 1952.

Bando's first full season revealed his durability (he played in 162 games) and aggressive, hard-nosed defensive play, which invited comparisons to the best third-sacker in the game. "He's got his body moving forward," said Bando of the difference between him and the Baltimore Orioles' Brooks Robinson. "He keeps his hands up. I keep mine down. My glove's webbing is touching the ground because I can bring my hands up [easier] instead of down."[7] Often described as stocky, the 6-foot-tall, 200-pound Bando may not have appeared as lithe and graceful as Robinson, and did not cover as much ground, but he made up for it with his quick release and hard throw to second and first base; and the ball typically had a low trajectory. "Bando has such a strong arm," raved A's beat reporter Ron Bergman writing for *The Sporting News*, "that he can run down the ball after taking it in the chest and get the runner out."[8] Although he never won a Gold Glove, Bando annually ranked in the top five in putouts, assists, and double plays.

Bando took full advantage of Major League Baseball's decision to lower the pitching mound to ten inches in 1969 in an effort to stimulate offense by belting five home runs and driving in 17 runs in 19 games in April, including his career day at the plate (3-for-4 with two home runs, seven knocked in). Bando credited Joe DiMaggio (an A's executive vice president and occasional bench coach in 1968 and 1969) for his improvement. Bando had a wide stance with his right foot placed at the back of the batter's box; the Yankee Clipper suggested that he close his stance and keep his head down to generate more power.[9] The results were immediate: by the All-Star break Bando had 18 home runs and 64 RBIs.

In what was described as the "biggest upset of the American League players' voting," Bando's peers chose him over Robinson to start the Midsummer Classic in Washington.[10] In the AL's 9-3 loss, Bando smacked a single off Bob Gibson for his only hit in three at-bats. Bando slumped after the All-Star Game, but enjoyed the most productive month in his career in September (9 HRs and 29 RBIs in 30 games) to set career highs in home runs (31), runs batted in (113), hits (171), and runs (106). He also played in every inning of every game.

Pressure and increasingly high expectations came with the A's new-found success. Manager Hank Bauer named Bando team captain in May 1969 to help the young team forge an identity, and he held the title throughout his tenure with the A's. "[Bando] has capabilities of being a leader out there on the field," said Bauer. "He deserves the job on the basis of baseball instinct and knowledge."[11] Just 25 years old, Bando got along with his teammates well, had earned their respect for his hustle and willingness to play through injuries, and put winning above personal statistics and fame, but was not a rah-rah type. "I was a leader by example not by talking," said Bando later in his career. "You don't tell a (Reggie) Jackson, a (Jim) Hunter, or a (Joe) Rudi what to do. You lead by example, by giving 100 percent, by giving a continuous effort. A successful individual is one who is dedicated, on and off the field."[12]

With their fourth different Opening Day manager in four years, the A's began the 1970 season edgy after Bando's harsh contract negotiations with owner Charley Finley and Reggie Jackson's holdout. The poor start under John McNamara made clubhouse tensions even worse. Bando was the team's hottest hitter through the All-Star break, almost replicating his numbers from the previous year (17 HRs and 56 RBIs), but the team languished in third place, 9½ games behind the Minnesota Twins. For the first time since 1957 fans voted for the position players at the All-Star Game. Bando was neither selected nor named by the coaching staff as a substitute. His "lack of recognition," suggested *The Sporting News*, was a product of playing in Oakland and not in a traditional bastion of baseball.[13] Despite Bando's horrendous second half (just three home runs and 19 runs batted in 75 games), the A's finished in second place.

The A's had played sloppy, uninspired ball under McNamara; consequently, it was no surprise that he was replaced at the end of the season. The choice of his successor raised eyebrows and hopes: Dick Williams, who had transformed the hapless Boston Red Sox into the AL pennant winners in 1967. "We need a guy to kick us in the rear every now and then," said Bando. "[Mac] said he just wasn't the type to jump all over guys and we liked that. We knew if we made a mistake, it wouldn't be too bad. But we didn't learn from our mistakes; we didn't take them seriously. I think that hurt us as the season wore on."[14] Williams arrived with a reputation as a tough-as-nails disciplinarian; players hoped he would stand up to Finley and his constant meddling.

In 1971 the A's captured their first of five consecutive AL West crowns behind a nucleus of players who came up through the team's farm system: Bando, Bert Campaneris, Joe Rudi, and Jackson, and pitchers Catfish Hunter, Vida Blue, and Rollie Fingers. Avoiding the Jekyll-and-Hyde act of the previous year, Bando had a consistent if not spectacular year, clouting 24 home runs and leading the team with 94 runs batted in. He finished second in MVP voting, behind teammate Blue. In their first postseason series since the franchise's World Series loss in 1931 when they were still located in Philadelphia, the A's lost three consecutive games to the Orioles in the ALCS. Bando was one of Oakland's lone highlights, going 4-for-11 with a home run off Jim Palmer in Game Three, and scored three of the club's seven runs.

Dick Williams and Bando developed a mutual trust and respect during the manager's tumultuous three-year tenure (1971-1973) with the team. Bando often claimed that the A's could win without the star players (Jackson, Hunter, and Blue), but not without Williams, who struck a visceral chord with the players. His intensity for winning, fundamentally sound baseball, and a team-first attitude matched Bando's. In his autobiography, *No More Mr. Nice Guy*, Williams wrote, "[Bando was] the only player I ever socialized with. I'd invite him to my hotel suite after games or during an offday, and we'd just talk baseball. The rest of the team saw this and figured I must be all right."[15]

Player salaries and pensions dominated offseason discussion and led to the first major-league-wide players strike in baseball history in 1972, the cancellation of 86 games, and a 13-day delay for Opening Day. While the A's got off to a torrid start, Bando unexpectedly struggled offensively for most of the season, reaching bottom over a 25-game stretch in late August through mid-September when he hit just .141 (11-for-78); however, Williams considered Bando's value to the team more than just with the bat and refused to bench him. "We can't afford not to play Sal," said Williams, whose team was in a fierce division race with the upstart Chicago White Sox in September.[16] Bando finished with 15 home runs and led the team with 77 runs batted in, but his batting average dipped to .236.

The A's defeated the Detroit Tigers in five games in the ALCS to set the stage for a World Series of polar opposites, dubbed the "Hairs vs. the Squares." The outsized personalities of the "Swinging A's" shunned baseball tradition by proudly sporting mustaches and beards ("We got a $300 bonus for growing a mustache,"

said Bando)[17] and faced the more traditional, clean-shaven, staid, and favorite Cincinnati Reds. The A's overcame the absence of Jackson (who injured his hamstring in the ALCS) with the slugging of Gene Tenace (four HRs) and pitching brilliance. Bando (7-for-26 in the series) knocked in only one run, but it gave the A's their third and final run in their 3-1 Game Seven victory.

Bando was an outspoken critic of Finley's constant meddling in players' matters and lives, the lack of a television contract to broadcast A's games in the Bay area, and general fan apathy. "In another town, someplace back East, we might be heroes," said Bando in May 1973. "Here we're not even something special."[18] The A's ranked eighth and 11th (among 12 AL teams) in attendance in 1973 and 1974 despite the championships while the Coliseum was derided as the "mausoleum" for its mortuary-like atmosphere. "The Oakland Coliseum is the worst park in baseball," Bando said. "The weather is terrible, there's too much room beyond the foul lines, the ball doesn't travel well, the players lack good parking facilities, and the security for our families and ourselves is poor."[19]

The A's encountered a difficult adversary in the Kansas City Royals en route to their third consecutive AL West crown in 1973. They fell into second early in August, but the team's sluggers and three 20-game winners (Ken Holtzman, Hunter, and Blue) proved too much for the inexperienced Royals. Bando was at his best during the last month of the season, batting .390 (39-for-100), scoring 26 times, and driving in 29 runs in 29 games. For the third of four times in his career, Bando led the league in games played (162), and also belted 29 home runs, knocked in 98 runs, and batted .287 to finish fourth in MVP voting. Bando socked two home runs and drove in three in Game Two of the ALCS against the Baltimore Orioles, but was otherwise quiet with the bat (3-for-18) in Oakland's five-game victory.

The A's exciting, yet emotionally draining World Series triumph over the New York Mets in seven games was overshadowed by Finley's stifling control culminating with his attempt to have second baseman Mike

Andrews declared medically unfit to play after he committed two costly errors in Oakland's loss in Game Two, at home. Even before that incident Dick Williams informed the team of his plan to resign at the end of the season. Upon the team's arrival in Game Three at Shea Stadium, Bando led an open revolt against Finley by suggesting that the team wear black armbands in Andrews' honor. As the brouhaha escalated, Commissioner Bowie Kuhn intervened and denied Finley's request to replace Andrews with Manny Trillo. "It's been a long season," said a depressed and mentally exhausted Bando after the A's lost two of three in New York. "Guys are looking forward for it to end."[20] The A's rode on the back of regular season and Series MVP Reggie Jackson to win Games Six and Seven and capture the title.

Bando's offseason was marred by rumors of his impending trade and a bitter salary dispute ultimately settled by an arbitrator. "As the success of the team developed," Bando said years later, "[Finley] became more difficult to deal with. He became an adversary of the players."[21] Reports that Bando would succeed Williams as manager incensed Finley, who named former A's skipper Al Dark to pilot the team. Bando (and many teammates) were displeased with the choice, especially in light of Williams's success and support of the players. Dark was seen as a company man, much like McNamara. Bando's displeasure with Dark came to a head on June 19 when he said. "Dark couldn't manage a flipping meat market" with his skipper standing behind him.[22] They ultimately reconciled their relationship, and Bando accepted and respected Dark's new-found sedate approach.[23]

While internal struggles threatened to consume the team, the A's cruised to yet another AL West crown. "On a team in which trouble bubbles like a live volcano" wrote A's beat writer Ron Bergman, "Bando, more than anyone else, keeps teammates relaxed and thinking about baseball."[24] Bando led the team with 103 runs batted in and belted 22 home runs. He was named to the All-Star Game for the third consecutive year, but did not play due to a foot injury. The star of the ALCS against the Orioles, Bando hit a home run off

Jim Palmer in Game Three that accounted for the only run in a 1-0 victory; and he scored both of Oakland's two runs in the deciding Game Four victory. The A's defeated the prohibitive favorite Los Angeles Dodgers in five games in the World Series, but Bando's bat was silent (1-for-16) though he scored a team-high three runs and drove in two. Bando was one of 13 A's players who participated on all three championship teams.[25]

Bando's relationship with Finley hit its nadir in the offseason when he filed for arbitration seeking a salary increase to $125,000. "[Bando is] a popoff and one of the worst fielding third baseman in baseball," said Finley, taking his fight with Bando public.[26] After winning the arbitration hearing, Finley triumphantly announced, "There are too many players in baseball who want unjustified, astronomical salaries. It is my obligation to … stop these shenanigans."[27] Dark guided the A's to their fifth consecutive AL crown, but Bando struggled all season at the plate. Batting just .198 with a month left on the season, Bando hit .354 in his final 29 games with 29 runs batted in to salvage his year. The A's dynasty ended at the hands of the Boston Red Sox, who swept them in the best-of-five ALCS.

In his final season in Oakland, Bando was one of seven players (the others were Blue, Rudi, Don Baylor, Campanaris, Tenace, and Fingers) who refused to sign a contract in order to be declared free agents at the end of the season. Finley summarily cut their salary by the maximum 20 percent allowed, and declared his willingness to sell any of his unsigned players for one million dollars.[28] Tempers came to a boil after Bowie Kuhn voided Finley's sale of Rudi and Fingers to Boston and Blue to the Yankees at the June 15 trading deadline. Finley subsequently filed a lawsuit against Kuhn and refused to permit new skipper Chuck Tanner to play the three. "We went about ten days in June without them," said Bando. "Finally I had to tell [Finley] that we were striking if he didn't start using them. Marvin Miller (then executive director of the Players Association) called me and said, 'Don't walk out.' But still we voted to walk out just before a game against Minnesota [on June 27] and were ready to forfeit it."[29] Sensing the gravity of the players' threat, Finley acquiesced. Bando rebounded in 1976 to belt a team-high 27 home runs (second most in the AL) and knocked in 84 runs, but the A's finished in second place.

Bando's "value to the team transcends what he does on the field," wrote Ron Bergman of the *Oakland Tribune*.[30] In an offensively depressed era, Bando was extremely durable, averaging 156 games played, 23 home runs, and 90 runs batted in for the A's from 1969 through 1976. Though he batted just .257, his on-base percentage (a statistic not as valued at the time) was .366. Advanced sabermetric statistical analysis may help shed light on just how valuable Bando was. In a five-year period (1969-1973), Bando's WAR (33.6) was the highest in all of baseball, besting Joe Morgan, Johnny Bench, Reggie Jackson, and Pete Rose.[31]

Bando was granted free agency at the end of the 1976 season and signed a five-year contract worth a reported $1.5 million with the Milwaukee Brewers. Team president Bud Selig saw Bando as a veteran leader who could serve as a mentor to the young players and in the words of *Milwaukee Sentinel* writer Lou Chapman end the "loser image" of the team.[32] After a sixth-place finish in Bando's first season, the Brewers slugged their way to 93 wins in 1978 for the first of a franchise-record six consecutive winning seasons.

Bando contributed with 17 home runs and about 80 runs batted in each of his first two seasons while playing in excess of 150 games each year. After playing in 130 games and hitting just nine home runs in 1979, Bando was named player-coach for his last two seasons (1980 and 1981) while still occasionally playing third base and serving as designated hitter, but batted just .197 and .200 respectively. Bando enjoyed a last hurrah of sorts when the Brewers faced the New York Yankees in the 1981 League Division Series following the strike-shortened season. Starting at third base in all five games, Bando went 5-for-17 with three doubles in the team's first-ever postseason appearance. He declined an invitation to return to the team in 1982 and concluded his 16-year big-league career with 242 home

runs, 1,039 RBIs, and a .254 batting average in 2,019 games. In 44 postseason games he hit .245 (39-for-159) with five round-trippers and 13 runs batted in.

Bando was well-prepared to transition to life after his playing days were over. A constant source of support and grounding was his wife, the former Sandy Fortunato, a New Jersey resident he met while playing in the Puerto Rican winter league, and married in 1969. They had three sons, Sal Jr., Sonny, and Stefano. During his playing days, Sal had invested shrewdly, lived within his means, and regularly had offseason jobs, most notably as a sports radio host and in banking. In retirement he founded a successful investment company with former Milwaukee Bucks player Jon McGlocklin.

Financially secure, Bando served as special assistant to Brewers GM Harry Dalton from 1982 to 1991. It was a part-time position that allowed Bando to maintain his close ties to baseball and remain living in the Milwaukee area, where he had established firm roots. His primary responsibilities were to serve as a liaison between players and management, periodically visit minor-league affiliates, and offer insights about players and teams.

Bando was named the Brewers GM in October 1991 and served in that position until August 1999. During his eight years as GM, the team had only one winning season (1992). Operating in the smallest market in baseball, Bando and the Brewers struggled to field competitive teams as salaries skyrocketed throughout the decade, especially before Major League Baseball instituted revenue sharing in 1996 to stimulate competiveness. In a public-relations nightmare evoking memories of Charley Finley, Bando allowed fan favorite Paul Molitor to depart via free agency after the 1992 season. Robin Yount retired the following season leaving a void in team leadership. Dale Hoffmann of the *Milwaukee Journal-Sentinel* wrote, "When mediocrity becomes not so much a goal, as a dream, it takes more than a stern lecture from a new voice to correct the problem."[33] Bando was replaced by Dean Taylor, but the Brewers waited eight more years before their next winning season, in 2007.

As of 2013 Bando lived with his wife in the Milwaukee and Phoenix areas. He was the CEO of Middletown Doll Company, which had a host of investment businesses associated with it. Though he no longer had formal ties to any professional baseball team, the 69-year old Bando remained close to the game as a fan.

SOURCES

Newspapers

Chicago Tribune

Cleveland Plain Dealer

Milwaukee Journal

Milwaukee Sentinel

Milwaukee Journal-Sentinel

New York Times

Oakland Tribune

The Sporting News

Radio Interviews

With John Lund and Greg Papa on July 15, 2013, for 95.7 FM (San Francisco): media.957thegame.com/a/78170288/sal-bando-looks-back-on-his-time-with-the-a-s-in-the-70s.htm

With Jimmy Scott for *Jimmy Scott's High and Tight:* http://www.jimmyscottshighandtight.com/node/118

With Thetford and Ashby for 104.3 FM (Lubbock, Texas): double1043.com/content/thetfordashby/story/Sportstalk-Interview-Sal-Bando/KGBGqfQsPoC_Vf3DwcI5Qg.cspx

Other

Sal Bando player file, National Baseball Hall of Fame, Cooperstown, New York

NOTES

1   Hal Lebovitz, "Hal asks: What's behind a big leaguer?," *The Plain Dealer* (Cleveland), April 4, 1982, [no page]. Player's Hall of Fame file.

2   Ed Leavitt, "The Year of the Mule," *Oakland Tribune*, August 30, 1971, 58.

3   *The Sporting News*, September 24, 1966, 16.

4   *The Sporting News*, March 30, 1968, 6.

5   Ibid.

6   *The Sporting News*, April 13, 1968, 44.

7   *The Sporting News*, July 27, 1968, 5

8   *The Sporting News*, July 27, 1968, 5.

9   *The Sporting News*, June 14, 1969, 4.

10   Ron Bergman, "Stars Will Gaze at Reggie, Sal," *Oakland Tribune*, July 10, 1969, 37.

11   "Capt. Bando Takes Duty in Stride," *Oakland Tribune*, June 1, 1969, 3C.

12   "Bando. Looking Forward to '78 Season Following Hectic First Year With Club," *Brewers Scorebook*, 1978, 11.

13   *The Sporting News*, July 11, 1970, 19.

14   *The Sporting News*, December 12, 1970, 56.

15   Dick Williams, *No More Mr. Nice Guy* quoted from Bill James, *The New Bill James Historical Baseball Abstract* (New York: Free Press, 2001), 548.

16   *The Sporting News*, September 23, 1972, 7.

17   *The Sporting News*, February 24, 1973, 41.

18   *The Sporting News*, May 26, 1973, 20.

19   Ibid.

20   Ron Bergman, "Depressed A's Face Met 'Believers,'," *Oakland Tribune*, October 10, 1973, 13E.

21   Interview with Jimmy Scott for Jimmy Scott's High and Tight. jimmyscottshighandtight.com/node/118.

22   Ron Bergman, "Sal Says Dick Can't Manage," *Oakland Tribune*, June 20, 1974, E37.

23   Dark was a hot-headed manager with the A's in the late 1960s; however, when he returned to the club in 1974 his personality had changed radically. A self-described born-again Christian, Dark was no longer the screaming, tantrum-throwing firebrand. He openly talked about Christianity. Bando credited Dark with leading him to his religious awakening (Sal Bando, "The Big Slump," *Guideposts*, July 1980).

24   *The Sporting News*, May 18, 1974, 23.

25   The 13 players who were on all three World Series teams are Sal Bando, Vida Blue, Bert Campaneris, Rollie Fingers, Dick Green, Ken Holtzman, Catfish Hunter, Reggie Jackson, Darold Knowles, Angel Mangual, Blue Moon Odom, Joe Rudi, and Gene Tenace; Knowles did not pitch in the 1972 or 1974 World Series, and Jackson did not play in the 1972 World Series.

26   "Bando is Worst Fielding 3rd Baseman in Baseball," (Associated Press) *Sarasota Herald-Times*, February 17, 1975, 2-C.

27   "Charley's Happy to Beat the Band-o," (Associated Press), *Binghamton* (New York) *Press*, February 20, 1975, 9-B.

28   *The Sporting News*, July 3, 1976, 8.

29   Sid Bordman, "Sal Bando says A's glory days should have been even better," *Kansas City Star* [no date]. Player's Hall of fame file.

30   *The Sporting News*, September 14, 1974, 21.

31   Wins Above Replacement, an advanced sabermetric statistic, presents, in the form of a single number, the number of wins the player added to the team above what a replacement player (e.g., Triple-A player) would add.

32 *The Sporting News*, March 5, 1977, 20.

33 Dale Hofmann, "Hold the door open for Bando," *Milwaukee Journal-Sentinel*, August 12, 1999 [no page]. Player's Hall of Fame file.

Vida Blue

By Richard J. Puerzer

Vida Blue burst onto the scene in major-league baseball as a fireballing left-hander for the Oakland A's and served as one of the primary characters in the A's streak of five division championships and three World Series championships. His career, which spanned from 1969 to 1986, would see high points, including the multiple World Series championships and outstanding pitching performances, as well as dark days, such as his suspension from the game for drug use and his involvement in one of the most publicized contract holdouts in the history of the game. In many ways, the ups and downs of Blue's baseball career, both on and off of the field, reflected the times during which he played perhaps more than any other of his contemporaries.

Vida Rochelle Blue, Jr. was born on July 28, 1949, in Mansfield, Louisiana, a small town in the northern part of the state. He was the eldest of six children born to Vida Blue, Sr. and Sallie Blue. His father was a laborer, and Blue remembered having everything he needed, although not everything that he wanted, as he grew up.[1] He recalled Mansfield as a town that was still segregated, with a white high school and a black high school, DeSoto High, which Blue attended. As a youngster Blue played baseball and football with his peers. He was a good athlete, and could throw a baseball very hard when he was still quite young.

When he entered high school, the school did not have a baseball team. However, the principal recognized Blue's talent and formed a school baseball team around him.[2] Blue's pitching prowess got the attention of scouts, including Kansas City A's scout Ray Swallow. Despite Blue's wildness—he once pitched a no-hitter and struck out 21 in a seven-inning game, but lost the game due to ten walks—his skill was evident. Blue was equally renowned as a high-school football player, starring as a quarterback. He was recruited by major

colleges, including Notre Dame, Purdue, and Houston. Houston was recruiting Blue to play quarterback at a time when there were no African-Americans playing quarterback for major colleges. But Blue's father died during his senior year in high school, and he decided that he needed to support his family. Baseball would provide that support sooner than football might. He was selected by the Kansas City Athletics in the second round of the 1967 draft and was offered a two-year contract a $12,500 per year. Although he later said he had a stronger desire to play football than baseball, Blue signed with the A's.

Blue's professional baseball career began in the Arizona winter instructional league in 1967. He pitched in nine games, striking out 26 batters while walking 22 in 34 innings. At age 18, he reported to spring training with the A's for the 1968 season, then was assigned to the Burlington Bees of the Class A Midwest League. Blue started the season opener against the Quad City

- 37 -

Angels and struck out 17 while giving up only three hits in eight innings. On June 19, in the first game of a doubleheader, Blue pitched a no-hitter in the seven-inning game. Throughout the season, Blue developed his curveball to go along with his dominant fastball, and improved his control. He finished with a record of 8-11 in 24 games, pitching 152 innings and striking out 231 while walking 80.[3]

For the 1969 season, Blue was assigned to Double-A Birmingham. He pitched in 15 Southern League games, going 10-3, with 112 strikeouts and 52 walks in 104 innings. Oakland A's owner Charlie Finley was anxious to bring Blue up to the majors, seeing him as his next pitching star. Blue was called up in July, and made his major-league debut on July 20, starting against the California Angels. He lost the game, pitching into the sixth inning and giving up home runs to Aurelio Rodriguez and Jim Spencer. He started three more games, including a win on July 29 over the New York Yankees, before being sent to the bullpen for the rest of the season. In his first major league season, he finished with a record of 1-1, pitched 42 innings, struck out 24 while walking 18, and finished with an earned-run average of 6.64. Joe DiMaggio, then a coach with the A's, said of Blue, "It was a shame to bring up a kid like that when he hasn't pitched two pro years. He throws as hard as anybody, but he hasn't learned to pitch yet."[4]

Blue was sent to the Triple-A Iowa Oaks (American Association) to start the 1970 season. There he crossed paths with fellow pitcher Juan Pizarro. Blue learned a great deal from the veteran Pizarro, and later said that "[Pizarro] helped me more than any single person in my career."[5] With Pizarro's help, Blue made adjustments in his delivery that helped him to achieve greatness. He was rested for a few weeks in the middle of the season because of an injury, but came back to finish the season. In 17 games, Blue put together a record of 12-3 while striking out 165 in 133 innings.

He was called up to the A's in September, and started the first game of a Labor Day doubleheader against the White Sox in Chicago's Comiskey Park. Although he helped himself by hitting a three-run home run,

he was knocked out of the game after giving up four runs in less than five innings. However, in his next outing he pitched a complete-game one-hitter against the Kansas City Royals, giving up a single to Pat Kelly with two outs in the eighth inning. After a lackluster start against the Milwaukee Brewers, Blue faced the division-leading Minnesota Twins on September 21. He was matched against Jim Perry, who would win 23 games and the Cy Young Award that season. Blue was the star that night, however, throwing a no-hitter and walking only one batter. Finley telephoned the locker room after the game to congratulate his new star pitcher and tell him he would receive a $2,000 bonus for the performance. Blue made two more starts that season and finished the season as one of the young star pitchers in baseball. Along with Catfish Hunter, Blue Moon Odom, and Rollie Fingers, the A's pitching staff was one of the primary reasons the A's would have high expectations for the next few seasons.

Although Blue made a spectacular splash in 1970, his 1971 season ranked among the great pitching seasons of all time. The A's made the franchise's first postseason appearance since 1931. It may have been their best season of the 1970s despite the fact that they won the World Series in the following three seasons, 1972-1974.

Blue pitched the 1971 season opener for the A's in Washington against the Senators, and took the loss, pitching only into the second inning. He then won ten straight games, including nine complete games, and over the course of the season received the attention of the nation. He appeared on the cover of *Sports Illustrated* and *Time*. As a hard-throwing left-hander, the press compared Blue favorably to Sandy Koufax. However, this comparison was clearly difficult for Blue as Koufax was one of the greatest pitchers ever, and his prowess was nearly impossible to match. Veteran player Tommy Davis was one of Blue's best friends and a roommate that season. Davis helped him to navigate through the heavy load of press requests, as well other demands for his time. Anything Blue did drew the attention of the press. For example, it became known that he carried two dimes in his pocket when he pitched. Although it was likely a charm Blue used in his pursuit of winning 20 games, he would not verify that to the press, which drew even more attention.

Blue's start on July 9 against the California Angels was perhaps his best performance of the season. Although he did not get a decision in the game (he was going for his 18th win), he went 11 innings, gave up seven hits, no walks, and no runs while striking out 17 batters. The A's eventually won the game 1-0 in 20 innings. In his next appearance, Blue started the All-Star Game for the American League. Although he gave up home runs to Henry Aaron and Johnny Bench, he was the winning pitcher, the youngest in All-Star Game history. Blue's performance declined slightly in the second half of the season. He won his 20th game on August 7, and won his next two starts, raising the question of whether he could win 30 games for the season. But after number 22, he won only two and lost four of his last nine starts of the season. Surely he tired as the season wore on. The previous season, between the minors and majors, Blue pitched only 171 innings. In 1971, he pitched 312 innings. He finished the season with a record of 24-8 and a league-leading ERA of 1.82, and allowed the fewest runners per inning in the American League.

In the American League Championship Series, Blue faced off against the defending champion Baltimore Orioles and pitcher Dave McNally in Game One in Baltimore. The Orioles matched the A's in wins, with 101, and the opening game would be a test of Blue. He had a 3-0 lead going into the bottom of the fourth inning, but gave up a run in that inning, and four more in the eighth to lose the game. The A's were swept in three games, bringing an anticlimactic close to Blue's magical season.

Despite his dominant regular-season performance, Blue had competition for the American League Cy Young Award. Detroit's Mickey Lolich had surpassed Blue in wins with 25 to Blue's 24, and in strikeouts, 308 to 301 (although Lolich pitched a staggering 376 innings). However, Blue edged out Lolich to win the Cy Young Award. Blue actually had an easier time winning the American League Most Valuable Player

Award, finishing well ahead of teammate Sal Bando in the voting.

In 1971 Blue became involved in his first controversy with owner Charlie Finley. Finley offered Blue $2,000 to change his middle name legally to "True." The always creative Finley saw the nickname as another way to market his pitching superstar. Blue declined the offer. He liked his name, thought it unique as it was, and had no desire to change it. Finley however would not let the idea rest. When Blue pitched, his name appeared on the scoreboard as "True Blue." Finley instructed the A's radio and television announcers to refer to Blue by the nickname. Blue asked them to stop, and also asked the team's public-relations people not to refer to him as True Blue in press releases or to use the name on the scoreboard. This situation began the friction between Blue and Finley that blew up after the end of the season.

After his spectacular 1971 season, Blue demanded a pay raise. In 1971 he had made $14,750 in salary and $6,365.58 as his share of the postseason money, and also got a Cadillac as a bonus from Finley. Finley offered a raise, but not nearly what Blue wanted. Bob Gerst, an attorney representing Blue, presented an opening offer to Finley of $115,000. Later he told Finley that Blue would accept $85,000, which was a little less than the average salary paid to the top ten highest paid pitchers in baseball. Finley said he would pay Blue no more than $50,000. Finley held firm, making the negotiations public and declaring that Blue would not be seeking so much if he had not hired a lawyer to represent him. Both sides made their case to the press and the public, and the acrimonious situation became referred to as "The Holdout." The situation also served to elevate scrutiny of the reserve clause, which was under new attack by the players. Marvin Miller, director of the Players Association, was critical of Finley and the reserve system. The holdout extended into spring training. On March 16 Blue and Gerst held a televised press conference to announce that Blue was withdrawing from baseball to take a position with the Dura Steel Products Company. While Blue actually did work for the company for a time, this was obviously an effort to combat Finley as it was clearly Blue's desire to play baseball.

When the season started, Blue was placed on the restricted list, meaning he could not play for the first 30 days of the season. The major-league season was delayed ten days by a players strike in spring training, and opened on April 15 without Vida Blue. In late April Commissioner Bowie Kuhn organized a meeting between Finley, Blue, and Gerst. They reached an agreement on a $63,000 deal. However, Finley and Blue couldn't agree on the wording of the announcement of the agreement. Finley did not want to appear as conceding anything, and insisted that he was paying Blue $50,000, an additional $5,000 signing bonus, plus $8,000 for Blue's college fund. Blue wanted the deal to state what it was: payment of $63,000. Finally, on May 2, Blue signed for the package.[6]

Although Blue had missed only 18 playing days, he had not been conditioning and practicing as he would have during spring training and was not ready to pitch. He did not make his first appearance, which was only one inning long, until May 24. The 1972 season was tough for Blue. Although he did post a relatively good ERA of 2.80 and allowed only 165 baserunners in 151 innings, he finished with a disappointing record of 6-10. His team, of course, won the American League West and faced the Detroit Tigers in the League Championship Series. Blue pitched exclusively out of the buillpen, pitching middle relief in Games One, Three, and Four. In each appearance, the games were in the balance, and Blue acquitted himself well. In the fifth and decisive game, Blue relieved Blue Moon Odom in the sixth inning of a 2-1 game, and pitched the final four innings for the save. In the World Series against the Cincinnati Reds, Blue pitched in relief in Game One, picking up the save, as well as in Games Three and Four. With the A's leading three games to two, he started Game Six. He was not as sharp as a starter as he had been in relief, and allowed three runs, including a Johnny Bench home run, in 5⅔ innings, and took the loss. The A's won Game Seven,

In 1973 Blue returned to form as an All-Star-caliber pitcher. He went 20-9, with an ERA of 3.28. While he was not the power pitcher that he was in 1971, striking out 158 in 263⅔ innings, he was described by many as a smarter pitcher. A *Sports Illustrated* article quoted teammate Sal Bando as saying, "In the first part of 1971 Vida was overpowering everybody, now he is overmatching them."[7] The article described Blue's pitching style: "He jogs out to his position and works with quick efficiency, throwing his left-handed darts out of a fluid, high-kicking motion." Blue's pitching repertoire included his highly regarded fastball as well as a good curveball and changeup.

For the first four months of the 1973 season, Blue pitched well, but was often inconsistent. He hit his stride in August, winning six straight starts, including four complete games. He put together another streak of five consecutive wins in September, helping to lead the A's to a division win over the Kansas City Royals. In the American League Championship Series, Blue started Game One against the Baltimore Orioles' ace, Jim Palmer. Blue did not make it out of the first inning, giving up three hits and two walks before being relieved by Horacio Piña. Baltimore got four runs in the inning, and won, 6-0. Blue again faced Palmer in Game Four and pitched much better. Through six innings he shut out the Orioles, giving up only two hits as the A's held a 4-0 lead. However, after getting one out in the seventh, Blue gave up a walk to Earl Williams, a single to Don Baylor, an RBI single to Brooks Robinson, and a three-run home run to Andy Etchebarren, tying the game, 4-4. He was relieved by Rollie Fingers, who went on to lose the game, 5-4. In the World Series against the New York Mets, Blue's postseason troubles continued. He started Games Two and Five, both against Jerry Koosman. In Game Two, a high-scoring affair, Blue gave up solo home runs to Cleon Jones and Wayne Garrett. He was relieved in the sixth inning after allowing two baserunners who would later score. The Mets went on to win the game 10-7 in 12 innings. In Game Five, Blue gave up two runs in 5⅔ innings and lost to Koosman who, with reliever Tug McGraw, shut out the A's, 2-0. The A's won the Series, softening the effects of Blue's lackluster pitching.

In 1974, although his won-lost record was not as impressive as in 1973, Blue pitched equally well. He finished with a record of 17-15 and an ERA of 3.25. He was durable, making 40 starts, and struck out 174 batters in 282⅓ innings. The A's faced off again against the Orioles in the AL Championship Series. With the series tied one game apiece, Blue started Game Three, matched up again against Jim Palmer. Unlike 1973, Blue pitched brilliantly. He pitched two-hit, no-walk shutout, striking out seven in the 1-0 win. In the World Series against the Los Angeles Dodgers, Blue started Games Two and Five, matched up against Don Sutton in both games. In Game Two he was bested by the Dodgers, giving up a run in the second and a two-run homer to Joe Ferguson in the sixth, taking the 3-2 loss. In Game Five Blue pitched five shutout innings before giving up two tying runs in the sixth. After allowing a walk in the seventh, Blue was relieved by Blue Moon Odom, who went on to win the game for the A's.

The 1975 season was Vida Blue's best since his masterful 1971 season. He started the All-Star Game and finished the season with a record of 22-11 and an ERA of 3.01. With the departure of Catfish Hunter to the Yankees, Blue and Ken Holtzman starred on the A's pitching staff and helped to lead the A's to their best record since 1971. Among his pitching highlights that season, Blue was the starter and one of four A's pitchers to pitch a combined no-hitter against the California Angels on September 28, in the last game of the season. However, after three straight World Series championships, the A's were swept in the AL Championship Series by the Boston Red Sox. Blue started Game Two against Reggie Cleveland. He gave up a two-run home run in the fourth inning to Carl Yastrzemski and two more hits before being relieved. Although he had ten more seasons in the major leagues, this was Blue's last postseason appearance. Over his career, his postseason numbers were unexceptional, with a record of 1-5 and an ERA of 4.31 in 17 appearances.

The 1976 season was another controversial year in Blue's career, although the controversy was not of his doing. Starting with the departure of Catfish Hunter

to the Yankees before the 1975 season and the trade of Reggie Jackson and Ken Holtzman to the Orioles before the 1976 season, the dynastic A's were being dismantled. Through mid-June, the A's were in fifth place in the West Division, 11 games behind the Royals. Blue had a record of 6-6 in 15 starts, with an ERA of 3.09. Then, just a few hours before the June 15 trade deadline, Charlie Finley announced that he was selling Blue to the New York Yankees for $1.5 million, and Joe Rudi and Rollie Fingers to the Red Sox for $2 million. However, the transactions were held up by Commissioner Bowie Kuhn. Kuhn and Finley had battled over a number of issues over the years, but this event brought their rancorous relationship to a breaking point. In retrospect, the attempted sale of these players was yet another step in the process of transitioning from the rule of the reserve system and moving toward free agency for players. It foreshadowed transactions in the years to come. Kuhn justified his concern with the transactions, stating: "The issue is whether the assignment of the contracts is appropriate or not under the circumstances. That's the issue I have to wrestle with. I have to consider these transactions in the best interest of baseball."[8]

On the 18th Kuhn announced that the sale of the three players would not be in the best interests of baseball, and disallowed them. Blue thus remained with the A's. However, with all of the legal threats made by Finley after Kuhn's ruling, Blue did not pitch again until July 2. Both he and the A's improved over the remainder of the season. Blue finished 1976 with a record of 18-13 and an ERA of 2.35, and the A's finished in second place, 2½ games behind the Royals.

In 1977 the team was truly dismantled, not by Finley's actions, but by his inaction in signing his players who were now eligible for free agency. Joe Rudi, Rollie Fingers, and Sal Bando, who had all been with the team throughout the championship years, left the A's via free agency. However, Blue had signed a three-year contract before the "trade" to the Yankees, and was ineligible for free agency. The 1977 season was a forgettable one for Blue. He led the league in losses with a record of 14-19, and had an ERA of 3.83. The A's

Also tried to sell to Reds
in 77 + was vetoed
Dec 77 - before 78 season

finished last in the American League West, behind even the expansion Seattle Mariners.

During 1978 spring training, Blue was traded to the San Francisco Giants, giving him a new opportunity. For Blue the A's got seven players and $300,000. The new environment with the Giants and distance from Charlie Finley helped to restore his career as he became the ace of the Giants' pitching staff. The Giants were a solid squad, and were in first place as late as August 15 before fading and finishing in third for the 1978 season. Blue started the All-Star Game for the National League, making him the first pitcher to start the game for both leagues. He had a very good year overall, going 18-10 with a 2.79 ERA. He finished third in the balloting for the NL Cy Young Award and was named *The Sporting News* National League Pitcher of the Year. Although he was only 28 years old and his career would extend on for several years, 1978 was Blue's last great year. In 1979 he and the Giants saw a significant decline. Blue finished the season with a record of 14-14 and an ERA of 5.01 while the Giants finished 19½ games under .500 and in fourth place. In 1980 Blue rebounded a bit, with a record of 14-10 and an ERA of 2.97. In the strike-shortened 1981 season, he went 8-6 with a 2.45 ERA. It was the first full season in Blue's career in which he did not win 14 or more games. He did pitch and get the win in the All-Star Game, becoming the only pitcher to win the game for each league.

On March 30, 1982, at the end of spring training, Blue was traded with another player to the Kansas City Royals for four players. He pitched pretty well for the Royals, with a record of 13-12 an ERA of 3.78, and led the pitching staff in strikeouts. He did fade at the end of the season. After throwing a one-hitter against the Mariners on September 13, Blue started four more games, losing his last three decisions while his ERA grew from 3.36 to 3.78. In 1983 Blue struggled mightily. After seven starts and a record of 0-3 he was relegated to the bullpen. He stayed in the pen and made spot starts, but did not pitch well in either role. With a record of 0-5 and an ERA of 6.01, he was released by the Royals on August 5.

At the time, Blue's problems on the field paled in comparison with his problems off the field. Blue and Royals teammates Willie Wilson, Jerry Martin, and Willie Mays Aikens were implicated in buying cocaine. Blue pleaded guilty to cocaine possession and served 81 days in prison. On December 15, 1983, he was suspended for a year by Commissioner Kuhn. He was out for the 1984 season, then after being reinstated he signed with the Giants in the spring of 1985. Considering that he had missed a full season, Blue pitched respectably as both a starter and reliever, going 8-8 with a 4.47 ERA in 1985. In 1986, he returned to the Giants, pitching exclusively as a starter, and went 10-10 with an ERA of 3.27. Blue was a free agent after the season and signed with the A's for 1987, but abruptly retired during spring training. It was rumored that he had tested positive for drugs and retired rather than face another possible drug suspension. In announcing his retirement, Blue suggested that he still struggled with drug addiction, stating, "I reached the point where I had to choose between baseball and life."[9] In an autobiography published in 2011, he indicated that he had struggled with substance abuse for much of his career: "Along with all the glory that I'd achieved, there was a growing darkness reaching for me. And the light began to dim as early as 1972."[10] It makes one wonder what his career might have been but for his struggle with drugs.

In 1992 Blue became eligible for election to the Baseball Hall of Fame. He received a modicum of support in the four years he was considered, with his highest vote total, 8.7 percent, occurring in 1993. He was automatically removed from the ballot in 1995 because of his low vote totals. Some have wondered why Blue did not receive more serious consideration for the Hall of Fame, considering that his career numbers are quite similar to those of his former teammate, Hall of Famer Catfish Hunter. Perhaps the negative impressions created by his drug problems led to his lack of consideration. Regardless of his worthiness for the Hall of Fame, Vida Blue was one of the top pitchers of his time. In his 2001 *Historical Baseball Abstract*, Bill James ranked Blue as the 86th best pitcher in the history of baseball. Blue finished his career with 209 wins and

161 losses, 2,175 strikeouts, three 20-win seasons, a Cy Young Award, and a Most Valuable Player Award in his 17-year major-league career.

After retirement Blue retained a close association with baseball. He played in the Senior Professional Baseball Association in 1989 and 1990. He became active in philanthropic work, and spoke to a number of audiences about his struggle with substance addiction. Most recently, Blue served as a television analyst for the San Francisco Giants.

SOURCES

Blue, Vida, as told to Marty Friedman, *Vida Blue: A Life* (Nashville, Indiana: Unlimited Publishing LLC, 2011).

Clark, Tom, *Champagne and Baloney: The Rise and Fall of Finley's A's* (New York: Harper and Row, 1976).

Clark, Tom, *Baseball: The Figures* (Berkeley, California: Serendipity Books, 1976).

Clark, Tom, *Blue* (Los Angeles: Black Sparrow Press, 1974).

Clark, Tom, *Fan Poems* (Plainfield, Vermont: North Atlantic Books, 1976).

James, Bill, *The New Bill James Historical Baseball Abstract* (New York: The Free Press, 2001).

James, Bill, and Rob Neyer, *The Neyer/James Guide To Pitchers* (New York: Fireside, 2004).

Kuhn, Bowie, *Hardball: The Education of a Baseball Commissioner* (New York: Times Books, 1987).

Libby, Bill, and Vida Blue. *Vida: His Own Story* (Englewood Cliffs, New Jersey: Prentice-Hall, Inc., 1972).

Markusen, Bruce, *A Baseball Dynasty: Charlie Finley's Swingin' A's* (Haworth, New Jersey: St. Johann Press, 2002).

Neyer, Rob, and Eddie Epstein, *Baseball Dynasties* (New York: W.W. Norton and Company, 2000).

baseball-reference.com

NOTES

1   Bill Libby and Vida Blue, *Vida: His Own Story*, 16.

2   Libby, 20.

3   Libby, 43-45.

4   Libby, 49.

5   Libby, 51.

6   Libby, 231-248.

7   Ron Fimrite, "Vida's Down With the Growing-Up Blues," *Sports Illustrated*. September 10, 1973.

8   Ron Fimrite, "Bowie Stops Charlie's Checks," *Sports Illustrated*, June 28, 1976.

9   Ron Fimrite, "Oakland A's Pitcher Vida Blue," *Sports Illustrated*, May 19, 1997.

10 Vida Blue, as told to Marty Friedman, *Vida Blue: A Life*, 55.

Bert Campaneris

By Rick Schabowski

Bert Campaneris had a distinguished 20-year major-league career that included six All-Star selections, six American League stolen-base crowns, and a major role in the Oakland Athletics' three world championships in the 1970s.

Dagoberto Campaneris was born on March 9, 1942, in Pueblo Nuevo, Cuba. His father was a mechanic in a factory. Campaneris had three brothers and four sisters. He attended Jose Tomas School in Pueblo Nuevo.

Campaneris was gifted with incredible speed and quickness, but the only sport he played was baseball. He competed in a Cuban Little League at the age of 11, and later was a catcher for a semipro team. He said he loved baseball so much that he even assisted as a groundskeeper. Reflecting on his childhood, Campaneris said, "I never worked in Cuba. All I did was play baseball. I play, I play, I play, I like to play."[1] At the Pan-Am Games in Costa Rica in 1961, he drew the attention of Kansas City Athletics scout Felix Delgado, who persisted in efforts to sign him. Eventually Campaneris signed a contract that called for a $1,000 bonus, payable only if he remained with the A's organization for at least 60 days. Campaneris was one of the last players to leave Cuba for the United States before the Castro revolution made emigration extremely rare.

Campaneris split the 1962 season between Daytona Beach (Florida State League) and Binghamton (New York) of the Class A Eastern League. Campaneris was eager to play at every position, and was ambidextrous. Once with Daytona Beach, he pitched both right-handed and left-handed in a two-inning relief appearance. He faced a switch-hitter during his stint on the mound, and changed over when he faced him.

Campaneris spent two months of the 1963 season on the disabled list with a sore arm but got into 48 games with Lewiston of the Northwest League and Binghamton where he caught, and batted .308 as the leadoff hitter. He spent the offseason playing for the A's team in the Florida Instructional League.

Campaneris began the 1964 season with Double-A Birmingham and batted .325. Playing shortstop, he was named to the Southern League all-star team.

On July 22, 1964, Campaneris was called up after A's shortstop Wayne Causey injured his elbow. After an overnight plane trip, he arrived in Minneapolis the next day two hours before the start of the A's game against the Twins, and had an unforgettable major-league debut. Playing shortstop and batting second, he sent a pitch by the Twins' Jim Kaat over the left-field fence in his first at-bat. In the seventh inning he hit another home run. He turned in a brilliant defensive play, singled, and stole a base in the A's 11 inning victory.

Campaneris became the second major leaguer to hit two home runs in a debut game, after the St. Louis Browns' Bob Nieman, who did it in 1951.

Campaneris finished the season batting .257 for the A's with 10 stolen bases in 67 games, and earned a spot on the Topps Major League Rookie All-Star team. He was in the major leagues to stay, though he spent the offseason playing for the Caguas Criollos in the Puerto Rican League.

In 1965 Campaneris battled his second cousin, Angels outfielder Jose Cardenal, for the American League stolen-base title. (Cardenal said in an interview that they played baseball together constantly during the youth.[2]) Campaneris won the stolen-base title with 51, besting Cardenal's second-place total of 37. He batted .270 with 23 doubles, a league-leading 12 triples, and 6 home runs.

Campaneris was honored with a "night" at Kansas City's Municipal Stadium on September 8, 1965. He marked the occasion by playing all nine positions in that night's game against the Angels. He started at shortstop, went to second base for the second inning, then successively played third base, each outfield position, and first base. He pitched the eighth inning, yielding a run, and caught the ninth inning. The 5-foot-10, 160-pound Campaneris injured his shoulder in a collision with Ed Kirkpatrick at home plate in the ninth and had to leave the game. He was out of the lineup for five games. He spent the offseason playing for Caracas in the Venezuelan League.

In 1966 Campaneris teamed with second baseman Dick Green, and their great range gave the A's a very dependable double-play combination. Green remarked, "I had never played with a shortstop who threw the ball that hard."[3] Campaneris led the league with 259 shortstop putouts. Again he led the league in stolen bases, pilfering 52 in 62 attempts.

In the A's last season in Kansas City, 1967, Campaneris captured his third consecutive stolen-base title with 55. On August 29 against Cleveland he belted three triples. His batting average for the season slipped to .248.

In 1968, the A's inaugural season in Oakland, Campaneris raised his batting average to .276, aided by a 15-game hitting streak between August 4 and 18 (including a five-hit game on the 9th). He captured his fourth consecutive stolen-base title with a career-high 62 thefts (he was caught stealing 22 times), and led the league with 177 hits and 642 at-bats. On August 29 he repeated his feat against Cleveland, again belting three triples. Of his success at the plate, Campaneris said, "Now, I'm trying to hit to right field. I was swinging too hard trying to hit it too hard."[4] He spent the offseason playing for Lara in the Venezuelan League, where he batted .335.

Campaneris had 62 steals in 1969, but his four- year reign as the AL stolen-base leader ended as came to an end in 1969 as Tommy Harper of the Seattle Pilots stole 73. Campaneris missed most of July after he fractured his right index finger while taking a double-play relay throw at second base in a game against Seattle on July 3. The injury kept him out of the lineup until July 25. For the season, Campaneris batted .260, and along with Reggie Jackson, Catfish Hunter, and a host of others led the A's to a contending role in the AL West. Oakland finished with an 88-74 record, nine games behind the division champion Minnesota Twins.

During the season Campaneris married Norma Fay, a Kansas City native. Afterward, the shy player said, "I had no one in the United States. I was so lonely. Now I got somebody to take care of me."[5]

In 1970 Campaneris batted .279, posting career highs in home runs (22) and RBIs (64). The A's finished second again with an 89-73 record, nine games behind the Twins.

The A's won the American League West title in 1971, by 16 games over the Kansas City Royals. Campaneris experienced a power outage that season, hitting only five round-trippers while batting .251. Two of his homers came in a game in Cleveland on May 12 off Sam McDowell. On September 6 Campaneris was thrown out of a game by home-plate umpire Russ Goetz after burying the plate with dirt while protesting a called third strike. Two days later, after stealing second he broke the base loose from its mooring, chased it five feet, and wrapped his arms around it so he wouldn't be called out. In the American League Championship Series, Oakland was swept by the Baltimore Orioles.

Campaneris had a great season in 1972, leading the league in chances (795), at-bats (625), and stolen bases (52). He finished second to Boston's Luis Aparicio in balloting for the All-Star Game. Even after Aparicio broke a finger and couldn't play, AL manager Earl Weaver selected Texas shortstop Toby Harrah. Harrah was also unable to play because of a sore shoulder, and Weaver then selected Orioles shortstop, Bobby Grich, who played the entire 10 innings in the game, much to Campaneris's chagrin. Three weeks later Campaneris responded to the All-Star snub in a game at Baltimore: After collecting his third stolen base of the game in the fifth inning, he went to third on a throwing error by Orioles catcher Andy Etchebarren, then coaxed Jim Palmer into a run-scoring balk. While heading home, he looked into the Orioles dugout and tipped his hat to Weaver.

On the last day of the season, Campaneris led by two in the stolen-base race, and was going to sit out the season finale. After the A's broadcasters found out that Dave Nelson of the Texas Rangers had stolen three bases in his game, Campaneris entered the A's game in the fourth inning as a pinch-runner. He stole second and third, denying Nelson the title, and also spoiling Nolan Ryan's bid for his first 20-win season. Of Ryan, Campaneris said, "I know I can steal on that guy. He pitches so slow."[6] Campaneris was referring to Ryan's deliberate motion, not his velocity.

The A's finished the 1972 season with a 93-62 record, winning their division by 5½ games over the Chicago White Sox, earning them a berth in the ACLS against Detroit. After the A's won Game One, 3-2, fireworks erupted during Game Two. In the bottom of the seventh, Campaneris who was already 3-for -3 with two stolen bases and two runs scored, was hit in the ankle by a pitch from Lerrin LaGrow. Campaneris threw his bat toward LaGrow, who ducked to avoid being hit.

With Detroit manager Billy Martin in the lead, the Tigers went for Campaneris. (Afterward, Martin said of his role in the fracas, "You bet I was after him! There's no place for that kind of gutless stuff in baseball. That's the worst thing I've ever seen in all my years of baseball. I would respect him if he went out to throw a punch, but what he did was the most gutless thing of any man to put on a uniform. It was a disgrace to baseball."[7]) Three umpires held Martin back, and home-plate umpire Nestor Chylak ejected LaGrow and Campaneris. Explaining his actions, Campaneris said, "My ankle hurt so bad. I knew he was going to throw at me, but people now tell me it's better to go and fight. I don't know. I just lost my temper."[8]

Oakland's Joe Rudi said he thought LaGrow threw at Campaneris because "Campy had run the Tigers ragged in the first two games, and when (Billy) Martin gets his ears pinned down, he's going to do something about it."[9] Teammate Mike Hegan said he thought Martin "wanted to light a fire under his ballclub, and Campy was the guy that they were going after because he was the guy that set the table for us. There's no question that Billy Martin instructed Lerrin LaGrow to throw at Campaneris."[10]

American League President Joe Cronin suspended Campaneris for the remainder of the ALCS, fined him $500 and left the decision about a possible World Series suspension to Commissioner Bowie Kuhn. Kuhn ruled that Campaneris could play in the World Series, but would be suspended without pay for the first seven games of the 1973 season.

The incident did indeed spark the Tigers; without Campaneris in the A's lineup, they tied the series. But the A's won the fifth and deciding game, 2-1 and went to the franchise's first World Series since 1931, when they were in Philadelphia.

The underdog A's, playing without Reggie Jackson, who had ruptured a hamstring during the Tigers series, captured the world championship, defeating the Cincinnati Reds in an exciting seven-game Series.

The A's led the Series three games to two, but Cincinnati stormed back in Game Six, tying the Series with an 8-1 drubbing of Oakland. When Campaneris came to bat in the eighth inning he told Reds catcher Johnny Bench, "We never lose three in a row!" Bench replied, "You've never faced the Big Red Machine!"[11]

Campaneris batted only .179 in the World Series, but it was a defensive, pitching-oriented affair in which each team batted .209. Campaneris scored the run in Game Seven that gave the A's the lead for good, coming home on Gene Tenace's double in the top of the sixth inning.

In 1973 Campaneris became the first A's player to be offered a two-year contract by owner Charlie Finley, signing a deal for a reported $65,000 a season. Campaneris sat on the bench the first five games (the seven-game sentence had been reduced on appeal) and watched Dal Maxvill play shortstop. On May 25 the A's returned to Detroit and Campaneris was welcomed back to a loud chorus of boos from the fans who had not forgotten the LaGrow incident. Tigers catcher Bill Freehan took out Campaneris in a play at the plate, and Campaneris suffered a shoulder injury that forced him to miss six games. In the 11 games Campaneris missed as a result of the suspension and injury, the A's record was 2-9. For the season, Campaneris batted .250, had 34 stolen bases, and was selected as the American League's starting shortstop for the All-Star Game.

The A's won the American League West with a 94-68 record and faced the AL East champion Baltimore Orioles in the ALCS. Before the series, Orioles pitcher Jim Palmer commented, "I think the key to beating Oakland is keeping Campaneris off base."[12] The Orioles failed miserably in Game Two, as Campaneris reached base three times in five plate appearances, hitting a home run to lead off the game, stealing a pair of bases, and scoring two runs in the A's 6-3 victory. He hit a walkoff home run in the 11th inning of Game Three. The A's wound up winning the series three games to two.

Against the New York Mets in the World Series, Campaneris batted .290, stole three bases, and hit a two-run home run in the third inning of Game Seven which along with Reggie Jackson's two-run homer in the same inning, gave the A's a lead they did not relinquish in a 5-2 victory. Reggie Jackson (.310, 6 RBIs) was named the Series Most Valuable Player. Campaneris (.290, 3 RBIs) was disappointed that he did not get the award, but said, "Reggie is my friend."[13]

The A's returned to the World Series in 1974, their third straight appearance. Campaneris again represented the American League in the All-Star Game. He batted .290 and stole 34 bases for the season. He missed 15 games between July 29 and August 11 when he suffered a severely sprained left ankle.

After defeating the Orioles three games to one in the ALCS, the Athletics faced the National League champion Los Angeles Dodgers in the World Series, and won the Series in five games. In Game One, a 3-2 victory, Campaneris laid down an excellently executed squeeze bunt on which Ken Holtzman scored. Campaneris batted .353 in the Series, stole a base, and contributed sparkling defense. He was also named to *The Sporting News* AL All-Star Team for the second consecutive season.

Campaneris received a substantial raise for the 1975 season, reported by various sources at $20,000, $25,000, or $35,000. He batted .265 and stole 24 bases. Despite the loss of Catfish Hunter to free agency, the A's won the AL West division, but were swept by the Red Sox in the ALCS.

The A's entered a difficult period in 1976. The team was aging and many members were passing their prime. And free agency had become a factor in contract negotiations, something Charlie Finley had difficulty dealing with. Campaneris was among the players who sought big raises. Finley offered $90,000, but Campaneris asked for a five-year contract at $120,000 per year, or $135,000 for one year. (According to *The Sporting News*, Campaneris wound with a salary of $72,000.[14]) Campaneris batted .256, made 23 errors in 149 games, and stole 54 bases in 66 attempts, including a club-record five in a 12-7 victory over Minnesota on May 24. Despite the loss of Reggie Jackson and Ken

Holtzman to free agency, the A's posted an 87-74 record and finished in second place in the AL West, just 2½ games behind Kansas City.

A free-agency re-entry draft was held after the season and Campaneris was selected by the maximum of 12 teams. After considering all the offers, he signed a contract worth a reported $750,000 for five years and became a Texas Ranger. Rangers general manager Dan O'Brien said Campaneris "adds two dimensions to our team—speed and defense."[15] The signing meant that Toby Harrah would be moved to third base. (Harrah commented, I consider it a pleasure to play next to him in the infield."[16]) To comments that he was now 35 years old, Campaneris said, "I think I know what I can do and how long I can do it. … I plan on playing seven, eight more years. Who knows, maybe more than that."[17] Campaneris had a decent season, batting .254 and stealing 27 bases, and his veteran leadership was a contributing factor in the Rangers' rise from fifth place a year earlier to a second-place finish with a 94-68 record.

Despite his confidence, Campaneris began a downward slide in 1978, batting only .186 and playing in only 98 games. After being benched in early August, he voiced his displeasure: "This is the first bad year that I've had and it's because they've taken me out of games for pinch-hitters, and now I don't play. I'm not going to say anything the rest of this year. I'll do the best I can when I do play, but I'll tell you one thing—I'm not going to go through this again next season."[18]

Rookie Nelson Norman was named the Rangers starting shortstop for the 1979 season, sending an unhappy Campaneris to the bench. On May 4 the Rangers traded him to the California Angels for infielder Dave Chalk. The Rangers also made the trade to rid themselves of Campaneris's $190,000 annual salary, which ran through the 1981 season. With the Angels, Campaneris split time at shortstop for the next two seasons with Jim Anderson and Freddie Patek, batting .234 with 12 stolen bases in 85 games in 1979. On June 20 he got a measure of revenge by stealing three bases in a 5-4 Angels victory over the Rangers.

Campaneris batted .252 with 10 steals in 1980 and had a good stretch in midseason; in September Angels manger Jim Fregosi praised him, commenting, "Over the last six weeks, Bert Campaneris has been our best player."[19] However, Campaneris realized his role when 22-year- old Dickie Thon was called up by noting, "They want a young kid, someone to stay around another two years. Maybe we can be like Baltimore with (Kiko) Garcia and (Mark) Belanger. I can help the kid."[20]

Campaneris played in 55 games in 1981 for the Angels, 46 of them as a defensive replacement at third base, and batted.256. He had five stolen bases. After the season he was granted free agency.

After an unsuccessful tryout at the Orioles' camp during 1982 spring training, Campaneris played for Veracruz and Poza Rica in the Mexican League, batting .277 in 104 games primarily as a third baseman. He still loved playing, and said, "I'll play as long as my legs and arms allow me."[21]

On February 24, 1983, the 40-year-old Campaneris signed as a free agent with the New York Yankees, who invited him to spring training in Fort Lauderdale, Florida. The Yankees had to pay $5,000 to obtain his release from Poza Rica. Happy to be getting another major-league shot, Campaneris said, "All my life I've thought about one day playing for the Yankees. Everybody wants to play for the Yankees. That's why I came here first."[22]

Campaneris was one of the final players in camp that was cut, and he was sent to Triple-A Columbus, where he batted .333 in 13 games, with seven runs batted in and three stolen bases. When Yankees second baseman Willie Randolph was injured, Campaneris was called up to the Yankees on May 4, and in his first start on May 6, playing second base, he had four hits, stole a base, and took part in four double plays. Campaneris played in 60 games, batting a career-high .322 and was a valuable backup at second and third base for the Yankees.

Released by the Yankees after the season, Campaneris was hired by the Angels as a minor-league bunting and baserunning coach. One of his special projects was working with Angels speedster Gary Pettis. He also had stints as a coach with the Houston Astros and the San Francisco Giants. In 2014 he libed in Scottsdale, Arizona, and was a frequent participant in old-timer's games. He conducted baseball camps and was actively involved in the charity golf tournaments held by the Major League Baseball Players Alumni Association.

The highest praise for Campaneris may have come from his old boss and antagonist, Charlie Finley, who said in 1980, "You can talk about Reggie Jackson, Catfish Hunter, and Sal Bando, all those great players, but it was Campy who made everything go."[23]

NOTES

1   Ron, Bergman, "Quiet Campy Stealing Thunder … and Bases," *The Sporting News*, June 25,1970

2   Joe McGuff, "Campaneris Thrills Kaycee Fans With Exploits as Bandit," *The Sporting News*, July 31, 1965.

3   *The Sporting News* August 26, 1967

4   Ron Bergman, "Kennedy Turns Campy Into the Wild West Gunslinger," *The Sporting News*, August 17, 1968.

5   "Ouiet Campy."

6   Ron Bergman, "Oakland Fans Welcome Their Hero — Speedy Campy," *The Sporting News*, October 28, 1972.

7   "Oakland Fans."

8   "Oakland Fans."

9   Bruce Markusen, *A Baseball Dynasty* (Haworth, New Jersey: St. Johann Press, 2002), 133

10 Markusen.

11 Markusen, 162.

12 Markusen, 234.

13 Dave Anderson, "Bert Campaneris Is Still Hurt," *New York Times*, February 28, 1974

14 *The Sporting News*, January 8, 1977.

15 Randy Galloway, "Rangers Land Campaneris With a $750,000 Package," *The Sporting News*, December 4, 1976.

16 Randy Galloway, "Campy's Arrival Convinces Harrah to Switch to Third," *The Sporting News*, March 26, 1977.

17 Randy Galloway, "Campy Looks for Fountain of Youth in Texas," *The Sporting News*, April 16,1977

18 Randy Galloway, "Campy Counting His Bucks on Ranger Bench," *The Sporting News*, September 9, 1978.

19 Peter Gammons, "A.L. Beat," *The Sporting News*, September 13, 1980.

20 Dick, Miller, "Angels Will Test Trade Winds, but Not Free-Agent Market,"

21 Class AAA Notes, "Campy Going Strong at 40," *The Sporting News*, June 14, 1980.

22 Murray Chass, "Campaneris, at 40, Tries to Be a Yankee," *New York Times*, March 4, 1980.

23 Gammons, Peter, "A.L. Beat" *The Sporting News*, October 4, 1980.

Rollie Fingers

By Dale Voiss

Rollie Fingers was clearly excited as he caught a leaping Ted Simmons, his catcher, after Fingers struck out Detroit's Lou Whitaker to nail down the victory and the second-half American League East title for his Milwaukee Brewers in 1981. (The unprecedented split season was devised after the players' two-month strike was settled.) The Brewers were in the postseason for the first time in their 13-year history. They lost in the first round to the first-half champion New York Yankees, three games to two, but Fingers, whose 28 saves that season preserved 45 percent of the Brewers' 62 victories, won not just the Cy Young Award but the American League Most Valuable Player award as well. Only four pitchers (Don Newcombe, Sandy Koufax, Bob Gibson, and Vida Blue) had done that before Fingers, and only three (Willie Hernandez, Roger Clemens, and Dennis Eckersley) did it after him, as of 2014.

Roland Glen Fingers developed his mustache, perhaps the most colorful in major-league baseball, on his own. But he credited his father with teaching him how to pitch. Roland was born on August 25, 1946, in Steubenville, Ohio, to George and Pearl (Stafford) Fingers. His father, a steelworker, had pitched in the St. Louis Cardinals farm system for four years and had been a roommate of Stan Musial.

One day, after returning home from a tough day in the steel mill, George Fingers said, "That's it, we're moving to California," Roland Fingers recalled in a TV appearance with Tim McCarver in August 2010. He sold his house for $1,500, bought a car, and moved the family to Cucamonga, California, where he went to work in yet another steel mill. On the drive west, the family couldn't afford to stay in hotels, and they were forced to sleep in sleeping bags by the side of the road.

At Upland High School (Upland and adjoining Cucamonga are east of Los Angeles), Fingers played left field and pitched on the baseball team. He also played American Legion baseball for the Upland Post. In August 1964, after graduating from high school, Fingers pitched his Legion team to the national American Legion title and was named the tournament's player of the year. After winning local and regional tournaments, Upland went to the national tournament in Little Rock, Arkansas. Playing the outfield, Fingers belted three hits and made two running catches in Upland's victory over a Detroit team in the opener of the round robin. He pitched a three-hitter against a team from Charlotte, North Carolina, to wrap up the title. For the Legion season he finished with an 11-2 record, a 0.67 earned-run average, and 102 strikeouts in 81 innings. In the regional and national tournaments, he batted .450 (18-for-40).

After the tournament Fingers returned home to California to discuss his baseball future with his parents. The free-agent draft hadn't been instituted yet, and Fingers had already received offers from more than a dozen major-league organizations. He was prepared to turn them all down to attend Chaffey Junior College at Alta Loma, California.

The Los Angeles Dodgers offered Fingers a $20,000 bonus to sign a contract. But because they already had a solid pitching staff, led by Fingers' boyhood heroes Sandy Koufax and Don Drysdale, he felt it would take him years to make the majors with the Dodgers. Instead, he accepted a $13,000 offer from the Kansas City Athletics, signing the contract on Christmas Eve of 1964.

The Athletics originally wanted Fingers as an outfielder but decided in his first spring training to have him pitch. At Leesburg, in the Class A Florida State League in 1985, he won 8 games and lost 15, with a 2.98 ERA. In late August he went to Cooperstown, where in a ceremony at the Baseball Hall of Fame he received the American Legion player of the year award from the previous summer.

Fingers spent the 1966 season with the Modesto Reds of the Class A California League. Still a starter, he went 11-6 in 22 games with a 2.77 ERA. Among his teammates that season were future Hall of Famers Reggie Jackson and Tony La Russa.

In the spring of 1967, Fingers married his high-school sweetheart, Jill Cutler, who had been the statistician for the Upland High School baseball team. He moved up the A's ladder again, to Birmingham of the Double-A Southern League. Pitching on Opening Day, he suffered a fractured cheekbone and jawbone, and lost some teeth when he was hit by a line drive off the bat of Fred Kovner of Evansville. Fingers' jaw was wired shut for five weeks. He returned to the mound in two months and finished the season with a 6-5 record and a 2.21 ERA. After Birmingham's season ended, to get in some more work, Fingers pitched for the Athletics' entry in the Arizona Fall Instructional League.

The Athletics moved from Kansas City to Oakland after the 1967 season, but Fingers stayed in Birmingham in 1968 for a second straight year. He started the season with eight straight victories, including a two-hit, 5-0 shutout of Evansville, and ended the season with a 10-4 record and a 3.00 ERA. This performance earned him a call-up to Oakland in September, and Fingers would never again pitch in a minor-league game. He pitched just once for the A's after his call-up, allowing four runs on four hits in relief in a 13-0 loss to the World Series-bound Detroit Tigers on September 15. The four hits included a home run by Tigers catcher Bill Freehan.

In the winter of 1968-69, Fingers pitched for the La Guaira club of the Venezuelan Winter League, and worked on developing a slider to supplement his "out" pitch, the fastball.

In 1969 the Athletics' new manager, Hank Bauer, installed a four-man starting rotation—Blue Moon Odom, Chuck Dobson, Catfish Hunter, and Jim Nash—and said that to keep the starters on four days' rest, Fingers would start when the A's played more than four straight days. Fingers made his first start of the season on April 22 in Minnesota. He shut out the Twins on five hits, 7-0, facing just 32 batters. He made his next start five days later in Seattle, going 8⅓ innings and allowing five runs on six hits in a 13-5 win over the Pilots. Seven days later he started against Seattle again, this time at Oakland, and lost, 6-4, giving up 11 hits in six-plus innings. He didn't start again until May 30, when he was shelled by the Cleveland Indians, lasting just one-third of an inning in a 9-2 loss. For the next 3½ months, Fingers worked out of the bullpen; he did not start again until September 15, when he lost to the Twins. In the remaining two weeks of the season he made three more appearances as a starter. In 60 games, including eight starts, Fingers was 6-7 with 12 saves.

Hank Bauer was fired in September and replaced by third-base coach John McNamara, who had been Fingers' manager at Birmingham in 1967. Under McNamara in 1970, Fingers got 19 starts and made 26 relief appearances, posting a 7-9 record.

Dick Williams replaced McNamara for 1971. Fingers began the season in the rotation and started eight games, winning one and losing three. His last start of the season came on May 15, after which Williams made Fingers the closer. Except for two starts early in the 1973 season, Fingers was a closer for the next 15 years. In that 1971 season he earned 17 saves in 20 opportunities, the fourth highest saves total in the American League.

The A's won 101 games that year to win the American League's West Division by 16 games over the Kansas City Royals, but were swept by the Baltimore Orioles in the American League Championship Series. Fingers pitched in two games in the series, allowing two runs in 2⅓ innings.

The division championship in 1971 was the first of five straight for the A's. Their rise to the top was fueled by the talent they got out of their minor-league system in the 1960s, players like Fingers, Reggie Jackson, Bert Campaneris, Joe Rudi, Sal Bando, Catfish Hunter, Blue Moon Odom, and Vida Blue. As these players came together, they jelled as a team and brought success to Oakland. The A's appearance in the 1971 ALCS was the first postseason play for the franchise and its predecessors since the Philadelphia Athletics lost the 1931 World Series to the St. Louis Cardinals.

In 1972-74 the A's won three straight World Series. Over that span, in a time when the semiautomatic ninth-inning closer was not as much of a fixture as it became two decades later, Fingers had 61 saves and a 27-22 won-lost record with an ERA of 2.34. In each of those seasons he pitched between 111 and 126 innings — numbers unheard of among closers of the 21st century. He made the American League All-Star team in 1973 and 1974. (He was also an All-Star in 1975, 1976, 1978, 1981, and 1982.)

Reggie Jackson, Oakland's star outfielder, showed up for spring training in 1972 with a mustache. His teammates did not like the idea of Jackson with a mustache so they all started growing facial hair to protest. Team owner Charles Finley, instead of making everyone shave, as the players hoped he would, offered a cash prize to the player who could grow the best facial hair by Opening Day. Finley felt the look would help sell tickets. Fingers grew a handlebar mustache that curled at the tips. It won the contest, and the mustache became his trademark look.

After the 1972 season Finley sent Fingers a contract calling for a $1,000 raise for 1973. Fingers phoned Finley to argue about the contract. Finley would not budge, so Fingers slammed down the receiver and vowed never to talk to Finley again. He hired agent Jerry Kapstein to represent him in negotiations with Finley and kept his word never to speak to Finley again.

In each of the three seasons from 1974 to 1976, Fingers pitched in at least 70 games, leading the league in appearances in 1974 and 1975. During that span, he saved 62 games for Oakland and had a better than 3-to-1 strikeout-to-walk ratio.

In June 1976, anticipating that he might lose them to free agency after the season, Finley sold Fingers and Joe Rudi to the Boston Red Sox, and Vida Blue to the New York Yankees for a total of $3.5 million ($1 million each for Fingers and Rudi and $1.5 million for Blue). Baseball Commissioner Bowie Kuhn rescinded the deals, saying they were not in the best interests of baseball. Finley's argument had been that if the three became free agents at the end of the season, he would not get anything in return if they signed elsewhere. Kuhn, on the other hand, said that if he allowed the sale to go through, "the door would be opened wide to the buying of success by the more affluent clubs." Finley sued Kuhn for restraint of trade but lost the suit.

After the 1976 season, with Fingers and several teammates eligible for free agency, Finley chose not to sign them and they all went their separate ways. In an attempt to prevent teams from making offers to Fingers, Finley stated that he was washed up, but the San Diego Padres signed Fingers anyway, for a salary of slightly over $250,000, almost triple his highest salary as an Athletic. (The Dodgers, Cardinals, Giants, and Pirates had also wooed Fingers.) Among the players leaving Oakland that winter were Don Baylor, Joe Rudi, Sal Bando, Bert Campaneris, and Gene

Tenace, who also signed with the Padres. In signing, Fingers said he was glad to move to the National League because he was a low-ball pitcher and NL umpires were more likely to call the low-ball strike. Fingers' signing with the Padres came shortly after his wedding to the former Danielle Lamar on November 14. (His first marriage had ended in divorce in 1974, and this one would, too.) A former A's teammate, pitcher Ken Holtzman, was Fingers' best man at the ceremony in the Oakland suburb of Lafayette.

On the Padres, Fingers was reunited with former Athletics manager John McNamara. But McNamara, who took over the Padres in 1974, was fired 48 games into the 1977 season and was replaced by Alvin Dark. At the time Fingers signed, many believed that McNamara would move him into the rotation. This would leave the closer role to Butch Metzger, who had saved 16 games for the Padres in 1976 and earned the NL Rookie of the Year Award. McNamara surprised many by giving the closer job to Fingers and using Metzger in middle relief.

In San Diego, Fingers joined a staff anchored by 1976 Cy Young Award winner Randy Jones. Jones had won 22 games for the Padres in 1976, but an arm injury in September threatened his 1977 season. Jones recovered enough to start the season but went a disappointing 6-12 in 27 games. Meanwhile, Fingers saved 35 games, more than half of the Padres' 69 wins.

Fingers spent four years in San Diego as the Padres' closer, going 34-40 while earning 108 saves in 265 outings. The Padres had just one winning season in the four years and never finished higher than fourth in the six-team National League Western Division. Fingers could hardly be blamed; during his stay in San Diego he won the unofficial National League Fireman of the Year Award three times, in 1977, 1978, and 1980. In his final year in San Diego, Fingers surpassed Hoyt Wilhelm's career record for saves. (As an indication of how the use of closers has changed over the years, Fingers' career total of 341 put him, as of the beginning of the 2014 season, only 11th among closers; the leader as of that year was Mariano Rivera, with 652.)

After the 1980 season Fingers returned to the American League. The Padres traded him, Tenace, and pitcher Bob Shirley to the St Louis Cardinals for seven players; then the Cardinals sent Fingers, catcher Ted Simmons, and pitcher Pete Vuckovich to the Milwaukee Brewers for outfielders Sixto Lezcano and David Green and pitchers Lary Sorensen and Dave LaPoint. When Fingers arrived in Milwaukee, the Brewers were coming off three straight winning seasons. They were led by an explosive offense that included future Hall of Famers Robin Yount and Paul Molitor. But they struggled to find a consistent closer. Fingers was seen by many as the final piece of the puzzle that could send the team to their first postseason appearance. Fingers did not disappoint. In what was regarded as one of the greatest seasons a relief pitcher had up to then, he saved 28 of the team's 62 victories as the Brewers sailed to the second-half American League East title in the strike-shortened 1981 season. Fingers' dominating performance, which included a minuscule 1.04 earned-run average, landed him not only the Cy Young Award but the MVP award as well. Fingers had one victory and one save as the Brewers fell to the Yankees three games to two in the divisional playoffs.

In 1982 Fingers saved 29 games through late August as the Brewers led the American League East for most of the season. The team had really taken off when hitting coach Harvey Kuenn replaced Buck Rodgers as manager in early June. Rodgers' removal had been precipitated by the team's poor play (the Brewers were 23-24 when he was fired) along with criticism of Rodgers by several players, including Fingers.

On August 30 the Brewers obtained right-handed pitcher Don Sutton from the Houston Astros in exchange for three prospects. Sutton, a future Cooperstown inductee, joined the team the next day and started the second game of a doubleheader September 2 against the Cleveland Indians. The Brewers lost the game, 4-2. The loss, however, was not the worst news the team received that night. In the first game of the doubleheader Fingers tore a muscle in his right forearm. The injury kept him out of action for the remainder of the season. Rookie Pete Ladd replaced him as the closer, and the Brewers, without Fingers, advanced to the World Series, which they lost to the Cardinals in seven games.

This tendinitis injury left Fingers sidelined for the entire 1983 season. He returned to form for the Brewers in 1984, saving 23 games for a team that disappointed nearly everyone by finishing 67-94, last in the American League East, under manager Rene Lachemann.

In 1985 Fingers, now 38 years old, returned to the Milwaukee bullpen but clearly wasn't his old self. He saved 17 games but had eight blown saves and finished with a 1-6 record and a 5.04 ERA. The Brewers released him after the season. He received overtures from the Cincinnati Reds, but a team rule against facial hair would have forced him to shave his trademark handlebar mustache, so he declined the Reds' offer and retired.

Fingers went to work for a communications company in the San Diego area, where he worked for about a dozen years. He followed that with a short stint at a printing company, also in the San Diego area.

In January 1992, on just his second appearance on the ballot, Fingers was elected to the Baseball Hall of Fame, along with pitcher Tom Seaver. Before his induction the Brewers retired his uniform number, 34. The following year the Athletics followed suit by also retiring number 34.

Golf became a major passion for Fingers in retirement. He carried a handicap of 2 to 3 for most of his adult life. Fingers played over a decade, with several other pro athletes, on the Celebrity Golf Tour, where he was known to finish as high as third.

In 1999 Fingers moved from his home in California to Las Vegas, where he took a job with Billy Walters, who owned several golf courses in the area. After less than a year he left Walters Golf and later got involved with a golf company that developed a product which helps clean up lakes.

In January 2007 the state of Wisconsin listed Fingers as number eight on its list of tax delinquents. The state Department of Revenue alleged that he owed nearly $1.5 million in income tax from his days as a pitcher for the Brewers. In July the state filed documents saying that two of the three cases it had filed against Fingers had been satisfied, with the third case, for more than $58,000, still pending. The next month Fingers said that his name had been cleared and he had never been delinquent.

As of 2014 Fingers still resided in Las Vegas. Of his five children, a son, Jason, was drafted by the Kansas City Royals in the tenth round of the June 2000 amateur draft. He pitched for Spokane of the Class A Northwest League in 2000 and Burlington in the Class A Midwest League in 2001 before ending his baseball career. During the summer of 1970 Fingers' younger brother, Gordon, pitched in eight games for Coos Bay-North Bend, Oakland's entry in the Northwest League.

SOURCES

Wisconsin State Journal (Madison, Wisconsin), November 4, 1981.

The Sporting News, September 12, 1964, August 7, 1965, April 27, 1967, November 25, 1967, November 16, 1968, January 11, 1969, February 8, 1969, April 19, 1969, July 3, 1976, December 11, 1976, March 12, 1977.

Armour, Mark, Charles Finley biography at SABR BioProject website.

Fingers' Hall of Fame induction speech, 1992

Online interview with Fingers by Jimmy Scott, at jimmyscott-shighandtight.com/node/824

"Fingers still takes pioneer route," at lasvegasgolf.com/departments/features/rollie-fingers-golf-326.htm

Dick Green

By Rory Costello

Second base was a revolving door for the Oakland A's during their 1972-74 dynasty—the team used 17 players at that position. The closest thing to a regular was steady veteran Dick Green. Though he missed most of 1972 after surgery on a herniated disc in his back, he recovered in time for the postseason. Green—who wore uniform number 1, as befit the senior man in terms of service with the club—remained Oakland's primary second baseman in '73 and '74, during the regular season, playoffs, and World Series. Despite going hitless in the '74 Series against the Dodgers, he was a strong MVP candidate because of his superb fielding.

There were many other excellent glove men among Green's American League peers, which explains in part why he never won a Gold Glove during his career. Despite that, he was universally recognized as one of the best in the business, and the available advanced metrics confirm that he was well above average in the field. Green had some power before his back became a problem, but his hitting was up and down—moderate at best. "I'm lucky, the caliber ballplayer I am, to get my eight or nine years in," he said ahead of the 1972 season. "I work very hard for everything. I've got to concentrate so much."[1] Still, all in all, he was an integral part of Oakland's success.

Ted Kubiak, Green's most frequent backup, gave insight in 2013. "Dick was well liked by Mr. Finley and rightly so. He was probably as surehanded an infielder as you'd find. He rarely made an error, positioned himself well and turned the double play as well as anyone. He gave the pitchers a comfort level because of his consistent defensive play year after year. He played through a lot of back trouble. Our club had players who did maybe not a lot of things well but excelled consistently in others. The composite skills of everyone made for a team that didn't make a lot of mistakes."[2]

Richard Larry Green was born on April 21, 1941, in Sioux City, Iowa. He was the first of Mick and Millie Green's three children; a sister named Patty followed, then a brother. Mick Jr., also a second baseman, signed with the A's in 1966.[3] The younger Green never actually played pro ball, however, even though Dick said on several occasions that he thought Mick was better.

Sioux City lies on the Missouri River, near Nebraska and South Dakota. Young Dick lived there for about five years, and then his family moved to Yankton, South Dakota, about an hour's drive northwest.[4] One of his childhood friends there was future NBC anchorman Tom Brokaw.[5]

"I always went to the games growing up in Yankton," Green remembered in 2003. "I'd go see the Yankton Terrys play."[6] From 1953 through 1973, there was a high-quality regional circuit called the Basin League that operated mainly in South Dakota. Well over 100 of its players (mostly college men, but some pros) went on to the major leagues, including Hall of Famers Bob Gibson, Jim Palmer, and Don Sutton. Green became one of them.

Partway through high school, Green moved to Mitchell, another South Dakota town about an hour and a half northwest of Yankton. His father had been in the shoe business, which brought about the moves. Mick Sr. later operated a North American Van Lines franchise in Rapid City, in the western part of South Dakota.[7] As an adult, Dick joined this business—which became known as Green's Moving & Storage—and remained in it for many years. This was the main reason that he did not play winter ball, except for some Instructional League in Florida during his time in the low minors.

At Mitchell High, Green was all-state in football as a quarterback. He was also a standout in basketball and track. As a senior, he was named South Dakota's prep athlete of the year. "We had no baseball team," he said in 1969. "It was too cold to play baseball during the school year. Baseball is strictly a summer game in Mitchell. So I played Babe Ruth and American Legion ball."[8]

Green had always loved baseball. "I played midget, junior Legion and summer league, and anywhere else I could," he said in 1961.[9] However, many years later, he observed, "Football was probably my best sport. I was on Mitchell's first undefeated team in school history. I was thinking about going to college. I got an offer to go to Florida State and also had a full ride at Michigan. At both places I was going to play football and baseball."[10]

The local baseball scene, however, was fruitful. Mitchell had a team in the Basin League from 1953 through 1960, and Green played with the Kernels after graduating from high school in 1959. At that time he was a

shortstop. "[Manager] Joe Lutz called me and wanted me to try out," Green remembered in 2003. "So I tried out and provided a little hometown flavor. I was very fortunate to have played in the Basin League. When I played, teams got to put up to three major leaguers on their teams. I remember getting to watch some great players growing up and playing against some great players. It was a great experience."[11]

With Mitchell, Green had at least one teammate who made it to the majors. That was Dean Look, who played in three games for the Chicago White Sox in 1961. (Look, a college football star, also played in one game in the American Football League in 1962 before going on to a long career as a referee in the NFL.)

Green said that as a Kernel, "I was really raw. I made a few errors and I didn't hit very well, as I recall."[12] However, Marv Olson, a scout with the Athletics (then based in Kansas City) had been following him for years. Olson, a South Dakotan who played in the majors from 1931 to 1933, had played for Yankton as late as 1956 (he was also the manager). Olson signed Green to a contract, and the $12,000 bonus was enough to make him forsake football.[13] Green never played for any other organization.

During his first season in the minors, Green hit just .228 with 8 homers and 54 RBIs for Sanford of the Class D Florida State League in 1960. He led the league's shortstops in fielding, though, and got attention for making sharp plays.[14] So he jumped to Class B in 1961. However, the organization shifted him from shortstop to third base with Lewiston of the Northwest League.

Before going to Lewiston, Green had attended Black Hills Teachers College in Spearfish, South Dakota, for one quarter. He concentrated in physical education. "But I've got a six-month Army tour to go through," he said as the season started, "and I enjoy playing winter ball, so I don't know if I'll go back or not."[15] As it developed, he did not.

Green noted, "Any ballplayer will tell you that a slider, properly delivered, is the toughest pitch to hit."[16] He was confident in his batting, though — indeed, he set a personal best with 18 homers for Lewiston, while hitting .273. Thus, he moved up to Double-A for 1962. He remained at third base for Albuquerque of the Texas League, but he played in only 90 games. A mysterious injury to his right hand bothered him all season; it turned out to be a hairline fracture of his thumb.[17] Nonetheless, he hit .285-10-52.

The A's switched Green to second base at their early instructional camp in 1963. In spring training, he impressed many observers.[18] The Sporting News wrote, "[He] showed an immediate aptitude for the new job. One of Green's greatest assets is his determination. He fields ground balls for 30 or 40 minutes at a stretch and gave Jimmie Dykes so much exercise with the fungo bat that Dykes started to lose weight."[19]

Kansas City had Jerry Lumpe at second base and Ed Charles at third, both coming off good seasons. The organization wanted Green to play regularly, and so he finished his minor-league seasoning that year with Portland of the Pacific Coast League (Triple-A). Everyone in the front office was convinced, though, that he would be back.[20] He hit .234-15-65 for the Beavers, slumping after a strong start. Coach Bill Posedel thought Green had trouble with the outside pitch, but the following spring, Green himself said he thought it was more a matter of confidence, and that he didn't like it much at Portland.[21]

The A's kept Green at second base for the bulk of the season at Portland, though he still played a bit of third. He noted that the hardest things about his new position were the different spin of the ball and especially learning to make the pivot. "It took me about three months before I really got it down," he said. "I got hit pretty good while I was learning." Bill Posedel said, "He makes the double play very well. He has quick hands and a good arm for a second baseman. He moves well and covers a lot of ground."[22]

Kansas City called Green up after the Beavers' season ended, and he made his debut at Municipal Stadium on September 9. Pinch-hitting for Tom Sturdivant, he drew a walk off Steve Hamilton of the Yankees and came around to score. He got into 13 games for the A's that month, moving to short from second while Wayne Causey was injured, and hit .270 in 37 at-bats. On September 25 he hit his first homer in the majors. It came at Fenway Park off Jack Lamabe of the Red Sox. He wound up with 80, a franchise record for second basemen that stood until Mark Ellis — a Rapid City native — broke it in 2010.

Toward the end of the '63 season, The Sporting News discussed the team's needs — in particular, lack of power. "If the A's do trade a front-line infielder, they probably will have to count on rookie Dick Green as a replacement. This is an admitted gamble."[23] The team took that gamble, though, sending Jerry Lumpe to Detroit in a six-player trade that brought in Rocky Colavito. After the trade, A's general manager Pat Friday said, "Second base is a wide open shot, with Green the leading candidate. We know he can do an excellent job defensively. We also know he has power. It's just a question of whether he can make contact with the ball frequently enough against major league pitching."[24]

Green never did go back to the minors after 1963, and he did take over as Kansas City's starting second baseman in 1964. He had a fine training camp with both bat and glove; manager Eddie Lopat credited the help of coach Luke Appling.[25] During the regular season, Green was hitting around or below .200 into early July, but the outlook was good because of his hard work and determination. Indeed, he finished strongly (.264-11-37 in 130 games), despite nagging problems with both thumbs.

Fielding was not a concern. Green's range and effort impressed the likes of Phil Rizzuto and Jerry Coleman, who saw him while broadcasting for the Yankees.[26] He played unusually deep at second (except if the batter's speed or turf conditions were factors) and had the arm and agility to make it work.[27] Green drew favorable comparisons to another longtime Yankee, incumbent Gold Glover Bobby Richardson, and graciously thanked Richardson for sharing his knowledge and experience.[28]

Green remained the A's starter in 1965, when he reached a big-league high with 15 homers. Two of the three big-league games in which he homered twice came that year. His average declined to .232, however; in 1966, Green said, "We were having a lot of problems on the club and I let them affect me."[29]

In October 1965 Green married his first wife, Carol Tomlinson. She was a show-horse fancier, and Green became interested in the animals too, eventually owning several.[30] He and Carol had two children—a daughter named Kim and a son named Mike—but were divorced in 1978.

Alvin Dark became the A's manager for the 1966 season. In spring training he rhapsodized about Green's range and hands, saying, "Heck, there isn't anything he can't do." Green had actually considered quitting over the winter, because the previous year's disappointment was lingering and there was also a pay conflict with Charles Finley. He thought he could do just as well working with his father, but the A's finally made him an acceptable offer.[31] Green's talk of retirement became a running theme in future years.

Luke Appling wanted Green to stop swinging for the fences, although in Dick's opinion, he got his homers when he was rested and he wasn't trying. He did think, though, that he could lift his average by looking to bunt more and hitting to all fields. He wound up at .250-9-62. As usual, he made numerous sensational plays in the field. At age 25, he was also named team captain after Wayne Causey was traded in late May.[32]

In 1967 Green got off to a slow start at the plate. A's broadcaster Monte Moore later alluded to a family problem, but Dick discounted that as the reason. John Donaldson, who had been hitting well at Triple-A, was brought up. Green moved to third base, where Sal Bando had not yet come into his own, but his batting continued to languish. He later said, "I think my hitting just fell off when I didn't get to play. I lost my sharpness and ability to concentrate on the pitch."[33] He also lost his captaincy; according to a 1972 account, his batting slump was one reason.[34] A 1969 story suggested, however, that Green was caught in the

middle of the August 1967 squabble among the A's players, Alvin Dark, and Charlie Finley that led to Dark's firing.[35]

In 1968, after the A's moved to Oakland, Green got into just 76 games. He played just 11 times during April and May; one of his roles was bullpen catcher. Near the beginning of the year, he was pressed into service behind the plate for an inning in an actual game. It was something he said he wasn't cut out for (though he was needed once more in this capacity in 1970).[36] Green was dispirited; he was simply looking to get enough time in to qualify for his pension. "Then I was going to get my lunch pail and go home to work for my dad," he said in 1969. "I was through with baseball. I didn't think I had the goods any more."[37]

After about a month of military service, Green remained a reserve in July—but in August, manager Bob Kennedy benched John Donaldson. Donaldson's fielding was worrisome and his hitting had gone south, so Green was back at his best position.[38] In 1969 he went on to have his best year overall with the bat (.275-12-64, .427 slugging percentage, .779 OPS). That was despite badly bruising his knee in mid-June. He missed a couple of weeks, and A's beat writer Ron Bergman observed that August, "It took him quite a while to get his timing back at the plate, although he continued to field spectacularly."[39]

Green fell off sharply at the plate again in 1970 (.190-4-29). Late that July, Ron Bergman wrote, "It wasn't until late June that Green began to show flashes of the glovework that made him the American League's top fielding second baseman in 1969. But he still couldn't raise his batting average to the .200 mark, nor recall the power he displayed." Manager John McNamara first benched Green, then platooned him with John Donaldson, who had been reacquired from Milwaukee.[40] Tony La Russa also got the most extended audition of his big-league career that year.

After the 1970 season, Dick Williams succeeded McNamara and made noises about using Dwain Anderson at second base. Green announced his retirement in February 1971, saying he doubted that he could bounce back, was disinclined to travel, and would stay in Rapid City with the moving business.[41] He even sent back his travel expense check before changing his mind and reporting.[42] Charlie Finley himself phoned Green at the office in Rapid City and lured him back. His hitting bounced back (.244-12-49) and his fielding once again earned raves. Perhaps Ron Bergman's most interesting observation there concerned Green's way of moving around in the field to disguise where he would wind up playing a hitter.[43]

From that point on, though, Green hit just five more homers in his career. He started each of Oakland's first seven games in 1972—but on a cold day at Yankee Stadium, he hurt his back while running to first base. The original diagnosis was a pinched nerve, and he went into traction.[44] He went on the disabled list and underwent surgery for removal of a herniated disc on May 18.[45]

Green returned in mid-August, ahead of schedule. He played in 19 games the rest of the way, though he saw no action from August 30 through September 16. He went back on the DL when Dal Maxvill was acquired.[46] Nonetheless, when it came to the postseason, Green started every game in both the ALCS against the Tigers and the World Series against the Reds. Though Dick Williams continued to play musical chairs at second base, frequently pinch-hitting, Green was still 6-for-18 with two doubles against Cincinnati.

He also showed his toughness in the field, as Bruce Markusen (author of the A's book *Baseball's Last Dynasty*) wrote. "If you've ever seen tape of Hal McRae's vicious slide into second base during the 1972 World Series, it is Green who is on the receiving end of his rolling block. Two innings later, Johnny Bench knocked down Green with a vicious takedown. Green hung in on each play, didn't complain either time, and actually claimed to enjoy being in the middle of such heavy contact."[47]

After Oakland became champions, Rapid City declared "Dick Green Day" on November 3. South Dakota's governor, Dick Kneip, joined the mayor for the banquet.[48]

In 1973 Green started 128 games at second during the regular season, though he admitted that his back was stiff in the early going because of cold weather.[49] He hit .262-3-42 in 332 at-bats, and though Dick Williams thought that Green might have lost a step in the field, he committed just seven errors. One of his increasingly rare home runs, on May 17 at Anaheim Stadium, was noteworthy because it was the play on which Bobby Valentine badly broke his leg while giving chase.

Once again, Green started every game for the A's in the postseason, although he went just 2-for-29 altogether against the Orioles and Mets. He showed his professionalism after making an error in Game Four, denying that there was any extra pressure on him after owner Finley made a scapegoat of fellow second baseman Mike Andrews for costly errors in Game Two. "I'm out there to do a job," Green said. "You don't concentrate on the bad stuff. The ball was hit right to me. I knew what I was gonna do with it, but I didn't do it."[50]

Green mulled retirement again that offseason, even sending a formal letter to Charlie Finley.[51] But Finley didn't forward the letter to the league office and was able to talk the second baseman into reporting once more. Alvin Dark, who was back as A's manager, also telephoned and said, "You're the guy we need to win the pennant."[52]

However, Green was able to start just 95 regular-season games in 1974. In the fourth game of the season, he hurt the arch of his right foot while turning a double play, and he wound up missing nearly all of April and May. He spent another stretch on the DL in July. His hitting tailed off to .213-2-22 in 287 at-bats.

Yet again, however, Oakland relied on Green when October came. He started all four games as the A's swept Baltimore in the ALCS and all five in the World Series against the Dodgers. He went just 2-for-9 against the Orioles and was hitless in 13 trips versus Los Angeles, yet he won the Babe Ruth Award as most valuable player in the postseason. In Game Three of the Series, he started three double plays, including a crucial one in the eighth when the Dodgers were threatening. He was perfectly positioned to grab Steve Garvey's liner and double Jimmy Wynn off first base. The savvy vet said, "We studied the scout report two days before the Series started and our pitchers can hit the spots, so you know where you should play."[53] Then in the eighth inning of Game Five, he choked off another Dodger rally by nailing Bill Buckner at third base with a perfect relay throw.

"That was one helluva throw he made," said A's captain Sal Bando. "That, in my mind, was the biggest play of the Series, even bigger than all those double plays Greenie took part in." Charles O. Finley said, "No one deserved the [World Series] Most Valuable Player award more than Green." Reggie Jackson added, "In my mind Dick Green was responsible for our winning. … the Little General is our big man." Green himself said simply, "I'm just a fringe ballplayer on a great team, and a lot of other things happen, and I can sit back and enjoy it."[54]

That offseason he also said with a laugh, "I got more recognition in that World Series than I got in all of the last 15 years." The bigger topic, though, was the perennial talk of retirement. Green told Ron Bergman that in the past he got "itchy feet and maybe a little more money" when spring training came around—but this time he said, "I'm just not going to come back. … I've had enough. I'm done." He had a beautiful home and the moving business was booming, but a big factor for Green was the loss of Catfish Hunter to free agency. He thought the A's couldn't win without the ace pitcher.[55]

To reflect losing a potential World Series share, Green made what appears to be a largely symbolic request for a salary hike of $20,000, to $80,000. "I'm asking for more than I'm worth," he said.[56] In early March, the A's released Green—he hadn't bothered to send in the formal retirement letter.

Dick Williams, who had become the Angels' manager in mid-1974, went so far as to say the A's would miss Green more than Hunter in the long term. Williams called Green the stabilizer in the infield and was another of those who thought the second baseman

deserved to be MVP of the 1974 World Series.[57] In 2002 Green echoed a common sentiment toward Williams, stating, "I played for 11-12 managers, and as far as liking managers, he was near the bottom of that list, maybe at the very bottom. But he was the smartest baseball man I played for."[58]

Ever after quitting, Green remained in Rapid City, cherishing the quiet lifestyle. He married Cecelia "Lia" Meirose on August 19, 1982. They did not have any children. As of 2013, Dick was the grandfather of three. He stayed involved with the moving business until 1997, when he sold out to his partner and retired. "I love fishing, traveling, hunting, and a little golf," he said in 2008. "I hate public speaking. … I don't even answer the phone."[59]

Lia Green made her career in the radio business, rising to become president of New Rushmore Radio in Rapid City. Darrell Shoemaker, who wrote about the Basin League in a series of articles for the *Rapid City Journal* in 2003, said, "On any given day you can walk into the radio station where Lia is general manager and find Dick chatting and sitting behind the front desk handing out radio prizes to listeners."[60]

Green also liked to take part in team reunions; in 2013 he added, "I talk to Joe Rudi now and then." When asked about his favorite career memories, his answer was simple: "The World Series."

SOURCES

Thanks to Dick Green for his input (handwritten responses on draft copy, mailed August 20, 2013), Lia Green, and Darrell Shoemaker. Continued thanks to Ted Kubiak.

Internet resources

baseball-reference.com

retrosheet.org

comc.com (online sports card market with repository of images)

Dick Green page at South Dakota Sports Hall of Fame website (sdshof.com/inductees/dick-green/)

Basin League history by SABR member David Trombley (usfamily. net/web/trombleyd/BasinMenu.htm)

NOTES

1 "Like grass, A's Green sprouts for 8th year," Newspaper Enterprise Association, April 9, 1972.

2 E-mail, Ted Kubiak to Rory Costello, July 20, 2013.

3 *The Sporting News*, September 24, 1966, 16.

4 Darrell Shoemaker, "Hills players filled Basin League lineups," *Rapid City* (South Dakota) *Journal*, August 18, 2003.

5 Tom Brokaw, *What Baseball Means to Me* (Curt Smith, editor) (New York: Hachette Brook Group, 2002). The Yankton High School 1956 yearbook shows them in the same photo.

6 Darrell Shoemaker, "Opportunity knocked; not everyone answered," *Rapid City Journal*, August 18, 2003.

7 Jim Scott, "Green Is Making A's Rivals See Red," *The Sporting News*, May 24, 1969, 7.

8 Scott, "Green Is Making A's Rivals See Red."

9 "Green Sharpens Batting Eye After Making Mark In Field," *Lewiston* (Idaho) *Morning Tribune*, April 27, 1961, 10.

10 Mike Carroll, "Green to throw first pitch at Pheasants game Saturday," *Huron* (South Dakota) *Plainsman*, May 5, 2010. Originally published in 2008.

11 Shoemaker, "Opportunity knocked; not everyone answered."

12 Shoemaker, "Opportunity knocked; not everyone answered."

13 Scott, "Green Is Making A's Rivals See Red."

14 Jack Slayton, "Tribe Triumphs; Saints Here Tonight," *Lakeland* (Florida) *Ledger*, August 5, 1960, 5.

15 "Green Sharpens Batting Eye After Making Mark In Field."

16 "Green Sharpens Batting Eye After Making Mark In Field."

17 *The Sporting News*, June 9, 1962, 47. "Green's Fracture Dukes' Break?," *The Sporting News*, July 21, 1962, 39.

18 Edgar Munzel, "Dodger Whiz Rated Best of Florida Crop," *The Sporting News*, April 13, 1963, 5.

19 Joe McGuff, "Spring Surprise — A's Show Off Trio of Snazzy Rookies," *The Sporting News*, April 13, 1963.

20 McGuff, "Spring Surprise — A's Show Off Trio of Snazzy Rookies."

21 Joe McGuff, "If Dick Green Stumbles, A's Face a Crisis," *The Sporting News*, March 21, 1964, 23.

22 McGuff, "If Dick Green Stumbles, A's Face a Crisis."

23 Joe McGuff, A's Will Scan Trading Lists for HR Belter," *The Sporting News*, September 28, 1963, 6.

24 Joe McGuff, "Rookie Green Leading Candidate to Plug Kaycee Gap at Keystone," *The Sporting News*, November 30, 1963, 18.

25 Joe McGuff, "Three Flashy Rookies Splash A's Picture with Brighter Hue," *The Sporting News*, April 25, 1964, 27.

26 Joe McGuff, "Rivals Envy A's — Green Makes Flashy Plays as Keystone Kid," *The Sporting News*, June 20, 1964, 7.

27 Joe McGuff, "Gambler Green Robs Sluggers by Playing Deep at Keystone," *The Sporting News*, August 29, 1964, 18.

28 "Trio Helped Dick Win Spurs," *The Sporting News*, March 19, 1966, 5.

29 Joe McGuff, "Dick Green: K.C. Keystone Emerald," *The Sporting News*, March 19, 1966, 5.

30 Scott, "Green Is Making A's Rivals See Red."

31 McGuff, "Dick Green: K.C. Keystone Emerald."

32 "Dick Green Captain of Kansas City A's," *Chicago Tribune*, May 31, 1966, C3.

33 Scott, "Green Is Making A's Rivals See Red."

34 "Like grass, A's Green sprouts for 8th year."

35 Ira Berkow, "A's Dick Green Almost Settled for Lunch Pail," Newspaper Enterprise Association, May 31, 1969.

36 Scott, "Green Is Making A's Rivals See Red."

37 Berkow, "A's Dick Green Almost Settled for Lunch Pail."

38 Scott, "Green Is Making A's Rivals See Red."

39 Ron Bergman, "Up, Down … A's Shuttling Chattels Like Chessmen," *The Sporting News*, August 30, 1969, 16.

40 Ron Bergman, "Donaldson Blue as Green Takes Job," *The Sporting News*, July 25, 1970, 11.

41 "A's Green Retires," *The Sporting News*, February 20, 1971, 47.

42 Ron Bergman, "A's Feared Mailed Fist, But Got Velvet Glove From Williams," *The Sporting News*, March 6, 1971, 38.

43 Ron Bergman, "Green's Glove One of A's Shattering Weapons," *The Sporting News*, September 25, 1971, 5.

44 Ron Bergman, "Bitter Vida Unloads a Tirade at Finley," *The Sporting News*, May 20, 1972, 21.

45 Ron Bergman, "Green Has Disc Removed; May Return in September," *The Sporting News*, June 3, 1972, 25.

46 Ron Bergman, "Green Right at Home as A's Moving Man," *The Sporting News*, November 25, 1972.

47 Bruce Markusen, "A baseball card mystery: Who's sliding into Dick Green?," *The Hardball Times*, January 1, 2013.

48 Bergman, "Green Right at Home as A's Moving Man."

49 Ron Bergman, "'Smooth' Awaiting A's Call To Cover Green's Pasture," *The Sporting News*, May 5, 1973.

50 "Over Early," *The Sporting News*, November 3, 1973, 7.

51 Ron Bergman, "Finley to Try Green-Edged Charm on Balky Keystoner," *The Sporting News*, January 5, 1974.

52 "Green a Hitless Wonder," United Press International, October 18, 1974.

53 Lowell Reidenbaugh, "Accurate Scouting Reports Help A's to 2-1 Advantage," *The Sporting News*, November 2, 1974, 9.

54 "Green a Hitless Wonder."

55 Ron Bergman, "'A's Cannot Repeat,' So Green Retires Again, *The Sporting News*, January 11, 1975, 31.

56 Ron Bergman, "Finley Clear-Cut Winner Over His Angry A's," *The Sporting News*, March 15, 1975, 37.

57 Ron Bergman, "A's Bold Forecast—'We'll Win It Without Catfish," *The Sporting News*, April 19, 1975, 5.

58 Glenn Dickey, "Saluting Finley's champs," *San Francisco Chronicle*, July 14, 2002.

59 Carroll, "Green to throw first pitch at Pheasants game Saturday."

60 E-mail from Darrell Shoemaker to Rory Costello, August 30, 2013. Shoemaker, who became a top staffer for Tim Johnson, US Senator from South Dakota, added, "I was 12 years old when Dick Green gave a bunch of Boy Scouts, myself included, autographed baseballs signed by the World Series champions."

Dave Hamilton

By Tom Hawthorn

Dave Hamilton, a left-hander, was scheduled to start for the Iowa Oaks on a spring Sunday in 1972, another game in the long march to make the major leagues.

Hamilton already had six seasons in the minors to his credit and was deep into the second month of his seventh. He was 24, the future still looked promising, some recent wildness a minor setback. The pitcher was mentally preparing for the day's work ahead when the telephone rang.

He answered to a familiar voice—Charlie Finley, owner of the Oakland A's.

"I know you didn't look too sharp your last couple of starts and I was thinking," the boss said. "Maybe this league's too fast for you. Maybe you might like to try Birmingham for a while."

"No sir," the pitcher replied. "I think I can pitch in the big leagues."[1]

That was what the owner wanted to hear. He told Hamilton to get on an airplane, as he was to pitch the second game of a doubleheader the following day at Arlington, Texas. The pitcher left Des Moines and landed in Dallas that evening via Kansas City and Oklahoma City.

The next day—Memorial Day—Hamilton made his debut, his pregame jitters eased by the bats of his teammates. "I was nervous at first," Hamilton said after the game. "But getting five runs in the first really helped."[2] He lasted 6⅓ innings, pitching out of a two-on, one-out jam in the third inning by striking out the Texas Rangers' Frank Howard and Rich Billings. The A's prevailed, 7-1, to sweep the double-header and give Hamilton a victory in his first appearance. He had been called up on the cusp of the A's facing 32 games in a 31-day stretch, during which

Oakland manager Dick Williams planned to use him as a long reliever and spot starter.

In the end, Hamilton appeared in 25 games (12 of which he started), going 6-6, a fill-in who performed adequately though not spectacularly. He was on the roster for all three of Oakland's championship teams from 1972 to '74, though he got to pitch in only three postseason games.

Hamilton had a brief and unhappy appearance in the American League Championship Series in 1972. Leading the best-of-five series two games to one, the A's scored two runs in the top of the 10th inning of Game Four to go ahead by 3-1. The Tigers rallied in the bottom of the inning, pushing across a run and chasing two pitchers before Hamilton was called to the mound with the bases loaded and still none out.

He walked Norm Cash (tying the score, 3-3) before Jim Northrup's single prolonged the Tigers season. Oakland's Bob Locker took the loss. "We didn't do the job," manager Williams said after the game. "It's as simple as that."[3]

Despite that poor performance, Hamilton was entrusted with the ball twice in the 1972 World Series. He pitched in the ninth inning of Game Five after the Cincinnati Reds pushed across a run to go ahead, 5-4. With one out, Pete Rose on second, and Dave Concepcion on third, Hamilton faced Joe Morgan at the plate. Morgan flied out to right with the runner at third tagging on the play. Matty Alou threw to Gene Tenace to nail Concepcion at the plate and end the inning. The 9-2 double play gave the A's a chance to rally, but the home team failed to score.

With Oakland trailing 3-1 in Game Six, Hamilton was brought in to work the seventh. He managed to record only two outs while being touched for three singles and an intentional walk (issued to Rose), and was charged with four earned runs in a game the Reds won, 8-1. He'd never again be entrusted to throw in a postseason game.

David Edward Hamilton was born in Seattle on December 13, 1947. He pitched for Edmonds High (now Edmonds-Woodway) in Edmonds, Washington, and was selected in the fifth round (No. 82 overall) of the 1966 amateur baseball draft by the Kansas City Athletics. (The Athletics took Reggie Jackson with the second overall pick.) Hamilton spent four seasons pitching in Single-A for the Lewiston (Idaho) Broncs; Burlington (Iowa) Bees; Peninsula Grays of Hampton, Virginia; Leesburg (Florida) A's; and Lodi (California) Crushers. He then went 8-6 for the Double-A Birmingham (Alabama) A's of the Southern League over the 1969 and 1970 seasons.

A 12-4 campaign in Des Moines with the Iowa Oaks in 1971 followed by a 5-1 start to the 1972 season led to the Sunday-morning telephone call from Finley.

Despite his contributions to Oakland's championship, Hamilton spent part of the 1973 season back in the minors. He completed six of 14 starts for the Tucson Toros with a record of 8-5.

After two seasons as a spot starter, Hamilton was at last integrated into the Oakland rotation as a fifth starter in 1974. He won his first four starts, followed by three no-decisions and a loss. The loss was a mess of fielding misjudgments, dubious umpiring verdicts and a pitcher who lost his composure.

Oakland pitching coach Wes Stock asked relief pitcher Darold Knowles to talk to the anxious starter. "Hammy, don't worry about the umpires, or errors, or bloopers," Knowles told his fellow hurler. "Just do what I do. Step off the mound and take a deep breath."[4] Soon after, on June 26, Hamilton had a no-hit bid against the California Angels broken up in the sixth inning when, after walking Mickey Rivers, he was touched for a single by Dave Chalk. The hit was followed by another walk. The starter followed Knowles' advice by stepping off the mound, recovering to survive the bases-loaded challenge and finish the only complete-game shutout of his career. He gave up two hits and four walks in the 5-0 victory.

Hamilton preferred Alvin Dark as manager to his predecessor, saying, "I don't want to knock Dick Williams, but I don't think he was good for me. … When I lost, he never told me what I was doing wrong. He wouldn't even talk to me. If I had a bad game or two, I was out of there."[5] Dark did not call on Hamilton in the 1973 or '74 postseason.

On June 15, 1975, Hamilton and Chet Lemon were traded to the Chicago White Sox for Stan Bahnsen and Skip Pitlock. In Chicago he was used out of the bullpen, earning 25 saves before being traded to the St. Louis Cardinals after the 1977 season. In 1978 he had no decisions in 13 games of early-season mopup duty with the Cardinals before being sold on May 28 to the Pittsburgh Pirates, for whom he appeared in 16 games. Hamilton then signed with the A's as a free agent for the 1979 season. He performed adequately on a dismal squad, going 3-4. His career ended with a 1980 season split between the A's and the minors, with a final four games of inconsequence played in 1981 with the minor-league Tacoma Tigers.

The left-hander was 39-41 over nine major-league seasons with four teams. He appeared in 301 games with 57 starts and 31 saves, and a career earned-run average of 3.85. In 704 innings pitched, he issued 317 bases on balls while striking out 434.

A son, Jon Hamilton, born on October 23, 1977, spent eight seasons in the minors after being drafted by the Cleveland Indians in the fifth round (like his father before him) of the 1977 amateur draft. The son spent time in the Chicago Cubs, White Sox, and Cardinals organizations before ending his playing career in 2004.

In 1996 Dave Hamilton became baseball coach for the Grizzlies at California High School in San Ramon, California, a position he held until 2004. He had also worked as a foreman for a local roofing contractor.

SOURCES

In addition to the sources reflected in the notes, the author also consulted:

Mitch Stephens, "Ex-A's pitcher enjoying titles on a different level," *San Francisco Chronicle*, May 14, 2002.

calhigh.net/championships.

Retrosheet.org.

Baseball-Reference.com.

NOTES

1   William P. Oppel, "Instant Fame for Finley Rookie," United Press International, *Beaver County* (Pennsylvania) *Times*, May 30, 1972.

2   Ibid.

3   "We didn't do the job," *Palm Beach Post*, October 12, 1972, E4.

4   Ron Bergman, "Hamilton curbs wildness, wins starter job with A's," *The Sporting News*, July 20, 1974, 5.

5   Ibid.

James "Catfish" Hunter

By Jeff English

For someone who always preferred the simple things in life, James Augustus Hunter was a complex man. To most of the world, he was Catfish, the big-game, big-money, right-handed ace who anchored an Oakland A's pitching staff that won three straight World Series titles from 1972 to 1974. It was Catfish who in May 1968 pitched the American League's first perfect game in 46 years. He won 20 or more games for five straight seasons, and captured the American League's Cy Young Award in 1974. It was Catfish who, after being declared a free agent by an arbitrator in December 1974, was made baseball's highest-paid player by the New York Yankees. He paid immediate dividends with the Yankees, winning 23 games in the first year of his new contract, and then contributed to three straight pennant-winning seasons, 1976-1978.

But to those who were closest to him, had grown up with him, and knew him best, he was just Jimmy. It was Jimmy who was born and raised in little Hertford, North Carolina, the youngest and most athletically gifted of eight children. As a boy he used to catch and sell frogs to local restaurants to earn enough money to buy baseballs. It was Jimmy who earned state title victories in football, track, and baseball at Perquimans County High School. He married his high-school sweetheart, lived on a modest farm, and drove an old Ford pickup around town, even after he was baseball's highest-paid player. And it was Jimmy who chose to sign with the Yankees despite more lucrative offers elsewhere, in large part due to New York's relative closeness to his farm in Hertford. Those best acquainted with Catfish often resorted to words like "artist," "control," or "competitive" in discussions of the man and his career. Those who best knew Jimmy were more likely to use words such as "humble," "modest," "low key," or "down to earth." Hunter was a country boy who excelled on the biggest stages in the game of baseball, without ever losing sight of

where he came from or who he was as a person. And it endeared him to his teammates, fans on both coasts, and seemingly all of the state of North Carolina, where after his death he continued to be revered as a legendary native son.

Jim Hunter was born on August 8, 1946, in Hertford, North Carolina, a farming town with a population at the time of about 2,000. He was the youngest of eight children, five boys and three girls crammed into a modest four-bedroom wood-frame home on 30 acres just a couple of miles from town. His father, Abbott, was a tenant farmer and logging foreman and his mother, Millie, a homemaker, and they worked hard to instill a strong work ethic and sense of discipline in their children. Abbott loved the outdoors and taught all of his children to hunt and fish at a young age. Jim

proved especially receptive to the instruction and frequently trumpeted his enjoyment of the outdoors for the rest of his life.

Hunter learned the game of baseball as a boy by playing with his brothers. When they were not in school, they were expected to perform chores around the house or work in the fields with Abbott. But time allowances were made for baseball. Sometimes that meant piling in the back of Abbott's 1959 Ford for trips to Baltimore so Jim could see his favorite pitcher, Robin Roberts. Usually it meant at least a couple of hours playing games in the backyard after a long day of work. As Hunter recalled in his 1988 autobiography, "The lessons learned in those backyard games stayed with me the rest of my career. The biggest one: If you don't throw strikes to your brothers, you don't play. It was that simple."[1] As they got older, the Hunter boys organized neighborhood teams made up of Jim and his three of his older brothers (Marvin, Ray, and Pete), as well as boys from the surrounding area. Jim's brother Edward played catcher in local semipro leagues. By the time he reached his teens, Jim had developed a reputation as a good all-around ballplayer, both on the mound and at the plate. He perfected a side-arm style of delivering the ball to hitters. According to childhood friend, occasional opponent, and high school teammate, Francis Combs:

"Jimmy matured early. I think it was all the playin' he did with his brothers, all the hard work on the farm. He just worked harder than anyone else coming up. Mechanically, he threw hard, always with pretty good control, and he had a good curveball. I remember how intimidated, how scared some of those hitters were. You could actually see kids' knees shakin' when they batted against him."[2]

Jim entered Perquimans County High School in 1960, and excelled on the gridiron, the track, and the diamond. He posted an 8-5 record on the mound his sophomore year, and followed that up with 13 wins against only one loss to lead his team to the state Class AA title his junior season. In one 12-inning game, he struck out 29 batters. He went on to throw two no-

hitters in American Legion ball that year, garnering the attention of a number of major-league scouts.

One scout in particular took a liking to Jim and made himself a regular visitor to the Hunter home. Clyde Kluttz was born in Rockwell, North Carolina, and owned a farm in nearby Salisbury. He scouted for the Kansas City Athletics. He caught over 500 games in the big leagues for five different teams throughout the 1940s and early '50s. With over 25 years in the game in one capacity or other, Kluttz liked what he saw from Jim on the mound. Like a lot of others, he eagerly awaited what Jim had in store for his senior season of high school.

Jim's senior year began well enough. He made all-state in football while contributing to a 33-0 victory in the Class AA state title game. He was the 440-yard dash state champion in track and field. But on Thanksgiving Day in 1963, an accident occurred that threatened to bring Jim's athletic career to a sudden end. As they returned from a hunting trip, his brother Pete's shotgun accidentally discharged, hitting Jim's right foot and causing significant injury. He lost his small toe and suffered numerous broken bones as dozens of pellets lodged in his foot. Recalling the incident in 1974, Hunter joked, "My brother still doesn't know what happened, but his shotgun went off accidentally and got me in the foot. Then he went and had the nerve to faint on me. I had to slap his face to wake him up."[3] At the hospital, doctors were able to remove six of the 45 or so pellets they found in Jim's right foot. He had no feeling in his fourth toe, and over the next few months had multiple visits to the doctor to have additional pellets removed. He recovered in time for the start of baseball season, but news of the injury caused many scouts to question Jim's future on the mound. But not Clyde Kluttz. When he heard about the accident, he immediately went to visit Jim and became an even more frequent guest at the Hunter home than he had been the previous season.

Although 30 pellets remained lodged in Jim's right foot, the injury did not seem to detract from his effort on the hill. The team began the season by shutting out its first eight opponents, including a 5-0 perfect game by Jim against rival Elizabeth City on April 15, 1964. It was his second no-hit performance in a row. By season's end, he had compiled an impressive 13-1 record with five no-hitters. In his final two seasons at Perquimans County High School, Jim's record was 26-2. Any doubts observers had about the injured foot seemed a thing of the past, as scouts were once again taking notice.

But Clyde Kluttz had always been there. He believed in Jim before the injury and never doubted him afterward either. As Hunter recalled, "Seeing his face was certainly no surprise; by now he'd almost earned himself a spot in the family portrait, stopping by as he pleased, having dinner, talking to my daddy in the fields and my mom in the kitchen."[4] Kluttz, convinced of Hunter's ability, recommended signing him to Athletics owner Charlie Finley. Finley arrived in Hertford in June, watched Jim pitch in the state championship game, and then offered him a $75,000 bonus to sign with Kansas City. A few days later, Jim agreed to become a member of the Athletics.

Catfish Hunter was born inside the mind of Charlie Finley. Finley was a successful businessman, and part of being a successful businessman requires understanding how best to market a product. On a telephone call at the time of Hunter's signing, Finley asked Jim if he had a nickname. Hunter relayed the story in a 1991 interview with Edvins Beitiks of the *San Francisco Examiner*:

"He told me, 'A player's got to have a nickname,' and he asked me what I liked to do. 'Hunting and fishing,' I said, and he said, 'Let's call you "Catfish."'... The story is, when you were 6 years old you ran away from home to fish and by the time your parents got to you you'd caught two catfish and were just about to bring in a third. Got that? Now you repeat it to me.'"[5]

Shortly after signing, Hunter was dispatched to Finley's farm in LaPorte, Indiana, to rest. Arrangements were made for him to travel from there to the Mayo Clinic in Rochester, Minnesota, where 16 more pellets and bone fragments were removed from his right foot. He healed well enough to participate in fall instruc-

tional ball in Bradenton, Florida, under the watchful eye of camp coordinator Clyde Kluttz.

Nineteen-year-old Jim Hunter was a $75,000 bonus baby fresh out of high school with no real track record to speak of. Nineteen-year-old Catfish Hunter was a fireballing, can't miss, right-handed phenom whose nickname was ready-made for memorable headlines. Expectations were high despite the fact that Hunter had not pitched since before he visited the Mayo Clinic. He made his debut with two scoreless innings of relief work against the White Sox on May 13, 1965. His first start came against the Tigers in Detroit and resulted in four earned runs in just two innings of work. He finally earned his first big-league victory in his sixth start, on July 27 at Boston. He yielded five earned runs in five innings as the Athletics scraped out a 10-8 victory.

Hunter finished the 1965 season with a record of 8-8, a 4.26 ERA, and 82 strikeouts in 133 innings pitched. As a club, the A's were young, inexperienced, and losers of 103 games, resulting in a tenth-place finish in the standings. But despite mediocre numbers, Hunter impressed with his competitiveness and a maturity that belied his 19 years. A's pitching coach Ed Lopat told the *The Sporting News*, "He's made a believer out of me now. The thing that impresses me about Hunter is the way he reacts after someone has hit a home run against him. ... Hunter doesn't scare. He keeps on throwing strikes."[6] Hunter's development into a Hall of Fame-caliber pitcher would take several seasons, but the faith shown him by the likes of Kluttz, Finley, and the A's organization would be generously rewarded.

Over the next several seasons, Hunter continued to improve. He did not possess an overpowering fastball, instead succeeding largely on the basis of pinpoint control and a willingness to challenge hitters with pitches in the strike zone. In 1967 he reached double digits in wins for the first time with 13, while striking out 196 batters, the highest single-season total he achieved in his career. The following season, the A's moved from Kansas City to Oakland and won 82 games to finish over .500 for the first time since 1952. The highlight of the season was 22-year-old Hunter's perfect game against the Minnesota Twins on May 8 in Oakland. He struck out 11 batters and helped himself at the plate by driving in three runs with three hits in the 4-0 win. Teammate Jack Aker told the *Oakland Tribune*, "There was just one thing he did wrong. He flied to center field once."[7] While the team finished in sixth place, expectations continued to grow with the improvement of a core of young players that included Hunter, Reggie Jackson, Blue Moon Odom, and Sal Bando.

Catfish won a personal-best 21 games in 1971 as Oakland won 101 games and the American League West title. They were swept in three games in the League Championship Series by the Baltimore Orioles, who went on to win the World Series. In his first shot at postseason glory, Hunter took the loss in Game Two of the ALCS, 5-1. Of his performance, he quipped, "And I only made four mistakes. Naturally, all four ended up in the seats. Two home runs by Boog Powell, one each by Brooks Robinson and Elrod Hendricks."[8] Oakland's appearance in the postseason was the first by the Philadelphia-Kansas City-Oakland franchise since 1931. Most observers felt the club, with all of its accumulated talent, would compete for the pennant again in 1972.

Hunter entered the 1972 season as the ace of the Oakland staff and one of the unquestioned leaders on a team full of big characters and bigger egos. His country-cool attitude and all-out effort garnered respect from his teammates, who were always confident when Catfish was scheduled to take the mound. He equaled his previous season's victory total with 21, to go along with a 2.04 ERA, third best in the league. The club won 93 games to finish 5½ games ahead of the Chicago White Sox. Oakland won, three games to two, over the Detroit Tigers in a hotly contested ALCS in which three of the five games were decided by a single run and two went into extra innings. Hunter failed to earn a decision in either his Game One or Game Four start, but he pitched well, allowing just two runs in 15⅓ innings. Oakland won the first game in 11 innings, 3-2, and lost Game Four in ten innings by the same score.

The 1972 World Series pitted the A's against the National League's Cincinnati Reds. The A's took Game One. 3-2. Catfish got the start in Game Two and delivered 8⅔ innings, allowing just one run while notching six strikeouts. Reliever Rollie Fingers was called upon to record the final out to give Oakland a two-game lead over Cincinnati. The Reds narrowly took Game Three, 1-0, but Oakland rebounded the next day to win 3-0. Up three games to one, the A's looked to Hunter to close out the series in Game Five.

It was apparent early on that Hunter did not have his best stuff. Recalling Game Five in his autobiography, he lamented, "It was all up to me now. Game Five. It wasn't to be. Pete Rose, just one for fifteen up to that point, hit my first pitch of the game over the 375-feet sign in right."[9] Cincinnati won the game, 5-4. The Reds took Game Six as well, an 8-1 blowout to set up a decisive Game Seven showdown. In that game, Hunter was brought in to relieve starter Blue Moon Odom with one out in the fifth inning. He yielded just one run in 2⅔ innings while striking out three. Hunter was credited with the win while Rollie Fingers earned his second save to give the Athletics franchise its first World Series title since 1930. Hunter finished fourth in the American League Cy Young voting and received enough consideration from voters to place 11th in the Most Valuable Player balloting. He was now a two-time 20-game winner and a World Series champion.

Oakland repeated as World Series champions in 1973, defeating the New York Mets in seven games. Hunter's season record was remarkably similar to the numbers he posted the previous year. He again managed 21 victories while earning a spot on his fifth All-Star team. He was masterful in the postseason, winning two games against the Orioles in the ALCS and outdueling Mets ace Tom Seaver, 3-1, in Game Six of the World Series, to avoid elimination and force a Game Seven.

In February of 1974, Hunter signed a new two-year contract with Oakland that called for him to receive $100,000 per season. A stipulation in the agreement called for half of each season's salary to be deferred into insurance annuities. By most accounts, A's owner Charlie Finley agreed to the arrangement, and Hunter began to make preparations for the 1974 season.

Oakland finished five games ahead of the Texas Rangers in the American League West, and dispatched the Baltimore Orioles three games to one in the ALCS to secure its third straight American League pennant. Catfish turned in what was perhaps his finest season on the mound, with a league-leading 25 wins, a 2.49 ERA and a league-best 0.986 WHIP (walks and hits per inning pitched). In the World Series, the A's faced the Los Angeles Dodgers, who had won 102 games during the regular season, the most in baseball. Oakland did not require any extra motivation for the Series, but the Dodgers provided it anyway. According to Hunter, "Dodger first baseman Billy Buckner helped matters along by suggesting to all the world that only a few of our guys could make their precious little Dodger roster. Riiiight. We didn't say so at the time, preferring to keep our words to ourselves, but Buckner made a big mistake by telling us we couldn't play."[10] The A's took the series in five games, with Catfish earning a save in Game One and a win in Game Three, in which he allowed only one run in 7⅓ innings. Afterward, Buckner remarked, "I thought I should have hit the ball hard every time."[11] The A's were World Series champions for the third straight season. For his efforts, Hunter won the American League Cy Young award and finished sixth in the MVP vote. Texas Ranger Jeff Burroughs won the MVP award, but some felt Hunter's contributions to the A's were more valuable. Reggie Jackson offered that he "would give Cat the Cy Young Award, the Most Valuable Player Award, the Academy Award, and the kitchen sink."[12] For his part, Hunter had other things to concern himself with immediately after the season concluded.

In August Hunter's hometown attorney, J. Carlton Cherry, began sending letters to Charlie Finley requesting compliance with the terms of Hunter's contract. At issue was the fact that Finley had not yet made arrangements to pay the deferred compensation portion of the agreement. Failing to receive a satisfac-

tory response, Cherry took the case to the Major League Baseball Players Association. On October 4, a telegram arrived at Finley's office, stating:

"Pursuant to paragraph 7(a) of contract between Mr. Hunter and the Oakland Club, please be advised that contract is terminated due to Club's default in making payments in accordance with said contract and its failure to remedy said default within ten days after receiving written notice thereof. Because of the impending playoffs and World Series, the effective date of termination shall be the day following the last game played by the Oakland Athletics in 1974."[13]

The telegram was signed by Dick Moss, general counsel for the union. Hunter, his representatives, and the MLBPA were contending that since Finley had failed to honor the specifics of the agreement, Hunter deserved to be declared a free agent, available to the highest bidder of his choice. Despite Finley's protests, the case was sent to an independent arbitrator under the rules of the union contract. On November 26, at the MLBPA offices in New York, the case was heard before a three-person panel: Marvin Miller, executive director of the MLBPA; John J. Gaherin, an attorney representing the club owners; and Peter Seitz, an independent arbitrator. On December 16 Miller and Seitz voted in Hunter's favor, effectively freeing him from Finley's grasp and leaving the pitcher's future in the hands of the open market. Hunter could sign with any team willing to have him. As it turned out, almost every club in the big leagues wanted him for their pitching staff.

In a series of scenes that can only be described as bizarre, executives and other representatives from 23 major-league teams descended upon the town of Ahoskie, North Carolina, to negotiate with Cherry for Hunter's services. Every team except the San Francisco Giants attempted to sign him. It soon boiled down to just a handful of clubs with a serious shot at landing Catfish. Among them were the San Diego Padres, the Kansas City Royals, and the Cleveland Indians. Some of them sent former teammates to visit Hunter at home in order to persuade him to sign. But one club had an ace up its sleeve in the form of Clyde

Kluttz, the former Oakland scout who had convinced Finley to sign Jim in 1964.

Kluttz now scouted for the Yankees. They had not qualified for the postseason since 1964. In the offseason, Kluttz and Hunter enjoyed hunting together, as they had remained close since Hunter's days in high school. George Steinbrenner, the Yankees' owner, was not allowed to participate in the negotiations because he was serving a two-year suspension imposed by Commissioner Bowie Kuhn after an indictment on charges related to illegal campaign contributions. But general manager Gabe Paul had strict orders from his boss: "When his unfortunate suspension was invoked, he told me, 'Anytime you have the opportunity to buy the contract of a player for cash, I want you to go ahead whenever, in your judgment, it would be advantageous to the Yankees.'"[14] Ultimately, Jim agreed to become a Yankee, and a press conference was held on New Year's Eve 1974 to announce the deal to the world. The agreement called for Hunter to receive $3.2 million over five years, making him the game's first free agent to cash in for big money on the open market. The influence Kluttz had on Hunter's decision to sign with the Yankees can't be understated. He was offered more money by several other teams, but said, "I don't think I would have signed with the Yankees if anybody but Clyde had contacted me for them. Clyde never lied to me about anything and I knew he wouldn't now."[15] The loss was devastating to the A's, many of whom wished the best for their former ace while decrying the effect his absence would have for the ballclub. Catcher Gene Tenace expressed a common sentiment, saying, "I'm tickled to death for him. It couldn't happen to a better guy. I'm glad he was able to get all he could. But his loss will definitely hurt our club."[16] Finley continued to insist that Hunter was a member of the Oakland club, contractually speaking, and filed a lawsuit to have the arbitrator's decision overturned. His relationship with his former Cy Young Award winner was irreparably damaged. The resentment Hunter held toward Finley was the result of a long list of questionable decisions and minor injustices the A's owner had committed over Hunter's 10 years in Oakland.

Catfish made his debut with the Yankees on April 11, 1975, against the Detroit Tigers and promptly lost, allowing five earned over nine innings. He proceeded to lose his next two decisions as well before finally beating the Milwaukee Brewers on April 27. As the season wore on, Jim warmed up to his new surroundings. By season's end he had compiled 23 wins and a 2.58 ERA in 328 innings pitched. He made his seventh All-Star team and finished second to Baltimore's Jim Palmer in the Cy Young voting. He rose to the occasion and met the pressure of his new contract head-on, turning in one of his finest seasons in the big leagues. But the Yankees as a team regressed from their wins total the previous season, and any postseason promise implied in Hunter's signing was left unfulfilled.

In 1976 the Yankees returned to the postseason after an 11-year absence. Hunter won 17 games in the regular season, and beat the Kansas City Royals in Game One of the ALCS, going the distance and allowing a single earned run. In the World Series the Yankees were swept by Cincinnati's Big Red Machine. Hunter took the loss in Game Two, allowing 10 hits and walking an uncharacteristically high four batters. During the regular season, he pitched 298⅔ innings, a total he would not come close to approaching in any of the three years remaining on his contract.

The Yankees won two straight World Series titles in 1977 and 1978. Hunter appeared in only 43 games over the course of the two seasons, with an overall record of 21-15. He suffered from arm fatigue, and was diagnosed with diabetes in February of 1978. He lost his only postseason start in 1977, allowing three home runs in 2⅓ innings in Game Two of the World Series. In 1978 he posted a respectable 12-6 record, and pitched especially well in the thick of the pennant race in August, winning six games to go with a 1.64 ERA in the month. In the final postseason appearance of his career, he beat the Dodgers in Game Six of the World Series to give the Yankees their second straight title.

For Hunter, 1979 was a devastating year personally and, as it turned out, his final season in the big leagues. On May 12 Clyde Kluttz, the man Jim most admired in baseball, died from a blood clot just one day after insisting to Jim on a telephone call that he was doing fine and was just tired. On July 26 Hunter was making preparations to pitch when manager Billy Martin called him into his office to inform him that his father, Abbott, had died after a long battle with cancer. On August 2 Yankee catcher Thurman Munson, Hunter's closest friend on the team, was killed when his twin-engine plane crashed at an airport where he was practicing landing. Acknowledging the toll the losses took, Hunter said, "Dealing with three deaths in a span of three months was beyond belief. You try not to let it affect you; you know you've got a job to do, a game to play, but Lord, it's a lot to ask of a man."[17] On the field, Hunter turned in his worst season in the big leagues. He finished the season with a 2-9 mark and an ERA of over five. The Yankees finished in fourth place.

Catfish made it clear before the 1979 season that it would be his final one in a major-league uniform. After the season, in an interview that appeared in *The Sporting News* in October 1979, he said, "When I signed my contract with the Yankees, I told them I would play these five years and call it a career no matter what happened. Fifteen years is enough."[18] His primary motivation for doing so was to spend more time with his family, and more time outdoors, hunting and fishing.

George Steinbrenner declared Sunday, September 16, 1979, Catfish Hunter Day at Yankee Stadium. Hunter's number 29 was retired by the club, and teammates and fans had an opportunity to celebrate his career accomplishments. In his speech to the crowd, Hunter spoke of wishing his father, Abbott, his friend Clyde Kluttz, and his teammate Thurman Munson could have been there to celebrate. He was leaving the game with a heavy heart, but he was just 33 years old, financially secure, and had a loving family who looked forward to having him around the house full-time.

At the time of his retirement, Jim's wife, Helen, was pregnant with their third child. Helen was Jim's high-school sweetheart, and they were married on October 9, 1966. In October 1979 she gave birth to their second son, Paul, who would join 10-year-old Todd and 6-year-old Kimberly as the lights of Jim's life. The new baby helped ease Jim into retirement. But between diaper changes and coaching Todd's Little League team, he made plenty of time to fit in as much hunting and fishing as he could manage. While he always professed that he was happiest on a pitcher's mound, those who knew him best found it hard to believe he could be any happier than when he was outdoors in North Carolina. He owned a 1,000-acre farm, where he grew corn, soybeans, and peanuts on a portion of the land. He leased the rest of it to other growers. He kept a kennel full of hunting dogs, and remained an avid outdoorsman for the remainder of his life.

In 1987 Hunter was inducted into the Baseballs Hall of Fame. He won 224 games, had five straight seasons with 20 or more wins, and collected five World Series rings. In his induction speech, he thanked Charlie Finley and George Steinbrenner for giving him the opportunity to play. He spoke about the guidance Clyde Kluttz provided to him over the course of his career, and called his election to the Hall "the greatest honor that any guy could ever receive."[19]

Hunter lived a quiet life on his farm with his family. In September 1998, after having difficulty lifting his arms to fire his hunting rifle, he visited a hospital in Baltimore, where he was diagnosed with amyotrophic lateral sclerosis, also known as Lou Gehrig's disease. His last public appearance was in Tampa, Florida, at the Yankees' first spring-training game in March, 1999. He died at his home in Hertford on September 9, 1999, at the age of 53. He was buried in Cedar Wood Cemetery in Hertford, just behind the field where he had starred as a high-school pitcher. In a tribute to the type of competitor Catfish Hunter was on the field, and the type of man Jim Hunter was off the field, George Steinbrenner remarked, "Catfish Hunter was the cornerstone of the Yankees' success over the last quarter-century. We were not winning before Catfish arrived. He exemplified class and dignity and he taught us how to win."[20] Jim Hunter was survived by his wife, Helen, their three children, and one grandchild.

NOTES

1   Jim "Catfish" Hunter and Armen Keteyian, *Catfish: My Life in Baseball* (New York: McGraw-Hill Book Company, 1988), 19.

2   Hunter and Keteyian, 21-22.

3   Phil Elderkin, "Catfish Hunter: Hooked on Pitching," *Baseball Digest*, March 1974, 58-60.

4   Hunter and Keteyian, 29.

5   Edvins Beitiks, "Catfish Hunter: A Lifetime of Happy Baseball Memories," *Baseball Digest*, November 1991, 72-74.

6   Joe McGuff, "Catfish Best Catch in A's Pitching Net," *The Sporting News*, September 18, 1965.

7   Ron Bergman, "Catfish Is 'Perfect,' First In 46 Years," *Oakland Tribune*, May 9, 1968.

8   Hunter and Ketevian, 98.

9   Hunter and Keteyian, 111-112.

10 Hunter and Keteyian, 132.

11 Joe Gergen, "Catfish Hunter: A 'Money' Pitcher From the Start," *Baseball Digest*, June 1975, 53.

12 Bill Libby, *Catfish: The Three Million Dollar Pitcher* (New York: Coward, McCann & Geoghegan, Inc., 1976), 132.

13 Libby, 130.

14 Libby, 27.

15 Phil Pepe, "Yankees' $2.85 Million Land Catfish," *The Sporting News*, January 18, 1975.

16 "Catfish Feels Like Million, or Three," *Oakland Tribune*, January 1, 1975.

17 Hunter and Keteyian, 206.

18 Phil Pepe, "Yankee Era Ends With Hunter's Retirement," *The Sporting News*, October 6, 1979.

19 baseballhall.org/node/11219

20 sportsillustrated.cnn.com/baseball/mlb/news/1999/09/09/hunter_obit_ap/

Reggie Jackson

By Ted Leavengood

Reginald Martinez Jackson was born on May 18, 1946, in Wyncote, Pennsylvania, a largely white suburb north of Philadelphia's central city. His father, Martinez Jackson, ran a dry-cleaning and tailoring business. As a grown man, Reggie claimed he still knew how to cuff a pair of slacks.[1] His father was a veteran of World War II who flew a P-51 Mustang fighter during the North Africa campaign and used his Army Air Corps savings to start his business in a modest two-story structure, home to both family and business.

Reggie's father was a significant presence in his early life who provided a working-class environment amid somewhat more affluent surroundings. His mother, Clara, left with three of the children when he was 6 years old. His father raised Reggie, older brother James, and an older half-brother, Joe. Martinez continued to provide important stability until Reggie's senior year in high school.

Jackson was often one of the few black students attending his school. His background differed greatly from that of other black major leaguers of his generation who came of age in segregated communities and learned early the importance of a low profile. His comfortable demeanor among whites of relative affluence was at times a source of problems with other players, the press, and ownership.

Jackson starred in high-school sports including football, basketball, baseball, and track, and his games attracted many scouts. Martinez father wanted his son to get a college education and urged him to eschew a professional contract. When Reggie graduated from high school and made his way to Arizona State University on a football scholarship, the most important figure in his life was not present. Martinez Jackson had been arrested and jailed near the end of Reggie's senior year in high school for making moonshine in his basement.

Later, when he played for the Baltimore Orioles, Jackson reconnected with his mother and sisters Tina, Beverly, and Delores, who lived in Baltimore. He maintained a relatively close relationship with both sides of his family during his adult years.

With his father imprisoned, Jackson found important new mentors at Arizona State. The football coach was Frank Kush, who later was inducted into the College Football Hall of Fame. Jackson said Kush taught him toughness in relentless, physically demanding drills for the football team. An excellent football player, he could run the 60-yard dash in sprinter speed, 6.3 seconds.[2] By the beginning of his sophomore year he was a starting defensive back and the defensive captain in a Top 20 program.

Jackson found baseball more by accident than by intent. He had asked permission to play baseball as part of his scholarship agreement, but had to maintain a B average to do so. In the spring of his freshman year, he arranged a tryout. He displayed the tape-measure power he had even as a young man and was asked to join the freshman team. His skills were still rough and coach Bobby Winkles suggested that he play baseball in the summer with a Baltimore amateur team to sharpen them. It was an all-white team run by a Baltimore Orioles scout, Walter Youse.

Neither Youse nor anyone else on the team understood Reggie to be black until he showed up for the tryout. Youse watched the tryout and told Reggie years later, "The more I saw you that day, the whiter you got."[3] After a summer playing competitive baseball almost every day, Jackson returned for his sophomore year at Arizona State and claimed the starting job in center field.

The position had been manned the prior year by Rick Monday, who Jackson said "was a big league ballplayer when he was 19."[4] Monday was the best college player in the country when he left Arizona State and signed a $100,000 bonus contract with the Kansas City Athletics at the end of Jackson's freshman year. Reggie opined that replacing Monday in center field was like "replacing the sun and moon."[5]

Jackson had a remarkable sophomore baseball season and was drafted by the A's, the second player chosen in the June 1966 draft. What followed was the first of many protracted negotiations between Jackson and Athletics owner Charles O. Finley. Jackosn and his father (nowout of jail), traveled to Finley's Indiana farm, where they agreed to a contract with an $85,000 bonus.

Jackson began at Lewiston (Idaho) of the low Class A Northwest League, but was quickly moved to Modesto of the high-A California League, where he met many of players with whom he would share some of the greatest moments of his early years in the majors. Rollie Fingers, Joe Rudi, and Dave Duncan played for Modesto and were a cut above the rest even then.

When the team traveled to Bakersfield for a series, the local paper's headlines read, "Call Out the National Guard, the Modesto Reds Are in Town."[6]

The next season the foursome continued as the backbone of Birmingham in the Southern League. It was Jackson's introduction to the unique cultural institutions of the South as they existed in 1967. Segregation was enforced unofficially in many aspects of life in Alabama and Jackson said that he felt the "uncomfortableness, the awkwardness, the fear ... in the heart of Dixie."[7] He played well enough for the Birmingham A's to earn a midseason promotion to Kansas City.

In his first exposure to the majors, Jackson hit only .178 and was sent back down. The demotion was difficult for him emotionally, but Birmingham manager John McNamara provided important support. McNamara managed Jackson again in Oakland and Anaheim, and Jackson said his help was essential for a 21-year-old trying to grow up and handle both success and failure in a Deep South environment.

Jackson started the 1968 season with Oakland, where Finley had relocated the Athletics. He shrugged off the tentative emotions from his prior "cup of coffee" and started the season strong. At the end of April he was hitting .309 with four home runs. He cooled off and saw his average drop to .231 in early June. In May he hit only one "dinger," as he liked to call his home runs.

Then in June Jackson found his power stroke again. He ended the season with 29 home runs and batted .250. His ability to hit the long ball established him as a permanent feature in a lineup anchored by Sal Bando, also from Arizona State, Joe Rudi, and Bert Campaneris, the dynamic basestealer who hit at the top of the lineup. Rick Monday was in center field, but it was Bando, Jackson, Campaneris, and Rudi who became the backbone of the Oakland Athletics teams that dominated the American League in the 1970s.

The '68 Athletics finished sixth, winning 82 games. They were on a slow ascent and the next year Jackson was at the center of it all. He became a national celebrity during the 1969 season as he put up home run numbers that compared to those of Roger Maris and Babe Ruth. By July 5 he had 34 home runs; Frank Howard and Harmon Killebrew had 30 and 22 respectively.

"Microphones were shoved in my face for the first time. ... Fans grabbed and screeched for autographs," Reggie said, acknowledging that he was not ready for the pressure his success had created.[8] He was only 23 years old and described himself as "tired and beat up" by the end of the season. Managing only a single home run in September, he ended the season with 47 home runs, third behind Killebrew with 49 and Howard (48). Jackson led the league in slugging, at.608, and the 47 home runs were his career best.

The next season was one of the worst in Jackson's early life. He hit .237 with only 23 home runs. He and his wife, Jennie, whom he had met at Arizona State and married in 1968, divorced. Very little went right during the year and Reggie decided to play winter ball in Puerto Rico in hopes of finding his swing. At Santurce he played for future Hall of Famer and inveterate tough guy Frank Robinson, who was a positive influence and helped Jackson put his life back on track.

In 1971 the Athletics began to establish their dominance in the American League. They won 101 games and won the West Division. Sal Bando most often was the dominant force in the clubhouse and just as important in the lineup. Jackson said of him, "When Sal talked, people listened."[9] The atmosphere in the clubhouse was pugnacious at times and it took a strong personality to keep order. According to Reggie that decorum led to execution on the field."Just do it," was Bando's motto. No whining, no excuses, just get the job done.[10]

With Bando, Jackson, and Mike Epstein at its heart, the A's offense was potent, but the pitching was even better. The 1971 season saw the emergence of Vida Blue (24-8, 1.82 ERA), who won both the Most Valuable Player Award and the Cy Young Award. Catfish Hunter won 21 games and had an ERA of 2.96.

The Athletics were swept in the 1971 American League Championship Series to the Baltimore Orioles. From that near-miss, the Athletics and Jackson began a historic run, winning three straight World Series, 1972-1974. No franchise other than the New York Yankees has achieved a similar level of dominance. For a team that defined the term "small-market franchise," it was a remarkable feat.

In 1972 Jackson set a goal of winning the MVP, but failed, hitting only .265 with 25 home runs. First baseman Epstein led the team with 26 home runs and Joe Rudi (.305) was the only Athletic to hit over .300. The A's won the pennant because they featured the best combination of hitting and pitching, finishing second-best in the American League in both runs scored and fewest runs allowed.

In the ALCS the A's beat the Tigers in the playoffs in a tight five-game series where pitching dominated. Jackson was not a deciding factor in any of the games, but played well. In the fifth and final game, Oakland manager Dick Williams called for a double steal with Jackson on third base, Epstein on first, and one out. On the pitch Gene Tenace swung and missed for the second out, and Freehan fired for second base. As soon as the ball went past the pitcher, Jackson bolted from third. Epstein beat the throw and shortstop Woody Fryman threw back to home. Jackson felt his hamstring give 20 feet from home.[11] Despite doing serious damage in the process, Jackson continued down the baseline and executed a perfect slide around Freehan to score what proved to be the winning run. His determination gave Oakland its first American League championship, but he had to be carried from the field with a torn hamstring.

His foot in a cast, Jackson missed the World Series between Oakland and Cincinnati's Big Red Machine. With Reggie watching on crutches from the dugout, the A's defeated the Reds in seven games. The Series MVP was Gene Tenace who had four home runs and hit .348. Though Jackson missed the World Series, he was still in the spotlight and he wanted more. In 1973 he would grab it in earnest.

Early in 1972 Jackson said in an interview, "I want to make me $100,000." He believed he could become an MVP-caliber player and told the interviewer, "I want to be hitting .300 and some change, hitting 35-40 homers, and driving in 100-110 runs."[12] He did not have that kind of year in '72, but it was coming.

In 1973 Mike Epstein was gone and Gene Tenace took over at first base with Ray Fosse catching most games. Tenace had a fine season, hitting 24 home runs with a .259 average. Bando had one of his best years with 29 homers and a .287 average. But this was the first season that Reggie Jackson's name was written into the heart of the lineup without fail every day. Manager Williams also moved him from center field to right, where he would face fewer defensive pressures.

With their strong pitching and Brooks Robinson a third, the Orioles had the best regular-season record in 1973. But in the ALCS Oakland had too much firepower and pitching. Catfish Hunter threw a shutout in the fifth game to win the pennant for the Athletics. Jackson batted only .143 against the Orioles. His fame as the postseason player who became known as Mr. October was still to come.

In the 1973 World Series, Oakland drew the New York Mets, who had surprised Cincinnati for the NL crown. Oakland got the best of it and won in seven games, giving the A's back-to-back titles. Jackson hit his first World Series home run in Game Seven. He hit .310 for the Series, drove in six runs, and was named Series MVP.

It was the first of many honors Jackson won for his 1973 season. He led the league with 32 home runs and 117 RBIs. He batted .293 and stole 22 bases. The collective numbers gave him the MVP season he had sought the year before. He was a unanimous selection, joining an elite group of five other players who had been elected unanimously: Hank Greenberg, Al Rosen, Mickey Mantle, Frank Robinson, and Denny McLain. In January, *The Sporting News* made Jackson its Player of the Year.[13]

Joining such select company was precursor to an almost certain contract war with Charlie Finley. Jackson credited Finley with putting the team together and keeping the squad playing at a high level. But Finley was a one-man operation, filling the jobs of general manager and others to cut his administrative budget to the bone. Jackson said that Finley was a sharp businessman who taught him many things about the world of business, but said above all else, "he was cheap."[14]

Finley issued each player two Oakland A's hats and 24 bats to last the season. During the postseason, when other teams provided a separate plane for press and families, Finley paid for one plane and anyone who could fit. When the trainer taped his ankles, Jackson said, he used tape sparingly and saved whatever was left of each roll, never throwing anything away because there might not be a replacement.[15]

The tight-fisted Finley made contract negotiations high drama. After his MVP season in 1971, Vida Blue held out in April 1972, saying he would retire before taking the $50,000 contract Finley offered. For Jackson the negotiations were just as contentious. Finley drew the line at $100,000, saying he could not pay Jackson more than he paid Catfish Hunter. Jackson was sensitive to the needs of others on the team, saying, "I suppose I could shoot for $175,000 or $200,000, but that would lower the take for the other guys."[16] He maintained that he would not play for less than $125,000. The impasse was resolved in baseball's newest institution, salary arbitration, where the arbitrator bridged the difference at $135,000.

Jackson described the 1974 Athletics as a team that could "win at will."[17] The comment papered over clubhouse angst that began to surface around him that season. A serious physical confrontation with center fielder Bill North stung Jackson because of North's allegations that Jackson spent too much time with whites, especially white women. Jackson's mood soured over the course of the season and during a game he angrily threw a bat into the stands, where it narrowly avoided injuring manager Alvin Dark's wife and two young boys.[18]

Despite the tensions, the deeply talented Athletics team won the Western Division handily and faced the Orioles again for the pennant. As in the previous year, the talented pitching of Jim Palmer, Mike Cuellar, and Dave McNally provided problems, but Oakland won in four games. The A's won the World Series against the Los Angeles Dodgers in five games. Jack had a good Series with the bat, though nothing to rival the previous year. This time it was a great defensive play that defined his contributions to Oakland's third consecutive World Series win.

In Game Five, with the A's leading 3-2 in the eighth inning, Bill Buckner hit a single that North misplayed in center field. Buckner took second and was headed to third with the tying run. Jackson had backed up North and, corralling the ball, he threw a bullet to cutoff man Dick Green who fired to third baseman Bando. Bando applied a sweep tag and Buckner was out, erasing the Dodgers' last threat.

During the offseason, Finley's dynasty began to crumble. Catfish Hunter was awarded free agency by arbitrator Peter Seitz because Finley had failed to make a payment to an annuity as required under Hunter's contract. Hunter signed with the Yankees for $2.85 million over five years. Finley then traded reliever Darold Knowles to the Chicago Cubs for Billy Williams, and Blue Moon Odom to Cleveland. Oakland's diminished potency was underscored when Hunter faced his former teammates for the first time and shut them out, 3-0. Jackson went 0-for-3 and began to question whether he too should be looking for greener pastures and bigger paydays.

As if to make a case, Jackson began an assault on American League pitching that carried him to another home-run title and the Athletics to another West Division title. He was aided by a newcomer, Claudell Washington, Finley's rookie sensation, whose natural position was the same as Jackson's: right field. Neither Washington nor Jackson could get the A's past the Boston Red Sox in the ALCS. Jackson and Sal Bando tore up the Red Sox pitching staff, but Oakland missed Catfish Hunter and was swept by Boston in three

games. There was no World Series in Oakland for the first time in three years and there would be more bad news in the months to come.

In December 1975 arbitrator Peter Seitz expanded his prior year's finding for Catfish Hunter by declaring Andy Messersmith and Dave McNally free agents, thus nullifying the reserve clause. Finley, who had been shopping Jackson in 1975, began a more serious attempt to trade Jackson and other players who would be hitting the free market at season's end.

Seven days before Opening Day of 1976, Finley traded Jackson and pitcher Ken Holtzman to the Orioles. Despite wanting to test the free agent market and often asking Finley to trade him, Jackson was devastated by the news. He had made his life in Oakland and considered it home. Despite fights with teammates and Finley's tight-fisted oversight, he said of his time there, "The eight years I spent in Oakland were the best baseball years of my life."[19]

Jackson took his frustrations out on the Orioles, laboring to reach a suitable deal with GM Hank Peters and owner Edward Bennett Williams over the first few weeks of the season. His holdout impressed neither the Baltimore fans nor the players and when he finally signed at the end of April, he was out of shape. He started the season slowly and on June 13 his batting average was .208 with a paltry four home runs. He started to hit for power late in the month and wound up with 27 homers. The Orioles were never able to close the gap on the Yankees, finishing second in the AL East, 10½ games back. Jackson put a positive spin on his time playing for Earl Weaver and the Orioles in 1976. "Weaver is a great manager," he said. "He made you get more out of yourself."[20]

Still, Jackson resolved to taste free agency and the riches it promised. After the season he listened to offers from the Orioles and the Montreal Expos, but signed with the Yankees—not only were they the best team with the most money, but they were the Yankees, home to baseball's Pinstripe tradition. Owner George Steinbrenner paid him $2.96 million to play five years for New York. It was more than Catfish

Hunter got, and more than any of the veteran Yankee players were making at the time.

Players like Graig Nettles and Thurman Munson had carried New York to the World Series in 1976 and like manager Billy Martin they believed they could do it again without Jackson. Many in the Yankee organization had argued against signing him, saying that the team had Nettles and Chris Chambliss and didn't need another left-handed bat. But the idea of bringing Jackson's huge personality to the Big Apple appealed to owner Steinbrenner. Tension with his teammates began almost immediately. Jackson described the Oakland clubhouse as being "like a college frat house," yet was never part of the club with the '77 Yankees.[21] Billy Martin was particularly problematic. The volatile Martin had once knocked out one of his pitchers at Minnestoa, Dave Boswell. A similar confrontation was narrowly averted between Jackson and Martin in 1977.

On June 18 the Yankees were in Boston playing the Red Sox at Fenway Park in a nationally televised game. Late in the game Jackson misjudged a pop fly off the bat of Jim Rice that fell for a hit. Martin believed Jackson was loafing and the simmering feud that had started with Jackson's signing reached a critical mass.

Martin was angry enough to pull Jackson from the game in mid-inning. When his right fielder entered the dugout, Martin confronted him with pugnacious obscenities. Jackson responded that he wasn't loafing, but escalated the rhetoric when he told Martin, "You never wanted me on this team," and followed it up by calling Martin an "old man."[22] The two came dangerously close to blows and a fistfight was avoided only when Yankee coaches Yogi Berra and Elston Howard strained to keep the two men apart. Much of the scrum was captured on national television, and media attention boiled over in the following days. Despite numerous rumors that Martin would be fired because of the fracas, Steinbrenner and Yankees general manager Gabe Paul and brought the two men together to make peace.

According to Jackson, New York City hosted an ongoing media circus that was a major factor in the difficulty he experienced over his five-year tenure with the Yankees. Jackson said off-handed and off-the-record comments that would not have been printed in other cities regularly became public in New York.

Despite the lack of comity among the star players on the team, the Yankees won the AL East in 1977. Jackson's season was typical: 32 home runs, 110 RBIs, and third in the league in slugging. But Steinbrenner had brought him aboard to win the World Series, to revisit the glories that Yankees teams had not experienced since 1962.

Jackson went 1-for-14 in the first four games of the Championship Series against the Kansas City Royals and Billy Martin benched him for the final game. Insulted and incensed, Jackson still drove in a key run with a pinch-hit single late in the game. New York beat the Royals to earn a match against the Dodgers in the World Series.

Jackson started the Series slowly, going 1-for-6. But in Games Four and Five he hit home runs, helping give the Yankees a three-games-to-two lead as the Series moved to New York. With the Dodgers ahead 3-2 in the fourth inning of Game Six, Jackson faced Burt Hooton, who had handcuffed the Yankees in Game Two. With Thurman Munson on base, he hit a fly ball that just made the right-field stands to give the Yankees the lead. He hit two more homers, in the fifth and eighth innings, drove in five of the victorious Yankees' eight runs—and listened gleefully to deafening chants from the crowd of "Reggie, Reggie" as New York City found itself a new hero.

The press made much of Jackson's World Series, comparing him with Babe Ruth, even calling him the "black Babe Ruth."[23] Jackson made good on Steinbrenner's investment, winning the Series MVP award for the second time in his career. The nickname "Mr. October" stuck to him.

In 1978 the Yankees defeated the Dodgers in the World Series againm with Jackson and Graig Nettles leading the way for the powerful New York lineup. The following season was very different. Team captain Munson died in a crash of his airplane on August 2. The loss devastated the team and Jackson as well. Jackson had smoothed over the tempests of 1977 with Munson and had flown with Munson just days before the crash.

The Yankees never regained their form without Munson, finishing fourth in 1979. Billy Martin was fired after the season. Martin's fall from grace buoyed Jackson, who had his best season in 1980, batting .300 for the first time and hitting 41 home runs. It was good enough to help the team to a first-place finish in the AL East, but the Yankees were swept by the Royals in the ALCS.

In the strike-shortened 1981 season, Jackson played less of a role, but he and the Yankees made it to the World Series one last time. He continued to earn his reputation as a clutch player in October, but he did not lead his team to the championship; the Dodgers beat the Yankees in six games. Jackson missed the first three games with a calf injury.

With that Series loss, Jackson's five years as a player with the Yankees were over. Looking back, he told a biographer that signing with New York and playing in the city had been a huge mistake. Asked if he would do it again, he said, "I would not have signed with them in a million years. Not a chance."[24] Aching to get out of New York and return to his home in California, he signed a five-year deal with the California Angels starting in 1982. Playing that year for Gene Mauch, he had a fine season, hitting 39 home runs and driving in 101 runs. The veteran Angels lineup won the American League West title but did not advance in the postseason.

In his second year with the Angels, 1983, Jackson was pleased to be reunited with former manager John McNamara, but had the worst year in his career. He was 37 years old and hit only .194 for the season with 14 homers. He was more productive the remaining three years of his Angels contract, but the team failed to make the postseason.

His time with the Angels done, Jackson chose to close out his career in Oakland. He was 41 for his final season and numerous teams marked his last appearance with special Reggie Jackson days. It was one final time for fans to chant, "Reggie, Reggie," and a victory lap for one of the most talented and colorful players of his era. After 21 seasons in the majors, Jackson hung up his spikes at the end of the 1987 season with 563 home runs, good enough at the time for sixth on the career list.

Jackson prided himself in his investments and his business acumen. He had wealth from endorsements, real estate, and other investments. But he was not ready to dedicate himself to life in business. He wanted to try his luck as a manager, but was unwilling to work his way up the ladder from the minors. He served in Oakland as a broadcaster and hitting coach, but it wasn't enough. He wanted to call the shots, to own a team, but that remained beyond his reach.

On January 5, 1993, Jackson was voted into the Baseball Hall of Fame on the first ballot. His plaque in Cooperstown has him in the uniform of his first team, the Athletics. His father, Martinez, who had been so important to the young Reggie, lived long enough to see his son inducted, but died the next spring. (Part of Jackson's dream of owning a baseball team had been making his father a scout for the team.)

Having his own family and closing the gap with his mother, father, and siblings were the most elusive thing Jackson ever set his sights upon. He remained unmarried, but a woman friend gave birth to his child, a daughter named Kimberly. She became an important and enduring presence in his life, his most meaningful ownership stake to date.

SOURCES

Jackson, Reggie, and Kevin Baker, *Reggie Jackson, Becoming Mr. October,* (New York: Random House, 2013).

Jackson, Reggie, and Mike Lupica, *Reggie: The Autobiography* (New York: Villard, 1984).

Perry, Dayn, *Reggie Jackson* (New York: Harper Collins, 2010).

Bergman, Ron, "A Bunt or a Home Run, A's Jackson Can Deliver," *The Sporting News*, May 6, 1972, 9.

Bergman, Ron, "Reggie Jackson Named Player of the Year," *The Sporting News*, January 12, 1974, 29.

Pepe, Phil, "Peace Pipe or Exit Sign for Yanks' Martin," *The Sporting News*, July 2, 1977, 19.

Spander, Art, "Reggie Is a Man for His Times," *The Sporting News*, November 5, 1977, 14.

NOTES

1 Reggie Jackson and Mike Lupica, *Reggie, the Autobiography*, 16.

2 Jackson and Lupica, 44.

3 Jackson and Lupica, 45; Dayn Perry, *Reggie Jackson*, 21.

4 Jackson and Lupica, 41.

5 Jackson and Lupica, 47.

6 Jackson and Lupica, 54.

7 Jackson and Lupica, 58.

8 Jackson and Lupica, 73.

9 Jackson and Lupica, 82.

10 Jackson and Lupica, 82.

11 Jackson and Lupica, 89; Perry.

12 Ron Bergman, "A Bunt or a Home Run, A's Jackson Can Deliver," *The Sporting News*, May 6, 1972, 9.

13 Ron Bergman, "Reggie Jackson Named Player of the Year," *The Sporting News*, January 12, 1974, 29.

14 Jackson and Lupica, 72.

15 Jackson and Lupica, 71; Perry, 103.

16 Jackson and Lupica, 71.

17 Jackson and Lupica, 100.

18 Perry, 125.

19 Jackson and Lupica, 86.

20 Jackson and Lupica, 123.

21 Jackson and Lupica, 148.

22 Jackson and Lupica, 169-173; Perry, 190-191; Phil Pepe, "Peace Pipe or Exit Sign for Yanks' Martin," *The Sporting News*, July 2, 1977, 19.

23 Art Spander, "Reggie Is a Man for His Times," *The Sporting News*, November 5, 1977, 14.

24 Jackson and Lupica, 151.

Ted Kubiak

By Rory Costello

"Being a utility player wasn't a pleasant way to spend your time in the major leagues," said Ted Kubiak in 1987. "But it was a living."[1] Twenty years later, he said, "There's no doubt in my mind that my ten-year major-league career was because of my defensive ability."[2] In 2011 he expanded further. "It took quite a while for me to be comfortable with the role and I don't think I ever really did. I hit enough to keep a job but it was my glove that made my career."

The infielder hit a mild .231 with just 13 homers from 1967 to 1976. Even so, he made a useful contribution to the Oakland A's dynasty that won three straight World Series from 1972 through 1974. The highest praise came from a former teammate in Oakland. In 1980 Tony La Russa said, "I always thought Kubiak was the most valuable player on that team because he could fill in for Dick Green at second or Campy Campaneris at short or Sal Bando at third and the team would go on winning."[3]

Starting in 1989, Kubiak began molding young players as a minor-league manager and instructor. "When I quit [in 1977], I wasn't interested in staying in the game," he said in 2011. "I'd had enough of the contractual battle in San Diego and having my salary cut the full 20 percent after being told I'd done a great job for them was the last straw. When they refused to even talk to me about it, that was all I needed to end it. I was 34 years old, wasn't happy with how I was playing and was struggling with being able to keep my abilities sharp, something that used to be so easy for me. But after being away from the game for 12 years I decided it was still something I loved. I made a couple of phone calls and was hired by my old Oakland club. It was a good decision because I enjoy managing and working with and developing the young players."

Theodore Rodger Kubiak was born on May 12, 1942, in New Brunswick, New Jersey. His family lived in nearby Highland Park, a small borough that provided a great place in which to grow up.[4] "I don't know how old I was when I would play catch with my dad when he got home from work, but at the age of 7 I was invited to play on an unofficial Little League team in Highland Park." Growing up an hour from New York, he was a fan of the Yankees. In 2011 he said, "Even with the Dodgers and Giants in New York, the Yankees got all the media coverage, plus they won the World Series every year, so I naturally gravitated to them and Mantle in particular. He was an amazing player and though I got to know a little of his personal life, reading the latest biography of him revealed just how hard it was for him to play the game every day because of his leg problems. That made everything he accomplished

so much more amazing. It was eventually incredible to play against him in the major leagues."

"I was on our high-school basketball team but didn't play much. As a shortstop at Highland Park High, I didn't think I was anything special, just one of the guys, trying to do the best I could. Somehow I hurt my back as a junior and had a terrible year, but my senior year saw me chosen as the MVP of the team. When my name was called for that honor in our school assembly, I was shocked and the cheers from the audience a complete surprise."

Kubiak was invited to a tryout camp by the Kansas City Athletics while playing in a tournament game his final year. While on the bench between innings, he was tapped on the shoulder and turned around to face Ray Sanders, a Kansas City scout, who issued the invitation. He was shocked and couldn't believe what he'd just heard. Sanders worked with scout Tom "T-Bone" Giordano, who played 11 games in the majors for the Athletics in 1953, when they were still in Philadelphia. "Tom was active with the Indians organization at the same time I was and I still keep in touch with him." After his pro career ended, Tom was a high-school teacher in Copiague (Long Island), New York, but baseball proved to be his enduring livelihood. Fifty years after he signed Kubiak, Giordano was still active, in the Texas Rangers organization.

"I would have signed for nothing, but when I hesitated Tom offered a modest bonus of $500. I was going to Pratt Institute to become an architect but with Instructional League and winter ball, I never did get back, which I regret." Even without a college degree, though, this man's flair for language was apparent. He embarked on a book about his life in baseball, its changes over his 40-plus years in the game, and its effect on him as a person and a man. The format of the book centers on the 300-page infield manual he developed for the Cleveland organization when he was their defensive coordinator for five years.

Kubiak's apprenticeship in the minors lasted six seasons. While with the Sarastoa Sun Sox, he made the Florida State League All-Star team during his first year, leading the league in putouts, assists, chances accepted, and double plays. His batting was solid enough too at .253, and though he did not hit any home runs, he had 53 RBIs. He went to spring training with the Athletics in 1962, which was quite a thrill, and jumped to Binghamton in the Double-A Eastern League.

Against the higher competition, the young pro's batting slipped to .203. "Kansas City jumped me three levels in 1962 and I was way over my head. At the end of the season I began switch-hitting, hoping to lessen the effect of the breaking ball, and it was a good decision. In 1963 they sent me to Lewiston, where I hit .295. Switch-hitting complemented my glove work enough to help me stay in the major leagues for ten years."

Kubiak was a Northwest League All-Star in 1963, but he was still developing. During each of his first three years, he made more than 40 errors at short. In a 2007 interview with David Laurila of *Baseball Prospectus*, Kubiak said, "I received one suggestion—the smallest amount of instruction—in my first spring training, and after that, everything I learned, I taught myself. In order to make myself into a good defensive player, I had to dissect what I was doing and make changes on my own. I had to determine how to maximize my talents while judging what my talents were."[5] He did so successfully, cutting his errors down to the high 20s from 1964 through 1966.

He also showed just enough with the bat to keep advancing. The 1964 season was another step back (.214 in 105 games in the Texas League and .171 in 16 games in the Pacific Coast League). But he stepped forward in 1965 (.281/7/38 with Birmingham in the Southern League) and held his own when he returned to Triple-A in 1966 (.260/2/38 with Vancouver). He was one of four PCL players to appear in every one of his team's games that year. Vancouver manager Mickey Vernon said, "He is an excellent competitor. He has great hustle and is a major league shortstop all the way. I think he can hit quite well in the majors."[6]

In the spring of 1967 Kubiak made the Kansas City roster, and he never appeared in another minor-league game. He played sparingly (hitting just .157 in 117 plate appearances in 53 games) behind Bert Campaneris at shortstop and John Donaldson at second base. Occasionally he filled in at third, where Sal Bando was trying to unseat Danny Cater. "When I got to the majors I had to learn how to play second and third base," Kubiak said in 1987. "A more important thing I had to learn was how to sit on the bench and keep myself mentally prepared to come into a game if I was needed. That was something to which I really had to adjust."[7]

The following winter Ted went back to the Dominican Republic. It was his third taste of winter ball; he had played 14 games in Venezuela for Tigres de Aragua in 1965-66 and was with the Dominican club Estrellas Orientales in 1966-67. "In Venezuela, I dislocated my thumb tagging a runner in a rundown," Kubiak recalled in 2011. "So I was only there about a month. The Venezuelan and Dominican Leagues are very good—the competition is on a major-league level. I was a rookie just trying to get along and did well enough to get invited back, which tells you something."

The return to San Pedro de Macorís, cradle of short-stops, was very satisfying. Estrellas won the league championship in 1967-68. The team's biggest local star was Rico Carty. The pitching staff was led by Cuban Mike Cuéllar—who faced just 28 men as he threw a one-hitter in Game Six of the finals versus Escogido—and Larry Dierker.[8]

"The Dominican was great," said Kubiak. "The people down there are great. I've gone back in recent years for work. The league has blown up so much, although there is still the poverty. But the people are still as nice and friendly as can be. One of my good friends now is Minnie Mendoza, who also works for Cleveland and was the third baseman on our Estrellas team. We gloat over the team never having won again for the past 40 years."

Kubiak continued in his reserve role for the A's, who had moved to Oakland, during 1968. Campaneris remained a fixture at short—he held the position for 12 straight years with the A's—but for three games in April, manager Bob Kennedy experimented with the Cuban in left field because he wanted to get Kubiak in the lineup. Campy hated the change, though, and was soon back at his familiar spot. Kubiak was often the subject of trade talks. That year the Baltimore Orioles were interested in acquiring him because they were worried that Mark Belanger's unit might be called into service in Vietnam. Ted himself was serving in the National Guard, which he had joined in 1967.[9]

A natural shortstop, Kubiak didn't play second base until he got to the big leagues. "Everything was backwards at second base, and it took time to separate the two positions, but second base was so much easier." One rival pitcher said, "Ted Kubiak is the best short-stop OR second baseman in either league."[10] In 1969, however, smooth-fielding Dick Green reclaimed his natural second-base position. Kubiak's starting opportunities typically came when either Campaneris or Green was injured. His hitting had picked up to .250 in 1968 and remained at .249 in '69. On June 22, 1969, he hit his first big-league homer, off Minnesota's Jim Kaat.

On December 7, 1969, Oakland traded Kubiak and pitcher George Lauzerique to the Seattle Pilots for Ray Oyler and Diego Segui. "I knew when I was traded from Oakland the first time the team was eventually going to do well," Ted said in 1987.[11] Segui had been the Pilots' best pitcher, but "the weeping need was for a shortstop who can play every day. Kubiak can; Oyler could not. Ted is 27, Oyler is 31. Ted batted .249, Oyler hit .165."[12]

The 1970 season marked Kubiak's career highs in just about every category and it was that year that convinced him he was a major-league player; nothing more than an average player but one nonetheless. After the Pilots moved to Milwaukee, he played in 158 games for the Brewers—but he started 88 times at second base and just 68 times at short. In June manager Dave Bristol decided that he needed a new second baseman. Kubiak got the call, and in 2011 he said, "I hated the change at first. I'd lost much of the edge I had in 1967, my first year in the majors, because I had to sit on the bench and did so for three years before the trade to Seattle. I was never as good as I was after my Triple-A season. The year in Milwaukee was giving me a chance to maybe regain some of my ability, but then I was moved to second. It was a battle." In August 1970 he had said, "I suppose I should be grateful for the change because at least I'm a regular in the big leagues."[13]

Given regular duty, Kubiak hit 4 homers, drove in 41 runs, and hit .252. He also enjoyed his finest day at the plate in the majors on July 18, 1970, at Fenway Park. He was 4-for-5, driving in seven of the Brewers' runs (and tying the club's single-game record) in a 10-5 win over the Red Sox. The highlight was a ninth-inning grand slam off Ed Phillips, a righty whose big-league career consisted of 18 games with Boston that year. Kubiak had also reached him for a homer at County Stadium on May 6. In 2011 Ted quipped, "Phillips was unfortunately sent down; I guess they figured if I could hit home runs off him, he didn't have quite enough."

Ted played much the same role for the Brewers during the first four months of the 1971 season—except in reverse. Dave Bristol switched him back to short in June. On July 29 Milwaukee traded Kubiak and minor leaguer Charlie Loseth to the St. Louis Cardinals for José Cardenal, Bob Reynolds, and Dick Schofield. "I was glad to be going to a good club," said Kubiak after the trade. "Here they don't let you play—there's too much pressure on you. I knew I was going to be traded, but I didn't expect it now at this stage in the season."[14] Ted didn't stay long in St. Louis, though, as the Cardinals sent him to the Texas Rangers on November 3 for pitcher Joe Grzenda. Ted Williams, then the Rangers manager, liked Kubiak as a second baseman and inquired with St. Louis. Cardinals general manager Bing Devine said, "You know, we had tried for a couple of years to get Kubiak. He did his job with us, but it was just one of those things—we needed an experienced left-handed reliever so badly." But before they could spare Kubiak, they obtained another utilityman, Marty Martinez, from the Astros.[15]

Ted was in Texas for only a few months as well. On July 20, 1972, the Rangers dealt Don Mincher and him to Oakland for Vic Harris, Marty Martinez, and a player to be named later (Steve Lawson). "I could see a big change when I returned," Kubiak said in 1987. "I was pleasantly surprised to see some of the guys I had come through the minors with had matured so much and at the right time."[16]

Dick Green missed nearly all the season with a herniated disc before coming back in mid-August. He was replaced by Larry Brown, who hurt his back. Tim Cullen played more second base than anyone for Oakland that year, but when he pulled a hamstring, the A's needed depth. Kubiak stepped in and started 15 straight games at second. At the end of August Dal Maxvill came in through the revolving door. Seven different men started at the position for the team that year.

Kubiak offered interesting insights into the A's contentious clubhouse atmosphere and owner Charles O. Finley. Author Bruce Markusen, who has chronicled the A's dynasty in a book and many articles, quoted Ted. "A lot had to do with the intensity of the ballclub and the fact that the players were there to win games. I think Charlie Finley had something to do with that because he was so outspoken. I don't know whether it was his design or whether it was just his method or just his personality, but he allowed the players to speak out also. There were guys who'd get pissed off at him, get angry and say things in the papers."[17]

The manager of the A's, Dick Williams, was another forceful personality. "I really liked playing for Dick," said Kubiak in 2011. "I can't say I had much contact with him, but I thought he managed extremely well. I always liked playing for someone like Dick was. He was hardnosed and commanded respect. I had questions about some of my other managers—although Ted Williams was a great guy—but on the A's, everybody knew their job and did what it took to get the job done."

Kubiak made it to the postseason for the first time in 1972. In the AL Championship Series against Detroit, he appeared in four games and went 2-for-4. He added a single in three at-bats against Cincinnati during the World Series.

Mainly backing up Dick Green, Kubiak got into 106 games during the 1973 season, though he came to the plate just 198 times (.220-3-17).[18] During the postseason, Kubiak got into three games in the ALCS against Baltimore, going 0-for-2. In the World Series, he appeared in four games versus the New York Mets, going hitless in three at-bats. However, he scored the winning run in Game Three at Shea Stadium. He drew a one-out walk off Harry Parker in the top of the 11th inning, advanced on a dropped third strike by Jerry Grote, and scored on a single by Campaneris.

The most notorious moment in the Series was Finley's scapegoating of another second baseman, Mike Andrews, whose errors helped lose Game Two after he had replaced Kubiak in the eighth inning. In 2011 Kubiak still remembered well how Finley tried to remove Andrews from the roster and replace him with Manny Trillo. "I was in shock. We were on the plane getting ready to fly to New York and we realized Mike wasn't with us. We eventually heard what was happening but eventually Mike made the plane. The next day during our workout in New York, we wore black armbands with Mike's number as a show of support." The Mets fans gave Andrews a standing ovation in Game Four when the reinstated player entered as a pinch-hitter.

In between the 1973 and 1974 seasons, Kubiak was part of a pioneering group: the first 29 major-leaguers who went to salary arbitration with the owners. The amounts were peanuts by today's standards. The biggest demand came from Reggie Jackson, who asked for (and got) $135,000 instead of Charlie Finley's offer of $100,000. Ted, who had made $30,000 in 1973, asked for $42,500. He had to settle for $37,000.[19]

Kubiak remained a frequent fill-in for Dick Green in 1974, also spelling Campaneris on occasion. He said, "Sure it bothers me, but over the years, I've become accustomed to being a utilityman and I contribute as best I can." He added, "As soon as Greenie is ready,

even on one leg, he's in there. There are times when I get ticked off, but if I go out there and try to play like that, I can't do as good a job. Maybe it's maturity, but I can separate my play now from my feelings."[20] In part because of some long idle stretches, his hitting languished (.209/0/18 in 220 at-bats).

Ted "sat out the [1974] playoff with a swollen left ankle and hurt feelings. Although he was in uniform in both Oakland and Baltimore, he said back then that the A's wouldn't allow him to be introduced with his teammates before the game."[21] "I have no recollection of that," said Kubiak in 2011. "But I was hurt. I was upended trying to turn a double play in Chicago about three weeks before the playoffs [on September 22]. My leg was all swollen; it took a long time for the blood to get out of it and I was on crutches for a while. I was (on the active roster) in the World Series, I just didn't get in the games because of the way they went." Dick Green, though he went hitless in the Series, was outstanding in the field. Dal Maxvill, who had returned to Oakland, subbed briefly for Green in the first two games.

On May 16, 1975, Oakland traded Kubiak to the San Diego Padres for pitcher Sonny Siebert. He joined the Padres when their infield was a shambles as a result of illness and injuries. "Ted will do a good job for us at third or second and he can fill in at short if we need him," said San Diego manager John McNamara, who had managed Kubiak at Binghamton, Dallas, and Oakland.[22] "Why they figured I was going to be a regular third baseman with no home-run power, I couldn't figure," Ted said in 2011. "Once again, I was asked to play a position on a daily basis that I really never played before and it was not easy." He played mainly third for the remainder of the year, since 22-year-old Mike Ivie really wasn't suited for the hot corner.

In 1976 Kubiak filled in behind the Padres' new third baseman, Doug Rader, and behind Tito Fuentes at second. Both years in San Diego, his hitting numbers were right around his career average: .224 and .236. The Sporting News commented, "Kubiak has been a first-rate fill-in for the Padres, but they don't feel he could play every day for any length of time."[23] Heading into the 1977 season, he and the Padres could not come to terms by the March 10 deadline, so the Padres renewed his $38,000 contract at the maximum pay cut. He "walked out of the Yuma spring training camp on March 30 … was never heard from again and was placed on the disqualified list."[24]

That was it: Ted Kubiak never played another game in the majors. In 2011 he commented, "I didn't like the experience. They treated me exactly the way they treated most of us in those years. They wouldn't say anything—take it or leave it. But I was 34 then, it was probably time to go."

In the 1978 season, Kubiak returned to the A's, doing some color work on TV broadcasts along with Hank Greenwald. "That was just spot appearances, fill-in color jobs. Finley called me up." He was then involved in various other businesses before returning to real estate, renovating houses and apartment buildings. Back in 1971, he had taught real estate in Milwaukee; he went into that business in Oakland in 1973. But he hoped to get back into baseball, perhaps as a scout.[25]

In 1989 he returned to the field, again with the Oakland organization. It's tempting to think that Tony La Russa (then managing the A's) might have had a hand in this, as he had previously with Joe Rudi's return to the team as a coach. But Kubiak said, "No. I sent out two résumés and made two calls: one to the Giants and one to the A's, because I was living in the Bay Area. The A's sounded like they were going somewhere with Sandy Alderson. I also still had some friends in the organization, like Wes Stock. He called up Karl Kuehl, the farm director, they interviewed me and offered me a position."

Kubiak started with Southern Oregon in the Northwest League (rookie ball) and then took over in midseason for Lenn Sakata at Modesto, an A's affiliate in the California League. After four more seasons with Modesto, he moved to the Cleveland Indians organization in 1994, managing at the Double-A and A levels through 2003.

When asked if he had ambitions of becoming a big-league manager, Kubiak responded, "Because I'd left the game for 12 years, the game was not being run any more by my contemporaries. So often in the game you need a friend to take you along with him, so I was a very new face to the new people. I had a lot to learn when I first began managing and don't think I even presented myself as managerial material. As the years have gone by, I've learned a lot more and it would be interesting to do so—but the game has changed so much, I wouldn't fit in with the new technology and computerized look everyone seems to think is so important now. The game is very different."

From 2004 through 2008, Ted served as the minor-league defensive coordinator for the Indians. Each of his infielders and staff members received the 300-page personalized infield manual that he wrote. [26] In the interview with David Laurila, he offered many intriguing observations—notably on how well-conditioned legs are the foundation of a good infielder, influencing all other parts of body positioning. He called Omar Vizquel "the consummate infielder of these times."[27]

In 2011 he added, "There are some very acrobatic players in the major leagues these days. I see things that would be helpful to many of them, but there's no doubt today's player is a better athlete than we were. Not smarter but better athletes, and that doesn't mean their fundamental play is better. Look at the mistakes made in the game today. I played in an era when there were many of the best players of all time. It's hard for me to comment on anyone specific because I just don't see them enough. I did get to watch Vizquel when he was with us in Cleveland, and he and Roberto Alomar were as good as they were said to be."

Kubiak returned to managing in 2009 with Cleveland's rookie-ball club in Arizona. In 2010 and 2011 he managed the Lake County Captains in the Midwest League; they won the league championship his first year. "There's not as much pressure as when I was a player. It wasn't easy at first because there is so much you have to be aware of, but everything has fallen into place and I love it," he said in 2011. "I love the puzzle of the game, battling the other teams. Winning is a huge part of development, and playing for our Oakland club and the St Louis Cardinals taught me a lot about winning." In 2012 the Indians made him the manager of the Mahoning Valley (Niles, Ohio) Scrappers of the short-season New York-Penn League, and he was still at the helm in 2014.

At 70-plus, Ted Kubiak was still filled with energy and desire. "It's not really a job. Baseball is still the game I enjoyed when I was a kid. It's a great game. In many other ways it's changed a lot, but it's still the same game on the field. I work out every day, I keep in shape, and hearing from the people who've been under my tutelage and gone on—that's an energy boost. They're going to have to take the uniform off me."

Grateful acknowledgment to Ted Kubiak for his memories (telephone interview, September 12, 2011, plus extra input via e-mail, October 11, 2011). Thanks also to Tom Barthel for the introduction.

SOURCES

baseball-reference.com

retrosheet.org

NOTES

1   Randy Schultz, "Where Are They Now?" *Baseball Digest*, March 1987, 83.

2   David Laurila, "Prospectus Q&A: Ted Kubiak." Baseball Prospectus website, April 22, 2007 (baseballprospectus.com/article.php?articleid=6131)

3   Bob Markus, "Pryor Waxing Hot Over His Utility Billing," *The Sporting News*, August 16, 1980, 27.

4   Ted was the only child of Theodore Kubiak (no middle name), a traffic manager for Gerber Plumbing, and Margaret "Marge" Pochinski.

5   Laurila.

6   Joe McGuff, "A's Offer Swap Bait In Spare DP Duo-Kubiak, Donaldson," *The Sporting News*, December 24, 1966, 32.

7   Schultz.

8   Juan Carlos Musa, "Recuerdan la conquista de la corona de las EO en 1968," *Hoy* (Santo Domingo, Dominican Republic), February 2, 2011.

9   Ron Bergman, "Kubiak Leads Rising A's," *The Sporting News*, June 15, 1968, 17.

10   Ibid.

11   Schultz.

12   Hy Zimmerman, "Milkes Gambles to fix Pilots' Defense," *The Sporting News*, December 27, 1969, 36.

13   Larry Whiteside, "Heise a Blue-Chip Shortstop, Brewers Will Drink to That," *The Sporting News*, August 21, 1971, 10.

14   "Kubiak Sent to St. Louis by Brewers," Associated Press, July 30, 1971.

15   Neal Russo, "Bird Bullpen Lists Sharply to Portside," *The Sporting News*, November 20, 1971, 47.

16   Schultz.

17   Bruce Markusen, *Baseball's Last Dynasty: Charlie Finley's A's* (Indianapolis: Masters Press, 1998), 139.

18   That year, he also married the daughter of former big leaguer Irv Noren, who was one of the Oakland coaches. Bruce Markusen, "Here's What Happened to '73 World Champion Oakland A's," *Baseball Digest*, October 1998: 69. Kubiak's two children, Justin and Kristi, are from a prior marriage.

19   Jerome Holtzman, "Arbitration a Success, Players and Owners Agree," *The Sporting News*, March 16, 1974, 53.

20   Ron Bergman, "Kubiak, Gilt-Edged Utilityman, Pays Handsome Dividend to A's," *The Sporting News*, August 10, 1974, 22.

21   Ron Bergman, "Player Barbs and Pressure Fail to Jar A's Pilot Dark," *The Sporting News*, October 26, 1974, 11.

22   Phil Collier, "Kubiak Plugs Big Hole at Padres' Hot Corner," *The Sporting News*, June 14, 1975, 13.

23   Phil Collier, "Padres Back Off on Talk About Metzger Deal," *The Sporting News*, January 1, 1977, 36.

24   Phil Collier, "Padres Give Blessing to 'Reborn' Hendrick," *The Sporting News*, April 16, 1977, 11; Collier, "Novice Gives Padres the Look of a Champion," *The Sporting News*, April 23, 1977, 9.

25   Schultz.

26   David Hall, "The Sleeper," *Kinston* (North Carolina) *Free Press*, April 6, 2008. Subject: Carlos Rivero, then an Indians prospect.

27   Laurila.

Blue Moon Odom

By Greg Erion

When you review how professional baseball integrated, it is easy to begin and end with the story of Jackie Robinson's struggles. Scant attention is given the fact that African Americans faced tremendous resistance to their presence throughout the 1950s and 1960s, especially in the Deep South. One such player who experienced this was Blue Moon Odom. Often remembered solely for his colorful nickname, this stalwart pitcher for the Oakland A's played his first year of professional baseball on a minor-league team that represented one of the last bastions of segregated baseball. Already under pressure to succeed because of the large bonus he received, Odom now had to pitch in an environment of great racial tensions.

Johnny Lee Odom was born on May 29, 1945, in Macon, Georgia, the son of Elish and Florine Odom. John was the youngest child in the family, two sisters and a brother preceding him. His father, a laborer, died when John was 5, the victim of lung cancer. Florine became the breadwinner in the family. She cleaned, washed, cooked, and did whatever else her employer, a family in Macon's upper class, asked of her.[1]

It might be thought that "Blue Moon" was a nickname contrived by A's owner Charlie Finley. After all, he had tried to persuade Vida Blue to change his name to True Blue, but Odom's nickname came earlier.[2] As Odom related it, "I received my nickname in the fifth grade in Macon, Georgia. A classmate of mine named Joe Morris started calling me 'Moon Head' and a few days later, he started calling me 'Blue Moon.' He said he could not call me 'Yellow Moon' because of my complexion; and Black Moon would not sound right. So he decided to call me 'Blue Moon.' I used to hate that name but now I love it."[3]

Odom had two ambitions: to become a professional singer or a baseball player. Life as a singer seemed tangible; Otis Redding and Little Richard had pre-ceded Odom from Ballard-Hudson High to successful careers in the entertainment industry.[4] This option dissolved when Odom's voice changed.[5] That left sports, and he excelled in them all. By the time he graduated from high school in 1964, he had lettered in baseball, basketball, football, and track. He had gained a reputation as the best high-school pitcher in Georgia, compiling a 42-2 record including eight no-hitters.[6] He had a wicked fastball and serviceable curve. His fastball was even more effective because of its movement, "a sinking fastball." Along with his natural ability was an intense competitiveness. Winning was everything and Odom pushed himself to the nth degree, as sports was one of few ways a black man in Georgia could succeed.

Jack Sanford, a former major leaguer with the Washington Senators and now a regional scout for

the Kansas City A's, was fully aware that several teams were following Odom. Knowing competition for Odom's services would be keen once he graduated from high school, Sanford contacted Finley and alerted him to Odom's potential. Finley directed Haywood Sullivan, manager of the Birmingham Barons (an A's farm team), to watch Odom pitch. Sullivan, with Sanford, happened to pick a day when Odom threw one of his eight no-hitters.[7] With that, Finley decided to meet Odom.

Charles O. Finley, who had built a thriving insurance business based in large part on an overpoweringly persuasive personality, put it to work in pursuing Odom. He flew to Macon, the only team owner to do so in pursuit of Odom. As recounted in *Charlie O.*, he waited his turn on the appointed day among the scouts to make his pitch.[8] Finley arranged for a truck to deliver food to the Odom family. He met and charmed Florine, at one point going into her kitchen to help cook. That, and Odom's opportunity to deal directly with Finley rather than with intermediaries, contributed toward his selecting the A's. Odom received a $75,000 bonus, the largest given up to then to a black athlete.[9] He would report to the Barons, the A's team in the Double-A Southern League.

Today that might seem an innocuous assignment, but in 1964 it was of major significance. While Robinson broke the color barrier in 1947, baseball did not fully integrate until 1959. Robinson's trials were daunting, but perhaps not as severe as they could have been because most of his games were in Northern surroundings and not in the Deep South. The minors, especially in the South, generated tremendous resistance to integrating the game. In 1953 the Cotton States League actually took action to bar two brothers, James and Leander Tugerson, from playing.[10] Numerous African-Americans who played in the 1950s and 1960s attested to how difficult it was for them to play when their presence was not welcomed, assigned to teams in the region out of ignorance as to what they had to endure. Only in 1961 did Major League Baseball force all minor-league teams to integrate.[11]

Odom was going to play in a city at the epicenter of the civil rights movement. A year earlier, in May 1963, events at Birmingham proved pivotal in the effort to eliminate discriminatory actions. The nation was first stunned, then enraged, by a confrontation between blacks and the Birmingham police, which escalated when high-pressure fire hoses and police dogs were used. Later that year, the 16th Street Baptist Church was bombed, and four girls were killed; the Ku Klux Klan was implicated in the incident. This was where Odom would start his professional career.

Larry Colton's *Southern League* begins with Odom being pulled over by a Birmingham policeman who, only after realizing who he was, decided to let him go without giving him a ticket for a nonexistent traffic violation. Yet he gave a warning, "This is Birmingham, Alabama. It's real important you stay in the 'N———' part of town."[12]

That the Barons even fielded a team was an offshoot of several factors, the civil rights movement and Police Chief Bull Connor, a noted racist, being two of them.[13] Another factor, a positive, one was team owner Albert Belcher, a baseball-loving local businessman who decided Birmingham's image needed to be something other than obstinacy on civil rights that had severely tarnished its image.

Odom joined the team with a great deal of hype, mostly of Finley's making. The team, with a tenuous hold on first place, saw Odom as a distraction. The pressure to do well was high, a natural expectancy born out of his huge signing bonus. Odom was joining good company, as the Barons had a lot of talent: 12 members of the team would play in the majors at one time or another. The star of the team was Campy Campaneris, who in his third year of play had already established himself as a basestealing expert.

Odom did not do well initially. In his first game, he struck out seven in 5⅓ innings but gave up seven hits and seven walks.[14] Over the next several weeks, there were few bright spots in his performance. The patient A's avoided the temptation to over-coach him. All could see he had a great arm, but his experience in the art of pitching was limited. There was more to the game than blowing a fastball past a hitter.

Several weeks after Odom's debut, Kansas City sent Bill Posedel, a former major-league pitcher and the A's minor-league pitching instructor, to Birmingham to work with Odom. Posedel saw raw talent, an intense desire to succeed, and a willingness to learn. He started with basics, teaching Odom how to field his position and how to hold a runner on first.[15] At first Odom did not progress after Posedel's visit—too many walks. However, on the verge of being sent down to Lewiston in the Class A Northwest League, he began to improve.

This all played out in an environment rife with racial tension. The Civil Rights Act was working its way through Congress, creating tremendous backlash in the South. Only 150 miles from Birmingham, near Philadelphia, Mississippi, three civil-rights workers disappeared; their bodies were discovered in an earthen dam 44 days later. That was the time when Odom made his professional debut.

Race was never far from the consciousness of the Barons. Blacks had to stay in "their" part of town. They were forbidden to use restrooms in various establishments and often refused service at restaurants. At one such restaurant, as the players began to take seats, the owner announced, "I'm sorry. The colored boys will have to eat out back." Odom told his teammates, who were seated, "Anyone who don't get back on the bus right now gonna have a problem with me." Within a few minutes, the team bus was back on the road.[16]

After Odom's poor start, he reeled off five straight wins. Finley, anxious to show Odom off in the big leagues, called him up. For Birmingham, he ended 6-5 with a 4.14 ERA in 16 starts. His first start with the Athletics would be against the New York Yankees on September 5, 1964, in Kansas City. The Yankees were in a tight pennant race with the Baltimore Orioles and Chicago White Sox. The A's were in last place.

A crowd of 18,759 came to see the debut of Georgia's pitching phenom. Anyone late to the game missed Odom's efforts. After Tony Kubek singled and Bobby

Richardson walked in the first inning, Odom got Roger Maris to hit into a force play. Odom now faced Mickey Mantle, who was enjoying his last solid season. After Odom threw a wild pitch, Mantle hit his 30th home run of the season. It didn't get any better in the second as three more Yankee runs scored before manager Mel McGaha took Odom out of the game. It was not an auspicious debut.

Despite his drubbing, Odom was on the mound six days later facing the Orioles, who were clinging to first place. Facing the likes of Boog Powell and Brooks Robinson, Odom threw a two-hit shutout and posted his first major-league victory, 8-0. That victory, over one of the American League's best teams, offered the hope of things to come; Odom started three more games and was hit hard in each one. He ended the season 1-2 with a 10.06 ERA. Whether his victory over Orioles was an anomaly remained to be seen.

It was obvious Odom needed more seasoning. He was assigned to Lewiston for the 1965 season. During the offseason, he married Perrie Washington, whom he had met while in high school. They later had a son.[17]

At Lewiston, Odom came under the tutelage of Posedel, who began the season as manager of the Broncs. His performance was mediocre, 11-14 with a 4.27 ERA, with too many hits and walks to be effective as a pitcher. Called up at the end of the season, he pitched one inning of relief against the Washington Senators. In 1966 he was back in the Southern League, this time with the Mobile A's under John McNamara. He improved; for the first time he gave up fewer hits than innings pitched and sharply decreased his walks allowed.

Called up to Kansas City at the end of July, Odom made 14 starts and threw four complete games, two of which were shutouts in a ten-day span against the Cleveland Indians. He recorded a 5-5 record to go with a sparkling 2.47 ERA. Odom regressed in 1967, though, posting a 3-8 record and a 5.04 ERA with no complete games in 17 starts. The A's, sent him down to the minors to straighten himself out. Once again Odom hooked up with Posedel, this time working on his windup and delivery motion. Posedel's efforts must have helped straighten Odom out. While his demotion to the minors proved to be a blessing in disguise, he did not forget that A's manager Alvin Dark had sent him down. When Dark moved on to manage the Indians the next season, Odom pitched against them with a bit of an edge, beating them five times over the next two seasons, four on shutouts.

Odom blossomed in 1968. Inserted into the Oakland A's rotation (they had moved from Kansas City after the 1967 season), he led the team in victories with 16 and posted a 2.45 ERA, ninth in the league. Included in his victories was a one-hitter against Baltimore on June 7. He was picked for the All-Star Game and threw two innings of scoreless ball in a 1-0 win for the National League, the eight hits between both teams epitomizing how pitching dominated the game in the late 1960s.

Like most pitchers, Odom enjoyed hitting. On June 12, while fashioning a shutout over Cleveland — again — Odom hit his first major-league home run. During his career, he hit 12 home runs, including five in 1969.[18] He was also an accomplished baserunner and appeared as a pinch-runner in 105 games during his career, scoring 31 runs in that role.

Long a doormat in the American League, the A's began showing signs of improvement. Catfish Hunter, signed within a week of Odom, was beginning to show the form that would mark him a Hall of Fame pitcher. Chuck Dobson and Rollie Fingers also provided solid pitching. Sal Bando, Reggie Jackson, Joe Rudi, and Odom's teammate from the Barons, Campy Campaneris, generated solid defense and offensive efforts. In 1968, their first year in Oakland, the A's ended at 82-80. Not since 1952 had they finished above .500.

The A's further improved in 1969, finishing second to the Minnesota Twins in the American League West with an 88-74 record. Odom shined, tying with Dobson for the team lead with 15 wins, finishing 15-6 with a 2.92 ERA. He was also picked for the All-Star team again although he was roughed up in the one inning

he worked, giving up five runs, four earned in one-third of an inning. The chief blow was a two-run homer by Willie McCovey, the first of two McCovey hit that day.

Odom's success derived from his sinking fastball. While there was talk in the league that the pitch might be a spitter, most observers of Odom's game felt he had a "heavy" fastball that just dropped coming to the plate. "I don't know where it's going," Odom said. "It's kind of hard for me to be a control pitcher because my ball moves so much. Some games it just moves a lot. Other times it doesn't move as much. It takes me about the first or second inning to see how it's going. I'll either have a good sinker or I have to pitch to spots."[19]

The 1970 season was almost identical to 1969; the A's improved their record by one game, as did the Twins, Oakland again coming in second. Odom had an off-year, however, finishing 9-8 with a 3.80 ERA. His elbow gave him problems and he missed six weeks, pitching only 156 innings after having thrown 230-plus the previous two years. After the season he had a bone chip removed from his elbow at the Mayo Clinic.[20]

In 1971 Oakland won 101 games to finish 16 games ahead of the Kansas City Royals before they lost the league championship in three straight games. Vida Blue and Hunter combined to win 45 games and were backed by Dobson's 15 wins and Diego Segui's 10. Odom, whose recovery from surgery prevented him from pitching until mid-May, posted a mediocre 10-12 record. His arm was giving him enough problems that he stopped pitching in late September, thus missing the championship series against Baltimore, in which the A's were swept three straight. He underwent physical therapy at the Mayo Clinic to rebuild strength in his arm, his dipping fastball having deserted him.[21]

The A's had turned into a juggernaut team that won three straight World Series from 1972 through 1974. While Odom contributed to this run, and to the drama that constantly surrounded the team, he was lucky to be part of the effort — an encounter with three thieves nearly ended his career, and life.

On the afternoon of January 6, 1972, Odom's wife, Perrie, noticed several youths breaking into a house near their offseason home in Macon. She called the police and Odom, who was working as a clerk in a nearby liquor store during the offseason. The fleeing youths ran past the store. Odom gave chase. One turned and shot at him, hitting him once in the neck and side, dropping him to the sidewalk. Perrie, who had followed their escape, came on the scene and—seeing her husband wounded—put him into the car and drove straight to the hospital. Odom was lucky; neither wound was life-threatening and three days later he was released from the hospital. Soon thereafter, the three young men were arrested; Odom identified them at their trial. They were convicted on several charges.[22] By the time spring training began, Odom had fully recovered.

Odom had the best season of his career in 1972, fashioning a 15-6 record and a 2.50 ERA, ninth in the league. He joined Ken Holtzman and Hunter to give Oakland a solid trio of pitchers, leading to their second straight division championship. The A's bested Detroit in five games in the ALCS. Odom led the way with a three-hit shutout in Game Two and five innings of effective pitching in Game Five, giving up an unearned run before Blue came in to shut out Detroit to save Odom's 2-1 victory. Odom's line for the championship series read 14 innings, one unearned run, five hits, and only two walks.

During the A's championship years, the team always seemed to be embroiled in controversy. Perhaps it was the mix of talent, perhaps it was dealing with Charlie Finley's constant machinations; whatever it was, nothing seemed to go smoothly. Barely had the A's beaten Detroit when Odom and Vida Blue got into an argument. Blue, who disappointed that season, finishing with a 6-10 record, had been demoted to the bullpen. He began to kid Odom about having had to save his win. The kidding turned serious, quickly escalated into a shouting match, and almost got physical.[23]

The A's faced Cincinnati in a hard-fought World Series that went to seven games. Odom started two games and although he gave up only two runs in 11-plus innings, one of the runs was in a 1-0 loss in Game Three. He appeared in two games as a pinch-runner. His speed was not enough when he ran for Gene Tenace in Game Five. With the A's down 5-4 in the ninth, Odom tried to score from third on a popup to Joe Morgan—a make-or-break play. Morgan nailed Odom on a close play at the plate to end the game. The play was close, and Odom got into an intense argument with umpires Bob Engel and Jim Honochick. He bumped Engel and was fined $500 for misconduct.[24]

Two days later Odom started Game Seven, pitching into the fifth nursing a 1-0 lead. When he tired, Hunter relieved him with runners on second and third. Hunter gave up the tying run, but Oakland broke the tie in the sixth inning with two runs that held up for a 3-2 victory and the world championship. Odom had topped off a fine season with an even better postseason. His share of World Series earnings came to $20,705.01.[25] He had reached the height of his career at the age of 27.

Oakland started slowly in 1973. By late May, although slightly over .500 at 23-21, they were languishing near the bottom of their division. On May 28 the Tigers knocked Odom out of the game in the fifth inning and won, 4-3, Odom having given up all four runs. At this point, he was 1-8 with a 6.75 ERA. Manager Dick Williams took him out of the rotation. "He's been getting behind a lot of hitters. He walks quite a few," Williams said. "I'm concerned enough that we're going to put him in the bullpen."[26] Although Odom got back into the starting rotation, going 4-4 the rest of the way and somewhat regaining his control, the regular season disappointed as he finished 5-12 with a 4.49 ERA. In six relief appearances and 18-plus innings, he did not give up any runs. His performance out of the bullpen must have registered with the A's as he exclusively relieved against Baltimore during the Championship Series and against the New York Mets in the World Series. Odom gave up three runs in nine-plus innings in three World Series games. The A's beat New York in seven games, earning their second straight World Series and Odom earning over $24,000 for his postseason efforts.

In 1974 Odom again got off to a slow start. This time his old nemesis, manager Al Dark, who replaced Williams, did not wait long to take Odom out of the rotation and put him in the bullpen. Odom made five starts and 29 relief appearances for the year, going 1-5 with just one complete game. The A's beat Baltimore in the ALCS once again and went after their third straight World Series title.

But not before Odom got into another fight, this time with teammate Fingers on the eve of the opening World Series game against the Los Angeles Dodgers. The altercation made coast-to-coast headlines. Fingers was having marital difficulties, spawning ribbing from several teammates. Odom pushed Fingers too far and the two went at it, Fingers ending up needing several stitches in the back of his head. The A's took it in stride. As Coach Bobby Winkles said, "Just a normal day."[27]

The incident had little effect on either player; Fingers recorded two saves and a win and Odom won Game Five. The Series was a close one; one run settled four of the five games. Odom had pitched one scoreless inning through the first four games and got a crucial out in Game Seven.

The score was tied 2-2 in the top of the seventh when Blue gave up a two-out walk to Steve Yeager. He was on the verge of walking pitcher Mike Marshall when Dark called for Odom. Odom completed the walk and got Davey Lopes to ground out, ending the threat. Joe Rudi led off the bottom of the inning with a home run and Fingers came in to hold the lead, giving Odom the victory and Oakland its third straight world championship.

Despite their success, the A's had peaked. Hunter was embroiled in a dispute with Finley that resulted in his being declared a free agent. He signed with the Yankees for 1975, the first of the core A's to leave Oakland. Dick Green, the A's second baseman, was released before the 1975 season began. The next to go was Odom. Off to another poor start, he was 0-2 with a 12.27 ERA when he was traded to the Indians for Dick Bosman and Jim Perry—three dominating

pitchers in their time, each at the end of his career. Less than a month later, Odom went to the Atlanta Braves after pitching only three games for Cleveland, one of which was a two-hit shutout over the Royals. It was the last of Odom's 15 career shutouts and his last complete game. With Atlanta, Odom proved as ineffective as he had been in his beginning for the A's. He pitched in 15 games—ten starts, no complete games, a 1-7 record, and a 7.07 ERA. This was enough for Atlanta to assign Odom to Triple-A Richmond.

Odom was 4-3 as a starter with Richmond before being traded to the Chicago White Sox in June. Chicago sent him to the Triple-A Iowa Oaks, where he won his three starts before being recalled in July. With Chicago, he pitched in eight games and was ineffective in all but one. However, that one game produced baseball history. Ironically, it was against the A's.

Starting against Oakland on July 28 at the Coliseum, Odom held the A's hitless through the first five innings. He also walked eight batters. When he walked Billy Williams to lead off the sixth, manager Paul Richards had enough. He brought in Francisco Barrios to relieve. Barrios pitched the last four innings, walking just two—and not giving up any hits. A combined no hitter. After having come close to pitching one several times, Odom finally achieved it, even if partially. In the clubhouse he watched Barrios on TV. "I couldn't take it, man. I was here pacing. Wow. This was like the World Series. Really exciting. This is the greatest experience I've ever had. It tops them all." A's manager Chuck Tanner was incredulous: 11 walks and a no-hitter. "It was not your typical no-hitter, that's for sure," he said.[28] It was the last of Odom's 84 major-league wins. Attendance was 3,367, less than half of the number who had watched him pitch his first professional game in Macon 12 years earlier.[29]

Odom's next start also came against Oakland. This time he was ineffective, removed after giving up four runs in less than three innings. He made his last major-league appearance on August 17 against Boston and gave up six runs before leaving in the fourth. The loss made his major-league record 84-85. Chicago did not use Odom the rest of the year and he was released the following January. He hooked on with the A's farm club in San Jose for the 1977 season, then moved on to the Mexican League, where he played in 1977-78 for the Mexico City Tigres and Tabasco Plataneros before retiring.

Odom's professional career had been marked with colorful incidents, and life after baseball generated more of the same. Now divorced from Perrie, he remarried and appeared to have adjusted to a nonbaseball life, obtaining a job with Xerox in Southern California as a computer maintenance operator, never missing a day of work for six years. All went well until 1985, when Odom was arrested for selling cocaine to a co-worker. He lost his job and while waiting for his day in court, he became depressed. With financial strains mounting, he began to drink.

In December 1985 Odom threatened his wife with a shotgun. The police were called and after a tense scene with a SWAT team, he released her. Several hours later, with negotiations at a standstill, police discharged teargas into his apartment. Odom surrendered. He spent several weeks in an alcohol rehabilitation program. Later, he served 55 days in jail on two counts of selling cocaine. These incidents proved to be life-changing. Looking back years later, Odom reflected, "What happened in the past probably happened for the best. It made a better man out of me." He gave up drinking and smoking, dealing with what in part created a crisis in his life.[30]

Odom eventually went back to work, painting houses for a living, doing business as Blue Moon Odom's Paint Service. He divorced and remarried, then retired to live on his major-league pension. As of 2014 he lived with his third wife, Maureen, in Fountain Valley, California, and enjoyed participating in baseball-related golf tournaments and autograph-signing sessions. After retirement, accounts of Odom reflected a man who was at peace with himself, or as writer Larry Colton put it in *Southern League*, one whose "pleasing and pleasant personality" came back.[31]

NOTES

1 Larry Colton, *Southern League: A True Story of Baseball, Civil Rights, and the Deep South's Most Compelling Pennant Race,* (New York: Grand Central Publishing, 2013), 17.

2 Finley's effort to change Blue's name is described in G. Michael Green and Roger D. Launius, *Charlie Finley: The Outrageous Story of Baseball's Super Showman* (New York: Walker & Company, 2010), 149.

3 Samuel J. Skinner, Jr. "On the Way Back," *Black Sports,* June/July 1972. From Odom's file at the Baseball Hall of Fame.

4 Colton, 20.

5 "Voice Changed, Robbed Moon of Singing Career," undated, unidentified publication in Odom's Hall of Fame file.

6 Colton, 117. The only two games Odom lost were on passed balls by his catcher.

7 Colton, 117.

8 Herbert Michelson, *Charlie O., Charles Oscar Finley vs. the Baseball Establishment* (New York: Bobbs-Merrill Company Inc., 1975), 153.

9 Colton, 1.

10 "Hot Springs Options Negro Pair to End Cotton States Controversy," *The Sporting News,* April 29, 1953, 28. Numerous other articles in *The Sporting News* that year covered the legal machinations concerning the Tugersons.

11 Colton, 75.

12 Colton, 4.

13 Colton, 75-84.

14 Colton 168-170.

15 Colton 214-215.

16 Colton 236-237.

17 Colton, 297.

18 Once Odom was helping a charity effort at spring training in Scottsdale, Arizona, signing autographs. When asked by the author to choose from among several pictures to sign, without hesitation he chose one of him sliding into third with a triple, rather than the several others showing him on the mound.

19 Ron Bergman, "Blue Moon Mystery—Fast Ball That Sinks," May 31, 1969, unidentified publication in Odom's Hall of Fame file.

20 Ron Bergman, "New Moon…," July 3, 1971 (full title of article not available), unidentified publication in Odom's Hall of Fame file.

21 Skinner, "On The Way Back," Odom's Hall of Fame file.

22 Ron Bergman, "Shots Fail to Alter Odom's Comeback Plans," January 1972, unidentified publication in Odom's Hall of Fame file; Colton, 296. Several descriptions of the incident in articles

and books describe the incident, with varied versions of what took place.

23 "Athletics Blue Not Happy," *The Phoenix*, October 14, 1972, 13.

24 "Odom of A's Fined $500 For Misconduct In Series," November 17, 1973, unidentified publication in Odom's Hall of Fame file.

25 *1981 Baseball Guide* (St. Louis: The Sporting News), 281.

26 "Wild Blue Moon Banished to Bullpen," May 29, 1973, unidentified publication in Odom's Hall of Fame File.

27 "Fingers vs. Odom Latest Fighting A's bout," October 27, 1973, unidentified publication in Odom's Hall of Fame File. Fingers

and Odom had engaged in a shouting match the year before, when Odom was defending, of all teammates, his former antagonist, Vida Blue. "A's Snap at Each Team Up to Hoist," Hall of Fame file.

28 "1976 Sox no-hitter no walk in park," Unidentified publication in Odom's Hall of Fame file.

29 Colton, 296-297.

30 Ron Kroichick, "Blue Moon' Risen, *San Francisco Chronicle*, October 14, 2001, from Odom's Hall of Fame file; Colton 297.

31 Colton, 297.

Joe Rudi

By Rory Costello

Solid left fielder Joe Rudi was a core member of the Oakland A's 1972-74 dynasty. He was the runner-up for the American League Most Valuable Player twice during this period, and he also won three straight Gold Gloves (1974 through 1976). Rudi's numbers with the bat don't look dazzling today, but he did lead the AL in total bases in his best offensive season, 1974. He also hit .300 in 70 World Series at-bats and made one of the top catches in Series history in 1972.

It took Joe several years and a lot of hard work to mature as a major leaguer. This and his quiet, low-key nature on a team with many flashy characters gave him a reputation as "underrated." As Bill James wrote in his *New Historical Abstract*, "the press … continued to say this for years after it was no longer true. … Rudi himself finally put an end to it."[1] Joe said in 1974, "Sometimes all I get is ink about not getting ink. I wish people would just concentrate on the job I do on the field."[2]

Joseph Oden Rudi (the family name is Norwegian) was born on September 7, 1946, in Modesto, California. His father, Oden Rudi, was born and raised in the small town of Waterford, about 20 miles east of Modesto. Oden met his wife, Bessie Courtney, while he was stationed in Georgia with the Air Force in World War II. Joe was the second of their three children; he had an older sister, June, and a younger brother, Paul. Oden was originally a meatcutter, but he mainly worked in the Sharpe Army Depot while Joe was growing up.[3] Bessie was employed by Sears as a bookkeeper and later went to work for Stanislaus County.

Joe served as a Little League batboy at the age of 5 and joined the team at age 7 "because a lot of times they didn't have nine guys to play." The lad stood 6 feet tall at the age of 11.[4] "Other managers would not

believe my age," he said in 1967. "I had to carry a birth certificate around to prove it to them."[5] Size was probably one reason he pitched from ages 10 to 14.

Rudi first went to Oakdale High School in Waterford, but he transferred to Downey High in Modesto after his family moved there in 1961.[6] Joe starred in three sports at Downey. He was a heavyweight wrestler, played football in his freshman and senior years, and starred in baseball, bouncing back and forth between third base and shortstop. He was known more for batting than fielding, hitting .320 as a sophomore and .436 as a junior. Coach Jerry Streeter said in 1964, "He has the grades to go to college but professional offers can be tempting." Already Rudi was projected as a first baseman or outfielder. Streeter added, "When a kid can swing the bat like Joe can, they can find a place for him."[7]

Yet his father would not come out to see Joe play. "He kept telling me to stop this foolishness and concentrate on preparing myself for a real career," Rudi recalled in 1975. "He would remind me over and over again that in Norway young men worked hard learning to be shipbuilders or fishermen or engineers and didn't waste time fooling with bats and balls."[8]

Joe's senior season was cut short in April 1964. Pat Jacquez of Stagg High in Stockton (who pitched in two games for the 1971 Chicago White Sox) ran a ball in on the righty swinger. It broke a small bone in Rudi's left hand, and he wound up in a cast for three months. Amazingly, he stayed in the game, hitting a two-run homer.[9] But after the injury, "his father became more convinced than ever that sports was his son's ruination."[10] A number of pro scouts also shied away. The one who remained most interested was Don "Ducky" Pries of the A's (then still based in Kansas City), who had watched Rudi in American Legion ball as well. He signed Rudi for a modest bonus; "I think it was $15,000," Joe said in 2011. "Not much." In 1967 he said of Pries, "I liked him and he was very honest with me."[11] In 1972 he added, "Other organizations offered me more money, but I signed with the A's because of him. Also, he told me the players in Kansas City then were old, more or less hangers-on."[12]

Because his hand was still healing when he signed, Rudi reported first to Kansas City so the club could evaluate the progress. After his first pro season, *The Sporting News* put Rudi in "the doubtful category."[13] Teammate Skip Lockwood later said, "He was a big kid but he hadn't matured. He was always so strong that you knew if he ever found his coordination, it would really be awesome."[14]

To start the 1965 season, Rudi was actually on Kansas City's major-league roster, but under the constraints of the "first-year player" rule, the A's then worked an end run around the system with the Cleveland Indians and a prospect named Jim Rittwage (who eventually pitched in eight games for the Tribe in 1970). Rudi played for Dubuque, a Class A Cleveland farm club, in 1965; he then rejoined the Oakland organization. By good fortune, the A's had a Class A farm club in

Modesto, and in 1966, Rudi had an excellent year in front of the hometown folks. "His solid hitting made him a town favorite and induced his father to begin attending his games." Said Joe in 1975, "He converted and became such a fan that now you can't keep him away from the ballpark."[15]

On May 9, 1966, Rudi married his high-school sweetheart, Sharon Nickerson (whose original family name was Howell until her mother remarried). Sharon's stepfather, Gilbert "Gib" Nickerson, was a real-estate man in Modesto. He got the newlyweds involved in that business, which continued to provide their livelihood into the 21st century.

In spring training 1967, Joe impressed manager Alvin Dark. He made his big-league debut on Opening Day at Kansas City's Municipal Stadium, starting in left field. "It was a really tough time," Rudi recalled in 2011. "My biggest problem was that I hadn't played the outfield much. Going from the small minor-league ballparks to the big-league parks was a big adjustment. It was like playing in the Grand Canyon." He appeared in just eight games before the team sent him down to Double-A, where he played mainly first base. "The farm director, Bill White—not the Cardinal, but also a first baseman—gave me his glove," Rudi said in 2011. "Taking all that infield practice and throwing hard every time really strengthened my arm for when I returned to the outfield." He was recalled to the majors in September.

The A's moved to Oakland for the 1968 season, and Rudi started the year at Triple-A Vancouver. After an impressive 16-game stint, he was brought up in early May—and in his first return appearance, Catfish Hunter threw his perfect game ("a little nerve-wracking!" Rudi said in 2011). Joe spent the rest of the season with Oakland but struggled. One highlight came on July 15, when he hit his first of 179 big-league homers, off Boston's Dick Ellsworth.

In the winter of 1968-69, Rudi got his only taste of baseball in a foreign land, joining the Magallanes Navigators of the Venezuelan league. He played both first base (which Al Dark had thought might be his better position) and the outfield. He hit .221 with 8 homers and 21 RBIs in 59 games, in part because he had a back problem from carrying his newborn son around Caracas.

For 1969, the A's assigned Rudi to their new Triple-A affiliate, Iowa. There again he played mainly first base. In early June, he was hitting .395—better than anyone else in Organized Baseball at the time—with 59 RBIs. Thus, Oakland recalled him. Herb Michelson of the *Modesto Bee* wrote, "The A's immediately used him in left. And Joe felt laden with instant pressure. He didn't produce in a couple of weeks, was benched and then, on Aug. 4, returned to Iowa in the first corn boat."[16]

Though he cooled off to .354 overall at Iowa, Rudi returned in September and never played again in the minors. Yet the Oakland brass was still doubtful. "We know Joe is better than he's shown so far," said manager John McNamara. "But it's hard to say what his future might be with the team. There are a number of question marks. … I'm playing Joe now because I want to look at him. But I haven't looked ahead to next spring."[17]

"I just got really frustrated those first few years," Rudi said in 2011. "In 1969, I just never hit it off with [manager] Hank Bauer. I never got to stay in the lineup consistently."

In December 1969 the A's acquired Felipe Alou from Atlanta, and they made him their primary left fielder in 1970. However, Rudi (who had also hit .402 in the Arizona Instructional League) felt like he was on firmer footing. "I got a chance in spring training that year," he said in 2011. "Reggie Jackson had 47 homers in 1969, and he got in a salary dispute with Charlie Finley and held out, and Johnny McNamara used me." He also blossomed as a hitter, thanks to noted batting coach Charlie Lau, who (in his only season with the A's) cut down Rudi's long swing and put him in a very closed stance. In 1972 Joe said, "Charlie Lau changed my whole theory on hitting and what I was trying to do with the ball. … It was like being in the boonies all your life and walking into a big city and finding a metropolitan library."[18]

In April 1971 Oakland traded Felipe Alou and made Joe the full-time left fielder. He hit fairly well, but his power disappeared after a two-week stint with the Marines in late July and early August. Joe said, "I missed more than 30 games because of the service. Those two- and three-day weekend breaks hurt too. They disturb your rhythm."[19] In 2011 he gave more insight. "You *couldn't miss* a meeting in the Marines. You had to check in at 5:00 at night on Friday, and you were released at 5 P.M. on Sunday. That meant you had to leave Thursday and fly back Monday."

After returning from his offseason job selling insurance out of his home, Rudi made the All-Star team for the first of three times in 1972. He led the AL in base hits with 181 and triples with 9. He was runner-up to Dick Allen as league MVP, modestly noting, "I think it would have been unjust if anyone but Dick had won it after the year he had."[20]

That June also featured one of owner Charles O. Finley's promotional gimmicks: Mustache Day. Joe said in 2011, "I've never shaved it. Sharon liked it. I guess it'll stay with me until she gets tired of it."

Rudi attained national prominence during the 1972 World Series against the Cincinnati Reds. In Game Two at Cincinnati's Riverfront Stadium, his third-inning solo homer stood up as the margin of victory as Oakland won 2-1. He preserved the lead with a great catch in the ninth inning. Roger Angell, in one of his many brilliant images, described it best: "Rudi, in pursuit of a very long drive hit by Denis Menke, plastered himself belly-first against the left-field wall like a pinned butterfly and somehow plucked down the ball."[21] It was right at the end of the webbing of Joe's glove; in fact, some fans thought it had bounced free. At the time, Tony Pérez was on first, and if Joe hadn't made his leaping backhanded grab, Pérez would have scored. A's manager Dick Williams proclaimed that the catch was better than either Willie Mays's in 1954 or Al Gionfriddo's in 1947 (though that may have been hyperbole).

In a postgame interview, Rudi credited Joe DiMaggio with teaching him how to go back on balls. It's hard to imagine the Yankee Clipper in anything but pin-stripes, but he wore Charlie Finley's garish green and gold getups as a coach with Oakland in 1968 and 1969. "I loved him," Rudi said in 2011. "He was totally different to what everyone thought: funny, a prankster, he loved to rib guys—he was one of the guys. But he was hounded so much, they had to make special arrangements for him to get in and out of the stadium. Everyone wanted a piece of him. But he was a great guy. It was a real blessing with him there. Working with him and Bob Kennedy [Oakland's manager in 1968] made all the difference in the world."

Rudi's production dipped in 1973. Slipping on wet outfield grass at Minnesota in late July, he severely jammed his left thumb and missed nearly a month. For the season, he appeared in just 120 games. Down the stretch, though, he was one of the A's hottest hitters. In the ALCS against Baltimore, he hit just .222, but his three RBIs all came in important situations. During the World Series against the Mets, he hit .333 and enhanced his reputation as a clutch hitter, while again playing well in the field.

Rudi was runner-up to Jeff Burroughs of the Texas Rangers for AL MVP in 1974. He went just 2-for-13 in the ALCS against the Orioles but hit .333 once again in the World Series. His seventh-inning homer off Mike Marshall in Game Five gave the A's a 3-2 win and finished their rout of the Los Angeles Dodgers. This moment showed Rudi's intelligence as a player. The start of the inning had been delayed because fans in the left-field bleachers at Oakland had showered Dodgers left fielder Bill Buckner with objects. "Like thousands of spectators, Rudi noticed and wondered about Marshall. Unlike other pitchers in similar circumstances, Iron Mike did not 'stay loose' during the interruption, nor did he take warm-up pitches when action resumed. When Rudi stepped into the batter's box, Marshall had not made a pitch for several minutes.

"I sorta expected an inside fastball," said Rudi, "and that's what I got. Before the delay I thought he was going to throw a screwball or a slider, but then when he didn't take any warm-up pitches, I figured he would

try to sneak one by on the inside, because they were jamming me (the previous game)."[22]

In 1975 the A's decided to put Claudell Washington—promising as a 19-year-old rookie the previous year—in left field, shifting Rudi back to first. Bemused, he said, "It's kind of funny that after playing left field eight years and finally winning a Gold Glove there, I'm moved."[23] Yet, Joe won another Gold Glove in '75 despite playing only 44 games in the outfield. He continued to hit well.

By this time, however, things were going sour with Charlie Finley. Rudi had made $84,000 in 1975 as he settled with Finley out of arbitration. He asked for $400,000 over three years, not an outlandish amount, but "Finley ignored the request, did not negotiate and, because Rudi did not sign once the season had started, cut the contract the maximum 20 percent."[24]

On June 15, 1976, Finley decided to sell Rudi and Rollie Fingers for $1 million apiece to the Boston Red Sox, while peddling Vida Blue to the Yankees for a reported $1.5 million. As Herb Michelson wrote, "Joe was annoyed by Boston's treatment of him. 'Boston started off by lying to us,' said Joe. 'Telling us no deal had been made yet. Then they said they wouldn't restore my 20 percent salary cut. I'd asked for that as a sign of good faith so [agent] Jerry [Kapstein] could negotiate with them. But they wouldn't do it. Here they'd spent a million dollars to get me and they wouldn't spend another $15,000 as a gesture of good faith.'"[25]

A few days later, Commissioner Bowie Kuhn voided the sales as "not in the best interest of baseball." Rudi finished playing out his option with the A's. He broke out of his slump of June and July, and had another solid year (.270-13-94), even though "I reached the point this season where I just didn't enjoy going to the ballpark anymore." Despite its disadvantages, Oakland was home, but the time had come to leave—which was really saying something. Rudi was by all accounts the nicest and most upright guy on the club. In 1972, he gave the ball that he caught to end the World Series to Finley, saying, "He's waited a long time for this."[26] After that season, when his contract was mentioned, Joe said, "Mr. Finley has always been fair to me."[27] Now he voiced his discontent to Herb Michelson at length, feelings best summed up by the line, "I'm just tired of Charlie's bullbleep."[28]

Rudi entertained various offers, and while money was certainly a prime consideration, he said, "I just want to go to a good organization where it's fun to play, where they treat you first class, where there's no bickering and hollering. Where you won't be harassed."[29] On November 17 he signed with the California Angels and owner Gene Autry. "Another great man—a wonderful guy," said Rudi of The Cowboy in 2011. "I used to have a golf tournament in Modesto for charity. One year he came up and I didn't even know he was coming. He was the main speaker. Win or lose, he'd come around the clubhouse. He never said a derogatory word."

Rudi's years in Anaheim were productive—when injuries didn't keep him out of the lineup. The 1977 season was shaping up as potentially his strongest, but it was derailed after 64 games by an injury like the one he suffered back in high school. On June 26 Nelson Briles of Texas hit Joe's hand with a pitch, chipping the second metacarpal, behind the index finger.

"It was the only time I ever saw Gene Autry get mad," Rudi recalled in 2011. "Briles had hung a slider to Don Baylor that inning, and Baylor hit it out. When I came up, he threw the ball behind my head. I ducked, and I still had the bat in my hand. Autry was just seething. He knew it was on purpose. It was so obvious it was ridiculous." The hand went in and out of casts over the next couple of months but failed to heal properly. Finally, Rudi underwent surgery on September 2 to remove bone fragments, ending any thoughts of a comeback that year.[30]

The hand still wasn't 100 percent until well into spring training 1978, but as it turned out, that was the only season approaching a full one for Joe in Anaheim. He started well but slumped badly. Former President Richard Nixon, always a keen baseball fan, then offered his support after a visit to Anaheim Stadium. It's easy to imagine Tricky Dick saying, "Let me say this about

Rudi. Although he hasn't hit well, he has saved some games in the field. He will be the glue to get this team back together if he gets his swing back."[31] Rudi proceeded to hit two grand slams in the span of nine days. (He finished his career with 12.)

Assorted leg injuries marred Rudi's 1979 season. While running out an infield hit in Detroit on August 15, he hurt his right Achilles tendon. The initial estimate was that he would be out for "at least three weeks," but he was done for the year. As a result, Joe did not appear in the postseason for the Angels, who won the AL West with Don Baylor as their primary left fielder.

The 1980 season was Rudi's last with the Angels; calf and hamstring pulls hampered him. Yet again his season was cut short prematurely. In a game at Minnesota's Metropolitan Stadium, Joe left with a strained left calf, and he did not return. In January 1981 the Angels traded him along with pitchers Jim Dorsey and Frank Tanana to the Red Sox for outfielder Fred Lynn and pitcher Steve Renko.

After the trade, Joe told Peter Gammons of the *Boston Globe*, "I've got some good days left."[32] Just a few of them came during his lone year in Boston, though, including a two-homer game at Fenway Park on August 12—his last of nine such games in the majors. Overall, it was not an enjoyable season. He became a free agent again on November 13.

On December 4, 1981, he signed a two-year contract with Oakland, returning to the scene of his triumphs. "There were many reasons why we signed Rudi," said A's president Roy Eisenhardt, "not the least of which was sentiment. Joe Rudi brings character, community, and a sense of team with him." He compared Joe's veteran experience to that of Lou Piniella, who had helped the Yankees to beat Oakland in the AL playoffs that year.[33] It was no coincidence that the A's manager was Billy Martin, who had preferred Rudi to Reggie Jackson when both were free agents in 1976.[34]

Joe played his final big-league season in '82, mainly at first base. The A's expected him at spring training in 1983, but chronic soreness in both Achilles tendons kept him at the family's new home, a 300-acre cattle ranch in the northeastern Oregon town of Baker City. "The team doctor told me, 'If you hurt your Achilles again, you won't be able to do things with your kids,'" said Rudi in 2011. "I still kept trying to get back, but I never could." Rudi spent the entire '83 season on the disabled list, and Oakland chose to release him that October.[35]

Rudi started the baseball team at Baker High School. In 1986 and '87, however, manager Tony La Russa, a close friend from their minor-league days, brought him back to the A's as a batting and outfield coach. Among others, Joe worked with José Canseco, seeking to make the hulking slugger a "complete" player. "It was homestands in '86, I'd come down from Baker and then go back to check on things at the ranch. In '87, I was gone about four-fifths of the time. Tony wanted me as hitting coach in '88, but the stress of being gone was too much. I wanted to be there for Sharon and my second son in particular." He then assisted at Baker for another couple of years.

Joe and Sharon had four children: Michael (the infant who was with them in Venezuela), Scott, Heather, and Shaun.[36] Shaun was good enough in baseball to be a 48th-round draft pick in 1998. That year the Rudis moved back to Modesto to be nearer their elderly parents; they worked for a real-estate firm there. Former teammate Carney Lansford bought the ranch in Oregon.[37] In the fall of 2001, however, they returned to Baker City after concluding family business. "Team Rudi" remained very active in the local real-estate business; Joe did some instructing at a local baseball academy and sponsored tournament play with wooden bats. His main leisure pursuit was ham radio, which he took up in his playing days.[38]

Looking back on his baseball career in 2011, Joe Rudi said, "It's all I ever imagined doing when I was younger. It was the focal point of my younger years. It was an amazing journey, a group of guys who came up together from Single-A to Birmingham to the majors. We were a really young ballclub in '68, Finley threw us out there every day and we got our butts kicked. Then we matured. I talk to Gene Tenace, I talk to Reggie once

in a while, I see some of the other guys at alumni golf tournaments, though we don't travel much any more. But the relationships you develop—when we get back together, it's like we've never been apart at all."

Grateful acknowledgment to Joe Rudi for his memories (telephone interview, April 17, 2011).

SOURCES

baseball-reference.com

retrosheet.org

purapelota.com (Venezuelan statistics).

NOTES

1 Bill James, *The New Bill James Historical Abstract*. New York: Simon & Schuster, 2001), 697.

2 Ken Rappoport, "Uonbtrusive Joe Rudi Is Making Big Noise at Plate," Associated Press, August 9, 1974.

3 Joe Rudi telephone interview with Rory Costello, April 17, 2011; M.S. Vasche, "The Folks Back in Modesto Are Staunch Rudi Rooters," *Modesto Bee*, October 19, 1973, A-10.

4 Steve Ames, "Joe Rudi: The A's Unheralded Star," *Baseball Digest*, March 1973, 25.

5 Joe McGuff, "Sweet-Swinging Rudi Wins A's Left Field Job," *The Sporting News*, April 22, 1967, 29.

6 Ibid.

7 Bernie Flynn, "Slugging Downey Hi Infielder Joe Rudi Breaks Hand, Will Miss Rest of Season," *Modesto Bee*, April 16, 1964, C-1.

8 Barry Abramson, "Joe Rudi: His Father Disapproved of 'That Baseball Foolishness,'" *Family Weekly*, September 20, 1975.

9 Flynn, op. cit.

10 Abramson, "Joe Rudi: His Father Disapproved."

11 McGuff, "Sweet-Swinging Rudi Wins A's Left Field Job."

12 Ron Bergman, "New Swat Style Working Wonders for Rudi," *The Sporting News*, July 22, 1972, 3.

13 Joe McGuff, "A's Start Youth Drive, Put Nine Kids on Roster," *The Sporting News*, October 31, 1964, 20.

14 Ames, "Joe Rudi: The A's Unheralded Star."

15 Abramson, "Joe Rudi: His Father Disapproved."

16 Herb Michelson, "Joe Rudi Homers Twice in A's Win," *Modesto Bee*, September 26, 1969, A-14.

17 Ibid.

18 Bergman, "New Swat Style Working Wonders for Rudi."

19 Ron Bergman, "Rudi's Not a Super Star—But He's Solid A's Belter," *The Sporting News*, February 12, 1972, 28.

20 Ron Bergman, "Banquet Requests Pour In; Rudi Prefers Home Hearth," *The Sporting News*, December 16, 1972, 51.

21 Roger Angell, *Five Seasons* (New York: Simon & Schuster, 1977), 55.

22 Lowell Reidenbaugh, "Joe Rudi's Bat Signals Lights Out for Dodgers," *The Sporting News*, November 2, 1974, 11.

23 "Hunter-less A's Still Tough." Associated Press, March 19, 1975.

24 Herb Michelson, "Tormented Season Chased Rudi to Angels," *Modesto Bee*, November 18, 1976, B-1.

25 Ibid.

26 Ames, "Joe Rudi: The A's Unheralded Star."

27 Bergman, "Banquet Requests Pour In; Rudi Prefers Home Hearth."

28 Michelson, "Tormented Season Chased Rudi to Angels."

29 Ibid.

30 "Rudi out for Rest of Year," Associated Press, August 26, 1977.

31 Mike Tully, "Joe Rudi Backs Up Nixon's Endorsement," United Press International, June 28, 1978.

32 Peter Gammons, "Rudi All Ready: 'I've Got Some Good Days Left,'" *Boston Globe*, January 27, 1981.

33 "Oakland Signs Joe Rudi," United Press International, December 5, 1981.

34 Roger Kahn, *October Men* (New York: Harcourt Books, 2004), 123.

35 Kit Stier, "Sore-Armed Krueger Stays Home," *The Sporting News*, November 14, 1983, 52.

36 Kelvin C. Bias, "Joe Rudi, All-Star Outfielder," *Sports Illustrated*, July 10, 2000.

37 Bruce Markusen, "Here's What Happened to '73 World Champion Oakland A's," *Baseball Digest*, October 1998, 69.

38 Gene Menez, "Loud and Clear," *Sports Illustrated*, July 2, 2007.

Gene Tenace

By Joseph Wancho

The Cincinnati Reds did not seem a bit concerned about their opponent from the junior circuit. The Big Red Machine were the bullies on the beach, waiting to kick sand in the face of their rival, the Oakland Athletics. Pete Rose viewed the coming 1972 World Series as anticlimactic. "The real World Series was between the Reds and Pirates," said Rose of the Reds' opposition in the NLCS.[1] Cincinnati skipper Sparky Anderson chimed in, "If I said the American League was as good as the National League, I'd be lying."[2]

The Athletics franchise was appearing in the Series for the first time in 41 years. Slugger Reggie Jackson was sidelined with a hamstring injury, and the Reds were overwhelming favorites.

Catcher Gene Tenace was penciled into the seventh spot in the batting order in Game One at Cincinnati's Riverfront Stadium. Tenace, despite having got just one hit in the League Championship Series against Detroit, felt that he was seeing the ball very well. "The balls that I was hitting were right on the nose, but right at somebody," he recalled.[3]

Tenace may have been on to something with his analysis. After a walk to George Hendrick in the third inning, Tenace sent a Gary Nolan pitch into the left-field bleachers for a 2-0 Oakland lead. In the fifth inning he homered again off Nolan, giving the visitors a 3-2 advantage. That was the final score.

Tenace became the first major leaguer to homer in his first two at-bats in the World Series. "I never hit two home runs in one game before," he exclaimed. "The first one was on a fastball out over the plate. The second was on a hanging curve."[4]

He was not finished, as he added round-trippers in Games Four and Five. He had hit only five home runs in the regular season, and had four in the Series. The four home runs tied a major-league mark for home runs in a World Series. After number 4 the scoreboard at the Oakland Coliseum delivered this message to Tenace, and the 49,000-plus fans: The mark equaled those of Babe Ruth, Duke Snider, Lou Gehrig, and Hank Bauer. "I don't belong with those guys," Tenace remembered thinking to himself.[5]

Cincinnati catcher Johnny Bench credited Tenace with taking advantage of mistakes. "Any time a batter hits a home run, he hits a pitcher's mistake—and I see a lot of that behind the plate," Bench said. "Tenace hit a curveball that hung and a couple of sliders that didn't slide. But Gene knew what to do when he got those mistakes, and that's what counts."[6]

Tenace, who batted .348 in the Series and knocked in nine runs, was named the Series' Most Valuable Player,

an honor that earned him a sports car from *Sport* magazine. Tenace brushed off the honors, claiming that there were 25 heroes on the team, not just one. Always humble and reserved, he was happy to be a face in the crowd.

Fury Gene Tenace was born on October 10, 1946, in Russellton, Pennsylvania, the second of three children born to Fiore and Ethel Tenace. He had an older sister, Nadine, and a younger sister, Serena Kay, who was killed in an auto accident at the age of 21. His original name was Fiore Gino Tennaci. But his maternal grandfather, who had emigrated from Italy, wanted to Americanize the family name. It was also his grandfather who gave the youngster the nickname Steamboat, because of his block-like build.

Gene's father dropped out of school at the age of 16 and joined the Merchant Marine. He enlisted in the Navy when World War II began and also served in the Korean War. After he was discharged, Tenace moved his family to Lucasville, Ohio, where he found work as a laborer, and then as a union truck driver.

Fiore Tenace put tremendous pressure on young Gene to become a ballplayer. Fiore had played semipro ball around the Ohio-Pennsylvania border area. Ethel Tenace recalled her husband berating the youngster in front of others. "'Didn't I always tell you to swing at a third strike? How come you didn't swing?' his father used to scream. Gene, he didn't say anything except, 'I don't know.' If Gene would ever attack back at his father he probably would've got a slap across the mouth. His father used to say, 'No kid who lives under my roof is goin' to sass me. If he's going to be a ballplayer, he'll do as I say.'"[7]

Because of this treatment, young Gene suffered from ulcers. He couldn't play baseball for a year, and was restricted to a special diet. When he recovered enough to return to the diamond, he asked his father not to come to his games because it made him too nervous.

Tenace eventually grew into a fine ballplayer at Valley Local High in Lucasville. He was a two-sport star, excelling in football and baseball, earning all-state

honors while playing shortstop. He also played on an American Legion team that featured future major-league stars Al Oliver and Larry Hisle, both of nearby Portsmouth, Ohio. "We could put some runs on the board, but we just didn't have the pitching to get past the state playoffs," recalled Tenace.[8]

After graduating from high school in 1965, Tenace was drafted by the Kansas City Athletics in the 20th round of the June amateur draft. He puttered around the Athletics organization as a utility player. Once, while with Peninsula of the Carolina League, Tenace played all nine positions in one game as part of a promotion. "I pitched the first inning and got out of it, though I nearly got the third baseman killed," he remembered. "I caught the second inning, then moved around the horn each inning and ended up in right field. It was fun till I got to the outfield. There was no action there."[9]

In 1969 Tenace was promoted to Birmingham of the Double-A Southern League. Manager Gus Niarhos, known for his skill at developing young receivers, went to work on his newest pupil. "I'd call Tenace an adequate catcher now," said Niarhos near the beginning of the season. "His arm is good. The biggest thing is getting him to relax. When he does, and if he keeps hitting, he'll be up there. That could be next year — that's how much I think of his chances. Tenace wants to know. He asks, too. He's a good student."[10] Tenace showed that his progress was ahead of the timetable Niarhos had set, when he was promoted to Oakland after backup catcher Jim Pagliaroni was sold to Seattle and Dave Duncan was called into military service. Tenace made his big-league debut on May 29, 1969. Tenace played in five games as a backup for Phil Roof. His first major-league hit was a single off Cleveland's Luis Tiant on May 30. His second was a solo home run off Detroit pitcher Earl Wilson on June 6.

The A's acquired catcher Larry Haney from Seattle on June 14, and returned Tenace to Birmingham. He had a solid year there, batting .319 with 20 homers, and 74 RBIs. Behind the plate, he fielded a respectable .988 with 46 assists in 80 games. He capped off his season when he was recalled to the varsity after the

Southern League season. Tenace was dispatched to Iowa of the Triple-A American Association to begin the 1970 campaign. He flourished again, and was recalled to the Athletics for the last two months of the season. Gene saw more action, hitting .305 in 105 at-bats. (He did not come near .300 again in his career.)

In 1971 the Athletics' third season in the Bay Area after relocating from Kansas City, the team broke through to end Minnesota's hold on the American League's Western Division. Other than pitcher Vida Blue, the A's star players had all begun their careers in Kansas City. Now Charlie Finley's team was about to get a taste of the postseason.

Tenace was Dave Duncan's backup at catcher. Manager Dick Williams favored Duncan, who was a better defensive player, possessed a stronger arm, and had the intangibles such as success in handling the pitching staff. But Baltimore swept the A's in the League Championship Series, claiming the American League pennant for the third straight year.

If their quick exit from the playoffs taught the A's anything, it was that they needed to bolster their pitching staff. After the season the A's traded promising outfielder Rick Monday to the Chicago Cubs for pitcher Ken Holtzman. With Blue and Catfish Hunter, the Oakland rotation was suddenly a force. But their offense, outside of Reggie Jackson and Joe Rudi, was anemic at times. Their pitching staff was the cornerstone that Oakland rode to three straight world championships, beginning in 1972.

Dick Williams realized that his team needed an infusion of offense. Tenace provided a bit more than Duncan. "He wasn't doing it with the bat," Williams said of Duncan. "It began to affect his catching,"[11] Williams then went against his normal thinking of playing the better defensive player, and inserted Tenace in the lineup for the last two months of the season. Oakland was in a fight with the White Sox all season, outlasting them by 5½ games. The League Championship Series against the Tigers went the full five games, and Tenace knocked in outfielder George Hendrick with the go-ahead run in the fourth inning

of Game Five. The 2-1 win was Blue Moon Odom's second victory of the series. Tenace's game-winning blow was his only hit in 17 at-bats, but a key one nonetheless.

The World Series was a tightly matched battle between Oakland and Cincinnati, with six of the seven games being decided by a single run. Oakland prevailed in seven games, starting a dynasty such as the Bay Area had never seen before.

An interesting story developed before Game Six, as the Series moved back to Cincinnati. A woman waited in line to purchase standing-room tickets. She overheard a man remark, "If Gene Tenace hits a home run today, he won't walk out of the ballpark."[12] The woman alerted police, and Finley and Williams requested extra security. They decided not to tell Tenace of the threat until after the game. The man, who carried a loaded gun and a bottle of whiskey, was arrested during the game.

The next year Dave Duncan was a holdout as spring training commenced. Tenace took over the catcher duties. As late March approached, Duncan was still unsigned. Rather than deal with the contract issue, Finley traded Duncan and George Hendrick to Cleveland for catcher Ray Fosse and infielder Jack Heidemann. Fosse, an excellent fielder (Gold Gloves in 1970 and 1971) but lacking on offense, became the starting catcher. But the Athletics were anxious to keep Tenace and his bat in the lineup. They asked Mike Hegan, who was a defensive specialist at first base, to tutor Tenace on the finer points of becoming a first sacker. "All the time Mike was doing this," said Tenace, "he was pushing himself further and further away from the job. He knew it and I knew it, but he still kept helping me."[13] Hegan was sold to the Yankees during the season.

Besides starting at first base, Tenace sometimes filled in for Fosse, who was often injured. He hit 24 home runs In 1973, the first of four straight seasons in which he smacked at least 20 homers. Despite medkiocre batting averages Tenace proved to be a valuable offensive commodity. In 1974 he batted only .211 but led the league in walks (110). He was the starting first baseman for the American League in the 1975 All-Star Game.

The Athletics were a strong team, dominating the American League's West Division. They dispatched Baltimore two years in a row in the ALCS, and topped the New York Mets in the 1973 World Series and the Los Angeles Dodgers in 1974 to win three straight world championships.

The major-league owners locked the players out of spring-training in 1976 until a new contract could be reached. The gates were finally opened in mid-March, and Finley sent out the obligatory contracts, cutting each player's salary by 20 percent. Sensing that free agency was imminent, Finley dealt Holtzman and Jackson to Baltimore a few days before the season began. Thus began the fire sale as the trade deadline approached in June. Finley offered all of his starters to all interested parties for the right price. The players were willing to play out the year, hoping to cash in at the end of the season when free agency was granted. Finley's attempts to sell or trade his stars were doused by Commissioner Bowie Kuhn.

The players were correct in their assumption that the moolah would be coming their way. Tenace, who made a salary of $40,800 in 1976, signed a six-year contract with San Diego for a total of $1.85 million. Fingers joined Tenace in the Padres' fold.

Despite owner Ray Kroc's attempt to bolster the Padres, they were not a competitive team. The Dodgers, Astros, and Reds fought it out at the top of the Western Division. Each team had its way with the weaker Padres. San Diego signed Tenace to be the starting catcher, even though his skills may have been better suited for first base. As it turned out, he split time between the two positions. His power numbers tailed off; he reached 20 home runs only once in his four years at San Diego. Kroc was dissatisfied with his free-agent acquisition. "Tenace kept saying if he played every day he'd improve. Well he's been in there every day and he hasn't done a damn thing," the owner said.

"All he wants to do is walk. Well, we can't win games waiting for walks. He's being paid to hit and he can't hit. Nobody in either league wants him and we're paying a premium price."[14] For his part, Tenace did not respond negatively to Kroc's criticism; he acknowledged that he was not playing well and said Kroc's tirade was intended to stir up the Padres.

On December 10, 1980, Tenace was part of an 11-player deal, going with Fingers, pitcher Bob Shirley and catcher Bob Geren to St. Louis. The principal player among seven Cardinals going to San Diego was catcher Terry Kennedy. During the 1981 season Tenace went back and forth between first base and catcher, backing up Darrell Porter and Keith Hernandez.

In 1982 Tenace broke a bone in his right thumb in spring training. Later in the year, he broke a bone in his right hand diving into third base. Despite these setbacks, Tenace played a key role among the reserves, always encouraging them. "Gene Tenace keeps my head above water," said outfielder Tito Landrum. "If I start having a letdown, he comes over and kicks my rear end. Literally. He pulls no punches. He lets you know."[15] Tenace preached to the bench players to always be ready because they never knew when they would be called upon to enter a game.

The Cardinals won the 1982 World Series, topping Milwaukee in seven games. Tenace, who had hit his 200th career home run during the season, went hitless in six at-bats with one walk in the Series.

Tenace became a free agent after the season and signed with Pittsburgh. He played sparingly (78 plate appearances) and quit as a player after the season. He retired with a .241 batting average, 201 home runs, and 674 RBIs. He had a respectable fielding percentage of .986 as a catcher, and .993 as a first baseman. Tenace served as a minor-league instructor for the Boston Red Sox and also coached in the majors, primarily with Toronto. He was the bench coach on Cito Gaston's staff that won back-to-back world championships in 1992 and 1993.

Tenace retired from baseball after the 2009 season. As of 2013, he and his wife, Linda, lived in Redmond, Oregon. They have two daughters.

The 1972 World Series was not all rosy for Gene Tenace. The Reds swiped 12 bases in the Series, taking advantage of Oakland pitchers' inability to hold baserunners. Tenace did not have the strongest of throwing arms, which did not aid the cause. Asked after the A's victory in Game Seven if he thought he might be elected the MVP of the Series, Tenace responded, "What the hell, even if I do, the Reds'll steal it from me."[16]

SOURCES

Berkow, Ira, *Beyond the Dream: Occasional Heroes of Sports* (Lincoln, Nebraska: Bison Books, 1974).

Green, G. Michael, and Roger D. Launius, *Charlie Finley* (New York: Walker Publishing Company, 2010).

Markusen, Bruce, *A Baseball Dynasty: Charlie Finley's Swingin A's* (Haworth, New Jersey: St. Johann Press, 2002).

Sport magazine, October 1973.

The Sporting News

Tenace's file from the Giamatti Library, National Baseball Hall of Fame.

baseball-reference.com

baseball-almanac.com

retrosheet.org/

sabr.org/

NOTES

1 Bruce Markusen, *A Baseball Dynasty: Charlie Finley's Swingin A's* (Haworth, New Jersey: St. Johann Press, 2002), 143.

2 Ibid.

3 Markusen, 144.

4 Ibid.

5 Markusen, 158.

6 *The Sporting News*, November 11, 1972, 14.

7 Ira Berkow, *Beyond the Dream: Occasional Heroes of Sports* (Lincoln, Nebraska: Bison Books, 1974), 6-9.

8 *Sport,* April 1973.

9 Ibid.

10 *The Sporting News*, May 31, 1969, 41.

11 *The Sporting News*, November 11, 1972, 36,

12 Markusen, 162,

13 Markusen, 181.

14 *The Sporting News*, July 1, 1978, 23.

15 *The Sporting News*, August 9, 1982, 14.

16 *Sport,*, October 1973.

Strike One: Spring Training 1972

By Matthew Silverman

The Oakland A's were the pride of the American League West as winter turned to spring in 1972. The 1971 A's had become just the second team to win the Western title, after the Minnesota Twins claimed the honor in the first two seasons following the adoption of

divisional play in 1969. But the A's didn't just win the AL West in 1971, they ran away with it—claiming the division by 16 games. They never led by fewer than 13 games after beginning August with seven straight wins, the first of two streaks of that length during the month.

But October 1971 arrived with a thud. The 101 wins were the same number as the AL East champion Baltimore Orioles, yet the A's were no match for the O's in the League Championship Series. Oakland allowed five runs per game; Baltimore surrendered half that many. It was clear to A's owner and general manager Charles O. Finley that if Oakland wanted to compete with Baltimore—the class of the American League after appearing in three straight World Series—the A's needed an upgrade. But not even the self-assured A's owner could have imagined his team would appear in the next three World Series, and win them all.

The new Athletics, the Swinging A's, the only team besides the New York Yankees to win three straight world championships, came together in spring training 1972, clean-shaven and raring to go. Well, clean-shaven except for one slugger with something to prove.

No major-league player had worn a mustache in the regular season since World War I. Now, in the wind-down of the divisive Vietnam War, with so many other weighty issues going on in the country and the world,

finally came a breakthrough on the hirsute baseball front: Reggie Jackson wasn't shaving.

Iconoclast slugger Dick Allen, then of the Cardinals, had arrived in Florida with a mustache and muttonchops for spring training in 1970, but he shaved before departing St. Petersburg for St. Louis.[1] Now, two years later, Jackson, never at a loss for words, was at a loss for putting his razor to use.

No player had donned a mustache past spring training since another A's regular on a pennant-winning team: Wally Schang, catcher for Connie Mack's 1914 American League champions. Facial hair was out of fashion in the 1910s and Schang—and the rest of the major leagues—remained clean-shaven through two World Wars and then two wars in Asia. But by the 1970s, hair was in again. Even Broadway was in on it, with the musical *Hair* in the midst of a four-year run while simultaneously running in nine US cities as well as London.[2] So it only made sense that the counterculture enclave of Oakland, home of the Black Panthers, Cal Berkeley, Hell's Angels, and John Madden's Raiders, would be the launching pad for hair on big-league faces.

When Jackson showed up to spring training in Mesa, Arizona, sporting a 'stache, Finley did not like the idea initially. He wanted Reggie to shave before the season started, just as Dick Allen had—not to mention Frenchy Bordagaray, whose mustache lasted only through Brooklyn's spring training in 1936.[3] Oakland's owner, famous for getting under the skin of his players, took a new tack during spring training, however. Finley fashioned himself quite the showman, having introducing everything from the mule press conference (no comment from Charlie O the mascot, but plenty of words from Charlie O. the owner) to ballgirls (enjoyed by players and fans alike in Oakland). So why not bring the mustache back to baseball?

Accounts differ whether Finley first encouraged players to grow mustaches as reverse psychology to get Jackson to shave, or if the players came up with the plan on their own.[4] What is beyond dispute is that the A's broke the 58-year-old facial-hair barrier as a team. The Mustache Gang was led by a furry trio who eventually made the Hall of Fame and had their numbers retired in Oakland: Rollie Fingers and his legendary handlebar mustache; Catfish Hunter, who sported a debonair farmer's mustache; and Jackson, of course, in beard, mustache, and machismo. Like his three star players, manager Dick Williams, who joined the mustachioed masses on his '72 team, even sported a 'stache on his Hall of Fame plaque in Cooperstown.

Nearly every A's player who could physically grow facial hair did so in the spring of '72 in order to extract a bonus from the notoriously tight-fisted Finley. The $300 bonus went to any player who grew the mustaches by Father's Day, or Mustache Day, as Finley rechristened June 18. And those mustaches looked great with the new uniforms.

It was not as if the A's didn't already have the most colorful uniforms in the game, but Charlie Finley outdid himself. Kelly green and Fort Knox gold had been the team colors since Finley introduced them to the stunned American League in 1963, and though garish at the time—"It makes them look like grasshoppers," said Yankees manager Ralph Houk—the new uniforms were a step through the looking glass … and avoiding the mirror was not necessarily a bad thing.[5]

Gone were button-up tops. In their place: double-knit pullover shirts. "No buttons. No zippers," Finley crowed. "Imagine—a baseball uniform without buttons."[6] The team wore white pants, home or away, along with the pullover tops in either green or gold, though the latter color seemed almost fluorescent. The team wore green undershirts with the gold jerseys and vice versa; the stirrups were green with gold socks. Striking! Long before any team thought of alternate

uniforms for special days, the A's had their Sunday whites. And not just your run-of-the-mill white every other team wore at home, but, to borrow a phrase from Procol Harum, an English rock group of the day, "a whiter shade of pale." Finley called it "polar bear white,"[7] while team captain Sal Bando later referred to them as "wedding gown whites."[8] In any event, the whites were special, reserved for Sunday games.

What was really special was the A's pitching staff, which boasted a potential ace every day of the week. The team entered the year with two pitchers coming off 20-win seasons: Vida Blue had had a tremendous 24-win campaign, while Jim "Catfish" Hunter had enjoyed the first of five straight 20-win seasons.

John "Blue Moon" Odom, who, like Hunter, had been signed by Finley as a teenager in 1964, was no longer a sure thing in the rotation. Odom, who had started at least 25 games each of the previous four seasons, had been shot in the neck and chest in January 1972 while foiling a burglary near his mother's home in Macon, Georgia. One might think Odom's life—never mind his career—had been placed in serious jeopardy. But incredibly, each bullet passed through his body without doing serious damage to any organs.[9] Odom would be fine and pitch five more years in the majors. He finished 1972 with a 2.50 ERA and placed second in the AL to Hunter in winning percentage (.714). But in March of 1972, Charlie Finley didn't know that. All he knew was that right-handed starters Odom and Chuck Dobson were question marks due to health issues. (Dobson would not pitch at all in the majors in '72 because of elbow problems.) So Finley replaced two pitchers who'd combined for 25 wins with a 30-game winner.

Denny McLain was only 28 in '72, but he seemed a long way from 30. The first pitcher in 34 years to win 30 games, McLain had actually gone one better with a 31-6 mark for the 1968 world champion Tigers. He won the Cy Young Award in both '68 and '69 (sharing the award the latter year with Baltimore's Mike Cuellar), but he subsequently dropped off a cliff—of his own making. He showed plenty of wear and tear after averaging 23 wins and 290 innings a season from 1966 to 1969, compounded by his treating his body like a rental and treating those around him like dirt. McLain could, and often did, drink a case of Pepsi per day—an endorsement deal with the bottler included delivery of ten cases to his house per week—but his cola obsession was the least of his poor habits. He invested in a Michigan bookmaking operation and was suspended for half of the 1970 season. He then drew additional suspensions for carrying a gun on a team flight and pouring buckets of water on two Detroit writers.[10] Despite McLain's tremendous success on the mound, the Tigers were willing to part with their award-winning headache. Barely a week after the 1970 season ended, Detroit traded him to the Washington Senators, where he clashed with manager and legend Ted Williams. McLain led the league in losses instead of wins.

On March 4, 1972, with two pitchers hurt and Vida Blue holding out, McLain didn't look so bad from where Charlie Finley sat. Still, the A's owner wasn't about to pay full price. Bob Short, who had relocated his team from Washington to Texas over the winter, was prepared to pay one-third of McLain's $75,000 salary to get rid of him, but he wasn't willing to take damaged goods in return for spoiled goods. Short passed on both the injured Odom and Dobson and insisted on pitching prospects Don Stanhouse and Jim Panther. McLain proceeded to get into a shouting match with a TV reporter the day he arrived in Arizona and then surrendered ten runs in his spring debut for the A's.[11] He would make his last major-league start that August—as an Atlanta Brave.

Finley had far better luck with Ken Holtzman. He was one of the National League's top lefties, pitching no-hitters for the Cubs in 1969 and 1971, and slotting in behind the 1971 Cy Young winner Ferguson Jenkins in the Cubs rotation. Though he was coming off his worst year (9-15, 4,48 ERA), Holtzman, like McLain, was still in his 20s, but unlike McLain, his best years were ahead of him.

Holtzman's biggest problem with the Cubs was his manager, Leo Durocher. Old school Leo the Lip used

a motivational technique from his playing days in the 1920s and 1930s, belittling players and making them mad to get the most out of them. In the 1970s it wasn't working, at least not with Holtzman, especially given that many of the barbs dealt with his faith. "I think Jewish athletes tend to be stared at more often because they defy a commonly held stereotype of nonphysical, academic-minded nerds who strive to become doctors, lawyers, etc.," Holtzman reflected long after his career ended. "While some of this stereotype is perhaps justified, it never hindered my pursuit of both disciplines."[12]

Holtzman asked for a trade after the 1971 season and the Cubs found a willing partner in Charlie Finley. The A's owner/GM spent most of his time in Chicago and knew all about Holtzman's talent. He also knew that the A's had been caught short in the rotation in the previous year's ALCS, facing a Baltimore rotation that included the last quartet of 20-game winners in history. With Blue, Hunter, and Holtzman, the 1973 A's would become the last team to have three 20-game winners on one staff.

Finley had the perfect bait to procure Holtzman from the Cubs: Rick Monday, a power-hitting center fielder who could fill one of the weak links in the Cubs lineup. Monday had been the first-ever pick in the 1965 amateur draft, but A's manager Dick Williams grew frustrated with his lack of success against lefties and had resorted to a platoon with right-handed Angel Mangual in center field late in the 1971 season.

Trading for Holtzman was arguably the best deal among the myriad moves by Charlie Finley during Oakland's championship run. Holtzman fit in superbly with his new club, immediately buying into the winning vibe in the Oakland locker room. And he very much appreciated his new manager. "Dick Williams had complete trust and faith in his starting pitchers and let them pitch out of trouble on occasions where Leo might have pulled them from the game," Holtzman reflected.[13]

The A's players did not, however, have that level of trust in their owner. Especially when it came to contract negotiations. The two biggest seasons by A's players since their 1968 move from Kansas City—and, to be honest, since their 1955 move from Philadelphia—had been achieved in the last three years by high draft picks who vaulted through the A's farm system and became young stars on the big-league stage. In 1969 Reggie Jackson, just 23, had crushed 37 home runs by the All-Star break. He tailed off in the second half but his 47 home runs and .608 slugging hadn't been touched by anyone in an A's uniform since Hall of Fame slugger Jimmie Foxx for Connie Mack's Philadelphia Athletics in the 1930s. In the spring of 1970, Jackson asked for his salary to be tripled, to $60,000. The two sides finally reached an agreement of $45,000 shortly before the season began, but they continued feuding after Jackson got off to a slow start.[14] The acrimonious public fight between player and owner soured their relationship for the rest of Reggie's time in Oakland. Next up: Vida Blue.

Blue had been truly sensational in 1971. After losing on Opening Day, he won 16 of his next 17 decisions. He tossed 40 innings in a four-start span in July, including two 11-inning no-decisions, not to mention three innings pitched as the starting (and winning) pitcher in the '71 All-Star Game that ended the AL's eight-year losing streak. By mid-August he was 22-4 with a 1.70 ERA and 245 strikeouts. McLain's magic number 30 was not out of the realm of possibility.

Blue tailed off down the stretch, but he still finished 24-8 with a 1.82 ERA and 301 strikeouts in 312 innings. An overnight sensation at age 22, he appeared on the covers of *Time* and *Sports Illustrated* and was the youngest Cy Young Award winner in history. (New York Met Dwight Gooden later garnered that distinction, but Blue remains the youngest AL pitcher to claim the award.) Blue also captured the Most Valuable Player trophy, also becoming a trivia answer as the last switch-hitter to be named league MVP—hitting was the one area in which he did not excel in '71 (just a .118 BA).

Blue's lawyer, Bob Gerst, started contract negotiations the first week of January 1972. Blue had made $14,500 during his remarkable '71 season. Gerst asked for

$115,000; Finley offered $50,000. They had a long way to go.

Gerst lowered his client's asking price to $92,000, but Finley stayed at $50,000. Spring training opened, Blue stayed home. Finley acquired McLain, a 22-game loser, and planned to pay him the same $50,000 sum (after Washington's share) as Blue, a 24-game winner. Vida Blue announced he would quit baseball, go into acting, go to Japan, go into the steel business. None of these came to be. Even Vida had a hard time keeping a straight face. Finley dispatched players to Oakland to try to get Blue to sign. No dice. The impasse continued.[15]

The Major League Baseball Players Association called the first work stoppage in major-league history on April Fool's Day, abruptly ending spring training with the A's record at 9-11.[16]

The issue of the players' pension fund delayed the regular season and seven games wound up cut from Oakland's schedule; they were never made up because the owners refused to pay the players for the games missed. Finley was far from the only stubborn man sitting in an owner's box.

When it came time to cut down to a 25-man roster, the A's released two-time batting champ Tommy Davis, a .324 hitter the previous year off the bench. Yet the more painful move was placing the previous year's Cy Young Award winner and MVP on the restricted list.[17] Ken Holtzman's Oakland debut was as Opening Day starter. Would Blue ever don the green and gold again? Yes, but it would take pressure from both the commissioner of baseball and president of the United States for it to come to pass.

"It would be a great tragedy if a young player with all that talent stayed out too long," stated Richard Nixon, who would find tragedy on a much grander scale following a botched break-in at the Watergate Hotel in June of 1972. As for Commissioner Bowie Kuhn, he had troubles of his own.

After enduring the game's first strike—and the players claiming victory—Kuhn's next move was to settle this Blue business. Both pitcher and owner were pretty bitter when summoned to the Drake Hotel in Chicago; Kuhn's room but Finley's turf. It turned into a 22-hour negotiating marathon. "I had never felt so much like a Louisiana bayou sheriff," Kuhn later wrote, which may have explained why the Louisiana native Blue was so hostile toward the commissioner.[18]

As the sun came up, the two sides finally agreed on $63,000. It still took three days and more threats to get them in a room to sign the deal. When Finley initially refused to go to American League President Joe Cronin's office in Boston for the May 2 meeting, Kuhn responded that if the A's owner didn't show, Kuhn would make his star pitcher a free agent. Both sides signed, reluctantly. As a result of the ramping up of the Finley-Kuhn feud, the A's owner drew a $500 fine from the commissioner, the maximum fine allowed at the time.[19] After Dick Williams used a three-man rotation of Holtzman-Hunter-McLain (until Blue Moon Odom replaced the demoted Denny),[20] Vida Blue finally made his first start of 1972 during the final weekend of May. By then the owner was angrier at Kuhn than he was at Blue, but his team was finally whole—and dominant.

SOURCES

Author Interview

Sal Bando, September 14, 2011.

Ken Holtzman, May 3, 2012.

Books

Green, G. Michael, and Roger D. Launius, *Charlie Finley: The Outrageous Story of Baseball's Super Showman* (New York: Walker & Company, 2010).

Kuhn, Bowie, and Marty Appel (Editorial Assistant), *Hardball: The Education of a Baseball Commissioner* (New York: McGraw-Hill Book Company, 1988).

Markusen, Bruce, *Baseball's Last Dynasty: Charlie Finley's Oakland A's* (Indianapolis: Masters Press, 1998).

Newspapers and Magazines

Meyers, Jeff, "Frenchy Bordagaray, an 82-Year-Old Grandfather Living in Ventura, Shocked the Baseball Establishment in the 1930s With Such Gimmicks as Racing a Horse on Foot and Growing a Mustache, But His Flair Made Him a Media Darling," *Los Angeles Times*, December 25, 1992. articles.latimes.com/1992-12-25/sports/sp-2588_1_frenchy-bordagaray

Rushin, Steve, "The Hirsute of Happiness: How Facial Hair Brought Joy to the Red Sox," *Sports Illustrated*, September 30, 2013.

"They Said It," *Sports Illustrated*, April 29, 1963. sportsillustrated.cnn.com/vault/article/magazine/MAG1074724/index.htm

Websites

baseball-almanac.com

baseball-reference.com

hairthemusical.com/history.html

oakland.athletics.mlb.com/oak/downloads/y2011/2011_media_guide.pdf

Armour, Mark, "Denny McLain," SABR BioProject, sabr.org/bioproj/person/6bddedd4

NOTES

1   Steve Rushin. "The Hirsute of Happiness: How Facial Hair Brought Joy to the Red Sox." *Sports Illustrated*, September 30, 2013.

2   James Rado, "Hairstory: The Story Behind the Story," February 14, 2009. hairthemusical.com/history.html

3   Jeff Meyers, "Frenchy Bordagaray, an 82-Year-Old Grandfather Living in Ventura, Shocked the Baseball Establishment in the 1930s With Such Gimmicks as Racing a Horse on Foot and Growing a Mustache, But His Flair Made Him a Media Darling," *Los Angeles Times,* December 25, 1992. articles.latimes.com/1992-12-25/sports/sp-2588_1_frenchy-bordagaray

4   Green and Launius, *Charlie Finley*, 159.

5   "They Said It," *Sports Illustrated*, April 29, 1963. sportsillustrated.cnn.com/vault/article/magazine/MAG1074724/index.htm

6   Green and Launius, *Charlie Finley*, 158.

7   Ibid.

8   Author interview with Sal Bando, September 14, 2011.

9   Bruce Markusen, *Baseball's Last Dynasty: Charlie Finley's Oakland A's* (Indianapolis: Masters Press, 1998), 77-8.

10 Mark Armour, "Denny McLain." SABR BioProject. sabr.org/bioproj/person/6bddedd4

11 Markusen, *Baseball's Last Dynasty*, 81.

12 Author interview with Ken Holtzman, May 3, 2012.

13 Ken Holtzman interview.

14 Green and Launius, *Charlie Finley*, 133-34.

15 Markusen, *Baseball's Last Dynasty*, 81-84.

16 oakland.athletics.mlb.com/oak/downloads/y2011/2011_media_guide.pdf

17 Markusen, *Baseball's Last Dynasty*, 88.

18 Bowie Kuhn and Marty Appel (Editorial Assistant), *Hardball: The Education of a Baseball Commissioner* (New York: McGraw-Hill Book Company, 1988), 132.

19 Kuhn and Appel, *Hardball*, 131-133.

20 Markusen, *Baseball's Last Dynasty*, 93.

Jerry Adair

by Royse Parr

Kenneth Jerry Adair was born to Kinnie and Ola Adair on December 17, 1936, at Lake Station, an unincorporated area named for a station on a trolley-car line between the northeastern Oklahoma cities of Sand Springs and Tulsa. Jerry claimed Sand Springs as his hometown. He was a fair-skinned, blond-haired descendant of mixed-blood Cherokee tribal leaders who once were the warlords of the southern Appalachians. The strong "will to win" of Cherokee warriors was exemplified in the life of Jerry Adair, who was an exceptional multisport competitor.

A notable Adair who lived with the Cherokee tribe in the 18th century was an Irish trader, James Adair. He wrote a lengthy book about his belief that the unique, dignified Cherokees were one of the biblical lost tribes of Judah. In 1838 a majority of the Cherokees under the terms of an onerous treaty with the United States government were forcibly removed on the Trail of Tears to Indian Territory. Thousands of Cherokees died along the way. In 1907 Indian Territory and Oklahoma Territory were combined to form the state of Oklahoma.

Bordering on the state of Arkansas in the flint hills of northeastern Oklahoma, Adair County is named for one of Jerry Adair's Cherokee family members of the Civil War era, Judge William Penn Adair. Jerry's grandfather George Starr Adair was enrolled in a tribal census as a 28-year-old member of the Cherokee Nation in 1900 in what became Adair County, Oklahoma. His son, Kinnie Adair, spoke Cherokee when he visited with friends and relatives from Adair County. Today, heavy concentrations of the inhabitants of the county are descendants of the original Cherokee settlers.

Jerry Adair's life was described by the *Tulsa World's* sports editor Bill Connors as "an experience of two lifetimes." Connors' obituary after Jerry's death in 1987 surmised, "The first half was exaltation. The second half was tragedy." He described Jerry as "the best athlete to come out of the Tulsa area in his lifetime." He would not have stretched the truth if he had stated that no athlete from Oklahoma had a more storied pre-professional career than Adair, not even Mickey Mantle, who was 5 years older than Adair. Mantle had close relatives who were Cherokee; his grandmother was born in Indian Territory, but he was not a mixed-blood American Indian.

Jerry's father played sandlot baseball on his employer's teams in the Sand Springs area. Like Mantle's father, Kinnie Adair always had time after work to play ball with his son. A tool grinder by trade, Kinnie also coached Jerry's Little League teams. Jerry told Ray Fitzgerald, a *Boston Globe* sports columnist, about his Little League days when he "did a lot of pitching. Anybody who could throw a curveball was a pitcher, and I was a pretty good one."

Kinnie Adair died in 1986, one year and three days before Jerry's death. He had remarried after Jerry's mother died in 1952 and had a son, Dennis, who died in 2005. Jerry's only sister, Joyce, who was born in Adair County, still lived in Sand Springs in 2014.

Adair's high-school coach, Cecil Hankins, was a legendary football and basketball player at Oklahoma A&M College, now Oklahoma State University, in Stillwater, Oklahoma. Hankins regarded Jerry as the greatest all-around athlete he ever coached. Jerry earned nine letters at Sand Springs High School, three each in football, basketball, and baseball. During his high-school years, he earned the nickname "Iceman" because of his coolness. He is particularly remembered for his coolness during the football game against Ponca City during his senior year. Ponca City grabbed a 20-0 lead in the first quarter. Playing quarterback, Jerry scored just before halftime and kicked the extra point to cut the deficit to 20-7. In the third quarter, he engineered a scoring drive and kicked another extra point for a 20-14 score. Late in the fourth quarter, Jerry scored a touchdown and kicked the extra point to win the game 21-20 for Sand Springs. Bill Connors once wrote, "Adair demonstrated All-American possibilities as a high school quarterback at Sand Springs."

After football season in the fall of 1954, *Daily Oklahoman* sportswriter Ray Soldan telephoned coach Hankins to tell him that he had selected Jerry for the all-state football team. For many years Soldan made Oklahoma's all-state team selections. Only seniors were eligible and a player could be selected for only one sport. Coach Hankins spoke with Jerry, who said he did not want to make all-state in football; he wanted to make it in basketball. Soldan said he would give no assurance that Jerry would be selected for basketball, but Jerry said he would take the chance. Another player was named to replace him on the all-state football team. After basketball season, Jerry was selected on the all-state basketball team. Playing in the state all-star game in the summer of 1955, he was selected as the most outstanding player in the game.

Jerry also played Ban Johnson League baseball during the summer of 1955. He was scouted by Toby Greene,

the longtime head baseball coach at Oklahoma State. Jerry's team was leading 1-0 in the bottom of the ninth inning, but the opponent had loaded the bases with no outs. Greene watched as the manager motioned for Jerry to pitch. Jerry nodded and walked to the mound from his third-base position with a big cud of tobacco in his mouth. He threw two balls to the catcher and announced he was ready. Greene thought this was the cockiest player he had ever seen. Jerry struck out the three batters he faced. Greene later declared to Coach Hankins, "I'll take him—he can play anywhere." Jerry Adair was one of Coach Greene's seven All-Americans at OSU.

Adair entered OSU in the fall of 1955 on an athletic scholarship to play basketball and baseball. Freshmen were not then eligible for varsity competition and played only limited schedules in all sports. Adair's first varsity competition was during the 1956-1957 basketball season under Hall of Fame coach Henry Iba. A rare sophomore starter at OSU, the 6-foot, 175-pound Adair was the team's playmaking guard and second leading scorer on the nation's top defensive team. During his junior year, he was again the team's second leading scorer. Bill Connors once wrote, "Longtime Iba watchers say Adair was one of the few players who was not yelled at by Iba. 'There was no need to yell at Jerry,' Iba said at the time. 'He does everything right.'"

The 1957 OSU baseball season was essentially "called on account of rain." Nine games were canceled because of rain or unplayable fields. The year's record for OSU was 12-3. When three consecutive days of rain prevented the Missouri Valley conference championship series from being played, Bradley University was given the NCAA tournament bid because of its better conference record.

Regarded as a "converted basketballer," sophomore Jerry Adair was the starting shortstop on the experienced 1957 OSU baseball team. Two of his senior teammates signed professional contracts at season's end. Center fielder Mel Wright, who was the other starting basketball guard with Adair during the 1956-1957 season, signed with the Kansas City Athletics.

He had four undistinguished seasons in the minor leagues. Pitcher Merlin Nippert signed with the Boston Red Sox, with whom he had a cup of coffee in 1962 before finishing his career in the Pacific Coast League.

Competing in the Big Eight conference in 1958 for the first time, OSU was rained out of its last two games of the year with champion Missouri, which thus backed into the NCAA tournament bid. OSU's record for the year was 17-6. Junior shortstop Adair was the team's leading hitter with a .438 batting average. He was the first player from OSU named to the All-Big Eight team. He was also named to the All-American second team by the American Baseball Coaches Association.

On August 24, 1957, Jerry married his high-school sweetheart, Kay Morris. They had met in an English class at Sand Springs High School. While he was playing semipro baseball during the summer of 1958 for Williston, North Dakota, in the Western Canada Baseball League, Kay gave birth in Tulsa to Kathy, their first of four children.

Adair won the batting title with a .409 average. He tied for the lead in home runs and finished close behind the RBI leader. Jerry was the league's top fielding shortstop. He was the starting pitcher in three games and was credited with the victory in each. He batted .444 in 14 playoff games and led his team to the league title.

Adair was signed by Baltimore Orioles scout Eddie Robinson for a reported $40,000. The Boston Red Sox offered him a larger signing bonus than Baltimore, but Adair figured he would move up the ladder more quickly with the Orioles. He made his major-league debut at shortstop for the O's on September 2, 1958, in a 4-3 loss to the Senators in Washington. At third base for the Orioles was future major-league manager Dick Williams, who would be Adair's future ticket to participate in three World Series.

(The news that Adair had signed a professional baseball contract came as a complete surprise to OSU's athletic director and basketball coach, Henry Iba. He had understood that Jerry would return to OSU for conferences with him before making a definite commitment to a major-league club. Iba had once counseled OSU's baseball and football star, Allie Reynolds, to take a baseball contract offered by the Cleveland Indians instead of one offered by the New York Giants in Allie's then favorite sport, football. As to Adair, Iba was quoted in the *Tulsa World* as saying "He has an excellent chance in baseball, I believe, for he is a fine baseball player and a boy with a great competitive spirit." With his playmaking guard not in the lineup for the 1958-1959 season, Iba was to suffer through his first losing basketball season (11 won, 14 lost) since his arrival at OSU in 1934.)

After playing only as a late-inning substitute in 11 games with the Orioles in September 1958, with just 19 at-bats, Adair was shipped in the spring of 1959 to the Amarillo Gold Sox, the Orioles' farm team in the Double-A Texas League. His Amarillo manager, George Staller, told the *Tulsa World* that Adair was a surefire major leaguer but needed a season of Triple-A experience. At the beginning of the season, Adair batted around .275 and failed to cover much ground. Suddenly he caught fire, both at bat and in the field. Staller credited Adair with being instrumental in Amarillo's surge from 17 games below .500 to four over that mark. Recalled Adair in a *Tulsa World* article, "My fielding improved when my hitting got better and I learned to play the batters. That's the big difference. When you're hitting, everything seems to go well. Knowing the hitters is the key. That's why I didn't do so well with Baltimore."

In 146 games, mostly at shortstop, for Amarillo in 1959, Adair batted .309. Called up at season's end by Baltimore, he batted .314 in 12 games, playing second base or shortstop, mostly as the starter. After playing in an instructional league in the fall of 1959, he batted .266 in 1960 for the Miami Marlins of the Triple-A International League. He was named the league's all-star shortstop.

Adair had an excellent 1961 spring training with the Orioles to make the club, but by Opening Day was still unable to dislodge veterans Ron Hansen at short-stop or Marv Breeding at second base. But as the season progressed, he replaced Breeding as the regular second baseman and substituted occasionally for Hansen at shortstop. Batting .264 for the season, he outhit both Hansen and Breeding and played 107 games at second base, 27 games at shortstop, and two at third base. He hit nine home runs and drove in 37 runs. During the seasons 1961-1965, Adair was recognized as one of the premier fielding infielders in the American League. In 89 games from July 22, 1964, to May 6, 1965, he handled 458 chances at second base without an error, a major-league record.

In 1964 and 1965, Adair led American League second basemen in fielding percentage. He shares an American League record (as of 2014) with Bobby Grich and Roberto Alomar for the fewest errors in a season by a second baseman (five in 1964). For his career he had a better fielding percentage (.985) than all three Hall of Fame second basemen of his era: Nellie Fox, Bill Mazeroski, and Red Schoendienst. However, on the Orioles he was overshadowed by their spectacular third baseman, future Hall of Famer Brooks Robinson.

Adair batted .258 from 1961 to 1965, above the league average for middle infielders. Although he was known primarily for his glove, he told the *Boston Globe's* Ray Fitzgerald in August 1967 that his biggest moment in the major leagues came in late August 1962 when the Orioles swept a five-game series against the New York Yankees and he had 13 hits in the series. His best day came in a twi-night doubleheader that opened the series when he was 3-for-4 in the first game and 5-for-6 (with a double and a triple) in the second game.

When Orioles manager Hank Bauer gave the second base job to rookie Dave Johnson, Adair demanded a trade—more than once—and was finally dealt to the Chicago White Sox for pitcher Eddie Fisher on June 13, 1966. The trade cost Adair the opportunity to be with the Orioles when they defeated the Los Angeles Dodgers in the 1966 World Series, and cost him about $12,000 World Series money.

After hitting .243 for the White Sox in 1966, Adair shared second base with Wayne Causey early in the 1967 season. After he had missed out on a pennant in 1966, things balanced out when on June 2, 1967, the White Sox traded him to the Boston Red Sox. Dick Williams was glad to get him; the two had been teammates for several years in Baltimore and author Bill Reynolds said that Williams viewed him as "the ultimate professional." Adair's toughness appealed to Williams. Reynolds recounted a 1964 doubleheader when Adair was hit in the mouth by a throw in the first game, received 11 stitches, then played in the second game. He described Adair as having "a face right out of the *Grapes of Wrath.*" Jerry was hitting only .204 with the White Sox when the trade was executed, but hit .291 in 89 games while playing three infield positions for the Red Sox. The Red Sox were 22-21 before he joined them but were 70-49 afterward.

Adair filled in for the injured Rico Petrocelli at short-stop for a solid month, playing errorless defense. He played pivotal roles on offense in several games, too, but his biggest single day was likely the Sunday double-header at Fenway Park on August 20. Adair was 3-for-3 in the first game, a 12-2 rout of the Angels. In the second game California got off to an 8-0 lead after 3½ innings. The Red Sox crept back, and Adair's single in the bottom of the sixth tied the game, 8-8. In the bottom of the eighth his leadoff home run gave the Red Sox the lead and the 9-8 win. As Herb Crehan wrote in *Lightning in a Bottle*, "Role players like Adair seldom get their moment in the sun. But in the summer of '67 every Red Sox fan thought of Jerry as a hero."

In the final game of the season, Adair was 2-for-4 at the plate. He singled and scored the tying run in the bottom of the sixth, but his big play of the day came in the top of the eighth as Jim Lonborg worked with a 5-2 lead. Pinch-hitter Rich Reese singled to lead off the inning, and Cesar Tovar grounded to second. Adair charged in on the ball, sweeping it up with his glove, tagging the oncoming Reese, and firing accurately to George Scott at first, though spiked so severely that he had to leave the game and have several stitches. Red Sox broadcaster Ken Coleman called Adair "Mr.

Clutch" and wrote that if there had been a Tenth Player Award in 1967, he would have deserved it.

After the wild clubhouse celebration when the Red Sox clinched the American League pennant on the last day of the season, Jerry telephoned his sister to say that manager Dick Williams had just kissed him and other Red Sox players. In the World Series that was won by the pitching heroics of Bob Gibson for the St. Louis Cardinals in seven games, Adair appeared in five games, starting the first four (all against right-handers), but had only two hits in 16 at-bats. He did have Boston's only stolen base of the Series and had one RBI. Williams started Mike Andrews in Game Five against lefty Steve Carlton, then stuck with Andrews in Games Six and Seven.

Neil Singelais of the *Boston Globe* quoted 1967 Red Sox catcher Russ Gibson as saying, "No one could pivot as well as Jerry on a double-play ball. He could play anywhere and he was a tough guy to get out." Jim Lonborg, the 1967 pitching ace of the Red Sox staff, added that the trade that brought Adair to Boston "was like adding a gem to a beautiful necklace. He did such a magnificent job for us. He was a quiet guy around the clubhouse. He was so invaluable, older and more experienced."

In 1968 Adair had a poor year at the plate for the Red Sox, batting only .216 in 74 games while filling a journeyman's role and playing all four infield positions. In the 1968-1969 offseason, he was selected by the Kansas City Royals in the American League expansion draft. He was the regular second baseman for the Royals in 1969 and batted .250 for the season. On April 8, in the first game the Royals ever played, Adair hit second and knocked in their first-ever run: Lou Piniella led off with a double, and Jerry singled him home.

In 1970 the Royals awarded the second-base position to Luis Alcaraz, and Adair played sparingly. In May the Royals abruptly released Adair as he boarded an airplane. He had spent most of the spring with his daughter, Tammy, who died of cancer shortly after his release. Jerry resented the Royals not taking his family problems into consideration at the time of the release.

Later that season, Adair played near his hometown with the Tulsa Oilers of the Triple-A American Association, the top Cardinals farm club.

In 1971 Adair joined the Hankyu Braves in Japan and batted .300 for the season. The Braves won the pennant in the Pacific League, but were defeated by the perennial champion Yomiuri Giants of the Central League in the Japan Series. In 1972 and 1973 he earned World Series rings as a coach under his friend, manager Dick Williams of the Oakland Athletics. Williams quit as manager of the A's after the 1973 World Series. Jerry earned another World Series ring in 1974 as a coach for manager Alvin Dark of the A's, who won their third straight World Series. In 1975 and 1976 he was a coach for manager Dick Williams of the California Angels. The major-league coaching doors were closed to Jerry after the Angels fired Williams during the 1976 season.

Adair's wife, Kay, died of cancer in June 1981. Personal and financial problems forced Jerry, always an introvert, into a shell. A cancerous mole was removed from his arm in 1986. Prior to gall-bladder surgery, it was discovered that the cancer had spread to his liver. As former OSU basketball players made plans to have a banquet in Stillwater, Oklahoma, honoring Henry Iba, Jerry was out of the hospital and optimistic for a new treatment for his disease. The night before the banquet, he was readmitted to the hospital. At the very hour of the event that Iba called the happiest of his life, Adair's condition worsened. He died on Sunday morning, May 31, 1987. Jerry was survived by his sister, Joyce; his half-brother, Dennis; and three children, Kathy, Judy, and Michael. Graveside funeral services were held at Woodlawn Cemetery in Sand Springs.

Sand Springs friend Ron Dobbs helped perpetuate Jerry's memory by putting up a display of his sports memorabilia at Dobbs's pizza restaurant in Sand Springs. Many of the items were still on display years later. Adair's fierce competitive nature was evident early on, according to Dobbs. Like the Dodgers' Pee Wee Reese, Jerry was regarded by his friends as a world-class marbles shooter in grade school. He was said to have more marbles at his house than any other kid in Lake Station. Dobbs and one of Adair's former Sand Springs teammates, Oklahoma State Representative David Riggs, helped get the Sand Springs Little League complex named in his honor. In 1992 Adair was inducted into the Sand Springs Sandite Hall of Fame. In 2001, he was inducted into the OSU Baseball Hall of Fame.

SOURCES

I interviewed Jerry Adair's only surviving sibling, Joyce Bachus, and a close friend, Ron Dobbs, both of Sand Springs, Oklahoma. They also reviewed and provided helpful comments as to my draft of this article. Like Jerry, I have a Cherokee heritage and was a student at OSU when Jerry was making his records in basketball and baseball.

In addition, I made use of the following sources:

Bischoff, John Paul, *Mr. Iba: Basketball's Aggie Iron Duke*, (Oklahoma City: Oklahoma Heritage Association, 1980).

Burke, Bob, Kenny A. Franks, and Royse Parr, *Glory Days of Summer: The History of Baseball in Oklahoma* (Oklahoma City: Oklahoma Heritage Association, 1999).

Coleman, Ken and Dan Valenti, *The Impossible Dream Remembered* (Brattleboro, Vermont: Stephen Greene Press, 1987).

Crehan, Herb, with James W. Ryan. *Lightning in a Bottle* (Wellesley, Massachusetts: Branden Publishing, 1992).

Echohawk, Rodney, "Jerry Adair, Sandite Athlete Without Equal," *Sand Springs Leader*, May 31, 2001.

Ehle, John, *Trail of Tears: The Rise and Fall of the Cherokee Nation* (New York: Doubleday, 1988).

Hankins, Cecil, "Adair," in *Sand Springs, Oklahoma: A Community History* (Sand Springs, Oklahoma, Museum, 1994).

Parr, Royse, "Jerry Adair," in Richard King, ed., *Native Americans in Sports* (Armonk, New York: Sharpe Reference, 2004).

Parr, Royse, *Allie Reynolds: Super Chief* (Oklahoma City: Oklahoma Heritage Association, 2001).

Reynolds, Bill, *Lost Summer* (New York: Time Warner, 1992).

Woodward, Grace Steele, *The Cherokees* (Norman, Oklahoma: University of Oklahoma Press, 1963).

Prepared by the Commission and the Commissioners of the Five Civilized Tribes, *The Final Rolls of Citizen and Freedman of the Five Civilized Tribes in Indian Territory*, 1907.

1957 Redskin and *1958 Redskin*, yearbooks of Oklahoma A&M College.

Press book, *Oklahoma State 1999 Cowboy Baseball*.

Numerous articles and game reports from the sports section of the *Tulsa World* on microfilm at the Tulsa City-County Library, particularly writings by its sportswriters Bill Connors and John Cronley, 1956-1987.

Boston Globe, August 7, 1967, with articles about Kay Adair by Laura Holbrow and about Jerry Adair by Ray Fitzgerald.

Internet sources last viewed for Jerry Adair information in January 2006 included findagrave.com, baseballlibrary.com, thebaseballpage.com, thedeadballera.com, and attheplate.com/wcbl.

Matty Alou

By Mark Armour

Most famous today for being the second of three baseball-playing brothers, Matty Alou was part of the first wave of Dominicans who helped change the very culture of American baseball in the 1960s. After years of sporadic playing time, often competing with his brothers, he finally left them and became a batting champion, and one of baseball's unique and interesting stars.

Mateo Rojas Alou was born on December 22, 1938, in Bajos de Haina, San Cristóbal, not far from Santo Domingo on the southern coast of the Dominican Republic. His father, José Rojas, was a carpenter and blacksmith who built the family home and many of the others in the neighborhood. Rojas fathered two children with his first wife, who died young, then six more with Virginia Alou. Mateo was her second of four boys. Virginia was white, though Mateo and his siblings did not think of themselves as belonging to any race—they were Dominicans. They were also poor, as José's income was dependent on the local economy and the ability of his customers to pay him. The Rojas family had a house, but they did not always have food.

The subject is known in his home country as Mateo Rojas Alou, informally Mateo Rojas, and he and his brothers are known as the Rojas brothers. Early in Felipe's minor-league days he began to be called Felipe Alou (also mispronounced "Al-oo" instead of "Al-oh"), and the mistake was never corrected. The brothers Felipe, Mateo, and Jesús are therefore all known in the US as Alou, and Mateo was often Anglicized to Matty in the States. For this article, the subject will be referred to as Mateo or Matty Alou.

Mateo later said that his father played baseball as a boy until he saw a friend die after being struck by a ball, though Felipe did not remember this. "I can say for sure my father never threw a ball to me," Felipe recalled.[1] The boys spent hours in the nearby ocean

fishing for grouper or snapper, helping out their father in his shop, or playing ball in their yard. Their ball was often a coconut husk or half a rubber ball, their bat a tree limb, and their gloves made from strips of canvas. Unlike Felipe, who planned to be a doctor and spent a year in college, Mateo left school after the eighth grade and hoped to become a sailor. In the meantime he caddied at the Santo Domingo Golf Club and played more baseball.

In 1956 the 17-year-old Mateo Alou played for Aviación Militar, the Dominican Air Force team, sponsored by General Ramfis Trujillo, the son of the Dominican dictator Rafael Trujillo. Alou's teammates included future major-league teammates Juan Marichal and Manny Mota. Although they were all members of the Air Force, they were mainly ballplayers recruited

because the younger Trujillo wanted to field the best baseball team in the Caribbean. "We were soldiers," laughed Mota. "The only thing, we have no guns." It was still serious business—when the team lost a doubleheader in Manzanillo, the General launched an investigation, and accused the players of drinking (a charge Marichal denies). The entire team was put in jail for five days.[2]

In late 1955 Felipe had signed a baseball contract with Horacio Martínez, a former Negro Leaguer who worked as a bird dog for the New York Giants scout Alejandro Pómpez. With the considerable help of Pómpez and Martínez, the Giants got a jump on the rest of baseball in the Caribbean, especially the fertile Dominican Republic, inking Marichal, Mota, and eventually all three Alou brothers. Mateo signed in the winter of 1956-57, at the age of 18.

Unlikely many blacks and Latinos of the era, Mateo Alou spent the bulk of his minor-league days outside of the Deep South. But even in Michigan City, Indiana, where he began his career in 1957, he and Manny Mota were turned away from a restaurant because of their skin color. During spring training in Florida one year, Mota and Alou were placed in a police lineup because a white woman said a black ballplayer had molested her.[3] The Dominicans had not encountered much racism in their own country, but in the US they had to do so while also not understanding the language. "The ballplayers always treat us good," Alou recalled. "The only trouble we had was in the streets, the restaurants, the hotels, all those things. We used to cry but we didn't fight."[4]

Alou hit just .247 for Michigan City in full-time play in 1957. He then played winter ball at home in the Dominican League for the first time. Promoted to St. Cloud of the Northern League in 1958, he recovered to hit .321 for the first-place club and made the postseason All-Star team as an outfielder. For 1959 he reached Class A Springfield, Massachusetts, playing with several future major leaguers, including Mota, Marichal, and Tom Haller. Springfield won the Eastern League championship, with Alou contributing a .288 average and 11 home runs to the cause.

Unlike older brother Felipe, who grew to a chiseled 6-feet and 200 pounds, or his younger brother Jesús, who was even taller, Mateo was later listed officially at 5-feet-9 and 160 pounds as a major leaguer (though he was likely shorter and lighter, especially in the minors).[5] Unlike his brothers, he was left-handed, and got a lot of bunt singles and infield hits. "Nobody taught me how to play ball, nobody taught me how to hit," Alou recalled. " But I practiced, I had good reflexes, was quick moving. Good eyes. And it came natural."[6]

Alou spent the 1960 season with the Tacoma Giants of the Pacific Coast League. This was another good club filled with future major-league players, and Alou hit .306 with 14 home runs as the center fielder. In September he earned a call-up to San Francisco, and appeared in four games at the end of the year. In his first big league at-bat, he singled off the Dodgers' Larry Sherry.

Alou's rise to stardom was slow and sometimes frustrating, and he believed he was not given the opportunities he deserved. In truth, he faced some pretty stiff competition, including Willie Mays in center field (Alou's best position) and his brother Felipe in right field. In 1961 Alou made the club and played parts of 81 games in the outfield or as a pinch-hitter, batting .310 with 6 home runs in 200 at-bats. He was just 23 years old and behind a few other players on his team, but after the season farm director Carl Hubbell suggested he would not trade Matty Alou for the Dodgers stars Willie *and* Tommy Davis.[7]

The next season Alou played the same role, batting .292 in 195 at-bats, and had a big part in the National League pennant chase. In the last seven games of the regular season, he played six complete games, and hit 14-for-27 (.510). In the decisive game of the three-game playoff series with the Dodgers, with the Giants trailing 4-2 in the ninth inning, Alou led off with a pinch-hit single that launched the game-winning rally. He played in six of the seven World Series games, getting 4 hits in 12 at-bats. In the ninth inning of the final game, with the Giants down 1-0 to the Yankees, Alou led off with a pinch-hit bunt single, advanced to third base on Willie Mays' two-out double, but was stranded there when Willie McCovey lined out. There was talk over that winter that third-base coach Whitey Lockman should not have held Alou at third on Mays' hit, but most observers, including Alou himself, felt that he would have been out easily at home plate.

Alou's transition to the big leagues was aided immeasurably by the presence of so many other Latino players on the Giants. Besides his brother Felipe, his teammates included Dominicans Marichal and Mota and Puerto Ricans José Pagán and Orlando Cepeda, all of whom were very close. When he first arrived in San Francisco Mateo and Marichal lived in the home of an older woman named Blanche Johnson, who taught them to speak English, and cooked both American and Dominican food for them.[8]

On October 24, 1962, Mateo married María Teresa Vásquez in the Dominican Republic. During the 1963 season he, Felipe, Marichal, and their three wives lived together in a house in San Francisco. "We got along very, very well together," recalled Marichal. "Felipe is the godfather of my oldest daughter, Rosie, and I am the godfather of a daughter of his. And Mateo is the godfather of my second girl, Elsie, while I'm the godfather of his daughter [Teresa]. That is a serious obligation for a Dominican, to be a godfather."[9] The couples spent a lot of time together away from the park. Mateo, the former caddy, taught the others to play golf, while the wives helped each other make their way in a strange country. After the season, they all returned to their homeland for the winter baseball season.

In spring training of 1963, working hard in hopes of earning more playing time, Alou badly hurt his knee running to first base during an exhibition game in El Paso, Texas. He played through it, but struggled all summer long. Felipe, who often acted as the reserved Mateo's spokesman with club management, urged the Giants to send his brother to a doctor. Instead, in early August, they sent him to Tacoma. He returned in September, but it was a lost year: 11 hits in 76 at-bats for a .145 batting average. The only good memory from the season came in September, when younger brother Jesús joined the Giants and helped form an all-Alou

outfield late in the game on September 15. The three played in the same game a few other times, but their time as teammates was brief—after the season, Felipe was dealt to the Milwaukee Braves.

Heading into the 1964 season, Mateo had been passed by Jesús on the Giants depth chart. With Willie Mays and Willie McCovey in the outfield, and the veteran Harvey Kuenn still productive, Mateo returned to his fifth-outfielder/pinch-hitter role. Hitting just .219 on June 2, Alou was struck on the wrist by a pitch from Pittsburgh's Bob Veale, breaking a bone, and spent five weeks home in the Dominican Republic. He hit better upon his return (.282), so well that he was used fairly regularly in September. He managed to get into 110 games, including 49 starts, and hit .264. For a man who had very little power and drew few walks, the batting average was too low for an outfielder even in the 1960s.

Even so, based on his strong second half, in 1965 new manager Herman Franks gave Alou a lot of playing time—but he did not hit. "'65 was my worst year in baseball," recalled Alou, "because they gave me a chance and I didn't do anything." He hit just .231 in 324 at-bats. His most memorable game that season came on August 26 at Pittsburgh's Forbes Field when he pitched the final two innings of an 8-0 loss. He allowed no runs and struck out three, including Willie Stargell twice. "I just threw him slow curve, slow curve," Alou said. "And I know I would get him out again if I faced him."[10]

Despite his star turn on the mound, it came as no surprise when the Giants traded Alou to the Pirates on December 1, 1965. In later years the Giants were criticized for their handling of Alou, although they gave him 1,131 plate appearances and he had not contributed much since 1962. Alou welcomed the deal, later saying, "My brother didn't tell me anything about Willie Mays. I just signed because I liked to play the game."[11]

Pittsburgh manager Harry Walker had coveted Alou, and had big plans for him. Walker spent many years as a hitting instructor in the game, usually trying to get everyone to choke up, and hit the ball down and to the opposite field, as Walker himself had done as a player. This approach backfired with many people, but Alou was his best and most famous success story. "The Hat" worked tirelessly with Alou, getting him to stop trying to pull the ball and instead hit nearly everything up the middle or to left field. To force this, he gave Alou a much bigger bat—38 ounces—and asked him to stroke down on the ball and use his speed. As a pull hitter, Alou had held the bat low and swung with an uppercut. Walker had him hold the bat high and straight up, forcing him to swing downward on the ball. Walker set up a platoon in center field with Alou and old friend Manny Mota, giving the left-handed Alou most of the at-bats, and hit Alou in the leadoff position whenever he played.

Alou took to the new batting style extremely well. Bunting and slapping singles, he put up a league-leading .342 batting average, more than 100 points higher than his effort in 1965. Since Mota was also hitting very well, finishing at .332, the platoon in center field remained—Alou started 121 games, just twice against a left-handed starter, but managed 535 at-bats. Finishing second was Atlanta's Felipe Alou at .327. Mateo still did not walk much or hit for power, but at a time when the league's on-base percentage was .313, Alou's .373 mark was eighth highest in the league, and tops among players who primarily hit leadoff for their teams.

Alou's sudden fame raised a lot of questions about what had changed for him. He credited Walker's tutelage, escaping San Francisco's challenging Candlestick Park, and platooning with Mota, which allowed him plenty of rest. Late in the season, when it appeared that one of the Alous might win the batting title, Felipe allowed that he was rooting for his brother. "It would be a wonderful thing for Matty to win it," said Felipe. "Wonderful for the Alous, and wonderful for baseball in the Dominican Republic. We always sort of took care of Matty because he was so small. Now look at him leading all of us in hitting!"[12]

Alou's next two years were nearly carbon copies of 1966. He continued to platoon with Mota, his room-

mate and best friend, and both men continued to hit. In 1967 Alou hit .338 (third in the league) in 550 at-bats, starting just four times against left-handers, while Mota hit .321, also backing up the other outfield positions. (Walker could not easily play both of them—his left fielder was Willie Stargell, and his right fielder was Roberto Clemente.) The acquisition of Maury Wills moved Alou out of the leadoff spot in the order, and by 1968 he was often hitting third or fourth. In 1968 Alou hit .332, just three points behind Pete Rose for the batting title, in 558 at-bats. He also played in his first All-Star Game, legging out an infield single off Sam McDowell in his only at bat.

After the 1968 season the Pirates lost Mota to the Montreal Expos in the expansion draft. Although Alou had faced lefties a bit more in 1968, the next year he became a full-time player for the first time in his career. Playing in 162 games, he led the league in at-bats, hits (231), singles (183), and doubles (41), while hitting .331 at the top of the order. He played the entire All-Star Game in center field, garnering two hits and a walk in five appearances in the NL's 9-3 win. The 30-year-old Alou, after hitting .330 or higher for four straight seasons, had become a full-fledged star and one of the more interesting players in the game. He was a leadoff hitter who did not walk much—just 42 times in 1969—yet he was valuable because he was able to maintain his high batting average. His 698 at-bats set a major-league record, since broken.

Although he faced occasional criticism for his defense, especially for being shy about crashing into fences, Alou had a strong and accurate throwing arm and often was among the league leaders in outfield assists, finishing first with 15 in 1970. "I play deep because this is a big park and the ball carries deep. I'm not fence-shy. They said that in San Francisco. You know, sometimes everybody want you to be Willie Mays. Sometimes they say, 'Why aren't you like Willie Mays?' Well, there is only one Willie Mays."[13]

In 1970 Alou slipped to .297, but still finished with 201 hits, fifth best in the league. The Pirates had been a good team for a few years but finally broke through and won the Eastern Division, and Alou finished

3-for-12 in the three-game loss to the Reds. During the offseason the Pirates, wanting to make room in center field for youngster Al Oliver, sent Alou to the Cardinals in a four-player deal. Thus, Alou missed out on the Pirates' championship season of 1971. "I think of myself mostly as a Pirate," Mateo said years later. "Because they gave me confidence. They treat me good, and I had the best years of my life there."[14]

Alou spent most of the next two seasons for the Cardinals and played well. He hit .315 in 1971, with 192 hits, playing center field for half the season and (after the recall of rookie José Cruz) mostly first base in the second half. In 1972 he switched between first base and right field and hit .314. In late August he was traded to the Oakland A's, a young team on the verge of winning their first of three straight championships. He played nearly every day the rest of the season in right field, hitting .281. He played well in the ALCS (.381 with four doubles), but slumped in the World Series (just 1-for-24). Still, after just missing in 1962, Alou finally tasted the champagne of a World Series victory.

Not long after the Series, Alou was traded again, this time to the New York Yankees, reuniting with his brother Felipe. He hit well in New York, .296 in 123 games as the regular right fielder, but when the team fell out of contention they sold him back to the Cardinals, who were in contention for a division title, on September 6. (On the very same day, the club sold Felipe to the Montreal Expos.) Mateo was not thrilled with the trade, delayed reporting for a few days, and was used solely as a pinch-hitter in the waning weeks of the pennant race. After the season the Cardinals sold him to the San Diego Padres, but after hitting just .198 in 81 at-bats, he drew his release in July 1974, ending his major-league career. He ended with a .307 career average over 15 seasons, with three All-Star appearances and two trips to the World Series.

The 35-year-old Alou next took his career to Japan, spending the rest of the 1974 season and two more with the Taiheiyo Club Lions in the Nippon Pro League. He hit .312 in his first half-season, then .282

and .261 his next two years. He finished with a .283 lifetime average in Japan. "I didn't like playing there really," Alou recalled. "I played there because I had to. I had three kids to support. It was too hard there. Too much practice, too much traveling, had to travel almost every day."[15]

Alou returned home. A star for 15 seasons with Leones del Escogido in the Dominican Winter League, h had a .327 career average there, second only to Manny Mota's .333. He won batting titles in 1966-67 (.363) and 1968-69 (.390). He later coached and managed in the league for many years. While the Alou brothers gained fame for manning the same outfield for the Giants for a parts of a few games in 1963, this was not such a big deal to the Rojas brothers — in the Winter League for many seasons they formed the Escogido outfield, and still dominate the all-time leader boards for the club. For the 1961-62 and 1962-63 winters, when political unrest shut down the Dominican league, Mateo played winter ball in Venezuela.

Although Alou spent most of his post-playing years in his homeland, he worked for several major-league organizations over the years. He scouted for the Tigers for a while in the late 1980s. He spent many years as the Dominican scouting supervisor for the San Francisco Giants. He coached a single season (1994) for a club in the Dominican Summer League (a circuit affiliated with the US minor leagues). In 2007 he was honored at San Francisco's AT&T Park, celebrating his induction to the Hispanic Heritage Baseball Museum Hall of Fame. Brother Felipe, then manager of the Giants, had been inducted in 2003.

Mateo remained a private person who was not often in the news in the States. His 1962 marriage to Teresa lasted the rest of his life. They raised three children, Mateo Jr., Matías, and Teresa, primarily in their homeland. Mateo died at age 72 in Santo Domingo on November 3, 2011, from complications of diabetes. He had stopped working for the Giants a few years earlier for health reasons. He was survived by his wife of 49 years, his three children, four grandchildren, three brothers and two sisters.

SOURCES

Thanks to Rory Costello for his assistance.

NOTES

1   Michael Farber, "Diamond Heirs," *Sports Illustrated,* June 19, 1985.

2   Rob Ruck, *The Tropic of Baseball* (Lincoln: University of Nebraska, 1998), 70-71.

3   Rob Ruck, *Raceball—How the Major Leagues Colonized the Black and Latin Game* (Boston: Beacon Press, 2011),

153-4.

4   Mike Mandel, *SF Giants. An Oral History* (Santa Cruz, California: self-published, 1979), 123.

5   Charles Einstein, "Alou Alou," *Sport*, September, 1962, 25.

6   Mike Mandel, *SF Giants*, 123.

7   *The Sporting News*, May 2, 1962.

8   Juan Marichal with Charles Einstein, *A Pitcher's Story* (New York: Doubleday, 1967), 100-101.

9   Rob Ruck, *The Tropic of Baseball*, 78.

10   Mike Mandel, *SF Giants*, 124.

11   Mike Mandel, *SF Giants*, 123.

12   *The Sporting News*, September 24, 1966.

13   Lou Prato, "Matty Alou: 'Wait, Wait, Wait,' *Sport*, October 1968, 38.

14   Mike Mandel, *SF Giants*, 124.

15   Mike Mandel, *SF Giants*, 125.

Brant Alyea

By Charlie O'Reilly

Garrabrant Ryerson Alyea, IV, a free-swinging right-handed batter and one of just nine players to hit a home run on the first pitch he saw in the major leagues, was born on December 8, 1940, in Passaic, New Jersey,, to a family of Dutch heritage that had been in the northern New Jersey area since the 17th century. The name was originally French; an ancestor, Peter Aliee, who was born in Hackensack, New Jersey, in roughly 1688, changed the name to Alyea, a more phonetic spelling, by the time he married Margritie van Voorhees, whose parents were Dutch, in 1715 in Hackensack. By the mid-19th century, much of the Alyea family had settled in the part of southern Bergen County that became the Borough of Rutherford in 1881.

Alyea's great-grandfather, the first Garrabrant Ryerson Alyea, was a co-founder of the Hillside Cemetery Association in adjacent Union Township (now Lyndhurst) in 1883, and he also served as Rutherford's postmaster. This Alyea was married to Martha Brinkerhoff, a member of another Dutch family long established in northern New Jersey. Brant himself was the son of Garrabrant III (1918-92), who drove the Inter-City Lines bus from Paterson to New York that ran through Rutherford,[1] and the former Janet Olcott (1924-90), a legal secretary.[2] Garrabrant III and Janet had four other children.

Early in his life, Brant was known as Ry, from his middle name, to distinguish him from his father and grandfather, who variously went by Gary and Brant. By the time he reached college, he was known as Brant, but articles chronicling his athletic career in the local newspapers continued to show him as Ry through his high-school career.

Already tall at the age of 12, Alyea took the field as a first baseman for the Rutherford National all-star team in the 1953 Little League tournament, batting fourth. The team opened play against a neighboring league, Lyndhurst East. That contest, begun on Monday, July 27, turned into a marathon that was played over two days. Alyea's first hit tied the game, 2-2, in the third inning, and the contest stayed deadlocked well past its scheduled six-inning length. The umpires stopped play for darkness after 10 innings and brought both teams back the next evening to complete the game. Finally, catcher Eugene Cole homered over the center-field wall in the top of the 17th to give Alyea's team a 3-2 victory. The writer for the *South Bergen News*, Rutherford's weekly paper, credited Alyea, who finished 2-for-7, with "several circus-day scoop-ups at first."[3] Alyea's counterpart in the cleanup slot, Lyndhurst center fielder Tom Longo, went 4-for-7. He went on to play three seasons as an NFL defensive back for the New York Giants and St. Louis Cardinals.

Alyea lettered in three sports at Rutherford High School, playing quarterback for the Bulldogs and starring in basketball and baseball. He accepted a scholarship to Hofstra College in Hempstead, New York, a seemingly perfect fit as the small Long Island institution was established on a campus bequeathed by a Dutch lumber magnate, William Hofstra, in the 1930s, and their athletic teams were known as the Flying Dutchmen. More significantly, Hofstra would give Alyea the opportunity to play basketball as well as baseball. The basketball team was then coached by another Dutchman originally from New Jersey, Butch van Breda Kolff. Alyea and the Dutchmen enjoyed significant basketball success in the NCAA College Division. In the 1959-60 season, they finished 23-1, losing only to Wagner College of Staten Island by two points in January, but that loss cost them the conference title and they were not selected for post-season play.[4] The next year, Alyea led the Dutchmen in scoring and rebounding, and Hofstra was selected for the small-college tournament, in which the team was eliminated by Albright College.[5]

In baseball, Alyea's play, especially his power, attracted the attention of scouts. He had the opportunity to sign after he hit 13 home runs in 30 games for a team that won its conference championship, but he stayed at Hofstra for another season to play basketball. He eventually signed with the Cincinnati Reds in the spring of 1962. By then Alyea had grown to his full height of 6-feet-5. The Reds assigned him to Geneva (New York) of the Class D New York-Penn League, and he clubbed 32 home runs while hitting .319 in 105 games. Those healthy numbers made Alyea a prime target in the Rule 5 draft, which at that time covered all first-year players who had not been placed on the 40-man roster, and Alyea was snatched up by the Washington Senators.

Over the next two seasons, Alyea moved up the ladder, playing for the Peninsula Pilots of the Carolina League and then the York White Roses of the Eastern League. In those two seasons he hit just 29 home runs, but his right-handed power again manifested itself when he got to Triple-A. He hit 27 homers while batting .269

as an outfielder and first baseman for the Hawaii Islanders in 1965. That performance earned Alyea a call-up to Washington at season's end, and his major-league "debut" came on September 11 against the California Angels at D.C. Stadium, when he was announced as a pinch-hitter for pitcher Mike McCormick in the sixth inning with two on and two out. But when the Angels brought in Bob Lee to replace George Brunet, Senators manager Gil Hodges countered by sending up Jim King to hit for Alyea. King hit a three-run homer to give Washington a 4-3 lead, but the Angels rallied to win 6-5.

Alyea's first trip to a major-league batter's box came the next day. The Senators came into the day 18 games under .500, and only 840 fans showed up for the Sunday afternoon game on a day that saw the nation's capital receive nearly two-thirds of an inch of rain. With runners on first and second, one out and the Senators leading 3-0 in the sixth inning, Hodges again turned to Alyea, this time to pinch-hit for lefty-hitting second baseman Don Blasingame. Alyea crushed left-handed pitcher May's first pitch over the left-field wall, doubling the Senators' lead.

In the waning days of the 1965 season, Alyea played in six more games, pinch-hitting in four and starting at first base in two others. He managed just two more hits in 12 at-bats, both coming in one game; one was a three-run homer against John O'Donoghue of the Kansas City A's on September 28.

After the season Alyea played in winter leagues in Nicaragua and Venezuela. This became a staple of his life both before and after he became a major-league regular.

Alyea returned to Honolulu for 1966, but he batted just .218 although he did hit 21 home runs. That performance saw him demoted to York for 1967, and he spent two-thirds of the season there and the remainder on loan to the Montgomery Rebels of the Southern League, then a Tigers farm club. For the entire year at Double-A, he batted .229 with 14 homers, although he drew 54 walks and cut his strikeouts from a 164 in 1965 to 110. That was enough to persuade the Senators to move Alyea back up to Triple-A for 1968, and at Buffalo he hit .253 with 31 homers, earning a call-up on July 26. For the rest of that season, he batted .267 and hit six home runs for the Senators, earning 33 outfield starts.

Ted Williams took over as Senators manager for 1969, and Alyea had a productive season, playing a career-high 104 games, mainly as a corner outfielder although he did appear a few times at first base. The next spring the Senators dealt him to Minnesota in return for pitchers Joe Grzenda and Charlie Walters. With the Twins in 1970, Alyea made an immediate impact with his bat, as he smacked two home runs and drove in seven runs in an Opening Day 12-0 Twins victory over the White Sox at Chicago.[6] That April he was also involved in a very unusual play, described by Don Mankowski of SABR in 2000:

"Earl Wilson, who pitched for the Boston Red Sox and Detroit Tigers between 1959 and 1970, was an excellent hitter as pitchers go. He hit 35 home runs in an 11-year career. And, once, he almost homered while striking out. After a fashion.

"Wilson's Tigers trailed the Twins 2-1 in the seventh inning of an April 25, 1970, game at Bloomington, Minnesota. Batting against Jim Kaat, Wilson swung and missed a third strike, and it looked as if the inning were over.

"But not so fast! Kaat's catcher Paul Ratliff didn't hold on to the ball and umpire John Rice refused to call Wilson out. Ratliff rolled the ball back toward the mound and made himself scarce. Noting that the entire Minnesota team had left the field, Wilson took off around the bases.

"Two Twins [is that redundant?] had the semblance of mind to hurry back on the field as Wilson tore around third. Brant Alyea grabbed the ball and threw to Leo Cardenas, covering at home plate. Wilson was caught between third and home, and retired by Cardenas' return throw to Alyea. Wilson, who was throwing a three-hitter, pulled a hamstring muscle on the play and had to leave the game.

"The Tigers managed to tie the game at 3-3 in the top of the ninth, but afterward Harmon Killebrew singled home Tony Oliva to win the game.

"Because Alyea just happened to be the left fielder and Cardenas the shortstop, the play on Wilson had to be scored K767, that is, Strikeout: putout left fielder to shortstop to left fielder. Ratliff got an error in there, so maybe that's not quite correct."[7]

Alyea delivered career highs in the three Triple Crown categories, batting .291 with 16 homers and 61 RBIs in 94 games. He was on the Twins' postseason roster in 1970, appearing in all three games of their American League Championship Series loss to the eventual World Series champion Baltimore Orioles. Starting twice in left field, he went hitless in seven at-bats, although he scored a run in Game One.

That winter Alyea returned to Venezuela and set a record there by clubbing 15 home runs in a 55-game season. But back home in 1971, Alyea's production dropped significantly. The Twins dropped him from their 40-man roster at season's end, after Alyea hit just .177 with two home runs in 79 games.

The Oakland Athletics claimed Alyea in that winter's Rule 5 draft, and in the spring of 1972 he played in 10 games for the A's, going 3-for-13, before being shipped to the St. Louis Cardinals in a trade for infielder Marty Martinez on May 18. With the Cards he played in 13 games, batting .158 (3-for-19). He also played in 11 games for the Triple-A Iowa Oaks, batting .410 in Triple-A. The A's brought him back on July 23, and he went 3-for-18 the rest of the season with one home run. But his season ended prematurely; in a game at Baltimore's Memorial Stadium, he hit a ball into the gap off Jim Palmer and Alyea pulled a muscle in his groin while rounding first on what turned out to be a double. Although he played in four more games, that injury effectively finished Alyea for the year, as the A's signed Matty Alou for the stretch run that led to the first of their three straight World Series titles.

Alyea attempted to rehabilitate his injury without surgery. He was sent to the Texas Rangers in November to complete a trade for pitcher Paul Lindblad, but his nagging injury left him unable to make the team. He finished his professional career with 48 games for the Pawtucket Red Sox in 1973, playing the newly created position of designated hitter. He underwent surgery a few years later, and contemplated a return to the game in 1977 at the age of 36, but never made it to Florida to try out.

Like most players of his era who did not earn a full pension for playing 10 seasons, Alyea had to find regular work after his playing days. By 1986 he was a pit boss at an Atlantic City casino. That spring, he learned that a son he had fathered at the end of the 1966-67 winter season in Nicaragua was a prospect who had been discovered by the Toronto Blue Jays. That led to a reconnection with the young man, Brant Jose Alyea, whom he had not seen since the Central American nation was plunged into unrest in the 1970s.[8] The younger Alyea spent six seasons in pro ball, briefly reaching Triple-A with the Texas Rangers and hitting .281 with 49 home runs, including 25 with Gastonia of the South Atlantic League in 1988.

After his time with the casino, which lasted just over a decade, Alyea hooked on with an automobile dealer-ship near Philadelphia for another decade or so. As of 2014 he was retired and living in the Philadelphia suburbs.

SOURCES

Baseball-Reference.com

Retrosheet.org

New York Times

Sports Illustrated

NOTES

1   *The Record* (Hackensack, New Jersey), October 10, 1992, A-10..

2   *The Record*, March 6, 1990, A-9.

3   *South Bergen News* (Rutherford, New Jersey), July 30, 1953, 17.

4   George Vecsey, "A Shot That Sank a Season," *New York Times*, March 1, 2012, B18.

5   Hofstra University men's basketball media guide 2004-05, 122, 132,

6   Dave Wright, *162-0: Imagine a Twins Perfect Season: The Greatest Wins!* (Chicago: Triumph Books, 2010).

7   Don Mankowski, "Odd Strikeout," post to SABR mailing list, May 10, 2000.

8   Peter Gammons, "A New Land, an Old Bond," *Sports Illustrated*, June 30, 1986, 66.

Dwain Anderson

By Clayton Trutor

Dwain Anderson was a utility infielder who played in 149 major-league games over the course of four seasons between 1971 and 1974. He threw and batted right-handed and was a versatile infielder, playing second base, third base, and shortstop over a ten-year career in professional baseball. Frequently included in early 1970s trades, Anderson played for four major-league teams during his brief career: the Oakland Athletics (1971-1972), the St. Louis Cardinals (1972-1973), the San Diego Padres (1973), and the Cleveland Indians (1974). Anderson's major-league career peaked in 1972 when he hit .267 in 57 games for the St. Louis Cardinals, leading to his inclusion on the Topps 1972 All-Rookie Team.[1] He was also a member of the 1972 world champion Oakland Athletics club. A combination of nagging injuries, managerial ambiguity about Anderson's role on the roster, and erratic play in the field led to an abrupt end to his professional baseball career.

Dwain Cleaven Anderson was born in Oakland, California, on November 23, 1947. His mother, Louise (Jackson) Anderson, and father, Cleaven Anderson, an Army veteran of World War II, raised their two children, Dwain and Gwendolyn, in nearby El Cerrito.[2] Dwain played shortstop for the El Cerrito High School Gauchos, a traditional baseball power in the Bay Area that has produced six major-league ballplayers, including former Boston Red Sox infielder Pumpsie Green and former St Louis Cardinals and Chicago Cubs pitcher Ernie Broglio. In 1965 the Kansas City Athletics signed the 17-year-old Anderson and assigned him to the Burlington (Iowa) Bees of the Class A Midwest League. In 1966 and 1967, Anderson bounced around the Athletics' Class A affiliates, spending most of 1966 with the Lewiston (Idaho) Broncs of the Northwest League and most of 1967 with the Peninsula Grays (Hampton, Virginia) of the Carolina League. Anderson missed the last

week of the 1966 season after injuring his hand trying to field a groundball bare-handed during pregame warm-ups. He required four stitches for a cut he suffered between his thumb and forefinger. Anderson's absence from the already-depleted Lewiston lineup left the team with only eight position players for the final seven games of the season.[3]

In 1968 Anderson, then 20, spent all season as the shortstop for the Grays, batting .254 in 122 games. The Athletics organization, now in Oakland, promoted him to Double-A Birmingham (Southern League) for 1969. Despite missing two months with a broken foot, Anderson excelled in the field and put up solid numbers at the plate. In 87 games, he put together a .269 batting average with 6 home runs and 38 RBIs. Several times during the season, *The Sporting News* made note of Anderson's defensive work at shortstop and the fine double-play combination he made with second baseman Rusty Adkins.[4]

Anderson was invited to the A's 1970 spring training in Yuma, Arizona, where he impressed with his hitting. He nearly earned a spot on the Opening Day roster as a utility infielder, but uncharacteristically erratic defensive performances, particularly at second base, cost him a spot on the big-league club. Growing up in El Cerrito, Anderson had always played shortstop. He continued to play primarily shortstop in the early years of his minor-league career, but as Anderson ascended the A's ladder, the organization tried to convert him into a utility infielder capable of playing second, third, and shortstop. With the Triple-A Iowa Oaks (Des Moines) in 1970, he "moped around a bit," according to *The Sporting News*, but turned in a fine performance for the season, hitting .252 and displaying unprecedented power with 15 home runs and 69 RBIs.[5]

Entering the spring of 1971, the Athletics considered Anderson one of the top prospects in their farm system.[6] New manager Dick Williams put Anderson in a competition for the second-base position with veteran infielder Dick Green. Anderson lost out on the competition and was sent back to Des Moines.[7] He had an unspectacular year but received a September call-up to the AL West-leading Athletics. He made his major-league debut on September 3, 1971, in the second game of a doubleheader against the Minnesota Twins at Metropolitan Stadium in Bloomington, Minnesota. Anderson, who batted leadoff and played his traditional shortstop position, went 2-for-5 with two singles, a run scored, and two strikeouts in a 2-1 Twins victory.[8] Over the course of September, Anderson appeared in 16 games, playing primarily shortstop, but also appearing as a second baseman, third baseman, and pinch-hitter. He hit .270 with 3 RBIs in 37 at-bats. The A's left Anderson off the playoff roster in the American League Championship Series, in which they were swept by the eventual world champion Baltimore Orioles.

Anderson began 1972 back in Triple-A Iowa, but was recalled by Oakland in early May to replace the injured Dick Green.[9] After playing in just three games for the Athletics, he was traded to the St Louis Cardinals on May 15 for left-handed relief pitcher Don Shaw.

Anderson's brief presence on the world champion A's 1972 roster earned him a $100 share of the winners' portion from the World Series.[10] The willingness of the Cardinals to surrender Shaw, a 27-year-old who had gone 7-2 with a 2.65 ERA the previous season, for Anderson indicates the latter's perceived high value at the time of the trade.[11] During the 1972 season, Anderson lived up to the Cardinals' confidence in his abilities, hitting .267 in 57 games while platooning at shortstop with the aging Dal Maxvill and occasionally filling in for Joe Torre at third base. On September 13 Anderson was hit by a pitch during batting practice in Montreal and suffered a hairline fracture in his left arm, bringing an end to his season.[12] Anderson was a bright spot on a disappointing 75-81 Red Schoendienst-managed Cardinals team, earning a spot on the 1972 Topps All-Rookie Team.[13]

In Anderson, the Cardinals believed they had found their replacement for the veteran Maxvill. The organization assigned their legendary former shortstop Marty Marion to teach Anderson the nuances of the position, but Anderson's arm injury limited the amount of fieldwork they did together.[14] Anderson's inability to stay healthy and his poor defensive play during spring training in 1973 relegated him to a backup utility-infield position behind shortstop Mike Tyson. He played infrequently during the first two months of the 1973 season, filling in occasionally at shortstop, but more often pinch-hitting or -running. In May 1973 the Cardinals experimented with him briefly in center field.[15]

On June 7, 1973, the Cardinals traded Anderson to the San Diego Padres for veteran infielder Dave Campbell. Padres manager Don Zimmer said, "He has a few tools. ... I know he can run and he has some sock with the bat."[16] Anderson was the Padres' starting shortstop for most of June, filling in for the injured Derrel Thomas, before being relegated to backup status for the remainder of the season. He batted a mere .121 for the Padres and did not register an extra-base hit in 123 plate appearances. After the season the last-place Padres traded Anderson to the last-place Cleveland Indians for middle infielder Lou Camilli, who had already played in what proved to be the last of his 107 major-league games.

Anderson started the 1974 season in Triple-A with the Indians' Oklahoma City 89ers farm team. He played in 18 games for the 89ers before being called up to Cleveland in May. Anderson played in two games for the Ken Aspromonte-managed Indians. On May 17 he ran for catcher Dave Duncan in a 4-3 loss to the Detroit Tigers, and on May 28 he replaced Jack Brohamer at second base in an 8-0 road victory over the Texas Rangers. He went 1-for-3 in what proved to be his final major-league appearance, singling off Jim Shellenbeck. Three weeks later the Indians traded Anderson to the New York Mets for shortstop Brian Ostrosser. It was Anderson's fourth trade in little more than two years. The Mets assigned Anderson to tTriple-A Tidewater, where he spent the remainder of the season. After the season Anderson left Organized Baseball. In 1978 he married Seneca Joshua of Los Angeles. The couple settled down in the Bay Area along with rest of the Anderson family. As of late 2013, Anderson resided in suburban Contra Costa County, east of Oakland.

SOURCES

New York Times

The Sporting News

Washington Post

Baseball-Reference.com

Baseball-Almanac.com

El Cerrito High School Athletics: elcerritogauchos.net/athletics

NOTES

1 "Fisk, Matlack Lead All-Rookie Team," *New York Times*, November 27, 1972, 49; "Fisk Leads in Voting for Yearling All Stars," *The Sporting News*, December 2, 1972, 40.

2 Thanks to Bill Mortell for his help finding Dwain Anderson's family through his research on ancestry.com and genealogybank.com.

3 "Broncs' Ranks Dwindle," *The Sporting News*, September 17, 1966, 43.

4 "A's Shortstop Injured," *The Sporting News*, June 27, 1969, 53; "Change for Edmonson," *The Sporting News*, May 10, 1969, 41; "Rain Affecting Gate," *The Sporting News*, May 31, 1969, 41.

5 "Anderson to Get Another Chance," *The Sporting News*, November 21, 1970, 48; "Some Rookies Take Jobs from Veterans," *Washington Post*, March 29, 1970, C2

6 Ron Bergman, "A's Anderson Eager for Keystone Fit," *The Sporting News*, January 16, 1971, 54.

7 Ron Bergman, "Ailing Odom A's Big Question Mark," *The Sporting News*, February 27, 1971, 18; Ron Bergman, "Happy Reggie Is Making Enemy Pitchers Moan," *The Sporting News*, April 3, 1971, 31.

8 "Green's Glove One of A's Shattering Weapons," *The Sporting News*, September 25, 1971, 5.

9 "Athletics' Green Out," *Washington Post*, May 6, 1972, D5.

10 "Rich Gravy for A's and Reds in Record Series Pot," *The Sporting News*, November 25, 1972, 45.

11 Neal Russo, "Dealer Devine Shakes Up Plummeting Redbirds," *The Sporting News*, June 3, 1972, 15.

12 "Redbird Chirps," *The Sporting News*, October 7, 1972, 14.

13 "Fisk, Matlack Lead All-Rookie Team," *New York Times*; "Fisk Leads in Voting for Yearling All Stars," *The Sporting News*, December 2, 1972, 40.

14 "Cards Flash Full Speed Ahead with 'SS' Busse," *The Sporting News*, December 30, 1972, 36.

15 Neal Russo, "Defense Strikes Blue Note in Redbirds' Spring Sonata," *The Sporting News*, April 21, 1973, 10.

16 "Padres, Cardinals Swap Infielders," *Washington Post*, June 8, 1973, D1.

Curt Blefary

By John Henshell

Curtis Le Roy Blefary is best remembered for winning the American League Rookie of the Year award in 1965. He had three productive seasons for the Orioles before his intertwined personal demons, alcohol and anger, overcame his terrific natural ability. Blefary was a key contributor to the Orioles' pennant in 1966. The left-handed hitter was an outfielder during his three solid seasons, then subsequently became a regular catcher and first baseman.

Blefary was born in Brooklyn, New York, on July 5, 1943, and grew up in Mahwah, New Jersey. His father, an AT&T employee, named him after Curt Davis, a pitcher who won 158 major-league games and was pitching for the Brooklyn Dodgers when Blefary was born.

The *Bergen Record* honored the Mahwah High School ballplayer as a member of its "Best of the Century" team. Blefary was a third baseman until his senior year, when he was converted to catcher. He was also an all-state halfback on the football team. After high school he starred for the Wagner College Seahawks football team in the fall of 1961.

The New York Yankees signed Blefary to a contract in 1962. (The free-agent draft didn't begin until 1965.) *Baseball: The Biographical Encyclopedia* says that Blefary received a $40,000 bonus,[1] but Blefary's high-school classmate Richard E. Robbins said it was $18,000. "His dad let him buy a car for a few thousand and made him invest the rest in AT&T stock," Robbins said, adding, "Apparently he sold the stock somewhere along the way. If he hadn't, he wouldn't have had any money worries later in life." In addition to the bonus, the Yankees agreed to pay Blefary's tuition and expenses at Wagner during the offseasons.

The Yankees sent Blefary to Greensboro (Carolina League) in 1962 and tried him as an outfielder. He hit two home runs in his first full game. His first-year performance (.240 batting average, 13 home runs, 39 RBIs, and 8 eight stolen bases in 66 games) did not earn him a promotion for the 1963 season. His attitude might have concerned the Yankees more than his batting average. He scared everyone by throwing bats and helmets. Joe DiMaggio was bemused by Blefary's intensity in spring training, but expressed confidence in his future.

At Greensboro in 1963 Blefary hit 25 home runs, but was sold to the Baltimore Orioles early in the season on first-year waivers in a transaction that was never adequately explained by the Yankees. The Yankees acquired veteran utilityman Harry Bright from the Reds on April 21. Blefary had been protected on the 40-man roster, but had stitches in his leg at the time

Bright was purchased. Blefary was relegated to pinch-hitting duty while his leg healed. Various accounts of why the Yankees risked losing Blefary have been reported. In one version, Yankees general manager Ralph Houk said Blefary was "expendable,"[2] an explanation that strains credulity given the Yankees' investment in Blefary. No documentation suggests that the Yankees attributed Blefary's behavioral problems to anything but immaturity, so his behavior wasn't a factor. Another reported theory is that the Yankees made a technical mistake and were surprised when the Orioles claimed Blefary. *Sport* offered a plausible but convoluted explanation, writing that New York's front office, in an effort to exaggerate the severity of Blefary's injury, told him to sit in the stands while he was on waivers. Blefary defied orders to keep quiet and told a Baltimore scout that he was fine.[3] Regardless, the promising slugger was crushed by the deal; he claimed he had turned down more money from other teams because he wanted to play for the Yankees.[4]

Baltimore initially kept Blefary at Greensboro, where he hit .289 and slugged 25 home runs with 67 RBIs in 88 games. In 40 games with Elmira in the Eastern League he hit .247. Blefary also played first base and had his first professional experience as a catcher. The Elmira trainer nicknamed him "Cadillac Curt" because of his grandstanding home-run trots. Blefary basked in success and fired equipment at the dugout wall when unsuccessful.

Baltimore sent Blefary to the Florida Instructional League in the fall of 1963. Orioles scout Dee Phillips counseled him to control his temper if he wanted to reach the majors. Blefary thought he was ready to jump to the majors in 1964, but the Orioles sent him to Triple-A Rochester. "Nothing depresses me; I will be back," he asserted. Playing first, second, and third base as well as the outfield for Rochester, Blefary batted .287 with 31 homers and led the International League with 102 walks. In January 1964 Curt married his high-school sweetheart, Eileen Fitzgerald.[5]

In spite of complaining to the media that manager Hank Bauer didn't play him enough in spring training, the 6-foot-2, 195-pound Blefary made the 1965 Orioles.

He explained, "Sometimes my mouth would get into gear before my brain was engaged. I did not get to the big leagues being shy. I got the attitude from my father. He said, 'Do not even try to make it, son, unless you really believe you are the best. Otherwise you are going to be heartbroken.'"

In each year of his career, Blefary had a chip on his shoulder about something. His issue as a rookie was platooning. Casey Stengel had platooned Bauer, and the Orioles manager was a believer in the merits of the system. Powell and Norm Siebern split first base equally. Blefary and Boog Powell split left field; Blefary and Sam Bowens split right field. Powell had an off-year, and Blefary led the Orioles with 22 home runs and 88 walks. He finished third in the league in on-base percentage (.381) and ninth in slugging percentage (.470). Setting a trend, he batted .367 with six home runs against the Yankees. Bauer loved Blefary's hustle and competitiveness. He earned the Rookie of the Year award.

Blefary wanted to control his temper and improve his statistical performance in 1966. "The so-called sophomore jinx is just a lot of horseradish," he swore. "It's all mental. I don't expect to have any jinx." With the addition of Frank Robinson, the promising Orioles ran away with the American League pennant. Blefary did avoid the jinx and compiled on-base and slugging percentages that were within a few points of his rookie marks, and again ranked in the top 10 in the league. In his only World Series, a sweep of the Los Angeles Dodgers, Blefary went 1-for-13 with a pair of walks.

Blefary hit five more home runs against the Yankees in 1966. He told *Sports Illustrated*, "Those seats in right field [at Yankee Stadium] … were made for me."[6] Eventually he earned a level of respect unwarranted by his performance against other teams: New York pitchers walked him a total of seven times in consecutive games.

Articles about Blefary continued to document his temper tantrums on and off the field. Oddly, he seemed to be a compliant source for those stories. His unusual eating habits were also fodder for celebrity-hungry journalists. He loved the celebrity lifestyle and enjoyed the nightclubs. The unique young man had the capacity to drink at night and get up and have clam chowder and hamburgers for breakfast. At the same time, his cocker spaniel, Long Ball, would be treated to scrambled eggs and Coke.

Blefary was an inexperienced and graceless outfielder when he reached the major leagues. Teammate Frank Robinson nicknamed him Clank, after the sound of the ball rebounding from his glove. When the team bus passed a pile of scrap iron, Robinson told Blefary, "Go get yourself another glove." Although the legend was exaggerated, his range was poor for someone with average speed. His error totals were always close to the league average. He had a strong but not necessarily accurate throwing arm.

While Blefary was a better outfielder than Boog Powell, Baltimore entered 1967 with three left-handed sluggers, none of whom could help the team in the outfield. Mike Epstein, *The Sporting News* 1966 Minor League Player of the Year, was a poor defensive first baseman. The Orioles sent him to the Florida Instructional League to learn left field. The experiment continued in spring training, but Blefary still got his at-bats. Hank Bauer tried him as a catcher after Powell accidentally stepped on backup catcher Charlie Lau's toe. Blefary also experimented with switch-hitting. He had been a switch-hitter in high school. He asserted that he had more power right-handed. Presumably Bauer wasn't impressed.

Trade rumors, especially in the *Sporting News*, were rampant. Years later, Jim Palmer said the Cubs were willing to trade Billy Williams for Blefary and Epstein. Palmer claimed that owner Jerry Hoffberger told general manager Harry Dalton, "You can make that trade, but you'd better be right."[7] He would have been: Williams outlasted both much younger players and had the seasons that created the mold to cast his Hall of Fame bust in 1970 and 1972. *The Sporting News* also claimed that Dalton turned down offers from the White Sox for Bruce Howard or Joel Horlen for Blefary.

Blefary's batting average declined to .242 in 1967, but he played a little more and drove in a career-high 81 runs. He ranked in the top 10 in the AL in hojme runs (22) and RBIs. The Orioles skidded to sixth place with a losing record, primarily due to key injuries to the pitching staff.

Spring training in 1968 was eventful for Blefary again. In mid-March, Bauer suddenly moved him to catcher. Andy Etchebarren had thrown out 29 percent of would-be stealers in 1967, which was 12 percent below the league average. Bauer said the move was no more than an experiment. The fact that Etchebarren batted right-handed must have entered into his thinking. Blefary noted, "I came to the Yankees as a catcher, but when they sent me to Greensboro the catcher there was off on a hitting tear. So they used me as a first baseman. The next spring I was spiked at home plate and I couldn't squat. So back I went to first again."

The experiment was successful enough to entice Bauer to use Blefary as a catcher, outfielder, and first baseman in much the same way the Yankees used their catchers in the late 1950s and early '60s. He caught in 40 games; one of them was a no-hitter pitched by Tom Phoebus against Boston on April 27. Blefary's batting average plunged to .200 (actually .199556) in "The Year of the Pitcher." He said his hitting suffered from playing too many positions. His batting average had declined in each season, but so had the league's. Blefary still exceeded the league average on-base percentage in 1968 (.301 to .297). However, in the previous three seasons he had exceeded the league average on-base and slugging percentages by huge margins.

Earl Weaver, who had managed Blefary in the minors, took over the Orioles during the 1968 season. The team, which had won just 76 games while finishing a disappointing sixth in 1967, rebounded to win 91 games.

When Weaver told the media that Blefary would have to compete for an outfield job in 1969, that triggered a tirade and a trade. The O's made a deal with Houston that was subsequently regarded as an extremely unbalanced trade. Blefary and minor leaguer John Mason went to the Astros for pitcher Mike Cuellar, prospect

Enzo Hernandez, and minor leaguer Elijah Johnson. The trade helped the Orioles become as good as any team ever in 1969. Cuellar was the co-winner of the Cy Young Award (with Denny McLain of the Tigers) and averaged 21 wins per season from 1969 to 1974.

After the trade, *The Sporting News* reported that Blefary said, "Weaver and I don't see eye-to-eye, period. He was a decent guy in the minors, but now he's speaking out of turn. He's a coach half a year and then he becomes a manager and crucifies me." He added, "So I had a bad year. ... I had three good ones before this."[8]

Blefary became the Astros' first baseman. Pitching kept the team in the National League West race, but eventually Houston dropped to .500 and finished fifth. Although Blefary had hit in the .170s against left-handers in 1967 and 1968, manager Harry Walker played him almost regularly. He hit only .195 against left-handers, but had a decent .253/12/67 season. Remarkably, he didn't hit a home run until the Astro' 44th game. He had career highs of 26 doubles, 7 triples, and 8 stolen bases; and slugged .393. His 77 walks ranked 10th in the NL and contributed to a .347 on-base percentage. He exceeded the league's batting, slugging, and on-base averages, but not by significant margins for a poor-fielding first baseman. However, considering his ballpark, Blefary's numbers were respectable and represented a comeback.

Regardless, Curt was unhappy in Houston. Fortunately for him, the Yankees also had a problematic, controversial player in Joe Pepitone, whom they accused of loving off-the-field excesses more than baseball. Both teams wanted to trade their misfits and loved the potential of the other team's player: An even swap was consummated on December 4, 1969, exactly a year after the Astros acquired Blefary.

After the trade, *Houston Chronicle* sportswriter John Wilson blasted Blefary in *The Sporting News*: "Blefary has failed to see eye-to-eye with his last two managers, Harry Walker at Houston and Earl Weaver at Baltimore. He showed a lack of restraint in expressing displeasure with the way he was being handled and asked to be traded from both teams."[9] Walker responded that Blefary hurt himself by blaming his troubles on others. "He ought to grow up and take a good look at himself," Walker asserted. Walker claimed he taught Blefary bat control and discipline with high pitches. His philosophy was right for the Astrodome, and Blefary hit to all fields as instructed, but he longed to hit long balls. Trading for a slugger and turning him into a line-drive hitter is somewhat analogous to trading for a player and converting him to a different position: For the strategy to fully succeed, the player has to have right attitude about it. Blefary had a gung-ho attitude and aggressive style of play that any manager could love, but his pride and short temper were unmanageable in his era.

Blefary wore number 13 in Houston. The choice was iconoclastic and controversial in that era. However, his willingness to room with Don Wilson was far more daring. The duo were probably baseball's second pair of interracial roommates. The 1960s were the most volatile period for race relations in American history. Legislation mandated integration, but members of various races were slow to accept each other as peers. In that era, white people who openly embraced members of other races were often victims of covert and overt discrimination, especially in the south. You could argue that Blefary played the most significant role in integrating the game of any white player in baseball history, but the case is hard to make simply because his role has been so minimally documented.

Blefary felt the trade to New York was the best thing that had happened in his career in a long time. "It was like an early Christmas present," he said. The *Yankee Yearbook* quoted him as saying, "I know it sounds corny, but I always wanted to play for New York. It's my home and wearing the pinstripes and standing in the same batter's box where Babe Ruth stood do something to me." On Opening Day, he enthused, "This is a lifelong dream come true at last. I'm finally playing at Yankee Stadium as a Yankee."

The Yankees knew they were getting a Yankee-killer who had hit very well in their ballpark. In four years with Baltimore, Blefary hit .299 with a dozen homers against New York. Only half of the homers came in the Bronx, but he hit .324 there. The 1970 Yankees had a deep pitching staff and an exciting nucleus of young talent led by Roy White, Bobby Murcer, and Rookie of the Year Thurman Munson. Veterans Blefary and Danny Cater were expected to solve weaknesses.

Under different circumstances, Yankee Stadium might have been a panacea for Blefary. Ralph Houk's laissez-faire management style gave Curt the same type of release that a student of a repressive teacher might experience with a substitute. He abandoned tying to hit singles and doubles in favor of trying to hit every pitch he swung at out of the park. As a result, he failed to do either. Hickoksports.com quoted Blefary as once saying, "Home runs are the root of all evil. You hit a couple and every time up, you're looking to hit the ball out. Next thing you know, you're in a slump."[10] As in 1969, Blefary went an amazingly long stretch before hitting his first home run of the season. He hit it on June 2 against the Kansas City Royals off former Orioles teammate Moe Drabowsky. Afterward, Blefary praised Ralph Houk: "He really has been great all through my long slump. He just kept telling me to hang in there and it would come." But he finished the season at .212 with 9 home runs and 37 RBIs, and lost playing time in right field to Ron Woods, Jim Lyttle, and others. and finished 9-37-.212 (and 43 walks) in 269 at-bats. The Yankees won 93 games, but didn't challenge the Orioles. The Yankees needed a slugger in right field. Former number-one draft choice Ron Blomberg appeared to be a solution for New York. Blefary was 7-for-36, primarily as a pinch-hitter, when the Yankees traded him to the Oakland Athletics for left-hander Rob Gardner May 26. Oakland used him as a pinch-hitter and utilityman. He caught in 14 games (his first experience in that role since 1968), and played second base, third base, and the outfield. Overall, Blefary hit a familiar .212 in just 137 at-bats.

With tough Dick Williams as his manager, Blefary understood that he was in no position to complain. As spring training began in 1972, he told *The Sporting News*, "I've got three things to do this spring. I'm going to get in shape, take my swings, and keep my mouth shut."[11] Instead, as spring training ended, he reprised

his "play-me-or-trade-me" refrain. He had 5 hits in 11 at-bats when the A's honored his request on May 17. They shipped Blefary, left-hander Mike Kilkenny, and a player to be named later (minor leaguer Greg Schubert) to San Diego for right fielder Downtown Ollie Brown. Brown, then 28, was off to a horrendous start for the Padres; both teams may have perceived that they were trading problems, and salaries may have been a factor.

Blefary, with his fifth team in five years, was reduced to being a journeyman utilityman. He filled the same role for struggling San Diego as he had for pennant-winning Oakland. He hit .196 in 102 at-bats and was released by the Padres in December. A month later, he was signed by the Atlanta Braves, but was released by the Braves during spring training of 1973. Just 29 years old, Blefary could not get a job with another team. In 1986 he told John Eisenberg of the *Baltimore Sun*, "Evidently, I did something to somebody during my career, because there is no way a 29-year-old left-handed-hitting catcher cannot hook up with someone, not even in Japan. No one has ever told me what it was. For me to be through then was ridiculous. I had 10 years left. I have never known what happened. There are several things I can touch on: I was very outspoken; I let my mouth get me into trouble even though I knew I was right. There might be times when you have been partying too much and someone sees you and puts a label on you. It could have been different things. No one will tell me."[12]

Blefary hit .237 with 112 home runs and 382 RBIs in 974 games in his eight-year career. He was devastated by the abrupt loss of his baseball career. His personal life suffered a similar downward spiral. His marriage ended in divorce. He wore blue collars, white collars, a sheriff's uniform, and a bartender's apron, but couldn't find satisfying work. For years, he and baseball avoided each other. Blefary later sought baseball jobs, but never got one. He returned to New Jersey and tried several occupations. He sold cars and insurance. He served customers in bars and fast-food restaurants. He took a temporary agency job at $4.25 per hour. He drove a truck. Eventually, he and his second wife, Lana, settled in the Virgin Islands and Florida. He owned a nightclub, Curt's Coo Coo Lounge in Dania, Florida.

By the mid-1980s, Blefary found solace in old-timer's games and autograph events. He loved getting together with other former ballplayers. He served as a volunteer coach for the Northeast High School team in Fort Lauderdale, the longtime spring training home of the Yankees. He wrote an instructional booklet, *Curt Blefary's "Way to Play,"* which he hoped to have published, but self-published instead. Even as his health failed in his later years, he hoped to secure a professional coaching job. Lana Blefary said, "He was a lifelong student of the game." Curt reveled in his past glory. He cherished his World Series ring. Lana reflected, "He gloated about it for the rest of his life. He loved Baltimore, and he loved his fans."

Blefary experienced a variety of health and financial problems. He had hip replacement surgery in late 1994 or early 1995. The surgeon performed the work pro bono.

In February 1995 Jennifer Frey of the *New York Times* conducted a revealing interview with the former player. For the first time, Blefary publicly documented his drinking problem. He admitted that his reputation as a drinker and carouser kept him out of the game. "In the big leagues, I was out of control," he confessed.[13]

Blefary explained, "I was a drinker for 33 years. I started when I was 18. By Triple-A, I was drinking hard liquor." Blefary believed that his drinking was encouraged by society, and perhaps his peers as well. "I had a problem," he said, "but nobody ever had the guts to tell me." With financial help from the Baseball Assistance Team, he completed Sam McDowell's alcohol rehabilitation program in 1994. He had regularly attended Alcoholics Anonymous meetings for 11 years, but that didn't work.

In the *Times* article, Blefary offered prophetic warnings to Dwight Gooden and Darryl Strawberry, who were both dealing with substance-abuse problems and trying to resurrect their careers. "It seems like everybody is telling them that it's going to be all right, and they believe it," Blefary said. "Well, it ain't going to be all right, not if they're still in denial. I've been there. I know."[14] Like Blefary, the former Mets stars let their addictions destroy their careers, even though they played in a more enlightened era.

In the last years of his life, Blefary suffered from chronic pancreatitis. The disease and the problems it caused eventually took his life. According to the National Digestive Diseases Information Clearinghouse, a service of the National Institutes of Health, "Chronic pancreatitis occurs when digestive enzymes attack and destroy the pancreas and nearby tissues, causing scarring and pain. The usual cause of chronic pancreatitis is many years of alcohol abuse, but the chronic form may also be triggered by only one acute attack, especially if the pancreatic ducts are damaged. … Damage from alcohol abuse may not appear for many years, and then a person may have a sudden attack of pancreatitis. In up to 70 percent of adult patients, chronic pancreatitis appears to be caused by alcoholism. This form is more common in men than in women and often develops between the ages of 30 and 40."

Curt Blefary died on January 28, 2001, at his home in Pompano Beach, Florida. "It's good that his suffering is over now," the AP obituary quoted Lana Blefary as saying. He was survived by his wife, two daughters, a son, three grandchildren, and two sisters.

At one time, Blefary expressed a desire to be buried in Baltimore's Memorial Stadium. However, Curt outlived the demolition of most of the ballpark. With help, Lana was able to honor his last wish to scatter his ashes in Memorial Stadium. The ceremony was held on May 24, 2001. The Babe Ruth Museum supplied the home plate used in the last game at the defunct stadium and located it in the precise spot where it had been used. Curt told Eisenberg in 1986, "I am a damn ballplayer, and I will go to my grave that way."[15] He did.

SOURCES

Angell, Roger, *The Summer Game* (New York: Viking Penguin, 1972).

Bouton, Jim, *Ball Four*, (New York: World Publishing, 1970).

Honig, Donald, *American League Rookies of the Year* (New York: Bantam, 1989).

Brown, Doug, "The Man With the Cadillac Trot," *Sport*, June 1966, 42-43.

Barker, Barbara, "Comeback Year," *Bergen Record* (Hackensack, New Jersey), February 12, 1995.

Brown, Doug, "Blefary Has Curt Reply: 'I'm No Peck's Bad Boy,'" *The Sporting News*, December 21, 1968, 34.

Martindale, David, *Biography,* October 1998, 24-25.

Drebinger, John, "DiMaggio Has Wonderful Time Teaching at N.Y. Rookie Camp," *New York Times,* March 22, 1963.

Eisenberg, John, "Building a Life After Baseball," *Baltimore Sun,* September 1986.

Frey, Jennifer, "I've Walked in Their Shoes," *New York Times,* February 26, 1995.

Goldstein, Richard, "Curt Blefary, 57, Outfielder and A.L. Rookie of the Year," *New York Times,* January 30, 2001.

Ogle, Jim, "Trade Winds Puff Out Yank Muscle," *The Sporting News,* December 20, 1969, 31.

Schneider, Russell, "Indians Stalk New Prey—Phil Slugger Richie Allen," *The Sporting News,* October 26, 1968, 25.

Schneider, Russell, "Tribe's Bid For Sock Runs Into Roadblock," *The Sporting News,* December 21, 1968, 28-29.

Wiebusch, John, "Angels Talk Deals, Seek Curt Blefary," *The Sporting News,* December 7, 1968, 36

Wiebusch, John, "Angels Whiff On Allen Deal, Try Callison," *The Sporting News,* December 21, 1968, 45.

Wilson, John, "Astros Proud of Off-Season Overhaul Job," *The Sporting News,* December 21, 1968, 35.

Wilson, John, "Clank, Cuckoo; By Either Name Blefary Can Hit," *The Sporting News,* January 4, 1969, 44.

Wilson, John, "Hat's Figures Offset Blefary's Blast," *The Sporting News,* April 4, 1970, 8.

Wilson, John, "Trades Add New Zing to Astro Attack," *The Sporting News,* February 15, 1969, 39.

Associated Press, November 22, 1965, January 29, 2001.

Bergen Record, various issues.

"Blefary Dies," *USA Today Baseball Weekly,* January 31, 2001, 14.

New York Times, March 21, 1968.

Sports Illustrated, July, 11, 1966, June 13, 1968.

"The Year of the Rookie," *Time*, June 4, 1965, 68.

Time, July 22, 1966.

astrosdaily.com

baseball-almanac.com

baseballguru.com

BaseballLibrary.com

Baseball-Reference.com

Biography.com

hickoksports.com

Historicbaseball.com

Retrosheet.org

Brief conversations with Curt Blefary, 1968-1971

Newspaper and magazine clippings with no source documentation.

NOTES

1   The same figure was stated as fact by Doug Brown in the June 1966 issue of *Sport* and by Richard Goldstein in the January 30, 2001, *New York Times*.

2   *New York Times*, January 30, 2001.

3   Doug Brown, "The Man With the Cadillac Trot," *Sport*, June, 1966, 42-43.

4   He once said, "Because I was born in Brooklyn, I always rooted for the Dodgers, but the team I wanted to play for was always the Yankees." *New York Times*, January 30, 2001.

5   *The Sporting News*, May 8, 1965.

6   *Sports Illustrated*, July, 11, 1966.

7   *The Sporting News*, February 2, 1998.

8   *The Sporting News*, December 12, 1968.

9   *The Sporting News*, December 20, 1969.

10 Hickoksports.com (Website no longer functioning).

11 *The Sporting News*, April 7, 1972.

12 *Baltimore Sun*, September 1986, date unknown.

13 *New York Times*, February 26, 1995.

14 *New York Times*, January 30, 2001.

15 *Baltimore Sun*, September 1986, date unknown.

Robert "Bobby" Brooks, Jr.

Thomas Ayers

Although he displayed a strong batting eye and some extra-base power during his minor-league career, Bobby Brooks had a relatively brief major-league career over parts of four seasons. Nicknamed "The Little Hammer," Brooks may have been hurt by his short stature (he stood 5-feet-8 and was listed at 165 pounds), which may have led some observers to determine prematurely that he would never be an offensive contributor in the majors.[1] After his playing career, Brooks became well-known in his community for coaching Little League baseball, but he was stricken with multiple sclerosis and died at the age of 48.

Robert Brooks, Jr. was born on November 1, 1945, in Los Angeles to Robert E. and Flaxie (Phillips) Brooks. One of four children born to the couple, he had two brothers, Chris and Nicki, and a sister, Paulette. Religion played an important role in Brooks's life. He was baptized at a young age by the Reverend Dwitt Bradley at the Union Baptist Church.[2]

Brooks started playing Little League baseball at 8 years old and went on to play Babe Ruth League and American Legion baseball. A talented athlete, he went to Narbonne High School in Harbor City, California, after having attended Normont Elementary School and Alexander Fleming Junior High School. At Narbonne, Brooks lettered in baseball, football, and track and field.[3] He was one of three big leaguers to have graduated from Narbonne High School, along with pitchers Paul Pettit and Chad Qualls.

After performing as a standout athlete at Narbonne, Brooks attended Los Angeles Harbor Junior College in Wilmington, California, where he played baseball and football. He was twice named to the All-Western State Conference baseball team and once to the All-Conference football team.[4]

On March 17, 1967, at the age of 21, Brooks married his 20-year-old high-school sweetheart, Valorie Marie Coleman.

Brooks's performance in his two years at junior college attracted the attention of scout Art Mazmanian of the Kansas City Athletics. In 1965 the Athletics drafted Brooks in the 15th round. Brooks got his first taste of professional baseball with the St. Cloud Rox of the Northern League. The Rox, an affiliate of the Minnesota Twins, finished 43-23 and won the Northern League title by 12 games. Brooks hit .294 with a .506 slugging percentage in 66 games.[5] He led the league with 16 doubles, 46 RBIs, and 51 walks (along with 78 strikeouts). He also tied for the league lead with 8 home runs and 119 total bases.

Brooks began the next season with the Athletics' Modesto affiliate in the Class A California League. After batting .264 in 110 at-bats, he was promoted and spent most of the season with the Burlington Bees in the Midwest League, where he wasn't able to replicate his success with Modesto and only posted a .234 batting average, although he did display extra-base power with 14 doubles and 16 home runs.

In 1967 Brooks returned to the Bees for a full season. He hit .274 and posted a .461 slugging percentage, with 20 doubles and 15 home runs. That year also marked the birth of daughter Jaime Louise Brooks, Bobby and Valorie's first child, on November 11, 1967 in Los Angeles

Brooks stayed in Class A in 1968, at the Peninsula Grays (Hampton, Virginia) in the Carolina League. He batted .256 and hit 26 home runs. He also stole a career-high 22 bases. Not a particularly strong defensive player during his career, Brooks displayed some defensive prowess that season, leading Carolina League outfielders in assists (22) and double plays (9). He was selected for the midseason league All-Star game and named to the end-of-season league All-Star team.[6]

That season set the stage for the following year, which could be considered Brooks's breakout year, as the outfielder announced his presence in the upper levels of the minor leagues and finished the year in the majors. Brooks began the year with the Birmingham A's in the Double-A Southern League, where he played a career-high 140 games, hit .292, posted a .408 on-base percentage, and hit for a .503 slugging percentage. He led the league in runs scored (102), homers (23), and bases on balls (92), and tied for the lead in RBIs (100). It was the only time Brooks broke the 100 RBIs and 100 runs scored threshold in his career. Brooks was also second in the Southern League in total bases (243) and was fifth in batting average (.292). Brooks was one of seven A's farmhands to make the Southern League All-Star team and play an exhibition game against the Atlanta Braves.[7] He was named to the National Association Class AA-East All-Star team.

After the Southern League season, Brooks was called up to Oakland. The 23-year-old made his major-league debut on September 1, 1969, against the Boston Red Sox at Fenway Park. The A's sat 5½ games behind the Minnesota Twins in the battle for the American League West championship. Brooks pinch-hit in the top of the fifth inning for pitcher Jim Roland with the A's trailing 5-2 and smacked a double to center field off Lee Stange.

On September 3 the A's and Red Sox played a doubleheader. In the first game Brooks struck out as a pinch-hitter. In the second game he got his first major-league start, in left field. Batting seventh, Brooks went 0-for-2 with a strikeout, but he reached base twice by drawing a walk and being hit by a pitch.

After making several more pinch-hitting appearances, Brooks was handed his second major-league start on September 11 in Oakland against the Seattle Pilots. Batting third and playing left field, Brooks went 2-for-3 with a pair of doubles, two runs scored and a walk in a 6-3 victory. He contributed defensively with his first major-league assist, as he threw out Steve Hovley at home plate.

Brooks then started every game for the Athletics through September 28, playing both ends of a doubleheader twice. On the 14th he hit his first major-league home run, off Gary Peters of the Chicago White Sox. He had several other multihit games, including going 3-for-5 with a home run in a 3-2 ten-inning victory against the Kansas City Royals in Kansas City. Brooks was instrumental in that victory, as he hit a solo homer in the top of the third inning, singled in the top of the eighth inning to advance Bert Campaneris to third with two out and then singled Campaneris home in the top of the tenth with the A's and Royals tied 2-2. On September 23 against the White Sox, Brooks came up in the bottom of the sixth with the A's losing 2-1 with two runners on and hit a three-run homer off Bart Johnson. The next time Brooks came to bat, he was intentionally walked for the only time in his major-league career.

Brooks had a .241 batting average during his month in the majors, but posted a .396 on-base percentage and a .418 slugging percentage. He went 19-for-79 with five doubles and three home runs. This accounted for more than half of his career major-league at-bats.

Upon arriving in the big leagues, Brooks acquired the nickname "The Hammer." After he was asked about it, Brooks stated, "Listen … Henry Aaron's The Hammer. They call me the Little Hammer because they know I admire the man." Brooks later allowed, "I guess I'm The Hammer of the American League."[8]

Despite a relatively strong rookie season, Brooks was sent to the Triple-A American Association to play for the Iowa Oaks in 1970. In 124 games, Brooks hit .286 with a 397 on-base percentage and a .459 slugging percentage. Displaying his trademark strong batting eye, Brooks drew 82 walks to lead the American Association and finished second with 28 doubles. With his 128 hits, 72 runs scored, and 205 total bases all ranking fifth in the American Association that season, Brooks earned an Honorable Mention to the league All-Star team.

Brooks was called up to the A's in August and struck out in a pinch-hit appearance on August 11. He was sent back to Iowa shortly thereafter, but was recalled when the rosters expanded in September. Brooks started each of Oakland's last four games and got a hit in each game. In two of those contests he went 2-for-4 with a home run and two RBIs. Brooks finished the year with a .333 batting average and a .722 slugging percentage.

In 1971 Brooks was the last player cut from the A's in spring training, as he had been the previous season.[9] However, he didn't let this disappointment of returning to Iowa affect him on the field; he had one of his best seasons in professional baseball, batting .272 with a .488 slugging percentage, a .402 on-base percentage, 14 doubles and 23 home runs. He led the American Association in bases on balls (83) and was third in home runs and was named to the American Association All-Star Game. Brooks posted those numbers despite missing about a month with a broken bone in his hand

after he was hit by a pitch on May 24. Brooks was just thankful he avoided more serious injury. He said, "It could have been worse. I should be thankful that I got my hands up in time to keep from getting hit in the head."[10]

With the A's winning 101 games and the AL West title and having a strong starting outfield of Joe Rudi, Rick Monday, and Reggie Jackson, with Angel Mangual as the primary reserve outfielder, Brooks wasn't recalled to Oakland in September. This was despite the fact that he ended the year on a hot run, collecting five singles, a double, a home run, and ten RBIs during a five-game series in Denver during mid-August and batting .350 over an 18-game stretch in August.[11] Brooks's hot spell at the plate coincided with a switch from a 35-ounce bat to a 31-ounce model, because "I wasn't getting around quick enough when the pitcher threw one in my kitchen."[12] That offseason, Brooks and his wife had their second child, son Robert Ethan Brooks on January 3, 1972, in Los Angeles. Given that he was Robert Brooks, III, the son often went by the name Ethan.

Facing a crossroads in his career, Brooks was told on the first day of spring training in 1972 by manager Dick Williams that he'd either make the A's or the team would get him another major league job. Brooks said that was all right with him and that he was glad for the certainty, but also felt short-changed because he hadn't received more of an opportunity in the major leagues. "I've been playing with these people a long time—seven years. It's been a long, hard grind. I feel I deserved a shot long before," he said.[13] One wonders if his relatively diminutive size was a factor in not being given a longer look in the major leagues.

While all but one of his previous major-league at-bats had come in September, Brooks got his shot from the beginning of the year in 1972, as Oakland released Tommy Davis and Mangual suffered a torn leg muscle that was slow to recover. Brooks hit .344 in spring training with three home runs and 11 RBIs in 18 games. Williams announced that Brooks would be Oakland's Opening Day center fielder.

Brooks played the entire game in the A's first 11 contests of the season. On April 30, after those 11 games, he was hitting .171 with no extra-base hits, although he had drawn eight walks and was posting a .326 on-base percentage. During that first month, a highlight for Brooks probably came on April 26 at Yankee Stadium. Batting fifth, Brooks reached base three times off Mike Kekich, with two hits and a walk. It was Brooks's last multihit game in the majors, and one of the two hits was a two-run single with two out in the seventh inning that drove Kekich from the game. Brooks also reached base three times against Kansas City in Oakland-Alameda Coliseum on April 19. He drew two walks and added a two-run single off Dick Drago in a 4-0 Oakland win.

However, when Brooks failed to seize the opportunity given to him at the beginning of the 1972 season, it may have effectively ended his major-league career. He was relegated to pinch-hitting duty in May and made his last appearance for the A's on May 13 in a 9-6 loss to the Red Sox when he struck out as a pinch-hitter. Two days later he was sold to the Detroit Tigers, ending his eight seasons in the A's organization, and the Tigers sent him to the Triple-A Toledo Mud Hens in the International League.

Although he was optimistic that the trade might give him a new start in a fresh environment, Brooks was quite unhappy with the way he had been treated by the A's and their owner, Charlie Finley. He said, "Charlie has sent players to other clubs before and then brought them back. If that happens to me, I'm not going back."[14]

Although he didn't have a great year in Toledo, Brooks had a nice three-game series from July 7-9 in Syracuse. He hit three home runs in three games, slugging a round-tripper in the first inning of each game[15] In 90 games with Toledo, Brooks hit .220, but posted a .372 on-base percentage and a .379 slugging percentage. He drew 65 walks, struck out 65 times, and finished the year with 10 home runs.

On March 25, 1973, Brooks was traded by Detroit to the California Angels for Bruce Kimm. The Angels apparently acquired Brooks primarily to serve as minor-league depth, as he was sent to Salt Lake City in the Pacific Coast League as spring training drew to a close. However, on May 23 Brooks was called up from Salt Lake City to replace an injured Bobby Valentine. He made a pinch-hit appearance that evening and reached on an error.

The Little Hammer's last major-league start came on May 29 against the Boston Red Sox in Fenway Park. Brooks started in left field and batted second. He singled off Bill "Spaceman" Lee in his first plate appearance of the game for his last major-league hit, but the Angels wound up losing the pitchers' duel, 2-1. His last major-league game was on June 5, when he pinch-hit and struck out against John Hiller of the Tigers.

With Salt Lake, Brooks hit .246 with 14 doubles and 12 home runs. He posted a .356 on-base percentage and a .431 slugging percentage. There is no further record of Brooks playing professional baseball again in the United States.

In 1975 Brooks played in the Mexican League for both the Chihuahua Dorados, alongside former major leaguers Roy Foster and Norm McRae, and the Aguascalientes Rieleros, with Jimmy Ray Hart, Horacio Pina, and Santiago Rosario and future major leaguer Angel Moreno.

After he retired, Brooks remained active in baseball and was well-known in the community for coaching in both the Harbor City and Lomita Little Leagues. He was named to the Harbor City Hall of Fame, and the Harbor City Little League renamed its senior baseball diamond Bobby Brooks Field. Brooks and Valorie divorced on August 10, 1978.

On October 11, 1994, Brooks died from multiple sclerosis in Harbor City.[16] He was survived by his ex-wife, Valorie; their two children, Jaime and Ethan; two granddaughters; a grandson; his mother; his sister; and his two brothers. Valorie paid tribute to her ex-husband, saying, "He was so giving to this community.

He was strong and a tremendous athlete and was loved by everybody."[17]

Brooks was buried in Inglewood Park Cemetery, and a homegoing ceremony was held for him on October 19 at St. Margaret Mary Church in Lomita, California.[18]

SOURCES

Bobby Brooks player file from the National Baseball Hall of Fame in Cooperstown, New York. All quotes are taken from clippings in the file.

NOTES

1 Ron Bergman, "A's Nail A.L. Foes With The Hammer," *The Sporting News*, October 11, 1969.

2 Unidentified clipping, Bobby Brooks National Baseball Hall of Fame File.

3 Bobby Brooks, 1971 Oakland Athletics Press Guide, Bobby Brooks National Baseball Hall of Fame File.

4 Ibid.

5 Ibid.

6 Ibid.

7 "Birmingham Puts Seven on Southern's All-Stars," *The Sporting News*, June 28, 1969.

8 Ron Bergman, "A's Nail A.L. Foes With The Hammer," *The Sporting News*, October 11, 1969.

9 Ron Bergman, "A Seven Year Battle Ends in Triumph for A's Brooks," *The Sporting News*, April 22, 1972.

10 Unidentified clipping, Bobby Brooks National Baseball Hall of Fame File.

11 "Oaks' Hendrick Gone—But His Bat Lingers On," *The Sporting News*, September 4, 1971.

12 Ibid.

13 Ron Bergman, "A Seven Year Battle Ends in Triumph for A's Brooks," *The Sporting News*, April 22, 1972.

14 Unidentified clipping, Bobby Brooks National Baseball Hall of Fame File.

15 Unidentified clipping, Bobby Brooks National Baseball Hall of Fame File.

16 "Bobby Brooks, former Angel, dies at age 48," *The Daily Breeze*, Redondo Beach, California, October 14, 1994.

17 Ibid.

18 Unidentified clipping, Bobby Brooks National Baseball Hall of Fame File.

Larry Brown

By Gregory H. Wolf

A gritty and hard-nosed middle infielder, Larry Brown debuted as a 23-year-old with the Cleveland Indians in 1963. Once described by *The Sporting News* as "one of the top shortstops in the league," the 150-pound Brown proved that a rifle arm, sure hands, defensive versatility, and sheer determination could lead to 1,129 games in a productive 12-year major-league career despite a .233 career batting average.[1] After primarily starting during his tenure with the Indians (1963-1971), Brown served as a veteran utilityman with the Oakland A's (1971-1972), Baltimore Orioles (1973), and Texas Rangers (1974).

Larry Leslie Brown was born on March 1, 1940, in Shinnston, a small coal-mining town in the Appalachian hills of north-central West Virginia, about 35 miles from Morgantown. His parents were Raymond and Dora (Jones) Brown. "My dad was a coal miner and I would have been one also, but we moved to Florida when I was 2 years old," Brown told the author.[2] At the suggestion of a physician, the family relocated to Lake Worth in Palm Beach County on the Atlantic coast where the year-round warm climate benefited Brown's mother, who suffered from arthritis and was confined to a wheelchair. His father opened a country grocery store with a gas pump in front and the family's living quarters in the rear.

Brown started playing baseball by the age of 10, influenced by his only sibling, Dick (five years older) and another neighborhood kid, Herb Score. "I was a follower of those guys," he said honestly. "I wanted to be a pro baseball player by the time I was 12 or 13 years old when Herb and Dick signed with the Cleveland Indians [in 1952 and 1953 respectively.]" Gifted with speed, agility, and natural athleticism, the right-handed Brown progressed through Little League and Pony League, and later starred as an all-conference basketball and baseball player at Holy Name High School in Lake Worth. "I don't remember any scout at my games until I was a senior," said the 5-foot-10 Brown. "I pitched and played shortstop, and talked to maybe four or five scouts."

In an era when scouts were not permitted to sign high-school prospects, Brown anticipated signing his first professional contract the day he graduated in 1958. "I went to my graduation dance and kept calling home asking my dad if anyone called," Brown reminisced with a chuckle. "I was disappointed that no one did."

Brown's agonizing wait ended in July when the Cleveland Indians invited him to a tryout at Municipal Stadium. "It was the first time I was ever on an airplane," said Brown of his life-changing event. "I worked out with the Indians for a week. Frank Lane was the general manager and Joe Gordon was the manager, but nobody said a word to me. I dressed with the players in the locker room, took batting practice, and took infield practice like I was with the team. I

was finally told that they are going to sign me to a contract."

Just 18 years old, Brown signed with Cleveland scout Mike McNally and was assigned to the Cocoa Indians in the Class D Florida State League earning $200 per month in 1958.[3] He inaugurated his professional baseball career by smashing a home run in the second at-bat of his first game. Over the course of 65 games, Brown hit at a respectable .264 clip, and more importantly "scintillated defensively" at shortstop (in the poetic words of *The Sporting News*).[4]

After batting a career-best .300 with the Selma (Alabama) Cloverleafs in the Class D Alabama-Florida League in 1959, Brown impressed Cleveland brass in the Florida Instructional League in the fall of 1959, earning a promotion to the Reading (Pennsylvania) Indians in the Class A Eastern League in 1960.[5] Though his average dipped to .236, he hit a career-high 15 home runs to tie another hot shortstop prospect, the New York Yankees' Tom Tresh, for eighth-most in the league.

Brown parlayed a productive showing in the Florida Instructional League (he batted .298 and was named second-team all-star) into an invitation as a nonroster player to his first big-league spring training in 1961.[6] "It really wasn't a big deal," said Brown. "I never thought about making the ballclub and wasn't in awe of the players." After a look-see, Brown was assigned to the Triple-A Salt Lake City Bees (Pacific Coast League).

Despite his success, Brown's future as shortstop with the Indians seemed cloudy. Hard-hitting slugger Woody Held occupied the position with the parent club and prospect Jack Kubiszyn (who batted a combined .330 in Double-A and Triple-A in 1960) made the Opening Day roster. When Kubiszyn was optioned to Salt Lake City in midseason, it had a ripple effect in the organization. "The Indians sent me back to A-ball in Reading (Pennsylvania) in midseason in 1961," said Brown, who suffered a broken bone in his hand and batted just .214 in 68 games with the Bees. "They told me, 'We think you'll have a better chance

at making it if you play second base.'" Brown made a seamless transition to his new position and improved his average to .299 in the Eastern League.

Brown spent the offseasons throughout his baseball career in the West Palm Beach area. In January 1962 he married Helen Boynton, a transplant from Atlanta, who was in the insurance business. Together they raised three girls, and celebrated their golden anniversary in 2012.

Brown displayed his rifle arm at the keystone position for the Triple-A Jacksonville Suns of the International League in 1962. After the Indians added Brown to their 40-man roster in the offseason, he subsequently missed spring training with Cleveland in 1963 while he finished a six-month tour of duty with the army as the Vietnam War played havoc with rosters throughout Organized Baseball.

"I opened the season in Jacksonville at second base in 1963," said Brown. "Cleveland had two players get hurt: (shortstop) Dick Howser, and Held broke his finger. The Indians called me up. Gabe Paul, the general manager, told me that I might be up for a while. I was 23 and it was time to either make it or break it."

Brown debuted on July 6, 1963, against the New York Yankees in front of almost 58,000 spectators at Municipal Stadium. Pinch-hitting for left fielder Tito Francona, he struck out against Al Downing in the sixth inning and then took over second base in the seventh. He bunted for his first big-league hit, walked in his second at-bat, and scored twice in the Indians' 11-6 loss. "I hadn't played shortstop in two years," said Brown, "and wound up playing 46 games at short and 27 at second base for the rest of the season."

Brown's first big-league round-tripper was part of an AL record-setting four consecutive home runs in the second game of a doubleheader against the Los Angeles Angels on July 31. After Held, pitcher Pedro Ramos, and Francona victimized reliever Paul Foytack in the sixth inning, Brown came to the plate. "In those days, you had to think that you were going down," said Brown bluntly. "Foytack threw the first two balls right down the middle. Now I had to hit. He threw another down the middle and I hit it out of the park." Praised for his "good bat control," Brown finished the season with a surprising .255 average (63-for-247) for the fifth-place Indians.

Indians beat reporter Hal Lebovitz described Brown's fieldwork as "acrobatic" and "flashy," yet the 24-year-old infielder was relegated to the bench to start the 1964 campaign.[7] Management questioned whether he was strong enough to hold up during a 162-game season. "I had never thought about my size as a handicap," said Brown matter-of-factly. When Held was moved to center field to replace the injured Vic Davalillo on May 6, Brown took over the keystone sack. Brownie (as he was known throughout his career) displayed surprising pop in his bat, smashing a career-high 12 home runs. Against the Detroit Tigers in May, he hit two home runs in a game for the only time in his career. Boils on his right knee limited his play over the last five weeks of an otherwise promising season during which he played in 115 games and batted .230.

Brown was the Indians' Opening Day second baseman in 1965. "We were in Boston on our first road trip (on May 9) and Howser got sick," said Brown. "I hear from manager Birdie Tebbetts, 'Brownie, you're playing shortstop.' I went 5-for-10 and made some good plays in the hole even though I had hadn't played (much) shortstop for two years." Brown became the everyday shortstop after the All-Star Game when Howser suffered a sprained ankle. "I had a better arm than Howser," said Brown. "I wound up taking his job and stayed at shortstop until 1970. I always say, 'Don't ever get out of the lineup because someone is going to take your job.'" Brown was batting a robust .285 in early September when tragedy struck. His daughter was run over by a car. She fortunately recovered fully; but Brown said it was difficult to concentrate on baseball in light of the event. He lost more than 30 points off his average in the month and finished with a respectable .253 (league average was .242) in 124 games, registered a career-best 22 doubles, and matched his career high of 40 RBIs from the previous season for the fifth-place Indians.

"I liked playing shortstop and the long throw," said Brown when asked which middle infield position he preferred. "Second base was easier. The only hard thing is when you have a left-handed hitter and you've gotta go left to the bag to make a double play. At second base you can knock the ball down, spit on it, play with it, and still throw the guy out at first. At shortstop you got to field the ball cleanly and get rid of it."

Throughout his tenure with the Indians, Brown had a reputation as a player's player with a positive team-oriented attitude. He was blessed with a good voice, and he and teammates Fred Whitfield and Chuck Hinton were known to strum guitars and sing country music in the clubhouse. Brown's boundless enthusiasm and hard-nosed play made him a fan favorite. Good-natured and modest, he was honored in the spring of 1966 with the Golden Tomahawk award given annually by the Cleveland chapter of the Baseball Writers Association of America to the most underrated player on the team.

Notwithstanding the award, 1966 proved to be a forgettable year for Brown. On May 4 at Yankee Stadium he collided violently with muscular left fielder Leon Wagner and suffered a fractured skull, nose, and cheekbones. He required operations on both cheekbones, was hospitalized 18 days, and missed six weeks. "I probably came back too soon and wasn't in midseason shape," said Brown, who also lost ten pounds. He finished the season with a .229 batting average in 105 games.

"I was a dead pull hitter," said Brown. "I wanted a fastball and swung at the first pitch. I liked the ball high like most small guys." Though Brown never fulfilled the promise his batting average and home-run totals his first two years suggested, he worked tirelessly on his batting stance and swing throughout his career. "Hoot Evers, our farm director, would tell me, 'Brownie, just get jammed every once in a while.' What he meant was that I had to hit the ball to the opposite field," said Brown.

Brown was brutally honest about his struggles at the plate. "I'd get a sinker or slider down and away and hit a sharp grounder right down the third base line, instead of learning to slice the ball over the first baseman's head or hitting it foul. I'd just try to hit the ball hard. That's how you hit .230 in your career. If I had my career to do all over again, I'd learn how to hit to the opposite field."

Brown's "value to the Indians certainly isn't reflected in the cold, cruel statistics," wrote Indians beat reporter Russell Schneider.[8] At no time was that more evident than in 1967 and 1968 when an injury-free Brown started 150 games each season at shortstop. In an offensively depressed era, Brown batted .227 and .233 respectively; however, the figures corresponded to the league averages of .236 and .230 in that pitching-dominant era. Brown provided invaluable infield stability, helped develop his travel roommate, Vern Fuller, into a starting second baseman, and ranked among the league leaders in putouts (fourth both seasons) double plays (second in 1967), and assists (fourth in 1967). Brown was often removed for a pinch-hitter in the late innings, but provided some insightful context to his perceived hitting woes. "When I played for (manager) Joe Adcock in 1967, he told me, 'Brownie, I don't care what you hit. Just go and catch the ball.' But he also took the bat out of my hands," explained Brown. "I never swung when I was ahead of the pitcher. I always had to take the pitch. That means that I was hitting with a full count or behind the pitcher. And your average goes down."

Reporter Russell Schneider wrote that Brown had "to prove himself year after year" to Indians managers and was under constant pressure to earn a starting job. "When manager Al Dark came to Cleveland in 1968, he told me, 'Brownie, you're gonna be a great utility infielder.' I told him that I don't want to be a great utility infielder. I want to be a mediocre regular and want to get dirty every day," said Brown. Annual trade rumors swirled around Brown after his collision with Leon Wagner, and intensified after Dark's arrival. Even though Brown played in a team-high 306 games in 1967-1968, he was made available in the major-league expansion draft in October 1968 (but was not drafted).

"He's not spectacular, but he can do everything well," said Vern Fuller of Brown in 1969.[9] However, Dark was not convinced about Brown's ability. "All I'm asking for is a fair shake to win the job," said Brown when Dark all but promised offseason acquisition Zoilo Versalles the starting shortstop job in 1969.[10] Brown beat out Versalles as the Opening Day starter, but ultimately lost the job to 22-year-old rookie Eddie Leon in mid-July. Consequently, Brown saw his playing time radically reduced over the last ten weeks of the season (July 16 to October 1). Among his 42 appearances, he started only 28 times, including 21 at third base—where he had never played in his entire professional career. "Not good," said Brown when the author asked about his relationship with Dark. "Al Dark wanted to control everything. I'd been in the big leagues for five years, but I had to look at Dark on every pitch and he would move me (in the field). When you control the players, you inhibit them."

As a versatile utility infielder in 1970, Brown started games at shortstop (19), third base (9), and second base (8), and saw action as a late-inning defensive replacement among his 72 games. Less than a week after Opening Day, his brother Dick, a scout with the Baltimore Orioles and a former big-league catcher (1957-1965), died tragically at 35 from a brain tumor. While 20-year old rookie shortstop Jack Heidemann struggled at the plate (batting .211) and in the field (his 23 errors ranked second-most in the AL), Brown showed he could still play despite his age (30). In the first game of a doubleheader on July 26 against the Kansas City Royals, he tied a big-league record with five double plays from the shortstop position and also recorded a season-high three hits in a 6-5 victory.

In a tumultuous offseason, Brown instigated his eventual trade to the Oakland A's by his incendiary comments at an awards banquet. "I was unhappy about not playing, but Dark wanted me on the bench as a utility player. I loved Cleveland and was an Indian by heart," he said. "Dark got up and said that we have a set group of starters. Well, it didn't include me. In front of everyone, I said that unfortunately for me, Dark is the manager and I won't get a chance to play shortstop in spring training. Nobody said a word to me in spring training."

Heidemann was injured in spring training, and Brown was unexpectedly Cleveland's Opening Day shortstop in 1971. In the third game of the season, he went 2-for-4 and knocked in a career-high five runs in victory over the Boston Red Sox. "I think I've done pretty well as a fringe player," Brown told *The Sporting News* sarcastically. "Here I am in my eighth year in the majors. Not bad."[11] Two weeks later he was sold to the A's for a reported $50,000.[12] "[Trades] are one of the bad things about being a ballplayer," said Brown, who added that they take an economic and psychological toll on the family. Brown made starts at shortstop (25), second base (16), and third base (4), but batted only .196 for the A's.

"I went to Oakland and never was happy," said Brown honesty. "I was an outsider on that team and never really felt part of it. I wasn't one of the guys who came up through their minor leagues or played in Kansas City."

Brown replaced second baseman Dick Green, who was suffering from an ailing back, in the second week of the 1972 season. He started 44 of the team's 45 games from April 26 to June 18, but was running on fumes physically. "My legs started hurting and I had a bad back," said Brown, "and finally landed on the DL in mid-June." In excruciating pain, Brown heard from Chicago White Sox third baseman Bill Melton about an experimental treatment involving the injection of enzymes made from papaya. "I had the injection in my lower back and was in the hospital for about a week," said Brown. "Three weeks later I was running the bases and fielding groundballs. It was late August and the season was winding down and I think I am going to play. (Manager) Dick Williams told me I'll be activated."

Brown's excitement about his recovery and the possibility of playing in his first postseason was met with frustrating news. "It turns out that I am on the 60-day disabled list. I'm through for the season—I can't play. Williams tells me I can work out with the team, but

that I could also leave the team and go back to my wife and kids in Florida." With no role on the team, no chance to play, and an invitation to leave, Brown's fate was sealed.

More than 40 years after the event, Brown still felt insulted by the way the A's treated him. Despite his contributions to the team, he was not invited to the World Series. To top it off, notoriously cheap team owner Charlie Finley sent Brown a package with a faux World Series ring. Upon reading the enclosed card praising the ring as "finest quality synthetic white sapphire," Brown called Finley to voice his objection. As with most situations, Charlie O didn't budge. Brown wasn't surprised by his release in the offseason.

Brown was invited to Miami to participate in the Orioles' spring training in 1973. He had contacts in the organization owing to his brother Dick's association as a player and scout with them. "On the first day of spring training, Earl Weaver asks me how my back is," said Brown. "I tell him fine and then he says that I'm on the team."

The Orioles Gold Glove-winning infielders were remarkably healthy in 1973. Second baseman Bobby Grich started all 162 games, shortstop Mark Belanger played in 154, and third baseman Brook Robinson played in 155. "You gotta be at the right place and the right time," said Brown with a laugh. "I only batted 28 times the entire season." Among his seven hits was his last big-league round-tripper, a two-run shot off reliever Lindy McDaniel in Baltimore's 9-6 victory over the Yankees in the Bronx. After 11 seasons in the majors, Brown's long wait to play in his first postseason game came to an end on October 7 at Municipal Stadium against the A's in the AL Championship Series. In the Game Two loss, Brown took over third base in the final frame for Brooks Robinson, who had been lifted for a pinch-runner.

In the offseason Brown refused a minor-league contract for $14,000 with the Rochester Red Wings. "I was making $30,000," he said. "I told (Orioles GM Frank) Cashen that if I can't make it in the big leagues I'm retiring."

Brown was not quite ready to hang up his spikes. "I called (manager) Billy Martin," he said. "The Rangers played in Pompano, not far from my house. I hit a double in my first spring-training game and Martin told me that I'm on the club." The 34-year-old Brown provided veteran leadership on a young club en route to its first winning season since its move to Arlington, Texas. Used primarily as a defensive replacement, Brown batted .197 in 76 at-bats.

The Rangers did not invite Brown to spring training in 1975, thereby bringing the versatile infielder's professional baseball career to a close. In 12 big-league seasons, Brown batted .233 (803-for-3449) with 47 home runs and 254 RBIs. He batted .262 in six years in the minors.

Brown's transition to his post-playing career was not as easy as he anticipated. "I spent 17 years worrying about what I was going to do, but when it was over, I still wasn't sure what I'd do," he said candidly. From the late 1960s until 1982 he coached in baseball clinics in the offseason and had a cerebral approach to the game. "I think Billy Martin wanted to groom me as a coach, but I couldn't support my family on a minor-league coach's salary," said Brown, noting that he turned down offers from major-league clubs to serve as a minor-league instructor. Brown found his niche in his hobby. An avid tennis player, he devised a specialized tennis visor and began a small business producing and selling them. He operated the company for almost two decades.

As of 2014 Brown resided with his wife, Helen, in the Palm Beach area. As trim as he was in his playing days, Brown revealed his passion and youthful enthusiasm when he talked about baseball from his era. "Big old Municipal Stadium was a great place," he said nostalgically. "The best sound in the world was when I'd walk down the hill from the hotel to the ballpark and I'd hear someone taking batting practice in an empty stadium. The sound of the bat and that crack—that was amazing."

SOURCES

Schneider, Russell, *The Cleveland Indians Encyclopedia*, 3rd edition (Champaign, Illinois: Sports Publishing LLC, 2005).

———— *Whatever Happened to Super Joe? Catching Up With 45 Good Old Guys from the Bad Old Days of the Cleveland Indians* (Cleveland: Gray and Company, 2006).

The Sporting News

Author's interview of Larry Brown on October 7, 2013, and subsequent correspondence.

BaseballReference.com

Diamond Mines. National Baseball Hall of Fame. scouts.baseballhall.org/scout?s-sabr-id=f0429c9e

Retrosheet.org

MLB.com

SABR.org

NOTES

1 *The Sporting News*, August 12, 1967, 11.

2 The author expresses his gratitude to Larry Brown for his interview on October 7, 2013. All quotations from Brown in the biography are from this interview unless otherwise noted.

3 Diamond Mines. National Baseball Hall of Fame. scouts.baseballhall.org/scout?s-sabr-id=f0429c9e

4 *The Sporting News*, August 6, 1958, 39.

5 *The Sporting News*, December 9, 1959, 21.

6 *The Sporting News*, December 14, 1960, 37.

7 *The Sporting News*, May 30, 1964, 9.

8 *The Sporting News*, October 28, 1967, 27.

9 *The Sporting News*, January 14, 1969, 42.

10 Ibid.

11 *The Sporting News*, April 24, 1971, 26.

12 *The Sporting News*, May 8, 1971, 32.

Ollie Brown

by Andy Sturgill

There is a charm to being the first of anything. Most people know that Neil Armstrong was the first man to set foot on the surface of the moon. Far fewer people know that Buzz Aldrin was the second. The first commissioner of baseball and the first to break baseball's color line are also remembered much more widely than their successors. Toward that end, Ollie Brown is a first: the first player in the history of the major-league San Diego Padres.

Ollie Lee Brown was born on February 11, 1944, in Tuscaloosa, Alabama. The middle of three boys born to Willie Frank Brown, Sr. and Mayola Washington Brown, he grew up in a home of athletes. Older brother Willie was a running back at the University of Southern California and played three years (1964-66) in the NFL with the Rams and Eagles; younger brother Oscar played in the major leagues for the Atlanta Braves in parts of five seasons (1969-73).

In the mid-1940s, looking to provide better opportunities for their two young boys, the Browns left Tuscaloosa for Long Beach, California, where Oscar was born in 1946. The Brown boys attended Long Beach's Polytechnic High School, which boasts among its alumni actress Cameron Diaz, rapper Snoop Dogg, tennis great Billie Jean King, and major-league stars Tony Gwynn and Chase Utley.[1] Ollie excelled on the baseball and basketball teams at Long Beach Poly, and attended Long Beach College for one year after graduation. He signed with the San Francisco Giants in 1962, three years before the onset of the free-agent draft.

Because of his powerful throwing arm, when Brown signed with the Giants there was some uncertainty about whether he would pitch or play the field. In his first season, 1962, Brown split his time between Salem (Virginia) of the Class D Appalachian League and Decatur of the Class D Midwest League. Between the two teams he posted a .227 batting average in 278 plate appearances. In 1963 he started 21 games as a pitcher for Decatur, throwing a no-hitter but compiling a 4.76 earned-run average (he walked 132 batters in 123 innings), and also playing in 59 games as an outfielder.

The story of how Brown advanced to Decatur after only a few games at Salem, however, is more complicated than just a hotshot prospect advancing through a team's minor-league system. This was 1962. And Ollie Brown was an African American from Southern California. And this was the Appalachian League, six teams in Virginia, West Virginia, Kentucky, and Tennessee. On a trip to West Virginia, the Salem team bus pulled up to a hotel where the white players got off the bus and stayed in the hotel, while the black

players were taken to the home of a local black family who housed them.

The incident occurred at the beginning of a two-week road trip, one that saw the 19-year-old Brown lose ten pounds. When the team returned to Salem, he confronted his manager and gave an ultimatum to the Giants organization – move him to another team in the organization or he would quit professional baseball and return home to California. The Giants accommodated Brown's demand and moved him to Decatur, Illinois, where he played the rest of 1962 and all of 1963.[2]

As a 20-year-old at Class A Fresno in 1964, Brpwn belted 40 home runs while hitting .329 in 133 games. The big season gave rise to his enduring nickname, Downtown Ollie Brown. The outfield fences in Fresno were in the direction of the city's downtown area, so Brown's power display produced the natural nickname. (Having Brown as a last name probably helped too. It's hard to imagine the nickname would have stuck if he were Downtown Ollie Jones.)

After strong seasons at Fresno (Class A California League) and Tacoma (Triple-A Pacific Coast League) in 1964 and '65, Brown was called up by the Giants at the tail end of the 1965 season. Only 21 years old, he made his debut on September 10 against the Cubs, starting in right field and going 0-for-3. He played in five more games before the rest of the season, going 2-of-6, with his first hit a double off Billy O'Dell of the Milwaukee Braves.

Brown spent almost all of 1966 with the Giants, hitting .233 with seven home runs and 33 RBIs in 115 games. He managed to stay with the Giants for the entire 1967 season too, posting a .267 average with 13 home runs and 53 RBIs in 120 games. Ken Henderson had opened the season as the Giants' regular right fielder, but a .205 average in May got him benched in favor of Brown. On May 12, shortly after replacing Henderson in the lineup, Brown was hit in the jaw by a fastball thrown by the Astros' Claude Raymond. After receiving a few stitches to close a cut on the inside of his mouth, Brown returned to the lineup the next day, saying, "It was tough enough to get in the lineup in the first place. And I don't want out."[3]

Over the next month after the beaning, through June 26, Brown hit .290 with 11 home runs and 24 RBIs, including a walk-off home run off the Astros' Raymond just two days after getting hit by Raymond. Brown suffered a groin injury shortly after this stretch and was unable to get going in a similar vein the rest of the season, adding only two more home runs and 26 RBIs.

Entering the 1968 season Brown was still only 24 and had 241 major-league games under his belt. However, he started only 21 games through the end of June and was sent to Triple-A Phoenix because there was no room for him in the in the Giants outfield, with Willie Mays still posting MVP-level numbers, Jesus Alou holding down one corner spot, and 22-year-old sensation Bobby Bonds making his debut in late June. Recalled in September, Brown played briefly.

The Giants elected not to protect Ollie in the 1968 National League expansion draft that helped stock the new teams in Montreal and San Diego. (A separate American League expansion draft was held for the new Seattle Pilots and Kansas City Royals.) After getting himself into the Giants' doghouse by not immediately reporting to Phoenix when he was sent down the year before, Brown anticipated that he might be made available for the expansion draft.

Seeing the opportunity to grab a 24-year-old outfielder with a strong arm, power potential, and significant major-league experience, San Diego made Brown its first pick in the expansion draft, making Brown the first major-league Padre. "I'm very serious about doing a good job for San Diego," Brown said.[4]

As Brown joined the Padres for their inaugural 1969 season, he recognized as much as anyone that his career was at a crossroads. "I've been in the majors for three years off and on without much happening," he said during spring training.[5] His new manager, Preston Gomez, thought Brown had all the requisites to be an elite player. "I told Ollie when he reported that he can be as good as he wants to be," said Gomez. "He has all the tools – he can hit, run, and throw." Gomez said he thought that Brown lacked in confidence and hoped that the chance to play consistently would help him.[6] "It was a good deal," Brown said in 2005. "If I was going to get some playing time in the big leagues, it was a good thing they had that expansion draft because that opened up some positions for a number of players at that time."[7]

Brown played in 151 games for the Padres in their inaugural campaign. He led the team with a .264 batting average and was second to Nate Colbert with 20 home runs. (Colbert had 24.) Unsurprisingly, the team struggled to a 52-110 record. In 1970 the Padres improved 11 games to 63-99, and Brown enjoyed his finest all-around season. He played in 139 games, hit .292, and posted career highs in home runs (23) and RBIs (89) as well as in hits, runs scored, doubles, and total bases. He came back with an effective campaign in 1971, but saw his power dip significantly, as his home run total fell to 9 and his slugging percentage plunged over 100 points

While Brown was growing into a solid major leaguer at the plate, one aspect of his game was ever present – his powerful throwing arm. While patrolling right field from 1968 through 1970, he had double-digit numbers in assists. "I think Brown has the best throwing arm in the business," said Preston Gomez. "If I were a fan, I'd come to the ballpark early just to see him throw."[8] Cincinnati Reds scout Ray Shore thought Brown's arm was the best he had ever seen, and other scouts considered him the equal of the great Roberto Clemente.[9]

As the 1972 season dawned, Brown was 28 years old and in a mood for reflection. In an interview before spring training he vowed to give 100 percent of himself to the game. "I hope it's not too late to change," he said. "I'm just beginning to realize what this game is all about. ... I know there were games last year where I didn't give 100 percent. Some players have desire right away and some take longer. It has taken me this long to mature. I wish it had happened sooner."[10]

In the same interview Brown said he had thought he was going to be traded during the offseason. The Padres had several outfielders, and plenty of holes elsewhere. Oakland A's owner Charlie Finley had long coveted Brown, offering $200,000 and four players to the Padres for him after the 1969 season. (The Padres declined.) But in May of 1972, with Brown hitting .171 in half-time duty for the Padres and the A's needing a right-handed-hitting outfielder, Brown was traded to Oakland for three players, none of them a front-liner.

Brown joined the defending World Series champions and played a few games in the outfield. But only six weeks later, in late June, he was sent to the Milwaukee Brewers in what was first announced as a cash transaction, but eventually resulted in the A's getting the rights to Billy Conigliaro from the Brewers.

Brown spent the rest of 1972 and all of 1973 with the Brewers. He hit a respectable .279 in 1972 and .280 in 1973, and along the way added another first to his résumé. On Opening Day 1973 at Baltimore, Brown's became the Brewers' first designated hitter. He went 0-for-3 that day; 314 of his 333 plate appearances that season came as a DH.

After the season Brown was part of a nine-player deal that sent him to the California Angels. Late in spring training he was sold to the Houston Astros. He played in only 27 games for the Astros before moving on in late June to Philadelphia, the last leg of his professional baseball career.

The Phillies were stirring in 1974 after several woeful seasons. The team had begun to get results from its impressive farm system in the likes of Mike Schmidt, Bob Boone, Larry Bowa, and Greg Luzinski. Now 30 and never a part of a playoff team (save for his six weeks in Oakland), Ollie Brown moved into a situation in which he was ideally suited to help a club win. "The years I was there we had real good ballclub," Brown recalled in 2005. "The situation I was in there, I played outfield, but I was part of a platoon system. Most of the time it was Jay Johnstone. Whenever there was a right-handed pitcher, he would play, and whenever there was a left-handed, pitcher I would play. The two of us did real well together.".[11]

The Phillies went 80-82 in 1974, then won 86 in 1975 before capturing the National League East championship in 1976 and 1977, winning more than 100 games both years. As the right-handed half of the platoon with Johnstone, Brown hit .264 with a .334 on-base percentage in his four years with the Phillies, achieving career highs in batting average (.303) and on-base percentage (.369) in 1975. He got his only taste of the postseason, getting five plate appearances in the Phillies' National League Championship Series losses to the Reds in 1976 and the Dodgers in 1977. "The years I was there, we won a couple of division titles, but in the National League that's when the Big Red Machine was going along, and they had one of the best teams in baseball and we couldn't get past them when we hooked up in the playoffs. We always fell short of getting to the World Series," Brown said of his time with the Phillies.[12]

After the 1977 season, though he was only 33 year old, Brown retired from professional baseball. He had played 13 major-league seasons and had had enough. "It gets to the point in everybody's career where some guys realize it and other guys don't," Brown said years later. "It's a cycle, and sooner or later, your turn is going to come up. You realize that this is the end, and you have to accept it and move on."[13]

Brown returned home to Southern California with his wife, Sandra (they had married in 1967), their son, Troy, and their daughter, Danielle. The family suffered tragedy in 2000 when Troy was killed in an auto accident at the age of 32. leaving behind two young daughters.

In his early 70s as of 2014, the Browns lived in Buena Park, California, near Anaheim. Ollie helped Sandra run a promotional products company called Zoe Designs, and spent time with family. "We see our grandchildren often, and that keeps us busy," he said[14]

On April 16, 2015, at his home in Buena Park, Brown died from complications of mesothelioma.

He was 71 years old.

SOURCES

Special thanks to Bill Mortell for his extremely important assistance in tracking down Ollie Brown's family information.

In addition to the sources listed, the author consulted Baseball-Reference.com and Retrosheet.org.

http://www.latimes.com/local/obituaries/la-me-0516-ollie-brown-20150516-story.html

NOTES

1   "One High School, So Many Future NFL Players," *USA Today*, April 22, 2008, 2C.

2   Dan Durbin, " 'Downtown' Ollie Brown Boxing With Giants, aisms.uscannenberg.org, August 5, 2013.

3   Bob Stevens, "Even a Beaning Can't Brake Brown," *The Sporting News*, July 8, 1967, 19.

4   Paul Cour, "Padres Boast Trade Bait, Seek Flyhawk, Backstop," *The Sporting News*, November 2, 1968, 41.

5   Paul Cour, "Brown Rewarding Padres Faith," *The Sporting News*, March 29, 1969, 22.

6   "Brown Rewarding."

7   Mike Scarr, "Downtown Will Always Be No. 1," MLB.com, February 22, 2005.

8   Paul Cour, "Padres Brown Brings Runners to Their Knees," *The Sporting News*, August 9, 1969, 20.

9   Bruce Markusen, *Baseball's Last Dynasty*. (Dallas: Masters Press, 1998), 98.

10 Phil Collier, "Padres Brown Vows to Give His All in '72," *The Sporting News*, February 26, 1972, 41.

11 Scarr.

12 Scarr.

13 Scarr.

14 Scarr.

Orlando Cepeda

By Mark Armour

When Orlando Cepeda stood on the podium in Cooperstown, New York, on July 25, 1999, it is likely that no man had followed a more difficult path to the Baseball Hall of Fame, or that any man was any happier to attain the honor. Cepeda had escaped the slums of Puerto Rico to attain stardom at a very young age, and he overcame numerous injuries during his career, and even worse personal difficulties after leaving baseball. Although he had two remarkable comeback seasons in his baseball career, he had his biggest and most impressive comeback years later, when after a decade of humiliation he again stood on a ball field and listened to the roar of a crowd.

To know Orlando, one must first know his father. Pedro "Perucho" Anibal Cepeda, born in 1906, was one of the greatest ballplayers the island of Puerto Rico ever produced, starring in leagues in the Dominican Republic and Puerto Rico from the mid-1920s until 1950, when he was 45. He came up as a shortstop, and his strong hitting (he won numerous batting titles) and aggressive baserunning earned him the nickname "The Babe Cobb of Puerto Rico."[1] Perucho resisted many overtures to play in the Negro Leagues because he did not want to endure the segregated culture of the United States. So he stayed home, earning no more than $60 a week as a ballplayer and a bit more working for the San Juan Water Department.

Orlando Manuel Cepeda Pennes was born in Ponce, Puerto Rico, on September 17, 1937, to Carmen Pennes, a tiny (4-feet-11), beautiful woman, and Perucho Cepeda. (Per the custom in many Latino countries, each parent contributed half of his double surname, with the father's half being used in everyday life.) Orlando Cepeda was preceded by Pedro, born four years earlier, and he also had sisters born to his father's girlfriends, sisters whom Cepeda grew close to.

Although surrounded by love, Cepeda grew up in stifling poverty—his father made little money, and often gambled what he made—and by crime and drugs, habits Orlando participated in. "What saved me," he later wrote, "was baseball—and the talent I inherited from my father. Had it not been for baseball and the legacy of Perucho Cepeda, I could have followed my boyhood pals into a world of crime, violence, and hate."[2]

His family moved a few times before settling in Santurce, a district of San Juan. The son of a baseball star, Cepeda had a childhood dominated by the game, including visits from famous ballplayers—like Satchell Paige, his father's friend. Orlando played a lot of baseball, but suffered the first of his many knee injuries playing basketball when he was 15. During his long recovery, he grew six inches and added more than 40 pounds to his previously scrawny frame. "Before I was in the hospital we had a short wall. I couldn't hit over

it. But afterward, whoosh!"[3] He soon grew to 6-feet-1 and 210 pounds, and was playing mainly first base.

In late 1953 the 16-year-old was scouted by Pete Zorilla, who ran the Santurce Crabbers in the Puerto Rican Winter League. Zorilla asked his friend Perucho if Orlando could serve as the Crabbers' batboy and work out with the club. The next winter, Zorilla arranged for the young Cepeda and a few other islanders (including future big-league teammate Jose Pagan) to go to a New York Giants tryout camp in Melbourne, Florida. Because they were all underage, and had never left the island, they were accompanied by the 20-year-old Roberto Clemente, on his way to spring training with the Pirates. Cepeda impressed at the camp, and signed a contract that included a $500 bonus.

Just days before Orlando's first professional game, with the Salem Rebels of the Appalachian League, the 49-year-old Perucho died after a long bout with malaria. Cepeda returned home and used his bonus money for the funeral. He returned to Virginia but struggled on and off the field. "I lived in the black part of town, and on Sunday mornings I'd hear the people singing gospel music in the church across the street. I'd sit by the window in my room listening, and I'd cry from misery and loneliness."[4]

After a month with Salem, where he hit just .247 with one homer, he was released but picked up by the Giants' Kokomo, Indiana, club. The 17-year-old starred there, batting .393 with 21 home runs in just 92 games. The next year, in St. Cloud, Wisconsin, all Cepeda did was win the Northern League Triple Crown, with 26 home runs, 112 RBIs, and a .355 batting average. In 1957 he made it all the way to Minneapolis, the Giants' Triple-A affiliate in the American Association. It was at that spring that he first met Felipe Alou, a Dominican outfielder who became a lifelong friend. Alou was demoted to the Eastern League, but Cepeda became the club's first baseman and had another fine season: 25 home runs, 108 RBIs, .309 average. "If he ever learns the strike zone," said Red Davis, his manager, "he'll be murder up there. He's tough enough now."[5] Cepeda drew just 27 walks, and he would always be known as a free swinger.

In 1958 the Giants moved from New York to San Francisco. After winning the World Series in 1954, the club had slid to sixth place in both 1956 and 1957. But help was on the way. When Cepeda arrived at spring training in 1958, he was joined by fellow prospects Felipe Alou, Leon Wagner, Willie Kirkland, Willie McCovey, Jim Davenport, and Jose Pagan. The Giants had an opening at first base because Bill White was serving a two-year stint in the Army. Whitey Lockman had held the position in 1957, but manager Bill Rigney asked him to work with the 20-year-old Cepeda that March. The youngster had a tremendous spring, crushing home runs, fielding his position well, and running the bases. "Hey, Rig," said Lockman one day to Rigney. "This kid Cepeda is three years away." Rigney was startled, until Lockman added, "from the Hall of Fame."[6]

On April 15, 1958, the Giants hosted the Los Angeles Dodgers at Seals Stadium, in the first major-league game ever played in California. Cepeda played first base and batted fifth, joining right fielder Kirkland and third baseman Davenport, also playing their first big-league games. The Giants prevailed, 8-0, behind Ruben Gomez, with Cepeda hitting his first home run, off Don Bessent. This was the start of a magical season for the 20-year-old, as he hit .312 with 25 home runs and a league-leading 38 doubles. After the season he was the unanimous winner of the NL Rookie of the Year award.

Cepeda and San Francisco were a perfect fit. While Willie Mays had starred in New York before the Giants moved west, the provincial San Franciscans considered Cepeda to be one of theirs. And the feeling was mutual. "Right from the beginning, I fell in love with the city," Cepeda said. "There was everything that I liked. We played more day games then, so I usually had at least two nights a week free. On Thursdays, I would always go to the Copacabana to hear the Latin music. On Sundays, after games, I'd go to the Jazz Workshop for the jam sessions. At the Blackhawk, I'd hear Miles Davis, John Coltrane. … I roomed then with Felipe Alou and Ruben Gomez, but I was the only one who liked to go out at night.

Felipe was very religious and quiet, and Ruben just liked to play golf, so he wasn't a night person. But I was single, and I just loved that town."[7]

Cepeda's stardom, which he sustained, was considerably complicated in 1959 by the arrival of Willie McCovey, another young hitting phenom who, like Cepeda, played first base. Though Cepeda had another great year in 1959 (27 homers, .317), McCovey's extraordinary four months in Phoenix (29 homers, .372) forced the Giants' hand. When McCovey debuted on July 30 (hitting two singles and two triples), Cepeda played third base. After four games there, manager Bill Rigney moved Cepeda to left field, which he played for the rest of the season.

The Giants spent most of the next five years dealing with the problem of having two All-Star first basemen. Though McCovey had a great two months in 1959, he was plagued by inconsistency and struggles against left-handed pitchers for a few years. Cepeda, regardless of his position, kept playing and kept hitting. But his reluctance to play the outfield became a matter of controversy. "I just wasn't ready mentally," Cepeda said years later. "I know I could've played left field if I'd put my mind to it, but I was only 21 years old and very sensitive. Friends and other players kept telling me I should demand to play first. It was all pride with me. And ignorance."[8]

"I could understand his reluctance," Rigney recalled. "But Cepeda was the better athlete, so I thought he could make the move to another position more easily. But he would come up to me and say, 'Bill, I'm the first baseman not the left fielder.' What could you do? He was the most popular San Francisco Giant. It was very hard not to like Orlando Cepeda. But this became an unresolvable situation."[9] McCovey was back in the minor leagues briefly in 1960, which got Cepeda his first-base job back, and the two shuttled between the outfield and first base in 1961. In 1962 manager Al Dark moved McCovey to left field and Cepeda was back at first base. Cepeda kept hitting, but McCovey did not become a consistent star as long as he and Cepeda remained teammates.

Most of Cepeda's offensive seasons look alike, but his 1961 stands out as a singularly great year; he led the league with 46 home runs and 142 RBIs while hitting .311. Baseball held two All-Star games each season from 1959 to 1962, and Cepeda was named to the team all eight times, starting in five of them. In his career he was named to 11 All-Star teams, playing in nine of them but hitting just 1-for-27. Although he continued to play, Cepeda hurt his right knee in a home-plate collision in 1961 and never had another day without pain.

After a few years of criticism for their underachieving, the Giants broke through in 1962 to win their first pennant in San Francisco. After tying the Dodgers at 101-61 through the regular schedule, they prevailed in a best-of-three pennant playoff, before falling to the New York Yankees in seven games in the World Series. Cepeda had another excellent season, batting .306 with 35 homers and 114 RBIs. The season was not without its problems—he was fined by Dark in August for not hustling, then hit just .231 with three homers after August. In the regular season final, Dark benched him, though Cepeda had four hits the day before in a doubleheader. He played in all three playoff games (3-for-13 with a home run) and hit just 3-for-19 in the World Series.

Cepeda's final years in San Francisco were clouded by his terrible relationship with Dark. Cepeda believed that Dark did not like blacks or, especially, Latinos. Dark did not approve of the Giants' many Latino players speaking Spanish, and he believed their loud Latino music and laughter to be indicative of not taking the game seriously.[10] Moreover, Dark developed his own plus-minus rating system, in which he gave people positive or negative points for what they did on the field. While Mays, unsurprisingly, led the 1962 team with over 100 points, Cepeda came in at negative 40. "There are," said Dark, "winning .275 hitters and losing .310 hitters."[11] That Dark kept such a system and publicly used it to denigrate one of his players is astonishing.

In the remaining two years of his stewardship of the Giants, Dark had run-ins with Cepeda numerous times for what the manager believed was a lack of hustle and what Cepeda claimed was a hurt knee. "The knee hurt me all the time," said Cepeda, "and I always aggravate it when I slide or stretch or even hit. Some people think that because we are Latins—because we did not have everything growing up—we are not supposed to get hurt. But my knee was hurt. Dark thought I was trying not to play. He treated me like a child. I am a human being, whether I am blue or black or white or green. We Latins are different, but we are still human beings. Dark did not respect our differences."[12]

Through it all, Cepeda continued to hit. He batted .316 with 34 home runs in 1963, then .304 and 31 in 1964. Through the first seven years of his career, he had hit .309, with a .353 on-base percentage and .537 slugging percentage. His 222 home runs were three more than Henry Aaron had through his first seven seasons. At the end of the 1964 season, Cepeda was still just 27 years old.

His return to first base full-time in 1962 surely helped his knee, but when he reported to spring training in 1965 he could barely put any weight on it. New manager Herman Franks, like Dark, felt that Cepeda was dogging it, so Cepeda tried to tough it out. After hobbling through the spring, Cepeda was used mainly as a pinch-hitter for the first month of the season (three singles in ten at-bats) before finally going on the disabled list in May. He returned as a pinch-hitter in August, but finished just .176 in 34 at-bats for the year. After the season he had surgery on his right knee.

When he returned in the spring of 1966, McCovey was finally fully entrenched at first base. Playing mostly left field, Cepeda started slowly but was hitting .286 with three homers in 19 games on May 8. On that date, he was traded to the St. Louis Cardinals for pitcher Ray Sadecki. Though Cepeda was shocked and upset by the trade, he was joining a team that had a gaping hole at first base, the only position he wanted to play. In fact, Cepeda never played the outfield again. Batting cleanup for the rest of the year, he homered in his first game and finished the season hitting .301 with 20 home runs in 123 games.

After years of discomfort in San Francisco, Cepeda was beloved by his teammates and manager Red Schoendienst. He became a jokester in the clubhouse, and his taste for jazz and Latin music earned him the nickname Cha Cha. Cepeda noted the change. "You know," he said, "if I do all this in San Francisco they would give me a funny look all the time and everyone would think there is something wrong with me."[13] In 1967 he completed his comeback in style, hitting .325 with 25 home runs and a league-leading 111 runs batted in. After two straight losing seasons, the Cardinals rolled to the NL pennant and victory over the Red Sox in the World Series. After the season Cepeda was unanimously named the league's Most Valuable Player.

After his MVP season in 1967, the 30-year-old Cepeda followed up with the worst full season of his career, batting just .248 with 16 home runs. The 1968 Cardinals returned to the World Series, this time losing to the Detroit Tigers in seven games. After hitting poorly in the Series in both 1962 and 1967, this time Cepeda hit .250 and slugged two home runs.

Cepeda returned to spring training in 1969 hoping for a comeback year with the Cardinals. But on March 17, he received the unwelcome news that he had been traded to the Atlanta Braves for star catcher-first baseman Joe Torre. Cepeda loved St. Louis and his teammates, and he was uncomfortable with the idea of playing in the South. In the end, he enjoyed his time in Atlanta, which reunited him with his good friend Felipe Alou and allowed him to play with the great Henry Aaron.

His first year in Atlanta was a struggle personally and professionally (.257 with 22 home runs) but a big success for the team, which finished first in the NL West in the first year of divisional play. Cepeda hit .455 in the playoff series against the Mets, with a home run off Nolan Ryan in Game Three, but the Mets swept the three-game series. Cepeda came back with a vengeance in 1970 (.305, 34 home runs, 111 RBIs), though the Braves dropped to fifth place.

Cepeda started 1971 as good as ever—on June 1 he was slugging .584 with 13 home runs, among the league leaders in both categories. Later that month, in the act of getting up to answer the telephone at home, his left knee—up until then, his "good" knee—collapsed. The Braves doctor told him the knee was "finished."[14] He hobbled out to first base for a few weeks before finally shutting it down in late July. He underwent another knee surgery in September and went home to Puerto Rico.

A hobbled Cepeda showed up in the spring wanting to play. He played only twice in April, hit .350 (but with little power) playing half-time in May, and hit just .182 in June. On June 29 he was traded to the Oakland A's for pitcher Denny McLain, another recent MVP who looked to be nearing the end of the line. He pinch-hit three times for Oakland, before shutting it down. After the season he was released. With two bad knees, Cepeda's career looked to be finished.

On January 11, 1973, the American League agreed to a three-year trial run of the designated-hitter rule, allowing a batter to hit in place of the pitcher throughout the game. Along with its strategic consequences, there was suddenly a place in the game for good hitters who could not play the field. A week later the Red Sox signed Cepeda with this role in mind. For the 1973 season, Cepeda played 142 games, never once playing in the field. He hit .289 with 20 home runs and 86 RBIs, and was the first recipient of the Designated Hitter of the Year award (later named the Edgar Martinez Award).

Just before the 1974 season, new manager Darrell Johnson decided he wanted to make room for younger players, and he released Cepeda and veteran shortstop Luis Aparicio, surprising most observers. Cepeda was crushed, and remarkably was unable to find another job. He played briefly in Mexico before finally being signed by the Kansas City Royals in August. He hit just .215 in 107 at-bats before drawing another release. This time he was finally through after 17 seasons and 379 home runs.

Cepeda had married Annie early in his career and fathered Orlando Jr., but after years of his infidelity, and at least one child with another woman, they di-

vorced in 1973. He married Nydia in 1975 but his behavior did not improve. In December 1975 he was arrested for taking delivery of 170 pounds of marijuana. Although he admitted to being a marijuana user, he claimed that he was expecting only a small amount for himself, and that he was not a dealer. Puerto Rico had made Cepeda a hero after the tragic death of Roberto Clemente three years earlier, but his arrest made him a pariah on the island. He and his family received death threats. He lost all of his money on his legal case, which caused him to miss child-support payments and led to more legal trouble. He finally stood trial in 1978, was found guilty, and was sentenced to five years in prison. He served ten months in a minimum-security facility in Florida.

Upon his release Cepeda continued to struggle. Still shunned at home, he had trouble finding and keeping work. He got a job as a minor-league hitting coach for the White Sox, but failed to show up a few times and was let go. In 1984 he, Nydia and their two children moved to Los Angeles so he could conduct baseball clinics, but after a few months of fighting, his family moved back home, leaving Orlando with Orlando Jr., who had joined him in LA.

Orlando credited his embrace of Buddhism in the 1980s for turning his life around. It allowed him to take responsibility for the mess he had made of his life, to get control of his shame and his anger, and to help him find a path forward. He also met Mirian Ortiz, a Puerto Rican woman who eventually became his third wife. He and Mirian moved to the Bay Area, close to where his baseball journey had begun 30 years earlier. In 1987 he took part in a Giants Fantasy Camp in Arizona. "Of all the ex-players we had there," recalled a team official, "Orlando was the approachable idol. I couldn't believe it; I kept waiting for the flaws to show in that great personality. But there were no flaws. He is such a genuine person, such an emotional person, that you feel like hugging him. You get this sense that people just want to love him. I asked him if he'd be interested in coming back to work for the Giants."[15]

The next year Cepeda started by making trips for the team to scout or help with instruction. In the 1989 NLCS, he was asked to throw out the first ball before the third game, listening from the pitcher's mound as the cheers rained down on him. For more than 25 years Cepeda acted as a humanitarian ambassador for the club, showing up wherever and whenever they wanted him to, including inner-city schools throughout the country. He also made appearances in Puerto Rico, his native island that once again embraced him.

In 1999 Cepeda was inducted into the Baseball Hall of Fame, 25 years after his last at-bat. "I wasn't ready to get in before," he said. "I still had work to do in healing myself."[16] That same year the Giants retired his number 30. In September 2008 the Giants unveiled a statue of Cepeda outside the 2nd Street entrance of AT&T Park. "When things like this happen to you, that's when I say to myself, 'Orlando, you're a very lucky person,'" Cepeda said after seeing his bronze likeness, holding a ball and first baseman's mitt.[17]

As of 2014, Cepeda lived in Fairfield, 35 miles northeast of San Francisco, with Mirian, and still worked for the Giants. He had five sons, Orlando Jr., Malcolm, Ali, and Karl and Jason.

NOTES

1 Orlando Cepeda and Herb Fagen, *Baby Bull: From Hardball to Hard Time and Back* (Dallas: Taylor Publishing, 1998), 2.

2 Cepeda and Fagen, 7.

3 Robert Creamer, "Giants—A Smash Hit in San Francisco," *Sports Illustrated*, June 16, 1958.

4 Ron Fimrite, "The Heart of a Giant," *Sports Illustrated*, October 16, 1991.

5 Cepeda and Fagen, 31.

6 Roy Terrell, "The Sa-fra-seeko Kid," *Sports Illustrated*, May 23 1960.

7 Fimrite, "The Heart of a Giant."

8 Fimrite, "The Heart of a Giant."

9 Fimrite, "The Heart of a Giant."

10 Peter Bjarkman, *Baseball With a Latin Beat—A History of the Latin American Game* (Jefferson, North Carolina: McFarland, 1994), 138.

11 Richard Boyle, "Time of Trial for Alvin Dark," *Sports Illustrated*, July 06, 1964

12 Mark Mulvoy, "Cha Cha Goes Boom, Boom, Boom!" *Sports Illustrated*, July 24, 1967.

13 Mulvoy, "Cha Cha Goes Boom, Boom, Boom!"

14 Cepeda and Fagen, 161.

15 Fimrite, "The Heart of a Giant."

16 William Nack, "From Shame to Frame," *Sports Illustrated*, July 26, 1999.

17 John Shea, "Cepeda Honored With His Own Statue at the Ballpark," *San Francisco Chronicle*, September 7, 2008.

Ron Clark

by Andy Sturgill

Some men hang around professional baseball for a long time because they possess a skill given to longevity. One may be a good catcher, or a left-handed relief pitcher, and he parlays this ability into lengthy playing careers. Some men hang around professional baseball for a long time because they're great players, and long after they've retired they still trade on their fame to get them work, or at least to make money doing appearances and signing autographs. Still others hang around professional baseball for a long time because it's all they've ever known, and they do whatever jobs need to be done to stay connected to the game. Lifers, you may call them. For example: Ron Clark.

Ronald Bruce Clark was born on January 14, 1943, in Fort Worth, Texas, one of three sons (Mike and Charles were the others) born to Marvin Randolph Clark and Marjorie Geneva Clark, who went by her middle name. Marvin was an aircraft machinist for General Dynamics. Charles was a good amateur pitcher, good enough to be offered a contract by the Cleveland Indians, which he declined.[1]

Ron began playing baseball at an early age. His father was instrumental in youth baseball programs in the Fort Worth area. "My dad started me at 6 years old," Clark recalled. "It seems I've always had a bat in one hand and a baseball in the other."[2] He attended Brewer High School in nearby White Settlement, where he was a four-sport star. He played quarterback and halfback on the football team and guard on the basketball team, and ran the 440-yard relay event in track. On the diamond, Clark earned all-district honors as a sophomore while playing shortstop and as a catcher in his junior season. He split his senior year among second base, shortstop, third base, and catching. He overcame a knee injury suffered playing football in 1958 that required a pair of surgeries to correct.

After graduating from high school in the spring of 1961, Clark signed a contract with the Philadelphia Phillies and made his debut with the Bakersfield (California) Bears of the Class C California League. The 18-year-old hit only .202 but with a respectable .359 on-base percentage in 39 games split between second base and third base. After that, a convoluted series of transactions led to his being property of the Minnesota Twins.

Over the next four seasons Clark worked his way up the Twins' minor-league ladder, playing for Class C San Jose, Class A Wilson (North Carolina), and Double-A Charlotte. He continued to split time between second and third base, and also played 36 games as a shortstop for San Jose in 1962. He never

hit higher than .295, but drew walks and provided stellar infield defense.

Many players who aspire to become big leaguers would probably say that they'll make it even if it kills them. In 1964 Ron Clark's journey to the majors nearly did just that. While with Charlotte, he was hit in the chest by a batted ball during fielding practice. A coach was attempting to hit a fly ball to the outfield, but instead hit a line drive right at Clark, who did not see the ball and could not react to it because he was fielding a groundball hit to him by another coach. The ball drilled Clark in the left side of the chest, just above the heart. "Blood gushed out of his nose, ears, and mouth," remembered teammate Frank Quilici. "We thought he was dead." "It knocked me to my knees, but I didn't know I was hurt until I bent over. Then the blood spurted out," Clark said.[3] The ball had knocked a bronchial tube loose, but while scary, the injury kept him out of the lineup for just a few days. Toughness was one of the hallmarks of the young Texas. As a youth he spent a lot of time around the rodeo circuit, and was well acquainted with riding the horses himself. He notched 104 victories in 111 bouts as a Golden Gloves boxer. He wore cowboy boots, Stetsons, and Western clothes, and spoke with a Texas drawl. He also overcame a number of injuries—to his knees, to his bronchial tubes, and to his throwing arm.

Clark spent most of the 1966 season with the Denver Bears of the Pacific Coast League, the Twins' Triple-A affiliate. Late in the season he was called up and played in five games. He made his major-league debut on September 11 against the Baltimore Orioles, pinch-running for Harmon Killebrew after the slugger had singled in the eighth inning. Clark was later thrown out at home to end the inning, but the Twins won 11-6 anyway. He got his first major-league hit in his last at-bat of the 1966 season, singling off George Korince of the Tigers after replacing Killebrew at third base.

Clark had a real chance to take over the hot corner for the Twins in 1967. The team had prioritized defense at third base, and Clark had won a minor-league Gold Glove the previous season at Denver. He had also

improved with the bat, sharing the Pacific Coast League RBI title with 94. Clark's most likely avenues to a spot on the big-league roster were at third or as a utility player. On winning a big-league job, Clark simply said, "It's up to me to prove I can do it."[4]

Clark didn't get a start until April 30, following an injury to regular third baseman Rich Rollins. Rollins was out for more than three weeks, and Clark got the lion's share of time at third base in his absence. He posted 11 RBIs in 15 games over this span, but he struggled to a .175 batting average and Rollins re-entered the lineup immediately upon his return. Clark played in only three more games the rest of the season, limited in part by surgery at the Mayo Clinic to remove a fingertip-sized bone chip from his right elbow.

At spring training in 1968 the feeling was that Clark was the best bet to be the everyday third baseman. He started there on Opening Day, and another 54 times while appearing in 104 games overall, both career highs. As might be expected, Clark also established career highs in most offensive counting stats

After playing in five games for the Twins in April 1969, Clark was sent to Denver. In mid-July, he was sold to the expansion Seattle Pilots, and he got into 57 games in a utility role for the Pilots in their first and only year before they moved to Milwaukee. Clark was mentioned in *Ball Four*, Jim Bouton's classic memoir. Commenting on a game in which Clark collided with Boston slugger George Scott and needed 13 stitches in his lip to repair the damage, Bouton called Clark a "tough, gutty ballplayer" and wrote that he "has a baby face, two tattoos on his arm, smokes big cigars—and when he has thirteen stitches in his lip he drinks beer out of the side of his mouth."[5]

In January of 1970, before the Pilots even knew for sure where they would play the coming season, Clark and Don Mincher were traded to the Oakland Athletics for four players ("warm bodies," Bouton would call them later in *Ball Four*).[6] Clark spent all of 1970 and virtually all of 1971 (save for two games in April) with the A's Triple-A affiliate Iowa Oaks of the American Association. When he finally did get a chance for significant playing time with Oakland in 1972, he became one of 12 players the eventual World Series champions used at second base during the season. Clark appeared in 11 games at second for the A's. (Tim Cullen played the most, 65 games.) In mid-June he was traded to the Milwaukee Brewers in mid-June for utilityman Bill Voss. He lasted a month in Milwaukee before he was shipped to the California Angels, who sent him to the minors.

By 1974 Clark's major-league career appeared to be over, and he just short of qualifying for a full player's pension. Phillies scout Hugh Alexander arranged for Clark to spend enough time with the Phillies to qualify.[7] Clark played in nearly 250 games for the Phillies' Toledo farm team in 1974 and 1975, and joined the Phillies for the end of the '75 season. He made one appearance, striking out against the New York Mets in the third to last game of the season.

After the 1975 season, Clark's career as a player was over. But that didn't mean he was finished with baseball. He remained in the Phillies organization in the late 1970s as an assistant to the player-development staff and a minor-league manager. As a manager (including part of a season as skipper at Triople-A Oklahoma City), Clark helped guide the development of such future stars as Ryne Sandberg, George Bell, Julio Franco, and Mark Davis. (As it turned out, those four players achieved their success with other teams. That undoubtedly drove the old-school scouting and development man in Clark crazy.)

During his post-playing days, Clark managed winter-ball teams in the Caribbean and also managed in the Cubs' minor-league system. He made it back to the major leagues in the late 1980s and early '90s as a coach for the Chicago White Sox, Seattle Mariners, and Cleveland Indians. Once off the field, Clark settled in with the Kansas City Royals for more than a decade in a variety of positions, including major-league advance scout and roving minor-league infield instructor.

In his early 70s in 2014, Clark was retired to Florida after nearly 50 years in professional baseball.

SOURCES

In addition to the sources listed, the author consulted Baseball-Reference.com and Retrosheet.org.

Special thanks to Bill Mortell for his extremely important assistance in tracking down Ron Clark's family information.

NOTES

1 Arno Goethel, "Tough Ron Clark Born to Play Ball," *The Sporting News*, March 30, 1968; 7.

2 Goethel.

3 Goethel.

4 Max Nichols, "Rookie Rod Carew Stakes Out Claim to Twin Keystone," *The Sporting News*, March 25, 1967, 27.

5 Jim Bouton, *Ball Four: The Final Pitch* (New York: Macmillan General Reference, 1990), 276.

6 Bouton, 398.

7 Daniel Austin, *Baseball's Last Great Scout* (Lincoln: University of Nebraska Press, 2013), 130.

Tim Cullen

By J.G. Preston

San Francisco Bay Area native Tim Cullen signed with the A's during spring training in 1972, returning to the region where he had been a two-sport star in high school and helped Santa Clara University become the nation's top-ranked college baseball team. He did not play in the 1972 World Series and retired after the season, but he helped the A's through a rough stretch in mid-season after two of their second basemen suffered long-term injuries.

Timothy Leo Cullen was born in San Francisco on February 16, 1942, the third of four children (all sons) born to Joseph Murtha and Catherine (O'Leary) Cullen. Joseph Cullen worked for the Internal Revenue Service, and he was transferred to Reno, Nevada, in 1954. That's where Tim started playing Little League baseball, which had not yet come to where the Cullens had lived in the Bay Area. When the family returned to the Bay Area the next year Tim stayed in Reno for another year because he wanted to keep playing baseball. He lived with another family through a Knights of Columbus program.

When Joseph Cullen returned to the Bay Area it was as district director in charge of the IRS's San Francisco office. The family lived first in Palo Alto and then in Burlingame, a community near San Francisco International Airport. Tim was educated in Catholic schools and attended Junipero Serra High School in San Mateo, where he was a star athlete, earning all-Catholic Athletic League honors twice in baseball and once in basketball before graduating in 1960.[1] Future major-league star Jim Fregosi played shortstop while Cullen played third base; after Fregosi graduated in 1959, Cullen moved to short as a senior. Serra's left fielder was Fregosi's classmate Gary Hughes, who went on to have a long career as a scout and executive for several major-league teams (as this was written he was still employed as a scout for the Red Sox). Serra

is best known for having produced all-time home-run leader Barry Bonds and three-time Super Bowl-winning quarterback Tom Brady.

Cullen also played football until his father persuaded him to give up the sport as a senior. "He said, 'Tim, I don't know if I'm going to be able to afford to put you through college. You've got a chance to get a scholarship, but it ain't going to be in football,'" Tim recalled. "He wanted me to concentrate on my other sports, and he also wanted me to spend football season working on my grade average."

Joseph Cullen's advice paid off, as Tim improved his grades enough to get college scholarship offers. Loyola (now Loyola Marymount) University of Los Angeles offered a full basketball scholarship (basketball was the sport Tim said he preferred at the time), but Cullen

accepted a combined basketball-baseball scholarship from Santa Clara, not far from his Burlingame home. He had the opportunity to follow his high-school teammate Jim Fregosi's path and go into pro baseball, but on his father's advice he chose college instead.

"The Giants wanted to sign me," Cullen said. "Before they offered me a contract they asked if I wanted to work in their clubhouse. The deal was I would go to the ballpark and work out with them, put on a uniform and shag flies and take batting practice and take groundballs before the game like one of the players, and then when the game started I'd clean up the clubhouse, then go out and sit on the end of the bench. And I got paid for it. But when they offered me a contract, I already had the scholarship offer from Santa Clara, and my dad wouldn't let me sign. He said, 'You could be out of baseball in two, three years with no education.' And I agreed with him 100 percent. So I told the Giants I was going to Santa Clara, and they've never talked to me since. They didn't even offer me a contract when I got out of college. I think I ticked them off."

Before heading to Santa Clara Cullen played in the Hearst Sandlot Classic on August 18, 1960, at Yankee Stadium. Cullen started at third base and batted third for the United States All-Stars, who defeated the New York Journal-American Stars, 6-5. Future major leaguers Bill Freehan, Mike Ryan, and Mike Marshall were among Cullen's teammates.[2]

At Santa Clara Cullen joined a baseball team that already had two other stars from Bay Area Catholic schools, both of whom also went on to play in the majors: Ernie Fazio, who had gone to St. Elizabeth High School in Oakland, and John Boccabella, who attended Marin Catholic High School in Kentfield. Cullen's freshman-year roommate (and baseball and basketball teammate) was Bob Garibaldi, who signed a big bonus contract with the Giants after the 1962 College World Series and went directly to the majors. Garibaldi's older brother, Dick, was Santa Clara's freshman baseball and basketball coach.

Cullen was the second leading scorer on the freshman basketball team (behind Garibaldi) and tied for the lead on the freshman baseball team in home runs (freshmen were not allowed to play varsity sports at that time under NCAA rules). As a sophomore in 1961-62, the 6-foot-1 Cullen was a key reserve guard on the Bronco basketball team that posted a 19-6 record. And then came a baseball season that was even better.

Santa Clara had tied for last in the California Intercollegiate Baseball Association in 1961, despite excellent seasons from Fazio and Boccabella. But with Cullen and Garibaldi joining the varsity in 1962, the Broncos took off, winning the conference title and taking the number-one national ranking into the College World Series. Santa Clara reached the championship game before losing a 15-inning epic to the University of Michigan.

Cullen had two hits and drove in three of Santa Clara's four runs in the title game to cap an excellent season. His .365 batting average in conference play led the CIBA—a league that included Southern California, Stanford, UCLA, and Cal Berkeley—and he led the Broncos in triples. He was named to both the all-CIBA and all-NCAA District 8 (Pacific Coast) teams.

Cullen's sophomore year was notable aside from sports as well. He met Lindy Frisbie, a freshman from Seattle who was part of the first class of female students at the previously all-male Santa Clara. Tim and Lindy were still together as this was written more than 50 years later.

As a junior Cullen averaged 10 points a game as a starting guard for the basketball team. The Broncos went into the final game of the season March 9, 1963, at the University of San Francisco tied with USF for the West Coast Athletic Conference lead. With the conference championship and an NCAA tournament berth on the line, Santa Clara lost by one point. The next afternoon Cullen was back at USF—this time with the baseball team for a game against the Dons.

Cullen played in summer baseball leagues after each of his first three seasons at Santa Clara, thanks to Broncos coach John "Paddy" Cottrell, who used connections he had made as a scout prior to coaching at Santa Clara. In 1961 Cullen, along with Fazio and Boccabella, played for the Saskatoon Commodores, champion of the Western Canada League; all three were named to the league all-star team.[3] On July 26, in a tournament game at Lacombe, Alberta, Cullen hit grand slams in consecutive innings.[4] In 1962 he played for a team in Everett, Washington, along with future major-league pitchers Jim Lonborg and Wally Bunker.[5] In 1963 Cullen returned to the Western Canada League, this time with the Calgary Giants, and led the loop in batting average (.365), home runs (19), RBIs (62), and doubles (19) in a 70-game season.[6]

In his senior year Cullen stopped playing basketball. Dick Garibaldi had taken over as the varsity head coach the year before, when Bob Feerick left Santa Clara to coach the NBA's San Francisco Warriors. "We didn't get along very well," Cullen said with a chuckle, talking about Garibaldi. "He had too much information about what I used to do in my off time from when I roomed with his brother." Able to be with the baseball team from the start of the season for the first time, Cullen was named second-team All-America at third base by the American Association of College Baseball Coaches. After he received his degree in business he signed with the Boston Red Sox and scouts Bobby Doerr and Glenn Wright for a $15,000 bonus. "First thing I did was buy a car," Cullen said, shaking his head. "Stupid."

He continued: "Almost every club in the big leagues came through my house. My dad was kind of my agent, and we just set up shop at home in Burlingame. Houston came in late and offered me double the money, but that wasn't the biggest concern. I decided I wanted to start at Triple-A; I didn't want to go to the lower minors and get lost. Boston was the only team that would agree to that. People thought I signed with Boston because their Triple-A team was in Seattle and that was where my girlfriend was from, but that wasn't it. I just wanted to start at Triple-A, anywhere.

"I flew to Seattle and went right to the ballpark to join the team. Wilbur Wood came over and said, 'Hey, rookie, how ya doin', shook my hand and he had a big wad of tobacco in it."

Cullen finished the season as the Rainiers' third baseman, batting .254. His former summer-league teammate Jim Lonborg (who had been a college opponent at Stanford) was also with the Rainiers, and they roomed together at a downtown hotel. After the season Cullen married Lindy in Seattle, on September 19, with Lonborg as one of the groomsmen.

Under the rules of the time, first-year professional players had to be protected on the major-league team's 40-man roster or else be made available to the other teams in the majors for just $8,000. The Red Sox didn't protect Cullen, and the Washington Senators snapped him up in the first-year-player draft.

"I was unhappy, but Lindy was ecstatic, because their Triple-A team was in Hawaii and that's where I was going to go," Cullen said. "We would go to the beach every day. I'd be exhausted when I got to the ballpark and I hit .221."

Cullen was the everyday shortstop at Hawaii in 1965, and when he returned there the next year his batting average perked up to .295. He also picked up a nickname, "The Worm," which he said he earned when he dirtied a new uniform while groveling in the dirt for a groundball.[7]

The call to the big leagues came in August 1966, and Cullen made his debut with the Senators on August 8, striking out as a pinch-hitter against Detroit veteran Johnny Podres. His first start came on August 14, at third base, and his first hit came two days later off Cleveland's Gary Bell. Then on September 4, he made his first appearance at second base, a position he had never played in high school, college, or the minors.

"Gil Hodges was the manager. When I joined the team he called me into his office and said, 'You ever played second base?' Of course I said, 'Heck, yeah, all my life!' I wound up playing most of my career at second base, but I learned in the big leagues."

The highlight of Cullen's 1966 season came on September 25, when he got four hits and scored four runs in a doubleheader sweep of the White Sox on the same day his first child, daughter Anna, was born.[8] He also played the night his second child, Tim, was born, September 3, 1968, after staying up until 3:30 a.m. for the delivery. He got a pinch-hit two-run single to give the Senators a 2-1 win over the White Sox.[9] (No paternity leave for ballplayers in those days.)

Cullen was named to the Topps All-Star Rookie Team in 1967 as a shortstop. He started 64 games there, plus 34 at second base and 12 at third, and batted .236 (exactly the league average). But in February 1968 he was traded to the White Sox as part of a package for shortstop Ron Hansen. Hansen was expendable because the White Sox had just acquired Luis Aparicio to play shortstop, and Cullen was expected to take over at second. Cullen was excited about the prospect of going to a team that had been in the pennant race until the final days of the 1967 season.

The White Sox were managed by Eddie Stanky, a former major-league second baseman to whom Cullen had been compared as a player by *Washington Post* writer George Minot, Jr.[10] "Eddie Stanky really liked me," Cullen remembered. "I was a spark-plug type of guy. But it just didn't work out. We lost the first ten games and Stanky got fired just before the All-Star break."

Cullen made history of a sort on May 26, 1968, when he started at second base and batted ninth in a game at Yankee Stadium. Stanky put pitcher Gary Peters in the sixth spot in the lineup in an effort to shake up the White Sox offense. It didn't work, as Chicago lost 5-1, but Cullen was the last nonpitcher to be in the lineup batting ninth in an American League game prior to the adoption of the designated hitter.

The White Sox wound up trading Cullen back to Washington on August 2—for Hansen, neither player having had a very good season with his new team (Cullen was batting .200 at that point, Hansen .185). Al Lopez had succeeded Stanky as Chicago manager,

and Hansen had been his shortstop from 1963-65 when he previously managed the Sox.

Cullen recounted the day of the trade: "The White Sox were playing the Senators that night, in Milwaukee [where the Sox hosted a number of games during the 1968 and 1969 seasons]. Ed Short, the Sox general manager, called me at home in the morning and told me I'd been traded back to Washington. I was happy about that, and we chatted for a while, then I asked him, 'How am I getting to Milwaukee?' He said, 'I didn't think about that.'

"He called me back and said, 'We're not going to announce this trade until before the game, so don't say anything.' So I rode up to Milwaukee on the bus with the White Sox! I used to like to have a little fun, so I made sure I sat next to Tommy John, who was starting that game, and I said to him, 'Let's go through the hitters. How are you going to pitch this guy, and that guy, and Frank Howard. …' We did that all the time anyway." Cullen took the results of his interrogation to his new team, and the Senators knocked John out of the box in the fourth inning en route to an 11-6 victory, Cullen delivering a single as the last batter to face John. Cullen got three hits that night and Hansen two.

"When the bus got to County Stadium, I started heading to the first-base clubhouse and I see this guy walking toward me, and it's Ron Hansen. He's got his equipment bag, I've got my equipment bag. I said, 'What do you think about this?' He said, 'I'm happy.' I said, 'So am I!' So we shook hands and said best of luck."

Cullen played at least 119 games for the Senators each season from 1969 through 1971, despite never having a batting average higher than .214 in any of them. But he did a fine job in the field and in 1970 he led American League second basemen with a .994 fielding percentage, making just three errors in 112 games. His fielding percentage was just two-tenths of a point below the then-major-league season record for second basemen, set by Jerry Adair in 1964 (the mark has been topped many times since).[11] In 1971 Cullen started a career high 123 games, 69 at second base, at 54 at shortstop.

After the 1971 season the Senators moved to Texas, and Cullen wore a Texas Rangers uniform … but not in Texas. He was released on March 1, with the Rangers at spring training in Florida. "Cullen is a hell of a fielder," Senators manager Ted Williams told reporters, "but we have to make room for the kids in our organization."[12] Cullen said he thought the release might have been related to his status as the team's union representative; many teams' player reps were traded or released in that era, including Cullen's two predecessors with the Senators, Jim French and Jim Hannan.[13] (His successor, Don Mincher, was traded to Oakland before the season was over.)

Cullen did not have a telephone where he was staying during spring training, so when he learned of his release he went to teammate Paul Lindblad's hotel room to use the phone to start looking for another team to sign with.[14] Lindblad, a former member of the A's, gave Cullen the phone number of A's owner Charles Finley. "Finley was the only guy who would talk to me," Cullen said. "That's one of the reasons he was an outcast, because he was the only guy who would break the unwritten rule about signing player reps. He talked to Dick Williams at their training camp in Arizona and called me back the next day and said, 'There's a plane ticket waiting for you at the Miami airport. You've got an opportunity with us, come on out.'

"Lindy's with me, and our two little kids, we'd driven all the way to Florida, now I've got to tell her I'm getting on a plane and she's got to pack up everything and drive to Arizona. Then when she got there, she went to the ballpark and they told her I was in the hospital with pneumonia. When she found me I thought she was going to punch me, and I wouldn't have blamed her; she had two kids, no place to live, and I'm in the hospital."

Cullen finally made his first appearance in an A's uniform on March 14. He made the Opening Day roster (an Opening Day that was delayed by a brief players' strike, the first ever to affect regular season

play), but two days after the season started the A's acquired pitcher Joe Horlen on waivers, and when Horlen was activated two days later on April 19 the Cullen family was on the move again. "Dick Williams told me they were sending me to Des Moines, Iowa [where the A's had their Triple-A affiliate], and I thought Lindy's going to punch me this time for sure." But Lindy and the kids went to Des Moines with him and the family got an apartment there.

Playing in the minors for the first time in six years, Cullen played shortstop and hit .266 for the Iowa Oaks. "I learned to hit in those few months in the minors," Cullen said. "I concentrated out of terror, and it made me a better hitter."[15]

Dick Green opened the season as the A's second baseman but lasted only a week before a herniated disc that required surgery sent him to the disabled list. Larry Brown moved into the lineup in Green's place, until a similar back injury put him out of action for the rest of the season on June 18. The call went to Cullen, who learned he was heading back to the big leagues with the Oaks on a road trip. "I had mixed emotions," Cullen recalled. "I'm in Indianapolis, Lindy's in Des Moines, and I'm not going back there, I've got to call and tell her she's got a find a way to Oakland."

Cullen rejoined the A's on June 20 and moved right into the lineup, starting 27 of the next 29 games until he too went down with an injury, a pulled hamstring, on July 18. "I took myself out of the game right away and went to the trainer's room. Finley called to ask how I was. I said, 'Charlie, I'll be fine after a couple of days. Don't make a deal, because I'll be back out there real quick.' He said, 'Good, that's the attitude I like. I won't do anything.' Later that night he traded for Ted Kubiak. That really disheartened me."

Cullen was back in the starting lineup for 11 straight games from August 5-14 until Green returned to action, then Cullen started just five more games the rest of the season. He saw frequent action, though, as manager Williams regularly pinch-hit for his second basemen, with Green, Kubiak, and Dal Maxvill also part of the rotation. Two hits in his final game of the season lifted Cullen's batting average to a career-high .261.

During the 1972 American League Championship Series, Cullen came off the bench to make brief appearances in the two games the A's lost to Detroit, both times playing shortstop as Bert Campaneris had been suspended for throwing his bat at Tigers pitcher Lerrin LaGrow in Game Two. Cullen was one of two A's, along with Maxvill, who was eligible but did not play in the World Series against Cincinnati.

Cullen received $15,528.76 as his share of the A's postseason pot, a three-quarters share reflecting the fact that he had not been with the team all season.[16] That check helped him make the decision to walk away from the game at age 30. He had begun laying the groundwork for his career after baseball soon after he got out of college, working in the offseason learning how to trade stocks for the Walston & Co. brokerage company in San Francisco. While playing for the Senators he trained at Walston's New York office and became a licensed stockbroker.

"I had a meeting with Finley and I said, 'I've had a pretty rough year. I'd like to settle down somewhere, this is my home town. What are your plans?' He told me he was working on a trade that I might be part of. I had my broker's license, I was working in San Francisco trading stocks on a part-time basis, I had a job there if I wanted it, I had a check in my hand that would allow me to put down a down payment on a house, and I just thought I couldn't put Lindy through this anymore. I loved the game and I wish I could have played longer, but I just couldn't do it with the family. I had a pretty good career in the securities industry for years, ended up at Morgan Stanley in San Francisco."

Cullen did get back into baseball as part of a group that owned minor-league teams in the 1990s. He ran the team in Greensboro, North Carolina, in 1993 (a team that featured Derek Jeter and Mariano Rivera), then went to Madison, Wisconsin, in 1994 before deciding to return to California. Later he was vice president of a group that bought the Tucson franchise

in the Pacific Coast League, moved it to Fresno in 1998, and built a ballpark there, but after a few years in Fresno Cullen retired and moved back to the Bay Area. As of 2014, he and Lindy lived in Benicia, about 40 miles northeast of San Francisco, and he kept active by playing golf several times a week. His two children also were in the Bay Area, and his grandson was a freshman in high school who "loves baseball," according to his grandfather.

Tim Cullen finished his major-league career with a .220 batting average and 9 home runs in 700 games, a World Series ring, and many friends. "The Worm had next to no tools," his Senators teammate Frank Howard said. "But everybody admired him."[17]

Thanks

Unless otherwise indicated, quotes from Tim Cullen are taken from an in-person interview December 31, 2013, in Benicia, California. Thanks to Joey Karp, associate director of media relations for the Santa Clara University athletics department, for providing team media guides from when Tim Cullen was on campus there. Thanks to Erin Louthen, Santa Clara University archivist, for directing me to where the school's yearbooks are available online (scholarcommons.scu.edu/handle/11123/178). Some information about Cullen's college experience came from the Official Collegiate Baseball and Basketball Guides of 1962-65 published by the National Collegiate Athletic Bureau.

NOTES

1 serrahs.com/page.cfm?p=2542.

2 Morrey Rokeach, "Lefty Howie Kitt Sets Whiff Mark in Hearst Classic," *The Sporting News*, August 31, 1960, 26.

3 attheplate.com/wcbl/1961_1.html.

4 "Playoffs Are All-WCBL Affair," *Medicine Hat* (Alberta) *News*, July 27, 1961.

5 attheplate.com/wcbl/1962_1g3.html.

6 attheplate.com/wcbl/1963_2.html.

7 George Minot, Jr., "Cullen Makes Hit With Nats," *Washington Post*, May 21, 1967, D4.

8   Bob Addie, "Nats, Balancing Books for '66, Find Heavy List on Debit Side," *The Sporting News*, October 25, 1966, 19.

9   Merrell Whittlesey, "Lemon Promises New Nat Twist," *The Sporting News*, September 21, 1968, 12.

10 George Minot, Jr., "Cullen Makes Hit With Nats."

11 baseball-reference.com/leaders/fielding_perc_2b_season.shtml.

12 George Minot, Jr., "'Worm' Won't Be Used as Trade Bait," *Washington Post*, March 2, 1972, H3.

13 Ibid.

14 Ron Bergman, "Ranger Cast-Off Cullen Plugs A's Keystone Gap," *The Sporting News*, July 29, 1972.

15 Thomas Boswell, *How Life Imitates The World Series* (New York: Penguin, 1982), 111.

16 "Rich Gravy for A's and Reds in Record Series Pot," *The Sporting News*, November 25, 1972, 45.

17 Thomas Boswell, *How Life Imitates The World Series.*

Dave Duncan

By Paul Hofmann

David Edwin Duncan's ascent to becoming the most respected and successful pitching coach of his generation began in Dallas, Texas. He was born on September 26, 1945, to Clarence Edwin and Evelyn Louise (Rabun) Duncan. Clarence was a Dallas firefighter who operated a small plumbing company on the side, and Evelyn was a homemaker who later became an accountant.[1]

Dave started playing baseball on the sandlots of Dallas. When he wasn't attending school, Duncan was on the field across the street "playing in any pickup game that was going on."[2] His parents divorced when he was 13 years old and in 1960 he moved with his mother and three siblings (he was the second of four children) to San Diego. Evelyn took a job as an accountant with a company in San Diego and Dave attended Crawford High School, where he took an interest in drafting classes and starred as a standout player for the baseball team. By this time, Duncan had his sights set on a major-league career.[3]

Duncan signed with the Kansas City Athletics in 1963 for a reported $65,000 bonus. After signing, the 17-year old catcher was sent to Los Angeles to join the big-league club for a week before being sent to the Daytona Beach Islanders of the Class A Florida State League. The short stint with the parent club proved fortuitous. It was on his very first day in professional baseball with the A's in Los Angeles that he met Tony LaRussa, a fellow A's bonus baby, who was with the parent club under the same rules that would keep Duncan on the roster in 1964.[4] The two established a friendship that later evolved into what proved to be one of the longest manager-pitching coach relationships in baseball history. Over the years LaRussa often credited Duncan as being a key factor in the success of the teams he managed over a period of 30 years.

After his one-week stint with the parent club, Duncan reported to Daytona Beach. Despite hitting a homer

in his first professional at-bat for the Islanders, he struggled the remainder of the season and finished with a .145 average with only four home runs in 47 games. His performance at Daytona Beach did little to cool the A's on Duncan as a big-league prospect and in an effort to protect him from draft rules governing the signing of bonus babies, the A's carried Duncan on the roster for the entire 1964 season. As an 18-year-old prospect, the youngest player in the American League that year, Duncan played in only 25 games with the Athletics. However, the A's gave him a long look in late September and early October, when he played in 13 of the team's final 17 contests. He finished the year with a .170 batting average, with one home run and 5 RBIs. He did not appear in another major-league game until June 9, 1967.

Duncan's minor-league maturation began in earnest in 1965 when he was assigned to the Lewiston Broncs of the Class A Northwest League. There he joined future Athletics John "Blue Moon" Odom, Chuck Dobson, and Rick Monday, the 1965 number-one overall draft choice. Duncan appeared in 55 games, 51 behind the plate, and compiled a .277 average with nine home runs before being promoted to the Birmingham Barons of the Double-A Southern League, where he appeared in 61 games. Despite hitting six home runs and driving in 20 runs, Duncan struggled hitting for average. In 192 at-bats he managed a .208 batting average, 19 points below the league average, in the pitching-rich Southern League. His call-up to Birmingham in 1965 was the first time he became a teammate of Tony LaRussa's.

Like many other professional baseball players during the Vietnam War, Duncan enlisted in the Marine Reserve. After the 1965 season he spent an initial 30-day stint in the Marines and was subsequently required to serve two days per month and two weeks per year of activity duty.[5] This typically occurred during midsummer and required the A's to use a backup catcher or call up another catcher. or carry an additional receiver on the roster. Reflecting on how his military service affected his career Duncan said, "It didn't help any and in 1972 it cost me my job."[6]

Duncan spent the entire 1966 season at Class A Modesto of the California League. Joining future A's All-Stars Reggie Jackson, Joe Rudi, and Rollie Fingers on a star-studded roster, it was Duncan who shined brightest at the plate as he led the league with 46 home runs and improved his batting average to .271. His performance, coupled with a lack of depth at the catching position, put Duncan on the fast track for a return to Kansas City.

The 1967 season saw Duncan split time between Double-A Birmingham and the parent club. He started the season with the Barons and was called up to the Athletics in early June. After getting off to a torrid start in his first three games with the Athletics (he batted .417 with 2 home runs and 5 RBIs), Duncan quickly cooled off. In his next 18 games he hit only

.140 with one homer and three RBIs before being sent back to Birmingham, where he finished the year with a .241 average, 13 home runs, and 48 RBIs before earning a September call-up to the A's. His third stint with the big-league club was similar to his first two. While he exhibited the ability to hit for power, he continued to hit below .200 and finished his season hitting .188 with 5 home runs and 11 RBIs.

Duncan started the 1968 season with the Vancouver Mounties of the Triple-A Pacific Coast League. In 35 games he batted .313 with 6 homers and 21 RBIs before earning another call-up to Oakland. He appeared in 82 games, 79 behind the plate, with the Athletics. Although he continued to demonstrate that he could hit for power — he belted seven home runs — he continued to struggle to hit for average. In 247 at-bats, Duncan raised his average above .200 for a few brief days in June and July and one day in September before finishing the season at .191.

The Athletics broke camp in 1969 with Duncan and Phil Roof slated to handle the bulk of the catching duties. Duncan started the season opener and started the majority of the games in April, but again failed to hit for average. He was mired in a season-long slump and his average stood at .094 as late as September 8. He finished the season at .126 with 3 home runs and 22 RBIs. His lack of offensive production, in part, kept the Athletics unsettled at the catcher position. In addition to Duncan and Roof, the A's used Larry Haney, Gene Tenace, and Jim Pagliaroni behind the plate during the 1969 season.

In 1970 Duncan had a breakout season — for him — offensively. He split the catching duties with Frank Fernandez, with a little help from Gene Tenace. Duncan finished the season with a career-high .259 with 10 home runs and 29 RBIs and appeared well positioned to become the A's top receiver for 1971 — at least until Duncan, one of the more outspoken A's, publicly spoke out against Finley's handling of the team. After the 1970 season, Duncan assigned responsibility for the team's failure to win the American League West to A's owner Charles Finley. Duncan felt the A's didn't win the division title because the atmosphere created by Finley didn't foster cohesiveness among the team. Duncan felt, "There's no spirit, no feeling of harmony. We should be close like a family, but it's not here."[7]

Despite being outhit by fellow catching candidate Gene Tenace during spring training, Duncan started the 1971 season as the A's number-one receiver. While the first half of the 1971 season was not his greatest stretch offensively, Duncan's 11 home runs and 27 RBIs, coupled with his defense, were enough to earn him a berth on the 1971 American League All-Star team along with fellow A's Reggie Jackson and Vida Blue. Duncan did not played in the game (held in Detroit) and was never named to another All-Star team. Dave picked up his average in the second half of the season and finished 1971 with a .253 average, 15 home runs, and 40 RBIs.

Duncan's first taste of postseason play came in the 1971 American League Championship Series, against the Baltimore Orioles. In Game One, he went 2-for-3 with a second-inning double that scored Angel Mangual and staked the A's to a 2-0 lead. Duncan was sacrificed to third before being thrown out at home on a failed suicide squeeze attempt by Vida Blue. In Game Two, Duncan drove in Sal Bando with a fourth-inning single to center for the A's lone run. For the Series Duncan finished 3-for-6 with two RBIs.

The Athletics broke spring training in 1972 with an eye on a World Series title and with Duncan as the team's everyday backstop. Although his batting averaged dipped to .218, he contributed 19 home runs and 59 RBIs, both career highs. On July 12 he registered the only five-hit game of his career when he collected four singles and a homer against the visiting Boston Red Sox. But during his 1972 stint in the Marines Duncan lost his starting job to fellow catcher and first baseman Gene Tenace when the A's were looking for additional run production.[8] In the postseason he played in five games, collecting a pinch-hit single in the bottom of the ninth of Game Five of the World Series against Cincinnati. Gene Tenace, for his part, caught fire and was named World Series MVP. Duncan

ranked catching Game Seven of the 1972 World Series as his most memorable moment in baseball.[9]

In the spring of 1973, Charlie Finley offered Duncan a contract for $40,000 for the coming season. Dissatisfied with the offer, Dave decided to hold out. The salary dispute was just one of a series of disagreements Duncan had with Finley. In reflecting on his negotiations with Finley, Duncan had less than fond memories; he simply stated he had "personal" differences with Finley.[10] Bruce Markusen shed some light on the origins of these differences in *Baseball's Last Dynasty: Charlie Finley's Oakland A's*: "That's the one area where I might have a little bit of resentment," the book quoted Duncan as saying, "because negotiations of those contracts was always very difficult." In the pre-free-agent era at that time, "you had no alternative to sign the contracts they were offering. (Finley) certainly wasn't going to do you any favors when it came to contracts. He was pretty difficult that way."[11]

Finley, for his part, was known for not giving in easily and carrying grudges. On March 24, 1973, he sent Duncan to the Cleveland Indians, along with young outfielder George Hendrick, in exchange for former All-Star catcher Ray Fosse and utility infielder Jack Heidemann. Duncan's relationship with Finley was over.

Duncan's trade to the Indians was life-changing in more ways than one. During his first spring training with the Indians, in Tucson, Dave met Jeanine Grove. They married in Cleveland in 1974 and had two sons, both of whom played in the majors.[12] David Shelley Duncan was born in 1979 and played parts of seven major-league seasons with the Yankees, Indians, and Rays as an outfielder, first baseman, and designated hitter. Chris Duncan, born in 1981, spent five seasons as an outfielder and first baseman with the St. Louis Cardinals, and became a sports personality for ESPN radio in St. Louis.

In his initial season with the Indians, Duncan was the number-one catcher and was backed up by John Ellis. However, Duncan missed two months of the season with a broken wrist and played in only 95 games. He hit .233 with 17 home runs and 43 RBIs. The next season he played in a career-high 136 games with the Indians, 134 behind the plate, and finished with a .200 batting average, 16 home runs, and 46 RBIs. His .976 fielding percentage for the 1974 season was the fourth-worst (as of 2013) in the major leagues since 1946 among catchers who played in 125 games or more.[13]

During spring training 1975, the Indians dealt Duncan along with the Indians' 1969 first-round draft pick, outfielder Al McGrew, to the Baltimore Orioles for pitcher Don Hood and aging first baseman/designated hitter Boog Powell. Powell went on to enjoy his last big year in a major-league uniform while Duncan spent two relatively uneventful years with the Orioles. He spent the entire 1975 season hovering around the .200 mark and finished at .205 with 12 home runs and 41 RBIs. In 1976, he hit .204 with four home runs and 17 RBIs.

On November 18, 1976, Duncan was traded by the Orioles to the Chicago White Sox in return for former All-Star outfielder Pat Kelly. The trade turned out to be decisively in favor of the Orioles. Kelly played four seasons with the Orioles while Duncan was released at the end of spring training in 1977. At the age of 31, he had played his last major-league game.

In an 11-year major-league career, Duncan appeared in 929 games. Though widely regarded as a light-hitting catcher, a reputation based on his .214 career batting average, Duncan possessed good power. He hit 109 home runs in 2,885 at-bats, one for every 26.5 at-bats—a ratio better than those of Hall of Famers Carl Yastrzemski, Cal Ripken, and George Brett, names rarely associated with the light-hitting category.

Despite his relatively modest numbers at the plate, Duncan was widely regarded as one of the best defensive catchers in the game. He was known as a catcher with a deep knowledge of the game, a strong throwing arm, and the ability to handle a pitching staff. Although his .984 fielding percentage was slightly below the league average of .986 for the same 11-year period covering his career, he was widely considered one of the better defensive catchers of his generation.

His baseball career behind him, Duncan began looking for opportunities outside of the game. In 1977 he started a baseball novelties company with former A's teammate Ed Sprague, Sr.[14] The company was not successful and Duncan soon found himself looking for work back in baseball. He began his coaching career in 1978 with the Cleveland Indians. He served as the Tribe's bullpen coach in 1978 and 1979 under manager Jeff Torborg and later Dave Garcia before becoming the team's pitching coach for the 1980 and 1981 seasons. In 1981, Duncan's second season as pitching coach, the combined ERA of the Indians' pitching staff dropped from 4.68 the previous season to 3.88.

In 1982 Duncan became the pitching coach of the Seattle Mariners, a franchise in just its sixth year in existence. He had an immediate impact on the pitching staff. The Mariners' staff ERA dropped from 4.23 the previous year to 3.88; the pitchers led the American League in strikeouts, and finished second in saves and shutouts. The staff's relief pitchers saw an even more dramatic improvement as the bullpen's ERA fell from 4.26 in 1981 to 3.31. In three short years, Duncan had established a reputation as one of the best up-and-coming pitching coaches in the majors.

After the 1982 season, Duncan bumped into old friend and former teammate Tony LaRussa at Seattle's Swannies Comedy Underground nightclub during a roast of then-Mariners manager Rene Lachemann.[15] At the comedy club, LaRussa, then the manager of the White Sox, and Duncan discussed the pitching coach's future. Duncan shared with LaRussa that he was seeking a $5,000 raise and hoped to make $35,000 for the coming season. The Mariners, however, were unwilling to meet his salary demands. The next day, LaRussa approached Lachemann to ask permission to pursue Duncan. Soon after, Duncan left the Mariners to join LaRussa as the White Sox pitching coach at $50,000. It was the start of a close baseball partnership that spanned the next 30 years.

As with his stints with the Indians and Mariners, Duncan's presence brought immediate results to a White Sox pitching staff that featured a rotation of LaMarr Hoyt, Rich Dotson, Floyd Bannister, Britt

Burns, and Jerry Koosman, and a strong bullpen by committee. The White Sox staff led the team to the American League West title and finished first in fewest walks allowed, second in saves, third in team ERA, and third in total strikeouts. With the team slumping early in the 1986 season, LaRussa and Duncan were fired by White Sox vice president Ken Harrelson.[16] Less than three weeks later, the two were hired by the Oakland A's.

Less than two years after the duo's arrival in Oakland, the A's made the first of three consecutive World Series appearances. While this was largely due to the offensive power supplied by Jose Canseco and Mark McGwire, the effect of the A's new pitching coach on Dave Stewart can't be underestimated. Prior to the 1986 season, Stewart had won only 30 games over parts of seven major-league seasons and was on the path to being a career journeyman. However, his midseason acquisition by the A's and his relationship with Duncan transformed his career. Stewart posted four consecutive 20-win campaigns in 1987-1990, notching 84 victories over that time period. Somewhat humbly, Duncan attributed Stewart's success to his hard work and willingness to be coached.[17] From 1988 through 1990, his Oakland pitchers had the lowest ERA in the American League

After the 1995 season, both LaRussa and Duncan left the A's to assume their respective positions as manager and pitching coach for the St. Louis Cardinals. The success of the Cardinals during the LaRussa-Duncan years is well documented: NL Central Division titles in 1996, 2000, 2001, and 2002, and World Series titles in 2006 and 2011. Looking back on his years with the Cardinals, Duncan fondly recalled the performance of Woody Williams. Williams, who was acquired in midseason 2001, compiled a 45-22 record with 3.53 ERA over 3½ seasons with the Cardinals under the tutelage of Duncan, far better than the seven games below .500 record he compiled over the other 11½ seasons of his major-league career. True to form, Duncan credited the transformation to Williams himself.

Duncan is credited with having coached four Cy Young Award winners: LaMarr Hoyt (Chicago White Sox) in 1983, Bob Welch (Oakland A's) in 1990, Dennis Eckersley (Oakland A's) in 1992, and Chris Carpenter (St. Louis Cardinals) in 2005. However, in many ways Duncan revolutionized the role of a pitching coach. As part of his duties, he maintained records on every opposing hitter. His files indicated the type of pitch each batter hit, the location of the pitch, and the description of where the batter hit the ball. While many experts attributed his success to his innovative methods, Duncan himself ascribed his achievements as a pitching coach to his ability to deal with a wide range of personalities and approaches to the game. As a catcher he learned early on that differences in personality often required different approaches to the game. Armed with this knowledge, Duncan was able to get the most out of his pitchers.

Andy Benes' tale of a Duncan visit to the mound in a bases-loaded, no-out situation illustrated Duncan's uncanny ability to refocus his pitchers. Benes recalled, "(Duncan) comes out and the first thing he says is, 'OK, what is the worst thing that can happen if you get the next three guys out?' I said, 'Well, they could score two runs.' He said, 'Two runs aren't going to beat you.'"[18]

Duncan continued to serve as pitching coach of the St. Louis Cardinals until the end of the 2011 season. In January 2012 he took an indeterminate leave from the team to spend time with his wife, Jeanine, who had been diagnosed with glioblastoma multiforme, a rare form of cancer. Jeanine died on June 6, 2013, at the family's home in Kimberling, Missouri.

True to his nickname during his playing days, the Silent Assassin, Dave Duncan remained a very private man who didn't talk about himself a great deal. As of 2014 he was in semiretirement, serving as a pitching consultant for the Arizona Diamondbacks.[19] Asked to reflect on his baseball career, the private Duncan summarized his experience by thankfully stating, "I've been very fortunate to be employed in a field for as long as I have."[20] He said his hope was to continue working in baseball on a part-time basis for as long as he continued to enjoy it.[21]

SOURCES

Markusen, Bruce, *Baseball's Last Dynasty: Charlie Finley's Oakland A's* (Indianapolis: Masters Press, 1998).

Society for American Baseball Research, *The SABR Baseball List & Record Book*. (New York: Scribner, 2007).

DiMeglio, Steve, "LaRussa, Duncan still a team as baseball evolves around them," *USA Today*, May 5, 2006. Retrieved from usatoday30.usatoday.com/sports/bbw/2006-05-10-cover-larussa-duncan_x.htm

McNeal, Stan, "Best Pitching Coach," *The Sporting News*, January 18, 2010, 234(2), 33.

Jeanine C. Duncan (July 23, 1948-June 6, 2013) obituary. Retrieved from greenlawnfuneralhome.com/fh/obituaries/obituary.cfm?o_id=2114115&fh_id=12076

"White Sox Fire LaRussa and Pitching Coach," *Los Angeles Times*, June 21, 1986. Retrieved from articles.latimes.com/1986-06-21/sports/sp-19683_1_white-sox.

Baseballlibrary.com/ballplayers/player.php?name=Dave_Duncan_1945

Baseball-reference.com.

Personal correspondence with Dave Duncan, February 24 and March 5, 2015.

NOTES

1 Personal correspondence with Dave Duncan, March 5, 2014.

2 Personal correspondence with Dave Duncan, February 24, 2014.

3 Personal correspondence with Dave Duncan, February 24, 2014.

4 Personal correspondence with Dave Duncan, February 24, 2014.

5 Personal correspondence with Dave Duncan, March 5, 2014.

6 Personal correspondence with Dave Duncan, February 24, 2014.

7 Bruce Markusen, *Baseball's Last Dynasty: Charlie Finley's Oakland A's*, 2.

8 Personal correspondence with Dave Duncan, February 24, 2014.

9 Personal correspondence with Dave Duncan, February 24, 2014.

10 Personal correspondence with Dave Duncan, February 24, 2014.

11 Markusen, 190.

12 Personal correspondence with Dave Duncan, March 5, 2014.

13 *The SABR Baseball List & Record Book*.

14 Personal correspondence with Dave Duncan, February 24, 2014.

15 Steve DiMeglio, "LaRussa, Duncan still a team as baseball evolves around them," *USA Today*, May 5, 2006.

16 "White Sox Fire LaRussa and Pitching Coach," *Los Angeles Times*, June 21, 1986.

17 Personal correspondence with Dave Duncan, February 24, 2014.

18 Stan McNeal, "Best Pitching Coach," *The Sporting News*, January 18, 2010, 33.

19 Dave Duncan (baseball).

20 Personal correspondence with Dave Duncan, February 24, 2014.

21 Personal correspondence with Dave Duncan, Febraury 24, 2014.

Mike Epstein

By Ted Leavengood

Sports writer Phil Jackman once called Mike Epstein "Babe the Blue Ox with brains."[1] The name did not stick, but it was an apt description of the brawny man's prodigious power and academic bent, traits that Epstein carried throughout a baseball career that featured nine seasons in the major leagues.

Michael Peter Epstein was born on April 4, 1943 in the Bronx, New York. His parents, Jack and Evelyn, moved the family to Hartsdale, New York, in Westchester County to provide better educational opportunities for Mike and his two sisters, Linda and Carole. Mike's uncle Irving took him to watch the Yankees play and was the first to start Mike dreaming of playing big-league baseball.

Opportunity came knocking for Jack Epstein in 1957 when he opened a new office for his company in Los Angeles. Epstein remembered the two-week drive across the country to his new life, and the palm trees that greeted them as they entered the city. The California sunshine provided Mike his first chance to play sports all year long.

Epstein played ball at La Cienega Park, near his house, and honed skills that led him to a productive career at Fairfax High School, where he starred in all sports. His high-school football team won only two games in three years, but Epstein excelled. He played fullback on offense, also played on defense and was "in on 90 percent of the tackles."[2]

He was a pitcher on the baseball team, coached by Frank Schaffer, who had mentored big leaguers Larry and Norm Sherry, Chuck Essegian, and Barry Latman. In Epstein's sophomore year his arm gave out and instead of a bonus to pitch in the big leagues, it was football that provided a lucrative scholarship for him at the University of California at Berkeley.

He had great success on the gridiron at Berkeley, playing for future NFL coach Marv Levy. As a sophomore running back, Epstein was the number-two ground gainer in a backfield that included future All-American and NFL quarterback Craig Morton. At that juncture in his career Epstein believed firmly that playing with Morton, "we would both make All-American before we were through."[3]

A chance occurrence led Epstein back to baseball. Walking back from spring football practice, he and other football players made their way past the baseball field, where the freshman team was warming up. Their coach, Al Mathews, needled them about the average football player's lack of real athletic talent. "Not one of them has the athleticism to hit a baseball," he said loudly.[4]

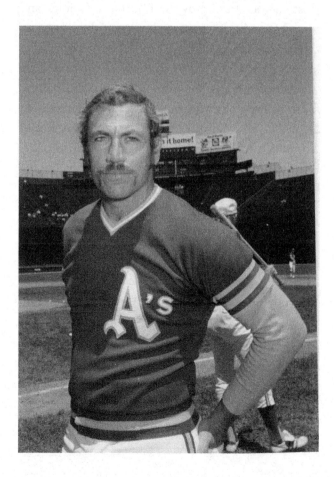

Epstein yelled back that he could hit anything the coach could throw. Mathews took him up on the notion, and though Epstein struggled to make contact initially, he finally started to drive one ball after another over the fence. Varsity coach George Wolfman was handed his star player for that season and the next.

The next fall Epstein quit football and focused on baseball, fearing the gridiron was only a chance for injury. During his junior season Epstein became a college all-star, hitting .384. He had only five home runs, but in a stadium where it was 420 feet to the right-field wall, which stood 80 feet high.

Epstein played in 20 games for the US team in the 1964 Tokyo Olympics. The team was coached by the legendary Southern Cal coach Rod Dedeaux. Epstein led the team in hitting. He credited Dedeaux and the other instructors he had in his collegiate career with making him into an All-American slugger in a relatively short period. But his greatest experience learning from the best was yet to come.

Epstein was drafted by the Baltimore Orioles and signed for a bonus estimated at more than $20,000. Orioles general manager Harry Dalton said, "He's a kid who could hit 50 home runs." Epstein's work ethic was one of two attributes that impressed those in his first spring-training camp with the Orioles. "As Emerson said, 'Nothing great was ever achieved without enthusiasm,'" Mike said. His desire to quote literary figures earned Epstein a new nickname, Egghead.[5]

Epstein quickly converted his college success into an all-star minor-league career. He was assigned to Stockton, in the Class A California League. Batting .338 with 30 home runs, he was voted the Most Valuable Player in the league. His 30 homers tied a league record set by Vince DiMaggio.

At Stockton the nickname "Superjew" first surfaced. The term could have a pejorative connotation, but Epstein warmed to the sobriquet when Rocky Bridges applied it for the first time after Epstein hit a prodigious home run. When asked whether it was spelled

as one word or two, Epstein replied, "Well, you spell Superman with one word."[6]

Epstein's manager at Stockton, Harry Malmberg, was the first to raise questions about his finesse with the glove, saying his slugging first baseman needed to "improve around first base, especially on pop flies."[7] Years later Epstein admitted that his eyesight was never good enough to follow a pop fly, especially during night games.

The next season was no less successful as the Orioles jumped Epstein to Triple-A Rochester. He started the season slowly but made quick progress in May, hitting .456 for the month with six home runs in a nine-game stretch. He credited his sudden surge to adjusting his stance. He was quick to credit others with coaching tips, including manager Earl Weaver and former Cleveland Indians and Negro League star Luke Easter, who was serving in public relations for the Red Wings after a stint as hitting coach. Joe Altobelli, a longtime coach and manager in the Orioles' and other teams' organizations, was another who offered wisdom, telling Epstein, "Always be content, but never satisfied."[8]

Epstein was working hard on his fielding as well, and in one article was described as an agile fielder. "The harder you work, the more breaks come your way," he quoted Branch Rickey as saying.[9] He was also making strides in his personal life. He married Barbara Gluskin while playing for Rochester. The two had met in Stockton, where her father was the president of the synagogue that Epstein attended briefly. Epstein brought his bride back to Rochester where she began her career as a baseball wife, one that has lasted for 47 years as of 2013.

Epstein was named International League Player of the Month in June 1966. Writers noted his major-league potential, but added that he was blocked effectively by Boog Powell, who was well-established as the slugging first baseman for the Orioles. By the end of the 1966 season Epstein had a .309 batting average, 29 home runs, and 102 RBIs. The numbers earned him recognition by *The Sporting News* as the

Minor League Player of the Year, as well as a September call-up to the Orioles.

With Powell firmly entrenched at first base for the Orioles, rumors surfaced that the Orioles might trade Epstein. Speculation centered on a possible trade to the New York Yankees for Mel Stottlemyre. The trade never happened. Epstein went to the instructional league after the season to learn to play the outfield. But in spring training in 1967, it was evidence that despite his effort, no amount of hard work was able to make Epstein into an outfielder. His trouble judging fly balls around the first-base bag was warning enough that he was not a good fit chasing them full time in the outfield.

Epstein believed, however, that all the minor-league success and hard work had earned him a shot at the majors. Shortly after the 1967 season began, the Orioles decided to send Epstein to Rochester again and he bristled at the news. Rather than report, he and his wife went to New York, where they stayed with Epstein's grandmother.[10]

General manager Dalton tried to lure Epstein back. Epstein asserted that Dalton had promised him a trade if he failed to make the big-league roster. In late May Baltimore sent Epstein and pitcher Frank Bertaina to Washington for Senators pitcher Pete Richert.

Washington manager Gil Hodges made Epstein the everyday first baseman and Epstein had some initial success, hitting a grand slam against the Orioles. But he was unable to hit with consistency, managing only a .226 batting average with nine home runs in 297 at-bats. (He did set a fielding record, getting 32 putouts in a 22-inning game against the Chicago White Sox.)

The next season started with the same disappointing production and in May the Senators sent Epstein to Buffalo, their Triple-A affiliate. Epstein acknowledged that this demotion was "an entirely different set of circumstances" than the prior year when he had refused to report to Rochester.[11] He showed that there was nothing left for him to learn in the International

League, hitting .400 with five home runs in 11 games. When he came back in June he had only slightly better results than in his rookie season. He hit only 13 home runs for the year and his .234 batting average was well off the minor-league figures that had made him such a "can't-miss" prospect.

Epstein's career took a fortunate turn in 1969 when Ted Williams became the Senators' manager. He proved the best of all the instructors Epstein worked with. Mike became Williams's special project. Beginning in 1969 spring training, Williams subtly remade Epstein's approach at the plate.

Williams knew the importance of Epstein to the Senators' offense and said of him, "Epstein has the tools. He should be a great hitter."[12] Cutting through all the theories about how Epstein could make the most of his talents, Williams told him to go back to the swing that had made him Minor League Player of the Year. He suggested that Epstein shorten his swing, saying, "Why the big swing? With his power, if he connects, it's gone."[13] Citation needed As he did with all of the Senators' hitters, Williams preached to Epstein the need to be more selective at the plate. Epstein recalled the constant refrain from the dugout to the Senators as they came to the plate: "Come on, Bush, get a good pitch to hit."[14] Like the rest of the Senators, Epstein learned to swing at strikes and make the most of his opportunities at the plate. His spring tutelage was a resounding success and he started to hit major-league pitching with gusto. By the end of May Epstein was batting .267 and he had a dozen home runs.

One game in Chicago was especially sweet for Epstein. The Senators were playing in Comiskey Park for the first time under Williams, who told Epstein it was the toughest park for him to hit home runs in. Meanwhile Williams told reporters that Epstein was going to be a slugger who would "hit 40 home runs some day." Encouraged by his manager's confidence, Epstein hit three home runs that day off Sammy Ellis and Wilbur Wood. Williams was not pleased. Having told Epstein of his own problems hitting home runs in Comiskey Park, he saw the young player as attempting to show him up. Williams refused to speak to Epstein when he returned to the dugout after the final home run and again after the game. But Williams was unaware that the walls had been moved in for the 1969 season, and quickly forgave Epstein. The two remained friends for many years after they were no longer active in baseball.

Much of the friendship was based on the sense of gratitude Epstein had toward Williams for bringing him to life as a power hitter. Epstein had 30 home runs for the year and hit a respectable .278, both career highs. Perhaps most impressive of all was the success he had putting Ted Williams' advice into play about swinging only at strikes. His on-base percentage of .414 was perhaps his most impressive accomplishment, and it was another career mark.

Williams earned Manager of the Year honors from *The Sporting News* for his work with sluggers Frank Howard and Epstein. But Ted was concerned that Epstein could not repeat his 1969 performance and encouraged team owner Bob Short to trade him. During much of the 1969 season, Williams had platooned Epstein and was concerned that he could not handle left-handed pitching. In '69 Epstein hit .259 against lefties while hitting .283 against right-handers. Williams's analysis proved prescient as Epstein fell off as a hitter in 1970 (.256, 20 home runs). Much of the fall-off was due to the fact that he faced left-handed pitching more often, and managed only a .199 batting average against them. The Senators' offense overall was far less successful in Williams's second year.

Bob Short was convinced that Williams had been correct in his assessment of Epstein, and in May of 1971 the Senators traded Mike and relief pitcher Darold Knowles to the Oakland Athletics for three players and an undisclosed amount of cash. (It may have been the money that prompted the trade, as Short needed funds to pay on the borrowed money he had used to purchase the Senators.)

Epstein was back at home in California as an Oakland Athletic and it showed in his immediate performance for his new team. When he was traded, his batting average stood at a meager .247 and he had but a single home run. In his first six weeks in Oakland he batted over .300 and had ten homers and seven doubles. "You take more pride with a first-place club," Epstein said, acknowledging that the atmosphere in Washington had quit being conducive to a player's top performance. Epstein was no longer being platooned. Manager Dick Williams had him hitting against all comers. But the long season wore on Epstein. In July his batting average neared .300, but the August heat wore on him and he failed to hit a homer in the month. His average sank to .243. Tommy Davis began playing first for Oakland against left-handed pitching. By season's end Epstein's batting average was down to pre-Ted Williams levels: .237, with 19 home runs.

In October Epstein saw his first postseason action with Oakland. It was the American League Championship Series against his old team, the Orioles. Although Epstein had found motivation in prior years playing against his old team, his hitting funk now continued. He played in only two games and managed just a single in five at-bats. The Athletics were swept in three games.

The next season Epstein started strong again. He lost weight—30 pounds, according to press accounts—and was more nimble around the first-base bag as a result.[15] In the first half of the season Epstein had 18 home runs and his batting average held just below .300. He hit fifth in the lineup, behind Reggie Jackson and Sal Bando, and provided essential support for the pair who were the heart of the Athletics team. He continued his strong numbers against both right- and left-handed pitching throughout July, and Dick Williams was no longer platooning him. "Mike's a totally different player than he was last year," Williams said.[16] Again Epstein's numbers fell off as the season dragged through the August heat. But he still had one of his best seasons as a hitter. He led the Athletics with 26 home runs, more than either Jackson or Sal Bando. He established himself as an integral piece in the Oakland lineup. He hit .270 and had 70 RBIs.

With a rejuvenated Epstein, the Oakland Athletics were primed for the American League Championship

Series against the Detroit Tigers. The A's defeated the Tigers in five games. Epstein started every contest, even against the tough left-handers Mickey Lolich and Woody Fryman. He had his best games against Lolich, going 2-for-3 against him in the first game and hitting a solo home run in the fourth game that Oakland lost in extra innings.

The Athletics moved on to face Cincinnati's Big Red Machine in the World Series. Oakland won the first two games, but Epstein, batting cleanup, went hitless in both games. In Game Two manager Dick Williams took Epstein out of the game for a pinch-runner in the sixth inning. Epstein had made an error the inning before. Epstein and Williams got into a shouting match on the plane back to Oakland and the fracas made the press.

Oakland won the Series in seven games with Epstein starting at first base in the first six. He remained hitless during the Series and in Game Seven, Williams replaced him with Gene Tenace at first base. It proved to be a deciding factor as Tenace went 2-for-3, knocking in two of victorious Oakland's three runs. Epstein believed that there was lingering ill will, not with manager Williams, but from a locker-room altercation with Reggie Jackson late in the season when the two men came to blows and Reggie missed several games. Owner Charley Finley sided with Jackson. He traded Epstein back to the Senators franchise, which was now in Texas. Finley said that Gene Tenace had lingering shoulder problems that would mean he could play only first base, making Epstein expendable.

Epstein was not pleased by the trade. "What is shocking is that I am going from a good ballclub to a bad ballclub," he said. "I am going from the best ballclub in the world to the worst in the world."[17] Bob Short helped ease the pain for Epstein by giving him a new contract worth $60,000, making him the highest-paid member of the Texas Rangers. There were rumors that Short was trying to trade his expensive new slugger and that Finley wanted him back in Oakland. Whatever options Short may have had, Epstein did not stay long in Texas. He was traded to the California Angels early

in May with his batting average just north of .200 and a single home run to his credit.

In 312 at-bats with California in 1973, Epstein's numbers were the worst in his career. He hit only .209 and the slugger that Ted Williams had predicted would hit 40 home runs in a season managed only nine in 1973. Epstein also did not get along with manager Bobby Winkles, who had managed the Arizona State University team that produced Oakland stars Sal Bando, Reggie Jackson, and Rick Monday, but had trouble adapting to professional athletes who did not have patience for his college approach. But it was more than Winkles. After he started the 1974 season hitting at an even more anemic pace, Epstein was released by the Angels on May 6. He still drew a full year's salary under new rules negotiated by the Major League Players Association.[18]

Epstein said that at this point in his career he was just burned out. He was only 31 years old and players would earn free agency at the end of that year. But Epstein walked away from the game and the pending explosion in salaries. It was several decades before he returned to baseball.

Epstein made a successful transition into the world of business. He turned around a small company that refined and traded precious metals and had less than a million dollars in annual sales. Two years later the firm grossed $25 million.[19] He started his own commodities trading company and had success before selling the business for a profit.

After moving to Colorado Epstein got back into baseball to stay. His son Jake proved to have real baseball talent. Epstein coached a youth team for 11- and 12-year-olds called the Denver Reds that played their way to the National Championship tournament in Atlanta and finished second. Both father and son were hooked.

Epstein moved his family to Orange County in Southern California, where his son could play year-round. Jake's team won three consecutive national championships in the Amateur American Baseball

Congress. Epstein coached the team, that included future major leaguers Eric Chavez, Nick Punto, and Ty Wigginton.

Epstein's success earned him a shot with the Milwaukee Brewers, who made him their minor-league manager in Helena, Montana. But Epstein's theories of hitting learned from Ted Williams went against the grain at a time when the Charley Lau theory of hitting was still popular. Leaving Helena, Epstein established his own hitting school in Southern California in 2000. In 2003 Jake joined the business after playing college ball at the University of Missouri and California State Fullerton. He signed with the Angels but quit after one season to concentrate on a burgeoning family. Jake Epstein was one more believer in the wisdom of Ted Williams, teaching the same approach that his father had learned in 1969.

In 2013 the Epstein School of Hitting was operating in Colorado. It has certified 600 instructors who have taken back to their homes the Ted Williams approach at the plate. It is the best legacy Teddy Ballgame could ever have, helping kids of all ages take their game to the next level. And Mike Epstein said he was proud that he could still keep his old coach in the game.

Epstein has been inducted into the National Jewish Sports Hall of Fame. Summing up, he said his baseball career "was a great ride," adding, "How often can a nice Jewish kid from the Bronx bat fourth on a winning World Series team? I have been truly blessed."[20]

SOURCES

Telephone interviews with Mike Epstein, June 15, 2007, and September 4, 2013.

Leavengood, Ted, *Ted Williams and the 1969 Senators* (Jefferson, North Carolina: McFarland and Company, 2009).

The Sporting News, 1966-1974.

NOTES

1   Phil Jackman, "Orioles Will Be Sitting Pretty If Epstein Cuts It as Flyhawk," *The Sporting News*, March 18, 1967, 7.

2   Doug Brown, "Egghead Epstein: the Slugging Scholar," *The Sporting News*, April 3, 1965, 5.

3   Ibid.

4   Telephone interview with Mike Epstein, July 15, 2007.

5   Brown, "Egghead Epstein."

6   Doug Brown, "Orioles Slugger Epstein: A Bomb Ready to Go Off," *The Sporting News*, November 13, 1965, 22.

7   Ibid.

8   Epstein interview, September 4, 2013.

9   Epstein interview, September 4, 2013.

10 Doug Brown, "Epstein Insists He's Earned Wings—But Not Red Variety," *The Sporting News*, May 27, 1967, 12.

11 George Minot, "Senators Farm Epstein to Buffalo," *Washington Post*, May 23, 1968, C1.

12 Merrill Whittlesey, "Ted Tutors Promising Pupil Epstein," *The Sporting News*, March 22, 1969, 23.

13 Ibid.

14 Epstein interview, July 15, 2007.

15 Ron Bergman, "Epstein Meets Cepeda Challenge With Hot Bat," *The Sporting News*, July 22, 1972, 4.

16 Ibid.

17 Rob Bergman, "Epstein Exit Traced to Tenace Shoulder Ailment," *The Sporting News*, December 23, 1972, 37.

18 Dick Miller, "Epstein to Get Big Payoff," *The Sporting News*, May 18, 1974, 30.

19 Telephone interview Mike Epstein, September 4, 2013.

20 Epstein interview, September 4, 2013.

Adrian Garrett

By Alan Cohen

"It would be hard to say I am not a typical minor leaguer. I've spent 11 years in the minors, practically my whole career. It doesn't feel good to say I am a typical minor leaguer. It doesn't feel good to say it at all, but I suppose it's the truth. I still keep hoping for a break that will get me back up there. Something, just something."[1]

So said Adrian Garrett in 1972, more than halfway into a professional career that would see him hit more than 400 home runs, all but 11 at something other than the major-league level. At that point, he had appeared in just 21 major-league games and had gone 3-for-27, mostly as a pinch-hitter. His many travels would prompt Bob Verdi, in 1975, to suggested that Garrett's "baseball biography will be ghosted by Rand McNally."[2] Oddly enough, in 1975 Garrett's travels still had a long way to go.

He was Sarasota, Florida's first home-grown product to make it to the major leagues. Henry Adrian "Smokey" Garrett, Jr. was born in nearby Brooksville on January 3, 1943, the oldest of three brothers, all of whom grew up to play professional baseball. Each was signed by the Milwaukee Braves. Jimmy made it as far as Shreveport in the Double-A Texas League, and Wayne, after being traded to the Mets, was on their 1969 and 1973 championship teams. His parents, Henry Sr. (a machine operator) and Iva, also had two girls.

The Garrett family moved to Sarasota when Adrian was 6 years old. Baseball success came early for the young man. In 1955 local papers reported him pitching his Little League team to a 3-1 victory. In 1957, at the age of 14, he led his team to the regional Babe Ruth League championship. At Sarasota High he starred in baseball and football.

Garrett modeled his swing after that of Ted Williams and was picked to be in a commercial with the Splendid Splinter when he was in junior high school. For his efforts, Garrett received an autographed bat, ball, and glove.

Although Garrett never attained significant fame as a player beyond the minor leagues, his minor-league career was something special.

After graduating from high school in 1961, he was signed by Zack Taylor of the Milwaukee Braves for a $35,000 bonus and began his trek through the minor leagues. He was still traveling through minor-league cities more than 50 years later as a hitting instructor.

Garrett's travels took him to many ports, and he hit home runs in five countries (US, Canada, Japan, Dominican Republic, and Venezuela). He won four home-run titles in three minor leagues and when he went abroad, he topped the Dominican Republic

winter league and finished second in the Japanese Central League.

Garrett's first stop was in Palatka (Florida State League), where, he remembered, "there was only a sink in my hotel room, no toilet, no shower."[3] Stops in Davenport (1961) and Cedar Rapids, Iowa (1962), were next on his path. Since Davenport was close to Milwaukee, he got a chance to be seen by the Braves.

In 1962 at Cedar Rapids, in his second year of professional baseball, Garrett finished third in the Class D Midwest League in home runs and RBIs. He had a league-leading 18 outfield assists. From there it was on to Boise, Idaho, where he batted .317 in 1963; Austin, Texas (1964); and a couple of Instructional League stops, before arriving in Atlanta with the International League Crackers in 1965. He was in spring training with the Mets in 1964, and also spent time in the Florida East Coast Instructional League at West Palm Beach after the 1964 season.

Garrett's 1963 season in Austin resulted in his acquiring both a nickname and a wife. He roomed there with Walt Hriniak, who was from Massachusetts and who noted that Adrian bore a resemblance to Smoky Joe Wood, whose picture hung at Fenway Park in Boston. Hriniak began calling Garrett Smokey. In May 1964 Hriniak was involved in an automobile accident in which teammate Jerry Hummitzsch was killed. Hriniak was badly injured and his teammates, in an expression of support for Hriniak, also took to calling Garrett Smokey.

In Austin in 1963, Garrett met Linda Jean Thurman. They were married on September 5, 1968, and made their home in Austin. Their son Jason, born in 1973, was drafted by the Florida Marlins in 1995. He played four seasons in the Marlins organization but did not make it past Class A. The Garretts also had a daughter, Angela, and as of 2014 there were three grandchildren.

After batting .280 for Austin in 1964 and leading his team in doubles (23), triples (11), total bases (184), and slugging percentage (.437), Garrett was promoted to Triple-A Atlanta. For the 1965 Crackers, he slugged

a team-leading 20 homers, placing him second in the International League. In July Garrett was selected for the league's All-Star game. However, he slumped toward the end of the season and his batting average dropped to .224.

A good spring training in 1966 earned him a spot on the roster of the Atlanta Braves as they opened their first season in the South. He appeared in four games for the Braves in April, three as a pinch-hitter and one as a defensive replacement. In his first major-league at-bat, he faced Vernon Law of the Pittsburgh Pirates and popped out to the catcher. His last two at-bats came against the L.A. Dodgers' Don Sutton and Don Drysdale, and he struck out each time. Manager Bobby Bragan wanted Garrett to be "more than a pinch-hitter," and on April 30 he was sent down to Richmond for the balance of the season.

Writer Furman Bisher of the *Atlanta Constitution* fell in love with Garrett's swing. In 1991 Bisher reminisced that "they speak of sweet swings, as sweet a swing I ever saw was that of a Braves rookie of the '60s, Adrian Garrett."[4]

Garrett spent another three seasons in the Braves organization. In 1967 he returned to Austin (Texas League) for the third time. Although he batted only .254, his slugging percentage was .481. He was an All-Star selection and finished second in the league in homers (27) and RBIs (90). He led his team in runs scored (73). But he was mired in the bushes.

In 1968 Garrett split his time between Evansville and Richmond, and in 1969 he was back in the Texas League, with Shreveport. Teamed with his brother Jimmy, he batted .261 and won the first of his four minor-league home run crowns, slugging 24 to go along with a team-leading 75 RBIs.

Despite the power he had shown, the Braves released Garrett at the end of the 1969 season. He caught on with the Chicago Cubs and spent the 1970 season back in the Texas League, this time with San Antonio, where he was selected to play in the All-Star game.

He won his second consecutive league home-run title, this time with 29.

At the end of the 1970 season, Garrett got his second taste of major-league action, appearing three times as a pinch-hitter for the Cubs and striking out each time, once against Bob Gibson of the Cardinals. He was sent to Triple-A Tacoma for the 1971 season. He began the season as the fourth outfielder, but when Gene Hiser was called into the Army Reserve, Garrett got his chance and made the most of it.[5] He garnered Player of the Month honors in June. For the season he batted .289 with career highs in home runs (43) and RBIs (119). His RBI and total base (292) totals were Tacoma team records, and he led the team in walks (90) and slugging percentage (.649). His home-run championship was his third in as many minor-league seasons. His 43 homers were the most in the Pacific Coast League since PCL legend Steve Bilko banged out 56 in 1957.[6] He was named to both the Triple A and Pacific Coast League All-Star teams. In 1993 Garrett was inducted into the Tacoma Hall of Fame.

Near the end of the season, Garrett was traded to the Oakland A's, for veteran catcher Frank Fernandez. In his first game with the A's, on September 1, he went got his first major-league hit, a single off the California Angels' Andy Messersmith. After 12 hitless at-bats, on September 19 he collected his first major-league home run, off Bill Parsons of the Milwaukee Brewers. Rollie Fingers caught the home run ball in the A's bullpen and presented the ball to Garrett. The homer was Garrett's final hit of the season. His A's batting average was .143 (3-for-21).

Winter ball became a regular part of Garrett's life beginning with the 1971-72 offseason, when he played in the Dominican League with Aguillas Cibaenas, posting a .307 average with six homers and 35 RBIs. Aguillas won the Dominican playoffs and finished second in the Caribbean Series to Ponce, Puerto Rico. During the Caribbean Series, Garrett led all players in home runs.

Garrett split 1972 between Oakland and Triple-A Des Moines. He began the season in Iowa and was called up to the A's at the end of May. With the A's he went 0-for-11 and spent his down time in the bullpen where, at manager Dick Williams' suggestion, he donned the catching gear, warming up pitchers in the bullpen. On occasion, he caught during batting practice, but saw no game activity behind the plate with the A's. By August he was back in Iowa.

Garrett returned to the Dominican League after the 1972 season, playing for Estrellas Orientales and leading the league in homers (9) and RBIs (42). The A's sold him to the Cubs and he he earned a spot on the Opening Day roster. That year, he got into 36 games, mostly as a pinch-hitter, and made four starts behind the plate. He batted .222 with 3 home runs.

Garrett began the next season with the Cubs, and was 0-for-8 before being sent down to Wichita, where he clubbed 26 homers, securing his fourth minor-league home-run title. He was back in winter ball in 1974-75 and once again was the home-run leader in the Caribbean Series, this time playing with Tigres de Aragua.

In 1975 Garrett was called up to the Cubs on April 25. He had a game-winning home run against San Diego. But not long after, Garrett was sent down to Wichita. On July 31 he was sold to the California Angels, where he was reunited with Dick Williams, for whom he had played in Oakland. On August 2 he homered off the Texas Rangers' Bill Hands. The next night he homered again, giving him home runs in consecutive games for the first time in his major-league career. That kept him in the lineup, and one day later, he had amassed six RBIs in four games. It was the first time in his major-league career that Garrett had played four consecutive games.[7] His first three-hit game as a major leaguer came on August 9 in an 8-1 win over the Yankees. Pinch-hitting in the 16th inning of a scoreless thriller with the White Sox on September 22, he hit a walk-off three-run homer. It was his 11th and last major-league home run. (When Garrett entered the game, he was the only position player left on the Angels' bench.)

The following season, 1976, Garrett's position with the Angels was precarious. He was the third-string catcher, fourth first baseman, fourth designated hitter, and seventh outfielder.[8] He played 15 games behind the plate that year, making it 25 for his career. It was Garrett's last season in the majors. In his final game, on July 11, he pinch-hit in the seventh inning and caught the last two innings as the Angels, with Nolan Ryan pitching, lost 3-1.

Despite playing parts of eight seasons in the majors, Garrett's time on the field was minimal. He got into 163 games, and at the time of his final major-league game was still 100 days shy of qualifying for the pension plan.[9] His major-league line was none too stellar. In parts of eight seasons, he batted .185 (51-for-276) with 11 homers and 37 RBIs.

On July 15 the Angels sent Garrett to Salt Lake City, but he was quickly shipped to Hawaii in the San Diego organization. With Hawaii, he banged the last nine of his 280 minor-league home runs. (Seven of the 280 came during an 11-game stretch in August 1975.)

After the close of the Pacific Coast League season, it was off to the Venezuelan Winter League. Playing for the Caracas Lions, Garrett broke a 25-year-old league record, hitting in 28 consecutive games.[10]

In 1977 Garrett took his home-run bat to Japan and played for the Hiroshima Toyo Carp of the Japanese Central League. In his first season in Japan, he batted .279 with 35 home runs and 91 RBIs. In 1978 he homered in of his team's first four games (five homers in all) to set a Japanese record,[11] and had seven through eight games. His 15 homers in April tied the mark set by Sadaharu Oh and two others for the most in a month. He earned Player of the Month honors for April and went on to slug 40 homers that season, the second most in the league. He had 97 RBIs and a .271 batting average.

Garrett was named to the league All-Star team and hit three home runs in the first game of the three-game All-Star series. His home runs accounted for six runs as his team won the game, 7-5. Garrett was the first player to homer three times in a Japanese All-Star game.[12] (All-Star teammate Masayuki Kakefu of the Hanshin Tigers hit three home runs in the third game of the same series.)

Thanks in large part to Garrett, Hiroshima became the first team in the Japanese professional leagues to have more than 200 home runs in a season.

Garrett retired as a player after the 1979 season with Hiroshima. During his three years in Japan, he had 102 homers with 247 RBIs and played on the 1979 Nippon Series champion. Hiroshima wanted to cut his pay after a .225 season with 27 homers but only 59 RBIs. Garrett held out for more money, but Hiroshima signed Mike Dupree to take his place.

After his playing days, Garrett stayed in the game with positions ranging from managing in the minors to coaching in the majors. Garrett and White Sox manager Tony LaRussa had roomed together with the Cubs and had played against each other in high school in Tampa. From 1982 through 1985, Garrett was in the White Sox organization as a manager, coach, and minor-league hitting instructor. In 1982 he managed Appleton of the Class A Midwest League to the league championship.[13] (He was elected to the Appleton Baseball Hall of Fame in 2008.)

In 1983 he was moved up to manager of Double-A Glens Falls (Eastern League). Although the team fared poorly in the standings, Garrett understood his role in the organization, stating, "It's never easy because, usually they (the major league organization) take a guy going good for you. Losing a player who is helping you win is the frustrating part of this game. But it's more important that I teach and prepare players for the next step, rather than worry about the won-loss record."[14]

Garrett began the 1984 season coaching at Denver in the American Association and was named manager on July 3, relieving Vernon Law.[15] Under Garrett, the Bears went 37-31, and finished the season in third place with a 79-75 record. They swept the last four games of the regular season against Wichita to make the playoffs, but lost in the playoffs to Louisville. Bobby Winkles was the White Sox farm director, and was happy with Garrett, but Adrian elected to stay home in 1986.

During his time in the White Sox organization, Garrett made the acquaintance of John Boles, who had succeeded him as manager at Appleton and Glens Falls. In 1987 Boles was appointed farm director for the Kansas City Royal, and hired Garrett. He was hitting instructor at Omaha in 1987. He joined the Royals as third-base coach in 1988, and in 1991-92, he took on the additional duties of hitting coach.

Garrett was dropped by the Royals after the 1992 season, and Boles, who had moved on to the new Florida Marlins franchise, hired him as a minor-league hitting coach. Boles subsequently said of Garrett, "He's the best. If you had to say who you'd like your sons to grow up to be like, it'd be Adrian Garrett."[16]

Garrett spent the next nine seasons as a Triple-A hitting instructor for the Marlins, in 1993-94 with Edmonton in the Pacific Coast League and with Charlotte, in the International league in 1995-98. He was promoted to hitting instructor with the Marlins in 1999 and remained with them through 2001, when everyone was let go after a change in ownership.

In 2002 Gary Hughes, who had been the assistant general manager of the Marlins when Garrett was there, hired him as the hitting coach for the Cincinnati Reds' Louisville farm team. He remained with the Bats through 2011, then became a roving hitting instructor for the Reds, working in spring training, the instructional league, and with the team's minor-league affiliates. During the 2012 and 2013 seasons, he worked about a week each month in that role. He and his wife, Linda, continued to make their home in Austin, Texas.

SOURCES

Author interview with Adrian Garrett, August 21, 2013.

In addition to the sources cited, the author consulted the book *Mendoza's Heroes* by Al Pepper (Clifton, Virginia: Pocol Press, 2002).

BaseballReference.com

NOTES

1   Milton Richman, "Garrett Typical of Minors," *Sarasota Herald Tribune,* June 2, 1972, D-1

2   Bob Verdi, "Cubs top Padres on Garrett's Clout," *Chicago Tribune,* May 19, 1975, E1

3   Richman, "Garrett Typical."

4   Furman Bisher, *Atlanta Constitution,* July 31, 1991, E1.

5   *Sarasota Herald Tribune,* June 1, 1971

6   *Spokane* (Washington) *Spokesman Review,* August 25, 1971, 18.

7   *Los Angeles Times,* August 5, 1975, D1.

8   Alan Lassilla, "Adrian Garrett Hanging on for Pension," *Sarasota Journal,* June 7, 1976, 2-D.

9   *Sarasota Herald Tribune,* March 2, 1977.

10 *The Sporting News,* February 5, 1977, 47.

11 *Hartford Courant,* April 5, 1978, B64.

12 *Hartford Courant,* July 23, 1978, C9.

13 *The Sporting News,* September 20,1982, 58.

14 Terese Karmel, *Hartford Courant,* July 20, 1983, D1.

15 Mike Kiley, *Chicago Tribune,* July 4, 1984.

16 Baseball-reference.com/bullpen.

Larry Haney

By Austin Gisriel

A backup catcher who amassed only 984 plate appearances in 12 seasons, Wallace Larry Haney nevertheless was a member of some historic teams, including the 1974 Oakland Athletics. Upon retiring as an active player, the right-handed hitting Haney spent an additional 34 years in professional baseball as a coach and scout, and his dedication to the game is exceeded only by his love of family. In fact, when asked to recount his most cherished moment in the game, it is not the home run he hit in his first major-league contest or being a member of two world championship teams or playing with Hall of Famers.

"The biggest thrill I had was getting to see my son Chris pitch at [the big league] level," said Haney in his mild Southern drawl.[1]

Haney, who was born on November 19, 1942 (he was christened Wallace Larry Haney), and his two older brothers, George and Wayne, grew up on a farm in Barboursville, Virginia, near Charlottesville, along with their sister, Jeanette. George, who pitched as high as Triple-A in the Yankees' system before hurting his elbow, was the superior athlete, according to Haney, who himself played four sports at Orange County High School. "Probably because I didn't want to work on the farm," he joked.

"Without the support my mom and dad gave us as young kids and the support they gave our baseball habits, I wouldn't have had the opportunity to do what I did over 46 years in the game," said Haney, who helped repay that support immediately upon embarking on his pro career when he bought his parents, George and Janice, a house with part of the $60,000 bonus money he received from the Baltimore Orioles upon graduation.

Haney, who considered himself a better football player than a baseball player, had accepted a full scholarship to play quarterback at Virginia Tech, but several baseball clubs came calling. "My parents didn't have a lot of money, of course, growing up on a farm, and a number of clubs called me the day after I got out of high school. I had made up my mind that if I didn't get a certain amount of money, that I was going to go to Virginia Tech and play football. Obviously, I got [the amount I was looking for] and maybe a little more. It was something I was able to help my parents out with and buy a house for them and do some things for them that they wouldn't have been able to do on their own."

The Orioles sent Haney, who as an amateur played primarily third base and shortstop and caught occasionally, to Bluefield in the Appalachian League, where he was immediately converted into a full-time catcher.

"I guess they thought I couldn't play anywhere else! I had good hands and a plus arm, so maybe they thought that was my best opportunity to play at a higher level."

Two years later Haney was already playing regularly at Double-A Elmira for an incredibly talented team that included infielders Davey Johnson and Curt Blefary, as well as pitchers Tom Phoebus, Darold Knowles, and Frank Bertaina. The pitching staff also included a couple of interesting left-handers: Pat Gillick and Steve Dalkowski.

"I used to tell Pat later on when I'd run into him in Toronto or Philadelphia or wherever, that the best thing about his pitching was he'd walk a guy and pick him off first! He had a great move; plus the fact that Pat Gillick was one of the sharpest guys I think I ever met in baseball. He's very intelligent. He would get on the bus and read *The Sporting News* from cover to cover and remember everything in it."

As for Dalkowski, "Steve was Steve." The legendary fireballer hurt his arm late in spring training in 1963 while pitching against the Yankees in a game Haney recalled clearly. "He was going through the Yankees, who had Mantle and Maris and Elston Howard and Boyer and all those guys, and he was pitching great when all of a sudden he just threw one up on the screen; and the next pitch he threw up on the screen, and he walked off the mound holding his elbow."

Dalkowski's arm was never the same. According to Haney, he was "down to 94 [mph]. There's no telling how many pitches he threw back then. He would have to go to the bullpen and warm up for half an hour just to try to wear his arm down a little bit to where they thought he could come in and throw strikes."

In addition to Elmira's talent on the field, prowling the dugout was future Hall of Fame manager Earl Weaver.

"Earl was very fiery in the minor leagues; one of the most knowledgeable baseball managers as far as match-ups. I think his game management was as good as anybody I've ever seen. He was able to maximize ability and get the most out of players. He did it a little differently maybe; he intimidated some players, but he knew the right buttons to push."

Five years into his pro career, Haney married Connie Deane in 1965. "I've known her family and I've known her ever since we were 10 or 11 years old, I guess. We went to the same church, the same high school, but didn't really start dating until I was a few years into pro ball. I don't know why she chose me, because she had a lot of opportunities!" The Haneys had three sons, Chris, Kevin, and Keith.

By 1966, Haney and Weaver were at Triple-A Rochester as the Orioles were beginning a reign that would see them win four pennants in the next six years. Haney's former roommate Andy Etchebarren established himself as Baltimore's primary catcher that year, but the Birds used several backups, including Charlie Lau, who missed the rest of the season after undergoing elbow surgery in May, Camilo Carreon, and Vic Roznovsky. When Etchebarren suffered a broken bone in his right hand, Haney was summoned to Baltimore and made his major-league debut on July 27. He actually took Wally Bunker's spot on the roster, as the Orioles were suffering from a slew of injuries to the pitching staff as well.[2]

Haney started that night and in his second at-bat, the right-handed hitter drove a John O'Donohue pitch into the left-field stands at Memorial Stadium for a two-run homer in what proved to be a 7-1 victory over the Cleveland Indians. Haney would hit only 11 more homers in his big-league career, but he remained the only Oriole to homer in his first game until 2013, when Jonathan Schoop did it.

Haney got into 20 games for the Orioles that year and made the World Series roster, but didn't play in the Series. Of course, many Orioles never played in Baltimore's four-game sweep of the Los Angeles Dodgers, as the Birds used only one extra position player (Russ Snyder and Paul Blair platooned in center field) for the entire series. In fact, Haney never had much of a chance to even catch anyone in the bullpen because Baltimore used only one reliever, Moe

Drabowsky, in Game One and none in the next three games.

"To have the opportunity to go the World Series and play the Dodgers and see Koufax and Drysdale and Wills and all those guys. I mean, I was a big fan of a lot of those guys, and I was a fan during the Series because that's all I did was sit there and cheer for our club!"

Haney made the Orioles coming out of spring training in 1967, and on April 30 found himself involved in one of the strangest no-hitters in major-league history. Baltimore lefty Steve Barber had held the Detroit Tigers hitless through eight innings in the first game of a doubleheader, but had walked seven and hit two batters. He entered the ninth with a 1-0 lead thanks to a Luis Aparicio sacrifice fly in the bottom of the eighth, but promptly walked Norm Cash and Ray Oyler. After a sacrifice bunt and a foul out to Haney, who had entered the game in the ninth, the southpaw got ahead of Mickey Stanley 0 and 2. Barber then "bounced the ball four feet in front of the plate and over catcher Larry Haney's head, enabling the tying run to score."[3]

When Barber walked Stanley to reload the bases, manager Hank Bauer brought in Stu Miller, who induced a groundball to shortstop Aparicio. He flipped to Mark Belanger at second. In keeping with the absurdity of the game, Belanger, who would win eight Gold Gloves at shortstop, dropped the ball.

The Orioles lost the combined no-hitter, 2-1, and then lost the second game as well, 6-4. It was a portent of a disastrous season following Baltimore's first world championship, although Haney's .268 average in 164 at-bats was the highest of his career.

Haney got into only 38 games in 1968 and the Orioles were shopping him around.[4] A trade became a moot point when Haney was selected as the 32nd pick in the expansion draft by the Seattle Pilots.

"I was happy to go somewhere to get an opportunity to play," said Haney. "Not that I wanted to leave Baltimore, but I knew it wasn't going to happen there."

The opportunity to play never materialized in Seattle either. Haney found himself backing up once again, this time for Jerry McNertney. Just 2½ months into the season, the Pilots traded Haney to Oakland on June 14 for second baseman John Donaldson. Haney received regular playing time under former Oriole manager Hank Bauer, who was now in Oakland, but an injury derailed this opportunity.

"Got a foul tip that broke my right toe and really never had a chance to catch a whole lot after that. We were winning and Bauer says, 'Even with a broken toe, you're going to play!' and I tried, but it didn't work. I ended up hurting my arm a little bit trying to play with a broken toe."

Haney did find himself taking part in another Baltimore no-hitter that year, however, when on August 13 he was the final out in Jim Palmer's no-hitter.

"Palmer reminds me of that all the time," laughed Haney. "He said he walked the bases loaded to get to me because he knew I'd hit a groundball to the short-stop." [Haney did, resulting in a fielder's choice.]

Apparently, the Baseball Gods were listening to the prayers of a certain Oriole fan in Barboursville.

"It's tough to get a hit when your mother roots against you," recounted Haney. "My mom told me later on: 'I'll have to be honest with you. I was hoping you wouldn't get a hit because Jimmy needed a no-hitter worse than you needed a base hit.' I said, 'I don't think you've been reading the papers, Mom!'"

Appearing in only two games for Oakland in 1970, Haney was loaned out to Montreal's Triple-A affiliate which began the year in Buffalo, but ended in Winnipeg. "Gene Tenace was catching at Des Moines, and they didn't want both of us to be on the same club to split catching time," Haney explained.

Haney spent the entire 1971 season at Iowa (Des Moines), Oakland's Triple-A affiliate, and the vast majority of 1972 at Honolulu, San Diego's Triple-A affiliate, after the A's sold his contract to the Padres on May 30. Oakland bought him back in September of that year, but he did not appear on the postseason roster. It was back to Triple-A in 1973, this time in Tucson, Oakland's latest Triple-A affiliate, and once again Oakland sold the soon-to-be 31-year-old backstop, to St. Louis on September 1.

"They wanted someone that could back up Ted Simmons in case they needed a body because [Tim] McCarver couldn't throw at that time. I was there the last month of the season, and I got in two ballgames. Simmons caught probably 157 games that year in that heat in St. Louis; Simmons was an animal, really. [Simmons appeared in 161 games for the Cardinals in 1973, starting 151 games at catcher.]

"I went to spring training with the Cardinals the next year, and they basically told Jeff Torborg and myself that 'One of you is going to be the backup catcher; whichever one has the best spring.' At the end of spring training, they let Jeff Torborg go, and a couple of days later they sold me back to Oakland, which was a blessing in disguise because that was the '74 season when we beat the Dodgers in the World Series in Oakland." [Tim McCarver was the primary backup for St. Louis in 1974, as Simmons caught in "only" 141 games.]

Haney remained on Oakland's roster for the entire season in 1974, appearing in 76 games while sharing the catching duties with Ray Fosse and Gene Tenace. During the World Series, he appeared in two games defensively, but never got an at-bat.

"A great pitching staff," recalled Haney of the A's that year. "One of the best and most competitive pitchers I caught at [the major-league] level was Catfish Hunter. He had great command of the strike zone with all pitches. Also on that staff was another Hall of Famer, Rollie Fingers. Ken Holtzman and Blue Moon Odom were two other starters, and with Bando, Campaneris, Green, Tenace, Fosse, Rudi, North, and Jackson, this club from '72 to '75 was one of the best in the game.

"They had speed, defense, pitching, and a Hall of Fame manager in Dick Williams, followed by Alvin Dark

in '74-75 who, along with Earl Weaver, I consider one of the better managers I played for."[5]

Haney spent two more seasons in Oakland, catching in 47 games while garnering only 27 plate appearances in 1975, as Oakland won its fifth consecutive AL West crown, and playing in 88 games in 1976. On December 6 of that year, his contract was sold to Milwaukee. He appeared in 63 games for the Brewers in 1977. Released by Milwaukee on March 30, 1978, he remained with the team as the bullpen coach, but was activated when rosters expanded on September 1, appearing in another four games before retiring as an active player for good. As a Brewers coach, Haney again went to the World Series, this time in 1982, when future Hall of Famers Robin Yount and Paul Molitor, along with Haney's former St. Louis teammate Ted Simmons, led Milwaukee against the Cardinals, ultimately losing in seven games.

Haney remained with the Brewers as the bullpen coach until 1990, when he was named Milwaukee's pitching coach. The next year, 1991, Chris Haney made his major-league debut for the Montreal Expos on June 21. Like any parent, Larry Haney found it nerve-wracking when it came to watching his child play.

"Oh yeah, without a doubt. I had control over what I did; I had no control over what he did. All you can do is sit there and hope for the best!

"His first start was in Cincinnati, who had won the World Series the year before. I couldn't go because I was the pitching coach in Milwaukee. It was really tough on me, sitting there watching my pitcher and watching the scoreboard trying to figure out what was going on. [Chris started the game, gave up four runs in four innings, and took the loss.] I did get to see him pitch a number of times in pro ball when I was doing pro scouting."

Sal Bando became Milwaukee's general manager after the 1991 season, hiring Phil Garner to manage the club. Naturally, Garner brought with him an entirely new coaching staff, and Haney was relieved of his coaching duties. Bando, however, had an assignment for his former Oakland teammate, and named Haney a major-league scout. With no big-league players to evaluate during the 1994 strike season, Haney was asked to look at amateur talent around the country. He continued to scout both major leaguers and amateurs until his retirement in 2006.

Haney said he felt very fortunate for the support that his wife, Connie, gave him throughout his career.

"Without Connie and her ability to handle the needs of the family and moving around the country, none of my baseball ventures would have been possible," he said. "She would film [our sons'] games and keep me updated on what was going on with the boys. She is one strong lady and someone I will be forever thankful for."[6]

The Haneys celebrated their 48th wedding anniversary in 2013.

"I didn't get a chance to see [any of our three boys] play in Little League, high school, or college; they all played at [each of] those levels. Chris had a little boy, and I decided I wanted to watch him play. I decided it was time to pack it in and watch Jake play all of his sports," said Haney, explaining the reason for his retirement.

Jake, Larry and Connie's only grandchild, attended Orange County High School, as did his father and grandfather. Although he had retired from professional baseball, Larry remained in the game, helping Chris coach Little League, and also starting an American Legion team, which the father-son duo coached for three years.

Larry and Chris continued to coach through their business, Old School Academy, which offered private lessons and clinics. As of 2013 the academy sponsored four travel teams. Chris took on most of the teaching duties. Larry said in 2013 "I still go up to the building in the afternoons if Chris is teaching some kids up there. I just sit there and second-guess him now!"

Larry was honored by his alma mater when the Orange County Hornets inducted him into its Hall of Fame

on May 10, 2013. His Milwaukee jersey was hung next to Chris's Kansas City jersey in the Hornets' Sports Center.

Living about a mile from where he grew up, Haney said he still wondered if he could have successfully quarterbacked Virginia Tech. "I miss the fact that I didn't get a chance to play football in college, to find out whether I could have played at that level. Just having that competitive nature, you always want to find out if you could have done it.

"[However] being in baseball for 40-some years, meeting all the people that I've met … I was very fortunate; I wasn't a good player, but [had] the opportunity to play on clubs that had great players. Not good players, but *great* players. You look at Baltimore, you look at Oakland; I was with St. Louis for a month, the Hall of Famers, Bob Gibson, Lou Brock, guys like that. And I even look at Ted Simmons, who should have had a shot at the Hall of Fame, when you look at his numbers. To have an opportunity to play with guys like that … and to play against the great players … guys you admired from afar, and you get a chance to see them up close and personal. I had a chance to play against Mickey Mantle. It was his last two years in New York, and he was just a shell of himself, but … guys that I idolized as a little kid and to see those guys …"

Haney recalled a play by Willie Mays, not from his own playing days, however, but from his childhood, in a game that he and his dad attended.

"Willie Mays was in the Army, I think during the Korean War. He was playing for one of the forts, either Fort Lee or Fort Eustis, but they played a local team in a tournament. … There was a fence that ran kind of parallel along the highway on an angle. Willie was playing center field. Some guy hit a ball up over the fence. Willie went up over the fence with his back to the infield, caught the ball, turned, and threw a seed to second base. I see highlights of the play that he made in the Polo Grounds and all these others, but that to me … when I was 10 years old, or whatever I was. My dad had taken me to the game, but it stuck out all these years as one of the greatest catches I've ever seen a guy make in the outfield."

From seeing Willie Mays with his dad to coaching his grandson, Larry Haney could lay claim to one of baseball's best numbers: part of four successive generations who have passed the love of the game and the encouragement to play from father to son.

SOURCES

Books

Beard, Gordon, *Birds on the Wing: The Story of the Baltimore Orioles* (New York: Doubleday & Co., 1967).

Eisenberg, John, *From 33rd Street to Camden Yards: An Oral History of the Baltimore Orioles* (Chicago: Contemporary Books, 2001).

Weaver, Earl, *Winning*. Edited by John Sammis (New York: William Morrow & Co, Inc., 1972).

Online

baltimoresun.com

Baseball-Reference.com

dailyprogress.com (Orange County, Virginia)

Personal correspondence

Telephone interview with Larry Haney, October 16, 2013

E-mail from Larry Haney, October 25, 2013

NOTES

1   All quotations are from October 16, 2013 telephone interview with Larry Haney, unless otherwise noted.

2   Gordon Beard, *Birds on the Wing: The Story of the Baltimore Orioles* (Doubleday & Co., New York, 1967), 73.

3   Doug Brown, "No-hitter ruined by walks, Barber now drives a bus," *The Sun* online, August 17, 1995.

4   Earl Weaver, edited by John Sammis. *Winning* (William Morrow & Co, Inc., New York, 1972), 70.

5   Email, October 25, 2013.

6   Email, October 25, 2013.

Mike Hegan

By Joseph Wancho

During the summer of 1954 the Cleveland Indians visited New York to play a three-game series against the Yankees with both teams in contention for the American League pennant. The story of the second game wasn't the Yankees' 4-1 victory, or Eddie Lopat outdueling Mike Garcia, but the 12-year-old batboy in the Cleveland dugout, Mike Hegan. Mike, the son of Indians starting catcher Jim Hegan, was pressed into service because the normal visiting team batboy, Mike Morton, was absent. The Little Leaguer became a celebrity when Red Barber interviewed him on his pregame TV show. The Yankees' batboy, 18-year-old Joe Carrieri, heaped praise on his younger counterpart, saying, "Considering his lack of experience, Mike showed some real promise."[1] Little did Mike Hegan know that he would make his major-league debut ten years later in the same stadium.

James Michael Hegan was born on July 21, 1942, in Cleveland, the son of Jim and Clare Hegan. Jim Hegan, a five-time All-Star, played on Cleveland's last world championship team, in 1948. One of the best defensive catchers ever, he was a fan favorite in Cleveland for his all-out play and professionalism. His career lasted 17 years, 14 of them with the Indians.

During Mike's early years, the Hegans made their offseason home in Lynn, Massachusetts, Jim's hometown. In the summer it was common to see Mike hanging around the clubhouse or shagging fly balls in the outfield at Cleveland Municipal Stadium.

In 1954 Jim and Clare Hegan relocated their family of three children (Mike, Patrick, and Catharine) to Lakewood, Ohio, after Jim entered a business venture with Cleveland Browns quarterback Otto Graham. Their business was called Hegan-Graham Inc., and later became Hegan-Graham Appliance, a store in downtown Cleveland that sold appliances, sporting goods, luggage, and jewelry and urged customers to "get the right pitch, before you buy."

In 1956 Mike enrolled at St. Ignatius High School in Cleveland. He excelled in football, basketball, and baseball. On the baseball team he pitched and played first base, and made several local and state all-star teams. (In 1989 he was elected to the St. Ignatius High School Athletic Hall of Fame.)

After high school Hegan accepted a football and baseball scholarship at from Holy Cross College in Worcester, Massachusetts. He passed up offers from Notre Dame, Stanford, Syracuse, Maryland, and Wisconsin to play for Holy Cross's legendary baseball coach, Jack Barry, who had been a shortstop for the Philadelphia Athletics from 1908 to 1915 and started in Connie Mack's famed "$100,000 Infield." As a

freshman Hegan played freshman football and baseball, and hit .510 while playing first base for a baseball team that finished 6-10.

In August 1961 Hegan was offered contracts by 15 major-league clubs, and signed with scout Bill Skiff of the New York Yankees even though two other teams offered more money. He felt the short distance down the right-field line at Yankee Stadium would be to his advantage since he was a left-handed pull hitter, so he accepted the Yankees' offer of a minor-league contract with "a substantial bonus."The following year, he was off with the rest of the Yankees for spring training in Fort Lauderdale, Florida. General manager Roy Hamey said of Hegan, "We'll play him as high as we can."[2]

As Hegan's playing baseball career was beginning, his father's had just ended. After 14 years with the Indians and short spells with four other teams, Jim Hegan was hired as the bullpen and catchers coach for the Yankees. "I felt I had to be better to justify being the coach's kid," Mike said. "But Dad treated me just like any other player."[3]

Mike returned to Cleveland to continue his college education and enrolled at John Carroll University. "My father and mother told me that when you take that step to play professional baseball, you'd better have something to fall back upon," he said. "One of their stipulations was that I finish my college education."

Mike thought of his father as a disciplinarian, but fair. "He didn't yell or scream, but when he gave you that look, you didn't go any further." Mike was living at home when he came in one morning at 2:30. "When I pulled into the driveway, I saw a light on in the kitchen," Mike said. "My father was sitting at the table."Jim was not happy and let Mike know it. "You've got your whole career in front of you, and I don't want to see you start screwing up," Jim said. "I don't want to see you coming home this late again."[4] Mike understood his father's message.

Playing first base in his first pro season, with Fort Lauderdale in the Class D Florida State League in 1962, Hegan hit .306 and walked 100 times in 121 games. Said Yankees assistant general manager Dan Topping, Jr., "He's got terrific determination and great coordination." Everybody who saw him in his first year as a pro agrees he's a big-league fielder right now."[5]

In 1963 Hegan was promoted to Idaho Falls of the Class C Pioneer League. In 126 games, he hit .323, smacked 28 home runs, had 98 RBIs, and had a league-leading 123 runs scored. He was named to the league's All-Star team. Idaho Falls won the league title, besting Billings two games to one in the final series. After the season, on October 12, he and Nancy McNeill were married at St. Pius Church in Lynn.

The next season Hegan played for Double-A Columbus (Southern League) and was a late-season call-up to the Yankees. He made his major-league debut on September 13, 1964, against the Minnesota Twins as a pinch-hitter for Whitey Ford and flied out to right field. He was 0-for-5 with one walk in five games, and was added to the Yankees' World Series roster when Tony Kubek suffered a sprained wrist. In Game One against the St. Louis Cardinals in St. Louis, Hegan ran for Johnny Blanchard at second base in the eighth inning and scored on a Bobby Richardson single. The Yankees lost, 9-5, and eventually lost the Series in seven games. Hegan had the distinction of scoring a run in a World Series game before getting his first regular-season major-league hit.

Hegan returned to Columbus in 1965 and earned a midseason promotion to the Triple-A Toledo Mudhens. He returned to Toledo in 1966, led the International league in triples and walks, and was a late season call-up by the Yankees. He collected his first major-league hit on September 15, 1966, two years and two days after his debut with the Yankees. Batting leadoff against the Washington Senators, Hegan singled in the fifth inning and eventually scored on Clete Boyer's hit. In the seventh inning he singled and scored on a hit by Joe Pepitone.

When the 1967 season began, Hegan was completing his active duty with the Army National Guard and did not join the Yankees until May 12. He hit his first major-league home run on September 1 off of Dick Lines of the Washington Senators in the 12th inning to provide the Yankees with a 2-1 win.

On February 23, 1968, Mike and Nancy welcomed their first son, Shawn Patrick, three days before Mike was to report for spring training. First base was becoming crowded with Mickey Mantle starting and Andy Kosco and Joe Pepitone backing him. At the end of spring training the Yankees assigned Hegan to Syracuse, where he hit .304 with 11 homers and 39 RBIs, while mostly stationed in right field. He was selected to play in the International League All-Star Game, but was unable to play because of military reserve commitments. On June 14 the Yankees sold Hegan to the expansion Seattle Pilots for $25,000. The one caveat to the deal was that Hegan finish out the year in Syracuse.

Hegan was the first player to sign with the Pilots, who would begin play one year later in 1969 in Seattle's Sick's Stadium. He was thrilled to join the expansion Pilots. "It's a mental lift to be with the Pilots," Hegan told *The Sporting News.* "While I was with the Yanks, I put a lot of time into the service and couldn't get rolling. And then I always had to back another first baseman. When I came up, they had Moose Skowron. Then they had Joe Pepitone. Then I was a fill-in when they shifted Mickey Mantle to first. What if Mantle retires? Then I would have to back Pepitone again. Here I may be in a similar situation with [Don] Mincher on first. But I played more outfield than first in Syracuse, so right field would suit me fine."[6]

Hegan found familiar faces in Seattle. Also coming over to the Pilots from the Yankees were pitchers Jim Bouton, Steve Barber, Dooley Womack, and Fred Talbot, infielder John Kennedy, and outfielder Steve Whitaker. Garry Roggenburk, also from St. Ignatius High School, was on the Pilots' pitching staff. Scout Bill Skiff, who had originally signed Hegan, was now a scout with the Pilots. Former Cleveland broadcaster Jimmy Dudley was the radio voice of the Pilots.

Managing the Pilots was Joe Schultz, who came to Seattle from the St. Louis Cardinals, where he had been the third-base coach for the 1968 National League pennant winners. Schultz emphasized a running style with the Pilots, who led the American League in 1969 with 167 stolen bases. Unfortunately for the expansion club, the team batted .234, grounded into 111 double plays, and led the American League with 1,015 strike-outs. The pitching staff yielded 172 home runs.

But Hegan had his finest year to date in the major leagues. He hit the first home run for the Pilots on Opening Day off Jim McGlothlin of the California Angels. He led the Pilots in batting average (.292), slugging percentage (461), and on-base percentage (427), and was chosen for the All-Star Game, but had to withdraw in favor of Don Mincher because of a hamstring injury. Hegan missed 67 Pilots games, partly due to injuries.

Just before the 1970 season the Pilots were sold to Milwaukee car dealer Bud Selig, who moved the club to his hometown, where they became the Milwaukee Brewers.

On September 24, 1970, Hegan began a streak of playing in 178 consecutive games at first base without making an error, and the streak went into 1973, when he was a member of the Oakland Athletics. The record stood as the major-league mark for 12 years, and was the high-water mark in the American League until 2010, when it was broken by Seattle's Casey Kotchman.

Also in 1970 Hegan got a glimpse of his career after baseball. During the offseason he began doing drive-time sports reporting and TV interviews for WTMJ-TV in Milwaukee.

On June 14, 1971, Hegan was sold to the Oakland Athletics. A month before, on May 18, Nancy gave birth to their second son, James Joseph (known as JJ).

It was a break of sorts for Hegan to go from the struggling Brewers to the A's, who won their first of five consecutive AL West Division crowns in 1971.

In 1972, the A's adopted the moniker "The Mustache Gang." Reggie Jackson reported to spring training with a full-grown mustache. Although no official rule banned players from wearing facial hair, it was more or less an unwritten rule. A's owner Charlie Finley didn't like the look of Jackson's mustache, but instead of making him shave it off, he told a couple of other players to start growing mustaches. It was Finley's hope that Jackson would not feel like an individualist, and would shave his whiskers. Instead, the strategy backfired, and all the players grew mustaches. Finley began to like the idea and offered a cash incentive to any player who grew a mustache by Father's Day, or "Mustache Day." True to his word, the players found $300 apiece in their lockboxes after the game. In addition, Finley extended his idea to the fans, and any fan bearing a mustache was admitted free on Father's Day.

Hegan shaved his mustache off shortly thereafter, giving into a higher authority than Finley: his wife Nancy. "My wife didn't like it," he admitted.[7]

On the field the Athletics stormed through the American League West, winning 101 games despite 49 players going through a revolving door on the roster. After they defeated Detroit in the American League Championship Series, the National League champion Cincinnati Reds awaited them in the World Series. Hegan played in six of the seven games, mostly as a defensive replacement for first baseman Mike Epstein. At the plate he got a single in Game Five, his only hit of the Series, won by the A's in seven games. It was the first of three straight world championships for Oakland.

Jim and Mike Hegan claimed a first by becoming the first father-and-son combination to each win a World Series. There have been six other such combinations since.

As the 1973 season commenced, Hegan was again a backup at first base, this time to Gene Tenace. On June 3 Hegan's streak of consecutive errorless games at first base ended. The error occurred in the eighth inning against the Boston Red Sox on a groundball by Carl Yastrzemski to Hegan, who threw late to pitcher Vida Blue covering first base.

On July 18 in Baltimore, a glimpse of Mike Hegan's future was on display. A's radio announcer Jim Woods was ailing, and Oakland manager Dick Williams instructed Hegan to report to the radio booth to call three innings. After three innings, he went to the clubhouse, put on his uniform, and reported to the dugout.

On August 18 Hegan was reunited with his father when the Yankees Yankees purchased his contract. Jim was still the Yankees' bullpen coach. Mike, a left-handed hitter, batted mostly against right-handed pitchers, and hit .275, with 6 homers, 14 RBIs, and 36 runs scored. On September 30 he became a bit of Yankee trivia as the last batter in Old Yankee Stadium when he flied out to center field in an 8-5 loss to the Tigers.

Hegan opened the 1974 season platooning at first base with Bill Sudakis until April 26, when the Yankees acquired first baseman Chris Chambliss from the Cleveland Indians. Chambliss commanded most of the playing time, and Hegan asked the Yankees to move him to one of three teams: Boston, where Nancy's family lived; Milwaukee, where they made their off-season home; or Detroit, where his father had become the Tigers' bullpen coach. The Yankees granted Hegan's request and sold him to the Brewers, where George Scott was getting most of the playing time at first base.

In 1975 and 1976, Hegan split his time between first base, designated hitter, and the outfield. He became only the sixth player (all left-handed batters) to pinch-hit for Hank Aaron, on July 8, 1975, against Kansas City at Royals Stadium. On September 3, 1976, Hegan became the first Brewer to hit for the cycle by going 4-for-5 with six RBIs against Detroit's Mark Fidrych, at Tiger Stadium.

As the 1977 season unfolded, Hegan was dissatisfied with his diminished playing time, and with the direction of the team under manager Alex Grammas. On

July 8 he played in his last major-league game, getting his release from the Brewers a week later.

Hegan had done the sports news at WTMJ-TV during the offseason in 1976, and had decided to stay in broadcasting. Ten days after his release, he was in the broadcasting booth with sportscaster Ray Scott, providing color commentary for Brewers games, and the next season he started doing some play-by-play. In all, he handled Brewers games for 11 seasons.

Broadcasting major-league baseball was not all that kept Mike Hegan busy. For 15 years he owned Grand Slam USA in suburban Milwaukee, which housed indoor baseball and softball batting cages, and pitching machines. Grand Slam USA also offered instruction in hitting, pitching, and fielding.

In 1989 Hegan returned to Cleveland to broadcast Indians games on WUAB-TV. A generation of Tribe fans grew up listening to him describe the action for the Indians. Later he moved to the radio broadcast team. He called play-by-play and color on both television and radio. Hegan retired from broadcasting after the 2011 season.

Hegan died of heart problems on December 25, 2013. He was survived by his wife of 50 years, Nancy; their sons, Shawn and JJ; and four grandchildren.

SOURCES

Rosen, Byron, *Washington Post*, July 13 and July 16, 1977

Shippy, Dick, "Hegan Returning as an Estabished Pro." *Akron Beacon Journal*, April 2, 1989

baseball-reference.com/bullpen/IdahoFalls Yankees

ignatius.edu

retrosheet.org

thebaseballcube.com

Author interviews with Mike Hegan on May 19 and August 1, 2007

Photo Credit

The Topps Company

NOTES

1   *New York Times*, September 2, 1954.

2   *New York Times*, August 10, 1961.

3   Bob Dolgan, *Heroes, Scamps and Good Guys* (Cleveland: Gray and Company, 2003), 35-36.

4   Ibid.

5   *The Sporting News*, December 1, 1962, 10.

6   *The Sporting News*, March 29, 1969, 26.

7   Historical Hot Stove, "Thirty Years Ago … Birth of the Moustache Gang", March 13, 2002.

George Hendrick

By Joseph Wancho

Perhaps no other sport offers redemption to a player more often, or more quickly, than baseball. It can be a dangerous motivator for a young ballplayer. This is especially true for one who has been given his first opportunity to play every day. Or for a player who has been lauded for his skill on the baseball field Often, his attempts at salvation are detoured, and his downward plight continues.

Such was the case with George Hendrick, a 23-year-old outfielder who was trying to make the most of his first season with the Cleveland Indians. Most young players, even those who were given the "can't-miss" tag, have suffered through the peaks and valleys of their early careers. Indeed, the majors could be quite humbling. Hendrick had just arrived on the shores of Lake Erie via a trade with Oakland. Even though he was a bench player with the Athletics, his talent could not be doubted and Cleveland considered him the key player in the four-person swap.

The trade launched an odyssey that saw Hendrick play for six teams in a mildly controversial 18-year major-league career in which he was sometimes accused of lack of hustle and criticized for refusing to talk to the media.

Om June 19, 1973, Hendrick was in a mild 0-for-8 slump, including three strikeouts. Two of the K's had been at the hands of Detroit's Jim Perry, the starting pitcher the night before in the Tigers' 5-1 victory. The Indians center fielder may not have been trying to avenge his performance, but he unleashed an offensive show on the 19th that had Cleveland Stadium buzzing.

Stepping to the plate in the bottom of the first inning, Hendrick sent an offering by the Tigers' Woodie Fryman over the fence just inside the left-field foul pole. He duplicated his power display with home runs off Fryman in the fourth and sixth innings, both sailing high over the fence in right-center field. All three round-trippers were of the solo variety. A Charlie Spikes solo homer sent Fryman to the showers in the sixth, but the Tribe still trailed, 7-4.

Hendrick was not done. He worked his way for a walk in the eighth inning against reliever Mike Strahler, and scored on a home run by John Ellis that knotted the affair, 7-7. Then, with the outcome hanging in the balance, Hendrick delivered his biggest hit of the evening. His single with two out and two on in the bottom of the ninth scored Jack Brohamer from second base.

"George always swings the same way," said teammate Walt Williams. "The ball just jumps off his bat. When you're tall and you make good contact and you hit the ball in the air, there's a good chance it will go out."[1] Tribe coach Rocky Colavito, who had banged out four

home runs in a game 14 years earlier, saw the raw talent in George. "He's got such great God-given talent," said Colavito. "It's just whether or not he can make it work for him."[2]

What was George Hendrick's reaction to all the fanfare? "I got lucky," he said.[3]

George Andrew Hendrick was born on October 18, 1949, in Los Angeles. He was raised in the Watts section of South LA and attended Fremont High School. George did not play organized sports in high school. When he was asked why, he merely replied, "I just didn't."[4]

Hendrick's first love may have been the hardwood, as he preferred basketball to baseball. But it was his talent playing semipro baseball that caught the eye of Whitey Herzog. "I remember I saw him on a Saturday before the very first Super Bowl," recalled Herzog, who was the director of player development for the New York Mets at the time. "I saw George in a sandlot game in Watts. He was the only guy there of any consequence. He had great tools. If Oakland hadn't picked him, we would have gotten him in a minute."[5]

Based on the recommendation of their Southern California scout, Bob Zuk, the Athletics made Hendrick their number-one pick in the January 1968 free-agent draft. Their selection made Hendrick the first overall pick as well.

Playing for Burlington (Iowa) of the Class A Midwest League in 1968, Hendrick led the league in hitting with a .327 average and was named to the all-league team. He was one of the top prospects in the Oakland organization, ripping the cover off the ball at each level. Hendrick stood 6-feet-3 inches tall and weighed near 200 pounds. The Oakland front office was confident that he had the same potential as Rick Monday and Reggie Jackson, both of whom had similar builds.

In 1971, his fourth year in the Athletics' farm system, Hendrick crushed 21 home runs and drove in 63 runs in only 63 games at Triple-A Iowa (Des Moines). In a brief call-up to the A's, he made his major-league debut against the Washington Senators on June 4,

1971, and got his first major-league hit in a 21-inning affair won by the Athletics, 5-3. He returned to Iowa after appearing in two games, He was recalled to the big leagues in mid-July, and except for a brief stretch with Iowa in 1972, was in the majors to stay.

Hendrick spent most of the 1972 season as a reserve outfielder. The A's were on a roll. They won the second of what would be five consecutive Western Division titles. An offseason trade of Monday to the Chicago Cubs for pitcher Ken Holtzman solidified a pitching staff that already had Catfish Hunter, Blue Moon Odom, and Vida Blue. Manager Dick Williams's lineup was stocked with good young talent, including Sal Bando, Joe Rudi, Bert Campaneris, Mike Epstein, and Reggie Jackson.

The A's cruised through the season and faced Detroit in the American League Championship Series. In the second inning of Game Five, Jackson scoring from third base on a delayed steal that tied the score, 1-1, slid feet first into Tigers catcher Bill Freehan and pulled a hamstring. Hendrick, who had pinch-hit in each of the first four games, assumed Jackson's spot in center field.

In the fourth inning Hendrick reached base on an error by Tigers shortstop Dick McAuliffe. Bando bunted him to second, and he scored the go-ahead run on a single by Gene Tenace. It turned out to be the winning run, as Odom made the 2-1 lead stand. The Athletics were returning to the World Series for the first time in 41 years.

With Jackson sidelined for the Series, the A's were considered heavy underdogs as they met the Cincinnati Reds. Hendrick started five of the games in center field in the closely contested series in which six of the seven games were decided by a single run. The A's rode supreme pitching and four home runs by Tenace to their first of three straight world championships.

Hendrick credited teammate Joe Rudi for his development: "It was Joe Rudi who took me under his wing. He's a super fantastic person and a totally unselfish team player. Everything you see him doing on a field, you know he developed through hard work. If I were starting a new team and had a chance to pick any player in baseball, the first guy I'd choose is Joe Rudi—that's how much I think of him as a player and a person."[6]

Hendrick was not without detractors. He played his outfield position with an easy, effortless gait. Some characterized his play as nonchalant or lazy, while others believed that he quickly learned how to position himself in the outfield, so consequently had less ground to cover. At times he was criticized for "lollipop" throws to the cutoff man. New York Yankees coach Elston Howard was one of Hendrick's detractors. "He's a real dog," said Howard. "You could see that the way he played against us. Half-trying. What a shame."[7]

When spring training dawned in 1973, Hendrick balked at the notion that he should be sent down to the minors. He had accomplished all he could, and felt that he had contributed enough to the A's success the previous year to earn his stay. Oakland had acquired Billy North from the Cubs to play center field. On March 24 Hendrick and catcher Dave Duncan were sent to Cleveland for catcher Ray Fosse and infielder Jack Heidemann.

For Hendrick, the move across the country was a fresh beginning. Cleveland skipper Ken Aspromonte inserted him into the center-field position. The position was Hendrick's to lose. Despite missing the last six weeks because of a broken wrist, Hendrick was still second on the club in homers (21), RBIs (61), and batting average (.268). Hendrick was dubbed "Silent George" for his uneasiness in talking to the media. He often said that when he had something to say, he would say it. "Man, I gave up caring about what the world thinks about George Hendrick a long time ago," he said. "The people only believe what they read and what they want to believe. I'm happy the way I am. I have my friends and family, and that's the way it's going to stay."[8]

Hendrick was a solid contributor in the Tribe's lineup. He was one of the few power hitters and RBI men on the team. He was selected for the All-Star Game in 1974 and 1975. Still, Hendrick was criticized for not hustling and for what was perceived as a lackadaisical approach to the game. "There was a game right at the end of his career with the Indians where Gaylord [Perry] had a 2-1 lead in New York in the ninth inning," recalled Cleveland broadcaster Joe Tait. "Bobby Murcer hit a high fly ball to center field. There were a couple of Yankees on base. George Hendrick went back for the ball—he was really nonchalanting it. The ball dropped over his head and two guys scored. Game, set, match. After the game Gaylord went over to Hendrick's locker, stood in front of him, and said, 'I never want this son of a bitch in center field when I pitch again.' Then he walked away, and Hendrick never said a word. No one did."[9]

Personality conflicts affected Hendrick's playing time. On August 8, 1974, he suffered a hamstring pull and played only intermittently for the next few weeks. An exasperated Aspromonte would not play Hendrick full-time until George told him he was 100 percent. The problem was that neither was talking to the other. "I wanted to play, but I wasn't going to talk to the man," said Hendrick. "I am not going to talk to him. I don't have anything to say to him. It's no secret I don't care for the man, but I don't want to get into the reasons. I don't want to attack anybody. I just want to leave it at that."[10]

Cleveland acquired Frank Robinson from California on September 12 to help in the stretch run. Robinson recalled a conversation he had with Hendrick in Boston on the last day of the season. "Hendrick came into the locker room early, as I did. He hung his suit bag in the locker next to mine, then went to check the lineup posted on the wall. He came back, slung the suit bag over his shoulder and said, 'I'm out of here.' I said, 'What do you mean, George? We have a game to play.' Hendrick replied, 'He's got me in the lineup, and I'm not playing with Perry pitching. I'm gone.' I said, 'Are you sure you want to do that?' Hendrick answered, 'Yeah I'm catching a plane,'"[11]

Robinson succeeded Aspromonte as manager of the Indians the following year. The appointment of the first black manager in the major leagues may have had a positive effect on Hendrick on the field. In 1976 he belted 25 of the team's 85 home runs. "We, the Indians, have come a long way since Frank became manager," said Hendrick. When he was asked if he should be a motivating voice for the young Indians team, Hendrick replied, "In my opinion, the less I expose myself, the better. I feel I have the respect of the guys on the team, and that's the important thing. Because I have their respect, I can do my bit for motivation, but I can't stand up and be a holler guy, if you know what I mean. That's not me."[12]

The front office felt that it was time to move Hendrick, and on December 8, 1976, he was traded to San Diego for outfielder Johnny Grubb, catcher Fred Kendall, and infielder Hector Torres. The Padres' director of player personnel, Bob Fontaine was pleased about acquiring a player of Hendrick's capabilities for three bench players. "Getting Hendrick was our best possible deal," said Fontaine. "He's a better all-around player than (Richie) Zisk, (Gary) Matthews, or (Jeff) Burroughs. He's a better runner, fielder, and thrower than any of the three and he has their power."[13]

Hendrick led the team in hitting in 1977 with a .311 batting average, and was second in homers (23), RBIs (81), and hits (168), and tied for second in runs scored (75). Despite his insistence on not speaking to the media, the San Diego Chapter of the Baseball Writers Association voted him the team's MVP.

(Syndicated columnist Mike Royko, in an offhand way, lauded Hendrick for his silence. He urged other professional athletes, who he said babbled the most public nonsense next to politicians and sports broadcasters, to emulate Hendrick.)

Hendrick got off to a slow start in 1978. He was moved to right field and Dave Winfield took over in center. Hendrick was platooned with Oscar Gamble. The platoon system that manager Roger Craig employed did not work, prompting Gamble to suggest that either he or Hendrick be traded. Hendrick, and his three-year, $1 million deal were shipped to St. Louis on May 26 for relief pitcher Dennis Rasmussen.

"When I played against the Cardinals my observation was that if they had someone in the lineup who could protect Ted Simmons and hit 20 home runs and drive in 80 or 90 runs, I thought they could contend. I'm not saying I'm that guy, but I'm going to try to be," Hendrick in response to the trade.[14] He lived up to his vow. In his first six years as a Cardinal, he averaged 19 homers and 85 RBIs. He had a big day on August 25, 1978, when he powered the Cardinals to an 11-10 win in Atlanta. He smacked two homers and had a career-high seven RBIs.

In 1980 Hendrick smacked 25 home runs and 33 doubles, and driving in 109 runs while batting .302. He won *The Sporting News'* Silver Slugger award for most homers by a National League right fielder, and the paper named him to its NL All-Star Team. It seemed that George's bat was doing his talking.

"I don't think you'll find a better hitter in the National League with men on base than Hendrick," said St. Louis coach Red Schoendienst. "What makes George so tough is that he hits all kind of pitching so well. If an adjustment has to be made between pitches, he'll make it almost without thinking about it."[15]

Whitey Herzog replaced Ken Boyer as the Cardinals manager halfway through the 1980 season. Herzog had success in Kansas City, winning three straight division titles (1976-78), only to be eliminated by the New York Yankees in each ALCS. Under Herzog's leadership, the Cardinals were back in the playoffs in 1982, finishing first in the National League's Eastern Division. Hendricks' 19 homers and 104 RBIs easily led the Redbirds, who were a team built mostly on speed. The Cardinals swept the Atlanta Braves in the League Championship Series and returned to the World Series for the first time since 1968.

Their opponent was the Milwaukee Brewers. The Series went down to Game Seven, at Busch Stadium. Trailing 3-1, St. Louis scored three runs in the sixth inning and took a lead they never relinquished. Hendricks' single drove in the go-ahead run. The Mound City celebrated the Cardinals' ninth world championship. The following season, after playing his whole career as an outfielder, Hendrick reinvented himself by learning the skills of a first baseman. His mentor in spring training was the Cardinals' slick-fielding first sacker Keith Hernandez, whom he subsequently replaced when Hernandez was dealt to the New York Mets in June. Hendrick again received *The Sporting News* Silver Slugger Award and won a place on its NL All-Star team (18 HR, 97 RBIs, .318 average).

Whitey Herzog may have had something to do with Hendrick's turnaround. "When I got here in the middle of 1980, George loafed down the line once," the manager said. "We had a little talk. About six weeks later, he loafed again. We had a little longer talk. I have not had one bit of trouble with him since."[16]

Still, in December 1984, Hendrick was traded to Pittsburgh for pitcher John Tudor and outfielder Brian Harper. He did not stay in the Steel City long. On August 2, 1985, he was shipped to the California Angels with pitcher John Candelaria in a five-player deal. By now in his mid-30s, he spent most of his tenure with the Angels as a part-timer. He retired after the 1988 season with a career batting average of .278, 267 home runs, 1,111 RBIs, and 343 doubles.

After his playing days, Hendrick stayed close to baseball. He made stops in St. Louis, Los Angeles, and Anaheim, working as a hitting or a first-base coach. In 2002 he managed the Lake Elsinore Storm of the Class A California League, a Padres farm club, to the league championship series. He had become friends with Joe Maddon, the Angels' bench coach, and when Maddon was appointed manager at Tampa Bay in 2006, Hendrick went with him as first-base coach, a position he still held as of 2014.

Jim Frey, first-base coach for the Mets in 1983, told of his first encounter with Hendrick, wo was playing first base for the Cardinals. "I didn't know him, but for ten years I'd heard these stories about him—how he didn't talk to the press, stuff like that. But I'm a friendly sort of guy, so I ask him, 'George, how do you like first base?' Now I'm expecting him to say something like 'What the hell does it matter to you?' Well out comes this voice that is soft and articulate-like. He says, 'Well Jim, my teammates have been so helpful, they've made the transition easy.' Now I'm knocking my head because I don't know if I'm hearing right. But I was—George was just something other than what people said he was."[17]

Indeed he is.

SOURCES

retrosheet.org/

baseballlibrary.com/homepage/

baseball-almanac.com/

baseball-reference.com/

sabr.org/

tampabay.rays.mlb.com/index.jsp?c_id=tb&tcid=mm_cle_sitelist

NOTES

1   *Cleveland Plain Dealer*, June 20, 1973.

2   Ibid

3   *Cleveland Press*, June 20, 1973.

4   *The Sporting News*, February 17, 1968.

5   National Baseball Hall of Fame, Players File.

6   *The Sporting News*, May 22, 1976.

7   Bruce Markusen, *A Baseball Dynasty—Charlie Finley's Swingin' A's* (Haworth, New Jersey: St. Johann Press, 2002), 186.

8   National Baseball Hall of Fame, Players File

9   Terry Pluto, *The Curse of Rocky Colavito* (New York: Simon & Schuster, 1994), 133.

10 *The Sporting News*, September 28, 1974.

11 Frank Robinson and Barry Stainback, *Extra Innings* (New York: McGraw-Hill Book Company, 1988), 109-110.

12 *The Sporting News*, May 22, 1976.

13 *The Sporting News*, December 25, 1976.

14 *The Sporting News*, June 17, 1978.

15 *Christian Science Monitor*, April 10, 1984.

16 National Baseball Hall of Fame, Player's File

17 *Sports Illustrated*, September 19, 1983.

Ken Holtzman

By Richard J. Puerzer

Upon his arrival in the major leagues, Ken Holtzman was promoted as the new Sandy Koufax. A hard-throwing, left-handed Jewish pitcher, Holtzman quickly became the ace of the Chicago Cubs staff and one of the best pitchers in the majors. He enjoyed a fine career, spending his best years with the tumultuous and talented Oakland A's. Holtzman was known as something of a thinking man's ballplayer — he was quoted as having read Proust's *Remembrance of Things Past* in the original French, and was a staunch union advocate and player representative during the nascent years of free agency. Holtzman's pitching career had a rocky ending and he retired at the age of 33, but he is remembered today as a very good, if still underestimated pitcher.

Kenneth Dale Holtzman was born on November 3, 1945, in St. Louis. Henry Holtzman, his father, was in the machinery business while his mother, Jacqueline, was a homemaker. Ken grew up in the St. Louis suburb of University City. He graduated in 1963 from University City High School, where he had an overall pitching record of 31-3. Holtzman then entered the University of Illinois, where he studied business administration and played baseball. Holtzman was selected in the fourth round of the 1965 amateur draft by the Chicago Cubs. The 6-foot-2, lanky left-hander was 19 years old and was in his sophomore year at Illinois. He was given a reported bonus of $65,000.[1] Holtzman joined the Cubs organization, but later graduated from the University of Illinois with a bachelor's degree in business administration and later earned a master's degree.

Holtzman joined the Treasure Valley Cubs (Caldwell, Idaho) in the Rookie Pioneer League. He started four games for the team, winning each and allowing only 21 baserunners in 27 innings while compiling an earned-run average of 1.00. He was quickly promoted to the Wenatchee (Washington) Chiefs of the Class

A Northwest League. There Holtzman started eight games and went 4-3 with an ERA of 2.44 in 59 innings. In his 86 innings of minor-league work, he struck out 114 batters.[2] Based on his success in the minors, albeit at the Class A level, Holtzman was called up to the Cubs. He made his major-league debut on September 4, called in to pitch the ninth inning with the Cubs down 6-3 to the San Francisco Giants. He promptly gave up a home run to Jim Ray Hart before retiring the side. Holtzman pitched in three games for the Cubs in 1965, and demonstrated that he would contend for a spot in the starting rotation the following season.

Cubs manager Leo Durocher wanted to put Holtzman into the starting rotation for the 1966 season. Holtzman later reflected that "[Durocher] gave me a chance right away at age 20."[3] After an early-season relief appearance, he made his first major-league start on April 24 in a matchup against Don Drysdale and the World

Series champion Los Angeles Dodgers. Holtzman pitched six shutout innings and got the win in the 2-0 Cubs victory. Despite a lineup featuring three future Hall of Fame players, Ernie Banks, Ron Santo, and Billy Williams, the 1966 Cubs were a terrible team. They won only 59 games and finished in the basement of the National League. In spite of the Cubs' poor season, Holtzman's rookie-year performance was not bad. He led the team with 11 wins and 171 strikeouts in 220⅔ innings pitched and showed great promise. One highlight was a late-season matchup between Holtzman and his boyhood idol, Sandy Koufax. Holtzman faced Koufax on Sunday, September 25, in a game that drew 21,659 fans to Wrigley Field. (In Holtzman's previous outing, four days earlier, the attendance at Wrigley was 530.) The 24th was Yom Kippur and neither Holtzman nor Koufax was in uniform as they both observed the Jewish holy day. The Cubs scored two runs in the first inning against Koufax, and Holtzman was stellar on the mound. He went into the ninth inning with a no-hitter before giving up singles to Ducky Schofield and Maury Wills. Holtzman got the complete-game 2-0 win, striking out eight Dodgers.

The 1967 season was an unusual one for Holtzman. He got off to a very good start, winning his first five decisions and posting an ERA of 2.33. He was then called up by the Illinois National Guard for a six-month tour of duty. Holtzman was sent first to Fort Polk in Louisiana and later to Fort Sam Houston in Texas. While in Texas, Holtzman learned that he would be allowed to get weekend passes so he could return to the Cubs to pitch. To help him prepare, the Cubs sent former catcher and coach (as a part of the "College of Coaches" approach that the Cubs took in 1961 and 1962) El Tappe to Texas to work with Holtzman when he was off duty. Beginning in mid-August, Holtzman was granted weekend passes, and flew to wherever the Cubs were playing. He pitched in four games, August 13 and 20 and September 3 and 30. He was extremely, and perhaps surprisingly, effective in each outing, winning all four. All told, he posted a record of 9-0 and an ERA of 2.53 for the season. Holtzman regressed a bit in the 1968 season, which

was again disrupted by military duty, including in August when his unit served guard duty during the stormy Democratic National Convention in Chicago. He was able to start 32 games and pitch 215 innings, and posted a record of 11-14 and an ERA of 3.35.

The 1969 campaign was both a breakthrough and heartbreaking season for Holtzman and the Cubs. He got off to a great start, including a span in mid-May of 33 innings without allowing a run. By June 10, Holtzman had a record of 10-1 and the Cubs held a seven-game lead in the National League East. His best performance of the season came on August 19, when he pitched a no-hitter against the Atlanta Braves and pitcher Phil Niekro. Holtzman was aided by a wind that blew in from center field and kept a seventh-inning drive by Henry Aaron in the park; left fielder Billy Williams caught it at the wall. Holtzman faced Aaron again with two out in the ninth inning, and induced a groundout that ended the game. The game was unique in that Holtzman did not strike out a single batter in the game.

For the Cubs, this game was unfortunately one of the final highlights of the season, as they went on to lose what seemed an insurmountable lead and the division to the "miracle" New York Mets. During their September swoon, Holtzman was not terribly effective on the mound; he went 1-5 as the Cubs collapsed. He finished the season with a record of 17-13 and a 3.58 ERA.

In 1970 Holtzman was the number-two pitcher in the Cubs rotation, with Fergie Jenkins as the team's ace. The Cubs had another good season, but finished second in the division again, this time behind the Pittsburgh Pirates. Holtzman finished the season again with 17 wins, posting a record of 17-11 and an ERA of 3.38. He struck out 202 batters, the only time in his career he exceeded 200 strikeouts in a season. This was likely a result of pitching 287⅔ innings. In 1971 Holtzman fell out of favor with manager Durocher. Between interruptions to his season for military duty and criticism from Durocher, Holtzman grew unhappy. Durocher rapped Holtzman in the press for not using his fastball enough and relying too much on his curve.

He insinuated that Holtzman was not making his best effort. Allegedly, Durocher also made anti-Semitic slurs about Holtzman. Holtzman struggled throughout the season, but did have one exceptional game. On June 3 he tossed his second no-hitter, this time against the Cincinnati Reds in Riverfront Stadium. He struck out six and walked four in the 1-0 win. His opponent on the mound was Gary Nolan, and the run he gave up was unearned. Aside from the no-hitter, the season was a difficult one for Holtzman. He finished with a record of 9-15 and an ERA of 4.48.

After absorbing the criticism of Durocher, Holtzman asked for a trade. While he had had a poor season, he was still only 25 years old and had not suffered any injuries. The Cubs followed through on his request, and on November 29, 1971, Holtzman was traded to the Oakland A's for outfielder Rick Monday. The trade took Holtzman from the hapless Cubs to an Oakland A's team on the cusp of greatness.

With the addition of Holtzman, the 1972 Oakland A's had a pitching staff that was even stronger than it had been in 1971, when the A's won 101 games. Holtzman joined fellow left-hander and 1971 Cy Young Award winner Vida Blue, as well as Catfish Hunter, and Blue Moon Odom in the A's pitching rotation. Because of Holtzman's struggles in 1971, A's owner Charlie Finley cut his pay from $56,500 in 1971 to $53,250 for 1972. But Holtzman had a much better chance to succeed in Oakland. Because of the players' strike, which delayed the opening of the 1972 season, and Vida Blue's contract holdout to start the season, the pitching rotation was not set at the start of the season. As a result, Holtzman ended up as the Opening Day pitcher. He faced the Minnesota Twins on April 15, pitching a strong eight innings before giving way to reliever Rollie Fingers with a 3-2 lead. Fingers blew the save and the win for Holtzman, but the A's came back to win in 11 innings.

Holtzman was a highly effective pitcher all season long. He was named to the American League All-Star team, although he did not pitch in the game. Holtzman had a fine September and October, winning his final five decisions of the season. He finished with a record

of 19-11 and an ERA of 2.51. In the League Championship Series, against the Tigers, Holtzman started Game Three, with the A's having won the first two games. He gave up two runs in the fourth inning, and was pinch-hit for in the fifth. The A's offense could not do much against Tigers starter Joe Coleman, and the A's ended up losing, 3-0.

Holtzman had better luck in the World Series. He pitched Game One, matched up against Gary Nolan of the Cincinnati Reds. Holtzman pitched well enough against the potent Reds offense to get the win, with relief help from Rollie Fingers and Vida Blue. Holtzman also started Game Four, facing Reds starter Don Gullett. Holtzman pitched well before leaving the game with a 1-0 lead in the eighth inning with two outs and Dave Concepcion at third. Reliever Vida Blue lost the lead, but the A's prevailed, scoring two runs in the bottom of the ninth. Holtzman pitched once more in the Series, making a relief appearance in the eighth inning of Game Seven. With the A's leading, 3-1, Holtzman relieved Catfish Hunter after Hunter allowed a leadoff single to Pete Rose. Holtzman gave up a double to Joe Morgan, putting the tying runs on base. Holtzman was then relieved by Rollie Fingers, who allowed Rose to score on a sacrifice fly by Tony Perez. But Fingers allowed no other runs and finished off the game, and the World Series.

After his and the A's success in 1972, Holtzman was given a raise by the penurious Charlie Finley, to $66,500. The 1973 season was another great one for Holtzman. He had a very strong first half, going 7-0 in May and putting together a record of 10-2 with an ERA of 1.56 by June 1. He hit a rough patch in June, going 1-6 for the month. Nevertheless, he was named to the All-Star team, and pitched in the game, relieving teammate and starter Catfish Hunter with one out in the second inning. After getting Johnny Bench to ground out, he give up a single to former Cubs teammate Ron Santo, then induced Chris Speier to ground out. Holtzman then gave way to a parade of relievers in the exhibition. He steadied his season in July and finished 1973 as a 20-game winner, with a record of 21-13 and a 2.97 ERA.

Holtzman pitched Game Three of the American League Championship Series against Orioles starter Mike Cuellar in Oakland with the series tied at 1-1. It was one of the most thrilling postseason games ever played. Holtzman gave up a solo home run to Orioles first baseman Earl Williams in the second inning, then matched Cuellar in shutting down the opposition. The A's tied up the score, 1-1, in the eighth inning, and both Holtzman and Cuellar continued to pitch as the game went into extra innings. Holtzman continued to shut down the Orioles through 11 innings before Bert Campaneris hit a game-winning home run in the bottom of the inning. Holtzman pitched 11 innings, giving up only three hits and one walk, and pitching through three errors by the A's to earn the 2-1 win.

In the World Series, against the New York Mets, the A's leaned heavily on Holtzman, who started Games One, Four, and Seven, matched up against Mets starter Jon Matlack in each game. In Game One Holtzman gave up one run in five innings and got the win. In Game Four, he gave up a three-run home run to Rusty Staub in the first inning, then walked John Milner and gave up a single to Jerry Grote, and was taken out after getting only two outs in the first inning. A's manager Dick Williams did not lose faith in Holtzman, however, and started him in Game Seven. Holtzman pitched well and also helped himself at the plate. In the third inning of the scoreless game, Holtzman doubled and later scored on a Campaneris home run that was a part of a four-run rally. Holtzman pitched 5⅓ innings, and got the win as the A's won their second World Series in a row.

The next season, 1974, was another great year for both Holtzman and the A's. Before the season, Holtzman won his arbitration case, securing a $93,000 contract, $13,000 more than Finley had offered. Holtzman was again the number three starter in the A's rotation behind Hunter and Blue, although all three hurlers would have been the ace on many other teams. He finished the season with a record of 19-17 and an ERA of 3.07, helping the A's to their fourth consecutive postseason appearance. The A's faced the Orioles again in the League Championship Series. After the A's lost the first game of the five-game series, in Oakland, Holtzman faced Dave McNally in Game Two. Holtzman pitched brilliantly, throwing a complete game and shutting out the Orioles, 5-0. He allowed five hits and two walks, with only one Oriole batter getting as far as second base.

Holtzman continued his dominant pitching against the Los Angeles Dodgers in the first all-California World Series. The pitching matchup for Game One of the Series was Holtzman and Andy Messersmith. Holtzman pitched 4⅓ innings and allowed one unearned run before giving way to Rollie Fingers, who picked up the win. In addition to his pitching, Holtzman doubled off Messersmith in the fifth, advanced to third on a wild pitch, and scored on a bunt single by Campaneris. It was the second run of the game for the A's, who went on to win by a score of 3-2. Holtzman and Messersmith faced off again in Game Four, and again Holtzman helped himself at the plate, this time hitting a home run in the third inning of the scoreless game. He pitched 7⅔ innings and allowed two runs before handing over a 5-2 lead to Fingers. Holtzman earned the win, the fourth and final World Series victory of his career.

After the season Holtzman had acrimonious contract negotiations with Finley. They again went to arbitration, with Finley offering $93,000, the same as Holtzman earned in 1974, and Holtzman asking $112,000. After the arbitration hearing, much to the chagrin of Holtzman, Finley went public with a statistical analysis of what he deemed Holtzman's shortcomings. Finley won the case. The dealings with Finley greatly frustrated Holtzman, who spoke of retiring and joining a Chicago investment firm, perhaps even before the end of the season.[4]

Although his record was 3-6 at the end of May, Holtzman had a fairly strong start to the 1975 season, allowing three runs or more in only two of his first 12 starts. On June 8, against the Tigers, he came tantalizingly close to pitching his third no-hitter. In the fourth inning, Holtzman walked a batter, who was immediately erased by a double play. Then, after 8⅔ hitless innings, the 27th Tiger to come the plate, weak-hitting shortstop Tom Veryzer doubled to break up the no-hitter. Holtzman proceeded to strike out the next batter, Ron LeFlore, and won the game, 4-0. Holtzman pitched effectively for the remainder of the season, finishing with a record of 18-14, and an ERA of 3.14.

In the postseason for the fifth consecutive year, the A's faced the Boston Red Sox in the League Championship Series. Holtzman pitched Game One, matched up against Red Sox ace Luis Tiant. The Red Sox took a quick lead, scoring two unearned runs in the first inning. Then in the seventh, Dwight Evans and Rick Burleson doubled off Holtzman, knocking him from the game, as the Red Sox scored five runs in the inning. Holtzman was charged with the loss as the Red Sox won the game 7-1. After an A's loss in Game Two of the series, Holtzman was called upon to start Game Three on just two days' rest. He pitched valiantly, but in the top of the fourth the Red Sox scored an unearned run to take the lead. Then in the fifth, the Red Sox knocked Holtzman from the game and went on to win, 5-3, and sweep the series.

After the 1975 season, major-league players and owners were negotiating a new contract and agreed to suspend the arbitration process. As a result, Finley offered Holtzman and eight other A's contracts with 20 percent pay cuts, the maximum allowable cut. Holtzman and several other players chose to remain unsigned and report to spring training in an effort to become free agents after the season. He was becoming increasingly disenchanted with Charlie Finley's negotiating tactics and his approach to his players. On April 2 Holtzman was freed from Finley. In a blockbuster deal, Holtzman, Reggie Jackson, and minor-league pitcher Bill Von Bommel were traded to Baltimore for pitchers Mike Torrez and Paul Mitchell and outfielder Don Baylor. Holtzman pitched well for the Orioles, holding an ERA of 2.86 in mid-June. However, his stay in Baltimore ended abruptly. At the trading deadline, June 15, he was a part of a ten-player trade between the Orioles and the New York Yankees. Holtzman, along with pitchers Doyle Alexander, Grant Jackson, and Jimmy Freeman, and catcher Elrod Hendricks were traded to the Yankees for catcher Rick Dempsey

and pitchers Scott McGregor, Tippy Martinez, Rudy May, and Dave Pagan. Holtzman provided a solid left-handed starter for the Yankees. However, the Yankees had traded to their division rivals several players who would later star for the Orioles.

The trade reunited Holtzman with Catfish Hunter, and for a time it was thought that Vida Blue would also be a Yankee. But Finley's sale of Blue to the Yankees was disallowed by Commissioner Bowie Kuhn. Holtzman stepped into the Yankee pitching staff, but was not nearly as strong as he had been in previous years with the A's. By season's end, he had with a record of 14-11 (9-7 with the Yankees), but with an uncharacteristically high ERA of 3.65. His strikeout totals for the season were significantly lower than in previous years, only 66 in 246⅔ innings. And although the Yankees won their division, Holtzman, who of course had a tremendous amount of postseason pitching experience, pitched in neither the League Championship Series nor the World Series.

In the offseason Holtzman got a five-year, $825,000 contract. He began the season in the starting rotation. However, after a few starts, including a particularly disastrous one on May 16 in which he could get only one out before being relieved, Holtzman found himself in Yankee manager Billy Martin's doghouse. For most of the remaining season, Holtzman pitched out the bullpen and rarely when the game was on the line. He was essentially unable to strike out batters, amassing only 14 whiffs in 71⅔ innings. He finished the season with a record of 2-3, with his last decision coming in mid-May. As in 1976, Holtzman again did not appear in the playoffs or World Series.

Much has been made over the years of Billy Martin disliking Holtzman, and perhaps displaying a streak of anti-Semitism in his treatment of the pitcher. Likewise, George Steinbrenner seemed to dislike Holtzman both for his performance on the field, especially after just getting a large contract, and also for his work with the players union as the player representative for the team. However, there is no question that Holtzman's performance on the mound was not close to what it had been in the recent past.

Holtzman started the 1978 season in the Yankees' rotation again, but lasted for only two starts before he was benched again. He did not pitch again for a month, when in mid-May he made a start, which was likely to showcase him for suitors in a trade. After two more relief appearances later in May, Holtzman was traded to the Cubs on June 10 for pitcher Ron Davis. Holtzman was both relieved to get away from Billy Martin and the Yankees, and happy to be going back to Chicago, where his career began and where he made his home. His pitching did not improve, however. Holtzman first pitched out of the bullpen for the Cubs, then joined the rotation for a few weeks, then went back to the bullpen. He was not terribly effective in either role, and between his time with the Yankees and the Cubs, finished the season with a record of 1-3 and an ERA of 5.60. In 70⅔ innings he struck out just 39 while walking 44.

Holtzman fared a little better for the Cubs in 1979. He worked as a fifth starter, although he made three relief appearances to go along with his 20 starts. He had two especially good outings against Houston. On May 12 and July 7, he shut out the Astros. However, after two rough starts in late July and early August, Holtzman was relegated to the bullpen once more. He made one more start, and pitched quite well, on September 19 against the St. Louis Cardinals. In seven innings he held the Cardinals scoreless, giving up four hits and two walks before giving way to reliever Bruce Sutter, who blew the lead for Holtzman. It was Holtzman's last major-league appearance. Immediately after the season, the Cubs released him. While the Yankees would pay his contract for two more seasons, Holtzman was out of baseball at the age of 33.

Holtzman finished his career with a record of 174-150 and an ERA of 3.49. He won nine more games in his career than Sandy Koufax, making Holtzman the winningest Jewish pitcher of all time. He received a handful of votes for the Hall of Fame in 1985 and 1986, the two years that he was considered for election into the Hall. After baseball, Holtzman worked as a stockbroker and in the insurance industry. In 2007 he briefly returned to the sport when he managed the Petah Tikva Pioneers in the new Israel Baseball League. He did not have a good experience with the team however; he was unhappy with how the league was run, and left the team before the season was complete.[5] As of 2014 Holtzman was retired and living outside St. Louis.

SOURCES

Clark, Tom, *Champagne and Baloney: The Rise and Fall of Finley's A's* (New York: Harper and Row, 1976).

Clark, Tom, *Baseball: The Figures* (Berkeley, California: Serendipity Books, 1976).

Clark, Tom, *Fan Poems* (Plainfield, Vermont: North Atlantic Books, 1976).

Feldman, Doug, *Miracle Collapse: The 1969 Chicago Cubs* (Lincoln, Nebraska: University of Nebraska Press, 2006).

Gold, Eddie, and Art Ahrens, *The New Era Cubs: 1941-1985* (Chicago: Bonus Books, 1985).

James, Bill, and Rob Neyer, *The Neyer/James Guide To Pitchers* (New York: Fireside, 2004).

Markusen, Bruce, *A Baseball Dynasty: Charlie Finley's Swingin' A's* (Haworth, New Jersey: St. Johann Press, 2002).

Neyer, Rob, and Eddie Epstein, *Baseball Dynasties* (New York: W.W. Norton and Company, 2000).

baseball-reference.com

NOTES

1   Eddie Gold and Art Ahrens, *The New Era Cubs: 1941-1985,* 143.

2   Ibid.

3   Doug Feldman, *Miracle Collapse: The 1969 Chicago Cubs,* 38.

4   Tom Clark, *Champagne and Baloney: The Rise and Fall of Finley's A's,* 306.

5   Joel Greenberg, "Israeli Baseball League Turns Sour For Holtzman," *Chicago Tribune,* September 19, 2007. (The league folded after one season.)

Joe Horlen

By Gregory H. Wolf

A name can sometimes be confusing. Four years into his major-league career, Joel Edward Horlen said that though the news media and fans knew him by his proper name, Joel, "All my friends call me Joe and that's what I go by. When I got into baseball, it became Joel somehow. I guess because that's how I sign my contract."[1] Often overlooked as one of the best pitchers of the 1960s, Joe Horlen led all American League pitchers with a 2.32 ERA over a five-year period (1964-68) as the right-handed ace of the Chicago White Sox. (Chicago led the AL in team ERA for three of those five seasons.) After pitching for the notoriously weak-hitting South Siders for his first 11 years, Horlen concluded his career as a reliever and spot starter for the world champion Oakland Athletics in 1972. With a career record of 116-117, Horlen could lay claim as one the best pitchers with a losing record in major-league history.

Born on August 14, 1937, in San Antonio, Texas, to Kermit and Geneva Horlen, Joel Edward Horlen wanted to be a major-league pitcher from the time he was child. His father, a former semipro catcher, played in a Sunday beer league where Joe, as his parents called him, and his younger brother, Edward, were introduced to the game. Kermit, an executive at an insurance company, played an active role in Joe's development as a pitcher and coached him from the time he started playing organized baseball through his high-school days. "My dad [built] a pitching mound in the backyard and [hung] a tire on a rope by the shed that we had," Horlen said. "My mother gave us an old rug and we put it over the tire and just threw to it all day long."[2] By the time he was about 10 years old, Joe began playing for his father on a YMCA team, and in 1952 was on the first-ever PONY League national championship team. At Burbank High School in San Antonio, he earned letters in basketball, football, and golf, but his school did not field a baseball team. A small, quick, and versatile athlete, Joe played shortstop on his American Legion team (led by future major-league pitcher Gary Bell) and pitched occasionally, and also honed his pitching skills in Sunday beer leagues.

After graduating from high school in 1956, Horlen was picked to play in the national Hearst Baseball Sandlot Classic.[3] The Cleveland Indians sought to sign him, but Horlen was recruited by baseball coach Toby Greene of Oklahoma State University and enrolled there, intending to play baseball and study geology. In 1959, as a junior, he posted a 9-1 record, including three victories in the NCAA tournament, and led the Cowboys to the championship, upsetting the University of Arizona. "Every major-league scout in the Southwest was on his trail," *The Sporting News* reported.[4] White Sox scout Ted Lyons had been following Horlen for two years by the time the Cowboys

made it to the College World Series in Omaha, and Chicago sent Jack Sheehan, the team's farm director, to scout the tournament. "Jack talked with me and all he asked was that before I signed with anyone that I'd promise that he'd be the last person I talked with," Horlen said.[5] In the wake of the Cowboys' victory celebration, Horlen contacted Sheehan at 2:30 A.M. and accepted the team's contract offer, which included a reported $30,000 bonus.[6]

Horlen was hit in the pitching arm by a line drive in his first game for the Lincoln (Nebraska) Chiefs of the Class B Illinois-Indiana-Iowa League, but nevertheless started four times, relieved once, and pitched 41 innings in a 13-day span to begin his professional career. "My arm wasn't sore or anything," he said of the initial heavy workload that led to a disappointing 1-9 record, "but it was just dead for the rest of the year!"[7] With a 5.64 ERA in 91 innings (13 starts), Horlen was sent to the Florida Instructional League after the season. Promoted to the Charleston (South Carolina) White Sox in the Class A South Atlantic League to start the 1960 season, he was forced out of the starting rotation by a sore arm. After 26 appearances (12 starts) and a 2.92 ERA in 120 innings, Horlen's season was cut short when the White Sox medical staff determined that he had a pinched nerve in the arm.

After playing again in the Instructional League in 1960, Horlen was added to the White Sox' 40-man roster and went to his first big-league spring training in 1961. A coachable, hard-working, and intense pitcher, Horlen was assigned to the San Diego Padres in the Pacific Coast League. He credited managers Bob Kuzava at Charleston and Bill Norman in San Diego with helping him learn to set up hitters and develop into a bona-fide major leaguer. At San Diego Horlen posted a 12-9 record on a losing ballclub. Norman praised Horlen's ambition and considered him the best pitching prospect he had seen since Mike Garcia in the late 1940s. With a 2.51 ERA (second in the league) in 197 innings, Horlen attributed his new-found stamina to his close work with Herb Score, who was attempting a comeback with the Padres.

A September call-up, Horlen joined the White Sox in Minnesota and was slated to start against the Twins on September 5, but was surprised when he was called to relieve Cal McLish to start the fourth inning on the 4th. "I was sitting in the bullpen wearing my warm-up jacket because I was a little embarrassed (his uniform with his number and name on the back had not arrived) and the guys were giving it to me," said Horlen. "Then during the middle of the game the phone rings and Al Lopez said to get me up and ready. [When] I'm ready to throw my first pitch in the majors, Twins manager Sam Mele called time and went out to talk with the home-plate umpire … and shrugs his shoulders like 'Who the heck is that guy?' Everyone got a good laugh out of it including myself and it might have helped me since it relieved the tension."[8] Horlen pitched four scoreless innings, surrendering just two hits, and earned the victory in his major-league debut. But he was hit hard in four subsequent starts, and finished with a 1-3 record and 6.62 ERA.

Manager Al Lopez and pitching coach Ray Berres were convinced that Horlen would be successful as soon as he learned to control his "big roundhouse curve," which came in head-high and dropped to the batter's knees.[9] Playing after the season for the Mayaguez Indians in the Puerto Rican Winter League, Horlen began throwing his curveball faster to lessen the break. With his hard curve, a fastball with good movement, and a sinker, Horlen emerged as one of the league's best pitchers. Pitching an unfathomable 401 innings in a 12-month period (186 with Mayaguez, 197 with San Diego, and 18 with the White Sox), Horlen was tabbed the "likely rookie pitcher of the year" for the 1962 season by *The Sporting News*.[10]

Named to the White Sox' starting rotation in 1962, Horlen opened the season by pitching an impressive five-hitter against the California Angels on April 12, allowing just one run. The game foreshadowed his career with Chicago in the 1960s: The light-hitting White Sox were shut out and Horlen's reputation as a "tough-luck loser" was in the making. In his next start he pitched his best game of the season, blanking the Twins on six hits. The 24-year-old Horlen was benefiting from working with coach Berres, who taught him how to set up hitters, keep his pitches low in the strike zone, and let the batters get themselves out. "Ray was an absolute stickler for mechanics," Horlen said. "He'd watch you when you were throwing on the sidelines and he'd keep reminding you about little things … things that made a big difference, like your arm swing, staying on top of the ball and the position of your body."[11] Not an overpowering pitcher, Horlen learned to approach pitching and batters cerebrally; no longer concerned about hitting the corners, he let his natural abilities come to the surface. Finishing May with two consecutive complete games that pushed his record to 5-2, Horlen seemed to fulfill preseason projections, but after enduring a rough June (19 earned runs in 18⅓ innings), he tore a muscle in his pitching shoulder and missed ten weeks. Returning in September to win two of three decisions, Horlen finished the season with a 7-6 record and a 4.89 ERA. In the offseason he worked for the White Sox' ticket office.

Now tabbed the "best young pitcher" in baseball, Horlen began the 1963 season with a new-found sense of confidence.[12] But after winning his first start, against the Angels, Horlen was plagued by wildness in his next four starts and lost his spot in the rotation after a disastrous outing against the Angels on May 12 in which he got just one out in the first inning and gave up three hits before Lopez yanked him. Struggling with his command out of the bullpen and as a spot starter, Horlen finally was optioned to the Indianapolis Indians in the American Association in early July to work on his curveball and regain his confidence. Overpowering the competition with three wins and a 1.74 ERA, he was recalled and defeated the Detroit Tigers on July 25 in his first start back. Four days later, pitching against the Senators in Washington, he had a no-hitter and a precarious 1-0 lead going into the ninth inning. After losing the no-hitter on a one-out single by Chuck Hinton, Horlen lost the game when Don Lock crushed a two-out walk-off home run. Horlen concluded the season with four consecutive victories, posting an 11-7 record and 3.27 ERA on a staff considered the best in the league.

After leading San Juan to the Puerto Rican Winter League title in 1963-64, Horlen was a contract holdout and paid his own expenses to spring training before finally signing a contract at the end of camp. In his season debut he gave up four runs in three innings in a 4-1 loss to the Boston Red Sox. Losing his patience with his young hurler, Lopez sent him to the bullpen, where he saw action in just four games in the next five weeks. After a spot start on May 24 against the Senators in which Horlen gave up two earned runs in five innings in a 3-0 loss, Lopez put him back into the rotation and Horlen pitched well but with little luck. Though he posted a 1.84 ERA in 44 innings in June, he won just two of five decisions as the White Sox provided him a total of seven runs in his six starts in the month. Then he turned things around, concluding the first half of the season with three consecutive complete-game victories. He struck out a career-high ten batters against the Senators on July 1 and hurled a four-hit shutout against the Indians on July 5. With his "souped-up curve," the slender right-hander was the hottest pitcher in baseball.[13] "I like to work hitters in and out, up and down," said Horlen, "but never have I been able to put the ball so well where I want."[14]

Despite Horlen's third consecutive month with a sub-2.00 ERA in July, critics pointed to his one complete game in eight starts as proof that he "tires in late innings" and lacked stamina.[15] Unknown to most at the time, Horlen suffered throughout the month from a recurrence of pain in his right shoulder that required cortisone shots. From a career perspective and in context of pitching in the 1960s Horlen did not pitch many complete games (59 in 290 starts) and reached double figures only once (13 in 1967). However, managers Lopez and Eddie Stanky, for whom Horlen pitched from 1961 through 1968, had reputations for being "quick hooks" and were also blessed with deep and extremely effective and efficient bullpens with knuckleballers Hoyt Wilhelm, Eddie Fisher, and Wilbur Wood, as well as Bob Locker. A nervous type on and off the mound, Horlen credited veteran Wilhelm with helping him to learn to relax while pitching and to throw naturally instead of leading his pitches or aiming at the corners.

Pitching his best in September when the White Sox needed it most, Horlen posted a 1.07 ERA with four complete games and won three of four decisions. Duplicating his career high of ten strikeouts in a victory over the Indians on September 5, Horlen gave the White Sox a surprising one-game lead over the New York Yankees, whom they battled the entire season in an exciting pennant race. The White Sox relied on their Big Three pitching stars—20-game winner Gary Peters, 19-game winner Juan Pizzaro, and Horlen. Pitching on three days' rest for almost the entire month of September, Horlen tossed a complete-game victory against the Athletics on September 27 and a two-hit shutout over the A's on October 3 to give the White Sox their eighth consecutive victory, but the they could not overtake the Yankees, who went 24-9 down the stretch to win the pennant. "We thought we were going to win [the pennant]," Horlen said.[16] Provided just nine runs of support in his nine losses, Horlen won 13 games, was second in the AL with a career-low 1.88 ERA, and limited hitters to a .190 batting average by surrendering a league-low 6.1 hits per nine innings.

With a crew-cut hairstyle and brown eyes, Horlen lived in the offseason in his hometown of San Antonio with his wife, Catherine, whom people called Kitty, and raised a daughter and a son. Quiet and soft-spoken, he worked for an insurance company and had the reputation of investing wisely and eschewing grand expenses. Balking at Chicago's 1965 contract offer for "less than $14,000," Horlen was a holdout for the second year in a row, finally reporting in mid-March.[17]

Horlen pitched consistently all season and led the team with 34 starts, a 2.88 ERA, 219 innings pitched, and four shutouts, yet finished with just a .500 record (13-13) on a team that won 95 games and finished in second place behind the surprising Minnesota Twins. (It was Al Lopez's tenth second-place finish.) The White Sox scored two runs or fewer in eight of Horlen's losses and four runs or more just twice.

Accepting his contract the day before 1966 spring training opened, Horlen was greeted by new manager

Eddie Stanky, who had replaced the easygoing player's manager Lopez. Stanky, known as the Brat in his playing days, pushed his players and instituted an aggressive, hit-and-run-style game uncommon in the 1960s. On a weak-hitting team (last in the AL with a .231 average), the small and quick Horlen was used a pinch-runner 27 times. "I learned more about baseball from Eddie than any other manager I ever played for," he said. "He was tough, some guys just didn't get along with him. Eddie would walk up and down the dugout during a game and he'd often stop by a guy and ask him, 'What's the count?' If you didn't know it you'd be fined $25."[18]

Beginning with a complete-game 2-1 loss to the Angels on April 14, Horlen lost six of his first seven decisions despite owning a stellar 2.64 ERA at the end of May for the 19-21 Sox. In June and July he won six of ten decisions, and tossed his first shutout of the season on July 2, against Boston. He suffered from another bout of shoulder pain in August and failed to make it out of the second inning in two of four starts. Demoted to the bullpen, Horlen made six appearances, the last of which marked an improbable reversal of his season. In relief of Gary Peters on September 9, he held the Washington Senators to three hits over six innings in a scoreless game before giving way to Hoyt Wilhelm in the tenth inning. That earned Horlen his first start in three weeks, and he hurled a three-hit shutout against the first-place (and eventual World Series champion) Baltimore Orioles on September 16. Then he blanked the Yankees for seven innings to earn his tenth and final victory of the season on September 22, and threw eight more scoreless innings in a no-decision against Boston. Horlen's scoreless streak reached 32 innings before the Yankees ended it and dealt him his last loss of the season on October 1. Finishing with an 83-79 record, the White Sox set an AL record for the lowest team ERA post-1920 (2.68). Gary Peters led the league with a 1.98 ERA, and Horlen was second, posting a 2.43 ERA in 211 innings. Provided three runs or fewer in 11 of his losses, Horlen saw his record fall to 10-13, his first losing season as a starter.

Confident in his abilities and in the best shape of his life after undergoing a rigorous offseason exercise regimen and officiating at local basketball games, the 29-year-old Horlen braced for a career year in 1967. "If you can stay loose and relaxed," he said, "you won't be pressing and you'll retain your rhythm. If you have your rhythm, you'll have good motion. That means you'll have good control."[19] Horlen had a peculiar way of staying loose: He chewed a wad of tissue. Explaining that he got sick when he tried to chew tobacco and felt bloated when he chewed gum, Horlen began chewing tissue because "it relaxes me."[20]

Dogged by criticisms that he lost concentration in games, Horlen got off to the best start in his career in 1967.[21] With two different fastballs (a sinker and one that broke away from right-handers) and a hard curve, Horlen tossed two complete-game victories over the Senators in a week, the latter being his fourth and final career two-hitter, a 1-0 shutout in front of just over 4,100 Washington fans on April 22. Regularly accused of throwing a spitball, Horlen denied the charge, but years later admitted, "I threw about 20 spitballs in one game but it was just to see if I could get away with it."[22] With a team-leading ten wins for the first-place White Sox in early July, Horlen was named to the American League All-Star team for the first (and only) time, but did not pitch in the game.

Horlen won four of five decisions to begin the second half of the season, and his 3-1 victory over the Orioles on August 18 pushed his record to 14-3 and kept the White Sox in an exciting four-team pennant race with the Twins, Tigers, and Red Sox. After losing his last three starts in August, Horlen ditched his slider (which he thought negatively affected his fastball because of its delivery), threw his curveball one out of three pitches, and relied even more on his fastball. He pitched a no-hitter against the Tigers on September 10. Horlen's only blemishes were a hit batter. and an error by first baseman Ken Boyer. Then, pitching on short rest, he tossed consecutive shutouts over the Angels on September 19 and the Indians (a three-hitter) on September 23, his 19th victory of the season. In third place one game behind the Twins with five

games to go, the White Sox lost those five games to two second-division teams, the Kansas City Athletics and the Senators, and finished in fourth place at 89-73. Horlen was the loser when the A's shut out the White Sox 4-0 on September 27, effectively ending the team's pennant hopes, and then failed in his bid to win his 20th game in the final, meaningless match of the season. In his best big-league season, Horlen posted career highs with 19 wins, 258 innings pitched, 13 complete games, and a league-leading six shutouts and 2.06 ERA. Holding opponents to a .203 batting average, Horlen walked just 58 batters and led the AL with a 0.953 WHIP.[23] The White Sox staff set a major-league post-Deadball-Era record with a 2.45 ERA.

Coming off an exciting and emotionally draining season in 1967, the White Sox lost their first ten games of 1968 on their way to a tumultuous 67-95 season during which Stanky and his replacement, Les Moss, were fired and 60-year-old Al Lopez was brought back for the last seven weeks of the season. Horlen pitched inconsistently and lost his first five starts. Bothered by calcium deposits on his shoulder all season, he struggled to pitch deep into games and had only four complete games. One of those came on May 17 when he pitched ten innings in a four-hit, 1-0 shutout of the Oakland A's. He held the Orioles scoreless for seven innings and the Yankees scoreless for 8⅓ in his next two starts, both no-decisions, and ran his scoreless streak to a career-best 37 consecutive innings before giving up a run in a complete-game 3-1 victory over the Orioles on May 29. With Gary Peters suffering an off-year and Tommy John injured, Horlen was the workhorse of the staff, finishing with a 2.37 ERA in 223⅔ innings, but a 12-14 record. The White Sox scored only 16 runs in his losses.

After an offseason procedure to remove calcium deposits in his shoulder and heal "atrophied areas of his deltoid muscle," Horlen began spring training in 1969 in good health.[24] "I didn't have any arm strength," he said of the previous season, and had "active pain every time I pitched."[25] The White Sox finished with 94 losses (only four less than the expansion Seattle Pilots). Horlen started 35 games for the third consecutive season and paced the team with 13 wins, but lost a career-high 16, and posted a 3.78 ERA in 235⅔ innings, the sixth consecutive (and final time) he exceeded 200 innings in a season.

A pilot as well as a ballplayer, Horlen flew his own plane to spring training in Sarasota in 1970.[26] After losing his season debut, Horlen defeated the Angels for his 100th career victory on April 14. He was 5-2 on May 15, but then entered the most frustrating period in his career. Pitching for the worst team in White Sox history (loser of 106 games), Horlen won only one of his next 15 decisions. His season appeared to be over when he discovered that he had torn cartilage in his right knee after a start on July 28.[27] But Horlen showed "tremendous determination" by coming back five weeks later to make four appearances in September, and finished the season at 6-16 with a career-worst 4.86 ERA.[28]

After venting his frustration at team officials who questioned his work ethic and commitment to baseball during the disastrous 1970 season, Horlen felt more comfortable with new White Sox skipper Chuck Tanner and pitching coach Johnny Sain. As fate would have it, Horlen tore cartilage in his left knee sliding into second base in the last preseason game. "I was going to do a 'pop-up' slide," he said, and "when I threw my left leg back as I hit the dirt I heard a loud pop in my knee. The leg was locked into a 90-degree angle. I just couldn't bend it back."[29] After knee surgery on April 5, Horlen made it back on the field in just 29 days when he pitched two innings of scoreless relief against Boston. Lauded by Tanner for his "true grit," Horlen split his time between starting and relieving and posted an 8-9 record with a 4.26 ERA for the surprising White Sox, who finished 79-83.[30]

Horlen was the White Sox' union representative in 1971 and 1972, and argued in favor of the players' strike in 1972. He clashed with White Sox general manager Stu Holcomb, and was released at the end of spring training, on April 2, the day after players voted for the strike. At a meeting of the Players Association as the team representative (the players had not had time to elect a new one), Horlen was told that Oakland had attempted to acquire him in an offseason trade.[31] He called A's owner Charley Finley. "He asked me about being waived and how my legs were," Horlen said. "I told him that they were fine. He said, 'I've been keeping up with the strike. It's not going to last more than ten days. After five days we're going to send you a plane ticket to come to Oakland.'"[32]

Pitching primarily in long relief, Horlen logged 84 innings and notched a 3.00 ERA for the world champion A's. He appeared once in Oakland's seven-game World Series victory over the Cincinnati Reds, relieving Dave Hamilton in the seventh inning of Game Six (an 8-1 Oakland loss) and giving up two hits, two walks, and a wild pitch before settling down to record three consecutive outs. It was the last time Horlen pitched in the major leagues. Released in the offseason, he announced his retirement. He finished with a 116-117 record and a 3.11 ERA in 12 seasons.

Horlen began working as a building contractor in San Antonio, but was persuaded to join the San Antonio Brewers, the Double-A affiliate of the Cleveland Indians, in midsummer as a pitcher and mentor to the team's young staff.[33] He won six games and lost just one, then worked as a roving minor-league pitching instructor for the Indians for two years before returning to San Antonio, where he owned and operated construction and roofing companies. After a divorce, Horlen married Lois Eisenstein in 1981 and converted to Judaism. He helped start a golf program at the University of Texas at San Antonio.[34] Persuaded to return to baseball in 1987, Horlen served as a minor-league pitching coach and roving pitching instructor over the next 14 years in the farm systems of the New York Mets, Kansas City Royals, San Francisco Giants, and San Diego Padres.

"I had only one goal and that was that I never wanted to embarrass myself out there on the mound," said "Hard Luck Horlen" as he was often known during his years with the White Sox in the 1960s. "I had pride, that's the way I was my whole career. I couldn't control how good or bad the team was, I could only control myself."[35] Still a resident of his hometown in 2013,

Horlen followed baseball closely and was involved with special events and anniversaries of the White Sox.

SOURCES

Joe Horlen player file at the National Baseball Hall of Fame

Ancestry.com

BaseballLibrary.com

Baseball-Reference.com

New York Times

Retrosheet.com

The Sporting News

NOTES

1   *The Sporting News*, February 13, 1965, 5.

2   Mark Liptak, "Flashing back . . . with Joel Horlen," White Sox Interactive.com., whitesoxinteractive.com/rwas/index.php?id=2755&category=11

3   *The Sporting News*, August 8, 1956, 38.

4   *The Sporting News*, March 14, 1962, 8.

5   Liptak.

6   *The Sporting News*, March 14, 1962, 8.

7   Liptak.

8   Liptak.

9   Liptak.

10   *The Sporting News*, April 11, 1962, 46.

11   Liptak.

12   *The Sporting News*, April 20, 1963, 14.

13   United Press International, July 22, 1964. In Horlen's Hall of Fame file.

14   Ibid.

15   *The Sporting News*, September 26, 1964, 5.

16   Liptak.

17   *The Sporting News*, February 13, 1965, 5.

18   Liptak.

19   *The Sporting News*, August 13, 1966, 13.

20   *The Sporting News*, June 17, 1967, 27.

21   *The Sporting News*, May 6, 1967, 7.

22   Gary Herron, "Horlen was a classic, good-pitch/no-hit hurler," *Sports Collectors Digest*, March 17, 1995, 139.

23   WHIP refers to the total number of walks and hits given up dived by innings. A WHIP of 1.0 means that the pitcher surrendered an average of nine hits and walks per nine innings.

24   *The Sporting News*, February 8, 1969, 42.

25   Ibid.

26   *The Sporting News*, April 11, 1970, 58.

27   *The Sporting News*, August 8, 1970, 12, and August 15, 1970, 15.

28   *The Sporting News*, December 5, 1970, 51.

29   Liptak.

30   *The Sporting News*, June 12, 1971.

31   The Sporting News, April 22, 1972, 14

32   Liptak.

33   "Horlen Signs with Brewers" [no publisher; 1972]. In Horlen's Hall of Fame file.

34   Herron, 139.

35   Liptak.

Vern Hoscheit

By Jimmy Keenan

Vern Hoscheit's career in professional base-ball spanned six decades. Signed as a catcher by the New York Yankees in 1941, he had little hope of making the major-league roster with Bill Dickey and later Yogi Berra ensconced behind the plate. The Yankees front office took notice of Hoscheit's leadership potential and made him a player-manager for its McAlester (Oklahoma) club at the age of 26. Although Hoscheit never was called up to the big leagues, he ended his minor-league career with a solid .283 batting average. Then he made his mark in the majors as the bullpen coach on four World Series winners. One of baseball's true unsung heroes, he taught the fundamentals of the game to hundreds of players in five different major-league organizations, as well as scores of youngsters in American Legion ball.

Whitey Herzog, who played for Hoscheit in the minors, told *The Sporting News*, "He was a good manager for young people, a good teacher. He drove the bus, handed out meal money, did the laundry. He'd catch and he'd pitch. He was really the only extra guy we had. I think we carried 16 guys, one for each position, plus the pitchers."[1]

Player and manager Davey Johnson wrote about Hoscheit in his book on the 1985 Mets, "Vern, whom all the players call 'Dad,' is the greatest coach of catch-ers I have ever known. We have been friends since I was in the Baltimore organization, where he trained Andy Etchebarren, Larry Haney, and Curt Blefary. He gave Curt an extra three or four years in the big leagues. When he was hired by the Oakland A's, he made Adrian Garrett into a catcher for manager Dick Williams and then his big coup was transforming outfielder Gene Tenace into a major-league catcher."[2]

Vernard Arthur "Bud" Hoscheit was born on April 1, 1922, in Brunswick, Nebraska. The first German fami-lies had settled in the rural farming community in

1879. By 1915 the town had a bank, a 30-room hotel, and a railroad depot supported by a population of 300. The 1930 US census shows Vernard and his younger sister, Delores, along with their parents, Walter and Elsie (Westerhoff) Hoscheit, living on the family farm in Brunswick.

Hoscheit played his first organized baseball with an American Legion team, the Neligh Antelopes. He graduated from Brunswick High School in 1939. The 5-foot-9, 190-pound Hoscheit was a natural catcher who also played both the infield and outfield. Known for his strong arm and defensive skills, he was also a good hitter with an instinctual knowledge of the game.

In 1940 Hoscheit was the star catcher for Concordia, Kansas, in the Ban Johnson League, and drew the attention of New York Yankees scout Lou Maguolo, who signed him to his first professional contract. Starting the 1941 campaign with the Norfolk Yankees

in the Class D Western League, Hoscheit hit .284 while catching and playing the outfield. Norfolk won the pennant and Hoscheit was named to the All-Star team.

The next year, Hoscheit moved up a rung on the Yankees' minor-league ladder to the Joplin Miners of the Class C Western League. On May 26, 1942, he married the former Helen Edwards in Joplin. That same night, the newlywed belted a grand slam in the bottom of the ninth to give the Miners a 9-8 victory.

In November 1942, he joined the Army Air Corps and was stationed at Lincoln Airfield. While serving at Lincoln, he caught for the base's baseball team. Discharged in January 1946. Hoscheit resumed his professional baseball career in 1947 with the Norfolk Tars in the Class B Piedmont League. After hitting .354 in 19 games, he was promoted to Binghamton (New York) in the Eastern League, where he finished out the season.

The following year, Hoscheit split time between Binghamton, Norfolk, and Triple-A Kansas City (American Association). Named player-manager of the McAlester Rockets in the Class D Sooner State League, Hoscheit batted .335 while guiding his team to the best record in the circuit. Grateful fans presented him with a new car at the end of the season. The Rockets were out of contention in 1949 but captured the playoffs in 1950-51. Hoscheit had the most productive year of his professional career in 1951, hitting .354 with 11 home runs and 109 RBIs. Future Yankee first baseman-outfielder Norm Siebern was a member of the 1951 McAlester club. The 17-year-old rookie credited Hoscheit with being a major influence on his baseball career.

Hoscheit was the first person, other than his immediate family, that Whitey Herzog thanked during his Hall of Fame induction speech in 2010. Herzog, who played for McAlester in 1949-50, wrote of his former minor-league manager in his autobiography, *White Rat: A Life in Baseball*: "Hoscheit was very good at his job. He could teach every phase of the game and he was just hard enough to make everyone a little scared of

him. He really taught me what being a professional baseball player is all about."[3]

Vern and Helen liked McAlester so much that they lived in town full-time during his four-year run with the team. In 1952 Hoscheit took over as manager of the Joplin Miners in the Class C Western Association. The Miners won the second-half title of a split season and then defeated Muskogee in the league playoffs.

Hoscheit's next managerial post was with the Quincy Gems in the Class B Three-I League in 1953. He was named general manager in 1955, serving as manager and GM of the Gems through the 1956 season. His last year with Quincy was his final season as an active player. Hoscheit told the *New York Times,* "I hit a ball off the center-field fence and barely made it into second base. Lee McPhail, who was in charge of the Yankee minor-league teams, told me it was time to retire."[4]

From there Hoscheit was assigned to Peoria, Durham, and finally Greensboro, where he held the dual roles of manager and general manager. In 1959 he left the Yankees organization and became a scout for the Baltimore Orioles. Soon after, he was notified that he had been elected president of the Three-I League. Although he neither sought nor applied for the post, he was voted in unanimously by all eight representatives of the clubs in the circuit. He resigned at the conclusion of the 1961 season after serving two terms as president.

In 1962 Hoscheit returned to the Orioles as a scout, covering Illinois, Iowa, and Wisconsin, while doing double duty as the club's minor-league coordinator. He managed Baltimore's rookie-league team for three years, winning the Florida Instructional League pennant in 1965. Vern also coached the Orioles in spring training during Hank Bauer's tenure as manager.

Late in the 1967 season, Orioles general manager Harry Dalton asked Rochester Red Wings manager Earl Weaver to recommend new coaches for the major-league club. Weaver said that Hoscheit would be his choice for bullpen coach because he was a no-nonsense kind of guy. On October 3, 1967, Hoscheit was hired, replacing Sherm Lollar, who had been released at the end of the season. Earl Weaver and George Bamberger were also brought on as coaches.

Orioles ace Dave McNally credited Hoscheit and pitching coach Bamberger with helping him battle through control problems. Hoscheit was responsible for the development of catchers Elrod Hendricks, Andy Etchebarren, and Larry Haney. He also tutored Curt Blefary on the finer points of catching when the Orioles decided to use the former Rookie of the Year behind the plate.

Hank Bauer was fired as Orioles manager in July 1968, and was replaced by Earl Weaver, who kept Hoscheit on as a coach. On September 29 Oakland A's owner Charlie Finley hired Bauer as manager, and Bauer chose Hoscheit as his bullpen coach. Hoscheit resigned from the Orioles coaching staff to take the job.

For the next few years in Oakland, Hoscheit worked under managers Bauer, John McNamara, Dick Williams, and Alvin Dark. Vern always backed up his players and that included bench-clearing brawls. On July 19, 1972, at County Stadium in Milwaukee, three Brewers batters hit catcher Dave Duncan with their backswings and finally Brewers pitcher Jim Colborn nailed him with a curve. Duncan charged the mound as both benches and bullpens emptied on to the field. The 50-year-old Hoscheit, attempting to join the fray, injured his arm while jumping over the high wall in front of the visitors bullpen. Although Hoscheit was unable to participate in the on-field scuffle, the A's players appreciated his game effort.

Oakland went on to defeat the Cincinnati Reds in the World Series. Hoscheit made sure that 64-year-old advance scout Al Hollingsworth received recognition for his spot-on assessment of the Reds players. "If this man does not get the credit he deserves, it is a real shame," Vern told the Associated Press.[5] Then, turning to Hollingsworth, Hoscheit said, "They did everything you told us they would."[6] Among many observations, the keen-eyed Hollingsworth noted that the Reds scored twice on a pair of two-out bunt singles during

their playoff series with Pittsburgh. A's manager Dick Williams took Hollingsworth's advice and played third baseman Sal Bando up to take away the bunt, which he did successfully throughout the Series.

During spring training in 1973, the A's had a double-header scheduled in Mesa, Arizona, but there were no umpires available. Hoscheit, who had done everything at the ballpark during his minor-league days from concessionaire to groundskeeper, went behind the plate for both tilts, earning an extra $200 from owner Finley

Hoscheit was instrumental in developing Rollie Fingers into one of the game's best relief pitchers. Dick Williams recounted how Fingers had difficulty as a starter: "The closer it got for him to start—and they went every fourth day not every fifth day—the more nervous and hyper he'd get. He'd last one inning or at the most two or three. Bill Posedel was our pitching coach at the time. We finally stuck (Fingers) in the bullpen. Vern Hoscheit was our bullpen coach and he made sure the reliever, whoever it was, knew who he was going to face. And he pumped that into Rollie. Then when Rollie got to the mound, I'd ask him, what did Vern say? He said, well, Vern said I was going to face so and so. I said how are you going to pitch him? He said Vern told me this way. Okay, as long as you know. He put him in some games that didn't mean anything, as the score indicated. He did well. Put him in a little tougher situation, he did well. Put him in a save situation—what they call a save situation now—and he did well. So that's how he became a relief pitcher. And he got better as he went along."[7]

Hoscheit tutored catchers Dave Duncan, Adrian Garrett, and Gene Tenace during his time with Oakland. He was able to take Tenace, an average outfielder, and turn him into an excellent defensive backstop.

After the 1973 World Series, Dick Williams shocked the baseball world when he resigned. He was replaced by Alvin Dark. On July 9, 1974, Charlie Finley gave Dark permission to fire Hoscheit and third base coach

Irv Noren. Oakland was in first place at the time. Dark had previous issues with Noren over the signals he was giving the batters from third base. In Hoscheit's case, he and Dark had been at odds over the team's policy requiring players to sign up days in advance for extra batting practice. Dark said, "This is no reflection on their ability. I want my own people as coaches."[8] Hoscheit said, "When you have to work for people like that it is time to get out. Dark is a horse feathers manager and Finley is no good either. He promised us a raise and he never kept his word." [9]

Reggie Jackson, in his book *A Season With A Superstar*, wrote that when Alvin Dark took over as manager, he rarely spoke to Hoscheit. The A's slugger found it odd that although Hoscheit kept notes on how to pitch to every hitter in the league, Dark never consulted him on pitching strategy. Aside from Wes Stock, the team was purged of every coach who had an allegiance to former manager Williams.

In October 1975, Hoscheit was reunited with Dick Williams, now the manager of the California Angels, who hired him as a coach. Hoscheit initially was the first-base coach. In July, he moved to third base when Norm Sherry took over for the fired Williams as manager.

Hoscheit retired from baseball after the 1976 campaign. He went back home to Plainview, Nebraska, where he ran a liquor store and managed the local American Legion team. But in 1983 he accepted an offer from the New York Mets to become the team's minor-league catching instructor. That same year, he managed the Mets' Sarasota team in the Florida Gulf Coast League. After the 1983 season Davey Johnson was hired to manage the Mets and he named Hoscheit as his bullpen coach. Johnson had known Vern since his days in the Orioles organization.

For the next few years, Hoscheit handled the Mets' bullpen duties while tutoring the backstops on the finer points of catching. On July 22, 1986, the Mets got into a fight with the Cincinnati Reds. Sportswriters noted that every player and coach, including the 64-year-old Hoscheit, got into the action, while Mets outfielder George Foster never left the bench. The Mets went on to defeat Boston in the World Series, giving Hoscheit his fourth World Series title as a bullpen coach.

Hoscheit was popular with the players but he meant business when it came to following team rules. His quote in the *1987 Mets Yearbook* said it all: "The bus leaves in ten minutes, be on it or under it."

Hoscheit retired again in October 1987. But his absence from baseball was short-lived; a few months later he was again named the Mets' minor-league catching instructor. Among his many duties he was called into help recently-acquired catcher Phil Lombardi, who was having difficulty throwing the ball back to the pitcher. Hoscheit advised the young catcher not to look at the ball before tossing it back to the mound. He was able to help Lombardi with his throwing, but the highly touted prospect was unable to adjust to major-league pitching and was soon out of baseball.

Hoscheit retired from professional baseball for good in 1991, returning home to Plainview. He stayed involved with the game, coaching in the local American Legion team. Hoscheit enjoyed hunting and fishing. He also owned a kennel of hunting dogs. One of his business interests was a celebrity fishing camp in Ocala, Florida, that he co-owned with Whitey Herzog and Davey Johnson.

After a long illness, Hoscheit died at Pierce Manor Nursing Home in Creighton, Nebraska, on June 11, 2007. His wife, Helen, had died in August of 2001. He was survived by his son, Billy Ray Hoscheit; two daughters, Sherri Ann Huigens and Cathy Jean Brodhaugen; a sister; eight grandchildren; and one great grandchild. He was buried in Plainview Cemetery.

SOURCES

Baseball-Reference.com

Wooldridge, Clyde, Hoscheit Obituary, *McAlester News-Capitol*, June 16, 2007. Posted on Frank Russo's Deadball Era website.

Gary Bedingfield's baseballinwartime.com.

Jackson, Reggie, with Bill Libby, *A Season With a Superstar* (Oakland: Playboy Enterprises Inc.) (Quote excerpted from the *Palm Beach Post* August 27, 1975, 30).

Markusen, Bruce, *Baseball's Last Dynasty: Charlie Finley's Oakland A's* (Indianapolis: Masters Press, 1998), 116, 211, 305-06.

Hummel, Rick, "Herzog Retraces his Steps to Cooperstown," *St Louis Post-Dispatch*, July 26, 2010.

Bergman, Ron, "A's Chopping Block Claims Noren, Hoscheit," *The Sporting News*, July 27, 1974, 27.

BR Bullpen, Sooner State League.

Telephone interview on August 10, 2013, with Lois Olson (Plainview Historical Society).

Vern Hoscheit obituary and tribute page, Brockhausfuneralhome.com.

Vern Hoscheit, Ultimate Mets Website, Ultimatemets.com

Eugene (Oregon) *Register Guard*

Gadsden (Alabama) *Times*

Lewiston (Idaho) *Evening Journal*

Milwaukee Journal

Milwaukee Sentinel

Observer Reporter (Pennsylvania)

Palm Beach Post

St. Joseph (Missouri) *Gazette*

Dubuque (Iowa) *Telegraph-Herald*

*The Hour (*Connecticut)

(Ontario, CAN) Windsor Star

Youngstown (Ohio) *Vindicator*

I would like to thank the following people who assisted me with this biography:

Lois Olson, historian at the Plainview Historical Society.

Lyle Spatz and Rod Nelson for providing the name of the Yankees scout, Lou Maguolo, who signed Hoscheit.

NOTES

1   Joe Gergen, "No Fish Tale: Herzog and Johnson in Same Boat," *The Sporting News*, July 13, 1987, 8.

2   Davey Johnson and Peter Golenbock, *Bats* (New York: G.P. Putnam's Sons 1986), 56.

3   Whitey Herzog with Bill Horrigan, *White Rat: A Life in Baseball* (New York: Harper and Row, 1987), 39-40.

4   Murray Chass and Thomas Rogers, *New York Times*, November 12, 1983.

5   "Super Scout Helped Beat Reds," *Observer-Reporter*, October 24, 1972, 16.

6   Ibid.

7   Fay Vincent, *It's What's Inside the Lines That Counts: Baseball Stars of the 1970s and 1980s* (New York: Simon & Schuster 2010), 69.

8   Associated Press, "Dark Fires A's Coaches After Oakland Tops Tribe," *Toledo Blade*, July 10, 1974, 17.

9   United Press International, "Dark Takes Charge, Fires Two Coaches," *Milwaukee Journal*, July 10, 1974, 20.

Mike Kilkenny

By Thomas Ayers

A cheerful southpaw from a small town in Canada, Mike Kilkenny determinedly forged an unlikely major-league career despite not having organized baseball activities in his hometown for most of his childhood. He was named Detroit's Rookie of the Year in 1969 and became known for his humor and community involvement. While his stubbornness may have cut his major-league career short, Kilkenny also made his mark in two other sports, as he had a stint as a harness racehorse owner and as a coach for a PGA tour golfer.

Kilkenny's forbears immigrated to Canada from Ireland in the 19th century and became lighthouse keepers in Caraquet, New Brunswick. After her husband and one of her sons were lost at sea in a storm, Kilkenny's great-great-great-grandmother moved west with her surviving son, who became a rider for the Pony Express and eventually settled in Bradford, Ontario, about 40 miles west of Toronto.

Mike's father, Keith, was successful in the furniture and appliance business established by the family. Keith and his wife, Gwendolyn, had two sons, Peter, born in 1941, and Mike, born on April 11, 1945. As a child Mike was much more focused on sports, particularly baseball and golf, than on academics. He developed a curveball in a childhood game by throwing a baseball over a hedge to his brother and trying to have it to drop to the ground before his brother could catch it.

When Mike was about 10, he pitched for a peewee baseball team in Bradford that went to the provincial finals in its division. The team disbanded at the end of the season. Mike was told he was too young to play in the Leaside Baseball Association in Toronto, but a team told him he could participate in drills and come to games. Toward the end of the season, Mike was allowed to pitch in a game the team was losing badly.

He struck out the side on nine pitches, struck out the side again the next inning and was given the start in the team's next game.

The next season Mike joined another team and, at the age of 15, became their primary starting pitcher. Despite the fact that many players in the league were around 21, Kilkenny struck out 177 in 81 innings and in one game he struck out 22 batters over seven innings. This opportunity to play was critical to his development, because Bradford District High School had no baseball team. Kilkenny played on the school's golf team, and won the school's golf championship twice.

Word spread of Kilkenny's prowess through bird-dog scouts and Kilkenny received contract offers from 19 of the 20 major-league teams. He signed with the Detroit Tigers in 1964. At the time his $15,000 signing bonus was a record for an amateur Canadian baseball player. Mike left high school before graduating and

soon married Carolyn Hughes, whom he had dated throughout high school.

Weighing 145 pounds, the 6-foot-3 southpaw began his professional baseball career as a starter for the Rookie League Cocoa (Florida) Tigers. Kilkenny was promoted to Lakeland of the Class A Florida State League midseason where, although he had a losing record at 3-4, he had a relatively low 2.47 ERA in 51 innings.

The next season, pitching for the Daytona Beach Islanders in the Florida State League, was a tale of two halves for Kilkenny. Midway through the season his record was 1-10. After a stern lecture from manager Al Federoff, Kilkenny had a much improved second half and finished with a 14-15 mark as the staff workhorse. In perhaps his finest game as a professional, he threw a no-hitter against Tampa on July 14, 1965. Kilkenny recalled that he got into a perfect zone during the game and "everything was in slow motion" for him; "I knew where I wanted to throw the ball and I knew exactly how to get it there."

In 1966 Kilkenny was promoted to the Montgomery Rebels of the Double-A Southern League. After injuring his left index finger fielding an infield fly in batting practice, he only pitched 21 games and had a 4.23 ERA, which was the highest of his minor-league career. Kilkenny recalled he had a difficulty regaining the feel of his pitches after injuring his pitching hand. He set a Southern League record by throwing five wild pitches in a game at Macon. Mike recalled that there was a foundry near the diamond beyond right field and, when the blast furnaces were cleared out, ash would sometimes drift into the playing field. During that game the ash covered the field and the game was delayed for an hour. Kilkenny attests most of his wild pitches resulted from the ash obstructing his catcher's view.

Kilkenny returned to Montgomery in 1967. His 39 relief appearances led the team and he posted an impressive 2.88 ERA. He struck out nearly a batter an inning, but continued to struggle with his control. That offseason, Kilkenny went to Florida for the second consecutive year to play in the Florida Instructional League.

Kilkenny returned to Montgomery in 1968. The players were given free tickets for friends and family members to the season opener. On a lark, Kilkenny sent a postcard to Alabama Governor George Wallace and his wife telling them he had left tickets for the governor at the ticket office. He was shocked when Governor Wallace came to the game. Governor Wallace left in about the sixth or seventh inning and, as he walked out of the stadium, he gave Mike a shout and a wave.

Kilkenny didn't mind spending a third straight season in Montgomery, as he loved the warm weather and played golf whenever he had the opportunity. His third stint with the Rebels was his best. He pitched in three straight games against the Evansville White Sox on June 16-18, and surrendered only one hit over nine innings. After posting a 1.20 ERA in 45 innings, Kilkenny was promoted to Triple-A Toledo. Mike posted a 2.32 ERA in 22 relief appearances with the Mud Hens. After the season, Kilkenny received a pair of World Series cufflinks; the Tigers had won the Series and Kilkenny had been at major-league spring training that year. After the season he worked as a furniture deliveryman in Bradford. He held a variety of odd jobs over the winters when he wasn't able to play winter ball, including one offseason he worked as a mail carrier.

Kilkenny made the Tigers out of spring training in 1969 and his major-league debut occurred on his 24th birthday, April 11, against the New York Yankees at Tiger Stadium. He came into the game with one out in the top of the ninth and the Tigers trailing 9-3. He said his most vivid memory of the moment was that, as he came onto the diamond and walked to the mound, third baseman Don Wert told him, "You're every bit as good as this guy or you wouldn't be here." This gave Kilkenny a boost of confidence and eased his nerves. He retired Gene Michael on a fly ball and then struck out Bill Robinson.

With Detroit's strong rotation, led by Denny McLain, Mickey Lolich, and Earl Wilson, Kilkenny pitched sparingly during his first few months in the majors. After his debut, he pitched only one inning in the next 13 days and he pitched only 1⅓ innings in May. He didn't give up a run until June 22, which was his 12th major-league appearance.

On July 10 Kilkenny had a 0.44 ERA in 20⅓ innings and had held opposing batters to a .130 batting average and a .174 slugging percentage. However, to that point he had been mostly utilized as a low-leverage reliever. He was given an opportunity to seize the fifth spot in the starting rotation and, after suffering two losses and a no-decision, on August 12 Kilkenny had one of the most memorable days of his life. Before the night was over, he had won a major-league start for the first time, thrown his first complete game, notched his first major-league hit, driven in his first run, and had become a father for the first time.

Kilkenny's wife, Carolyn, went into labor six weeks before their baby was due and gave birth to the couple's first child, a boy named Rory Erin Kilkenny in the early afternoon. Mike stayed with Carolyn until about 4 P.M. and then, he recalled, "I sent my wife some roses, let the dog out—he hadn't been out all day—took a shower, grabbed a sandwich and came to the ballpark." He proceeded to pitch a three-hitter against the California Angels, striking out ten, and added a run-scoring single, which was his first major league hit.

Aside from one relief appearance, Kilkenny remained in the rotation for the rest of the season. In his last nine starts, he threw four shutouts, including a three-hitter against the Oakland A's. Over his final four starts, Kilkenny posted a 1.36 ERA over 33 innings. He struck out 24 batters and held opponents to a .164 batting average and a .224 slugging percentage. After finishing the season with a 3.37 ERA in 39 appearances, which included 15 starts, Mike was named the Tigers' Rookie of the Year.

Kilkenny ascribed much of his success to his curveball, telling a sportswriter, "When I'm right, I feel I can throw my curve on 3-and-1 and 3-and-0 without thinking twice about it." He attributed his improved

command and control of the pitch to the lessons of Johnny Sain and Hal Naragon, who were the pitching and bullpen coach, respectively, for the Tigers for part of the season before Sain was let go and Naragon quit. Kilkenny said they both taught him how to pitch, instead of how to simply throw the ball.

During the season Kilkenny was part of a group of Tigers who visited the FBI Building in Washington, which led to him forging an unusual friendship. The group met with J. Edgar Hoover, who made an offhand remark to Kilkenny that he liked his blue seersucker jacket. A couple of months later, Kilkenny saw a similar blue seersucker jacket, which he bought and sent to Hoover. He was soon visited by an FBI agent who passed along Hoover's gratitude and extended an invitation for Kilkenny to meet Hoover for lunch. Kilkenny visited Hoover in his office in the FBI Building and the two got along very well. For the rest of Kilkenny's playing career, they would have lunch a couple of times a year when Kilkenny had a road trip to Washington or Baltimore.

With his exceedingly strong ending to the 1969 season, Kilkenny was given a larger role in the rotation in 1970 and made a career-high 21 starts. However, as the team's fourth starter, he still had to deal with periods of inconsistent usage. In April he went 22 days between pitching assignments and in August he threw 18 innings in six days, but then made only one appearance in the next three weeks. For the season, Kilkenny put up a 7-6 record with a 5.16 ERA in 36 appearances.

Kilkenny's repertoire consisted of a fastball, a curve, and a changeup. He could vary the speeds for each pitch and could also command them from three arm slots when he was going well. Mike primarily threw from a three-quarters arm angle, but could also throw straight overhand or side-arm. He enjoyed success against left-handed batters, whom he'd often attack with his strong curve. Kilkenny worked during the season on developing a screwball, but scrapped it after it didn't develop as he hoped.

In 1970, Carolyn gave birth to the couple's second child, a daughter named Dawn Michelle Kilkenny.

The offseason was also eventful in an unexpected manner, as on New Year's Eve Kilkenny went to Windsor Raceway with some friends. One owned a harness race horse and Kilkenny bet his friend that he could get a horse that could beat his friend's horse. He proceeded to buy a horse named Royal Pick, which he described as "a horse of little repute." He entered Royal Pick in a race in which his friend's horse was running and won the bet. This started Kilkenny's involvement in harness racing, which lasted for the better part of a decade. Kilkenny owned 31 horses at one point, before quitting the horse business in 1977 or 1978.

Just before spring training in 1971, Kilkenny won the Pasadena Major League Baseball Golf Tournament. He shot a 73 and tied Joe Horlen for the best score. Because of darkness, a playoff was impossible and Kilkenny was named the tournament's victor after a coin flip. He received a color television and trophy. Kilkennny also won the driving contest with a 310-yard shot, besting the more than 70 players in the tournament.

In 1971 Kilkenny continued to serve as a swingman for the Tigers. He started the fifth game of the year, but did not start again until the club's 43rd game. He picked up his first win of the year on June 11, when he limited the Minnesota Twins to one run in a complete-game victory. On September 13, he surrendered Frank Robinson's 499th major-league home run in a game against the Orioles. Over the season, Kilkenny threw only 86⅓ innings and posted a 5.00 ERA.

After the season Kilkenny went to Vietnam as part of a USO troupe, which included players Bobby Bonds and Jim Hannah and umpire Nick Colosi. At one point he was in a vehicle that was fired upon by the Viet Cong. As part of the tour, Kilkenny and the others were expected to return to the US and talk about how well the war was going, but after their firsthand experience they agreed amongst themselves to remain mostly silent about their trip. Kilkenny made a few brief statements about the hospitality and dedication of the troops. When he returned from the tour, Mike picked up his regular offseason community involvement, which included participating in the Tigers' winter tour.

Kilkenny's preparations for the trip to Vietnam revealed another reason why he may have struggled during the previous season. When he was receiving inoculations for the trip he was told by doctors that he was recovering from mononucleosis, which he didn't even know he had. "No wonder I was so tired last summer," he remarked. Kilkenny told a reporter, "I just didn't have any strength. I was always tired. Heck, I fell asleep a couple of times in the bullpen. But now … [a]ll I want is a chance to pitch."

Many trade rumors involving Kilkenny were floated that offseason, but they were consistently denied by Tigers general manager Jim Campbell. Despite that vote of confidence, Kilkenny only pitched in one game for the Tigers in 1972, which came on April 30 when he pitched an inning of relief and surrendered a homer. Manager Billy Martin was calling pitches from the dugout, which Kilkenny did not appreciate. After the game, Kilkenny and Martin, who didn't get along well, got into a shouting match in the clubhouse and Kilkenny threatened to punch Martin. He never pitched for the Tigers again.

On May 9, 1972, the Tigers dealt Kilkenny to the Oakland Athletics for first baseman Reggie Sanders. Kilkenny received news of the trade in a hotel room in Chicago, where he was napping after a long flight. When he went to the ballpark to get his belongings and say goodbye to his teammates, he found himself barred from entering and his bag waiting outside the clubhouse.

Kilkenny made his first appearance for the Athletics with a flawless inning pitched on May 13 against the Boston Red Sox in relief of his fellow ace golfer Joe Horlen. The two didn't get a chance to have a rematch on the links, as those would be the only batters Kilkenny faced wearing Oakland's green and gold. On May 17, only eight days after acquiring him, the A's dealt Kilkenny, Curt Blefary, and a player to be named later to the San Diego Padres for Ollie Brown.

Kilkenny made five appearances for the Padres, mostly in blowout losses. On June 11, the Padres dealt Kilkenny to the Cleveland Indians for infielder Fred Stanley.

Reflecting on being traded three times in just over a month, Kilkenny said, "It gets a little depressing to be moved along as much as I have been." He considered not reporting to Cleveland, but general manager Gabe Paul assured him that he wouldn't be dealt again. Reflecting later, Kilkenny said he felt that the Indians had wanted him all along and that his stops in Oakland and San Diego occurred as teams worked out other moving pieces in the trades.

On June 14, when Kilkenny entered a game against the California Angels, he tied a major-league record by pitching for four teams in a year. In a strange co-incidence, the trivia question on the back of one of Kilkenny's 1972 baseball cards, which was printed before the season began, was: "How many pitchers ever pitched for four teams in one season?" Upon real-izing the coincidence, Kilkenny remarked, "I can't believe it."

After joining the Indians, Kilkenny experienced im-mediate success and surrendered only one run in his first 14⅔ innings, including a start against the Yankees in which he pitched a four-hitter for a 5-1 win. Over the entirety of the 1972 season, Kilkenny totaled 64⅓ innings, all but 6.1 of them for Cleveland, where he posted a 3.41 ERA.

Kilkenny got into a dispute with the Indians over money in spring training in 1973, which spiraled into a verbal battle with manager Ken Aspromonte, who was threatening to send him to the minors. Kilkenny felt that managers didn't give him as many chances as he should have been granted, as his biggest strength was his breaking ball and managers preferred power pitchers. Mike eventually signed with Cleveland, but was demoted to the minors in early May.

After refusing to accept the demotion, Kilkenny was placed on the suspended list by the Indians. This precluded him from playing baseball elsewhere and he was effectively left in limbo. The Indians refused to give up on Kilkenny and carried him on their minor-league roster for the whole year, hoping he might change his mind.

However, Kilkenny wouldn't budge and he turned his attention to harness racing. Kilkenny told a newspaper reporter that he had basically invested his life savings into his horses. "I'm in this right up to my neck right now and it's costing me plenty," he said. By April 1973, Kilkenny and his trainer, Tom Pederson, had 16 horses. Kilkenny spoke of hoping to purchase a farm in Ohio. "You can't make any money unless you have your own facilities, your own pastures. It just costs too much to stable your horses at somebody else's barn all year."

Kilkenny was finally released by the Indians in 1975, although his career in major-league baseball was ef-fectively over. By this time, he was managing the golf shop and happily working as a pro manager at Llyndinshire Golf Club, near London, Ontario.

After his release, George Hall, the owner of the London Majors of the Intercounty Baseball League, asked Mike to pitch for the club. Happy with his emerging practice at Llyndinshire, Kilkenny reached an agreement that he would join the Majors, but would pitch only Friday night games in London and wouldn't travel with the team. This unique arrangement paid huge dividends for the Majors, as Kilkenny posted a 9-0 record in the regular season with a 2.31 ERA and 129 strikeouts in 96 innings pitched. He won the Intercounty League's Most Valuable Player Award and led the team to the league title.

Kilkenny didn't return to pitch for the Majors in 1976. He had moved to the Maple Ridge Golf and Country Club and was busy giving golf lessons and repairing clubs. He became so busy at Maple Ridge that he began selling his horses and divesting himself from his harness racing hobby.

Kilkenny's business at the pro shop picked up sub-stantially and around 1979 he started a business that was both a retail store and repaired clubs for golf shops across the province. It was focused on wood-headed clubs and, as metal heads became more popular in the

1980s, Kilkenny shut down the business at the end of 1984.

Meanwhile, Mike and Carolyn were going through a divorce. In 1983 he reconnected with Edie Hobbs, a woman he had met briefly while pitching for the Padres. A single mother of two children, Edie came to stay with him in March 1983. Despite the fact it was supposed to be a short trip, she didn't return to California until March of the following year.

That spring Kilkenny decided he could still compete in the Intercounty League, despite not having picked up a baseball in eight years. He threw a pitching session for the Majors and was invited to play for the team again. He had another undefeated season, posting a 9-0 record. Mike has fond memories of his second season with the Majors, as it was only time Edie and his children regularly saw him play baseball. In 1984, his divorce was finalized and later that year he and Edie were married.

After his golf business closed, Kilkenny took a job with Kert Chemicals in Toronto selling pool chemicals. Kilkenny described himself as a "nonresponsive employee." He would not complete paper reports or follow some of the company's other standard requirements, but he sold so much product that the company wouldn't do anything about it.

Kert was bought by a British company, Holt Lloyd International, which shifted him to selling bulk military specialized lubricants. After a couple of years, Holt Lloyd asked him to take over as head of its US division, which would have required Mike to move to Atlanta and spend about three-quarters of the year on the road. Mike and Edie turned down the offer. Mike felt that his career with the company was probably limited, so he resigned at the end of 1989.

In 1991, Kilkenny gave some golf lessons for a friend's clients. The lessons went well, and his reputation as a golf pro grew. He wound up spending nearly 20 years as a golf professional at the Fairview Golf Practice Facility, retiring for health reasons in 2010.

For the last 15 years, Mike has been a constant presence in the life of Ted Potter Jr., who has gone on to forge a professional golf career. After meeting Potter as a 15-year-old in Ocala, Florida, Kilkenny took him under his wing and began to help him with his golf game. Potter has been on the PGA Tour since 2011 and earned his first PGA tour win at the Greenbrier Classic on July 8, 2012.

Most memorably, Mike stayed with Potter for 13 days in August, Georgia, for the 2013 Masters. Kilkenny describes his relationship with Potter as "part-time swing coach, full-time mentor and all-time friend." He characterized the relationship as "very personal, but very low profile."

Kilkenny had left knee replacement surgery in 2008. That surgery did not go well, as he suffered an infection while recovering and he later had a mild stroke. Kilkenny also had a right knee replacement in 2012 and had his gall bladder removed in 2014. As of 2014, he was in good health.

Asked to reflect on the most memorable moment of his playing career, Kilkenny didn't respond with a specific moment, but instead recalled standing on the mound for the national anthem before a night game. He remembered those moments as wonderful and said he'd stand there and ask himself how a kid from Bradford, Ontario, could make it to start a game at a sold-out Yankee Stadium or Fenway Park.

Mike describes his father was the biggest influence on his playing career, given all the sacrifices he made to ensure that Mike had every opportunity to play baseball, such as driving him to Toronto multiple times a week to play in the Leaside Baseball Association during his childhood. "He took time out of everything," Mike recalled. "He was at every game, and he never got in the way, he never criticized me." Kilkenny's father died in 1988. His mother died in December 2005.

In February 2011, the Bradford West Gwillimbury Council renamed the main baseball diamond at Joe Magani Park the Mike Kilkenny Field. In 2012, the

London Majors retired his number 17. "It means more than a lot to me," Kilkenny said.

As of 2014, Mike and Edie divided their time between their homes in Belmont, Ontario, and Ocala, Florida.

SOURCES

Unless otherwise indicated, all quotations and attributable information relating to Mike Kilkenny come from an interview the author conducted with Kilkenny in Bradford, Ontario, on March 2, 2014.

Other sources

Chass, Murray, "Roundup: Blessed Events of All Kinds for Canadians," *New York Times,* August 14, 1969.

Crawford, Scott, "Baseball Night at the St. Mary's Lincolns Game," February 4, 2013; online: baseballhalloffame.ca/news/baseball-night-at-the-st-marys-lincolns-game/.

Green, Steve, "Majors Pay Tribute to Championship Legend," *London Free Press,* June 24, 2012, online: lfpress.com/sports/baseball/2012/06/24/19915746.html

Huff, Bruce, "Event Details: Oldtimers Sports Association Game," June 12, 2012; online: pointstreaksites.com/view/londonmajors/schedule/events_38278

Lang, Jack, "Kilkenny Shoots a 73 to Win Links Tournament," *The Sporting News,* March 13, 1971, p. 34.

Spoelstra, Watson, "Kilkenny Is Tough Pitcher in a Paradise for Swingers," *The Sporting News,* October 11, 1969.

Young, Rick, "Pitch and Putt Makes Great Team," *London Free Press,* July 18, 2012; online: lfpress.com/sports/golf/2012/07/17/19997576.html

"Bubble-Gum Kid Doubles A's Troubles," clipping from unidentified source dated August 28, 1969, in Kilkenny's file at the Baseball Hall of Fame, Cooperstown, New York.

"Former Major-Leaguer Mike Kilkenny to be Honoured at London Majors Game," London Metro News, June 18, 2012; online: metronews.ca/news/london/267428/267428/

"Has His Business Well in Harness," clipping from unidentified source dated January 7, 1973, in Kilkenny's file at the Baseball Hall of Fame, Cooperstown, New York.

"One Pitcher's Future Lies in Horsemeat, the Running Kind," clipping from unidentified sourced dated April 15, 1973, in Kilkenny's Hall of Fame file.

"Only a Job in Majors Could Pay for the Hay," clipping from undated, unidentified source in Kilkenny's Hall of Fame file.

London Health Sciences Centre, Orthopaedics Donor Update, "Former Baseball Pro 'Forever Grateful' to LHSC," September 2013.

Clipping from unidentified source dated July 1, 1972, in Kilkenny's Hall of Fame file.

The Sporting News, December 15, 1973.

Minor League Baseball, "This Day in Minor League Baseball History: April 25," milb.com/milb/history/tdih.jsp?tdih=0425&sid=milb

Darold Knowles

By Austin Gisriel

Darold Knowles, a left-handed reliever whose 16-year career spanned three decades, is best known for a World Series record that may be tied but will never be broken. He is the only pitcher to appear in all seven games of a World Series, accomplishing that feat with the 1973 Oakland A's. Knowles did not yield a run in 6⅓ innings in that Series while bookending saves in Games One and Seven.

"It's kind of my claim to fame," said Knowles. "The amazing thing to me is that it's been 40 years and no one else has ever done it."[1]

A native of Brunswick, Missouri, a small community on the Missouri River in the north central part of the state, Knowles was born to Ralph and Verna Anne Knowles on December 9, 1941, two days after Pearl Harbor was attacked. Among his many jobs, Ralph drove a bus and worked for both Kansas City Power and Light and the Missouri Cities Water Company. He served in the military during World War II and took part in the postwar occupation of Japan. Darold's only sibling, older brother Ralph Wayne, died one week prior to the author's interview with Knowles.

"I knew from when I was in Little League that I wanted to be a baseball player, and my parents were very, very supportive," he said. "They were not wealthy people at all, on the contrary; but I never missed a ballgame. Whatever they could do to get me there, they did."

A standout amateur player, Knowles played for Moberly in the Central Missouri Ban Johnson League, where on July 16, 1959, he struck out 32 batters in a 13-inning, 1-0 victory over of Boonville, giving up only four hits and two walks.[2]

"That was a big night; I can remember like it was yesterday. Bunny Brummel was the opposing pitcher and he struck out I think 18, and I just had one of those nights. … Hell, I'll always remember it. The scouts tried to sign me after that game and they didn't even see me pitch; [they wanted to sign me just based on] the results of it. There was one scout there and eventually I wound up signing with him, a guy named Byron Humphrey with the Baltimore Orioles."

Before signing, however, Knowles attended the University of Missouri at Columbia on a partial scholarship for one semester, but never played baseball for the school.

"Books and studies weren't my big thing," Knowles said. "I signed with the Baltimore Orioles for $5,000 and that was so much money that we spread (the payment) out over two years."

Knowles became part of a talented Orioles minor-league system beginning in 1961 with Class C Aberdeen, where he went 11-5, starting 22 games in 23 appearances. By 1963 he had moved up to the Double-A Elmira Pioneers, a team that featured two other notable lefties in Steve Dalkowski and Pat Gillick. Knowles chuckled at the mere mention of the former.

"Even before I played with Dalkowski, he was a legend. When he came to Elmira, he had hurt his arm and he wasn't throwing quite as good as he did at one time, but he had very good stuff. We used to get on him all the time, so much that we were talking about him throwing a ball through a fence and we went out to the right-field fence in Elmira. It was an old wooden fence and he did throw a ball right through it and I watched it. Steve said, 'Aw, it was old.' I didn't see him when he could really throw, but he was in the 90s then when I played with him."

Pat Gillick made quite an impression on Knowles as well. "I didn't see Gillick for 25 years and I was with the Phillies as a coach and we were in spring training or the instructional league in Dunedin, where the Blue Jays train, and he was general manager of the Blue Jays. I walked up to him and said hello and he remembered the street I lived on in Missouri! He had that kind of mind."

Gillick was famous among his Elmira teammates for reading *The Sporting News* and instantly remembering all that it contained. "We used to call him *Sporting News*. It obviously helped him in later life," recalled Knowles.

The 6-foot, 180-pound lefty worked his way up the Baltimore organizational ladder and made his debut on April 18, 1965, against the Red Sox in Boston. "I remember it very well. I was pumped about being in the big leagues obviously, and here I am at Fenway Park and I faced Felix Mantilla and struck him out on a 3-and-2 curveball looking. Had no business throwing a curveball 3-and-2 but I did and I happened to throw it over and he took it. And I did not record another out that day." Knowles actually pitched 1⅓ innings in his debut, but it may seem to him now as

if he never retired another hitter, as he walked three and hit a batter while yielding two hits and four runs.

The lefty pitched in only four more games for Baltimore that year, spending most of the season in Triple-A Rochester. After the season he was traded with outfielder Jackie Brandt to the Philadelphia Phillies for pitcher Jack Baldschun. (The Orioles immediately included Baldschun as part of a package for Cincinnati's Frank Robinson.)

Appearing in 69 games for the Phillies in 1966, Knowles notched 13 saves, but was again traded during the offseason, this time to the Washington Senators for outfielder Don Lock. Being traded two consecutive years did not rattle his confidence, he said.

"Trades are just a part of the game. I was happy to still be playing. I liked Philly. It was my first full year in the big leagues. Gene Mauch was the manager and gave me a chance to really prove that I could pitch so I'll always thank him for that, but at the end of the year he kind of got down on me. I finished very slowly and did not pitch well the last month of the season. Later on I found out that's why he traded me, because he just didn't think I was going to be strong enough to pitch that much, I guess."

Knowles established himself in Washington, never recording an earned-run average above 2.70 in his four full campaigns there. His 1968 season was interrupted when his Air National Guard unit was activated and sent to Japan.

"I went overseas in July of '68 … but I was still on the active roster of the Senators up until the time I went overseas. I think I pitched in 20-some ballgames before I went over there, but it was an exhausting period because I'd go to the military base all day and then have to go to the ballgames at night."[3]

Back from the service in 1969, Knowles was named to the American League team for the All-Star Game and pitched two-thirds of an inning of hitless relief.

"I really pitched well that year. I came back from overseas and missed the first month of the season and still made the All-Star team so I was really throwing the ball extremely well, and it just all came together for me in a short period of time. I was thrilled to even pitch in that game. We got beat pretty bad … but I think Frank Howard hit two home runs that day. I faced two hitters and got 'em both out, so I was pumped!"[4]

Knowles' 1970 season is proof that a pitcher's won-loss record is not necessarily indicative of how well he pitched. Despite 27 saves and a 2.04 ERA in 119⅓ innings, the southpaw recorded only two victories against 14 defeats.

"I felt and still feel that [1970] was probably one of the best years I ever had. I pitched well, I thought, but the results did not turn out real well sometimes. But I remember Ted Williams [Washington's manager] coming to me early in the season and saying, 'Every time we get to the seventh inning and we're tied or winning I'm going to give you the ball.' And he did. If we had a lead everything was fine, but it seemed like if we were tied, somebody would make an error or I'd give up a run and I wound up losing. It was a long, long year that way."

It was such a long year for Knowles that even his hotel-room assignment seemed to conspire against him one night in Milwaukee.

"I was 2-12; I'd just lost my 12th game [versus the White Sox, 4-3, on a Rich Morales sacrifice fly in the ninth]. We went to Milwaukee after the game and I walked up to my room and it was number 212. I thought, that's really great."

On May 8, 1971, Knowles and first baseman Mike Epstein were traded to Oakland, a move that initially disappointed Knowles.

"When I first got traded I was kind of down. I loved Washington; had a home there and even though we were a last-place club, I was the main cog out of that bullpen. I was the big guy, I was the closer, and I loved that. I went to Oakland and they had this other guy named Fingers, a guy with a mustache," Knowles said with a laugh. "It wasn't long, maybe ten days, two

weeks, and all of a sudden I said, 'We can win it all here.' Rollie was the horse, there's no question, but we complemented each other pretty well. Either he got the save or I got the save, it seemed like. If he'd get 30, I'd get 12."

Knowles appeared in 43 games for the A's during the regular season, winning five and notching seven saves. He made his first postseason appearance with one-third of an inning in Oakland's loss to the Orioles in the American League Championship Series.

Going 5-1 with a career-low 1.37 ERA in 1972, Knowles helped the A's to the pennant but missed the postseason, including the A's World Series triumph over Cincinnati, after he broke a thumb on September 27 against Minnesota. Batting against Bert Blyleven in the top of the tenth with Dick Green on first, Knowles hit a ball that he thought might fall in for a hit.

"It had rained the night before, which was a rarity in Oakland, and the field was not in great shape. Anyway, I hit a ball and I thought when I hit it that it had a chance to be a double. I rushed out of the box and slipped and I jammed my thumb into the ground and broke it. The guy [Cesar Tovar] caught the ball anyway. That was a low point in my life because if you play this game you want to get in the World Series; you want to perform in the World Series, but I missed it all. I was there, but I didn't have an opportunity to pitch."

Knowles more than made up for that lost opportunity in the 1973 World Series. He recorded nine saves in 99 innings that season but never made it into any of the ALCS games against Detroit. "It seemed like I was up throwing in every game [in the playoffs], but I didn't have to go in, but that was okay; it was all about the team."

In Game One of the World Series, however, with the A's clinging to a 2-1 lead over the New York Mets, Knowles came in with one on and one out in the ninth to relieve Rollie Fingers, who had pitched 3⅓ innings in relief of starter Ken Holtzman. Fingers had walked pinch-hitter Ron Hodges. Knowles retired pinch-hitter Jim Beauchamp on a pop fly to second baseman Dick Green and then got third baseman Wayne Garrett on a short fly to right fielder Reggie Jackson.

New York, with an 82-79 regular-season record, seemed no match for the powerful Oakland squad, but the Mets battled tenaciously and the Series came down to a deciding seventh game.

"When that Series started, my dream was to at least pitch in one game. As luck would have it, I relieved in the first game and got the save, so now I had pitched in a World Series game and I was pumped. And then I got in the second one and the third, fourth, and so on and nobody even knew; it wasn't even mentioned that no one had ever pitched in all seven games until that morning. I read it in the paper that if by chance I got in that game, I'd be the only one to do it."

It appeared that Knowles would not pitch in the seventh game and that Rollie Fingers would record his third save of the Series, but Fingers gave up a walk and a single in the ninth with the Athletics leading 5-1. With two down, first baseman Gene Tenace booted a groundball, allowing a run to score and bringing the tying run to the plate in the person of the left-handed-hitting Wayne Garrett, the same hitter Knowles had retired for the save in Game One. Manager Dick Williams brought in Knowles.

"I always thank Gino for that [error]! As far as Dick taking Fingers out; Fingers had already thrown two-plus innings in that game. Wayne Garrett was the hitter and that was kind of my thing, being able to get left-handed hitters out. [Williams] played it by the book and brought me in and I was lucky enough to get the out. That was the biggest thrill I ever had in baseball, getting that last out."

Indeed, Fingers had hurled 3⅓ innings in that final contest and 13⅔ for the Series. To put that total in perspective, starter Ken Holtzman amassed only 10⅔ innings in three games started.

Knowles laughed about relieving the future Hall of Famer with the World Series on the line. "I give Dick

Williams a lot of credit—that took some [guts] to take Fingers out of the game and bring me in."

The Athletics again won the AL West in 1974 and again Knowles did not appear in the ALCS against Baltimore. He never saw action in a World Series game either. Rollie Fingers was named Most Valuable Player in Oakland's thrashing of the Los Angeles Dodgers in five games, winning the first game and saving the fourth and fifth. The only other relief pitcher to see action for Oakland was Blue Moon Odom, who pitched 1⅓ innings in two appearances. According to Knowles, there may have also been another reason that he did not appear.

"I wasn't in Alvin Dark's good graces in '74 (Williams had resigned as manager after the 1973 season), to be honest and I didn't have a great year.[5] I can see why he got down on me a little bit. It seemed like I was up throwing in every game, I just didn't get in any of them."

Reflecting on those championship teams Knowles acknowledged that Oakland's reputation as "the fightin' A's" was well deserved. "Everything you read or heard about the Oakland As, the bickering the fighting (and all of it wasn't in the paper), it's probably all true, but I can honestly say this: When the game started everybody was a true professional. There was never anything carried over that would cost anything as far as the game was concerned. But yeah, there were a lot of ego differences, if you will, in that clubhouse and it was just part of it. Every day you'd wait to see what was going to happen and usually, it did! There was always something going on.

"I played for eight different major-league clubs and that is the only club that I played for that ever had anything like that. You put that many guys together for that long a time, there's some bickering and maybe a spat or two, but they weren't spats in Oakland, I mean there were some fisticuffs, and that was going on all the time. There were some pretty good [fights]. But it never prevented anybody from playing the game."

Shortly after the 1974 World Series, Knowles was traded to the Chicago Cubs along with pitcher Bob Locker and infielder Manny Trillo for outfielder Billy Williams. Two years in Chicago were followed by a year in Texas and then a year in Montreal, where Knowles recorded six saves, a 3-3 record, and a 2.38 ERA.

"I had a good year in Montreal and they wanted me to come back. They offered me a contract with a nice raise, but I just didn't like playing in Montreal. My kids were small, it was a French-speaking province, and my family didn't enjoy it. [It was a] good ballclub, but I thought, 'I got a chance to play out my option and become a free agent,' and I did. I took the chance and I wound up with the Cardinals which is where I always wanted to be my entire career, having grown up in Missouri. Unfortunately, it was at the tail-end of my career and I didn't have that much left. I didn't have the good stuff that I had earlier, but it was okay—I wound up playing for my boyhood dream team and loved every minute in St. Louis. And then went to work for them when I got out of the game."

Knowles' last appearance in the big leagues occurred on the 16th anniversary of his major-league debut. It was April 18, 1980, in Pittsburgh. In two-thirds of an inning, the left-hander surrendered two runs on three hits and took the loss in the Cardinals' 12-10 defeat.

Knowles was a roving minor-league pitching coach in the Cardinals' system from 1981 to 1988, a term that was punctuated by a six-week stint with St. Louis in 1983 when he filled in for Hub Kittle on the big club, whose wife was seriously ill. Knowles thoroughly enjoyed his time at Whitey Herzog's side during that month and a half.

"This is how good a manager Whitey Herzog is. We are in LA — I'll never forget this — it's in the sixth inning and I think Bob Forsch was on the mound and there's two out and nobody on. Somebody got a base hit up the middle and Whitey was just beside himself and I was standing there by him as the pitching coach and I said, 'That's all right, we got two out, Whitey.' And he said, 'Nah, now that damn Baker can beat us in the ninth.' Dusty Baker hit a three-run homer in

the ninth to beat us. I sat in the dugout for 20 minutes after the game thinking, 'How in the hell did he think of that three innings in advance?' And that's exactly what he said, 'Nah, that damn Baker can beat us now,' and he did."

Whitey Herzog was not the only legendary manager for whom Darold Knowles coached or played. "I was fortunate enough to play for some really good managers. Gene Mauch gave me my first full chance in the big leagues and I'll always appreciate that. Then I went to Washington and played for Gil Hodges the first year. He was a great manager as well; he handled pitchers as well as anybody I ever played for. … Let me just say this about Ted Williams: Ted Williams, when he came, was probably the worst manager I played for during those years, but he got a lot better because he was such a perfectionist. He thought he knew a lot about pitching and he didn't, but he was the most charismatic man I ever met in my life. I couldn't wait to get to the ballpark every day and just listen to him. Everybody would sit around and talk and he loved that. I'll never forget those days."

Knowles had high praise for Dick Williams. "Dick Williams demanded—*demanded*—that those guys play the game with respect when they played. I think that was one of his biggest attributes. He demanded that from you. It's probably one of the reasons it seemed like he had better results with a veteran club than he did with a young club because veteran players knew how to play and he made sure that they did that."

Knowles left the Cardinals organization in 1989 when Lee Thomas, who had been the farm director in St. Louis, was named general manager of the Phillies and asked him to become the pitching coach. After two seasons with the big club, Knowles was reassigned ("That's what they called it back then—'reassigned'") to the Phillies' Florida State League affiliate in Clearwater, where he spent ten seasons. From 2002 to 2005, Knowles was Pittsburgh's Triple-A pitching coach, but when the Pirates asked him to coach rookie ball, he left and signed with Toronto. Knowles was assigned to Dunedin in the Florida State League, which was a boon to the lefty because it was his home.

Knowles was to enter his ninth season as Dunedin's pitching coach in 2014. He still threw batting practice every day at the age of 72, but he wasn't not dropping in any curveballs as he did to Felix Mantilla at age 23.

"I didn't throw that curveball the last ten years I played. In the minor leagues I did throw it. Hell, I thought it was good, but it wasn't that good. The last one I threw in the big leagues, Chuck Hinton hit off the wall. I finally went straight to the slider.

"I'm probably one of the luckiest guys in the game. I work in baseball. I enjoy working with the kids — I know that's an oft-used saying, but it's so true — and I'm home every night. That's even better. I'm very fortunate."

As a result of his lengthy coaching career with both Clearwater and Dunedin, Knowles was inducted into the Florida State League Hall of Fame in 2011. In 2012 Knowles was inducted into the Missouri Sports Hall of Fame — "both tremendous honors," he said.

Knowles married three times. He had two daughters, Holly and Lori, by his first marriage; a third, Kali, by his second marriage; and a stepdaughter, Jamie, now deceased, by his third wife, Lynne.

In 2014 Knowles said he had no plans to retire from baseball any time soon. "It's all I've ever done. I'm sure I've made a lot of mistakes, but I'd like to think I've helped a hell of a lot of people, too. And I enjoy it! I love it!"

NOTES

1   All quotes are taken from a January 7, 2014, phone conversation with Darold Knowles.

2   "Pitchers in a Battle," *Kansas City Star*, July 17, 1959, 33.

3   Knowles pitched 41⅓ innings in 32 games with an ERA of 2.18.

4   The AL lost, 9-3. Frank Howard hit a home run off Steve Carlton in his only plate appearance. Knowles retired Matty Alou and Don Kessinger to close out the third inning.

5   Knowles amassed only three saves along with a 4.22 ERA in 53⅓ innings.

Allan Lewis

by Rory Costello

Allan Lewis was baseball's first "designated runner." Owner Charles O. Finley, on one of his many whims, put "The Panamanian Express" on his Kansas City and Oakland rosters for parts of six seasons from 1967 to 1973. "Mr. Finley's called me up every time," said Lewis in 1973. "No reports, no scouts, no managers—just him."[1] An outfielder by trade, Lewis played in 156 big-league games—but appeared just 10 times in the field, with three starts. The speedster scored more runs (47) and stole more bases (44) than he had plate appearances (31). Yet he was part of two World Series champions. Later, as a scout, he signed two solid major leaguers, Einar Díaz and Carlos Ruiz, from his homeland.

There are two ambiguities about the birth of Allan Sydney Lewis. Baseball references show that he was born on December 12, 1941, but at least two Panamanian sources show the year as 1937.[2] Since many ballplayers have shaved years off their age for professional purposes, there's reason to believe the earlier date. Also, his place of birth is listed as Colón, which could be either of two places. Rather than Panama's second biggest city (which lies near the Atlantic entrance to the Panama Canal), it was probably Colón island in the nation's northwest corner. This isle is part of the beautiful province of Bocas del Toro, on the Caribbean coast near Costa Rica. Its main town, also called Bocas del Toro, is where young Allan first played Little League ball.

"I love the game always since I was a kid," Lewis said. "When I was a kid in Bocas del Toro, I used to listen to baseball on Armed Forces Radio."[3] The sport was popular in the area, which proved to be a fertile source of talent. At least three of Panama's 53 major leaguers (as of year-end 2013) were born in Bocas del Toro town: Ivan Murrell, Sherman Obando, and Fernando Seguignol. Like Lewis, Chico Salmón's birthplace is listed as Colón without specifying, but stories from Panama make it clear that Salmón's roots were also in Bocas del Toro.

Information about the Lewis family is lacking, including the names of his parents and siblings. Since people use double surnames in Latin America, though, we know that his mother's maiden name was Elliott.[4] It is therefore likely that both sides of the family originally came from English Caribbean possessions. Jamaicans founded Bocas del Toro town in 1826, and more Jamaican immigrants followed as the area became a major center of banana plantations. Even today the town is known for its reggae-flavored ambiance.

Allan went to high school at Colegio Félix Olivares Contreras in David, the capital of Chiriquí, the neighboring province to the south. On December 12, 1959,

his birthday, he married Barbara Hall; they would go on to have nine children (six boys and three girls). The likelihood that he married at age 18 seems low, which also supports a 1937 birthdate.

Lewis represented his province in the 17th and 18th National Amateur Championships in 1960 and 1961, helping his team win the title the first year. The Kansas City Athletics signed him to a pro contract, thanks to their Latin American regional scout, Félix "Fellé" Delgado, and assigned him to Albuquerque in the Class D Sophomore League. After missing the early part of the 1961 season with an ankle injury, Lewis hit .271 with 2 homers and 20 RBIs. However, he then broke a leg in June and went back home to Panama.[5]

After recovering, Allan played most of the 1962 and 1963 seasons with Daytona Beach in the Class A Florida State League. He also saw action with another Class A affiliate of the A's, Lewiston in the Northwest League. He hit over .300 both years in Florida but showed little power. The injuries did not appear to have diminished his speed, though (9.5 seconds in the 100-yard dash).

Lewis first played winter ball in Panama in 1962. In the winter of 1963-64, after initial indications that he might play in Venezuela, he remained in his homeland with the Marlboro Smokers. The fourth Interamerican Series took place in February 1964 in Managua, Nicaragua, and Allan was named to the Panamanian team. He later recalled the biggest thrill of his early career as getting a hit off big leaguer Juan Pizarro in that series. That spring he returned to Daytona Beach, where he hit over .300 again but without any homers.

After another winter with Marlboro, Lewis returned for his fourth season in the Florida State League. Kansas City's entry was now located in the town of Leesburg. Though his average dipped to .280 and he again went homerless, Lewis stole 76 bases and was named a league All-Star. He earned the same honor in the winter of 1965-66 with Marlboro.

The Panamanian Express ran wild in 1966, stealing 116 bases for Leesburg. Lewis also led the league in

runs (92) and hits (156). That November he played in a different winter league—Nicaragua. He was supposed to return to Panama when the season opened there on December 1, but the league was reduced to just three teams. Thus he stayed with the Granada Sharks, where he tied with Doug Rader for the league lead in runs scored (40).

Lewis had captured Charlie Finley's fancy. "Finley dispatched his manager of the year, Alvin Dark, to Nicaragua to scout Lewis. Then the owner ordered them to make a command appearance. In a press conference, Finley grandly announced two things: 1. a new dimension in baseball in the pinch-running person of Allan Lewis, and, 2. that the Kansas City A's would wear white shoes for the first time." The club's fastest men, Bert Campaneris and Lewis, got special soft light pairs.[6] Newspapers carried the story of the albino kangaroo kicks—with a photo of a grinning Finley and Lewis—on January 17, 1967.[7]

"Dark seethed. ... '(H)e even tried to break camp without me, but Mr. Finley already had all that publicity out so Dark couldn't do it.'"[8] Thus Allan Lewis made Kansas City's Opening Day roster. In his debut, on April 11, Lewis ran for Ed Charles in the seventh inning—and Cleveland's Steve Hargan promptly picked him off first base. "The first time I went in ... everybody was waiting to see me. I took my lead, and [Hargan] picked me off, just like that. I froze. I just stood there and watched."[9]

In late April, though, Dark was toeing the party line: "A standout baserunner can give your team a tremendous lift during the eighth and ninth innings of a close game. He raises the devil with the opposition and sets up runs that can win you the squeezers. This is a specialized age. We can use specialized players."[10]

Lewis was optioned to Double-A Birmingham in late June (ostensibly because the team needed more pitching). He was recalled in July but sent down again in August, having stolen 14 bases in 19 tries. In the winter of 1967-68, Allan returned to Panama, joining Cerveza Balboa. "Beat[ing] out infield grounders and grass cutters," he won the league's batting title at .374, though he had just 91 at-bats in an abbreviated 22-game schedule.[11] Balboa was the champion that year, repeated in 1968-69 (as three teams played 26 games each), and added one more in 1970-71. By that time, coverage in *The Sporting News* had petered out. The original Panamanian League lasted until 1972.

The remainder of Lewis's US pro career resembled the 1967 season. A quick recap will suffice for the summers of 1968 through 1971:

1968: Birmingham through early August, then up to Oakland, where the A's had moved that year.

1969: Iowa Oaks (Triple A), Lodi (Single A), and stints with the big club in June, August, and September. "Al's speed and daring made him a great crowd-pleaser," said Oaks general manager Bob Morris that June.[12]

1970: Iowa, then Oakland in August and September. After Lewis got picked off base twice in September, one sarcastic newspaperman quipped, "The Panamanian Express is a local that stops between first and second."[13] However, on September 27, starting in left field at Anaheim Stadium, Allan hit his one major-league homer, off the Angels' Greg Garrett, in a 9-4 loss.

1971: Lewis broke an ankle in spring training and was reassigned to Double-A Birmingham.[14] He saw no big-league action that year.

The 1972 and 1973 seasons are worthy of more attention because Lewis got to appear in the postseason. In 1972 he remained at Birmingham until Oakland recalled him in September. His last of just six major-league hits came in a September 29 start. Lewis was not on the playoff roster, but after Bert Campaneris threw his bat at Tigers reliever Lerrin Lagrow, Finley called him in case Campy was suspended. Instead, Reggie Jackson tore his hamstring in the last playoff game while sliding home on a double steal, and Lewis went to the World Series.

Sharp-tongued manager Dick Williams jibed, "He's a switch-hitter. He batted .300 last year, .150 left-handed and .150 right-handed." Still, Lewis wasn't lacking in confidence. He boasted, "I'm not afraid of [Reds catcher] Johnny Bench. He should be worrying about me."[15] Williams sent his 25th man in to run for Mike Epstein in both of the first two games—which angered the hulking first baseman—and Bench cut Lewis down. *Sports Illustrated* writer Ron Fimrite said: "The Express ran on schedule in both Series games and both times he was derailed by perfect throws by Bench."[16] In Game Four, however, Lewis scored the tying run on Gonzalo Márquez's pinch single in the ninth. He appeared in six of the seven Series games, also scoring in Game Seven.

Lewis was back in Birmingham once more in 1973 after dislocating a shoulder near the end of spring training. Fans voted him the team's most popular player that year. Oakland called him up in June, irking captain Sal Bando, who stated that more fully rounded players were more deserving. (In retrospect, though, author Bruce Markusen noted that Bando and Williams both saw some merit to Finley's notion.) Allan was sent down at the end of July and once more recalled when the rosters expanded in September. Again he got to appear in the postseason as Finley pulled strings. As it turned out, Charlie O outmaneuvered himself. When he sought to banish second baseman Mike Andrews after two costly errors in Game Two of the World Series, Commissioner Bowie Kuhn denied Finley's request to replace Andrews with Manny Trillo.

According to a story by Ron Bergman in the *Oakland Tribune*, "The A's worked themselves into the predicament by selling [José] Morales to make room for pinch-runner Allan Lewis, a Finley favorite, on the 25-man roster. Two days later, Bill North sprained his ankle. The Baltimore Orioles allowed Trillo to replace North for the American League playoffs. When the A's found out the Mets wouldn't agree to the same switch, an attempt was made to get Morales back from Montreal. He didn't clear National League waivers because some team claimed him. Ironically, the Mets allowed the A's to replace North with Lewis."[17] He pinch-ran in three World Series games, scoring a key ninth-inning run to help send Game Two to extra innings.

After the A's won their second of three straight championships, they voted Lewis a one-tenth Series share. In December, though, the team assigned him outright to Tucson. He never played again. Around that time, Commissioner Bowie Kuhn was talking up the possibility of a designated-runner rule.[18] In March 1974, Charlie Finley signed Olympic sprinter Herb Washington to be Oakland's new pinch-runner deluxe.

Before the 1973 season, Lewis had said, "I'd like to go as far as I can with my role and then be a scout in Latin America. Being a Latin myself would help. I wrote Mr. Finley a letter last year telling him what I want to do."[19] Allan worked as an instructor in the A's minor-league system for several years but then decided to come home to Panama.[20] After his return he served as a scout for the Cleveland Indians. He recruited catcher Einar Díaz from Chiriquí for the Tribe in 1990.

In January 1997 the Philadelphia Phillies hired Lewis as a regional scouting supervisor along with Jesús Méndez and Fred Manrique. Allan's turf was mainly Panama and the rest of Central America, but he also beat the bushes in unusual destinations such as Ecuador. It's also likely that he spent time in Colombia, which shares a border with Panama. Lewis signed another *chiricano*, Carlos Ruiz from David, in 1998. As he had done with Díaz, he was responsible for converting the 2008 World Series star from infield to catcher.[21] His days of studying catchers as a baserunner gave him insight into the position.[22]

Lewis also did some coaching in Panama. In the winter of 2001-02, when the nation launched another winter league, he was with the Carta Vieja Roneros, based in Chiriquí. Despite the support of Major League Baseball, that league lasted just one season. In the 2009 World Baseball Classic, at the request of national team manager and fellow big leaguer Héctor López, he was on the staff of Panama's squad. He appears to have retired as a scout after that year; after 2010 stories out of Philadelphia referred to him as a "former Phillies scout." He lives in David with his wife Barbara.

Thanks also to SABR member Cliff Blau, whose research provided additional information (notably from the National Baseball Hall of Fame's clippings file).

SOURCES

Pérez Medina, Ramón G., *Historia del Baseball Panameño* (Panama: Dutigrafia, 1992).

Extracts from this book are presented on the website *El Pelotero*: espanol.oocities.com/elpelotero_online/biografextran/allan_lewis.htm

Allan Lewis interview from August 1, 2001, also on the website *El Pelotero*: espanol.oocities.com/elpelotero_online/entrevistas/allan_lewis01.htm

Blau, Clifford, "Leg Men," *Baseball Research Journal*, Society for American Baseball Research, 2009

paperofrecord.com (various small pieces of information from *The Sporting News*)

retrosheet.org

bocas-del-toro.org

Professional Baseball Players Database V6.0

Markusen, Bruce, "Cooperstown Confidential" online columns:

oaklandfans.com/columns/markusen/markusen157.html

oaklandfans.com/columns/markusen/markusen164.html

Davids, L. Robert, "Lewis Making Mark as Pinch Runner," *SABR Baseball Research Journal*, 1974.

NOTES

1   Ron Bergman, "The Freakish Role of Allan Lewis," *Oakland Tribune*, March 25, 1973, 24.

2   Lewis interview from *El Pelotero*. Gustavo Aparicio, "La leyenda Allan Lewis," *Día a Día* (Panama City, Panama), February 6, 2009.

3   Bergman, "The Freakish Role."

4   Panamanian telephone directory.

5   Carlos Salazar, "'Wheels' keep Lewis going," *Albuquerque Tribune*, July 21, 1971, 29.

6   Bergman, "The Freakish Role."

7   "A's To Wear White Shoes, Gold Batting Helmets in 1967 Season," *Raleigh Register* (Beckley, West Virginia), January 17, 1967, 7.

8   Ibid.

9   Maury White, *Des Moines Register*, May 9, 1969, 1-S.

10 Ed Nichols, "Shore Sports," *The Daily Times* (Salisbury, Maryland), May 3, 1967, 19.

11 Alberto Montilla, "Lewis Wins Bat Title—In Absentia," *The Sporting News*, February 17, 1968, 39.

12 Bill Bryson, "A's Nab Oaks' Lewis, Send Velazquez Back," *Des Moines Register*, June 17, 1969, 1-S.

13 Bergman, "The Freakish Role."

14 Salazar.

15 Ralph Bernstein, "Allan Lewis Can Start Eating Words," Associated Press, October 15, 1972.

16 Ron Fimrite, "A Big Beginning for the Little League," *Sports Illustrated*, October 23, 1972.

17 Ron Bergman, "Finley Reprimand by Commissioner," *Oakland Tribune*, October 15, 1973, E35.

18 "Kuhn: No designated runner yet," Associated Press, December 14, 1973.

19 Bergman, "Finley Reprimand."

20 Aparicio.

21 Ben Shpigel, "Phillies Catcher Delivers on a Game 3 Prediction," *New York Times*, October 26, 1998.

22 Aurelo Ortiz G., "¡Caza— Catcher!" Crítica en Línea (Panamanian online service), critica.com.pa/archivo/01112007/dep15.html.

Bob Locker

By Keith J. Scherer

Bob Locker threw 879 innings in the major leagues. His career earned-run average was 2.75. Pitching for the White Sox in the mid-1960s, he was an ace for a bullpen that led the league in ERA for four straight years. Oakland manager Dick Williams deployed him as his designated rally-killer in 1971, when the A's won 101 games, and 1972, when they became world champions. And yet Locker saw himself as a player of very limited ability. "I had no depth perception, I couldn't field, I couldn't hit," he said. "My job was to work at avoiding trouble, on not screwing it up for the other guys."[1]

The first child of Henry and Northa Locker, Robert Autry Locker was born on March 15, 1938, in George, Iowa. The Lockers grazed cattle and grew corn on pasture they owned at the edge of town. When he could, Locker played baseball as a child, but he spent much of his after-school time chopping corn. He adored his mom, "an absolute saint. She's the reason I turned out reasonably well."

Locker attended his mother's alma mater, Iowa State University, where he played baseball for legendary coach Cap Timm. Locker would credit Timm, who coached the Cyclones for over 30 years and whose name graces the team's ballpark, as the person who taught him the most about baseball. In high school Locker had been "a typical farmboy, trying to throw the ball through a brick wall. I had very little science and finesse. I was trying to impress myself, throwing harder and harder." Under Timm's guidance, Locker worked hard on his mechanics and grips, shortened his stride, and learned to hang onto the ball longer before releasing a pitch. When he finally put it all together, Locker developed a major-league-caliber sinker. "Those adjustments, coupled with my inflexible fingers, allowed me to throw the sinker with full fastball velocity," he said.

Tall (6-feet-3) and lean (200 pounds), and coming from a heavily scouted program, Locker was courted by three major-league organizations by the end of his fourth year at Iowa State. "The White Sox, Yankees, and Orioles made me offers," he recalled. "Even though the Yankees offered $12,000, I accepted the White Sox offer for $10,000." His rationale: By the time he was ready for the majors, Early Wynn and others would be retiring, so Locker decided to take short money in exchange for the faster path to the majors.

Locker pitched briefly in the low minors in 1960 before returning to school to finish his geology degree, and in 1961 he joined the Lincoln Chiefs, Chicago's affiliate in the Class B Illinois-Indiana-Iowa League. He led his team in ERA (2.57) and wins (15), and his 228 innings were most in the league. He spent 1962 and

1963 out of baseball fulfilling an Army ROTC service commitment. On leave in 1962, Locker married Judy Swalve, and in 1963 they had their first child. When Locker returned to baseball in 1964, Chicago rushed the 26-year-old to the Indianapolis Indians of the Pacific Coast League and he picked up where he left off. He led Indians starters in innings (226), ERA (2.59), and wins (16). He struck out 178 and walked only 57, a preview of the control he would have throughout his major-league career.

When Locker reported to his first major-league camp, in February 1965, he had military experience, a college degree, and a family. He arrived in boot-camp shape. He wore a weighted vest and spent much of his time doing finger exercises. He carried index cards everywhere he went so he could keep notes on hitters and umpires. "I keep tabs on just how umpires call pitches on me," he told a sportswriter. "I want to remember if they will give you that low strike or whether they're high-ball umps, whether they are good on inside or outside pitches. Someday, in a tight situation, it may be important."[2] Small things, perhaps, but Locker, assiduously self-critical, felt he needed every edge to close the gap between his talent and everyone else's.

Locker made the team but not as a starter. In the minors he had complemented the sinker with a changeup, a nickel-curve, and a fastball. But the White Sox were so impressed with the explosive sinker that they sent him to the bullpen and—in not so many words—ordered him to forget the rest of his repertoire and stick to the sinker.

"There are two kinds of sinker," Locker explained. "One is a roll-over sinker—Tommy John had one of those—a predictable pitch. I had a smothered sinker, which is a lot like a knuckleball. It's hard to predict. I had to fight it every day, every pitch. But when everything was right the ball had some pretty wicked downward movement. It offset my liabilities. You know that if you throw it and the guys get a couple of singles off it, you keep throwing it and they'll eventually hit it at someone and you'll get a double play."

In *Ball Four* Jim Bouton wrote that he heard rumors the White Sox kept the balls so cool and damp that they mildewed.[3] What's more, Locker remembered that the team kept the infield wet.[4] "Managers really want you to get the ball on the ground. The Sox liked the idea that I was a groundball pitcher, a good thing to be if you come into the game with runners on." When he became the team's manager in 1966, Eddie Stanky threatened to fine Locker $200 for any hit he gave up on a pitch other than the sinker. "Two hundred dollars was a lot of money to me then." Locker believed his place in the majors was far from secure and he had a family to take care of. And so, though he had misgivings and would come to regret the decision, Locker agreed.

He debuted on a cool, clear afternoon in Baltimore in front of a small house of 4,248 fans. With the White Sox trailing 3-0, Locker entered the game in the seventh inning to face the bottom of the Orioles' lineup. He gave up a single to the first batter, John Orsino, who stole second and then scored on a single two batters later. Locker got through the first two batters in the eighth, but the heart of the order—Brooks Robinson, Norm Siebern, and Curt Blefary—tagged him for two runs on three straight doubles.

If Locker's first game was rough, the next couple of weeks were a three-finger prostate exam. He surrendered runs in his first five games. It would be 12 days before he got into a sixth, but the break did him good: he didn't allow a run in 11 of his next 12 appearances, and he rolled for the rest of the year. Overall, the rookie threw 91⅓ innings and, despite the bad start, he finished 5-2 with a 3.15 ERA.

With all-star Eddie Fisher (2.40 ERA) and future Hall of Famer Hoyt Wilhelm (1.81) in the pen, White Sox manager Al Lopez could shield Locker by using him in low-pressure situations. Throughout the season, he was rarely used when the White Sox were ahead. From May 19 to July 10, Locker pitched 20 times; he entered with a lead only once. It wasn't glamorous work but it wasn't grunt work either. "It was Locker," Fisher said, "who went in to pitch the middle innings and keep the Sox in the game,"[5] a role that would come to define Locker's career. Led by great pitching—the bullpen's 2.54 ERA was the best in the majors—and great defense, Chicago won 95 games in 1965, but the offense couldn't keep up. The White Sox finished second, seven games behind the Minnesota Twins.

Overwhelmed by poor mental and physical health, Lopez didn't return the following year. He handed the team to Eddie Stanky. Compared with Lopez, Stanky wasn't known to be adroit with pitchers. The transition, though, didn't hurt the staff. The White Sox again had the majors' best ERA. The transition didn't hurt Locker, either. No longer an apprentice, he often got the ball with the game at risk. In late May Fisher told sportswriter Jerome Holtzman that Locker was the best reliever on the team. Despite pitching the last two months with a sore elbow, he dropped his ERA from 3.15 to 2.46. In 95 innings he struck out 70 and gave up only ten unintentional walks. He finished 35 games, up from 14 the year before. He saved two games in 1965, 12 in 1966. The White Sox had great pitching and defense, but a constipated offense kept them out of the playoffs once more. They finished fourth, 15 games behind the first-place Orioles.

Chicago finished in fourth again in 1967, held back again by its inept offense. For the third straight year the bullpen had the majors' best ERA. Locker had a breakout season. He didn't allow a run in 12 of his first 13 games. His ERA by month was 0.77, 2.35, 2.66, 2.92, 1.63, 1.80, and 0.00. He led AL relievers with 77 games and 124⅔ innings and had the most saves (20) and lowest ERA (2.09) of his career. He ended the season with five straight scoreless appearances.

Every year, scar tissue accumulated in Locker's pitching arm. Every spring, he spent the first few weeks of camp loosening it. In 1968 the tissue proved more stubborn than usual. He started the season with a sore elbow, and it showed. Batters hit .318/.391/.515 against him through the end of May. The pain began to subside, and Locker's performance improved to .257/.333/.314 for June. In July Lopez returned as manager and soon after the reunion Locker went 20 straight games without allowing a run. From June

through the end of the year he held hitters to .213/.268/.270, and his second-half ERA of 1.38 was the best half-season ERA of his career. Locker's great second half and another league-leading year for the bullpen couldn't save the White Sox from their first losing campaign in 18 years, however. They fell to ninth place, 36 games off the division lead.

In 1968 Locker continued to pitch well even as the team around him fell apart, but things were different in 1969. As the White Sox got off to a tepid start, Locker took several beatings. On April 3 the Seattle Pilots pelted him for five hits and four runs in less than an inning. At the end of May the Yankees got to him for four runs in just 1⅓ innings. A bad outing on the first of June swelled Locker's ERA to 7.23. He remembered that stretch as "the worst 45 days of my career." Locker's problem wasn't physical or mental. It was mechanical. "I lost the sinker," he recalled. The White Sox grew impatient and on June 8 sent Locker to Seattle, where he joined Jim Bouton and Mike Marshall in the notorious *Ball Four* bullpen.

Widely regarded as an offbeat, independent thinker, Locker immediately bonded with Bouton and Marshall. "Marshall was a genius," he said, "especially about pitching. And Bouton"—Locker had no idea a book was in the works—"was scribbling stuff down in his notebook all the time." Locker had been known to teammates as Wall or Foot. To Bouton he was Snot (a snot locker, explained Bouton, is a nose.[6]) They worked out together in the outfield before games, Bouton developing his knuckler; Marshall, his screwball; Locker, his sinker. They did more than toss baseballs back and forth. They pitched an eight-pound shot to each other. "People thought we were crazy, but it didn't hurt our arms. In fact, I think it strengthened all three. I think it might have had something to do with the success I had with my sinker that year." In addition to throwing an eight-pound ball, Locker did lots of finger exercises. "I had stiff, terrible hands and I needed strength and as much flexibility as I could get."

Within days of the trade to Seattle, the sinker came back. It returned a bit too exuberantly at first—in his second game for the Pilots, against the White Sox no less, he faced three batters and walked them all — but he quickly tamed the pitch, and over the next two weeks shrank his ERA from 7.12 to 4.09. Before the trade, his ERA was 6.55. Afterward, it was 2.18. Before the trade Locker had fewer innings pitched (22) than hits allowed (26). He had already given up six home runs. After the trade he allowed 69 hits and three homers in 78⅓ innings. It was some of the best work of his career.

For the Pilots, though, the year was a dud. Managed by Joe Schultz, they went just 42-70 after acquiring Locker, and finished in last place. Players loved Schultz but he wasn't much of a tactician — a manager more inclined to worry about the color of a player's sweatshirt than what pitch he was working on.[7] Schultz's haphazard management of the Pilots' bullpen got extensive treatment in *Ball Four*. Locker, a former military officer, hated the lack of defined roles in a bullpen. Under Schultz and every manager except Dick Williams, Locker never knew what his job was from one inning to the next. "In those days," he said, "the closer was the only defined role. Other jobs weren't defined." Even Al Lopez didn't tell the relievers, other than his closer, how he planned to use them. "Lopez was very good at handling pitchers but nobody knew what he was thinking. Sometimes I'd warm up in the second inning, then sit, then be called on late in the game. For a reliever there's nothing worse than spending the whole game on pins and needles with no idea whether you could be called on in the second inning or the ninth."

The Seattle franchise was moved to Milwaukee for 1970 and installed Dave Bristol as manager. "He didn't use me as he should have. I don't know why," Locker said. "With Seattle the year before, I was throwing as well as I ever had." And Locker started the year well — six games, no runs — but by the end of April he had allowed 19 baserunners in 10⅓ innings and an OPS (slugging average against plus total bases) of .873. He found himself working the back end of blowouts. By mid-June Locker had appeared in 28 games. The Brewers won five. At 18-41 and 20½ games out of first, the season was already a lost cause. And then,

for reasons that remain unclear, Milwaukee sold Locker to Oakland for an undisclosed, and presumably small, amount of cash. From a distance it's hard to imagine what was in it for Milwaukee. For Oakland, it was a matter of keeping an enemy close. In the previous three seasons, Locker had pitched 27 innings against the A's and held them to 12 hits and one home run, while striking out 20 and posting a 1.37 ERA.

When Locker arrived in Oakland he was in third place instead of last, six games out of first instead of 20. With Mudcat Grant as the new closer, Oakland's mediocre bullpen had become one of the league's strongest. As Locker saw it, the A's bullpen in the early '70s was the key to their success. "We always had three or four closers on that team," Locker said. "That's why we were so good, not because we had guys who could hit the cover off the ball. We were always in the game."

The Brewers, like the White Sox, gave up on Locker too soon. With Milwaukee he allowed 37 hits in 31⅔ innings; with Oakland, 49 in 56⅓. He gave Bristol an ERA of 3.41; Dick Williams, 2.88. The A's finished second but were on the verge of becoming a dynasty.

When the 1971 season began, Williams expected Locker to be the right-handed closer. It would be the first time he had a clearly defined role. On April 27 Locker entered a game in the eighth inning with the A's trailing 3-2. He put six runners on base that inning (two of them by intentional walks as Williams tried to set up a double play). Three runs scored, pushing his ERA up to 4.63.

Williams decided to give Rollie Fingers a chance to take Locker's place. Fingers had been with the A's for a while but mostly as a starter. "He had good stuff," said Locker, "but knowing he had to pitch every third day or so, he had problems with nerves." Fingers, who according to Williams "was the clubhouse patsy and the guy tricked into giving his money away or putting on the wrong uniform," got a chance to close.[8]

"Rollie went to the bullpen because I wasn't doing so well," Locker said. Fingers moved to the pen for good and took over as closer. Locker didn't have a problem with it. "Rollie had great confidence out of the bullpen. He went right at it. He was awesome."

Locker lost his job as closer, but he finally knew what his role was every day. When the A's were down by one or two runs, Locker's assignment was to make sure things didn't get any worse. "My job," he said, "was to stop the other team's rally and keep us in the game." Supported by a boisterous offense and great defense, Locker finished the year 7-2. Other than that, Locker was the same in 1971 as he had been in 1970. His walk rate came down a little (from 3.0 per nine innings to 2.4) but his strikeout rate, home run rate, ERA, and WHIP (walks and hits per inning pitched) hardly changed at all.

With Locker and Darold Knowles handling setup duty from the right and left sides, and Fingers reprising his role as closer, Williams expected his bullpen to be unstoppable in 1972. Was the pen as good as the ones Locker was part of in Chicago? "It's hard to compare our bullpen here with the one in Chicago," he said. "Over there, we all had trick pitches. Wilhelm and Wood threw those knucklers, and"—referring to his side-arm delivery—"I come from Port Arthur."[9]

The A's won four out of five to start the season, went 18-3 from May 20 to June 10, and went into July 43-23, four games ahead of the White Sox. Through July and August the A's hit poorly, pitched well, and essentially played .500 ball. Meanwhile the White Sox steadily gained ground. They began a 26-10 run on July 19 and surpassed Oakland by a half-game on August 27. But within 48 hours the A's reclaimed the lead and never gave it back.

Between August 6 and September 11, Locker pitched 17 times without allowing a run, the second longest scoreless streak of his career. He finished the year 6-1 with a 2.65 ERA. Overall, his hit, walk, strikeout, and home run ratios were the almost the same as they had been in 1970 and 1971.

From 1970 to 1972, Locker threw 206⅔ regular-season innings for the A's, with an ERA of 2.79. He allowed

four home runs—one every 51 innings—and 37 unintentional walks. He preserved enough winnable games in 1971 and 1972 to go 13-3.

Locker turned that performance upside-down in the playoffs. He pitched in four postseason games in 1971 and '72. Oakland was in every game when Locker came in, but they went 0-4. Of the 14 batters he faced, 11 were right-handed, an ideal setup for a right-handed specialist, but five of the 11 reached base and three scored. His career playoff ERA was 9.00.

"Williams wasn't enamored with me," Locker said of the 1972 postseason. He might have been on borrowed time even before the 1972 playoffs. "Dick was the best manager I ever had," he said, "but I don't think he liked me. If you asked him, he would say something not too kind about me, I imagine. I was a free spirit, or whatever you'd call it and Dick just didn't dig my vibe."[10]

Two months after the A's won the World Series, they flipped the 34-year-old Locker to the Chicago Cubs for coveted prospect Bill North. The A's were thrilled with the deal but Locker was so upset he threatened to quit. Some in Chicago didn't like it either. Jerome Holtzman wrote, "It could turn out to be [GM John] Holland's worst trade since he sent Lou Brock to the Cardinals in 1964."[11]

Locker was sullen and apprehensive when he reported for training camp in 1973. "I don't like the idea of coming here," he told Holtzman.[12] It was his first time in the National League. He didn't know his teammates and they didn't know him. Making matters worse, he had a sore arm. "My arm was so weak I couldn't break a pane of glass."[13]

Opening Day cheered him up. On a cool, sunny day at Wrigley Field, the Cubs beat the Montreal Expos 3-2 with a ninth-inning rally. Locker watched the comeback from the bench instead of the bullpen. "I was amazed to hear these guys yelling and cheering," he said. "And I don't mean the extra men. I mean stars—guys like Santo and Kessinger and Williams and Hundley and Beckert. They were yelling their heads off."[14]

Realizing his fastball wasn't what it used to be, and discovering that he was in a fastball-hitting league, Locker knew he had to expand his repertoire. At the time, he was infatuated with *Jonathan Livingston Seagull*, a fable about self-perfection. He turned to Bill Bonham, who owned the team's best changeup, for help. They worked out together, they roomed together, and before long Locker had his changeup back. "My goal was to throw three consecutive changeups for a strikeout," he said. "Eventually it worked." It worked especially well against lefties (.541 OPS in 1973), who had always given Locker more trouble than righties.

Locker carried a 1.96 ERA into June. He pitched with a lead—and under pressure—more than ever. He continued to pitch well and, despite a record of 64-69, the Cubs entered September only 3½ games behind the St, Louis Cardinals for the division lead. With the pennant an arm's length away, manager Whitey Lockman nearly doubled Locker's workload down the stretch, using him 17 times in the Cubs' final 28 games. Locker responded with a 2.61 ERA, five saves, and a 3-1 record, but it wasn't enough. The Cubs finished in fifth place.

Locker pitched 106 innings in 1973, his most since 1967. He saved 18 games and won ten. He had a 2.54 ERA, even though he worked in a hitter's park and had the league's worst defense behind him. In a sense, 1973 was his best year. He contributed more to his team's wins—measured by Wins Above Replacement and Win Shares—than any other team he had played for.

The 1973 season was Locker's last good year. Whitey Lockman's desperate push for the pennant cost Locker his elbow. He missed the entire 1974 season but midsummer surgery had him ready for spring training in 1975. Ever since he arrived at his first training camp wearing a weighted vest, Locker proved himself to be a fitness fanatic. When he was with the A's, he sprinted against younger players and Charley Finley's kids, and

he outran them all. As he saw it, fitness was just one more edge he needed to overcome his liabilities. He came to spring training in 1975 feeling stronger than ever. Even the elbow felt good. But a shoulder problem developed before the end of camp. By June 25, when the Cubs released him, Locker had more walks than strikeouts and a 4.96 ERA in 32⅔ innings. He took the flight home from Montreal and never returned to baseball.

Locker returned with Judy to the Bay Area, where they raised three boys and one girl. Having occasionally worked in real estate during his baseball career, he was able to build a second career in real estate and exterior design. After 40 years in the Bay Area, he retired to Montana in the late 2000s, became an inventor, and taught himself to write. He published two books, *Cows Vote Too* in 2013 and *Esteem Yourself* the following year. *Esteem Yourself*, he said, was meant to inspire young people. "If allowed to do what they want, they're going to do what they want. It's all what can I do to entertain myself, not what can I do to improve myself. Young people don't have self-esteem, because they haven't had to earn it. They haven't had to do something for someone and feel good about it." In addition to inventing and writing, Locker collaborated with Jim Bouton to create ThanksMarvin.com, a website in tribute to Marvin Miller.

Throughout his career, Locker played equally well for four organizations, no matter what kind of offense or defense he had around him, regardless of whether he was in a hitter's or pitcher's park. Consider this: His ERA was 2.68 for the White Sox, 2.54 for the Pilots and Brewers, 2.79 for the A's, and (excluding his abortive comeback in 1975) 2.54 for the Cubs. He frequently pitched in pain, but until his final year he never lost significant time to injury. He threw at least 88 innings in seven out of nine seasons between 1965 and 1973. Three organizations gave up on him, and he bounced back each time. Consistency, durability, resiliency—these traits, not just the sinker, made Locker an asset wherever he went. "The reality is that I was never a star, but when I got to the end of a career spent running scared, looking back I had good stats. The reason I was successful is that I avoided slumps. Other than the start of 1969, when I couldn't find my sinker, I never had a bad year. I never let a bad outing become a bad week, or a bad week become a bad month, or a bad month to become a bad year. I always fought back."

NOTES

1 All quotations, unless otherwise noted, are from interviews with Bob Locker in May 2014.

2 Edgar Munzel, "Rookie Dares to be Different—He Works Out in a Weighted Vest," *The Sporting News*, March 20, 1965.

3 Jim Bouton, *Ball Four Plus Ball Five: An Update 1970-1980* (New York: Stein and Day, 1980), 211.

4 Bob Locker, telephone interview, May 15, 2014.

5 Jerome Holtzman, "Bob Locker," *The Sporting News*, May 28, 1966.

6 Bouton, 210.

7 Bouton, 156.

8 Dick Williams and Bill Plaschke, *No More Mr. Nice Guy: A Life in Hardball* (San Diego: Harcourt Brace Jovanovich, Publishers, 1990), 132.

9 Ron Bergman, "No Wonder A's Are Tough: Their Bullpen Unbeatable," *The Sporting News*, May 27, 1972.

10 Ed and Meat's Sports on the Street, "My Interview With Bob Locker," November 17, 2009, sportsonthestreet.blogspot.com/2009/11/my-interview-with-bob-locker.html.

11 Jerome Holtzman, "Cubs Look to Locker to Turn Bullpen Key," *The Sporting News*, December 9, 1972.

12 Jerome Holtzman, "Suddenly Locker Likes Cubs—'No Reason Why We Can't Win,'" *The Sporting News*, April 28, 1973.

13 Holtzman, "Suddenly Locker Likes Cubs."

14 Holtzman, "Suddenly Locker Likes Cubs."

Ángel Mangual

By Geoffrey Dunn

On a team composed of several leading men and future Hall of Famers, Ángel Mangual was, at most, a minor actor in a supporting role on the great Oakland A's teams of the early 1970s, good for an occasional walk-on or cameo appearance. He was dubbed the "Little Clemente," but it was a billing he never lived up to. In recent years, one less-than-empathetic baseball blogger has opined, "I can think of no outfielder on any other dynastic team who was given so much playing time over such an extended period of time with such poor production."[1] It was a harsh but mostly accurate assessment; he could have also mentioned Mangual's erratic play in the outfield. But for one night in the fall of 1972, the spotlight shone brightly on the quiet 24-year-old outfielder from Puerto Rico. Headlines across the country blared out the following day: "Mangual Gets Winning Hit," "'Little Clemente' Puts A's One Game Away," "Athletics on the Wings of an Angel," and "Mangual Takes After Clemente." It would prove to be his moment in the sun.

With Oakland losing 2-1 to the Cincinnati Reds in the bottom of the ninth inning in the pivotal fourth game of the 1972 World Series, the A's mounted a last-ditch rally before an ecstatic crowd of 49,410 at the Oakland Coliseum. It proved to be a comeback for the ages. After left-handed-hitting first baseman Mike Hegan opened the frame off Reds reliever Pedro Borbón with a hard-hit groundout to third, A's manager Dick Williams leaned heavily on his bench. Gonzalo Marquez, a superb situational left-handed hitter, bounced one up the middle (he went 5-for-8 in postseason pinch-hitting roles that fall), bringing the partisan crowd to its feet. Reds manager Sparky Anderson then pulled some levers of his own. With a 2-and-1 count on A's catcher Gene Tenace and the tying run on first base, Anderson yanked Borbón in favor of his best reliever, Clay Carroll, who had set a major-league record with 37 saves during the season.

The A's hadn't touched him in any of his previous appearances in the fall classic.

Tenace, who had homered earlier in the game for his third round-tripper of the Series, slapped Carroll's second offering solidly into left field, sending controversial pinch-runner Allan Lewis, the "Panamanian Express," to second. Then pinch-hitter Don Mincher, the A's aging backup first baseman, roped a line-drive single into right-center field, scoring Lewis to tie the game and sending Tenace to third. The crowd went wild —the noise, according to one account, was "ear splitting"[2]— and the stage was set for yet another A's pinch-hitter, this time the right-handed-hitting Mangual. Williams pulled the final card from his sleeve, sending Blue Moon Odom in to pinch-run for the slow-moving Mincher.

Sparky Anderson might have had Carroll walk Mangual to load the bases and set up a possible double play. But the A's next batter was Campy Campaneris, a tough hitter to double up, and in Anderson's mind, he would later say, simply a tougher out.[3] Anderson directed Carroll to go after Mangual, who had hit only .246 with five home runs during the regular season. It was his first at-bat of the Series. Anderson's strategy backfired. With the infield playing in, Mangual, executing an inside-out swing, punched Carroll's first pitch — a fastball over the inside portion of the plate — beyond the reach of the Reds' second baseman Joe Morgan for a game-winning single, scoring Tenace, as Mangual was mobbed by his teammates after reaching first base.

It was the first time in World Series history that a team had collected three pinch hits in an inning. Williams, who had also used two pinch-runners in the bottom of the ninth, looked like a genius. "When I hit the ball," Mangual said after the game, "the first thing that came to mind was that it was a double-play ball. I know I got to run. I wouldn't even look at the ball. I just put my head down and prayed that it would go through."[4]

The underdog A's, scoring only 16 runs in seven games, went on to win the Series, the first for the franchise since Connie Mack led the Philadelphia Athletics to a world championship over the St. Louis Cardinals in 1930. And Mangual's heroics would mark the high point of his less-than-fabled career.

Ángel Luis "Cuqui" Mangual Guilbe was born on March 19, 1947, in Juana Díaz, Puerto Rico, a sugarcane center on the south coast of the island. He grew up in a family that worshipped baseball and the national idol, Roberto Clemente. Mangual's younger brother, José "Pepe" Mangual, and his older cousin, José "Coco" Laboy, also played major-league ball.

The 19-year-old Mangual was signed in 1966 by the Pittsburgh Pirates' legendary Puerto Rican scout, Francisco "Pancho" Coímbre, who had also persuaded the Pirates to draft Clemente. Mangual played his first professional season with the Clinton Pilots of the Class A Midwest League, batting a meager .228 in 80 games, with only four home runs. But he also got his first professional attention that season. An article in the *Muscatine* (Iowa) *Journal* in June noted that Mangual had hit a pinch-hit home run for the Pilots, in the same article that highlighted a young Graig Nettles for hitting a three-run home run for the Wisconsin Rapids Twins.

The following year, with Raleigh of the Carolina League (Class A), Mangual upped his average to .285, collecting 150 hits in 136 games; his defense, however, was terrible. He made 17 errors in the outfield for a dismal fielding percentage of .940.

The 5-foot-10 Mangual worked his way slowly through the Pirates' farm system. At York in the Double-A Eastern League in 1968, he batted a lackluster .249, but his fielding percentage improved to .981.

In 1969, at the age of 22, Mangual staged a breakout season at York. By midseason he was leading the league in hits, batting average, doubles, total bases, and RBIs. He wound up finishing second in the batting race with a .320 average, but led the league with 26 home runs and 102 RBIs in only 133 games. His stellar performance earned him honors as both Player of the Year and Most Valuable Player in the Eastern League, as well as a coveted end-of-the season call-up to the Pirates' Triple-A affiliate, the Columbus Jets, and then to the big-league Pirates, where he collected a double in four at-bats, and got a chance, if only for a brief moment, to rub shoulders with his boyhood idol Clemente.

Pittsburgh area papers began to take notice of the rising young outfielder. "The fact that York of the Eastern League ran away with the pennant was due largely to the sensational hitting exploits of Angel Mangual, named Player of the Year and MVP of the Eastern league," said one. "… (H)e has all the tools to develop into a major league star."[5]

Mangual must have begun believing the press. He was a holdout at training camp the following February, signing the day before the Pirates' 1970 spring training camp opened in Bradenton, Florida. He was the last Pirate on the team's 40-man roster to sign. He was competing for the Pirates' fourth outfield position, as a backup in center field to Matty Alou. Mangual actually told reporters that he didn't want the job. "I want to go somewhere I can play every day," he said.[6] Alou had led the National League with 231 hits in 1969 and had batted .331. When camp broke, Mangual was sent to Triple-A Columbus. He was the last outfielder cut from the team.

Mangual held his own on the Jets in 1970, starting in right field and batting a respectable .281 with 20 home runs, though he didn't receive a call-up to the Pirates at the end of the year. Instead, after the season the Pirates sent Mangual to the Oakland Athletics to complete a deal made on September 14, 1970, involving pitcher Mudcat Grant.

Mangual came to the A's with high hopes. Charles Finley believed that A's starting center fielder, Rick Monday, was "not going to be the star that everyone predicted"[7] and that Mangual was the A's center fielder of the future.

Many people forget how dominant a team the A's were in 1971, winning 101 games in the American League West and finishing 16 games ahead of the second-place Kansas City Royals. Mangual hit the first home run of his major-league career on April 27, breaking up a shutout being pitched by left-hander Dave McNally. But he was off to a slow start. By May 18, Finley was offering up Mangual as part of a trade for Sam McDowell. It didn't happen. Perhaps the rumor of a trade lit a fire under Mangual's feet. In early July, in the longest scoreless game in American League history, Mangual singled with two outs against the California Angels in the bottom of the 20th inning to drive home the winning run in a 1-0 victory. Finley called the A's clubhouse with "orders" for Mangual to go out and buy himself a $200 suit and charge it to Finley.[8] Manager Dick Williams indicated that Mangual "may get more chances to play in the second half of the season." At the time, Mangual was batting .322 against right-handed pitching, while Monday

was batting just .229. "He's earned it," Williams said of Mangual.[9]

While Monday started most games in center field that season (batting a mediocre .241), Mangual wound up playing in 94 games (the most among A's bench players), batting .286. His promising performance placed him third in the Rookie of the Year vote and second in *The Sporting News* balloting for top rookie. (Chris Chambliss of the Indians won both competitions.) He was named to the Topps All-Rookie team.

In a rare journalistic portrait of Mangual appearing in the April 1972 *Baseball Digest*—his limited English skills proved to be a barrier for sportswriters during that era—Steve Ames interviewed Clemente about his young countryman. "He has a quick bat," the Great One noted. "But it's a matter of confidence. He has the tools and he could be a hell of a ballplayer. Time will tell. It depends on his mind."[10]

Clemente described Mangual as "a pretty nice kid; listens to everybody; good fellow, good family." With Al Oliver and Willie Stargell coming up in the Pirates organization, Clemente called the trade to Oakland a stroke of good fortune for Mangual. "Look over our roster," he said. "The best thing was a trade. It was a break for Angel."

"I had played right field in the minors," Mangual told Ames in the article. "I thought someday I'd play, you know, right field for the Pirates. I knew I could play, you know. But no position for me in Pittsburgh. I'm glad to be here; A's give me a chance."

Mangual also paid homage to his hero, Clemente: "Roberto was a big help to me, show me, you know, how to hit, how to play outfield. He talked to me all the time. He said when pitcher throws hard you open your hips. For breaking pitcher, try to hit the ball to right field."

"I wish he don't try to be a long-ball hitter," Clemente interjected. "He got lots of power; not so much that he should try home runs."

"It is a credit to Mangual," writer Ames observed, "a scatter-shot hitter blessed with quick hands, that he is Mr. Relaxed prior to a game....He may be seen walking around the clubhouse twisting a foot-long steel rod to strengthen his hands or lying on the rug signing baseballs or talking with another player. He's good natured."

"We had a very strong outfield situation last year," A's manager Williams declared, "and even though we traded away a good center fielder in Monday, we feel that Mangual earned the job as a regular with an outstanding season."[11]

The experiment didn't work out. Mangual's defense was erratic; Reggie Jackson actually played 92 games in center field that year and only 43 in right. Mangual played 51 games in right field and 22 in center. He wound up collecting only 67 hits in 272 at-bats, scoring a mere 19 runs without a single stolen base. His celebrated pinch hit in Game Four of the Series was the highlight of an otherwise dismal year.

The following season, 1973, was no different. Finley kept Mangual on the roster, though he batted only .224 with three home runs. He also was a liability in the clubhouse. Midway through the season, Mangual got into a fight aboard an airplane flight with A's pitcher Blue Moon Odom, a well-known music aficionado who was playing a cassette loudly. "Shut it off," Mangual barked. "Hell no," Odom retorted, charging Mangual. The two had to be separated by teammates.[12]

On another occasion, Mangual threw his helmet to the ground in disgust when manager Williams ordered Jackson to pinch-hit for him in a game in which Mangual had started. Williams fined him $200. "I wasn't tossing my helmet because Reggie pinch-hit for me. I did it just to relax," an uncontrite (and unconvincing) Mangual told *The Sporting News*. "If Williams no like me, why doesn't he trade me?"[13] But given both his attitude and poor performance on the field, the real question is what the A's could get for their unhappy outfielder. Although they won the American League West again in convincing fashion,

there would be no heroics for Mangual in postseason play this time to compensate for a subpar season. He batted .111 in the American League Championship Series against Baltimore and went hitless in six at-bats during the World Series against the Mets.

The 1974 season proved to be more of the same. Mangual started erratically in all three outfield positions, and also served as the A's designated hitter in 37 games, batting a dismal .233 with only 9 home runs and 43 RBIs. During the playoffs he was reduced to an afterthought, collecting a single in four at-bats against Baltimore in the ALCS, and striking out in his only World Series at-bat against the Los Angeles Dodgers. Nonetheless, he collected his third World Series championship ring.

By 1975 the writing was on the wall. A sullen Mangual played in only 62 games during the regular season, collecting a mere 24 hits en route to a .220 average. His one highlight was winning the team bubble-gum blowing championship. The contests were sponsored by the Bazooka Gum Company and overseen by "gum commissioner" Joe Garagiola, but Mangual was replaced for the finals of the contest by Glenn Abbott. More significantly, he was left off the roster for the A's ALCS encounter with the Boston Red Sox. In September he was placed on waivers to make room for Cesar Tovar. "It's just a necessity when you are going for all the marbles," said Finley. "We felt that he was expendable. We just thought that Tovar could be of more help to us than Mangual."[14]

The following year, Mangual broke spring training with the A's Triple-A farm team in Tucson. He was called up to Oakland briefly in June, collecting a single and a double in a dozen at-bats, and his numbers in the Pacific Coast League weren't much better. He batted .274 at Tucson in 42 games, with two home runs. A nerve injury in his neck had left one of his hands feeling numb. What little power he had was gone. He also lost several fly balls in the desert sun—one of his miscues cost a Toro teammate a no-hitter—and the A's released him outright. As though adding insult to injury, both of his Toros baseball cards issued that season misspelled his last name as "Manguel."

Mangual bounced around in the lower minor leagues for three more seasons—he played with the Aquascalientes Rieleros and the Poza Rica Petroleros in the Mexican League, and later with the Puerto Rico Boricuas of the Inter-American League (batting a paltry .190 in a handful of games), but he never gained traction again as a player. His days in baseball were over—at the age of 32.[15]

For the next two decades, Mangual was off the radar of professional baseball, but in May of 1997 he made headlines again, this time of a different sort. According to several news accounts, Mangual "and 21 other alleged members of [a] drug ring [based in Puerto Rico], including a policeman and a prison guard, were taken into custody Monday by police officers and federal agents." A federal indictment accused Mangual of acting as "an intermediary between drug-buyers and sellers."[16]

Whether or not Mangual served time for his alleged activities is unknown. In August 2010, his personal 1972 world championship trophy, presented to all A's players by Finley, was sold at auction. His last recorded public appearance was in January of 2013, when he participated in SABR Day, sponsored by SABR's Orlando Cepeda Chapter at the Francisco "Pancho" Coimbre Sports Museum in Ponce, Puerto Rico, where he appeared with his cousin and former major leaguer José "Coco" Laboy.[17]

NOTES

1 Baseball-Fever.com. Thread: "70's A's—Angel Mangual," May 2010.

2 Associated Press, *Santa Cruz* (California) *Sentinel*, October 20, 1972, 19.

3 *Raleigh Register*, Beckley, West Virginia, October 20, 1972, 8. Anderson's exact quote was: "I'd rather pitch to Mangual than to Bert Campaneris, who was up next. I thought we could handle Mangual."

4 *Pittsburgh Press*, October 20, 1972, 29.

5 "Twelve Pirate Hopefuls Named Minor League All-Stars," Uniontown (Pennsylvania) *Evening Standard*, February 9, 1970, 19.

6 "Pirates to Open Friday," *Simpson's Leader-Times* (Kittanning, Pennsylvania), March 5, 1970, 14.

7 Mark L. Armour and Daniel R. Levitt, *Paths to Glory: How Great Baseball Teams Got That Way* (Dulles, Virginia: Potomac Books Inc.: 2004), 253.

8 *Kentucky New Era* (Hopkinsville, Kentucky, July 2, 1971, 12.

9 "Williams Promises Mangual More Work," *San Mateo* (California) *Times*, July 10, 1971, 6.

10 Steve Ames, "Mangual of the A's: An Angel with a Quick Bat," *Baseball Digest*, April 1972, 35-36. I have quoted Ames' article verbatim. He invokes a typical journalistic practice of the times, that of quoting Spanish-speaking players from Latin America in broken English rather in their native Spanish. It tended to make them sound illiterate. As such, it is important to understand Mangual's career in a larger framework that addresses the various ways in which Latino ballplayers at all levels of professional baseball were subjected to the racist and ethnic stereotypes of their times. See Adrian Burgos, Jr., Playing America's Game: Baseball, Latinos and the Color Line (Berkeley: University of California Press: 2007).

11 Ibid.

12 Hope (Arkansas) *Star*, July 13, 1974, 6.

13 Cited in "Cooperstown Confidential" Regular Season Edition, by Bruce Markham, Oaklandfans.com, June 12, 2003.

14 *Kansas City Star*, September 1, 1975, 9.

15 Mangual's statistics from playing in Puerto Rico's winter league are not available online.

16 *Toledo Blade*, May 7, 1997, 3.

17 According to Luis Machuca, president of the Orlando Cepeda SABR Chapter (Puerto Rico), Mangual as of 2014 resided in Ponce, Puerto Rico. Efforts to contact him via telephone for this profile proved unsuccessful.

Gonzalo Márquez

By Rory Costello

Gonzalo Márquez, one of the earlier Venezuelans in the majors, never played a full year in "The Show." From 1972 through 1974, he got into just 76 regular-season games with Oakland and the Chicago Cubs. Márquez's primary position was first base, and he was a good fielder—but he lacked power. Across his entire pro career, including play in the postseason and Latin American leagues, he hit home runs once in every 132 at-bats.[1]

Márquez was a contact hitter. He averaged exactly .300 in the minors and .288 during 20 seasons of winter ball in his homeland. Thus, he made his mark in post-season play as a pinch-hitter. During the 1972 AL Championship Series against Detroit, he was 2-for-3. He won Game One with a single in the 11th inning and scored a go-ahead run after singling in the tenth inning of Game Four. Márquez continued to deliver off the bench in the World Series, going 3-for-5. In Game Four, he ignited the game-winning rally in the bottom of the ninth.

Márquez played his last season in the US minors in 1974. He then spent two years in the Mexican League (1975 and 1978), followed by a stint in the short-lived Inter-American League of 1979. After that, he played on with the Caracas Leones of the Venezuelan League, his team for nearly all his career at home. He became a respected leader and was serving as a player-coach when his life was cut short in a postgame car accident in December 1984.

According to most baseball references, Gonzalo Enrique Márquez Moya was born on March 31, 1946. However, his birth certificate shows that the true date was March 31, 1940. He presented an ID that showed 1946 when he turned professional.

Márquez's birthplace was Carúpano, a small city in the state of Sucre. Sucre is in the northeastern part of Venezuela, along the coast of the Caribbean Sea. It has much natural beauty, including beaches—Carúpano's are lovely—and mountains. Carúpano is also famous for its annual carnival, the biggest of its kind in the nation. The *Lonely Planet* travel guide to Venezuela describes it as "quite possibly the most lively, boisterous, and crazy rave you'll ever experience."

Sucre is one of the poorer and less developed states in Venezuela. The local economy of Carúpano relies on trade and shipment of commodities, cocoa in particular. Gonzalo Márquez's father, Jesús "Chuíto" Márquez, was a merchant (the family also owned some farmland).[2] His mother, Edelmira Moya, was a dressmaker and housewife looking after six children (four brothers and two sisters), of whom Gonzalo was the second.

Márquez had happy memories of growing up in Carúpano. In 2012, Venezuelan baseball author Alfonso Tusa wrote, "I can't remember exactly whether it was in *Sport Gráfico* magazine or in a radio interview that I heard Gonzalo Márquez say that what he missed most from home were the arepas [a South American corn cake] with fresh mussels that were sold in the municipal market." Márquez also enjoyed playing the guitar and painting on canvas.[3]

Márquez developed his skills in amateur baseball with a club called Vigilantes. His professional baseball career began in the winter of 1965-66, when he joined the Caracas Leones. The nation's capital is about 250 miles west of Carúpano (as the crow flies). That team had a working agreement with the Athletics organization, then still based in Kansas City, so it's not entirely certain whether the A's noticed him with Caracas, or signed him first and assigned him to the Leones. At any rate, the man who signed him for Kansas City was Félix "Fellé" Delgado, the club's Latin American regional scout. He gave Márquez the nickname "Hurricane," though Gonzalo never knew why.[4]

The Leones then featured two of the all-time Venezuelan baseball heroes, Vic Davalillo and César Tovar. The 1965-66 squad also included several young A's. Pitchers Lew Krausse and Paul Lindblad led the staff, which also included 19-year-old Jim Hunter until he had to leave with a sore arm.[5] The shortstop was Bert Campaneris. Márquez got into 19 games, getting more of an opportunity after Caracas fired Ken "Hawk" Harrelson for playing golf when he was supposedly ill.[6]

Márquez played in the US for the first time in 1966. The lefty swinger spent three seasons at Class A, hitting for a nice average (.297) but with little extra-base pop (slugging percentage of .352, and just one homer). He also showed some base-stealing ability, swiping nine in ten games after becoming a leadoff hitter during the 1968 season.[7]

According to Alfonso Tusa, Márquez had an excellent glove at first base. He wasn't tall (5-feet-11), but he had quick reactions and was especially good at saving wild throws. Further support for Márquez's skill in the field comes from Jesús "Chalao" Méndez, who played in the US minors, Mexico, and Venezuela in the 1980s and 1990s before becoming chief scout in Venezuela for the Philadelphia Phillies. Méndez never reached the majors; like Márquez, he was a flashy fielder with very little power—"a shortstop who played first." In a 2010 interview, he called Márquez "my all-time idol" and "a guide for me to play first base."[8]

Márquez also developed enough with the bat to become the regular first baseman for Caracas in his second winter with the team, 1966-67. The Leones won the league championship that year and again in 1967-68, when Márquez hit a career-high .354 and tied a league record with eight RBIs in a playoff game on February 4. He eventually became a member of eight title winners at home.

In 1969 Márquez moved up to Double-A Birmingham. He had another pretty fair year (.297-3-34, .372 slugging percentage) but received no particular attention in *The Sporting News*. That December, he married Hercilia Rísquez. He also drew plans for the Venezuelan national telephone company while playing winter ball.[9]

A special career highlight for Márquez came in February 1970. After playing for Caracas in the regular winter season, he joined Navegantes de Magallanes to reinforce their roster for the playoffs (a common winter-league practice). Magallanes won the championship and thus went on to represent Venezuela in the Caribbean Series, which had been revived after a hiatus of nine years. The tournament was held in Caracas, and Venezuela took seven of eight games in the round-robin against the Dominican Republic and Puerto Rico. It was the nation's first Caribbean Series title. Márquez led all hitters with his .478 average (11-for-23) and was named series MVP.

Coming off this performance, Márquez earned another promotion in 1970. With Iowa of the Triple-A American Association, he had his best season as a pro (.341-6-60, .430 slugging). Márquez, who hit primarily to the opposite field or up the middle, benefited from manager Sherm Lollar's advice. Lollar said, "The defenses were beginning to play him like a right-handed pull hitter. I suggested that he keep 'em honest by taking a shot to that open area in right."[10]

During the summer of 1971, Márquez sat out the entire season. Reports varied as to why; one said he held out, another said he had a leg injury.[11] In 1972, though, Márquez himself said that he was taking care of his mother, who was very sick with gangrene in one foot. He later said, "It was a long year."[12] He returned in 1972, however, and displayed his usual contact hitting at Iowa (.309-0-27). Márquez was not unusually hard to strike out, but he did not walk very much either.

In August 1972 Márquez—thought to be aged 26, but really 32—got his first call to the majors. He made his debut on August 11 and struck out as a pinch-hitter against Cecilio "Cy" Acosta of the Chicago White Sox. He was just the 21st Venezuelan to appear in a big-league game.

Márquez did almost nothing but pinch-hit for the A's in 1972. Out of his 23 appearances, one came as a pinch-runner, and he stayed in the game at first base. His only start came in the season's last game. Overall, he was 8-for-21 (.381) with four RBIs.

Oakland put Márquez on the postseason roster—but he wasn't on the original list of 25 players that the team submitted. He had a plane ticket for Venezuela at the end of the regular season.[13] However, when reliever Darold Knowles broke his left thumb, manager Dick Williams chose Márquez to replace Knowles instead of lefty pitcher Don Shaw.[14] The skipper's thinking was something that would be unheard of today. "I added [Márquez] then," said Williams, "because I was quite content using eight pitchers in the playoffs and I wanted another bat to use with our second base situation."[15] The skipper was referring to the strategy of pinch-hitting for the club's light-hitting second basemen whenever they came up.

The decision to bring Márquez paid immediate dividends in the ALCS. In Game One, veteran Tigers star Al Kaline had given Detroit a 2-1 lead with a home run in the top of the 11th. In the bottom of the inning, Márquez came up with runners on first and second. He ripped a single to right off Chuck Seelbach, past a diving Norm Cash. The tying run scored and the winning run followed when Kaline made a throwing error. "It was the biggest hit of my life," said Márquez, through translator Bert Campaneris.[16] Previously he had told Campy, "If I get a chance to hit, I win the game."[17]

Márquez also started what could have been a game-winning rally in the tenth inning of Game Four. He scored with a diving slide that knocked the ball loose from Tigers catcher Bill Freehan, but had the wind knocked out of him. As a result, he did not remember rolling over to touch the plate. In the bottom of the tenth, though, three Oakland pitchers combined to give up a two-run lead. Márquez rubbed his aching chest as he was interviewed but said, "I can play if it's only as a pinch-hitter. Anyway, I want to [play]."[18] However, Williams did not call on his rookie as Oakland won Game Five and advanced to the World Series.

Against Cincinnati, Márquez was 1-for-2 in his first two appearances off the bench. Neither of those influenced the game's outcome—but the finest moment of his big-league career came in Game Four. Oakland trailed 2-1 going into the ninth inning. Williams sent Márquez up to pinch-hit for George Hendrick with one out and the bases empty. Reds manager Sparky Anderson later recalled, "The information which Ray Shore had provided on Márquez in his scouting report was right on the money. If we had followed it, we would have won that game—and the Series.

"The report said to bunch Márquez down the middle. That was where he hit the ball in any games that Shore saw him play. It just happened, though, that [Dave] Concepción, our shortstop, had played against Márquez in Venezuela.

"Dave told us, 'Skip, this guy hits everything to left.' As Alex Grammas, my infield coach, pointed out, Concepción had more opportunity to see Márquez than Shore had."

The account by *Toronto Star* columnist Milt Dunnell continued, "Márquez hit a high hopper over the hill. If Concepcion had been playing where the scouting report recommended, he would have taken the ball in his hip pocket. He almost made the out anyway."[19] The game-winning rally then unfolded. After spending the winter second-guessing himself, Anderson was still blaming himself for the decision in 1975.[20]

Márquez appeared twice more during the rest of the World Series. In Game Six, he got his third pinch hit, tying the World Series record then held by three men: Bobby Brown (1947), Dusty Rhodes (1954), and Carl Warwick (1964). Ken Boswell became the fifth (and as of 2013, the last to date) in 1973.

In the winter of 1972-73, Márquez won another championship with Caracas. He then made the Opening Day roster for the A's in 1973. Again he served almost exclusively as a pinch-hitter. The American League adopted the designated-hitter rule that year, but Márquez got just one start there—owner Charlie Finley thought the singles hitter didn't fit the bill.[21] He also was listed as the starting second baseman in back-to-back games on May 4 and 5. The first time, Márquez thought it was a joke.[22] On both occasions, though, Dick Green—a true second baseman—replaced him in the field in the bottom of the first inning. The A's used this strategy on various other occasions.

Márquez played only one inning at his true position for Oakland in 1973. He entered the game on May 18 after Bill North had been ejected for throwing his bat at Kansas City pitcher Doug Bird and charging the mound. Two days later, Márquez also played one inning in right field.

Despite his sporadic duty, Márquez did a fairly good job, going 6-for-23 (.261). The A's sent him down to Triple-A Tucson in early June, though, recalling pinch-runner Allan Lewis. "We don't have any use for Márquez as a pinch-hitter with the designated hitter rule," said Dick Williams.[23] Márquez was recalled in August and made two more pinch-hitting appearances. On August 29 Oakland traded him to the Chicago Cubs, even-up for another first baseman, Pat Bourque.

A's beat writer Ron Bergman commented, "Márquez lost his batting stroke through disuse. The A's then opted for someone with more power, and Bourque was available."[24]

In Chicago, Márquez finally got a chance for some regular action, at least against righties. He started 17 games that September, hitting .224. On September 21 at Wrigley Field, he hit his only homer in the majors. It was an opposite-field shot into the basket atop Wrigley's outfield wall, off Steve Rogers, then a rookie with the Montreal Expos.[25]

Before Márquez came to the Cubs, the team had given rookie André Thornton and veteran star Billy Williams looks at first base. Thornton played that position most frequently for Chicago in 1974, and Márquez (one of the last cuts after holding out) opened the season at Triple-A Wichita. He got back to the big club in early May, though, when little-used utilityman Adrian Garrett was sent down. Márquez remained with the Cubs through early June. During that month, he got into 11 games in the majors, all as a pinch-hitter. He went hitless in 11 at-bats and played one inning in the field at first. Chicago sent Márquez back to Wichita; he never made it back to the majors. All told, he hit .235-1-10 in 128 plate appearances.

In December 1974 Chicago sold Márquez's contract to Puebla of the Mexican League. He played in just 24 games for the Pericos in 1975 (.314-1-14); his family remembered that he didn't want to be separated from them. Márquez did not play during the summers in Mexico (or anywhere else) in 1976 and 1977, though he remained active at home in the winters. Márquez loved to play baseball—it bored him to watch on television. He returned to Mexico in 1978 and had a good year with Tampico. He set a personal high with 12 home runs, while driving in 61 runs and hitting .288 in 135 games.

In 1979 the Inter-American League started up. The IAL had two of its six franchises in Venezuela, which gave Márquez an opportunity to play at home in the summer too. He played 24 games for the Caracas Metropolitanos and two for the Maracaibo Petroleros.

However, the ill-starred league folded in June before its first season was complete.

Márquez played with Caracas for another six winter seasons. He had rejoined the Leones in the winter of 1976-77 after one season with Magallanes—the only other time he did not wear a Caracas uniform during the winter. During the regular season in Venezuela, he hit just 16 homers in 833 games and 2,932 at-bats.

Márquez appeared in the playoffs in 14 of his 20 years, though, and as he did in the US, he took his play up a notch in the Venezuelan postseason. He hit .300 with six homers in 96 games and 310 at-bats. He was part of four more league champions: 1977-78, and the "three-peat" teams of 1979-80, 1980-81, and 1981-82.

As a consequence of being on all those teams, Márquez was on hand for five Caribbean Series (the 1981 edition was not held because of a Venezuelan players' strike). He got to play in three, hitting .387 (24-for-62) overall and making the 1973 tournament all-star team. Winning the Caribbean Series is a matter of national pride, though—even highly regarded native players remain on the bench sometimes. In 1980 the primary first baseman for the Leones was Ken Phelps. In 1982 the great Venezuelan first baseman Andrés Galarraga had played a lot during the regular season. But he was still just 20 and inexperienced, as he graciously admitted.[26]

So manager Alfonso "Chico" Carrasquel used American Danny García in the 1982 postseason, and did so again in Hermosillo, Mexico. The Leones won five of six games there and brought the Caribbean title to Venezuela. García remembered, "I had led the team in hitting. I batted third in the lineup behind Eddie Milner and Steve Sax, followed by Venezuelan greats Tony Armas and Baudilio [Bo] Díaz batting fourth and fifth, with Dave Henderson batting sixth." He added, "I remember 'Gonzo' as a quiet, very smart teammate."[27]

Márquez was a mentor to Galarraga. "The Big Cat" played with the Leones for the first time in the 1978-79 season at the age of 17. In 1978 Márquez also helped mold another future Venezuelan star, Ozzie Guillén, then a skinny little 14-year-old. That came as Márquez and his former Caracas teammate Dámaso Blanco managed the national team.[28]

According to the Associated Press, Márquez also became a scout for the Los Angeles Dodgers in 1983.[29] He may have been affiliated with the club years before, though—the book *Los Leones del Caracas* states that Márquez discovered Leonardo "Leo" Hernández and brought him to Caracas for the 1978-79 season.[30] Hernandez, who played in the majors for parts of four seasons in the '80s, started his US pro career in the Dodgers chain in 1978. In October 1984 Márquez signed another of his countrymen for the Dodgers, Carlos Alberto Hernández. The catcher eventually played in the majors from 1990 through 2000.

Márquez's family said he had a hand in the signing of Óscar Azócar, another Sucre native. Azócar's first pro action came with the Leones in the winter of 1983-84; he signed with the New York Yankees in November 1983, originally as a pitcher.[31] After converting to the outfield, Azócar made it to the majors from 1990-92.

In the 1984-85 winter season, another of Venezuela's all-time greats joined the Leones as a youth of 17. That was shortstop Omar Vizquel, coming off his first year as a Seattle Mariners farmhand. Vizquel was another of the young ballplayers who affectionately called Márquez *Abuelo*, or Grandfather. In 2010, after Óscar Azócar died suddenly, Vizquel said, "His personality reminded me lot of Gonzalo Márquez. He was a very happy person."[32]

On December 19, 1984, Caracas played Navegantes de Magallanes in Valencia. Márquez did not have to play because he had some broken toes, but he stayed in the lineup—he was not one to complain. After the game, Márquez got in his car with Julio César, his 16-year-old son from a relationship before his marriage to Hercilia, and 12-year-old Gonzalo Jr., to drive back to the capital city. It was about halfway through the trip, in the city of La Victoria, when tragedy struck. In 1986 Andrés Galarraga told the sad story of what happened. "Some young people in a car were drunk and they came across the road and hit his car. We were right behind him in the team bus. We saw it happen and we had to pull his body out."[33]

Julio escaped the accident nearly unscathed, except for a nine-stitch cut in his arm, received as he got out of the car. Gonzalo Jr. was severely injured in the accident but pulled through.[34] In 2013 he related another sad twist of fate about the accident. "After the game, we always stopped to eat a *pernil* [roast pork shoulder] sandwich at a place called La Encrucijada [The Crossroads, a roadside eatery famous throughout Venezuela]. I remember as if it were yesterday that we were blocked by a car parked behind us and my father tried to get out for more than 10 minutes. This happened five minutes before the accident. If that car hadn't been there, the story would have a happy ending."

Márquez's death certificate put the time of death at around 1:00 on the morning of December 20. Several days after the accident, however, his wife, Hercilia, gained access to personal effects and noticed that the crash had caused his watch to stop at 11:45 P.M. on the 19th.

The loss of Márquez—who had helped young players with their skills and kept the team united—affected all the Leones deeply, but Galarraga in particular.[35] "He was my best friend," said El Gato in 1988. "He helped me more than anyone, and when he died I was left alone."[36] Galarraga remained a good friend to the Márquez family.

In addition to Hercilia, Márquez was survived by their four children, as well as Julio. Before Gonzalo Jr. came a daughter named Edjuly and after him was María Alexandra; they were then aged 13 and 7. There was also a baby of seven months named Jesús Enrique. "When Gonzalo died," said Hercilia in the late 1980s, "there were many problems because we had no insurance." As a result, the Gonzalo Márquez Foundation was established with the goal of helping Venezuela's professional ballplayers, retirees to begin with. Hercilia dedicated much time to this venture at first, but she

lived 25 miles from Caracas and could not continue. After the foundation's president, Gustavo "Gus" Gil, moved to the US, the need arose for someone to take charge.[37] Unfortunately, that did not happen, and the foundation ceased to operate.

In January 1985, shortly after Márquez's death, the Caracas Leones retired his uniform number 6 in tribute. The pregame ceremony was solemn and moving; in the ensuing game, Andrés Galarraga marked the occasion by hitting a home run.[38]

Estadio Gonzalo Márquez in Carúpano is named for the local hero, who entered the Hall of Fame of Venezuelan Sports on May 29, 2002.[39] He also became a member of the Venezuelan Baseball Hall of Fame on November 17, 2008. His widow accepted the honor.[40] Yet another fitting way to remember Gonzalo Márquez is by the title of respect that he earned in Venezuela. El Caballero del Béisbol—The Gentleman of Baseball—was known for his fine character on and off the field.

SOURCES

Books

Treto Cisneros, Pedro, editor, *Enciclopedia del Béisbol Mexicano* (Mexico City:

Revistas Deportivas, S.A. de C.V.: 11th edition, 2011).

Internet resources

baseball-reference.com

retrosheet.org

purapelota.com (Venezuelan statistics)

comc.com (online sports card market with repository of images)

Grateful acknowledgment to the family of Gonzalo Márquez for their support. Continued thanks to Marcos Grunfeld in Venezuela for his help with Caribbean Series statistics. Thanks also to Danny García.

NOTES

1   Major leagues (regular season and postseason), Venezuelan winter league (regular season and postseason), Mexican summer league, Inter-American League, and Caribbean Series.

2   Gonzalo Márquez birth certificate, courtesy of the Márquez family; Ron Bergman, "What Will A's Do With Pinch-Hitting Hero?," *The Sporting News*, November 18, 1972, 41.

3 Alfonso L. Tusa C., "Un gran momento de Gonzalo Márquez," Magallaneando blog, October 9, 2012 (magallanenando.blogspot. com/2012/10/un-gran-momento-de-gonzalo-marquez.html).

4 Bill Bryson, "Oaks Unleash Hurricane in Batter's Box: Márquez," *The Sporting News*, September 12, 1970, 27.

5 Eduardo Moncada, "Big Hassle Erupts as Sharks Demand a Ban on Cardenal," *The Sporting News*, December 11, 1965, 27.

6 Eduardo Moncada, "Caracas Fires Harrelson, Played Golf as Rest Cure," *The Sporting News*, January 1, 1966, 27.

7 *The Sporting News*, June 15, 1968, 39.

8 2010 interview with Jesús Méndez on the now-defunct Venezuelan website Batazos.com; glimpses of the story are still visible through Google search results.

9 Bryson, "Oaks Unleash Hurricane in Batter's Box: Márquez."

10 Bryson, "Oaks Unleash Hurricane in Batter's Box: Márquez."

11 Ron Bergman, "Blue Pitch for Long Green Leaves Finley Seeing Red," *The Sporting News*, February 26, 1972, 32. Pete Swanson, "Big Sticks Could Give Added Boost to A.A. Gate," *The Sporting News*, April 22, 1972.

12 "Williams wants pinch hitters," United Press International, October 8, 1972.

13 Lowell Reidenbaugh, "Late 3M Rally Boosts Athletics' Series Stock," *The Sporting News*, November 4, 1972, 7.

14 Clif Keane, "A's sting Tigers, 3-2," *Boston Globe*, October 8, 1972.

15 "Williams wants pinch hitters."

16 "Williams wants pinch hitters."

17 Hal Bock, "A's nip Tigers in 11th; rookie settles it," Associated Press, October 8, 1972.

18 Pete Bennett, "Relievers Didn't Do Job, says Disappointed Dick," Associated Press, October 12, 1972.

19 Milt Dunnell, "One Big Regret," *Toronto Star*, February 16, 1973, 15.

20 "No geniuses among managers—Sparky," Associated Press, October 12, 1975.

21 Ron Bergman, "Will DH Slash Hill Staffs? Not Finley's 10-Man Corps," *The Sporting News*, February 10, 1973, 37.

22 Ron Bergman, "New Rule, New Role: Johnson Enjoying Both," *The Sporting News*, May 26, 1973, 3.

23 "People in Sports," *New York Times*, DATE, 1973.

24 Ron Bergman, "Series Still the Big Thing to 20-Win Holtzman," *The Sporting News*, September 22, 1973, 8.

25 "Richard Dozer, "Cubs win," *Chicago Tribune*, September 22, 1973, A1.

26 Andrés Galarraga with Humberto Acosta, *Andrés Galarraga: Una Historia que Contar* (Caracas, Venezuela: Los Libros de *El Nacional*, 2009). Galarraga said he enjoyed the Caribbean Series experience even though he didn't get a single turn at bat.

27 E-mail from Danny García to Rory Costello, September 14, 2013.

28 Billy Russo, "Siempre tuve el sueño de ser pelotero," MLB.com, February 2, 2010 (mlb.mlb.com/news/article.jsp?ymd=20100201&content_id=8007352&vkey=ozzie_guillen&c_id=mia).

29 "Gonzalo Marquez, scout for Los Angeles Dodgers," Associated Press, December 22, 1984.

30 Rosa Alma John, *Los Leones del Caracas* (Caracas, Venezuela: Editorial Cejota, 1982), 205.

31 Other sources show that Fred Ferreira signed Azócar for the Yankees. See "Profiles of Coaches, Players on A-C Yanks 1988 Roster," *Schenectady Gazette,* April 6, 1988, 34.

32 "Falleció el ex-pelotero Oscar Azócar," Meridiano.com.ve, June 17, 2010.

33 Peter Hadekel, "The Big Cat," *Montreal Gazette*, May 31, 1986, G-4.

34 Bruce Markusen, "Remembering Gonzalo Márquez," Oaklandfans.com, May 6, 2004 (oaklandfans.com/columns/markusen/markusen174.html).

35 Hadekel, "The Big Cat."

36 Richard Justice, "Andres Galarraga Called Best in National League," *Washington Post*, July 3, 1988.

37 Carlos Lares Cárdenas, *Venezolanos en las Grandes Ligas. Sus Vidas y Hazañas 1939-1989* (Caracas, Venezuela: Nacho, 1990).

38 Alexis Salas H., *Los Eternos Rivales* (Caracas, Venezuela: Seguros Caracas, 1988), 301. Galarraga, *Andrés Galarraga: Una Historia que Contar.* The other ten numbers retired by the Leones belonged to Pompeyo Davalillo, Víc Davalillo, César Tovar, Tony Armas, Baudilio Díaz, Urbano Lugo, Alfonso "Chico" Carrasquel, Omar Vizquel, and Andrés Galarraga.

39 "Siete figuras del deporte nacional ingresarán al Salón de la Fama," *Notitarde* (Valencia, Venezuela), May 28, 2002.

40 "Exaltados nuevos miembros al Salón de la Fama del Béisbol Venezolano," Solodeportes.com, November 18, 2008 (solodeportes.com.ve/2008/11/1238/exaltados-nuevos-miembros-al-salon-de-la-fama-del-beisbol-venezolano/).

Orlando "Marty" Martinez

By Joseph Gerard

Orlando "Marty" Martínez Oliva was a major-league baseball player, coach, manager, and scout who was best known for scouting Edgar Martinez and signing him to a professional contract with the Seattle Mariners in 1982. Orlando Martinez played for six teams in the major leagues, beginning with the Minnesota Twins in 1962 and ending with the Texas Rangers in 1972. After his major-league playing career was over, Martinez played, coached, and managed in the Rangers minor-league system for four years before becoming player-manager of the Double-A Tulsa Drillers in 1977. He managed the Drillers for two years and won a first-half championship in 1977. Afterward, he became a scout and coach for the Seattle Mariners, and was named interim manager of the team for one day in 1986.

Orlando Martinez was born on August 23, 1941, in the Batabano section of Havana, Cuba, in what is now Mayabeque province. At the Instituto Civico Militar in Marianao, he lettered in baseball, track, and basketball. He set a national record for striking out 23 batters in one game and was named to the All-Cuba national team. In 1957 he traveled to Mexico with a team of Cuban high-school players, compiling a batting average of .306 during the trip.

After graduating from high school in 1959, Martinez attended the University of Havana for one year and the University of Mexico in Mexico City for another, but his academic studies came to an end when he was discovered by Joe Cambria, the scout who helped open up Latin America for the major leagues. Cambria signed hundreds of players, mostly of Cuban descent, to inexpensive contracts for the Washington Senators and their successors, the Minnesota Twins, including Bobby Estalella, Tony Oliva, and Camilo Pasqual.

Martinez signed with Cambria in 1960 and was sent to play for the Erie Sailors, the Senators' affiliate in the Class D New York-Penn League. He got off to an inauspicious start, hitting only .222 in 297 at-bats, but improved the following season with the Wilson Tobs (short for Tobacconists) of the Class B Carolina League, where he hit .265 with 24 extra-base hits (one a grand slam) and 56 RBIs. He led the league's short-stops in putouts and assists, and was named to the league All-Star team. The Tobs, managed by Jack McKeon—who went on to win more than 1,000 games as a big-league manager—captured the league championship by 11 games. (There were no playoffs.)

The former Washington Senators, in their second year in Minnesota, were impressed enough by Martinez to jump him straight to the big leagues in 1962. He spent all season with the Twins, though he got only 18 at-bats in 37 games. The Twins returned him to their farm system in 1963. He played briefly for Dallas-

Fort Worth in the Triple-A Pacific Coast League before being sent down to Double-A Charlotte of the South Atlantic League. He failed to hit .200 at either level and repeated Triple-A at Atlanta in 1964.

Martinez was assigned to Triple-A Denver in 1965, and spent two years with the Bears under manager Cal Ermer, who made a recommendation that resulted in Martinez returning to the big leagues, albeit with another team. In July of 1966, Ermer noticed the left-handed Martinez taking some swings right-handed in batting practice, and asked, "Why don't you try that in games, against left-handers?"[1] Despite an 0-for-14 start, Martinez said "Ermer stuck with me. When I started batting both ways, I was hitting around .218, as I remember, and I hit about .380 the rest of the way."[2] Martinez ended the season hitting .313. The Atlanta Braves took notice, and selected Martinez off the Twins roster in that winter's Rule 5 player draft. When Twins president Calvin Griffith trivialized the loss of Martinez, Braves manager Billy Hitchcock responded, "All I know is we weren't the only club interested in drafting Martinez. I know of at least two other clubs who wanted to make him their first draft choice."[3]

The Braves eyed Martinez as a late-inning defensive replacement at shortstop. During 1967 spring training Hitchcock said, "He has shown us here that he can make the plays, both at shortstop and second base."[4] The Braves manager also liked the enthusiasm and spirit that came to be known as Martinez's calling cards. "He's alive when he's in the dugout, too, always chattering and keeping everybody in the game," the manager said. "Little things like that are extremely important."[5] Martinez became a utility player with the Braves, a role he would fill for the rest of his major-league career. He appeared in 44 games, and hit .288 in 87 plate appearances before he hurt his left ankle while sliding into second base on August 26, an injury that ended his season.

After the season, the Braves sought a catcher to back up Joe Torre. After failing to land one at the winter meetings, they took the advice of Cal Ermer, Martinez's manager at Denver, who was now skipper of the Twins. Ermer told Braves manager Lum Harris at the winter meetings that Martinez could handle the backup catcher position. "He has the arm, he has the hustle and he is agile enough that he handles himself behind the plate well," Ermer said.[6] Bullpen coach Ken Silvestri seconded Ermer's opinion, as Martinez had filled in as both bullpen and batting practice catcher the prior year, and had done well catching Braves knuckleballer Phil Niekro. "When we get to spring training next February, Martinez will be our No. 2 catcher. That will be one of my first projects," Harris concluded.[7]

As it turned out, Martinez appeared in only 14 games behind the plate in 1968, but he was the Braves' primary infield reserve, amassing 395 plate appearances, his major-league season high. He hit .230 playing mostly at shortstop, third base, and second base.

After the season, the Braves traded Martinez to the Houston Astros in return for Bob Aspromonte, the last original member of the Colt .45s. In 1969 Martinez hit a personal high .308 in 213 plate appearances. However, his playing time diminished considerably over the next two seasons. In 1970 he had only 159 plate appearances and batted only .220, and in 1971 he was relegated to the bench for much of the season. After 67 games he had been to the plate only 52 times, and made known his desire to be traded. "I like Houston and the organization has been good to me. I have no complaints, but everyone wants to play," said Martinez.[8]

Houston manager Harry Walker meanwhile had let it be known that the team was beset by internal problems caused by what he called three to five troublemakers, and suggested that Martinez was one of them, despite the fact that no such assertion had ever been made by anyone else associated with the club. In fact, Martinez had begun a popular program that grew to include all of the Astros players, in which they made regular visits to hospitals. "We are a part of society," he said. "It is a chance to be a part of the community, to repay something for what we have."[9]

Not surprisingly, the Astros complied with Martinez's request and traded him in November to the St. Louis Cardinals in exchange for Bob Stinson. The 1972 season turned out to be Martinez's last in the major leagues. His stint with the Cardinals lasted only nine games before he was traded to the Oakland Athletics on May 18 for Brant Alyea. Martinez played only two months for the A's before he was traded to the Texas Rangers on July 20 with Vic Harris and a player to be named for Ted Kubiak and Don Mincher. (The trade was first announced on the afternoon of the 19th, yet Martinez played for the A's that night and got three hits in a 9-6 win over the Milwaukee Brewers. Brewers director of baseball operations Frank Lane filed a protest with the American League, but it was disallowed.)

While Martinez may have been denied an opportunity at a world championship with Charlie Finley's developing dynasty in Oakland, his time in Texas led to the next phase of his career. In 1973 Martinez became a player-coach for the Spokane Indians of the Pacific Coast League, a Rangers farm team. He batted .303 in 152 at-bats for the Indians, the last season in which he saw significant playing time.

In 1974 Martinez returned to Spokane as a coach, and in 1975 he was assigned to Pittsfield of the Double-A Eastern League. On July 24 he replaced Jackie Moore as manager. In 1976 he managed San Antonio, which had replaced Pittsfield as the Rangers' Double-A affiliate. The team kept him on as manager in 1977, when they relocated their Double-A team to Tulsa. The Drillers made the Eastern Division playoffs as a result of winning the first-half title, but lost the division championship series to the second-half winner, the Arkansas Travelers.

Martinez was involved in an unfortunate incident during the 1977 season that may have been representative of the racist tendencies still prevalent in the South at that time. A fan, Jerry Sterling, sued Martinez, the Drillers, and the Texas Rangers, alleging that Martinez and several players had punched him during a game on May 10 at Little Rock. In his defense, Martinez claimed that Sterling had been using racial invective against him throughout the game. The suit was settled two years later for $1,125.

Martinez left the Drillers after the 1978 season. In 1980, he began his association with the Seattle Mariners when he managed the Wausau (Wisconsin) Timbers of the Class A Midwest League to a 57-82 record. The Timbers were a co-op club whose roster was stocked by several teams, but was predominantly made up of Seattle prospects.

Martinez subsequently went to work for the Mariners as a minor-league instructor and scout, and it did not take long for his impact to be felt. In 1982 he spotted Edgar Martinez playing in a semipro league in Puerto Rico and arranged for a tryout. "He was a third baseman at the time and had great hands," Martinez said. "I honestly thought at the time that he would be a great second baseman. That shows how much I know. He was a good hitter, not a power hitter, and handled the bat well."[10]

Edgar Martinez, who was a college student and worked at a pharmaceutical company, signed a $5,000 bonus contract with the Mariners and turned out to be one of the best hitters of his era, but not without Marty Martinez's help. "He was a big part of my development throughout the minor leagues," Edgar said. "He was almost like a father figure to many of the Latin players, and anyone who played in the infield. They were all like his sons. He took his work very personally and very serious."[11]

Marty believed strongly in Edgar, and after Edgar hit only .173 at Class A Bellingham in 1983, Marty persuaded Mariners general manager Hal Keller to send the player to the instructional league in Arizona. Keller didn't see why he should, but later said, "I was wrong on Edgar. I never thought he'd hit in the big leagues."[12] Edgar, who hit .340 in Arizona, said, "Marty was fighting for me. He asked them to give me another opportunity. I'll always be grateful for that."[13]

Martinez also signed Omar Vizquel to a contract with the Mariners in 1984, and tutored him in the minor leagues. Vizquel had a 24-year major-league career, and his fielding percentage of .985 as of 2014 was the best ever recorded by a shortstop. Martinez was credited with assisting future Mariner major-league infielders Harold Reynolds and Spike Owen as well.

Martinez joined the Mariners coaching staff in 1984 under manager Del Crandall, and stayed on in 1985 when Crandall was replaced by Chuck Cottier. On May 8, 1986, Cottier was fired, to be replaced by Dick Williams. While Williams was in transit, Martinez was named interim manager for one game on May 9, which the Mariners lost to the Boston Red Sox, 4-2. Mariners president Chuck Armstrong remembered, "We felt like he would be a sentimental favorite among the players. Marty was so well-liked, no one could resent the fact we had asked him to do that for a game."[14]

Martinez was not included on Williams's coaching staff in 1987. In 1988 he managed the Triple-A Calgary Cannons after manager Bill Plummer was promoted to be the Mariners' third-base coach in midseason.

Martinez was named supervisor of Latin American Scouting for the Mariners in 1989, and held that role until 1992 when he became the Mariners' third-base coach under Plummer.

In addition to his scouting responsibilities, in 1993-94, Martinez managed the Mariners' Arizona League rookie team, based in Peoria, Arizona, where he helped develop a young Dominican player named David Ortiz.

After retiring, Martinez and his wife, Jessie Faye, split their time between homes in Tulsa, Oklahoma, and the Dominican Republic. He died in Santo Domingo of an apparent heart attack on March 8, 2007, at the age of 65. He was buried in Green Acres Cemetery in Skiatook, Oklahoma. At the time of his death, Martinez was reportedly attempting to find a new job in baseball

Chuck Cottier conferred Martinez with the nickname, Baseball Marty, and it soon stuck. "Just a wonderful, happy, guy," said Cottier. "He was, first and foremost, a great baseball man."[15]

SOURCES

Bisher, Furman, "Lum Catches Martinez," *Atlanta Journal*, December 2, 1967.

Minshew, Wayne, "Martinez Strikes Happy Tepee Note With Two-Way Bat, Glove," *Atlanta Constitution*, April 1, 1967.

Stone, Larry, "Baseball Marty Left Big Impression on Mariners," *Seattle Times*, March 19, 2007.

Wilson, John, "Just a Sub, Marty Leaves Mark on Astros," *The Sporting News*, July 10, 1971.

Street, Jim, "Mariners Fans Salute Martinez," Seattle mariners.mlb.com, seattle.mariners.mlb.com/sea/news/sea_news. jsp?ymd=20041003&content_id=880369&vkey=news_sea&fext=. jsp&c_id=sea. Accessed November 3, 2013.

Ancestry.com

Baseball-almanac.com

Baseball-reference.com

Retrosheet.org

Baseball Hall of Fame Library, player file for Orlando "Marty" Martinez.

NOTES

1 Wayne Minshew, "Martinez Strikes Happy Tepee Note with Two-Way Bat, Glove," *Atlanta Constitution*, April 1, 1967.

2 Ibid.

3 Ibid.

4 Ibid.

5 Ibid.

6 Furman Bisher, "Lum Catches Martinez," *Atlanta Journal*, December 2, 1967.

7 Ibid.

8 John Wilson, "Just a Sub, Marty Leaves Mark on Astros," *The Sporting News*, July 10, 1971.

9 Ibid.

10 Jim Street, "Mariners Fans Salute Martinez," *Seattle mariners. mlb.com*, October 3, 2004.

11 Larry Stone, "Baseball Marty Left Big Impression on Mariners," *Seattle Times*, March 19, 2007.

12 Ibid.

13 Ibid.

14 Ibid.

15 Ibid.

Dal Maxvill

By Loretta Donovan

In the history of the St. Louis Cardinals, there have been many wonderful shortstops. Think of the flamboyant Leo Durocher, the slick-fielding MVP Marty Marion, and the Hall of Famer Ozzie Smith. To their number add Charles Dallan Maxvill, who went from barely making the team to building a major-league career that lasted 14 years, most of them with the Cardinals. He earned four world championship rings and became a trusted major-league coach and finally the general manager of the Cardinals. Dal Maxvill lived a young boy's baseball dream.

The Cardinals had been Dal's favorite team since he was a youngster growing up in a St. Louis suburb, Granite City, Illinois, where he was born on February 18, 1939, to Harold and Eileen Maxvill. Harold was a steelworker. His parents took him to Sportsman's Park, where he saw the Cardinals legends of the 1940s and early '50s, including seven-time All-Star shortstop Marty Marion. When he was 11 years old, Dal wanted to play in the Khoury League, a youth baseball organization centered in the St. Louis area. Most of his friends' fathers were too busy working in the steel mills to coach his team, so Eileen volunteered to be the manager. Dal rode the handlebars of her bicycle taking the team's gear to the practices and games. Dal was always underweight, so his family tried to help him gain a few pounds. His grandmother financed a series of shots intended to improve his appetite. "But all I got out of the shots was a sore arm," he said.[1]

Dal played baseball at Granite City High School. A 5-foot-11, 135-pound infielder when he got out of school, he received baseball scholarship offers from the University of Missouri and Northwestern University.[2] He turned them down to attend Washington University in St. Louis, which had a good engineering school. The fact that his girlfriend, Diana Sinclair, was in St. Louis helped him make his college choice. Maxvill financed part of his college education by working at Granite City Steel as a laborer for several summers. He eventually received an academic half-scholarship, and graduated in 1960, after 3½ years, with a degree in electrical engineering and a senior-year .350 batting average on the Bears' university baseball team.

The major-league scouts considered Maxvill too small, but Irv Utz, his college coach, arranged a tryout with the Cardinals. By chance, one of the St. Louis affiliates needed a defensive infielder, so scout Joe Monahan signed him. Bing Devine, the Cardinals' general manager (also a Washington University graduate), assigned Maxvill to Winnipeg, a Cardinals affiliate in the Class C Northern League. He received a $1,000 bonus and a promise of $1,000 more if he lasted the full season. He did last the season, playing in 74 games

and batting .257 as the Goldeyes won the Northern League pennant. Maxvill began the 1961 season in Winnipeg, but was moved up to the Cardinals' Triple-A team in Charleston, West Virginia (International League), in time to play 88games there.

The Cardinals moved Maxvill to Double-A Tulsa (Texas League) to start the 1962 season, but brought him up after he batted .348 and fielded well in 47 games. He played in 79 games for the Cardinals and batted .222. In 1963 he started only five games at shortstop because Dick Groat, acquired from Pittsburgh and the regular shortstop, was having another All-Star year. At the beginning of 1964 the Cardinals sent Maxvill to Triple-A Jacksonville, where he fielded well but hit an anemic .140 in 38 games. The Cardinals sent him on loan to Indianapolis, a White Sox farm team, in June. While traveling to report to Indianapolis, Maxvill thought about quitting baseball and going home to work at Bussmann Fuse Company, his offseason employer. At the airport in Chicago he spoke by phone to his wife, Diana, who encouraged him to continue in baseball, and Maxvill decided to report to Indianapolis.

He made the right decision, because after playing in 45 games for Indianapolis, batting .285, and continuing to field well, he was called up by the Cardinals. After playing in only a half-dozen games as a backup to Groat, and getting only six hits in 26 at-bats, Maxvill started at second base in the all-important last game of the season against the New York Mets. Julian Javier, the regular second baseman, was out with a bruised hip. The Cardinals had lost the first two games of the three-game series in St. Louis. If they lost this game, there could be a three-way tie for the lead in the National League, or they could lose the pennant if the Reds won their game. A Cardinals win would give them the pennant, if the Reds lost to the Phillies.

Manager Johnny Keane told Maxvill the night before the big game that he would be the second baseman for the pivotal game. "All I could think was if somebody hit the ball to me, I wanted to get them out," Maxvill said after the game.[3] He got the hitters out, but also got two big hits in the game. He came up in the fourth with the score tied, 1-1, two out and Groat on second. Maxvill singled to center off Galen Cisco, the Mets hurler, to give the Cardinals the lead. The Mets went ahead, 3-2, in the top of the fifth. In the bottom of the inning the Cardinals went ahead, 4-3, and Maxvill came to bat again. He got another run-scoring single to make it 5-3. The Cardinals eventually won, 11-5, to clinch their first National League pennant since 1946. (Philadelphia had already defeated Cincinnati.)

Next came the World Series and the New York Yankees with Roger Maris and Mickey Mantle. Maxvill started every game at second base. (He was pinch-hit for in the late innings of three games.) Maxvill batted only .200 (4-for-20) but Keane was pleased with his play and the way the youngster handled the pressure. In Game Seven Maxvill singled home Mike Shannon in the fourth inning to make the score, 3-0, and he caught the ninth-inning popup by Yankee Bobby Richardson that ended the game and gave the world championship to the Cardinals.

But 1965 was a different season. Javier had healed and Groat was still the Cardinals' regular shortstop. As a result, Maxvill had only 89 at-bats in 68 games. No matter that in spring training general manager Stan Musial had called him the "take-charge leader of the Cardinals' infield."[4]

Maxvill continued to use his engineering degree by working in the offseason for Bussman Fuse Company. He usually traveled around the country demonstrating and selling fuse systems.

Groat was traded after the 1965 season but Maxvill did not automatically inherit the shortstop position in 1966. In spring training Jerry Buchek, Jimy Williams, and Phil Gagliano were the biggest competition to him. Coach Dick Sisler worked with Maxvill to improve his hitting, spending extra time in the batting cage with him. "Dick got me to wait on the ball better and hit to right field more consistently," Maxvill said. "He had me moving around better at the plate so I could handle certain pitches better."[5]

Finally, in early June, Maxvill became the regular shortstop. Red Schoendienst, his manager, felt that his defensive abilities made the infield stronger. Pitchers, especially Bob Gibson, wanted Maxie—as he became known—fielding behind them in every game. Although he batted only .244 for the season, Maxvill delivered numerous key hits and drew 37 walks to tie Shannon for the most on the team. After the season, Maxvill was selected Khoury Major Leaguer of the Year, beating out ten other major leaguers who started their baseball careers in the Khoury League organization.

Maxvill began spring training of 1967 knowing he was the starting shortstop. He was pleased, telling a sportswriter, "Not many players like to be picked up, or substituted for. I don't. I want to play every day, all the time. It's an old story in baseball—rest two days and maybe you rest five years."[6]

Things went well for regular shortstop Maxvill and the 1967 Cardinals. He played in 152 games and had 14 runs batted in during September. His fielding percentage at shortstop, .974, was tied for second-best in the league. He also appeared in seven games at second base, where he did not make an error.

The Cardinals again went to the World Series, this time against the Boston Red Sox. The Series went down to the seventh game at Fenway Park. Jim Lonborg, the Red Sox starter, had won 22 games in the regular season, and was the Cy Young Award winner in the American League. Lonborg had won Games Two and Five with commanding complete-game efforts. Maxvill led off the third inning with a triple off the center-field wall and scored the Cardinals' first run when Flood drove him in with a single. With nobody out in the ninth inning, Maxvill grabbed a hard groundball in the hole and teamed with Javier for a rally-killing double play. The Cardinals went on to win, 7-2, to claim their eighth world championship.

The 1968 season was another good one for Maxvill and the Cardinals. He was the National League Gold Glove winner at shortstop, and his .253 batting average was the highest of his major-league career. Maxvill

was the only Cardinal who started every game in the club's stretch of 59 games in 56 days after the All-Star break.[7] The Cardinals went to the World Series again, this time losing to the Detroit Tigers in seven games. Maxvill was 0-for-22 at the plate, a World Series record for futility.

The Cardinals had the highest payroll in baseball. In those pre-free-agency days, that brought criticism of the organization from elsewhere in baseball. But manager Schoendienst and general manager Devine defended the players. "Some highly placed baseball people believe that by paying so well the Cardinals are undermining the very structure of baseball," a *Sports Illustrated* writer said just before the World Series, adding a comment from Devine: "Almost every place I go … someone will ask me how Dal Maxvill can be making $37,500. It really seems to bother people, but if you have seen the way he has played shortstop this year and how he gets himself involved in the good things we do, his salary won't surprise you."[8] Indeed, Maxvill's salary went up to $45,000 in 1969.

High salaries and all, the 1969 and 1970 seasons were forgettable for Maxvill and the Cardinals. The team finished in fourth place both years, 13 games behind the division winners in the NL East. One bright spot for Maxvill came on April 14, 1969, when he hit the first major-league grand slam in Canada during a Cardinals-Montreal Expos game at Parc Jarry. But in the 1970 season he failed to hit a homer in 152 games and 399 at-bats. The Cardinals did better in 1971, winning 90 games but finishing in second place, seven games behind the Pittsburgh Pirates.

Maxvill was respected and popular among his teammates, who named him their union representative. The responsibility put Maxvill in a tough spot during the players' strike in the spring of 1972. He thought the fans did not understand the players' side of the squabble, which erased the first week of the season. On August 28 he was named Sportsman of the Year by the Southside Kiwanis Club in St. Louis. Two days later he was traded to the Oakland Athletics for two minor leaguers.

Maxvill played in most of the remaining games for his new club, usually at second base. He wanted to play every inning of every game, but the Oakland manager, Dick Williams, used a rotating second baseman system. Williams used 11 shortstops/second basemen that season. Most of the time, the second baseman who started the game would not be around to finish it. He would usually be taken out for a pinch-hitter early in the game. On September 28 Maxvill was the fourth second baseman the A's used against Minnesota. He batted in the bottom of the ninth with the game tied and a runner on first. His double to left field won the game, 8-7, and gave Oakland a six-game lead in the American League West, with five games to play Oakland had won its second successive American League West title. The A's finished 5½ games ahead of the Chicago White Sox for the West Division title, and went on to beat the Detroit Tigers in the American League Championship Series. Maxvill played in every game of that ALCS, starting three of them at shortstop. He was ineligible for the World Series, in which the A's beat the Cincinnati Reds, but was awarded a World Series ring and was voted a half-share of the World Series money.

Maxvill played only sporadically for the A's in 1973, and on July 7 he was sold to the Pirates, who ended up in third place, 2½ games behind the Mets. He started the 1974 season with the Pirates but was released on April 20 and went home to St. Louis to help operate Cardinal Travel, an agency he and former Cardinals teammate Joe Hoerner, along with other investors, had started in 1969. He did not stay there long, as the Athletics came calling on May 10, and he signed with them. He played in 60 games and had 52 at-bats and ten hits for the A's. The A's again won the AL West, and played Baltimore in the league championship series. Maxvill appeared in one game in the ALCS, with only one at-bat, in which he struck out. The A's went to the 1974 World Series and won over the Los Angeles Dodgers in five games. Maxvill played in two games, with no at-bats, and received his fourth World Series ring and a full World Series share. He was released after the season but re-signed as a coach and utility infielder, at a salary of $40,000. He played

in 20 games in 1975 and had two hits in ten at-bats. He was released by the A's on October 10, 1975. In November Maxvill officially retired from baseball. By this time he was 36 and ready to settle down in St. Louis and put his talents to work at the travel agency. In a few years, however, he was back in baseball as Joe Torre, now the manager of the Mets, signed him to coach third base for the 1978 season. Torre respected Maxvill's knowledge of the fundamentals of baseball, and thought that his former Cardinal roommate could help improve the play of his infielders. Maxvill resigned after the season, again to be closer to home and his travel business. But baseball called again, and quickly. In October, he and Red Schoendienst were hired as coaches for the Cardinals under manager Ken Boyer. Fans reacted favorably because both lived in St. Louis, and were well liked in the baseball community. By that time Maxvill had four children and appreciated the opportunity to have a baseball job close to home. He coached for the Cardinals in 1979 and 1980. Whitey Herzog became the Cardinals' manager in June 1980, hired his own coaches, and in 1981 Maxvill became a minor-league instructor.

When Torre became manager of the Atlanta Braves in 1982, Maxvill again became a coach for his good friend. After the 1984 season, Torre was fired and Maxvill was the only coach retained by the Braves.

The Cardinals fired their general manager, Joe McDonald, in January 1985. In February, during the Braves' spring training, the Cardinals came calling again, asking Maxvill, now 46, to interview for the position of general manager. The team was looking for someone with a good head for business and a working knowledge of baseball and of the Cardinals organization. Maxvill and team owner August Busch, Jr. talked on Busch's yacht off St. Petersburg. After the meeting, Busch asked Maxvill to leave for a while, so he could have a discussion with other team officials. Dal walked along the beach for a half-hour. When he returned, he was offered the position. He was officially named general manager on February 25, 1985. Maxvill was now the GM for Herzog, the man who had sent him down to coach in the minors.

Maxvill was enthusiastic about the opportunity to help shape the team he had followed since he was a boy. "It would be awfully nice to be humble," he said, "but I can handle the job. It will be fun, a challenge. If I thought I couldn't do the job, I wouldn't have talked to them when they approached me."[9] His contract would be for one year at a time. The team's chief operating officer, Fred Kuhlmann, would be in charge of business matters. Everything would have to be approved by the executive committee and then by Busch.

Maxvill's rookie season as general manager was a good one. In his first trade he acquired Jose Oquendo from the Mets for Angel Salazar, on April 2, 1985. For ten years Oquendo proved to be a valuable utility player for the Cardinals, and became a popular coach in 1999. In a surprising turn of events, the 1985 Cardinals, whom many picked to finish last in the NL East before the season started, won 101 games and defeated the Dodgers in the NLCS. They battled Kansas City in what became known as the I-70 World Series, for the interstate highway that connected the two cities. The Cardinals were two outs away from winning the Series in Game Six before the Royals rallied to win that game and then Game Seven. The next season, 1986, the Cardinals finished three games under .500 and ended the season 28½ games behind the Mets, but in 1987 they again won the NLCS, this time over the Giants, before losing the World Series to the Minnesota Twins in seven games. In 1988 St. Louis ended in fifth place, ten games under .500, in the NL East.

As general manager, Maxvill often voiced his concern about escalating salaries in baseball. He had to contend with a manager, Herzog, who freely offered his ideas on ways to improve the team. Before the 1989 season, pitchers Danny Cox and Greg Matthews were injured. Herzog wanted Mark Langston, a left-handed starting pitcher for Seattle. Even though Maxvill and Herzog agreed that the price for Langston was too high, the manager kept insisting on acquiring Langston. "When you're a manager, you want to have a club that can compete, that has a fair shake when you go out there. Last year we didn't have that from day one," Herzog

said.[10] Langston went to the Expos in a July trade and Herzog continued to have issues with the pitching.

The Cardinals finished the 1989 season in third place, seven games behind the division-winning Chicago Cubs. In late September the Cardinals also lost their primary backer at the brewery when August Busch, Jr. died at the age of 90. There was a restructuring of the team's top brass. Kuhlmann became the president and CEO, and August Busch, III, who had no interest in baseball, was the chairman of the board.

Another example of the difficulties escalating salaries posed Maxvill was his contract negotiations with Cardinals third baseman Terry Pendleton, who had been awarded a Gold Glove in 1989 and batted .264. The issue went to arbitration, and Pendleton was awarded $1.85 million, the second highest amount given to a player in arbitration to that point. As much as he would have liked to keep Pendleton a Cardinal, Maxvill could not afford to sign him to a long-term deal at that price, and Pendleton went to the Braves as a free agent after the 1990 season.

By June 1990 the Cardinals were last in the National League in batting with a .235 average. Maxvill insisted that he would not make changes just to "shake things up." He was in a bind because 11 of the players were going to be free agents at the end of the season. The management did give Maxvill an endorsement by extending his contract another year, even though the team lost 39 of its first 66 games.

On July 6, 1990, Herzog resigned as manager. The team was in last place and playing poorly. Herzog could not motivate them and no trade was imminent. The number of free agents also bothered Herzog. Joe Torre eventually became the new manager, but the Cardinals finished in last place in the NL East, 25 games out. During the winter they lost several players to free agency. Maxvill had to work within the conservative budget of the brewery to try to put a winning team on the field. He had to find inexpensive young talent to replace the expensive free agents they had to let go.

For the next two seasons, the Cardinals sang the familiar refrain. They would not go after free agents. After the 1992 season, they had ten players who could apply for free agency. They re-signed Ozzie Smith but let the others leave. The Cardinals finished in third place in 1993, ten games behind the Phillies. After the season, Maxvill admitted that the team needing pitching help but added, "Unfortunately, we are looking for a pitcher who doesn't make a lot of money."[11]

The 1994 season quickly disintegrated. The team was having trouble winning games, and then the players union went on strike on August 11, wiping out the remainder of the season. In August Mark Lamping, a former Anheuser-Busch executive, was hired as president of the Cardinals. In September he fired Maxvill. Dal continued to draw his salary through 1995, doing some specialized scouting. He was 55 years old. He did some scouting for the Yankees for a while. Otherwise, he stayed away from baseball.

SOURCES

Feldmann, Doug, *St. Louis Cardinals Past & Present* (Minneapolis: MVP Books, 2009)

Goold, Derrick, *100 Things Cardinals Fans Should Know & Do Before They Die* (Chicago: Triumph Books, 2010).

Allen, Maury, "Cards' New GM Rarin' to Rebuild." *New York Post*, April 11, 1985

Daley, Arthur, "Sports of the Times." *New York Times*, March 28, 1969

Herman, Jack, "Rookie Executive," *St. Louis Weekly*, July 19, 1985 (article from Maxvill player file, National Baseball Hall of Fame)

Chicago Daily News

St. Louis Globe Democrat

St. Louis Post Dispatch

St. Petersburg Times

Sports Illustrated

The Sporting News

National Baseball Hall of Fame, Cooperstown, New York

New York Mets Scorebook, 1978

St. Louis National Baseball Club, Inc.

St. Louis Mercantile Library at University of Missouri-St. Louis

Baseball-Reference.com

Retrosheet.org

NOTES

1   Neal Russo, "Dal Maxvill: Classy Card Minute-Man," *The Sporting News*, January 30, 1965.

2   Neal Russo, "Little Maxie Getting Big Cardinal Hits,," *The Sporting News*, August 24, 1968.

3   Milton Gross, "Dal Maxvill No Bat Boy," *Chicago Daily News*, October 5, 1964.

4   Jack Herman, "Musial High on Maxvill," *St. Louis Globe Democrat*, March 11, 1965.

3   Gross.

4   Herman, "Musial High on Maxvill.".

5   Neal Russo, "Alley Route Best for Me, Says Maxvill," *The Sporting News*, January 7, 1967.

6   Jimmy Mann, "Pickup Man Who Made Good," *St. Petersburg Times*, 1967.

7   Bob Harlan, St. Louis National Baseball Club, Inc. press release, February 18, 1970.

8   William Leggett, "Manager of the Money Men," *Sports Illustrated*, October 7, 1968.

9   Jack Herman, "Rookie Executive," *St. Louis Weekly*, July 19, 1985.

10   *The Sporting News*, March 27, 1989.

11   Rick Hummel, *The Sporting News*, November 8, 1993.

Denny McLain

By Mark Armour

On September 19, 1968, at Tiger Stadium, Detroit right-hander Denny McLain was cruising along in the top of the eighth with a 6-1 lead over the New York Yankees. He had won his 30th game five days earlier, and the Tigers had already clinched the American League pennant. When Yankees first baseman Mickey Mantle came to bat with one out and nobody on, McLain let Mantle know that he would give him whatever pitch Mickey wanted. After a few batting-practice fastballs were skeptically ignored or fouled off, Mantle signaled for a fastball letter high, McLain delivered it, and the Mick deposited it into the right-field seats. It was Mantle's 535th career home run, passing Jimmie Foxx for third place all-time. McLain was coy in the locker room, and later received a stern rebuke from Commissioner William Eckert, but freely admitted the circumstances of the event over the subsequent years.

It was classic McLain: charming, cocky, arrogant, reckless. Just 24 years old, and arguably the biggest star in his sport at that moment, McLain had played by his own rules his whole life, and as baseball's first 30-game winner in 34 years, he was not going to be changing any time soon. He had a prickly relationship with his teammates, managers, the fans, and the city of Detroit, all of which he was apt to criticize at the slightest provocation. Bill Freehan, his catcher, once wrote, "The rules for Denny just don't seem to be the same as for the rest of us."[1]

A virtual gunfighter on the mound, McLain pulled his hat brim down so low that he had to tilt his head backward to see the signs from his catcher. He worked fast and without deception, throwing pitch after pitch in the strike zone, even ahead in the count. Although he had a change and an overhand curve, he used

fastballs and hard sliders for the most part, challenging the hitter with every pitch, often throwing one letter-high fastball after another. If a batter hit the ball hard, the next time up McLain would just give him the same pitch in the same location. "Here you go," he seemed to say, "let's see you hit it again."

Off the field, McLain's life was equally carefree and, it would turn out, even more reckless. His idol was Frank Sinatra, not just for the legendary singing voice but because Sinatra exuded wealth and power. "Sinatra doesn't give a damn about anything, and neither do I," said Denny.[2] Likely due mainly to his pitching prowess, Denny had a successful side career as organist; he played on *The Ed Sullivan Show*, headlined performances in Las Vegas, and cut a pair of LPs. Not content with traveling like the rest of us, he bought his own airplane, and learned to fly it himself. *Time* magazine put McLain on its cover in 1968, comparing him to a "high-school wise guy."[3]

For his 31 victories and 1.96 ERA, McLain won the American League's Cy Young and Most Valuable Player awards in 1968, and his team won its first World Series in 23 years. He won the Cy Young again in 1969 (tying with Baltimore's Mike Cuellar) when he won 24 games. He made nearly $100,000 from the Tigers, and much more than that off the field. He was living the dream life. Until he wasn't.

Dennis Dale McLain was born on March 29, 1944, in Markham, Illinois, to Tom and Betty McLain, both Irish Catholics. Tom had been a star high-school shortstop in Chicago, but married Betty at age 18 in 1941, and adhered to her demand that he not travel around chasing a baseball career. When Dennis was born, Tom was in the Army in Europe; he later held jobs as a truck driver and insurance adviser, and made extra money giving electric-organ lessons.

Denny remembered Tom as a hard worker who chain-smoked and guzzled beer. Denny and his brother Tom lived in fear of their father's angry outbursts, which often resulted in beatings. Tom also got in frequent fistfights, on at least one occasion responding to the heckler at one of his son's Little League games. Denny did not try very hard to avoid his father's wrath, though –once, at age 12, taking the family car for a joyride. This behavior became more and more typical. Denny's memories of his mother are no better; he remained bitter over her failures to intervene on her children's behalf, and he has depicted Betty as a cold and heartless woman.

Tom encouraged Denny's baseball career, organizing the first youth baseball league in their hometown of Markham when Denny was 7, and a few years later driving his son to a neighboring town to play in a Babe Ruth baseball league. Denny dominated these leagues as a pitcher, just rearing back and throwing one fastball after another. Tom died suddenly of a heart attack at age 36 when Denny was a 15-year-old high school freshman. Betty quickly remarried, and Denny began doing whatever he pleased.

McLain attended Catholic schools, first at Ascension Grade School, then receiving a baseball scholarship to attend Chicago's Mount Carmel High School. An indifferent student who had trouble keeping quiet, Denny led his team to three city championships, amassing a 38-7 record on the mound. Upon his graduation in June 1962, McLain signed with the White Sox, receiving a $10,000 bonus, and another $7,000 if he made it to the major leagues. Days later he reported to Harlan, Kentucky, to play for the Smokies in the Class D Appalachian League.

McLain had a spectacular professional debut on June 28 against the Salem Rebels, tossing a no-hitter and striking out 16. He lost his second start, but allowed no earned runs and struck out 16 more batters. Though he was in Harlan only a couple of weeks, that was sufficient time for McLain to exhibit the reckless behavior that would become his trademark, defying team rules by making a 30-hour round trip to visit his girlfriend in Chicago on an offday. He figured, correctly, it would turn out, that throwing a no-hitter would entitle him to more leeway than other players. This notion had been applied growing up in Chicago, and would stay with him all the way to the major leagues. After just two games, with a 0.00 ERA and 32 strikeouts, McLain was deemed to have mastered the Appalachian League, and was promoted to the Clinton, Iowa, C-Sox in the Class D Midwest League.

The Midwest hitters weren't as overmatched by a pitcher who threw almost all fastballs, and Denny had to settle for a 4-7 record, but with 93 strikeouts in 91 innings. In Clinton he went AWOL on the team several times, costing himself several hundred dollars. On the mound, his promise was still apparent.

That offseason McLain began dating Sharon Boudreau, daughter of former star shortstop Lou Boudreau, then an announcer for the Chicago Cubs. The two had met in high school, but their relationship escalated enough that they were engaged by January 1963, and married the following offseason.

At the time, players with one year of service in the minor leagues were susceptible to a draft if not promoted to the major leagues. The White Sox were faced with this dilemma with McLain, along with fellow pitchers Bruce Howard and Dave DeBusschere. In the end, the White Sox chose to protect the other pitchers and not McLain, the local boy. The Detroit Tigers soon claimed McLain.

McLain did not take long to soar through the Detroit system. He began the 1963 season in the Class A Northern League with Duluth-Superior, and after 18 starts he was 13-2 with a 2.55 ERA, with 157 strikeouts in 141 innings. He then moved on to Knoxville in the Double-A Sally League, and finished 5-4 in 11 starts. In September he was in the major leagues.

McLain's major-league debut was almost as spectacular as his pro debut in Harlan. Taking the hill against the White Sox in Tiger Stadium on September 21, he came away with a 4-3 complete-game seven-hitter, starting the Tigers' scoring by belting a home run off Fritz Ackley in the fifth inning. This would be the only home run of his major-league career.

McLain began the 1964 season with Syracuse in the Triple-A International League, but he did not stay long. After fashioning a 3-1 record and a 1.53 ERA in eight starts, he was promoted to the Tigers in early June. Just 20 years old, Denny joined the rotation for the rest of the season, winning four of nine decisions for the fourth-place Tigers.

McLain later claimed he turned the corner as a pitcher in the winter of 1964-1965 when he pitched for Mayaguez in the Puerto Rican Winter League, finishing 13-2 to help his team to the championship. Back in the States, Denny's first full season resulted in a 16-6 record and a 2.61 ERA. McLain relied essentially on one pitch-a letter-high fastball with movement, a pitch that was a strike in the 1960s but would not be a generation later. Tigers manager Charlie Dressen advised McLain to just throw strikes, and said he'd get a lot of hitters out with his stuff. He struck out 192 in 220 innings, including a league-record seven in a row in a relief appearance on June 15.

His success continued in 1966. Starting the season 13-4, he was selected to start the All-Star Game in St. Louis and responded by retiring all nine National League hitters he faced. He did not pitch well after the break, but finished 20-14 with a 3.92 ERA, with 192 strikeouts. Dressen, whom McLain has always credited for his breakthrough, had to leave the team after suffering an early-season heart attack, and died soon thereafter. Denny would never find another manager to his liking.

McLain's outsized personality, combined with his pitching success, began to earn him a lot of money off the field. He played the organ, either by himself or with a group, in clubs around the Midwest, and earned a $25,000 endorsement deal with Hammond organs. McLain's biggest personal vice was his huge appetite for Pepsi-Cola, on the order of 24 bottles every day. When the company heard of his obsession, they signed him as a sponsor, paying him $15,000 a year, plus 10 cases (240 bottles) delivered to his house every week. By the age of 22, McLain was earning more money off the field than he was from the Tigers.

Detroit lost a heartbreaking four-team pennant race in 1967, due in large part to an offyear from McLain. He finished 17-16 with a 3.79 ERA, and was winless after August 29. After several poorly pitched games—no wins, two losses, 13 runs in 13⅔ innings in four starts—on September 18 McLain reported that he had severely injured two toes on his left foot. His foot had fallen asleep while he was watching television, he said, and he stubbed it getting up when he heard some raccoons that were getting into his garbage cans. In the heat of the pennant race, McLain did not pitch again for 13 days, until the very last game of the season. (If Detroit had won, the club would have forced a one-game playoff with the Red Sox for the American League pennant.) McLain was again ineffective, and the Tigers lost to the California Angels to fall one game short. His teammates were not happy about McLain's efforts that season, and many doubted his injury story.

Entering the 1968 season, the Tigers were considered a talented group of individuals who could not play together. They proceeded to debunk that theory by leading the league nearly wire to wire on the way to a 103-win season and an impressive 12-game margin over the second-place Orioles. The star of the team, and of all of baseball, was Dennis Dale McLain, who captured the attention of the sports world with his 31-6 record. No pitcher had won 30 games since Dizzy Dean in 1934, and by midsummer McLain's pursuit drew attention across the country. The 30th win came on September 14 on national television against the Oakland Athletics, a 5-4 victory. His 31st came five days later, the game in which he grooved the pitch to Mantle. In the Tigers' World Series triumph over the St. Louis Cardinals, McLain lost twice to Bob Gibson to help put the Tigers in a 3-1 hole, but won Game Six as the team pulled out the Series. Mickey Lolich won three times to lead the Tigers.

After the season, McLain won the American League Cy Young and Most Valuable Player awards, among many other honors. He spent the offseason flying around the country playing the organ, making money, and running his mouth. When asked during a performance in Las Vegas about teammate Mickey Lolich, who had saved the Tigers' season with his performance in the World Series, McLain responded: "I wouldn't trade (one) Bob Gibson for 12 Mickey Loliches."[4]

McLain had another big year in 1969, winning 24 games and capturing a second consecutive Cy Young Award (tying with Baltimore's Mike Cuellar). The best pitcher in the game, the 25-year-old McLain was also raking in money on endorsements, appearing on national talk shows, and performing as a headliner in Las Vegas. As the 1960s ended, Denny McLain had reached a level of fame that very few baseball players have ever reached. When considering his outside income along with his baseball salary, he made more money than anyone in the game, and he spent it as fast as it came in.

The good times ended very suddenly.

In February 1970 *Sports Illustrated* featured McLain on its cover next to the headline "Denny McLain and the Mob, Baseball's Big Scandal."[5] The mob? According to the magazine, in early 1967 McLain invested in a bookmaking operation based in a restaurant in Flint, Michigan; several of his partners were part of the

Syrian mob. When a gambler named Edward Voshen won $46,000 on a horse race, his bookie couldn't pay it off, suggesting instead that Voshen find the bookie's partners. One of his partners was McLain. Voshen spent several months trying to get his money, finally enlisting the aid of mobster Tony Giacalone. According to the magazine's sources, Giacalone met with McLain in early September and, while threatening much worse, brought his heel down on McLain's toes and dislocated them. This would have coincided with time of McLain's ankle-toes injury in September 1967. The magazine also reported that Giacalone had bet heavily on the Red Sox and Twins to win the pennant, and had made a large bet on the Angels in McLain's final start.

McLain denied most of the story. He admitted to investing in the bookmaking business to the tune of $15,000, but claimed that his partners reneged on him, causing McLain to withdraw his support. He told Bowie Kuhn, baseball's commissioner, that he was completely uninvolved in the ring at the time of the Voshen bet, but oddly admitted that he had loaned $10,000 to one of the partners to help pay off the debt. Furthermore, he had never met Giacalone, and McLain retold the story of his toe injury. (In subsequent years, McLain recalled that it was an ankle sprain, not injured toes.) Just prior to spring training, Kuhn suspended McLain indefinitely while he conducted an investigation.

The problem with all of these accusations was that many of the people making them were criminals and lowlifes, as *Sports Illustrated* acknowledged. Although he has continued to deny the allegations regarding his injury, his denials have been in themselves damning. In his 2007 memoir *I Told You I Wasn't Perfect*, he wrote that he was heavily distracted in September 1967. "I was spooked about the ghost of Ed Voshen and worried about being exposed," he wrote. "I kept expecting someone to tap me on the shoulder and say, 'Hey, where's my money?' or that my car was going to blow up."[6] This fear is precisely why baseball has a paranoia about gambling.

If these problems were not enough, McLain was also suddenly broke. Though his annual income was close to $200,000, McLain had entrusted it all with a lawyer, who either mishandled it or stole it before fleeing to Japan. Without his baseball income, McLain's financial problems caused him to file for bankruptcy. Claiming that all of his problems were due to poor business decisions, his petition listed debts of $446,069 and assets of only $413.[7]

On April 1, 1970, Kuhn announced his decision. He continued McLain's suspension until July 1, roughly half of the season. Kuhn's report, among other things, said: "While McLain believed he had become a partner in this operation and has so admitted to me … it would appear that he was the victim of a confidence scheme. I would thus conclude that McLain was never a partner and had no proprietary interest in the bookmaking operation."[8] Kuhn also absolved McLain from any charges that his actions had any effect on baseball games or the 1967 pennant race. (On the contrary, McLain's later recollection that he feared for his life in September 1967 suggests that the pennant race was quite affected.)

After Kuhn read his statement, a reporter asked him to explain the difference between McLain attempting to become a bookmaker, and actually becoming one. "I think you have to consider the difference is the same as between murder and attempted murder," responded the wise commissioner.[9] Reporters all over the country, and especially in Detroit, thought the decision was a whitewash. Denny's teammates seemed surprised as well. Dick McAuliffe spoke for many when he said: "If Denny's innocent, it should be nothing. If he's guilty, then this is not enough."[10] Jim Price, the Tigers' player representative, said that most Tigers thought McLain would get one or two years, or else nothing at all. Nonetheless, three months it was.

McLain returned on July 1 to a packed house, but struggled that night and for the next several weeks. On August 28, in what he claimed was a harmless prank, he doused two Detroit writers with buckets of ice water, earning a seven-day suspension from the Tigers. Before the week was up, Kuhn discovered that McLain had carried a gun on a team flight in August,

so Denny was declared through for the season. His 1970 record was 3-5 with a 4.63 ERA.

McLain had lived the past several years by his own rules, and his stunning success on the pitcher's mound allowed him tremendous leeway. He showed up late, flew his plane to music gigs after games, and popped off about teammates, management, the fans, the ballpark, or the city. When you win 31 games, all of this is forgivable. When you finish 3-5, you are a pain in the neck.

A few days after the 1970 season, McLain was traded to the Washington Senators in an eight-player deal. Although he was just 26 years old — and was just six months removed from being considered one of the best players in the game — the Tigers considered themselves fortunate to acquire pitchers Joe Coleman and Jim Hannan and infielders Aurelio Rodriguez and Eddie Brinkman. They were fortunate indeed.

In his one year in Washington, McLain carried on a yearlong battle with manager Ted Williams, and finished 10-22. He spent 1972 with the Oakland A's, the Birmingham Barons, and the Atlanta Braves, getting hammered at all three stops, before finally drawing his release by the Braves the next spring. He spent a few weeks with Shreveport and Des Moines in 1973, but the magic was long gone.

His baseball career was over, at age 29, four years removed from winning 55 games over a two-year period. How could this have happened? McLain claims to have suddenly lost his fastball in 1970, but one couldn't help but notice that he was putting on ten pounds of fat a year. At the time of his release, he was 29 and looked 45. Denny McLain had a remarkable right arm, but he did not seem willing to do the work necessary to stay in the game. He had time to fly around the country playing the organ, but he didn't have the time to stay in shape. The case of Pepsi he still drank every day likely did not help his waistline.

Without his baseball career to get in the way, McLain could now devote all his energies to his "successful" business ventures. Always looking for the fast buck, he invested in a big-screen-television business, ran a bar, wrote a book, opened a line of walk-in medical clinics. In the mid-1970s he was the general manager of the minor league Memphis Blues, who soon went belly up. McLain filed for bankruptcy again in 1977. His wife, Sharon, left him several times, but he always managed to get her back.

Denny made a living for a while hustling on the golf course. While involved with a financial services company in Tampa, he turned to loan sharking and bookmaking. With losses piling up, he and his colleagues got more adventurous. He once made $160,000 smuggling a fugitive out of the country in his airplane.

Eventually, the US Justice Department began to sniff around Denny's associates, several of whom were willing to talk. In March 1984 McLain was indicted on charges of racketeering, extortion, and cocaine trafficking. McLain was tried, convicted, and sentenced to 23 years in prison. Thirty months later, an appeals court threw out the verdict on procedural grounds, setting McLain free, and the government ultimately decided to not retry the case.

McLain spent the next several years putting his life back together. He wrote another book, appeared at card shows, worked for a minor-league hockey team, and got his own radio show. He was doing what he could have done all along — making a living being Denny McLain. It was a good living, reportedly making him $400,000 a year.

It wasn't enough. In 1993 McLain and a friend bought Peet Packing, a struggling 100-year-old meatpacking firm in Chesaning, Michigan. Within a month after the sale, $3 million was taken from the company's pension fund, and by 1995 the company was bankrupt. Though he denied knowledge of the financial illegalities, McLain and his partner were eventually convicted on charges of embezzlement, money laundering, mail fraud, and conspiracy. McLain spent seven more years in prison.

Released in 2003, McLain made appearances and lived a life as a former baseball hero. His wife, Sharon,

divorced him when he returned to prison, but they remarried when he got out. They raised four children: Kristen, Denny Jr., Tim, and Michelle. Kristen McLain was killed in an automobile accident in 1992 at age 26, a tragedy that McLain says caused his downward spiral that led to the debacle with Peet Packing. He continued to battle weight problems. When Sharon was diagnosed with Parkinson's disease, Denny decided he needed to get healthier to help take care of her. He underwent bariatric surgery and lost 156 pounds — 24 pants sizes. "I'm trying to get to my playing weight [about 200 pounds]," said McLain. "I would just love one more time to go out to Tigers Stadium and throw one pitch and kick my leg up ... and see what would happen."[11]

McLain was a great pitcher for a few years before his shocking downfall. He lived by his own rules, and hurt countless people along the way, including teammates, friends, and his own family. But for many people in Detroit, he remained a hero for what he did on the mound for their beloved Tigers.

NOTES

1   Bill Freehan with Steve Gelman and Dick Schaap, *Behind the Mask* (New York: World. 1970), 64.

2   David Wolf, "Tiger on the Keys and on the Mound," *Life*, September 13, 1968, 82.

3   "Tiger Untamed," *Time*, September 13, 1968, 76.

4   David Stevens, "Denny's Vegas Debut Called 'Less Than Smashing,'" *The Sporting News*, November 2, 1968.

5   Morton P. Sharnik, "Downfall of a Hero," *Sports Illustrated*, February 23, 1970.

6   Denny McLain with Eli Zaret, *I Told You I Wasn't Perfect* (Triumph: 2007), 73.

7   Jerome Holtzman, "Players, Umpires, Books, Law Suits ...," *Official Baseball Guide 1970* (St. Louis: The Sporting News), 1970, 263.

8   Holtzman, "Players, Umpires," 265.

9   Holtzman, "Players, Umpires," 266.

10 Holtzman, "Players, Umpires," 266.

11 "Ex-Detroit Tigers pitcher Denny McLain: I've lost over 150 pounds," *Detroit Free Press*, February 27, 2014.

Bill McNulty

By Chip Greene

It was a scene that even a Hollywood scriptwriter might find fantastic. As baseball's 1972 regular season entered its final week, the Oakland Athletics, preparing for their second consecutive American League division playoffs, wanted to give their regulars some much needed rest. So with the minor-league season over, management decided to call up one of the organization's premier young power hitters, Bill McNulty.

Only, they couldn't find him.

With the front office unable to reach McNulty by phone or telegram, the team's radio broadcasters resorted to the airwaves, sending out messages asking McNulty to immediately call the team. Upon hearing their pleas, McNulty's father, Raymond, called the club and told them his son had gone hunting in the Warner Mountains of Northern California. In no time, a Forest Service airplane was dispatched to try to track down the elusive slugger.

Eventually, McNulty was located. Four decades later, he recalled, "My friends and I were sitting around a campfire … it was cold … and in walked two guys, almost literally out of the dark. Two game wardens; didn't even see 'em coming."

"You must be Bill McNulty," they said.

"I am."

"We need you to come down to the sheriff's office with us," said the wardens.

And the next day, McNulty was in Oakland, wearing the green and gold Athletics uniform.

It wasn't the first time he'd put it on, but perhaps this time he'd wear it a little longer. If anyone appeared to possess the requisite skills for baseball stardom, it was 26-year-old William Francis McNulty. Born in Sacramento, California, and raised in the suburb of

Roseville, 20 miles northeast of Sacramento and about 80 in the same direction from Oakland, McNulty had been a three-sport star at Highlands High School, midway between Roseville and Sacramento, a school that also produced McNulty's "high school hero," fellow major leaguer Bob Oliver. (McNulty was a freshman when Oliver was a senior.) By the time he graduated in 1964, McNulty had been named Most Valuable Player of both the basketball and football teams, and had also been voted Highlands' Outstanding Athlete. Moreover, that year, too, he'd been named to Sacramento's All-Legion baseball team after leading his Haggin-Grant Post American Legion team to the district championship.

That McNulty, at 6-feet-4 and 210 pounds, owed much of his athletic success to natural ability was unquestion-

able, yet he had also been well-schooled in the fundamentals. His father, Ray, had been a minor-league star on the West Coast, playing primarily in Oregon, with Salem in the Western International League and Portland in the Pacific Coast League. Ray began his career as a third baseman, but his strong arm led to a shift to the mound, where, between 1946 and 1954, he won 85 games, an impressive complement to his .258 career batting average and 25 home runs.

Naturally, Ray exposed his son to the game at a young age. "In Dad's last year [1954]," remembered Bill in 2013, "I was 8 years old. He took me to the games and into the clubhouse. I used to shag balls during batting practice. I couldn't make the throw from the outfield to the infield." Such attention, of course, gave McNulty a leg up on the competition. "When it came to baseball I was always ahead of the other kids. I got into an 8- to- 11-year-old Little League when I was 7, and made the All-Star team." An important lesson imparted by his father was that "you never wanted to be the best player, because you never improved. You always had to find better competition. You have to go find older kids who are better than you." (After retiring from baseball Ray worked as a car salesman; his wife, Joyce, was a homemaker.)

Once graduated from Highland Hills, McNulty enrolled at American River College, a two-year institution in Sacramento. It proved to be a relatively short stay. In what turned out to be his only season at the school, McNulty once again played basketball and football, and his strong arm on the gridiron gave the school's baseball coach high hopes for the coming baseball season. However, a visit to McNulty's home by a friend of his father's soon altered McNulty's course.

By virtue of his own career, Ray knew all the local baseball scouts. One was Don Pries, a fellow career minor leaguer, who was then a scout for the Kansas City Athletics. One day, Bill recalled, "I think Don contacted my dad—this would have been around January or February of '65—and said, 'I'd like to come out to the house and talk to you about signing Bill.'" Accompanying Pries was John McNamara, then managing the Athletics' Double-A affiliate in Birmingham, Alabama. That day, Bill McNulty said, the two men who "had the biggest influence on what turned out to be an [Oakland] dynasty in the '70s" were "very persuasive": *Kansas City was in last place*, they said; *we're moving to Oakland in a year or two, just about the time you'll be ready to play in the big leagues*; and *you'll be playing 80 or 90 miles from your hometown.* Thus, McNulty joined the Athletics organization.

(There is one final anecdote about that afternoon. As Pries left, Ray asked "Where are you off to now?" "Well," replied Pries, "tomorrow I'm driving down to Modesto to sign this kid named Joe Rudi."

("That turned out pretty good," McNulty later recalled, with a chuckle.)

In his first season, 1965, the Athletics sent the 18-year-old McNulty (he turned 19 on August 29) to Leesburg in the Class A Florida State League, where, he recalled, he joined a "skinny kid from Cucamonga, California," named Rollie Fingers. In 133 games McNulty made an impression on both sides of the ball, finishing first in RBIs and second in home runs, while also pacing the league's third basemen in putouts and finishing second in double plays. Despite his .199 batting average, it was nonetheless a promising debut. That fall McNulty also fulfilled a military obligation. Beginning in October 1965, for the next six months he underwent Marine Corps Reserve training, beginning with boot camp at the Marine Corps Recruiting Department in San Diego alongside fellow players Rick Monday and Dave Duncan, then at Camp Pendleton, California, and finally to radio operator's school. McNulty satisfied his Reserve obligations for the next six years.

The next three seasons for McNulty were marked by a steady climb through the Athletics farm system. Along the way he played with many of the men who eventually formed the core of the Oakland A's championship dynasty. While he made occasional forays into the outfield, McNulty settled into third base and proved a better than average fielder with a rifle arm. Moreover, anchored in the middle of the batting order, the right-handed slugger also proved a powerful if sometimes inconsistent hitter.

Over that period, he made several stops. In 1966, at Burlington (Iowa), in the Class A Midwest League, McNulty was an All-Star. He led the league in fielding average and assists, and also delivered ten home runs and 60 RBIs. Promoted to Double-A Mobile for the final weeks of the season, he produced a blistering OPS (on-base average plus slugging average) of 1.413 in seven games. (Among the players on that team were Tony LaRussa, Rick Monday, Sal Bando, and Rene Lachemann.) The following season, in addition to playing in the Arizona Instructional League with such future stars as Reggie Jackson, Bert Campaneris, Vida Blue, Gene Tenace, and Fingers, McNulty also played 44 games with the Peninsula Grays (Class A Carolina League), where he excelled (.307/.398/.569), and 63 at Double-A Birmingham, where the going was a little tougher (.213/.273/.370). In 1968 he returned to both of those teams, to similar levels of success (.290/.355/.515 in 54 games at Peninsula; .188/.241/.324 in 48 games at Birmingham). In those three seasons combined McNulty produced 43 home runs and 189 RBIs. His powerful performance placed McNulty emphatically on the radar of the only man who mattered in the Athletics front office, owner Charles O. Finley.

Every once in a while the game's most promising prospects make the jump from Double-A to the majors. So it was with McNulty. Although he had struggled during his first two stints with Birmingham, in 1969 he opened the season there, and this time proved up to the challenge. By July 4 McNulty, on his way to being named the Southern League's All-Star third baseman, had become one of the leading hitters in the league, posting a slash line of .288/.347/.568 over 75 games, while also producing league-leading totals of 20 home runs and 67 RBIs. Then, on July 7 in Chicago, Athletics outfielder Tommy Reynolds suffered a broken finger that forced him to the disabled list. To replace him, Oakland called up McNulty. Perhaps surprisingly, the 22-year-old headed to the major leagues.

In 2013 McNulty recollected with levity the day he got that first call to join the A's. At the time Birmingham was in Charlotte, North Carolina, for a series with the Charlotte Hornets. In his hotel room around 7:30 A.M., McNulty and his roommate were awakened by a phone call. "I'm Joe Williams of the *Charlotte Observer* newspaper," the caller announced. "I understand you're having a great year, and I want to do a story about you." To which McNulty replied, "Catch me at the ballpark," and began to hang up. Just before he could do so, however, the caller said, "No, don't hang up; I've got a deadline here." To which McNulty responded, "What do you want?"

"Well, first of all, why aren't you in the big leagues yet?"

"I don't know. I guess I need a lucky break."

"Well," the caller countered, "you just got one. Tommy Reynolds broke his finger. My name's Charlie Finley and you're playing left field tonight in Chicago."

Skeptical, McNulty confirmed the promotion with his manager, Gus Niarhos, and immediately left for Chicago. That night when McNulty arrived at Comiskey Park, a smiling Finley said to the rookie, "I really had you going, didn't I, Bill?" and McNulty acknowledged the joke. In the clubhouse, manager Hank Bauer told McNulty, "Mr. Finley says you're starting in left field tonight." When McNulty protested that "I've never played left field in my life," Bauer retorted, "Well, if you're afraid, wear a helmet, because Rick Monday'll catch anything hit near ya." Finally, John McNamara, now an A's coach (he succeeded Bauer later in the season) counseled, "Bill, just hit the ball, don't worry about catching it." So on July 9, 1969, McNulty made his major-league debut.

If McNulty worried about playing left field, he nevertheless acquitted himself well. That first stint in the majors lasted five consecutive games; McNulty started each in left field and handled 11 chances (nine putouts and two assists) flawlessly. At the plate, he never got untracked; he went 0-for-17, with ten strikeouts. Over that span, he hit just one ball out of the infield. After his tenth strikeout, on July 13, Oakland sent McNulty to the Triple-A Iowa Oaks, where he was .198/.262/.333 in 26 games. It was three years before he returned to the major leagues.

In January 1970 *The Sporting News* reported that the A's had dropped McNulty from their 40-man roster.[1] At Iowa he re-established himself as a legitimate power prospect, as he batted .295, finished third in the American Association in home runs (22) and RBIs (73) and was named an Honorable Mention to the league All-Star team. It wasn't enough to impress the A's: After the season, they sold McNulty's contract to the Milwaukee Brewers. (The deal was for cash, "something over the Triple-A draft price," plus pitcher Gary Timberlake.[2])

Little could the slugger have foreseen the unexpected twist his career would take in 1971. With his confidence restored, he hit .333 with a home run and nine RBIs in 33 spring-training at-bats. McNulty thought he had done enough to make the team. Brewers manager Dave Bristol disagreed. In particular, he graded McNulty low in two phases: McNulty's "lateral range at third base isn't good enough," Bristol told *The Sporting News*;[3] and perhaps more damaging, Bristol concluded, "(T)he big thing against him is that he is lackadaisical. I've got to have players with fire."[4] It was a scathing assessment.

The worst was yet to come. In late March Milwaukee demoted McNulty to Triple-A Evansville. Before he left, Brewers general manager Frank Lane told him, "Young man, we'd like to have you work on becoming a pitcher at Evansville."[5] That suggestion did not interest McNulty. Recounting to the press his father's successful transition in the minors, he nonetheless protested, "I've never pitched in my life and I don't want to start at the age of 24. I want to hit—and I still think I can get to the big leagues as a hitter."[6]

In the end, he never had to attempt the change. That spring, McNulty ran into Ray Johnston, owner of the Iowa Oaks. "Can't you make a deal to get me back to Des Moines?" he said. "If I can't play in the big leagues, I'd rather play for the Oaks than anybody else. … I know they won't try to make a pitcher out of me."[7] Johnston, for whom McNulty had in 1970 led the Oaks in homers and RBIs, passed along McNulty's request to Charlie Finley, and Finley bought McNulty back from Milwaukee.

McNulty repaid the gesture in a big way, and also gained the admiration of Iowa's manager, Sherm Lollar, for whom he had produced so well the previous season. Later that 1971 season, told of Dave Bristol's opinion of McNulty's skills, Lollar, who had had the same impression the first time he'd seen McNulty, offered, "That seemingly nonchalant attitude of Bill's is misleading. It's just Mac's physical makeup to be kind of slow-moving and casual until he has to bear down. But he's really a good competitor and he hustles every time it counts. I tried last year [1970] to get Bill to move around more and show some fire, just to help liven up the infield. But it's just not his nature to holler and jump around."

Initially, Lollar had tried McNulty in the outfield, but once he moved McNulty to the infield, Lollar found him to be "just about the most exciting third baseman I've ever seen. Even when he didn't field the ball clean, he'd pounce on it after he knocked it down and throw out some of the fastest runners in the league. Lots of times, I'd think the batter was going to be safe for sure, but Bill would gun him down. … He's made it easier this year because he's been sure-handed. And he's been going a lot farther to make some real big league stops."[8] There wouldn't be a second McNulty on the mound.

McNulty finished the 1971 season with impressive production. Although his batting average lagged to .247, he led the league in home runs (27) and walks, compiled a .902 OPS and was voted to the American Association All-Star team. Some of his homers were what Lollar called "some real big league home runs—400 feet or more."[9] After some turbulent times, it appeared McNulty had righted the ship. But there were to be several more moves before the A's tracked him down at that campfire. Two days before the end of the 1971 season, the Chicago Cubs' Tacoma farm team, seeking help for the Pacific Coast League playoffs, purchased his contract from Iowa. Tacoma lost the five-game series, but McNulty was magnificent: 7-for-14, with three home runs and 7 RBIs. Based on that performance, he naturally assumed "there might be a chance for me with the Cubs" in 1972.[10] He was mistaken.

With Ron Santo entrenched at third base in Chicago, the Cubs had little use for McNulty. They shipped him out of the organization, ironically to Evansville. It was a move that appealed to McNulty. "I don't think I could tolerate sitting on the bench," he said. "Maybe if I have a good season, somebody will want me."[11]

McNulty did indeed have another good season and proved he was still a prospect. Playing primarily at third base, he overcame a slow start to finish second in the American Association in home runs (24) and fourth in RBIs (73). It was his third consecutive season with over 20 homers. But when Evansville's season ended, unsure what 1973 might bring, McNulty went to the mountains to hunt. And that's when the A's bought his contract and brought him back to Oakland.

Asked in 2013 to try to explain his brief major-league career, McNulty said, "I don't really know how to answer your question. I never felt overmatched. I should have stayed in the big leagues in '69; I would have been on all those championship teams, would have progressed like Joe Rudi, Gene Tenace, my buddy… but I didn't produce." Recalling his first big-league at-bat in 1969 (McNulty said it was against Tommy John; according to Retrosheet.org, it came against right-hander Billy Wynne), "I decided my first at-bat that I would take the pitch. It came in there. … It looked like a basketball coming in there, right down the middle. Next pitch, he threw something similar, I was so excited to see it that I swung and hit it in the upper deck, just foul, strike two. The next pitch, I took. Ed Runge was the umpire. Sal Bando told me, 'Don't ever look at Runge, because he'll run you out of the game.' Well, he [Runge] goes 'ball,' and that pitch was pretty good. And I reached down to grab some dirt and he leans over and he says, 'Don't ever take that pitch again, kid. I did it because it's your first at-bat.' Well, by then, I said, I'm swinging at the next pitch, I don't care where it is, and I swung and missed." (Note: according to Retrosheet.org, George Maloney was the home plate umpire; Runge was at first. Also, the final pitch was a called strike three.)

By October 4, 1972, the last of his four-game major-league swan song, it seemed McNulty had finally figured it out. In his three previous games (September 27, as a pinch-hitter against Bert Blyleven, and two subsequent starts at third base against the Royals), McNulty had gone 0-for-8, striking out just once and earning his first two walks. Then, on this night against the California Angels, McNulty faced perhaps the fastest pitcher of them all, Nolan Ryan, who was trying for his 20th win of the season. In the bottom of the second, Reggie Jackson doubled and catcher Dave Duncan walked. With runners on first and second, McNulty came to the plate for his first at-bat of the night. Ryan delivered, McNulty swung, and he drilled a line drive up the middle, a clean single to center, on which Jackson was thrown out at the plate. A final at-bat two innings later resulted in a fly out to left field, and McNulty's major-league career was over. He finished 1-for-27 over nine games, with 11 strikeouts and two walks.

McNulty hung on for a few more years, including one magical season back in his hometown. In October 1972 the A's traded McNulty and a player to be named later (Brant Alyea) to the Texas Rangers for left-hander Paul Lindblad. McNulty went to 1973 spring training with Texas and their new manager, Whitey Herzog, but the two didn't get along. So at the end of spring training, the Rangers traded McNulty to the New York Mets for infielder Bill Sudakis. That season, spent entirely at the Mets' Tidewater farm team in the International League, McNulty again delivered, finishing first, second, and third respectively in doubles, total bases, and home runs. But by then, he'd had enough. When the season ended, he decided to start the next phase of his life.

At home in Sacramento, though, McNulty got good news. Pacific Coast League baseball was returning to Sacramento. After a 14-year absence from the PCL, the Solons would return, as an affiliate of the Milwaukee Brewers. McNulty visited general manager John Carbray and told him, "I'd like to play in my hometown but I belong to the New York Mets, and in 1973 they had me in Tidewater."[12] The Brewers quickly purchased

McNulty's contract from the Mets, and he became a Solon for the 1974 season.

In one of the oddities of baseball stadium configurations, the Solons played that year at the Sacramento City College field, which featured a 40-foot-high fence that was just 233 feet away in left field. It was tailor-made for a hitter of McNulty's power. In 1974, playing in his hometown for manager Bob Lemon, McNulty hit 55 home runs, drove in 135 runs, and scored the same number. His slash line was .329/.438/.690, for a season's OPS of 1.128. The following year, through 40 games, McNulty was again on pace for a similar performance with the Solons, when he accepted an offer of roughly $70,000 to play the remainder of the season in Japan. He played his final 64 professional ball games with the Tokyo Lotte Orions in the Japan Pacific League, and then called it a career. In 11 minor-league seasons he'd hit 237 home runs.

With his baseball career over, McNulty returned to Sacramento and started to work. With a background in tools (while playing, he had invested in a hardware store in Sacramento), McNulty took a job with a chainsaw company and later became a salesman for a tool manufacturer, a position he still held in 2014.

Also, during his brief stay in Tacoma with the Cubs, McNulty met Sue Isekite; in 2014 they celebrated their 35th wedding anniversary. As of 2014 the couple resided in Eatonville, Washington; McNulty had two daughters and six grandchildren. Sue's father, Floyd "Lefty" Isekite, was a minor-league pitcher who won 61 games pitching on the West Coast. Their fathers' shared profession, McNulty said, was coincidental to the couple's meeting.

McNulty left one final thought on the outcome of his career: "If I had to tell a manager about me if I was still playing, I would say what I am is consistent. I won't get hurt. I'll be there every day. But it's going to average out over time. Be patient. But they don't do that in the big leagues; they want you to produce right away. I just think I needed the right guy to have a little patience. It is what it is."

SOURCES

The author expresses his sincerest appreciation to Bill McNulty for phone interviews on October 10 and November 22, 2013, as well as subsequent email exchanges. Unless otherwise noted, all quotations are drawn from those interviews.

Rose, George, *One Hit Wonders: Baseball Stories* (Lincoln: iUniverse, 2004).

(Galley proof) O'Connor, Alan, *Gold On the Diamond: Sacramento's Great Baseball Players 1886 to 1976* (Sacramento: Big Tomato Press, 2007).

The Sporting News

baseball-reference.com

retrosheet.org

McNulty player file, National Baseball Hall of Fame, Cooperstown, New York

NOTES

1 *The Sporting News*, January 17, 1970.

2 *The Sporting News*, August 21, 1971.

3 Ibid.

4 Ibid.

5 Ibid.

6 Ibid.

7 Ibid.

8 Ibid.

9 Ibid.

10 *The Sporting News*, June 3, 1972.

11 Ibid.

12 *The Sporting News*, August 31, 1974.

Don Mincher

By Marc Z Aaron

Donald Ray Mincher was a two-time member of the Oakland Athletics. In 1970 he was the team leader in home runs with 27. Before being traded for the second time to the Athletics on July 20, 1972, Mincher homered off Joe Coleman at Detroit on July 10. It was a personal career milestone, his 200th home run. It was also to be his last.

Minch,[1] as he was often called, "is the only man who played for both the original Twins and the original Rangers, 11 seasons apart. And, for that matter, he was the only player to see the end of both Senators' runs in Washington."[2]

Born on June 24, 1938, in Huntsville, Alabama, Mincher was of German-Irish-Indian descent. At Butler High School (Class of 1956) he played baseball, basketball, and football. In his senior year he captained both the baseball and football teams. He was a good enough football player to make both All-State and High School All-American. Mincher turned down a football scholarship at the University of Alabama to pursue his love of baseball.[3] At 6-feet-3 and 205 pounds, he was built for the sport. An American Legion baseball player, Mincher was signed by former major leaguer Zack Taylor to a Chicago White Sox contract for $4,000 after high school and was sent to Duluth-Superior of the Class C Northern League.[4] That year he married his high-school sweetheart, Patsy Ann Payne.[5] Mincher returned to Duluth-Superior in 1957 and led Northern League first basemen in putouts, assists, and double plays. In 1958, playing for Davenport in the Class B three-I League, he finished fourth in batting (.330) and was named to the league All-Star team.[6]

After spending the 1959 season at Charleston of the Class A Sally League (.272, 22 home runs), Mincher was sent on April 4, 1960, with Earl Battey and $150,000 to the Washington Senators for Roy Sievers.

On the 18th, Mincher was in the Opening Day lineup at first base, going hitless in front of the home crowd against the Boston Red Sox. In his third game, at Baltimore on the 20th, Mincher got his first two major-league hits. On the 25th, at home against Baltimore, he hit his first major-league home run, off Milt Pappas, to deep right field. In mid-May, batting .230 with 2 home runs, Mincher was sent to Charleston in the American Association. Recalled in late September, he had two hits in five pinch-hitting appearances.

Before the 1961 season the Senators franchise was moved to Minneapolis-St. Paul, to play as the Minnesota Twins. Mincher hit five home runs for the Twins but spent most of the season at Triple-A Buffalo. In 1962 he was back with the Twins. On April 28, playing at Cleveland, he hit a pinch-hit home run off

Ron Taylor, then, remaining in the game at first base, he homered for a second time, off Frank Funk. (Mincher was to finish his career with ten pinch-hit home runs, four of them in 1964.) Mincher had another two-home-run game on July 20, 1963, at Minnesota's Metro Stadium, taking starter Steve Ridzik of the expansion Senators deep twice as the Twins won 11-3. The next day he did it again, homering twice off Senators starter Don Rudolph as the Twins won 3-2. (Mincher, a left-handed batter, had no problem that day off the lefty Rudolph. However, throughout his career he always fared better against right-handers, and was often out of the starting lineup against left-handed starters.) Four days later, on July 24 at Cleveland Stadium, Mincher again hit two home runs, off Pedro Ramos and Jerry Walker.

Mincher made Ridzik a particular target. On August 26, 1963, he homered off the right-hander again, at D.C. Stadium, and on August 18, 1964, homered twice in consecutive at-bats off Ridzik, again in Washington.

Mincher settled in as the Twins' first baseman. He told an interviewer in 2010 that his biggest thrill in baseball came in the first game of the 1965 World Series when he hit a home run of the Los Angeles Dodgers' Don Drysdale. "To bat against Koufax and Drysdale when it really meant something," Mincher said. "I didn't realize what a big thrill it was until I got older and started thinking back on these things."[7] His wife, Patsy, knew Mincher was slightly nervous as he was extremely quiet as she drove him to the ballpark. Usually he was talkative.[8] In the bottom of the second inning, in his first Series at-bat, Mincher homered to deep right field off Drysdale. Mincher spoke of the feat often, his wife said.[9] In Game Two, Mincher tied a World Series record with four assists at first base. (Three of the assists were on groundballs by lefty Willie Davis.)

On June 9, 1966, Mincher was part of baseball history again when he was one of five Twins who hit home runs in one inning, an American League record. The Kansas City Athletics were the victims; the others besides Mincher to go deep in the seventh inning that day were Rich Rollins, Tony Oliva, Zolio Versalles, and Harmon Killebrew.[10]

After the 1966 season Mincher was traded by the Twins with pitcher Peter Cimino and outfielder Jimmie Hall to the California Angels for infielder Jackie Hernandez and pitcher Dean Chance. With the Angels Mincher had his best major league season in 1967. He hit 25 home runs and was selected to the All-Star team for the first time.

On April 11, 1968, in the second game of the season, Mincher was hit on the cheek by a fastball thrown by the Cleveland Indians' Sam McDowell. The blow was a glancing one and Mincher missed only nine games, but he was plagued by headaches and dizziness and struggled at the plate for the rest of the season.[11] On September 4, after he reeled backward while swinging at a pitch, he was removed from the game. X-rays and tests were inconclusive, but Mincher was given the rest of the season off.[12] Mincher's average for 1968 was .236, down from .273 in 1967; his home run and RBI production suffered likewise.

Though Mincher was cleared after tests at the Mayo Clinic, Angels manager Bill Rigney considered him damaged goods after his struggles during the season, and did not feel that the reports provided positive assurance as to Mincher's full recovery.[13] The Angels left Mincher unprotected in the expansion draft after the season and Mincher was selected as the Seattle Pilots number-one pick. He played in 140 games for the Pilots hit 25 home runs, and was named to the American League All-Star squad. Mincher was the Pilots player representative.[14]

On January 15, 1970, as the Pilots were becoming the Milwaukee Brewers, Mincher was traded to the Athletics with infielder Ron Clark for outfielder Mike Hershberger, pitchers Lew Krausse and Ken Sanders, and catcher Phil Roof. With Oakland he hit 27 home runs, his career high. His walk-off home run on August 2 off Horacio Pina of Washington with two outs in the ninth inning of a scoreless game in Oakland was one of 27 he hit that season—a career high.

The following season, on May 8, 1971, Mincher was traded by the Athletics along with catcher-outfielder Frank Fernandez, pitcher Paul Lindblad, and cash to the Washington Senators for first baseman Mike Epstein and pitcher Darold Knowles. On July 17 at RFK Stadium in Washington, Mincher, not in the lineup that day against the Twins, was in the outfield bullpen when in the fourth inning home-plate umpire Hank Soar motioned him to move away from the bullpen fence in center field, where he could pick up Minnesota's signs. Mincher's gesture in response 410 feet away was not to Soar's liking. In what could be a distance record for an ejection in baseball, Soar ejected Mincher without hesitation.[15] Patsy Mincher said that her husband was only motioning back to mean, "What do you want?," but it was taken differently by Soar.[16]

After the 1971 season the Senators moved to Texas to become the Rangers. On July 20, 1972, Mincher was traded back to Oakland with infielder Ted Kubiak for utilityman Vic Harris, infielder Marty Martinez, and pitcher Steve Lawson. Mincher was not too happy. "I'm not ready to sit on the bench," he said, noting that Athletics first baseman Mike Epstein was hitting well.[17] "I've been around a long time and I've learned to expect almost anything, but this trade knocked me off my feet," Mincher said.[18] But Epstein went out with an eye infection, and Mincher was placed at first base and in the cleanup spot. He got off to a poor start, going 2-for-22 with no home runs or RBIs. When Epstein returned, Mincher was relegated to pinch-hitting for the balance of the season.[19] He did contribute in the World Series; his pinch-single in Game Four drove in the tying run in the ninth inning against Cincinnati. The next batter, pinch-hitter Angel Manguel, singled home the game-winning run.

With little hope for his role to change in 1973, Mincher decided to retire. "I just have no desire to play the role I did last year," he said. "I don't care to be that kind of player. I enjoyed being on a world championships club, but I didn't want to sit on the bench watching my more mature years slip by."[20] (Patsy Mincher said in 2013 that Don's shoulder at this time hurt so much

that he could hardly comb his hair without being in pain.[21]

During Mincher's two stints with the Athletics he played in 210 games, hit 29 home runs (27 of them in 1970 that led the club), knocked in 87 runs and batted .236. Described by one sportswriter as "intense and introverted,"[22] Mincher may have been his own worst enemy. He admitted in 1968 to putting too much pressure on himself both when he was doing well (worrying about keeping it going) and when he was not (staying in the slump). He applauded his supportive wife, Patsy, for spending long nights listening to him spilling his guts out.[23]

After 13 seasons Mincher's retirement allowed him to spend more time with his wife and three children at home in Huntsville. It also provided Mincher with time to pursue his hobbies, which included fishing and hunting.

Mincher ran a sporting-goods store, specializing in trophies and awards for about ten years before returning to baseball in 1985 as the general manager of the Huntsville Stars of the Southern League.[24] The Stars were an Athletics affiliate from 1985 to 1998. When there was a chance in 1994 that the franchise might be moved out of the city, Mincher put together a group of investors to buy the team from owner Larry Schmittou. After the 1998 season the Stars and Athletics parted ways and the Milwaukee Brewers became the Stars affiliate. During Mincher's time with the Stars they won two Southern League championships. During all these years Patsy worked with him at the ballpark. In October 2000 Mincher was elected interim president of the Southern League when Arnold Fielkow left for the NFL. His interim position was made permanent before the start of the 2001 season. Later Mincher and his group sold the Stars to a New York attorney. During his time with the Stars, Mincher was twice elected Executive of the Year and in 2008 was inducted into the Alabama Sports Hall of Fame.

Mincher had a deep interest in the development side of baseball. He made it the mission of the Southern

League to promote minor-league baseball as wholesome family fun and entertainment at a reasonable cost.[25]

In October 2011 Mincher stepped down as president of the Southern League. In January 2012 he felt pain in both arms that proved to be symptoms of serious heart problems. He underwent surgery to take care of blockages. Then pneumonia kicked in. He died on March 4, 2012.[26] He is buried in Maple Hill Cemetery, Huntsville, Alabama.

Mincher was preceded in death by his parents, George and Lillian. He was survived by his wife, Patsy; and three children, Mark (head baseball coach for almost 30 years at Huntsville High before becoming principal), Lori Lumpkin, and Mincherna Hopper; and many grandchildren and great-grandchildren. At the 2012 Winter Meetings Patsy was honored as "The First Lady of Southern League Baseball." Not only had she worked at the ballpark during Mincher's tenure with the Huntsville Stars but she also handled the logistics and much of the child-rearing during Mincher's major-league career.[27]

NOTES

1   1974 player file fact sheet contained in Mincher's Hall of Fame Library Player file. (Hereafter cited as HOF file).

2   John Branch, "A Twin, a Ranger and, Most of All, a Senator," *New York Times,* October 6, 2010.

3   Telephone interview with Pat Mincher on December 10, 2013. (Hereafter cited as Pat Mincher interview.)

4   Maury Allen, "Mincher Enjoys HR and Series Chance," *New York Post,* October 7, 1965.

5   Pat Mincher interview.

6   1974 player file fact sheet.

7   John Branch, "A Twin, a Ranger and, Most of All, a Senator."

8   Pat Mincher interview.

9   Pat Mincher interview; Oakland Athletics Press Release; HOF file.

10 Max Nichols, "Mele's Maulers Tie Mark, Clout Five HRs in Innin,g" *The Sporting News,* June 25, 1966.

11 John Branch, "A Twin, a Ranger and, Most of All, a Senator"; Hy Zimmerman, "Pilots Looking Toward Mincher to Get Em over *The Sporting News,* Choppy Seas," *The Sporting News,* February 1, 1969; Hy Zimmerman, "Mincher Fired Up to Clip Angel Wings," April 19, 1969.

12 "Mincher Goes to Hospital, Suffers from Dizzy Spells," *The Sporting News,* September 21, 1968; John Wiebusch, "Mincher Dismayed, Excited on Leaving Angels for Pilots," *The Sporting News,* November 2, 1968.

13 John Wiebusch, "Mincher Dismayed."

14 Hy Zimmerman, "Krausse Wants to be Starter ... Pilots Will Give him a Chance," *The Sporting News,* January 31, 1970.

15 "Soar's Vision Sharp," *The Sporting News,* August 7, 1971.

16 Pat Mincher interview.

17 Randy Galloway, "Critics Fault Ranger 'Suicide' Youth Drive," *The Sporting News,* August 5, 1972.

18 Ibid

19 Ron Bergman, "Mincher Weary of Bench Duty, Retires as 200-Homer Belter," *The Sporting News,* January 13, 1973.

20 Ron Bergman, "Mincher Weary of Bench Duty."

21 Pat Mincher interview.

22 Ross Newhan, "Mincher Sings Happy Tune With Long Bow to Rigney," *The Sporting News,* March 30, 1968.

23 Ibid.

24 John Branch, "A Twin, a Ranger and, Most of All, a Senator"; Pat Mincher interview.

25 Southern League website.

26 Mark McCarter, April 13, 2011: al.com/sports/index.sst/2011/04/opening_night_remains_special.html.

27 Mark McCarter, December 5, 2012: al.com/sports/index.ssf/2012/as/pat_mincher_proclaimed_first_l.html

Irv Noren

by Alan Cohen

In October 1935 Perry Noren of Jamestown, New York, drove his sons, Everett and Irving, to Detroit for the opening game of the 1935 World Series, and they saw Schoolboy Rowe pitch for the Tigers. The next time the family attended a World Series, Irv was playing in it.

Perry, a native of Sweden, owned a Swedish bakery in Jamestown. In 1936, when Irving was 12, the family moved to Pasadena, California, where Perry opened a bakery. Son Everett took over Noren's Hillcrest Bakery in 1955 and ran it through 1988. Irv, on the other hand, did the family proud on athletic playing fields.

Irving Arnold Noren, the Athletics' third-base coach from 1971 until mid-1974, was born on November 29, 1924, in Jamestown, the middle of three children born to Perry and his wife, Victoria. Everett was four years older and Irving's sister, Janet, was four years younger.

At Pasadena High School, Noren was a pitcher. He also competed in American Legion ball for Post 13 in Pasadena. After finishing high school, where he also starred in basketball and was named California Interscholastic Federation Player of the year in 1942, Noren went to Pasadena Junior College (now Pasadena City College), starring on both the basketball and baseball teams. As a pitcher he went 10-2 in 1942. In basketball, during his second year on the team, he set a school game scoring record of 29 points. His studies were interrupted by World War II. He entered the Army in March 1943.

During basic training at Fort Ord, California, Noren injured his knee and required surgery. It wouldn't be the last time. Still, he got to play baseball. And on March 23, 1945, he married Veda Mae Mewes, who worked in the telegraph office near Fort Ord. They

were married almost 68 years when she died of a heart attack on February 7, 2013. (On their 60th anniversary Vee said they were actually married for 30 years because Irv was on the road half the time.)

Noren was discharged from the Army in 1946 and returned to Pasadena Junior College, where he again excelled at basketball as a point scorer, including a record 37 points against Dixie College of Utah in the Western States College Tournament.[1]

While on leave from the Army, Noren had played semipro ball as a first baseman in Salinas and Monterey, California. On March 15, 1946, Brooklyn Dodgers scout Tom Downey signed him to a contract for a $5,000 bonus. Noren went to Fort Worth, Texas, for spring training and was dispatched to Class C Santa Barbara in the California League, where he was converted to an outfielder. He batted .363, with a league-leading 188 hits, 33 doubles, 14 triples, and 129 RBIs.

That fall Noren played professional basketball with the minor-league Los Angeles Red Devils, alongside future major-league baseball players Jackie Robinson and George Crowe.[2] On November 22-23, 1946, the Red Devils faced the Chicago American Gears of the National Basketball League in a two-game exhibition. The Gears' top player was George Mikan. Noren later remembered that he "had to pull on the bottom of Mikan's pants, so I could outjump him. He didn't like it too much"[3] Noren and two teammates joined the Gears on December 13.[4] He got into three NBL games, and scored one point. That was the end of his basketball career, as Dodgers general manager Branch Rickey told him to concentrate on baseball.

Noren's performance at Santa Barbara earned him a promotion to the Double-A Fort Worth Cats. In 1947 he batted .271 and was fourth in the league in hits (162) and doubles (33). He was back at Fort Worth in 1948 and was named the league's Player of the Year, as he batted .323 for the first-place Cats and edged out Houston second baseman Solly Hemus for the honor. The Cats, managed by 32-year-old Bobby Bragan, in his first managerial assignment, won the Texas League playoffs but lost to the Southern League champion Birmingham Barons in the Dixie Series.

In 1949 Noren went to spring training with the Dodgers at Vero Beach, Florida, then was assigned to the Hollywood Stars of the Pacific Coast League. Playing for manager Fred Haney, Noren was the league's MVP as he batted .330 with 29 home runs and 130 RBIs as the Stars won the the league playoffs. Al Wolf of the *Los Angeles Times*, in casting his vote for MVP, chose "that ball-hawking, hard-hitting, ever-dangerous rookie outfielder — Kid Noren."[5] Noren was also selected by the fans as the most popular member of his team.

Noren's path to a position with the Brooklyn club seemed clear, but on September 30, 1949, he was sold to the Washington Senators for $70,000. Noren later suggested that the sale was due in part to losses suffered by the Dodgers in a professional football venture that did not work out. This was indeed the case. The organization had lost $500,000 on the Brooklyn Dodgers

football team, which played for three seasons (1946-48) in the new All-American Football Conference, going 8-32. The league folded after the 1949 season, with Cleveland, San Francisco, and Baltimore absorbed into the NFL. Noren was one of ten Dodgers traded and sold by Rickey to recoup some money. Among the others were Chico Carrasquel (to the Chicago White Sox), Danny O'Connell (to the Pittsburgh Pirates), Sam Jethroe (to the Boston Braves), and Preston Ward (to the Chicago Cubs).

Washington's interest in Noren was heightened by reports from Bucky Harris, who had seen him while managing San Diego in the PCL and was en route to manage the Senators in 1950. In his first year with Washington, Noren batted .295 with 18 homers and 98 RBIs. He finished 15th in MVP balloting. On Opening Day, Noren's father traveled cross-country to see him play. In his first major-league at-bat, Noren singled off Carl Scheib of the Philadelphia A's, driving in Gil Coan with the Senators' first run. Noren subsequently scored and, as he was heading back to the dugout, President Truman cheered him on from the stands.[6]

While with Washington, Noren did particularly well against the Yankees. His first big game against New York came on April 28, 1950, at Griffith Stadium. In the third inning, he tripled off Fred Sanford to drive in a run, and then scored the tying run. In the seventh inning he hit his first major-league homer, victimizing the Yankees' relief ace Joe Page. It was a two-run blast that tied the game at 4-4. Washington went on to win 5-4. Not long thereafter, on May 11, Noren suffered appendicitis and missed 14 games, returning to action on May 27. Manager Harris said, "We need him if we're to get up in the race."[7]

On June 29 Noren once again excelled against the Yankees, this time in New York, and both his bat and glove were on display. He hit a three-run homer in the fourth inning to put the Senators in front, then in the bottom of the inning, he robbed Jerry Coleman of an extra-base hit by making a diving, tumbling catch in deep left-center field.

During that season Noren put together consecutive-game hitting streaks of 17 (July 23-August 10) and 20 (August 22-September 8) games. During the latter steak, he raised his batting average to .311, then tailed off at the end of the season, going hitless in his last 14 at-bats to bring his final average to .295. Noren's 20 assists and five double plays led all outfielders, and in his 2001 *Historical Baseball Abstract*, author Bill James assessed Noren being as worthy of a Gold Glove that season.[8]

In his first few games against the Yankees in 1951, Noren continued to impress Yankees manager Casey Stengel. In five games over a span of three series, he went 10-for-21, with two hits in each of the five games. On April 29 Noren gunned down Eddie Lopat, who was trying to score from second on a single. He made catches to rob Mickey Mantle and Joe DiMaggio of extra-base hits.[9]

After playing in all of the Senators' first 100 games and batting .290, Noren missed three games in early August with the flu and a knee injury resulting from a collision with teammate Gil Coan. Then on August 11 at Fenway Park in Boston, he suffered a fractured jaw while stealing second when he was hit by catcher Aaron Robinson's throw. He missed 22 games, and by season's end, Noren's average had slipped to .279 with 8 homers and 86 RBIs.

On May 3, 1952, Noren was traded to the Yankees, who needed him in the outfield because Joe DiMaggio had retired, Mickey Mantle was slow in recovering from offseason knee surgery, and Jackie Jensen had gotten off to a slow start. The Yanks sent Jensen, pitcher Spec Shea, infielder Jerry Snyder, and outfielder Archie Wilson to Washington for Noren and shortstop Tom Upton.

Noren's performance had the Yanks and manager Casey Stengel wondering about the merits of trading away Jensen. He batted .235 in 93 games with New York, but rescued his season by batting .350 as the Yankees won five of six games and won the pennant over Cleveland. In the World Series against Brooklyn, Noren played in four games, going 3-for-10. Still, he

spent the 1952 offseason on the trading block, but there were no takers. At a two-week pre-spring-training camp near Stengel's home in Glendale, California, the manager sought to modify left-hander Noren's batting stance so he would pull the ball more, definitely a plus at Yankee Stadium. Stengel encouraged Noren to stand further away from the plate, relax, and be ready to drive the ball.[10]

Noren proceeded to have a great spring training, and earned himself a roster spot as the fourth outfielder behind Mantle, Hank Bauer, and Gene Woodling.[11] In Stengel's platoon system, the Noren got into 109 games and raised his batting average to .267.

Stengel had high praise for Noren, saying, "Noren is the greatest fourth outfielder in the American League. He is playing much better ball now than he played last year. I put him in there regularly against right-handed pitching. His fielding is excellent. He's hitting. He came to me as a center fielder. Now he can play right field and left field. It is amazing to me how he has mastered all three."[12] In a year defined by streaks (the Yankees won 18 straight during late May and early June, and followed it up by losing nine in a row in late June), New York established a big lead and cruised to its fifth consecutive pennant. In the World Series against Brooklyn, Noren walked and popped up in two pinch-hitting appearances.

In 1954 the Yankees acquired veteran Enos Slaughter from the St. Louis Cardinals, prompting Noren to declare, "I've been slaughtered again." He began the season slowly, but his fortunes changed. Injuries to Mantle, Woodling, and Slaughter gave him the opportunity to play, and he took full advantage. In 59 games from May 1 through July 18, he batted .381 with 8 homers and 35 RBIs. During a three-game stretch in July, Noren went 9-for-13 to take the lead in the batting race. On July 18 he league-leading batting average stood at .366, and manager Stengel chose him for the American League All-Star team.[13] In Noren's only All-Star Game appearance, a wrist injury suffered on the eve of the game hampered his swing so much that he was unable to bat when manager Casey Stengel asked him to pinch hit in the eighth inning. However, in the ninth inning he replaced Ted Williams in left field. Noren finished the 1954 season with a .319 batting average, fourth in the league. His 12 homers and 66 RBIs were his best in a Yankee uniform. Cleveland, with 110 victories, beat out the Yankees (103 victories) for the pennant.

That season Noren further refined his batting stance, working with Yankees hitting coach Bill Dickey to become a line-drive threat. Most of all, pitchers were no longer able to get ahead of him by getting him to chase high pitches early in the count.

In the second game of the 1955 season, at Boston, Noren, running from second, was gunned down trying to score the tying run. Noren did not agree with the call, bumped umpire Bill McKinley, was thrown out of the game. When Noren's replacement, Elston Howard, entered the game, it was the first time a player of color had played for the Yankees in a regular-season game.[14] (It was also the first time Noren had been thrown out of a game. He was ultimately fined $100 and suspended for three days.)

That season Noren hit a rare inside-the-park grand slam. On May 15 he came to bat against the Kansas City Athletics' Ray Herbert with the bases loaded in a 1-1 game. His drive to left-center field eluded a dive by Suitcase Simpson and rolled to the wall as four runs scored. putting the Yanks ahead 5-1.[15] They went on to win 8-4.

For the year, Noren batted .253 with 8 homers and 59 RBIs. By season's end, he was hobbling on two bad knees, the result of running into a wall chasing a fly ball. In the World Series Noren produced only one hit and one walk in 17 plate appearances as the Brooklyn Dodgers won the Series.

In 1956 Noren's knees continued to give him problems. He missed much of the season, and did not play in the World Series. Noren did well as a pinch-hitter during the season. In 21 plate appearances he went 4-for-13 with eight walks. During a postseason tour of Japan, the pain in his knees became unbearable, and he returned early to have surgery on both knees.

Before the 1957 season, Noren was traded to Kansas City. He was not surprised. Noren was part of a 13-player exchange that resulted in Art Ditmar, Bobby Shantz, and Clete Boyer going to the Yankees, and the A's receiving virtually nothing in exchange. After batting only .213 with the A's, Noren was placed on waivers and was picked up by the St. Louis Cardinals on August 31. His bat came alive in the National League. With the Cardinals, Noren had a great September, batting .367 (11-for-30) in 17 games to help the team to a second-place finish. During spring training in 1958, Noren ran into a wall and saw less action for the Cardinals, batting .264 (47-for-178) in 117 games. During that 1958 season there were five outfielders ahead of the 33-year-old Noren on the Cardinals.

In 1959 Noren was used sparingly early in the season, and on May 19 he was traded to the Chicago Cubs, for whom he ended the season batting .321 (50-for-156) during a fifth-place campaign. The only other Cub with a .300 average was Ernie Banks. Nevertheless, he was released in June 1960 after mostly coming off the bench. Noren latched on with his hometown Los Angeles Dodgers, getting into 26 games, mostly as a pinch hitter, batting .200 and hitting the last of his 65 major-league homers on August 28 against Cincinnati. The Dodgers released him after the season. Noren concluded his 11-year career with a batting average of .275, and appearances in three World Series and one All-Star Game.

In 1962 and '63, Noren managed the Hawaii Islanders, the Los Angeles Angels' Triple-A affiliate. He played in 92 games over the two seasons, batting .240 (36-for-150). He even brought himself in to pitch in nine games, going 1-0 with a 5.73 ERA. He was replaced by Bob Lemon as manager after the 1963 season.

Noren scouted for the Washington Senators in 1964, and was out of baseball from 1965 to 1969. After managing the Niagara Falls Pirates of the Class A New York-Penn League in 1970, he was chosen by longtime friend Dick Williams to serve as the Oakland A's third-base coach in 1971.

Noren remembered the A's fighting in the clubhouse but being all business once they were on the field, although there were occasional brawls with the opposition. At age 48, Noren was not excluded from the fisticuffs. On August 22, 1972, the A's were playing the Detroit Tigers. A brawl broke out in the seventh inning and Noren's eye was cut open when he was blindsided by Detroit's Tom Timmerman.[16] Dick Williams, who had become disillusioned with Charlie Finley, left the A's after the 1973 season. Noren and the new manager, Alvin Dark, did not get along well in 1974. Noren was fired two weeks after the 1974 All-Star Game and joined the Chicago Cubs at third-base coach in 1975.[17]

While playing with the Yankees, Noren saw that Phil Rizzuto and Yogi Berra had enjoyed success operating a bowling alley in New Jersey, and used his World Series winnings from 1956 to invest in a bowling alley in Pasadena.[18] He also owned a liquor store in Arcadia, California, and two sporting-goods stores in Pasadena.

In 1985 Noren was honored in his hometown of Jamestown, New York when he was inducted into the Chautauqua Sports Hall of Fame. He received the Legends Award from the Pasadena Sports Hall of Fame in 2010, and was honored with a Distinguished Alumni Award from Pasadena City College. As recently as 2004, he served as president of the local Homeowners Association. At age 89 in 2013, Noren was not about to slow down. Between talking baseball at Brooklyn Boyz, a local pizza restaurant, and going to Del Mar and Santa Anita race tracks to watch his thoroughbreds owned with two partners, he found plenty to keep him busy. Many of the partners' first horses had baseball-inspired names, including Glove Man, Extra Quick, Delayed Steal, and Midnight Curfew."[19] Later he had success with Pinstripe Kid. He and his late wife, Vee, had a son and three daughters and, as of 2014, 15 grandchildren and six great-grandchildren.

SOURCES

Books

Golenbock, Peter, *Dynasty: The New York Yankees 1949-1964* (New York: Prentice Hall, 1975).

James, Bill, *The New Bill James Historical Baseball Abstract* (New York: Free Press, 2001).

Kelley, Brent P., *They Too Wore Pinstripes: Interviews with 20 Glory Days New York Yankees* (Jefferson, North Carolina: McFarland, 1998).

Madden, Bill, *Pride of October: What It Was to Be Young and a Yankee* (New York: Warner Books 2003).

Schumacher, Michael, *Mr. Basketball: George Mikan, the Minneapolis Lakers, and the Birth of the NBA* (Minneapolis: University of Minnesota Press, 2007).

Williams, Dick, *No More Mr. Nice Guy: A Life of Hardball* (New York: Harcourt, Brace, Jovanovich, 1990).

Articles

Bergman, Ron, "A's Chopping Block Claims Noren, Hoscheit," *The Sporting News*, July 27, 1974, 27.

Daniel, Dan, "Hat's Off: Irv Noren," *The Sporting News*, July 21, 1954, 21.

Dexter, Charles, "Irv Noren—20-Win Hitter: Baker's Son, Senators' New Bat Star, Finds Oppposing Pitching Easy as Pie," *Baseball Digest*, May, 1951, 13-18.

Dyer, Braven (Ray Canton interviewing Stengel and Noren) "Sports Parade," *Los Angeles Times*, June 9, 1953, C1.

Epstein, Ben, "Stand-In Becomes Standout: Understudy Outer Gardener Blossoms in Bronx," (four-part series), *New York Mirror*, July 1954.

Everett, Hap, "There's Nothing New About Noren," *Los Angeles Times*, April 18, 1949, C3.

Heft, Herb, "Nats Nip Bosox 6-5, As Ump Okays Disputed Run," *Washington Post*, August 14, 1950, 10-11.

Hyde, Frank, "Noren, Born Here, Arose Quickly to Major Leagues; Now With Yankees, *Jamestown* (New York) *Post-Journal*, June 24, 1953.

Kelley, Brent P., "Irv Noren Played with Mantle and Mikan," *Sports Collectors Digest*, June 23, 1995, 180-181.

Kindberg, Scott, "An Amazing Life," *Jamestown* (New York) *Post-Journal*, January 23, 2013.

Munzel, Edgar, "Irv and Earl Used Big Bats as Bruin Belters," *The Sporting News*, December 30, 1959, 17.

Povich, Shirley, "Noren, New Nat, has Way of Making Good," *Washington Post*, March 5, 1950, 1C.

Rosenthal, Harold, "New Noren Makes Ol' Case Look Good," *The Sporting News*, August 11, 1954, 3.

Sherman, Lola, "Baseball Holds Great Memories for World Series Veteran," *North County Times* (Escondido, California), May 2, 2012.

Siegel, Morris, "Fracture of Irv Noren's Jaw Puts Squeeze on Nats' Firth Place Dream," *The Sporting News*, August 22, 1951, 9.

Spink, J.G. Taylor, "Looping the Loops: Noren's Proud to be a Yankee," *The Sporting News*, May 28, 1952, 2.

Tarantino, Anthony, "Hair Affairs," *San Diego Union-Tribune*, April 24, 2006.

Zimmerman, Paul, "Noren Can't Hurt, Can Help Dodgers," *Los Angeles Times*, June 8, 1960, C1.

"Health Is Wealth: Noren Hopes Bad Luck Skips Him for Change," *Los Angeles Times*, March 15, 1952, B2.

"Noren Gets Player of the Year Award," *Dallas Morning News*, September 5, 1948, II, 4.

Boston Globe

Chicago Tribune

Dallas Morning News

Los Angeles Times

New York Mirror

New York Times

New York World-Telegram

Riverside (California) *Daily Press*

San Diego Union-Tribune

The Sporting News

Syracuse Post-Standard

Washington Post

Personal Correspondence

Interviews with Irv Noren, August 9, 2013, December 12, 2013, December 20, 2013. Unless otherwise noted, all Noren quotations are from these interviews.

Online

Ancestry.com

BaseballReference.com

Genealogybank.com

Newspapers.com

NOTES

1   Bob Wiede," In the Bullpen," *Riverside* (California) *Daily Press*, March 8, 1949, 14.

2   Brent P. Kelley, "Irv Noren Played with Mantle and Mikan," *Sports Collectors Digest*, June 23, 1995, 181..

3   Michael Schumacher, *Mr. Basketball: George Mikan, the Minneapolis Lakers, and the Birth of the NBA* (Minneapolis: University of Minnesota Press, 2007), 75-76.

4   *Chicago Tribune*, December 13, 1946.

5   Al Wolf, "Sportraits," *Los Angeles Times*, August 22, 1949, c2.

6   Brent P. Kelley, *They Too Wore Pinstripes: Interviews with 20 Glory Days New York Yankees* (Jefferson, North Carolina: McFarland, 1998), 143.

7   Charles Dexter, "Irv Noren — 20-Win Hitter: Baker's Son, Senators' New Bat Star, Finds Oppposing Pitching Easy as Pie," *Baseball Digest*, May, 1951, 14.

8   Bill, James, *The New Bill James Historical Baseball Abstract* (New York: Free Press, 2001), 726.

9   Dexter, 13.

10   Dan Daniel, "Special Courses for Carey, Noren by Prof. Stengel," *The Sporting News*, February 11, 1953, 11.

11   Dan Daniel, "Noren Steps off Block, Nails No. 4 Yank Picket Job," *The Sporting News*, April 8, 1953, 10.

12   Braven Dyer, *Los Angeles Times*, June 9, 1953, C1.

13   Dan Daniel, "Hats Off: Irv Noren," *The Sporting News*, July 21, 1954, 21.

14   Bill Madden, *Pride of October: What It Was to Be Young and a Yankee* (New York: Warner Books 2003), 153.

15   Louis Effrat, "Yankees Divide Doubleheader with Athletics," *New York Times*, May 16, 1955, 29.

16   Dick Williams, *No More Mr. Nice Guy: A Life of Hardball* (New York: Harcourt, Brace, Jovanovich, 1990), 138.

17   Ron Bergman, "A's Chopping Block Claims Noren, Hoscheit," *The Sporting News*, July 27, 1974, 27.

18   Zimmerman, Paul, "Noren Can't Hurt, Can Help Dodgers," *Los Angeles Times*, June 8, 1960, C1.

19   Ed Reddy, *Syracuse Post-Standard*, March 27, 1990.

Bill Posedel

By Gregory H. Wolf

Most commonly remembered as the pitching coach-guru who helped develop the dominating staffs for the Oakland A's championship teams of 1972-1974, Bill Posedel had a career in Organized Baseball spanning six decades, from the late 1920s to the 1970s. He debuted in the big leagues with the Brooklyn Dodgers in 1938 as a hard-throwing 31-year-old right-handed pitcher after more than eight grueling years in the minors. He was the top winner for manager Casey Stengel and the Boston Bees in 1939 and 1940, but suffered an arm injury in 1941 and never regained his form. After four years in the US Navy and a return to Boston in 1946, Posedel established his legacy as an insightful scout, coach, and expert evaluator of talent.

A lifelong career in baseball was far from foretold when Bill Posedel was born on August 2, 1906, in San Francisco, less than four months after the great earthquake and resulting fires destroyed about 80 percent of the city. His parents, Joseph and Johanna Posedel, German-speaking immigrants from Austro-Hungary, arrived in the United States in 1901 and had settled in San Francisco by 1904. Bill, the third of the couple's six children, is listed as Wilhelm Johann on US census reports from 1910 and 1920. In light of World War I and its aftermath, many German-American families Americanized their names and quickly assimilated. Wilhelm Johann became William John. The Posedels lived in Candlestick Cove, an industrialized section in the southern part of the city (near where Candlestick Park was later built), but during the war moved to Vallejo, a small town 30 miles north on the San Pablo Bay, where Joseph worked as a riveter in the burgeoning Navy shipyard. By all accounts an athletic youngster, the right-handed Posedel recalled in an interview with *The Sporting News* that he played baseball year-round in the temperate climate of Northern California and pitched in local sandlot leagues. "[I] was torn

between two ambitions," Posedel recollected upon graduation from St. Vincent High School.[1] He wanted to play baseball, but the ships he saw daily in the harbor unleashed a more alluring passion for traveling the world and escaping his prosaic surroundings.

Posedel enlisted in the Navy, but never strayed far from baseball. Traveling throughout the Pacific, he pitched for various fleet teams and achieved his greatest success when he led the USS Saratoga to the championship of Pacific Fleet B Division.[2] According to Posedel, upon his discharge in 1929, after four years of service, he had a stroke of luck. He met Tony Rego, catcher for the Portland Beavers of the Pacific Coast League, while the team was in Los Angeles. Accepting Rego's invitation to work out for the team at Wrigley Field, Posedel impressed manager Bill Rodgers and club president Tom Turner, who offered the 23-year-old pitcher a contract in August.[3] Posedel debuted in the

final weeks of the season and posted a 2.65 ERA in 17 innings.

Posedel returned to the Beavers in 1930, but struggled, surrendering almost two baserunners per nine innings in 26⅔ innings. "I was green as grass," said Posedel. "I soon found out that I didn't even know how to stand on the mound."[4] He was dispatched to the Pueblo (Colorado) Braves of the Class A Western League, where he logged 95 innings and posted a 5.12 ERA.

Success did not come as easily in professional baseball as it had in the Navy for Posedel, who acquired the sobriquets Sailor Bill, Barnacle Bill, and Ole Porthole from sportswriters (teammates often called him Posey). At one point during his minor-league career, he even contemplated quitting baseball to work full-time as a shipbuilder in Vallejo, but he persevered.[5] With a "high fast one with a wicked break," the 5-foot-11, 175-pound Posedel tried to blow past the hitters, but veteran PCL batters, many with big-league experience, waited for his heater.[6] After Posedel posted a 7-6 record but an unsightly 5.12 ERA in 131 innings in 1931, the Beavers traded him to the Wichita Aviators of the Class A Western League for 25-game winner Art Jacobs, and he was subsequently transferred to the Tulsa Oilers of the same league.

Posedel pitched for Tulsa from 1932 through early 1935 and helped lead the Oilers to the league championship in 1932 by posting a 16-10 record. "[In 1932 and 1933] I was still a Navy pitcher trying to pitch ball in the better minor leagues," said Posedel years later about his maturation process as a pitcher and his breakout season as a workhorse in 1934 (15 wins, 45 appearances, and 270 innings). "Art Griggs was president-manager of the club and a great baseball man. He was patient with me and finally made a pitcher out of me."[7] Notwithstanding his 1-7 record, Posedel was traded back to Portland in June 1935 for outfielder George Blackerby.[8]

Posedel experienced his biggest professional pitching success for the Beavers from 1935 through 1937. A 12-7 record after his trade suggested even greater heights

in 1936, but Posedel got off to a slow start, winning just three of his first ten decisions. He then caught fire, winning 17 of his final 20 starts to finish with 20 victories (sixth-most in the league). Before the season ended the Cincinnati Reds purchased his contract on a contingent basis.[9] Posedel won three more games in the Beavers' march to the league title. *The Sporting News* reported that Posedel was "not a pitcher of the sensational type … [but] has lots of stuff [and] improves under fire."[10]

The 30-year-old Posedel arrived at his first big-league training camp where he battled young, hard-throwing phenom Johnny Vander Meer and fellow PCL standout Dick Barrett for the chance to break into the rotation. After a good start, Posedel came down with arm problems. Dejected and suffering from homesickness, he requested to be returned to Portland, where he thought he could recover better. Cincinnati acquiesced, and Posedel responded with another outstanding campaign, setting career highs in wins (21) and innings (300), and once again attracted big-league scouts. On the recommendation of scout Ted McGrew, the Brooklyn Dodgers purchased Posedel's contract for an estimated $10,000 and sent outfielder Eddie Wilson and catcher Elmer Klumpp to complete the deal.[11]

Posedel joined a second-division club whose most obvious glaring weakness was starting pitching. Dodgers beat writers optimistically predicted that Posedel and a fellow rookie, Tot Pressnell, would match the success of the Boston Bees rookie duo of the previous year, 20-game winners Lou Fette and Jim Turner. Posedel made his major-league debut on April 23 by replacing Fred Frankhouse in the third inning against the New York Giants at Ebbets Field. Yielding just three hits over 5⅓ innings but collared with the loss, Sailor Bill fell victim to shoddy defense, which surrendered three unearned runs. Posedel earned his first win four weeks later when he tossed an eight-hit complete game to defeat the St. Louis Cardinals, 8-4, at Sportsman's Park. Used as a spot starter through June, Posedel made seven consecutive starts in July, won four of them, including his first shutout, a seven-hitter against the Philadelphia Phillies. But his success was fleeting. A horrendous August (1-5 with a 7.31 ERA) led to his demotion to the bullpen in September. His 8-9 record in 140 innings was tempered by the league's highest ERA (5.66) for pitchers with at least 100 innings. To make matters worse, Posedel broke his jaw on the last day of the season while warming up in the bullpen.

As a rookie Posedel clashed with Dodger veteran Leo Durocher, who wanted Sailor Bill to ease off the ball when he threw batting practice. Posedel refused, arguing that grooving the ball would throw off his timing in games.[12] When Durocher was named skipper of the team in 1939, tensions between the two were palpable. In a move generally described as a surprise by the press, Posedel was traded to the Boston Bees for catcher Al Todd, on March 31, 1939. Boston, coming off its second consecutive winning season, was led by a pitching staff that ranked second in team ERA the previous season, but was also the second oldest staff in the league. Casey Stengel, in his second year piloting the club, viewed 32-year-old Posedel as a cagey veteran despite his relative lack of big-league experience. Essentially a two-pitch pitcher (fastball and hard curve) with a high leg kick and a three-quarters to overhand motion, Posedel worked on developing a change-of-pace (and later slow curve) and the results were immediate.[13] On Opening Day, Posedel pitched three hitless innings of relief to earn the win in a dramatic 7-6 victory over Philadelphia in 12 innings.

Having earned the confidence of Stengel, Posedel entered the starting rotation on May 1 and proved to be one of the NL's biggest surprises over the next four months, completing 16 of 24 starts and winning 14 games for the underachieving Bees. During his most productive stretch as a big leaguer, he tossed five shutouts, including the best game of his career, a one-hitter against the Pittsburgh Pirates in which he surrendered only a fifth-inning single to Pep Young. "Casey taught me plays I never knew were in the book," Posedel said of his success, and he credited his skipper and especially catcher Al Lopez for giving him confidence in his pitches and helping him relax.[14] Posedel seemingly tired at the end of the season, losing

his last four decisions to finish at 15-13, but still led the seventh-place Bees in almost every pitching category, including wins, innings (220⅔), starts (29), and complete games (18). His five shutouts tied for second most in the league, behind teammate Lou Fette's six. Posedel's season was a study in contrasts: In his 15 wins he pitched brilliantly with a sparkling 1.75 ERA; however, he was equally dismal in his other 18 appearances posting a 6.68 ERA.

The Bees duplicated their seventh-place finish in 1940 and Barnacle Bill once again led the team in wins (12, tied with Dick Errickson), starts (32), and complete games (18), and was second in innings (233). A veritable Jekyll and Hyde on the mound, Posedel was commanding in his 12 wins (a stellar 1.73 ERA), but posted an alarming 6.08 ERA in his 17 losses. He struck out a career-best 11 in a six-hit win over the Pirates on June 17, but indicative of his season-long inconsistency, allowed 24 hits and 15 runs (included a career-worst ten against Brooklyn) in his next two starts. Unlike the previous season, Posedel finished the campaign in strong fashion, winning six of his last ten decisions, including a career-best ten-inning complete-game victory against Philadelphia at Shibe Park, 3-2, on September 7.

The elder statesman of the staff in 1941, Posedel arrived at spring training in San Antonio refreshed from a monthlong stay at the thermal spas in Hot Springs, Arkansas. Held out of the rotation the first two weeks of the season to spare him from pitching in the cold weather of the Northeast, Posedel responded by tossing complete-game victories in his first two starts of the year. The success proved to be illusory. After his next start he came down with a sore arm, then developed leg problems trying to overcompensate, and never fully recovered. He logged just 57⅓ innings and won four of eight decisions for the Braves, who finished in seventh place for the third consecutive year.

Given his arm and leg injuries, the 35-year-old Posedel was at a crossroads in his career when the Japanese bombed Pearl Harbor on December 7, 1941, striking fear in Americans and initiating a profound patriotic response. He was also a bachelor once again as his marriage to Erma Pyke, a Vallejo woman whom he married in 1933, had ended in divorce by 1940. Consequently, his military classification changed from 3-A to 1-A, making him eligible for the draft. On January 31, 1942, Posedel re-enlisted in the navy and was stationed at the naval bases Mare Island in Vallejo and Treasure Island in San Francisco, but spent most of the war as a chief of gun crews on merchant ships throughout the Pacific Theater. After almost four years of service, he was discharged on August 30, 1945.

Posedel was unsure if he would attempt a big-league comeback after his discharge. But Denny Carroll, nationally renowned trainer for the Detroit Tigers, whom Posedel knew from their days together in San Francisco, encouraged him to give it one shot.[15] Boston general managers Bob Quinn and his son John Quinn, who succeeded Bob following his retirement after the 1945 season, also felt a sense of duty to Posedel, and invited the 39-year-old pitcher to spring training in 1946. The team had undergone a drastic transformation in Barnacle Bill's four-year absence. First-year skipper Billy Southworth led a club deep in pitching (Johnny Sain, Warren Spahn, and Mort Cooper) and poised to challenge for the NL pennant. Southworth recognized Posedel as a student of the game who had also begun umpiring in the Navy, and gave him his first informal coaching job. In spring training Posedel served as first-base coach for intrasquad and split-squad games. Though Sailor Bill's productive pitching days were behind him (he made 19 relief appearances and posted a 6.99 ERA in 28⅓ innings), he served as a mentor to young pitchers.

Posedel planned on retiring at the conclusion of the 1946 season to embark on an umpiring career, but changed his mind when he was sold to the Seattle Rainiers in the PCL with the extra duties as serving as pitching coach.[16] Pitching beyond his 41st birthday, Posedel won 12 of 20 decisions and logged 131 innings for the Rainiers before retiring as a player at the end of the season. He finished with a 41-43 record and 4.56 ERA in 679⅓ innings in his five-year big-league career and also won 119 games in his minor-league career.

Posedel embarked on a career spanning four decades as an acclaimed scout, coach, and pitching instructor when the Pittsburgh Pirates named him a scout for the Rocky Mountain area in 1948. As with most big-league coaches at the time, Posedel was poorly paid and his professional life was in constant fluctuation; coaching staffs turned over as managers came and went. During the first half of his post-playing career, Posedel served on the staffs of the Pirates (1949-1953), St. Louis Cardinals (1954-1956), Philadelphia Phillies (1958), and San Francisco Giants (1959-1960), and scouted for the Cleveland Indians (1961). Along the way he built a reputation as a tireless and dedicated pitching instructor capable of helping young hurlers like Bob Friend and Vern Law of the Pirates develop into aces, and helping veterans like Sam Jones of the Giants resurrect their careers. Posedel's big-league coaching career was interrupted for one year when he took over the helm of his former team, the Portland Beavers, in 1957 after their manager, Bill Sweeney, died six games into the season.

Posedel is often seen as one of the architects of the dominant Oakland A's pitching staffs of their World Series years (1972-1974). His association with the team began in 1962 when the club was still in Kansas City. The long-suffering franchise hired Posedel as a scout, pitching supervisor, and organizational pitching coach. During his five years in that capacity (1962-1967), he helped develop such prospects as Catfish Hunter, Blue Moon Odom, Chuck Dobson, Lew Krausse, and Jim Nash. That quintet led the A's in their inaugural year in Oakland (1968) to their first season over .500 since 1952 (when the team was still owned by legendary Connie Mack and located in Philadelphia) by starting a combined 157 games, winning 64, and pitching in excess of 1,100 innings. Coincidence or not, 1968 also marked the first of five consecutive years that Posedel served as the team's pitching coach. The A's posted winning seasons in all five of those campaigns, and continued the streak for four more years after Posedel retired.

Posedel was universally praised by his players as a player's coach who led by example and not wrath.

"He's got great patience," said Dobson.[17] He was amiable, good-natured, and approachable, and called everyone "Chief." In turn, his players affectionately called him Chief. "Sometimes I feel more or less like a father," Posedel said of his relationship to his pitchers. "They're all pretty good kids and I'm always pulling for them to get ahead."[18]

"He's gets the best out of the pitchers," said former A's manager Bob Kennedy of Posedel's ability to coax maximum effort from his charges.[19] Posedel was an expert in noticing slight flaws in delivery and follow-through; Odom and Hunter credited him for helping their windup and delivery. When the pitching mound was lowered to ten inches in 1969 to stimulate more offense, Posedel taught his pitchers to bend their left knee for a more effective delivery. He encouraged his pitchers to bring their arms high above their heads in order to generate more power. Along with manager Dick Williams, Posedel is credited with helping convert the notoriously nervous Rollie Fingers from a mediocre reliever and spot starter into the era's foremost fireman and backbone of the A's relief corps during their five consecutive AL West crowns (1971-1975). Hunter paid Posedel an especially insightful tribute, stating that the coach endeared himself to players by letting them learn from their mistakes. "Posedel offer[ed] suggestions on mechanics, not lectures," said Catfish.[20] Barnacle Bill stressed physical fitness, made his pitchers run, and pitched batting practice well into his 60s.

Prior to Oakland's tension-filled march to their first championship, in 1972, Posedel announced his intention to retire from baseball. At the age of 66, he finally reached the pinnacle of team success when the A's defeated the Cincinnati Reds, 3-2, in Game Seven of the World Series. In the offseason, he was feted in Oakland by current and former players who paid tribute to his contribution to their success. Posedel's retirement was temporary; he agreed to serve as the team's minor-league pitching instructor for one more season.

Posedel was lured out of retirement again in 1974 when close friend John McNamara, who had piloted the A's in 1970, was named manager of the San Diego Padres. Posedel was on the staff for just one season, but maintained his association with the Padres, serving as pitching coach emeritus and instructing regularly at the team's spring training through the late 1970s.

A lifelong resident of the Bay area in California, Posedel retired to San Leandro with his second wife, Della Irene (Locker), with whom he one daughter. Confined to a wheelchair in the last few years of his life, Posedel died in Livermore, California, on November 28, 1989, at the age of 83 after a long battle with colon cancer.[21] He was cremated and his ashes were scattered at sea. In 2006 he was inducted into the Vallejo Sports Hall of Fame.[22]

SOURCES

Bill Posedel player file, National Baseball Hall of Fame, Cooperstown, New York

The Sporting News

Ancestry.com

BaseballLibrary.com

Baseball-Reference.com

Retrosheet.org

NOTES

1   *The Sporting News*, August 31, 1939, 3.

2   Harold Seymour, *Baseball: The People's Game*. Volume 3 (New York and Oxford: Oxford University Press, 1991), 354.

3   *The Sporting News*, August 31, 1939, 3.

4   Ibid.

5   Tommy Holmes, "Rookie Reds Discarded Viewed as Young Man Of Great Possibilities," *The Eagle* (Brooklyn, New York), 1938. [no date]. [Player's Hall of Fame file].

6   *The Sporting News*, August 20, 1931, 3.

7   *The Sporting News*, August 31, 1939, 3.

8   *The Sporting News*, August 1, 1935, 1.

9   *The Sporting News*, September 17, 1936, 1.

10 *The Sporting News*, November 12, 1936, 2.

11 *The Sporting News*, September 9, 1937, 13.

12 Dan Daniel, "Daniel's Dope," *New York World-Telegram*, August 25, 1939 [no page number]. [Player's Hall of Fame file].

13 *The Sporting News*, March 16, 1939, 6.

14 *The Sporting News*, August 31, 1939, 3.

15 From the personal correspondence of Hy Hurwitz, sports reporter for the *Boston Globe*, April 25, 1945 [Player's Hall of Fame file].

16 *The Sporting News*, December 11, 1946, 12.

17 *The Sporting News*, September 28, 1968, 18.

18 Michael Hagerty, "Posedel Begins 42nd Year in Baseball," Oakland A's News Release, 1971 [Player's Hall of Fame file].

19 Ibid.

20 Paul Hensler, *The American League in Transition, 1965–1975. How Competition Thrived When the Yankees Didn't* (Jefferson, North Carolina: McFarland, 2012), 166.

21 Bill Lee, *The Baseball Necrology* (Jefferson, North Carolina: McFarland, 2003), 322.

22 Ken Hart, "Vallejo's pioneering pitcher," *Times-Herald Sports* (Vallejo, California), March 19, 2006. timesheraldonline.com/sports/ci_3619210.

Jim Roland

By Gregory H. Wolf

Signed by the Minnesota Twins in 1961, left-hander Jim Roland debuted as a 19-year-old in a September call-up the following season and tossed a three-hit shutout in his first big-league start, in 1963. "[He] has a blazing fast ball and is effectively wild," wrote Twins beat reporter Arno Goethel.[1] Battling injuries and control issues throughout his ten-year big-league career, most notably with the Twins and Oakland A's (1962-1972), Roland never realized the potential his inaugural start suggested and was relegated to the unglamorous role of long reliever and mop-up artist. He was also unlucky: Seven years after Roland missed the Twins' pennant in 1965 when he spent the year in Triple-A, the A's sold him to the New York Yankees in 1972, the season they won their first of three consecutive World Series.

James Ivan Roland, Jr. was born on December 14, 1942, in the small town of Franklin, nestled in the Smoky Mountains of western North Carolina. His parents were James Ivan Sr., a pipefitter by trade, and Florence Virginia (Henson) Roland. By the time Jim was in the fourth grade in the early 1950s, the family had relocated to Raleigh, more than 300 miles to the east, where Jim Sr. found employment as a guard and maintenance man at a local prison. Like many youths, Jim Jr. got his start on the diamond in a local Little League. By the time he was a junior at Broughton High School in Raleigh, the tall (6-feet-3), yet thin (160-pound, though he grew bigger) hard-throwing southpaw had the attention of scouts. On the recommendation of scout Al Evans, Minnesota Twins executive vice president Joe Haynes signed Roland upon his graduation in 1961 for a $50,000 signing bonus. It was widely reported that the hefty financial incentive was the largest the Twins/Senators ever paid to a pitcher.[2] (The Washington Senators relocated to Minnesota for the 1961 season.)

Just weeks removed from high school, the 18-year-old Roland began his professional baseball career in the Class B Carolina League with the Wilson Tobs, a team located less than 50 miles from his hometown. Roland impressed the Twins brass by winning seven of 13 decisions and posting a fine 3.15 ERA in 123 innings for the first-place Tobs. After the season, he was added to the Twins' 40-man roster and sent to the Florida Instructional League to work on his control (4.9 walks per nine innings) with manager Del Wilber, a former big-league catcher and respected developer of young pitching prospects.[3]

Roland, coming off an ankle operation in the offseason, reported to Minnesota's spring-training facility in 1962. The Twins had finished with a lackluster 70-90 record (seventh place) in the first year of expansion in the AL, and desperately needed a hard-throwing

lefty to compete with the likes of the New York Yankees and Detroit Tigers. With less than a full season of Class B ball under his belt, Roland was sent along with other prospects (outfielder Tony Oliva and another hard-throwing lefty, Gary Dotter) to the Class A Charlotte (North Carolina) Hornets of the South Atlantic League (Sally). Roland struggled against more experienced competition (1-3, 4.17 ERA in 41 innings) and was reassigned to Wilson. Roland excelled for the below-.500 club. Named to the league's all-star team, he sported only a 10-8 record, but was the hardest-to-hit hurler in circuit (5.4 hits per nine innings), ranked second in ERA (1.98), and was third in strikeouts per nine innings (10.6). Twice the southpaw struck out 14 batters in a game to go along with 12 and 13 punchouts in two other contests,

Roland's performance with the Tobs earned him a late-season look-see with the Twins. On September 20 he made his major-league debut (and his only major-league appearance of the season). In relief of Jim Kaat, Roland tossed two scoreless innings, yielding a hit and striking out one.

The young lefty was back with Del Wilber in the Florida Instructional League in the fall of 1962. For all of his potential, Roland also walked 6.1 hitters per nine innings for the Tobs. Along with teammates Oliva, Orlando Martinez (infield-utility), and Joe McCabe (pitcher), Roland was named to the league's all-star team. He was also chosen as the "Rookie Pitcher" in the Florida Instructional League. He was widely expected to be the Twins' fifth starter in 1963.[4]

Roland made a big splash in his second camp with the Twins. "[He's] blossomed as the surprise of spring training," praised *The Sporting News*.[5] The newspaper also tabbed him as the "Best Young Pitcher" and the "Most Personable Newcomer" in light of his constant smile, talkative personality, and infectious enthusiasm.[6] "Lots of good natural stuff," said manager Sam Mele of his youthful prospect.[7] Roland earned his first big-league win in a wacky game on April 16, 1963, at Metropolitan Stadium. The eighth Twins pitcher of the contest, he tossed the last two frames against the Los Angeles Angels. He gave up a go-ahead run in

the 13th inning, but was bailed out by the powerful Twins offense in the bottom of the frame. Roland tossed a masterful three-hit, 144-pitch shutout in his first major-league start, on April 21 against the Chicago White Sox at Comiskey Park. He whiffed seven, but also walked nine, and got out of bases-loaded jams in the first and fifth innings. After struggling in his next four starts, Roland hurled a complete-game five-hitter on June 1 to defeat the Detroit Tigers, and seemed even stronger in his next outing, on June 5, when he held the Kansas City A's to just two hits in seven innings. However, that game proved to be disastrous for his career. "Something snapped," said Roland about the pain he felt in elbow after a pitch in that game.[8] "My elbow was swollen so much I couldn't wear a suit coat because the sleeve wouldn't fit over the elbow."[9] Save for a brief one-third-inning outing six weeks later, Roland was inactive for the rest of the season. Team physician Dr. Bill Profitt diagnosed the injury as ripping "scar tissue in his muscle," but not a tear, and prescribed rest.[10]

Sportswriter Arno Goethel, described Roland as "one of the biggest question marks in the Twins camp" in 1964.[11] The question mark got even bigger when Roland arrived in camp more than 40 pounds overweight — at about 223 pounds — drawing the ire of Mele.[12] The Twins had two dependable left-handed starters, Jim Kaat and Dick Stigman; consequently, Roland was tabbed as a swingman. He had counted primarily on his overhand fastball, curve, and effective changeup through his first three years in the pro ball, but added a slider to his repertoire in spring training. He unveiled the pitch in a spot start against New York in Yankee Stadium on May 19. He hurled a career-high 12 innings (and faced 50 batters), holding the eventual pennant winners to seven hits and two runs, while striking out eight and walking six. He was replaced by pinch-hitter Lenny Green in the 13th inning when the Twins exploded for five runs, making Roland the winner. Roland's 12-inning effort has been surpassed only twice in Minnesota Twins history (Camilo Pascual went 12⅔ innings against Cleveland in 1963 and Jim Merritt logged 13 innings against the Yankees in 1967.) "I've never seen a pitcher pick up [the slider] any faster," said pitching coach George Maltzberger about Roland's outing.[13] Two starts later the southpaw tossed an overpowering two-hitter against the Boston Red Sox, but struggled thereafter, losing four of his next five starts and his spot in the rotation. Confined to mop-up duty for the remainder of the season, Roland posted a 2-6 record and a 4.10 ERA in 94⅓ innings, while battling control problems (6.0 walks per nine innings).

Roland's once promising career had been marred by injuries (ankle and elbow), and by 1965 he seemed washed up at age 22. Dabbled as trade bait in the offseason, Roland struggled in spring training in 1965 under new pitching coach Johnny Sain. A pulled thigh muscle set him in further back in competition with Dwight Siebler, Dave Boswell, and Jim Merritt for a spot on the staff. He was optioned to the Denver Bears of the Triple-A Pacific Coast League, where a series of immature incidents made manager Cal Ermer question his commitment to the game. Roland injured his knee jumping in protest of a call by a first-base umpire in July. And he committed the cardinal sin of walking off the mound on several occasions while Ermer was on his way to remove him.[14] In primarily a starting role, the left-hander won eight, lost six, and posted a 3.81 ERA in 156 innings. He was recalled by the Twins in September but did not pitch.

Called a "problem kid" by Twins beat reporter Max Nichols, Roland reported to the Twins' spring training hoping for a new beginning.[15] He had been "disillusioned and discouraged" by his year in Denver, but appeared stronger and healthier in 1966.[16] "Roland is throwing the way he did in 1963 — hard and low," said team owner and general manager Calvin Griffith optimistically.[17] Roland also donned spectacles for the first time, claiming that poor depth perception had contributed to his erratic pitching. Despite the praise, Roland couldn't crack the deep Twins staff, and was sent back to Denver to start the season. Splitting his time with the Bears and the Syracuse Chiefs of the International League, Roland endured a horrific campaign, winning just six times, leading all Triple-A hurlers with 19 losses, and finishing with an unsightly

4.80 ERA in 163 innings. A September call-up, Roland made his first big-league appearance in more than two years by tossing two scoreless innings of mop-up duty in his only outing with the Twins.

Out of player options, Roland stuck with the Twins in 1967 and 1968. During spring training in 1967, an Associated Press story described Roland as "one of the most disappointing investments Calvin Griffith ever made."[18] Relegated to the unceremonious role of mop-up man, he logged only 35⅔ innings spread over 25 relief appearances in 1967 and 61⅔ innings (in 28 games) in 1968. His final win in a Twins uniform was a complete-game five-hitter (one of his four starts in the 1968 season) against the Washington Senators on August 27.

During those two years, the Twins tried everything to help Roland rekindle the magic his first start suggested. He joined less experienced prospects in the Florida Instructional league in 1967 in order to work extensively with Twins pitching coach, Early Wynn. The little-used Roland had developed bad habits and poor mechanics. "He's been bending his waist," said the future Hall of Fame pitcher, who admitted that it might be too late to reform the lefty.[19]

Roland's approach to life changed radically during his season with Aragua in the Venezuelan winter league in 1967-1968. He pitched well (5-3 with a 2.24 ERA, plus three more victories in the playoffs), but lying awake at night in his one-room accommodation made him take stock in his career and purpose in life. "Suddenly I felt that if I couldn't have my family with me, I needed somebody else on my side. I became a believer," he told Arno Goethel. "Since I've become more serious about Christianity, I've eased my mind."[20] For the remainder of his life, Roland was guided by his religious convictions.

The sale of Roland to the Oakland A's on February 24, 1969, merited little press coverage. In parts of six big-league seasons he had posted a 10-9 record and logged just 244⅔ innings. Nonetheless, the A's were willing to take a chance on the hard-throwing left-hander, especially since he was just 26. After 13 consecutive losing seasons in Kansas City (1955-1967), the A's were a team on the rise. In their maiden season in Oakland (1968), they enjoyed their first winning campaign since 1952, when they were located in Philadelphia and still owned by Connie Mack. Led by a young pitching staff including Catfish Hunter, Chuck Dobson, Blue Moon Odom, Jim Nash, Lew Krausse, and Rollie Fingers, the A's seemed poised for an even better season in 1969.

In his first year with Oakland, Roland enjoyed his best season in the big leagues. While right-hander Fingers and left-hander Paul Lindblad were the first two firemen out of the bullpen, Roland was assigned to long relief and often pitched in mop-up games. The A's lost 27 times in his 36 relief appearances (the team's overall record was 88-74), but Roland sparkled with a 2.82 ERA in 60⅔ innings out of the bullpen. With the pennant out of reach, manager John McNamara gave Roland a chance to start. The southpaw responded by winning a career-best three consecutive starts, beginning with a complete-game four-hitter against the California Angels in Anaheim on September 21. "This is the best year I've got control of both my slider and fastball every time I go out there," he said.[21] Roland will forever hold the distinction of pitching the final game against the Pilots in their brief, one-year tenure in Seattle. In the 162nd game of the season, Roland limited the Pilots to seven hits and matched his career high with nine strikeouts in a 3-1 victory in front of just 5,473 spectators in the final major-league game in Seattle's Sick's Stadium. An atrocious hitter, Roland also recorded his last hit in the big leagues (he went 6-for-84 with one RBI in his career). A's beat reporter Ron Bergman described Roland's showing as a starter as "impressive," while team brass promised to take a closer look at him as a fifth starter the next season.[22] He finished the season with a 5-1 record and career- and staff-low 2.19 ERA in 86⅓ innings.

Breaking into the A's starting rotation was easier said than done. The trio of Hunter, Dobson, and Odom had started 102 games between them and logged 713⅔ innings in 1969. However, the team lacked a left-handed starter. In spring training Roland competed for a job with hard-throwing Al Downing, acquired in the offseason from the New York Yankees. But Roland had an awful camp, struggled with mechanics, and was back in long relief, save for two ineffective starts.[23] Downing won the job, but was ineffective, and ultimately was sent to the Milwaukee Brewers at the trading deadline. Ron Bergman called Roland "one of the best (long relievers) in the business" and noted that the role is "one of the least respected jobs in baseball."[24] Roland hurled 2⅓ and 3⅔ innings to earn victories in August, but the latter win was costly. In that game, on August 11, he collided with the Cleveland Indians' Ray Fosse at home plate and tore ligaments in his right knee. "It was like hitting a wall," said Roland, who tried to jump over Fosse, instead of barreling over the catcher as Pete Rose had done about a month earlier in the All-Star game.[25] Roland landed on the disabled list and pitched just twice after that, finishing with a robust 2.70 ERA in 43⅓ innings spread over 28 appearances. His injury opened the door for the highly-touted prospect lefty Vida Blue, who was summoned from Triple-A Iowa.

With the triumvirate of Fingers, Bob Locker, and rubber-armed lefty Darold Knowles firmly ensconced as the A's relievers, Roland occupied his position at the far end of the bullpen bench in 1971. Manager Dick Williams called on him 31 times, and 26 of those were in mop-up losses. Roland went 1-3 with a 3.18 ERA in 45⅓ innings.

Plagued by recurring arm pain, Roland was a baseball nomad in 1972. After just two appearances for the A's, he was sold to the New York Yankees on April 28. A little more than four months (and 16 mainly ineffective appearances) later, he was traded to the Texas Rangers for pitcher Casey Cox. A combined 5.28 ERA in 30⅔ innings earned Roland his outright release from the Rangers. At just 29 years of age, Roland's professional career was over.

Roland chalked up a 19-17 record over parts of ten seasons, and compiled a 3.22 ERA in 450⅓ innings. In four seasons in the minor leagues, he went 32-42 with a 3.48 ERA in 651 innings.

After his playing days, Roland returned to North Carolina and began a long and successful career as a business representative for a sporting-goods company. He was active in the Elizabeth Baptist Church in his hometown of Shelby, North Carolina. Diagnosed with cancer, he retired from his job in January 2010. On March 6, 2010, Roland died in Shelby. He was survived by his wife, Vicki (Whiten) Roland, and four adult children, James III, Jan, Lori, and Megan.[26] He was buried in Oakland Cemetery, in Gaffney, South Carolina, his wife's hometown, about 20 miles from Shelby.

SOURCES

Chicago Tribune

New York Times

The Sporting News

Ancestry.com

BaseballAlmanac.com

BaseballCube.com

BaseballLibrary.com

Baseball-Reference.com

SABR.org

NOTES

1   *The Sporting News*, February 1, 1964, 22.

2   *The Sporting News*, May 4, 1963, 9.

3   *The Sporting News*, October 11, 1961, 26.

4   *The Sporting News*, April 13, 1963, 5.

5   *The Sporting News*, April 6, 1963, 2.

6   *The Sporting News*, April 20, 1963, 14.

7   *The Sporting News*, May 4, 1963, 9.

8   *The Sporting News*, February 1, 1964, 22.

9   Ibid.

10   *The Sporting News*, December 7, 1963, 22.

11   *The Sporting News*, February 1, 1964, 22.

12   *The Sporting News*, March 26, 1966, 12.

13   *The Sporting News*, June 4, 1964, 8.

14   *The Sporting News*, July 17, 1965, 50.

15   *The Sporting News*, March 26, 1966, 12.

16   Ibid.

17   Ibid.

18   Associated Press, "Jim Roland May Yet Repay Twins," *The Daily Republic* (Mitchell, South Dakota), March 28, 1967, 9.

19   *The Sporting News*, October 28, 1967, 20.

20   *The Sporting News*, September 21, 1967, 9.

21   *The Sporting News*, September 27, 1969, 16.

22   *The Sporting News*, October 18, 1969, 36.

23   *The Sporting News*, April 18, 1970, 12.

24   *The Sporting News*, September 5, 1970, 10.

25   Ibid.

26   Obituary, *Shelby* (North Carolina) *Star*. legacy.com/obituaries/shelbystar/obituary.aspx?n=jim-roland&pid=140499740.

Diego Segui

by Joanne Hulbert

On October 16, 1975, in the eighth inning of Game Five of the World Series, the Red Sox trailed the Reds 5-1. In the bottom of the eighth, Dick Pole walked Johnny Bench and Tony Perez. Diego Segui, one of Boston's two Cuban pitchers, replaced Pole and inherited a tough situation: two men on, no outs, George Foster advancing to the plate, and a crowd of 50,000 in Cincinnati not satisfied with the comfortable lead. Later, Dick Pole was asked what he thought about while out there during the few minutes of his World Series mound appearance. He said it was exactly what he didn't want to have happen, and he'd have to live with that memory.

No one asked Diego Segui, who relieved Pole, about his performance: how he got Foster, a formidable hitter during the regular season, to hit a fly ball to Dwight Evans, with Bench moving over to third and Perez waiting it out at first; then allowed Dave Concepcion to drive home Bench with his own fly to Evans.

For there is little glory in it for the relief pitcher. Their brief mound appearances provide scant inspiration to reporters prowling for after-game stories. Diego Segui had traveled a long way in the major leagues before he found himself on the mound in his only World Series appearance. And yet there is a great story to be told about him.

Born on August 17, 1937 — or 1938 by other reports — in Holguin, Cuba, " la tierra de campeones." Although a right-handed pitcher, he was a southpaw in every other activity of daily living, writing, eating; and, if required, could pitch that way too. "Not too well, though," he said in an interview with Hy Zimmerman in the *Seattle Daily Times* in 1969. "Been throwing other way too long. I was changed when I was [a] little boy in Cuba. It was so long ago, I do not remember who or why. But I changed. Maybe they needed

a right-hander. I grew up on [a] farm. Not many kids in the neighborhood. We played baseball in fields with small teams. Maybe five, six boys on a side. I was [a] good hitter. I thought I would get to baseball that way. But I throw hard. So they make me a pitcher."[1]

Diego Segui was signed by the Cincinnati Reds in 1958 after being scouted by Al Zarilla. But the Reds released Segui in April and he spent the season pitching for Tucson, a team in the Class C Arizona-Mexico League with no major-league affiliation. At the end of September Tucson sold him to the Kansas City Athletics. The next three seasons Segui pitched in the Athletics farm system and spent the offseason with teams around Central America and Venezuela, prompting concern that he would squander his pitching arm on meaningless games, instead of saving it for the major leagues. But Segui considered the off-

season an opportunity to stay in shape. When Fidel Castro canceled the Cuban Winter League season in 1961, players were confronted with a choice between returning to Cuba and joining amateur leagues or professional baseball outside their homeland. Segui had not been back to Cuba after 1960. His parents and sister were still there. His brother Dario, a pitching prospect, had a 13-4 record in the Florida State League until he hurt his arm. "He was better pitcher than I. Much too bad." Among the notable players who did not return to Cuba were Tony Oliva, Jose Cardenal, Cookie Rojas, and Frank Herrera.

In 1960, US players had been barred from playing in games in Havana, where the winter league had long attracted many major-league prospects. Cuban sports commissioner Jose Llanura struck the final blow in 1961 when he announced that any Cuban player who failed to return to Cuba by the end of November would lose all his property and be required to have a 1962 contract in order to receive a visa. Among those who chose to remain outside Cuba and pursue their major-league aspirations were Luis Tiant with the Mexico City Tigers and Diego Segui, the ERA leader for Hawaii of the Pacific League.

Segui worked his way up the Athletics minor-league system until the 1962 season, when he joined Kansas City, finishing 8-5 in 37 games (13 starts). After three more years as a starting pitcher for a dreadful team, Segui was sold to the Washington Senators as the 1966 season got under way but was reacquired by the Athletics (for pitcher Jim Duckworth) on July 30. At the time of that deal he was pitching in the minors and finished the season with Vancouver, the A's Pacific Coast League affiliate. Many fans as well as reporters were enthused about his highly anticipated return to Kansas City. At spring training at Bradenton, Florida, in March, 1966 pitching coach Cot Deal, interviewed by Joe McGuff of the *Kansas City Star*, said, "You know, I think this guy has as much stuff as Juan Marichal. Naturally, he doesn't have the control Marichal does, but Marichal's stuff isn't any better. Segui's forkball is outstanding. I'd say it's almost as good as Lindy McDaniel's, and McDaniel has the best one in the business. Segui's fastball is good, his slider is good and his curve is getting better."[2]

But, Deal was asked, if Segui's stuff is so outstanding, why did he have so much trouble winning games? After his 8-5 record in 1962, he was 9-6 in 1963. There was an opinion brewing that Segui was on his way to a record pitching career, but he dropped to an 8-17 record in 1964, and the next year, he posted a dismal 5-15 record. Dissatisfied with Segui's performance, Ed Lopat, the Athletics' executive vice president, cut his salary.

Coach Deal opined that Segui's lack of effectiveness was all a matter of control and a need to improve his delivery. (Deal thought Segui kicked too much with his left leg and brought his arm back too far, making it easier for runners to steal on him and upset his pitch delivery.) Deal was confident that Segui could work out these problems, but for 1966, Diego Segui was just another pitcher fighting for a spot on the Athletics' roster, and Deal decided to make him a special project, spending extra time in an attempt to improve his control and delivery. But the special attention did not pay off. Segui was put on waivers before the start of the 1966 season, and he was picked up by the Washington Senators, for whom he had a 3-7 record in 1966 with an ERA of 5.00. He returned to the Athletics in 1967, and moved with them to Oakland in 1968, all the time posting mediocre records.

In the expansion draft after the 1968 season, Segui was taken by the new Seattle Pilots. With the ill-fated Pilots in 1969, he had a good season, winning 12 games and losing 6 while pitching mostly in relief, and was named the Pilots' most valuable player. Charlie Finley, owner of the A's, regretted losing Segui, believing the A's would have won the American League West division if he'd stayed in Oakland. When the Pilots folded after the 1969 season and the team was sold to a Milwaukee group, Finley got him back in a trade.

The A's intended to turn Segui into their primary right-handed reliever in 1970, but in late June they team made him a starter. Segui went 8-6 the rest of the season, finishing with a 10-10 record and leading the American League with a 2.56 ERA.

Segui's repertoire of pitches and mound quirks exasperated batters and umpires. He took his time, rubbed the ball between each pitch, and defended himself against allegations of using a spitball when he blew on his hands. He took leisurely strolls around the edge of the mound while blowing through his right fist, and rearranged the dirt in front of the pitcher's rubber with his right foot. At times he paused between pitches by standing still, staring at the outfield while working on the ball, in deep contemplation as tension at home plate rose to an unnerving level. Joe Garagiola criticized Segui's pitching performance before the 1975 World Series and described his delivery as "like spreading ether over the ballpark," prompting the outraged pitcher to confront Garagiola before Game Five and attempt to get an apology out of him for the insult. Segui's teams put up with his rituals, as they valued his work ethic and variety of pitches. He never complained whether he was a reliever or a starter, or called in for only part of an inning. And he could throw a very decent forkball. "It goes somewhere all the time. … It acts like a screwie. It drops and sometimes acts like a screwball—sometimes."

Segui learned to throw the elusive forkball at a farm in Cuba, where a left-handed pitcher from a semipro team taught him to throw the traditional southpaw pitch. In a Cuban cow pasture he perfected his signature pitch, called the "tenedor." But was Segui's forkball truly a forkball? Or was it really a Pedro Ramos "Cuban forkball," a pitch that was suspected as a spitball? After all, the doubters hinted, Segui spent such a long time working over the ball before the windup. Such an accusation was vehemently denied by Diego. "Definitely not!" he said. "Maybe it reacts a little like a spitter, but it isn't."[3]

After 2½ seasons in Oakland, the A's sent Segui to the Cardinals in June 1972 for future considerations, and he played the next year and a half for St. Louis. In December 1973 he was traded to the Boston Red Sox with pitcher Reggie Cleveland and infielder Terry Hughes for pitchers John Curtis, Mike Garman, and Lynn McGlothen. The Red Sox were in dire need of bullpen help, and asked those in the know around the National League who were the best right-handed relievers. Segui's name came up frequently enough to corroborate a scouting report from Haywood Sullivan and Frank Malzone.

Although many within the Red Sox organization looked forward to his arrival in the bullpen, Segui wondered. As the MVP of the Pilots in 1969, the ERA leader in the American League in 1970, and owning respectable stats overall, why was he trade material year after year? In a March 1974 interview with Boston *Globe* reporter Clif Keane during spring training at Winter Haven, Florida, Segui said: "I sit and wonder each time that I have been traded, have I done something wrong? Did I not get along with the people? Why don't they like me, so that I have to go from one team to another so much? If you are confused about it," he said, "you can say that I am more confused than anyone else."[4]

Segui pitched regularly early in the 1974 season with great success. By early June he developed calluses on two fingers of his throwing hand, causing a control problem that nagged him until late August. An epidemic of bumps, bruises, and sore shoulders swept through Boston's bullpen, forcing the starters into leading the league in complete games. In early September Segui lost a couple of crucial games in late innings and ended the season with a 6-8 record and 10 saves. Manager Darrell Johnson expressed confidence in Segui's ability to come back in 1975 in good condition.

In 1975 Segui resumed his role as a short reliever, willing to pitch anytime, anywhere he was needed. When Luis Tiant's shoulder came up lame in July, Segui was ready to jump in as a starter, a role he had not played since May 1972. On the 29th he started, and lost a complete game, 4-0, to Milwaukee. "(Segui) pitched a hell of a game," said Darrell Johnson. He gave up 10 hits, but struck out 11. Three solo home runs, two by Don Money and one by Darrell Porter, were the key blows.

Throughout the 1975 season, the Red Sox pitchers kept everyone on edge. Bill Lee and Diego Segui didn't want the paying customers to be bored, wrote Peter Gammons in the *Boston Globe*. Yet the hitting, fielding and pitching brought the team to an American League pennant as well as the World Series, and Diego Segui made his one and only appearance on the mound at the World Series in the eighth inning of Game Five.

Just before the start of the 1976 season, Segui was released. He was not picked up by another major-league team and instead signed with the Hawaii Islanders of the Pacific Coast League. In September he was suspended by the club after a legal entanglement over money he claimed was owed him. When the Seattle Mariners began organizing their roster for their inaugural 1977 season, Segui's memorable year with the Pilots was recalled, and he not only made the Mariners, he was anointed the Opening Day starter. On April 5, 1977, Segui faced the California Angels with a crowd of over 57,000 in the Kingdome loudly applauding his return to Seattle. The win was not to be his; the Angels shut out the Mariners in their inaugural game, 7-0. Over and over Segui tried but could not get his pitches to sing again for him. His arm, that arm that he once called "the funniest one in the world," was not giving him much to smile about. He finished the 1977 season no victories, seven defeats, and an ERA of 5.69. He had some good moments that year, like when he struck out ten Red Sox, a record that stayed on the Mariners' books for a long time. He tried hard to make his famous forkball work, but it remained incorrigible, and Segui's year with the Mariners had an unfortunate ending when he was released. After 20 years in professional baseball, he was without a job. He wanted to continue the work he had spent most of his life practicing, and since he had a family to provide for, he returned again to the minor leagues with the hope he could work his way back.

In 1978 Segui had a very successful year with Cordoba, Mexico, where, in his 21st year of professional pitching, he achieved the first no-hitter of his career and did it, no less, with a perfect game. Segui would not have any more major-league service, but there was another

Segui working his way up. His second son, David, was showing interest and talent in baseball. He became a first baseman for the Baltimore Orioles in 1990. A part of Diego Segui had returned to major-league baseball.

There are baseball players who earn fame from their statistics, for achieving great things on the field, and they can leave their mark upon sports history in any number of ways. Diego Segui has done so. Other players may be merely a footnote, or notable as an answer to some obscure baseball trivia question. Diego Segui can claim that as well. In 1984, when the crew of the space shuttle Discovery was circling Earth, the ground crew at the Johnson Space Center in Houston made baseball trivia a routine part of the program in order to keep the astronauts' minds sharp with something to ponder other than keeping the shuttle aloft. Reporters at NBC Sports in New York also had a hand in feeding questions to the shuttle crew, and they all sent questions they were sure would stump them. When the astronauts returned, they cornered George Abbey, director of flight-crew operations, their baseball trivia nemesis — and a native of Seattle — and challenged him with their own question. Who was the only man ever to play for both the Seattle Pilots and the Seattle Mariners?

"I told him it was Gorman Thomas," said Abbey. "In fact, I insisted that it was Gorman. But now I'm not so sure it wasn't Diego Segui."[5]

SOURCES

The Baseball Encyclopedia. Ninth Edition (New York: Macmillan Publishing, 1993).

Bergman, Ron, "Reliever Segui Saving A's With Slick Starting Jobs," *The Sporting News*, August 15, 1970.

Gammons, Peter, "Bosox Feel Secure With Segui in Relief, *The Sporting News*, March 16, 1974.

Gammons, Peter, "Segui, Garagiola in Heated Exchange," *Boston Globe*, October 19, 1975.

Kachline, Clifford, "Cuban Standouts Shun Own Land, Play Elsewhere," *The Sporting News*, November 29, 1961.

Keane, Clif, "Wise, Segui Ponder Reasons for Trade," *Boston Evening Globe*, March 6, 1974.

Keane, Clif, "Red Sox, You Ask?" *Boston Sunday Globe*, March 17, 1974.

McCoy, Bob, "Baseball Trivia in Space," *The Sporting News*, September 17, 1984.

McGuff, Joe, *Kansas City Star*, March 7, 1966.

Red Sox Notebook, "Tiant's Sore Shoulder Gave Segui the Start," *Boston Globe*, July 30, 1975.

Zimmerman, Hy, "Can Bolin Polish Pilot Swap Image?" *The Sporting News*, January 3, 1970.

Zimmerman, Hy, "So Long to Ancient Mariner," *The Sporting News*, November 19. 1977.

Zimmerman, Hy, "Segui's Jammed Thumb Pained Joe Schultz Worse," *Seattle Daily Times*. April 6, 1969.

Box Score, Game Five, World Series, *Boston Globe*, October 19, 1975.

National Baseball Hall of Fame File, Diego Segui.

Tiant, Luis, Interview by author, July 15, 2005.

NOTES

1   *Seattle Daily Times,* April 6, 1969.

2   *Kansas City Star,* March 7, 1966.

3   *The Sporting News,* March 16, 1974.

4   *Boston Globe,* March 17, 1974.

5   *The Sporting News,* September 17, 1984.

Art Shamsky

By Eric Aron

In the locker room celebration after the New York Mets won the 1969 National League pennant, he was quoted by the *New York Daily News* as saying, "I'll walk down the street in New York now and people will say, 'There's Art Shamsky of the Mets.' People used to laugh. They won't anymore."[1] Indeed, after his performance in the 1969 National League Championship Series, a three-game sweep of the Atlanta Braves, nobody would laugh. His seven hits in the NLCS led both teams and, had the honor been bestowed, Shamsky might well have been named Most Valuable Player. He hit .300 during that Miracle Mets season and became a fan favorite, particularly among the area's large Jewish population.

Art Shamsky played professional baseball for 13 seasons, between 1960 and 1972, eight in the major leagues. Nicknamed Sham and Smasher, the lanky left-handed outfielder-first baseman began his career with the Cincinnati Reds organization and later became a key part of the 1969 world champion Mets' offense. In addition to his contributions to the Mets, Shamsky is perhaps best known for his four consecutive home runs in August 1966 while he was with Cincinnati. He is one of 17 players to hit four straight homers over a span of two games and the only major leaguer to hit three home runs in a game without being in the starting lineup.

Arthur Louis Shamsky was born in St. Louis on October 14, 1941. He grew up in a predominantly middle-class Jewish area of University City, son of William and Sadie Shamsky. William's family came from the Ukraine while Sadie's family originated from Poland. His father ran a scrap-iron business. Art, the only son, had an older sister, Delores. "We were Jewish but we weren't very religious," he told an interviewer. "We observed the holidays but we didn't make a big thing out of religion. About all I did as a player in recognizing the religion was to take off the major Jewish holidays."[2]

"As a young boy growing up, my life was basically two things, following the St. Louis Cardinals or playing baseball with my friends," Shamsky said.[3] He told another interviewer, "We used to put a quarter in the light machine at tennis courts just to hit some fungoes at night. We played every day, we played in the rain, we played every chance we got."[4] He listened to Harry Caray call Cardinals games on the radio and his biggest hero was Stan Musial.

Shamsky was an outstanding basketball and baseball player at University City High. Famous alumni of the school include playwright Tennessee Williams, southpaw Ken Holtzman (who is the winningest Jewish pitcher in the major leagues and was a teammate of Shamsky's on the 1972 Oakland A's), and one-time Mets outfielder Bernard Gilkey. Shamsky didn't try

out for baseball until his senior year in high school. He played two games at Busch Stadium during the state high-school playoffs, getting hits in both, but University City lost in the championship game.

"I wasn't spectacular," Shamsky said. "I hit only about .300, and I didn't consider pro ball right away. I was only 16 when I graduated from high school."[5] After graduating in 1958, Shamsky attended the University of Missouri for a year and played baseball. He then decided to leave school to play professionally.

Shamsky got offers from many teams, and signed with the Cincinnati Reds on September 9, 1959. "My father would have preferred that I had gone into business, but he was into baseball and I think he was thrilled when I signed," Shamsky has said. "My mother certainly wanted me to go to college and become a doctor, of course. What else is a Jewish boy supposed to do?"[6] (Shamsky's sister became a lawyer.)

Shamsky hit a home run in his first professional at-bat, for the Geneva Redlegs in the New York-Penn League. He was a teammate of Tony Perez and Pete Rose (whom he roomed with while with Geneva). For the season, playing in 119 games, Shamsky hit .271, with 18 home runs and 86 RBIs, making the league all-star team. He led the league's outfielders in assists, with 24. Despite the presence of the two baseball superstar teammates, Shamsky said, "That Class D team was so bad that we got our manager fired with a third of the season left." In a move Shamsky considered somewhat ironic, he was promoted to Class B Topeka while his teammates Rose and Perez remained in Class D. In a piece he wrote for the *New York Times* in 1986, Shamsky said in jest, "I guess, though, when you stop to think about it, somebody knew something because they're still playing and making a lot of money and I'm watching."[7]

Shamsky hit .288 with 15 home runs and 66 RBIs in 116 games for the Topeka Reds of the Three-I League in 1961. Dave Bristol, who managed him in the minor leagues in 1961 and 1962 and later with the Reds, remembered the left-handed hitter's power. "It's Artie's wrists," said Bristol. "Watch Artie's wrists when he

whips a bat and you won't be surprised by the long balls he hits. . . . They had a big barn behind the fence in right-center at Topeka. Artie's the only player I ever saw bounce a homer off the roof of that barn."[8]

Shamsky's 1962 season was spent with the Macon Peaches in the Class A Sally League. He started out strong, hitting six homers in the first 13 games, but went on the shelf for seven weeks with a hand injury. He ended up on the disabled list when he had surgery to remove calluses from his left hand. In 81 games, he hit .284 with 16 home runs and 61 RBIs. Shamsky was promoted to the Reds' Triple-A affiliate San Diego Padres, where he spent two seasons in the Pacific Coast League. In 1963 he played in 150 games, batting .267 with 18 home runs and 68 RBIs. In 1964 the Padres, including Shamsky and teammates Tommy Helms, Don Pavletich, Tony Perez, and other future major leaguers, won the PCL championship. Shamsky hit .272, slammed 25 home runs, and drove in 69, setting the record for the longest home run hit in the Padres' park, a tape-measure shot of 500 feet.[9]

Shamsky was now ready for the major leagues. "Art Shamsky has great potential," said San Diego general manager Eddie Leishman, who was named Minor League Executive of the Year after Shamsky and Co. took the '64 league title. "He certainly has the tools to make the grade and go far in baseball. He has the swing and actions of the Yankees' Joe Pepitone."[10]

Shamsky made his major-league debut on April 17, 1965, against the very team he loved growing up as a child, the St. Louis Cardinals. In front of family and friends at Busch Stadium, he batted for pitcher Gerry Arrigo in the seventh inning of a game the Cardinals won, 8-0. Shamsky had no easy task for a debut, as he was called upon to hit against one of the greatest pitchers of all time. "I had to pinch-hit against Bob Gibson, a great pitcher, and I was really nervous. I ended up striking out and I was very upset. However, I got over it, and the next time I faced him I pinch-hit a home run."[11]

Shamsky's first hit came five days later, at Wrigley Field against the Chicago Cubs, when he lined a pinch-hit single to right in the ninth inning off Ted Abernathy. His first major-league home run was launched in the first game of a doubleheader against the Mets on May 2. It was a pinch-hit two-run blast off Mets reliever Tom Parsons in the bottom of the fifth inning. The batter he hit for was the great Frank Robinson, who was in his final season with the Reds.

It was also during his rookie season that Shamsky got to face fellow University City High alumnus Ken Holtzman, four years his junior and also a rookie in the big leagues. Shamsky walked and sacrificed in his only two career plate appearances against the Cubs southpaw, an example of the strict platooning that Shamsky endured during his career. (He hit .223 with three home runs in 112 career at-bats against lefties and .255 with 65 homers in 1,574 at-bats against righties.)

Shamsky did not end up as a regular outfielder in 1965, but instead became the top pinch-hitter on a team boasting a lineup of All-Stars and future Hall of Famers. Pete Rose played in all 162 games and was the National League's starting second baseman in the All-Star Game; Frank Robinson belted 33 home runs, and Tony Perez hit .260 in his rookie year. Cincinnati had two 20-game winners, Sammy Ellis and Jim Maloney. The 1965 Reds finished in fourth place at 89-73, eight games behind the Los Angeles Dodgers.

After playing for Santurce in the Puerto Rican Winter League in the winter of '65, Shamsky returned to Cincinnati the following spring. He appeared in 96 games for the Reds, again serving primarily as a pinch-hitter and reserve outfielder. His team finished in seventh place in the National League with a record of 76-84, falling to 18 games behind the Dodgers.

During the 1966 season, Shamsky made history on August 12 and 14. Over the span of two games at Crosley Field in Cincinnati, he homered in four consecutive at-bats. On the 12th, the Reds and the Pittsburgh Pirates played an extra-inning affair in which 11 home runs were hit. The Pirates were ahead six times and the Reds three. With the Pirates ahead

7-6 in the eighth inning, Shamsky came into the game to play left field.

In the bottom of the inning, with a runner on base, Shamsky homered off Al McBean to give Cincinnati an 8-7 lead. The Pirates tied the game in the ninth and took the lead in the 10th on a Willie Stargell home run. In the bottom of the frame, facing pitcher Roy Face, Shamsky hit another shot into the right-field seats to tie the game again. Finally, in the home 11th, with Pittsburgh up 11-9, Shamsky faced pitcher Billy O'Dell. On a 3-and-1 count, he homered a third time, another two-run blast to tie the game at 11-11. Teammate Pete Rose called it "one of the greatest clutch-hitting exhibitions ever seen." [12]

In the end, however, despite Shamsky's heroics, the Pirates came away with a 14-11 victory in 13 innings. After the game, he took the loss hard and declined an opportunity to go on a Cincinnati post-game radio show, *Star of the Game*.. "How can you be a star when your team loses?" he commented. [13]

Despite Ahamsky's becoming the first player to homer three times after not starting, Cincinnati manager Dave Bristol sat him out for the second game of the series, against Pittsburgh lefty Woodie Fryman. The Reds won that game 11-0, a contest that was called during the sixth inning after a 50-minute rain delay. He then sat out the start of the rubber game of the series on the 14th, against right-hander Vernon Law. When Bristol sent Shamsky up to bat for catcher Johnny Edwards in the seventh, he connected for a two-run shot against Law that gave the Reds a brief 2-1 advantage. After the game, a 4-2 loss to the Bucs, the wild speculation and media circus began. Could he do it again? Could he make it five in a row?

Shamsky said he wasn't even aware he had tied a major-league record. "I didn't know a thing about it until the Cincinnati public address announcer made mention of it after my fourth homer. I can't say I tried to hit any of them. ... It's a funny thing. They come pretty easy when I don't try." [14]

Shamsky's teammates made light of the event. "Just think," kidded Sammy Ellis, "a few days ago Artie was just an average bench warmer. Today he's a national hero." Outfielder Tommy Harper said, "Artie's act sure is a tough one to follow. I struck out after three (actually, two) of those four homers. No one noticed it, though, they were still cheering Artie." Shamsky himself said, "If I do hit the fifth straight one, there will be champagne for everyone—on me." [15]

After the Pirates series, the Reds moved on to Los Angeles to play the Dodgers. Shamsky sat against Dodgers lefty Claude Osteen on the night of August 15, but in the eighth inning he stepped up to the plate to bat for Tony Perez against righty reliever Bob Miller with no outs and nobody on base, and lined a single to right field. "If I was going to hit one out of the park that would have been the pitch," he said. Sportswriter Jack Disney wrote the next day, "By lining a base hit to right in the eighth inning at Dodger Stadium, the Cincinnati outfielder was stopped three bases short of immortality." The *Los Angeles Herald-Examiner* ran a parody of "Casey at the Bat" that concluded, "But there is no joy in any town—just tears and sadness mingled; After four straight homers, mighty Shamsky only singled." [16]

Shamsky's four consecutive home runs put him in impressive company. Other players to hit four home runs in four straight plate appearances over multiple games include Albert Pujols, Troy Glaus, Shawn Green, Manny Ramirez, Bo Jackson, Larry Herndon, Deron Johnson, Mike Epstein, Bobby Murcer, Johnny Blanchard, Jimmie Foxx, Mickey Mantle, Hank Greenberg, Ralph Kiner, and Shamsky's hero Stan Musial. That season Shamsky hit 21 home runs in just 234 at-bats, finishing second on the team behind Deron Johnson's 24 in more than 500 at-bats. Despite his .521 slugging percentage, Shamsky finished the season batting only .231 with just 47 RBIs.

The next season, 1967, was Shamsky's last with the Reds. He had had an injury-riddled year, struggling primarily with back issues that would plague his entire career. He hit only .197 with just 13 RBIs and hit onlt three home runs all season. Shamsky was traded to the Mets on November 8 for utility infielder Bob Johnson.

Initially, Shamsky was not happy about the trade. He learned the news while recovering from surgery in St. Louis to have a cyst removed from his tailbone. Reds general manager Bob Howsam called him at home, and Art expected to be asked how he was feeling. He immediately said he felt great and was looking forward to next season. "That's good," said Howsam, "because we just traded you to the Mets."

Shamsky was leaving an organization and teammates he had been with his entire career for the team with the worst record in baseball in five of its six years of existence. After Howsam called, Mets GM Bing Devine phoned to reassure Shamsky about coming to New York. Devine was previously general manager of the Cardinals and had known Shamsky growing up. Things were different, he told Art, and the fans were great. "Two days later I picked up the St. Louis newspaper and read that Bing Devine was just named general manager of the Cardinals. ... Two days earlier he had told me how good the Met organization was and how great New York City was, and now he left to come back home. It was the longest winter of my life." [17]

Still, in 1968 things were looking brighter for both Shamsky and the Mets. Three weeks after Shamsky was traded to New York, the Mets acquired manager Gil Hodges in a trade with Washington. Johnny Murphy, who helped negotiate the Hodges deal, succeeded Bing Devine as general manager and brought up young talent from the minors that—combined with Hodges at the helm—brought a winning atmosphere to a team that had known only misery in its brief existence. Upon arriving in New York, Art joked that, like Sandy Koufax in 1965, he would miss any World Series game that fell on a major Jewish holiday. Everybody laughed; no one could have predicted the miracle to come one year later.

The 1968 New York Mets were the one of the youngest teams in the major leagues, with an average age of 25.9. (Only the Astros had younger hitters, 25.6, and only the Cubs had younger pitchers, 25.4.) The Mets had a core of returning position players in shortstop Bud Harrelson, first baseman Ed Kranepool, catcher Jerry Grote, and outfielders Ron Swoboda and Cleon Jones. The team also now had young players like Tommie Agee and Al Weis, both brought over in a trade with the Chicago White Sox, and Ken Boswell made the club for the first time out of spring training. Boswell, like Shamsky part of a left-handed platoon, became Art's close friend and roommate.

It was pitching, however, that would carry the team to a world championship. Flamethrower Nolan Ryan won the job as a starter in spring training, and rookie Jerry Koosman, arguably the greatest southpaw in Mets history, made the team despite a mediocre September call-up in 1967.. Koosman finished second in Rookie of the Year voting to the Reds' Johnny Bench in 1968. Then, of course, there was Tom Seaver, who himself had won the Rookie of the Year award the previous season. Though the Mets barely avoided the basement in the final season with a 10-team National League, the 1968 Mets had a different look and feel than their predecessors.

Even with a mediocre .238 average, Shamsky hit 12 home runs with 48 RBIs. "While we weren't breaking any records in 1968, we were competitive," Shamsky said. "We were a little less than a .500 ballclub through the middle of the season. The one thing we did have, though, was harmony. It was a clubhouse filled with people who generally liked each other. We had a few 'characters' and some loners, but, all in all, the 1968 Mets were a team that pulled for each other." [18]

Shamsky, a bachelor, also spent his first offseason in New York. "The city had put its claws on me. I learned that New York City is really one of a kind. … The city energizes you. There is never a dull moment in New York City. After a few months I fell in love with the city. And I got used to 'Auttie.' It's Artie in New York City lingo. I was okay with it now." [19]

The next season, 1969, was the first year of divisional play and new National League teams were added in Montreal and San Diego. Gil Hodges, who had suf-

fered a heart attack right before the end of the 1968 season, predicted that the Mets would win 85 games. His club won 100.

Yet the season could not have started any worse for Shamsky. After he had played in only three spring-training games, his back went out. "I was about to play first base that afternoon (March 15, 1969), and we were taking batting practice on the other field. When we finished our swings, I said to Kenny [Boswell], c'mon down in the right-field corner and throw me some grounders. He did, and about the 15th one, I bent over and felt something snap in my back. It was like somebody had taken a gun and shot me. I felt this pain shoot all the way down my left leg." [20] After what was initially thought to be back spasms, Shamsky was diagnosed with a slipped disk, which was pressing against the sciatic nerve. Doctors told him to get plenty of bed rest, take pain medications, and even wear a protective corset. He was unable to get out of bed for a week. One doctor even told him he might never play again. His condition began to improve, however, and he soon felt strong enough to pick up a bat.

After three weeks Shamsky was given permission by the medical staff to work out, but he played the entire 1969 season in pain, even taking pain medications throughout the playoffs and World Series. [21] Just before the Mets were to leave St. Petersburg and head north in April, Shamsky was informed by Hodges and GM Johnny Murphy that he was going on the disabled list. After three weeks on the DL, rehab games at Triple-A Tidewater would follow.

Shamsky did not take the news well. The last thing he wanted was to get sent down by a ninth-place team. He even considered retirement. He didn't know if he would ever be recalled to the Mets and was given no guarantees by Hodges. He was placed on the disabled list on April 8 and came off on April 29. He was optioned to Tidewater and flew to Syracuse for a game against the Chiefs. In his first game he got three hits, including a grand slam, to highlight a 10-run first inning in a 13-2 Tidewater victory. Mets farm director Whitey Herzog saw him hit the grand slam and said, "What the hell are you doing here?" [22]

After batting .289 with five doubles, four homers, and 12 RBIs in 11 games with the Tides, Shamsky was recalled by the Mets on May 13. In his first game back, he hit a pinch-hit RBI single against the Atlanta Braves at Shea. From his time rehabbing, he had learned how to become a better hitter, using a heavier bat and hitting to all fields. He adjusted his swing to make better contact and cut down on his strikeouts. In 1969 he struck out only 32 times in 302 at-bats

With the Mets Shamsky became part of a crowded outfield with Ron Swoboda, Tommie Agee, Cleon Jones, and Rod Gaspar, who'd come north with the club after Shamsky went down. Gil Hodges liked to platoon his players, using as many of them as possible. For the left-right combo in right field, Shamsky shared time with Swoboda, and he made the most of it. He began swinging the bat with power and was hitting nearly .350 in August.

Shamsky got the game-winning RBI five times that season. None came bigger than on June 6. He lined an eighth-inning pinch-hit single off pitcher Gary Ross to break a 3-3 tie in San Diego. The Mets won, 5-3, a franchise-record eighth in a row. They wound up winning 11 in a row. After trailing the Chicago Cubs by 9½ games on August 13, New York took over first place for good on September 10 and clinched the National League East title on September 24. Shamsky played in 100 games and for only time in his professional career, he hit .300 — exactly that figure — to place second on the team to Cleon Jones's .340. He was also second on the team in home runs with 14, behind Tommie Agee's 26.

Shamsky indeed sat out Rosh Hashanah with the Mets battling for first place late in the season. In typically miraculous fashion of the final push that month, the Mets won both ends of a September 12 doubleheader by identical 1-0 scores with the pitchers driving in the only run in each game. The Mets won again the next day with Shamsky still sitting it out in the hotel. Back on the field on Sunday and batting cleanup … the Mets lost. In 11 games after sitting out the Jewish holiday, Shamsky batted .306 with a homer and six RBIs — with the Mets losing just three times

with him in the lineup (and one of those defeats came after the Mets had clinched the division).

In the National League Championship Series, against the Atlanta Braves, Hodges continued his platoon system and Shamsky was in the starting lineup to face right-handed pitching — batting cleanup — for all three games of the best-of-five series. He went 7-for-13 at the plate (.538), but had only one RBI.

After the three-game sweep of Atlanta, the Mets faced the heavily favored Baltimore Orioles in the World Series, winner of 109 regular-season games. With left-handers Mike Cuellar and Dave McNally making four appearances for the Orioles, Shamsky sat for four of the five games. In Game Three, against right-hander Jim Palmer, he started and batted fourth. He entered Game One as a pinch-hitter with two outs in the ninth inning. The Mets trailed 4-1 and had runners on first and second. "I would be lying if I didn't say my heart was beating as fast as it could," he said. "Even though I had hit over .500 in the playoffs and was swinging the bat well, I was nervous."[23] Shamsky grounded out to second baseman Davey Johnson to end the game. The Mets won the next four games to win the Series, but Shamsky had no hits in six at-bats.

While the 1970 Mets were unable to repeat as NL East champs, Shamsky was almost as solid as in 1969. Splitting time between first base and right field, he led the team in hitting with a .293 batting average, with 11 home runs and 49 runs batted in. His RBIs and 122 games played were career highs as a major leaguer. But 1971 was another injury-plagued season, as he lost his platoon positions at first base and right field to left-handed hitters Dave Marshall and Ed Kranepool. Playing in 68 games, Shamsky hit only .185 with five home runs and 18 RBIs. On October 18, 1971, the Mets traded Shamsky along with three minor-league pitchers to the Cardinals for four players, including Harry Parker and Jim Beauchamp.

Shamsky did not survive spring training, however, and was unconditionally released by the Cardinals on April 9, 1972. He signed as a free agent with the Cubs but played in only 15 games, hitting .125 with no home runs and one RBI. The Oakland A's purchased his contract in June but released him on July 18 after he had appeared in eight games with no hits in seven at-bats. "This time I decided to quit," he told an interviewer. "Three teams didn't want me. That was enough." [24]

While still with the Mets, Shamsky had opened restaurants with former Yankee and Met Phil Linz, and later became a real-estate consultant. He was a play-by-play and color broadcaster for the Mets in 1980 and 1981. In 1980 he worked alongside Bob Goldsholl for cable, and in '81, he did radio and cable TV with Ralph Kiner, Bob Murphy, and Steve Albert. In a 1999 episode of the sitcom *Everybody Loves Raymond*, Shamsky appeared as himself along other 1969 teammates. (The dog on the show was named Shamsky and others, including comedian Jon Stewart, have followed suit in their pet naming.) In 2004 Shamsky wrote a book with Barry Zeman called *The Magnificent Seasons*. It is the story of the three championship sports teams in New York in 1969 and 1970, the Mets, Jets, and Knicks.

In 2007 it was announced that Shamsky, Ken Holtzman, and Ron Blomberg would manage in the new Israel Baseball League. "I decided to get involved in the new Israeli Baseball League because I like the challenge of starting something at the very beginning … particularly in a country that is just beginning to develop the game of baseball," Shamsky was quoted as saying in *Mets Inside Pitch*. "Managing is something I thought I would never be interested in, but this situation is different. There are many transplanted New Yorkers in Israel, and many New York Mets fans. I'm hoping that my credibility will help the new league get off on the right track."[25] Shamsky's team, the Modi'in Miracle, finished in third place in the six-team league, at 22-19. Although the league halted operations after one season, Shamsky continued to be active in the Israel Association for Baseball, making frequent visits to Israel to promote hardball in the Holy Land.

For his eight-year major-league career, Shamsky hit .253 with 68 home runs and 233 RBIs. He married twice and had two daughters and, as of 2009, five grandchildren. As of 2014, he was still a New York resident. Shamsky is a member of the New York Jewish Sports Hall of Fame and was inducted into the National Jewish Sports Hall of Fame in 1994. The bat he used to swat four straight homers is on display at the National Baseball Hall of Fame.

Shamsky expressed pride in what the 1969 Mets accomplished. "History will show that a team that was a 100-to-1 long shot at the beginning of the season became the toast of the sports world seven months later," he said "I have always said that the 1969 New York Mets probably weren't the greatest baseball team to win the World Series, but they were certainly one of the most memorable." [26]

SOURCES

Allen, Maury, *After the Miracle: The 1969 Mets Twenty Years Later* (New York: Franklin Watts, 1989).

Burick, Si, "Shamsky lets his stick do the Swaggering," *Dayton Daily News*, August 15, 1966.

Disney, Jack, "End of Shamsky Era," *Los Angeles Herald Examiner*, August 16, 1966.

Epstein, Andy, "Out of Left Field: With a Miracle Met," *Mets Inside Pitch*, May 2007.

Lawson, Earl. "Shamsky Equals Record, Hitting 4 HRs In Row." *Cincinnati Post*, August 27, 1966.

Lawson, Earl, "Shamsky Looks Like Comedian—N.L. Pitchers Wish He Were," *Cincinnati Post*, May 28, 1966.

Shamsky, Art, "Rose and Perez Can Do It, So Why Not Me, Too?" *New York Times*, April 6, 1986.

Shamsky, Art, with Barry Zeman, *The Magnificent Seasons* (New York: Thomas Dunne Books, 2004).

Young, Dick, "Disabled and Displaced … Art Swings Back," *New York Daily News*, July 19, 1969.

Young, Dick, "Shamsky Plays With Pain," *New York Daily News*, March 2, 1970.

"Art Shamsky's Long Drive for Majors May Be Over," *St. Louis Post Dispatch*, April 16, 1965.

"Shamsky Bat to Fame Hall," *Cincinnati Post and Times-Star*, August 16, 1966.

Art Shamsky clip file, National Baseball Hall of Fame.

NOTES

1   Art Shamsky with Barry Zeman, *The Magnificent Seasons* (New York: Thomas Dunne Books, 2004), 142.

2   Maury, Allen, *After the Miracle: The 1969 Mets Twenty Years Later* (New York: Franklin Watts, 1989), 198.

3   Shamsky and Zeman, 255.

4   Allen, 199.

5   "Art Shamsky's Long Drive for Majors May Be Over," *St. Louis Post Dispatch*, April 16, 1965.

6   Allen, 199.

7   Art Shamsky, "Rose and Perez Can Do It, So Why Not Me, Too?" *New York Times*, April 6, 1986.

8   Earl Lawson, "Shamsky Looks Like Comedian—N.L. Pitchers Wish He Were," *Cincinnati Post*, May 28, 1966.

9   Ibid.

10 "Art Shamsky's Long Drive."

11 Clipping in Shamsky's file at theNational Baseball Hall of Fame. The quote is not quite accurate. Shamsky did hit a pinch-hit home run off Gibson on June 8, but not the next time the two faced each other, on April 23. In that game he got a pinch-hit single off Gibson.

12 Lawson, Earl. "Shamsky Equals Record, Hitting 4 HRs In Row," *Cincinnati Post*, August 27, 1966.

13 Si Burick, "Shamsky Lets His Stick Do the Swaggering," *Dayton Daily News*, August 15, 1966.

14 Jack Disney, "End of Shamsky Era," *Los Angeles Herald Examiner*, August 16, 1966.

15 Ibid.

16 Disney, "End of Shamsky Era."

17 Shamsky and Zeman, 96.

18 Shamsky and Zeman, 99.

19 Shamsky and Zeman, 102.

20 Dick Young, "Disabled and Displaced ... Art Swings Back," *New York Daily News*, July 19, 1969.

21 Dick Young, "Shamsky Plays With Pain," *New York Daily News*, March 2, 1970.

22 Allen, 204.

23 Shamsky and Zeman, 155.

24 Allen, 201.

25 Epstein, 21.

26 Shamsky and Zeman, 186.

Don Shaw

By Gregory H. Wolf

Which pitcher earned the first win for the expansion Montreal Expos in 1969? If you said left-handed reliever Don Shaw, you would be correct. Besides the Expos, Shaw, a journeyman pitcher, applied his craft in parts of five seasons between 1967 and 1972 for the New York Mets, the St. Louis Cardinals, and the Oakland A's, making 138 appearances, and winning 13 games.

Shaw was born on February 23, 1944, in Pittsburgh, but grew into a hard-throwing left-hander and good-hitting pitcher for Grover Cleveland High School in Reseda, California, about 25 miles northwest of Los Angeles. The balmy, temperate climate of Southern California offered the Steel City transplant an opportunity to play baseball almost year-round. Shaw a sturdy 6-footer weighing 180 pounds, tossed a no-hitter in his senior year in high school, and pitched for Chatsworth in the local American Legion league.

After high school Shaw accepted a baseball scholarship to play for longtime coach Charlie Smith at San Diego State College (now San Diego State University) of the California College Athletics Association. San Diego State's baseball team was a regional powerhouse in the 1950s and won the NAIA baseball championship in 1958. During his four years with the Aztecs, Shaw was an unheralded, raw pitcher, and led the team in walks once. The New York Mets chose him in the 35th round (the 636th player overall) of the inaugural major-league draft, in 1965. Shaw's teammate Graig Nettles, was chosen by the Minnesota Twins in the fourth round. Shaw reported to rookie ball with the Marion (Virginia) Mets of the Appalachian League in 1965, joining among others 18-year-old Nolan Ryan. Mets farm director Eddie Stanky thought that the rubber-armed Shaw would be ideally suited as a reliever and the young prospect eagerly obliged. "If you want to get to the big leagues," Stanky told Shaw, "you better become a short relief man."[1] Groomed to be a reliever,

Shaw made 14 appearances (including one start), showing surprisingly good control and yielding about a hit per inning. At the conclusion of the short season, the Mets moved him up to the Auburn (New York) Mets in the Class A New York-Pennsylvania League. Shaw continued his success, surrendering just six hits in 15 innings. "I learned more about pitching and the whole game of baseball from Stanky than I did from anyone else," Shaw said later in his career.[2]

With a stellar 2.49 ERA in 49 innings in his first year of professional baseball, Shaw was a nonroster invitee to the Mets' spring-training camp in St. Petersburg, Florida, in 1966. Given the opportunity to pitch on the side and become acquainted with big-league coaches, Shaw was subsequently assigned to the Greenville (South Carolina) Mets in the Class A Western Carolinas League. While teammate Ryan gathered most of the headlines with a 17-2 record, Shaw developed into the league's best and most durable

reliever. He appeared in 51 games (one behind the league leader) and carved out an impressive 2.74 ERA. Shaw was moved up to the Double-A Williamsport (Pennsylvania) Mets in the Eastern League and then to the Jacksonville Suns of the Triple-A International League at the end of the season, and made nine consecutive scoreless appearances. The Mets added him to their 40-man roster after the season.

Shaw arrived at spring training in 1967 with two other highly touted rookies, Tom Seaver (his roommate) and Jerry Koosman. Still considered a long shot to make the team, Shaw had an impressive camp with the Mets, who were in dire need of a left-hander in the bullpen. (Tug McGraw was with the team at the time but was being groomed as a starter.) "[Our] young hurlers … really impressed," wrote Mets beat reporter Jack Lang in *The Sporting News*. "[Shaw] throws a sinker which Yogi Berra calls a 'worm killer,'"[3]

The Mets took 11 pitchers north, including rookies Seaver, Bill Denehy, Koosman, and Shaw; the latter two were the only lefties on the staff. Shaw had a rude welcome in his major-league debut on Opening Day, April 11, at Shea Stadium. In relief of Don Cardwell in the ninth inning of a 3-3 game with a runner on second and no outs, Shaw gave up two hits, issued a walk, and permitted an inherited runner to score (collaring Cardwell with the loss). After struggling in his first 11 appearances (with an ERA approaching 6.00), Shaw proved that he was big-league ready, posting a 2.08 ERA in his last 29 appearances (39 innings) while limiting batters to a paltry .201 batting average. He notched his third of four victories when he tossed three-hit ball over five scoreless innings of relief while striking out five against the Houston Astros on August 1. His season came to a premature close on August 13 when he was required to report to the military for a six-month tour of duty stateside as the Vietnam War wreaked havoc on baseball rosters. Not only did Shaw have an unexpectedly successful season (a 2.98 ERA in 40 appearances), he and his wife, Sandra, also welcomed the birth of their son in July.

Shaw proved to be a hot commodity in the offseason. Mets GM Bing Devine returned to the St. Louis Cardinals as GM in 1968, and tried to pry Shaw loose. Eddie Stanky, manager of the Chicago White Sox since 1966, coveted Shaw as well. But Mets GM Johnny Murphy steadfastly refused to trade his prized left-hander, not even for White Sox reliever Hoyt Wilhelm, or to include him in a package deal for Tommie Agee.[4]

Poised to become the left-handed reliever the Mets needed, Shaw suffered a sprained back in spring training. With little chance to prove his value to new manager Gil Hodges, Shaw was optioned to Jacksonville, but was recalled twice as a temporary replacement for pitchers who fulfilled weekend military reserve obligations, and was a September call-up when rosters expanded. He posted a fine 2.07 ERA in 61 innings (in 45 games) in Jacksonville, and made seven appearances for the Mets, concluding with ten consecutive scoreless innings, yielding just one hit in his five outings in September.

The Mets had an abundance of young, talented arms in 1968; starters Seaver, Koosman, Ryan, and Dick Selma were all under 25. Ron Taylor and Cal Koonce were proven, dependable relievers. It came as no surprise when the Mets made Shaw available in the expansion draft. On October 14, the Montreal Expos chose him with their 20th pick.

Expos manager Gene Mauch penciled in Shaw as the team's closer to inaugurate the first season of big-league baseball in Canada. As fate would have it, the Expos opened their season on April 8 at Shea Stadium. In a wild contest, Shaw entered the game in the bottom of the sixth inning with the scored tied 6-6. Montreal scored five unanswered runs, including one by Shaw (his second of three career runs). Shaw pitched three scoreless frames, then came undone in the ninth, yielding four runs to his former teammates before Carroll Sembera relieved him. Sembera saved the victory for Shaw, the first in Expos history. Shaw had difficulty replicating his success from the previous two years (2.56 ERA), struggled with his control, walking 37 in 65⅔ innings, and posted a 5.21 ERA. His season was interrupted by a two-week stint in the reserve in

July and a three-week option to the Vancouver Mounties (Pacific Coast League) in August. He finished with a 2-5 record in 35 appearances.

Shaw arrived at the Expos' spring training facility in Daytona Beach in 1970 no longer guaranteed a spot on the Opening Day roster. He battled journeymen pitchers Gary Waslewski, Mike Wegener, and Sembera for a roster spot, but was optioned to the Buffalo Bisons of the International League. After 12 early-season appearances, Shaw's contract was sold to the St. Louis Cardinals, whose GM, Bing Devine, considered him a reclamation project worth the risk. Shaw was assigned to the Tulsa Oilers of the American Association, where manager Warren Spahn was supposed to impart his wisdom. But Shaw broke his left hand in a game only two weeks after the trade and logged just seven innings for the Oilers, and 17 innings overall.

Shaw pitched in the Dominican Winter League in 1970-71 to prepare for his first spring training with the Cardinals. He had an excellent spring, tossing 12 scoreless innings at one point. But as fate would have it, he was one of the few pitchers with an option and was assigned to Tulsa. Though Shaw appeared in only two games for the Oilers in 1970, he credited his discussions about pitching with Spahn as one of the reasons for his unexpected comeback in 1971. "Spahnie would work with me as I warmed up," said Shaw. "He'd keep suggesting various things I might try in the course of a game under certain situations."[5]

Shaw was recalled to the Cardinals in late April to replace the recently released Fred Norman. With little fanfare and even fewer expectations, Shaw pitched ten scoreless innings spread over eight appearances to commence his career as a Redbird; he gave up his first earned run after 12⅔ innings. His confidence grew exponentially after just his second appearance when he relieved Reggie Cleveland with the bases full and one out in the seventh inning of a 2-2 game against his former team, the Expos. Shaw retired all eight batters he faced and earned the win when Jose Cardenal knocked in the winning runs.

"[Shaw is] among the cogs that make up the Big Bird machine," wrote Neal Russo in *The Sporting News*.[6] The Cardinals took over first place in the NL East during Shaw's commanding stretch. Shaw seemed like an ideal reliever: He could warm up quickly and could handle a heavy workload (he pitched in a career-high 13 games in June). His success seemed to dispel his doubt about his ability. "Even though I missed most of last season because I was hurt," he told *The Sporting News*, "I got to wondering whether I really was able to pitch. When you get into the regular season, it's entirely different."[7] Arguably the team's most effective reliever, Shaw finished the season as one of the hottest pitchers in all of baseball. In his last 26⅔ innings (23 appearances) he surrendered just one earned run (0.34 ERA) while winning five of seven decisions. While the Cardinals finished in second place to the eventual World Series champion Pittsburgh Pirates, Shaw set career-best marks in appearances (45), wins (7), and ERA (2.65). At just 27 years old, his future looked bright indeed.

With the threat of a players' strike looming, Shaw suffered from shoulder tenderness during spring training, but was apparently in good health when the season began. However, he unexpectedly struggled, blowing saves in three of his first six appearances. The Cardinals struggled, too, and occupied last place in the NL East when Devine decided to make a change. On May 15 he shipped Shaw (who had pitched just three innings in a month) to the Oakland A's for utility infielder Dwain Anderson.

The A's bullpen was excellent and deep; rubber-armed Rollie Fingers, Bob Locker, and Darold Knowles made at least 54 appearances each in 1972 and none posted an ERA higher than 2.65. Shaw's tenure with the A's was brief. In just his third appearance he had the kind of game that can leave scars on relievers: in three innings of mop-up relief duty against the Kansas City Royals, he surrendered nine hits (two home runs), nine runs, two walks, and a wild pitch. It proved to be his last game in the big leagues. He was optioned to the Iowa Oaks in the American Association, where he once again put up numbers expected of him: a 2.31

ERA in 32 appearances. Shaw was recalled in the last week of the season to replace Knowles, who had fractured his thumb. However, Shaw did not pitch and was dropped from the postseason roster in favor of rookie pinch-hitter Gonzalo Marquez.

Shaw was traded to the Detroit Tigers for catcher Tim Hosley on April 3, 1973. He spent his final year in professional baseball with the team's affiliate in the International League, the Toledo Mud Hens, for whom he made 38 appearances and carved out a 3.82 ERA. Now 29 years old, Shaw decided to transition into his post-playing career.

Once described by *The Sporting News* as easygoing, quiet, and always smiling, Shaw gradually drifted away from baseball. He became a regional manager of an employee benefits company, and was involved with insurance for more than 20 years. As of 2013, Shaw lived in St. Louis, where he ran his own health-insurance agency.

SOURCES

Associated Press

Independent Press-Telegram (Long Beach California)

Oakland Tribune

Van Nuys (California) *News*

The Sporting News

NOTES

1   *The Sporting News*, June 19, 1971, 11.

2   Ibid.

3   *The Sporting News*, April 8, 1967, 23.

4   *The Sporting News*, March 9, 1968, 22.

5   *The Sporting News*, June 19, 1971, 11.

6   Ibid.

7   Ibid.

Bill Voss

By Rick Schabowski

William Edward Voss had an eight-year major-league career playing outfield for the Chicago White Sox, California Angels, Milwaukee Brewers, Oakland A's, and the St. Louis Cardinals.

Voss was born in Glendale, California, on October 31, 1943. When he was a youngster, his baseball idol was Mickey Mantle. In 1968 he commented, "I think he's a great ballplayer. I've walked by him a few times, but I've never said anything. I imagine someday, if I'm lucky, I'll get on first base and say hello."[1]

When he played in the majors, the 6-foot-2 Voss weighed around 160 pounds. When Voss was a high-school freshman in Los Angeles, one of his coaches jokingly said, "We could always use you as a fungo bat."[2] After Voss's family moved to Newport Beach, California, he played baseball and basketball at Newport Harbor High School. Voss also played American Legion baseball. After graduating from high school in 1961, he attended Orange Coast College for two years, led the Eastern Conference in batting with a .450 average in 1962, and helped lead the team to California state junior college finals. Later he attended Long Beach State College.

Drafted by the Detroit Tigers in 1963, Voss batted .295 in 76 games for Lakeland of the Class A Florida State League, and .280 in 42 games with Knoxville in the Double-A Southern League. But the Tigers failed to protect him in the first-year draft, and the Chicago White Sox grabbed him at a cost of $8,000. Playing in 1965 for the White Sox' Southern League farm team at Lynchburg, Voss batted .284 with 73 RBIs and was named to the Southern League All-Star team. He was called up to the White Sox in September and made his major-league debut on September 14 when he pinch-ran for Smokey Burgess. Voss got his first major-league hit on the 21st, a home run off the Tigers' Denny McLain in the seventh inning at chicago.

Facing McLain again in the ninth, he tripled. Voss finished with a .182 batting average 6-for-33).

Commenting on his swift rise to the majors, Voss said in 1966, "It seems that I always have a good day or a good series when someone important is watching. I did when some of the (White Sox) front-office people were watching me at Lynchburg last year, and then when I came up to Chicago in September I hit the ball pretty good."[3]

A confident Voss said as he reported to spring training in Sarasota, Florida, in 1966, "I wouldn't be surprised if I made it. I wouldn't have signed if I didn't think I could play in the majors."[4] He impressed manager Eddie Stanky with his hard play (He's a good outfielder, he can hit with occasional power, he has a strong arm, and he's fast.")[5], but after getting only two

plate appearances in three weeks, he was sent down to Indianapolis of the Pacific Coast League.

At 160 pounds, Voss's playing weight was a concern. Voss tried a number of approaches and commented, "My wife gave me malted milks when I got up for breakfast, and she gave me malted milks before I went to bed at night."[6]

Voss's season with Indianapolis ended on August 26 when he broke a finger on his right hand in a collision with Denver's Marty Martinez. He was batting .252 at the time. After spring training in 1967, he was sent back to Indianapolis again. In a game against Oklahoma City in May, he was hurt sliding into second base. The injury turned out to be a ruptured tendon and a torn calf muscle, and he was out for a month. When Voss returned to action, he battered PCL pitching, finishing the season with a .320 batting average in 92 games. He was called up to the White Sox in September but didn't see much action.

Voss began the 1968 season with the White Sox' new Pacific Coast League affiliate in Hawaii. On April 28 he was recalled to the White Sox to replace Walt (No Neck) Williams, who was being sent down. Before reporting to Chicago, Voss set a PCL record by making 11 outfield putouts in a game against Vancouver on April 21. Voss struggled with the White Sox and was hitting just .115 on June 1. Manager Stanky kept Voss in the lineup, prompting the grateful player to say, "He's been good about it. He keeps telling me, 'Stay with it.' I'm happy I'm still playing." Voss remained confident and had some good moments for the White Sox, including a pinch-hit triple that drove in both runs in a 2-1 victory over the Indians on June 17, and a grand-slam on June 30 that helped the White Sox to a 12-0 victory over Detroit.

Voss suffered a major setback on July 4 when a pitch thrown by Baltimore's Pete Richert fractured his jawbone. Voss was out until September 14 and batted only 14 more times the remainder of the 1968 season, finishing with a .156 average.

On January 20, 1969, Voss was traded with rookie southpaw Andy Rubilotta to the California Angels in exchange for right-hander Sammy Ellis. Voss welcomed the trade because he lived just a few minutes from Anaheim Stadium. "It's really perfect," he said.[7] Voss said he knew it would be tough winning a starting job, "but I have confidence that I can do the job no matter where they put me."[8]

The Angels assigned Voss to Hawaii but invited him to spring training. Voss worked hard at spring training, led the Angels with a .477 batting average, and in the Angels' home opener he was the starting right fielder. "He came to play and he knows how to play," commented manager Bill Rigney.[9] Voss was elated — "This was my big opportunity. How many guys get a chance to play for their home team?" he said. "I made up my mind that I'd break my neck to make this team."[10] Voss had also regained weight. After fracturing his jaw he had been unable to eat solids and his weight dropped to 140 pounds, but he was now up to 165.

Voss had a slow start, and on May 27, when Rigney was fired, Voss was batting only .152. New manager Lefty Phillips still considered him "a solid hitter," and said, "He simply needs a chance to play."[11] Twenty-eight games later, the left-handed hitting Voss had raised his average to .239, batting .300 over that span. "It's simply a matter of finding a groove," he said.[12] In a three-game series against the Red Sox on August 8-10, Voss went 6-for-12, and drove in seven runs. He finished the season with a .261 batting average, and in the outfield made only one error in 187 chances. He also threw out 11 baserunners, and assisted in three double plays.

In 1970 the starting job for the Angels' right field spot was a battle between Voss and Rick Reichardt. After a great spring training, in which he batted .385, Voss got the job. He had a big series against the Milwaukee Brewers to open the season. On April 7 he drove in two runs with a triple, and he followed that up the next day with a 4-for-5 performance and four RBIs. On April 18 against the Kansas City Royals, Voss hit the first Angels grand-slam in the five-year history of Anaheim Stadium.

After Reichardt was traded to the Washington Senators on April 27, it seemed likely that Voss would get even more playing time. However, a concerned manager Lefty Phillips said, "Bill is a very valuable player to us, but he just doesn't have the stamina to play every day."[13] Things got worse for Voss when he was hit by a line drive during batting practice on May 28 and suffered a fractured left wrist. The injury kept Voss on the disabled list until mid-July, and he was platooned for the remainder of the season, winding up with a .243 batting average and 30 RBIs.

After the season, the Angels acquired outfielders Tony Conigliaro and Ken Berry, and Voss became expendable. On January 28, 1971, the Angels traded him to the Milwaukee Brewers for pitcher Gene Brabender. A pleased Brewers manager Dave Bristol said, "He'll give our club speed, defense, and a good left-handed bat. I just hope he gets off to a fast start as he had in other years. Good defense will make your pitching just that much better."[14]

Voss had a bad case of the flu toward the end of spring training and missed the beginning of the season. He was platooned for most of the season and batted .251 with 30 RBIs, but his a career-high 10 home runs.

In 1972 the Brewers outfield was loaded with potential starters. Besides Voss they were Billy Conigliaro, Joe Lahoud, Curt Motton, Brock Davis, and Dave May. Voss was ready for the challenge, saying, "I ran a mile each morning before I came down here. We've got good competition for jobs this year and I wanted to make sure I was in real good shape. In fact, I can see now it would have really hurt my chances if I wasn't in shape."[15] Dave Bristol was in his corner, saying, "Bill's a good guy to have on the club. ... Voss can play three outfield positions, and I love a guy who is versatile."[16]

Voss made the team, but his playing time was very limited. Before being traded to Oakland on June 20 for infielder Ron Clark, he started in only five games, batting .083. Oakland used Voss in the fifth spot in the batting order against right-handed pitching. He played in 40 games for Oakland, batting .227 before being traded on August 27 along with pitcher Steve Easton to the St. Louis Cardinals for outfielder Matty Alou. Voss played in just 11 games for Oakland, batting .267. After the season he was traded to the Cincinnati Reds for pitcher Pat Jacquez. He was in spring training with the Reds as a nonroster player but was released, and retired from baseball.

As of 2014 Voss was an assistant pastor for Vineyard Christian Fellowship in Cottonwood, Arizona. Voss and his wife, Donna, worked to help people through rocky family and marriage issues, and also did ministry work.

NOTES

1   Jerome Holtzman, "Slumping Rookie Voss Gets a Lift From Patient Stanky," *The Sporting News*, June 15, 1968.

2   Ross Newhan, "V Means Victory ... and Battler Voss," *The Sporting News*, April 19, 1969.

3   Jerome Holtzman, "Rookie Voss Gives Chisox Speed, Vigor," *The Sporting News*, March 26,1966.

4   Ibid.

5   Edgar Munzel, "V Stands for Victory—and Bill Voss," *The Sporting News*, March 4, 1967.

6   Holtzman, "Rookie Voss."

7   John Wiebusch, "Happy Voss Joins Angels' RF Battle," *The Sporting News,"* February 8, 1969.

8   Ibid.

9   Newhan, "V Means Victory."

10 Ibid.

11 Ross Newhan, " V Stands for Voss ... And Vigorous Bat," *The Sporting News*, July 19, 1969.

12 Ibid.

13 John Wiebusch, "Con Man? Phillips Builds Angel Egos," *The Sporting News*, June 6, 1970.

14 Larry Whiteside, "Lane Retains Old Touch—Three Quick Brewer Deals," *The Sporting News*, February 13, 1971.

15 Larry Whiteside, "Brewers' Voss Hard as Nails, Ready to Hammer A.L. Hurlers," *The Sporting News,"* March 18, 1972.

16 Ibid.

Gary Waslewski

by John Cizik

Gary Waslewski awoke in his Peabody, Massachusetts, apartment on the morning of October 11, 1967, as the starting pitcher in Game Six of the World Series. "I was reading the papers, and one guy wrote Waslewski has as much chance of winning as Custer had of beating the Indians," he said. "It didn't bother me. I just went out and tried to do my job." His major-league experience to that point consisted of 12 games, eight starts, a 2-2 record, and a 3.21 earned-run average. He had made his major-league debut four months earlier. He hadn't won a game since July 2; hadn't started one since July 29. He had never pitched a major-league complete game, and was declared eligible for the World Series only two days before Game One, after Darrell Brandon was placed on the injured list.

Gary Lee Waslewski was born on July 21, 1941, in Meriden, Connecticut, the first child of Michael and Adelaide (Lee) Waslewski. Michael was a master tool and die maker at a silversmith plant in nearby Wallingford. Adelaide died in early 1970, a cancer victim at 51. The family heritage was pure Polish on Michael's side, and a mixture of German and Cherokee Indian on Adelaide's.

Gary's younger brother, Michael, was born in 1943. "We played a lot of baseball in the open fields because there was nothing much else to do," Gary said. There was no Little League in Berlin, Connecticut, where they lived when Gary was younger, so childhood baseball consisted simply of those games in the cow fields and games of catch with his parents. "I would sometimes go out and have a catch with my mother," Waslewski recalled. "My father would come home from work at 6 at night and he'd catch for a while if I wanted to pitch, until it got to the point where I was throwing too hard and he couldn't handle me anymore." Finally, when Gary was about 13, organized ball came to town. Waslewski always remembers always being a pitcher.

Berlin's Little League ended at age 15. Without some motherly intervention, Waslewski's career might have ended there. "My mother had grown up in Meriden," Waslewski says. "And she went down to some friends of hers, guys she had gone to school with, who were running the Meriden Intermediate League, and asked them to make an exception to let me play there." While playing in the Meriden league, Gary was also recruited by the semipro Meriden Knights of Columbus. He pitched a lot during this period, usually throwing one game of a doubleheader for the Knights on Sunday, one or two games with the Intermediate League during the week, and maybe an American Legion game on Friday.

After pitching for the Berlin High School team (10-0 in his junior year as Berlin won the State Class C championship, Waslewski attended the University of

Connecticut on a partial scholarship. After his freshman year in 1960, it was back to playing ball for the Knights. "We played [a game] against a bunch of college all-stars that were barnstorming around," Waslewski recalled. "And there were a couple of good players on the team I was told that they were being scouted by some local scouts. I beat them 9-0, struck out 13, 14 guys, got four hits myself, and after the game [Pittsburgh Pirates scout] Milt Rosner, who was there to watch somebody else, came down and said, 'Gee, would you consider playing ball?' I probably wasn't going to go back [to UConn] because I just wasn't into the schooling and stuff." Bird-dog scout Rosner contacted his superiors, and Chick Whelan came down to sign Waslewski.

The right-hander was off to the Rookie Class D Appalachian League Kingsport Pirates. Of the 164 players in that rookie camp, only four survived the minor leagues. With about a month to go in the 1960 season, Waslewski was 4-2 with a 2.86 ERA. He was called up to play for the Sophomore League (Class D) Hobbs Pirates, where he went 0-1 with a 7.36 ERA as Hobbs made the playoffs. It was back to Hobbs in 1961. The team went 77-48 to lead the league. Waslewski was 12-7 with a 4.10 ERA

In 1962 Waslewski was moved up to Kinston of the Class B Carolina League. Teammate Steve Blass was an all-star, and the team won the championship. Waslewski was 7-8, with a 3.76 ERA. Back in Kinston in 1963, he went 1-1 with a 4.13 ERA before being called up to Reno of the Class A California League. The team went 71-69, finished fifth, and drew only 17,182 fans. Waslewski went 13-5 for the Silver Sox (3.83 ERA.)

It was back to Kinston and manager Pete Peterson for the 1964 season—not a demotion; the Carolina League had become Class A. Kinston took first place again, and Waslewski was 12-1 with a stellar 1.64 ERA. He wasn't around for the postseason, having been promoted to Asheville of the Double-A Southern League with around a month to go in the season. He went 5-5 for the Tourists, with an ERA of 3.84.

After the season the Pirates left Waslewski unprotected, and he was taken in the Rule 5 draft by the Red Sox. Waslewski did not make the Red Sox roster, and they had to offer him back to the Pirates. "Luckily, the Pirates said, 'We don't want him' or my career might have ended right there," Waslewski told author Jack Lautier.

The Sox sent Waslewski to Pittsfield of the Double-A Eastern League to start 1965. Waslewski went 6-2 with a 2.45 ERA, and was called up to Triple-A Toronto before season's end. He won only five games for the Maple Leafs, but his biggest win came off the field. "I went to a party … [with] two stewardesses from Air Canada." One of his teammates went with a girl named Nancy. "[He] kind of ignored her, and the two girls I was with ignored me, so we were just kind of sitting there, started talking, and started going out!" Nancy was a big baseball fan, and often attended Leafs games. They were married in September 1966.

In 1966 Boston's faith in the lanky right-hander paid off. The Leafs won the league championship, and Waslewski won Pitcher of the Year honors. He went 18-11 with a 2.52 ERA. He threw 200 innings, gave up only 143 hits, walked 84, and struck out 165.

After the season, it was off to Caracas in the Venezuelan League, and a honeymoon for the Waslewskis. With winter ball, and the 200 innings for Toronto, by spring training in 1967 Waslewski had thrown more innings than he was used to. "I ended up with tendinitis, inflammation in the shoulder." He had to stay behind with the Toronto club as spring training ended. Billy Rohr got off to a terrific start with the Sox, but became less effective. Eventually Rohr was sent to Toronto, and Waslewski was called up.

Waslewski's first start came in the second game of a June 11 doubleheader against the Washington Senators. Two errors in the first inning led to three unearned runs and a trip to the showers after three-plus innings. Waskewski's second start was a big improvement: He shut out the Chicago White Sox for nine innings before he had to leave in the tenth with a muscle pull behind his left shoulder,.

Waslewski was back on the hill in Minnesota on June 27, facing the Twins. An RBI single by Reggie Smith in the seventh helped give Waslewski his first major-league win. He won his next start, against Kansas City, throwing a 2-1 three-hitter with "nothing but a high-school curveball." In 26⅓ innings, Waslewski had allowed only three earned runs, and was 2-0.

"The main thing in our offense was Carl Yastrzemski," Waslewski said. "It was like — let's get on base so Yaz can knock us in. He was just incredible." Sal Maglie was the Sox pitching coach, but not a lot of help, according to Waslewski. "Jim Lonborg and I one day asked him about how to pitch to the Twins, and he told us how to pitch to the Dodgers! 'Well you know, Campy was kind of like Killebrew, and I would do this with Campy…' and he was telling us about throwing a slow curveball, and Lonborg and I were saying, 'We're just trying to get the curveball to break, never mind different speeds!' Sal was just … he was just there."

Waslewski had four more starts and a relief appearance in July, none worth writing home about. When his record fell to 2-2 after a start against the Twins on July 29, he was sent back to Toronto. After a September 3 start for the Maple Leafs, and Bill Landis's departure for military service, Boston brought him back. He made three relief appearances, pitching a total of eight innings, as Boston held on to win the pennant. Waslewski assumed his season was over, as he was not on the Series eligibility roster, but two days before Game One in Boston, he replaced injured pitcher Brandon.

Game Three, in St. Louis, began badly for the Red Sox. Gary Bell, the starter, immediately gave up a Lou Brock triple and a Curt Flood single. In the second Tim McCarver led off with a base hit, and Mike Shannon followed with a home run. Bell got out of the inning, but manager Dick Williams called on his rookie to stop the bleeding. "I remember walking in from the bullpen," Waslewski said. "And I felt like the matador walking into the ring." The first batter he faced was the speedy Lou Brock, who struck out. "I remember saying to myself, if I screw up, everybody in the world is going to see it! You screw up, it's not

just a local thing anymore!" Flood grounded out, Roger Maris flied to right, and the rookie had a perfect inning. He followed it with a perfect fourth, striking out Orlando Cepeda, and a perfect fifth, fanning Julian Javier. The Red Sox lost, 5-2, but Waslewski impressed his manager. "I think it was after that game that Dick came and said something about starting the sixth game if we have a sixth game. And I said, 'OK.'" Williams hoped to save his ace, Jim Lonborg, for a seventh-game appearance against Bob Gibson.

Fellow rookie Dick Hughes, Game Two loser, started Game Six for St. Louis. "Trailing three games to two," Leonard Koppett wrote in the *New York Times*, "the Boston Red Sox will rely on the least experienced pitcher ever to start a World Series game…" "So what?" said Dick Williams. The media scrutiny was intense. "The day of the game," Waslewski recalled, "somebody was up at the apartment in Peabody at about 6 o'clock in the morning. They wanted to come in, watch you shower. … What are you eating? More reporters. I remember answering the same questions over and over and over and over again!"

The Cardinals couldn't touch Waslewski in the first. Brock struck out, Flood grounded out, and Maris went down swinging. In the second, Waslewski got Cepeda, McCarver, and Shannon. Petrocelli's home run made it 1-0 after two. Julian Javier doubled to lead off the Cardinals' third. Brock drove him in with a single and stole second. Flood drove in Brock with a hit and the Red Sox trailed 2-1. Boston took the lead, 4-2, with a record-breaking fourth inning, as three players (Yastrzemski, Smith, and Rico Petrocelli) homered.

Maris walked on four pitches to start the sixth. Cepeda flied out to right, and McCarver walked on four pitches. The tying runs were on base. John Wyatt came in and got out of the inning. St. Louis tied the game in the seventh, but Boston won to force a seventh game, which a weary Lonborg lost. "Waslewski did one heck of a job," Williams said. "He had no starting jobs for quite a while, but he did it today. He was marvelous. I told him that when I went out there to take him out. He had thrown his best for as long as he could. I wanted six innings out of him and he came pretty close." "I just ran out of gas," Waslewski said. "I'm not especially proud of my performance. I'm glad we won, but I'd rather pitch nine innings. I was boiling inside, because I was so nervous."

After the season the Red Sox paid Waslewski and Bell "to go around with a group sales worker "and shake hands" at companies that the Red Sox hoped would buy tickets. That helped him pad his $8,500 salary and support his wife and newborn son. In 1968 he had a good spring. An unexpected spot was open in the rotation because of Lonborg's off-season skiing accident. Williams penciled Waslewski in as the fourth starter after he ended spring training with a string of 18 shutout innings and a 1.13 ERA. He won his first game of the season in Cleveland, 3-1, and then in Boston defeated the Indians again, 9-2, pitching his first major-league complete game. "And then I think I lost five in a row after that." He was removed from the rotation. He stayed with the Red Sox all year, pitching mainly out of the bullpen, and wound up 4-7 with a 3.67 ERA. On June 15 at Cleveland, he picked up his first major league save, mopping up for Ray Culp with 3⅓ innings of scoreless relief in a 9-3 Boston win.

After the season the Red Sox, who needed a backup infielder, traded Waslewski to the Cardinals for Dick Schofield. "That was a shocker," he said of the trade. "That was like having your wife come up and say, 'I want a divorce.'" Waslewski was in the competition to be the fifth starter but lost out to Dave Giusti. And on April 14 Waslewski became the answer to a trivia question. At Parc Jarry in Montreal, he relieved Nelson Briles in the fourth inning with the Cards up 7-6. An inherited runner scored to tie the game. In the Expos' seventh, they took an 8-7 lead off Waslewski. The score held up, and Waslewski became the first pitcher to lose a major-league game played outside the United States.

By June 2 Gary had appeared in 12 games for St. Louis, with an 0-2 record and a 3.92 ERA. On June 3 he was traded to the Expos for veteran Jim "Mudcat" Grant. Waslewski was reunited with former manager Dick

Williams, an Expos coach. After a string of ten scoreless innings out of the bullpen, manager Gene Mauch tabbed him to start against the Philadelphia Phillies at Connie Mack Stadium. "I had a good sinker that day, the bottom was dropping out of it," he recalled. Waslewski won, 5-0, a one-hit shutout in which he faced the minimum 27 batters.

In his next start, at Forbes Field against Pittsburgh, Waslewski's scoreless-innings streak ended at 25. He came out after the tenth inning, and didn't get the decision as the Expos fell, 2-1. Waslewski bounced between the rotation and the bullpen for the rest of the season, winding up 3-7 with the Expos, with a 3.29 ERA.

Waslewski began the 1970 season in the Expos bullpen, but moved to the rotation in late April. After four mediocre starts and an 0-2 record, he was placed on waivers. On the advice of a former Red Sox battery-mate, Elston Howard (then a Yankees coach), New York picked him up. Waslewski pitched in 26 games, with five starts. His ERA was good at 3.11, and his record was 2-2. His last career start came on Sunday, July 5, against Washington at Yankee Stadium, and he didn't survive the first inning, giving up two walks, a hit batsman, and a Del Unser home run. His last career victory was in a relief outing against the Detroit Tigers at Yankee Stadium on August 7.

Waslewski got his final major league save on June 19, 1971, at Memorial Stadium in Baltimore, throwing a perfect 11th inning. On July 6 he came into a game in Detroit, replacing Gary Jones with the Yankees trailing the Tigers 10-7 in the fifth inning. He was still in there to start the seventh. The Tigers' Willie Horton and Jim Northrup singled. Dick McAuliffe hit a groundball to first. The throw went to second base for a force out. Waslewski ran to cover first. Waslewski remembered, "[Felipe Alou] threw it to [shortstop] Gene Michael at second for one out, and Gene … threw me one of those sinkers down … and I'm running to the bag. I hit the bag and turn to go get his throw, and it's going to short-hop me. I'm thinking, if I don't block this ball, it bounces right into the stands because the stands are close, and the guy on second scores. So if I can at least block the ball and keep it in play, we're going to have first and third and I can get the next guy and we'll be out of the inning. As I tried to turn to block it, something locked in my knee, and I heard POP!

Waslewski's season was over. "I qualified for the pension plan at Lenox Hill Hospital," he joked. "I got my four years in." The Yankees had him pitch some batting practice near the end of the season, but manager Ralph Houk didn't want him injuring the knee again in a game.

Waslewski started the 1972 season with the Yankees' Triple-A club in Syracuse. He had no decisions with the Chiefs and a lofty 8.18 ERA when he was traded to the Oakland A's for infielder Ron Klimkowski. In August Waslewski was called up and reunited for a third time with Dick Williams, this time as an Oakland Athletic. His first appearance for the A's would be in—of all places—Boston on July 21. His last major-league appearance was in Oakland-Alameda County Coliseum on September 28 against the Minnesota Twins. The last batter he faced, Cesar Tovar, grounded to third. With the Athletics he pitched in eight games, all in relief, and was 0-3.

In 1973 the A's moved their Triple-A team to Tucson. Waslewski spent the entire season in the desert. "Not a good place for pitchers, because the air is very light," he said. He pitched well in relief for the Toros, helping them to the Eastern Division title. They lost to Spokane in the Pacific Coast League playoffs.

Near the end of spring training in 1974, Waslewski fell victim to owner Charlie Finley's penny-pinching ways. The word came down that Finley's wife had just served him with divorce papers, and he wanted everyone making more than $2,000 a month released. No other major-league job materialized. Back in Connecticut, he pitched in the Hartford Twilight League. He had obtained his securities and insurance licenses during his tenure in Boston, and he began to look for work. Career decisions were postponed when the Red Sox came calling. They signed Waslewski to a minor-league contract to replace some injured prospects at Triple-A Pawtucket. He never made it back

to the majors, winding up with no decisions and a 3.32 ERA. He knew the end had come, and began what turned out to be a 24-year career with the Hartford insurance company.

This biography is an abridged version of an article on SABR's BioProject website.

SOURCES

Books

Buckley, Steve, *Red Sox: Where Have You Gone?* (Champaign, Illinois: Sports Publishing, LLC, 2005), 28-31.

Johnson, Lloyd, and Wolff, Miles, eds. *The Encyclopedia of Minor League Baseball*, 2nd ed. (Durham, North Carolina: Baseball America, 1997).

Lautier, Jack, *Fenway Voices* (Durham, New Hampshire: Yankee Books, 1990),123-127.

University of Connecticut 2005 Media Guide

Newspapers

Addie, Bob, "Waslewski, Hughes Pitch Critical Sixth Game Today," *Washington Post*, October 11, 1967, E1.

Anderson, Dave, "Waslewski's Mound Problem Is Self-Control," *New York Times*, October 11, 1967, 52.

Bergman, Ron, "Joining A's? Better Keep Your Bags Packed," *The Sporting News*, August 12, 1972, 21.

Blackman, Ted, "Amaro Still a Glove Magician?" *The Sporting News*, March 21, 1970, 28.

Claflin, Larry, "Success as Tourists to Determine How Far Red Sox Can Go," *The Sporting News*, July 1, 1967, 4.

Claflin, Larry, "Bosox Pitching Not as Bad as Pictured, Says Williams," *The Sporting News*, December 9, 1967, 37.

Claflin, Larry, "Only Hub Question Marks Center on Lon and Con," *The Sporting News*, March 2, 1968, 4.

Claflin, Larry, "Those 6-1 Odds Don't Scare Bosox," *The Sporting News*, April 13, 1968, 12.

Dunn, Bob, "Woodie Wonder: Expo Lefty Ace," *The Sporting News*, May 17, 1975, 20.

"Gary, Not Denny," *The Sporting News*, June 3, 1972, 38.

Kahan, Oscar, "Red Sox Come Alive, Bury Cards Under 4-HR Salvo," *The Sporting News*, October 28, 1967, 7.

Obituaries, *The Sporting News*, March 14, 1970, 32.

Ogle, Jim, "Munson Makes Hit With Yankees Despite Slump," *The Sporting News*, June 6, 1970, 17.

Ogle, Jim, "Cater Edges Toward Yank Auction Block," *The Sporting News*, October 2, 1971, 22.

Ogle, Jim, "What Yankees Want in '72 — Just a Few Good Breaks," *The Sporting News*, January 8, 1972, 38.

Powers, John, "Former Players Felt a Kinship," *Boston Globe*, October 31, 2004.

Prell, Edward, "Boston Banks on Waslewski Today," *Chicago Tribune*, October 11, 1967.

"Red Sox Lose Rohr; Conigliaro Returns," *Washington Post*, June 2, 1967.

Reidenbaugh, Lowell, "Gibson, Redbirds — Second to None!" *The Sporting News*, October 28, 1967, 5.

Yantz, Tom, "Waslewski Delivered in Two Roles," *Hartford Courant*, October 26, 2004, C5.

Young, Dick, "Young Ideas," *Chicago Tribune*, October 11, 1967, E1-2.

"Waslewski Picks Up Red Sox," *Washington Post*, July 4, 1967, D2.

"Waslewski Sure to Pitch: Almost," *New York Times*, October 10, 1967, 59.

"Williams: 'Waz' Should Have Victory," *Chicago Tribune*, October 12, 1967, C1.

Other

Armour, Mark, "The Impossible Dream: How the 1967 Red Sox Won the Pennant," baseball-analysis.com/article.php?articleid=1711, March 17, 2003.

retrosheet.org

thebaseballcube.com

baseball-almanac.com

nmb.gov/publicinfo/airline-strikes.html

Author's interview with Gary Waslewski, Southington, Connecticut, December 29, 2005.

DVD: St. Louis Cardinals Vintage World Series Film, Major League Baseball Properties, Inc. 2002.

Dick Williams

By Eric Aron

Dick Williams was regarded as one of baseball's premier managers and turnaround artists. He was only the second skipper to win pennants for three different teams — Boston, Oakland, and San Diego.[1] As a rookie manager in 1967, Williams led the Red Sox from ninth place the year before to the World Series. Both personally and tactically, he took a no-nonsense, aggressive approach, which electrified several teams that he managed. His A's won back-to-back World Series, and he pushed the Padres to their first-ever postseason.

As a manager Williams compiled a record of 1,571 wins and 1,451 losses in 21 seasons, 20th on the career victory list as of 2014. Williams also enjoyed a fine playing career. As a versatile utilityman, he played with five teams in 13 seasons. After an appearance in the 1953 World Series with the Brooklyn Dodgers, Williams had three separate stints with the Baltimore Orioles, playing for manager and key mentor Paul Richards.

Richard Hirschfeld Williams was born on May 7, 1929, in St. Louis. He and his brother, Ellery, were raised in their grandfather's house during the Great Depression. Dick's father, Harvey, quit high school to join the Navy, and afterward found jobs delivering fish, cleaning brewery vats, and collecting insurance debts. Dick had fond memories of attending Browns and Cardinals games at Sportman's Park.

"I belonged to the Knothole Gang in St. Louis, and the seats were in left field. So (Browns left fielder) Chet Laabs and (Cardinals left fielder) Joe Medwick were my favorites," he said.[2]

When the elder Williams found regular employment, the family moved to Pasadena, California. Dick graduated from Pasadena High School and Pasadena Junior College, lettering in seven sports and even winning a city title in handball. Baseball, however, was his first love; he was 6 feet tall, weighed 190 pounds, and threw and batted right-handed.

In 1945, while playing a junior college football game, Williams suffered a leg injury. His father ran on to the field to check on him, only to suffer a fatal heart attack. Williams blamed himself for his father's death and never forgot how he felt that day. Harvey Williams left a lifelong impression on his son. A stern man, he accepted nothing but excellence from his boys, at times even physically abusing them. Consequently, Williams never accepted losing and constantly had to prove to himself that he was not a failure. Despite it all, he loved his father.

While playing for Pasadena Junior College, Williams was spotted by Brooklyn Dodgers scout Tom Downey and signed his first professional contract in 1947. After

graduation he reported to Santa Barbara in the Class C California league. In 79 games he hit .246 with 4 home runs and 50 RBIs, playing the outfield and third base.

The next season Williams was invited to spring training with the Dodgers. Through repetition and systemization, the Dodgers drilled young players in basics like bunting, hitting the cutoff man, and breaking up double plays. As a manager, Williams himself stressed those details. He began the 1948 season in Santa Barbara (California League), earning a promotion to Double-A Fort Worth (Texas League) after batting .335 with 16 home runs and 90 RBIs. He played mainly the outfield, with a few games at third while playing for Fort Worth.

Williams played in Fort Worth again in 1949, under the tutelage of another influential manager, Bobby Bragan, and was a Texas league all-star, thanks to 23 home runs, 114 RBIs, and a .310 batting average. Although Bragan bore a losing record in the major leagues, Williams credited him for all of his own victories. Bragan taught Williams about discipline, winning at all costs, and not being afraid to demonstrate how much you hate losing.

Williams said, "Players give you 100 percent not because they want something, but because they hate something. Me I gave a hundred percent because I hate losing … for the ones who treated losing and failure lightly, I figured I'd better get something ever better to hate. Me."[3]

Despite his progress, Williams had a hard time getting promoted in the Dodgers' deep organization. In 1950 he was back In Fort Worth, and in 144 games he hit .300 with 11 home runs and 72 RBIs. After the season, he played winter ball in Havana, and faced a young pitcher named Fidel Castro in batting practice. That winter he was drafted into the US Army, but with two weeks left in basic training, he reinjured his knee during a camp baseball game and got a medical discharge. Missing all of 1951 spring training, Williams expected to play at Triple-A St. Paul, but baseball,

trying to maintain competitive balance, required that minor leaguers returning from the service had to go through waivers. Both the Pirates and the Cardinals claimed Williams, so the Dodgers had to put him on the Brooklyn roster to keep him in the organization. As a returning serviceman, he was the 26th man on the 25-man roster and, not surprisingly, was first relegated to the bench. But he worked hard to earn playing time, and his opportunity finally came.

Williams made his major-league debut in the first game of a doubleheader against Pittsburgh at Ebbets Field on June 10, 1951. Pinch-hitting for Gene Hermanski, he grounded out to the pitcher. He started the second game in left field, batting leadoff, and went 4-for-5 with three singles and a triple. With an outfield of Carl Furillo, Duke Snider, and Andy Pafko, however, there simply wasn't a lot of playing time for Dick. He played in only 23 games in 1951, hitting .200 with one homer and five RBIs.

In 1952 Williams was on the verge of succeeding Pafko as left fielder but was injured again.[4] On August 25 in St. Louis, he suffered a shoulder separation while diving for a ball. Unable to play the rest of the season, he sat on the bench during the 1952 World Series against the Yankees.

In 1953 Williams played for Brooklyn and Triple-A Montreal. The Dodgers won the pennant again. Williams batted three times as a pinch-hitter in the World Series, getting a hit and a walk as the Dodgers fell in six games.

In 1954 Williams again spent time with the Dodgers but also played for Triple-A St. Paul. He spent the entire 1955 season back in Fort Worth, where he hit .317 and, in a season-ending doubleheader on September 5, he won the first game with an inside-the-park grand slam, and played all nine positions in the second game, pitching a scoreless eighth inning.[5]

On June 25, 1956, while playing for Triple-A Montreal, Williams was sent on waivers to the Baltimore Orioles. He became the team's starting center fielder, batting .286 with 11 home runs. In 1957 Williams was a true utility guy for the first time, playing all three outfield positions by first base and third base for the Orioles before being traded to the Cleveland Indians for outfielder Jim Busby in June. He continued to play multiple positions for the Indians, as he did the rest of his career.

Just before the 1958 season, Williams was traded back to the Orioles, with outfielder Gene Woodling and pitcher Bud Daley, for outfielder Larry Doby and pitcher Don Ferrarese. He went on to play 128 games, all over the diamond, hitting .276. After the season, Williams was traded to the Kansas City Athletics for shortstop Chico Carrasquel. Playing multiple positions, A's he batted .266 with 16 home runs and 75 RBIs.

Once again, the Orioles felt compelled to call for Williams's services. Early in the 1961 season, he was on his way back to Baltimore, traded with pitcher Dick Hall for catcher Chuck Essegian and pitcher Jerry Walker. He did poorly this time, batting .206 in 103 games. Back the next season, he raised his average to .247 in 178 at-bats.

On October 12, 1962, Williams was sold to the Houston Colt .45s, then in December he was traded to the Boston Red Sox in exchange for outfielder Carroll Hardy. Williams spent the last two years of his big-league playing career in Boston, as a utility player. The Red Sox teams of 1963 and 1964 hardly reminded him of the "Boys of Summer." He even claimed that Boston management did not expect the players to win. Moreover, he observed that players were treated differently depending on team status, aggravating natural resentments between highly competitive athletes.

"The place was a country club," Williams said. "Players showed up when they felt like it and took extra work only when it didn't interfere with a card game."[6]

During the winter of 1964, Williams was named manager of Boston's Triple-A affiliate in Toronto. He led the Maple Leafs to records of 81-64 in 1965 and 82-65 in 1966, winning Governors' Cup championships in both seasons. While in Toronto he managed players who would later come with him to Boston, including

Billy Rohr, Mike Andrews, Joe Foy, Russ Gibson, and Reggie Smith. Foy was the batting champion and MVP of the International League in 1965. Smith led the International League in hitting the following season, batting .320.

After the 1966 season, Red Sox general manager Dick O'Connell promoted Williams to replace Boston manager Billy Herman. At 37, he was the youngest manager in the American League.

Williams inherited a club that had grown complacent. In 1965 the team finished ninth in the 10-team American League with a dreadful mark of 62-100. In 1966 the Red Sox finished ninth again, 26 games behind the Orioles, although they played well in the second half. The 1967 Red Sox were considered a young team with talent, but no one could have predicted that they would win the pennant. Signing a one-year contract, Williams felt that he had a lot to prove. Remembering his own years with the Red Sox, he understood the country-club atmosphere and had a wealth of ideas about turning it around.

At spring training in Winter Haven, Florida, Williams made it perfectly clear that there would be only one person in charge—him—and that he would bring many changes to management's processes and rules. He began by stripping Carl Yastrzemski of his captaincy. All unmarried players were required to lodge at the team hotel. If players were late, they were fined. Williams stressed fundamentals, pitching, and defense. He was one of the first managers to use videotape to improve the adjustments.

Williams required his pitchers to play volleyball in the outfield to develop footwork skills while pushing their competitive instincts. Winning teams had to do only half of their post-workout sprints. When the great Ted Williams, incensed over the "boot camp" approach, walked out of spring training, the manager did not seem to mind.

In Las Vegas, Jimmy "The Greek" Snyder rated the Red Sox a 100-to-1 shot at winning the pennant. Williams promised that "we will win more games than we lose."[7] Opening Day at Fenway Park drew only 8,324 fans. The Red Sox were among the youngest teams in the league. Led by Yastrzemski, Jim Lonborg, Rico Petrocelli, Tony Conigliaro, and George Scott, these still-young veterans were surrounded by ex-Maple Leafs Foy, Smith, Gibson, and Rohr.

Williams was not afraid to exert his authority. If someone played poorly, he was benched and even embarrassed in front of his teammates. Williams chastised first baseman George Scott for being overweight, and described discussions with Scott as "talking to cement."[8] So many players were in the skipper's doghouse that it became a gag. One player said, "Listen, this thing is so full we're lucky we can field a team."[9]

On July 24 the team had rattled off a 10-game winning streak, including six on the road. Returning to Boston, the Red Sox were greeted wildly by thousands of fans. "I will never forget that night we landed at Logan Airport with that wild reception," Williams said later. "… I felt the franchise was practically reborn."[10]

Despite the odds, the Red Sox kept on winning, even overcoming Tony Conigliaro's beaning on August 18 that which sidelined the slugger for the remainder of the season. All season, it was a tight race. On October 1, the last day of the regular season, the Red Sox won the pennant by beating the Minnesota Twins. In the World Series, the Red Sox lost to the Cardinals in seven games. After the amazing season, Lonborg won the Cy Young Award, Yastrzemski, who won the Triple Crown, was voted MVP, and Williams won *The Sporting News'* Manager of the Year Award.

For re-establishing the team as a winner, Williams received a three-year contract extension. In 1968 Boston's pitching staff was decimated by injuries to Lonborg and Jose Santiago, and Conigliaro missed the entire season. The team finished in fourth place at 86-76, 17 games behind pennant winner and World Series champion Detroit.

In 1969 the Red Sox improved their victory total by one. Williams, however, was fired with nine games remaining in the season. His dismissal was attributed primarily to his acrimonious relationship with owner Tom Yawkey. Williams believed Yawkey was undermining his authority; pampering players after Williams had disciplined them. Media reports also claimed that Yawkey considered Williams disrespectful and unrealistic. In a game on August 1, Williams benched Yaztrzemski and fined him $500 for not hustling. Williams did not give special advantages to his star players. Rather, he was tougher on them *because* they were stars.

Williams spent the 1970 season with the Montreal Expos as Gene Mauch's third-base coach. That winter, he accepted an offer from Oakland owner Charlie Finley to manage the A's, becoming the 10th manager of the Athletics in Finley's short regime. John McNamara had been fired after leading the A's to a second-place record of 89-73. Finley charged that McNamara seemed unable to prevent bickering among his players. Backup catcher Dave Duncan remarked, "There's only one manager who manages this club — Charlie Finley … and we'll never win so long as he manages it."[11]

Right from the beginning, Williams knew he had talent on his team. There were outfielders Reggie Jackson and Joe Rudi, third baseman Sal Bando, shortstop Bert Campaneris, and pitchers Vida Blue, Blue Moon Odom, Catfish Hunter, and Rollie Fingers. Williams said, "This club is head and shoulders above the Boston club I had in '67."[12]

Oakland finished the 1971 season 16 games ahead of the Kansas City Royals, winning 101 games. Williams once again won the Manager of the Year award. Hunter went 21-11, and Blue finished a remarkable 24-8, winning both the Cy Young and MVP awards. But the A's didn't make the World Series: They were swept in three games by Baltimore in the American League Championship Series.

The 1972 A's were famous for their facial hair. It began when Reggie Jackson arrived at spring training sporting a mustache. When others decided to follow Jackson's lead, Finley seized another marketing opportunity, offering to pay anyone a $300 bonus if he would grow a mustache by Father's Day. The Mustache Gang was born. By now, Williams had changed as both a manager and a person, growing a mustache himself. Sal Bando said, "I think a lot of things are mislabeled on Dick, I mean, he was a strong disciplinarian, in terms of fundamental baseball and what he expected. … [But] as far as being a disciplinarian in terms of your curfew, your dress, your hair, Dick was very flexible there."[13]

The A's finished the season 93-62, winning the West by 5½ games over the Chicago White Sox. They won the League Championship Series by defeating Detroit three games to two.

In the World Series, the Oakland A's were matched up against the Big Red Machine, Sparky Anderson's Cincinnati Reds. With the hippie-like A's and the cleancut, conservative Reds, the Series was dubbed "the Bikers against the Boy Scouts."[14] Sparky and Williams had been friends since they were teammates in the Dodgers organization. The A's led the Series two games to one when in Game Four, Williams' aggressive managerial moves paid off. With Oakland trailing 2-1 in the bottom of the ninth, Williams used two pinch-runners and three pinch-hitters for a 3-2-comeback victory. The A's lost Games Five and Six, but rallied in Game Seven to win the Series.

In 1973 Oakland had three 20-game winners, Ken Holtzman, Vida Blue, and Catfish Hunter. The team won the American League West with a 94-68 record, and then defeated Baltimore in the ALCS, three games to two. The World Series against the New York Mets, however, marked the beginning of the end of Williams's tenure in Oakland. In Game Two, with the score tied, 6-6, in the 12th inning, Oakland second baseman Mike Andrews made two costly errors that gave the Mets four runs. After the 10-7 loss, Andrews blamed himself for his mistakes. Remembering his own experience with the death of his father, Williams consoled Mike. Mental errors upset Williams, not physical ones.

After the game Finley told Williams that Andrews should be placed on the disabled list with a shoulder injury. In reality, Finley was trying to add Manny Trillo to the postseason roster. Andrews was coerced into signing a medical statement indicating that he was injured, and did not accompany the team to New York.

Before Game Three Finley announced that Andrews was officially unable to play. Sal Bando, the team captain, retaliated by asking all of his teammates to wear Andrews' number 17 on armbands to show their support. Finally, Commissioner Bowie Kuhn intervened, arguing that a player could be replaced on a postseason roster only after suffering a new injury. Kuhn added, "The handling of this matter by the Oakland club has had the unfortunate effect of embarrassing a player who has given many years of able service to professional baseball."[15]

In Game Four, Williams sent Andrews up as a pinch-hitter to a standing ovation from the 54,817 fans at Shea Stadium. For Williams, the Andrews incident was the last straw; he told his team in the locker room that he would resign immediately after the Series. After the A's defeated the Mets in Game Seven, 5-2, Finley announced that he would "not stand in [Williams's] way" should he decide not to return as manager.[16] (Finley later said he meant not standing in the way of NON-baseball-related activities.)

It was no secret that Williams wanted to fill the managerial vacancy for the New York Yankees, and it was no secret that they wanted him. Before baseball's winter meetings, Yankees general manager Gabe Paul asked Finley for permission to talk to Williams. Since Williams had one year remaining on his Oakland contract, Finley demanded player compensation. Eventually American League President Joe Cronin intervened, determining that Finley was acting within his rights in retaining his manager. The Yankees hired Bill Virdon as their manager.

Williams left baseball to work for John D. MacArthur, one of the richest men in America, but realized that he missed baseball. California Angels general manager Harry Dalton persuaded Finley to allow him to hire Williams as manager. Williams replaced Bobby Winkles and interim manager Whitey Herzog on

July 1, 1974. He took the job despite having been warned by former Tigers manager Mayo Smith against accepting it, saying, "I've scouted them and I know: They've got no talent in the major leagues and nothing in the minor leagues. Nothing … But enough about me. Good luck."[17]

Nine of the Angels' first 13 seasons had resulted in losing records, and 1974 was no exception. Behind Nolan Ryan, Frank Tanana, and an aging Frank Robinson, Williams led the Angels to a 36-48 record the remainder of the season. The team finished last in the American League West at 68-94, 22 games behind the eventual three-peat world champion A's. The Angels fared no better in 1975, again finishing in last place at 72-89. The entire infield consisted of rookie or sophomore players: first baseman Bruce Bochte, second baseman Jerry Remy, shortstop Orlando Ramirez, and third baseman Dave Chalk.

Williams's frustration was epitomized by a 1976 incident. While talking to sportswriters in Chicago on June 30, he accidentally penciled Nolan Ryan in as the game's starting pitcher. Although it was not Ryan's turn in the rotation, league rules stipulated that the starting pitcher must face at least one batter. After Ryan retired Chicago's leadoff hitter, Chet Lemon, Williams yanked him. Unable to cope with the Angels' losing attitude, Williams was fired on July 24.

After three disappointing seasons in California, Williams got an offer to return to Montreal to manage the Expos. The 1977 Expos had nowhere to go but up. The previous season they had lost 107 games. Williams knew that a promising farm system generated the opportunity to build a winner. Montreal's young outfield consisted of future Hall of Famer Andre Dawson, Warren Cromartie, and Ellis Valentine. Larry Parrish was at third base and Tony Perez at first. Chris Speier was shortstop. And then there was a catcher nicknamed "The Kid": future Hall of Famer Gary Carter.

The team finished in fifth place in 1977 at 75-87. In 1978 the Expos were one game better at 76-86, rising to fourth place in the National League East. In his autobiography Williams recalled, "As we entered the

1979 season, [we] helped put together a team that would make people actually come to the park to watch baseball."[18]

The biggest pitching star in Montreal was Steve Rogers, who pitched his entire 13-year major-league career for the Expos. Montreal also had Ross Grimsley, who had won 20 games in 1978, and added Bill Lee, who had broken in under Williams with the 1969 Red Sox. The team was in the divisional race until the final weekend of both 1979 and 1980. In 1979 the Expos finished at 95-65, two games behind Pittsburgh, and in 1980, they went 90-72, just one game behind Philadelphia. Attendance soared, and pennant fever arrived in Montreal.

The strike-shortened season of 1981 was split into two halves. In the first half, the Expos finished 30-25 for third place behind Philadelphia. In the second half, the team was 14-12 when Williams was fired on September 8. Team president John McHale cited "lack of communication with players and poor clubhouse skills."[19] The team went on to win the "half-pennant," making the playoffs for the only time in franchise history, but after defeating the Phillies in the division series, the Expos lost to the Dodgers in the NLCS.

Williams's next stop was San Diego. In their first 13 seasons, the Padres had finished over .500 only once, in 1978. In 1981, the team finished 26 games out of first place. Credit for building the Padres into a pennant contender belonged to Jack McKeon, general manager since 1980. In 1982 McKeon gave Williams a three-year contract as manager, asking him to turn a franchise into a winner. Williams said in his autobiography, "At all my managerial stops I'd molded winners out of players already present. Doing it the San Diego way was perhaps a more difficult feat, considering that there was a chance that guys wouldn't just hate me, but hate each other."[20]

McKeon drafted outfielders Kevin McReynolds and Tony Gwynn in 1981. He traded shortstop Ozzie Smith to the Cardinals for Gary Templeton in 1982. He also signed Dodgers first baseman Steve Garvey as a free agent in 1983. Additional trades netted Carmelo

Martinez and Craig Nettles. McKeon also signed closer Goose Gossage.

Under Williams, the Padres finished 81-81 in 1982 and 1983. They started the 1984 season poorly, losing seven consecutive games in May. They moved into first place on June 9, however, and never looked back. The Padres clinched the National League West on September 20.

On August 12, 1984, the Padres were involved in one of the ugliest scenes in major-league history. A brushback game in Atlanta resulted in two bench-clearing brawls, 16 ejections, and five fan arrests. On the very first pitch of the game Atlanta starter Pascual Perez plunked Padres second baseman Alan Wiggins in the ribs. For the rest of the game, the Padres tried to retaliate. By the time Perez was struck in the eighth inning, Williams had long been ejected from the game. For his role in the brawl, Williams was suspended for 10 games and fined $10,000, while Braves manager Joe Torre was suspended for three games.

The 1984 National League Championship Series against the Chicago Cubs provided the Padres with one of the greatest comebacks in playoff history. In Game One of a best-of-five series, the Cubs blanked the Padres, 13-0. After losing Game Two, 4-2, the Padres faced elimination. Only the 1982 Milwaukee Brewers had rebounded from a two-game deficit to win a best-of-five series. In a scene similar to the '67 welcoming at Logan Airport in Boston, the Padres were greeted by thousands of fans upon arriving in San Diego.

The Padres won Game Three, 7-1. In Game Four, Steve Garvey hit a walkoff home run in the ninth to win, 7-5. Game Five completed the comeback as the Padres, after trailing 3-0, won 6-3. Meeting Williams's old foe Sparky Anderson again in the World Series, the Padres were clearly overmatched by a Detroit team that had won 104 games during the regular season, and fell in five games. Still, Williams finished third in voting for National League Manager of the Year.

In 1985 Williams led the Padres to an 83-79 record, 12 games behind the division champion Dodgers.

However, constant struggles with management forced him to resign on the first day of spring training in 1986. He wasn't out of work very long. A few weeks into the season, Williams accepted an offer to manage the Seattle Mariners. Knowing that it was likely his last chance at managing, he wanted to prove that he could still turn a bad team around. He signed a three-year deal to pilot a club for whom 76 wins marked a record high. He took over a 9-20 team (led by manager Chuck Cottier and Marty Martinez) and finished the 1986 season in last place at 67-95.

In 1987 Williams led Seattle to a then record finish of 78-84, seven games behind West Division champion Minnesota. However, he resented management for preventing him from replacing Billy Connors with a pitching coach who he felt would not coddle players or offer preferential treatment. Moreover, he lambasted pitcher Mark Langston for asking to be removed early from games rather than "tough it out." Clearly, Williams's hard-nosed management style had lost its effect. With the Mariners in sixth place at 23-33 on June 6, 1988, Seattle owner George Argyros fired him. Williams never managed again in the major leagues.

Williams became a skipper in the short-lived Senior Professional Baseball Association in Florida. Beginning play in November 1989, the eight-team league was made up of former players 35 and older. Williams managed the West Palm Tropics, who featured former A's Rollie Fingers and Dave Kingman.

In retrospect, a league consisting of aging stars seemed rather silly. As Williams remarked, "With pitchers who could barely throw and runners who could barely run [practice] games took nearly six hours."[21] Williams enjoyed the spirit of the game, however, as his Tropics led the league with a 52-20 record. They came within one game of winning the championship, losing 12-4 to the St. Petersburg Pelicans. The league folded after its second season.

Williams worked as a scout for the New York Yankees until 2002. He also broadcast games for the University of Nevada-Las Vegas and the Las Vegas 51s of the Pacific Coast League. On November 9, 2009, Williams was inducted into the Red Sox Hall of Fame for managing the Impossible Dream team of '67.

Williams got the call from the National Baseball Hall of Fame just a year earlier. On July 27, 2008, after being voted in by the Veterans Committee, Williams was enshrined in Cooperstown along with Rich Gossage.

Williams, who had been married to his wife, Norma, since 1954 and lived in Henderson, Nevada, died on July 7, 2011, of a ruptured aortic aneurysm. He was 82. Besides his wife he was survived by three children, Kathi, Marc, and Rick, and five grandchildren.

Rick Williams was a Red Sox batboy for his father in 1967, and later pitched college ball under coach Eddie Stanky at the University of South Alabama. He was drafted by the Montreal Expos out of school. In 1977, he went 3-1 with a 2.90 ERA for the GLC Expos, and 1-0 in four innings for the Jamestown Expos. In 1978, he reached Triple-A, pitching for the Denver Bears, but an arm injury derailed his career. He was the first pitching coach of the Florida Marlins and Tampa Bay Devil Rays. He was an assistant to the Tampa Bays general manager and scouted for the Yankees. As of 2014, he worked for the Atlanta Braves as a special assistant to the general manager for pitching development.

SOURCES

Chandler, Bob, with Bill Swank, *Bob Chandler's Tales From the San Diego Padres* (Champaign, Illinois: Sports Publishing LLC, 2006).

Crehan, Herb, *Red Sox Heroes of Yesteryear* (Cambridge, Massachusetts: Rounder Books, 2005).

Reynolds, Bill, *Lost Summer: The '67 Red Sox and the Impossible Dream* (New York: Warner Books, 1992).

Arbel, Allen, "Dick Williams Can Remember Baseball's 'Angry Days,'" *Baseball Digest*, July 1980.

baseball-almanac.com

baseballlibrary.com

baseball-reference.com

NOTES

1 The first was Bill McKechnie, who won pennants with the Pirates, Cardinals, and Reds.

2 Phone interview with Dick Williams by Jeff Angus, January 2006.

3 Dick Williams and Bill Plaschke, *No More Mr. Nice Guy* (New York: Harcourt Brace Jovanovich, 1990), 78.

4 Williams, 62.

5 *The Sporting News*, September 14, 1955, 42.

6 Williams, 71-72.

7 "Dick Williams; Sox Skipper for Impossible Dream Season" (obituary), *Boston Globe*, April 8, 2011.

8 Williams, 93.

9 Bill McSweeny, *The Impossible Dream: The Story of the Miracle Boston Red Sox* (New York: Coward McCann, 1968), 186.

10 Glenn Stout and Richard Johnson, *Red Sox Century* (Boston: Houghton Mifflin, 2004), 323.

11 Bruce Markusen, *A Baseball Dynasty: Charlie Finley's Swingin' A's* (Haworth, New Jersey: St. Johann Press, 2002), 1.

12 Markusen, 6.

13 Markusen, 117.

14 Markusen, 171.

15 Markusen, 248.

16 Markusen, 263.

17 Markusen, 183.

18 Williams, 206.

19 Williams, 225.

20 Williams, 233.

21 Williams, 316.

1972 A's: A World Champion Worth The Wait

By Curt Smith

For those of you keeping score, the Oakland Athletics' 1972-74 infield consisted largely but not exclusively of Sal Bando, third base; Bert Campaneris, shortstop; Tim Cullen and Dick Green, second base, 1972 and 1973-74, respectively; and Mike Epstein and Gene Tenace, first base, 1972 and 1973-74, respectively. Left field was Joe Rudi's. Reggie Jackson and fleet Billy North patrolled center field in 1972 and 1973-74, respectively. Jackson moved to right field in 1973-74, replacing 1972's Angel Mangual. Dave Duncan caught most of 1972, then was traded. Tenace, Ray Fosse, and Larry Haney crouched behind the plate in 1973-74. Designated hitter Deron Johnson preceded 1974's Jesus Alou. Mike Hegan, Ted Kubiak, and Mangual gave new connotation to utilitymen. The brightest star, an Arcturus or Cassiopeia, was pitching: Catfish Hunter, Ken Holtzman, Blue Moon Odom, Vida Blue, and relievers Dave Hamilton, Joel Horlen, Bob Locker, Darold Knowles, Paul Lindblad, Horacio Pina, Greg Abbott—and Rollie Fingers.

The dynasty began with a most interesting 1972. It, in turn, began with a players' lockout that cost 13 days, fairness (Boston lost seven games, Detroit six), and attendance (before August, many teams drew sparsely). The Phillies had a 59-97 record. Incredibly, their ace, Steve Carlton, won 27 games. Roberto Clemente got his 3,000th and final hit, but died on New Year's Eve on a mercy mission to help earthquake victims in Nicaragua. According to *Total Baseball: The Official Encyclopedia of Major League Baseball*, the American League batted an overall .240, leading to 1973's designated hitter. The 1972 A's lost seven games to the strike, also hit .240, but led the AL with 134 homers and were second with 604 runs. The A's began wearing solid green or solid gold jerseys with contrasting white pants. Owner Charlie Finley officially changed the team name to "A's," banning "Athletics." Either way, Oakland had a brilliant 2.58 ERA, topped the league with 43 saves, and had a 93-62 record.

The A's vaulted to a 42-20 start, then lost three of four games to the second-place White Sox. This augured a banal July and August of barely .500 baseball—Oakland was 30-28—before the A's forged a 20-11 September-October record, winning the American League West by 5½ games over Chicago. Rudi led the "Junior Circuit" in hits (181) and triples (9) and trailed only the Yankees' Bobby Murcer in runs (94 to 102). He had 32 doubles, 288 total bases, and a team-high .305 average that A's voice Monte Moore dubbed "phenomenal" in the 1972 World Series vs. Cincinnati. Given the AL's lack of offense, Moore may have had a point. He had an Okie twang: also, a hankering for hyperbole, terming "miraculous" Green's survival of a Reds block at second base in October. Campaneris hit .240, but led the league in steals (52) for the sixth and final time. Epstein had 26 home runs, 70 runs batted in, and a .490 slugging average. Jackson hit .265, had 25 home runs, and added 75 RBIs; Bando, .236, 15, and 77; Duncan .218, 19, and 59. Paraphrasing Earl Weaver, the A's lineup had "deep depth."

At one time or another, Connie Mack is said to have claimed that pitching is 75 or 90 percent of baseball. All apply to the club a/k/a The Mustache Gang. Finley offered any player $500 to grow a mustache by Father's Day. In that very different salary age, each player complied. One, Catfish Hunter, had a 2.04 earned-run average and won 20 games (21-7) for the second of five straight years, leading in 1972 win percentage (.750). Cooperstown '87 retired 224-166 with a 3.26 ERA. "There was no one like him to win the big one," said manager Dick Williams. Few equaled Fingers' handlebar mustache, or his genius in relief. Once

Finley voided a major pay hike by giving Rollie a year's supply of mustache wax. Fingers repaid him in 1972-74 with 61 saves, including 1972's third most in the league's 21 with a 2.51 ERA in 65 games. Holtzman was 19-11; Odom, 15-6; Blue, 6-10; and swingmen Dave Hamilton 6-6 and Joel Horlen 3-4. Relievers Bob Locker and Darold Knowles finished 6-1 with 10 saves and 5-1 with 11, respectively. The A's fought like other teams played pepper. "So what else is new?" said Fingers of a Jackson-North brawl. "Being on this club is like having a ringside seat for the Muhammad Ali-Joe Frazier fights."

The A's clinched their division in September. The AL East Division was stickier. On October 2 the Red Sox readied for a year-ending series—three games at Detroit. "That schedule!" said Boston announcer Ken Coleman. "The strike made us play one fewer game than the Tigers." The Sox led their division by a meaningless one-half game, needing two of three to win. Instead, base-running bungling—two Sox simultaneously landed at third base—cost Boston the first game, 4-1. A day later Detroit's Al Kaline's single scored the division-winning run, 3-1. The 1972 League Championship Series began October 7 at the Oakland-Alameda County Coliseum before 29,536. Before it was over the LCS reminded you of the Capulets vs. the Montagues. Sparta.

The Game One prologue to the World Series was tied, 1-1, for the first ten innings. In the top of the 11th, Kaline took Fingers deep: 2-1 Tigers. In the bottom half, pinch-hitter Gonzalo Marquez singled to tie, right fielder Kaline threw the ball away, and Gene Tenace scored the winning run: A's, 3-2. The next day 31,088 saw Odom blank the Tigers, 5-0, on three hits in a match recalled for another kind of hit. In the seventh inning, Campaneris batted, having already singled thrice and scored and stolen a base twice. Lerrin La Grow's first pitch plunked him in the ankle, after which Campy flung his bat toward the mound, narrowly missing the reliever; at which point a bench-clearing brawl began; whereupon Tigers skipper Billy Martin had to be restrained from attacking Campaneris. Like the year's regular-season atten-

dance—921,323—the crowd was so loud as to compensate in volume for what it lacked in size.

Behind two games to none, the Tigers flew home to "the corner of Michigan and Trumbull," as their great announcer, Ernie Harwell, dubbed Tiger Stadium. Joe Coleman kept Detroit alive, fanning an ALCS record 14 in a seven-hit 3-0 victory. Next day the teams played the playoff's most riveting game. Tied 1-1 after nine, the A's scored twice in the top of the tenth inning on a Matty Alou double and a Ted Kubiak bloop single. Ahead 3-1, Dick Williams asked Bob Locker to uncork the champagne in the A's clubhouse. Instead, Locker, Joel Horlen, and Dave Hamilton yielded two singles, two walks, a wild pitch, were pricked by an error, then allowed another single by Jim Northrup to score Gates Brown with the winning run: Tigers, 4-3. The noise in the ancient chamber, opened in 1912, was almost insupportable. Twice playing extra innings, the two combatants had split the first four ALCS games.

Tiger Stadium hosted the best-of-five's decisive game. The score was 1-all entering the fourth inning. "Here's the pitch to Tenace," said Moore's partner, the gravelly Jim Woods. "Line drive into left field—this may be tough to score on. Here's [George] Hendrick around third. Here's the throw coming on into the plate. The ball is dropped—ball is dropped by [catcher Bill] Freehan! And Oakland moves into the lead, 2 to 1, on Gene Tenace's first hit of the playoffs!" The same 2-1 score held forth in the ninth. Left-handed Blue, relieving, faced Detroit's Tony Taylor: one on, two out, a 2-2 count. "Vida gets set," said Moore. "He kicks high, he throws. There's a drive into center field. Back goes Hendrick. He is under it! The Swinging A's have won the American League championship! The Oakland A's are champions!" Odom got the win, Blue the save, the A's the franchise's first pennant since 1931.

For Oakland, the LCS had been, as Wellington said of Waterloo, "a close-run thing." You could also say that of the National League titlist that emerged from *its* League Championship Series. Born in 1969, five of the first six best-of-five LCS had ended in a sweep. The 1972 Pirates-Reds series, like the A's, went the maximum length. In Game Five Pittsburgh led, 3-2,

Johnny Bench batting in Cincinnati's last of the ninth inning. "Change—hit in the air to deep right!" said Reds voice Al Michaels. "Back goes Clemente! At the fence—she's gone! Johnny Bench—who hits almost every home run to left field—hits one to right! The game is tied!" With two out, the pennant—George Foster—led off third base. Hal McRae pinch-hit. "In the dirt—it's a wild pitch!" Michaels bayed. "Here comes Foster! The Reds win the pennant [4-3]! Bob Moose throws a wild pitch, and the Reds have won the National League pennant!"

Would the Series be as close as either LCS? Many wondered. The A's had lost Jackson for the Series, No. 9 tearing his hamstring in the LCS. It further lengthened the long Classic odds that the Big Red Machine would flatten the A's. Baseball's oldest professional team entered the Series running on every cylinder. The Reds finished 95-59, winning the National League West by 10½ games. Catcher Johnny Bench hit an NL-high 40 homers, had 125 RBIs, and was the MVP. Pete Rose led the league with 198 hits. Second baseman Joe Morgan had an NL-best 122 runs and 115 walks, stole 58 bases, and with shortstop Dave Concepcion turned the double play so fast it was as though the ball was radioactive to their gloves. Starters Jack Billingham, Ross Grimsley, and Gary Nolan went 41-25. Manager Sparky Anderson was named "Captain Hook" for pulling them. He had ample reason: a brilliant bullpen. Clay Carroll, Pedro Borbon, and Tom Hall compiled 60 saves.

Beyond baseball, the Series acquired a cultural coloration. The A's were rebellious, often fought, and had a counter-culture air. The clean-shaven Reds were a metaphor for the Silent Majority itself. In fall 1972, Middle America was in the saddle. The economy was booming, President Nixon having frozen wages and prices, cut taxes, and severed the dollar's link to gold. Said the *New York Times:* "The United States is in the midst of a new economic boom that may prove to be unrivaled in scope, power, and influence by any previous expansion in our history." Earlier that year Nixon had ended a quarter-century of estrangement between America and the People's Republic of China, visiting in February; signed the first agreement of the nuclear age to limit strategic arms, in May in Moscow; and two weeks after the Series ended won statistically America's greatest landslide re-election, taking 49 states and 60.7 percent of the popular vote. June 1972's break-in by Republican officials at D.C.'s Watergate offices seemed an asterisk. Nixon appeared invulnerable.

So did the Reds. "The A's were lightly regarded," Ron Fimrite wrote on the eve of the World Series. We should have recalled Yogi Berra: "In baseball, you don't know nothin'." Gene Tenace had hit five homers in the regular season. October's Hero twice went yard his first two at-bats in the Series—a Fall Classic first. In the second inning, the .225 part-time catcher/first baseman bashed a two-run stiletto. Cincinnati tied the score, 2-all, in the fourth. Then: "One out in the Oakland fifth," said NBC Radio's Jim Simpson. "Hits this one a long way to left field down the line! Rose looking up! It is—gone! Home run, Tenace!" His second home run gave the A's their final 3-2 edge. The next day Hunter singled in a run and pitched 8⅔ one-run innings. Rudi homered, and in the ninth robbed Dennis Menke of a potential game-tying blast, leaping face-first against the green board fence at Cincinnati's Riverfront Stadium. "I didn't think I had a chance," he said. "I thought it was gone." A's win, 2-1. Gone was the Reds' invulnerability, down two games to none, the Series moving west.

Before 1976, each rival home-team announcer aired the World Series. Thus, in 1972-74 Moore did half of each NBC TV and radio game at Oakland and away, respectively. Monte recalls Jack Billingham beating Odom in Game Three, 1-0—especially the eighth inning. With Reds runners on second and third base, a 3-2 two-out count on Bench, Williams asked for time, went to the mound, called catcher Tenace and third baseman Bando over, talked, sauntered back to the bench, and pointed to first base. Fingers, Tenace, and Bando nodded at Williams' *diktat*: clearly, an intentional walk. Bench readied. Fingers set and looked at second base. Said Bench: "I thought they were putting me on." As Fingers kicked, Tenace suddenly squatted behind the plate and nabbed a slider that caught its outside corner—called strike three!—that left Bench vowing, "I'll never be set up like *that* again."

Next day's *affaire* was just as close: Six of seven Series games, in fact, were decided by one run. In the fifth inning, Tenace homered: 1-0 A's. Bobby Tolan knocked in Concepcion and Morgan in the eighth: 2-1 Reds. In the bottom of the ninth inning, four straight singles, including three pinch-hits, set a World Series first and brought Oakland within a game of another first—a title. A's win, 3-2, leading the Series three games to one. How could Cincinnati survive? Courageously, as it happened. In Game Five the Reds braved that man again. "McGlothlin is ready, throws," Jim Simpson said of Tenace, batting with two A's on base. "Long drive—left field! Back goes Rose, looks up. Home run! His fourth of the Series! It's 3 to 1, Oakland!" The Reds rallied one run at a time, Rose's ninth-inning single giving them a 5-4 edge. In the bottom of the inning Morgan's great throw doubled pinch-runner Odom at the plate—the potential tying run. Cincy was alive—till when?

Game Six was a clunker: Reds, 8-1. The finale, though, was taut and exhausting, like the whole. Tolan's first-inning error gave the A's a run. Hal McRae's sacrifice fly tied things in the fifth. An inning later Tenace and Bando each doubled in a run: 3-1, A's. Cincinnati scored its second run in the eighth inning, but Fingers said *no mas.* "Rose steps in," Simpson said in the ninth. "He is two-for-four today and has made great contact all four times. The other two were driven deep to the center-field wall … Fly ball, deep left field! Rudi goes back near the warning track, is there. The World Series is over! And on one pitch, Rose is out, and the underdog Oakland Athletics win their first world championship since they were in Philadelphia in 1930! The A's win it, 3 to 2!" Neither team pitched a complete game. The two teams hit an identical .209. Oakland

was outscored, 21-16. Fingers relieved in six games. Tenace, the Series MVP, had four homers, 9 RBIs, and a .348 average.

The contrast was indelible: Kiwanis vs. camp, Main Street vs. Woodstock, gray/white vs. green and gold. A Series to shout about. A classic Fall Classic. Its last tableau was unforgettable. On the roof of the A's dugout, Charlie Finley and Dick Williams kissed their wives, the straw-hatted A's Swingers Band playing Finley's favorite song. "Sugartime" lyrics went: "Sugar in the morning, sugar in the evening, sugar at supper time. Be my little sugar, and love me all the time."

At that moment, Oakland loved Charles O. Finley. "Mr. Finley has been wonderful to me," Williams said, full-heartedly. One year later, he pined to punch Charlie in the nose.

SOURCES

Virtually all material, including quotes, is derived from Curt Smith's books *Voices of The Game, Storied Stadiums, Voices of Summer, The Voice, Pull Up a Chair, A Talk in the Park,* and *Mercy! A Celebration of Fenway Park's Centennial Told Through Red Sox Radio and TV* (published, in order: Simon & Schuster 1992; Carroll & Graf 2001 and 2005, respectively; the Lyons Press, 2007; and Potomac Books 2009, 2010, and 2012, respectively).

Books

Fimrite, Ron, *The World Series: A History of Baseball's Fall Classic* (New York: Time Inc. Home Entertainment, 1997).

Lowry, Philip, *Green Cathedrals: The Ultimate Celebration of All Major League Ballparks* (New York: Walker & Company, 2006).

Silverman, Matthew, *Swinging '73: Baseball's Wildest Season* (Guilford, Connecticut: The Lyons Press, 2013).

Thorn, John, Peter Palmer, and Michael Gershman, *Total Baseball: The Official Encyclopedia of Major League Baseball* (Kingston, New York: Total Sports Publishing, 2001).

Websites

Baseball-reference.com

Life in the Good Old A's, or Growing Up Finley

By Matthew Silverman

Nancy Finley grew up in the Oakland Coliseum, occupying a seat in her father's office every day after school while the Swingin' A's went about their work of dominating baseball. A teenager and Oakland High School student during Oakland's legendary run, Nancy was the daughter of Carl Finley, who ran the A's front office. Carl, the cousin of A's owner and general manager Charlie Finley, served in numerous capacities, but he was Charlie's man on the ground in Oakland while the owner spent most of the year two time zones away. Charlie, who wanted to maintain his business and home base in Illinois and Indiana, had persuaded favorite cousin Carl to leave his job with the Dallas school system to be his eyes and ears in Kansas City. Then Carl moved to Oakland along with the franchise in 1968. He was not alone.

Carl's daughter, Nancy, lived with him in an apartment not far from the Oakland Coliseum. Nancy had lived in Dallas with her mother following an acrimonious divorce, but her father gained custody and she moved to Oakland at 14. As the A's grew up, so did Nancy. She ran errands, stuffed envelopes, sat in on meetings, peeked in at Pink Floyd doing a sound check at the adjoining Oakland Coliseum Arena, processed postseason ticket requests, visited Charlie O. the mule at his stable, and watched some of the best baseball played during the 1970s. It was a childhood many would envy, but it was just the way things were for a shy high-school student whose family name was constantly in the press—and not always favorably.

It was the time of her life, which she has been working into book form. Her story includes never-before-seen documentation and perspective from her family's side of a story that has often been told only one way in the press of the day and in the books and documen-taries that have followed. Still a resident of the East Bay, and raising her own family, Nancy Finley fondly recalls the A's glory days.

1) How old were you when you started working in the A's offices?

Nancy Finley: Working? At a very young age, someone in one front office would ask me to take a note to someone in another front office. They thought it was cute. I would have to say that I was paid for my work starting with our championships, because of how serious it was. I never worked full time during those years, though—I was only 14 in 1972.

2) There have been a lot of stories about how few people worked for the A's front office compared to other teams. Can you paint a picture of what it was like behind the scenes with the A's?

Finley: I still have a December 24, 1974, *Oakland Tribune* article, where a well known entertainment columnist, Perry Phillips, wished all of his friends happy holidays. I remember this columnist well. He was a friend of Dad's.

This columnist mentions the Raiders staff (including front office), many Bay Area restaurants (I recognize most names), and our A's staff. He names Al Dark, Dad, Charlie, and Charlie's secretary. That is it. With the Raiders, the list is much longer. [Editor's Note: The list has 32 Raiders names, to be exact.]

We were the smallest front office in baseball, but we were also the best.

3) Did you have any input with the yearbooks?

Finley: No. If I had, my name would have appeared. Dad never wanted my name here. There were too many kidnapping threats (à la Patty Hearst) in the

1970s. Dad had 99 percent of the input in the yearbook. Dad often beefed up our front office by adding names twice, or, inserting other relatives.

4) There's an interesting story about you handling the A's postseason tickets. Can you describe what the task was like in the age before computers and credit cards?

Finley: I remember we had to start taking orders for postseason tickets soon after Labor Day. It may have even been slightly earlier. Whoever was in first and second place a certain amount of time before the end of the season had to have championship tickets pre-printed. Seeing printed World Series tickets in mid- to late September added stress.

During our radio and TV broadcasts, our announcer would tell fans that if they wanted to purchase tickets for playoffs or World Series, they needed to send a check to a PO box in Oakland. Only Dad had this POB key.

Fans could call our ticket office for pricing. Everything was paid via check, money order, or cashier's check, via "snail mail" to that address. I spent all day, from about 7 or 8 a.m. until it was dark, opening envelopes. Sometimes, cash fell out instead. Sometimes, gift certificates fell out. Sometimes, jewelry fell out—nothing bulky, usually a thin gold chain. Bribery did not work in getting better seats, though I never knew what happened to the excess people sent in.

5) Did you ever work the ticket booth?

Finley: On occasion, I helped inside our ticket front office. I did not work behind the ticket booth at the Coliseum. Again, it was for security purposes.

6) Did you help with any promotions?

Finley: Yes. I remember being around the family during brainstorming sessions at a very young age. I'll always have fond memories of this. It electrified the room. As a pre-teen, just about every business dinner I attended with Dad and Charlie turned out to be a brainstorming session. No one's idea was ever laughed at in a bad way. This taught me to be open-minded.

As a teenager, I was brought into this group. It just happened. I could offer what my generation thought. It was during one of these brainstorming sessions that Charlie said he really liked the way I thought. Charlie told dad that I was now an A's VP. Unofficially, my father made sure.

7) Can you explain how you were related to Charlie Finley?

Finley: My grandfather and Charlie's father were brothers. They were the eldest of the Finley siblings. After World War I (most Finley males were drafted), Charlie's father married and lived close to his parents and siblings in Birmingham, Alabama. My grandfather did not want any part of working in the local steel mill. He moved to Dallas, Texas, for a better employment opportunity. My grandfather became a salesman of anything, as I call it. Mostly he sold used cars. Dad never had the typical Depression-era stories, since they always had food on the table.

Granddad used to call Charlie his "favorite nephew," and "like a son." I have heard how Charlie was more like my grandfather than Dad was. Dad was more like Charlie's father, Uncle Oscar. Uncle Oscar was mellow. Charlie certainly was not.

In the late 1930s the Birmingham steel mills were closing. Uncle Oscar had worked in these steel mills. At this time, steel-mill jobs were opening in Gary, Indiana. Charlie did not want to move. He asked to live with Granddad while his parents settled in Gary.

After Uncle Oscar was settled in Gary, my other uncles—I call them "the brothers"—and Granddad visited Gary often. They were very close.

Dad and Charlie each had one younger brother. These were not close relationships. Charlie and Dad, and through all of the other "brothers," stayed in touch. I don't know if this is just a Southern thing, although I notice my older cousins refer to themselves as my "aunt" or "uncle." This is what my children now call them. I remember in Kansas City, being in a large crowded room, with Charlie squatting down, his arms held out, and saying, "Come to Uncle Charlie!"

8) Did you enjoy baseball or other sports before your father, Carl, became associated with the A's?

Finley: I was too young to know about other sports. I used to think our Kansas City players changed into Chiefs uniforms in the winter, and played football.

9) Since there are so many stories about Charlie Finley, can you provide a better picture of what he was like behind the scenes with his team and his family?

Finley: If you can believe it, he was very private with his family. He was also down to earth. He did not like pretentious people. He appreciated being asked for advice. Sometimes he was in a mood to say something, to see if a reporter would pick up on it. This backfired at times. It was written as fact, when he was actually bluffing. He absolutely loved animals.

10) Did you spend much time with the fabled mule, Charlie O.?

I spent a lot of time visiting Charlie O. in Kansas City, at Benjamin Stables, where he was boarded. Howard Benjamin gave me my own pony, slightly larger than a standard pony. Everyday after school, I was at Benjamin Stables to ride, and visited Charlie O., with carrots or sugar cubes.

In Oakland, the only boarding stable was Skyline Ranch in Oakland Hills, about five miles from the Coliseum. It appeared Skyline Ranch wasn't familiar with mules, though this was just my intuition. I visited Charlie O. as much as possible. I really yearned for Benjamin Stables.

11) What was it like living in the Bay Area and going to Oakland High School during such a turbulent time in the city's history?

Finley: When I moved to Oakland, I didn't realize this area was in the middle of so many movements. I moved from Dallas, where girls were not allowed to wear pants in public schools. Suddenly I was enrolled in an Oakland public school without many dress restrictions. Dad and Charlie were strong believers in the public-school system.

I never realized how my school was fully aware of who I was, and my father's position. I did see clues. It was difficult to make friends. I was very shy, and it seemed like most of my schoolmates knew each other from elementary school. I do remember some mornings when "Finley" would appear as the main headline on the front page. This was the actual front page, not the sports section. I was worried about classmates saying something. A few did come up to me, and demand to know why we did such and such. This was a scary feeling. Dad said he might look into a private school. I said no, since it felt like I had changed schools so often. I was determined to learn to deal with these comments.

I stayed to myself. After school each day, Dad or someone in our front office would pick me up and drive me to our front office. This is where I felt the most comfortable. I often did my homework sitting near the top of our upper deck and watching the sun set over the Bay, toward San Francisco. The view from our box seats had the backdrop of the Oakland Hills to the east. This was before the Coliseum renovations in 1996, which took away the view of the east hills.

12) What do you think was the secret to Charlie and the A's success? Was it really Sweat plus Sacrifice?

Finley: One secret, I recently discovered, is synesthesia. Massachusetts Institute of Technology defines synesthesia as "an involuntary joining in which the real information of one sense is accompanied by a perception in another sense." To put it another way, people with synesthesia can taste shapes or smell colors. This has been proven to be genetic. Charlie meets all of the criteria. And how many times have I read the word "color" or "colorful" in the same sentence with Charlie's name.

Charlie, and, I believe Dad—they discussed everything—had an instinct for finding talent. I remember when Charlie would call Dad, and be very excited about a new prospect. He had that immediate feeling. He would ask Dad, "What do you think?"

Dad said Charlie's description of this new talent was always amazing.

I believe our key to success was instinct, with a little common sense thrown in.

I refer to this instinct as the fourth "S" in the formula: Synesthesia.

13) Who was your favorite A's player? Do I recall correctly that some of the players' families babysat you as a child in Kansas City?

Finley: My favorite players have changed year to year. I have never had just one favorite player.

In Kansas City, Dick Green's wife babysat me. I think he demanded too much money afterward. Ha!

14) What was the adjustment like for you and your family going from Kansas City to Oakland?

Finley: Interesting. I was living in Dallas when the team made the move from K.C. to Oakland. This may have been a good thing at the time. When my parents divorced in late 1966, I moved back to Dallas with Mom. Dad stayed in K.C. My parents' divorce was adversarial.

Before the divorce, I remember hearing about the team moving to Dallas/Fort Worth, if it had to move. This was the desired place to move. It also made sense for the family, since several family members had moved to Texas.

I remember hearing about other city locations, if a move had to happen. Oakland and Atlanta were the

other places. I had heard of Atlanta, although I didn't know where Oakland was.

While living in Dallas, about mid-1968, I finally heard about the team moving to Oakland. I remember wondering how everyone was doing, what it was like in Oakland. I missed Dad so much. I missed everyone. I wanted to be with Dad.

In early 1970, when I was 11, Dad gained sole custody of me. I was so happy. The first thing I wanted to do was see the Oakland Coliseum, and visit the front-office staff.

15) After working for the A's during their three straight world championships and five straight division titles, what did you do for an encore?

Finley: After our 1975 AL West Division title, I began to spend more hours inside our front office. I remember trying to recruit former classmates who seemed trustworthy. Dad and Charlie preferred hiring people we knew and could trust, which is probably one of the reasons we had fewer employees than other teams.

By the mid-1970s our office at the Coliseum still wasn't finished. This was promised when the team moved to Oakland in 1968. According to Dad and Charlie, Oakland was the only city they looked at that had a "ready to move into" stadium. So Oakland was chosen. Charlie would not spend his money on the Coliseum office, since he spent about $400,000 to remodel the old Kansas City stadium, and felt burned. The unfinished Coliseum front office became contentious.

In 1976 Charlie and Dad decided to rebuild another dynasty. They sounded very confident that they could do it. They kept this to themselves. I remember how curious the press seemed about what was happening with us in the late 1970s. Behind the scenes, we were making it happen again.

Then, about March 1979, I remember when we were served with a complaint by the city, county, and Coliseum board. I remember reading the "Causes of Action." Even I could see these were silly, and meaningless. It was as if it was meant to harass.

This complaint was filed in federal court, with higher costs than municipal courts. What a waste of taxpayer money. Within four months, the federal-court judge dismissed this suit, in our favor. I remember Charlie saying he couldn't understand why this would be filed against us, after so many championships. Someone on the Coliseum board replied, "It isn't all about winning." We were all perplexed by this statement.

Dad said this suit made him have a lengthy talk with Charlie. They both agreed it was probably time to sell the team. This suit impacted morale.

We hired Billy Martin for our 1980 season. That was a wonderful year. The new ownership did not happen until the end of 1980, so 1981 was the first season under the new ownership. The new owners took over the players we'd scouted, brought through the farm system, and broken in for the major leagues.

Dad was asked to remain with the new ownership in a VP/Mentor position. What happened in 1981? We won the 1981 AL West Division title! This was our rebuilding!

If only Charlie and Dad could have been together with the A's for this series; 1981 was like our first 1971 division title. It made me wonder if we could have had a repeat, with '82, '83 and '84, if only Charlie hadn't sold the team.

Junkyard Dogs

By Ted Leavengood

In his autobiography, Reggie Jackson said that the championship Oakland Athletics "were the meanest junkyard dogs who ever played the game."[1] He believed that Charlie Finley's legendary cheapness, which confronted them at every turn, made them tough and hungry. "We were like a pickup team from the baseball ghetto and nobody wanted to come into our neighborhood and play," Jackson said. "We were always mad at Charlie because we were the best baseball team in the world and we knew he was paying us slave wages."[2]

Whatever the source of the anger, the Oakland Athletics were a fighting and feuding bunch. The index to Dayn Perry's biography of Jackson has a listing for "fights (fighting)" with six references that only begin to detail the many memorable confrontations, some of which included Reggie, though he was hardly a lone actor.[3] The first reference leads the reader to a confrontation between Jackson and reliever Dick Woodson of the Minnesota Twins in 1969 when Billy Martin—legendary for his own brawling behavior—was the Twins' rookie manager. As a very successful college football player, Jackson believed he played the game with a higher level of intensity than many, and so when he charged Woodson after the pitcher threw at him, he proudly said he executed a "form tackle that would have made Frank Kush (legendary Arizona State coach) proud."[4]

From the perspective of the modern game, it is difficult to recall fully the way the game was once played by rough-and-tumble personalities like Billy Martin. Before free agency opened the financial floodgates and players started getting paid like movie stars, tough guys like Martin and Jackson were less concerned that needless injury from fighting might cut into their seven-figure paydays. Back in the day—pre-1975—when teams poured onto the field after a beaning, the odds that a punch would be thrown were

far greater, and one of the last great teams celebrated for their pugilism almost as much as their baseball talent was the Oakland Athletics. And their anger found a home at least as often in their own clubhouse as it did on the field against the opposing team.

The press gave internal strife within the Oakland clubhouse a prominent role in crafting the competitive edge of the Oakland Athletics, or at least were complicit in airing the private squabbles publicly. Wells Twombly of *The Sporting News* wrote about the rivalry between Billy North and Angel Mangual under the heading, "Civil Strife Brings Out Best in A's." Mangual and North literally fought for playing time in center field during the '73 midseason, but the more pugnacious of the two, Billy North, won the job by TKO. Sal Bando, captain of the team and chairman of the "morale committee," told Twombley that total candor in the clubhouse "is a tradition with us. ... The owner screams at the players. The manager screams at the players and the players scream right back."[5]

Jackson was the most notorious of a wild bunch and his remarks about fights within the clubhouse provide much of the available information on them. However, the other protagonists have invariably clarified key points in the Jackson narrative. Jackson's reputation took off during the first championship season in May 1972 when he and Mike Epstein had one of the more serious confrontations of any that ensued.

Jackson had anchored the defensive backfield at Arizona State and Mike Epstein had played fullback for the University of California Golden Bears before turning to baseball. Epstein was a big, burly man whose 230 pounds were stretched over a 6-foot-3 frame and he was used to hitting the line with enough brute force to gain his three yards in a cloud of dust. Charlie Finley gave Jackson authority over distributing the tickets given to players for each game that were then doled out to family and friends. Epstein—whose family lived in the Bay Area—asked for tickets in late May and Jackson asked who the tickets were going to. "It's none of your business," Epstein shot back.[6] According to Epstein, the fight was a short one as the fullback knocked the defensive back unconscious.[7]

Besides the two footballers, the A's boasted two diminutive players with quick tempers. Cuban-born Bert Campaneris stood only 5-feet-10 and was known for having a short fuse.[8] In the American League Championship Series against the Detroit Tigers, the A's were once more up against manager Billy Martin. In Game Two of the series, Campaneris had gone 3-for-3 and Martin ordered his pitcher, Lerrin LaGrow, to throw at Campaneris. When the ensuing pitch hit the feisty Cuban in the ankle, he got up and whipsawed his bat toward the mound where the helicoptering projectile "narrowly missed the top of his head."[9] The benches emptied and though few punches were actually thrown, Martin was physically removed from the field of play screaming at Campaneris to come out and fight him. The Oakland players remained uncharacteristically placid in response, but Campaneris was fined $500 and suspended for the rest of the ALCS.

The other player in the Oakland clubhouse whose small size hid a large fist was Billy North, who led off for Oakland during his six-year tenure with the A's. He fought numerous times with opposing pitchers. Reggie Jackson described an   incident in which North charged the mound after Doug Bird of the Kansas City Royals threw him a strike. The pitch seemed to have no special message attached to it, but according to Jackson, Bird had beaned him three years earlier and North had not forgiven the offense until that very moment when he "walked to the mound and dropped Bird with a right to the jaw and then just started banging away on him."[10]

As Jackson put it, "It was always something."[11] Reggie recounted fights between Rollie Fingers and Blue Moon Odom, Bert Campaneris, and Vida Blue. There was the time that "Blue Moon Odom went after reserve outfielder Tommy Reynolds with a coke bottle."[12] But the worst of them all may have been the

numerous accounts of the fight between Billy North and Reggie Jackson.

The confrontation is said to have occurred in the shower, where the slippery conditions contributed to the injuries suffered by Jackson. The most objective accounts of the fight lay the blame on Reggie's failure to come to terms with the clubhouse cliques that had sprung up racially. Billy North was part of a group of African American players who did not mix as easily with the white players as Reggie did. Reggie had grown up in a white neighborhood in Philadelphia and is said by Dayn Perry in his biography of Jackson to have been boasting of dating a "gorgeous white chick," when North asked if she might have a friend for him.[13]

With racially loaded language that Mike Epstein claimed was all too common for Reggie Jackson, the slugger told North that the woman did not date African Americans, though he chose his words less carefully. North was quick and got the better of the larger man with surprising force. Jackson was injured in the fight, as was Ray Fosse, who tried to break it up. Fosse ended up in the hospital, Jackson merely missed a few innings, but according to Perry's accounts, the aftermath of the fight bothered Reggie for weeks and hindered his performance on the field.

Ironically, Charlie Finley was always quick to try to bring the feuding parties together, as he did with North and Jackson. Whether Finley was an underlying irritant who kept the pot boiling or not, he went to considerable lengths to keep his star slugger happy. He held a "Reggie Jackson Day" several weeks after the fight with North and showered Jackson with gifts. However, the effects of the confrontation became cumulative and the expanding reservoir of ill will may have ultimately led to Jackson's leaving Oakland. For all of the camaraderie that Jackson enjoyed playing in Oakland, the clubhouse animus that built up over the years from the "Junk Yard Dogs" lingered in his final years with the team.

The next fight, between Blue Moon Odom and Rollie Fingers, also took a toll. "Odom walked with a limp and Fingers needed six stiches in his scalp."[14] Jackson saw the fights as building a combative spirit that ultimately helped the team win its final World Series triumph against the Los Angeles Dodgers in 1974. Though they won the Series, the team began to come apart in the offseason that followed.

Reggie Jackson painted a sanguine face on the inner turmoil of the team and said it helped nurture the players' winning ways. Others saw something darker, and ultimately Charlie Finley may have been moved by more than the money demands of his star-filled lineup to let them go. Mike Epstein believed he was traded at the end of the 1972 season because of the bad blood with Reggie Jackson. That fissure healed easily enough, but Finley's inability to resolve the endless disputes between himself and his cast of All-Stars, and those between the players themselves may have provided additional motivation when he let the Yankees sign Catfish Hunter in 1975 and then traded Reggie Jackson and Ken Holtzman to the Orioles for the 1976 season. There may have been a precarious chemistry that fueled the fighting Athletics, but the same pugnacious character that marked relationships between so many involved with the team may have ultimately helped undermine their staying power as a team.

SOURCES

Telephone interviews with Mike Epstein, June 15, 2007, and September 4, 2013.

Jackson, Reggie, with Kevin Baker, *Becoming Mr. October* (New York: Doubleday, 2013).

Jackson, Reggie, and Mike Lupica, *Reggie: The Autobiography* (New York: Villard, 1984).

Perry, Dayn, *Reggie Jackson.* (New York: Harper Collins, 2010).

The Sporting News, 1966-1974.

NOTES

1 Reggie Jackson and Mike Lupica, *Reggie, the Autobiography*, 78.

2 Jackson and Lupica, 72.

3 Dayn Perry, *Reggie Jackson*, 317.

4 Perry, 51-52.

5 Wells Twombly, *The Sporting News*, October 27, 1973, 14.

6 Perry, 84.

7 Epstein interview.

8 Perry 86.

9 Perry, 86-87.

10 Jackson with Baker, 23,

11 Lupica, 83.

12 Ibid.

13 Perry, 122.

14 Jackson with Baker, 23.

"The Bikers Against The Boy Scouts"

The 1972 World Series and the Emergence of Facial Hair in Baseball

By Maxwell Kates

The date was October 14, 1972.

Families across North America gathered around their wood-paneled television sets to watch Game One of the World Series that Saturday afternoon. Many fans in the televised audience had not seen the Oakland A's or the Cincinnati Reds in a regular-season contest. There stood the Reds along the first-base line wearing businesslike white outfits with minimalist red graphic design, black shoes, short hair, and shaven faces. Meanwhile, the A's were dressed in green caps, yellow jerseys, white shoes, long hair, and every combination of facial hair imaginable.

"That was a focal point of the media," analyzed Sal Bando, third baseman and captain of the A's. "You had more of a radical personality in Charlie Finley, and we had the long hair and the mustaches. And then you take this very conservative, very inflexible Sparky Anderson and the Cincinnati Reds and their short hair and their high socks and their nice pants. It was a contrast between two different styles."[1] Bando imagined that "you probably had the youth of the day rooting for the A's ... [and] the older population rooting for the Reds."[2] True enough, households watching the game probably had more in common with the cartoon Boyles of "Wait Till Your Father Gets Home" than the idyllic families portrayed in television serials from the recent past.

To anyone attending Opening Day at any ballpark during the 1960s, the game appeared untouched by the social changes occurring elsewhere. The attire and attitudes of the players represented a throwback to the Eisenhower era, precisely what the Lords of the Realm wanted. Baseball teams were governed by a cabal of wealthy, conservative older white men. In their estimation, the players were paid to throw strikes and hit curveballs, not to write philosophy or criticize the establishment. Paul Daugherty of the *Cincinnati Post* illustrated the owners' fears of being infiltrated by "those stubbly, pinko subversives who thought the Vietnam War worked best as a concept."

Upon his appointment as general manager of the Cincinnati Reds in 1967, Bob Howsam became the first baseball executive to prohibit his players from growing facial hair.[3] Besides banning mustaches, beards, and long hair, players were instructed to wear only black shoes, pants legs at the knee, jackets and ties at all times in public, and to refrain from drinking alcohol on airplanes.[4] Many of the managers shared Howsam's paternalistic stance on player grooming, including George "Sparky" Anderson. Hired by Cincinnati in 1970, Anderson demanded that hirsute players report to the unofficial team barber, relief pitcher Pedro Borbón.[5] Many of Borbón's teammates challenged the rules. As a long-haired rookie in 1971, pitcher Ross Grimsley was ordered to get four haircuts before being allowed to work out with the team.[6] Pete Rose expressed his dissatisfaction with the rule by attending the 1972 winter meetings wearing a Vandyke beard.[7] Rose asked Anderson, "Do you think Jesus Christ could hit a curveball?" When Anderson replied to the affirmative, Rose rebutted, "Not for the Cincinnati Reds he couldn't—not with that beard."[8]

By 1970, other teams had copied the Reds' dress code, including, paradoxically, the Oakland A's. During the

1971 American League Championship Series, it was obvious that the Oakland right fielder was growing a mustache.[9] Reginald Martinez Jackson was everything a baseball player was not supposed to be in 1971: university educated, outspoken, and articulate. Of mixed African American and Puerto Rican heritage, Reggie claimed that the New York Mets deliberately overlooked him in the 1966 amateur draft because he dated a "white" girl.[10] He referred to himself in the third person and he stopped to watch his home runs before jogging gingerly around the bases. Now he was flouting the team rules with his mustache.

Reggie Jackson was hardly the first baseball player to grow a mustache. In the 19th century, they were commonplace. However, by 1913, when catcher Wally Schang wore a mustache as a member of the Philadelphia Athletics, it was considered an oddity by standards of that time.[11] After Schang, attempts to grow mustaches and beards in the majors were scarce. The Washington Nationals signed former House of David pitcher Allen Benson to a contract in 1934, and he retained his beard.[12] In 1936 outfielder Frenchy Bordagaray arrived at the Brooklyn Dodgers' training camp sporting a goatee. Manager Casey Stengel was not impressed, insinuating that "if anyone is going to be a clown on this club, it's going to be me."[13]

In the postwar era, an anecdote shared by Tommy Davis was emblematic of the attitude toward facial hair among his peers. In 1966 he arrived in New York from the Dodgers wearing a Fu Manchu mustache. Davis was greeted by Mets teammates Jack Fisher and Ed Kranepool with a razor and shaving cream. Though Davis later grew a mustache, in 1966 he conceded, "Whoever heard of a ballplayer with a mustache?"[14]

Toward the end of the 1960s, Davis's question was no longer rhetorical. Late in the 1968 season, the year before he was traded to the expansion Montreal Expos, Astros outfielder Rusty Staub grew a mustache. The manager in Houston was Harry Walker, an ardent traditionalist who "hated hippies and long hair."[15] According to John Wilson of the *Houston Chronicle*, "If Rusty had not grown that mustache, that … trade

would [never] have been made."[16] In 1969 Dick Allen of the Philadelphia Phillies wore a mustache and an Afro during the regular season.[17] He too was traded, to the St. Louis Cardinals. Jim Bouton grew a mustache one offseason but shaved, predicting, "What's standing between me and my mustache is about twenty wins."[18]

Despite their mod image, the 1971 Oakland A's were otherwise no less conservative than any other team. Their owner, Charles O. Finley, proclaimed that "sweat plus sacrifice equals success." His manager, Dick Williams, earned his reputation as a rigid disciplinarian with the Boston Red Sox. An insurance magnate based in Chicago, Finley imposed a dress code not only on his players, but also on the front-office staff. In 1972 Reggie arrived at spring training with a beard, much to the chagrin of his manager. Mike Hegan remembered:

"Charlie [Finley] didn't like it … so he told Dick to tell Reggie to shave it off and Reggie told Dick what to do. This got to be a real sticking point."[19] As Williams remembered the situation, the other A's players were becoming upset that Reggie was ignoring team protocol. Catfish Hunter, of all people, decided to take matters into his own hands aboard an early-season flight:

"Catfish walked to … where Charlie [Finley] was sitting," recalled Williams in his autobiography. "'Charlie,' he announced, 'Reggie Jackson has facial hair … and we don't think it's fair.' 'Oh really?' he answered."[20] Using reverse psychology, he refused to reprimand Reggie and instead offered $300 to any player who grew a mustache by June 18.[21] Father's Day in Oakland was to become Mustache Day.[22]

Anyone associated with the Oakland A's was familiar with Charlie Finley's penury. When the players were offered $300 merely for growing a mustache, most jumped at the occasion. Rollie Fingers grew a handlebar mustache that became his trademark—when his gross biweekly earnings were $1,200, how could he refuse a $300 bonus? As Fingers once told Phil Pepe, "For $300, I'd grow one on my rear end."[23] He even managed to negotiate for Finley to include $100 for mustache wax in his contract.[24]

Not all of the A's were enthusiastic about the promotion, including Sal Bando:

"There were three guys that didn't want to do it, Larry Brown, Mike Hegan, and myself. Finley called us in and convinced us … he wanted us to do it."[25] Hegan was the last holdout. "I finally grew a mustache, did it for about six weeks … and then shaved it off," explaining that "my wife didn't like it."[26] After a bitter contract negotiation with Finley, Vida Blue refused to engage. As Williams remembered, "The players were so confused by Charlie's edict that most of them [also] decided to grow their hair long."[27] By Father's Day, all the A's except Vida wore a mustache. Mike Epstein grew muttonchops and a Fu Manchu mustache. Dave Duncan grew a beard. Even the coaching staff participated.

"I took the lineup card to the umpire and he said it didn't look very good," reported third-base coach Irv Noren. "It took a month or two to grow but $300 was $300 in 1972." Along with the rest of the A's, Noren returned from the game to find a check in his locker, though he admitted that "I shaved as soon as the check cleared."

At a time when per-game attendance barely exceeded 11,000, the Oakland A's sold 26,000 tickets to Mustache Day.[28] In addition, fans wearing mustaches were admitted free. Several of the A's besides Noren shaved immediately after the game, only to grow their mustaches back during the pennant drive. As Sal Bando explained, "We had success as a team so everybody stayed with it."[29]

The Reds were favored to win the 1972 World Series. It was a close series that went the full seven games. Game Seven was tied, 1-1, after five innings. Gene Tenace, who had homered for Oakland twice in Game One, broke the deadlock with an RBI double off Pedro Borbón. Then Sal Bando drove in an insurance run with another double. With the score now 3-2, Rollie Fingers was called in from the bullpen for the ninth inning. When he enticed Pete Rose to fly out to left field for the third out, the Bikers had beaten the Boy Scouts.[30] The A's had established themselves as the pre-eminent team in the American League West, winning a division title each year from 1971 to 1975. Their prominence on the field, however, did not signify an instant eradication of dress codes elsewhere. Other teams retained their opposition, especially the Cincinnati Reds.

Despite playing barely .500, the Montreal Expos found themselves in an unexpected pennant race in 1973. General manager Jim Fanning acquired veteran outfielder Felipe Alou from the New York Yankees. As John McHale reminisced in 1993, "Now you have to understand that we did not allow mustaches on the team at that time. When Felipe arrived, he had this beautiful mustache. We didn't know what to do and in this case, we decided to allow him to keep his mustache. By the time we were ready to tell him, he had already shaved in the clubhouse."[31]

Ironically, the Expos were less charitable when younger players Steve Rogers, Tim Foli, and Dale Murray arrived at spring training with mustaches. Bob Dunn of the *Montreal Star* witnessed McHale's reaction and compared it to "Louis Pasteur discovering a stream of bacteria loose in the lab."[32] Foli shaved grudgingly, arguing that he "wouldn't want to take it to court but I probably could have."[33]

Foli was referring to a controversy from 1973 involving Cincinnati outfielder Bobby Tolan. As the Reds fought the Los Angeles Dodgers for their division title, Tolan stopped shaving. Sparky Anderson ordered him to "shave or take off that uniform."[34] Tolan refused and was suspended for the rest of the season without pay.[35] Then he filed a grievance through Marvin Miller and the Players Association. At the hearing, the union lawyer asked Anderson if he objected to Tolan's Afro and his beard. The manager replied, "No, but he's not wearing the uniform."[36] Tolan won the hearing and the Reds lost the pennant to the New York Mets. By December, both Tolan and Grimsley were traded to other teams.

The Oakland A's won their third consecutive World Series in 1974, over the Los Angeles Dodgers. Owned by one Walter (O'Malley) and managed by another

(Alston), the Dodgers allowed mustaches but not long hair or beards. So did the Yankees. From the time he purchased the Yankees in 1973, George Steinbrenner was paranoid about the image beards and long hair would convey to the public. At his first spring training with the Yankees, Lou Piniella remembered Steinbrenner barked at Bobby Murcer and Gene Michael to "put those caps on [and] look like Yankees—and you, Michael, get a haircut!"[37] Bronx Bombers felt free to grow their hair long during Steinbrenner's subsequent exile from baseball. When Steinbrenner returned in 1976, he was incensed about player photographs he saw in the team yearbook. Marty Appel was the director of public relations at the time:

"Look at this!" Steinbrenner screamed at Appel as he pointed at the players, "Hair's too long! Hair's too long! Hair's too long! Hair's too long! I can count twenty players with their hair too long in the photos you chose. Now I'm not saying that I'm putting you out on the street over this, but I am saying you better get it fixed."[38] Rather than affront Yankee tradition, Appel recalled the entire press run. The yearbooks were not reissued until June, thereby forfeiting two months of sales. Oscar Gamble joined the Yankees in 1976 wearing a legendary afro. Mindful of the Bobby Tolan grievance, team president Gabe Paul worried about how to approach Gamble to trim his afro. To Paul's surprise, Gamble had no objection. Finding a barbershop open in Fort Lauderdale on a Sunday morning, on the other hand, was a far more difficult task.[39] Reggie Jackson, Thurman Munson, Goose Gossage, Dave Winfield, and Don Mattingly were among the Yankees who attempted to test Steinbrenner's patience by allowing their hair or beards to grow.

Many teams soon followed Oakland's lead in reversing their dress codes. The Angels dropped theirs in 1974 when they hired Dick Williams. According to batboy Paul Hirsch, they could not impose one set of rules for the players and another for the manager.[40] Steve Rogers and his teammates could grow beards however they wanted by 1977 as Williams left Orange County for greener pastures in Montreal. What if Dick Williams had managed Cincinnati instead? The Reds continued to be the most stubborn team on the issue of grooming standards. Meanwhile, as Sparky Anderson's coaches received promotions to manage other teams, they took the Reds' dress code with them.

In 1976 third-base coach Alex Grammas left Cincinnati to manage the Milwaukee Brewers. His new club featured several players with Fu Manchu mustaches, including Jim Colborn,

Darrell Porter, George Scott, Robin Yount, Gorman Thomas, Kurt Bevacqua, and Pete Broberg.[41] All were required to shave under Grammas. A year later, Vern Rapp left the Reds to manage the St. Louis Cardinals. Asserting that he "didn't come here to be liked," Rapp drove a wedge against Al Hrabosky and Ted Simmons, when he prohibited mustaches and long hair.[42] "The Mad Hungarian" was famous for his pitching antics and credited his intimidating presence to his Fu Manchu mustache. The long-haired Simmons was the player representative and with his support, Hrabosky threatened to file his own grievance. Hrabosky relented and shaved his mustache before posting a ghastly ERA of 4.38.[43] Grammas was released in 1977 and Rapp barely lasted through April 1978.

Meanwhile, after nine years in Cincinnati, Sparky Anderson re-emerged in June 1979 to manage in Detroit. Already familiar with his feelings on facial hair; many Tigers shaved without being asked, including Reds alumnus Champ Summers.[44] If Anderson banned mustaches on the Tigers, someone failed to notify Jason Thompson or Aurelio Rodriguez.[45] Both players *did not* shave and were playing for different teams in 1980.

By the end of the 1970s, many of the attitudes viewed as radical or subversive a decade earlier were accepted as mainstream. To paraphrase Herb Tarlek from *WKRP in Cincinnati*, the battle between the dungarees and the suits had largely been won. Nobody bothered to alert the Reds that the white flags had been drawn. Only on February 2, 1999, when the Reds traded for outfielder Greg Vaughn to Cincinnati, was their facial hair ban repealed.

The 1972 World Series marked a turning point in the evolution of grooming standards in baseball. Facing the conservatively dressed Cincinnati Reds, the underdog Oakland A's won a tightly fought seven-game Series wearing long hair, mustaches, and green and yellow polyester. As is the case with any form of social evolution, attitudes in baseball toward self-expression among the players did not change overnight. Opposition among managers and executives remained, particularly on the Reds, whose policy against facial hair remained intact until the final year of the 20th century. Did "the Mustache Gang" define the Oakland A's players and if so, did they envision themselves as vanguards of change? Not if you asked Sal Bando, they did not. When interviewed on the subject, Captain Sal admitted that "we might have worn our hair longer and had mustaches but probably in today's political climate most of us were conservative anyhow."[46] Perhaps the greatest legacy of the 1972 World Series was what transpired on the diamond 12 Octobers later. The San Diego Padres faced the Detroit Tigers in 1984, a World Series rematch between Dick Williams and Sparky Anderson. Many of the Padres players wore long hair and mustaches, as did several of the Tigers. And nobody noticed.

SOURCES

Appel, Marty, *Now Pitching for the Yankees: Spinning the News for Mickey, Billy, and George* (Toronto: Sport Media Publishing, 2001).

Bouton, Jim, *Ball Four: The Final Pitch* (North Egremont, Massachusetts: Bulldog Publishing Inc., 2000).

Epstein, Dan, *Big Hair and Plastic Grass: A Funky Ride Through Baseball and America in the Swinging '70s.* (New York: St. Martin's Press, 2010).

Gallagher, Danny, and Bill Young, *Remembering the Montreal Expos* (Toronto: Scoop Press, 2005).

Green, G. Michael, and Roger D. Launius. *Charlie Finley: The Outrageous Story of Baseball's Super Showman* (New York: Walker Publishing Company Inc., 2010).

Hill, Art, *I Don't Care If I Never Come Back: A Baseball Fan and His Game* (New York: Simon and Schuster, 1980).

Jackson, Reggie, and Kevin Baker, *Becoming Mr. October* (New York: Random House LLC, 2013).

Kashatus, William, *September Swoon: Richie Allen, the '64 Phillies, and Racial Integration.* (State College, Pennsylvania: Penn State University Press, 2004).

Kates, Maxwell, "Alex Grammas," in Mark Pattison and David Raglin, eds., *Detroit Tigers 1984: What a Start! What a Finish!* (Phoenix: Society for American Baseball Research, 2012).

Markusen, Bruce, *A Baseball Dynasty: Charlie Finley's Swingin' A's* (Haworth, New Jersey: St. Johann Press, 2002).

Miller, Marvin, *A Whole Different Ball Game: The Sport and Business of Baseball* (New York: Carol Publishing Group, 1991).

Piniella, Lou, and Maury Allen, *Sweet Lou* (New York: Putnam Publishing Group, 1986).

Posnanski, Joe, *The Machine: A Hot Team, a Legendary Season, and a Heart-Stopping World Series — the 1975 Cincinnati Reds* (New York: Harper Collins Publishers, 2009).

Reston, James, *Collision at Home Plate: The Lives of Pete Rose and Bart Giamatti* (New York: Harper Collins Publishers, 1991).

Robertson, John, *Rusty Staub of the Expos* (Scarborough, Ontario: Prentice-Hall of Canada Ltd., 1971).

Williams, Dick, and Bill Plaschke, *No More Mr. Nice Guy: A Life of Hardball* (Orlando: Harcourt Brace Jovanovich, 1990).

Daugherty, Paul, "Reds Keeping Stiff Upper Lip," *Toledo Blade,* March 10, 1992: 15.

Goldstein, Richard, "Frenchy Bordagaray is Dead; The Colorful Dodger was 90," *New York Times,* May 23, 2000).

Grayson, Harry, "Wally Schang, One of Catching Greats, In Six Fall Series," *Evening Independent,* September 18, 1943, 10.

Kay, Joe, "Reds Lift Ban on Facial Hair," *Bryan* (Ohio) *Times,* February 16, 1999, 13.

Pepe, Phil, "Fingers, Reds Losers in Mustache Dispute," *Ottawa Citizen,* March 26, 1986, B2.

Tarantino, Anthony, "Hair Affairs," *San Diego Union-Tribune,* April 24, 2006.

"Maury Means Pirate Flag, Says Ex-Teammate Tommy Davis," *Baltimore Afro-American,* December 20, 1966, 11.

"Allen Benson," Washington Senators Press Photo, 1950.

ACKNOWLEDGMENTS

Jim Charlton, Dan Epstein, Paul Hirsch, Sean Lahman, Bruce Markusen, Scott Schliefer, Fred Taylor.

NOTES

1 Bruce Markusen, *A Baseball Dynasty: Charlie Finley's Swingin' A's,* 171-172.

2 Markusen, 172.

3 Daugherty, 15.

4 Joe Posnanski, *The Machine: A Hot Team, a Legendary Season, and a Heart-Stopping World Series — the 1975 Cincinnati Reds,* 60.

5 Posnanski, 60.

6 Dan Epstein, *Big Hair and Plastic Grass: A Funky Ride Through Baseball and America in the Swinging '70s,* 174.

7 James Reston, *Collision at Home Plate: The Lives of Pete Rose and Bart Giamatti,* photo insert.

8 Posnanski, 115-116.

9 Markusen, 85.

10 Reggie Jackson and Kevin Baker, *Becoming Mr. October,* 9. The "white girl" referred to, Jennie Campos Jackson, was actually a light-skinned Mexican American of Mestizo ancestry).

11 Harry Grayson, "Wally Schang, One of Catching Greats, In Six Fall Series," *The Evening Independent,* September 18, 1943, 10.

12 "Allen Benson," Washington Senators Press Photo, 1950.

13 Richard Goldstein, "Frenchy Bordagaray is Dead; The Colorful Dodger was 90," *New York Times,* May 23, 2000.

14 "Maury Means Pirate Flag, Says Ex-Teammate Tommy Davis," *Baltimore Afro-American,* December 20, 1966, 11.

15 John Robertson, *Rusty Staub of the Expos,* 18.

16 Robertson, 18.

17 William Kashatus, *September Swoon: Richie Allen, the '64 Phillies, and Racial Integration,* cover.

18 Jim Bouton, *Ball Four: The Final Pitch,* 20.

19 Markusen, 85.

20 Dick Williams and Bill Plaschke, *No More Mr. Nice Guy: A Life of Hardball,* 136-137.

21 Williams, 137.

22 Williams, 137.

23 Phil Pepe, "Fingers, Reds Losers in Moustache Dispute," *Ottawa Citizen,* March 26, 1986, B2.

24 Markusen, 102.

25 Markusen, 101.

26 Markusen, 101.

27 Williams, 137.

28 Epstein, 173.

29 Markusen, 101.

30 Markusen, 171.

31 John McHale's speech at the Montreal Expos' 25th-anniversary gala dinner, January 14, 1993.

32 Danny Gallagher and Bill Young, *Remembering the Montreal Expos,* 42.

33 Gallagher, 43.

34 Daugherty, 15.

35 Marvin Miller, *A Whole Different Ball Game: The Sport and Business of Baseball* , 241.

36 Daugherty, 15.

37 Lou Piniella and Maury Allen, *Sweet Lou*, back cover.

38 Marty Appel, *Now Pitching for the Yankees: Spinning the News for Mickey, Billy, and George*, 235-236.

39 Appel, 181-182.

40 Correspondence with Paul Hirsch, January 18, 2014.

41 Maxwell Kates, "Alex Grammas," in Mark Pattison and David Raglin, eds., *Detroit Tigers 1984: What a Start! What a Finish!*, 201.

42 Epstein, 176.

43 Epstein, 176.

44 *Art Hill, I Don't Care If I Never Come Back: A Baseball Fan and His Game,* 190.

45 Hill, 191.

46 Markusen, 172.

Postcard: Mesa, March 1973

by Matthew Silverman

While the New York Yankees had a wife swap between pitchers Fritz Peterson and Mike Kekich in Florida in March of 1973, the Oakland A's went about the business of getting ready to defend a world championship in Arizona. The only snag was that the A's had no experience as world champions.

The organization had not gone into spring training as World Series champions since 1931, when Connie Mack's Philadelphia Athletics won their second straight title. But as winter gave way to spring in 1973, Connie Mack was long gone, and the Athletics had been sold and twice moved, first to Kansas City, then Oakland. And the team was owned by a man who threatened any employee who called his team any name other than the A's, Athletics be damned.

Not that Charles Oscar Finley wasn't generous. Coming off his 1972 world championship, the A's owner was as generous as he would ever get. In fact, Finley drew the ire of the other owners in baseball for his benevolence. And when he developed the best team in baseball, those who would criticize his methods and flair looked as though they had a mouthful of sour grapes.

Manager Dick Williams was the one who jury-rigged a World Series lineup without Reggie Jackson, ordered a fake pitchout that caught Johnny Bench looking with two men on, navigated six one-run games in a seven-game Series, and made so many trips to confer with his pitchers that the rules on postseason mound visits became more rigidly enforced,[1] but it was Finley who spent all winter being feted. In addition to nights in his honor in both Gary, Indiana, and his adopted hometown of LaPorte, Indiana, the A's owner also picked up "Hoosier of the Year" from the Indiana Society of Chicago. More than a thousand people came to a "Thank You Charlie Finley" gala in Oakland.[2] And to top it off, Finley became the only team owner ever named *The Sporting News'* Sportsman of the Year — it not being lost on the recipient that the newspaper was the traditional "baseball bible." Finley gave interviews to any and all who asked, taking *Parade Magazine* on a tour of his 21-room, 1,280-acre LaPorte spread and tossing out pearls of wisdom: "If anyone will pay the high price of success, he can attain it. But the price is high. You have to do more work than your competitor, and sacrifice some of your competitor's enjoyments."[3]

Finley was on top of the world when he arrived in Mesa, Arizona, for spring training in 1973. Unlike some owners who spent all of spring training — and most of the season –around their clubs, Finley operated at a distance of about 2,100 miles from his team. Even while serving as its general manager.

Yet Charlie Finley got to 1973 spring training ahead of several players — holdouts Vida Blue, Dave Duncan, and Ken Holtzman, plus Joe Rudi and team captain Sal Bando, signed but not yet delivered (the former moving his family and the latter driving cross-country). Finley wanted to be on hand to personally hand out 1972 World Series rings to his world champion ballplayers. And what rings they were.[4]

Each A's World Series ring, valued at about $1,500 in 1973 (roughly $8,100 in 2013 dollars), was individualized with the player's name while "WORLD CHAMPIONS 1972" encircled a full carat diamond. The teams that Oakland defeated to claim the pennant (Detroit Tigers) and World Series (Cincinnati Reds) were listed on each side of the ring. Underneath Charlie Finley's signature was his motto: "S + S = S," Finley's self-proclaimed and oft-quoted formula of "Sweat plus Sacrifice equals Success." The high price for success he told the *Parade* reporter about was now displayed on his finger — and the fingers of his employees.

Finley also provided players with full-sized replicas of the World Series trophies and charm bracelets with a half-carat diamond for each ballplayer's wife.[5] All this largesse infuriated the other major-league owners, whose taste for jewelry selection had never approached this level of ostentation or expense. That only made the equation even more successful by Finley's reckoning.

A shrewd businessman, Finley had raised himself up from humble beginnings in the steel mills to business tycoon by selling affordable group disability insurance to doctors, making as much as $43 million in premiums per year.[6] Finley did not get where he was by being afraid of change. He and his wife, Shirley, came up with the kelly green and Fort Knox gold uniforms that ended a decades-long embargo on garish baseball threads; he paid a $300 mustache bonus in '72 to each of his hirsute A's, ending a half-century without facial hair in the game; he kept fans' eyes on the field by hiring beautiful ballgirls to man Oakland-Alameda Coliseum's expansive foul territory; and he had plenty of ideas about how to shake up the game in fair territory as well, proposing everything from orange baseballs to night World Series games to designated hitters and designated runners. The only thing that bothered the other owners more than Finley's showmanship and uncompromising manner was that his ideas not only worked, they made them all more money. Well, except the designated runner—and the orange baseballs. The balls proved hard for players to grip and were abandoned after three spring-training games in '73 at the behest of the commissioner.[7] Finley would, however, get the day-glow balls in the hands of players warming up at the 1973 All-Star Game in Kansas City, a colorful calling card as if to say that the owner had not forgotten Kansas City—or his dislike for the place.[8]

March of 1973 marked the A's fifth spring in Arizona. Finley relocated the team's spring home from Bradenton, Florida, to Rendezvous Park in Mesa in 1969, one year after he relocated the club's summer home from Kansas City to Oakland.[9] Finley bought the Kansas City franchise in December 1960, after the death of Arnold Johnson, who'd bought the Philadelphia Athletics from Connie Mack and moved them to the Midwest. The Kansas City A's were bad under Johnson and were worse under Finley. He grew frustrated with the stadium, the city, the league, and the confines that forced him to remain in a struggling market. After the A's stuck it out for 13 seasons in Kansas City—seven of them under Finley—he finally coerced the American League into allowing him to move the team. He'd looked all over the country, but Oakland was a fresh market—albeit one with the San Francisco Giants nearby—and, most importantly, Oakland had a new stadium. Yet it was not exactly love at first sight, for owner or audience. Though they played better than the team ever had in Kansas City, Oakland attendance never approached one million in the club's first five seasons by the Bay.

Though coming off a championship season, the 1973 A's did not draw any better in Arizona than they had in Oakland. The A's had their highest spring-training attendance since their move from Florida: 21,206 … for the month. That translates to 1,515 fans per spring-training home game.[10] The 1972 world champion A's drew 921,323 in Oakland, only 14th among the 24 major-league teams. The attendance situation was a sore enough point that World Series hero Gene Tenace discussed it with the press in Mesa. "Sometimes I find myself feeling sorry for [Finley] because we don't draw better in Oakland," said Tenace. "I hope attendance picks up this year, but I won't believe it until I see it."[11]

Sympathy, however, was an emotion rarely articulated by A's players about their boss. And while many players received raises for the coming season, playing hardball was the way Finley generally did business: alternating a hard-line approach between platitudes in his unique brand of salesmanship that launched a mountain of insurance policies. Though Ken Holtzman soon came to terms for 1973, Finley still had holdouts in catcher Dave Duncan and star hurler Vida Blue. Duncan told the press that this was only the latest money squabble in a cycle that dated back to 1963, when he turned down 17 other clubs to sign with Finley.[12] Blue's problems were more recent and more bitter. The lefty's

1972 contract negotiation had been so acrimonious that Commissioner Bowie Kuhn had stepped in—Finley referred to it as butting in. Kuhn made the 22-year-old star and the 54-year-old tycoon stay in a room until they agreed on a figure. Even after they decided on $63,000, the two fought over how it would be announced to the press.[13] So after a down year by Blue in '72, Finley was looking to cut the southpaw's pay.

Also unhappy in camp in '73 was George Hendrick. The outfielder, who had started five games in center field during the World Series in place of injured Reggie Jackson, came to Mesa in the spring to once again serve as a spare outfielder. If he was lucky. Finley told Hendrick to expect to remain in Arizona, playing for Triple-A Tucson. The first overall major-league draft pick in 1968, Hendrick would become the first player to win a Silver Slugger award at two positions, but at age 23, he was hitting just .200 in his first 100 major-league games. He did not endear himself to his owner by asking for a trade.

Though Finley publicly bluffed that he would trade Blue, he wasn't about to chuck away a 22-year-old Cy Young and MVP winner, no matter what happened in '72 or how much each person loathed the other's business practices. Blue and Finley agreed on a $53,000 contract in the final week of '73 spring training.[14] A blue-chip stud pitcher was gold in the days before free agency, when players were indentured to a team for as long as the owner saw fit. Or as long as a team could afford them, now that salary arbitration had just entered the game as the result of an 11-day lockout at the start of spring training in February of '73.[15] Even with arbitration entering the game—it would hit Finley especially hard in the coming years—Vida Blue was irreplaceable. Not everyone on the roster was indispensable, however. "If we have to get along without Duncan," the owner said as he headed back to the Midwest, "I'm sure we can."[16]

So Duncan, who'd turned up his nose at Finley's $40,000 contract offer, wound up the Opening Day catcher … in Cleveland. On March 24 Finley sent Duncan and Hendrick to the Indians for catcher Ray Fosse and spare infielder Jack Heidemann. (It turned out that Heidemann, not Hendrick, spent the summer of '73 in Tucson; he never played an inning in Oakland before being sold back to the Indians a year and a day after Finley acquired him.)

In Fosse the A's received a better bat behind the plate. Though he was never the type of hitter he'd been before Pete Rose slammed into him in the 1970 All-Star Game, Fosse was an experienced backstop revered by Cleveland's pitching staff. The trade also assured that Gene Tenace would be an everyday player in 1973. A part-time catcher who played in just 82 games during the 1972 season, Tenace became the starting catcher for the postseason. He responded by hitting four World Series home runs, single-handedly out-homering the Big Red Machine and becoming the Series MVP. But Tenace's arm was exposed by the Reds, who stole 11 of 13 bases against him. Dick Williams moved Tenace to first base and Duncan took over behind the plate for Game Seven, cementing Tenace's reputation as a good backup catcher but not good enough to be an everyday receiver for a championship club.

Finley spun stories about a bad shoulder as the explanation for shifting Tenace to first base in 1973, then the owner reversed course during Duncan's spring holdout because the A's needed someone to catch. Sure, bringing in a new catcher for a world-championship pitching staff in the final week of spring training was a risky move, but Charlie Finley liked taking risks—he'd already taken plenty since his club claimed the world championship.

Barely a week after the 1972 World Series ended, Finley went about reimagining the Swingin' A's. He acquired Paul Lindblad, a 31-year-old southpaw who grew up outside Kansas City and had been signed by Finley when the team was still there. (Finley had traded Lindblad, Don Mincher, and Frank Fernandez to the Washington Senators in May of 1971 and got back Mike Epstein and Darold Knowles.)

After getting Lindblad back, Oakland's owner/GM then shipped out 34-year-old reliever Bob Locker to the Chicago Cubs to bring in outfielder Bill North, ten years younger than Locker. North, unhappy and unproductive in Chicago, had been displaced in his natural center-field position by Rick Monday, whom Finley had shipped to Wrigley Field after the 1971 season in exchange for Ken Holtzman. Finley, who spent most of his time in Chicago, kept tabs on the Cubs throughout the year, including their numerous exhibition games at Mesa. Finley fleeced the Cubs for two of the keys to his A's dynasty: Holtzman, who with Catfish Hunter and Vida Blue gave Oakland three aces in its rotation; and North, who supplied speed to track down balls in center field while combining with Bert Campaneris to give the A's a lethal top of the batting order.

As happened with Dave Duncan in March, Finley passed another personal headache on to someone else. First baseman Mike Epstein, a vocal foe of Finley's in the Oakland locker room, was shipped to Texas a month after the 1972 World Series. The A's got back reliever Horacio Pina, the second deal in a month for a durable Rangers reliever. Pina's 15 saves and 60 appearances for the Rangers, not to mention Texas teammate Lindblad's league-leading 66 games, added two veteran arms to an already outstanding A's bullpen headlined by Rollie Fingers and Darold Knowles. The A's came into 1973 with four solid relievers who had been among the top ten either in saves (Knowles), appearances (Lindblad), or both (Fingers and Pina). And this was an era when a team was fortunate to have one or two reliable relievers.

Never one to stand still, Finley kept dealing. By the time the 1973 season began, the A's had a dozen players who had not been on the team the previous season. Among those shipped out was Matty Alou. The 33-year-old outfielder-first baseman was sent to the Yankees in return for Rich McKinney, a versatile if not overly successful contact hitter. As if to show that the owner had nothing against the Alous—he'd dumped brother Felipe after only two games in 1971—Finley acquired the third Alou brother, Jesus, in July 1973 and he played a key role in the '73 postseason.

Constantly bringing in new veterans meant that old hands had to be dispatched. Finley released infielder Larry Brown plus relievers Joel Horlen and Marcel Lachemann, but among the released veterans was one name better known than the rest, and whose absence would be felt in 1973.

Orlando Cepeda, an 11-time All-Star and a future Hall of Famer, had batted .289 in 91 plate appearances for the Braves before being acquired for Denny McLain on June 29, 1972, in a deal of former MVPs both seemingly on their last legs. Literally. Cepeda had such knee trouble that it was nearly impossible for him to play the field; he appeared in an Oakland uniform in just three games—all as a pinch-hitter in July. Cepeda's physical issues and his place in the upper salary tier for the early 1970s at $90,000, explain Finley's considerations for the release of "Baby Bull" on December 18. For Cepeda's part, even though he played just three games for the A's, he had endured more than enough from the Oakland owner. When Finley, a phone addict decades before the cellular phone, insisted that Cepeda call him from Puerto Rico or be released, Cepeda opted to end his A's tenure.[17] Exactly one month after his release, Cepeda joined the Red Sox as the first player ever signed to the position many were still calling the designated pinch hitter.

Finley had long lobbied for the designated hitter, but when it was finally approved in the American League on January 11, 1973, he was caught without someone on his team equipped for the role. In spring training the A's lost several chances to experiment with the new position because the National League refused to allow the DH in any games they were involved in, and three of the other seven Cactus League teams hailed from the NL. Finley, not surprisingly, was outraged at the Cubs, Giants, Padres, and especially National League President Chub Feeney: "When will they wake up?"[18]

With fewer games to get the hang of the new rule, the A's seemed to wing it when the season began. Speedy Bill North was Oakland's DH choice on Opening Day, becoming the first designated hitter to bat leadoff. Manager Dick Williams would use five other players who combined with North to bat just .231 with two home runs and six RBIs in the newly created position over the first month of the season before Finley acquired the Phillies' Deron Johnson, who had collected 194 homers in a little over 5,000 plate appearances, and had also played for Finley in Kansas City in the early 1960s.

Johnson filled what became the prototypical DH profile: a veteran slugger with something left in the tank who was better off without a mitt. Johnson hit 19 homers and knocked in 81 runs while batting .251 and hardly missing a game for the A's. But Oakland discard Orlando Cepeda hit .289 with 20 homers and 86 RBIs for Boston in '73 to earn the first Outstanding Designated Hitter Award.

Finley couldn't win 'em all. At least until October.

SOURCES

Parts of this story were adapted from the author's book on the 1973 season, *Swinging '73: Baseball's Wildest Season*, published in 2013 by Lyons Press, Guilford, Connecticut.

Books

Clark, Tom, *Champagne and Baloney: The Rise and Fall of Finley's A's* (New York: Harper & Row, 1976).

Green, G. Michael, and Roger D. Launius, *Charlie Finley: The Outrageous Story of Baseball's Super Showman* (New York: Walker & Company, 2010).

Markusen, Bruce, *Baseball's Last Dynasty: Charlie Finley's Oakland A's* (Indianapolis: Masters Press, 1998).

Rosengren, John, *Hammerin' Hank, George Almighty and the Say Hey Kid: The Year That Changed Baseball Forever* (Naperville, Illinois: Sourcebooks, 2008).

Williams, Dick, and Bill Plaschke, *No More Mr. Nice Guy: A Life of Hardball* (San Diego: Harcourt Brace Jovanovich Publishers, 1990).

Newspapers and Magazines

Associated Press, "Rule Will Limit Trips to Mound by Dick Williams," *Schenectady* (New York) *Gazette*, October 3, 1973.

Bergman, Ron, "Finley Denies Blue Trade Rumor," *Oakland Tribune*, March 5, 1973.

Bergman, Ron, "Finley Leading A's Holdouts 4 to 3," *Oakland Tribune*, March 3, 1973.

Levitt, Ed, "Finley and Feeney," *Oakland Tribune*, March 13, 1983.

—————————, "Pressure on Tenace," *Oakland Tribune*, March 5, 1973.

Orr, Robin, "Sports Millionaire Charles O. Finley," *Parade Magazine*, January 28, 1973.

Websites

baseball-almanac.com

baseball-reference.com

oakland.athletics.mlb.com/oak/downloads/y2011/2011_media_guide.pdf

sports.espn.go.com/mlb/news/story?id=2635604

springtrainingonline.com/teams/oakland-athletics.htm

throughthefencebaseball.com/1973-the-last-time-kc-hosted-the-all-star-game/23892

NOTES

1   Associated Press, "Rule Will Limit Trips to Mound by Dick Williams," *Schenectady Gazette*, October 3, 1973.

2   G. Michael Green and Roger D. Launius, *Charlie Finley: The Outrageous Story of Baseball's Super Showman* (New York: Walker & Company, 2010), 180.

3   Robin Orr, "Sports Millionaire Charles O. Finley," *Parade Magazine*, January 28, 1973.

4   Ron Bergman, "Finley Leading A's Holdouts 4 to 3," *Oakland Tribune*, March 3, 1973.

5   Ed Levitt, "Pressure on Tenace," *Oakland Tribune*, March 5, 1973.

6   Robin Orr, "Sports Millionaire Charles O. Finley," *Parade Magazine*, January 28, 1973.

7   Green and Launius, *Charlie Finley*, 182.

8   Eric Aron, "1973: The Last Time Kansas City Hosted the All-Star Game," throughthefencebaseball.com/1973-the-last-time-kc-hosted-the-all-star-game/23892, July 9, 2012.

9   springtrainingonline.com/teams/oakland-athletics.htm

10 2011 Oakland A's Media Guide, oakland.athletics.mlb.com/oak/downloads/y2011/2011_media_guide.pdf

11 Ed Levitt, "Pressure on Tenace."

12 Ron Bergman, "Finley Denies Blue Trade Rumor," *Oakland Tribune*, March 5, 1973.

13 Green and Launius, *Charlie Finley*, 157-8.

14 Bruce Markusen, *Baseball's Last Dynasty: Charlie Finley's Oakland A's* (Indianapolis: Masters Press, 1998), 193.

15 espn.go.com/mlb/news/story?id=2635604

16 Ron Bergman, "Finley Denies Blue Trade Rumor."

17 Markusen, *Baseball's Last Dynasty*, 182-3.

18 Ed Levitt. "Finley and Feeney." *Oakland Tribune*, March 13, 1983.

Glenn Abbott

by Clifford Corn

For Glenn Abbott, his days in the major leagues were filled with stories and memories and good feelings.

In an interview, the former American League pitcher conjured up a past filled with recollections of warm summer days in big-league cities around the country. And although he played his last major-league game in August 1984—when the Detroit Tigers cut him after a terrible stretch after the All-Star break—he continued to make his presence felt by coaching up-and-coming young pitching arms.

Abbott's tale is an interesting one: a leap from being a member of the World Series-winning Oakland A's of the 1970s to the expansion Seattle Mariners to the impressive Tigers teams of 1983 and '84.

William Glenn Abbott was born on February 16, 1951, in Little Rock, Arkansas. "When I was a kid, everybody played baseball," he told an interviewer in 2008. "I always loved it. When I was 14 or 15, we'd ride bicycles over to the baseball fields and would play a little workup or something and then help prepare the field. It's just what kids did then.

"The Cardinals were big in Little Rock. I can remember when Dick Allen came to Little Rock; he was the first black to play there. I remember Ferguson Jenkins and guys like that who played there. ... I've always loved it and played the game. This is not a job to me. I really enjoy what I do. It's my 39th season, and I love it. I like working with the young kids."[1]

In his early days with the sport, Abbott played the infield and caught as well as pitched.

That changed when he entered high school. "I realized that I had the chance to go on beyond high-school ball," he said. "I realized that I had some ability and didn't want to take a chance of breaking a finger or something like that."

Abbott played baseball and basketball in high school and had planned to continue with both sports in college. But he was drafted out of high school in the eighth round by the Oakland A's in June 1969, and signed immediately. He was 18 years old. For a couple of years during the offseason, he attended State College of Arkansas, now called the University of Central Arkansas. He made the big leagues when he was 22.

Starting in the Rookie-classification Northwest League, Abbott quickly worked his way through minor-league ball and made his debut with Oakland on July 29, 1973, when he started against the Texas Rangers. He was taken out in the fourth inning with Oakland leading 4-2, and Texas runners on second and third. (The A's eventually won, 7-4.)

Though Abbott's major-league pitching record was just 62-83, with a 4.39 earned-run average, he had his moments. September 28, 1975, the last game of the season, was a good example. Abbott was the second of four pitchers who combined to throw a no-hitter against the California Angels. Abbott pitched one inning and retired the side in order.

Abbott said the A's were preparing for the playoff series against the Boston Red Sox, and the manager, Alvin Dark, already had decided that Vida Blue would start but pitch no more than five innings. Abbott was slated to pitch the sixth, Paul Lindblad would throw the seventh inning, and Rollie Fingers would wrap things up in the eighth and ninth, regardless of the score.

"When I went out to take the mound in the sixth inning, the home crowd was booing—people were booing," Abbott said. "But they weren't booing me. They were booing because Vida Blue came out of the game and he was pitching a no-hitter. I said to myself, 'Lord, please don't let me give up a hit.'" And he didn't.

Abbott pitched for Oakland for four seasons and compiled a 13-16 record with a 4.08 ERA.

His years with the A's brought a lot of smiles. "I was on a team where you hear all the stuff about how wild they were, with all the fights and stuff. But the players were all-for-one when they were at the ballpark and on the field. They expected to win. In my first year we won the league championship." Oakland went on to win the World Series as well.

His next stop in an 11-year major-league career was with the Seattle Mariners, when he became the 24th pick in the 1976 expansion draft.

Abbott viewed the change from winning a title in Oakland to moving to an expansion team in Seattle as a positive experience as well.

"I went from a team that expected to win to a team that didn't have a lot of confidence," he said. "They thought they could win but weren't sure. It was a big adjustment. In expansion, you always have a bunch of Triple-A players who never had a chance to play in the majors. It's a big step to make. If you can play Double-A ball, you can pretty much play Triple-A ball. But they don't understand the jump to the majors. It's like daylight and dark. A lot of guys can't comprehend that."

Abbott's promise was realized in the 1977 campaign, the first of the Mariners' existence. He compiled a 12-13 record with a 4.45 ERA, fanning 100 batters. He was the longest-serving of the original Mariners players—his last game for Seattle was on August 21, 1983. His record with the Mariners was 44-62 with an ERA that ranged from 3.94 to 5.27.

Abbott missed the 1982 season because of floating bone chips in his elbow. His arm problems were compounded by a serious bout of viral meningitis. He lost 30 pounds, as well as some vision and hearing, and still had repercussions from the illness into June 1983. He was finally able to pitch again in midsummer of 1983.

Abbott was purchased by the Tigers on August 23, 1983, for $100,000, and stayed with Detroit for parts of two seasons.

"Detroit is a good baseball town, and I wanted an opportunity to go to a winning ballclub," he said during an interview at PGE Park in Portland, Oregon, his baseball home in 2008, where he was the pitching coach for the Portland Beavers, the San Diego Padres' Triple-A affiliate. "You really appreciate a chance like that. It's huge to get that opportunity."

He was released by the Detroit organization on August 14, 1984, during the height of the championship run to the World Series. Abbott immediately started a coaching career that topped his pitching career for longevity.

Standing 6-feet-6, Abbott had a playing weight of around 200 pounds, and added a few pounds after his coaching career started. To an interviewer, his native Arkansas showed up in his easy drawl: the word "four" became a two-syllable word when it left Abbott's mouth.

In talking about the differences between the two leagues, Abbott made a definitive observation about his playing days: "National League umps were far more consistent back then," he said, though he wouldn't comment on the current umpiring situation in the major leagues.

"I wish I could have played in the National League as a pitcher," he said. "I like the game a lot better. There's more things going on, more decisions to be made, pitcher having to hit, et cetera. It's also a better league to pitch in. The designated hitter means that teams like Boston and New York have no weaknesses in the lineup."

The right-hander's feelings about his time with the Tigers? "I knew I had a chance to go to a contending ballclub, and you don't realize how important that is until later. I was very fortunate," he said.

He made his Tigers debut on August 27, 1983, pitching seven innings against Toronto and leaving with the scored tied 2-2. His best game for the Tigers that season was a 5-0 shutout of the Cleveland Indians on September 14. His mark with the Tigers in '83 was 2-1 with a 1.93 ERA in seven starts

"The Tigers made a run in '83 and came up a game or two short [actually six games behind Baltimore]. I pitched well for them then, with Sparky [Anderson, the manager,] and Roger Craig as the pitching coach. And in '84, that team started 35-5 and set a record. We set the [American League] record in Anaheim for the most consecutive games won on the road and got a standing ovation.

"But I was in the bullpen and wasn't getting a chance to pitch much because the starters were so good. It made it really difficult; it's difficult to perform at a high level if you don't get the chance to play. But Jack Morris and Dan Petry and those guys were just dealing."

Abbott took the second loss of the '84 season when the Tigers were 16-1 but recalled few details of the 19-inning game in his interview, despite the fact that he committed two errors that contributed to the loss.

"Two errors? That's bad. Maybe that's why I can't remember," he said.

During Detroit's wire-to-wire American League East championship run in 1984, Abbott pitched in 13 games, eight of them starts, with a 3-4 record and a 5.93 ERA before he was cut. His best game that season was a complete-game victory over the Chicago White Sox on July 16, in which he gave up only four hits and one walk.

Abbott had fond recollections of his teammates from that charmed 1984 season, even though it was a truncated one for him.

Of Sparky Anderson, he said: "He didn't talk to you much. He would say hi, but that's the way managers were then. I had no problems with Sparky at all. He was a pretty positive guy. He had some good players on the team. It was amazing; those guys came to play. They never even complained about playing charity games against Cincinnati on an offday."

Roger Craig, the Tigers' pitching coach during Abbott's tenure in Detroit, "was one of the most positive people I've ever been around. He was always telling you how good you were. You have to be positive with the guys, and Roger was always that way."

Abbott said Jack Morris, the Tigers' acknowledged ace throughout the 1980s, "had tremendous confidence. He was probably the best pitcher of that decade — or one of the best, I'll say that. He was just getting better and better at the time. Jack was a winning-type pitcher. He threw a no-hitter in April in one of the first televised games [of the season] in Chicago. I remember a fan was yelling after every inning, 'Hey Morris, you got a no-hitter going'—trying to get him off stride. And about the eighth inning, Jack said back to him, 'Damn right. Stay right there 'cause you're gonna see one.' He was a quality pitcher."

Dan Petry, considered the number-two man in Detroit's rotation for most of the 1980s, "didn't say a lot," Abbott said, "but he was very consistent. You knew what you were going to get every time you went out there."

Abbott also had good words for two relievers who not only saved his bacon on more than one occasion in1984, but that of other Tigers hurlers during the championship season. Guillermo Hernandez, the 1984 AL Cy Young Award winner and Most Valuable Player, "couldn't do anything wrong," he recalled. Aurelio "Senor Smoke" Lopez, who notched a 10-1 record and 14 saves in the midst of Hernandez's spectacular season, "also was very consistent," Abbott said.

Alan Trammell, Detroit's shortstop and the World Series MVP in 1984, "was just as solid as they come. He was a ballplayer. He could handle the bat so well. He was underrated at that time. Howard Johnson was coming along at that time, too, playing third base. They were all very professional, and they expected to win. There was a lot of confidence—a good atmosphere to be in.

"Darrell Evans did a good job. It was the end of his career, but he was very consistent and made a tremendous impact on the club. Whitaker and Trammell and Lance Parrish and Kirk Gibson and Dave Rozema—it makes a difference when your players come up together. You've got to have talent, but you need chemistry, too, and it all fell together with the Tigers."

Abbott said he got a ring and a share of the World Series money that year, even though he left the team in August.

"It might have been a three-quarter share; I can't remember. It just makes you feel good that your teammates appreciate you," he said.

His time in the majors flew by, but the memories lingered.

"I had never seen a no-hitter in professional games, and in the first three years I was in the league, I saw one every year, including being involved in the one against the Angels when I was with Oakland. (It was actually four.) The Angels at that time were a bad ballclub, but Vida Blue was on that day. It was just five innings, but he walked through them.

"I had a chance to play with guys like Catfish Hunter. They made a big impression on me. They were very professional about the way they approached the game."

One of his greatest thrills was pitching in Yankee Stadium for the first time. "It was really an experience to go see those monuments for the first time. If you love baseball, that is really something. That's why I hate to see Yankee Stadium moving. It's one thing that bothers me. There's so much history. If you think of the people who played there, Yankee Stadium is like hallowed ground. You hate to see that happen, but I understand it when teams have to go to larger parks.

"The dugouts in Tiger Stadium were so small that everybody couldn't sit down when you came off the field. It was like a bunker in the bullpen."

As for Detroit's fans: "The Tigers have great fans. Everywhere you go you'd hear people talking about the Tigers. Every night they had big crowds. It was really a unique experience. It was really a cool deal there. I really enjoyed that—very much."

Abbott began a career as a pitching coach with the Little Falls Mets in 1985, the year after the Tigers cut him loose. He spent five years with the Mets' organization before joining the Athletics. He logged 13 years at various levels with the A's. Then Abbott was a pitching coach for five years in the San Diego Padres system, and spent four seasons in the Texas Rangers organization. In 2011 he returned to the Mets' organization, as the pitching coach for the Savannah Sand Gnats of the South Atlantic League. In 2012 he joined the Binghamton Mets of the Double-A Eastern League. As of 2014 he was still with Binghamton.

Abbott was married in 1973. He and his wife, Patti, lived in Arkansas in the offseason, and wherever he was working during the season. The eldest of their three children, Todd, pitched in the Oakland minor-league system from 1995 through 1998 and became a high-school teacher and baseball coach in Bentonville, Arkansas. Their second son, Jeff, also became a teacher, in Bolivar, Missouri. There is also a daughter, Amy.

SOURCES

The author relied on baseball-reference.com for the statistical data presented in this article.

NOTES

1 Clifford Corn interview with Glenn Abbott on April 21, 2008. Unless otherwise indicated, all quotations from Glenn Abbott come from this interview.

Jesus Alou

By Mark Armour

He enjoyed a 15-year career in the major leagues and has spent more than a half-century working in baseball, but Jesús Alou is destined to be remembered as the third brother in an extraordinary baseball family. He might have accomplished less as a player than his two All-Star siblings, but those comparisons are unfair. Jesús had a fine career in his own right as part of the first great wave of Dominican players who came to the major leagues in the late 1950s and early 1960s. Jesús Alou was the 13th Dominican in the majors, though just third in his own family.

José Rojas and Virginia Alou raised six children (Felipe, María, Mateo, Jesús, Juan, and Virginia) in their small home in Bajos de Haina, San Cristóbal, near Santo Domingo on the southern coast of the Dominican Republic. Rojas, a carpenter and black-smith who built their home and others in the neighborhood, also fathered two children with a previous wife who had died. Though José was black and Virginia white, this was not unusual in the Dominican and the children knew little racism in their homeland—they were Dominicans. The family was poor, like most people they knew. "We all helped [our father] in the shop," recalled Jesús, "but no money was coming in because everyone was poor around there. I was happy, though, just thinking about where my next meal might come from."[1]

Jesús María Rojas Alou was born on March 24, 1942. In keeping with the Latino custom, each parent contributed half of his double surname, but he is known in everyday life as Jesús Rojas in his homeland. While Felipe was playing in the US minor leagues, a team official mistakenly began identifying him as Felipe Alou, and he did not feel empowered to correct the error. When Mateo and Jesús followed him to the States, they used the Alou surname in order to associate with Felipe.

If this were not enough, many American writers and broadcasters were uncomfortable with his first name (properly pronounced "hay-SOOS"). Although there have been more than a dozen players named Jesús in the major leagues, Jesús Alou was the first, and is still the most prominent. Before his first season with the Giants, a San Francisco writer asked local religious leaders about the situation, and they all agreed that he needed a nickname, that reading "Jesus Saves Giants" in the morning paper would not do. The paper asked readers to write in with their suggestions, which many did.[2] His Latino teammates often called him Chuchito, but the writers often called him Jay. "What," the subject asked in 1965, "is wrong with my real name, Jesús? It is a common name in Latin America like Joe or Tom or Frank in the United States. My parents named me Jesús and I am proud of my name."[3] Thankfully, by the end of his career, everyone, even the writers, called him Jesús.

When Jesús was born, Felipe was nearly 7 years old, while Mateo (later known mainly as "Matty" in the US) was 3. Unlike his older brothers, Jesús came to baseball slowly and somewhat reluctantly. "I wouldn't even go and watch Felipe and Mateo play on the lots around our home," he recalled. "I went fishing."[4] When he did play, the brothers used bats that they made on their father's lathe.[5] In fact, it was mainly his brothers' success that led Frank (Chick) Genovese, who managed the other Rojas brothers on Leones del Escogido in the Dominican Winter League, to pressure Jesús to give baseball a try. Genovese's cause was joined by Horacio Martínez, a former Negro Leaguer who worked as a bird dog for New York Giants scout Alejandro Pómpez and helped run the Escogido team. In late 1958 the 16-year-old Jesús signed to be the team's batting practice pitcher.

At about the same time, Genovese signed Jesús for the San Francisco Giants organization, as he had done a few years earlier with Felipe and Mateo. The man who would now be known as Jesús Alou had very little experience playing on organized teams and the Giants' optimism was largely based on the talents of Felipe, who had made the major leagues, and Mateo, who had hit .321 for St. Cloud the previous year. Jesús was assigned to Hastings, Nebraska, which had a team in the short-season Nebraska State League. Alou pitched in just two games, allowing 11 runs in five innings, though he did manage to finish 2-for-3 as a batter. "I don't win. I don't lose," Alou recalled of his summer in Nebraska. "I don't do much of anything except brood."[6]

The next winter Alou hurt his arm throwing batting practice for Escogido, and thought his reluctant baseball experiment might have ended before he turned 18. He reported to the minor-league camp for the Giants in 1960, and was assigned to Artesia (New Mexico), a Class D affiliate. Manager George Genovese, the brother of Chick, wanted Alou to give up pitching and play the outfield, like his brothers. Again Alou balked, suggesting instead that he just go home. He finally agreed, and played the entire year in center field. His hitting was great (.352 with 11 home runs and 33 doubles), though his outfield play was a bit raw due to his sore arm. "It was a tougher year on Gil Garrido, our shortstop, than it was for me," Alou remembered. "My arm was so bad that every time a ball was hit out to me Garrido had to race almost to my side to take the cutoff throw."[7]

Tough year or not, Garrido, a future major leaguer from Panama, hit .362 to win the batting title, while Alou led the league with 188 hits. Both were named to the league's postseason all-star team. After the Artesia season was over, the 18-year-old Alou played a few games with Eugene (Oregon) of the Northwest League, where he hit .350 in 20 at bats.

Alou's remaining years in the minor leagues were equally successful. Spending the 1961 season in Eugene, he hit .336, led the league in hits, and was named a postseason all-star. The next year in El Paso (Texas League), the 20-year-old Alou hit .343. Finally reaching the top rung of the ladder (Triple-A Tacoma) in 1963, Alou hit .324 with 210 hits (a total that broke Matty's former Tacoma record). He was an all-star at every level, and had done everything he could to earn a spot with the Giants. On September 10, 1963, he finally made it, pinch-hitting against the New York Mets and grounding out against Carlton Willey to lead off the eighth. Willey then retired Mateo and Felipe for a 1-2-3 inning. The three brothers also played the outfield together briefly five days later. During his call-up, Jesús hit .250 in 24 at bats.

As his major-league career was starting, many people believed that Jesús would surpass both his brothers as a player. Among the believers were his brothers. "Jesús represents our family now," said Felipe. "He has the right approach to baseball. Matty and I are, how you say it? We're satisfied. We're in the majors doing the best we can. But Jesús, he is a restless man. If he can't be supreme, he doesn't want to be at all. He has to be the greatest."[8] As evidence, people could point to his performance with Escogido, where the three brothers had formed the outfield over several winters. As early as 1961, Alejandro Pómpez had said, "Jesús Alou hits the curveball twice as good as most kids who have been around much longer. The day will come when he'll outshine both Felipe and Matty."[9]

Jesús had already outgrown both of his brothers, reaching 6-feet-2 and 190 pounds by the time of his debut. George Genovese, who had managed Jesús a few times in the minors, was optimistic. "He has live hands and a fast bat and he attacks the ball with great aggressiveness," he said. "When he puts on another 15 pounds, he will have more power than Felipe."[10] Added manager Al Dark, "We think young Alou is one of the finest players our farm system has developed in recent years."[11]

Thoughts of an all-Alou outfield in San Francisco were unrealistic, however. The team already had star performers in center field (Willie Mays), left field (Willie McCovey), and first base (Orlando Cepeda). Felipe Alou had established himself as a good player in right field, while Matty Alou was behind Harvey Kuenn among the extra outfielders. After the season the Giants partly dealt with the logjam by trading Felipe to the Braves. They announced that Jesús, and not Matty, would get first crack at the right-field job.

The biggest flaw in Jesús's game, then and later, was his inability to take a walk. Even in the 1960s this was remarked upon, though more as a curiosity than a flaw. In 1963 baseball increased the dimension of the strike zone from the bottom of the knee to the top of the shoulders, which did not affect Jesús at all. As a Tacoma writer remarked, "Jesús has a personal strike zone which far exceeds anything considered by rulesmakers."[12] Teammate Juan Marichal remembered, "One time ... a pitch [came in] about level with Jesus's head. Jesus swung at it and hit a home run to right field. He was that type of hitter."[13] But the Giants were ready to live with his approach. "He swings at quite a few bad balls," admitted farm director Carl Hubbell, "but I call him one of those 'they shall not pass' hitters. If he can reach a ball, he'll swing."[14]

Alou played fairly regularly in 1964, hitting .274 but with little power (three home runs) or plate discipline (13 walks). On July 10 he enjoyed the game of his career, when he went 6-for-6 with a home run in a Giant victory in Chicago's Wrigley Field. His season ended abruptly on September 2 when he was spiked at second base by New York's Ron Hunt, resulting in 91 stitches in his foot, ankle, and calf. He came back the next year to play 143 games, batting .298 with 9 home runs. At a time when the league hit just .249, his average was impressive, but his 13 walks gave him only a .317 on-base percentage, just over the league average. With Alou's skill set, he was going to have to hit .320 to be a star, and most observers believed that he would. He turned just 23 in 1965.

Alou reported in 1966 determined to improve his batting eye. "I know pitchers are getting me to swing at bad pitches," he admitted. "I try to cut it down this year. Sometimes maybe I forget, but I am going to cut it way down, I think."[15] Instead, he took a step back, and when he was hitting just .232 with two walks in nearly full-time play on June 13, he was optioned to Phoenix for two weeks, ostensibly because of a sore arm. He hit better upon his return, and got his average up to .259. It was a big year for the other Alou brothers: Matty, traded to the Pirates the previous winter, hit .342 to capture the league batting title; and Felipe, playing for the Braves, finished second at .327 while also clubbing 31 home runs. The talk of Jesús being the best of the Alou brothers had quieted down.

After the 1966 season, Jesús allowed that he wanted to be traded, reasoning that his brothers had found success after leaving San Francisco's Candlestick Park, whose cold winds created difficulties for both hitters and outfielders. During the winter meetings, the Giants reportedly talked to other clubs about Alou, but held on to him.

In 1967 Alou played more or less full-time, and returned to his 1965 levels of hitting: .292 in 510 at-bats, though again with little power (five home runs) and few walks (14). Oddly, the Giants used Alou as their primary leadoff hitter. As manager Herman Franks explained, Alou's swinging and missing at so many bad pitches made him a bad hit-and-run guy, so he didn't like him up with men on base. "So," said Franks, "the leadoff position is where he can do the least harm and definitely the most good."[16] Alou hit .308 as the leadoff batter, and hit .337 when leading off innings.

The 26-year-old Alou played left and right fields for the Giants in 1968, starting 97 games and playing parts of 23 others. He regressed a bit from his 1967 comeback, hitting just .263 with no home runs and nine walks in 436 plate appearances. This turned out to be his final go-round with the Giants, as on October 15 Alou was selected by the Montreal Expos in an expansion draft to stock the two new National League teams.

Montreal reportedly turned down several trade offers for Alou, including one from the Astros for Mike Cuellar. After several weeks of speculation, on January 22 the Expos dealt Alou and Donn Clendenon to the Astros for outfielder Rusty Staub. Six weeks later Clendenon announced that he would retire rather than report to Houston, nullifying the trade for a few weeks. Eventually the Expos substituted two pitchers and some money to get the deal done. Houston manager Harry Walker coveted Alou, as he wanted more speed in the outfield. Walker had long fancied himself a hitting guru, and his biggest success story had been Matty Alou, who became a consistent .330 hitter after joining up with Walker in Pittsburgh in 1966.

Jesús Alou began the 1969 season as the Astros' right fielder and leadoff hitter, and stroked three hits in his first game. He then went into a long slump that lasted most of the year, though his season was partly saved by hitting .328 after the start of September. On June 10, while playing left field, Alou was involved in a brutal collision with shortstop Héctor Torres. His teammate's forehead hit Alou's face and caused him to swallow his tongue. Pirates trainer Tony Bartirome may have saved the unconscious Alou's life when he pried open his mouth, inserted a rubber tube and breathed into it, which opened Alou's air passage enough so that he could resume breathing. Alou and Torres were each carried off the field and taken to the hospital—both players suffered concussions while Alou fractured his jaw. He missed six weeks of action. For the season, he hit just .248.

Alou was not a regular to start the 1970 season, but his consistent hitting eventually got him an everyday role. He ended up hitting .306 in 117 games, with a career-high 21 walks. "To me, hitting .300 is not all

that big an issue," he said late in the year. "What is important for me as the leadoff hitter is to get on base. I think I've been good, actually, ever since I came out of the hospital last year."[17] Once again he excelled as a leadoff hitter—he hit .392 leading off games, and hit .328 when leading off an inning. In 1971 he started even hotter, hitting over .350 into June before slowly dropping off. A bad September left him at .279 for the season.

Through it all, baseball people liked having Jesús Alou around. Jim Bouton, an Astros teammate in 1969 and 1970, described him in his second book, *I'm Glad You Didn't Take It Personally*. "We called him J. or Jesus, never hay-soos . . . . J. is one of the most delicate, sensitive, nicest men I have ever met. He'd walk a mile out of his way to drop a coin in some beggar's cup." Bouton then went on to describe how Alou's sensitivity made him a comic foil for practical joker Doug Rader's most disgusting antics.

"Alou is popular with his teammates because of his inherent good nature and philosophical way of looking at things," said another writer in 1971. "And Alou is interesting to watch during a game." He drew much comment throughout his career for all his mannerisms in the batter's box—he held the bat vertical directly behind his right ear, then repeatedly rotated his neck. "People write letters asking why I jerk my neck," Alou said. "I can't answer except to say it's not a back problem. It's just a mental problem."[18] Early in his career Dodger pitcher Don Drysdale thought Alou might be trying to steal the catcher's signs, and subsequently knocked Alou down with a pitch.[19] Yet the habit remained.

Alou also had a very self-deprecating sense of humor. Late in his career he failed to reach a fly ball in the outfield, and observed, "Ten years ago, I would have overrun it."[20] When reminiscing about his years in the game, he would often recall moments when he forgot how many outs there were or the time he overran a base.[21] Despite his relatively modest accomplishments, he stayed in the game a long time because his managers and teammates liked him so much. He was quiet and dignified, and often could be seen reading a Bible at his locker.

As Jimmy Wynn recounted in his autobiography, though, Harry Walker's inveterate tinkering with hitters and their approach at the plate managed to infuriate even "The J. Alou"—as Jesús jocularly referred to himself. "The Hat" went so far as to break Alou's bat in order to make sure that his player used a Harry Walker model. Another clubhouse incident a few days later finally set Alou off, and Wynn wrote, "We are laughing in shock over the discovery that he is capable of anger at this level."[22]

With the emergence of Bob Watson and Cesar Cedeño, and the presence of Wynn, Alou no longer had a regular job after the 1971 season. He hit .312 in 1972 as a reserve outfielder and pinch-hitter, but just .236 in the same role the following season. On July 31, 1973, his contract was sold to the Oakland Athletics.

The A's had won the World Series in 1972 and would repeat the next two seasons. Alou played 20 games over the last two months of the 1973 season, mainly in left field, and hit .306. When regular center fielder Bill North sprained his ankle that September, it opened the door for Jesús to play in the postseason. He hit 2-for-6 in the ALCS, but just 3-for-19 in the World Series. The next year he stayed with the A's the entire year and got 232 plate appearances, mainly as a designated hitter, hitting .262. He hit just twice in the postseason, including a pinch single in the first game of the ALCS. Matty Alou had helped win a World Series for the A's in 1972, and now Jesús had won back-to-back with the same club.

The next spring Alou was released. "Maybe I'm overrating myself," he said. "I think this team needs a guy who does the type of job I can do."[23] He was soon picked up by the New York Mets. "I was offered more money to play with my brother, Matty, in Japan," Alou said, "but I prefer to play in the United States." Alou served as a reserve outfielder and pinch-hitter, hitting .265 in 108 plate appearances.

In March 1976 he was released again, and this time he headed back to the Dominican, where he remained for two years. Besides playing winter ball in his homeland, he and a friend tried to start a business. "We were going to start a watch-assembly plant in the Dominican Republic," he recalled. "We would buy the parts in other countries and assemble the watches there. But the government down there didn't like the idea."[24] After two years away, Alou returned to the major leagues with the Astros in 1978, and hit .324 in a reserve role. When he returned the next year, the 37-year-old took on the added role of batting coach. He hit .256 this time around in just 43 at-bats, though his relatively high walk total (6) gave him a respectable .347 on-base percentage.

After the 1979 season Alou drew his release, and his major-league career was over. He finished with a respectable .280 batting average, but his walk rate of just 3 per 100 plate appearances was the lowest in the 20th century for someone who played 1,000 games. He played parts of 15 seasons in the majors, and won two World Series. In the Dominican, he starred for many years for Escogido with his two brothers. He was Rookie of the Year in 1960-61. His lifetime stats at home were .302 with 20 homers and 339 RBIs in 20 seasons (12 for Escogido and 8 for archrival Licey). He played in five Caribbean Series (1973, 1974, 1977, 1978, and 1980), hitting .351 with two homers and 13 RBIs. One of his highlights in a Dominican uniform came during the 1973 edition in Caracas, Venezuela, when he was 12-for-24 (.500) as Licey won the tournament.[25]

Jesús Alou married Angela Hanley in the late 1960s, and the couple raised five children –Angela, Jesús Jr., María de Jesús, Claudia, and Jeimy— in the Dominican Republic. After his playing career ended, Alou moved back home and remained there, still fishing and swimming in the nearby waters in the summer. He lived not far from where he grew up, and not far from the homes of his brothers and sisters. "I guess we look much richer to the people here than we really are," he once observed.

Although he did some managing in the Dominican winter league, Alou turned to scouting when his pitching coach with Escogido, Bob Gebhard, became an executive with the Montreal Expos. Jesús said, "I imagine he saw me working with kids. Even when I was a player, I liked to work with kids." In typical form, he added, "I have very high blood pressure. I don't think I can stand managing."[26]

He continued to work for American baseball, moving from the Expos to the Marlins. In 2002 he became the Dominican scouting director for the Boston Red Sox. He has also served as director of the team's Dominican Summer League operations, much the same role as he had held with the Marlins' Dominican academy.

Jesús came back to San Francisco in 2003 for Opening Day, joined by his two brothers, one of whom (Felipe) was now managing the Giants. They had all accomplished so much in the game, 40 years after playing in the same outfield. "I have never dreamed anything in baseball," Jesús said. "Everything has been a surprise. Every day is a new surprise. Felipe being manager in San Francisco makes me proud. It's another surprise."[27]

Dominicans have come to play a huge role in American baseball, following in the giant footsteps of Felipe, Mateo, and Jesús Alou. Late in his career, Jesús was asked to compare the skills of the three Alous. "Felipe is a very tough guy in baseball," he said, "tougher than all of us. Matty was smaller and had to take more advantage of his ability, the guy who does more thinking. Me, I wasn't as tough as Felipe or as thinking as Matty. One thing we had in common: we didn't like to strike out too much, maybe because we used to play with rubber balls in our backyard. As long as a guy didn't strike out, he could keep batting, and we all liked to bat."[28] The brothers played over 5,000 major-league games between them.

Jesús Alou spent many years in the game as a player, and as of 2014 was still involved in finding players for the major leagues. He was a vital part of a great baseball family, and his legacy will live on.

SOURCES

Thanks to Rory Costello for his editing and for adding a few additional stories to the article. Thanks also to Gabriel Schechter, Rod Nelson, and Matías Alou.

NOTES

1   Joseph Durso, "We Band of Brothers," *New York Times*, August 14, 1975.

2   Prescott Sullivan, "Wanted — Name for New Right Fielder!" *San Francisco Examiner*, March 6, 1964.

3   Bob Stevens, "Jesús Alou Could Be the Best in Family," *The Sporting News*, July 3, 1965, 7.

4   Bob Stevens, "The Little Alou," *Sport*, September 1965, 81.

5   Jack McDonald, "No. 3 Alou May Gain No. 1 Spot," *The Sporting News*, April 6, 1963, 10.

6   Stevens, "The Little Alou," 81.

7   Stevens, "The Little Alou," 81.

8   Stevens, "The Little Alou," 80.

9   Jack McDonald, "Giants Phenoms Train in Lap of Luxury," *The Sporting News*, April 12, 1961, 9.

10 McDonald, "No. 3 Alou May Gain No. 1 Spot," 10.

11 Jack McDonald, "Giants," *The Sporting News*, February 22, 1964, 24.

12 Ed Honeywell, "Jesús Alou Gives Up Passes to Hit Away," *The Sporting News*, August 10, 1963, 33.

13 Juan Marichal with Lew Freedman, *Juan Marichal: My Journey from the Dominican Republic to Cooperstown* (Minneapolis: MVP Books, 2011), 114. Marichal's memory was fuzzy about the details. He recalled it as being in San Francisco against Jim Bunning of the Phillies, but SABR's Home Run Log shows no such record.

14 Jack McDonald, "Giants Paint Pennant Picture With Jesús Alou and Jim Ray Hart." *The Sporting News*, January 4, 1964, 10.

15 Jack McDonald, "Those Bad Pitches Look Too Juicy for Jesús Alou to Resist," *The Sporting News*, April 2, 1966, 17.

16 Bob Stevens, "Alou a Goliath in Giant Leadoff Spot," *The Sporting News*, July 1, 1967, 16T.

17 John Wilson, "Jay Alou Giving Brothers Lesson in Swatting Art," *The Sporting News*, August 29, 1970, 17.

18 John Wilson, "A Sizzling Bat Pushes Alou Into Astros' Lineup," *The Sporting News*, June 26, 1971 24..

19 Stevens, "The Little Alou," 80.

20 Gordon Verrell, "Dodgers Tap Rookie Wall to Add Bullpen Depth," *The Sporting News*, January 10, 1976, 28.

21 Mike Mandel, *SF Giants. An Oral History* (Santa Cruz, California: self-published, 1979), 149.

22 Jimmy Wynn and Bill McCurdy, *Toy Cannon: The Autobiography of Baseball's Jimmy Wynn* (Jefferson, North Carolina: McFarland & Co., 2010), 121-122.

23 Ron Bergman, "Happy Charlie Does Jig Over Hippity-Hoppy," *The Sporting News*, April 19. 1975, 5.

24 Harry Shattuck, "Bat Artist Alou Doubles as Astro Bat Tutor," *The Sporting News*, March 17, 1979, 51.

25 Gustavo Rodríguzez, "Jesús Alou: Ganó la triple corona en SC en 1973," *Hoy* (Santo Domingo, Dominican Republic), January 26, 2012.

26 Gordon Edes, "Alou Acts as Scout, Dreams as a Player," *South Florida Sun-Sentinel* (Fort Lauderdale), February 8, 1994.

27 Associated Press, "Alou Reunion Takes Place in San Francisco," *Albany Times-Union*, April 8, 2003.

28 Joseph Durso, "We Band of Brothers," *New York Times*, August 14, 1975.

Mike Andrews

By Saul Wisnia

From his key contributions as a rookie on the pennant-winning Boston Red Sox of 1967 to his final games spent entangled in one of the most controversial incidents in World Series history, Mike Andrews packed plenty of memorable moments into seven-plus big-league seasons. And while his baseball career may not have lasted as long—or ended—as he envisioned, it led directly to a second vocation that the former All-Star second baseman considered even more rewarding than playing on two AL championship teams.

As chairman of the Jimmy Fund of the Dana-Farber Cancer Institute, located less than a mile down Brookline Avenue from Boston's Fenway Park, Andrews spent 30 years before his 2009 retirement helping to raise hundreds of millions of dollars for research and treatment into childhood and adult cancers. Rather than spin tales of his athletic feats during his many public appearances, he spokeof the dedicated scientists, caregivers, and patients engaged in the cancer fight at Dana-Farber—"true heroes" whom he first encountered as a rookie.

Andrews was the perfect man for the job. The Jimmy Fund has long been a favorite charity of the Red Sox, and Mike was accustomed to quietly turning in clutch performances that helped others shine. All Red Sox fans worth their weight in Big Yaz Bread know who led the club in hitting down the stretch of the 1967 American League race, but it's a forgotten footnote that rookie Andrews was second to Carl Yastrzemski among regulars with a .342 batting average during that pressure-packed September.

"Just today, I had an electrician at my winter house in Florida, and when he found out who I was, he named the entire starting lineup from '67," Andrews recalled in 2006.. "That happens all the time. It was just a magical team; 2004 was great, but I'm not sure everybody will remember all the individuals the same way because players move around so much now. Plus, the Red Sox are always contending, whereas the team had been bad for years before we came along—and the excitement kept building each month. That season brought baseball back in New England."

Andrews was in the region so long with the Red Sox and the Jimmy Fund that many likely assume he is a New England native himself, but he's in fact a Southern California boy. Born on July 9, 1943, in Los Angeles, he grew up in nearby Torrance rooting for the Pacific Coast League's Los Angeles Angels and Hollywood Stars.

Andrews got his early big-league fix from television's *Game of the Week,* and after the Dodgers fled Brooklyn for the West Coast during his teenage years, he followed the exploits of their pitching aces Sandy Koufax and Don Drysdale. His athletic genes came from his father, Lloyd, who played football and basketball at

the University of Montana and owned Callahan's Bar in nearby Hermosa Beach. Mike starred in football, baseball, and basketball at South Torrance High.

The 6-foot-3, 195-pounder initially chose the gridiron—accepting a full scholarship to UCLA that required his attending one year of junior college to complete the necessary foreign-language requirement. Andrews earned JC All-American honors as a split end at El Camino College, but then came a life-altering decision for the 18-year-old.

The Pirates and Red Sox had scouted him, and he wanted to marry his high-school sweetheart, Marilyn Flynn, and start a family. Several more years of college football without a paycheck seemed like forever, and Boston scout Joe Stephenson was offering him a cash bonus of $12,000 plus $4,000 more if he made the big-league roster. Andrews took it in December 1961, got engaged early the next spring, and shortly thereafter reported to Boston's Class A club in Olean, New York. (Stephenson's son, Jerry, would later be one of Mike's teammates on the Red Sox.)

Up the ladder

Like many young prospects, Andrews' first taste of professional baseball was humbling. All around him on the '62 Olean squad were other former high-school hotshots, and as he later recalled for the *Boston Globe*: "I didn't think much of my chances. So all I could do was give it everything I had." Perhaps this self-deprecating attitude took the pressure off at the plate, as Andrews hit .299 with 12 home runs and 89 runs scored in 114 games as the club's starting shortstop.

Moved up the chain to Winston-Salem for 1963, he hit just .255 there, but .323 after a midseason switch to Single-A Waterloo. He cut his error total at shortstop by (more than 50 percent, and the Red Sox boosted him again the next year, to Double-A Reading. There he batted .295, raised his fielding percentage again, and in 1965—while still just 21 years old—earned an invitation to Red Sox spring training in Scottsdale, Arizona, from new manager Billy Herman.

Farmed out for the regular season to Triple-A Toronto, the top of Boston's minor-league ladder, Andrews had a disappointing year (.246, 4 homers) toiling for a fiery young manager named Dick Williams. It was Williams who played a part in Andrews' winter-league switch to second base (Rico Petrocelli already held the starting shortstop slot in Boston), and Mike excelled when he returned to Toronto for a second season in 1966. He played solid defense at his new position, boosted both his batting average (to .267) and home-run output considerably (to 14), and led the International League in runs scored with 97.

The performance earned Andrews a September call-up to the ninth-place Red Sox, where he started five games in the waning days of the season. He batted seventh in his first major-league contest, against his hometown Angels at Fenway Park on September 18, and went 0-for-4 with a run scored. His next action came a week later at New York, and on September 24 he notched his first big-league hit, a single off Fritz Peterson at Yankee Stadium in a 1-0 Sox loss.

"Mickey Mantle was one of my idols," Andrews recalled of the event. "When he said, 'Nice job, Mike,' that was terrific." Overall Andrews was 3-for-18 in the trial, with his other two safeties coming in the season finale at Chicago.

After Herman was fired and Williams named Red Sox manager for 1967, the new skipper announced before spring training that the starting second base job was "Andrews' to lose." Mike had hurt his lower back lifting weights in the offseason, however, and the lingering injury affected his defensive range in exhibition play. The tough-talking Williams was not sympathetic.

"We can't wait any longer," the manager stated flatly after two Andrews errors on March 26. "He has a bad back and he can't bend. If he can't bend, he can't play." Even though Mike had notched a five-hit game and was batting close to .400 in the exhibition season, Williams announced that day that he was moving fellow Southern Californian rookie Reggie Smith from outfield to second base and putting Andrews on the bench.

This was still the arrangement when the regular season started two weeks later, but it didn't last much longer. Smith had his own defensive troubles at second, while the center field platoon of Jose Tartabull and George Thomas that replaced him was batting less than .200. On April 19, with Andrews' back improving, Williams reinstated Smith in center and Mike at second. With very few exceptions, Mike Andrews would be the Red Sox' starting second baseman for the next four years.

Key contributor

Once he got his chance, Andrews made the most of it. He hit .321 during the rest of April, and settled in with Petrocelli to provide strong middle-infield defense for the surprising Red Sox. On April 25 he hit his first major-league home run, a three-run shot off the Senators' Pete Richert in a 9-3 Boston victory at DC Stadium. Later in the same contest, he had his first big-league stolen base and scored on a Carl Yastrzemski double.

A solid May (.281, including a 17-for-37 stretch) followed for Mike and featured the team's first trip to his home state for a series with the Angels. A contingent of 90 family members and friends made the 45-minute drive to Anaheim on two buses originating from his dad's bar, and Andrews received rousing applause from the sign-waving group even when he drew a walk in one of the games — thus earning him several weeks of ribbing from his teammates. A home run followed the next day, however, and Mike went on to enjoy several more clutch performances in front of his biggest fans over the years (including another homer at Anaheim later in the season). Briefly in May, the rookie was among the American League's top ten in hitting.

Andrews' batting average dropped off as the season wore on, but even while hitting below .240 each month from June through August, he was consistently in the thick of things as the Red Sox and their fans enjoyed Boston's first true pennant race in more than a decade.

Most often used as a leadoff man in front of players like Tony Conigliaro, Yastrzemksi, and George Scott, he also hit quite often in the second, seventh, and eighth slots.

July offered a prime example of Mike's value; he batted just .236 but scored 18 runs in as many games to help the team to a 15-3 stretch. He was a key man in a ten-game winning streak July 14-23 that many signaled as the turning point of the season, with two hits (including a three-run homer) in a 6-4 win at Baltimore July 19 and three more safeties (with another homer) in a 4-0 shutout at Cleveland on July 22 that drew Boston to within a half-game of the first-place Chicago White Sox. Happy with Andrews' contributions, owner Tom Yawkey quietly gave him a midseason salary boost from $11,000 to $15,000.

Making Andrews' performance all the more impressive were two factors — he was a 24-year-old rookie playing 3,000 miles from home, and (unbeknownst to all but his teammate and close friend Russ Gibson), he was the subject of a death threat late in the season. A Chicago fan who had apparently wagered a bundle on the White Sox winning the pennant sent Andrews and fellow AL second basemen Rod Carew and Dick McAuliffe (all from contending teams) menacing letters threatening their lives.

"Dick Williams called me into his office," Andrews recalled, "and (general manager) Dick O'Connell and an FBI guy were in there. The FBI guy says, 'We don't think it's a valid threat, but there have been one or two correspondences, so we want to watch it closely.' I believed that there probably wasn't anything to worry about, so I didn't even tell my wife right away. But I remember looking around the stands at Fenway when I first ran on the field for the next game."

By August, with a four-team scramble under way for the AL lead, every game was a huge one — and Andrews continued to deliver. August 1 through 3 he went a combined 7-for-12 with two homers, five RBIs and five runs scored in three games (the Red Sox won two), and, all told, had eight multihit games during the month. This was just a warm-up for September, when he hit.342 (25-for-73) and along with Yastrzemski and Dalton Jones kept the team in the hunt while others slumped. Mike was actually well over .400 for the month until an 0-for-9 skein, and after this manager Williams—who liked to go with the "hot hand" whenever possible—sat him in favor of veteran Jerry Adair for several games down the stretch.

Then, with the Sox needing to sweep Minnesota in two games on the season's final weekend for a chance at the pennant, Andrews came through again. On Saturday he was 2-for-3 in the leadoff slot with a key infield single ahead of Yaz's game-breaking three-run homer, and after starting on the bench in Sunday's finale, he played a significant defensive role subbing for Adair, who had suffered a spike wound to his leg while turning an eighth-inning double play. Two straight Minnesota hits immediately brought the tying run to the plate in a 5-2 game, and Bob Allison hit a hard liner off Jim Lonborg into the left-field corner for what looked like a double and two RBIs. The shot did score one run, but it also became the inning's third out when Yastrzemksi threw a bullet to Andrews just in time for a sweeping tag on the sliding Allison.

Now down 5-3, the Twins got the leadoff man on in the ninth, but Andrews turned a clutch "tag 'em out, throw 'em out" double play on a Rod Carew grounder to set the stage for Petrocelli's catch of Rich Rollins' popup and the bedlam that followed. Andrews and Scott were the first to reach pitching hero Lonborg, and managed to hoist him to their shoulders for a few moments before thousands of charging fans turned the team's celebration into the city's.

Andrews finished the regular season with a .263 average, 8 homers, and 40 RBIs in 142 games after his late start. He led the league with 18 sacrifice hits, and was runner-up to Rookie of the Year Carew among second basemen in voting by major-league players, managers, and coaches for the Topps All-Star Rookie Team. As the Red Sox readied for the World Series, the *Boston Record American* featured a huge front-page photo of Marilyn Andrews and the couple's 2-year-old son, Michael, in the window of their Peabody home, waving a "GOOD LUCK RED SOX" banner.

It's unclear if Dick Williams saw the newspaper and photo, but he again benched Andrews in favor of Adair during the first four games against the St. Louis Cardinals. Adair went 2-for-16, however, and after two pinch-hitting appearances (and one hit) Andrews was back in the starting lineup for Game 5—where he remained the rest of the Series. He wound up batting .308, but the Red Sox and a weary Lonborg lost to Cardinals ace Bob Gibson in the seventh game. "The script was there, but it just wasn't meant to be," Andrews said of the setback. "It was like, 'You guys have had your fun, now welcome back to the world. Here's reality.'"

Shining on field and off

Reality hit hard in 1968, as the team fell to a distant fourth place and the offensive output for many Boston hitters dropped off markedly. Andrews was an exception. In the Year of the Pitcher, during which Yastrzemski was the only everyday AL player to hit .300 for the season, Andrews battled for the league batting lead until Labor Day before finishing at .271 (12th in the circuit) with 7 homers and 45 RBIs. He topped his rookie totals with 22 doubles and 145 hits, and his tiny dip from 79 runs scored to 77 was much more a factor of Tony Conigliaro's yearlong absence due to his horrific '67 beaning and George Scott's anemic .171 average than a sophomore slump. After a few crucial errors early in the season, Andrews was steady on defense, and he was developing into a team leader. Boston sportswriters named him the club's "Unsung Hero" for the season.

None of this was lost on Red Sox coach Bobby Doerr, then the top second baseman in the team's history, who told *New York Times* columnist Arthur Daley of Andrews: "This kid will be around for a long while. What I like best about him is that he's a natural athlete who won't fall apart when he has a bad day. He has the ideal throwing arm for a second baseman, whipping it across his body. He's capable of .285 with 20 homers once he gets settled." Daley was similarly impressed, writing, "The Bostonians have been searching for a second baseman of Doerr's superlative skills ever since

Bobby retired in 1951. It could be that Mike will become that long-sought successor."

Off the field Andrews was shining as well. During his rookie year, he had become aware of the Jimmy Fund's status as the team's official charity—its billboard in right field was the only one allowed at Fenway Park by owner Tom Yawkey for years—and along with his teammates voted a full 1967 World Series share to the charity. Like other players, he also periodically met with young cancer patients brought to Fenway by Jimmy Fund executive director Bill Koster. One day such a visit gave him a reality check of a different kind.

"I was busy warming up, but I spent a few minutes with the kid, who was a Little League star looking forward to playing the next year after his treatment was done," recalled Andrews. "I wished him luck. Bill came up to me afterward and said, 'Thanks, Mike. That meant a lot. There isn't much we can do for that boy. We're sending him home.' That made me realize that an 0-for-4 day at the plate really doesn't mean too much in the scheme of things."

Andrews became a Jimmy Fund regular and in 1968 was named Man of the Year by the BoSox Club (the team's official fan club) for "contributions to the success of the Red Sox and for cooperation in community endeavors." He didn't know it at the time, but the seeds of his future career had been planted.

Mike made Doerr and Daley look prophetic in '69. Now batting second in Boston's lineup more often than leadoff, he firmly established himself as one of the most productive second basemen in the majors when healthy. He had a .293 average (tenth in the league), 15 homers, and 59 RBIs despite missing nearly 40 games in midseason after being hit in the hand by Minnesota pitcher Dave Boswell and suffering a blood clot that required extensive treatment. When a bad back kept Baltimore's Davey Johnson from going to the All-Star Game, Mike took his place and backed up starting second baseman Rod Carew. (Andrews played the last four innings for the American League and grounded out off Jerry Koosman in his only plate

appearance.) The Red Sox were again unable to recapture the magic of two years earlier, and with a third-place finish assured, Dick Williams was fired in the waning days of the season.

A change of Sox

The young lineup that was expected to lead the Red Sox to several pennants was still quite potent—Boston's 203 home runs in 1970 led all big-league clubs—but without the pitching to compete with the Baltimore Orioles, it was not enough. Back atop the batting order exclusively, Andrews reached new offensive heights himself that summer. He had 28 doubles, 17 homers, and 65 RBIs, and led off four games with homers—giving him eight leadoff clouts in his career. He topped AL second basemen with 19 errors, but even if management had big changes in store after a second straight third-place finish, Mike's spot with the club seemed safe.

On December 1, 1970, however, one day after Dick O'Connell was quoted as saying "Andrews is not available for trade," Mike and backup shortstop Luis Alvarado were sent to the woeful Chicago White Sox for Luis Aparicio, a future Hall of Famer. Aparicio would be slated to play short alongside newly acquired second baseman Doug Griffin in Boston, with Petrocelli moving to third. "The way I understood it, O'Connell was looking either for a shortstop or a third baseman," said Andrews. "If they got a third baseman, they'd leave Rico at short and me at second. But Aparicio became available, so they went that route."

He would later joke in his self-deprecating style that "at least I was traded for a Hall of Famer, even if he was 55 at the time" (Aparicio was actually 36), but the move "crushed" Mike—who had a wife and three young children happily settled in the suburb of Peabody. The majority of fans interviewed were also upset, both because of Andrews' reputation as a heady, tough athlete and Aparicio's age.

Like Fred Lynn and Mo Vaughn in later years, Mike was a popular ballplayer whose career and luck never seemed the same after he left the Red Sox. He made headlines in Chicago by holding out during his first spring training, but won Comiskey Park fans over with his grittiness. He homered in his first series back at Fenway Park as a visiting player, but suffered from arm, shoulder, back, and wrist injuries at various points during 1971.

When Andrews inexplicably developed problems with his throws to first base as well, he tried playing through the struggles; after that didn't work, he moved to first himself. "I never figured out what caused it," Andrews said. "It was identical to what Chuck Knoblauch and Steve Sax later went through, and I just couldn't work my way out of it." Despite these travails, Mike's hitting was better than ever during a late August spree in which he tallied four homers in a seven-game stretch. But then on September 1 he fractured his left wrist in a collision at first with Harmon Killebrew, the fifth time that year he had been knocked from a game by injury. Out for the season, Andrews finished with a .282 average, 12 homers and 47 RBIs in 109 games to help the team improve from 56-106 to 79-83.

Things looked promising for Andrews and the White Sox the following spring training. Manager Chuck Tanner gave him back his second-base job when the club picked up slugging first baseman Dick Allen, and Andrews said he felt better than ever after dropping some weight and giving his body time to heal. The White Sox shot out to a fantastic start and suddenly found themselves fighting with the Oakland A's for the AL West crown. It was a baseball revival on Chicago's South Side much like that experienced at Fenway Park five years before, with Comiskey Park attendance reaching its highest levels in 20 years amid the excitement of Allen's MVP season and a 24-win performance from knuckleballer Wilbur Wood.

Andrews could not match his team's resurgence. He batted just .200 in April, and after rebounding in May (.291), never hit higher than .245 in any other month. He was part of some big moments, most including Allen, but his final average of .220 (with 7 homers and 50 RBIs) was the worst of his career. In the field he was vastly improved, but still led AL second basemen in errors for the third straight year. Of some consola-

tion was that the White Sox wound up with a fine 87-67 record, just 5½ games behind World Series champion Oakland.

Oakland odyssey

Still just 29 years old going into the 1973 season, Andrews looked for a bounce-back year at a position new both to him and to baseball: designated hitter. The first DH in White Sox history, he seemed to thrive in the role with a .417 start (15-for-36) through 10 games. A dreadful slump followed, however, and by July 4, Mike's average had fallen below .200.

On top of this, Andrews was engaged in a heated dispute with general manager Stu Holcomb. The GM had wanted to cut his $60,000 salary a full 20 percent before the season, and Mike was still playing without a contract when on July 10 he asked to be released. Holcomb complied, and later that same month he himself resigned amid controversy over this and other player squabbles.

Here Dick Williams—by then manager of the A's—resurfaced in Andrews' life. Williams had reportedly attempted to trade for his former rookie standout upon first taking the Oakland job back in 1970. Now, with his defending champs trying for another pennant, he picked Mike up as a free agent on July 31. Andrews hit just .190 in 18 games, but the A's won the West and Williams saw fit to leave the veteran on his club's playoff roster.

Mike was hitless in two official pinch-hit appearances against Baltimore in the AL Championship Series (although he did lay down a sacrifice bunt in a third time up), and then was given the same task in the eighth inning of Game Two of the World Series against the New York Mets at Oakland-Alameda County Coliseum on October 14. Grounding out for Ted Kubiak, he stayed in the game at second base. Then the nuttiness began.

The score was 6-6 in the top of the 12th when the Mets scored four runs, due largely to two straight errors by Andrews—the first on a bad-hop grounder by John Milner, the second (one batter later) on a low throw that appeared to cause first baseman Gene Tenace to pull his foot off the bag. Replays indicated the umpire missed the second call, and Dick Williams thought Tenace deserved an error, but the damage was done. A rally in the bottom of the inning fell short, and New York won, 10-7.

Even before the game was over, meddling A's owner Charlie Finley was on the phone with the team physician, Dr. Harry Walker, and behind closed doors in the locker room after the contest Andrews received an impromptu medical exam from Walker. Mike was then asked to sign a document stating that he had a "chronic" shoulder injury and was going on the disabled list. Feeling pressured, he signed it.

Andrews flew home to Boston as Finley schemed to add rookie Manny Trillo to the roster, but teammates who had seen Finley meeting with Mike rightfully suspected something was up. The story made national headlines, and prompted A's players to affix Andrews' No. 17 to their uniforms with athletic tape as a sign of solidarity. Within a few days Andrews said in a press conference that he had been forced into signing the document.

"Finley told me, 'If you want to help this team, the best thing you can do is step aside and let us put Manny [Trillo] in there,'" Andrews recalled. "He kept beating me down, and finally I just signed it." Commissioner Bowie Kuhn ordered that Andrews be reinstated for Game Four, and he earned a standing ovation at Shea Stadium when he came up as a pinch-hitter in the eighth. After grounding out to third, he received another one.

Now pitching for Jimmy

That would be Andrews' last at-bat in the major leagues. He didn't expect the A's to keep him after the '73 season, and once Dick Williams quit after Oakland's World Series victory, Mike's fate was likely sealed. Released on October 26, he failed to catch on with another club. He spent that year working around his Peabody home and then took a big-money offer to

play in Japan during 1975 with the Kintetsu Buffaloes. "I was one of two gaijin [non-Japanese] players on the team, along with our top slugger, Clarence Jones. Even though we were both starters and playing well, they cut us before the playoffs with no explanation."

At this point, Andrews quit pro ball for good. Still popular in New England, he took a position as an agent with the Mass Mutual Insurance Company and followed the big-league exploits of his brother Rob, a second baseman with the Astros and Giants from 1975 to 1979. Then he received a surprising phone call from Ken Coleman, the Red Sox broadcaster who also was executive director of the Jimmy Fund.

"Mike had always been helpful to the Jimmy Fund during his days with the Red Sox, and he was the type of intelligent and personable individual whom I thought could be a great asset as we attempted to grow our fundraising program," Coleman recalled shortly before his death in 2003. "We needed more people, and he was at the top of my list."

Signing on as Coleman's part-time assistant director in 1979, Andrews needed just a few months to realize "this is what I wanted to do" and gave up insurance altogether. He succeeded Coleman as the charity's director in 1984.

For the next 25 years, Mike was often seen at Fenway Park for Jimmy Fund events and check presentations. He participated in both the Ted Williams memorial in 2002 (which benefited Dana-Farber) and the World Series ring ceremony on Opening Day of 2005, and delighted in showing off his own 2004 championship ring to young Jimmy Fund Clinic patients. The 18-hour WEEI/NESN Jimmy Fund Radio-Telethon became an annual staple of New England's summer fundraising calendar, and in his last year as chairman, the 2009 event raised more than $3.3 million. His popularity as the public face of the charity led to *Boston Sports Review* magazine naming Andrews one of the city's most powerful sports figures.

Mike and Marilyn sold their Peabody home late in his Dana-Farber tenure, but they stayed in the Boston area. His boyish good looks and California smile remained intact, with only a full head of white hair hinting that this grandfather many times over couldn't be just a decade or so removed from the majors. When Andrews started talking about the rapidly improving survival rates for various children's and adult's cancers, he seemed younger still.

"When Mike Andrews hung up his baseball cleats, he took his talent and competitive spirit and applied it to beating a foe much more formidable than any Fenway Park will ever see," said Larry Lucchino, Boston Red Sox president/CEO and a two-time cancer survivor, upon Andrews' retirement. "Through his tenacity and vision over the last 30 years, he has had a gigantic impact on the lives of countless adults, children and families who have been treated for cancer at Dana-Farber Cancer Institute."

More than 40 years after his rookie exploits, Mike Andrews was still helping make Impossible Dreams come true.

SOURCES

Mike Andrews quotes from author interviews of March 2006 and earlier, unless otherwise noted.

Ken Coleman quotes from author interview, 2003.

Coleman, Ken, and Dan Valenti, *The Impossible Dream Remembered* (Brattleboro, Vermont: Stephen Greene Press, 1987).

Boston Globe and *Boston Herald,* 1966-1973.

Chicago Tribune, 1971-1973.

Los Angeles Times, New York Times, Washington Post, and Associated Press articles, 1966-73.

Wisnia, Saul, "The Impossible Dream Team," *Red Sox Magazine,* 1992.

Wisnia, Saul, Andrews profile, *Red Sox Magazine,* 2004.

Interview with Andrews on Red Sox Nation website (redsoxnation.net), 2005.

Interview with Andrews on White Sox fan website (whitesoxinteractive.com), 2002.

Larry Lucchino quote from Jimmy Fund press release by author, 2009 (jimmyfund.org/abo/press/pressreleases/2009/former-red-sox-player-mike-andrews-to-retire-as-jimmy-fund-chairman.html).

Pat Bourque

By Clayton Trutor

Pat Bourque was a first baseman who played in 201 major-league games between 1971 and 1974. Looking something like a mustachioed Ted Kluszewski, Bourque was a powerfully built 6-foot-tall, 220-pound left-handed slugger whom *The Sporting News* once described as being "built like the village blacksmith."[1] Throughout his six-season minor-league career (1969-1974), Bourque posted excellent power numbers and was widely considered a top major-league prospect. Bourque spent four seasons in the major leagues with three teams: the Chicago Cubs (1971-1973), the Oakland Athletics (1973-1974), and the Minnesota Twins (1974). Afterward Bourque played in the Mexican League for the Mexico City Diablos Rojos (1975-1978), where he became one of the league's biggest stars.

Patrick Daniel Bourque was born on March 23, 1947, in Worcester, Massachusetts, the fourth of Antonette and Roland Bourque's five children. He grew up in the nearby bedroom community of Shrewsbury and attended St. John's Prep High School, a Catholic institution run by the Xaverian Brothers, in Shrewsbury. Following in the footsteps of his older brother, Mike, who pitched briefly in the New York Mets organization, Bourque starred on the St John's baseball and football teams. He accepted a scholarship to play football and baseball at the College of the Holy Cross in Worcester. Bourque played linebacker for the Holy Cross Crusader football team and served as a three-year starter in the outfield for the Holy Cross baseball team (1966-1969). The 1967 team reached the NCAA Tournament, the college's 11th appearance since 1952. Bourque was the baseball team's captain in his senior season and was named to the District 1 All-New England team.[2] The Cubs drafted him in the 33rd round of the 1969 amateur draft and assigned him to the Huron (South Dakota) Cubs of the Class A Northern League.

Bourque excelled at Huron, hitting .281 with a .398 on-base percentage, 5 home runs and 34 RBIs in 65 games. In 1970 the Cubs elevated Bourque to their affiliate in Quincy (Illinois) of the Midwest league and moved him from the outfield, where he had struggled for Huron in 1969, to first base. Bourque earned a spot on the Midwest League All-Star team with a .326 batting average, a .439 on-base percentage, 13 home runs and 77 RBIs. The Cubs invited the hard-hitting prospect to their 1971 spring training in Mesa, Arizona, then placed him in Double-A San Antonio for the start of the season.[3] Bourque transitioned well to Double-A ball, hitting .279 with 15 home runs and 83 RBIs for the San Antonio Missions

of the Dixie Association. On May 3 he drove in eight runs in a game against Albuquerque Dodgers.[4] Topps named Bourque its Dixie Association Player of the Month for that month.[5] In June *The Sporting News* profiled Bourque, commenting on his "village black-smith" physique and describing him as one of the most promising prospects the Cubs had produced in years.[6] Bourque made a brief stop at Triple-A Tacoma late in the 1971 season before being elevated to the major leagues in a September call-up along with pitchers Burt Hooton, Larry Gura, and Jim Colborn.[7]

Bourque made his major-league debut on September 6, 1971, against the Pittsburgh Pirates at Three Rivers Stadium, striking out against Bob Moose as a pinch-hitter. Bourque played in 14 games and hit .189 with one home run (off Rick Wise of the Philadelphia Phillies) and three RBIs in 37 at-bats.

After an up-and-down spring training in 1972, the Cubs sent Bourque to the Wichita Aeros of the Triple-A American Association. He missed more than a month of early-season action with a back injury, but returned in late June and went on a tear that lasted for the rest of the season.[8] "The village blacksmith" led the Aeros to the West Division championship and won the American Association's Most Valuable Player award. Bourque hit .279 with 20 home runs and 87 RBIs in 119 games for the Aeros. He started at first base for the West team in the American Association All-Star Game. On August 7 Bourque put the finishing touches on a 5-4-3 triple play, the first triple play in Aeros' history.[9] After the Aeros were swept by the Evansville Triplets in the American Association play-offs, Bourque was called up by the Cubs and played in 11 games, hitting .259 with five RBIs in 27 at-bats.

In an interview with Jerome Holtzman after the 1972 season, Bourque said he was ready to be a full-time major leaguer.[10] Unfortunately for Bourque, the Cubs roster had a backlog of aging players vying for time at first base, including Billy Williams, Joe Pepitone, and Jim Hickman. In April 1973 Bourque was one of the final two players cut from the Cubs' Opening Day roster.[11] He was sent back to Wichita, where he continued his assault on American Association pitching.

Bourque hit six home runs in a four-day stretch between May 10 and 13, 1973.[12] The Cubs recalled Bourque on May 19 after they traded Joe Pepitone to Atlanta. When Bourque arrived in Philadelphia for a game against the Phillies, the Cubs' clubhouse staff did not have a uniform large enough to fit him. A size 48 jersey was airmailed from Chicago for Bourque just in time for the next evening's game, which he was scheduled to start, but which ended up being rained out.[13]

Bourque impressed Cubs fans and management alike during his first month with the club, more than making up for the departure of Pepitone. In his first 15 games in 1973, he belted four home runs and hit .304 for a Cubs team that took an early lead in the National League East race over the St. Louis Cardinals and New York Mets. "I'm not overmatched," he told Jerome Holtzman in a June 1973 interview. "If I couldn't handle big-league pitching it would have shown up right away."[14]

Bourque failed to keep up that pace at the plate. He slumped through the second half of June and all of July. His average dropped to .197 through the end of July. Bourque's struggles mirrored those of the Cubs, who had led the National League East by eight games at the end of play on July 1, but had fallen 3½ games behind the Cardinals by August 1. Through August the Cubs struggled to stay in the race and Bourque struggled to keep his average over .200. On August 29, the Cubs traded him to the defending world champion Oakland Athletics for pinch-hitter/infielder Gonzalo Marquez. The Athletics, in need of a power-hitting left-handed bat who could serve as their designated hitter. Marquez had been a pinch-hitting hero for the A's in the 1972 American League Champion Series and the 1972 World Series.[15]

Bourque played in 23 games for the A's in August and September 1973, frequently as a pinch-hitter. He continued to slump at the plate, hitting .197 with two home runs and nine RBIS for the A's, who clinched their second consecutive division title on September 22. For the season as a whole, Bourque hit .204 with 9 home runs and 29 RBIs. A's manager Dick Williams put Bourque on the roster for both the American League Championship Series and the World Series. During the A's five-game victory over the Baltimore Orioles in the ALCS, Bourque went 0-for-1 in three plate appearances. He was walked twice, once intentionally. During the A's seven-game victory over the Mets in the World Series, Bourque played in two games. In the A's 3-2 victory in Game Three at Shea Stadium in New York, Bourque pinch-hit for catcher Ray Fosse in the seventh inning and took over for Gene Tenace at first base. In two at-bats, Bourque went 1-for-2, reaching base on a bunt single off Ray Sadecki in the top of the ninth inning. In the Mets' 2-0 victory in Game Five, Bourque came in as a defensive replacement at first base in the bottom of the eighth inning, but he did not come to the plate. For his role on the A's 1973 championship team, Bourque received $4,923.52.[16]

Bourque started the 1974 season on the A's roster. During April and May, he served primarily as a pinch-hitter, putting together a .286 batting average with seven RBIs, but failed to hit any home runs. On June 2 the A's demoted Bourque to Triple-A Wichita, to the surprise of his teammates. "There are other guys on the team who are contributing a lot less than Pat Bourque," an unnamed teammate was quoted as saying by *The Sporting News*.[17] On June 15 the A's brought Bourque back to Oakland but he was unable to match his early-season success as a pinch-hitter. By the middle of August, Bourque's average had fallen to the .220s and he had hit only one home run in 96 at-bats. On August 19 the A's traded him to the Minnesota Twins for first baseman/outfielder Jim Holt. A change of location did not end Bourque's struggles at the plate. He hit .219 in 64 at-bats for the Twins in August and September.

After the 1974 season, the Twins traded Bourque back to the Athletics for outfielder Dan Ford and minor-league pitcher Dan Myers.[18] The A's cut Bourque during spring training in 1975, optioning him to Wichita. Bourque refused to report to the minor leagues and was released by the A's.[19] He continued his career by signing on with the Mexico City Diablos

Rojos of the Mexican League. He played for the Diablos Rojos for four seasons (1975-1978) and appeared in three Mexican League All-Star Games. He won the Mexican League batting title in 1975 and earned a Silver Bat Award from Louisville Slugger for his performance. The Diablos Rojos won the 1976 Mexican League championship and were the runners-up in 1977 during Bourque's tenure with the team.[20] He became a fan favorite in Mexico City. In 1977 he donated money to keep an orphanage open in the city.[21]

Bourque left professional baseball after the 1978 season and moved his family full-time to his offseason home of Flagstaff, Arizona. He worked for Waste Management Inc. for many years. As of 2014 he served in a managerial position for the city of Flagstaff's Public Works Department. Bourque has also worked as a private hitting coach in Arizona for a number of years.

SOURCES

New York Times

The Sporting News

Washington Post

Baseball-Reference.com

Baseball-Almanac.com

The College of the Holy Cross Athletics Department: goholycross.com

City of Flagstaff: Official Website: flagstaff.az.gov/

NOTES

1   John Hines, "Bourque Built Like the Village Blacksmith; He's San Antonio's RBI Belter," *The Sporting News*, June 5, 1971, 41.

2   "2013 Holy Cross Baseball Yearbook," *Holy Cross Athletics: Baseball Site*, accessed on December 2, 2013: goholycross.com/sports/m-basebl/2012-13/files/13-base-yb.pdf; John Hines, "Bourque Built Like the Village Blacksmith," 41.

3   Jerome Holtzman, "Wrigley Tells Cubs to Accent Youth," *The Sporting News*, January 2, 1971, 40.

4   "Eight RBIs for Bourque," *The Sporting News*, May 22, 1971, 42.

5   "Grimsley No.1 Topps Star," *The Sporting News*, June 19, 1971, 34.

6   John Hines, "Bourque Built Like the Village Blacksmith," 41.

7   Edgar Munzel, "Bruin Briefs," *The Sporting News*, September 25, 1971, 17.

8   "Aeros Bolstered," *The Sporting News*, July 15, 1972, 36.

9   "Wichita, Indy Players Dominate A.A. Stars," *The Sporting News*, August 19, 1972, 35; "Manager, Player Kudos to Marshall, Bourque," *The Sporting News*, September 23, 1972, 32; "One Pitch, Three Outs," *The Sporting News*, August 26, 1972, 34.

10 Jerome Holtzman, " 'I'm Ready for Majors' Says Bourque," *The Sporting News*, October 28, 1972, 21.

11 Charlie Feeney, "Two Garden Gaps, Keystone Hole to Test Virdon Genius," *The Sporting News*, March 3, 1973, 18 Jerome Holtzman, "Bruin Briefs," *The Sporting News*, April 28, 1973, 10.

12 "Bourque Spreads Homers," *The Sporting News*, June 2, 1973, 38.

13 "N.L. Flashes," *The Sporting News*, June 9, 1973, 26.

14 Jerome Holtzman, "Belter Bourque Making Cub Fans Forget Pepi," *The Sporting News*, June 30, 1973, 9.

15 "A's Exchange Marquez for Cubs' Bourque," *Washington Post*, August 31, 1973, D2; Ron Bergman, "Series Still the Big Thing to 20-Win Holtzman," *The Sporting News*, September 22, 1973, 8.

16 Lowell Reidenbaugh, "Hahn's Triple Trips up A's; Mets Go Ahead in Series," *The Sporting News*, November 3, 1973, 8; "Players Split Up Record Playoff-Series Pot," *The Sporting News*, December 1, 1973, 30.

17 "A's Defend Bourque," *The Sporting News*, June 22, 1974, 22.

18 "Athletics," *The Sporting News*, November 9, 1974, 56.

19 "Big League Clubs Begin Their 1975 Name Dropping," *Washington Post*, March 27, 1975, F5; "A's Acorns," *The Sporting News*, April 19, 1975, 8.

20 "Mexican League," *The Sporting News*, July 26, 1975, 32; Roberto Hernandez, "Volkening and Bourque Star in Mexican League's Playoffs," *The Sporting News*, August 30, 1975, 38; "Pactwa Named Mexican League MVP," *The Sporting News*, September 27, 1975, 33; "The 1975 Silver Bat Awards," *The Sporting News*, December 4, 1975, 44; Roberto Hernandez, "The 'Bald Magician' Leads Reds to Mexican Flag," *The Sporting News*, September 25, 1976, 38.

21 "Bourque's Bat Booms," *The Sporting News*, May 21, 1977, 36.

Rico Carty

by Wynn Montgomery

In 1964, a 24-year-old Dominican strongman named Ricardo Adolfo Jacobo (Rico) Carty burst into the major leagues like a tropical storm. After two hitless at-bats in 1963, Carty's batting average (.330) in his first full season was the second highest in the majors. Only Roberto Clemente hit better, and only a phenomenal year by Philadelphia's Richie Allen prevented Carty from being voted Rookie of the Year. He had exceeded the high expectations created by a stellar four-year minor-league apprenticeship and quickly became "one of the most popular players ever to wear a Milwaukee uniform."[1] After the Braves relocated, his popularity grew in Atlanta, where the left-field stands became known as "Carty's Corner."[2]

Lofty predictions regarding Carty's future did not materialize due to an unfortunate combination of illness, injuries, ineptitude on defense, and a reputation as a troublemaker. Concerns about Carty's prowess in the field plagued him throughout his seven seasons with the Braves. His 1973 move to the American League –which included an abbreviated appearance with the Oakland Athletics—coincided with the birth of the designated hitter, which most baseball people thought fit Rico like a glove, but Carty initially resisted.[3] Poor performance in his first year as a DH seemed to have ended his career, but a good season in the Mexican League earned Carty the chance to resurrect his career.

Rico Carty's baseball journey began in San Pedro de Macoris, Dominican Republic, where he was born on September 1, 1939, one of 16 children. His mother, Olivia, was a midwife; his father, Leopoldo, worked in the sugar mill and played club cricket.[4] Rico played pick-up baseball until he was 15, when he followed the example of four uncles and turned to boxing. He won his first 17 bouts (12 by KOs), but turned to baseball full-time after one embarrassing ring defeat.[5]

In 1959 Carty joined (as a catcher) the Dominican team that played in the Pan-Am Games in Chicago, and he attracted considerable attention. Eight major-league teams and four Dominican League clubs offered him contracts, and the naïve youngster signed them all. George Trautman, head of minor-league baseball at the time, resolved the resulting dispute in favor of Milwaukee.

Carty's professional baseball career began in 1960 with Davenport/Quad Cities in the Class D Midwest League. He struggled both with the English language and with minor-league pitching, but moved up to Class C Eau Claire in 1961. In 1962, at Class B Yakima, Carty showed the hitting skills that would ensure his future success. He also showed the penchant for injury that would limit that success. His .366 average was leading the Northwest League when he tripped over first base, pulling a leg muscle and ending his season. He lost the batting race but made the year-end league

All-Star team and was the Topps Class B All-Star catcher.

Carty started the 1963 season at Triple-A Toronto, where he was hailed as "the best catching prospect … in 10 years."[6] Even so, he was sent down to Double-A Austin to be converted into an outfielder because the Braves had a bevy of young backstops. The only blemish on Rico's season, and perhaps another portent of the future, came when he decked a spectator for heckling him.

Despite his late arrival, Carty ended the season among Texas League leaders with a .327 average, 27 home runs, and 100 RBIs. He made his major-league debut on September 15, 1963, striking out as a pinch-hitter. The future looked bright for Carty, who was now being touted as "the best young hitting prospect in the [Braves] organization."[7] He had an outstanding 1963-64 season in the Dominican League and then married Gladys Ramirez de Jacobo. They would have six children, who produced 16 grandchildren.[8] One son, Rico Jr., played 16 games as a Seattle Mariner farmhand.

After Carty's fine winter season, Braves farm director John Mullen compared him to Orlando Cepeda,[9] and his Grapefruit League performance justified the praise. He hit .408 and led the team with 13 RBIs. Carty made the Braves' 1964 Opening Day roster, but did not play regularly at first as manager Bobby Bragan tried to balance playing time among his outfielders (Hank Aaron, Felipe Alou, Lee Maye, and Carty). When Alou was hurt in late June and Rico took over in left field, the Braves won 16 of their next 23 games. In late August, he ended a rare batting slump in dramatic fashion, delivering two 5-for-5 days within a week. He led the Braves in batting (.330) and slugging (.554), and made Topps' Rookie All-Star Team.

In January Carty became the first Brave to sign his 1965 contract (for a salary of $17,500).[10] He had a strong season in winter ball and reported for spring training, where Bragan was determined to transform him into a first baseman. Rico never mastered the new role and injured his back while trying to do so. Carty's back

ailment kept him out of the lineup often throughout that season; he never played more than a week at a time. He complained that Bragan often jerked him from the lineup late in games, undermining his confidence,[11] but Carty's fielding lapses often justified the manager's actions. Late in the season, a doctor discovered that Carty's right leg was slightly shorter than his left and prescribed a corrective shoe, quieting those who had accused the slugger of exaggerating his back pain.

While the 1965 season was disappointing, Carty hit when he played, compiling a .310 average in 83 games (all in left field). He also demonstrated his willingness to speak out when he thought he'd been wronged. Both traits continued throughout his career—as did frequent trade rumors, which began to circulate during that offseason.

Carty spent the winter of 1965-66 in a new environment, playing winter ball for the Aragua Tigers in the Venezuelan League. He wore his new orthopedic shoe and led the league with a .392 batting average and 13 home runs, a new season record. When he returned to the US, he was again headed for a different setting—the Braves' new home in Atlanta—and renewed enthusiasm about his potential to become "the next great hitter in the National League"[12] Even so, he was the Braves' fourth outfielder, behind Aaron, Alou, and Mack Jones.

On June 4, 1966, Carty was inserted into the lineup as the starting catcher, and the Braves promptly won seven consecutive games as Rico went 12-for-24. But after nine games, he was back in left field. Trade rumors continued, but Carty was in the lineup to stay. He played in 151 games, even filling in at first base and third base, and hit .326 (third in the NL). During the offseason, Carty was the Brave most sought after player in trade, but the team now saw him as "the next NL batting champ."[13]

Before returning to the Dominican League for winter ball, Rico signed his 1967 contract (in the $25,000 range). He had another good season with the Estrellas Orientales, but his temper flared again, garnering him a $50 fine for insulting an umpire, and his injury jinx reappeared as he was hurt in a car crash.

The 1967 season began with optimism in Atlanta. The team had finished fifth in 1966, but had compiled a winning record (33-18) after Billy Hitchcock replaced Carty's nemesis Bragan. Those hopes faded quickly, however, as both the Braves and Rico had dismal seasons. The Braves fell to seventh place, and Carty had his first sub-.300 season in the majors, although he was relatively injury-free. The low moment of the season came on June 18, when Carty engaged in a "brief but heated scuffle" with Hank Aaron.[14] At the time, details were scarce, but Aaron later said that he was angry because Carty had loafed on a ball into the outfield and had called him a "black slick."[15] At season's end, the Braves were actively seeking trades, and Carty was "among the most likely to go."[16]

Carty won the 1967-68 Dominican League batting title (.350) and led Estrellas to the regular-season title and the playoff championship. He reported for spring training down ten pounds to his "fighting weight" of 190 and downplayed teammate Clete Boyer's offseason criticism (echoing Aaron's) that Carty "doesn't give 100 percent."[17]

Three weeks into 1968 spring training, Carty's injury jinx struck with a vengeance. He was diagnosed with tuberculosis. While the disease was "not as serious as first suspected," Rico was lost to the Braves for the season.[18]

When he reported for spring training in 1969, a rejuvenated Carty tied for the team lead in batting (.333) during the spring, but a dislocated shoulder put him on the disabled list on Opening Day. He finally got into a game on May 2 as a pinch-hitter and responded with a game-tying sacrifice fly. In his first start, on May 18, he re-injured that troublesome shoulder and missed another two weeks.

Carty was in and out of the lineup for much of the season, but returned to spark the Braves in their stretch drive to the first NL West division title. He had hits in 19 of the final 21 games (17 Atlanta wins), averaging .383 and driving in 22 runs. He drove home the game-winning run in the division-clinching game and finished the season with a team-leading .342 average in 104 games.

The Braves lost that first League Championship Series in three straight games to the New York Mets, but Carty played well in what would be his only postseason appearance, hitting .300 and compiling a .462 on-base percentage and a .500 slugging average, but with no RBIs. He finished a surprising second to Tommie Agee as the NL Comeback Player although, as Hank Aaron observed, Agee "only came back from a bad year [while] Rico came back off a hospital bed."[19]

Carty hit .333 in the Dominican League that winter. He was also fined $50 and suspended for three days for shoving an umpire. Major League Baseball later added a $500 fine for "inexcusable and intolerable" conduct.[20]

Carty opened the 1970 season even better than he had ended 1969. He would have been a shoo-in for All-Star selection by the fans, but his name wasn't on the ballot. The list of 48 candidates in each league had been compiled during spring training, and Carty wasn't included. The fan voting period began on May 16, the day that saw the end to Rico's 31-game hitting streak, a team record that lasted until 2011. More than 2 million fans voted, and Rico received 552,382 votes (67,000 more than Pete Rose) to join Hank Aaron and Willie Mays in the NL's starting outfield as the first "write-in" All-Star.

Carty injured his wrist just before the All-Star Game, but started the game, batting twice (a walk and a groundout) before being replaced. In the latter half of the season, he suffered other injuries (a pulled leg muscle and a chipped bone in his finger caused when he was hit by a pitch), but he led the NL in batting average (.366) and on-base percentage (.454). In the midst of his best season ever, however, Rico was involved in another fight with a teammate—pitcher Ron Reed. Carty insisted afterward that "it was just a misunderstanding,"[21] but he was on the trading block despite having the highest career batting average among active players.[22] Sports columnist Dick Young suggested that Carty was an excellent choice for any team "looking for a big bat and willing to accept a big headache."[23]

On December 11, 1970, a different form of physical conflict took Carty off the market; he collided with Dominican League teammate Matty Alou and suffered a fractured knee and ligament damage. He was flown to Atlanta for surgery on what a team doctor called "as bad a knee injury as an athlete can have."[24] With his career in jeopardy, he returned home to recover — after signing a contract that included a raise over his 1970 salary of $45,000.

Carty reported for 1971 spring training with his leg in a brace, and he hobbled out of the dugout on Opening Day to a standing ovation. He took batting practice on July 18 and hit the first pitch he saw off the top of the fence in left field. He was scheduled to return to the lineup on August 5, when the first 15,000 fans would receive buttons that read "SMILE — the Beeg Boy's Back."[25]

But a blood clot in his damaged leg ended any hope of a comeback, and Carty missed his second full season in four years. His bad luck didn't end there, however. On August 24 he and his young brother-in-law were involved in a fight with two off-duty Atlanta policemen when Rico took umbrage at a racial slur. Atlanta Mayor Sam Massell labeled the incident "blatant brutality" and suspended the officers.[26]

Although Carty played only sporadically during spring training and seemed destined to start the 1972 season as a pinch-hitter, he received a $50,000 contract after a trial period imposed by the Braves because of concerns about his physical condition. He hit well when he played, but developed elbow tendinitis and went on the disabled list with a pulled hamstring. He played in only 86 games that season and hit just .277. Though his career batting average (.315) was still the highest among active players,[27] in October the Braves traded him to the Texas Rangers.

Neither the Atlanta press nor Braves fans were happy about the trade, but Rico said he was not surprised because he and new manager Eddie Mathews were not on good terms.[28] Rangers GM Joe Burke admitted that some would call the trade a gamble, but expressed confidence that Carty had matured and was eager to play.[29] New Rangers manager Whitey Herzog emphasized that he was looking for "ballplayers, not Boy Scouts" — a description that certainly fit Rico Carty. [30] Then Carty suffered another Dominican League injury; a pitch from Pedro Borbon fractured his jaw.

There was good news, however. The American League had adopted the designated-hitter rule, and Herzog called Carty "the perfect man for such a role."[31] Rico did not agree. The man whose defensive skills had been described as "amusing at best"[32] and who had accumulated more outfield errors (40) than assists (31) wanted to play on defense.

During 1973 spring training, Rico took a parting shot at the Braves, again singling out Eddie Mathews for criticism.[33] Word leaked out that Carty had won a $20,000 judgment against the Braves, whom he accused of shortchanging him by not sharing the funds the team received (under an agreement between MLB and the Dominican League) after his 1971 knee injury.[34]

On the field things were not going well for Carty. By early June his .203 average had cost him the Rangers' DH job. He was back in left field and feuding with his manager.[35] When he was sidelined after breaking a small bone in his foot sliding into second base on July 19, Rico's initial foray into the American League was over. He was hitting only .232 with three homers and 33 RBIs in 86 games for the Rangers when the Chicago Cubs acquired him on waivers on August 13.

Carty made his Cubs debut the following day, grounding out as a pinch-hitter in a loss to the Braves. The next day, he was batting cleanup and did so for most of his time with Chicago. His best day as a Cub came on August 28 in his first game as a visitor at Atlanta-Fulton County Stadium; he hit a two-run homer in his first at-bat and later singled to drive in two more runs in a 9-6 Cubs win. That was his only home run for the Cubs and half of his RBIs, and on September 11, after 22 games with the Wrigleyites, Carty was sold to the Oakland Athletics. He again demonstrated his willingness to attack local legends, blaming his demise in Chicago on Ron Santo, whom he called a "selfish ballplayer."[36] The more likely reason was his .214 batting average and .257 slugging percentage—both career lows.

The Athletics were leading their division by six games when they acquired Carty "for reasons unclear to outside observers," and they finished the season in the same position.[37] Rico appeared in seven of the Athletics' final 18 games, hitting .250 (2-for-8) and getting his only RBI with a solo home run. The A's went on to win the World Series, but Rico was not eligible for postseason play. When he was released on December 12, Rico complained that he had gotten only a termination telegram from the A's, who "didn't give me a Series share, a ring, a handshake—nothing at all."[38]

Everyone except Carty thought his career was over. He played winter ball in Mexico and then signed with Cordoba in the Mexican League, where his performance justified his self-confidence. He hit .354 (second in the league) with 11 home runs and 72 RBIs in 112 games,[39] and the Cleveland Indians, who were in a tight divisional pennant race, signed Rico to a $72,000 annual contract through the 1975 season. After 11 hitless at-bats, his first Tribe hit was a two-out, ninth-inning, game-tying RBI single. He then fought through a pulled hamstring to hit .363 in 33 games as a designated hitter and first baseman.

Carty was back with Cleveland in 1975, and the 35-year-old hit .308 and tied for the team lead in game-winning RBIs (9). He was even better in 1976, hitting above .400 until injuries once again shelved him. He played in a career-high 152 games, compiled a .310 batting average, and led the team with 83 RBIs. He had even become a fan of the DH rule, and Cleveland's baseball writers voted him Man of the Year.[40]

Despite this performance, the Indians did not protect Carty in the 1976 expansion draft. The Toronto Blue Jays made him their fifth pick but quickly traded him

back to the Indians. In 1977 he was the highest-paid Indian, making an estimated $90,000, but he started slowly.[41] He was hitting .200, and the team was in the division cellar (4-9) when he accepted the Wahoo Club's 1976 Man of The Year award with "one of the strangest acceptance speeches in history," criticizing manager Frank Robinson, who shared the head table, for "lack of leadership."[42] Carty had taken his reputation for confrontation to a new level, and when Robby fined Rico for "insubordination" after a June 6 dugout clash, local writers speculated that Carty would soon be traded.[43]

Instead, less than two weeks later, Robinson was fired. Carty finished the season hitting "only" .280 while leading the team in RBIs (80). He signed on with Cleveland for 1978, but when the Tribe acquired Willie Horton, Carty became expendable and was traded to the Blue Jays during spring training.[44]

Carty had 19 RBIs in April for Toronto. His troublesome hamstring again put him out of action briefly, but in a seven-game August homestand, Rico hit three homers and drove in six runs, bringing his season totals to 20 and 68, new franchise records. That was his farewell performance for the Jays, who soon traded Carty to Oakland for Willie Horton, whose arrival in Cleveland had led to Rico's departure.

Carty quickly made the trade look extremely one-sided in favor of the A's. After going hitless in his first game, he went on a 15-game hitting streak—two short of the club record. He hit eight homers in his first 19 games with Oakland and continued to top Horton's Toronto performance in every important offensive category. Carty's 31 homers for the season were his career high and set a new record at the time for designated hitters.

Carty made it clear that he intended to test the free-agent market in 1979 and indicated that his next team would be his last. Even so, the Blue Jays reacquired Rico, believing they could sign him because they could play him every day.[45] When Carty was granted free agency, four teams sought him, but the Blue Jays signed him to a five-year partly-guaranteed contract for $1.1

million plus an immediate loan of $120,000 — not bad for a 39-year-old player with a history of frequent injuries.[46] Carty's 31-page contract was described as "probably the bulkiest in the history of baseball."[47]

After skipping winter ball, Carty pulled a calf muscle in spring training and hit under .200. The regular season saw no major improvements. In early June he was hitting only .250 and was the target of boos from Toronto fans. On July 1 he was benched after hitting only one homer in almost two months. Carty blamed his slump on a "freakish injury" — a swollen hand caused when he accidentally stabbed himself with a toothpick.[48] That 1979 season had few highlights for Rico, but on August 6 he hit his 200th career home run, becoming the oldest player (at 39 years, 339 days) to achieve that milestone. Overall, however, it was his worst season except for 1973, when he had shuttled among three teams. When Jays manager Roy Hartsfield was fired after that season, he observed that it had been "hard to live with Rico Carty's virtual life-time deal."[49]

Hartsfield's successor did not have that challenge. Carty hit poorly in winter ball, where he was again hampered by a leg injury, and was still favoring his calf when spring training started. He was unconditionally released on March 29, 1980. His "lifetime" deal as a player had lasted one year, although he still worked for the Blue Jays as a Latin American scout.

Carty's major-league playing days were over, and his lifetime batting average had dropped to .299. Early visions of superstardom had not been realized, but, despite losing two entire seasons to illness and injury, he had played 13 seasons in the majors. He was big (6-feet-2) and slow, but he was a natural-born hitter. The flamboyant, self-described "Beeg Boy" made more comebacks than a boomerang, and few who saw him play will ever forget his aggressive right-handed swing and his trademark one-handed catches. He was a study in contrasts — known for his infectious grin and also for his fierce glare at the plate; popular because of his cheerful banter with fans yet branded a troublemaker. Carty argued that the latter reputation was unfounded, claiming he simply "stood up for his rights."[50] The

record shows that he defended those rights frequently and that he was an equal-opportunity combatant, engaging in physical and/or verbal conflicts with teammates, managers, umpires, fans, local police, and at least one front office.

Rico Carty remained a hero in his homeland, where he lived as of 2014. During his playing days, he returned to the Dominican Republic almost every year to play winter ball, saying, "I owe my country a lot."[51] He retired as the Dominican League's all-time home run leader (59). That record was eclipsed, but Carty's legend survived. He didn't get to Cooperstown, but he is enshrined in two Halls of Fame, the ones honoring heroes of Caribbean Baseball (1996's inaugural class) and Latino Baseball (2011). He is an honorary general in the Dominican Army,[52] and he once thought he had been elected mayor of his hometown until a recount proved otherwise.[53]

Baseball gave Carty financial security,[54] and he stayed active in the game at home and elsewhere. In 1988 Rico led the Dominican team to a third-place finish in the first Men's Senior Baseball League World Series and won the home run contest in the 40-plus age bracket. League founder Steve Sigler said, "He's still an amazing hitter [at age 49], and he was the only one using a wooden bat."[55] He may have summarized Rico Carty's career: The "Beeg Boy" could hit … and he did things his way.

SOURCES

Aaron, Hank, with Lonnie Wheeler, *I Had A Hammer* (New York: Harper-Collins, 1991).

Kurlansky, Mark, *The Eastern Stars: How Baseball Changed the Dominican Town of San Pedro de Macoris* (New York: Riverhead Books, 2010).

Ruck, Rob, *The Tropic of Baseball: Baseball in the Dominican Republic* (Lincoln, Nebraska: Bison Books, 1999).

——— *Raceball: How the Major Leagues Colonized the Black and Latin Game* (Boston: Beacon Press: 2011).

Atlanta Braves Illustrated Yearbooks (1966-1972)

Chop Talk, the official monthly magazine of the Atlanta Braves

Milwaukee Braves Yearbook, 1964

Milwaukee Journal

Sarasota Herald-Tribune

The Sporting News

Sports Illustrated

baseball-almanac.com

baseballprospectus.com

baseball-reference.com

hardballtimes.com

MLBlogsNetwork (mlb.com)

retrosheet.com

Author's Note: I regret that this biography was completed without input from the subject. Extensive efforts to locate Rico Carty were fruitless. One representative of the Atlanta Braves said that Rico "has dropped off the map." Obviously, there is plenty of information on his career; I hope I have done him justice. If not, I'm sure he will let me know.

NOTES

1 Bob Wolf, "Rookie Rico Set Off Tom-Tom Beating by Braves' Faithful," *The Sporting News*, July 25, 1964.

2 Wayne Minshew, "Friendly Rico Rates Tops on Tepee List," *The Sporting News*, July 12, 1969.

3 Randy Galloway, "Carty Shuns DH Job—I'm No Invalid," *The Sporting News*, March 24, 1973.

4 Rob Ruck, *Raceball*, 202-204.

5 Mark Kurlansky, *The Eastern Stars: How Baseball Changed the Dominican Town of San Pedro de Macoris* (New York: Riverhead Books, 2010), 202-204.

6 "Leafs Rave Over Kid Carty," *The Sporting News*, April 20, 1963, 33.

7 Bob Wolf, "Braves Examine Hot-Shot Kids In 1964 Blue Print," *The Sporting News*, September 28, 1963.

8 Chris Boone, "Carty Still Loves the Braves," *ChopTalk*, April 26, 2006.

9 Bob Wolf, "Carty Rated Excellent Chance to Crash Braves Picket Party," *The Sporting News*, January 18, 1964.

10 Bob Wolf, "Braves Load Their Bench With Wallop in Oliver Bat," *The Sporting News*, January 16, 1965.

11 Bob Wolf, "Carty Lets Out Yelp In Bragan's Doghouse," *The Sporting News*, August 28, 1965.

12 Furman Bisher, "Ache-Free Carty May Put New Punch In Tepee Bats," *The Sporting News*, March 19, 1966.

13 " 'Everybody at Convention Eyed Carty,' Says McHale," *The Sporting News*, December 17, 1966, 30.

14 "Aaron-Carty Feud Explodes on Plane After No-Hitter," *The Sporting News*, July 1, 1967, 12.

15 Hank Aaron, with Lonnie Wheeler, *I Had a Hammer*, 190.

16 Wayne Minshew, "Braves Cut Price Tags, Seek Deals," *The Sporting News*, October 7, 1967.

17 Jay Searcy, "Clete Takes Verbal Jab at Rico; 'He Loafs,' Claims Third Sacker," *The Sporting News*, February 24, 1968.

18 Wayne Minshew, "TB Kayoes Carty for Year," *The Sporting News*, April 13, 1968.

19 Wayne Minshew, "Same Old Rico—He's Hitting a Ton," *The Sporting News*, February 14, 1970.

20 *The Sporting News*, February 21, 1970, 49.

21 "Reed, Carty Have Fight Before Game," *Milwaukee Journal*, August 21, 1970.

22 Frank Eck, "Two-Year Tempo of .356 Lifts Carty to Lofty .321 for Career," *The Sporting News*, November 14, 1970.

23 Dick Young, "Young Ideas," *The Sporting News*, September 12, 1970.

24 Wayne Minshew, " 'With God's Help, I'll Be Back'—Carty," *The Sporting News*, January 30, 1971.

25 "Smile—That Beeg Boy's Coming Back to Braves," *The Sporting News*, August 7, 1971: 30.

26 "Carty Beaten; Atlanta Policemen Suspended," *Sarasota Herald-Tribune*, August 26, 1971.

27 Bob Fowler, "Killer, Oliva Express Doubt Over DH Rule," *The Sporting News*, February 3, 1973.

28 Wayne Minshew, "Braves Swapping of Carty Puts Mathews on Hot Seat," *The Sporting News*, November 18, 1972.

29 Merle Heryford, "Rangers Get Carty to Beef Up Attack," *The Sporting News*, November 11, 1972.

30 Randy Galloway, "Herzog Seeking 'Ballplayers, not Boy Scouts," *The Sporting News*, December 23, 1972.

31 Oscar Kahan, "DH's May Give Needed Hypo to AL," *The Sporting News*, January 27, 1973.

32 Peter Carry, "Player of the Week," *Sports Illustrated*, September 14, 1964

33 Wayne Minshew, "Carty Fires Volley at Mathews," *The Sporting News*, April 7, 1973.

34 Jerome Holtzman, "Reuschel Hungry for 20-Win Season," *The Sporting News*, May 19, 1973.

35 Merle Heryford, "Rico-Whitey Spat Ends in Truce," *The Sporting News*, June 23, 1973.

36 Ron Bergman, "A's Acorns," *The Sporting News*, October 6.

37 Ron Bergman, "A's Have a Credo: Do Jobs the Hard Way," *The Sporting News*, October 27, 1973.

38 *Sarasota Herald-Tribune*, August 25, 1974 (UPI wire story).

39 Cleveland Indians roster, *The Sporting News*, March 15, 1975.

40 On his sentiments regarding the DH rule, see Russell Schneider, "Carty's Ex-Bosses Wince—But Injuns Grin at Hot DH," *The Sporting News*, June 12, 1976.

41 Milton Richman, "Average Regular's Pay Rockets to $95,149," *The Sporting News*, April 23, 1976.

42 Russell Schneider, "Tepee Totters From Oral Blasts at Robinson," *The Sporting News*, May 14, 1977.

43 Russell Schneider, "Carty Exit Almost Certain After Hassle With Robby," *The Sporting News*, June 25, 1977.

44 Neil McCarl, "Jays Get Carty and Bosetti to Beef Up Anemic Attack," *The Sporting News*, April 1, 1978.

45 Neal McCarl, "Jays Miss Goal, Post 102 Losses," *The Sporting News*, October 21, 1978.

46 Murray Chass, "Ten Aging Free Agents Hit $15 Million Jackpot," *The Sporting News*, March 3, 1979.

47 Murray Chass, "Carty's Pact 31 Pages Long," *The Sporting News*, March 3, 1979.

48 Neil McCarl, "Howell Returns With Hot Bat and Tongue," *The Sporting News*, July 21, 1979.

49 Stan Isle, "Kroc Also Big in Milk—Milk of Human Kindness," *The Sporting News*, November 17, 1979.

50 Russell Schneider, "Rico's Bat a Bargain Buy for Indians," *The Sporting News*, September 14, 1974.

51 Rob Ruck, *The Tropic of Baseball: Baseball in the Dominican Republic*, 161.

52 Bruce Markusen, "Card Corner: Rico Carty," *Hardball Times*, October 8, 2010.

53 Bruce Markusen, "Cooperstown Confidential," MLBlogsNetwork, July 6, 2005 (mlb.com).

54 Rob Ruck, *The Tropic of Baseball*, 161.

55 Bob McCoy, "Keeping Score: Never Over the Hill," *The Sporting News*, November 21, 1988.

Billy Conigliaro

By Bill Nowlin

In 1970 Billy Conigliaro played all three outfield positions for the Boston Red Sox, the majority of them in left field. His brother and teammate Tony played right field almost exclusively. Together they hit 54 home runs (Tony hitting 36 and Billy half as many—18), the combined total setting a major-league record for homers by brothers on the same team. Billy hit for a slightly higher batting average, .271 to Tony's .266, but (as in homers) Tony drove in twice as many runs, 116 to younger brother Billy's 58. In many respects it was the best year for both brothers—Tony (born in January 1945) and Billy (born on August 15, 1947, also in Revere, Massachusetts). The Red Sox may have realized that medical problems were hovering for Tony, in the aftermath of the horrific beaning he had suffered in August 1967. Right after the 1970 season they traded Tony to the California Angels. Tony hit only four homers for the Angels in 1971, while Billy—still with the Red Sox—was upset with the ballclub for trading his brother and saw his own offensive numbers decline significantly across the board. After their respective times with the Red Sox, neither brother excelled again. Billy ended his career as a part-time outfielder for the 1973 Oakland Athletics.

Both Conigliaro parents encouraged their boys at baseball, as did their uncle Vinnie Martelli, who was head of Little League in Revere. The two brothers worked out with each other, the way kids sometimes did, with two taped-up balls. Tony wrote, "Billy would threw me the two baseballs and I'd hit them. I'd hit them as far as I could, go get them, come back, then I'd pitch the two balls at him. He'd hit them as far as he could, come back, then throw to me again. We'd do this back and forth all day long."[1]

Tony graduated from St. Mary's High School in Lynn, Massachusetts. The family moved to bordering Swampscott and Billy graduated as a three-sport star from Swampscott High. There was a third brother, Richie, born in 1951, but as the boys' mother, Teresa Conigliaro, later acknowledged, after what had happened to Tony, "We kind of discouraged the third one, Richie, from baseball. I couldn't take having another boy in baseball."[2]

Richie did play some ball in school, but there was a lot to try to live up to. Billy knew the problem. In his school days, he told writer Herb Crehan, "When I would strike out, some fan was sure to yell, 'Hey Conigliaro, you're a bum, just like your brother Tony!'"

It was even harder for Richie. "There I am trying to play high-school baseball, and I've got one brother starting in right field for the Red Sox and the other brother starting in center field. When I would strike out they would yell, 'Hey Conigliaro, you're a bum, just like your brother Tony *and* your brother Billy!'"[3]

Teresa and her husband, Sal, who worked at Triangle Tool and Die, attended every game they could, though Sal had his job to hold down. Theirs was a true working-class family. The boys grew up playing ball in the streets of East Boston, Billy once explaining, "My mother could never find a broom handle. We were always cutting them off for stickball."[4] They even played in the parking lot of nearby Suffolk Downs racetrack. Sal had worked in a zipper factory at the time of Tony's birth. He also ran a doughnut shop with Vinnie Martelli and raised chickens in the backyard. The job he settled into was at the tool and die shop and he worked there from the middle 1950s, eventually becoming plant manager.[5]

Tony was scouted by the Red Sox and signed in 1962, making his major-league debut in April 1964, at age 19. He homered in his Fenway Park debut and had a spectacular rookie year, hitting 24 homers for the eighth-place Red Sox, with a .290 average. Not many days after Tony's debut, Billy threw a no-hitter against Winthrop High School.[6] He threw a couple of one-hitters, too, striking out 28 batters over a 14-inning stretch, while batting over .400.

In June 1965, with the major-league draft now in place, the Red Sox selected Billy in the first round, the fifth pick overall. An estimated $50,000 bonus facilitated his signing. He was 17 and the Red Sox foresaw him only as an outfielder. Billy was assigned to the Waterloo (Iowa) Hawks in the Midwest League, playing 70 games of Class A baseball and — after a slow start — hitting .272 with five home runs. At age 18, in 1966, he started playing close to home for the Eastern League's Pittsfield (Massachusetts) Red Sox. For Pittsfield, he hit a home run in his first game, and hit for a .226 average over 82 games, but during the middle of the season was "demoted" to Class A, where he played 24 games for the Class A Winston-Salem Red Sox in the Carolina League, hitting .313.

Billy perhaps needed more seasoning and in June 1967, after he completed Army service at Fort Knox, Kentucky, he was started again at Single-A. He had played some for the Fort Knox team before his discharge. He was assigned to the Greenville Red Sox

(Western Carolinas League) and hit .274 but appeared in only 35 games in what remained of the 1967season.

This was the year the Boston team enjoyed the "Impossible Dream" season, leaping from a half-game out of last place the year before to win the pennant and take the World Series to a seventh game. Had Tony Conigliaro still been with the team for the Series, they might well have won it, but Tony had been hit in the head by a pitch in August and was unable to play again for more than a year. Billy, unfortunately, was in the stands, a witness to the event. In September Tony returned to Fenway when there was no one in the stands and had Billy pitch some to him, but it was clear he hadn't yet recovered his vision sufficiently to play ball.

The Red Sox staged a joint signing for the two brothers on February 14, 1968. The two played together in several spring-training games. Tony was medically unable to play baseball in 1968, however. Billy played a full season that year, again with Pittsfield, hitting only .238 but starting to show a little home-run power; he hit seven. He was still only 20 years old until that August. During the offseason, he worked as a host at the well-known Anthony's Pier 4 restaurant in Boston.

Billy played exceptionally well in 1969 spring training. "Billy has put himself in the picture." said manager Dick Williams.[7] He debuted in the big leagues on April 11, 1969. He pinch-ran in his first appearance and filled in on late-inning defense in his second game, on the 15th, and struck out in his first at-bat. He was given his first start on April 16, playing right field, and struck out again his first time up. The Baltimore Orioles had a 6-4 lead when he came up to bat for the second time, in the bottom of the fourth. He hit a leadoff home run into the net atop Fenway Park's left-field wall, off Baltimore starter Dave Leonhard. It was a slider on a 2-and-2 count. Billy also led off the sixth inning, and Leonhard served another pitch to his liking, this time a fastball. He homered again. In the seventh, reliever Dick Hall struck him out. He conceivably could have batted again in the ninth; it was a high-scoring game, 11-8 in the Orioles' favor, but rain brought the game to an end after one out in the bottom of the eighth. Tony had not taken part in the game. He was suffering a sore knee. Billy was in effect filling in for him in right field.

After the game, the two brothers posed for some photographs and Rico Petrocelli, watching the shoot, said, "Come on, Billy. Smile." Billy's response: "We lost." He did nonetheless muster up a smile.[8]

Tony said, "I guess I better go to Pittsfield and learn how to play another position."[9] The Red Sox figured out a way to work both of them into the outfield.

Sal Conigliaro missed Billy's first two home runs. He was working at the tool and die shop in Lynn, but co-workers kept him up to date. When Tony had homered in his own debut, Billy had heard it on the radio. He was working out with the Swampscott High squad at the time.

For Billy Conigliaro, it was either a K or a HR through his first three games, and the pattern continued when future Hall of Famer Jim Palmer struck him out his first two times up the day after his two-homer game. But Billy hit a home run—another leadoff home run—into the Red Sox bullpen when he led off the fifth. In the seventh, Billy finally did something else—singled off Palmer. He doubled in the bottom of the ninth, a 3-for-5 day.

Billy played in 15 April games but after the May 1 game, batting .313 with two more homers and a total of six RBIs, he was sent to Louisville to play Triple-A ball for the Colonels. Tony was far from pleased "Billy has worked so hard. I think it's rotten."[10] Red Sox manager Dick Williams said he wanted to see Billy get more playing time than he otherwise would. Billy was so upset, though, that he said he didn't care to be brought up to the Red Sox as long as Williams was managing.[11] "I don't think he's an honest manager," he said.[12] Billy hit .298 with 13 homers and drove in 81 runs for Louisville, and was recalled to the Red Sox in September, playing in another 16 games—though both Williams and Billy C steered clear of each other.[13] His minor-league years were over.

In his September stint with the Red Sox, Conigliaro hit no more homers and drove in only one run. He was 13-for-48 at the plate. He finished the season with a .288 major-league batting average.

In 1970 Billy got in a full season with the Red Sox; it was the year he hit 18 homers and he and Tony combined for 54.

Though the two brothers grew up together, and overlapped in tenure with the Red Sox, they didn't spend a lot of time together during the 1969 season. In his autobiography Tony wrote, "While I feel very close to Billy it has always been hard for me to show it." He knew it troubled Billy, but couldn't help himself. "I guess I never believed that brothers should do things together," he said, detailing an incident in a bar during spring training and that he realized, "When I'm out with Billy it makes me feel overprotective."[14]

Close or not, the family always stuck together and when Tony returned from California in January 1982 to audition for a position as color commentator on Red Sox broadcasts. Billy was driving him back to the airport when Tony had his heart attack, as Billy rushed him to the hospital. And it was Billy who devoted so much time to taking care of Tony after he was incapacitated. It was Billy who flew to California to close up Tony's place there and arrange for the sale of his car and other possessions.

That was a dozen years in the future, however, as the 1970 season unfolded. Many wondered how Billy could possibly fit into a Red Sox outfield patrolled by Carl Yastrzemski, Reggie Smith, and Tony Conigliaro. He had no options left. At first, injuries to one or the other of the regulars gave Billy playing time, and he proved himself. The problem was ultimately solved when Yaz moved to play first base, freeing up a spot. Eddie Kasko was the Red Sox manager. He'd managed Billy in Louisville and stuck by him when Billy was struggling: "You're going to play every day, Bill, no matter what. So be ready to be in there every single game. I know you want to be up with the big team, but this is going to help you, wait and see."[15]

The April 12 *Boston Globe* featured twin columns, one under Billy Conigliaro's byline and the other under Tony's. Each praised the other.

Billy C played in 114 games in 1970 with 444 plate appearances. He hit .271 with those 18 homers. He drove in 58 runs and scored 59. With Tony's 36 homers, the two set their record for the most homers by a pair of brothers in a season despite both of them having to take a couple of weeks off for Army Reserve duty during the course of the summer. Billy might have had a better shot at Rookie of the Year honors had he maintained the .298 average he'd had after the September 1 game but he faded during the final month of the year while Thurman Munson came on exceptionally strong, batting .350 after the All-Star break.

Tony took exception when Fred Lasher of the Indians hit him during the second game of a doubleheader on July 12 (he'd homered in the first game) and Tony charged the mound. Lasher stood ready with his fists, but Tony karate-kicked him and set off a brawl. Tony was ejected from the game. The first batter up in the top of the second was Billy Conigliaro, who hit Lasher's first pitch into the second deck in left field.

Billy was a late signing in 1971, only coming to terms in late February.

When failing eyesight forced Tony to announce his retirement during the 1971 season, Billy pointed fingers at one of his own teammates for Tony having been sent to the West Coast in the first place. "Tony was traded because of one guy—over there," he said as he pointed to Yastrzemski. "You can quote me, because I don't care. I know I'm next."[16] He claimed that Yaz was running the ballclub. Red Sox GM Dick O'Connell shot back, "That's a lot of bull. I wouldn't be bothered to dignify it any further."[17] Reggie Smith spoke up, saying the Red Sox should take action against him, adding, "I don't want to play with Billy Conigliaro any more. . . . I don't want to play with a quitter."[18] Yaz said more or less the same thing, adding, "Billy is just alibiing for his lack of ability."[19] A couple of days later, both Conigliaros and Carl Yastrzemski held a press conference at which Billy apologized to both Yaz and

Reggie Smith.[20] He finished the season with a .262 average in 380 plate appearances, with 11 homers and 33 RBIs.

There was a sense abroad that Billy was one of the most likely players on the team to get traded over the winter. And it didn't take the Red Sox long to trade him. They didn't even wait until after the World Series. Billy was one of six players (Jim Lonborg and George Scott were two others) sent to Milwaukee for four from the Brewers, on October 10. Billy was far from pleased. On his way out the door, he charged that Yaz and team trainer Buddy Leroux had pretended Yaz was injured so that he wouldn't have to play the final games of the season.

In April 1972 Red Sox owner Tom Yawkey made a couple of comments on team harmony and added, "All the guys we have now seem to be pulling together and I like that." It was, wrote the *Record*'s D. Leo Monahan, "an obvious reference to the malcontents—Billy Conigliaro, George Scott, and Joe Lahoud—who were shipped to Milwaukee."[21]

Billy wasn't used as much with the Brewers. His biggest game of the year came in Boston, when he tripled and homered and drove in four runs on May 29. The one day provided a quarter of his RBI total—he played in 52 games, hit .230, with 16 RBIs, and homered seven times. He would have played more, but he was apparently discouraged with his play and jumped the club on June 25. (The Red Sox were in Milwaukee, and had lost the first two games of four. Billy had not hit safely and was left out of the lineup for the games on June 24 and 25.)

"We had no indication that he was really that uptight until today," said Brewers manager Del Crandall.[22] Neither had the Red Sox; it was only in the fourth inning of the first game on June 25 that they learned Conigliaro was not in uniform. It had caught everyone by surprise; an AP story led by describing him as "a problem player at Boston but until Sunday a model of hustle for the Milwaukee Brewers."[23] Conigliaro said that his whole life had been tied up in baseball "but it has become an unhappy chore."[24] He was suspended without pay.

On June 28 Theresa Conigliaro was the first to let the world know that her son Billy had decided to retire. Brewers GM Frank Lane was still holding out hope that Billy would change his mind, but confirmed the news. Billy returned to what was described as "a family recreation business near Boston."[25] The family owned a golf course and cocktail lounge in the town of Nahant. Reasons for his departure were later succinctly described as "bad weather, small crowds and a losing team."[26]

A report in November said that Conigliaro had been traded to the Oakland Athletics four days after going AWOL from the Brewers, on June 29 for Ollie Brown.[27] Billy started talking about his desire to return to baseball, and Oakland manager Dick Williams — despite his problems with Conigliaro in the past — said, "The past is the past. Billy Conigliaro is a ballplayer of great talent and potential. We need an outfielder. There is no reason in the world why Billy could not have a fine season playing for us."[28]

In February 1973 Conigliaro applied for reinstatement. He was hoping to play for the reigning world champion Athletics. On February 14 a deal was finalized and Oakland sent an undisclosed amount of cash to the Brewers.

Billy proved himself in spring training and won the starting slot as center fielder for the A's. At the end of April he was hitting .300, though without a homer and with only five RBIs. He'd injured his right knee sliding into second base, and tried and failed to play through the injury. He was placed on the disabled list with cartilage damage in early May, had surgery in Cambridge, Massachusetts, and didn't get back into a game until July 10. His knee had bothered him as far back as when he was with the Red Sox and had stepped in a sprinkler hole during a game in Oakland.[29]

After his return, Conigliaro singled in the winning run in the July 28 game and had some successes here and there, but his batting had fallen off significantly and he finished the season with a .200 average, without a home run, and with only 14 RBIs. In each of his four last seasons in the majors, his average had progressively fallen from the .288 he hit in his first year. He hadn't been happy working under Dick Williams; he didn't feel the manager was using him properly.

Conigliaro was on the postseason roster of the 1973 A's and, though 0-for-4 at the plate, made one superb play on defense in the first inning of the third game of the American League Championship Series against Baltimore, robbing the Orioles of at least one run and perhaps more. "That catch by Conigliaro cost us a run," Orioles manager Earl Weaver declared.[30] Oakland won the game, 2-1, in 11 innings. Conigliaro played in three games of the World Series, coming on for defensive purposes in each of the three games. He had one at-bat in each game, but without reaching base safely. It was the only time a Conigliaro made the postseason. The Athletics beat the New York Mets in seven games. Billy earned himself a World Series ring. He hadn't committed an error at any point in 1973, neither the regular season nor the playoffs.

Conigliaro had another knee operation in December 1973. As spring 1974 approached, he was a holdout, the only one on the A's. On March 27 the team placed him on waivers for the purposes of giving him his unconditional release. "I guess they figure my knee is vulnerable to injury," he said. "That's the only thing I can think of."[31]

Tony attempted a comeback with the 1975 Red Sox, and Billy signed with the New England entry in the proposed World Baseball Association. He had worked at Tony C's restaurant and lounge in Nahant, but the business suffered a fire in 1975 and was closed for a few months. In December the two brothers opened the Tony C in Providence, where Tony was working as a TV broadcaster.

Billy attempted a comeback in 1977 with the Athletics and hit a homer in his first at-bat, in an intrasquad game. The A's asked him to start the season with their Triple-A team in San Jose, but he declined and said he would travel back east to see if he could get a job with a minor-league team closer to home.[32] He was 30-odd days short of qualifying for a pension.

After baseball, Billy had run a camera shop in Rockport and gone into the construction business, remodeling homes and then reselling them.

It was in January 1982 that Tony suffered his heart attack, as Billy was driving him to the airport in Boston. Tony was hospitalized, and in March he was moved to a rehab facility where he stayed for almost 15 months. Near the holidays at the end of 1983, he was moved to his home but he was on a respirator and required 24-hour nursing care. For the six years that he lived, it was either with his parents or at Billy's house. Tony's longtime friend Bill Bates, who served for more than ten years as head trainer for the New England Patriots, said, "Billy was there every single day for him. Every single day. He gave up his life to take care of his brother."[33]

It was heart-wrenching and it was unremitting. As biographer David Cataneo wrote, "Good days meant that Tony hadn't thrown up, or gotten agitated and wrestled a nurse, or had a coughing fit." Cataneo also said that Billy began to envision the relief that would come to Tony if he were to die. "I felt so bad for him. He couldn't eat. He couldn't talk. He'd have spams. He'd grab you and shake you and he'd look you in the face and there was terror in your eyes. It was such torture for him."[34] A nurse friend talked Billy out of thoughts of ways he could help out Tony without himself having to go to jail.

Noted Hollywood producer Peter Guber met with Billy and talked about doing a television movie. "It would be the story of Billy's belief in his brother, his dream and the support he's given Tony. It's about a love between two men."[35]

On April 15, 1983, there was a "Benefit for Tony C" at Symphony Hall in Boston that raised a couple of hundred thousand dollars to help with the bills for Tony's care. Ted Williams, Willie Mays, and Joe DiMaggio were among baseball alumni who attended.

In February 1990, Tony died. The ordeal he and the whole family had borne was over.

After leaving baseball Billy got involved in a number of self-employed ventures, from a fitness center named The Body Shoppe to photography, construction, and building maintenance.

As of 2013, Billy's wife, Keisha worked at La Chic Modeling and Charm School, and served as the leader of La Chic Mentoring Plus, an organization that gave lessons in self-esteem, self-confidence, etiquette, public speaking, and interpersonal skills.[36] From time to time, Billy appeared during the baseball season at Fenway Park's Autograph Alley and fans enjoyed having the opportunity to meet him and share a word or two.

SOURCES

In addition to the sources reflected in the notes, the author also consulted the *Encyclopedia of Minor League Baseball*, Retrosheet.org, and Baseball-Reference.com. Thanks to David Cataneo and Linda Huber for assistance.

Williams, Dick, with Bill Plaschke, *No More Mr. Nice Guy* (San Diego: Harcourt Brace Jovanovich, 1990).

NOTES

1 Tony Conigliaro with Jack Zanger, *Seeing It Through* (New York: Macmillan, 1970), 130.

2 David Cataneo, *Tony C: The Triumph and Tragedy of Tony Conigliaro* (Nashville: Rutledge Hill Press, 1997), 204.

3 Herb Crehan, *Red Sox Heroes of Yesteryear* (Cambridge, Massachusetts: Rounder Books, 2005), 180.

4 Cataneo, *Tony C.*, 13.

5 Conigliaro, *Seeing It Through*, 119-122.

6 *Boston Herald*, May 1, 1964.

7 *Hartford Courant*, March 16, 1969.

8 *Boston Globe*, April 17, 1969.

9 Conigliaro, *Seeing It Through*, 206.

10 Conigliaro, *Seeing It Through*, 210.

11 *Boston Herald*, August 11, 1969.

12 *Boston Globe*, August 11, 1969.

13 The awkward first day back was described by Clif Keane in the September 10, 1969, *Boston Globe*.

14 Conigliaro, *Seeing It Through*, 233.

15 *Boston Globe*, September 25, 1969.

16 Associated Press story appearing in many newspapers, including the *Springfield* (Massachusetts) *Union*, on July 22, 1971.

17 *Boston Herald*, July 11, 1971.

18 *Boston Record American*, July 12, 1971.

19 *Washington Post*, July 12, 1971.

20 *New York Times*, July 15, 1971.

21 *Boston Record American*, April 18, 1972.

22 *Boston Herald*, June 27, 1972.

23 Ibid.

24 *Boston Globe*, June 27, 1972.

25 *Boston Herald*, August 23, 1972.

26 *Boston Herald*, February 9, 1973.

27 *Boston Herald*, November 1, 1972, citing a story by Larry Whiteside in the *Milwaukee Journal*.

28 *Boston Herald*, November 27, 1972.

29 *Boston Herald*, May 15, 1973.

30 *Boston Herald*, October 10, 1973.

31 *Springfield* (Massachusetts) *Union*, March 29, 1974.

32 *Boston Herald*, April 5, 1977.

33 Cataneo, *Tony C.*, 253.

34 Cataneo, *Tony C.*, 254.

35 *Boston Herald*, December 3, 1982.

36 *Lynn* (Massachusetts) *Journal*, June 11, 2103.

Vic Davalillo

By Rory Costello

The Los Angeles Dodgers had a pair of antique dueling pistols in the late '70s. Yet despite their age, Vic Davalillo and Manny Mota were in great condition — and the fire of these small arms was often deadly. Davalillo's big-league career had seemingly ended in 1974, but after more than three years in the Mexican League, the wiry little outfielder (5-feet-7 and 150 pounds) returned at the age of 41 in 1977. He remained active in the US through 1980 and continued to play winter ball in his native Venezuela until the remarkable age of 50.

Davalillo — known as "Vítico" at home and in other Spanish-speaking lands — was a good major-league player. Although he became a semi-regular or reserve after 1968, his sixth season in the majors, he was a valuable journeyman. He won World Series rings with the Pittsburgh Pirates in 1971 and the Oakland A's in 1973. The lefty never had much power, but he made contact, batting .279 lifetime and striking out in less than 10 percent of his plate appearances. He was a fine pinch-hitter; he was long credited with 24 pinch-hits in 1970, and even his true total of 23 that year remains high on the list of single-season bests. Vic's 1967 Topps baseball card called him "one of the league's toughest men to get out because of his ability to go with the pitch."

This skill was really on display in the Venezuelan League, where Davalillo as of 2013 was the all-time leader in batting average at .325. He hit .400 or better three times at home and won four batting titles. He was also the lifetime leader in various other categories, including games played (1,249), base hits (1,505), and RBIs (483). In a place with a passion for baseball, Vítico is a national legend.

When Ichiro Suzuki came to the US, his slap-and-run style brought Davalillo to mind. They had other things in common. Davalillo was also very fast, a deft bunter,

and a Gold Glove center fielder in 1964. His arm was another plus — in fact, Vic was a pitcher for his first four years in the pros. He continued to take occasional turns on the mound at various points during his career.

Víctor José Davalillo Romero was born on July 31, 1936. As with many ballplayers, he was long billed as being several years younger. Up through 1974, his baseball cards showed 1939 or even 1940 as his year of birth. This was finally corrected after Vic's comeback in 1977 — even though he stuck by 1939 at that time, saying, "I don't care what anyone says."[1] Also, many baseball references — both at home and in the US — show Davalillo's birthplace as Cabimas, a town in Venezuela's northwestern state of Zulia, on the shores of Lake Maracaibo. In 2006, however, he told Asdrúbal Fuenmayor, who has written several pocket biographies of Venezuelan stars, that he was actually

born in Churuguara, in the neighboring state of Falcón.[2]

Víctor was the fifth of Martireño Davalillo and Angelina Romero's six children, all boys. The family moved to Cabimas a few days after he was born — and this was why the baby's birth was registered there. Martireño was a laborer, helping truck drivers to load and unload their vehicles in the oil businesses of the Maracaibo region.[3] He died around 1944.[4]

All the Davalillo brothers enjoyed baseball, but the only other one who wanted to be a pro was Pompeyo Davalillo.[5] The shortstop, who was even more diminutive than Vítico at 5-feet-3 and 140 pounds, played from 1952 through 1964 in the US, Cuba, Mexico, Nicaragua, and of course Venezuela, coming back for two final games in the winter of 1966-67. "Yo-yo" (his nickname in the US) got into 19 games for the Washington Senators in 1953 but never made it back to the majors. He suffered a broken ankle and kneecap playing at home late that year and missed the entire 1954 summer season.[6] He later became a successful manager in Mexico and at home.

Vítico started playing ball at the age of 8 with his older brothers. The lads would play numerous games a day. He was a first baseman to start with, but turned to pitching in the sixth grade; his teacher gave him a chance when the regular pitcher didn't show up.[7]

In 1956 Vítico had a chance to turn pro, but his family said no because he was too young (or so he said in 1965). He was then also studying to be a mechanic.[8] In October 1957, though, he joined the Caracas Leones of the Venezuelan League (Liga Venezolana del Béisbol Profesional, or LVBP). Brother Pompeyo had already been with the Leones for five seasons. The younger Davalillo would spend the next 16 of his record 30 Venezuelan winter seasons with this club, but he got into just nine games that season, including 17 innings in six relief-pitching appearances. He also experimented with switch-hitting, but gave it up when he realized he was losing a step running down the line to first base. The records didn't show it, Vítico said in 2007, because news reports focused only on his

pitching and the fact that he was Pompeyo's brother. His batting was an afterthought then.[9]

The Cincinnati Redlegs (as they were then still known) signed Davalillo in 1958. A year before, Pompeyo Davalillo had become the shortstop for the Havana Sugar Kings of the International League, the Reds' top farm club. As he had done in Caracas, Pompeyo opened the door for his jockey-sized kid brother — and, as they told Asdrúbal Fuenmayor, at this time he altered the birthdate on Vítico's documents. "Looking more like Pompeyo's son than his brother ... Vic, who hardly weighed more than 120 pounds ... dogged his brother's footsteps into the Havana training camp. Following his introduction to O[rganized] B[aseball] by his big brother ... the olive-skinned kid was immediately shipped out to California — Visalia — as a pitcher."[10]

From 1958 through 1961, Davalillo remained primarily on the mound. Yet despite his small stature, he was not a finesse artist in the Bobby Shantz mold. With Palatka of the Florida State League (Class D) in 1959, Vic struck out 150 batters in 147 innings. His all-around ability was also attracting attention, though. In 1959, he pitched in 53 games but appeared in 73 altogether. In 1960 he pitched 52 times in 90 total games; in 1961 his mound appearances dipped to 38 in 81 games. The latter two years featured brief stints at Triple-A with Havana and (after the Sugar Kings finally left Cuba) Jersey City. Pompeyo Davalillo was still with the club.

On February 25, 1961, Davalillo was married to Luisa Ramona Barrera. She was from the city of Valera, which is about 100 miles southeast of Cabimas. For many years, though, he has been with the woman who became his second wife, Zoraida Caravallo. He fathered three children.[11]

The International League dropped Jersey City as a location in October 1961. The owner, Cuban baseball man Bobby Maduro, held onto the franchise in its new home, Jacksonville, Florida. He established a new working agreement with the Cleveland Indians, who purchased Vic Davalillo's contract. Maduro had signed Vic to the US minors back in Havana in 1958.[12] Since he was his own general manager in Jacksonville, he almost certainly was responsible for this deal too.

In the winter of 1961-62, Davalillo batted over .400 in the Venezuelan League, becoming the first man to do so for a complete season. He was 56-for-138 (.406) in 43 games—but since he fell eight plate appearances short of the required 158, the batting title went to fellow Lion Tony Curry at .346.[13] That season was also Vítico's busiest and most successful as a pitcher at home. He was 10-4 with a 2.46 ERA in the regular season, and though he lost a game in the semifinals, he had a complete-game win in the seventh game of the finals. Caracas, thanks also to two wins from playoff reinforcement Bo Belinsky, defeated Oriente.[14] The Leones then went on to represent Venezuela in the second Inter-American Series.

That was Davalillo's second Venezuelan championship; the previous year he had joined Valencia as a playoff reinforcement. Caracas made the finals six times in eight years from 1961-62 through 1968-69, winning four titles. All told, Vítico was a member of seven champion teams during his 30 winter seasons.[15] Perhaps his only regret as a player is that he never was on a team that won the Caribbean Series.[16] The tournament was on hiatus from 1961 through 1969, which deprived him of five chances.

Under manager Ben Geraghty, Davalillo made the transition to full-time outfielder with Jacksonville in 1962. He still pitched in six games, though, one reason being the International League's 20-man roster limit, which put a premium on versatility.[17] Harry Fanok, who led the International League in strikeouts that year with the Atlanta Crackers, remembered his opponent well. "Vic Davalillo had to be the first Ichiro!" Harry said in 2010. "The guy used a big ole bat, ran like the wind, had an excellent batting eye and had a good arm.

"I remember one day [September 2] we had a doubleheader with Jacksonville. They had Vic pitch—against me! I got the win, and we were fortunate to come away with it." Davalillo had entered in the first inning of the opening game after Tommy John failed to retire a batter. He pitched seven scoreless innings and tripled in a run to help even the score at 2-2. He took the loss, though, as the Crackers scored two in the eighth. "The dude could pitch, as the score would indicate," Fanok added. "However, his calling had to be his play in the outfield and at the dish."[18]

Davalillo won the International League batting title with an average of .346, hitting 11 homers and collecting 69 RBIs. He showed speed and surprising extra-base pop, and worked to add a drag bunt to his adept push bunting and all-fields hitting.[19] The Suns finished first in the IL, then lost to Atlanta in the seventh game of the playoff finals. Fanok remembered the pennant race. "Late in the '62 season, it was going down to the wire. In a late series with them, down in Jax, I recall something that I had never seen before. Every time Vic came out on the on-deck circle, the fans would give him a standing ovation. He could have run for mayor down there and won! He was one hell of a ball player, that's for sure."[20]

During the season, Bobby Maduro turned down attractive offers from several big-league clubs for Vic.[21] Yet even though the Indians were on their way to a mediocre sixth-place finish, Cleveland general manager Gabe Paul did not want to call the hot prospect up. Paul, an old friend of Maduro's, said, "You know now why I didn't want to take Davalillo away from him when his team was doing so well. Hadn't Castro taken enough from him already?"[22]

Instead, under the terms of the working agreement with the Suns, the Indians claimed Davalillo for $15,000 at the end of the season.[23] Coming off a winter in which he hit .400 on the nose for Caracas—this time he got enough plate appearances to win the batting crown—Vic became Cleveland's starting center fielder in 1963. He was the eighth Venezuelan to make it to the majors. As early as May 29, the Associated Press wrote that he and Ron Hunt of the Mets "probably would win hands down if the 1963 Rookie of the Year poll were to be taken now." But just a couple of weeks later, on June 12, lefty Hank Aguirre of the Detroit Tigers broke Vic's forearm with a pitch. He missed nearly two months, and by various accounts, he was never quite the same hitter.[24] He had a tendency to step in the bucket or even bail out.

Umpire Pam Postema, who grew up in Ohio, wrote in her book, "Whenever Vic Davalillo would come up to the plate, we'd start yelling, 'Chicken! Chicken!' Davalillo would always back away from any pitch that came within a yard of him. He was so afraid of getting hit."[25]

In 1965 Bob Sudyk of the *Cleveland Press* wrote about "Davalillo's Fight Against Fear." Vic himself said, "Everybody talk about it and I begin to worry. I lose my confidence last year and I swing at everything. Then I really afraid, you know?" Birdie Tebbetts, who had also backed Davalillo as Rookie of the Year in 1963 even after the injury, returned as Indians manager in July 1964 (he had suffered a heart attack near the end of spring training). He worked closely with Vic on trying to overcome "one of the most trying times in a baseball player's life." Tebbetts talked about how Vic had lost his knack of setting up a pitcher because he was pressing. He also observed that Vic had a natural fallaway batting style against righties as well as lefties.[26] Davalillo's other notable trait at the plate was "an exaggeratedly high leg kick, perhaps the most noted since Giants great Mel Ott."[27]

The 1965 season was a successful one, as Davalillo finished third in the American League in hitting at .301 behind Tony Oliva and Carl Yastrzemski. He might have placed higher if he could have managed more than .248 against lefties. Vic was also the AL's starting center fielder in the All-Star Game, going 1-for-2. That was his only appearance in the midsummer classic, though; from 1966 onward, he was largely a platoon player. At least in the majors, Davalillo faced righties in just about 80 percent of his plate appearances.

It's quite likely that Vítico was more comfortable playing at home. He won his second and third Venezuelan batting titles at .351 in 1963-64 and .395 in 1967-68. He might have become the only man to win three straight in the LVBP, but his .389 mark in 1964-65 was only good enough for third that winter.[28]

Davalillo was always intensely patriotic. In June 1965 he spoke of how he wanted to win a US batting championship mainly to inspire the young boys growing up playing ball in his homeland. It seems remarkable today, but at that time there were only two Venezuelans active in the majors: Luis Aparicio and Vic.[29]

On June 15, 1968, the Indians traded Davalillo to the California Angels even-up for Jimmie Hall. He hit well for the Angels: .298, raising his average to .277 overall in the Year of the Pitcher. A quote that July summed up his approach well: "You can't get base hits if you don't swing."[30]

Vic started poorly in 1969, though—perhaps he was still getting back in form after suffering a nervous breakdown while playing in Caracas. Brother Pompeyo denied the breakdown story, though, saying that it was acute gastroenteritis.[31] Near the end of May, California dealt Vic to St. Louis for Jim Hicks. In his first at-bat for the Cards, he hit a three-run homer to ice an 11-3 win, but his .265 average with St. Louis was only enough to lift his 1969 mark to .219. He also made his only two big-league pitching appearances that year, both in the span of a week in June and July as the Amazin' Mets blew out St. Louis. Vic failed to retire any of the four batters he faced and allowed one earned run, which left him with an ERA of infinity.

In 1970 Davalillo started just 23 games while pinch-hitting in 74. Some sources still show him with 24 pinch hits that year, which ostensibly tied Dave Philley's single-season record from 1961. However, in later years the record was re-examined, and the correct total proved to be 23—two separate scoring nuances clouded the original count.[32] At the time, Vic said, "The record isn't that important to me."[33]

In the winter of 1970-71, Davalillo won his fourth and final Venezuelan batting title at .379. While he was down there, he got the news that he had been traded on January 29 to the Pittsburgh Pirates, along with Nelson Briles, for Matty Alou and George Brunet. Alou had a very good year for St. Louis in 1971, but Brunet pitched only seven more games in the majors (though he would pitch well into his 50s in Mexico). The deal turned out very well for the Pirates, as Briles gave them three good years and Davalillo became a key reserve. He hit .285 for the world champions, even starting 14 games at first base. However, he was just 1-for-5 in his first taste of postseason play.

Vic enjoyed one of his best years in 1972 with Pittsburgh, hitting .318 in 403 at-bats and even leading the club in stolen bases. He did not fare well in 1973, though: .181 in just 83 at-bats. The Pirates brought up rookie Dave Parker to stay in July, and so Davalillo's action became even more limited.

The Oakland A's purchased Vic's contract on July 31, picking him up along with Jesús Alou and Mike Andrews for the stretch run. Although he hit just .188 in 67 plate appearances during the rest of the regular season, he saw extensive postseason action after Bill North was injured. Davalillo got into four games in the AL playoffs against Baltimore, starting two, and went 5-for-8 with a key triple in the decisive Game Five. He then played in six of seven games against the Mets in the World Series, again starting twice, though he got just one hit in 11 at-bats. After the A's won their second of three straight championships, they voted Vic a one-third Series share.

One of Davalillo's teammates in Oakland that year was José "Shady" Morales, who also became known as a pinch-hitter deluxe. Morales broke the single-season pinch-hit mark with 25 in 1976, and two years later Vic remarked (likely tongue-in-cheek), "I played one year with Morales. I taught him everything. And look what he does. He breaks my record."[34]

Davalillo remained with the A's to start the 1974 season, but owner Charles O. Finley released him on May 3 with a .174 batting average (4-for-23). There was more to the story, though; in August 1975, A's star Reggie Jackson told about it in a guest column for the *Los Angeles Times*. The team was flying home after a tough loss to the Yankees at Shea Stadium on May 1.

"The flight back to Oakland was a busy one and came to a bad end. Vic Davalillo is a good guy who goes bad when he drinks. He doesn't drink much but when he does he can't handle it. The guys tend to drink a little on the long air rides. The guy who handles the charter flights for United came to me on this flight and said Vic had had too much to drink and maybe I might do something to settle him down. … Today when we got to the ballpark, we heard that Finley had found out and had released Vic."[35]

At the time, Davalillo was actually more displeased with manager Alvin Dark (though he was by no means alone on the club).[36] Just how much Vic liked to imbibe, though, may have been more than Reggie thought. Pirates coach Don Leppert told a story—which is subject to confirmation—about how Vic went in to pinch-hit once for the Cardinals after a heavy night out. He went into his high leg kick and landed on his backside; manager Red Schoendienst had to send in another batter.[37] In later years Dodgers manager Tommy Lasorda said, "You know, I never knew that he drank until I saw him sober."[38]

At any rate, Vítico then joined the Córdoba Cafeteros in the Mexican League. He hit very well for the remainder of 1974: .329-4-27 in 71 games. Another fine season followed with Córdoba in 1975 (.355-9-70 in 114 games) and a third with Puebla in 1976 (.333-8-63 in 123 games). Moving on to Aguascalientes for the 1977 season—brother Pompeyo was skipper—Davalillo was hitting at a tremendous clip again. He was at .384 (198-for-516) with 6 homers and 78 RBIs when he got his ticket back to the majors. Veteran baseball man Charlie Metro, then a scout for the Dodgers, told the story in his book:

"Al [Campanis, the Dodgers' general manager] said, 'Charlie, we need a left-handed pinch hitter.' Somebody said something about Davalillo down in the Mexican League. Al said, 'Go down there and take a look at him.'" Although Metro had reservations when he saw "wine bottles all over" Vic's room, he still went out and saw "Davalillo put on one of the darnedest exhibitions I'd ever seen." Metro proceeded to make "a heck of a recommendation on him. I called Campanis and said, 'Al, this guy can help us.'"[39]

Indeed, Vic—who also served as a stopgap center fielder—went 15-for-48 (.313) down the stretch for the Dodgers. The at-bat that had lasting significance, though, was his only one in the playoffs against the Phillies. In the top of the ninth inning of Game Three, reliever Gene Garber had retired the first two men to face him. Davalillo, whose speed was still intact, saw that the right side of the infield was playing deep. He "recognized that he was being given a gift ... decided to take what was being given him ... and dragged a perfect bunt past the mound."[40] Manny Mota followed with a fly ball to left that a lurching Greg Luzinski couldn't hold; it fell for a double. A game-winning three-run rally ensued, propelling LA into the World Series.

Although the Dodgers lost the Series to the Yankees, Vic went 1-for-3 with an RBI in three pinch-hitting appearances. He did the same in the 1978 World Series, following a .312 performance (24-for-77) in the regular season. In its issue of June 24, 1978, *The Sporting News* pictured Davalillo (looking rather like a Venezuelan Keith Richards) and Mota on its cover, arms around each other's shoulders. "I don't care how old those two guys are," Tommy Lasorda said of his lefty-righty tandem. "They can still hit." Vic even still pinch-ran on several occasions. After one of those appearances, Dusty Baker (who had come out with a pulled muscle) said, "That's when you know you're getting old."[41]

Davalillo remained on Lasorda's squad to start the 1979 season, but in mid-June, having gone just 3-for-17 off the bench, he showed the good grace to return to Triple-A ball for the first time in 17 years. He hit .317 in 51 games for the Albuquerque Dukes, also pitching three times in relief. He then went 4-for-10 as he returned to the big club in September.

After the 1979 season the Dodgers released Davalillo. That winter, the ageless Vítico established another Venezuelan mark: he was the first to record 100 hits in a season. He batted .339 in his fourth season with Tigres de Aragua. (His long association with Caracas had come to an end after the 1974-75 season. The Leones then merged with Tiburones de La Guaira

for one season to form a club called "Tibuleones" de Portuguesa.)

Vítico returned to Aguascalientes in 1980. He flirted with .400, posting a batting line of .394-6-50 in 94 games. Al Campanis reached out for Davalillo again that summer, and he reported once more to Albuquerque (.287 in 36 games, including three more mound appearances). Facing a tight race with the Houston Astros in the NL West, LA recalled the 44-year-old vet, and he got his last six big-league at-bats in September and October. His last base hit came on September 22 as he legged out an infield hit to second. The opposing pitcher was Gene Garber.

Vítico's Mexican sojourns concluded in 1981, as he went .307-2-14 in 40 final games with Aguascalientes. For his career south of the border, he finished with a batting average of .357 (782-for-2190), with 35 homers and 302 RBIs in 577 games.

Still, Davalillo played on at home. In 2009 he said, "It's true that before ballplayers didn't make as much in the big leagues and they supplemented their earnings in Venezuela, but the principal reason that I always came was because I loved to play here."[42] He surpassed the .400 mark once again in 1981-82, going 43-for-104 (.413) for Aragua. As late as 1983-84, he still hit .306.

After ten seasons with the Tigres, Vítico returned to the Caracas Leones. At the end of the 1986-87 season, he said, "Now's the time to retire, there are so many good kids. I'm just getting old. My legs are not the same, and I'm losing my eyes already. My bat is getting slow." Even so, he finished with a respectable performance for a man of 50: 21-for-92 (.228) in 41 games. Caracas manager Bill Plummer said, "He can still bunt for a base hit, and I've used him in the outfield some. He can still catch the ball. He's not a one-dimensional ballplayer. Plummer added of his unofficial coach, "He's a pleasure to have on the team. He's a true professional. He just goes about his business and gets the job done."[43]

Davalillo went out on a high note as the Leones won the league championship that winter. His final action as a player came in the 1987 Caribbean Series, held in Hermosillo, Mexico. That year the ballpark in Cabimas was renamed Estadio Víctor Davalillo; Churuguara's facility did the same at some point.[44] The Most Valuable Player award in the LVBP is also named for this man, who entered his nation's Sporting Hall of Fame in 1991. When Venezuela established its Baseball Hall of Fame in 2003, Vítico was part of the inaugural class in 2003.

Back in August 1980, Davalillo had said, "When I retire as a player, I don't want to get into another profession. I will become a coach. And then, after I get some experience coaching, I might become a manager. I will always be in baseball."[45] For a time after his playing career ended, he directed an amateur team in Venezuela, but he then retired fully, drawing his pension.[46] Vítico (who had made Caracas his residence several decades before) stayed active by giving baseball clinics to the young people of his homeland. In his 70s, as wiry as ever, he was still doing so. He said in 2008, "I do it with great love and passion for Venezuela."[47]

Special thanks to Asdrúbal Fuenmayor (founder of Radio Deporte 1590 AM, a Venezuelan sports radio station) and to Marcos Grunfeld of beisbolvenezolano.net for confirming biographical details. Continued thanks to Harry Fanok for his memories.

SOURCES

retrosheet.org

baseball-reference.com

purapelota.com (Venezuelan statistics)

museodelbeisbol.org (Venezuelan Baseball Hall of Fame)

Peter C. Bjarkman. *Diamonds Around the Globe: The Encyclopedia of International Baseball* (Westport, Connecticut: Greenwood Press, 2005).

Pedro Treto Cisneros, ed., *Enciclopedia del Béisbol Mexicano* (Mexico City: Revistas Deportivas, S.A. de C.V., 1998).

NOTES

1   "Vic Oldest, Fairest." *The Sporting News*, September 24, 1977: 32. The 1969 *Sporting News Baseball Register* also showed 1936.

2   Asdrúbal. Fuenmayor. *Víctor Davalillo*. Caracas, Venezuela: Colección de Bolsillo Radio Deporte 1590 AM, 2006. Sr. Fuenmayor confirmed by e-mail to Rory Costello that Davalillo himself was the source.

3   Ibid.

4   Luis Bravo. "Pompeyo: béisbol y leyenda." Web forum of Águilas del Zulia baseball club, August 1, 2010 (aguilasdelzulia.foroactivo. com/noticias-del-portal-f3/pompeyo-beisbol-y-leyenda-t383. htm). This article lists Pompeyo Davalillo's year of birth as 1928, as does his web page on the Venezuelan Baseball Hall of Fame website.

5   Francis Stann, "Vic Davalillo May Prove He Was '63's Top Rookie in '64." *Baseball Digest*, December 1963, 57.

6   Bravo, "Pompeyo."

7   Russell Schneider. "Little Vic Big Gun in A.L. Batting Race." *The Sporting News*, June 26, 1965, 3.

8   Schneider, "Little Vic," 4.

9   "Vítico Davalillo Bateaba a Las Dos Manos en Sus Inicios." Double A Baseball of Zulia blog, October 22, 2007. (beisbola-adelzulia.blogspot.com/2007_10_01_archive.html)

10 Bob Price, "Power Hitting of Vic Davalillo Dazes Sun Foes" *The Sporting News*, July 21, 1962, 37.

11 *Sporting News Baseball Register*, 1967. Juan Pazos, "Si la selecciones criollas no practican perderemos contra todo el mundo." *Diario de los Andes* (Trujillo, Venezuela), November 19, 2007.

12 Frank Gibbons, "Battler Maduro: Castro Couldn't Strike Him Out," *The Sporting News*, November 24, 1962, 37.

13 Federico Rodolfo, "Skipper Otero Nabs 4th Flag in 5 Years." *The Sporting News*, February 7, 1962, 35.

14 Ibid.

15 Valencia—one (1960-61); Caracas—six (1961-62; 1963-64; 1966-67; 1967-68; 1972-73; 1986-87).

16 Pazos, "Si la selecciones."

17 Bill Reddy, "Davalillo Standout on Slab, in Garden." *The Sporting News*, June 30, 1962, 33.

18 E-mail from Harry Fanok to Rory Costello, December 18, 2010.

19 Price, "Power Hitting.".

20 E-mail from Harry Fanok to Rory Costello, December 18, 2010.

21 "Davalillo Skein Ends at 19," *The Sporting News*, June 23, 1962, 36.

22 Gibbons, "Battler Maduro."

23 "Davalillo Skein Ends at 19."

24 Russell Schneider, *The Cleveland Indians Encyclopedia* (Champaign, Illinois: Sports Publishing LLC, 2004), 157.

25 Pam Postema and Gene Wojciechowski, *You've Got to Have Balls to Make It in This League* (New York: Simon & Schuster, 1992), 25.

26 Bob Sudyk, "Davalillo's Fight Against Fear." Reprinted in *Baseball Digest*, June 1965, 15-16.

27 David Finoli and Bill Rainer, *The Pittsburgh Pirates Encyclopedia* (Champaign, Illinois: Sports Publishing LLC, 2003), 376.

28 The other back-to-back winners are Cito Gaston (1968-69 and 1969-70); Al Bumbry (1973-74 and 1974-75); and Luis Sojo, who has done it twice (1989-90 and 1990-91; 1993-94 and 1994-95).

29 Schneider, "Little Vic Big Gun in A.L. Batting Race." César Tovar was with the Twins at the beginning and end of the 1965 season but was in Triple-A from mid-May through August.

30 John Wiebusch. "A Swinging Davalillo Puts Angels Over, 3-2." *Los Angeles Times*, July 12, 1968.

31 "Davalillo, Outfielder, Suffers a Breakdown," *New York Times*, January 9, 1969. Eduardo Moncada, "Bo Cites Threats, Packs bags After a Spat with Pilot Reyes," *The Sporting News*, January 25, 1969, 47.

32 In the seventh inning on June 7, 1970, the Cardinals batted around against the Padres, and at first Vic got credit for two pinch hits. On August 31 he had seemingly broken the National League record of 22, which had been held by Sam Leslie (1932) and Red Schoendienst (1962). However, NL statistician Seymour Siwoff, of the Elias Sports Bureau, ruled that the second at-bat on June 7 did not count as a pinch-hitting appearance. In its July 1996 issue, *Baseball Digest* quoted Siwoff. "The man cannot pinch-hit for himself," he said.

There was a debate over the double-counting—the AL had said it would credit two pinch hits in such situations. Yet ultimately, Davalillo's pinch hit on August 31 proved to be his 21st, not his 22nd. A fourth-inning double on July 27 was originally credited as a pinch hit. (See *Sporting News* box score, August 8, 1970, 41; Neal Russo, "Vic Erases All Doubt with Pinch Hit No. 23," *The Sporting News*, October 3, 1970, 9). However, Vic had already replaced Jim Beauchamp in center field in the third inning. The pinch hits he collected on September 18 and October 1 were in fact numbers 22 and 23.

33 Neal Russo, "'I'm Not a Loafer!' Cardenal Protests," *The Sporting News*, September 19, 1970: 6.

34 Gordon Verrell, "Dodgers Turning Huge Profits in Spanish Antiques," *The Sporting News*, June 24, 1978, 3.

35 Reggie Jackson, "Fighting Champs," *Los Angeles Times*, August 25, 1975, D1.

36 "Davalillo, Released, Assails Dark," *New York Times*, May 12, 1974. Ron Bergman, "Anarchist A's Find It Easy to Fault Pilot Dark," *The Sporting News*, May 25, 1974, 19.

37 Finoli and Rainer, *The Pittsburgh Pirates Encyclopedia*, 377.

38 Charlie Metro and Thomas L. Altherr, *Safe by a Mile* (Lincoln, Nebraska: University of Nebraska Press, 2002), 360.

39 Metro and Altherr, *Safe by a Mile*, 359-60.

40 Mitchell Nathanson, *The Fall of the 1977 Phillies* (Jefferson, North Carolina: McFarland & Co., 2008), 197.

41 Verrell, "Dodgers Turning."

42 "Grandes diferencias entre ayer y hoy." *Lider en Deportes* (Caracas, Venezuela), June 28, 2009, 4. (liderendeportes.com/CMSPages/GetFile.aspx?guid=6ea6f959-86b2-499e-9a9c-6d30ef f27583&disposition=attachment)

43 "Vic Davalillo, 47 [*sic*], Still Going Strong," *Los Angeles Times*, February 8, 1987.

44 The Cabimas stadium hosted an LVBP team called Petroleros de Cabimas for the four seasons it existed (1991-92 through 1994-95). Later it was a temporary stadium for Águilas del Zulia. The Churuguara ballpark is a modest municipal stadium.

45 "Davalillo's Lifeblood," *The Sporting News*, August 16, 1980, 37.

46 Pazos, "Si la selecciones."

47 Eduardo Galindo. "Zona Central recibió Clínicas Béisbol y Amistad 2008." Blog of Eduardo Galindo, August 31, 2008 (eduardogalindoproducciones.blogspot.com/2008_08_31_ archive.html)

Chuck Dobson

By Gregory H. Wolf

Chuck Dobson might be best remembered as the first white player to room with an African-American on road trips, and as the first active player to admit using "greenies" (amphetamines) while playing. But that would be a disservice to the hard-throwing right-hander who seemed destined for a long career in the big leagues when he broke into the Kansas City Athletics' rotation as a 22-year-old rookie in 1966. He won 15 or more games for three consecutive seasons (1969-1971) and helped guide the A's to their first AL West crown in 1971. But as the A's were on the verge of three consecutive World Series championships, Dobson's career was derailed by chronic elbow miseries requiring surgery. He made only one brief appearance for the A's in the next two years (1972-73) and was out of the major leagues two years later.

Charles Thomas Dobson was born on January 10, 1944, in Kansas City, Missouri, the youngest of three children born to William James and Elizabeth Mary (Stahl) Dobson. "My mother came from good German stock," Dobson told the author, "but my father had the 'curse of the Irish.' He worked on an assembly line in a General Motors plant and gave the foreman hell for 42 years."[1] Dobson started playing baseball at the age of 12 when he picked up a ball and threw it through a wall. All of a sudden he realized he had a strong arm. "I grew up near the Municipal Stadium, where the A's played," he said. "It was at 22nd, I lived at 42nd and went to school at 39th Street. We played baseball every day." Dobson pitched in youth-league baseball with the 3-2 club in Kansas City and progressed to the Ban Johnson League, and also played American Legion ball.

A three-sport star at De La Salle High School, Dobson pitched on the baseball team and excelled on the hardwood. But his best sport may have been football. At 6-feet-4 and weighing about 200 pounds, he was

a highly recruited tight end and was offered a full scholarship to play football by such powerhouse programs as Notre Dame, Nebraska, and Missouri, and even Dartmouth. He chose the nearby University of Kansas in Lawrence, just about 40 miles from home. "I hurt my back during my senior year of baseball in high school in 1962," he said. "I asked Kansas if I could just play baseball and they agreed." Dobson never played football for Kansas; however, he played on the freshman basketball team and pitched for two seasons (1963-1964) for legendary Kansas coach Floyd Temple. In his sophomore season, he won six of eight decisions, led the Big Eight with 90 strikeouts, and was named all-conference. His teammate, pitcher Steve Renko, garnered most of the headlines.

After his freshman and sophomore seasons, Dobson pitched for the Valentine Hearts in the Basin League,

a semipro league based primarily in South Dakota where many collegiate stars and highly touted prospects played a short summer season of about 50 games. "It was a great break for me to go out to the Basin League," said Dobson. "You needed a scout's recommendation to play there. Floyd Temple managed [the Rapid City Chiefs] and he helped me out. It was a great league with great competition—Jim Palmer, Don Sutton, and Jim Lonborg pitched there." The league was heavily scouted by the major leagues. Dobson drew attention from several big-league clubs, especially the New York Yankees and Kansas City A's, as a hard-throwing strikeout artist and a unanimous selection to the league's all-star game in 1964.

Dobson signed his first big-league contract in late summer 1964 while pitching at the National Baseball Conference semipro tournament in Wichita. "Don't tell anyone that I signed then," Dobson joked with the author. "I was going to the Olympics late that fall and was still supposed be an amateur." During the Basin League season, Dobson had accepted an invitation from Rod Dedeaux, coach of the US national baseball team, to play in the Summer Games that October in Japan, where baseball was a demonstration sport. Dobson thought that in spite of his success in the Basin League, his value had gone down because of his back injury in high school. "But the A's Whitey Herzog [a scout at the time] didn't think so," he said. "He was after me in the Basin League and signed me before the Olympics, but we didn't announce it until afterward." In hindsight, Dobson admitted that he chose the A's for the wrong reasons. "I signed with the A's because they gave me more money, a $25,000 bonus. It was a big mistake," he said matter-of-factly. "I should have signed with the Yankees, but they offered $20,000. I got into a nickel-dime organization. I think my career would have been different with the Yankees."

Dobson counted his experiences with the Olympic team among the best in his baseball career. The Americans competed against college all-star and amateur teams during a monthlong tour in Japan and a few days in Korea. "I was probably a last-minute addition to the Olympic team," said Dobson, noting that a few of the scheduled players had turned pro. "But Dedeaux made me the number one pitcher on the team and I won four games."

From the spring of 1964 through the following summer, Dobson traveled the world and pitched for about 18 months without a chance to rest his arm. "I went from Lawrence to the Basin League, on to Wichita, to Japan and Korea, to the Florida Instructional League in the fall of 1964, to my first spring training with the A's in 1965, then on to the minor-league camp. Then I played in Lewiston, Idaho, and Birmingham, Alabama," he said. "I was never the same person after that."

The Kansas City A's were excited to have a hometown prospect in their organization. "He's not far away from being a major-league pitcher," said Herzog of Dobson during the Florida Instructional League. "He has an outstanding fastball and good rotation in his curve."[2] Dobson was a nonroster invitee at the A's spring training in 1965. "I knew I didn't have a chance to make it. My number was 98," said Dobson with a laugh." I worked out for three weeks but didn't pitch in any games. It was good experience and good to be around the major leaguers." The 21-year-old right-hander commenced his professional baseball career with the Double-A Birmingham Barons in the Southern League. He struggled, lost all six of his starts, and was subsequently transferred to the Lewiston Broncs of the Class A Northwest League. Displaying his potential, Dobson won ten of 17 decisions, averaged almost eight innings per start and carved out an impressive 2.90 earned-run average. The A's added him to their 40-man roster in the offseason.

It appeared as though Dobson was a year or two away from being big-league ready when he reported for his second spring training with the A's, in 1966. "I didn't think that I'd make the team," he said of those tension-filled days. "I went to the 12th hour before they let me know. (General manager) Eddie Lopat didn't want me to go, but (manager Al) Dark did. Dark and Lopat hated one another, by the way. I had a good spring but was told that I was going to Double-A. Then I was given another chance to pitch so Lopat could see me again and I pitched real well against the Washington Senators. Still no word. I think the team was going to break camp on Thursday morning and I was told on Tuesday night that I was going north with them."

Dobson joined a perpetually floundering team in Kansas City which had not enjoyed a winning season since its move from Philadelphia to start the 1955 season. And though the team racked up its 12th consecutive finish in the AL's second division in 1966, the A's had quietly assembled a cast of players who led them to respectability a few years later and to the height of the baseball world in the early 1970s. The core of their pitching staff in 1966 was a quintet, each 23 years old or younger: Catfish Hunter, Lew Krausse, Jim Nash, Blue Moon Odom, and Dobson. In the field, second baseman Dick Green and shortstop Bert Campanaris held down the middle infield; Sal Bando was drafted in 1965 and Reggie Jackson in 1966, while outfielder Joe Rudi had signed in 1964.

Dobson earned a victory in his major-league debut on April 19, 1966, against the reigning AL pennant-winning Minnesota Twins, 3-2, at Municipal Stadium. In a start that epitomized most of his career, Dobson displayed his heat, striking out five, but also his wildness, walking six in 5⅔ innings. Three starts later he hurled his first and only complete game of the season, overpowering the Washington Senators on just four hits in a 2-1 victory. Asked what he remembered about his rookie season, Dobson quickly answered, "My sore arm." By June, Dobson's shoulder was aching (it was eventually diagnosed as a serious strain of the Teres minor and major muscles) and he lost five consecutive decisions before winning his last two starts in June. "My arm gave out at the end of the season," said Dobson. "The team had me pitching too much between starts. I'd pitch a game and would then throw for a half-hour the next day. Lopat did that." Dobson, who won four of ten decisions and logged 83⅔ innings, was shelved at the end of June for the rest of the season.

Dobson's shoulder pain marked the first time in his life that he had experienced any kind of arm troubles, and he was understandably concerned. After pitching

in the Florida Instructional League following his rookie season, Dobson entered camp in 1967 as a question mark. "I still don't think I can throw as hard as I could before" he told *The Sporting News*, "but I know my arm is sound."[3] Dobson got off to a slow start (1-2 with a 4.57 ERA through May), but pitched better as the season progressed. On June 9 he hurled the first of his 11 career shutouts by blanking the Cleveland Indians on nine hits. But in an era when staff aces were expected to complete 40 to 50 percent of their starts, Dobson had a tendency to tire early or lose his rhythm late in games, and completed just four of 29 starts en route to a 10-10 record and a 3.69 ERA.

Dobson struggled at home despite playing in a pitcher-friendly park. In 1967 he won just three of nine decisions and posted a 4.06 ERA in Municipal Stadium; on the road he won seven of 11 decisions and carved out a good ERA (3.29). "After a while I didn't like playing in Kansas City," Dobson said as he attempted to explain the unexpected discrepancy in his pitching splits. "I couldn't handle the pressure. People always asked me for tickets. I was kind of relieved when we moved to Oakland." During the season he married Kay Marie Willard of St. Louis, whom he had met while a student at Kansas. They had one daughter, Andrea.

After years of poor attendance in Kansas City (they averaged less than 9,000 spectators per game in 1967), A's owner Charley Finley moved the club to Oakland for the 1968 campaign. On April 13 Dobson pitched a wobbly six innings against the Senators in Washington yielding eight hits and five runs (four earned), but picked up the first win, 9-6, for the new Oakland A's.

Free from pain in his shoulder and the pressure of pitching in front of friends, Dobson seemed to overcome his problems with concentration and began pitching deep into ballgames. In May he pitched three of the most dominant yet frustrating games of his career. On May 10 he pitched a complete game against the Chicago White Sox, striking out 11, then had his two longest career outings within a ten-day period to end the month. He tossed an 11-inning complete game against the Cleveland Indians and a 12-inning complete game with a career-high 13 strikeouts against the California Angels. But he lost each game as the weak-hitting A's scored just one run total while the big right-hander surrendered two, one, and three runs respectively in those games.

In the 1968 "Year of the Pitcher" when the AL posted a collective 2.98 ERA and teams scored just 3.41 runs a game, Dobson lost an inordinate number of close games. The A's scored three runs or less and a total of just 18 runs in 12 of his 14 losses. Nonetheless, the team's big-five pitching rotation (Dobson, Hunter, Nash, Krausse, and Odom) combined to start 157 games and logged more than 1,100 innings to lead the A's to their first winning season since 1952. "We all had friendly competition, and weren't envious and back-stabbing," recalled Dobson. "We ran around together after games, too. Hunter and I lived with our wives in the same apartment house." In his last start of the season, Dobson broke his ankle when he collided with first baseman Rich Reese of the Minnesota Twins while trying to beat out a bunt. He concluded the season with 12 wins and a career-best 3.00 ERA.

In 1968 Dobson broke a longstanding tradition by becoming the first white player in major-league history to room with an African American on the road. According to Dobson, it happened as a result of a different roommate and a bad outing. "Reggie [Jackson] would always come to me in spring training and ask if I wanted to be his roommate, but I was rooming with [Jim] Gosger at the time," said Dobson, explaining that Jackson was the 25th man on the team and had a single room. "After a late, knuckleball flight to Baltimore, we didn't get to the hotel until about 3 or 4 a.m. And I am supposed to pitch the first game of a doubleheader later that day (August 26) at 1. Well, I was woken up at 7:30 by my roommate who had a woman in his bed. I couldn't sleep after that, got dressed, and went to the park. I got shelled that day, gave up seven runs in the first inning. I went to Reggie and asked if he was ready to room together and he said 'sure.' I didn't say anything. I just got my suitcase and moved."

Dobson was a fiercely independent player, kept his own counsel, and never connected baseball talent to race and politics. Nor was he afraid of any backlash from teammates for a decision that was bound to have repercussions around the league. "The coaching staff didn't say much about us rooming together," said Dobson, but he added without mentioning names, "A few players asked 'Why do you want to room with that nigger?' That surprised me, but Reggie was becoming a star so there wasn't much anyone could say or do about the situation." They roomed for more than two years and developed a mutual respect.

In what seemed like an annual tradition, Dobson reported to spring training with questions about his health. Not only did he wear a brace on his right ankle that limited his flexibility, he had to get used to the new, lowered mound that Major League Baseball hoped would generate more offense. Dobson relied on his fastball (thrown from a three-quarters delivery), and a big overhand curve for his success. His concern about the effects of the mound seemed confirmed by his poor start (1-3 with a 6.41 ERA) to the season.

"I go out there and I'm King Kong mentally," he told *The Sporting News*. "I grimace so hard you can see my veins sticking out of my neck.[4] Throughout his playing career, his managers implored him to relax on the mound and throw the ball instead of trying to pinpoint it, which led to occasional bouts of wildness and a tendency to give up the gopher ball. But Dobson adjusted to the new mound and reeled off the most commanding stretch of his career thus far. In a span of 11 starts in May and June, he won eight of ten decisions, averaged a shade over eight innings per start and sported a 2.21 ERA while the A's battled the Minnesota Twins for first place in the AL West. Though Oakland fell off the pace in the second half of the season to finish in second place, Dobson enjoyed a breakout season and his first winning campaign. He tied for the team-high in wins (15) and starts (35), and paced the team with 11 complete games.

Dobson loved baseball, taking the mound, the competition with the batters, the suspense, and daily battles. And he had a reputation as a hard-working, committed, hustling player. But he revealed to the author another, more vulnerable side. "My problem in baseball was the lifestyle," he said. "I wasn't ready for it. I drank too much and became an alcoholic." Dobson suggested that baseball was a haven for alcoholics and drinking was tolerated if not encouraged. Players drank in the clubhouse, on the road, in the hotel, with teammates, and the list goes on. Alcohol abuse was an open secret that teams ignored as long as players performed. "A member of the coaching staff once told me to stop drinking so much," said Dobson. "But he was always drunk so it was hard to take the advice of someone like that." With brutal honesty, Dobson admitted that drinking affected his career, "It wasn't the alcohol; it was the alcoholism that kicked my ass."

Since the team's move to Oakland, Dobson had been bothered by pain in his right elbow. "My elbow hurt the entire year in 1970," he said. "The problem was that my elbow kept growing out of my arm. The bone was getting bigger and bigger and more extended from calcium deposits. That started to put more pressure on my forearm. But the trainers got me ready for every game and during heat of summer I could still loosen up quickly." Inconsistent through the first half of the season, he won seven games (all complete games), but lost ten with an ERA about 4.50. After the All-Star break, he commenced the most dominant streak in his career. In a span of 29 days (from July 16 to August 14), he won a career-high eight consecutive starts, tossed three, four-hit shutouts, and posted a minuscule 1.10 ERA. Batters hit just .162. Suffering from excruciating pain every time he threw the ball, Dobson pitched on three and four days' rest throughout the season, but managed only one more win after his streak. In spite of his elbow, he tied for the AL lead in games started (40) and shutouts (5), and established career highs in wins (16), complete games (13), and innings (267).

In his first six seasons with the A's (1966-1971), Dobson played for five different Opening Day managers (Al Dark, Bob Kennedy, Hank Bauer, John McNamara, and Dick Williams) and experienced two midseason managerial exchanges. He became accustomed to

Charley Finley's notoriously dictatorial ways, perpetual undermining, and cost-cutting approach. "Finley was the owner and general manager (after 1968)," said Dobson who compared him to the Dallas Cowboys' egomaniacal owner-general manager Jerry Jones. "We knew the managers didn't have much control. It was all Finley and he ruined things—until Dick Williams got there in 1971. We respected Williams because he gave the impression that he had some control." In interviews with A's beat reporter Ron Bergman of the *Oakland Tribune*, Dobson regularly voiced his frustrations with Finley's meddling, claiming the players had to get numb to Finley in order to concentrate on baseball.[5]

Articulate, opinionated, and brutally honest, yet never one to seek the limelight, Dobson made national news during spring training in 1971 when he became the first active big leaguer to admit to occasionally using greenies (amphetamines) on game days. In light of Jim Bouton's revealing and controversial book *Ball Four* detailing the everyday lives of baseball players (including the use of greenies) and the increased focus on illicit drug use in America at the time, Dobson's remarks were shocking. Like alcohol, amphetamines were tolerated in baseball and their widespread use ignored. "The whole league was taking amphetamines," Dobson told the author unequivocally. "Starting pitchers, at least. Not every game but at some time or another. They were common."

Dobson's admission to taking greenies spread like wildfire after the *Oakland Tribune* ran the headline "Dobson Defends Pills."[6] "I remember a game in California (May 28, 1970) when I was sicker than a dog," he remembered. "I had a 102-degree fever and broke out in cold sweats. I took an amphetamine and pitched a shutout. I told the writers about that game and they flew with it. It caused all kinds of flak." In attempt to preserve the last vestiges of a clean, all-American sport free from the evils of society, baseball executives acted quickly and forcefully. "Finley, (AL President) Joe Cronin, and (Commissioner Bowie) Kuhn called me up and told me that I gotta retract," Dobson said. "They put the fear of God in me. And

I did. I lied my ass off. I said to the press that that was the only time I did it. The whole situation quieted down after that." More than anything, Dobson recognized the precarious relationship between illegal drugs, on-field performance, and the rising salaries of the early 1970s; and his comments foreshadowed the discussion about steroids and performance-enhancing drugs (PEDs) 40 years later. "I don't see how [Kuhn] can stop [amphetamines] with the money involved," Dobson said in 1971. "One victory can mean thousands of dollars on your contract."[7]

Lost in the brouhaha about greenies was Dobson's aching elbow. After he missed most of spring training and all of April on the disabled list, Dobson's season was in doubt. But pitching on sheer determination and guts, and given some extra time between starts, he unexpectedly began the season by winning a career-high nine consecutive decisions. Though not quite as overpowering as in years past, Dobson was given better run support, helping him shed a reputation as a hard-luck loser. He had also added a "slurve," a slow breaking curveball, to his pitching repertoire. (He said he copied it from Catfish Hunter.) With the A's cruising to the first of five consecutive AL West crowns, Dobson improved his record to 15-3 by blanking the Angels on seven hits on September 1. Unbeknownst at the time, Dobson would not win another big-league game for three years and only two more in his career. "My arm crapped out on me and I really couldn't pitch the last month of the season," he said. He finished with a 15-5 record and a 3.81 ERA. He did not pitch in the A's three-game sweep by the Baltimore Orioles in the AL Championship Series.

During the offseason Dobson underwent elbow surgery at the Mayo Clinic in Minnesota. A quarter-inch piece of bone was removed from his elbow, which required additional muscle repair. The operation was not career-threatening, but ample recovery time was generally prescribed. "Finley's doctor in Oakland—not my surgeon—told me that I could come back and pitch in seven weeks," Dobson said with an air of disgust and disbelief more than 40 years later. "That was the beginning of the end for me. I ruined my arm.

And Finley blamed me!" In constant pain during spring training, Dobson cleared waivers in April and was sent to the A's Birmingham farm club. After pitching just 19 innings, he left without permission and returned home. "I roomed with Denny McLain, the world's craziest person," said Dobson, whose alcoholism, and excessive drinking with the former 30-game winner, took a toll on his physical recovery.

The A's, still sure that Dobson's elbow only needed time to regain its strength, sent him to Tucson in the Pacific Coast League in 1973. Notwithstanding his 5.23 ERA in 203 innings with the Toros, he was recalled in September but was shelled in his only start. Following a stint with Caracas in the Venezuelan Winter League, Dobson was released near the end of spring training in 1974.

"I was depressed when I got released," recalled Dobson. "I said screw baseball. But my arm was good enough and I could have stuck around playing somewhere. I figured I'd go into business." He was unable to resist an offer of $3,000 per month, however, and signed a contract with the Mexico City Lions. "I hadn't pitched in about a month and was out on the field and noticed there's no pain." Dobson said. "And then I thought, isn't this a hell of a situation. I'm down in Mexico and owned by them. All of a sudden I had my fastball back." Dobson won ten of 12 decisions and had a simple explanation for his unexpected success. "I was pretty dry, didn't drink too much, and didn't take amphetamines."

Dobson got a second chance when the California Angels signed him. He was assigned to the Salt Lake City Angels, and was a September call-up. In his first start he tossed a complete game against the Texas Rangers and got his first win in the big leagues in three years. After three rough outings, he enjoyed sweet revenge: He limited his former Oakland teammates to five hits and struck out nine in a 3-2 complete-game win. "I just went into the dugout after the game and cried." But he also noticed an undeniable change: "When I crossed the border to the US after I was signed by the Angels I lost my fastball again. I had my scotch again and access to amphetamines. My body just didn't respond." He pitched briefly for Salt Lake City in 1976.

"I didn't retire, I just quit," said Dobson about the end of his playing career in 1976. In his nine-year big-league career he won 74 games, lost 69, logged 1,258⅓ innings, and posted a 3.78 ERA. He won 38 times in the minor leagues.

In 1977 and 1978 Dobson coached in the Arizona Instructional League and was the pitching coach for Salt Lake City in 1977. "I worked harder than I ever did as a player and had more fun." he said. "I got my arm strong from pitching batting practice but I didn't have the heart to play. I loved the coaching." At the same time, his life was careening out of control and his marriage ended in divorce. He moved to St. Louis and became involved in television (he was a pitchman in local and national commercials) and radio, and was the sports director for KMOX-FM. "That was a great opportunity," he said, "but I blew it because of my drinking."

Dobson's story, however, is one of survival and triumph. "I've been sober since 1985," he proudly said of going into rehabilitation and turning his life around." He went back to college, finished his degree, and worked as an addiction counselor for more than a decade. At the same time, he became a house painter and traveled the world between jobs. He eventually relocated to Kansas City, and as of 2013 was retired and resided in the house he grew up in. In 2009 he suffered a stroke ("self-induced," he said matter-of-factly, "from strain, stress, and too much smoking"). He was partially paralyzed, but recovered and can walk and use his hands. "I never had ambition to be a big-league baseball player. It just happened," said Dobson.

SOURCES

Oakland Tribune

The Sporting News

Interview with Chuck Dobson on July 31, 2013.

NOTES

1   The author expresses his sincere gratitude to Chuck Dobson, who was interviewed on July 31, 2013. All quotations from him are from this interview unless otherwise noted.

2   *The Sporting News*, December 5, 1964, 34.

3   *The Sporting News*, August 26, 1967, 16.

4   *The Sporting News*, May 24, 1969, 23.

5   Ron Bergman, "McNamara's Fate Vague," *Oakland Tribune*, September 16, 1970, F4.

6   Ron Bergman, "Dobson Defends Pills," *Oakland Tribune*, February 23, 1971, 29.

7   "Dobson Defends Pills."

Ray Fosse

By Joseph Wancho

On June 24, 1970, the Cleveland Indians were visiting New York to play a doubleheader against the Yankees. Tribe catcher Ray Fosse went 2-for-4 with one RBI, one run scored and one walk as Cleveland won the first game 7-2 behind Sam McDowell's tenth win. Fosse was scheduled to sit out game two, but he was feeling strong, playing well, and was in the midst of a 23-game hitting streak. So Ray caught the second game as well. In the Yankees' fifth, with a runner at second base, New York pitcher Stan Bahnsen tried to bunt the baserunner to third, but missed the ball. Fosse threw the baseball back to Indian pitcher Mike Paul. As Fosse stood behind home plate, waiting for Paul to go to the pitcher's mound, a cherry bomb was thrown from the upper deck of Yankee Stadium. It exploded four feet from the ground and landed at the instep of Fosse's right foot. "I saw that thing land at my feet, but I didn't have time to do anything,"[1] he said. Fosse covered his head to protect his eyes as a reflex, but felt the pain, like a torch burning in his foot. The cherry bomb burned through his spikes and both pairs of socks. Indians trainer Wally Bock feared hat Fosse had been shot. But the catcher insisted that he return to the game. He was treated for ten minutes and continued to play. Nicknamed the Marion Mule, Ray was big and strong, could carry a team on his back, and was as stubborn as a mule. His career would be marked with injuries, some that he endured while playing, while others sidelined him for long periods.

Raymond Earl Fosse was born on April 4, 1947, in Marion, Illinois, the son of Wayne and Pauline Fosse. He had an older brother, Jerry, and a younger brother, Jim. Ray played the infield his freshman year at Marion High School, but his second year moved to catcher and was named the team's Most Valuable Player all three years. He hit .475 his sophomore year and .535

as a junior. In his last season, Fosse posted a .465 mark with four home runs and led Marion to the Illinois Regional Finals. Ray also lettered in football as a fullback and in basketball as a forward.

Several years later, as a tribute to Fosse, the City of Marion renamed its city park Ray Fosse Park. The park grew to have a number of baseball and softball fields, a miniature-golf course, a swimming pool, a children's play area, and a picnic area complete with shelters. Ray Fosse Park is used for everything from class reunions to the annual Easter Egg Hunt.

In June 1965 the Indians selected Fosse with the seventh pick of baseball's first-ever amateur draft. Advised by his high-school coach, Leroy Anderson, Fosse signed a $28,000 bonus contract with scout Walter Shannon within four days of the draft.

Fosse reported to the Indians Eastern League (Double-A) team in Reading, Pennsylvania, and batted .219 in 55 games to start his climb through the minor leagues. In 1966 he batted .304 in 116 games for Reno of the Class A California League, and the next season hit .261 in 75 games for Portland of the Triple-A Pacific Coast League before earning a call-up to the Indians in September.

Making his debut on September 8, 1967, batting eighth in the lineup, Fosse grounded out to shortstop in the first inning of a Cleveland 6-3 win over the Kansas City Athletics at Cleveland Stadium. On September 30 he collected his first major-league hit, a single off Baltimore pitcher Gene Brabender, his only hit in 16 at-bats in his first brief major-league stint.

Fosse returned to Portland for the 1968 season and hit .301 with 9 home runs and 42 RBIs for the Beavers. He joined teammate Lou Piniella on the postseason PCL All Star Team. Fosse would have liked to have played winter ball after the season, but had to fulfill a six-month commitment with the Army Reserve.

In 1969 catcher was a crowded position in Cleveland, with four men looking for playing time. Duke Sims and incumbent Joe Azcue were battling for the starting position, with Kenny Suarez and Fosse also looking to crack the roster. But on April 19 Azcue was dealt to Boston and Fosse was given the backup role behind Sims. On June 10 at Comiskey Park in Chicago, a foul tip exploded against Fosse's right index finger. Predictably, he stayed in the game. It was discovered later that the finger was broken, and Fosse was placed on the disabled list. He did not return to action until September, and played sparingly. For the season he played in only 37 games and hit just .172.

Duke Sims became the Indians' "Outstanding Player of the Cactus League" during spring training in 1970 and Fosse feared that his role would again be limited. Before the season he married Carol Mancuso, a Los Angeles schoolteacher he had met four years earlier when he played at Reno. Indians teammate Lou Klimchock served as the best man.

In the early part of 1970, Fosse and Sims platooned at catcher. On April 25 Fosse got the starting job and kept it until July 25, when he had to fulfill an Army Reserve obligation for a weekend. In the first half of 1970, Fosse hit .313 with 16 home runs and 45 runs batted in. He hit in 23 consecutive games beginning June 9, the longest AL streak since 1961. Fosse was rewarded with a spot on the American League All-Star Game roster by Baltimore manager Earl Weaver. (The town of Marion sent Fosse a congratulatory telegram with 1,713 signatures. His mother's name was at the top of the list.)

The All-Star Game, played on July 14 at Cincinnati's Riverfront Stadium, was scoreless when Fosse replaced Detroit's Bill Freehan in the bottom of the fifth inning. In the top of the sixth, Fosse singled to right field, was sacrificed to second base by Cleveland teammate Sam McDowell, and scored on a hit by Boston's Carl Yastrzemski. After the National League scored three runs in the bottom of the ninth inning, the game was deadlocked, 4-4.

In the bottom of the 12th inning, Pete Rose had singled and was on second base when the Cubs' Jim Hickman singled to center field. The Royals' Amos Otis fired the ball home to try to nail Rose. Fosse moved up the third-base line three to four feet to catch the throw from Otis when Rose and the baseball seemingly arrived at the same time. Rose crashed into Fosse's left shoulder to score the winning run, knocking the catcher's mitt off his hand and Fosse to the ground.

X-rays revealed that nothing was wrong with Fosse's shoulder. The Cleveland doctors figured it was a bad bruise. It was not until the following year that it was discovered that Fosse had a fracture and separation of his shoulder. The inflammation and swelling were such that the fracture did not show up on the original X-rays. Fosse kept playing. He started the first game after the All-Star break in Kansas City. He could not lift his arm up or out to catch the ball. Cleveland manager Alvin Dark was waiting for Fosse to tell him he was hurt. Fosse was waiting for Dark to ask him if he was hurt. On the other hand, Rose missed three games from the home-plate collision.

Fosse played on until September 3, when a foul tip struck his right index finger in a game against Washington. X-rays showed a fracture. For the rest of his career, Fosse developed the habit of double-clutching when he threw the baseball back to the pitcher. At times he had trouble getting a good enough grip the first time he tried to toss it back to the mound.

Fosse still batted .297 after the collision with Rose, but with only two home runs and 16 runs batted in. He was named to *The Sporting News* All-Star Team, won the Gold Glove Award for catchers in the American League, and was second in assists with 70. Fosse threw out 48 of 88 would-be basestealers. He shared Indians Man of the Year honors with Sam McDowell.

In the offseason Fosse played in the Florida Instructional League, and then in winter ball in Venezuela (as he had the previous year). On December 14, 1970, tragedy struck. Several members of the Magallanes team, including Herman Hill, Dale Spier, John Morris, Fosse, and their wives spent an offday swimming at Puerto Cabella Beach. A terrible current swept Hill into the sea, forcing the other team members to try to save him. Fosse saved Morris, who had gone in after Hill, but the players were not able to rescue Hill. Spier was also in difficulty, but managed to swim back to shore. Herman Hill was only 25, and had just been traded to the Cardinals from Minnesota after spending parts of two years in the majors.

Fosse was one of the few bright spots in 1971 for the Indians (60-102), who finished 43 games behind Baltimore. He hit .276 with 12 homers and 62 RBIs. On June 18, in a home game against the Tigers, Fosse charged the mound after getting hit by pitcher Bill Denehy. "I'm convinced he was throwing at me and any time a pitcher throws at a batter, he can expect something to happen,"[2] Fosse said. Both benches cleared and swarmed to the mound. Umpire Jim Honochick described the scene as "the bloodiest fight I've seen on a baseball field in 23 years."[3] Denehy

kicked Ray in his right hand, causing a gash that required five stitches and sidelined him for more than a week. When he returned, Fosse tore a ligament in his left hand while swinging through a pitch from the Senators' Denny McLain. It was a bad break, because Fosse had been voted by the fans to start the All-Star Game, but had to sit out because of the injury. Fosse did win his second Gold Glove.

Though he felt finally healthy in 1972, fully recovered from injuries, Fosse's batting average dipped to .241 with 10 home runs and 41 RBIs. New teammate Gaylord Perry finished 24-16 with a sparkling 1.92 ERA for a team that finished 12 games under .500. Perry won the first Cy Young Award ever awarded to a Cleveland Indian. He gave credit to Fosse, saying "I've got to split it up and give part—a big part—to my catcher, Ray Fosse. He kept pushing me in games when I didn't have good stuff. He'd come out and show me that big fist of his when I wasn't bearing down the way he thought I should."[4]

Fosse was traded to Oakland on March 24, 1973, along with shortstop Jack Heidemann, for outfielder George Hendrick and catcher Dave Duncan. Gaylord Perry was shocked by the news. "…[W]hy would we want to trade our quarterback?" he said.[5]

Fosse was thrilled to be going to Oakland, the reigning world champion. "I was shocked to say the least," he said of the trade. "Once I got my thoughts together, I was very happy. After all, the A's are a championship team and I couldn't go to a better club. I don't think I will have any trouble with the pitchers there because that staff is the best."[6] Another positive from the trade was that Oakland was only 40 miles from Tracy, California, the hometown of his wife, Carol.

In 1973 Oakland won the AL West by six games over Kansas City. Fosse played 143 games, the most of his career, and hit .256 with 7 home runs and 52 RBIs. The club featured three 20-game winners, Ken Holtzman, Vida Blue, and Catfish Hunter. The A's beat Baltimore in the League Championship Series. Fosse's defense stood out; he threw out four of five would-be basestealers in the series.

Fosse was involved in the most controversial play of the World Series. In the tenth inning of Game Two, in Oakland, the New York Mets' Bud Harrelson tried to score from third on Felix Millan's fly to left field. Joe Rudi made a perfect throw to Fosse, and umpire Augie Donatelli ruled that Fosse had brushed Harrelson with his glove after taking the throw. The Mets' Willie Mays, who had been in the on-deck circle, argued that Harrelson eluded the tag. "I had nowhere to slide," said Harrelson. "I saw a piece of the plate on the right side, so I went for it. He really had the plate blocked off. But I still don't think he touched me."[7] The Mets did go on to win the game, but the A's won the Series in seven games, coming from behind to win Games Six and Seven at home.

Oakland repeated in the AL West in 1974, this time by five games over the Texas Rangers. Injuries plagued Fosse again that season. On June 5 in Detroit, a fight broke out in the clubhouse before the game between Reggie Jackson and Bill North. Acting as a peacemaker, Fosse got caught in the middle and had surgery in July for a pinched nerve. He did not return to the starting lineup until August 26.

The A's again bested the Orioles in the ALCS to earn their third consecutive pennant. In Game Two, Fosse went 3-for-4 at the plate with a three-run home run in Oakland's 5-0 victory. The A's met the Los Angeles Dodgers in the World Series and won in five games. Four of the five games ended up 3-2, with Oakland winning three of them. Fosse hit a home run in Game Five off Dodgers starter Don Sutton, but was only 2-for-14 for the Series.

The A's claimed their fifth consecutive division title in 1975, finishing seven games ahead of Kansas City, but it was a frustrating year for Fosse. Gene Tenace, a better hitter, had become the starter while Fosse was sent to the bullpen to warm up pitchers. With only 147 plate appearances, Fosse batted a weak .140. The A's run of three consecutive pennants was snapped when they were swept by Boston in the ALCS.

Fosse was sold back to Cleveland after the season. Oakland owner Charles Finley brashly told the Indians they were getting damaged goods,[8] but Fosse felt that Finley was upset that he had taken the A's to arbitration the year before. Fosse lost, but now he was happy to be playing on a more regular basis and working with the Indians' young pitching staff.

Fosse again went on the disabled list with a spiked left hand after a collision at home plate with Boston's Jim Rice on April 13. Alan Ashby took over the catching duties, and when Fosse returned, the two players alternated. Fosse hit .301 for the fourth-place Tribe.

Before the 1977 season, Ashby was traded to Toronto, and Fosse got more regular work. The highlight of the 1977 season came on May 30, when Indians pitcher Dennis Eckersley threw a no-hitter against the California Angels, allowing only two baserunners. "Give Fosse a lot of credit too," said Eckersley after the 1-0 victory. "He called a hell of a game. I think I only shook him off three times."[9]

In June manager Frank Robinson was replaced by Jeff Torborg, and the new manager split the catching duties between Fosse and Fred Kendall, depending on the Indians' pitcher. Neither player was very happy with this arrangement. In September Fosse was traded to Seattle for pitcher Bill Laxton. He finished out the season with the Mariners and then signed a four-year deal with the Milwaukee Brewers. In spring training, Fosse tripped in a hole while running down the first-base line and suffered multiple injuries to his right leg. The most serious injury required the reconstruction of the ligament on the outside of the knee, and he missed the entire season. Fosse came to camp in 1979 battling Buck Martinez and Charlie Moore for the catching position, but was the odd man out and was relegated to bullpen duty. He played in only 19 games and had just 52 at-bats. In 1980 Ray was released by the Brewers at the end of spring training. Manager Buck Rodgers, a former catcher himself, said it was one of the hardest things he had to do because "Ray Fosse was the epitome of a catcher."[10]

After his release, Fosse retired as a player. As a major leaguer he batted .256 with 61 home runs and 324 runs batted in. He threw out 286 of 723 runners attempting to steal, just under 40 percent. Fosse had a career fielding percentage of .985.

After retiring, Fosse worked for TRS Video Sports Productions. He made instructional videos on how to play baseball, often using former teammates, among them the A's Sal Bando. Fosse then took a variety of positions in the Oakland front office. He ran the A's Speakers Bureau, then was director of sales and finally director of public relations. In 1986 Fosse joined the radio booth to provide color commentary for A's games as well as hosting a pregame show. In 2014 he was in his 28th season of providing insights to the game of baseball to A's fans in the Bay Area, both on radio and TV. In the offseason he and Carol lived in Phoenix, Arizona. They had two daughters, Nikki and Lindsey, and two grandsons, Matthew and Joseph.

In 2001, as a celebration of their 100th anniversary, the Indians named their 100 greatest players of all time. The players were selected by a panel of veteran baseball writers, executives, and historians. Fosse was selected as one of seven catchers on the all-time team.

SOURCES

Gammons, Peter, "Baseball Notes." *Boston Globe*, February 9, 1986

Van Dyck, Dave, "Baseball Notes." *Chicago Sun Times*, February 9, 1986

cleveland.indians.mlb.com/index.jsp?c_id=cle

oakland.athletics.mlb.com/team/broadcasters.jsp?c_id=oak

retrosheet.org/newslt16.htm

thebaseballcube.com/

NOTES

1   Terry Pluto, *The Curse of Rocky Colavito* (New York: Simon and Schuster, 2007), 121.

2   *New York Times*, June 20, 1971.

3   Ibid.

4   *Cleveland Plain Dealer*, October 16, 1972.

5   *The Sporting News*, April 14, 1973, 16.

6   *The Sporting News*, April 7, 1973, 34.

7   *The Sporting News*, October 27, 1973, 10.

8   *The Sporting News*, January 31, 1976, 43.

9   *Cleveland Plain Dealer*, May 31, 1977.

10 *Miami Herald*, March 3, 1985.

Rob Gardner

By Gregory H. Wolf

"I'm always the 11th man on a 10-man pitching staff," left-hander Rob Gardner told *The Sporting News* in 1972.[1] Gardner signed as an 18-year-old with the Minnesota Twins in 1963 and debuted with the New York Mets as a September call-up in 1965. In just his fourth big-league start, he dueled Chris Short of the Philadelphia Phillies for 15 scoreless innings in a game that was eventually called after 18 scoreless frames. Battling elbow and shoulder miseries for much of his 13-year professional baseball career (1963-1975), Gardner never achieved the success his career day in 1965 might have suggested. He went 14-18 in parts of eight seasons in the major leagues, pitching in seven different organizations, and also hurled for 12 minor-league teams.

Richard Frank Gardner was born on December 19, 1944, in Binghamton, New York, located at the confluence of the Susquehanna and Chenango Rivers in the state's Southern Tier, near the Pennsylvania border. Gardner went by the name Rob, as he explained to *The Sporting News*, "My mother used to call me Robin and I couldn't stand that. So it got shortened to Rob."[2] Growing up in a middle-class neighborhood and attending public schools in the advent of the Baby Boomer generation, Gardner's passion was baseball, and he seemingly played it whenever he could. Binghamton had always been a hotbed for baseball, with a storied history of minor-league ball, competitive industrial and semipro leagues, and well-developed youth leagues. According to Tom Ryan, a childhood friend of Gardner's, Rob was taller than most of the boys his age and had a strong arm even in Little League at Recreation Park on Binghamton's West Side. "Rob was a natural athlete and could have played any sport," Ryan told the author. "We'd play Wiffleball behind a school and Rob had all kinds of trick pitches. He enjoyed experimenting and seeing what a ball could do."[3] An astute observer, Rob was self-taught and learned to throw the curveball, the pitch that later

carried him to the major leagues, as a 10-year-old. "There was another kid in the neighborhood who could throw it," said Gardner. "I watched him and picked it up myself."[4]

Gardner was a standout pitcher at Binghamton Central High School, perhaps best known as the alma mater of science-fiction writer Rod Serling. In some ways, Gardner's 13-year professional baseball career with its unexpected twists and disappointments seemed ideally suited for one of Serling's *Twilight Zone* episodes. By his sophomore year, the 6-foot-1, 175-pound Gardner began attracting scouts. He graduated in midterm of his senior year and signed with the Minnesota Twins for a reported $12,500 bonus. "I had hoped to get a bigger bonus that that," Gardner said honestly. "Several other clubs were after me, including the Cubs, Reds, Senators, and Pirates. But two bad games right at the end of my high-school career ruined me."[5]

In 1963 Gardner was assigned to the Twins' new affiliate in the recently reclassified Class A Florida State League, the Orlando Twins (the minor leagues were reclassified and realigned for the 1963 season; Class B, C, and D were designated A). For an average team (64-59), Gardner excelled, winning 16 games, logging 235 innings (both second-best in the league), and leading the league with 213 strikeouts while posting a 2.22 ERA. "Rob did a fine job for us," Orlando manager Harry Warner told the author. "We didn't have pitching coaches back then or all the help the teams have today. The Twins would just send someone down to help out every once in a while. He learned on his own."[6] At the end of the season Gardner was transferred to the Wilson (North Carolina) Tobs of the Class A Carolina League, where he picked up another victory.

The Minnesota Twins gambled with Gardner, their biggest winner in the club's farm system, in 1963, and left him unprotected in the major leagues' first-year player draft in December 1963.[7] The New York Mets, coming off a record 231 losses in the franchise's first two seasons, drafted him for $8,000. The New York media quickly noted that Gardner (just weeks before his 19th birthday) was almost the same age as the Mets' batboy, Harvey Kamnitzer.[8] "I was disappointed," said Gardner about being drafted. "I liked the Twins and knew their staff wasn't very terribly strong. Then I thought about the Mets' staff, and believed there was no reason I shouldn't be able to make that club. By the time I went to spring training (1964), I was very enthusiastic."[9]

The Mets invited Gardner as a nonroster player to their spring-training camp in St. Petersburg, in 1964. One of 14 new players in camp, Gardner was exposed to major-league players and coaches and pitched on the side, but was optioned to Buffalo in the Triple-A International League. Gardner lasted only three starts with the Bisons. "I made the manager mad," said Gardner in an interview with baseball historian William Ryczek. "Back then if you were a teenage rookie, like I was, you were supposed to hold the party line and shut your mouth. I kind of annoyed [manager]

Whitey Kurowski with a couple of things I said."[10] Gardner's second year in professional baseball no doubt tested his commitment to the sport. After Buffalo, he was shipped across the country to Salinas, California, to play in the Class A California League, where he struggled on the field (1-3 with a 4.50 ERA) and in his new surroundings ("I hated Salinas. We would get fogged out," he said).[11] He was reassigned to the Class A Auburn Mets in the New York-Pennsylvania League. Playing just about 75 miles from his hometown, Gardner found his groove, won nine of ten decisions in less than two months with the team, and helped led them to the league title.

After his second look-see with Mets at spring training, in 1965, Gardner was assigned to the Williamsport (Pennsylvania) Mets of the Double-A Eastern League, where he was used almost exclusively in relief for the first time in his career. Gardner demonstrated his durability, appearing in 26 games, carving out a nifty 2.53 ERA in 57 innings in less than two months, and was promoted to Buffalo. Used as a starter again, Gardner was the best pitcher on the league's worst team, winning four of five decisions and posting an impressive 1.70 ERA in 69 innings.

The Mets, languishing in last place with the worst offense and pitching staff in the NL, purchased Gardner's contract and added him to their big-league roster effective September 1. "When I was called up from Buffalo they had me go straight to the hotel rather than the ballpark because I got in so late," Gardner said. "I was watching the game on TV and saw my name up on the scoreboard as tomorrow's starter. That's how I found out I was pitching."[12] Gardner had a rude awakening in his debut on September 1 in the second game of a doubleheader against the Houston Astros. In the first inning he yielded three hits and five runs (three earned) as the Mets' shoddy defense committed two errors and "butchered" another sure out.[13] He was removed at the end of the third inning after surrendering his second home run (and seventh run) of the game, and was charged with the loss. Three more mostly ineffective outings could not have prepared him or the Mets for one of the most unusual games in team history.

In just his fifth big-league appearance and fourth start, Gardner faced Chris Short and the Philadelphia Phillies in the second game of a doubleheader on October 2. In the game of his life, Gardner tossed 15 consecutive scoreless innings, yielding just five hits, walking two, and striking out seven, yet received a no-decision. The hard-throwing Short matched Gardner's feat and struck out 18 batters in 15 innings. Still a scoreless tie after 18 innings, the game was called at 12:50 A.M. due to a curfew and declared a tie. "I was almost out of the game," remembered Gardner, who had a 3-2 count on Dick Allen with a man on third base in the third inning. "I thought, I'm not going to walk this guy. I just threw the ball as hard as I could and he swung through it. As I walked off the mound, he looked at me and just shook his head."[14] The game marked the fifth and last time since 1920 that two pitchers each tossed at least 15 innings and allowed one run or less.

Gardner arrived at spring training in 1966 touted as a sure bet for the starting rotation. He worked closely with pitching coach Harvey Haddix, whom he credited for helping him relax and improve his concentration on the mound. "When things don't go as I would like, I start worrying whether I'm gripping the ball right, or breaking my wrists or other things connected to my technique. Harvey taught me to throw the ball without worrying."[15] In the early part of the season, Gardner seemed to fulfill sportswriters' lofty predictions for him. He followed an excellent outing (nine innings of one-run ball in an extra-inning no-decision) with his first career win, an impressive four-hit complete-game victory, 2-1, against the Chicago Cubs on May 6. Two starts later he hurled another four-hitter, defeating the San Francisco Giants, 6-1. Seemingly on top of the world, Gardner could not have imagined that his next start (his third complete game in four starts, a loss to the Giants on May 15) would be his last complete game in the major leagues for more than six years. He struggled in May (0-4, 6.54 ERA) and was relegated to the bullpen.

Gardner was not an overpowering pitcher; rather, he relied on his curveball and breaking balls for his success. "I always threw the ball on the outside of the plate with some movement, hoping to get a ground-ball," he said. "The first thing to go when you don't pitch a lot is control of your breaking ball. Going into the bullpen did not help me at all."[16] With just two starts among his 22 appearances after the All-Star break, Gardner logged 33 innings accompanied by a horrendous 7.36 ERA. In his only full season in the majors, he posted a 4-8 record and 5.12 ERA in 133⅔ innings.

Gardner pitched for Estrellas in the Dominican winter league and arrived at the Mets camp in 1967 thinking his job was safe. "I'll never be able to figure out what happened," he told *The Sporting News*. "It was about the next to last day of spring training when [manager] Wes Westrum told me that I had been waived out of the league. He floored me when he said 'I should have used you every fourth day last year, but I can't use you this year'."[17] The Mets loaned him to the Phoenix Giants of the PCL, where he surprisingly won four of five decisions and notched a 2.81 ERA in 48 innings. Recognizing Gardner's trade value, the Mets dealt him to the Chicago Cubs on June 12. "When I got to Chicago one mystery was solved," Gardner said. "[GM] John Holland's first question was, 'How's your arm?' After I told him fine, he added, 'When you were on the waivers list, the word was that you had a bad arm.'" In a half-season with the North Siders, Gardner went 0-2 in 18 appearances, including five starts, and logged 31⅔ innings.

During spring training with the Cubs in 1968, Gardner was sidelined with elbow and shoulder miseries that robbed him of much of his effectiveness during the next two seasons (1968-1969) and sent him on an unwelcomed baseball odyssey. On March 30, 1968, the Cubs traded Gardner to the Cleveland Indians, but he reported to the team only after GM Hank Peters threatened to suspend him. Other than a brief September call-up that year, Gardner spent his time toiling ineffectively with the club's PCL affiliate, the Portland Beavers, compiling a 9-12 record with an

ERA in excess of 4.00 until his trade to the New York Yankees in June 1969. He spent the latter half of the summer with the Syracuse Chiefs as a spot starter and reliever and gained exposure in the team's unexpected title run in the International League playoffs.

After a look-see with the Yankees as a nonroster invitee in spring training in 1970, Gardner was assigned to Syracuse, where he surprisingly had a career year. Relying on his curve, slider, sinker, and changeup, Gardner led the International League with 16 wins, 192 innings pitched, and four shutouts, accompanied by a stellar 2.53 ERA and 13 complete games in 24 starts. He was named the league's Most Valuable Player. In an interview with *The Sporting News*, Gardner was effusive in his praise of his manager. "You have to give the credit to Frank. Verdi got me in the groove. He let me pitch. Though things have been rocky at times, he had confidence in me."[18] En route to the Chiefs' league and Junior World Series titles, Gardner won three more games. Added to the Yankees' 40-man roster and called up in late September, Gardner made his one appearance count: he pitched 7⅓ innings to defeat the Washington Senators, 6-4, earning his first big-league victory in more than four years and recording his 20th triumph of the season.

Gardner's success in 1970 was not enough for him to earn a job with the Yankees during spring training in 1971. Four days after they optioned him back to Syracuse, they traded him and pitcher Ron Klimkowski to the pitching-rich Oakland Athletics on April 9 for outfielder Felipe Alou. After just four appearances with the A's, Gardner was sent back to the Yankees for utilityman Curt Blefary, and subsequently reassigned to Syracuse. Though Gardner did not duplicate his success from the previous year, he was arguably the Chiefs' most effective pitcher and won nine of 14 decisions. In another September call-up, Gardner made two brief relief appearances for the Yankees.

Gardner finally got his big break in 1972. After starting the season with Syracuse, he was recalled to the Yankees at the beginning of June as a "relief specialist."[19] Manager Ralph Houk used him as a spot starter in a host of doubleheaders in July. Gardner won all

three of his starts, including his first complete-game victory since 1966, a 7-1 six-hitter against Nolan Ryan and the California Angels. He hurled eight innings of two-hit ball in early August to defeat the Tigers 2-1 for his fourth consecutive win as a starter. *The Sporting News* hailed Gardner as an "unsung hero" who gave the staff a much-needed lift.[20] After two losses, Gardner earned victories in three consecutive starts, surrendering just four runs in 23⅓ innings (1.54 ERA), and emerged as the Yankees' most effective starter. On a fourth-place team, Gardner finished with an impressive 8-5 record in 20 appearances (14 starts), and a 3.06 ERA in 97 innings.

"In this game, you either have to have a lot of ability, be in the right place at the right time, or have a friend in high places to give you a break," Ron said matter-of-factly during his successful return to the big leagues in 1972.[21] Those words were prescient. As he prepared to pitch for San Juan in the Puerto Rican winter league (his fourth consecutive offseason pitching assignment), Gardner was unexpectedly traded on November 24 to the reigning World Series champion Oakland A's for outfielder Matty Alou.

Gardner expressed his frustration and anger to A's beat reporter Ron Bergman. "I just keep getting the feeling that Ralph Houk didn't particularly care for me for some reason. I pulled them out of a tough situation last year." However, he also questioned the A's motives for acquiring him, "Let's face it. They've got a pretty strong left-handed corps there."[22]

The Sporting News once described Gardner's career as like that of a man on a pogo stick.[23] And 1973, his last season in the big leagues, was no exception. After just three relief appearances with the A's (sandwiched around a stint with the PCL Tucson Toros), Gardner was sold to the Milwaukee Brewers. With elbow and shoulder pain resurfacing, he struggled as a reliever (9.95 ERA in 12⅔ innings) and was returned to the A's organization. He spent the rest of the season on the disabled list.

Gardner never overcame his arm miseries. He was given his outright release by the A's during spring training in 1974. He caught on with the Evansville Triplets, the Detroit Tigers' affiliate in the American Association, but made just four appearances. He returned to the site of his greatest success, Syracuse, and became the pitching coach for Bobby Cox and also made ten relief appearances in 1975. During the off-season, he had surgery on his arm, and prepared for a comeback with Syracuse in 1976. But in spring training he "blew out" his elbow, thus ending his professional baseball career needing only 70 days on an active major-league roster to qualify for a four-year pension.[24]

Gardner returned home to Binghamton, where he served as a longtime fireman and paramedic.[25] Throughout his baseball career, he was supported by his wife, Kathryn, whom he married in 1965. Together they had two children, Amanda and David. In 1999 the Syracuse Chiefs honored Gardner's legacy by adding him to their Wall of Fame at the baseball park.[26] He was inducted into the Binghamton Baseball Shrine in 2005.[27] As of 2013 Gardner enjoyed retirement in southern Florida.

SOURCES

Books

Ryczek, William J., *The Amazin' Mets 1962-1969* (Jefferson, North Carolina: McFarland, 2007).

Newspapers

New York Times

Syracuse Herald-American

Syracuse Herald-Journal

Syracuse Post-Standard

The Sporting News

Interviews

Tom Ryan (childhood friend of Gardner's) on August 10, 2013.

Harry Warner (Gardner's first professional manager, at Orlando in 1963) on August 11, 2013.

ACKNOWLEDGMENT

My sincerest appreciation to SABR member Bill Mortell for his diligent genealogical research.

NOTES

1   *The Sporting News*, September 9, 1972, 13.

2   *The Sporting News*, August 22, 1970, 37.

3   Interview with Tom Ryan (childhood friend of Gardner's) on August 10, 2013.

4   *The Sporting News*, May 21, 1966, 17.

5   Ibid.

6   Interview with Harry Warner (Gardner's first professional manager, at Orlando in 1963) on August 11, 2013.

7   Cliff Blau, "The Real First-Year Player Draft," SABR.org. sabr.org/research/real-first-year-player-draft.

8   *The Sporting News*, January 25, 1964, 14.

9   William J. Ryczek, *The Amazin' Mets 1962-1969* (Jefferson, North Carolina: McFarland, 2007), 115.

10 Ibid.

11 Ibid.

12 Ryczek, 116.

13 Joseph M. Sheehan, "Mets Top Astros, 4-1, Then Drop 13th of Season to Houston, 8-5," *New York Times*, September 2, 1965, 24.

14 Ryczek, 116.

15 *The Sporting News*, May 21, 1966, 17.

16 Ryczek, 117.

17 *The Sporting News*, September 9, 1972, 13.

18 *The Sporting News*, August 22, 1970, 37.

19 *The Sporting News*, June 22, 1972, 42.

20 *The Sporting News*, September 9, 1972, 13.

21 *The Sporting News*, September 9, 1972, 13.

22 *The Sporting News*, January 6, 1973, 30.

23 *The Sporting News*, September 9, 1972, 13.

24 "Gardner Makes Pitch for Chiefs Mound Job," *Syracuse Herald-Journal*, March 31, 1976, 42.

25 Matt Michael, "Ex-Chiefs Helped Each Other Reach Hall," *Syracuse Herald-Journal*, July 31, 1999, 13 C.

26 Syracuse Ball Wall of Fame. milb.com/content/page.jsp?sid=t552&ymd=20060725&content_id=110033&vkey=team2

27 Trio of Former Big Leaguers Headline Shrine Class of 2005. oursportscentral.com/services/releases/?id=3187347

Phil Garner (Scrap Iron)

By Norm King

What does Phil Garner have in common with Sir Edmund Hillary and Neil Armstrong?

The answer is that all three performed feats never before achieved by humankind. Sir Edmund was the first person to reach the summit of Mount Everest. Neil Armstrong was the first person to set foot on the moon. And Phil Garner boldly went where no Houston Astros manager had gone before when he led the team to its first World Series appearance in 2005.

Of course, that was not the only achievement of Garner's baseball career, but certainly one of the most significant in a career that included a World Series ring and three All-Star appearances in a 16-year playing career.

Philip Mason Garner was born on April 30, 1949, in Jefferson City, Tennessee, to Drew and Mary Francis (Helton) Garner. Both his father and grandfather were Baptist ministers. He grew up in Rutledge, Tennessee, 15 miles from Jefferson City. As a teenager, he went to Bearden High School in Knoxville due to the quality of the school's athletics and, upon graduating, accepted a baseball scholarship at the University of Tennessee.

Garner had a successful career as a Volunteer, both academically and athletically. He was twice named All-Southeast Conference and led the NCAA in 1969 with a 0.36 home runs per game average, based on 12 homers in 33 games. He graduated with a bachelor's degree in business.

The Montreal Expos drafted Garner in the eighth round of the 1970 amateur draft. The Expos showed minimal interest in their pick, so he didn't sign with them and became available in the January 1971 secondary draft. This time the Oakland A's, a dynasty in the making, scooped up the third baseman in the first round (third overall), signed him, and sent him to their A-ball affiliate, the Burlington (Iowa) Bees in the Midwest League.

Garner made a seamless transition from college ball to the pros. In 116 games, he hit .278, smacked 11 home runs, and drove in 70 runs. On the defensive side, the hot corner was proving to be a bit too toasty, as he committed 29 errors and had a .918 fielding percentage.

Garner married his wife, Carol, in 1971. They went on to have three children, sons Eric and Ty, and daughter Bethany.

Garner's fine 1971 season earned him a promotion for 1972 to the Birmingham A's in the Double-A Southern League, where he continued battering opposition pitching despite being on a bad (49-90, 29 GB) team. In 71 games, Garner hit .280, with 12 homers and 40 RBIs. These numbers earned him a midseason trip back to Iowa, this time with the Triple-A Iowa Oaks

of the American Association. He had more difficulty hitting at this level, as his .243 average in 70 games will attest. He hit nine home runs and had 22 RBIs. Defensively, Garner had better statistics at Triple-A than he did at Double-A. Handling virtually the same number of chances at each level, He had fewer errors at Triple-A.

The poorer offensive numbers at Iowa convinced Athletics management that Garner needed more seasoning, and they sent him to their new Triple-A affiliate, the Tucson Toros of the Pacific Coast League, in 1973. That season, he batted .289 with 14 home runs and 73 RBIs, but committed 35 errors and had a .913 fielding percentage. Defensive numbers notwithstanding, Garner received a September call-up to the A's, who were on their way to repeating as World Series champions. He appeared in nine games for Oakland, and went 0-for-5 at the plate with three strikeouts.

With Sal Bando as the team's regular third baseman, the A's weren't in any hurry to bring Garner up, so he returned to Tucson for another season in 1974. That season turned out to be frustrating for Garner. He was doing well in Tucson; he hit .330 in 96 games. However, in two stints with the parent club, he got into only 30 games, mainly as a defensive replacement. He hit a meager .179 in 28 at-bats and spent a lot of time on the bench.

With an incumbent at third and poor statistics to show for his time in the majors, Garner didn't have a lot to be optimistic about as spring training 1975 rolled around. Then, on March 6, 1975, the A's cut longtime second baseman Dick Green from their roster and Garner, who hadn't played second base since his university days five years earlier, was slotted into the position.

"I haven't seen anything look tough for him in the drills," said A's manager Alvin Dark. "We'll just have to see what happens when the buffaloes come toward him at second base."[1]

As it happened, Garner handled the buffaloes and any other wildlife that came his way quite well. By midseason it was clear that he could not only make the plays around second base, but that he was also a much better hitter than Green.

"I thought Phil would have trouble at the beginning of the season but he didn't," said Bando. "He's aggressive at the plate and in the field. He's a good ballplayer — a good, gutty ballplayer."[2]

The "good, gutty ballplayer" helped the A's overcome the loss of staff ace Catfish Hunter and win a fifth consecutive American League West title. Overall, Garner hit .246 with six home runs and 30 RBIs. Despite the plaudits he was receiving, he still had to improve on defense, as he led the league in errors with 26.

By 1976 A's owner Charlie Finley was in full dismantle mode as he began getting rid of the players from his dynasty teams. He traded Reggie Jackson, Ken Holtzman, and minor leaguer Bill VanBommell to Baltimore for Don Baylor, Mike Torrez, and Paul Mitchell. The A's nonetheless remained competitive, finishing in second place in the AL West with an 87-74 record under new manager Chuck Tanner. Garner's offensive numbers improved; he hit .261, with eight home runs and 74 runs batted in. He also displayed good speed by stealing 35 bases. His defense was a little better, as he cut his errors to 22, but that was still second-highest in the leagues. Overall, Garner played well enough to be selected to the American League All-Star team.

Finley continued divesting the A's of their good players prior to the 1977 season. Garner was fortunate to be one of them, as he was part of a trade that saw him go to the Pittsburgh Pirates with Chris Batton and Tommy Helms for Tony Armas, Doug Bair, Dave Giusti, Rick Langford, Doc Medich, and Mitchell Page. Garner contributed to the 96-66 Bucs, now led by Tanner, instead of languishing with the 63-98 A's. His numbers were similar to those of the previous season. He hit .260, showed more power with 17 home runs, drove in 77 runs, and stole 32 bases. He also showed flexibility on defense, for while he played primarily at third base (107 games), he also saw action at second base (50 games) and shortstop (12 games).

None of his defensive statistics, good or bad, were among the league leaders.

Garner's offensive numbers dipped slightly in 1978. He hit .261, but his home runs (10), RBIs (66), and stolen bases (27) were all down from the previous season, although he had a career-high .441 slugging percentage. Two of those home runs made baseball history.

On September 14 Garner hit a grand slam, the first of his major-league career, in a 7-4 Pirate win over the St. Louis Cardinals. Having quickly acquired a taste for grand salami, he hit another one the very next night in a 6-1 win over the Montreal Expos. It marked only the second time in National League history, and the eighth time in major-league history, that a player hit grand slams in consecutive games. The only previous National Leaguer to do it was James Sheckard of the Brooklyn Dodgers in 1901.

"I feel good I did it," Garner said after the second one, "but I wasn't trying to do that … when I went up there. At the time I was just glad we got a four-run lead out of it."[3]

Defensively, Garner split his time primarily between second and third, playing at each position in 81 games (as well as playing shortstop in four games). Perhaps the shifting of positions hurt his defense, because he ended up fourth in the league in total errors committed, with 28. Garry Templeton of the Cardinals led the league with 40.

Even Pittsburghers who hate disco love the song "We Are Family"—the anthem of the 1979 Pirates that rode the team's atmosphere and Willie Stargell's leadership to a World Series victory over the Baltimore Orioles.

Garner had arrived in Oakland too late to participate in any of the A's' ring ceremonies, but he played an important role in Pittsburgh's drive to the title. He had career highs in batting average (.293), hits (161), and on-base percentage (.359), and tied his career high in slugging (.441).

Garner also performed well under playoff pressure. He got five hits in 12 at-bats in the National League Championship Series with a triple, a home run, an RBI, and four runs scored. He batted .500 in the World Series with 12 hits in 24 at-bats, five RBIs, and four runs scored.

An Associated Press article on Garner just before the 1979 season illustrated what kind of ballplayer he was.

(The Pirates) took Garner, an All-Star second baseman in the American League and stationed him at third. But since then, because of various injuries, Garner has played third, shortstop and second base for the Pirates. He figures the switching does have a little effect on his overall performance, but dismisses (the effects) by saying it's the mark of a professional to adjust.[4]

Somebody in Pirates management must have agreed with the article, because the team allowed incumbent second baseman Rennie Stennett to leave via free agency after the 1979 season and handed Garner the keys to the keystone sack. In 1980 Garner played in 151 games at second base and responded with another All-Star season. His batting average dropped to .259 and his home run total dropped to five, but he drove in 58 runs and stole 32 bases. Despite not having to make the adjustments that come with switching positions, he led the National League in errors by a second basemen with 21, although he also led the league in assists (499) and double plays turned (116) at his position. He had a hit, scored a run, and stole a base in the All-Star Game as well.

Garner's 1981 season was an odd one. His offensive numbers dropped significantly that season, yet he made the All-Star team again. He also found himself with a new team; the Pirates traded him to Houston as he was about to become a free agent and contract negotiations with the Pirates were proving fruitless. Shoulder surgery in April 1981 had also hampered Garner defensively.

The Astros desperately needed help at second base. Incumbent Joe Morgan was injured, and the team had had more auditions than a Broadway chorus for an adequate replacement. Garner arrived on August 31, just in time to qualify for the Astros' post-season roster, in return for Johnny Ray and two players to be named later.

For the year, Garner hit only .248, with one home run and 26 RBIs. In the National League Division Series loss to Los Angeles, he had two singles in 18 at-bats.

Astros general manager Al Rosen was determined to sign Garner after the 1981 season and he succeeded, getting Garner's signature on a three-year, $1.85 million contract, plus a club option. Perhaps having the security of a contract helped Garner relax, because in 1982 he rebounded from his poor 1981 numbers. Playing primarily at second base, he hit .274 with 13 home runs and a career-high 83 RBIs. He stole 24 bases.

An oddity of his 1982 season was his performance against the Pirates. The Astros won nine of 12 games against the Bucs, and while Garner batted only .191, he made those hits count, by driving in 11 runs and having two game-winning hits.

The 1983 Astros overcame a 0-9 start to remain competitive in the National League West, finishing in third place with an 85-77 record, six games behind division champion Los Angeles. According to Garner, the team never let adversity stop them.

"These guys just don't face reality," Garner said. "When we were 0-9, these guys weren't thinking whether we would ever win a game. Everybody felt like we were fixing to run off a string of wins at any time."[5]

Garner's batting average for the year had fallen to .238, but he still had good production with 14 home runs and 79 RBIs. And while the hits didn't keep on coming, the errors did. Having returned to third base because incumbent Art Howe was out all season due to injury, Garner finished second in errors among National Leaguers at the position with 24.

It's hard to say whether Garner felt as if he was living in George Orwell's *1984* during the 1984 season, but he definitely wasn't happy. The scrappy player, who

had earned the nickname Scrap Iron for being a tough, gritty, sometimes brawling ballplayer, spent the 1984 season either on the bench or platooning at third base with Denny Walling.

"You remember Phil Garner," wrote Bob Hertzel in the *Pittsburgh Press*. "'Scrap Iron' they called him when he was here (Pittsburgh). In Houston, though, it's been more like 'Scrap Heap.'"[6]

He wanted to be traded but wasn't, and spent the entire season in Houston. It didn't help that team owner John McMullen said that other teams weren't "beating the doors down to get Phil Garner."[7]

Not surprisingly, Garner's production fell as a result. His batting average was a respectable .278, in 128 games, but he hit only four home runs and had 45 RBIs.

Considering Garner's subpar numbers and what McMullen said, it's surprising that the Astros exercised their option on him for 1985, but they did. Originally the plan was to have Garner and Walling platoon again, but Walling got off to a blazing start, batting .382 in April and finishing the month with an 11-game hitting streak. Walling therefore was moved to first base and Garner became the everyday third baseman for all or part of 123 Astros games that year. At the plate he hit .268, with six home runs and 51 runs batted in. No longer the speedster he once was, he stole only four bases and was caught stealing four times.

During the 1986 season, Garner achieved a personal milestone and the Astros had a highly successful season. On June 14 he not only hit his 100th career home run, but he did it in style, belting a grand slam that proved the difference in a 7-3 victory over the Giants. It was his first grand slam since the back-to-back clouts in 1978. The achievement was a bright spot in a campaign in which Garner was reduced to a part-time role, playing in only 107 games, many of them as a pinch-hitter. In 347 at-bats (his lowest total since the strike-shortened 1981 season), he hit .265 with nine homers and 41 runs batted in. His 37-year-old legs managed to steal 12 bases as Astros manager Hal Lanier brought the speed game to the team's offense.

That approach helped the Astros go 96-66 and win the National League West crown.

Houston played the New York Mets, a team that won 108 games, in the National League Championship Series, and put up a mighty struggle before losing the series in six games. Garner had two hits in nine at-bats during the series, with a double and two RBIs.

Garner's career wound down in 1987 and 1988. He was traded from the Astros to the Los Angeles Dodgers on June 19, 1987, and was a part-time player for both teams, hitting .206 for the season with five home runs and 23 RBIs. He signed with the San Francisco Giants for 1988 and although he didn't play much, he did live up to his Scrap Iron nickname. After having back surgery in April to repair two discs, he was able to come back when the Giants expanded their roster in September. He played his last game October 2, 1988, and got a base on balls as a pinch-hitter. It almost seems appropriate that Garner's last out came when he tried to steal second.

Garner wasn't unemployed very long. Art Howe hired him as a first-base coach when Howe became Astros manager for the 1989 season, and he stayed with the team for three years. He got his first managerial post with the Milwaukee Brewers in 1992 and guided them to a 92-70 record, four games behind the eventual world champion Toronto Blue Jays. Garner remained Brewers manager until August 1999, but never again achieved the same level of success that he had that first season. In fact, his Milwaukee teams never played .500 baseball after 1992. In eight years, his overall record was 563-617 (.477).

Garner took the helm of the Tigers in 2000, and after two losing seasons, he was fired six games into the 2002 campaign. His record in Detroit was 145-185 (.439).

In July 2004 Garner replaced Jimy Williams as manager of the Astros. Houston was only a .500 team under Williams at 44-44, but the team responded well under Garner, going 48-26 the rest of the way and finishing second in the NL Central with a 92-70 record, 13 games behind St. Louis. A seven-game

winning streak to close out the regular season proved a harbinger of things to come. The Astros made the NL playoffs as the wild-card team, and after defeating the Braves in five games in the NLDS, they took the NLCS to seven games before losing to the Cardinals.

The Astros repeated as the National League wild-card team in 2005 with an 89-73 record. It was déjà vu all over again as they defeated the Braves three games to one in the NLDS, and once again faced the Cardinals, who had won 100 games, in the NLCS. This time they were not to be denied as Roy Oswalt, the series MVP, pitched seven strong innings in Game Six, leading the Astros to a 5-1 win and the franchise's first-ever trip to the World Series.

Unfortunately for Garner and the Astros, they were victims of destiny. Their opponents in the Series that year were the Chicago White Sox, who last appeared in the fall classic in 1959, three years before the Houston franchise had even played one game. The White Sox swept the Astros in four straight, to win their first championship since the doughboys went to fight in World War I in 1917.

After an 82-80 record in 2006, the Astros fired Garner during the 2007 season after he compiled a 58-73 record in 131 games. Garner then entered the oil and gas business before coming full circle and joining his first team, the Oakland A's, as a special adviser in 2011.

No scrap heap for Scrap Iron.

SOURCES

Baseball-reference.com

fs.ncaa.org

mapquest.ca

news.google.com

paperofrecord.hypernet.ca.

NOTES

1   Ron Bergman, "A's Ticket Greenhorn Gardner for Green's Job," *The Sporting News*, March 29, 1975.

2   Bergman, "Garner Gleans 'Green' Laurels as A's Rookie," *The Sporting News*, July 26, 1975.

3   "Garner Makes Record Books," *Frederick* (Oklahoma) *Daily Leader*, September 17, 1978.

4   Associated Press, "Garner, Parker Keep Bucs On Their Toes," *Reading* (Pennsylvania) *Eagle*, April 4, 1979.

5   Associated Press, "Astros still fighting for pennant," *Bonham* (Texas) *Daily Favorite*, September 15, 1983.

6   Bob Hertzel, "Like old times as Garner comes through at Three Rivers," *Pittsburgh Press*, August 20, 1984.

7   Ibid.

Tim Hosley

By Neal Poloncarz

Right-handed-hitting backup catcher Tim Hosley came up through the Detroit Tigers farm system and broke in with the Tigers in 1970. Traded to Oakland, Hosley played for the 1973 and 1974 World Series champions, but spent much of those two seasons in Triple-A because the A's were deep in catching with Ray Fosse and Larry Haney. Sent back to the minors after the '74 season, he was drafted by the Chicago Cubs, but eventually returned to the Athletics for two additional stints, in 1976-1978 and 1981. For all his lack of playing time, he was described as having a strong work ethic.[1]

Born and raised in Spartanburg, North Carolina, Hosley was the son of Carrie Lee and Timothy Hosley. At George Washington Carver High School, he played football and basketball and, since the school did not have a baseball team, he played in a local Fast Pitch League.

Detroit scout Al Lakeman, a Spartanburg resident, first noticed Hosley. "I gave him a tryout and later took him to Asheville when Montgomery (a Tigers farm club) was playing there for another tryout. The reason I signed him was that he had a good arm, good speed, and was a good hitter. He hit three or four out of the park at Asheville that day. He'd got some ability."[2] An undrafted free agent in 1966, Hosley was signed by the Tigers. (The 1960s were a time when black catchers were about as rare as black starting pitchers.[3])

Hosley chose not to place any blame elsewhere for not being drafted, but instead pointed to his own inexperience. "I never played Legion ball or high-school ball," he said. "I just played a few sandlot games. Actually when the Tigers signed me, I probably had more experience playing softball than baseball."[4]

The 20-year-old catcher spent most of 1967 with Erie in the New York-Penn League, batting .255 with four

home runs. Behind the plate, he led the league's catchers in errors and passed balls.[5]

Moving through the Tigers' farm system, Hosley improved his batting, and in 1969, for Rocky Mount in the Carolina League, he led the league in hitting until the beginning of August.[6] By the time the season ended, Hosley was at .268; but was third in the league in home runs with 27 (his one-season high in Organized Baseball) and fourth in RBIs with 79. (Future major-league slugger Greg Luzinski led the league in both categories.)

In 1970 Hosley moved up to Double-A Montgomery (Southern League), where his batting average plunged to .215 but he hit 20 home runs and drove in 50 runs. This earned him a call-up to the Tigers at the end of the season.[7] Hosley made his major-league debut at

Tiger Stadium on September 8, 1970, in a 6-3 victory over Baltimore. He pinch-hit for pitcher Mickey Lolich. Facing Marcelino Lopez, he fouled out to first baseman Boog Powell.

Two weeks later, on September 26, at Yankee Stadium, Hosley made his first major-league start, and hit his first big-league home run, a solo shot to left off Fritz Peterson.

At Tiger Stadium in the season finale on October 1, Hosley caught John Hiller's two-hit, 11-strikeout 1-0 shutout over Cleveland. In his brief Tiger stint, he had appeared in seven games, going 2-for-12.

At the end of spring training in 1971, Hosley was assigned to Triple-A Toledo, where in 97 games he batted .239 and hit 23 home runs, tying George Kalaratis for the team lead. In September he was called up again after Tigers catcher Jim Price was injured. On September 5 at Yankee Stadium, in the fifth inning of a 6-5 Tigers defeat, Bobby Murcer crashed into Hosley at home plate. Removed from the field on a stretcher, Hosley was held overnight at the hospital for X-rays, but suffered no injury.[8]

On September 25 at Tiger Stadium, in his first multi-hit game in the majors, Hosley led Detroit to a 10-5 victory over New York, hitting two home runs off Mike Keikich and driving in five runs.[9]

Tigers skipper Billy Martin planned to carry Hosley as a backup to Bill Freehan and Tom Haller in 1972.[10] The tam liked his bat and considered him a potentially capable big-league slugger, at the very least a useful backup who could provide support at catcher and first base.[11] However, Hosley wound up being sent to the Tigers' minor-league complex. "We wanted him mainly for his arm, but he made three bad throws on steals down here," Martin said. "If you're going to carry a guy for defense, he has to be a specialist and Hosley hasn't done that yet.

"We expect a lot from him, but he isn't ready right now."[12]

After arriving late for a workout, Hosley was assigned to Toledo.[13] He hoped to hit for a better average and throw out baserunners. "I've got to make more contact and let the home runs take care of themselves," he told a sportswriter. "I know I don't have to swing hard to get the job done, but with me it's a lot easier said than done."[14] Playing in 132 games, Hosley led Toledo with 24 home runs and 67 RBIs, while hitting .243.

In the offseason the Tigers obtained catcher Charlie Sands from Pittsburgh, and had an abundance of catchers with Hosley, Bill Freehan, and Duke Sims.[15] At first base, the Tigers still had Norm Cash, backed up by Al Kaline, Frank Howard, and Ike Brown.[16] As a result, on April 3, 1973, Hosley was sent to Oakland for relief pitcher Don Shaw.[17] The trade was good and bad news for Hosley. On the one hand, he was joining the best team in baseball, a club positioned to repeat in the American League West. On the other, the A's featured a catching logjam similar to the Tigers', with Gene Tenace and Ray Fosse.[18]

Hosley began the season with the Tucson Toros of the Pacific Coast League, but was called up in May. He made his first appearance in an A's uniform on May 10 at Arlington Stadium. He drove in two runs on two hits, in a 17-2 rout of the Rangers. After a playing in 13 games, he returned to Tucson, where he hit .300 with 12 home runs.

Shortly after joining the A's, Hosley expressed some bitterness toward the Tigers organization. "I felt like I wasn't wanted at Detroit," he told the *Spartanburg Herald-Journal*. "At Oakland the guys have shown me that I'm wanted and it makes me feel a lot better."[19] While he liked his Oakland teammates, the good feelings did not translate into additional playing time. If there was a consolation, it was the opportunity to earn a pair of World Series rings as the A's repeated in back-to-back years.[20]

In July and August of 1974, Hosley got into ten games with the A's. At Tucson he hit .285 in 92 games with 17 home runs and earned an All-Star berth. After the season he was selected by the Chicago Cubs in the Rule 5 draft.

The Cubs needed help behind the plate. Catchers Steve Swisher and George Mitterwald were strong defenders but weak hitters. Cubs manager Jim Marshall loved Hosley's lively bat and his strong throwing arm. Hosley provided the Cubs another dimension. By May, Marshall moved Hosley into the starting lineup.[21]

For one of the few times in his career, Hosley spent an entire summer in the big leagues, free of a minor-league assignment. "I finally found a manager willing to give me a chance," he told sportswriter Jerome Holtzman.[22] In 62 games, he batted .255, hit six home runs, and slugged .433. On September 14 he hit his only career grand slam, against Philadelphia pitcher Randy Lerch at Chicago's Wrigley Field.

But despite a solid 1975 campaign, the Cubs placed Hosley on waivers early in the 1976 season. He was reclaimed by Oakland. In his second stint with the A's, Hosley received more playing time, but his numbers declined sharply. He spent much of the 1976 through 1978 seasons in the Pacific Coast League. At San Jose in 1977, he hit .321. In July he was recalled to Oakland after slugger Dick Allen was suspended, and batted .192 in 78 at-bats during the remainder of the season. In the minors again in 1978 (Vancouver and Charleston), Hosley didn't appear for the A's until September. He batted .304 in 23 at-bats, mostly as a pinch-hitter. In 1979 and 1980, Hosley was at Triple-A Ogden, and didn't play for Oakland. In 1980 he batted .301 with 26 home runs and 102 RBIs.

In 1981 season, Hosley was back with the A's. On April 29, in a 6-4 victory over California, Hosley came up as a pinch-hitter and bludgeoned a two-out, three-run homer off Andy Hassler. It was the final home run of his major-league career. On May 29 the players union went on strike, and the season didn't resume until August 9. Hosley didn't play after the strike, and he was released at the end of August. His major-league career was over. The next season he retired after playing in two games for Triple-A Tacoma.

In his nine-year up-and-down major-league career, Hosley played in 208 games, batted .215, hit 12 home runs, and collected 53 RBIs. His minoir-league numbers were more notable. He hit 208 home runs and had a .272 batting average. Hosley's skills were often unappreciated in his era, but are lauded by more recent analysts. In addition to his power, Hosley drew a lot of walks; he posted a .400 on-base percentage five times in the minors and had a career .373 OBP mark at that level.[23]

After a seven-year retirement, Hosley played one season for the Fort Myers Sun Sox in the short-lived Senior Professional Baseball Association. Many former MLB players played in this league.

In later years, Hosley was a hitting and pitching instructor, at Coach Dave's School of Hitting and Pitching in Boiling Springs, South Carolina. He was an ardent golfer and was involved with many charity fundraising events, and was a member of Macedonia Missionary Baptist Church. Hosley died on January 21, 2014. He was survived by his wife, Phyllis, and two daughters, Sharon Wilkins and Melissa Lee. He was preceded in death by an infant daughter, Alisha D. Hosley.[24]

NOTES

1   Bruce Markusen, "With the Tigers, Catcher Tim Hosley's Timing Was Bad," blog.detroitathletic.com/2014/01/31/tigers-catcher-tim-hosleys-timing-bad/, accessed January 31, 2014.

2   Lesley Timms, "A Cinderella Story," *Spartanburg Herald*, March 9, 1971, 10 (news.google.com/newspapers?nid=1876&dat=19710309&id=XXgsAAAAIBAJ&sjid=HswEAAAAIBAJ&pg=4974,1416213).

3   Markusen.

4   Markusen.

5   Markusen.

6   Lesley Timms, "A Cinderella Story," *Spartanburg Herald*, March 9, 1971; 10 news.google.com/newspapers?nid=1876&dat=19710309&id=XXgsAAAAIBAJ&sjid=HswEAAAAIBAJ&pg=4974,1416213.

7   Timms.

8   Markusen.

9   Dan McCourt, "September 25 in Yankee History; Take Him Downtown, September 25, 2012. takehimdowntown.com/yankee-history/september-25-in-yankee-history/.

10 Bill Fox, "Hosley Cut; Slot Open for Hurler," *Toledo Blade*, March 21, 1972, 28.

11 Markusen.

12 Fox, "Hosley Cut."

13 Markusen.

14 Bill Fox, "Hosley Tames His Swing: Mud Hen catcher Concentrating on Making Contact," *Toledo Blade*, April 24, 1972, 25.

15 Tom Loomis, "Hens Cause Helped by Detroit Dealings," *Toledo Blade*, April 3, 1973; 30.

16 Markusen.

17 Loomis.

18 Markusen.

19 Markusen.

20 Markusen.

21 Markusen.

22 Markusen.

23 Markusen.

24 GoUpstate.com

Deron Johnson

by John Vorperian

Deron Roger Johnson, labeled the "next Mickey Mantle," spent 16 seasons as a major-league slugger. His finest year was not as a Bronx Bomber but as a Cincinnati Red. A dual football and baseball interscholastic sports star, the San Diego native excelled on the gridiron. Johnson played end, linebacker, kicker, and punter for San Diego High School. In 1955 he scored 15 touchdowns for the Cavers as the team captured the Southern California championship. His high-school football coach, Duane Maley, said Johnson was "the top player I have ever coached…the easiest kid to coach you've ever met. If he has a bad habit, it's escaped me." He was indeed, as the *San Diego Union* wrote, a "coach's dream."[1] Johnson's baseball coach, Les Cassie, said the All-American end was among the top athletes ever to come out of San Diego High School.

Pursued by several colleges, Johnson was offered numerous football scholarships, including one from Notre Dame, but Johnson turned down the Fighting Irish and the other schools. Upon graduation from high school in 1956, having been also sought by the Yankees, Braves, Red Sox, Indians, and Pirates, Johnson signed with New York Yankees scout Gordon "Deacon" Jones to a Class-D contract for $1,000 a month.

Johnson avoided being a Bonus Baby, who by the rules at the time was someone who signed a contract for more than $4,000 and had to be kept on the major-league roster for two years. Brent P. Kelley in his book *They Too Wore Pinstripes* showed that New York skipper Casey Stengel simply did not play 1954's Frank Leja or 1955 signee Tommy Carroll. So by mid-1956 the Yankees front office opted out of the Bonus Baby game. Kelley wrote that Johnson had decided he would rather be in the minor leagues playing every day. The Kearney club of the Class-D Nebraska State League played only 63 games over two months. Thus, the net

deal "was essentially the major-league minimum ($6,000 a year)"[2] and with a good season Johnson could be given a raise. Johnson figured correctly.

At Kearney the 17-year-old outfielder led the league in total bases (167), runs scored (70), RBIs (78), and home runs (24). He was named to the circuit's all-star team. He also tied for the league lead in double plays by outfielders with four. The next year, the young phenom was promoted to Class-A Binghamton. Again he made the all-star team, and led the Eastern League with 279 total bases, 103 runs scored, and 26 home runs. In 1958, Johnson moved up to Triple-A Richmond (International League), where he clubbed 27 doubles, 5 triples, and 27 homers, and was selected as an IL all-star. In addition to the outfield, the Californian was called upon to handle third base. The year also brought the first of military duties that would occa-

sionally interrupt his ballplaying career. In 1958 and 1959 Johnson served in the US Army for six months under the Reserve Training Program. On the field, his 1959 and 1960 seasons were spent with Richmond (25 and 27 HRs respectively).

Called up to the Yankees in September 1960, Johnson made his major-league debut on the 20th. The 22-year-old pinch-hit in the ninth inning of a 1-1 tie game between New York and Washington with Bill Skowron on second base. Facing Senators southpaw Hal Woodeshick, Johnson advanced Skowron to third with a fly to center. The Yankees won, 2-1, in the 11th.

Overall, Johnson donned the pinstripes for 19 games in 1960 and '61. The Big Apple sports media had tagged him as a replacement for Mickey Mantle. But that never came about. On June 14, 1961, Johnson joined numerous other would-be Bombers in being sucked into the NY-KC trade pipeline. The Athletics got Johnson and right-handed pitcher Art Ditmar for lefty Bud Daley.

At Kansas City in 1961, Johnson batted .216. In October he was recalled to active Army duty and served until August 1962. The remainder of the 1962 season he batted a paltry .105. That October he wed Lucille DeMaria. They had three children, two sons, Deron Jr. and Dominick, and a daughter, Dena. In April 1963 Kansas City sold Johnson to the Cincinnati Reds, who assigned him to their San Diego Padres team in the Pacific Coast League.

At San Diego, 1963 was a honeymoon of a year. Johnson returned to his native California and was golden. He topped the Pacific Coast League with 33 home runs, tied for fifth with 91 RBIs, and was picked as the first baseman on the PCL all-star team. His performance pushed him onto the Reds' 1964 roster, where he remained for four seasons. Johnson later said of his full major-league season, 1964, "That was my first year. That was a hell of a pennant race. There was five teams right there: us, the Cardinals, the Phillies, the Braves, and the Giants. There was so many damned teams there, if you won one day you'd go from fourth to first. It was really fun. Once we were tied for first. Every

day you go you know it means something."[3] Cincinnati did not capture the NL flag. In 477 at-bats, as their starting first baseman, Johnson hit .273, with 24 doubles, 4 triples, 21 home runs, and 79 RBIs.

Johnson was moved to third base and had a banner year in 1965. He led the league with 130 RBIs, despite typically batting fifth or sixth in the order. He shared top rank in sacrifice flies with 10 and batted a career high .287 with 30 doubles, 7 triples, and 32 home runs. Johnson made *The Sporting News* and Associated Press all-star teams as a third baseman, and came in fourth for the NL MVP award. Johnson told Brent Kelley, "I had a good year. I was on a good ballclub. We had some good hitters. We had Pete Rose and Vada Pinson. I had Frank Robinson hitting in front of me. I had a hell of a year, really."[4]

After a .257 season in 1966, Johnson fell to .224 in 1967 with 13 home runs, 53 RBIs, and 104 strikeouts. After the season the Reds dealt him on October 10 to the Atlanta Braves for outfielder Mack Jones, pitcher Jay Ritchie, and first baseman Jim Beauchamp. Johnson hit .208 with Atlanta in 127 games and lasted just a season. On December 3, 1968, the Braves sold him to the Philadelphia Phillies in a cash deal.

The move to Philadelphia revived the slugger in Johnson. From 1969 to 1973, he clubbed 88 homers, had 304 RBIs, and hit 82 doubles despite playing in only 12 games in 1973 before being traded to Oakland. His most productive year was 1971; Johnson batted .265, garnered 95 RBIs, and hit 34 home runs. He homered 22 times at home, breaking Del Ennis's 1950 Philadelphia record. Further proof of Johnson's long-ball skill was evident on July 10 and 11, 1971, as he belted four consecutive home runs against the Montreal Expos, three of them coming on the 11th.

On May 2, 1973, after nearly a decade of playing in the National League, Johnson found himself back in the American League, as the Phils traded him to the Oakland A's for minor-league third baseman-outfielder Jack Bastable. Johnson clocked 19 homers and had 81 RBIs, for Charlie Finley's Athletics. The switch got him a World Series ring as the A's bested the New

York Mets in the '73 fall classic. Johnson entered baseball history as the first player to hit 20 home runs in a season divided between both leagues.

Johnson was 1-for-10 as the A's DH in the ALCS against the Orioles. He pinch hit in the first five games of the Series, collecting a double in Game Two and a single in Game Four, and played first base in Games Six and Seven, adding another single.

Johnson was on the A's disabled list for 15 days in April 1974. On June 24 he was released on waivers to the Milwaukee Brewers. (The Brewers later assigned hurler Bill Parsons to complete the transaction.) On September 7, 1974, the Brewers sold Johnson to the Boston Red Sox for the stretch drive. He hit .120 with two RBIs. The Red Sox released him after the season.

On April 5, 1975, as a free agent, the 36-year-old veteran signed with the White Sox. Chicago GM Roland Hemond said the Red Sox did not need Johnson because Tony Conigliaro had a successful spring comeback and they did not want to stand in the way of Johnson.

In 148 games for the White Sox in 1975, Johnson hit a team-leading 18 home runs and drove in 72 runs. On September 21, after Jim Rice had been hit by a pitch that broke his left hand, the Red Sox acquired Johnson from Chicago for cash and a player to be named later (catcher Chuck Erickson). Johnson's Red Sox role was to play first base and serve as designated hitter. He was 6-for-10 in the three games in which he appeared. The Red Sox went to the World Series but Johnson had joined the team too late to be eligible for the Series roster. He played sparingly in 1976 and was released on June 4, after which he retired as a player.

In all or part of 16 major-league seasons, Johnson played in 1,765 games and batted .244 with 245 home runs, 1,447 hits, and 923 RBIs.

A Poway, California, resident, Johnson owned a construction company in nearby San Diego and operated a 40-acre cattle ranch. Nevertheless he still maintained his contact with baseball. In 1978 he returned to the

Pacific Coast League and piloted Salt Lake City to a 72-65 second-place finish. The club lost in the playoff semifinals to Albuquerque.

In 1979 Johnson became a hitting coach for the California Angels. In addition to the Halos (1979-80 and '89-91), Johnson coached for the Mets ('81), Phillies ('82-84), Mariners ('85-86), and White Sox ('87).

In June 1991 Johnson was diagnosed with lung cancer. After a long fight with the illness, he succumbed on April 23, 1992. He was survived by his wife Lucy Ann, his sons Deron Jr. and Dominick, and a daughter, Dena. He is buried at Dearborn Memorial Park, Poway, California. Over his 28-year baseball life, he told Hall of Fame researchers, his greatest thrills were having played in the 1973 World Series for the Athletics and hitting four home runs in a row for the Phillies in 1971.

SOURCES

Kelley, Brent P., *They Too Wore Pinstripes* (Jefferson, North Carolina: McFarland & Company, 1998).

Pietrusza, David, Matthew Silverman, and Michael Gershman, eds., *Baseball: The Biographical Encyclopedia* (Kingston, New York: Total/Sports Illustrated, 2000).

Porter, David L., ed.. *Biographical Dictionary of American Sports: Baseball,* Revised and Expanded, Edition G-P (Westport, Connecticut: Greenwood Press, 2000).

Thorn, John, Pete Palmer, and Michael Gershman, eds., with Matthew Silverman, Sean Lahman, and Greg Spira, *Total Baseball*, 7th Edition (Kingston, New York: Total Sports Publishing, 2001).

New York Times, April 25, 1992, 12 (obituary).

San Diego Union-Tribune

National Baseball Hall of Fame library, Deron Johnson file.

John Pardon (minor-league information).

Baseballlibrary.com

Retrosheet.org

NOTES

1   *San Diego Union,* December 2, 1955.

2   Brent P. Kelley, *They Too Wore Pinstripes* (Jefferson, North Carolina: McFarland & Company, 1998), 94.

3   Brent P. Kelley, 95.

4   Ibid.

Jay Johnstone

By Rory Costello

The flake—"an odd or eccentric player; a kidder or comic"[1]—is an all-but-vanished species in major-league baseball these days. In 2003, writer Dave Joseph lamented, "Sadly, there are fewer creative thinkers these days in baseball. There are fewer flakes, if you will, who break up the monotony of an endless season played, for the most part, by robotic athletes afraid to express opinion or originality."[2]

Outfielder Jay Johnstone was one of the premier flakes in big-league history. As Dave Joseph added, a bunch of tattoos doesn't fill the bill. "You need talent. You need smarts. You need to have a mind of your own and give something to the game." Johnstone qualified on all counts. He was good enough to play 15 full seasons in the majors and parts of five others from 1966 to 1985. He was largely a platoon and role player, starting over 100 games in only three of those years—but he had a solid lefty bat, providing 102 career home runs and a .267 batting average.

He was also one of the game's craftiest pranksters and better storytellers, as he recounted in three entertaining books. His gags were innumerable, and among the best was trapping Tommy Lasorda (whom he liked to impersonate by padding himself with pillows) in the manager's room at Dodgertown by tying his doorknob to a tree and stealing the mouthpiece from his telephone. Johnstone's maxim was never to hang around to see the results of a prank, because that gives you away as the perpetrator. It's even better to frame someone else, as he did by surreptitiously wiping chocolate on Jerry Reuss's pants leg after sticking a gooey chocolate brownie in Steve Garvey's glove. "In perhaps his greatest stunt, he slipped into the team's Dodgertown clubhouse with carpenter's tools and cut Ron Cey's locker down to penguin size, putting a tiny stool in front of it."[3]

John William Johnstone, Jr. was born on November 20, 1945, in Manchester, Connecticut. His family moved to California when Jay was "just a three-year-old pup."[4] His father, Jack Johnstone, was in combat in the South Pacific with the US Army in World War II.[5] During the war, he met an Australian woman, Audrey Whebell, and they married. "At one time he was an accountant back east," said Jay in 2011, "but when we moved, he was with Supreme and Driftwood Dairy." Jack and Audrey had three children, of whom Jay was the first, followed by a brother and a sister.

In 1968 Johnstone recalled to Ed Rumill of the *Christian Science Monitor* that his father greatly influenced his competitive spirit. "I'd get three hits in a Little League game and be afraid to face him. He'd want to know why I didn't get four. I'd always know what his reaction would be."[6] Jack Johnstone was good enough to sign with the St. Louis Cardinals, but he

never got a chance to play pro ball because he went into the service.

For a while, the Johnstone family lived in Arcadia, a northeastern suburb of Los Angeles next to Pasadena. Then they moved to West Covina, which is about 20 miles east of downtown Los Angeles.[7] Author Kevin Nelson described Jay's early years in his book *The Golden Game: The Story of California Baseball*. "The lefty-hitting, righty-throwing Johnstone easily moved up through the youth ranks: Little League, Pony League, American Legion, and Edgewood High, where he starred in football and basketball in addition to baseball." He quoted Johnstone on "the carefree life of a suburban Southern California teenager: 'Crewcuts, Pendleton shirts, white socks, loafers, cars, hangin' out in the sunshine, listening to music, playing sports, and looking at girls. What else was there?"[8]

In 1976 Johnstone told Allen Lewis of the *Philadelphia Inquirer*, "I was a T-formation quarterback in football, and that might have been my best sport then. I had 35 college football scholarship offers, and I had already signed a letter of intent for one of them. Then the Angels came along and I decided to play baseball." On June 30, 1963, the 17-year-old signed for a bonus of $35,000 in progressive installments, "plus a smaller amount for my parents."[9] The scouts were Tufie Hashem and Ross "Rosey" Gilhousen, who reported to California Angels farm director Roland Hemond.

Johnstone reported to San José in the California League, where he batted .252 in 48 games. Returning to the Bees in 1964, he improved to .291 in 126 games. After that season, a month before his 20th birthday, Jay enlisted in the Marine Corps Reserve. He received basic training in Camp Pendleton and was able to play the 1965 season, moving up to El Paso in the Texas League (Double-A) after hitting .301 in 97 more games at San Jose. He then served at a naval base in Los Alamitos, receiving his discharge in the spring of 1966 without ever being called to serve "in country" in Vietnam.[10]

In 81 games for Seattle of the Pacific Coast League, Johnstone hit .340 with 7 homers and 42 RBIs in 1966.

The Angels called him up after they learned that Rick Reichardt was suffering from a congenital kidney blockage (Reichardt's right kidney was removed soon afterward, ending his season). Johnstone made his major-league debut on July 30, 1966. In his first three games, he went 6-for-12. His first RBI was a game-winner, a seventh-inning single to center at Anaheim Stadium against the New York Yankees. "I like everything I've seen of him," California manager Bill Rigney said.[11]

Though he is best remembered as a corner outfielder, Johnstone came up as a center fielder, and he was well regarded defensively. However, he picked up a lot of pointers on fielding from one of the best in the business at that time: his roommate, veteran Jimmy Piersall. "I thought I had outfielding all figured out," Johnstone told Ed Rumill. "He changed it completely. He taught me everything. I'd say that conservatively, he made a 50 percent improvement in my fielding."[12]

One wonders how much of Piersall's zaniness rubbed off on the rookie too — or if in fact there was further for Jay to go there. Eight years later, though, Johnstone said, "Jimmy Piersall once told me that as long as it's not derogatory, get your name in the paper any way you can. That's never been my goal, but I never minded all the talk about being a flake."[13]

Johnstone got off to a good start in 1967. As Bill Rigney recalled, "Then he fouled a ball off his ankle and never was right. In fact, he'd taken the center-field job away from José Cardenal, temporarily at least, when he was injured."[14] He slumped and fell below the Mendoza Line, and after Independence Day the Angels sent him down to Seattle. He returned for September and (after Cardenal had been traded) made the Opening Day roster again in 1968.

That May, Joe Gordon (then a special batting instructor for the Angels) said, "Jay has all the abilities you expect in a good young hitter. ... He may need a little more time. But he has a natural bat." Johnstone also gave credit to his minor-league manager, Rocky Bridges. "Rocky knocked the impatience out of me."[15] It was much the same story in 1968, though, as the Angrls optioned him to Triple-A again in June.

At some point during his early years with the Angels, Johnstone acquired a lasting nickname: Moon Man. Catcher Bob "Buck" Rodgers liked to tell one version of the story. "One day he lost a ball in the sun, but when he came back to the bench he said, 'I lost it in the moon.'"[16] The connections with outer space were fitting, especially when the whole nation was watching the Apollo missions. In 1981, though, Johnstone told Jim Murray of the *Los Angeles Times* that it came about as he sneaked back into his hotel room after curfew, cat-burglar style, and told another roommate, "Out of the way, you're standing in my moonlight."[17]

Johnstone got his first taste of winter ball in Puerto Rico in 1968-69, helping the Ponce Leones win the league championship. He told author Thomas Van Hyning about having to help push the team bus over mountain roads, adding, "I think I had a better experience, culture-wise, off the field than playing the game."[18]

Johnstone then set a personal high in games played (148) and at-bats (540) during the 1969 season. He posted a batting line that was not bad but not outstanding either: .270-10-59. He tailed off to .238-11-39 in 1970, and that November, the Angels sent him to the Chicago White Sox as part of a six-player deal in which they got back Gold Glove center fielder Ken Berry. "They never seemed willing to give me a steady job and say they'd give me time to develop no matter what I did," said Jay in 1976.[19]

Johnstone's first season with the White Sox was good: .260 with a career-high 16 homers. But as he said in 1976, "They told me they wanted me swinging for home runs after that, and I got all fouled up." His average dropped to an anemic .188 in 1972. He corrected his bad batting habits, though, with the help of coaching from Benny Lefebvre, father of Jim Lefebvre. "Benny put me on isometrics and weight training and he changed my stance completely. … He made me shorten [my swing] up, and become a line-drive hitter."[20]

During spring training 1973, Johnstone asked for his release after refusing to take the maximum 20 percent pay cut that the White Sox wanted to impose. At the end of March, he caught on with the Oakland A's; owner Charles O. Finley was the only one willing to give him a chance.[21] He was on the A's roster in April and early May, as well as July, but he also had to return to Triple-A for a while, playing 69 games for Tucson in the PCL. He was not on the postseason roster as the A's won their second of three straight World Series.

Returning to the Puerto Rican Winter League for the winter of 1973-74, Johnstone hit over .300 for the Caguas Criollos. He tied for the league lead in RBIs with Benny Ayala at 46. His manager was Bobby Wine, a coach with the Philadelphia Phillies. When spring training came around, since Oakland was overloaded with outfielders, Finley arranged a tryout with the St. Louis Cardinals. Jay hit well and looked to have made the club, but roster machinations kept him from playing a game for the Cards.

"I had a chance to go to Japan, for a lot of money," Johnstone said. "But I knew I could play in the majors and I wanted to prove it." Shortly thereafter, on Bobby Wine's recommendation, he signed a minor-league deal with the Phillies.[22] He played 57 games for their top affiliate, Toledo in the International League—but after that, he never had to go back to the minors. Mud Hens manager Jim Bunning recommended him to the big club, even though the two had nearly come to blows because Johnstone liked to push the no-nonsense Bunning's buttons with his little antics.[23]

Johnstone played some of his best ball in Philadelphia, just as the team was climbing from the cellar of the NL East and developing into the club that reached the playoffs in three straight years from 1976 to 1978. In 1975 the Phillies finished second, and Johnstone—coming off a .346-9-46 winter for Caguas—hit .329-7-54 in 122 games. He followed up with a .318-5-53 line for the 1976 club. During the playoffs against the Cincinnati Reds that year, it wasn't Jay's fault that the Phillies were swept in three games. He went 7-for-9 with a walk.

"I'm proving to a lot of people they were wrong about me," Johnstone told Allen Lewis after the season. "They're the reason I've worked so hard to get where I am." Lewis described the hours Johnstone put in taking extra batting practice and honing his swing by hitting the ball off a tee.[24]

Johnstone had another good year in 1977 (.284-15-59), but after a poor start the following year, Philadelphia traded him to the New York Yankees on June 14 with Bobby Brown for Rawly Eastwick. There he won his first World Series ring, although he saw no action in the playoffs and got into just two games without a plate appearance as the Yankees beat the Los Angeles Dodgers for the championship.

While he was with the Yankees, Johnstone played under manager Billy Martin, whom he described as "when it comes to strategy, the most astute man that I'd ever met."[25] Although playing time was again scanty for him in the first half of the 1979 season, that changed on June 15, when the Yankees dealt him to the San Diego Padres for reliever Dave Wehrmeister. Jay hit well for the Padres (.294 in 225 at-bats), though he had no homers. He became a free agent that November and signed about a month later with the Dodgers, where he spent two seasons and a fraction of a third—and his exploits as a prankster flowered fully.

Johnstone was part of his second World Series champion team during the strike year of 1981. He was hitless in two at-bats during the NL Championship Series against Montreal, but he went 2-for-3 against the Yankees, including a two-run pinch-hit homer in Game Four that brought the Dodgers to within a run at 6-5, in a game that they wound up winning 8-7. *The Dodgers Encyclopedia* said that it "may have been the key hit of the entire Series."[26]

Los Angeles released the veteran, by then 36 years old, in late May 1982. Within a week, though, he signed with the Chicago Cubs. He spent a couple of moderately productive seasons there, but his at-bats were halved in 1983 and again in 1984, when he served largely as a pinch-hitter (and his pranks failed to amuse manager Jim Frey). After obtaining Davey Lopes from Oakland, the Cubs released Johnstone in September 1984. Cubs general manager Dallas Green hoped to have him reinstated as a player, or bring him back as a coach, but he was deprived of another chance to go to the playoffs.

In February 1985 Johnstone returned to the Dodgers as a free agent. Tom Lasorda had a fondness for keeping veteran pinch-hitters at the end of his bench, men like Manny Mota, Vic Davalillo, and José Morales. The 39-year-old Johnstone spent the entire season with Los Angeles—albeit with a long stretch on the disabled list. He delivered two hits and a walk in 17 games without appearing once in the field. Despite such sparse activity, he remained on the postseason roster, going 0-for-1 against the Cardinals. At the end of October, the Dodgers released him, ending his big-league career.

Johnstone then focused on his auto-parts business, which he had been pursuing part-time for several years. Yet even while he was still active, he had begun to make good use of all the stories he had accumulated across his 20 big-league seasons. With co-author Rick Talley, he published his first book, *Temporary Insanity*, in 1985. *Over the Edge* followed in 1988, and 1990 brought the duo's last effort to date, *Some of My Best Friends Are Crazy*. This last was subtitled "Baseball's Favorite Lunatic Goes in Search of His Peers."

By then Johnstone had moved into broadcasting. He was the original host of the ESPN show *The Lighter Side of Sports* in 1987 and 1988. He hosted a couple of other shows in a similar vein, *Baseball's Funniest Pranks* and *Super Sports Follies*. He was also with the Yankees in 1989 and 1990 (working with John Sterling on WABC's radio broadcasts) and the Phillies in 1992 and 1993 (for the Philadelphia cable channel PRISM, with Chris Wheeler and former teammate Garry Maddox).

Johnstone left PRISM by mutual consent in 1994. He took three years off, visiting US troops in Saudi Arabia, Kuwait, and Germany. He also held clinics in Japan under the aegis of the World Children's Baseball

Federation and visited American children's schools in London, Paris, and Brussels.[27]

After that Johnstone has kept busy in a new variety of ways. In the late 1990s he helped started a part-time sports auction/charity fundraising business called Sporthings, which developed into Sporthings & More, handling items from other areas including entertainment and music. He also traveled the country as a speaker at both corporate and social events. He participated in baseball clinics, fantasy camps, and charity golf tournaments. In 1987 he began hosting his own Charity/Celebrity Golf Tournament every January on Martin Luther King's birthday to raise money for children in need. He also narrated several videos, including *The Hitter's Commandments*, and remained involved in broadcasting with the Fox network.

In 2006 Johnstone became part of a group that announced the formation of the independent Continental Baseball League. This circuit operated for four seasons (2007-2010) with four to six teams based in New Mexico, Louisiana, and Texas. He talked about the league in 2011. "Bob Ibach, who was a friend of mine and a PR man with the Cubs, started it with Ron Baron. The idea was to help players get back to the majors or reach a higher level. But it was always set back, either by some unusual act like a flood or by problems with financially unstable owners. They persevered, but it got to be too much. Ron Baron lost about half a million dollars. But it was a great idea for a while, a lot of fun."

August 2010 brought the news that Johnstone had become annual spokesman for Hope4Heroes, a nonprofit organization designed to benefit military veterans. Given his father's background and his own in the military (he served for four years total in the Marine Reserve), his support for this cause was not surprising. He said, "I am really, really excited about this. ... I wanted to come back and do my part to help out."

Johnstone and his wife, Mary Jayne Saunders, were married on November 25, 1967. Mary Jayne was an actress, starting as a girl of 5 in the late 1940s. Her career in movies and later TV continued until she got married, whereupon she retired from acting. The Johnstones had one daughter, Mary Jayne Sarah.

As far back as 1990, Johnstone saw flakes and pranksters passing from the major-league scene. He pointed to the media, saying, "[Players] can't afford to do anything crazy, because they're afraid it will end up in the papers and make them look bad. ... I couldn't have the overall, wide fun that I used to have when you were able to get away with a lot more. Times change, the game's changed."[28] Jay Johnstone, however, remained an easygoing and fan-friendly personality.

Grateful acknowledgment to Jay Johnstone for his memories (telephone interview, June 14, 2011).

Quotes on the Flakiness and Pranks of Jay Johnstone

"What makes him unusual is that he thinks he's normal and everyone else is nuts."

– Danny Ozark

"I don't rehearse anything. I just do what my instincts tell me to."[29]

"There are a lot of peaks and valleys in this game, and this was a way for me to come back up. Some guys to turn to drugs; some guys couldn't cope; some guys, the stress got to them. My way was to make people laugh. And laughter has helped me go on to the next level each time."[30]

SOURCES

baseball-reference.com

retrosheet.org

sporthings.net

imdb.com

Crescioni Benítez, José A., *El Béisbol Profesional Boricua* (San Juan, Puerto Rico: Aurora Comunicación Integral, Inc., 1997).

NOTES

1 Paul Dickson, *The New Dickson Baseball Dictionary* (New York: Harvest Books, 1999), 198.

2   Dave Joseph, "Baseball Aches for Flakes," *Baseball Digest*, August 2003, 64.

3   Gordon Edes, "Johnstone back in Dodger Blue, But Who Knows for How Long?" *Los Angeles Times/Washington Post* News Service, April 13, 1985.

4   Ed Rumill, "Johnstone Learns What 'Counts' in Playing Hitters," *Baseball Digest*, May 1968.

5   "Jay Johnstone steps to the plate for U.S. service veterans." Mysanantonio.com, August 2, 2010.

6   Rumill.

7   Rumill.

8   Kevin Nelson, *The Golden Game: The Story of California Baseball* (Berkeley, California: Heyday Books, 2004), 310.

9   Alle Lewis, "Jay Johnstone's Long Journey to Success," *Baseball Digest*, December 1976, 57.

10   Nelson, 310.

11   "Angels' Jay Johnstone Helps Only His Team," Associated Press, August 2, 1966.

12   Rumill.

13   Lewis, 61.

14   Rumill.

15   Rumill.

16   Paul Dickson, *Baseball's Greatest Quotations* (New York: HarperCollins, 2008), 384.

17   Jim Murray, "Jay Johnstone: The Man Who Fell to Earth," *Los Angeles Times*, September 4, 1981.

18   Thomas Van Hyning, *Puerto Rico's Winter League* (Jefferson, North Carolina: McFarland & Co., 1995), 39.

19   Lewis, 57.

20   Lewis, 58.

21   Lewis, 59.

22   Lewis, 59-60.

23   Frank Dolson, *Jim Bunning: Baseball and Beyond* (Philadelphia: Temple University Press, 1998), 168-170.

24   Dolson, 57, 60.

25   Brian Jensen, *Where Have All Our Yankees Gone?* (Lanham, Maryland: Taylor Trade Publishing, 2004), 139.

26   William F. McNeil, *The Dodgers Encyclopedia* (Champaign, Illinois: Sports Publishing LLC, 2003, second edition), 239.

27   Jensen.

28   Mike McGovern, "Jay Johnstone sees light side." *Reading* (Pennsylvania) *Eagle*, January 19, 1990, 11.

29   Verdi, Bob. "Pranks for the memories." *Chicago Tribune*, April 16, 1979: D4.

30   McGovern, op. cit., loc. cit.

Paul Lindblad

By Paul Hofmann

Paul Lindblad wasn't one of the Oakland A's most celebrated stars or eccentric personalities, but he was a valuable part of a formidable bullpen that contributed to the team's string of five consecutive division championships and three consecutive World Series titles. Though somewhat overlooked in the annals of Athletics history, Lindblad was without question an integral part of the Swingin' A's dynasty of the early 1970s.

Paul Aaron Linblad was born on August 9, 1941, to George and Helen (Walters) Lindblad in Chanute, Kansas.[1] He was the oldest of five boys. Chanute, a mill town in the southeast corner of the state, had 11,000 residents at the time. The Lindblads settled in Chanute after George was discharged from the Navy and went to work for the Santa Fe Railroad. The job required George to spend a great deal of time away from the family, commuting to and from Kansas City. George Lindblad was a strict and highly critical father.[2] Although he always wanted Paul to play professional baseball, he rarely encouraged him or was satisfied with his son's performance on the field. Over time, this contributed to a strained relationship between the two. Paul's mother was a homemaker.

Paul Lindblad's journey to the major leagues is a story of love, persistence, and faith. His baseball career began on the baseball diamond in Katy Park. He began playing Little League baseball, progressed to American Legion baseball, and was introduced to the world of semipro baseball on the Kansas prairies. It was there that he fell in love with the game of baseball and also the woman he would marry.

Paul, known as Junior, was a standout athlete.[3] He attended Chanute High School, where by all accounts he was a good student. He did well in math and drafting, subjects that would serve him well when he entered the construction business after baseball. Paul was a three-year letterman on the basketball team and

the 1959 state high school champion in the javelin.[4] The school did not have a baseball team.

American Legion baseball dominated the landscape of rural Midwest America and Lindblad led the Chanute Legion team to a regional title and a berth in the state tournament, where the team lost by one run in the first round.

After high school, Lindblad attended Chanute Junior College, which was conveniently located in the same building as the high school. He played semipro baseball, threw the javelin (he finished second at the National Junior College Championships in 1961), and continued his relationship with his high-school sweetheart, Kathy, who was still attending high school.

After earning an associate's degree in business from Chanute Junior College, Lindblad was awarded an

athletic scholarship to play baseball at the University of Kansas. He arrived in Lawrence, Kansas, in the fall of 1961 and found it difficult to be away from Kathy. He frequently made the 100-mile trip back home to Chanute to see her on weekends, and they decided to marry. The Lindblads were married on November 4, 1961. Soon after, Lindblad withdrew from school, moved to Kansas City, and took a job with the Sante Fe Railroad. He worked for the railroad for almost a year before signing a contract with the Kansas City Athletics prior to the 1963 season. His $2,000 signing bonus helped the young couple who by this time were the proud parents of a daughter they named Cindy.

The Athletics sent Lindblad to the Burlington Bees of the Class A Midwestern League, where the 21-year-old established himself as a bona-fide major-league prospect, winning 10 games with a 1.58 earned-run average before a sore elbow forced the Bees to shut him down. The elbow pain was severe enough for the A's to send Lindblad to the Mayo Clinic to have it checked. The pain was so severe, his wife said, that he questioned his future in baseball.[5] But there was no structural damage to his arm and a winter of rest was all that was required.

In 1964 Lindblad was assigned to the Birmingham Barons of the Double-A Southern League. The Barons were the first integrated professional sports team in Alabama, and Lindblad observed firsthand the segregation that continued to dominate the South. His teammates included future Athletics Bert Campaneris, Tommie Reynolds, and John "Blue Moon" Odom. (The team's story and the 1964 Southern League pennant race are chronicled in Larry Colton's *Southern League: A True Story of Baseball, Civil Rights, and the Deep South's Most Compelling Pennant Race*.)

Lindblad had an up-and-down season for Birmingham, winning his first five starts, then falling into a slump in June and dropping four straight. It was the first time the lefthander had to deal with the ebbs and flows of pitching professionally. Despite struggling in June, Lindblad earned a $1,000 promotion bonus after sticking with Birmingham for more than 90 days. The bonus again came in handy as the Lindblads were

expecting their second daughter, whom they named Paula. He finished 1964 with a respectable 11-8 season, 3.32 ERA, and 139 strikeouts, the highest strikeout total of his career. Lindblad was never an overpowering pitcher. His fastball topped out at around 90 mph and his best pitch was his slider. His greatest asset on the mound was his pinpoint control, the ability to put any pitch wherever he wanted it. Lynn Ranabargar, a longtime Chanute resident, said, "If he wanted a curveball low and outside, that is exactly where it was. If he wanted a fastball high and tight, all he had to know was how far off the chin they want it and that's where it went."[6]

Understanding that he was not an overpowering pitcher and that his future in baseball depended on his ability to stay healthy and be a fundamentally sound player, Lindblad jogged daily basis and ran extra wind sprints to keep himself in the best shape possible. He also took great pride in making sure he made the routine plays.

The 1965 season brought with it a promotion to Kansas City's Triple-A affiliate, the Vancouver Mounties of the Pacific Coast League. In 28 starts Lindblad posted a 12-11 record and a 3.67 ERA, which earned him a late-season call-up to the A's, a team on its way to and finishing last in the American League. On September 15, 1965, he made his major-league debut against the soon-to-be crowned American League champion Minnesota Twins. He tossed a perfect seventh inning, striking out Bob Allison and Jimmie Hall. He pitched in three more games for the Athletics that fall. On September 22 he suffered his first major-league loss after yielding a fifth inning, two-run homer to Washington Senators shortstop Eddie Brinkman. Despite an unimpressive 11.05 ERA in 7⅓ innings, he was in the major leagues to stay.

During his early years in professional baseball, Lindblad played winter ball in Venezuela and the Caribbean. During this time he became interested in collecting coins. When he wasn't playing ball, Lindblad explored his surroundings and often purchased old coins from the local people. Later he took his numismatic interests to the extreme of buying a metal detector, which he carried with him on road trips. Bruce Markusen wrote regarding Lindblad's penchant for searching for hidden treasures in *Baseball's Last Dynasty: Charlie Finley's Oakland A's:*

Don Mincher, who played with Lindblad in Washington, Oakland, and Texas remembered the left-handed reliever as a man of boundless energy, who always needed to keep busy. Mincher recalled Lindblad's trademark habit of searching for money with a metal detector. "He'd go to the ballparks and look for pennies and nickels all day long." By Lindblad's own estimation he collected an average of $11 per city on road trips and gave the money to his children, who like Lindblad himself enjoyed collecting coins. When the metal detector beeped, Lindblad used a small screwdriver to dig into the turf and warning track. Yet, Lindblad had to be careful not to dig too deep, for fear of striking a water hose or electrical line. Trips to Cleveland's Municipal Stadium posed a special problem, since groundskeepers Harold and Marshall Bossard took special pride in maintaining the grass field. "If I dig too deep into the Indians' field," Lindblad said, "those two guys would tan my hide."[7]

The A's broke camp in Bradenton, Florida, in 1966 with the 23-year-old Lindblad on the pitching staff. As a minor leaguer he had been used almost exclusively as a starter. However, his role with the A's was less defined and the next two seasons would go a long way toward shaping his role as a long and middle reliever. In 1966 and 1967 he started 24 games and worked in 60 as a reliever. On August 12, 1966, against the Minnesota Twins, Lindblad threw wild on a pickoff attempt at second base, allowing the Twins' Cesar Tovar to advance to third. Tovar then stole home off a rattled Lindblad. But the throwing error was noteworthy in that Lindblad would not commit another error until May 6, 1974, a record 385 errorless games streak that covered nearly eight years. He finished 1967 with a 5-8 record, with six saves and a 3.58 ERA.

On July 16, 1967, Lindblad tossed a three-hit shutout against the Chicago White Sox at Comiskey Park. It was the only complete game of his career. He made only 12 more starts the rest of his career. The Athletics struggled on the field and at the gate in 1967, winning only 10 of their final 40 games and drawing just 726,639 fans all season. Fearing a collapse of the franchise, baseball owners allowed owner Charles Finley to relocate the team to Oakland. The Lindblads were excited and nervous about moving their young family so far away from Kansas.[8]

Lindblad's first season in Oakland saw him settle into a role that would define the remainder of his major-league career. He appeared in 48 games, 47 in relief, and compiled a 4-3 record with two saves and a 2.40 ERA. He followed with two more solid seasons in 1969 and 1970. In 1969 he pitched in 60 games, winning nine and losing =six with a 4.14 ERA. Soon after the end of the 1969 season, Paul and Kathy welcomed their third child, a son they named Troy. In 1970 Lindblad made 62 appearances on his way to recording an 8-2 mark with three saves and a 2.70 ERA. Just as the 28-year-old Lindblad was establishing himself as a major leaguer, so too were the A's establishing themselves as contenders. The perpetual doormats of the American League finished 1970 in second place, nine games behind the Twins in the American League's West Division.

Early in the 1971 season Lindblad's career took an unexpected turn. On May 8 he was dealt with Frank Fernandez and Don Mincher to the Washington Senators for first baseman Mike Epstein and left-handed reliever Darold Knowles. Both players were key acquisitions that allowed the A's to get over the hump. After being an integral part of the Athletics rebuilding process, Lindblad now found himself playing for a Senators club that was battling the Cleveland Indians for last place in the American League East. A year later the team relocated to Arlington, Texas, and became the Texas Rangers. Lindblad spent two productive seasons with the Senators/Rangers franchise. In 1971 he appeared in 43 games for the Senators, finishing with a 6-4 record with eight saves and a 2.58 ERA. With Texas in 1972, he led all American League hurlers with 66 appearances and finished the season with a 5-8 mark, nine saves, and a 2.62 ERA. During these two years Lindblad solidified himself as one of the most reliable left-handed relievers in the American League. Meanwhile, his former teammates in Oakland were celebrating their 1972 World Series title.

In November 1972 Finley reacquired Lindblad in exchange for A's farmhand Bill McNulty and outfielder Brant Alyea. Finley's revolving-door style of managing player personnel often resulted in his reacquiring players he had previously traded, and when Finley dealt Lindblad to the Senators, he told Paul that he would try to reacquire him. Despite the many well-documented disputes Finley had with many of the players he employed, Kathy Lindblad said Paul's relationship with Finley was always friendly and respectful. The relationship extended beyond his playing days. Finley occasionally called Paul just to "catch up on things."[9] Lindblad's first season back with the A's was not one of his better ones. He pitched in only 36 games, making three spot starts. He finished the year 1-5 as his ERA rose more than a run per game, to 3.69. Heading into the postseason, Darold Knowles was the first left-handed option out of the bullpen and Lindblad did not appear in the A's five-game ALCS victory over the Baltimore Orioles.

Lindblad did pitch in three games during the 1973 World Series against the New York Mets. In Game Two he relieved in the 12th inning after the Mets had taken a 7-6 lead off Rollie Fingers. Lindblad induced back-to-back groundballs to second baseman Mike Andrews, both of which Andrews fumbled, leading to three more runs that put the game away.

In Game Three, also an extra-inning affair, Lindblad came on in the ninth inning, worked two innings, and earned the victory, one of the greatest moments of his life, according to his wife.[10] In addition to earning the victory, Lindblad became a footnote in baseball trivia when he became the last pitcher to face Willie Mays. In the bottom half of the tenth the Mets' aging slugger pinch-hit, and Lindblad got him to ground into a fielder's choice. The A's scored the winning run in the top of the 11th. The victory was Lindblad's only postseason win. He pitched once more in the Series, throwing a scoreless inning in Game Four.

Among the three World Series rings won by Lindblad, the 1973 ring was the one he was most proud of and routinely wore, despite the fact that it originally contained no diamonds.[11] He felt he had contributed more to this team's success than the other two teams that won World Series titles. The ring was lost when Lindblad placed it in a briefcase that was later stolen. Kathy Lindblad still has her husband's rings from the 1974 and 1978 World Series.[12]

The Athletics and Lindblad followed up their 1973 World Series title with another championship season in 1974. Lindblad pitched more than 100 innings for the first time since 1967 and had a 4-4 record with a career-low 2.06 ERA as he filled the void created by the struggles of fellow lefty Darold Knowles. However, his contributions ended at the conclusion of the regular season. The A's received such solid starting pitching performances throughout the American League Championship Series and the World Series that Lindblad didn't make a single postseason appearance.

The 1975 season was perhaps Lindblad's finest. With Knowles having been traded to Chicago, his workload increased significantly. He came out of the bullpen 68 times and pitched 122⅓ innings, both career highs, on his way to posting a 9-1 record with seven saves and a 2.72 ERA. The effort earned the attention of sportswriters across the country as Lindblad garnered a handful of votes and finished 18th in the American League MVP voting, during a season when the A's won their fifth consecutive American League West championship.

On September 28, 1975, the final day of the 1975 season, Lindblad combined with Vida Blue, Glen Abbott, and Rollie Fingers to toss a no-hitter against the California Angels. Lindblad pitched a 1-2-3 seventh inning, retiring Leroy Stanton on a groundout to third, striking out John Balaz, and getting Bruce Bochte to ground out to second. It was the first time in the major leagues that four pitchers combined for a no-hitter.

The A's were swept by the Boston Red Sox in the 1975 ALCS. Lindblad, who pitched in two of the three games, was one of the few A's pitchers who were remotely effective. In 4⅓ innings he allowed one run to a heavy hitting Red Sox lineup that included Carl Yastrzemski, Fred Lynn, and a host of other big bats.

The 1976 season was Lindblad's last in Oakland. The 34-year-old again proved to be a reliable member of the bullpen as he went 6-5 with a 3.06 ERA. The A's championship run ended as the team finished with an 87-74 record, 2½ games behind the Kansas City Royals. With many of the key pieces of the A's dynasty already departed, the franchise's glory days were clearly in the rear-view mirror. In an effort to cut costs, Finley sold off as many of the A's assets as possible. Lindblad still had value and before the start of the 1977 season he was sold to the Texas Rangers for $400,000.

Lindblad spent a little more than a season and a half with the Rangers before being purchased by the New York Yankees on August 1, 1978. The Yankees needed to bolster their bullpen in an effort to chase down the front-running Red Sox. The Yankees caught the Red Sox and went on to win a one-game playoff to advance to the American League Championship Series and eventually the World Series. Lindblad made his final appearance in the majors in Game One of the 1978 World Series. Coming on in relief in the fifth inning he pitched 2⅓ innings and gave up three earned runs as the Dodgers battered four Yankees pitchers for 11 runs in the opening game blowout.

The Yankees' acquisition of Lindblad reunited him with his good friend and longtime A's roommate, Catfish Hunter. In addition to collecting coins, Lindblad loved the outdoors, particularly hunting and fishing, activities he and Hunter relished together.

After the season the Yankees sold Lindblad to the Seattle Mariners, who released the 37-year-old left-hander at the end of spring training. After 14 seasons in the majors, Lindblad's career had ended, and he retired to his home in Arlington, Texas. Lindblad finished his career with a 68-63 record and 64 saves in 385 games, with a 3.29 ERA and the admiration of many who remembered him as the perfect teammate.

Lindblad became a custom homebuilder in Arlington. He returned to baseball as a minor-league pitching coach in the Milwaukee Brewers organization in 1987 and worked in that capacity until 1993, when he was diagnosed with early-onset familial Alzheimer's disease (FAD), the same disease that afflicted his mother and later three of his brothers. Early-onset Alzheimer's is a rare form of the disease that is known to be entirely inherited.[13]

The disease progressed rapidly and had a dramatic impact on Lindblad's behavior and his physical appearance. He began to get progressively more upset at little things and was unable to control his anger, often lashing out at Kathy.[14] According to Kathy, he didn't recognize her or his children and wasn't the same gentle, caring man she had married.[15]

In 1997 Lindblad was moved to a facility that specialized in assisted-living care for those suffering from Alzheimer's. Lindblad spent the final nine years of his life in Peach Tree Place in Arlingtons.[16] He died from complications of the disease on January 1, 2006. He was 64 years old.

After Lindblad's death, the field at Katy Stadium in Katy Park in Chanute was renamed Paul Lindblad Field. On October 5, 2008, Lindblad was inducted into the Kansas Sports Hall of Fame.

SOURCES

Colton, Larry, *Southern League: A True Story of Baseball, Civil Rights, and the Deep South's Most Compelling Pennant Race* (New York: Grand Central Publishing, 2013).

Markusen, Bruce. *Baseball's Last Dynasty: Charlie Finley's Oakland A's* (Indianapolis: Masters Press, 1998).

McDowell, Brian, "Legion tournament honors Lindblad's legacy," *Chanute Tribune*, July 5, 2013. Retrieved from chanute.com/sports/article_593e439e-e5c1-11e2-9e26-001a4bcf6878.html

Wolters, Levi. "Hall of Fame Induction Ceremony Sunday," *Wichita Business Journal*, October 2, 2008.

Chanute Area Chamber of Commerce and Office of Tourism (2012). Retrieved from chanutechamber.com

Chanute Historical Society. Retrieved from chanutehistory.org/

Chanute, Kansas. Retrieved from en.wikipedia.org/wiki/Chanute,_Kansas

Kansas City Athletics: Historical Moments. Retrieved from sportsencyclopedia.com/al/kcityas/kca_s.html

Markusen, Bruce, "Thinking of Paul Lindblad." Retrieved from bruce.mlblogs.com/2006/01/17/thinking-of-paul-lindblad/

Paul Aaron Lindblad 1941-2006. Retrieved from thedeadballera.com/Obits/Obits_L/Lindblad.Paul.Obit.html

Paul Lindblad. Retrieved from baseballlibrary.com/ballplayers/player.php?name=Paul_Lindblad_1941&page=chronology

Types of Alzheimer's: Early-Onset, Late-Onset and Familial (2013). Retrieved from webmd.com/alzheimers/guide/alzheimers-types

Wade Funeral Home, Arlington, Texas, Paul Aaron Lindblad August 9, 1941-January 1, 2006. [Funeral Program, 2006].

W.E. Alford, personal communications, December 10 and December 12, 2013

Lindblad, Kathy, personal communications, December 11, 16, and 17, 2013

NOTES

1   Wade Funeral Home, "Paul Aaron Lindblad 1941-2006."

2   Personal correspondence with Kathy Lindblad, December 17, 2013.

3   Personal correspondence with W.E. Alford, December 10, 2013.

4   Larry Colton, *Southern League: A True Story of Baseball, Civil Rights, and the Deep South's Most Compelling Pennant Race* (New York: Grand Central Publishing, 2013).

5   Personal correspondence with Kathy Lindblad, December 16, 2013.

6   Brian McDowell, "Legion tournament honors Lindblad's legacy," *Chanute Tribune*, July 5, 2013.

7   Bruce Markusen, *Baseball's Last Dynasty: Charlie Finley's Oakland A's* (Indianapolis: Masters Press, 1998), 177-178.

8   Personal correspondence with Kathy Lindblad, December 16, 2013.

9   Personal correspondence with Kathy Lindblad, December 11, 2013.

10 Personal correspondence with Kathy Lindblad, December 17, 2013.

11 Personal correspondence with Kathy Lindblad, December 11, 2013.

12 Personal correspondence with Kathy Lindblad, December 11, 2013.

13 Types of Alzheimer's: Early-Onset, Late-Onset and Familial (2013).

14 Colton.

15 Personal Correspondence with Kathy Lindblad, December 17, 2013.

16 Colton.

Rich McKinney

By John Vorperian

From 1970 to 1977, Rich McKinney was a utility player for all or part of each major-league season. His time in "The Show" was exclusively in the American League. He played for the Chicago White Sox, New York Yankees, and Oakland A's. Originally slated as an infielder, McKinney also handled the outfield and designated hitter positions.

Charles Richard McKinney was born on November 22, 1946, in Piqua, Ohio, to Charles E. and Barbara E. (Houser) McKinney. The couple also had a daughter, Carol. The elder McKinney was a farmer. The farm's primary crop was corn.

From 1962 to 1965, Rich McKinney attended Miami East High School in Troy, Ohio. A gifted athlete, he lettered in baseball, basketball, football, and track. McKinney quarterbacked and captained the football team, and was captain of the basketball team as well. In his senior year, as a hoopster, McKinney made all-state. A rebounding machine, he still held (as of 2014) the school's records for most career rebounds (707), season rebounds (327), and game rebounds (24), as well as the most career free throws (299).

On the baseball diamond, McKinney was the Vikings' field general at catcher. He was behind the dish for three years. Then in the spring of his senior year, McKinney was stricken with a mystery illness. For 2½ weeks he suffered with a 105-degree fever. Doctors initially thought the infirmity was leukemia, but medical tests did not bear that out. McKinney recalled, "They never did find out what I had. I lost 40 pounds and almost died. It was terrible."[1]

Though he didn't play much baseball in his senior year, out of all his collegiate recruiting offers, McKinney chose to go to Ohio University on a baseball scholarship. "I picked Ohio because of Coach Bob Wren,

and because I thought it was the best baseball school," he said.[2]

McKinney's assessment of the Bobcats baseball program and its skipper was on the mark. In 1949 Bob Wren was named head coach of his alma mater after being in professional baseball for six years with the St. Louis Browns organization. His first season, Ohio University went 14-10-1. During his tenure from 1949 to 1972, Wren's squads never had a losing season, and his .742 winning percentage ranks among the best in the NCAA record books. On September 22, 1997, the Athens, Ohio, school dedicated its new ballpark as Bob Wren Stadium.

McKinney's original plans were to be a two-sport star — baseball and football — for the Bobcats. He had regained most of his strength after his sickness and played quarterback and as a pass-catching flanker for the freshman football team. But a knee injury

suffered during a spring football match required surgery and put a stop to his gridiron aspirations. His athletic focus became solely baseball.

In his sophomore year, the 5-foot-11, 185-pound muscular ballplayer was abruptly switched from catcher to shortstop. He later said, "I didn't know anything about playing short."[3] McKinney credited Bob Wren with teaching him the position and making the transition to the infield a success.

At the plate, McKinney did not need any instruction whatsoever. In 1967 the upperclassman finished third in batting in the Mid-American Conference with a .392 average. He ranked third nationally in RBIs, fifth in home runs, and ninth in doubles. College baseball scribes and scouts labeled him one of the country's top collegiate sluggers. McKinney was named to First Team All-MAC in 1967 and 1968. His .697 slugging percentage in the 1967-68 season remains, as of 2012, an Ohio University record.

During the summer of 1967, McKinney played in the Carlings League. The amateur loop in Illinois was backed by the major leagues and stocked with college players who had not signed a pro contract. McKinney batted .308, fourth-best in the league.

A physical-education major, McKinney entered his senior year looking forward to playing in the big leagues. The All-American had already talked with about 15 organizations. His dream was to play for a West Coast team. "Ever since I was little, ever since I could see them play on television I've wanted to do that," he said.[4]

On June 7, 1968, McKinney was chosen in the first round (14th overall) of the major-league amateur draft, by the Chicago White Sox. Fred Schaffer, a longtime White Sox scout, had given positive reports on the prospect. In one of his reports to the team, Schaffer wrote of McKinney: "He has one of the best bats I've ever seen in the free-agent field."[5]

McKinney was the second collegian selected in the 1968 draft. The first (fourth overall) was also a MAC man, a catcher from Kent State University who went to the New York Yankees: Thurman Munson. Some others who were singled out in that initial round and made it to the majors were Tim Foli, Greg Luzinski, Gary Matthews, and Bobby Valentine.

McKinney received a $25,000 bonus and Chicago assigned the 21-year-old to the Double-A Evansville White Sox (Southern League). In 86 games at shortstop, McKinney had 307 at-bats and batted .261, with 12 doubles, 9 triples, and 37 RBIs.

McKinney split 1969 among three teams and military service. He found himself initially placed at the White Sox' Florida Instructional league outpost, then after 37 games there was moved to the Double-A Columbus White Sox (Southern League). Under manager Gary "Griz" Johnson, McKinney the shortstop was moved to center field. His stay at Columbus was for only 11 games. Promoted to the Triple-A Tucson Toros (Pacific Coast League), he completed the year there.

McKinney began the 1970 season with Tucson, where he batted .303 with 41 RBIs in 62 games. In late June he was called up to the White Sox. On June 26, 1970, at Comiskey Park in a night game against the Minnesota Twins, McKinney made his major-league debut before a home crowd of 9,486. Batting sixth, he started at third base, a position he had never played before professionally. The muscular right-handed batter scored his first major-league run in the second inning. He reached second base on an error by Twins center fielder Cesar Tovar, and a single by pitcher Bob Miller brought him home. In the fifth, McKinney got his first major-league hit, a single to right off Jim Kaat. In the 4-2 Chicago victory, McKinney handled his two fielding chances at the hot corner without any problem.

McKinney's first major-league home run came in an 8-2 loss on September 21, 1970, at Comiskey Park in the nightcap of a doubleheader against the Kansas City Royals. The gopher ball was given up in the eighth by Jim York, who was making his major-league debut. It was the first of four straight games in which McKinney hit a homer. He closed out the season with the four home runs but with a .168 batting average.

Before the start of 1971 spring training in Sarasota, Florida, White Sox manager Chuck Tanner was looking for another power hitter to add to the lineup. Discussing possible trade rumors, Tanner said, "It could be we might discover that extra power right in our own back yard in the person of Rich McKinney. … Rich showed us last fall that he has the potential power when he hit those four homers in four games. The only thing he has to prove is that he can handle major-league pitching consistently."[6]

After their 1971 home opener, the White Sox lost nine of ten games. Chicago scored only 18 runs in those games. McKinney had been used as a pinch-hitter in that stretch and in four successive plate appearances had hit safely. Skipper Tanner needed offense. He shook up the lineup and shuffled McKinney to the outfield. Later Tanner said, "He took to outfielding quite naturally."[7]

McKinney himself said, "I don't believe I have the ability to play shortstop in the major leagues. I just don't have the range and I don't do too well with the pivot. They had Luke Appling work with me, but I don't feel that's the spot for me. I'm in the right place now—the outfield. You don't have so many different plays to worry about out there and, therefore, can concentrate more on your hitting."[8] McKinney's prowess at the plate did improve; at one point in the season he even flirted with .400. As a pinch-hitter he ended the season 11-for-19 (.579).

Clearly 1971 was a career year for McKinney, with 114 games, 369 at-bats, a .271 batting average, 46 RBIs, and a .377 slugging percentage. McKinney's banner year raised his visibility among opposition advance scouts and general managers alike, and after the season New York Yankees general manager Lee MacPhail swapped pitcher Stan Bahnsen, who had been the American League Rookie of the Year in 1968, for McKinney.

Marty Appel was the Yankees' assistant public-relations director at the time of the trade. In his memoir, *Now Pitching for the Yankees*, Appel provided some insight as to why MacPhail had sought the deal: "No one had really secured the position since Clete Boyer was traded in '67. Five years of Charlie Smith, Bobby Cox, and Jerry Kenney—and it wasn't happening."[9] Appel wrote that Yankees scouts were impressed with McKinney and thought he would get better. "McKinney was our offseason big news, our new face, our new marquee star. He would take over third base." Appel recalled.[10]

To gain third-base experience, McKinney played winter ball for the Mayaguez Indians in the Puerto Rican League. An incident on December 17, 1971, may well have foreshadowed McKinney's Bronx Bomber career. At a beach party in Puerto Rico, he sustained second-degree burns to his right ankle. He returned to Troy, Ohio, for treatment. The Yankees said he was expected to be in spring training.

Before the 1972 season, the Yankees conducted their annual Winter Promotional Caravan. During this weeklong odyssey into parts of Connecticut, Pennsylvania, and upstate New York, the team would offer "meet and greet" opportunities to the local media as a marketing tool. On the first day of the tour, McKinney boarded a bus with general manager MacPhail, public-relations director Bob Fishel, manager Ralph Houk, and other club officials, including assistant PR director Appel.

Appel wrote, "Rich was 25, curly-haired. … I introduced myself to him. … It was clear to him, I'm sure ,.. that I was a club official."[11] During their exchange of pleasantries, Appel could not believe it when McKinney asked where he could buy some marijuana. Shocked, Appel could not believe a player would ask a team official for drug advice or tell a team official he smoked grass.

Although nothing further came of that peculiar incident, newly-minted Bomber McKinney had problems at the plate and at third base. On April 18, 1972, in his Yankee Stadium debut, batting second, he grounded into three double plays against Milwaukee Brewer starter Jim Slaton (twice) and reliever Frank Linzy. Later McKinney commented, "I didn't feel right in batting practice and I didn't expect to have a good night."[12] The team's spin cited the baseball strike as an impact upon McKinney's poor performance. (The first players' strike in major-league history ran from April 1 to April 13, 1972.)

Four days later, on the 22nd, McKinney found his swing. He had been dropped to the seventh slot in the batting lineup and went 3-for-4 with a home run. The homer came in the top of the fourth off Boston right-hander Sonny Siebert. In the field it was a different story. In the 11-7 loss at Fenway Park, McKinney made a record-tying four errors. In *The Sporting News* Jim Ogle wrote, "[I]t is doubtful any other player contributed nine runs to the opposition."[13] McKinney lamented, "They were all so easy. … If they had been tough chances, I wouldn't feel so bad, but I couldn't find the handle."[14]

Afterwards, teammates Bernie Allen and Johnny Callison took McKinney out to dinner. Allen said, "We had one primary purpose: to make him laugh and laugh and laugh. I knew how he felt. Any infielder knew how he felt, since we have all had rough days."[15] The outing was good but upon their return, they saw a local TV sports newscast that replayed each error in sequence. Allen recalled, "I'm surprised Mac didn't kick the screen in."[16] But manager Ralph Houk said, "One game doesn't make a season. It's not going to leave a mark on him. Rich is a hard-nosed kid with a lot of guts."[17]

McKinney's very next appearance was at Yankee Stadium; no boos were reported and the crowd gave him an ovation when he successfully handled a fielding chance in the second inning. But the home crowds were not so polite after that contest, and rumblings about "the trade" had begun.

Twenty games later McKinney had gone without an error, but by the end of May he was batting .216 and had only five RBIs. In late May the Yankees optioned McKinney to the Syracuse Chiefs, their Triple-A affiliate in the International League. Houk told *The Sporting News*, "McKinney got off to a bad start. … We still feel he has excellent potential, but things were just piling up on him."[18] Indeed they were, and had

been. McKinney, while in the pinstripes, had been playing with a bone chip in his elbow.

In 86 games at Syracuse, McKinney batted .299, with 16 home runs and 53 RBIs. During that interim, GM MacPhail went on the record to state, "There has been criticism of some of the deals we have made. … Just a word of caution here about criticism of the Rich McKinney deal. Neither Ralph nor I have given up on Rich, although we felt it best to send him out. He just got off on the wrong foot, had some personal problems and can't be judged on what he did this year."[19]

McKinney got a September call-up to the Yankees. He was an insurance policy to fill in for infielders Horace Clarke and Gene Michael, or could be placed in the outfield to cover for Johnny Callison, Bernie Allen, Ron Swoboda, or Hal Lanier. Offensively, McKinney put up no dramatic or magical batting numbers. He ended the year with a .215 batting average in 37 games with the Yankees.

Nonetheless, around the time of the World Series, rumors were reported that the Yankees were receiving inquiries from other clubs about the availability of two players: McKinney and catcher-first baseman Johnny Ellis. On November 24 the Oakland A's traded outfielder Matty Alou to New York for pitcher Rob Gardner and a player to be named later. On December 1 McKinney became that player.

In becoming an Oakland Athletic, McKinney fulfilled his childhood dream to play for a West Coast club. He started the 1973 season with the A's as primarily a role player. He was a backup for third baseman Sal Bando, a replacement second sacker for Dick Green and an occasional pinch-hitter or designated hitter. In one mid-June game, manager Dick Williams benched a slumping Joe Rudi and placed McKinney in left field.

In late July, the 26-year-old was sent to the A's Triple-A affiliate, the Tucson Toros (Pacific Coast League). He was recalled in September and he closed out the season with Oakland. In 48 games, he batted .246.

McKinney spent almost all of the 1974 season with Tucson, except for about two weeks with the A's in July. With Tucson he played in both the infield and the outfield. In 116 games his .285 batting average produced 26 doubles, 65 RBIs, and 7 home runs.

McKinney continued in Tucson in 1975, until he was called up by the A's in August. In 110 PCL games, he batted .297, repeated with 26 doubles, 13 home runs, and 74 RBIs.

In 1976 McKinney was with Tucson for the entire season. In 129 games, he batted .317, rapped 34 doubles and 6 triples, and had career highs of 95 RBIs and 22 home runs. The batting power scouts had touted about McKinney showed in his plate performance.

The nine-year professional had spent three straight seasons at Triple-A In 1977 the 30-year-old McKinney was prepared to leave baseball and take a job with a trucking company. That was the plan until Oakland owner Charlie Finley telephoned him. "Mr. Finley called me and told me it would be the best chance I had since I came to Oakland and I would be foolish not to report," said McKinney.[20]

In spring training McKinney surprised himself and sportswriters by hitting some home runs. Sportswriters commented on how typically McKinney wouldn't hit homers until midseason. Manager Jack McKeon planned to use him as a DH and first baseman. McKinney spent all season with the A's except for two weeks at Triple-A San Jose in th latter half of June. McKinney was in 86 games for the Athletics, 32 at first base, 18 as a DH, ten as an infielder and five in the outfield.

McKinney's last major-league game, on October 2, 1977, was a Sunday contest at Arlington Stadium against the Texas Rangers. McKinney started at third base and batted seventh in the 8-7 loss to the Rangers. In the top of the second against left-hander John Poloni, McKinney grounded into a double play. In the fifth he walked, and scored on a double and an error. In the seventh McKinney grounded out to shortstop. In the eighth, off reliever Roger Moret, he grounded into a double play.

McKinney's final season batting average was .177, with 21 RBIs and 6 home runs. In his seven-year major-league career, McKinney played in 341 games, batted .225, hit 20 home runs, and drove in 100 runs.

Upon his departure from baseball, McKinney drove semi trucks. In the 1980s he and his father owned some farms that produced corn and soybeans and stocked cattle. McKinney also worked some 16 years for Panasonic in one of its manufacturing divisions, from which he retired.

In 2008 Miami East High School, McKinney's alma mater in Troy, Ohio, inducted him into its Hall of Fame.

SOURCES

August 7, 2014, telephone call with Rich McKinney

Appel, Marty, *Now Pitching for the Yankees* (Kingston, New York: Total Sports Publishing, 2001).

Shatzkin, Mike, ed., *The Ballplayers* (New York: Arbor House William Morrow, 1990).

2012 Ohio University (baseball) *Media Guide.*

Chass, Murray, "On Baseball; The Orioles Lose Out From Coast to Coast," *New York Times,* January 23, 2005.

Markusen, Bruce, "Observations From Cooperstown: The Yankees and the 1971 Winter Meetings," December 19, 2011, at bronxbanter-blog.com/2011/12/19/.

"Former Bobcat baseball coach Bob Wren passes away," ohio.edu/news.

"Illness Nearly Curtails Rich McKinney's Career," *Athens* (Ohio) *Messenger*, date not certain, but circa May 10, 1968.

"Yankee Player Suffers Burns at Beach Party," *Virgin Islands Daily News*, December 20, 1971, 11.

baseball-almanac.com

baseball-reference.com

miamieast.k12.oh.us

news.google.com/newspapers?nid=1241&dat=19720331&id=H29TAA AAIBAJ&sjid=8IUDAAAAIBAJ&pg=4290,2721625

retrosheet.org

NOTES

1 "Illness Nearly Curtails Rich McKinney's Career,"*Athens* (Ohio) *Messenger*, date not certain but circa May 10, 1968.

2 Ibid.

3 Ibid.

4 Ibid.

5 Jerome Holtzman, "McKinney Mighty Big Chisox Plus" *The Sporting News*, August 21, 1971.

6 "Chisox Sitting Pretty—Catchers Are Swap Bait," *The Sporting News*, January 16, 1971, 60.

7 "McKinney Adding Muscle To Anemic Chisox Attack," *The Sporting News*, May 8, 1971, 17.

8 Ibid.

9 Marty Appel, *Now Pitching for the Yankees*, (Kingston, New York: Total Sports Publishing, 2001), 79.

10 Ibid.

11 Ibid.

12 -"Yanks' New Kekich—Thinking Pitcher," *The Sporting News*, May 6, 1972, 7.

13 Jim Ogle, "A Bad Day at Black Rock for a Fumbling McKinney," *The Sporting News*, May 13, 1972, 2.

14 Ibid.

15 Ibid.

16 Ibid.

17 Jim Ogle, "Yanks Admit Mistake on McKinney," *The Sporting News*, June 17, 1972, 16.

18 Jim Ogle, "Yanks' MacPhail Lashes at Baying Wolves," *The Sporting News*, June 17, 1972, 16.

19 Ibid

20 Associated Press, "Here's a Guy Who Likes Charlie Finley," *St. Petersburg* (Florida) *Evening Independent,* April 21, 1977, 19.

José Morales

By Rory Costello

José Manuel Morales was a master pinch-hitter. In 1976 he made his big-league reputation with 25 base hits in this role. This single-season record stood until Colorado's John Vander Wal stroked 28 in 1995; it remained the third best one-year total as the 2013 season ended. Morales—the seventh of 11 men from the US Virgin Islands to make the majors—still ranked eighth on the career list too, with 123.

In 1984, José's last year as a player, AP sportswriter Charles Cooper asked the veteran specialist—who had rarely started a game in the field since 1977—how he adapted to coming off the bench. Cooper observed, "The lack of playing time forces him to concentrate on the game on a much higher level."[1]

This cerebral approach to the demands of pinch-hitting was forged over 21 years as a pro. Playing every one of those winters in Puerto Rico was invaluable—though José had to tough it out for ten summers in the minors before he got his first call-up to "The Show" in 1973. But all of his experience led to a productive second career as a batting coach in the majors during the 1980s and '90s.

Morales was born on December 30, 1944, in Frederiksted, St. Croix. This small island is closely linked to its larger neighbor, Puerto Rico. The list of fellow big-league Virgin Islanders includes Valmy Thomas, whose mother bore him in a Puerto Rican hospital but immediately came home. It excludes Henry Cruz, who was born on St. Croix but returned to his family's roots in the city of Fajardo when he was an infant. Another special Puerto Rican case was José's good friend Julio Navarro, who was born on the island of Vieques, east of Puerto Rico, but grew up on St. Croix.

José's mother, Francesca Hernández, also came from Vieques. So did Angel Morales, the man who recog-

nized him with the family name. Unlike the Navarros, however, Francesca left her birthplace at age 7, around 1930, well before the US Navy started taking over most of the island. For a long time, the children of *viequenses* and other immigrants were never really accepted as Virgin Islanders even if they were born there—but José's case is different. His natural father was a Crucian named Stanley Latimer, whose father and mother came from Maryland and Barbados, respectively.

This Latimer was quite the *macho*. "My father has been married three times and he was a shoemaker going from door to door. So I have something like 18 half-brothers and half-sisters."[2] One of them turned up in 1979, when José got a letter that said, "If you have a brother named Ivan in the Virgin Islands and a father by the name of Stanley, then we have something in common. You and I are brothers." And so

Morales found he had a brother, Larry, living in St. Paul, Minnesota.[3]

In 1999 Morales recalled learning about baseball in the sleepy countryside near Frederiksted. "In them days, we used to just pick up the ball and play, nobody taught you anything like Horace Clarke and Elmo Plaskett [two other major leaguers from St. Croix who became government-paid baseball instructors when their playing days were over]. In Wheel of Fortune [a local neighborhood], Charlie Clarke, Horace's uncle, had a big cattle field that actually turned out to be my grandfather's property, and he cut out a field in the middle of the yard. And he brought the first balls and stuff and we all used to play there."

"From there I moved into town, and then I started playing Little League, and one thing led to another. I kept practicing, I used to go to the ballpark and throw a ball into a garbage can at second base, play by myself, run—you do that today, you're crazy."

While in the majors, José also offered some other glimpses of his shoestring baseball budget as a youth. "We didn't have enough money for weights. We would fill biscuit pans with concrete, and put them on each end of a bar. It weighed maybe 50 pounds and then we would pump those homemade weights. Then we would run two or three miles on the beach. Then we would hit."[4]

"I am right-handed and the only glove I had was left-handed. So I turned it inside out. One day my mother was angry and she threw it in the fire. I got it out but there was a big hole in it. So I cut a piece of sole from the bottom of my shoe and plugged the hole."[5]

José readily admitted that there were more naturally gifted players among his peers on St. Croix. Pitcher Norbert Rodgers played nine summers in the minors, including four in Mexico, and was on the staff of the Mayagüez Indios when they won the Puerto Rican championship in 1965-66. Infielder Miguel "Redhead" Santos was a fine hitter and glove man who opted for

family life after a brief taste of Class D ball with Elmo Plaskett in 1957. DeGold Francis, a slugging catcher-first baseman, led the Puerto Rican Winter League in home runs during the 1967-68 season. Why did Morales think he made it while they didn't? "I had a little thing different, I had determination."

The only place José played was in the sandlots. Elmo, Julio Navarro, and original Met Joe Christopher, all several years older, played ball for St. Patrick's Catholic School in Frederiksted. But Morales went to the public high school, which did not have a team. "Myself, I was introduced to a higher class by my brother Ivan Latimer. He had a team named the Giants. Then I started to develop a pretty strong arm, and I found out that Pedrín Zorrilla was coming to look for pitchers and catchers." Zorrilla was the owner of the Santurce Cangrejeros, Puerto Rico's most storied franchise. He was also a friend of New York Giants owner Horace Stoneham and served that organization as a scout.

Alfonso Gerard, the pioneer pro from the Virgin Islands, played many years for Zorrilla in Santurce. He then became a bird dog for his old boss on St. Croix and encouraged him to scout there. As it had several years before with Julio Navarro, this connection clicked again—the Giants signed Morales on September 13, 1963. However, the Pirates were also on the scent. José turned down Pittsburgh scout Chick Genovese's $500 offer (he wanted $1,000). Years later, Bucs' superscout Howie Haak—who made the V.I. part of his Caribbean beat—would say, "I just missed you."

José's arm also got him tagged "Shady" as a teenager. "I made a throw that went all the way into the outfield, under the shady tree, and from that time on … the guys are kidding around and you get pissed, and right away, that's it." (Joe Christopher suggested an alternate story—a lusty *al fresco* interlude; like father, like son!)

Morales noted, "I used to catch, I used to play all over, but I really didn't know that much about the game until I signed professional and went to play in Puerto Rico." When he first went to play in Caguas in late

1963, he was afraid to take the bus because he didn't know much Spanish. Over time, as Puerto Rican baseball man Luis Mayoral observed, José would become eloquent in his second language. But as a brand-new rookie, he walked to the town line, well beyond Yldefonso Solá Morales Stadium. He had not recognized the ballpark because he didn't realize it had lights.

Over his two decades-plus in Puerto Rico, José rose to third on the league's all-time RBI list with 467, behind Bob Thurman and Luis "Canena" Márquez. He also had 84 homers and a career average of .290 in 2,901 at-bats. He led the league three times in doubles, in 1974-75, 1975-76, and 1977-78. In the latter two seasons, he was the leader in base hits as well. Also among his notable feats: batting .402 for the San Juan Senadores in 1968-69, one of 19 men to break .400 in the PRWL. However, his 112 at-bats didn't qualify for the batting title—unsurprising, as he was backing up Johnny Bench.

In the 1978 Caribbean Series in Mazatlán, Mexico, Morales hit .421 and led Mayagüez (29-31 in the regular season!) to the title. René Lachemann, a teammate in the Oakland Athletics system along with Tony La Russa and Joe Rudi, was the manager, thanks to José's recommendation. "The fact I wasn't named MVP didn't bother me that much—we won."[6]

José did not rise to prominence quickly in Puerto Rico. But he had to claw even harder for every rung of the ladder stateside. He spent two summers in Class A ball (1964-65) and three more at Double-A (1966-68). The A's obtained him from the Giants via the minor-league draft in December 1968, and though Morales finally advanced to Triple-A in 1969, he remained with Iowa of the American Association for that season and the next two. Then he played on loan to Tidewater, the Mets' Triple-A affiliate, in 1972.

One main problem held up José's advance: He was a defensive liability, leading four different minor leagues in errors.[7] Indeed, during his major-league career, he appeared in the field in only 104 of his 733 total games, and he never had more than 242 at-bats in a season.

Broadcasters often referred to him as "a catcher by trade," though he played first most often in the majors.

José simply commented, "Once you have a bad reputation as a receiver, that's it. Nobody ever taught me how to catch, I just had a strong arm." He suffered occupational hazards such as a broken jaw and (before the flexible mitt) dislocated fingers and a broken thumb. "I concentrated on my batting and became known as an offensive player."

Finally, the A's summoned the 28-year-old in August 1973. Jim "Catfish" Hunter had suffered a hairline fracture of his right thumb in the All-Star Game on July 24. Oakland called Shady up once, sent him back down after a failed bid to put Hunter on the disabled list, and finally shipped out pitcher Dave Hamilton instead.[8] Morales had hit over .300 once before in the minors, posting a .306 mark in 1970. But he was hitting just too well to ignore—.355 for Tucson in the Pacific Coast League. Said Toros teammate Jack Heidemann, "José Morales hits the ball so well and so hard that I can't understand why he isn't hitting .400."[9]

Shady made his debut in Boston's Fenway Park on August 13, 1973. As the designated hitter, he went 1-for-4, reaching on a Danny Cater error in his first at-bat and doubling off Luis Tiant for his first hit in the ninth inning. José had 14 at-bats in six scattered games with the A's before they sold him to the Montreal Expos on September 18. This deal had repercussions in the World Series, but it is little remembered that Morales figured. After second baseman Mike Andrews committed two costly errors in Game Two, Oakland owner Charles Finley sought to replace him with Manny Trillo, but the Mets (as was their right) blocked the maneuver.

According to a story by Ron Bergman in *The Sporting News*, "The A's worked themselves into the predicament by selling Morales … to make room for pinch-runner Allan Lewis, a Finley favorite, on the 25-man roster. Two days later, Bill North sprained his ankle. The Baltimore Orioles allowed Trillo to replace North for the American League playoffs. When the A's found out the Mets wouldn't agree to the same switch, an attempt was made to get Morales back from Montreal. He didn't clear National League waivers because some team claimed him. Ironically, the Mets allowed the A's to replace North with Lewis."[10]

The further irony: While Allan "The Panamanian Express" Lewis pinch-ran in three Series games and was voted a one-tenth World Series share, José—who did not receive even a token share from the winners—was unaware of all the wrangling.

Morales played just 25 games for Montreal in 1974. He was back at Triple-A Memphis until July, and though he finished the year with the Expos, he missed by one day a signing bonus for spending 90 consecutive days in the majors.[11] On September 15, pinch-hitting for Larry Lintz in the seventh inning, José smacked his first major-league homer, off Pittsburgh's Ken Brett. The three-run blow gave the Expos a 5-4 win.

The next year, 1975, was Shady's breakthrough. He appeared in 93 games, batting .301. For the first of four times, he led his league in pinch hits, recording 15 in 51 at-bats (.294). José then went on to set his pinch-hit record of 25 in 1976, breaking the single-season mark of 24 established by Dave Philley in 1961 and tied by Vic Davalillo in 1970. Two years later, likely tongue-in-cheek, Davalillo remarked, "I played one year with Morales [with the '73 A's]. I taught him everything. And look what he does. He breaks my record."[12]

José posted a .316 average in '76, his major-league high, with 37 RBIs in just 158 at-bats. He hit 321 with 3 homers and 24 RBIs in his 78 pinch at-bats. As of 2014, the only man besides John Vander Wal who has had more pinch hits in one year since then was lifetime leader Lenny Harris (26 in 1999).

After the Minnesota Twins purchased Morales on waivers in March 1978, he became a very effective part-time DH. This had already been a frequent role for Shady in Puerto Rico too. Manager Gene Mauch, who was also his skipper in Montreal, said, "José's position is 'bat.'" Indeed, his weapon was almost part of him. "While with the Twins in the late 1970s, Morales insisted on taking his bat with him every-

where. At his hotel, he would stand in front of a mirror and practice his swing. Morales liked his bat so much he would sometimes kiss it."[13]

Pinch-hitting still remained his prominent *raison d'être*. In a feature article on Morales by Bob Fowler of *The Sporting News* that year, Mauch said, "We can use him as the DH often enough to keep him sharp."[14] Gene was as good as his word; it was in '78 that Morales recorded his single-season high of 242 at-bats, with a .314 average. He posted an AL-leading 15 pinch hits.

José's performance was not up to his standards in 1979 (.267, 2 homers, 27 RBIs), but he rebounded the next year, hitting eight homers (his most ever in the majors) and batting .303. His 13 pinch hits again led the AL. Even so, the Twins granted him free agency that October. In December he signed with the Baltimore Orioles, where he spent one season plus a month. General manager Hank Peters admired José's hitting ability, while manager Earl Weaver (always known for deep and flexible benches) liked the idea of having an emergency catcher/first baseman.[15]

Said, José, "I really liked that organization, it was the best one I played for." He drew an interesting comparison between Weaver and Mauch. "Mr. Weaver always really wanted to win, but in spring training, he focused on getting all the guys enough at-bats, getting them ready for the season. But with Gene Mauch, even if it was sandlot ball, he still wanted to win!"

However, after giving Shady just three at-bats in April 1982, the O's traded him to Los Angeles on April 28 for Leo Hernández. Morales hit .300 in 30 pinch at-bats—but did not play an inning in the field the whole year. Perhaps because carrying such a specialist was a luxury, Dodgers general manager Al Campanis wanted José to retire in 1983, but he said, "Nobody could get me out that spring training." Plus, he still had desire. "I was shooting for that Manny Mota record [150 career pinch hits, which Lenny Harris surpassed in 2001]," and manager Tommy Lasorda continued to spot him the same way. "But I got at least three hits thanks to Dusty Baker—he'd say, 'Hey, give José a chance!'"

In another *Sporting News* feature on his pinch-hitting prowess, Morales cited the helpful presence of Mota, who had become the Dodgers' first-base coach. "'We sit down and discuss a lot of things. We talk about hitters and situations. … I admire him as a good pinch-hitter who's done a lot to help me. I do pattern myself after his style. I feel if I do my job, the way I'm expected to, nature will take its course."[16]

Morales saw his only postseason action in 1983, going hitless in two pinch at-bats as LA lost the NL Championship Series to Philadelphia. The Dodgers brought José back again the next spring, but after he went just 3-for-19 off the bench, they released him on June 7, 1984, at age 39. He said, "That's the only thing I feel I didn't get a right break on."

Twelve days later, he signed again with the Expos as a free agent. He was offered jobs as a minor-league hitting instructor with Oakland, Toronto, and Los Angeles,[17] but accepted an assignment to Triple-A Indianapolis — his first time back in the minors in ten years, and almost unheard of for a player at that age. But after going .188 in 31 games, he retired. "I got a game-winning hit in the playoffs [for Indianapolis] that year. But they [the Expos] didn't give me a chance to come back. If I'd went back to Baltimore, maybe I'd have gotten a chance."

Morales finished his major-league career with a very respectable .287 batting average, including 26 homers and 207 RBIs. He struck out in only 13 percent of his plate appearances, a testament to his skill as a contact hitter. Like many batters of this type, though, he did not draw a great number of walks — 89 overall, bringing his lifetime on-base percentage to .332. José never stole a base in the majors, though he did swipe eight in Puerto Rico.

When asked about his toughest opponent on the mound in the late innings, José came up with a somewhat surprising choice. "Who was that black lefty pitcher, played with the Phillies and Pirates? Al Holland! He had that sneaky curve. I would say, 'Why I keep missing this guy?' By the time I got to see some video on him, it was too late." Indeed, the record shows

that Morales handled some great lefties well and good ones even better. He went 9-for-24 against Ron Guidry, 4-for-10 against Steve Carlton, and 13-for-22 against Larry Gura. Yet he was 0-6 lifetime against Holland.

Shady returned to the Orioles as a minor-league instructor in 1985. "Hank Peters said the day that I retired, he would like me to be with his organization." At the winter meetings that year, Roger Craig, the new manager of the San Francisco Giants, was looking for a hitting coach and found his man in Morales. "My 'godfather,' Gene Mauch, recommended me."

José also started coaching in the Puerto Rican Winter League during the 1985-86 season. Back with Mayagüez again, his star pupil was Wally Joyner, just before Wally's outstanding rookie year with the California Angels. That winter Joyner became just the third man to win the Triple Crown in the PRWL — the last, 35 years before, had been Elmo Plaskett. During spring training in March 1986, Joyner showed what he had learned in a lefty-lefty matchup against Giants reliever Mike Jeffcoat, singling with a shortened swing after falling behind in the count 0-and-2. "Morales, sitting on the San Francisco bench, gave himself away with a grin — a proud teacher's grin."[18]

Along with his intense observation and teaching, José had also come up with an innovative batting exercise: Players swung one-handed using a special short, heavy bat in order to hit more line drives.

"I invented that little bat when I was in the minor leagues with Baltimore because they were breaking so many bats. I could see that the kids didn't know how to use the regular wood bat, didn't know how to use their hands. I was playing pepper one day, and I said wait a minute, this s**t is different. I noticed how quick my hands reacted, and I came up with the little bat."

"But the only mistake, I didn't patent it. When I was with the Giants, a guy that made those aluminum bats, I can't remember his name, said, 'José, can I have a bat?' So I gave it to him, and the following year, he'd made a small bat, same size. He called me in spring training with the Giants, and I said, 'Hey, are you the sonuvabitch that used my bat?' and he hung up on me and I never heard from him again. That little bat made a lot of money for people, and now everyone's using it."

Morales spent three years in San Francisco, instructing Will Clark and Kevin Mitchell, among others. He then worked in the Indians minor-league system in 1989 — Hank Peters had become Cleveland's GM the previous year — and was hitting coach with the big club from 1990 to 1993. Kenny Lofton, for one, swore by him. "And look at Candy Maldonado. He went down the drain in San Francisco after I left. Then we got him in Cleveland [in 1990] and I helped him make the adjustments." Indeed, Maldonado enjoyed a rousing comeback; his two other best years (1986-87) were also under José's watch.

Another memorable anecdote from 1993 featured José's godson Jaime Navarro, son of Julio. The Indians in particular were feasting on Jaime during one of his slumps, and the reason? "Uncle José" could tell that Jaime was tipping his pitches. Since he worked for Cleveland, he kept his mouth shut and watched his godson get pounded. Only after Morales left the club did he tell the secret."[19]

However, Mike Hargrove wanted another man after that year, so Shady was out of baseball in 1994. He joined the Florida Marlins in '95, thanks to manager René Lachemann, "like a brother to me, he's good people." On the Florida roster was Jerry Browne, the man who picked up the baton for Virgin Islanders in the majors after Morales retired. They had fun bantering in the local patois, which nobody else could understand.

During the All-Star break in 1996, though, José lost his job along with Lachemann. The Marlins offense had been lagging, and Morales has a personal theory that Lach may have taken the fall out of loyalty because he did not want to see his coach made the scapegoat.

At every stop along his route, José used the original little bat. And he always took care of his team. "It's all about making the adjustments. If you don't see,

you can't hit. Your swing becomes too long. The players become like your kids — you gotta watch 'em."

Morales settled in the Orlando, Florida, area. On his property he set up a professional batting cage. He remained a keen observer of the game, willing to lend a hand when asked. Julio Navarro said, "But you gotta be serious! Shady will get you up at 8 in the morning. And he'll ask after that session, 'What are you doing in the afternoon?' He says, 'If you want me to teach, I'll teach. But if you don't, then don't come here.'"

In the winter of 1998-99, Carlos Baerga, another devoted former pupil from the Cleveland days, enlisted Shady's help. When St. Louis invited the second baseman to spring training, José came along. A roving minor-league post with the Cards was discussed but did not pan out. Another big Puerto Rican star who sought out Morales on the comeback trail was Juan González. "Igor really respects José," noted Navarro.

"Big-league hitters, they think you want something if you offer to help," Morales said. "But agents call me. Yorvit Torrealba's agent, he asked me to work with him." It is interesting to note that the Rockies catcher notched career highs in at-bats, home runs, and slugging percentage in 2006. "Yadier Molina — I worked with him on the side last year too."

Rockies general manager Dan O'Dowd, who worked with José in Cleveland as director of player development, interviewed him for the Rockies' vacant hitting instructor position in October 2006. He was also offered jobs at Triple-A, but turned them down. If Morales ever joins a team again, it will be on his terms. "Too much politics in the game — you gotta kiss ass. And I ain't gonna kiss no one's behind," he observed bluntly. "I got my pension, I don't need nothing."

José married his wife, Lyduvina (née Nieves), on January 21, 1968. Lyduvina's nephew, Melvin Nieves, was a big-league outfielder from 1992-98 and another godson of José's. They had three children, Patricia, José Miguel, and Eliut, and two grandsons.

Shady remained highly attentive to the needs of his ailing mother, whose home was close by. He occasionally visited family and friends in the Virgin Islands. In 2002 he remarked, "You get more recognition away from St. Croix than you do there. You're more of a king out of your kingdom. I'm always happy to see my friends, but they're always saying, 'I remember you when you were wearing no shoes!'"

This biography originally appeared on the website Baseball in the Virgin Islands (home.nyc.rr.com/vibaseball), from which it has been adapted. Grateful acknowledgment to José Morales for his personal memories (additional telephone interviews on December 13, 2002, and April 22, 2007). Continued thanks also to Julio Navarro.

José Morales on the art of pinch-hitting

"I've done it so often and for such a long time, I don't consider it a pressure job."

"I've always had success at coming off the bench to hit but I don't really know why. I think you've got to love to hit, and I do. And I believe you must always be ready, and I always am. For instance, when you pinch-hit, you may only see one fastball. Well, when it comes, you better be ready to hit it. You can't let that pitch get past you."

"If you go to the plate thinking the pitcher is good, there is no way you're going to get a hit. You have to have a positive attitude. So I bat thinking I'm going to get a hit every time. No one can bat 1.000. But I try. Then, if the pitcher does get me out, I have to admit he was the better man that time. But he doesn't destroy my confidence. I still feel I'll get him the next time."[20]

"You have to be thinking something when you go up there. You have to have a plan. You can't go up there cold."[21]

"There aren't many players that take the game home with them, but I do. Even the night before, I'll be thinking about what the pitcher is probably going to throw in different situations. You have to do a lot of mental preparation. That's the key. I always have my mind on the game."

"In this job you can't afford to miss…that's what they're paying you for. For me a slump is every time I don't get on base. Look, if I don't get a hit, that's my incentive to go out there the next time and bang one. I say to myself, 'Tough luck, José,' and try to do better the next time."

"The only difference between us is that he [a relief pitcher] comes in to close the line, and I go in there to open it up. We have pride in what we do."[22]

SOURCES

José A. Crescioni Benítez, *El Béisbol Profesional Boricua* (San Juan, Puerto Rico: Aurora Comunicación Integral, Inc., 1997), 275.

baseball-reference.com

retrosheet.org

Professional Baseball Players Database V6.0

NOTES

1   Charles Cooper, "Braun, Morales, Staub Come Through in a Pinch," Associated Press, June 24, 1984.

2   Augie Borgi, "Just for the Record: José Is OK in a Pinch," *New York Daily News*, September 28, 1976.

3   *The Sporting News*, May 12, 1979.

4   Patrick Reusse, "Morales' Tall Talk Tickles Twins," *The Sporting News*, August 2, 1980.

5   Borgi.

6   Thomas E. Van Hyning, *Puerto Rico's Winter League* (Jefferson, North Carolina: McFarland & Company, 1995), 130.

7   Mike Shatzkin, ed., *The Ballplayers* (New York: Arbor House/William Morrow, 1990), 759.

8   Ron Bergman, "Hunter Gets OK to Pitch This Week," *Oakland Tribune*, August 13, 1973, E31.

9   Regis McAuley, "Depression Catching," *Mansfield* (Ohio) *News Journal*, July 8, 1973, 8F.

10 Ron Bergman, "Finley Reprimand by Commissioner," *Oakland Tribune*, October 15, 1973, E35.

11 Bob Dunn, "Expos Could Present Ideal DH: Morales," *The Sporting News*, January 24, 1976, 45.

12 Gordon Verrell, "Dodgers Turning Huge Profits in Spanish Antiques," *The Sporting News*, June 24, 1978, 3. Davalillo's 1970 pinch-hit total was later corrected to 23.

13 Floyd Conner, *Baseball's Most Wanted II* (Dulles, Virginia: Brassey's, 2003), 122-23.

14 Bob Fowler, "Morales Is Mighty Tough as Twins' Pinch-Swinger," *The Sporting News*, June 24, 1978, 35.

15 Ken Nigro, "Two Big Bats Buttress O's," *The Sporting News*, January 10, 1981, 35.

16 Gordon Verrell, "Dodgers' Morales a Pinch-Hit Expert," *The Sporting News*, May 9, 1983, 18.

17 "Implausible Chiefs Pitching," *The Sporting News*, July 9, 1984, 35.

18 Tom Singer, "Joy Over Joyner in Angels Camp," *The Sporting News*, April 7, 1986, 41.

19 Mel Antonen, "Navarro's Godfather Doesn't Pitch Advice," *USA Today*, March 11, 1994, 4C.

20 Fowler.

21 Verrell, "Dodgers' Morales a Pinch-Hit Expert."

22 Cooper.

Bill North

By Tim Herlich

"The mentality of a basestealer is, when you get to first base, you see, you look around and say, 'Now they're in *my* ballpark.' Know why? Cause I can get a lead and take two steps. Pitcher ducks. Catcher's coming out. Shortstop's coming across. Second baseman's coming across. Center fielder's coming up. Cause I took two steps. And they couldn't stop me anyway! *That's* the mentality of a base stealer. You have to have that mentality. Look at these guys! Look at all that action! And they can't stop me anyway!"[1]

With determination, speed, toughness, swagger, and a resolve to never back down from conflict or confrontation, Bill North forged an impressive 11-year major-league career with the Chicago Cubs, Oakland A's, Los Angeles Dodgers, and San Francisco Giants.

North was the starting center fielder on four playoff teams, and earned World Series championship rings on two of them, the Oakland A's of 1973 and 1974. His fielding range was excellent; from 1973 through '76, he recorded more putouts than any other major-league outfielder. Despite a .261 career batting average, which was roughly on par with that of the league, his career on-base percentage of .365 was 43 points above the league average. Batting first or second in the lineup for most of his career, North racked up 395 stolen bases, leading the American League in 1974 and 1976, and narrowly missing a title in 1973 due to injury. Twice he was voted the outstanding player on his team by local sportswriters.

Yet North received very little national recognition. He never was selected to an All-Star team, or honored with a Gold Glove award. He received just two votes in league MVP balloting during his career. His postseason play was undistinguished, as he managed just 3 hits (but 8 runs) in 59 League Championship and World Series at-bats.

Perhaps North's best-known moment in the national spotlight was a celebrated clubhouse fight with superstar teammate Reggie Jackson in June of 1974. It typified the tumultuous times of the three-peat world champion Oakland A's of the early 1970s—a fractious collection of gifted ballplayers who attained the highest pinnacle of their sport despite frequent, sometimes violent, clashes of ego. The fight was one of several altercations that punctuated North's playing career.

William Alex North was born on May 15, 1948, in Seattle, the youngest of five children to Frances North, a strong woman who held the family together through all types of adversity. "Mom never raised us with any bitterness," he reflected. "I had a great childhood." He developed a passion for baseball at an early age and went to Sick's Stadium whenever he could to watch his hometown Rainiers of the Pacific Coast League.

He attended Seattle's Garfield High School, playing primarily second base, and in one game completed an unassisted triple play. But the diminutive infielder failed to attract the attention of big-league scouts, and after graduating in 1966 enrolled in Central Washington State College (now Central Washington University).

At Central Washington, North was mentored by new baseball coach Gary Frederick. "I was a pretty bad boy," he said in a 1972 interview. "I definitely had an attitude problem. But I was fortunate in having a very understanding coach in Gary Frederick. He helped straighten me out."[2] Said Coach Frederick, "All he could do when I got him was hit, run, and throw, and I taught him how to carry the chip on his shoulder."[3] In his sophomore year, North led the Wildcats to the National Association of Intercollegiate Athletics tournament finals, where they finished third. The following year, North hit .476 and was named an honorable mention All-American.[4] North elected to leave school after his junior year and was selected by the Chicago Cubs in the 12th round of the 1969 major-league draft. The scout who signed him was former major-league infielder George Freese.

North started his professional career that summer in Caldwell, Idaho. He led the Pioneer League in stolen bases with 42 and scored 67 runs on 50 base hits plus 61 walks. That fall he played in the Arizona Instructional League and won high praise from manager Lou Klein. "[Klein] predicted that the Cubs' next big hitter in the Banks-Santo-Williams mold will be outfielder Bill North," wrote Jerome Holtzman in *The Sporting News* the following summer.[5] North played most of 1970 with Quincy, Illinois, the Cubs' affiliate in the Class A Midwest League, and moved up to Double-A San Antonio in 1971. He led the Texas League with 91 runs scored and 47 stolen bases, and finished third in batting at .291. He earned a berth on the Texas League All-Star Team[6] and a September call-up to the Cubs, where he collected 6 hits in 16 at-bats.

North had made it to the big leagues strictly as a right-handed batter with some power, but was sent to the Arizona Instructional League after the 1971

season to learn to become a switch-hitter. Cubs manager Leo Durocher wanted to take advantage of North's speed. He led the fall league in runs scored, stolen bases, and walks,[7] and switch-hit his entire major-league career thereafter.

North hit over .400 in spring training in 1972[8] and appeared to have won a starting job in the outfield when the club broke camp in Arizona to play exhibition games against the White Sox at New Orleans' Tulane University football field. North looked at the concrete wall outside the running track that ringed the stadium and commented that he didn't like the field. According to North, pitching coach Hank Aguirre overheard and misinterpreted the comment and reported to manager Durocher that North didn't want to play. North rode the bench that night.

The next day, April 1, the Players Association called a strike against major league baseball that lasted until the 13th. When the strike was settled and the season began, North remained in Durocher's doghouse. He played sporadically before being optioned to Triple-A Wichita in May and again in July. Disheartened and defiant, North told the club he was quitting baseball to become a teacher, but acquiesced when Cubs vice president John Holland told him he'd be suspended indefinitely if he did not report. North batted over .400 for the Aeros with a 16-game hitting streak[9] and rejoined the Cubs on July 29. He ended his first season as a switch-hitter batting just .181, and was again sent to polish his skills in the Arizona Instructional League, where he was voted an all-star.[10]

Nonetheless, Chicago traded the promising young outfielder to the 1972 world champion Oakland Athletics that winter for Bob Locker, a 34-year-old relief pitcher. North made the A's roster as a fifth outfielder, but manager Dick Williams needed a leadoff hitter because shortstop Bert Campaneris was suspended the first week of the 1973 season. Williams inserted North into his Opening Day lineup as the A's first-ever designated hitter. North collected two hits and continued to DH until he moved to center field in late April.

Williams took an immediate liking to his new speedster, "the only player I've ever seen literally strut on to a world championship team. I saw North and thought, 'This will be fun.'"[11] It didn't take long for North to inject himself into the shenanigans of the Oakland clubhouse. The A's started the 1973 season with three straight losses, then flew to Chicago to play the White Sox. "On the bus ride from the airport to the hotel," Williams recalled in his autobiography, "I heard North and Blue Moon Odom sniping at each other, and then sniping louder, and I thought 'We're going to have our first fight before our first victory.'"[12] By May 2 North was leading the league with eight stolen bases, but hitting just .208, when Williams dropped him to ninth in the batting order. Over the next four weeks, North hit .397 to raise his season batting average to .303 and stole seven more bases. He hit his first major-league home run on May 17, off the California Angels' Rudy May. The next night, against Kansas City, North initiated a fight that earned him an ejection, a three-day suspension, and a $100 fine.

In that ruckus, the A's were leading 5-4 when North stepped to the plate in the bottom of the eighth against Royals rookie reliever Doug Bird. On Bird's first pitch, North swung and missed, and his bat sailed out near the mound. "Walking to the mound," Williams wrote, "just before he reached his bat, North stopped, turned, and nailed Bird with a right to the jaw. Bird dropped, but North didn't stop—he jumped on him and pounded him. What in the hell is Bill North doing pounding a guy after the guy throws him a strike? Did I have an insane man on my hands? I mean, more insane than the guys I already had?"[13]

Williams called North into his office after the game and demanded an explanation. North told the manager that in a Midwest League game in 1970, he came to bat after Bird surrendered back-to-back home runs. Bird knocked him down with his first pitch, then drilled him in the left ear with the next.[14] North had not forgotten the incident and vowed to get even. Williams chastised North for taking the game into his own hands. "Why didn't you at least tell us, and we would have gotten back at him some other way!"

Williams bellowed. "This is a team that doesn't just play together, it fights together!"[15]

The beaning by Doug Bird in 1970 was a defining moment in North's career. "I waited one pitch too long," he recalled later. "I should have stopped it when he knocked me down. And that's the way I felt about it the rest of my career." Later in 1973, the Angels' Dick Lange threw a pitch at North's legs. North responded on the next pitch with a drag bunt, hoping Lange would attempt to field the ball. Instead, first baseman Mike Epstein charged in and tagged North hard on the neck, but dropped the ball. Standing on first, North initiated a near-brawl with Epstein. Both benches emptied before order was restored.[16] "North's an aggressive player," said Dick Williams, admiring his combative style of play. "He can play for me anytime."[17]

After the suspension, North played in every one of the A's next 112 games. Manager Williams elevated him from ninth to second to leadoff spot in the batting order. The A's climbed back into contention, moving into first place in the American League West to stay by mid-August. On September 20 they were just days away from clinching the title. North was the offensive catalyst, batting .285 on that day, with an on-base average of .376, and leading the league in stolen bases (53) and runs scored (98). In the second game of a doubleheader that day in Minnesota, his fortunes turned. With a man on third, North hit a grounder to second base. Rod Carew fielded the ball and threw home. North took his eye off first base to follow the throw, and landed awkwardly on the side of the bag. He sprained his ankle so severely that he missed the rest of the season, including the American League Championship Series and the World Series. Boston's Tommy Harper and teammate Reggie Jackson nipped North the final week of the season to take the stolen-base and runs-scored titles, respectively.

The A's dispatched the Orioles to win the AL pennant, and then defeated the New York Mets in seven games in the 1973 World Series. Due to a blunder by owner Charlie Finley, the A's had only 24 eligible players on its Series roster. Finley petitioned the Mets and Commissioner Bowie Kuhn for accommodation but was denied. To accentuate his position that the A's were at a disadvantage playing shorthanded, Finley did not allow the injured North to suit up or sit in the dugout with his teammates, despite North's contribution to the team's success. "I was his pawn because of the beef that he was having with Bowie Kuhn," North recollected. Disconsolate, North watched Game Three from the Shea Stadium grandstand, with the players' families, then flew back home to Oakland. As a result, he was not in New York during the Mike Andrews controversy, nor in the A's clubhouse when Dick Williams announced he would resign after the Series. He did receive a World Series ring and a full share of the postseason bonus.[18]

North began the 1974 season under new manager Alvin Dark in the worst hitting slump of his career, collecting only two hits in his first 33 at-bats. He was coming back from the severe ankle sprain of the previous year and nursing a sore hamstring. By contrast, Reggie Jackson was off to a phenomenal start, batting over .400 and leading the league in home runs. Jackson had attained full-fledged superstardom the year before, being selected Most Valuable Player of both the regular season and the World Series. He had always gotten along with North. Sometime in mid-April, however, North failed to run hard to first on a routine groundout. When he returned to the bench, Jackson berated him in front of his teammates for not hustling. The seeds of The Fight were sown.

"I tried to set him up for a month," North recalled. He gave Jackson the silent treatment despite his torrid start, and refused to talk to him on or off the field. He would not congratulate Jackson after home runs. Gradually, North lifted his average to .228 and took the league lead in stolen bases. Jackson remained hot, batting .390 with a league-leading 15 home runs, and the A's were atop the AL West when they arrived in Detroit to play a night game against the Tigers on June 5.

In the locker room at Tiger Stadium, North made a remark that infuriated Jackson and ignited the brawl. The superstar, who was not even dressed for the game

yet, charged North and the two wrestled on the floor, in full view of teammates and sportswriters. Catcher Ray Fosse, pitcher Vida Blue, and others were able to separate the two, only to have the combatants tangle again a few minutes later. "It wasn't a regular clubhouse fight," said an A's teammate anonymously. "There was no backing off. They went at it hot and heavy—twice."[19] When the dust settled, Jackson ended up with a bruised shoulder and a battered ego. Fosse suffered a separated cervical disc in the melee and was out of action until late in the season. Owner Finley met the team in Milwaukee a few days later and chastised both combatants. For the rest of the June, Jackson batted .197 with just three doubles, no home runs, and four RBIs. Finally, North and Jackson met to clear the air and lift Jackson out of his funk. Reggie regrouped and finished the 1974 season with a .289 average, 29 home runs, and 93 RBIs. North finished with a league-leading 54 stolen bases, despite a foot problem that lingered all year long, a .260 average, and .347 OBP. He also compiled the finest defensive season of his career, recording 9 assists and making only 4 errors while finishing third in the league with 437 putouts

The A's won the AL West division for the fourth year in a row and defeated the Orioles again in the ALCS. The 1974 World Series pitted the defending champions against the Los Angeles Dodgers. First baseman Bill Buckner bragged about the Dodgers' seeming superiority: "If we played them 162 games, we'd win 100."[20] The A's went about their usual business, which included a North-Jackson-type scuffle between Rollie Fingers and Blue Moon Odom in the Dodger Stadium clubhouse the day before the Series began. "I learned my lesson," North said playfully at the time. "When Blue Moon and Rollie went at it, I moved to the other side of the clubhouse."[21] After the fracas, the A's vanquished the Dodgers in five games to win their third straight World Series title.

In his first postseason, North collected only two hits in 33 at-bats, but scored six runs, stole two bases, and played a hand offensively in all four of the A's World Series victories. Unlike 1973, he was able to celebrate on the field with his teammates, earning his second World Series ring.[22]

In 1975, despite losing Catfish Hunter to free agency, the A's won 98 games and a fifth straight AL West title. North batted .273 with a .373 OBP for the season, but his stolen-base total dropped to 30. Painful bone spurs that required surgery to his left ankle the following winter played a role. Also, manager Dark took away North's permanent green light, the only time that happened during his career. The impact of the loss of Hunter became evident in the postseason, as the A's were swept three straight by the Boston Red Sox in the ALCS. North went hitless in 10 at-bats.

In an afternoon game in Oakland on June 8, the center fielder failed to catch a deep line drive to left-center with two out in the ninth inning that some said he should have had, costing staff ace Ken Holtzman a third career no-hitter. "Every time I hear that, it pisses me off," North retorted in an interview. "We're supposed to pitch [weak-hitting Tom Veryzer] hard away. So I'm playing right-center field and shallow. [Holtzman] floated a damn changeup inside." Veryzer lined the ball into the left-center-field alley. In the Oakland Coliseum, the sun goes across from first base to third base, right behind home plate. "I'm running back. It's in the sun. If I had a clean run to it, I'd have had to dive for the ball to get it."

That winter the reserve clause that had stood in baseball since 1879 was struck down. North and teammates Jackson, Bando, Rudi, Campaneris, Holtzman, Fingers, Gene Tenace, and Vida Blue held out against owner Finley for better contracts. On April 27, 1976, North signed a two-year deal worth $75,000 per season, a substantial increase over his previous salary of $55,000.[23] The others remained unsigned, to become free agents at the end of the year. One week before the start of the season, Finley dropped a bombshell by trading Jackson and Holtzman to the Orioles. Without Jackson, new manager Chuck Tanner turned to the running game, and the A's stole a league-record 341 bases en route to a second-place division finish. North led the majors with 75 thefts, breaking Campaneris's Oakland club record. In his autobiography, teammate

Billy Williams recalled that when North was closing in on the record, "Campaneris would swing and foul every time Billy would take off to steal."[24] If not for Campaneris, North believed, he would have stolen 110 bases, easily setting a new American League record. North also led the team in runs, hits, and batting average, and was named Outstanding Player by the Bay Area sportswriters.

Before North joined the A's, Campaneris led the American League in stolen bases six times, including an Oakland franchise record of 62 thefts two years in a row. From 1973 through 1976, when they were together in Oakland, North stole more bases than Campaneris each year. North was successful on 71 percent of his career attempts, compared with Campaneris's success rate of 77 percent. "When I had a hitter hitting behind me, I had to steal second base on the first three pitches, or I'm taking the bat out of his hands," North said. "That's why I got thrown out quite a bit. But check the record from the seventh to the ninth [innings], on Campaneris, too. When the game's *on the line*." Indeed, from 1973 to 1976, North swiped 29 bases in 38 close-and-late attempts; Campaneris was 19 for 32.[25]

North and the A's would just as soon forget 1977. Only North and Blue returned to play for Oakland; the rest of the elite players became free agents and signed to play elsewhere. On Opening Day, North was the only returning starter from the previous year. Five weeks into the season, he missed nearly a month after severely cutting his foot when a shower door shattered at his health club. Shortly after returning to the lineup, he fractured his index finger on a sacrifice bunt and missed two more months. By the time he returned from the disabled list in late August, the team was hopelessly out of contention. North did not play after September 7 and finished 1977 with a .261 average and 17 stolen bases in 56 games. The A's sank to last in the AL West, with 98 losses.

Two weeks after attending the 1977 World Series in Los Angeles, North was arrested at his Bay Area home in a drug bust. Undercover police had bought cocaine from an acquaintance staying with North's roommate while North was out of town. On October 29, just before midnight, a vice squad burst through the front door. Drugs on the premises were seized, and North was charged with drug trafficking and possession of cocaine for sale, a felony carrying a maximum sentence of three to five years. A magistrate of the Oakland Municipal Court looked over the evidence and dismissed the charges. But the drug bust certainly did not enhance North's image.

The 1978 season was North's option year with the A's, his salary reduced to $64,000,[26] after which he would become a free agent. When Finley traded Vida Blue to the San Francisco Giants during spring training, North was the only player remaining from the A's championship years. On May 17, the day before his 30th birthday, Finley swung a waiver deal that sent North to the defending NL champion Dodgers for utility outfielder Glenn Burke. North scored 14 runs in his first 15 games with manager Tom Lasorda's crew. For much of the year, he batted over .280 with an on-base percentage well over .400 before tailing off to finish at .234 with a .371 OBP and 27 stolen bases, second on the team. North shared center-field duties with Rick Monday and helped the Dodgers win a second successive pennant before losing the World Series in a rematch against former teammate Reggie Jackson and the Yankees.

According to North, the Dodgers offered him a four-year $932,000 contract "but my agent suggested I go free agency. I was supposed to be one of the top free agents of the day." Instead, whether it was due to his drug arrest the previous year or other factors, North attracted almost no interest. "I had to go beg for a contract," he said. Finally, on March 9, North himself negotiated a one-year deal with the San Francisco Giants.

North had a fine season in 1979 for the Giants. Batting leadoff, he led the team with a .386 on-base percentage, 96 walks, 87 runs scored, and 58 stolen bases. He was named the team's outstanding player by the local sportswriters, and the Giants rewarded North with a three-year contract at more than $200,000 a year. The Giants as a team were a huge disappointment, falling

to a distant fourth place in the NL West after contending the year before.

North worked hard that winter with new hitting coach Jim Lefebvre, and got off to a great start in 1980, reaching base in each of the first 33 games he started. On April 17, trying to advance from first to third on a single, he unintentionally broke the nose of the Padres' Aurelio Rodriguez with an elbow-high slide. The 1980 Giants were expected to contend, but it was not to be. North barely played the last month of the season, and finished with a .251 batting average, a .373 OBP, and 45 stolen bases in 128 games.

The Giants hired Frank Robinson as manager for the 1981 season. At the time North publicly lauded the move, proclaiming, "He's a winner. He also has credibility as an individual and can make the Giants a cohesive unit."[27] Privately, the two had clashed earlier in North's career and Bill knew Robinson did not like him. When Robinson decided to platoon North with right-handed batter Jerry Martin, it didn't sit well. On May 8 in Montreal, North went 2-for-4 and stole three bases. The following night, off Expos ace Steve Rogers, he stroked the only grand slam, and the last home run, of his career, and drove in six runs, a career best. Despite the offensive explosion, North started only 10 of the next 22 games, and was hitting just .221, but with a .354 on-base percentage and 26 stolen bases, when the players' strike brought the season to a halt. When the strike was settled in August, North was released. Dispirited, he left baseball behind and did not pursue any potential opportunities to play the rest of the year.

North's old manager, Dick Williams, invited him to compete for a job with the San Diego Padres in 1982. If San Diego kept North on its roster, it would have to assume the final year of his contract with the Giants. At the end of spring training, Williams told North he did not make the team. His major-league career was over at the age of 33.

After baseball, North pursued different vocations before becoming a financial planner. He picked up the few remaining credits he needed to earn his bachelor's degree in sociology, attending commencement at Central Washington University in 1992. He began teaching the art of hitting to high-school, college and pro athletes. He and his wife, Pam, reside in Kirkland, Washington. They have a daughter, Ashley.

ACKNOWLEDGEMENTS

The author is indebted to Frances North, Gary Frederick, and especially Bill North and his family for consenting to the series of interviews that contributed to this work.

SOURCES

Dickey, Glenn. *Champions: The Story of the First Two Oakland A's Dynasties and the Building of the Third* (Chicago: Triumph Books, 2002)

Hunter, Jim, and Armen Keteyian, *Catfish: My Life in Baseball* (New York: Berkley Books, 1989)

Jackson, Reggie, and Mike Lupica, *Reggie* (New York: Ballantine Books, 1984)

Markusen, Bruce, *Baseball's Last Dynasty: Charlie Finley's Oakland A's* (Indianapolis: Masters Press, 1998)

Williams, Billy, and Fred Mitchell, *Billy Williams, My Sweet-Swinging Lifetime With the Cubs* (Chicago: Triumph Books, 2008)

Williams, Dick, and Bill Plaschke, *No More Mr. Nice Guy* (San Diego: Harcourt Brace Jovanovich, 1990)

Sporting News Baseball Guide, 1970 through 1982

The Sporting News, 1970-1983

retrosheet.org

Interviews with Bill North on February 23, March 15, May 31, and November 29, 2008, Frances North on November 17, 2007, and Gary Frederick on March 25, 2008.

NOTES

1   Interview with Bill North, March 15, 2008. All quotations from Bill North are from his interviews with the author in 2008 unless otherwise noted.

2   Edgar Munzel, "North's Torrid Bat Could Force Change in Cub Garden Forecast," *The Sporting News*, April 8, 1972, 27.

3   Interview with Gary Frederick, March 29, 2008.

4   Bergman, Ron, "A's Center Field Vacancy Interests North," *The Sporting News*, February 3, 1973, 36.

5   Jerome Holtzman, *The Sporting News*, July 4, 1970, 8.

6   "Caught on the Fly," *The Sporting News*, October 9, 1971, 35.

7   Ed Prell, "Cey Hey! Ron Dominant Figure in Arizona Loop," *The Sporting News*, December 4, 1971, 53.

8   Glenn Dickey, *Champions: The Story of the First Two Oakland A's Dynasties and the Building of the Third*, 56.

9   Ron Bergman, *The Sporting News*, February 3, 1973, 36.

10 Ed Prell, "Cactus Loop Picks 16-Man All-Star Squad," *The Sporting News*, December 2, 1972, 53.

11 Dick Williams and Bill Plaschke, *No More Mr. Nice Guy*, 156.

12 Ibid.

13 Williams and Plaschke, 157.

14 Ron Bergman, "A's Charge Double Standards in North Case," *The Sporting News*, June 9, 1973, 17.

15 Williams and Plaschke, 157.

16 Bruce Markusen, *Baseball's Last Dynasty, Charlie Finley's Oakland A's*, 228.

17 Markusen, 229.

18 "Players Split Up Record Playoff-Series Pot," *The Sporting News*, December 1, 1973, 30.

19 Markusen, 300.

20 Dickey, 84.

21 Dickey, 60.

22 "A's, Dodgers Divvy Up Record Series Swag," *The Sporting News*, November 23, 1974, 48.

23 Ron Bergman, "Unsigned A's See Break in Logjam," *The Sporting News*, May 15, 1976, 13; Milton Richman, "Average Regular's Pay Rockets to $95,149," *The Sporting News*, April 23, 1977, 29.

24 Billy Williams and Fred Mitchell, *Billy Williams, My Sweet-Swinging Lifetime With the Cubs*, 164.

25 Retrosheet.org.

26 Jerome Holtzman, *The Sporting News*, April 8, 1978, 43.

27 Nick Peters, "Older, Wiser Robinson Given Giant Welcome," *The Sporting News*, January 31, 1981, 47.

Horacio Piña

by Rory Costello and Francisco Rodríguez Lozano

This lanky pitcher was the first Mexican player to win a World Series ring. *El Ejote* — The Stringbean — was a member of the Oakland A's bullpen in 1973. His motion was quirky and memorable: Whipping the ball from a low side-arm/submarine angle, Piña then swung wide and landed hard with his trailing right foot. NBC's broadcasts of the 1973 World Series focused on the impact crater that Horacio created.

Piña pitched in 314 big-league games from 1968 to 1978, starting just seven times. After 1974 he then went back to Mexico, where he was a very effective starter in both summer and winter ball. His best season was the summer of 1978, highlighted by a perfect game on July 12. His 21-4, 1.94 record earned him a final two-game stint in the majors that September. Horacio then pitched on in Mexico through 1980 until he hurt his shoulder. He entered his homeland's Baseball Hall of Fame in 1988.

Horacio Piña García was born in Matamoros de La Laguna, in the state of Coahuila. This Matamoros is not the city directly across the Rio Grande from Brownsville, Texas (400 miles east, in the state of Tamaulipas). It is half an hour east of Torreón, the center of Mexico's ninth-biggest metro area. The Laguna region surrounds Torreón and its twin city Gómez Palacio, just across the Nazas River in the state of Durango.

Horacio's father was Roberto Piña Trujillo, a corn-mill operator on a communal farm called Ejido las Maravillas. On March 12, 1945, the fourth of Roberto and Nohemí García Castro's seven children entered the world.[1] Before Horacio came José, Óscar, and Silvia; after him were Cuca, Roberto, and Jaime.

Note the tilde (~) in the family name, which the American press left out in his playing days. He never had it on his uniforms in the US either; they read only

PINA. Looking back in 2009, though, Piña said it never mattered to him. "I had a lot of discipline. I came in running from the dugout to the field and I left running. What's more, I didn't know what that little thing above the 'n' was even called! It was only later I found out it's called a tilde."

Matamoros is a baseball-loving city, as is much of northern Mexico. Roberto Piña was a semipro pitcher (with a conventional overhand delivery). Horacio, however, barely touched bat and ball growing up — he favored soccer. He played goalie and sweeper because of his height. He only came to baseball by chance at age 17 after picking up a foul ball from a local field called Campo Cámara. His return throw was impressive enough to prompt someone to ask if he wanted to play ball. Horacio demurred, but the additional promise of 50 pesos — good money for the time — got him to join his first team. La Paletería Galindo (a

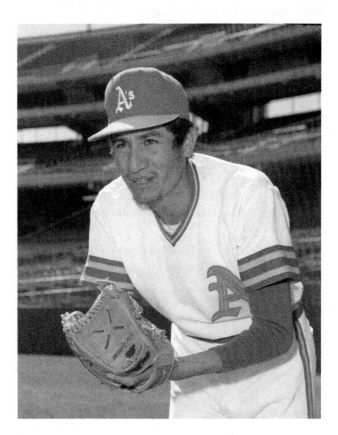

purveyor of paletas, or Mexican popsicles) was the sponsor.[2] He later pitched for another team called "Los Chicos del Once."[3]

There were other local clubs in Gómez Palacio. During a 1963 game there, the gangling teenager got nick-named for life. He stood well over 6 feet tall but then weighed little more than 150 pounds.[4] A friend named Joaquín Gómez first called him "slice of watermelon" and then Ejote. The latter tag stuck.[5]

In 1964 Piña played for the "Frankie" team of Gómez Palacio, as well as the Matamoros team in La Liga Mayor de Béisbol de La Laguna. After a regional championship game in the city of Guadalupe Victoria (also in Durango), scouts from the Puebla Pericos organization in the Mexican League approached him.[6] One was Nazario Moreno, who played just 32 games at the nation's top level but remained on the scene in various capacities, including manager. Horacio told them, "I don't know how to play." They replied, "We'll teach you there." His mother signed the contract, since his father had passed away.[7]

For the 1965 season, Piña joined Zacatecas in the Mexican Center League (Class A), a Puebla farm club also known as the Pericos (Parrots). He pitched 116 innings in 38 games, winning four and losing six. Control was a problem, as he walked 72 men, fueling a fat 6.60 ERA.

Horacio appeared in just six games with Zacatecas in 1966. He wanted to join the big club in Puebla, then managed by former Cleveland Indians star Beto Ávila (known as "Bobby" in the US). The Pericos reassigned him to the farm team, though, and so Piña went instead to the Monclova Acereros in La Liga del Norte de Coahuila. He also played for Matamoros in La Laguna's top league again.[8]

In 1967 Piña made the Puebla team. Even after he threw a 1-0 shutout, the Pericos had their doubts about whether he could be a starter. Horacio therefore decided to return to La Liga del Norte, but Cuban manager Tony Castaño persuaded him to stay.[9] Piña went on to win 16 games against 11 losses for the

last-place club, while posting a 3.28 ERA. The Mexican Baseball Writers Association did not make its annual MVP and Rookie of the Year selections that year, owing to an internal dispute. The Mexico City sports paper *La Afición* polled the league's managers, though, and they named Horacio top rookie.[10]

Regino "Reggie" Otero, a scout for the Cleveland Indians, was paying attention. Otero, a Cuban who had played briefly with the Chicago Cubs in 1945, had moved into scouting after serving as a coach with the Tribe in 1966. Cleveland worked out a deal with Puebla, and Horacio then joined Reno in the California League (Class A). There he went 1-0, 4.00 in 18 innings across three games.

After the summer season ended, Piña played winter ball at home for the first time in La Liga Mexicana del Pacífico (LMP). The owner of the Culiacán Tomateros, merchant Juan Ley Fong (known as "Chino" for his Chinese birth) brought him aboard. In December 1967 Horacio reeled off an impressive streak of 46⅓ scoreless innings, still (as of 2014) a league record. It started with 13⅔ innings in relief on the 12th; three straight shutouts followed before opponents finally got to him in the sixth inning of his next start. Piña also pitched a no-hitter that winter, winning 2-1.

Horacio pitched in spring training with the Indians in 1968. He opened the season on loan to the Portland Beavers, Cleveland's Triple-A affiliate, and made five sharp starts, including a one-hitter with nine strikeouts his first time out. Overall, he was 3-1, 0.69 in 39 innings before returning to Puebla in mid-May. That was the deal he made with the Indians front office—under threat of fine and/or suspension—because his salary was lower in Triple-A than the Mexican League.[11]

El Ejote continued to do well with the Parrots. He went 9-6, although he lost his last four decisions, with a 2.22 ERA. That prompted Cleveland to purchase his contract in mid-August. They were supposed to wait until after the Mexican League season ended on August 16, but manager Alvin Dark wanted his help.[12] "There was talk on the team that he was a racist," said

Piña in 2009, "but it wasn't certain, because there were various Latinos. He gave a chance to everyone, and those who got the job done, we got in."

Piña made his big-league debut at Cleveland's Municipal Stadium on August 14. In relief of Luis Tiant, he retired all six Detroit Tigers who faced him, striking out four. Three days later, again at home, he relieved his fellow Mexican Vicente Romo and picked up the last two outs against the Chicago White Sox. It was his first of 38 saves in the majors.

On August 21, Piña made his first big-league start, against the Boston Red Sox at Municipal Stadium. He allowed two runs (one unearned) in 8⅔ innings and left to a standing ovation from the crowd of 8,991. Vicente Romo returned the favor, finishing off the 8-2 victory. One point of interest was that the US papers listed his age as 21 rather than 23.

After the game, Horacio said, "I tired a little in the last inning and I believe this was the hottest night I have ever pitched. It is a little cooler in Mexico where I pitched this year. I was a little nervous at the start and also wild because I couldn't control my overhand fastball."[13] It is notable that he varied his motion in his earlier years. Also, one of his Latino teammates must have translated, because the rookie spoke little if any English then. Perhaps it was Luis Tiant; in 2009 Piña remembered how good the Cuban was to him. "In any way or whatever thing he would help us. On days off we would get together with the family—a very good person."

Author Bruce Markusen, who chronicled the Oakland dynasty of the early '70s, described Piña. "At six feet, two inches, and 160 pounds, the reed-thin right-hander .earned the nickname 'Ichabod Crane' during his early major league days. An impressive physical specimen he was not."[14] During the '70s, Horacio filled out to nearly 180 pounds. His wiry hair also grew quite bushy at times (as depicted on his Mexican Hall of Fame plaque and his bust at Campo Cámara).

Piña made the Indians staff in spring training 1969 and pitched in 31 games for them over the first four months, although he spent a brief spell with Portland in April. On the surface, his ERA was an unimpressive 5.21, but a couple of bad outings inflated that number. At the end of July, after the White Sox hit him hard, Cleveland sent Horacio down to Double-A Waterbury.[15] He did not appear in a single game there, though—rather, he went home. "I pitched more effectively than others, but I was demoted while they stayed," he said in 1990. "They (Cleveland) threatened to suspend me."[16] In fact, *The Sporting News* said he was suspended after refusing to report.[17]

On December 5 the Indians traded Piña along with pitcher Ron Law and infielder Dave Nelson to the Washington Senators. In return, they received Dennis Higgins and Barry Moore. The relatively minor deal received little attention at the time, as it was a busy day at the winter meetings and there was other news from the business side of the game: the move of the Seattle Pilots and a power struggle within the league offices.

That winter Culiacán won the first of two LMP titles during Horacio's time there (unfortunately, Mexico was not part of the Caribbean Series revival in 1970). He ranked these alongside his World Series as the best things that ever happened to him in baseball. About being a Tomatero, Piña said in 2007, "They were 12 unforgettable seasons. I don't forget that after each season in the big leagues, I arrived in my beloved Culiacán to defend the house of the Tomateros. We came to have the best pitching in the league for many years."[18]

Piña was late reporting to the Senators camp in 1970, until manager Ted Williams threatened to fine him $100 a day.[19] But when he did arrive, Williams became his benefactor. Although the general public was unaware back then, at least some of the Senators knew that Williams (who spoke some Spanish) had Mexican heritage. They did not know that it was on his mother's side, though, because Ted almost never spoke of family. Horacio has said that it was not a surrogate father-son relationship, yet the Splendid Splinter may still have seen something of his former self in El Ejote.

Piña described their rapport in *ProMex*, a San Antonio-based Hispanic sporting monthly of the early '90s. He told how "Williams became a close friend who helped him adjust to life in the United States. Since Pina didn't feel very secure about his English, he would get to the ballpark very early. Naturally the manager Williams was also there." Horacio also learned how to fish from the noted angler. He spoke fondly of "their talks while casting their rods into a tin can inside the dugout. '[Williams] would complain about guys like Frank Howard who were making a lot of money and weren't half as good as he was.'"[20]

In 2009 Piña added his memories of how Williams would invite him to the movies if a game got called. ("What are you doing?" "Nothing.") It would be just the two of them, and Ted would buy popcorn and a gallon of milk. They shared a lot of laughs even if they didn't understand the film. "I really appreciated him. He was a tremendous person and he gave me a job," said Horacio in summary.

Working strictly in relief, Piña appeared often with the Senators in 1970 (a career-high 61 games) and again in '71 (56 games). His stints were short by the standards of the day, as he totaled 128⅔ innings pitched. Though he continued to walk a good few batters, he was still generally effective.

Even so, author Thomas Boswell is fond of recounting one unflattering (yet funny) memory of an outing at Griffith Stadium. "Once, we saw the Senators' flamboyant submarine pitcher, Horacio Pina, as he caught his spikes and tripped in mid-delivery. He rolled down the mound in a sideways tangle as though he'd somehow nailed his own hand to the ground. For years, when somebody tried to be too flashy and fell on his face, my mother would intone, 'Horaaaacio Piiiina.'"[21]

Piña stayed with the franchise in 1972 as owner Bob Short moved it to Texas. That season he recorded a career-high 15 saves in 60 games. Though he had earned Ted Williams' confidence, Horacio said modestly, "I am just a mediocre pitcher. I could not be a starter,

but I could go in for a few innings and help the team. A relief pitcher has to throw strikes more than a starter and he has to use his brains more. … I just try to throw strikes aiming at the batter's weak points." The same article noted his "quick smile" and "friendly character"—and that he was making more money with Culiacán than he was with the Rangers.[22]

On November 30 the Rangers traded Piña to Oakland for a former Washington teammate, first baseman Mike Epstein. The A's sought room in their lineup for Gene Tenace, whose shoulder ailment was limiting his ability to catch.[23] The *Oakland Tribune* took a dim view of the deal—"Epstein [was] surrendered rather cheaply, it seemed"[24]—but it worked out well for the A's. The disgruntled slugger played only 27 games for Texas in '73 before they peddled him to the Angels, where he struggled for the rest of that season. "Superjew" was out of the majors after just 18 games with California in 1974.

On the other hand, Horacio was pleased. From Culiacán, he said, "Ted Williams was great to me and I was happy in Washington and in Texas, but pitching for the world champions will be something special."[25] He got off to a strong start in the East Bay, with some help from Oakland pitching coach Wes Stock. Bruce Markusen wrote:

"Initially, Pina had also failed to impress Stock, who noted his past inability to handle left-handed batters. Pina, an effective side-arming pitcher against right-handed hitters, seemed unwilling to use that style against lefties. 'He was coming over the top to left-handers and his ball always was up,' Stock explained to *The Sporting News*. 'His natural motion is side-arm, and his ball sinks when he throws it that way.'

"Stock quickly convinced Pina to rid himself of the overhand delivery and show courage in using his side-winding motion at all times. Pina had been given such advice in the past, but the recommendations never stuck—until now. With his long fingers and large hands, Pina already threw his best pitch, a sinking palmball, more effectively than most pitchers. Pina's palmball now became lethal to left-handed hitters, as well."[26] He had learned the pitch from bullpen mate Joe Grzenda with the Senators and mastered it in winter ball.[27]

In later years, Horacio commented, "I believe the submarine ball was a gift that God gave me ever since I started. When I went to the U.S., many people said they wanted me to change that style, but the reality is that they told me, "Forget it, you're getting outs and that's why we're keeping you with us.""[28]

Piña complemented Rollie Fingers, Darold Knowles, and Paul Lindblad nicely in the Oakland bullpen. He pitched in 47 games (6-3, 2.76) and picked up eight saves. Oddly enough, this was the first season since 1969 in which lefties had a higher batting average against him than righties.

In 2009 Horacio underscored how A's manager Dick Williams liked discipline. "He was good people but there was a lot of discipline, and that's why Oakland became champions. He didn't hang out with the team, just on the field, and outside he was apart."

He mentioned how Williams gave him chances to pitch, including various save opportunities when Rollie Fingers was not available. For a while, however, he was in Dick's doghouse. In a key situation against Baltimore, the skipper approached the mound and told him that he didn't want to see any curves or changeups, just fastballs. Piña disobeyed and gave up a home run. This appears to have been in Oakland on July 16, as aging Brooks Robinson hit a three-run homer in the seventh to give the Orioles a 7-5 lead that they then held.

"Dick Williams got mad. He had me a month [actually 11 days, but no doubt it felt longer], go warm up, sit down, warm up, sit down. He was right, I didn't pay attention. He told me, 'Here, what I say goes.' They told me that for this they could send me to Triple A."

Finally Piña returned to action on July 27 when Dave Hamilton got knocked out of the box in the first inning at Minnesota, following a doubleheader on the 26th. Williams came in and said, "Only fastballs." This time Horacio obeyed. In his view, the biggest

thing he learned from Williams was his sharp strategy in making changes. "He made some tremendous changes, good for the team and for winning."

Advancing to the postseason for the first time in the US, Horacio pitched in one game in the AL Championship Series against Baltimore. In Game Two, the Orioles knocked Vida Blue out in the first inning. Piña replaced him and pitched two scoreless innings, though he allowed one inherited runner to score.

The A's then faced the surprising New York Mets in the World Series. Horacio became the second Mexican to make it to the fall classic, following Bobby Ávila in 1954. In Game Two, Vida Blue was leading 3-2 in the sixth inning but put two runners on with one out. As Joseph Durso of the *New York Times* put it, "Blue was replaced, briefly and disastrously, by Horacio Pina and his right-handed, underhanded-whip delivery."[29] His first pitch hit Jerry Grote; he then gave up a 10-foot scratch single to Don Hahn. Bud Harrelson followed with a clean single and that was it for Piña. Darold Knowles then entered and got Jim Beauchamp to hit a comebacker that should have been a 1-2-3 double play. Instead, he slipped and threw it away, and two unearned runs were charged to Horacio. The Mets eventually won in 12 innings, 10-7, as Mike Andrews made two errors and became a scapegoat for owner Charles O. Finley.

Piña relieved for three innings in Game Four, which the Mets won 6-1. Mike Andrews, reinstated on the Oakland roster, pinch-hit for him in the eighth inning. Knowles and Fingers were the only relievers whom Dick Williams used after that. When the A's took Game Seven, though, Horacio pocketed a full winner's Series share: $24,617.57. He went home to the acclaim of all Mexico.

Not long after the Series ended (December 3), Oakland traded Piña to the Chicago Cubs, re-obtaining Bob Locker. It was a curious swap in a couple of ways. First, Locker was also a side-armer. In addition, "the trading of Locker fulfilled a promise the Cubs had made him when they swapped Billy North to Oakland for the veteran righthander [the previous offseason].

Locker ... had said he would not report unless the Cubs promised to trade him back to a Coast club."[30]

Charlie Finley, who acted as his own general manager, also apparently liked what Locker had done his first time around with the A's. Reportedly, however, Dick Williams was "dazed" by the deal, even though Piña had "fallen out of favor" with him. "How could Charlie make that trade?" Williams said. "He says he wants me back as manager and then he goes and trades Pina ... [who] is seven years younger."[31] Events would prove the manager mostly right. Locker missed the entire 1974 season after an elbow operation; Oakland then shipped him back to Chicago, along with Darold Knowles and Manny Trillo, for Billy Williams.

Meanwhile, in the National League for the first time, Piña appeared in 34 games for the Cubs in 1974. The team had envisaged him as their short reliever, but there were few save opportunities that year. Most of those went to Oscar Zamora after he was promoted to Chicago in June. Worse, Horacio had a sore shoulder (something that had also bothered him during 1973). On July 28 the Cubs traded him to the California Angels for lefty-hitting catcher Rick Stelmaszek, a Chicago native. Pitching under Dick Williams once again, he saw little action the rest of the way, pitching just 11⅓ innings in 11 games.

At the end of spring training 1975, the Angels released Piña (who had reported late). The A's reacquired him on waivers, but allegedly he refused to report because he didn't want to pitch in the minors.[32] According to Horacio, though, he was told that his fastball wasn't what it used to be. In addition, he refused to take a cortisone shot.[33]

Still not yet 30, the pitcher returned home to Matamoros. He wanted 40,000 pesos (US $3,200 at the prevailing exchange rate) and a Dodge Royal Monaco car to play in the Mexican League. His local team, Unión Laguna, wouldn't meet those conditions—but Aguascalientes did.[34] He paid dividends almost immediately, throwing a seven-inning no-hitter at Ciudad Juárez on May 1, 1975.

Piña would spend the next five seasons with the Rieleros, largely as a starter but also coming out of the pen, which was his primary role in 1977. From 1975 to 1977 he was only one game over .500 (32-31), but his ERAs were excellent, including a league-leading 1.70 in '77.

Horacio's second LMP championship with Culiacán came in the winter of 1977-78, and he got to play in the 1978 Caribbean Series in Mazatlán. Host nation Mexico went just 1-5, though, with Piña losing one game in relief to the Dominican Republic. His time with the Tomateros also ended after a run-in with Juan Manuel Ley, eldest son of Juan Ley Fong and the team's co-founder. "Three other players and I demanded of Chino Ley that he put us up on the beach and that he give us the $40 per diem that he gave the foreign ballplayers. But he got pissed off and ran us off the club. He sent me to Mexicali."[35]

Piña's greatest game came that summer in Aguascalientes, at Estadio Alberto Romo Chávez before a crowd of more than 25,000. He was aware he had a no-hitter—when the manager's young sons told him, he replied, "Go over there and bring me a coffee." However, he had no idea that the 86-pitch masterpiece was a perfect game, only the second of nine innings in league history. He was perhaps most pleased that he had set a career high with his 17th victory.[36] Horacio followed up by pitching six more perfect innings in his next start.[37] He capped his career year by helping the Rieleros win the Mexican League championship, although he lost a duel in the finals to Unión Laguna's ace, Antonio Polloreno.[38]

That September 14, the Philadelphia Phillies purchased Piña's contract. Rubén Amaro, Sr., then a Latin American scout with the Phillies, recommended him.[39] Horacio pitched in two games down the stretch for the NL East winners, but he was not on the postseason roster. After Philadelphia lost the NLCS to the Los Angeles Dodgers, they returned him to Aguascalientes.

In February 1979 one US article quoted Phillies manager Danny Ozark as unconcerned that Piña was not yet in camp,[40] suggesting that at some level he was still in the club's plans. He stayed with the Rieleros, though, and had a decent year (13-9, 2.80). Horacio's last full season in the pros was 1980; for the Yucatán Leones, he was 9-8, 1.51. That winter, however, he tore his rotator cuff while playing for Guaymas. Even though Dr. Eluterio Valencia operated, he knew it was a career-ender as it happened.[41]

Piña's final summer statistics in Mexico were 100 wins, 68 losses, and a 2.35 ERA. He started 160 of his 235 appearances, pitching 98 complete games and 24 shutouts. In 2007 the Mexican Pacific League celebrated its 50th anniversary and issued a list of the top 50 players in its history. One of those names was Horacio Piña.

After retiring, Piña served two seasons as a pitching coach for Unión Laguna.[42] He then stayed home in Matamoros. In addition to drawing his big-league pension, Horacio established a cantina alongside his house, together with one of his brothers. In his leisure time, he still spent many hours fishing.[43]

Piña and his wife, Zoila Ávila, whom he married in Matamoros in 1967, had six children: Horacio, Hilda Patricia, Rosa Isela, Roberto, Yazmín Anel, and José Iván. Sad to relate, they also lost an infant who was less than a month old. Horacio was away playing in the US at the time and he did not even know until the burial had already taken place. The same happened when his grandmother died. Piña suffered another tragedy when the son he had with a woman in Aguascalientes died at age 12 in a freak horseback riding accident. (He also had a daughter from this relationship.)[44]

In March 2009 Matamoros re-inaugurated La Unidad Deportiva Horacio Piña, the multisport facility that honors the town's best-known athlete. After several years of discussion, the center received much-needed government funding for repairs and upgrades, as time and the elements had taken a severe toll over three decades of use.[45] The young men of the city also play baseball in La Liga Municipal Horacio Piña.

By his early 60s, the once-skinny Ejote had put on a pleasing amount of weight (he liked his Corona beer). He remained lively, full of laughter, and interested in baseball. For example, he commented in 2007 that steroids don't make the ballplayer. "I'm going to put it to you very simply. To bat, first you have to hit the ball, and to get outs, first you have to throw strikes. Steroids don't give you either of those things."[46]

Looking back on his time in the majors—specifically with Oakland—Piña said in 2008, "They taught me to give it everything I've got, not to be wishy-washy, always give it your best shot, like the boxers."[47]

Francisco Rodríguez Lozano's article ("Horacio Piña: El hijo pródigo de Matamoros"), based on an interview at home with Piña, was originally published in the magazine Semanario Vanguardia (Saltillo, Coahuila, Mexico), August 4, 2008. It may be found with accompanying photos at semanariocoahuila.com/pdf_sem/semanario_131. pdf and also on Paco's blog (pacorolo.blogspot.com/2009/08/ el-hijo-prodigo-de-matamoros.html). Paco also re-interviewed Piña on November 25, 2009, and December 3, 2009, providing additional input.

Thanks also to Fernando Ballesteros of the Puro Béisbol website.

SOURCES

paperofrecord.com (other small pieces of information from *The Sporting News*)

retrosheet.org

ligadelpacifico.mx

salondelafama.com.mx

Treto Cisneros, Pedro, editor, *Enciclopedia del Béisbol Mexicano* (Revistas Deportivas, S.A. de C.V., 1998).

Bjarkman, Peter, *Diamonds Around the Globe: The Encyclopedia of International Baseball* (Westport, Connecticut: Greenwood Press, 2005).

Araujo Bojórquez, Alfonso, *Series del Caribe: narraciones y estadísticas, 1949-2001* (Colegio de Bachilleres del Estado de Sinaloa, 2002).

NOTES

1 "Pina Is Articulate Moundsman." Associated Press, August 11, 1972 (information on number of siblings and father's occupation); Rodríguez Lozano, Francisco, "Horacio Piña: El hijo pródigo de Matamoros." The photo of a plaque in Matamoros, on the blog version of Rodríguez's story, showed Piña's parents' names.

2 Rodríguez Lozano, op. cit.

3 "25 años de una hazaña perfecta." El Siglo de Torreón, July 12, 2003.

4 Ibid.

5 Fernando Ballesteros, "Desestima Piña los esteroides." Puro Béisbol website (purobeisbol.com.mx/content/blogcategory/10/28/), published in 2007.

6 Ibid.

7 Rodríguez Lozano, op. cit.

8 "25 años de una hazaña perfecta"

9 Ibid.

10 Roberto Hernandez, "Relief Star Suby Wins ERA honors," The Sporting News, September 9, 1967: 36.

11 Russell Schneider, "Gabe Nabs Another Tamale From Mexico in Horacio Pina," The Sporting News, September 7, 1968, 17.

12 Ibid.

13 "Tribe Scores Eight Times In Fifth inning For Win," United Press International, August 22, 1968.

14 baseballthinkfactory.org/files/cooperstown/discussion/markusen_2003-04-25_0/

15 "Cleveland's Indians Send Pina to Minors," Associated Press, August 1, 1969.

16 Raul Flores and Mario Longoria, "Mexican Hall of Famer—Horacio Pina," ProMex, issue unknown, 1990.

17 Russell Schneider, "Tribe Finds Relief From Bullpen Ache," The Sporting News, December 20, 1969, 40.

18 Ballesteros, op. cit.

19 Merrell Whittlesey, "Hot Tamales—Rodriguez and Pina Fuel Nats," The Sporting News, May 23, 1970, 33. During the 1970 season, before he was traded to Detroit, fellow Mexican Aurelio Rodriguez was Horacio's roommate both in a Washington hotel and on the road.

20 Flores and Longoria, op. cit.

21 "The Church of Baseball," in Geoffrey C. Ward and Ken Burns, Baseball: An Illustrated History (New York: Alfred A. Knopf, 1994), 191. In another telling of the story (Los Angeles Times, May 13, 2001, D-2), Boswell had a gust of wind blowing Piña sideways.

22 "Pina Is Articulate Moundsman."

23 Ron Bergman, "Epstein Exit Traced to Tenace Shoulder Ailment," The Sporting News, December 23, 1972, 37.

24 "Baseball Winds Up Big Week," Oakland Tribune, December 3, 1972, 51.

25 Tomás Morales, "Trade to A's Pleases Mexican Starter Pina," The Sporting News, January 6, 1973, 47.

26 Markusen, op. cit.

27 Ron Bergman, "Athletics Avoid Deep Water When Horacio Is on Bridge," The Sporting News, May 19, 1973, 13.

28 Ballesteros, op. cit.

29 Joseph Durso, "Mets Get 4 Runs in 12th to Beat A's, 10-7, and Even Series at 1-1." New York Times, October 15, 1973: 1.

30 "Giants, A's get relievers," United Press International, December 4, 1973.

31 Ron Bergman, "Williams Dazed by Finley Deal for Locker," The Sporting News, December 29, 1973, 29.

32 "A's Acorns," The Sporting News, April 19, 1975, 8.

33 Rodríguez Lozano, op. cit.

34 Ibid.

35 Ibid.

36 Ibid.

37 Sergio Luis Rosas, "Recibe homenaje Horacio 'Ejote' Piña," El Siglo de Torreón, November 4, 2007.

38 Claudio Martínez Silva, "De Jaboneros a Vaqueros," El Siglo de Torreón, March 21, 2008.

39 "25 años de una hazaña perfecta."

40 "Phils report for duty," Associated Press, February 28, 1979.

41 Rodríguez Lozano, op. cit.

42 "25 años de una hazaña perfecta."

43 Ballesteros, op. cit.

44 Ibid.

45 Joel Flores Maltos, "Inaugurarán obras en la UD de Matamoros," El Siglo de Torreón, March 3, 2009.

46 Ballesteros, op. cit.

47 Rodríguez Lozano, op. cit.

Wes Stock

By Tom Hawthorn

In the spring of 1972, Wes Stock worked as pitching coach for the Milwaukee Brewers, a four-year-old team with a roster of unproven throwers in need of tutelage. A year later, he had the same job with a different employer—the world champion Oakland A's.

"Wes Stock must feel like the auto mechanic who changes jobs from working in a back-alley garage with grease-covered floors to fixing Rolls-Royces in a spotless shop," Ron Bergman wrote in *The Sporting News.*[1]

Stock inherited a staff whose colorful monikers had become household names the previous October—Vida Blue and Blue Moon Odom, Catfish Hunter and Rollie Fingers, Dave Hamilton and Ken Holtzman. Hired to replace retiring 66-year-old Barnacle Bill Posedel, Stock was expected only to tinker with a staff in no need of an overhaul.

Stock signed a two-year contract with the A's, winning the World Series in both seasons. Stock would stay for four seasons in what would be the second of three stints with the club. He had been pitching coach for the Athletics earlier (in 1967, when the franchise was still in Kansas City) and he would return to Oakland for another three seasons beginning in 1984.

One of Stock's projects for the 1973 season was to rehabilitate Blue, a hard-throwing left-hander whose 24-8 record in 1971 was followed by a frustrating 6-10 in a 1972 campaign before which he had been a holdout. Stock's ambition was to transform Blue from a pitcher who could overpower batters to one who would overmatch them. "We've got him throwing a changeup and a hard-breaking ball," Stock said. "Vida's made up his mind he wants to be a good pitcher. Eighty percent of pitching is determination and he has all the determination in the world. He wants to prove that he's as good as he ever was."[2] Blue finished the 1973 season with a 20-9 record, joining Holtzman

(21-13) and Hunter (21-5) in the 20-win club. Stock and Hunter had been teammates in Kansas City when Catfish was a 19-year-old rookie in 1965.

While Catfish and other A's famously adopted a more hirsute look in the swinging '70s, Stock retained the close-cropped, military-style haircut of his playing days.

Wesley Gay Stock was born on April 10, 1934, in Longview, a mill town and port in southwestern Washington state. He grew up in Allyn, where his father operated a tavern, grocery, and service station that included a post office, for which his mother served as postmistress. He pitched for the local town team while attending Shelton High, graduating in 1952. His parents insisted he attend college before thinking about a baseball career.

Stock earned a spot as a walk-on with the Cougars at Washington State College (now University) at Pullman, coached by Buck Bailey. In 1955 he earned

honorable mention in balloting for his college division all-star teams. After three seasons of college ball, Stock signed with the Baltimore Orioles for $4,000 after being scouted by Don McShane.

The Orioles assigned Stock to the Class C Aberdeen (South Dakota) Pheasants, where the tall (6-feet-2) and lean (188 pounds) right-hander went 14-6. "I was just a young kid who threw hard and had pretty good control of the ball," Stock said in 2007.[3]

His career was interrupted by two years of Army service, but he exchanged his military uniform for a baseball uniform in time for the start of the 1959 season. Stock made his major-league debut with the Orioles on April 19, pitching the fifth and sixth innings in relief against the visiting Washington Senators, surrendering a bases-empty home run to Jim Lemon, the third batter he faced. He struck out two batters (first baseman Norm Zauchin and pitcher Russ Kemmerer, both looking) of the seven he faced. The O's lost, 4-2.

Six days later he earned his first save. The Orioles scored a run in the top of the 11th at Yankee Stadium to go up, 2-1, and Stock was summoned by manager Paul Richards with the heart of the order coming to the plate in the bottom of the inning. Mickey Mantle smacked a single to center, then stole second. Elston Howard went down looking. Moose Skowron grounded out to the second baseman with Mantle, the tying run, advancing to third. The game was decided when pinch-hitting Enos Slaughter was cajoled into popping up in foul territory, the ball caught by third baseman Brooks Robinson.

After just seven games (and 12⅔ innings) with the Orioles, Stock was optioned to the Triple-A Miami Marlins. Days later, he went on the disabled list with a sore shoulder. Later he was sent to the Vancouver Mounties of the Pacific Coast League, where he went 6-6 in 14 starts.

Stock began the 1960 season in Miami, where he showed promise. "It's tempting to bring up Wes Stock from Miami since he's going so well," Richards said in June. "But the best thing to do with that kid is to let him have a good year down there, bring him up next spring and let him fall into line."[4] In the end, he split the season between Miami (21 games) and Baltimore (17 games). After pitching in the Puerto Rican winter league in 1960-61, Stock found a permanent spot with Baltimore as a middle reliever, paired with left-hander Billy Hoeft as set-up men for the closer, Hoyt Wilhelm.

After 42 career relief appearances, Stock got the first start of his big-league career on July 6, 1961, at Griffith Stadium in Washington. He gave up two singles and a walk before leaving after five innings of a scoreless game with a blister on his finger. The Senators won, 1-0, Wilhelm taking the loss.

On June 15, 1964, Stock was traded to the Kansas City Athletics for catcher Charley Lau, going from first place to last. "It's a little tough to leave a club like Baltimore," he said, "but, after all, I get paid for pitching wherever I am."[5] Stock had gone a remarkable 19-4 with the Orioles over five-plus seasons and was riding a 10-game winning streak. At the plate, he had yet to record his first base hit, going 0-for-36 with 26 strikeouts.

The pitcher rolled his winning streak to 12 games before taking the loss in a 3-2 decision against the Chicago White Sox. He gave up a home run to opposing pitcher Gary Peters in the 13th inning, the homer coming only after the batter twice fouled on bunt attempts. Stock had not lost a game in two years—from July 12, 1962, to July 19, 1964.

More remarkably, he showed a hint of ability at the plate, stroking a run-scoring, bases-loaded single off Steve Ridzik of the Senators in his first at-bat after being traded. He went 3-for-15 for the A's in 1964.

In 1965 Stock attempted to add a screwball to his repertoire of fastball, slider, and changeup, but found that the pitch distorted his regular three-quarter delivery and he lost the control that had been the hallmark of his career. He was still a workhorse, but one without much success.

The A's released Stock in April 1966, and he rejoined Vancouver as a player-coach, pitching in one game before being recalled to Kansas City.

In 1967 he found himself to be an old-timer surrounded by young'uns like Hunter, aged 21, and Odom, 22. "When you have a staff of 22-year-olds," Stock said, "it's tough to be a 33-year old."[6] He was released, signed as a coach, and briefly put back on the active list (giving up three hits, two walks, and two earned runs in his only inning of work) before replacing Cot Deal as pitching coach in July. Over nine seasons with the O's and A's, Stock's record was 27-13 with appearances in 321 games, only three of them starts. Alvin Dark, who had hired him, was fired as manager and replaced by Luke Appling. Stock was told his contract would not be renewed.

He spent two seasons as a roving minor-league pitching instructor for the New York Mets before being hired as pitching coach by the brand-new Seattle Pilots. The franchise wound up moving to Milwaukee before season's start in 1970. Stock's philosophy about pitching mechanics was basic: "We try to teach all our young pitchers to throw pitches with the same motion."[7] Stock got strong reviews for his work with young pitchers including Skip Lockwood, Bill Parsons, and Jim Slaton. The A's lured Stock from the Brewers, where a week before the end of the 1972 season he was told his contract would not be renewed. He got some on-the-job introduction to the staff he would inherit the following spring.

After four seasons with the A's, Stock became the first pitching coach of the expansion Seattle Mariners in 1977, once again fashioning a staff from the chaff discarded by the established clubs. He worked under three managers over five seasons before leaving the playing field for the broadcast booth, where he provided color commentary on the Mariners for two seasons on KSTW-TV. "That was a real challenge," he said later. "I wasn't the best in English. I was a good ol' country boy."[8]

Stock returned to the A's as pitching coach in 1984, putting in another three seasons. He retired from baseball in 1994, at age 60. In 2014 he maintained a home on an island in Puget Sound, not far from where he grew up, and another in Scottsdale, Arizona. His two sons both played professional sports — Kevin Stock was a minor-league infielder in the Texas Rangers system, while Jeff Stock played soccer for the Seattle Sounders and Vancouver Whitecaps before going into business purchasing and operating theme parks.

SOURCES

In addition to the sources cited, the author also consulted:

"Ducks place six on All-ND team," *Eugene Register-Guard*, June 1, 1955, 2.

Retrosheet.org

Baseball-Reference.com

NOTES

1   Melvin Durslag, "Catfish Gives Stock Vision of an Angler's Paradise," *The Sporting News*, February 24, 1973, 41.

2   Ron Fimrite, "Vida's Down With the Growing-Up Blues," *Sports Illustrated*, September 10, 1973.

3   Dan Raley, "Where Are They Now? Wes Stock, Ex-Major League Pitcher, Coach," *Seattle Post-Intelligencer*, July 17, 2007.

4   *The Sporting News*, June 22, 1960.

5   *The Sporting News*, July 4, 1964.

6   *The Sporting News*, April 29, 1967.

7   *The Sporting News*, June 5, 1971.

8   *Seattle Post-Intelligencer*, July 17, 2007.

Manny Trillo

By Leonte Landino

Outstanding defense and strong character can be a short description for Manny Trillo's career. He was a slick-fielding second baseman who shined with a legendary Philadelphia Phillies team and played a huge part in the first title in almost 100 years of misery in one of the fieriest sports markets in the world.

Trillo is always remembered by fans for his distinctive fielding. A not untypical description of Trillo after getting the ball: "Seemingly stopping and reading the NL president's signature on the ball before firing it sidearm."[1]

But the path to an All-Star career that started with the power machine of the Oakland Athletics was not an easy one. The story began in the rural town of Caripito in northeastern Venezuela, where Jesus Manuel Trillo was born to Trina Trillo and Ismael Marcano on December 25 1950.

"My parents were separated since the day I was born and I always lived with my mother,"Trillo recalled in 2001. "My mother took care of me and my siblings Ismael, Eneida, and Zunilda. She was the mother and a father figure for us and she took good care of us. I was never too close to my father, we used to see him once in a while but we were never really close."[2]

Trillo's father was a worker in the booming oil industry, which widely promoted little league and other baseball programs. Young Jesús played on the teams and tournaments sponsored by these programs. Jesús grew up in Quiriquire, a small town in the oilfields, and during his middle-school years, his physical education professor, Rómulo Ortiz, took him under his wing, including him on organized teams and taking him to play local tournaments and competitions. Jesús saw Rómulo as a father figure who passed on to the boy his love for

the game. Ortiz used to call him Indio (Indian), making fun of the shy character and personality of his pupil. This nickname stuck with Manny for life.

As a youngster Jesús primarily played shortstop, where he developed quick hands and speed. He admired the two All-Star Venezuelan shortstops in the majors, Chico Carrasquel and Luis Aparicio, both local sports heroes. But one day the catcher for his team was injured and he was sent to play behind the plate. Jesús cried the whole game since he was afraid a foul ball was going to hit him. It didn't happen, and the joy and experience of calling and receiving pitches captured his attention. After that game, he became a catcher.

Jesús became passionate for the game, even skipping classes to go practice as a teenager. By the age of 14, he was determined to become a professional baseball player. His parents supported his diamond dreams.

Ortiz contacted Pompeyo Davalillo, who had recently retired as a player after a cup of coffee with the Washington Senators in 1953, and worked as a coach for Leones del Caracas of the Venezuelan League and a scout for the Philadelphia Phillies. In October 1965 Ortiz and his protégé traveled 10 hours Caracas to see him. Davalillo saw something special in him. He agreed to work with the youngster and, with his mother's permission, kept him in Caracas to train.

Trillo spent two years traveling from Caracas to Maturin, where he studied at Escuela Técnica Industrial. He participated in a tryout after an exhibition game in 1967 in Caracas between the Oakland A's and the Minnesota Twins. In January 1968 the Phillies signed him to a contract, and a few days later the 17-year-old flew to Clearwater, Florida, where the Phillies trained.

Facing a new language, a new culture and new challenges and being alone for the first time was ahead for a teenager from a rural oil town in Venesuela. "It was one of the hardest moments of my life," Trillo said. "I cried a lot and for and for many months. Leaving behind my mother was very hard but it was all worthy to try to achieve my dream of becoming a baseball player. And I wanted to play in the major leagues. I was determined."[3]

Jesús Manuel Marcano, his legal name in Venezuela, became Manny Trillo, a common mistake when processing legal paperwork between the US and Latin countries, where last names are usually confused with maiden names. "They started calling me Manny as a short for Manuel and they put my last name as Trillo, instead of Marcano. However that never bothered me since it was my mother's last name and I was proud of carrying her last name on my back. Although in Venezuela they kept using both of my surnames for the records, so it became Manny Trillo for the United States and Jesús Marcano Trillo in my country, even only Marcano Trillo. It was fine in any way for me."[4]

Trillo went to the Phillies camp as a catcher, but Dallas Green, who had just retired as a player and was to manage Huron (South Dakota) in the short-season Northern League, saw him fielding groundballs and realized his potential as an infielder. Trillo was assigned to Huron as a catcher, but after a few games Green decided to try him at shortstop and third base. "There was no way I was going to put this fragile, skinny kid behind the plate," wrote Green in his memoirs. "I found time to give Manny a little extra attention. He was one of the few Latin kids on the team. I could only imagine how difficult was for Manny at that time. In the lower minor leagues you make peanuts. I slipped Manny a few bucks here and there, because I knew he had nothing."[5]

Trillo played only 35 games at Huron, hitting .261 and performing well at shortstop. After the season he returned to Venezuela to play with Caracas and was already seen as an infielder.

Trillo spent the 1969 season with Spartanburg (South Carolina) of the Western Carolinas League, where he played mostly in the infield but put in some time behind the plate for the last time in his career. He improved with the bat, hitting .280 with 26 RBIs in 83 games, but seemed to attract little attention from the Phillies. But he caught the attention of Oakland owner Charlie Finley, and th Athletics drafted him in the minor-league phase of the 1969 Rule 5 draft. The A's assigned the 19-year-old to Double-A Birmingham (Southern League), where he played shortstop, second base, and third base in 1970 and shortstop and third base in 1971.

Trillo was viewed as a backup infielder, but with more playing time, his offensive performance improved consistently. In 1971 he batted .280 with 5 home runs and 44 RBIs. In the winter league he hit .291 in 35 games for Caracas.

In 1972 Trillo was assigned to Triple-A Iowa, where manager Sherm Lollar played him at shortstop, second, and thurd, and he batted a strong .301 in 133 games with 9 home runs. After the season, Trillo rejoined Leones of Caracas and played all 61 games of winter baseball as a third baseman, hitting .240 with 5 home runs. He played a huge role in helping his team to the league championship.

It was Trillo's first taste of championship, and he was also in a world championship organization, as the A's beat the Reds in the World Series while we was playing in his home country. (After winning the Venezuelan championship, Leones moved to the Caribbean Series (played in Caracas) and lost to Tigres del Licey from the Dominican Republic. For Trillo it was exciting to understand winning in baseball.

The world champion Athletics had Bert Campaneris at shortstop and Sal Bando at third base; so Trillo hoped to make the team as a second baseman. He was assigned to Triple-A Tucson.

"When we were in Triple A in 1973, my good friends Gonzalo Marquez and José Morales told me that the only chance I had to reach the majors with the A's was in second base," Trillo said in 2001. "So every day before each game in Tucson we went early to the park in our own time just to practice. They used to practice a lot of double plays with me and help me a lot with grounders. We did that for one or two hours each day before the team practice. Sherm Lollar saw our hard work and that I was focusing more on becoming a better second baseman and he gave me the chance to play that season every day on my new position."[6]

In 130 games, Trillo made 19 errors but gained confidence on the field and hit .312 with 8 home runs. He led the team with 78 RBIs. With such a solid performance, Charlie Finley saw his promising 22-year-old Triple-A second baseman as part of the team's future. On June 28, Trillo was called up to make his major-league debut, against Kansas City.

"I remember clearly my first at-bat since I hit the ball to right field and I drove in what eventually was our winning run, he recalled."[7] (Two batters later, Trillo was picked off by Kansas City pitcher Steve Busby, but another Oakland run scored in the process.) "Wearing for the first time a major-league uniform was the best sensation I had in my life. I had achieved my goal."[8]

Trillo played 17 games with Oakland and was 3-for-12. The A's advanced to the American League Championship Series, meeting the Baltimore Orioles for the second year in a row. Trillo was supposed to be on the roster but almost didn't. In error, his name was left off the roster submitted to Major League Baseball. Fortunately for Trillo, the Orioles allowed him to be added to the roster, along with Allan Lewis, substituting for the injured Billy North. In the end, Trillo didn't see any action in the ALCS, which the A's won in five games.

The story took a turn when the A's advanced to the World Series and had to petition the New York Mets for the roster changes. The Mets allowed Lewis for North but denied the addition of Trillo. (Before Game One an irate Finley had the PA announcer at the Oakland Coliseum tell fans to scratch Trillo from their lineup cards because the Mets had not allowed the roster adjustment, an action for which he was fined by the commissioner's office.)

Trillo started the 1974 season with the A's but was sent to back to Tucson after hitting .100 during the first month. He was recalled in September. He was included on the postseason roster and scored a run as pinch-runner in the ALCS against the Orioles, but did not play in the World Series, which the A's won over the Los Angeles Dodgers, their third title in a row.

Six days after the Series ended, Trillo was traded to the Chicago Cubs along with relievers Darold Knowles and Bob Locker for outfielder and future Hall of Famer Billy Williams.

Trillo was designated the starting second baseman, and never returned to the minors. In his first season with the Cubs, 1975, he hit .248 with 7 homers and 70 RBIs, but his defense was rough (29 errors). "My teammates used to make fun of me in Chicago saying that for me errors were like a vitamin … one a day," he joked. "But I worked hard on the position and little by little the errors were disappearing from my game."[9] Trillo was third in votes for the National League Rookie of the Year.

Trillo spent four seasons as the Cubs' primary second baseman. In 1977 he made the National League All-

Star squad as a backup to Joe Morgan. In February 1979 he was traded to his original club, the Phillies, in an eight-player deal. Philadelphia was seeking to upgrade its infield. It became one of the best trades the Phillies ever made. Under manager Dallas Green, Trillo shone. His improvement with the glove was evident; he made fewer errors, and showed flash and elegance in his defense. He won the first of his three Gold Gloves.

Trillo's trademark style was to catch a groundball and take a brief moment to look at the ball on his hand before making the throw to first base. "Some players used to tell me: Get rid of that ball faster! But I was just taking my time and watched the ball. Some people thought I was cocky, but no, maybe I was too serious on my job. I just like to do things right."[10]

After the 1979 season Trillo went back to Venezuela, where he had become a big star with Leones del Caracas. He hit .306 in 30 games and helped Caracas to win its third title in eight seasons. Trillo remained with the team to play the Caribbean Series in Santo Domingo, Dominican Republic, which was won by a Dominican team, Tigres del Licey.

In 1980 the Phillies under Green won 91 games and Trillo was on center stage, batting .292 with 7 home runs and 43 RBIs and winning the NL Silver Slugger award at his position. His momentum rolled over to the NLCS, in which the Phillies defeated the Houston Astros in five games. and Trillo (8-for-21, .381, four RBIs) was declared the NLCS MVP after a key RBI double in Game Four and a two-run triple in the clinching Game Five.

The Phillies advanced to the World Series against the Kansas City Royals. Trillo hit only .217 in the Series, he helped win Game Five with a great relay throw that kept the Royals from scoring a run, and got a ninth-inning infield hit that drove in the game's winning run. Two nights later, in Game Six, the Phillies won their first World Series title.

When Trillo returned to Venezuela, he stepped into controversy, fighting with Leones over its salary offer.

A league-appointed arbitrator couldn't settle the dispute and Trillo demanded a trade.[11] He was traded to Aguilas del Zulia, probably the biggest and most impactful trade in the history of the Venezuelan Winter League. Trillo became a leader of the team, which reached the playoff finals in 1981 and 1982.

The trade had a big impact on Trillo's career. "It's was painful for me to leave Caracas, but they received me so well in Zulia and they made me feel part of the team so fast that it became my new home," he said. "Also my wife was from Maracaibo and it made perfect sense for the family."[12]

In 1982 with the Phillies Trillo set a major-league record with 479 consecutive errorless fielding chances as a second baseman. When he finally made an error, it was on a high bouncer by Bill Buckner over the pitcher's head. "I thought the ball was going to hit the ground making it routine for me to catch it, but it hit the turf and the bound was higher and hit my elbow. I thought they were going to call it a hit, but my defensive game got people in Philadelphia used to seeing a hard play as an easy one and that tricked me that day." The official scorer took almost three minutes to make a decision and confirmed the error. The game stopped and the crowd gave Manny a standing ovation for over five minutes. "That was very special for me. I said, 'Wow! I made an error and people cheer at you!'"[13]

Trillo won his second consecutive Gold Glove, the third of his career. He was the starting second baseman for the National League in his third All-Star Game.

But happy times in Philadelphia came to an end. Baseball was changing and he understood the business. During his time with the Phillies his agent was David Landfield. In December 1982, while playing with Zulia, Trillo was traded to the Cleveland Indians along with George Vukovich, Jerry Willard, Julio Franco, and Jay Baller for highly-touted prospect Von Hayes. It was one of the worst trades in the Phillies' history, but trading two potential free agents to get a long-term player seemed to make perfect sense.

After the trade Trillo's former wife, Maria Elena, took over as his agent. She became the only female agent in the business, negotiating for her husband. For the Indians he hit .270 in the first half of the 1983 season and made the All-Star Game as the starter at second base.

By August, the Montreal Expos were looking for a solid infielder and they traded minor leaguer Don Carter for Trillo to help in a pennant chase they eventually lost. After the season Trillo became a free agent and signed with the San Francisco Giants. But his offense started to decline and after being used to playing with competitive clubs, he felt less motivation with the last-place Giants, hitting only .238 in 223 games over two seasons and making 18 errors.

In the meantime, Dallas Green had become the general manager of the Chicago Cubs; he needed infield backup, and acquired Trillo in December 1985 for infielder Dave Owen.

"As soon as I came back to Chicago Dallas told me to be ready to play all four infield positions," Trillo said. "It will be hard, but I`m 35. What the heck. The time comes for every ballplayer. I`m happy to be back, and I hope this will be my last stop. I only have one space left on my cap rack back home."[14]

Trillo became a mentor for younger Cubs players like Ryne Sandberg and Shawon Dunston. He was also a liaison between the Cubs and Zulia in Venezuela. The organizations had an unofficial agreement to exchange players that helped the Cubs develop prospects in winter ball. Trillo's relationship with the Venezuelan team grew stronger after he was activated for the 1984 Caribbean Series in San Juan, Puerto Rico, in which Zulia won its first international title.

Trilloplayed three seasons in his second stint with the Cubs. He was a solid backup, hitting .296 in 1986.294 with a career-high eight homers in 1987 while playing all the positions on the infield. He was a fan favorite and on his at-bats bleacher fans used to chant: "One-O!, Two-O!, Trillo!"[15]

For the 1987-88 winter ball season, Trillo returned to Zulia, this time with double duty as a player-manager. He played his last 33 games as an active player in winter ball, hitting.270 while managing the team to a record of 23-37. "I felt I could play a couple more seasons in Venezuela, but I thought it was time to give back to baseball," Trillo said. "I enjoyed more the coaching side than being a manager and after that experience I asked the team to allow me to continue as a coach." Zulia agreed and in 1988 Trillo became a full-time coach.

Trillo was released by the Cubs after the 1988 season but he got an invitation from the Cincinnati Reds to be a backup infielder. After playing in 17 games during the first two months of the season, he was released. At the age of 38, "I was ready to continue as an instructor," he said.[16]

Trillo's fielding elegance and clutch hitting were his trademarks. He played for seven teams in his 17-year major-league career, with 1,518 games as a second baseman. As of 2014 he had the best fielding percentage of any Phillies second basemen,.994 in 1982, with only five errors in 149 games.

Trillo's passion for teaching baseball and working in the minor leagues took him to work as a minor-league coach for the Cubs, Phillies, Brewers, Yankees, and White Sox. Ozzie Guillen, the White Sox manager, took him to the 2005 World Series as a guest coach.

In Venezuela Trillo continued to work with Aguilas del Zulia as a coach and special adviser. In his 19 seasons in the Venezuelan league he batted.277 with 29 home runs and 325 RBIs. In 2007 he was voted into the Venezuelan Baseball Hall of Fame. In 2012 Trillo was voted into the Latin Baseball Hall of Fame. He attended the induction ceremony in La Romana, Dominican Republic, joining inductes Tony Oliva, Bernie Williams, and Tony Peña among other Latin greats.

In 2014 Trillo had homes in Orlando, Florida, and Maracaibo, Venezuela. He enjoyed spending time with his family and playing golf. In September, Aguilas del

Zulia opens its training camp, he was there. "As long as I can and I'm capable, I'll be wearing the baseball uniform on the field," he said. "I enjoy being in the clubhouse, being around the guys and helping them to develop skills. … I am proud of what I did, I was serious about how I handled myself and I always respected the game and that is the biggest legacy of my career."[17]

SOURCES

Epstein, Dan, *Big Hair and Plastic Grass: A Funky RideTthrough Baseball and America in the Swinging '70s* (New York: Macmillan. 2012).

Green, Dallas, and Allan Maimon, *The Mouth That Roared: My Six Outspoken Decades in Baseball* (Chicago: Triumph Books, 2013).

Green, Michael G., and Roger D. Launius, *Charlie Finley: The Outrageous Story of Baseball's Super Showman.* (New York: Bloomsbury Publishing, 2010).

Westcott, Rich, *Tales From the Phillies Dugout* (Champaign, Illinois: Sports Publishing LLC, 2006).

Westcott, Rich, *Veterans Stadium: Field of Memories* (Philadelphia: Temple University Press, 2005).

Yellon, Al, Kasey Ignarski, and Matthew Silverman, *Cubs by the Numbers: A Complete Team History of the Chicago Cubs by Uniform Number* (New York: Skyhorse Publishing Inc. 2009).

Cárdenas, Augusto, "Un Indio con corazón zuliano," *Diario Panorama,* Maracaibo, Venezuela, December 9, 2009.

Chass, Murray, "Maria Trillo Acts in Family Interest," *New York Times,* November 11, 1983.

Serrano, Ignacio, "Manny Trillo repasa las anécdotas de su carrera," *El Nacional.* Caracas, Venezuela, December 9, 2013.

Landino, Leonte, *¡Aguilas … A la Carga! Episode 79* (Tripleplay Sports Productions, Maracaibo, Venezuela, December 30, 2001.

Lomartire, Paul, "Trillo Takes Heart Along, Leaves Gloom In S.F.," *Chicago Tribune,* January 12, 1986.

McNesby, Mike, "Hard to Believe!" Lulu.com. 2009.

Mitchell, Fred, "For Dunston, a Season Of Commitment," *Chicago Tribune,* March 2, 1986.

Megdal, Howard, "Jack of All Trades: Manny Trillo," MLBRumors. com, 2010.

Verdi, Bob, "Trillo Happy 2d Time Around," *Chicago Tribune,* March 6, 1986.

Diario Líder, Caracas, Venezuela, archives.

Diario La Verdad, Maracaibo, Venezuela, archives.

Baseball-Reference.com.

BR Bullpen, Baseball-Reference.com

New York Times archives.

Chicago Tribune archives.

Purapelota.com.

Retrosheet.org'

YouTube.com'

Landino, Leonte, personal interviews with Jesús Marcano Trillo in Maracaibo, Venezuela, November 18, 2012, and November 17, 2013; in La Romana, Dominican Republic, February 12, 2012; and in Bristol, Connecticut. March 28, 2014.

NOTES

1   Al Yellon, Kasey Ignarski, and Matthew Silverman. *Cubs by the Numbers, 120.*

2   *Águilasaa La Carga!, 79.*

3   Augusto Cárdenas, *Diario Panorama,* December 9, 2009.

4   *Águilas a La Carga!, 79.*

5   Dallas Green and Allan Maimon. *The Mouth That Roared: My Six Outspoken Decades in Baseball,"* 52.

6   *Águilas A La Carga!, 79.*

7   Augusto Cárdenas. *Diario Panorama.*

8   Ignacio Serrano. *Diario El Nacional.* Caracas, Venezuela. December 9, 2013.

9   Augusto Cárdenas. *Diario Panorama.*

10   Ignacio Serrano. *Diario El Nacional.*

11   Ibid. .

12   *Águilas a La Carga!, 79.*

13   Augusto Cárdenas, *Diario Panorama.*

14   Bob Verdi, "Trillo Happy 2d Time Around,"*Chicago Tribune.* March 6, 1986.

15   Yellon, Ignarski, and Silverman, 52.

16   Leonte Landino interview with Manny Trillo, Maracaibo, Venezuela, 2012.

17   *ÁguilasaA La Carga!, 79.*

1973 World Series: Two For The Money

By Curt Smith

In 1973 the movie *The Way We Were* earned awards, swelled receipts, and required Kleenex across the land. Baseball more resembled *One Flew Over the Cuckoo's Nest*, a film released two years later. In 1973 Yankees pitchers Fritz Peterson and Mike Kekich took the unusual step of swapping wives with each other. Commissioner Bowie Kuhn denounced their immorality. On April 6 the designated hitter debuted in the American League, New York's Ron Blomberg batting just ahead of Boston's Orlando Cepeda as baseball's first DH. The rule change helped the AL batting average soar 20 points to .260. Today the National League still hopes to revoke it, a cause as hopeless as King Canute trying to halt the tide. In 1973 the Mets' Willie Mays, 43, acquired from the Giants a year earlier, got his last hit, showing, he said, how "growing old is just a hapless hurt." His team won 82 games, baseball's ninth-best total, and somehow made the World Series. The Baltimore Orioles won baseball's most games, 97, and somehow didn't. In the fall classic, the A's error-prone Mike Andrews became a folk hero, his boss Charles O. Finley made Scrooge look beloved, and Oakland became the first team since the 1961-62 Yankees to win back-to-back World Series. After a while a cuckoo's nest looked stable.

Return to the 1972-73 offseason. Finley either traded or released Matty Alou, Mike Epstein, and, most notably, Cepeda, squandering baseball's first regular celebrity DH. In a major deal, the A's swapped one catcher, Dave Duncan, for another, Cleveland's Ray Fosse. Their Opening Day lineup read: catching, Fosse; pitching, Catfish Hunter; DH, Billy North; infield, third to first base, Sal Bando, Dal Maxvill, Dick Green, and 1972 Series titan Gene Tenace; and outfield, left to right, Joe Rudi, Billy Conigliaro, and Reggie Jackson, soon a/k/a Mr. October. What *The Sporting News*

called "the best lineup in the league" began 1973 by losing the first three games at home to Minnesota, soon seguéing to 4-8, then 9-12. On May 6 Oakland finally hit .500. A month later it was still even-steven at 28-28. The A's finished the year 15-14 in September. What won them the AL West was a .667 stretch between June 25 and August 29. The club compiled a 94-68 record, six games ahead of the team from its former home, second-place Kansas City.

A 1920s operetta, *Moon,* debuted the song "Stout-Hearted Men." The A's men were led by Jackson, the league MVP, who averaged a team-high .293 and topped the AL in home runs (32), RBIs (117), runs (99), and slugging average (.531). Bando was an iron man, leading in A's games (162) and hits (170) and ranking league-best in total bases (295) with George Scott and Dave May and doubles (32) with Pedro Garcia, third in slugging average (.498), fourth in home runs (29) and runs batted in (90), and fifth in runs (97). North was a revelation in center field, adding a .285 average to his team-high and AL-second 53 steals and runner-up 98 runs. Fosse hit .256, Tenace .259 with 24 dingers and 84 ribbies, and Rudi .270, down from 1972's .305. Designated hitter Deron Johnson batted the lowest of the starters, .246, with 19 homers and 81 RBIs. Campaneris hit a next-to-last .250, offset by a team-high 601 at-bats and 34 steals. Green averaged a surprising .262 and with Campy made the A's impregnable up the middle. For the first time a million regular-season customers—1,000,763—saw Oakland's likely best-ever defense.

A's pitching was almost as good, keyed by a starting hat-trick: Ken Holtzman 21-13, Catfish Hunter 21-5, and Vida Blue 20-9, compiling a 62-27 record and, in the first year of the DH, impressive ERAs of 2.97, 3.34, and 3.28, respectively. Catfish led the league with an

.808 winning percentage. Blue Moon Odom fell to 5-12, but Dave Hamilton was again an anchor: 6-4 in 16 games. Rollie Fingers had a deceiving 7-8 record and was third in the AL with 22 saves in 62 games. Darold Knowles, Horacio Pina, and Paul Lindblad graced 52, 47, and 36 games, respectively, saving a combined 19. The staff had a 3.29 ERA, trailing only the A's League Championship Series foil, the Baltimore Orioles. The Birds also were league-best in triples, stolen bases, walks, and fewest opponent hits, among other things. The ALCS, a five-year-old gateway to the World Series, promised to be, as Red Barber said, "as tight as a pair of new shoes on a rainy day." And was.

The then-best-of-five series began at Baltimore, the Orioles taking their tenth straight LCS victory dating to 1969, on a first-inning four-spot of four hits, two walks, and a hit batsman. Jim Palmer yielded five hits and fanned 12, the A's whimpering, 6-0. Following: a next-day bang, Campaneris, Rudi, and Bando (twice) homering, decking Dave McNally and two relievers, 6-3, and tying the series at a game apiece. The second game was nip-and-tuck through seven innings. Back at Oakland, Game Three was even tighter. A 1-0 O's lead forged by Earl Williams' second-inning homer lasted till the A's eighth, when Jesus Alou singled, pinch-runner Allan Lewis was sacrificed to second base by Mike Andrews, and Rudi's single tied the score. In the 11th, Campaneris, leading off, drove a home run over the left-field fence. A's win, giving them the game and Series lead, 2-1. Holtzman beat Mike Cuellar, each throwing a complete game, today a relic to rival the daguerreotype and corset zipper.

A day later the A's bombed Palmer with three runs in the second inning and one in the sixth. In the seventh catcher Andy Etchebarren socked a three-run homer to key a four-run Orioles rally. An inning later Bobby Grich went deep: Baltimore, 5-4, Fingers losing. The shock was apparently too much for Oakland — or was it too preoccupied with the National Football League Raiders? On October 11 Hunter yielded only five hits to blank the Orioles, 3-0, before a mere 24,265 at the Oakland-Alameda County Coliseum, winning the LCS. "How bad is this?" said Fingers. "Walk-up playoff

tickets are a breeze." Oakland's opponent in the World Series would be the Mets, whose .509 percentage winning the National League East was baseball's lowest-ever pennant record. What came then was a storm.

The fall classic opened the same week that Vice President Spiro Agnew, having enlarged America's vocabulary — e.g. "vicars of vacillation" and "effete corps of impudent snobs" — and split its public, resigned over charges of bribery as governor of Maryland. Someone called Agnew's fall the day's main headline. Kuhn disagreed, calling baseball's postseason preeminent. Already the year mocked credulity. The Watergate scandal plunged President Nixon from 68 percent approval in February 1973's Gallup Poll to 28 percent in October, when the Saturday Night Massacre, Nixon's refusal to turn over court-requested White House tapes, prompted first calls for impeachment. After hitting an all-time record high, the stock market fell 400 points in a year. Films like *Last Tango in Paris* mocked traditional values — less sensitive cinema about sexuality than pornography masquerading as art. An Arab oil boycott was about to make it very difficult for US drivers to find enough gas to fill their car. As Yeats said, the center would not hold.

Before the Series opener at the Coliseum, Holtzman, not batting all year, took extra batting practice. He doubled in the third inning, scoring when Campaneris's grounder went through Felix Millan's legs. Campy then stole second, scoring on Rudi's single. John Milner's single scored the only Mets run in a 2-1 loss. Jon Matlack was the loser, Holtzman, Fingers, and Knowles allowing only seven hits. Game Two was a corker — in a way, a metaphor for the year. "Sunshine turned every ball into adventure," said voiceover Curt Gowdy on the World Series highlight film, "helping produce" one of the "longest and weirdest games in Series history."

The "Metsies," in Casey Stengel's term, won, 10-7, in 12 innings and 4 hours and 13 minutes, the Series' then-longest game by 45 minutes. Willie Mays got his final hit, lost a fly ball in the sun, and missed another he once would have caught barehanded. Jesus Alou's double gave

Oakland a 2-0 first-inning lead. Next inning Rudi's single plated Campaneris, who had tripled. Cleon Jones and Wayne Garrett homered for New York: A's, 3-2. In the sixth inning, the Mets loaded the bases, at which point Don Hahn and Bud Harrelson knocked in two runs. Jim Beauchamp tapped to the mound, where Knowles threw to the plate trying for a 1-2-3 double play. Instead, his wild throw made the score 6-3. In the seventh Jackson doubled for a run, Mays lost Johnson's fly and fell down trying to catch it, and two singles tied the score at 6-6. Surprises vied: the game's ping-pong rhythm and Mays being mortal.

In the tenth Harrelson tried to score from third on Millan's fly to left. He appeared to avoid Fosse's tag at the plate, but umpire Augie Donatelli bayed *Out!* Mays, on his knees in the on-deck circle, proceeded to vainly and frenetically protest. Like falling down, it is how millions remember him. Two innings later, Harrelson, at third again, scored on Mays's two-out single—the final hit and RBI of his glorious career. Ahead 7-6, Milner bounced a bases-loaded grounder through the legs of Mike Andrews, the new Oakland second baseman replacing the slumping Green, and McGraw and Mays scored. Jerry Grote then grounded to Andrews, who threw past first baseman Tenace: 10-6—his second muff of the inning. In the last of the 12th inning, Mays lost another fly. The plot had turned surrealistic. George Stone finished, saving; McGraw pitched six innings, winning. The 10-7 loss, A's manager Dick Williams said later, made Finley "lose his mind."

Inexorably, Nixon drowned in the Watergate affair. Finley now authored the Andrews affair. After Game Two, the A's owner forced the second baseman to sign a false affidavit saying he was disabled, ruling him ineligible for the rest of the Series. Even Williams and A's players backed Andrews, making Kuhn order Finley to reinstate him, after which Andrews sued Charlie for libel and slander. Before the third game, the Series tied, the A's worked out at Shea Stadium, Andrews' number 17 taped to their uniforms, the

subject briefly back home in Massachusetts. Jackson said, "Half of my thoughts are on the mucking up that Finley has done and half my thoughts are on Tom Seaver." He had cause to worry: Seaver thrice fanned him. In the first inning Garrett homered and Millan scored on a wild pitch. In the sixth, two A's doubles scored a run. Rudi's eighth-inning single plated a tying Campaneris: 2-all. That man again: In the tenth, Mays pinch-hit vainly for McGraw—Mays's last big-league appearance. And *that* man, too: An inning later Campy's single beat the Mets, 3-2.

In Game Four, Rusty Staub pricked Holtzman for a first-inning three-run homer. Odom, then Knowles, relieved, the score soon 6-0. Matlack pitched eight innings, tying the Series. Williams had told Andrews, pinch-hitting, "They'll probably give you a standing ovation." Both laughed—until they did. Pinch-hitting, Andrews walked to the on-deck circle, identified by the number on his uniform. The Shea crowd roared as though reliving the Miracle Mets of 1969. Finley sat frozen, finally twirling an A's banner. Andrews grounded out, his last big-league at-bat, Charlie benching him for the rest of the Series. Next night Koosman beat Blue, 2-0. Milner's single and Don Hahn's triple scored the runs; McGraw got the save. New York led, three games to two as the Series returned to Oakland. "We'd come all the way from underneath everybody," said Seaver, "to one game from the top."

Oakland scored in the first inning in the Mets' first try to win their first Series since October 16, 1969: Jackson doubled, driving in Rudi. Two innings later Reggie doubled Bando home: 2-0. The Mets scored in the eighth, Ken Boswell singling, but Knowles, in a crucial Series at-bat, fanned Staub with two runners on. Fingers then got Jones to fly out to end the threat. In Oakland's half-inning, Jesus Alou's sacrifice fly scored Jackson as 3-1 insurance. Hunter beat Seaver, Fingers saving his second game. "It's like the fighter who has his opponent on the ropes and can't put him away," said Staub, who hit .279 with 76 runs batted in during the regular season but hurt his shoulder prior to the Series. "We let the A's get away." Next day the

Mets confronted Holtzman amid the feeling that they had treated momentum, to quote Ring Lardner, like a side dish they declined to order.

In the third inning Holtzman, as in the opener, doubled. Campy then lined the A's first Series dinger, to the opposite field: 2-0. Later that inning Jackson's long two-run homer found the right-center-field bleachers, Reggie triumphantly spiking home plate. Mets runs in the sixth and ninth innings were insufficient: 5-2. "There's a little looper out to Campaneris," said NBC-TV's Gowdy in the Mets' two-out ninth. "The A's are the world champs! Oakland has won it again!" Tenace's 11 walks tied Babe Ruth's record, set in 1926. Garrett, whose pop Campy caught, fanned 11 times to tie Eddie Mathews' record for futility, set in 1958. Knowles became the only pitcher to appear in every act of a seven-game series. Batting .310 with nine hits and six RBIs, Jackson became MVP. The Mets outhit the A's, .253 to .212, with four homers to two, but were unlikely to forget leaving a Series-record 72 men on base. Williams would never forget Finley's constant meddling in managerial personnel and strategy.

According to Matthew Silverman's book *Swinging '73: Baseball's Wildest Season*, the A's skipper had told Rudi, Bando, and Jackson that September that he was quitting. Andrews had been the final straw. In 1967 Williams and Andrews were Red Sox "Impossible Dream" rookie manager and infielder, respectively, linked forever in New England's heart. It enraged Williams for Finley to treat a player from that magical year like chattel. "He's a raving maniac," the A's manager said, announcing he would resign before the Series was even over. "A man can take only so much of Finley."

Finley got his pound of flesh by KO'ing Williams's acceptance of an offer to manage the Yankees in 1975, saying he still owed Oakland the last year of his contract—thus, couldn't work anywhere else. Later that year Finley finally let Williams manage the California Angels. In Charlie's view, Williams had been a hellion as A's manager and a 1950s Dodgers journeyman. In early 1974 Finley named his antithesis as once-and-again-A's manager: Alvin Dark, previously fired by the Giants and Indians and later canned by the San Diego Padres. Williams had won two A's titles for the money. Dark, a Bible-touting Baptist, would need every prayer he could summon to win a third for the show.

SOURCES

Virtually all material, including quotes, is derived from Curt Smith's books *Voices of The Game, Storied Stadiums, Voices of Summer, The Voice, Pull Up a Chair, A Talk in the Park,* and *Mercy! A Celebration of Fenway Park's Centennial Told Through Red Sox Radio and TV* (published, in order: Simon & Schuster 1992; Carroll & Graf 2001 and 2005, respectively; the Lyons Press, 2007: and Potomac Books 2009, 2010, and 2012, respectively.)

Books

Fimrite, Ron, *The World Series: A History of Baseball's Fall Classic* (New York: Time Inc. Home Entertainment, 1997).

Lowry, Philip, *Green Cathedrals: The Ultimate Celebration of All Major League Ballparks* (New York: Walker & Company, 2006).

Silverman, Matthew, *Swinging '73: Baseball's Wildest Season* (Guilford, Connecticut: The Lyons Press, 2013).

Thorn, John, Peter Palmer, and Michael Gershman, *Total Baseball: The Official Encyclopedia of Major League Baseball* (Kingston, New York: Total Sports Publishing, 2001).

Websites

Baseball-reference.com

Dark Spring:
1974 Auto Pilot Model

By Matthew Silverman

The 1972-73 A's were the first team not named the New York Yankees to win back-to-back world championships since, well, the A's. Some four decades and two franchise relocations earlier, Connie Mack's Philadelphia Athletics had claimed the 1929 and 1930 world championships. His team reached a third straight World Series in 1931, but the A's fell in seven games. Oakland's Charles O. Finley was not Connie Mack, who managed the team he owned and built. Tempted as it might have seemed to follow Mack into the dugout as the ultimate hands-on owner, Finley needed a manager for his championship team. Yet he was in no hurry after what happened with the last man to hold the position.

Manager Dick Williams had made up his mind to quit when the 1973 World Series ended, win or lose. Finley had been lambasted, reprimanded, and fined for his treatment of infielder Mike Andrews, who committed two errors in the 12th inning of Game Two. Finley pressured Andrews to sign a statement saying he was hurt, thus vacating his roster spot. With Andrews forcibly placed back on the roster by Commissioner Bowie Kuhn, Oakland rallied to beat the New York Mets in seven games. Williams then quit, true to his word. Finley's word was a different matter.

In the victorious locker room, NBC cameras running, the A's owner said he wouldn't stand in his departing manager's way of getting another job. Yet Finley refused to work out a deal to let Williams out of his contract to take over the Yankees. Finley dug in his heels even deeper when the Yankees held a press conference, dressed Williams in a pinstriped uniform, and introduced him to New York at a fancy media shindig. Outgoing American League President Joe Cronin upheld an existing A's contract, barring

Williams from going to New York. Ralph Houk, who'd left the Yankees and first-year owner George Steinbrenner, took over as the manager in Detroit. Former Pirates manager Bill Virdon was the afterthought choice to manage the Yankees. By the time manager musical chairs ended, the world champion A's were left waiting. For four months.

While Finley stayed silent on his managerial vacancy, others chimed in. Dick Williams –powerless to work in baseball yet still being paid by the A's — stated that team captain Sal Bando would make a fine player-manager. Bando, not yet 30 years old that winter, publicly turned down a job that hadn't been offered. Likewise mentioned in the press was Dave Bristol, who had preceded Sparky Anderson in Cincinnati and was the first manager of the Milwaukee Brewers prior to his 1972 dismissal by owner Bud Selig.[1] Bristol remained Montreal's third-base coach in 1974.[2] Frank Robinson, coming off a 30-homer year at age 38 with the Angels, was an intriguing name bandied by writers and by Oakland right fielder Reggie Jackson, who'd been managed by F. Robby in winter ball in Puerto Rico in 1971. Though Robinson would soon become baseball's first African-American manager, it would be with the Cleveland Indians in 1975.[3] Other names came and went, while those expecting Dick Williams to show up in Arizona, slip on an A's uniform, and finish out his contract would have a very long wait.

With spring training just days away, Finley got on the phone and summoned a manager he'd already unceremoniously fired. Now Alvin Dark was unceremoniously hired.

Finley offered Dark a one-year, $50,000 contract, with bonuses for winning the division, the pennant, and the World Series. Dark would be working for the man who'd fired him, rehired him, and fired him again in an eight-hour span because of a raucous Kansas City A's plane flight in August 1967. He would take the place of a man who preferred to quit a two-time world champion rather than put up with the owner for one more day.

The Bible-quoting Dark had been a football star at Louisiana State, Rookie of the Year shortstop for the pennant-winning 1948 Boston Braves, igniter of the ninth-inning rally that culminated in the 1951 "Shot Heard Round the World," a .400 hitter in two World Series as captain of the New York Giants, manager of the San Francisco Giants in the 1962 World Series, and, after his first term under Finley, manager and general manager of the Cleveland Indians for four years.[4] Dark called Finley's contract "better than I've ever had in baseball." Contract details later revealed that Finley essentially had Dark on a day-to-day string. Against standard baseball policy, the manager would not be paid the rest of his salary if he was fired during the season.[5]

Finley introduced Dark as A's manager on February 20, 1974, just three days before the start of spring training.[6] Good thing those games didn't count.

The first exhibition season since 1971 not interfered with by labor disputes saw the A's go 8-16, their worst exhibition mark in the six years since they changed their spring home from Florida to Arizona. At the same time, though, the two-time defending champions also set a new high with more than 2,200 fans per game at Mesa's Rendezvous Park.[7] Spring training records often have no correlation to the regular season, as evidenced by the three-time AL West champions finishing with losing records in two of the previous three springs — and that was with a manager *not* hired as spring training started.

Coming off two straight World Series victories, anything less than a world championship would be considered a letdown. Even if Dark won, Williams, Finley, and the players would get the credit. But Dark understood what he was getting into. Having managed the A's in 1966-67, he was not only familiar with the

unpredictable owner, he was familiar with several players. And not all of those players had fond memories.

Before joining the A's the first time in Kansas City, Dark had managed the San Francisco Giants for four seasons. He was not retained by San Francisco in the wake of a 1964 *Newsday* article featuring quotes not complimentary to the black and Latino stars on the Giants. In a matter of weeks he went from being a hot managerial commodity sought by both New York teams to not managing at all. He latched on with the A's as a consultant in 1965 and a year later took over in Kansas City as Finley's sixth manager in as many years.[8] It was a new start for Dark, but the stain on his reputation remained. After Blue Moon Odom was demoted from Kansas City to Vancouver in 1967, the outspoken pitcher accused his manager of racism.[9] Odom, who had a 5.15 ERA upon his demotion, returned to the A's starting rotation and lost a 14-1 blowout two games before Dark was fired in '67. Yet Odom did not forget the demotion. After Dark joined the Indians the following year, Odom took special delight in beating the Tribe. He tossed four shutouts plus a 2-1 victory against Cleveland in Dark's first two seasons with the Indians. "That man never gave me a chance," Odom told *Sports Illustrated* about Dark in 1969. "Man, every time I make a good pitch or strike out a guy on his team I look right at him in the Cleveland dugout."[10]

Odom was now in Dark's dugout and coming off a 5-12 season and 4.49 ERA in 1973. But Dark, reaffirmed in his religious faith, vowed to be less confrontational: "Being a born-again Christian, there is no color involved or race involved as far as love is concerned. He made a mistake, that's all."[11] Dark looked beyond past problems — and the pitcher's regression on the field — to anoint Odom as the team's fourth starter. But when Odom struggled during the season, Dark shifted him to long relief.

The back end of the rotation was a problem throughout '74, though when a team has starters like Catfish Hunter, Vida Blue, and Ken Holtzman — all 20-game winners in 1973 — the back end can look ragged. One pitcher who was not part of the mix was Chuck

Dobson. Elbow problems and ineffectiveness had kept him to only one major-league start the past two years. Faced with paying Dobson a major-league salary of $28,500 to stay in Triple-A Tucson in 1974, Finley released the right-hander in March. Dark had wanted to keep Dobson in the organization as insurance, but it was clear that the manager would not go against his owner's decisions.[12] Even when it came to pinch-runners.

Rosters in the 1970s generally had nine or ten pitchers, which allowed teams more backup infielders, outfielders, and catchers than seen on most 21st-century rosters. Even then, as now, it was generally accepted that a player needed to be able to play a position to merit a major-league roster spot. Unless Charlie Finley was calling the shots.

On March 16 Finley announced the signing of a new player—and a new position. Herb Washington, a former Michigan State sprinter and the owner of the indoor track record for the 50- and 60-meter dashes, became the A's "designated runner." Finley had long pushed for implementation of the designated hitter, which came into the American League the previous year, but he actually was one of four AL owners to vote against the DH rule because there was no proviso for a designated runner.[13] Finley maintained a soft spot for running specialists, no matter what the position was technically called. He had employed Allen Lewis as pinch-runner for parts of six seasons. "The Panamanian Express," scouted and signed in 1961, batted .282 in the minors over more than 4,000 at-bats. Promoted numerous times to the A's, Lewis stole 44 bases—in 61 tries—and even appeared in the previous two postseasons, though Reds catcher Johnny Bench threw him out in both of his steal attempts. Lewis did, however, score four runs in 11 postseason appearances. He appeared in the outfield in ten major-league games—even starting three times—and committed one error in 13 chances. A switch hitter, he batted .207 in 29 career major-league at-bats before being sent outright to Tucson in the winter of '74 (never to play professional baseball again). In summary, Allen Lewis wasn't good, but he was at least a legitimate ballplayer.

Herb Washington played no position. In fact, he hadn't played on a baseball team since the sophomore year of high school. He never appeared in the minors, but Washington became the first—and only—player to ever have a baseball card that designated his position as "pinch runner." Finley hired Maury Wills as Washington's personal instructor and they worked for a week in Arizona—with Wills wearing a Dodgers jersey during the sessions.[14] In the spring of 1974 Wills still was the record holder for steals in a season with 104 in 1962 for the Dodgers. He might have had more had the dirt around first base at Candlestick Park for a crucial August series not been a quagmire due to an infamous "busted hose." Then-Giants manager Alvin Dark, who always denied any part in a '62 plot, earned the name Swamp Fox for that bit of gamesmanship.

A dozen years later, the religious-minded Dark paid for his sins by dealing with Finley's latest pet project. Dark would use Washington 92 times. He never batted or played the field and is probably best remembered for getting picked off in the one World Series game the A's lost in 1974. During the season Washington scored 29 runs, stole 29 bases, and was caught 16 times. Teammate Bill North led the American League in steals (54) and times caught stealing (26), while Reggie Jackson had the league's best steal percentage (83.3 percent, 25 of 30 attempts). Though the A's led the American League in stolen bases (164) and times caught stealing (93), Lou Brock stole the show, literally. He swiped 118 bases for the '74 Cardinals to break the 1962 mark set by Herb Washington's baseball mentor, Maury Wills.

March 1974 marked the start of divorce proceedings by Shirley Finley, Charlie's wife of 32 years.[15] It was a long, acrimonious, and costly process that strained Finley's finances and made him ever moodier, something those close to Finley had noticed since his 1973 heart attack and especially in the wake of the "Andrews Affair" in the '73 World Series. Fortunately for his players, the arbitration process changed the way many of them did business with the owner. The new system was employed for the first time in 1974, a resolution from the brief spring-training lockout in 1973. While in the 21st century players and management have come to avoid an actual hearing, in the 1970s it was preferable to most A's players' experiences of sitting down with the A's owner—or arguing over the phone or through the newspapers. Arbitration helped prevent long holdouts like the 1972 impasse that kept Vida Blue from starting a game until almost Memorial Day, but it did little to keep player salaries under control.

Charlie Finley had warned his fellow owners about allowing an independent arbitrator to decide salaries: that they would creep up and up, even for players who lost their hearings. As usual, the other owners did not listen to Finley and agreed to arbitration. Nine of the 48 cases in the inaugural arbitration class of 1974 were Oakland A's. That represented 19 percent of the total arbitration cases and 36 percent of Oakland's 25-man roster.[16]

Finley was right: Arbitration did indeed drive up salaries. For an owner to have a chance at winning, the salary submitted should not be a lowball offer because that knocks down the odds that the lower salary will be chosen by the arbitrator. Though only five of nine A's won their 1974 hearings, every player except minor leaguer Jack Heidemann saw a salary increase. Arbitration pushed two A's stars past the $100,000 threshold: American League and World Series MVP Reggie Jackson received a $60,000 boost (to $135,000) and captain Sal Bando got a $40,000 increase to join baseball's previously exclusive $100,000 club—of which Catfish Hunter had been heretofore the lone Oakland member.[17] Seven of the arbitration-eligible A's received salaries that pushed past the $40,000 average major-league salary. Even rookie pinch-runner Herb Washington was making above-average money—though that didn't make him any more popular in the A's clubhouse.[18]

Yet even with the added salaries, the A's weren't any more popular in their home ballpark. They would draw 845,693 for 1974, third-lowest attendance in the major leagues. That number, plus the trickle over 1 million fans in 1973, and 921,323 in 1972, all marked the lowest attendance by a world champion since World War II.

Costs were up, revenue down, and Finley dithered in even getting the A's on the air. He hired recent college grad Jon Miller to work the radio booth. The inexperienced Bay Area native was dismissed after one season, but he later spent four-plus decades at the microphone and received the Ford C. Frick Award, annually given by the Hall of Fame for "major contributions to baseball." Oakland did not have a TV contract until weeks after the 1974 season started, and then to save money Finley teamed broadcaster Monte Moore with off-duty A's starting pitchers as color men in the booth—for no extra pay.[19]

Finley was feeling the pinch from both a slowing insurance business and a costlier baseball team. With a $1,135,400 payroll, the 1974 A's were the second-highest-paid club to the Yankees, a team Finley disliked so much he preferred to pay Dick Williams *not* to manage them. (Finley would permit Williams to manage the middling Angels halfway through the 1974 season.)[20] So, as much as Finley tried to prevent it, the A's were being paid like the baseball big shots they had become. It was almost enough to make an owner want to sell.

In January, shortly after the American League upheld Finley in the Dick Williams contract dispute, the owner stated that his doctors advised him to divest himself of his sports holdings because of the stress. Besides the A's, Finley also owned the National Hockey League California Golden Seals and the American Basketball Association's Memphis Tams. Both teams were as inadequate as the A's were successful, so it came as little surprise that Finley would want to get rid of them. His baseball team was a different matter.

Offers for the A's soon came in, ranging from $11.5 million to $15 million. Given that George Steinbrenner had paid $10 million the previous year for the revered New York Yankees, the two-time world-champion A's owner purred at the offers even while playing hard to get throughout the winter. And just as quickly, fickle Finley changed his mind about selling his most valuable asset. In a letter to season-ticket holders, he dashed the hopes of prospective buyers, not to mention many players and some fans who had become disillusioned with ownership despite two world championships. Finley flatly told season-ticket holders: "The A's will not be sold." And they weren't.

Showing that he hadn't lost his persuasive touch, in a six-month span Finley got the NHL to buy back the Seals for $6.5 million and the ABA to do the same for the Tams for $1.1 million.[21] He held onto his baseball jewel even as he doled out low-cost jewelry.

Finley, who a year earlier had infuriated the other owners by lavishing his players with the most expensive rings any world champion had ever seen, went the other way in 1974. Angered by the way his team banded against him for his treatment of Mike Andrews during the 1973 World Series, which directly led to the resignation of a future Hall of Fame manager, Finley took it out on the players' hardware. A year earlier Finley made a show of coming to Mesa to personally hand out the grandiose trinkets; in March of '74 an employee doled out the World Series rings. And then he ducked.

"These are trash rings," exclaimed Reggie Jackson.

"The worst World Series rings in history," opined reliever Darold Knowles.

"These rings are horsemeat," said Catfish Hunter, whose comments stung Finley most. "He promised us last year, standing right here at Rendezvous Park, that if we won again, he'd make the '72 rings look like babies. But this ring isn't even as good as a high-school ring."[22]

Finley's response? "Screw 'em." He told Dick Young of the *New York Daily News*, "The next time we win I won't give them a thing."[23] That much, at least, proved untrue.

While the rings given out in March of 1973 were valued at $1,500 and came with a full-carat diamond, plus half-carat pendants for the wives and World Series replica trophies, the new rings featured only a synthetic emerald with a value of around $400.[24] The rings also said '72 *and* '73 on them, so players acquired in 1973, like Ray Fosse and Jesus Alou, owned rings for a championship they did not win—and could only gaze fondly at last year's bling on the fingers of their teammates.

The 1974 A's, minus their manager, were almost the same cast of characters as the '73 version. Besides Herb Washington, the roster additions—reliever Bob Locker, backup catcher Larry Haney, and reserve infielder John Donaldson—had all been A's previously. They were aware of both the drawbacks and rewards of playing for Finley. No matter how bizarre things got off the field, a team that had reached the deciding game of four straight postseason series and won each time knew what it took to be the best again. "Once More in '74" wasn't just a saying on the cover of the A's yearbook; it was the team's goal. No matter what else was going on behind the scenes, the A's players would not be distracted from that objective.

"When you have that many guys living together for that amount of time, you're going to have disagreements," reliever Rollie Fingers reflected years later. "But once you cross that white line, if you have a different uniform on, we're going to beat you."[25]

SOURCES

Author Interview
Rollie Fingers, April 21, 2012.

Books

Clark, Tom, *Champagne and Baloney: The Rise and Fall of Finley's A's* (New York: Harper & Row Publishers, 1976).

Green, G. Michael, and Roger D. Launius, *Charlie Finley: The Outrageous Story of Baseball's Super Showman* (New York: Walker & Company, 2010).

Markusen, Bruce, *Baseball's Last Dynasty: Charlie Finley's Oakland A's* (Indianapolis: Masters Press, 1998).

Newspapers and Magazines

1974 Oakland A's Scorecard and Souvenir Yearbook

Oakland Tribune

Sports Illustrated

Websites

baseball-almanac.com

baseball-reference.com

bizofbaseball.com/index. php?option=com_wrapper&view=wrapper&Itemid=179

oakland.athletics.mlb.com/oak/downloads/y2011/2011_media_guide.pdf

oaklandfans.com

retrosheet.org

sabr.org/bioproj/person/15e701c9

NOTES

1   Bruce Markusen, *Baseball's Last Dynasty: Charlie Finley's Oakland A's* (Indianapolis: Masters Press, 1998), 271-72.

2   Retrosheet.org/boxesetc/B/Pbrisd801.htm

3   Markusen, *Baseball's Last Dynasty*, 273-74.

4   Eric Aron, "Alvin Dark," SABR BioProject, sabr.org/bioproj/person/15e701c9

5   Markusen, *Baseball's Last Dynasty*, 279-80.

6   Markusen, *Baseball's Last Dynasty*, 280.

7   2011 A's Media Guide, oakland.athletics.mlb.com/oak/downloads/y2011/2011_media_guide.pdf

8   G. Michael Green and Roger D. Launius, *Charlie Finley: The Outrageous Story of Baseball's Super Showman* (New York: Walker & Company, 2010), 96.

9   Markusen, *Baseball's Last Dynasty*, 280.

10 Herman Weiskopf, "Highlight," *Sports Illustrated*, May 26, 1969. sportsillustrated.cnn.com/vault/article/magazine/MAG1082451/index.htm

11 Markusen, *Baseball's Last Dynasty*, 280.

12 Markusen, *Baseball's Last Dynasty*, 288.

13 Bruce Markusen, Cooperstown, Confidential—Regular Season Edition, "Super Balls at the Stadium," June 12, 2003, oaklandfans.com/columns/markusen/markusen157.html.

14 *Oakland A's 1974 Scorecard and Souvenir Yearbook*, 72.

15 Tom Clark, *Champagne and Baloney: The Rise and Fall of Finley's A's* (New York: Harper & Row Publishers, 1976), 207.

16 Year in Review: 1974 American League, baseball-almanac.com/yearly/yr1974a.shtml.

17 Green and Launius, *Charlie Finley*, 195.

18 1974 Oakland Athletics Roster, baseball-almanac.com/teamstats/roster.php?y=1974&t=OAK.

19 Markusen, *Baseball's Last Dynasty*, 297.

20 MLB Salary Database, bizofbaseball.com/index.php?option=com_wrapper&view=wrapper&Itemid=179

21 Green and Launius, *Charlie Finley*, 202.

22 Clark, *Champagne and Baloney*, 203.

23 Markusen, *Baseball's Last Dynasty*, 285-286.

24 Clark, *Champagne and Baloney*, 203.

25 Author interview, Rollie Fingers, April 21, 2012.

Alvin Dark

by Eric Aron

President John F. Kennedy was said to have correctly answered a trivia question that had been floating around for years: Who is the only man to ever hit a home run off Sandy Koufax and catch a pass from Y.A. Tittle? The guess was always Alvin Dark. "It's not quite accurate, however," Dark always said. "Tittle played at LSU after I did."[1]

That JFK's answer was presumed true said it all about Dark—a terrific three-sport athlete at Louisiana State University who in baseball excelled at each phase of the game. Joe DiMaggio called him the "Red Rolfe type of hitter," meaning that he was ideal for the No. 2 spot, the type of batter who could "bunt or drag, hit behind the runner, or push the ball to the opposite field."[2]

One of the best shortstops in Giants history, Dark played in 14 major-league seasons with the Boston Braves, New York Giants, St. Louis Cardinals, Chicago Cubs, and Philadelphia Phillies before returning to the Braves, then in Milwaukee, to finish his career. A three-time All-Star, he started at shortstop for the National League in the 1951 and '54 contests. He was 24 years old when he broke into the big leagues with the Boston Braves on July 14, 1946, but was already nationally known for his collegiate exploits on the diamond and gridiron. A lifetime .289 hitter with 126 home runs and 757 RBIs, Dark, nicknamed the Swamp Fox, played on pennant winners with the 1948 Braves and '51 Giants, and also helped win a World Series title for New York in 1954. He was the Rookie of the Year in 1948 and was captain of the strong Giants teams of the 1950s.

Dark also had a successful managing career. He won a pennant with the 1962 San Francisco Giants just after his playing days, a world championship with the Oakland A's in 1974, and a division title for the A's in 1975. Accordingly, he became the first man to manage All-Star teams for both leagues: the National League

in 1963 and the American League in 1975. It was not quite a Hall of Fame career either on the field or in the dugout, but Dark was still one of the few men to reach the top of the heap in both roles.

Born on January 7, 1922, in Comanche, Oklahoma, Alvin Ralph Dark was the third of four children born to Ralph and Cordia Dark. Ralph was a drilling supervisor for the Magnolia Oil Company and a part-time barber. An amateur baseball star, he declined an opportunity to play in the Texas League to marry Cordia. Work brought the family, which also included son Lanier and daughters Margaret and Juanita, to Lake Charles, Louisiana.

Young Alvin battled malaria and diphtheria as a child, rendering him unable to attend school until he was 7. His athletic career blossomed at Lake Charles High

School, where he made all-state and all-Southern football teams as a football tailback; and his skills as a basketball guard were superlative enough to earn him the team captaincy. Lake Charles High lacked a baseball team, and Alvin played American Legion ball.

Dark reconsidered a basketball scholarship from Texas A&M University to play football at Louisiana State in 1940. Playing halfback as a sophomore for the Tigers in 1942, he carried 60 times for 433 yards and a 7.2-yard rushing average. He also played basketball and baseball for LSU that year, lettering in all three sports.

With World War II raging, Dark in 1943 joined the Marine Corps' V-12 program, which allowed him to continue his education for another year. The Marines sent him to the Southwestern Louisiana Institute in Lafayette, where he played for the greatest football team in the school's history. Undefeated at 4-0-1 (most Southern schools did not play a full schedule during the war), SLI beat Arkansas A&M University 24-7 to capture the inaugural Oil Bowl. In that game, played in Houston, Dark ran for a touchdown, passed for another from his tailback slot, and kicked three extra points and a field goal.[3]

In addition to playing football in the 1943-44 school year, Dark was a member of SLI's track, basketball, baseball, and even golf teams. His Marine V-12 obligations prevented him from playing the entire baseball season, but he made the most of his limited at-bats, going 12-for-26 (.462). After completing basic training at Parris Island and Camp Lejeune, Dark was commissioned at Quantico in January 1945 and was destined for service in the Pacific Theater. As he awaited orders at Pearl Harbor, he tried out for the Marine Corps baseball team, earning a berth on the lower-division squad.

In the end Dark never saw combat, but he still faced a pretty dicey situation. After the declaration of an Allied victory in the summer of 1945, he was sent to China that December to support the Nationalists against the Communists. He was dispatched to an outpost south of Peking (now Beijing) to guard the railroad and help transfer supplies to another station.

Although his platoon did not know it, they had to pass through a Communist-controlled town to complete their mission. "Our group ran the supply line for four months before being relieved," said Dark. "A month after I got back to the United States, I received word that the Marines who took our place were ambushed in the Communist town and massacred."[4]

When he returned home to Lake Charles, Dark learned that he had been drafted to play pro football for the NFL's Philadelphia Eagles. His first love was baseball, however, and Ted McGrew, a scout for the Boston Braves, had been watching Dark play in college. McGrew, who had helped engineer the trade of Pee Wee Reese from the Red Sox to the Dodgers, admired young Dark for his tenacity and competitive spirit in all sports. Spurning reported interest from several clubs, Dark signed with the Braves for $50,000: a $45,000 bonus and $5,000 to complete the season with Boston. The date was July 4, 1946.

Dark's obligations to the Marines prevented him from joining the Braves until July 14. That day, in the second game of a doubleheader against the Pittsburgh Pirates at Forbes Field, he pinch-ran for catcher Don Padgett in the ninth inning of a 5-2 loss. A month later, on August 8, Dark got his first hit, a double off Phillies' pitcher Lefty Hoerst at Philadelphia. Once again the Braves were defeated, as the Phillies triumphed, 9-8.

Dark played 15 games for the fourth-place Braves in 1946. Although he had just three hits in 13 at-bats, all were doubles—a nice harbinger of things to come (he wound up hitting 358 big league two-baggers). At spring training in 1947, Dark pleaded with manager Billy Southworth to retain him as a regular player. Southworth preferred to keep veteran Sibby Sisti as his starting shortstop, however, and optioned Dark to Milwaukee.

That summer, his only season in the minors, Dark hit .303 with 10 home runs, 7 triples, 49 doubles, 186 hits, and 66 RBIs. He earned American Association honors as All-Star shortstop and Rookie of the Year, and finished third in the Most Valuable Player balloting. Playing for manager Nick Cullop, Dark led the league in at-bats, runs, putouts, assists, and, dubiously, errors. His fielding, however, was considered solid; while not the flashiest of shortstops, he had good range and would become a good double-play man.

After the 1947 season Dark returned to Southwest Louisiana Institute to complete his degree in physical education. Although he wanted to compete in collegiate athletics, his request was denied because he had signed a professional contract. He did, however, serve briefly as the football coach's athletic assistant.

Dark made the Opening Day varsity for the Braves in 1948, but was relegated to the bench as veteran Sisti continued as the regular shortstop. Nevertheless, Dark persevered. His contributions as a reserve player eventually won him the starting job, and he wound up fourth in the National League in batting with a .322 average. He contributed 3 home runs, 39 doubles (third in the NL), and 48 RBIs from his No. 2 spot in the order, while fielding his position strongly (a .963 fielding mark, well above the league average). Initially, his tenure in 1946 disqualified him from the Rookie of the Year ballot. However, the Baseball Writers Association of America ruled that year that players with 25 games or less in previous seasons would qualify for the ballot. This allowed Dark to win Rookie of the Year honors for 1948, the last season both leagues combined to acknowledge one freshman player. He also finished third in the vote for NL Most Valuable Player, but was a letdown in his first World Series by batting just .167 with one double in 24 at-bats. The Braves lost to the Cleveland Indians in six games.

Dark's outstanding rookie campaign was augmented by the exploits of his keystone partner, second baseman Eddie Stanky. Known as "The Brat," Stanky had been traded to the Braves by the Dodgers during spring training. Not only were Dark and Stanky a great double-play combination for years to come, but they became close friends and roommates. Dark considered Stanky and Danny Murtaugh as his greatest mentors; as Dark remarked in his autobiography, "Stanky knew so much more about the game than anybody else. If there were ten possible percentage plays to make, most guys would know four or five. Stanky would know ten."[5]

Their strong double-play duo notwithstanding, the Braves had a disappointing 1949. They fell to 75 wins against 79 losses, good for just fourth place. Dark's batting average fell as well—to .276.

Just behind the Braves in the 1949 standings were the New York Giants, who finished a pedestrian fifth place at 73-81. New York manager Leo Durocher and team president Horace Stoneham attributed the shortcoming to inadequate speed and defense. To improve in these areas, the Giants traded outfielders Willard Marshall and Sid Gordon, shortstop Buddy Kerr, and pitcher Sam Webb to the Braves on December 14 for Dark and Stanky. The blockbuster deal was panned in Gotham, as the trade cost the Giants power hitters Marshall and Gordon—the latter a particularly strong fan favorite as one of the league's foremost Jewish sluggers. Fans at the Polo Grounds were also initially lukewarm to accepting Stanky, as he had previously played for the archrival Dodgers.

Dark, however, came with no such baggage, and Durocher immediately took to his new shortstop. As Dark later wrote, "Leo stuck by me in the early part of 1950, when I first came to the Giants and couldn't seem to get started ... yet Durocher stood by and kept telling me not to worry, that I would seem to come out of it."[6]

Durocher surprised Dark once again that first season by declaring the shortstop his team captain. Most sportswriters assumed that Stanky, not Dark, would get the nod. After all, it was the extroverted Stanky who emulated Durocher, in speaking his mind to the press and in the clubhouse. Yet Leo chose Dark, speculating that the position could easily build confidence in the mild-mannered infielder and help him emerge as a team leader.

"In my first year [as captain], all I did was take the lineup to home plate. After the success we had in 1951, I began taking on some responsibilities—automatic things, like consoling a guy after a bad day. After a while some of the younger players came around, and some of them, like (Willie) Mays, still call me 'Cap.'"[7]

In 1950 the Giants improved to third place with a record of 86-68. Playing in all 154 games, Dark batted .279 with 16 homers and 67 RBIs—by far his best power numbers to that point. It was in that season that the Giants made history.

Early in the campaign, the Giants promoted rookie outfielder Willie Mays from Minneapolis, and he was soon dazzling the league with his graceful catches and power. The Giants also boasted clutch-hitting outfielder Monte Irvin, who had 121 RBIs that year, 32-homer man Bobby Thomson in the third outfield slot, and pitchers Sal Maglie and Larry Jansen, each a 23-game winner. Dark, for his part, had a terrific year, hitting .303 with a career-high 196 hits, a league-best 41 doubles, 114 runs scored, and 14 homers. Defensively he led the league with 45 errors at shortstop, but he also was tops in assists (465) and double plays (114) in making his first All-Star team. Still, the Giants trailed the Dodgers by 13½ games as late as August 11. How was anyone to guess that they were about to complete one of the greatest pennant races in baseball history? The Giants won 37 of their last 44 games to tie the Dodgers at the end of the season and force a best-of-three playoff.

In the third game, with the teams tied, 1-1, Brooklyn had a 4-1 lead going into the bottom of the ninth at the Polo Grounds. With Dodgers ace Don Newcombe on the mound, Dark led off the inning with a single off the glove of first baseman Gil Hodges. "I must have fouled off six or seven pitches with two strikes before getting that hit," Dark recalled.[8] Four batters later, after Dark had scored, Bobby Thomson hit his legendary three-run homer to cap the "Miracle at Coogan's Bluff" and win the pennant, 5-4. Dark hit .417 with three doubles, a home run, and four RBIs in the World Series that followed, but the Yankees reigned supreme, winning in six games.

After the 1951 season, Dark's friend and teammate Eddie Stanky was traded to the St. Louis Cardinals. Without this sparkplug, and with Willie Mays in the Army most of the year, the Giants finished 1952 in second place, 4½ games behind the Dodgers. Meanwhile, Durocher had become impressed with

farmhand Daryl Spencer, who dazzled at shortstop while playing for Minneapolis. Durocher wanted to play Spencer at shortstop and move Dark to second or third base. Dark expressed his displeasure by intruding on a press conference orchestrated by Durocher. Things smoothed over, however, and Spencer departed for military service after the 1953 season. After his greatest season at the plate, in 1953, batting .300 with 23 home runs and 88 RBIs, Dark emerged as the undisputed shortstop for the New York Giants.

Perhaps the resolution of this conflict helped the club. After a disastrous 1953 season in which the Giants finished fifth, the team went on a roll the next spring. The press began referring to the squad as "Happy Heroes, Inc.," because they would always find a way to beat you, whether it was a pinch-hit home run or solid pitching.[9] Dark was reunited with erstwhile Braves teammate Johnny Antonelli, and the starting pitcher won 21 games after the Giants acquired him in a trade for Bobby Thomson. Center fielder Mays returned from the Army and emerged as a superstar, leading the National League with a .345 average while slugging 41 home runs and driving in 110 runs. The Giants finished five games ahead of the Dodgers, winning the pennant with a record of 97-57.

This time the Giants faced the Cleveland Indians, winners of 111 games, in the World Series. After hitting a solid .293 with 20 home runs and 70 RBIs during the year, Dark had another outstanding postseason with a .412 batting average on seven hits and a walk in 18 plate appearances. Boosted by his output and the incredible pinch-hitting of Dusty Rhodes (two homers, seven RBIs), the Giants surprised by sweeping the Indians. While Mays was the runaway choice as league MVP, Dark finished fifth in the balloting and even got one first-place vote.

An injury-plagued 1955 campaign was Dark's last full season as a Giant. After fracturing his rib in a game against Cincinnati on August 7, he separated his right shoulder against the Phillies on September 2. Dark's injuries limited him to 115 games, and he ended the year hitting .282 with 9 homers and 45 RBIs. New

York finished 18½ games behind the Dodgers, in third place.

The 1956 season started off dismally for the club, and by early June the Giants were settled into seventh place with a record well under .500. A shakeup was in order, and in an eight-player deal on June 14 the Giants sent Dark, Ray Katt, Don Liddle, and Whitey Lockman to the St. Louis Cardinals for Dick Littlefield, Jackie Brandt, Red Schoendienst, and Bill Sarni. New York wanted a second baseman (Schoendienst), and the Cardinals wanted a shortstop (Dark). It was initially a good move for Dark; the 1957 season, his last as a regular shortstop, was also his final pennant race as a player. He hit .290 as the Cardinals finished in second place, eight games behind the Milwaukee Braves.

Dark now became a third baseman—and a "traveling man." On May 20, 1958, the Cardinals traded him to the Chicago Cubs for pitcher Jim Brosnan; in his two seasons in Chicago, he hit .295 and .264 while playing alongside another standout shortstop, Ernie Banks. On January 11, 1960, Dark was swapped again, along with pitcher John Buzhardt and infielder Jim Woods, to the dismal Philadelphia Phillies for outfielder Richie Ashburn. Dark's first hit of the season in Philadelphia's home opener against the Braves on April 14, 960, was the 2,000th of his major-league career. He played 53 games at third base (hitting .242) before a June 23 trade for infielder Joe Morgan (later the Boston Red Sox manager) sent him to the Milwaukee Braves. Now 38, he was used primarily as a utility infielder, pinch-hitter, and occasional outfielder. Appearing in 50 games for the second-place Braves, Dark upped his productivity, batting .298 with one homer and 18 RBIs.

Still, it wasn't long before Dark was sent packing again. On October 31, 1960, he was traded for the sixth and last time when the Braves dealt him to the San Francisco Giants for infielder André Rodgers. With his future uncertain, Dark accepted a sales position with the Magabar Mud Company in Louisiana. He did not peddle mud for long, however, as he was named to replace Tom Sheehan as the Giants manager for 1961.

In his first press conference as skipper, Dark was asked if he retained any memento from the 1951 Miracle at Coogan's Bluff. "Yeah," the manager replied humorously. "Willie Mays!"[10] He demonstrated very quickly his ability and fortitude to make bold moves with his roster and in game situations, thereby emulating his mentor Leo Durocher. He intended to eliminate any racial cliques by reassigning clubhouse lockers that integrated whites with blacks. "We're all together and fighting for the same cause. This way we'll all get to know each other better," he said.[11] Dark also moved the Giants' bullpen across the field to better monitor pitchers who might not be focused on the game.

Although Dark earned a reputation for avoiding controversy as a player, he embraced it as a manager. Despite his strong religious views as a Baptist fundamentalist, he was prone to temper tantrums. To ventilate his anger after a 1-0 loss to Philadelphia on June 26, 1961, for instance, he flung a metal stool against the wall. In the process, he lost the tip of his little finger, requiring hospitalization for its repair. "I made up my mind two weeks ago not to take my anger out on the players. So, I guess I took it out on myself tonight," he said in jest.[12]

In his first season as manager, Dark guided the Giants to a third-place finish at 85-69, eight games behind pennant-winning Cincinnati. The next season, 1962, he led the Giants to a sparkling 103-62 record and their first National League championship in San Francisco. Mays, Felipe Alou, Orlando Cepeda, and Willie McCovey combined to hit 129 homers, and Jack Sanford led the pitching rotation with 24 wins.

The Giants' 1962 campaign was not without its controversy. Even as West Coast transplants, they retained their rivalry with the Los Angeles Dodgers. LA shortstop Maury Wills was en route to a then-record 104 stolen bases, and according to the Dodgers, the Giants were trying to slow him down. At one point during a three-game series at San Francisco's Candlestick Park in August, the infield was soaking wet around first base. The umpires had no choice but to douse the wet surface with sand, thereby preventing baserunners from stealing. For his alleged role in the situation, Dark earned the nickname "Swamp Fox." Dark responded to the incident with a "Who, me?" attitude. As he remarked to Baseball Digest some 40 years later, "I just remember that one day they had trouble with a hose that broke."[13]

Just as in 1951, the '62 NL pennant race came down to a tie finish and a three-game playoff with the Dodgers to decide a champion. The Giants triumphed again, and in another '51 rematch, they faced the Yankees in the World Series. Mickey Mantle and Roger Maris, sparked the Yankees' offense, complementing a rotation led by Whitey Ford and Ralph Terry. San Francisco took New York to the limit, but fell 1-0 in Game Seven at Candlestick Park. After this near-miss, the Giants returned to third place under Dark in 1963, posting an 88-74 record to finish 11 games behind Los Angeles.

Dark has been linked to a great urban legend involving Gaylord Perry, who pitched for the Giants' teams from 1962 to 1964 and was a notoriously weak hitter (.131 career batting average). Dark was said to respond to sportswriter Harry Jupiter's comments on Perry showing some pop in batting practice by saying, "There would be a man on the moon before Gaylord Perry would hit a home run." Sure enough, on July 20, 1969, Perry hit a home run in the third inning off Dodgers pitcher Claude Osteen. How long the home run came after Neil Armstrong stepped onto the lunar surface when the home run came is debatable. In any event, Perry hit five more homers before retiring.[14]

On June 7, 1964, during the last of a three-game series with the Phillies at Connie Mack Stadium Dark exemplified why the Bay Area had dubbed him the "Mad Genius" when he used four pitchers in the first inning.[15] He sent starter Bob Henley to the showers for surrendering two runs without retiring a batter, and when reliever Bob Bolin walked one man, he, too, was replaced, by Ken MacKenzie. MacKenzie retired a pinch-hitter before Gaylord Perry was summoned to record the final two outs of the frame. The craziness worked; 10 innings later, the Giants beat the Phillies 4-3.

Dark's Giants completed the 1964 season with a fine 90-72 record and a fourth-place finish. However, his role at the center of a controversial article numbered his days in San Francisco. Midway through the season, Stan Isaacs of Long Island Newsday asked Dark about the Giants' performance. The manager responded by accusing his players of making recent "dumb" plays.[16] Although he later insisted that his comments were specific to baserunning mistakes by Orlando Cepeda and Jesus Alou, it was already too late; because his team was made up primarily of African-American, Puerto Rican, and Dominican players, Dark was unfairly painted as a racist.

On August 4, 1964, Dark called a press conference at Shea Stadium in New York to explain that the newspapers had misinterpreted him, but it mattered not; Horace Stoneham fired him at the end of the season. Several high-ranking baseball officials declared their support for Dark, including Commissioner Ford Frick. Perhaps most significantly, former Dodgers great Jackie Robinson quickly rushed to Dark's defense. The two had been friends since their playing days, and Robinson told the New York Times that he had "known Dark for many years, and my relationships with him have always been exceptional. I have found him to be a gentleman, and above all, unbiased. Our relationship has not only been on the baseball field but off it. We played golf together."[17]

Surely boosted by this vote of confidence, Dark moved beyond the Giants and was subsequently hired as the third-base coach for the Chicago Cubs. Then, at the end of the 1965 season, Charlie Finley hired him to manage the Kansas City Athletics. Dark was already the sixth manager hired by the maverick Finley in the six years he had owned the team. The A's boasted an unknown young club with Catfish Hunter, Blue Moon Odom, and Lew Krausse in the starting rotation. After losing 103 games in 1965, the A's went 74-86 in 1966 during Dark's first season as skipper.

Despite considerable talent, lackluster baseball and personality issues caused the A's to fall back into the cellar in 1967. After an incident that alleged player rowdiness on an airline flight, Dark had the distinction of being fired, rehired, and fired again on August 20. Not even Hall of Famer Luke Appling could resurrect the A's as Dark's replacement. With two All-Star shortstops at the helm, the A's finished with a record of 62-99.

After the 1967 season, the Cleveland Indians hired Dark as manager and general manager. He led the team to its best record in nine years in 1968, with 86 wins and 75 losses. But in 1969 the Indians finished last, at 62-99. Without a substantial budget, they improved a bit in 1970 but returned to last place in 1971. With the team's record 42-61 on July 30, 1971, Dark was fired as manager and general manager, completing his four years at the Cleveland helm with a lackluster .453 winning percentage (in San Francisco, he had won at a .569 clip).

For the next two years, Dark lived in Miami, where he excelled as a regular golfer by winning local tournaments. He supplemented his savings as an after-dinner speaker at churches, lecturing on baseball and the Bible. By 1974, however, Dark missed managing. As spring training dawned on February 20, he accepted old pal Charlie Finley's offer to return to the A's, by now in Oakland, as their skipper.

Dark faced enormous pressure assuming the reins of baseball's most combative and successful team. Under Dick Williams the A's had won the World Series in 1972 and 1973. Although one year remained on Williams's contract, differences with Finley led him to resign. Dark accepted a one-year, $50,000 contract as Williams's successor, with incentive bonuses if he won the pennant or World Series. An Oakland reporter heralded Dark's arrival by writing, "The only thing worse than being hired by Charlie Finley [is] being hired by him a second time."[18]

Dark claimed that his renewed religious faith had made him a changed man. No longer would he berate his players or belittle them publicly. He vowed to accept Finley's suggestions, avoiding a renewal of their feud. Certain players, like Reggie Jackson, accepted Dark's new personality, while others, such as Vida Blue, were rather critical. A fellow Louisianan, Blue

"knew Alvin Dark was a religious man, but he's worshipping the wrong god—Charles O. Finley."[19]

The Oakland team Dark managed in 1974 had few weak spots. Catfish Hunter posted a record of 25-12, led the league with a 2.49 ERA, and won the Cy Young Award. Powered by a lineup featuring the likes of Jackson, Sal Bando, and Joe Rudi, the club captured its fourth consecutive division title by five games over the Texas Rangers. The A's pitchers proved dominant over the Baltimore Orioles in the League Championship Series, at one point tossing 30 consecutive scoreless innings. Oakland won the series, three games to one.

The 1974 World Series was the first to feature only California teams: the A's and manager Walter Alston's Dodgers. After defeating Los Angeles in five games for his first Series title as a skipper, Dark agreed to return to Oakland in 1975. And despite losing Hunter as a free agent, he guided the A's to yet another divisional title. With a record of 98-64, the A's paced the division with a comfortable seven-game lead over the Kansas City Royals, but the 1975 Red Sox swept Oakland in three games in the playoffs.

On October 17, 1975, Charlie Finley announced that Dark's contract would not be renewed. Dark returned to the Cubs as a coach for manager Herman Franks in 1977 before replacing John McNamara as the San Diego Padres' manager on May 28. Although the Padres played well under Dark, their second-half record could not lift them beyond a final mark of 69-93. Citing a "communication problem," Padres general manager Bob Fontaine fired Dark on March 21, 1978.[20] He was only the second manager in major-league history to be released during spring training.

Dark was inducted into the Oklahoma Sports Hall of Fame, the Louisiana Sports Hall of Fame, the Louisiana State University Sports Hall of Fame, and the New York Giants Baseball Hall of Fame. Dark married his childhood sweetheart, Adrienne Managan, in 1946, and the couple had four children, Allison, Gene, Eve, and Margaret. They divorced in 1969, and Dark was remarried a year later, to Jackie Rockwood, and adopted her children, Lori and Rusty. He returned to baseball as the farm-system evaluator for the Cubs in 1981, and in 1986 was hired as director of minor leagues and player development for the Chicago White Sox.

Dark was 92 years old in 2014, with 20 grandchildren and three great-grandchildren. He moved from San Diego to Easley, South Carolina, in 1983. He became involved with the Alvin Dark Foundation, which financially supports ministries,

As of January 2014, Dark was the oldest living manager of a World Series-winning, pennant-winning or post-season team.

SOURCES

Dark, Alvin, and John Underwood, *When in Doubt, Fire the Manager.* (New York: E.P. Dutton, 1980).

Markusen, Bruce, *A Baseball Dynasty: Charlie Finley's Swingin' A's.* (Haworth, New Jersey: Saint Johann Press, 2002).

Meany, Tom, *The Incredible Giants.* (New York: A.S. Barnes, 1955).

Stein, Fred, and Nick Peters, *Giants Diary: A Century of Giants Baseball in New York and San Francisco* (Berkeley: North Atlantic Books, 1987).

Boyle, Robert, "Time of Trial for Dark," *Sports Illustrated,* July 6, 1964, 26-31.

Bush, David, "Turn Back the Clock 1962: When the Giants Lost a Heartbreaker to the Yankees," *Baseball Digest.* October 2002.

Dark, Alvin, and John Underwood, "Rhubarbs, Hassles, Other Hazards," *Sports Illustrated,* May 13, 1974, 42-48.

McDonald, Jack, "Alvin Assigns New Lockers in Effort to Kill Cliques," *The Sporting News,* April 19, 1961, 26.

Stevens, Bob, "Dark Blows Stack—Loses Finger-Tip on Metal Stool," *The Sporting News,* July 5, 1961, 9.

Tourangeau, Dixie, "Spahn, Sain, and the '48 Braves," *The National Pastime* (SABR), 1998, 17-20.

"Dark's First Hit of the Season No. 2,000 for His Career," *The Sporting News,* April 27, 1960, 8.

Newell, Sean, "Did Neil Armstrong Help Perry Get His First Home Run?," Deadspin.com, August 12, 2010 (deadspin.com/5937875/did-neil-armstrong-help-gaylord-perry-get-his-first-career-home-run.)

Louisiana's Ragin' Cajuns Athletic Network, athleticnetwork.net

NOTES

1   Alvin Dark and John Underwood, *When in Doubt, Fire the Manager* (New York: E.P. Dutton, 1980), 32.

2   Tom Meany, *The Incredible Giants,* (New York: A.S. Barnes, 1955), 73.

3   Louisiana's Ragin' Cajuns Athletic Network (athletic-network.net).

4   Dark and Underwood, 36.

5   Dark and Underwood, 42.

6   Meany, 74.

7   Dark and Underwood, 59.

8   Interview with Alvin Dark, December 18, 2006.

9   Meany, *The Incredible Giants,* 76.

10 Fred Stein and Nick Peters, *Giants Diary: A Century of Giants Baseball in New York and San Francisco,* (Berkeley: North Atlantic Books, 1987).

11 Jack McDonald, "Alvin Assigns New Lockers in Effort to Kill Cliques," *The Sporting News,* April 19, 1961, 26.

12 Bob Stevens, "Dark Blows Stack—Loses Finger-Tip on Metal Stool," *The Sporting News,* July 5, 1961, 9.

13 David Bush, "Turn Back the Clock 1962: When the Giants Lost a Heartbreaker to the Yankees," *Baseball Digest,* October 2002.

14 There was a dispute over whether the words came from Dark or Perry, but the late umpire Ron Luciano said they were uttered by Dark. Ron Luciano with David Fisher, *Strike Two* (New York: Bantam Books, 1985). The controversy was also addressed by Sean Newell on Deadspin on August 25, 2012: (Sean Newell, "Did Neil Armstrong Help Perry Get His First Home Run?," Deadspin.com, August 12, 2010 (deadspin.com/5937875/did-neil-armstrong-help-gaylord-perry-get-his-first-career-home-run.)c

15 Robert Boyle, "Time of Trial for Dark," *Sports Illustrated,* July 6, 1964, 28.

16 Alvin Dark and John Underwood, "Rhubarbs, Hassles, Other Hazards," *Sports Illustrated,* May 13, 1974, 48.

17 Dark and Underwood, *When in Doubt,* 98.

18 Dark and Underwood, *When in Doubt,* 166.

19 Bruce Markusen, *A Baseball Dynasty: Charlie Finley's Swingin' A's,* (Haworth, New Jersey: Saint Johann Press, 2002), 289.

20 Dark and Underwood, *When in Doubt,* 230.

John Donaldson

By Gregory H. Wolf

Perseverance and a love for the game guided sure-handed utility infielder John Donaldson through a 12-year career in Organized Baseball (1963-1974), including parts of six seasons with the Kansas City/Oakland A's and the Seattle Pilots. The hard-nosed North Carolinian played in 405 big-league games and weathered trades, demotions, promotions, and outright releases, but looked back on his career with the same enthusiasm he exhibited as a player. "I'd do it all over again. It was the best time of my life," he told the author.[1] "Throughout my career, I think my managers saw my attitude. I wanted to play and worked extra hard—baseball's not easy. I tried to let my glove and bat do the talking."

John David Donaldson was born on May 5, 1943, in Charlotte, North Carolina, the eighth of ten children born to Walter Norris and Mary (Moore) Donaldson. Like many of their surrounding neighbors, the Donaldsons worked in the cotton mills of the rapidly urbanizing city of about 100,000 people. Walter, a World War I veteran, later worked for Johnston Manufacturing running cards in a cotton production line. "I was introduced to baseball by my three older brothers," John said. "We tossed and hit the ball on local sandlots." At the age of 9 he began playing Little League baseball at a local YMCA. "My coach was Fred Ashford, who was real good with mechanics," recalled Donaldson vividly. "He taught me the fundamentals of the game." Donaldson played in organized youth leagues through junior high school. By the time he was in high school, he worked part-time in a cotton mill and did not play for his school team. The summers, however, offered the enthusiastic youngster ample opportunities to play the game. "I started playing semipro baseball on a cotton mill team in Charlotte when I was 14 years old," said Donaldson. "We played against other mill teams in the area. I also played American Legion ball for three years in the

summer. Those leagues were highly competitive around here and fun."

Quick, agile, and athletic, Donaldson was 5-feet-11, weighed 160 pounds, and was blessed with great hand-eye coordination. "I always played infield even in semipro ball," he said. "I enjoyed playing shortstop the most, liked the long throw. I was converted to second base later in the minors. Playing second was awkward at first because you were always turned around, but I got used to it." The right-handed Donaldson batted left-handed. "I took that after Ted Williams," he joked, noting that his three older brothers also batted from the left side. "Williams and Stan Musial were my idols when I was a kid. I still remember listening to them on the radio and thinking that I'd be in the big leagues one day."

When Donaldson graduated from Garinger High School in 1961, scouts were not beating down his door to sign him. If fact, he followed his father's footsteps and began working in a mill, but continued to play semipro ball and never abandoned his dream about a career in baseball. And he had a stroke of luck. "I had been scouted by Red Robbins of the Minnesota Twins," said Donaldson. "He didn't think I was big enough to play and didn't want to sign me. But Phil Howser, general manager of the Double-A team of the Minnesota Twins in Charlotte, saw me play and thought I was good enough to join them in spring of 1963." Donaldson was sent to the Twins' minor-league camp in Fernandina Beach, Florida. "I had a real good spring," he said honestly. "Billy Martin was a scout for the Twins at the time and also taught the players fundamentals at spring training. He had the final say over me signing a contract." The Twins signed Donaldson, who was just shy of his 20th birthday. "I got a progressive bonus which was worth $7,500 altogether once I made it to the big leagues," he explained. When asked about his parents' reaction, Donaldson replied, "My parents were working people. My father didn't play baseball—he had a big family to support. But they always encouraged me because they knew I loved the game."

Donaldson's career with Minnesota did not last long. He was assigned to the Orlando Twins of the recently reclassified Class A Florida State League (Minor League Baseball was reclassified and realigned for the 1963 season; Class B, C, and D were designated A). The shortstop batted a respectable .251 and played in 121 of the team's 123 games. However, the Twins left him unprotected in Major League Baseball's First-Year Player draft in December 1963. On December 2 the Kansas City Athletics drafted Donaldson for $8,000 with the stipulation that he be added to the team's 40-man roster. "I went from semipro ball to the Florida State League to a major-league roster in just over a year. Can you believe that?" said Donaldson.

"I was young and full of myself," said Donaldson of participating in his first big-league camp in 1964. "It wasn't really overwhelming." Not ready to challenge

dependable Wayne Causey for the shortstop position, Donaldson was optioned to the Lewiston (Idaho) Broncs of the Class A Northwest League. He batted .315, showed surprising pop to his bat (ten home runs) and was named to the All-Star team.

Donaldson was assigned to the Vancouver Mounties of the Triple-A Pacific Coast League after spring training with the A's in 1965 and 1966. In Vancouver he came under the tutelage of former big leaguer Mickey Vernon, who became manager of the team in 1966 and had a profound effect on his career. "I loved Mickey Vernon. He took me under his wing and taught me how to approach hitting and work the pitchers," said Donaldson. "I came up as a pull hitter. He worked with me on my stance so I wouldn't lunge at the ball. He taught me to keep my bat back. I always got my front foot out too much." After batting a disappointing .231 in 1965, Donaldson improved his average to .298 and was named a second-team all-star in 1966. Donaldson's improvement accompanied a shift to second base. Kansas City's 24-year-old Bert Campaneris was a budding star and seemingly had shortstop locked up for the next decade. Consequently, the A's brass felt Donaldson's best chance to make it was at second base. "I had great instructors in the A's organization, like Alvin Dark and Al Vincent," said Donaldson. "They were patient and taught me how to play second base." Vernon was impressed with Donaldson's winning and team-first attitude and willingness to play through nagging, everyday injuries. "[He's] one of the gutsiest players in baseball," said the two-time former AL batting champ.[2]

After the 1965 season, Donaldson played winter-league baseball in the Caribbean for the first time in what became an annual tradition. "I played for Lara and Magallanes, and for (Baltimore Orioles shortstop) Luis Aparicio in Zuila, Venezuela, as well as with Escogido in the Dominican. It was kind of like a vacation, but the pay was good and I stayed in shape," said Donaldson. He relished playing baseball essentially year-round, but stopped after the 1971-72 season when it began to take a toll on his body.

The Kansas City A's noticed Donaldson's improvement and called him up to the parent club in late August 1966 before the rosters expanded to 40 players. He made his major-league debut on August 26 playing second base and batting leadoff against the California Angels. He went 0-for-5, but recorded two putouts and four assists in the field. He connected off the Angels Dean Chance the following game for his first big-league hit, an RBI single, and later scored on Jim Gosger's double. "I got a taste of the big leagues," said Donaldson, who managed just four hits in 30 at-bats.

The A's sent Donaldson and other top prospects like Reggie Jackson, Rick Monday, Cito Gaston, and Rollie Fingers, to the Arizona Instructional League in the fall of 1966. In his first six games, Donaldson rapped 20 hits, prompting sportswriter Frank Gianelli to gush, "[Donaldson is] one phenom who has been proving he can hit."[3] Eddie Robinson, a former big-league first baseman and then assistant general manager for the A's, noted, "I'm very impressed. ... [Donaldson] is a fine second sacker."[4] Despite the praise, Donaldson's promotion to the big leagues was blocked by Dick Green at second base and Campaneris; consequently, his name was bandied about as trade bait at baseball's 1966 winter meetings in Columbus, Ohio.[5]

Donaldson found himself in Vancouver for the third consecutive year after spring training with the A's in 1967. He continued his torrid pace from the previous autumn, putting together an 18-game hitting streak and earning the Topps Minor League Player of the Month award in June. On June 8 the A's called up the "hot-hitting star" Donaldson (batting .339) as well as Reggie Jackson and catcher Dave Duncan from the Birmingham Barons, and sent down third baseman Sal Bando, utility infielder Ossie Chavarria, and catcher Ken Suarez.[6] "I finally had my chance to play regularly in 1967," said Donaldson. "Dick Green was hurt at the time and manager Al Dark put me in. And I took off hitting and making the plays at second base. I got along with Dark really well. He was a good manager and you listened when he talked." Donaldson took over the keystone position on June 9 and pro-

ceeded to start 100 of the final 110 games. After a 3-for-4 performance with a career-high three runs batted in (achieved five times) in a 9-2 whitewashing of the reigning World Series champion Baltimore Orioles on June 14 at Municipal Stadium in Kansas City, Donaldson scored the winning run on Reggie Jackson's walk-off single in the bottom of the 11th to record the A's third straight victory over the Orioles, 6-5, the next day. With the majority of his at-bats in the two-hole, Donaldson was a streaky hitter. In his first month with the team, he recorded three hits in a game four times and had a career-high four against the Boston Red Sox.

For the last-place A's, Donaldson was a surprising bright spot. "The guy's a good hitter," said Dark. "He makes contact with the ball and keeps it moving around. I like his work at second base, too. He's a much better player than I thought he would be."[7] Donaldson led the team with a .276 batting average (104-for-377) and a .343 on-base-percentage. "Batting .276 was good back in those days," said Donaldson. "We faced a lot of good pitching and they had those high mounds." And then he told the author with a chuckle, "Of course, if you hit .276 at second base nowadays, you'd be out of a job unless you hit a ton of home runs."

After 13 losing seasons in Kansas City, the A's relocated to Oakland for the 1968 season. "Danny Cater, Jim Gosger, Lew Krausse, and I, and some others, went out to Oakland with Charlie Finley in the offseason to do some publicity and sell tickets," said Donaldson. "I looked forward to the season because I knew I'd be there the whole year. We had a good team with lots of young players. It was only a matter of time before we started winning. I roomed with Danny Cater mostly. We had a close team."

Donaldson began the season firmly entrenched as the A's second baseman. On April 18 he belted a walk-off sacrifice fly driving in Reggie Jackson in the bottom of the 13th inning to give the A's their first win at Oakland, beating Baltimore, 4-3. Six days later Donaldson came to the plate again with the bases loaded in extra innings, and delivered a walk-off single, this time knocking in Campaneris in the 11th inning to defeat the New York Yankees, 4-3. But despite the early-season heroics, Donaldson struggled at the plate, laboring to push his batting average to .200 through July 3. "I was having a problem with my stomach. It was acid reflux and making me sick. I wound up having offseason surgery," said Donaldson. He lost his starting job at second base at the end of July. "I wasn't hitting very well," he said, but added. "Bob Kennedy was the new manager and I think Finley talked him into putting Green back in." Donaldson was used primarily as a late-inning defensive replacement or pinch-hitter during the final two months of the season, finishing with a .220 average. In their inaugural season in Oakland, the A's posted a winning record for the first time since 1952 when they were still located in Philadelphia, and began a streak of nine consecutive winning campaigns.

Donaldson recalled that Joe DiMaggio (whom Finley persuaded to join the A's in 1968 as an executive vice president and consultant) was a good influence on the team. "DiMaggio enjoyed talking to the young players, like Bando, Monday, and Jackson, Joe Rudi, and me about hitting. We looked up to him and he taught us about winning. He and I got along well, too. We'd go out to dinner. He liked to hear my stories about growing up in North Carolina and playing semipro ball."

After playing just one game in the field in the first two months of the 1969 season, Donaldson was sent to the expansion Seattle Pilots for catcher Larry Haney on June 14. "I didn't anticipate the trade," he said. "Hank Bauer called me into his office and told me that they are trading me to Seattle." Then he joked with a tinge of seriousness, "I think it was Bauer. We had so many managers with the A's at the time, I can't keep 'em straight anymore."

In Boston at the time of the trade, Donaldson joined his new team in New York in time to pinch-hit against the Yankees. "Rich Rollins was hurt so Seattle moved Tommy Harper (who was playing out of position at second) to third base. I took over second base and played regularly for the rest of the year." Donaldson put together a career-best 11-game hitting streak (18-

for-40) in August and recorded 18 multi-hit games for Seattle en route to a .234 average, which matched the Pilots' team batting average. "John is not flashy," said Pilots beat reporter Hy Zimmerman. "He is steady, especially adept at going back in right field for shallow flies."[8]

Donaldson had fond memories about his season with the Pilots. "Manager Joe Schultz was a piece of work," he said, laughing. "After every game, he'd say, 'Pound that Budweiser, boys.' And I liked the uniforms, they weren't too bad. I know many people didn't, but I did."

"Playing in Sick's Stadium was like playing in the minor leagues, to be honest," Donaldson replied when asked what he thought about the Pilots' home field, which had a seating capacity of 25,420 and had an average attendance of 8,268, good for tenth place among 12 AL teams. "I played in the Pacific Coast League for years and knew the stadium well from the days I faced the California Angels Triple-A team there. It was really a minor-league ballpark."

The Pilots conducted spring training in Tempe, Arizona, in 1970, unsure about their future. "We didn't know where we were going to play—in Seattle or Milwaukee," said Donaldson. "The team had a new manager, Dave Bristol, and he liked a utility infielder named Gus Gil (whom he had managed in the Cincinnati Reds farm system). I didn't have a good spring. Two days before we broke camp, Bristol told me that I was being sent to Portland (Beavers of the PCL). I was upset because I had been on a major-league roster for the last three years. I was probably making as much as anyone on the team." After about a month in Portland, Donaldson was shipped to Oakland for utility infielder Roberto Pena. In his first game back with his former club, he started at second base against Bristol's team—now the Milwaukee Brewers—on May 19. "I got a bit of revenge later in the season when I had the game-winning hit against the Brewers in Oakland," said Donaldson. With two outs in the bottom of the ninth, he stroked a walk-off single to drive in Rick Monday for a 4-3 victory on July 12. In a season-long utility role, Donaldson batted .247 (22-for-89) in 41 games for the second-place A's.

Donaldson opened camp with the A's in 1971 but was optioned to the Iowa Oaks of the American Association to commence a three-year odyssey in the minor leagues before making it back to the big leagues in 1974. After batting a career-best .308 in 27 games with the Oaks, he was traded to the Detroit Tigers for pitcher Daryl Patterson on May 22. He was subsequently optioned to the Toledo Mud Hens (Triple-A American Association), where his .290 batting average ranked second on the team. Sent to the Baltimore Orioles for pitcher Bill Burbach in the offseason, Donaldson was acquired outright by the Hawaii Islanders of the Triple-A Pacific Coast League (a San Diego Padres affiliate) in 1972. He spent 1973 with the Islanders and split the 1974 season with the Islanders and the Wilson (North Carolina) Pennants of the Class A Carolina League.

"I loved the game and I was gonna stick around as long as I could," said Donaldson emphatically when asked why a 30-year-old former big leaguer would endure trades and insecurity, and keep playing. "I was making good money and I don't think I could have earned that much back in Charlotte. And I still felt like I could get back to the big leagues and I was determined to do so. I wasn't gonna quit."

Donaldson's career seemed as though it had reached its end in 1974. "I got released by Hawaii during spring training in Yuma, Arizona," he said. "I wasn't sure what I was gonna do. My wife called Charlie Finley and told him I needed a job. (Donaldson laughed). I'm serious. Finley liked me. I didn't have a problem with him. He gave me a job in Triple-A ball with Tucson."

Donaldson acknowledged that Finley got a lot of bad press and was known for being cheap, but said his generosity often went unreported. "He always treated me well. When I got married in 1967, Finley sent us on a honeymoon to Lake Tahoe and bought us a color TV."

Happy to have a job in Triple-A, Donaldson was sent to the Tucson Toros of the PCL in 1974. "A few weeks into the season, they called me up to Oakland," said

Donaldson with an air of incredulity in his voice. "I was 31 years old and hadn't played in the big leagues for three years. That upset a few young guys on the team, like (hot infield prospect) Phil Garner." *The Sporting News* reported that Donaldson needed only 53 days of active roster time in order to qualify for his four-year major-league pension.[9] In his second game with the club, Donaldson replaced pinch-runner Herb Washington in the ninth and took over third base against the Chicago White Sox in Oakland, on April 15. He led off the bottom of the 13th inning with a single and scored the dramatic winning run when Gene Tenace stroked a two-out walk-off single. The run proved to be the last in Donaldson's big-league career. On May 8 he was involved in a violent collision with center fielder Billy North trying to field a fly ball hit by Baltimore's Earl Williams. Both North and Donaldson were carried off the field (though North returned to the game). Donaldson was subsequently diagnosed with a separated shoulder.

After recuperating, Donaldson was back with the Toros and thought he had lost his chance of a four-year pension. But as A's beat writer Ron Bergman once noted, Finley had a "soft spot for former A's players."[10] Donaldson was recalled in September when the rosters expanded. He said his teammates and good friends lobbied for his return to the team. "I was tight with Catfish, who was from North Carolina, like me. He had a good relationship with Finley and Finley did what Catfish told him to do. Same with Reggie." Donaldson's only action that month was a pinch-hit appearance in the last game of the season. His addition to the roster of the reigning two-time World Series champions was a procedural and symbolic move with far-reaching ramifications. "My four years of service and pension mean so much. If anyone should be in the Hall of Fame, it should be Marvin Miller (former executive director of the Major League Baseball Players Association). He did more for players than anybody," said Donaldson, also paying tribute to Finley. Donaldson was not on the A's postseason roster.

Donaldson was released by Oakland in the offseason. "I could've gone to spring training with a big-league club in 1975 but didn't," he said. "The St. Louis Cardinals wanted me to sign a minor-league contract but that wasn't much money. So I went back to Charlotte. It was time to move on."The good-natured North Carolinian played in 405 games, batted .238 (292-for-1225), scored 96 runs, and drove in 86 runs in parts of six big-league seasons. In ten seasons in the minors, he batted .274 and hit 55 home runs in 1,055 games.

As of 2014 Donaldson still resided in Charlotte, where he has spent most of the four decades years since he retired from baseball. He owned a painting business and worked for a local trucking company, but as of 2014 enjoyed retirement. He is divorced from his wife, Barbara Brooks, with whom he had one child, John Jr. For anyone who has ever spoken with Donaldson about baseball, it is apparent that he never lost his passion for the sport. He has participated in old-timer's games and attended reunions of the Kansas City and Oakland A's, and kept in regular contact with many of his teammates. When asked about his greatest memory in his career, he thought for a moment and mentioned his first home run ("It was in Cleveland in 1968, and that's just something you don't forget") and going 4-for-4 against the eventual pennant-winning Boston Red Sox in 1967, but then stated unequivocally, "The highlight of my career was playing in Catfish Hunter's perfect game against the Minnesota Twins in 1968. I made a few plays for him in that game. I remember there were two outs in the ninth inning and I yelled to him, 'Hey Catfish, just make them hit the ball to me. I got it.' And then he struck out [Rich Reese] to end the game. Now that's baseball."

SOURCES

The author extends his sincerest appreciation John Donaldson, who was interviewed on January 26, 2014. He subsequently read this biography to ensure factual accuracy.

Sincere thanks also to SABR member Bill Mortell for his diligent genealogical research.

Oakland Tribune

The Sporting News

Ancestry.com

BaseballLibrary.com

Baseball-Reference.com

Retrosheet.com

SABR.org

NOTES

1 Interview with John Donaldson on January 26, 2014. All quotations from Donaldson are from this interview unless otherwise noted.

2 *The Sporting News*, August 20, 1966, 28.

3 *The Sporting News*, November 5, 1966, 41.

4 *The Sporting News*, December 24, 1966, 32.

5 *The Sporting News*, November 19, 1966, 35.

6 Associated Press, "Athletics Call Up Hot Hitting Stars From Farm Clubs," *Daily Capital News* (Jefferson City, Missouri), June 8, 1967, 10.

7 *The Sporting News*, August 5, 1967, 17.

8 *The Sporting News*, September 6, 1969, 20.

9 *The Sporting News*, June 1, 1974, 15.

10 Ibid.

Bobby Hofman

By Jeff English

Bobby Hofman spent a lifetime in baseball. Over a career roughly divided into three distinct phases, he played major-league baseball for parts of seven seasons, and then managed and coached at various levels, including Oakland, for the next 20. He transitioned from there into a career as a big-league executive until his retirement in 1989 at the age of 64. As a player, he displayed a great deal of determination which endeared him to teammates and fans alike, and he built relationships that served him well once his playing days had ended. As a minor-league manager and big-league coach, he was respected for his knowledge of the game and ability to identify talent. His penchant for organization and his demonstrated loyalty contributed to a successful career at the executive level, from part-time traveling secretary for the Athletics to director of player development for the New York Yankees.

Robert George Hofman was born on October 5, 1925 to Erwin and Sophia Hofman in St. Louis. His father grew up playing baseball with his four brothers, Louis, George, Arthur, and Oscar. They developed their skills under the watchful eye of their father, Louis Sr., who managed the local Mound City and Cold Storage team. All of the Hofman brothers played in the Trolley League, a semipro league with teams in Missouri and Illinois. Bobby's brother Arthur "Solly" Hofman enjoyed a 14-year big-league career as an infielder, outfielder, and noted utility player, and Oscar played briefly for Columbus in the American Association.

One of Bobby's teammates in American Legion ball was Lawrence "Yogi" Berra. Over the years, the origin of Berra's famous moniker has been attributed to Hofman, but it was actually their friend and teammate Jack Maguire who applied the name after the friends saw a movie travelogue about India one summer afternoon. Citing Yogi's own 1961 autobiography, Allen

Barra wrote, "When they walked out of the movie house, Jack (Maguire) said, 'You know, you look just like a yogi. I'm going to call you Yogi.'"[1]

Hofman and Maguire both played on the Beaumont High School baseball team. Their teammates included future major leaguers Jim Goodwin, Roy Sievers, and Bob Wiesler, and future Hall of Fame manager Earl Weaver. Initially an outfielder, Hofman switched to second base to accommodate his difficulty making long throws. One of his American Legion coaches was Gordon Maguire, Jack's father and a part-time scout for the St. Louis Cardinals. Gordon helped to develop Hofman's skills at second base. In 1944 Maguire became a full-time scout for the New York Giants, and although Hofman had dreamed of playing ball for his hometown Cardinals, he felt he owed Maguire a great deal for the guidance and coaching. One of the first players Maguire signed for the Giants was Hofman.

In 1944 Hofman quit school to join the Springfield Giants of the Class D Ohio State League. In 18 games, he batted .308, but his season was interrupted when in June he enlisted in the US Army at Jefferson Barracks, outside St. Louis. He served two years in the infantry, including 20 months in France and Germany, and fought in the Battle of the Bulge.

Discharged from the Army in June 1946, Hofman joined the Trenton (New Jersey) Giants of the Class B Interstate League, where he posted a .258 average in 59 games. Hofman returned to Trenton in 1947, playing in 130 games and batting a respectable .275. The club finished first in the standings, and in the playoffs Hofman drove in the winning run in the second game of a best-of-seven series against the Allentown Cardinals. (Despite jumping out to a two-game lead, Trenton dropped the next four games.)

For the 1948 season, Hofman was promoted from Class B Trenton to Class A Sioux City of the Western League. He enjoyed his best season yet, batting .319, slugging at a .475 clip, and reaching double digits in home runs for the first time. He missed some time in mid-August to attend to his father, who was seriously ill in St. Louis.[2] The following season began with a great deal of promise. After Hofman's strong showing at Sioux City, he was expected to be the Giants' starting second baseman in 1949. In spring exhibitions he played more than any other infielder. He swung the bat well. The Giants toured with the Cleveland Indians, playing a series of games in the run-up to the regular season. On April 15 in Richmond, Virginia, Hofman homered in a game won by Cleveland, 16-11. But he injured the middle finger of his throwing hand in the eighth inning, and when the season started, he spent a lot of time on the bench, going hitless in two plate appearances in the first 23 games.

On May 13 Hofman got his first opportunity to start at second base, against the Philadelphia Phillies at the Polo Grounds. He made the most of the opportunity by collecting four hits in five at-bats while driving in a run and scoring one. With five hits in 16 at-bats over the next four games, he was named the everyday second baseman. But Hofman's hot start did not last very long. He managed only one more hit in his next 25 at-bats while playing below-average defense. A costly error against the Cubs on May 24 contributed to four Chicago runs in the sixth inning of a game the Giants lost, 8-2. His playing time decreased significantly; he failed to get into a game between June 2 and June 12. On June 18 he was sent down to the Giants' Triple-A affiliate at Minneapolis of the American Association. It was three years before he reached the major leagues again.

Hofman's arrival with the Minneapolis Millers prompted the club to shift future Hall of Famer Ray Dandridge, the team's first African-American player and leading hitter, from second base to third. Hofman appeared in 92 games for the Millers and posted a .281 batting average with 9 home runs and 38 RBIs.

Hofman hoped to regain a roster spot with the Giants in 1950, but on April 13 he was optioned to the Triple-A Oakland Oaks of the Pacific Coast League. By mid-July, the Oaks were the league's best club, bolstered by an offense that finished the season hitting a league-leading .289 as a team. Hofman displayed a knack for timely hitting and teamed with shortstop Artie Wilson to form one of the best double-play combinations in the league.

On July 6 Hofman hit the first pitch thrown in the tenth inning out of Wrigley Field in Los Angeles to defeat the Los Angeles Angels, 3-2. By August the Oaks enjoyed a sizable lead in the standings. In early August, they hammered Los Angeles, 23-7. A week later, they beat the San Diego Padres, 17-6. Hofman went on a tear in September and finished the season with a .296 average, 15 home runs, and 83 RBIs. (To underscore how dominant the Oaks' lineup was at the plate, seven of Hofman's teammates finished ahead of him with averages above .300 as the Oaks claimed their second Pacific Coast League pennant in three years.)

Hofman had every reason to believe his chances to stick with the Giants in 1951 were good. An Associated Press article in January under manager Leo Durocher's byline said the team's bench had been "fortified" by players like all-star PCL shortstop Artie Wilson, Hofman, Davey Williams, Bill Jennings, and others.[3] Again Hofman hit well all spring, but still displayed some shortcomings defensively. He homered in the club's first intrasquad game, on March 4, but made an error against the Red Sox that proved decisive in a 2-1 loss two weeks later. On April 18 he was again optioned to the minor leagues, this time to Triple-A Ottawa (International League).

The local newspaper left no doubt that Hofman was highly coveted by Ottawa manager Hugh Poland. As early as April 3, stories began to appear suggesting as much: "Poland's chief hope, though he won't — or can't — say much about it, is that Hofman, who batted .296 for Oakland last year, may be moved to Ottawa. But he's only surmising this, though hoping would be a better word for it."[4]

Hofman did not immediately report to Ottawa, choosing instead to spend some time in St. Louis. This caused speculation in the media that he was not terribly anxious to go to Ottawa, perhaps preferring to return to Oakland, where he had enjoyed so much success the previous season. Poland dismissed the speculation as mere rumor, insisting that Hofman had simply returned home to settle some affairs prior to reporting to the club.[5] He arrived on April 26 and immediately made a good impression with some slick defensive plays. In all, Hofman played in 72 games for Ottawa, missing a handful of games in June with an ankle injury. He batted .274 with little of the power he had displayed in previous stops. In July he was moved back to Minneapolis, and the change of scenery improved his offensive output considerably.

The Millers were a good team prevented from possibly being great by the needs of the parent Giants, who indeed won the National League pennant in 1951. Their roster included three future Hall of Famers, Dandridge, pitcher Hoyt Wilhelm, and outfielder Willie Mays, who put up remarkable numbers in just 35 games before debuting in New York. As a team, they led the American Association in home runs, runs scored, and OPS (on-base percentage plus slugging average). In moving to the Millers, Hofman was replac-

ing Davey Williams, who had been called up to the Giants after appearing in 80 games for the Millers. Hofman supplied slightly better numbers than Williams, managing a .290 average with ten home runs in 67 games.

Hofman's success at the plate with the Millers left him in a good position to again compete for a major-league roster spot in 1952. In December the Giants traded starting second baseman Eddie Stanky to the Cardinals. Competition to replace Stanky was expected to be fierce, with Davey Williams considered to have the inside track over Hofman and Ronald Samford, an All-Star at Sioux City the previous year. Many saw it as primarily between Williams and Hofman, and while acknowledging that Stanky's leadership would be missed, conceded confidence that either would perform adequately. In February catcher Wes Westrum suggested that either Williams or Hofman could fill the bill at second base.[6] For his part, manager Leo Durocher insisted all spring that the competition was wide open. Williams was clearly better defensively, but Hofman offered a far more potent bat. Ultimately, a consensus evolved that Williams would be the primary second baseman and Hofman his backup, and that their combined strengths would be the equal or better of Stanky.

For the first half of the 1952 season, Hofman was primarily a pinch-hitter and late-inning replacement. He also was knuckleballer Hoyt Wilhelm's bullpen catcher. With playing time limited, Hofman never found any consistency, and by the end of July his average was a meager .133 in only 16 plate appearances. On August 23 he was involved in a bizarre double ejection in a game against the Cardinals. In the seventh inning, Giants third baseman Bob Elliott was ejected for arguing a called strike two. Hofman was called upon in the pinch to complete the at-bat, and when plate umpire Augie Donatelli called the next pitch strike three, Hofman launched into a tirade that led to his own ejection.

Even without Willie Mays for all but 34 games, the Giants were in a hotly-contested race for first place with the Brooklyn Dodgers. Hofman found considerably more playing time down the stretch. On September 12 he hit his first big-league home run, off Cincinnati pitcher Ken Raffensberger in the second inning of an 8-7 loss. The Giants ultimately fell short in their quest to repeat as pennant winners, finishing with 92 wins but 4½ games in back of Brooklyn. Despite his slow start, Hofman finished his first full season in the big leagues with a.286 batting average and above-average power for a middle infielder. But he appeared in only 32 games, and hoped to find more playing time the following year.

Hofman's playing career lasted parts of five more seasons, and along the way he proved invaluable as a part-time role player and pinch-hitter. In 1953 he emerged as one of the best pinch-hitters in the game, collecting 13 hits in 35 at-bats, a .371 average. He managed three pinch-hit home runs, tying Grady Hatton of Cincinnati for the National League lead. Of his role as a pinch-hitter, Hofman remarked, "When you come up to hit, your muscles are stiff from sitting on the bench, the pitcher is always bearing down against you and sometimes all you manage to get is one swing at the ball."[7] In 1954 his first two hits of the season were pinch-hit home runs, including a game-winning ninth-inning shot against Cincinnati on May 12. On June 20 against St. Louis, Hofman and Dusty Rhodes became the first teammates to homer as pinch-hitters in the same inning. In August Durocher said, "Every time we go bad, I call upon Rhodes and Hofman. They're my minutemen."[8] At season's end, Hofman again led the league with three pinch-hit home runs.

The Giants went on to win the pennant and sweep the Cleveland Indians in a memorable World Series. Unfortunately for Hofman, he never got to play. Durocher favored Rhodes, whose hitting exploits against Cleveland more than justified the decision.

On September 27, the day after the 1954 season ended, Hofman married Ruth Boston, 25, at Sacred Heart Roman Catholic Church in Clifton, New Jersey. All of his teammates attended the reception. The newlyweds settled in St. Louis at the end of the season.

In 1954 Hofman played 21 games at first base, ten at second base, and eight at third base. In spring training of 1955 he added catcher to his repertoire. He was brought in as a receiver after the starting catcher was ejected from a B-squad game against the Indians for arguing with the umpire. According to Fred Fitzsimmons, manager of the B-squad, "Sure, he was rough in spots, but nobody scored while he was in there. He blocked balls in the dirt well and he caught one difficult foul in high wind."[9] Hofman's first opportunity to catch in the regular season came against the Braves on April 27 when Ray Katt left the game with an injured finger. Hofman caught the last four innings, including two thrown by knuckleballer Wilhelm.

Hofman went on to appear in 19 games at catcher in 1955, to go with 24 games at first base, 19 at second base, and five at third base. He finished the season with an improved .266 average, 10 home runs, and 28 RBIs. On May 27 Hofman pinch-hit for Davey Williams and cracked his fourth home run of the season as the Giants beat the Dodgers 3-1 at the Polo Grounds. The home run was Hofman's third of the year as a pinch-hitter and the ninth of his career. It placed him in a tie with former slugger Cy Williams for the major-league record for career home runs as a pinch-hitter.

Despite his versatility in the field, Hofman was largely forgettable at the plate in 1956 and 1957. By the end of 1957 he had played his last game. His first career in baseball, as a player, was over. But his second career, as a coach and manager, began in earnest the following season.

In 1958 Hofman was appointed manager of the Danville Leafs, a Giants affiliate in the Class B Carolina League. He piloted the club to the pennant with a record of 80-59. In August the team won 13 consecutive games, the third longest winning streak in the league's history. The following year he was hired by the Kansas City Athletics to manage their Plainview, Texas, club in the short-lived Sophomore League. For the next six seasons, Hofman managed at various locations and levels in the Kansas City organization. In

1965, after beginning the season 18-7 and gaining a 3½-game lead for first place at Lewiston in the Northwest League, Hofman replaced Haywood Sullivan at Triple-A Vancouver when Sullivan succeeded Mel McGaha as Kansas City's manager.

In November 1965 Hofman was hired by Athletics owner Charlie Finley to replace Whitey Herzog on the Athletics' coaching staff. A month later Haywood Sullivan resigned as manager and was replaced by Alvin Dark. Hofman stayed on as a member of Dark's coaching staff and coached at third base until he was shown the door when Dark was fired by Finley in August 1967. Before the year was over, Hofman was hired to coach third base for the Washington Senators. Citing Hofman's coaching ability, manager Jim Lemon said, "…I watched him closely for two years when he was with the A's, and I was impressed with his work. I honestly don't think I saw Bobby make many mistakes."[10] After the season Hofman found himself once again hired by the Athletics organization, now located in Oakland. He joined manager Hank Bauer's staff and again coached third base. He remained with Oakland until October 1970, when John McNamara, Bauer's successor, was fired and replaced by Dick Williams.

The following month, the Cleveland Indians announced that Hofman had been hired at a salary of $15,000 to join manager Alvin Dark's staff as the third-base coach in 1971. He would also split the duties of traveling secretary with trainer Jim Warfield. The announcement was met with criticism that the Indians were trying to cut corners, but team vice president Jim Stouffer responded that it was "a matter of more efficiency," adding, "Here we have two people who are closely related to the team and living those jobs."[11] Dark nicknamed Hofman Fat Boy and the now shaggy-looking coach performed double duty for the entire season.[12] He was relieved of the traveling-secretary duties in November, and returned to coach third base for new manager Ken Aspromonte in 1972.

On June 28, 1972, Cleveland dropped a doubleheader in Milwaukee. After the game Hofman and fellow coach Warren Spahn went to a bar where the latter greeted the bartender by speaking German. As *The Sporting News* described the incident:

"Unfortunately, an obnoxious intruder, a nationalized German with a thick accent, broke into the conversation and began to relive World War II. Hofman, who was an infantryman in the Europe Theater, finally asked, 'Were you in the war?' 'Yah,' he replied, 'in Munich.' 'Then you were the one I didn't shoot,' Hofman told the fellow. 'Don't give me a second chance.'"

In 1973 Hofman managed at Triple-A Richmond, an Atlanta Braves affiliate. In June he was ordered by a doctor to step down from managing due to high blood pressure. By March 1974 his health had improved, and he accepted an offer to manage the Athletics' minor-league club in Lewiston. After just 24 games, he was promoted to the big-league coaching staff under manager Alvin Dark. In July Hofman was deployed full-time to scout the Boston Red Sox, who had taken seven of nine contests with Oakland thus far during the season. He returned to take over in the coach's box at first base for coach Jerry Adair, who was tasked with scouting the Yankees. Hofman was voted a half-share of the championship earnings money allotted to the A's who beat the Dodgers in five games in the World Series.

Hofman returned to coach under Dark in 1975. Oakland was swept by the Red Sox in the American League Championship Series, whereupon owner Charlie Finley made changes: Manager Dark was fired and replaced by Chuck Tanner. Hofman and several other coaches were replaced by Tanner's choices for a coaching staff. A year later Hofman was hired again by Finley to serve as the club's traveling secretary, a post he filled for the next two seasons, with a brief return to coaching in 1978.

Hofman was fired again by the Athletics in January 1980. The New York Yankees, who under George Steinbrenner were shaking up their front office, hired him almost immediately as director of scouting. Of his years working for Finley, Hofman said, "I got a lot of experience in Oakland. I have nothing but good things to say about Charlie Finley. He treated me great. He fired me four times, but he always hired me back."[13] Hofman was the Yankees' scouting director for five seasons. He went on to hold various positions with the club, including director of minor-league operations and director of player development until he was let go in December 1988. The next month he joined the Cleveland Indians as a scout in the Midwest. After a short stint in that job, he retired.

Hofman died on April 5, 1994, from cancer at St. Luke's Hospital in Chesterfield, Missouri. He was 68. He was survived by his wife, Ruth; a daughter, Deborah Ake; a brother, Jim Hofman; and a sister, Jane Berkmeyer. He had spent more than 40 years in baseball. In his varied career, he won World Series rings as a player and coach; he played with Willie Mays and for Leo Durocher; he coached alongside Hall of Famers Joe DiMaggio in Oakland and Warren Spahn in Cleveland; and he worked as an executive for both Charlie Finley and George Steinbrenner.

NOTES

1   Allen Barra, *Yogi Berra: Eternal Yankee* (New York: W.W. Norton & Company, 2009), 17.

2   "Soos Square Set," *Council Bluffs* (Iowa) *Nonpareil*, August 12, 1948.

3   "Lippy Admits He's Crazy—Over '51 Nine," *Fitchburg* (Massachusetts *Sentinel*, January 29, 1951.

4   W.G. Westwick, "Second Base Still Hugh Poland's Problem," *Ottawa* (Ontario) *Journal*, April 3, 1951.

5   W.G. Westwick, "The Sports Realm," *Ottawa* (Ontario) *Journal*, April 25, 1951.

6   "Westrum's Hands Are A-1," *Tucson Daily Citizen*, February 27, 1952.

7   Milton Richman (United Press), "Virgil Trucks Worried About Hitting Batters," *Lebanon* (Pennsylvania) *Daily News*, July 16, 1953.

8   Joe Reichler (Associated Press), "Manager Leo Durocher Up To Old Tricks," *Galesburg* (Illinois) *Register-Mail*, August 19, 1954.

9   "Hofman in Catching Debut When Grapso Is Thumbed," *The Sporting News*, March 23, 1955.

10 "Nat Pilot Lemon Picks Aids With Merit Yardstick," *The Sporting News*, December 2, 1967.

11 "'Quality, More Than Quantity'—Goal of Tribe Brass," *The Sporting News*, December 12, 1970.

12 "Mini-Hawk Set to Grab Tribe Utility Post," *The Sporting News*, March 6, 1971.

13 "Major Changes Sweep Yank Minor System," *The Sporting News*, January 19, 1980.

Jim Holt

by Norm King

When Jim Holt played for the Minnesota Twins, sportswriter Bob Fowler wrote that he was the type of ballplayer every winning team needed, one who knew how to play the game and was ready whenever called upon.

"Every team has an underrated player, a man who isn't a most valuable player but a most valued player," wrote Fowler. "Minnesota has one and his name is James William Holt."[1]

Holt was born in Graham, North Carolina, on May 27, 1944, the youngest of six children of Theodore and Emma Holt. Life in Graham, a town of approximately 5,000, likely meant working in a flour or timber mill, which wasn't a life that Holt wanted. Theodore was a laborer.

Holt began learning baseball a bit later than most, not really playing until he entered Graham High School. He had tryouts with the Cleveland Indians and Pittsburgh Pirates after he graduated, but neither team was interested in a 5-foot-11, 135-pound stringbean. With life as a mill worker as his only other option, Holt enlisted in the US Army in 1963, intent on a military career.

Army life helped Holt bulk up to 165 pounds, and he honed his baseball skills while stationed in Germany. One day in 1965, a player from an opposing team offered to write the Kansas City Athletics on Holt's behalf. After he attended spring training with the team in Bradenton, Florida, in 1966, the A's signed him. "If the A's hadn't signed me, I never would have left the service," said Holt. "I was going to make it a career. I was a field communications specialist."[2]

Holt's professional career got off to a pretty good start with the Leesburg A's of the Class A Florida State League in 1966. While that team only included one man who played on the three Oakland championship

teams of the 1970s, Gene Tenace, it nonetheless compiled an 87-44 record. Holt made his contribution, batting .286 with four home runs in 126 games. He also began learning how to play the outfield after starting out as a first baseman.

Holt continued his progression in 1967 with the Peninsula Grays of the Carolina League. In 129 games he batted .312 with eight home runs, 60 RBIs, and 12 stolen bases in 16 attempts. Those numbers didn't seem to impress the A's, but they caught the attention of the Minnesota Twins, who took Holt in the Rule 5 draft after the season.

Under the terms of the Rule 5 draft, the Twins had to keep Holt on the major-league roster or return him for half the price they paid for him. The Twins kept Holt. But being on the team doesn't guarantee playing time, especially for a rookie. The Twins had an off-year in 1968, going 79-83 after coming within one game of

winning the American League pennant the year before. With an established outfield of Bob Allison in left field, Ted Uhlaender in center, and Tony Oliva in right, plus Harmon Killebrew at first base, Holt's playing opportunities were few. He appeared in only 70 games, with 40 starts, and batted only .208 with no home runs and 8 RBIs.

Rookie numbers like that aren't going to keep you in the majors long, especially when you have a firebrand manager like Billy Martin, who became the Twins' skipper for the 1969 season. Holt was sent to the Denver Bears of the American Association. He blew away the opposition, both offensively and defensively. At the plate, Holt batted .336, second in the league, and added 11 home runs and 87 RBIs. He was second among league outfielders in assists with 27, including six double plays from the outfield between May 27 and June 22. And he did this while committing only six errors in 123 games.

Holt was among five late-season call-ups as the Twins held off Oakland to win the very first American League West Division title. He got five hits in 14 at-bats for a .357 average. He hit his first major-league home run on September 30, a game-tying solo shot off the Chicago White Sox' Danny Murphy in the eighth in a game that the Twins won 4-3.

After the season, Holt continued developing his skills in winter ball, hitting .357 with Magallanes of the Venezuelan League.

As spring training for the 1970 season began under new manager Bill Rigney—the firebrand Martin had been fired after the previous season—Holt's 1969 statistics gave him reason to be optimistic about finally becoming a regular major leaguer. The fact that the team had traded left-handed-hitting outfielders Uhlaender and Graig Nettles also improved Holt's chances at winning the numbers game.[3]

"If I do the job here they'll look at me," he said in evaluating his chances of making the team during spring training. "But I play exhibition games the same way I play regular-season games. If I go out and tighten up and press, I would hurt myself."[4]

Holt made the Opening Day roster and saw playing time in a platoon with right-handed-hitting Brant Alyea. Holt saw action in 142 games and hit .266 in 319 at-bats with three homers and 40 RBIs. The Twins repeated as American League West Division champions. They also repeated as losers to the Baltimore Orioles in three straight games in the American league Championship Series. Holt got his first taste of post-season action, appearing in all three games and going 0-for-5.

Both the Twins and Holt declined the next season. After back-to-back division titles, the Twins fell to fifth place in 1971 with a 74-86 record. Holt's average fell slightly to .259 in 340 at-bats, with only one home run and 29 RBIs.

Holt returned to spring training in 1972 only to be demoted to the Twins' Triple-A affiliate, the Tacoma Twins of the Pacific Coast League. There was some speculation that the demotion was racially motivated, as he would have been the team's fifth black player, and therefore required to room with a white player.[5]

Holt, for his part, wasn't surprised. "I didn't play much (in spring training)," he said. "I expected to be sent down."[6]

Despite the disappointment of returning to the minors, Holt made the best of the situation, hitting .333 with 8 home runs and 96 RBIs. Also, the world managed to survive Holt rooming with a white teammate, an Oklahoman named John Gelnar.

"I'm from the South but there isn't anything in the world I wouldn't do for him, and I think he'd do the same for me," said Gelnar.[7]

Tacoma management was also pleased with having Holt on the team, both on and off the field. "Off the field he has a big heart and a ready smile," said general manager Stan Naccarato. "If we need a player for a clinic or a speaker, he's always there—and he's usually an hour early. I wish we had a whole team of Jim Holts."[8]

Since Dolly the sheep hadn't been cloned yet, a whole team of Jim Holts wasn't possible, so Naccarato had to settle for the original. And as much as Tacoma appreciated Holt's contribution, it wasn't until September that the Twins thought Holt might help them. By that time Rigney was gone and Frank Quilici had the reins of a team heading toward a 77-77 record.[9]

Holt arrived at spring training in 1973 without any guarantees. He played very well in exhibition games and won a spot on the roster. That re-created the five-blacks-on-the-team conundrum, which was resolved when Larry Hisle, a black player, roomed with Danny Monzon, a Hispanic player from the Bronx.

Holt became a starter for the Twins, batting ninth and playing left field as the American League embarked on its newfangled designated-hitter experiment. Since the pitcher no longer occupied the ninth spot in the order, Quilici put Holt in there for strategic reasons.

"I wanted someone in that position who had good speed," the manager explained. "In the past, pitchers have led off a lot and with Holt being followed by Hisle and (Rod) Carew, we have three fast men batting ahead of Killebrew, Oliva, and (Bobby) Darwin."[10]

Holt got off to a good start, hitting a home run off the A's Catfish Hunter in his first at-bat. The solid play continued throughout the 1973 season, as he played in 132 games and set career highs in all offensive categories, including batting average, home runs, RBIs, and runs scored (.297, 11, 58, 52). His batting average was second on the team to Carew's league-leading .350. As Holt continued showing good numbers, his position in the batting order kept getting higher. He was hitting in the fifth spot by the end of the season.

Holt also held up his end defensively. While he played primarily in left field, he also saw action in center and right, and appeared in 33 games at first base. He made only two errors all season.

Holt's contribution was especially impressive because he played with sore feet all season. In the big-help department, his teammates acknowledged his tender tootsies by giving him footpads as a gift at a team party. The injuries were serious enough, however, to require surgery after the season; doctors shaved a bone growth from Holt's left big toe and removed a callus and a calcium deposit from his little toe.

Maybe Holt should have played using the footpads in 1974 instead of resorting to surgery because his production dropped precipitously. In 79 games with the Twins, the power he showed in 1973 disappeared completely (zero home runs, 16 RBIs), and his average dropped to .254. Disappointed in his production, the Twins traded him to the Oakland A's for first baseman Pat Bourque on August 19, 1974.

With the power in the A's lineup, Holt wasn't going to get much playing time. He played in 30 games, almost exclusively as a pinch-hitter and defensive replacement, and hit only .143. He was hitless in 24 consecutive pinch-hit at-bats during the season for both the Twins and the A's. His finest hour, though, was yet to come.

The A's faced the Los Angeles Dodgers in the World Series. They led two games to one with the score tied 2-2 in the sixth inning of Game Four. With Andy Messersmith pitching for Los Angeles, A's manager Alvin Dark batted Holt, who already had one pinch hit in the Series, for catcher Ray Fosse with the bases loaded and one out. Dark's face must have lit up when Holt singled to right, driving in two runs. Oakland won the game, 5-2, and claimed its third consecutive championship the next day. Holt finally had a World Series ring.

In 1975 Holt appeared in 102 games for the A's with only 20 starts, 18 at first base and two as DH. He hit only .220 with two home runs and 11 runs batted in. He donned the tools of ignorance for two innings in a game because the A's lacked depth at catcher and wanted to try him out. He didn't play very well, but the team was considering coaching him in 1976 to improve his skills. That idea ended when the A's demoted Holt to Triple-A Tucson. He hit .337 there and was brought up late in the season, getting two hits in seven at-bats. Holt's major-league career was over when the 1976 season ended. He played one last season for three teams in the Mexican League in 1977.

After his baseball career was over, Holt returned to Graham, North Carolina, a 30-minute drive from Greensboro. For seven years he was a fireman and policeman at Elon College. As of 2013, he worked for a company that sells firefighting equipment. Single, he had a daughter named Sarah.

SOURCES

Votano, Paul, *Stand and Deliver: A History of Pinch-hitting* (Jefferson, North Carolina: McFarland and Co., 2003)

Des Moines Register, August 26, 1969, 22

ourstate.com/lindleys-mill/

sportsencyclopedia.com/al/kcityas/kca_s.html

mlb.com/mlb/minorleagues/rule_5.jsp?mc=faq

baseball-reference.com/teams/MIN/1968.shtml

baseballlibrary.com/ballplayers/player.php?name=Jim_Holt_1944

Jim Holt, personal interviews, December 11 and 13, 2013

NOTES

1   Bob Fowler, "Whatever the Twins Need Hustling Holt Can Provide," *The Sporting News* May 29, 1971.

2   Ibid.

3   Although Nettles spent most of his career playing third base, in 1969 he started 44 games in left field and only 16 at the hot corner.

4   Mike Lamey, "Third Chance for Holt—Sink or Swim," *The Sporting News*, March 28, 1970.

5   The speculation appeared in an article in *The Sporting News* entitled "Nice-Guy Holt Thunderbolt with Twin Bat," on May 12, 1973.

6   Stan Farber, "Halting Holt—Season-Long Mystery for PCL's Pitchers," *The Sporting News*, September 16, 1972.

7   Ibid.

8   Ibid.

9   A players strike eliminated several games at the beginning of the 1972 season.

10 Bob Fowler, "Nice-Guy Holt Thunderbolt with Twin Bat," *The Sporting News*, May 12, 1973.

Leon Hooten

By Chip Greene

The 1974 Oakland Athletics pitching staff was a dominant bunch. Led by the trio of starters Catfish Hunter, Vida Blue, and Ken Holtzman, and the brilliant relief work of Rollie Fingers, the A's led the majors in six pitching categories, won 90 games, and claimed their third consecutive world championship. They were not without good fortune, however. During the season the team's hurlers largely escaped injury, and that circumstance combined with the trio's remarkable durability (they started 73 percent of the team's games and totaled 59 percent of the total innings) allowed Oakland to use just 11 pitchers over the course of the season, still another metric that was the lowest in the major leagues (tied with Baltimore).

Yet that number was somewhat misleading. In actuality, Oakland essentially relied on just nine pitchers during that championship season, as two men made only token appearances. In September right-hander Bill Parsons tossed two innings in the final four of what became 93 career major-league appearances. And over three weeks during April and May, 26-year-old right-hander Leon Hooten worked eight innings in six games.

They were the only innings of Hooten's major-league career.

Pitching for the A's represented for Hooten a homecoming of sorts. He was California-born and -bred, albeit in Long Beach, some 400 miles south of Oakland. Online references state that he was born in Downey, roughly 15 miles northeast of Long Beach; in 2013, however, Hooten explained in an interview, "I happened to be born at Downey Hospital, but we weren't living in Downey; we were living in Long Beach. My parents just happened to be passing through Downey."

His parents, Earl and Dorothy, were just 20 and 15 years old respectively when they married in 1942; it was World War II, and Earl was in the service. In addition to Leon, who was born on April 4, 1948, and christened Michael Leon ("I just always liked my middle name," he recalled), Hooten's parents also produced Leon's older brother, Hal, and sisters, Connie and Denise. Professionally, Earl Hooten drove a concrete mixer, and Leon remembered that while his father was not an athlete, he was nevertheless "a strong influence on my life." Dorothy always remained a homemaker.

By his own admission, Hooten, who eventually grew to a solid 5-feet-11-inches and 180 pounds, was a "late developer … pretty small," a trend that continued through college. At Long Beach's David Starr Jordan High School, the future major-league pitcher began his career as a position player, primarily a shortstop and outfielder (he was once named shortstop on the

All-Long Beach second team); in his senior season, he switched to the mound. While Hooten went un-scouted during his high-school career, he began to develop the pitching repertoire that later took him to Oakland. In that senior season, Hooten was named Jordan High's Player of the Year.

With no scholarship offers and limited financial re-sources, after his high-school graduation in 1966 Hooten enrolled locally at Long Beach City College, a renowned junior-college baseball powerhouse, where he came under the tutelage of legendary coach Joe Hicks. ("He's why everyone wanted to go there," Hooten said.)[1] There, as Hooten "started getting a little stronger and started throwing harder," over the next two seasons he dominated his competition, com-piling a 16-3 overall record. After the 1967 season Hooten was named both first-team All-Conference and the school's Most Improved Player; and in 1968, when his 6-1 record and 0.94 ERA in Metropolitan Conference play led the team to the state junior-college title, he was named second-team All-Conference and also received his school's Harry Macon Award as the team's hardest worker. Moreover, in both years Hooten also pitched for Long Beach in the California Collegiate League, where in '68 he made the league All-Star team after leading the circuit in innings pitched, wins, and complete games. Most importantly, though, Hooten's two-year performance brought him recognition by some of the country's premier four-year baseball programs. Accordingly, when the 1969 season got under way, Hooten was pitching in the prestigious Western Athletic Conference.

After graduating from Long Beach with an associate's degree, Hooten related 45 years later, he "had an op-portunity to get scholarships to many places." He chose to attend the University of Arizona, the Wildcats, in Tucson. It turned out to be a fortunate decision. Twenty years old when the 1969 season began, Hooten once again got to play for a highly accomplished coach: Frank Sancet had guided the Wildcats program for 20 years and had eight times taken teams to the College World Series, although his teams had never won. With

Hooten in his rotation, Sancet would once again return to that venue.

As Hooten's junior season ensued, he was much matured on the mound. When he began at Long Beach City College, he later related, "I had good control, wasn't throwing as hard. … I had a good overhand curve and a good changeup. I could really spot it." Now, at Arizona, Hooten added more speed to his repertoire, to excellent results. In his first season, as the number-two starter, Hooten was often over-powering, striking out 124 batters in 109 innings, while walking only 52, on the way to an 11-3 record and a 1.40 ERA. The following season he became the number-one starter, pitched the Wildcats' opening-day game, and finished the regular season with a 10-4 record. It was a season Hooten would never forget.

The 1970 Western Athletic Conference regular season ended in dramatic fashion, and Hooten was pivotal to the outcome. Throughout the year the Wildcats battled their archrival, the Arizona State Sun Devils (coached by Bobby Winkles) to a dead heat, and the season came down to a final three-game series between the two teams, to be played at Arizona's Hi Corbett Field. Hooten drew the starting assignment for game one, on May 15. If he wasn't at his best, nevertheless Hooten was the winning pitcher, as he scattered 13 hits, struck out eight, and walked four. Yet it was not his pitching that earned Hooten the most acclaim that afternoon; it was his hitting. Leading off the bottom of the third inning in a scoreless tie, Hooten blasted a 380-foot home run over the ballpark's green monster in right field that gave his team a lead it never relinquished, as the Wildcats beat the Sun Devils, 7-3. As Hooten rounded the bases, "players came from as far as the UA bullpen to greet him at home plate."[2]

Afterward, coach Sancet was equally elated. "Hooten's hit got us going," he said. "It was some lick. In fact, I don't believe I've ever seen a right-handed hitter put one over the right-field fence at Hi Corbett Field."[3]

The Wildcats' win left both teams with 9-7 conference records; a final doubleheader the next day would decide the league's Southern Division title. A sweep by either team meant a championship playoff against the North Division winner, Brigham Young University; while a split meant a coin flip to decide a winner. On May 16 the Wildcats swept the Sun Devils in the doubleheader and won the division title. A week later the Wildcats defeated North winner BYU, two games to one, to win the Western Athletic Conference championship; Hooten was the winner in Game Two. And the following week they defeated Denver University in a three-game series to win the NCAA District 7 title and advance to the College World Series. In that Denver series, Hooten won Game One, 4-2, at one point retiring 14 consecutive batters. In the big tournament, the Wildcasts lost to Iowa State, then on June 13, they lost to Florida State, 4-0, and were eliminated. Hooten pitched eight innings and took the loss, ending the Wildcats' season with a record of 44-17. It was Hooten's final intercollegiate performance.

Given the brevity of Hooten's big-league career, it's perhaps difficult for many except the most diehard Oakland fans or baseball historians to instantly recognize his name. More likely, on first consideration one may be apt to mistake him for the *other* pitching Hooton, Burt, who won 151 games, including a no-hitter, over a 15-season career. At one point, though, the two were teammates.

It happened in the summer of 1969. After his junior season at Arizona, Hooten played summer collegiate baseball as a member of the Boulder (Colorado) Collegians, in the semiprofessional Metro League. "They would give you a job to make a few bucks," Hooten recalled, adding, "It was good competition." Also on the Boulder squad was Burt Hooton, a pitcher for the University of Texas at Austin. "I just called him Brother Burt," Leon remembered. "I don't remember if he called me Brother Leon or not. I know people were always asking if we were brothers." Led by the pair of talented pitchers, Boulder posted a 20-2 record and won the state semipro tournament. (Also on that Boulder team was University of Texas quarterback James Street, father of major-league pitcher Huston Street. James Street died on September 30,

2013, three days before the author interviewed Hooten, who remembered his former teammate with fondness.)

Despite the end of Hooten's scholastic baseball career, he continued to play the game. It began in the upper Northwest. Unlike his Arizona teammates, shortstop Dave Jacome, who'd been selected in the 1970 draft by Cleveland, and fellow pitcher Jim Provenzano, chosen in the same draft by Houston, Hooten wasn't drafted. So after the Wildcats' season ended, he traveled with the rest of his teammates for an eight-game exhibition tour in Alaska. The region appealed to Hooten, so much so that when the tour ended, he stayed: Three weeks later, he was playing for the Bellingham (Washington) Bells, in the semipro Big West Conference. Hooten's stay there was brief, however, for soon he became a member of the Oakland organization.

Hooten joined the Athletics in the most rudimentary way: via a tryout. In 2013, he explained, "After college … my fourth year of school … at that time there was a military lottery draft, and my number came up. If I didn't get into the Army Reserves, I was going to be called up." So Hooten joined the Reserve.

Once enlisted, Hooten was sent to boot camp at Fort Ord, California, south of the San Francisco-Oakland area. A friend knew someone in the Athletics organization, and arranged for Hooten to try out with the team. "So I went down to Oakland," Hooten recalled, "and tried out." The A's were impressed, and in the spring of 1971 Hooten signed a minor-league contract.

Over the next 5½ years Hooten's rise and fall through the organization paralleled the A's own fortunes, as they captured five consecutive American League West titles and three consecutive world championships before the breakup of the team due to free agency ended their fabulous run.

Before he could begin his professional career, however, Hooten had to finish boot camp. When he was finally discharged midway through 1971, the minor-league season had already begun, so the A's sent him to their short-season Class A team in the Northwest League, the Coos Bay-North Bend A's. There, he made an immediate impact. Thrust into the starting rotation, Hooten proved a legitimate power pitcher, as he ended his abbreviated debut season with 67 strikeouts in 55 innings while surrendering less than a hit per inning. If his 5.4 walks per nine innings were at all problematic, his performance the following season appeared to allay any concerns.

In 1972 it took Hooten just 25 games to advance to Triple-A. That season he attended his first minor-league spring training. His initial assignment was to the Birmingham A's of the Double-A Southern League, where, over those 25 games, Hooten worked primarily in relief (but made seven starts) and again struck out more than a batter per inning. Clearly he had management's attention because in August, Hooten was promoted to the Iowa Oaks, in the Triple-A American Association. This time he was once again a starter, yet no less effective: In six starts he compiled a 2.61 ERA and 1.158 WHIP (walks plus hits per inning pitched). Perhaps surprisingly, the undrafted free agent showed bona-fide major-league potential. Even more, he was only a year away from getting there.

The year 1973 brought a change to the Oakland organization, one that returned Hooten to the scene of his past glory. After their first Oakland championship, the Athletics changed their Triple-A affiliate from the Iowa Oaks to the Pacific Coast League's Tucson Toros, who played their home games at the Arizona University home stadium, Hi Corbett Field. The '72 season had been disastrous for Tucson, as the Toros, aligned then with the Chicago White Sox, finished last in the league with a 60-88 record. After the season the Toros severed their agreement with Chicago and hooked up with Oakland. So in the spring of 1973, Hooten reported to Tucson.

By now the organization appeared to have decided on a permanent role for him. Asked by the press during spring training how Hooten would be used, Toros manager Sherm Lollar said the hard-thrower was being groomed for short relief.

"The A's feel that is his future," Lollar explained. "They want to make a stopper out of him—somebody who can come in when the going is tough and pitch strongly."[4]

For the first half of the season Hooten did just that. As the Toros, whose 84-60 record brought them the PCL's East division title (they eventually lost the league championship to West winner, the Spokane Indians), settled into first place, through the end of June, Hooten led the team with seven saves. Then he got hurt. While Hooten spent the second half of the season battling a tender elbow and pulled groin, Lollar gave the majority of closing opportunities to major-league veterans Gary Waslewski and Lew Krausse. After June 21, Hooten recorded just one save, and he finished the season with just 40 innings of work in 30 games.

Nevertheless, as Hooten later recalled, by the end of the 1973 season the 25-year-old "was probably right at my peak. I was throwing as well as anybody, I just wasn't consistent." By all appearances he was one of the organization's top prospects. Trade rumors abounded that fall in Oakland, as the press speculated that "some [veteran] players must go to make room for minor leaguers to move up," the latter a group that "could include Manny Trillo, Leon Hooten and Glenn Abbott."[5] Hooten's inclusion in that group was confirmed when in November he was added to the A's 40-man roster. The following spring he'd finally have a chance to make it to the big leagues.

As spring training opened in 1974, Hooten attended a major-league camp for the first time. He got off to a strong start, and, he recalled in 2013, "I think I was going to the big club." However, during hitting drills in the last days of February, Hooten sprained his right ankle when he stepped in a hole and crashed into the back of the batting cage. The injury kept him out for a week at the worst possible time; two weeks later, he was sent to Tucson.

He wasn't there for long. During the first week of the major-league season, while Hooten convalesced, two A's players, Dick Green and Deron Johnson, went on the disabled list. On April 13 Hooten and infielder John Donaldson were called up from the Toros to replace them.

For Hooten the promotion came as "pretty much a surprise." Given his injury, he explained, "I hadn't pitched a game yet" for Tucson. His arm, though, was sound, so manager Alvin Dark wasted no time getting Hooten into a game. The day of his call-up Hooten made his debut, versus the Texas Rangers in Oakland. It came in an A's blowout loss, but was memorable for one particular event.

"The first batter I had to face in the big leagues," Hooten recounted, "I hit him." (According to play-by-play accounts on retrosheet.org, it was the second batter.) With the A's trailing 8-3, Hooten came on to begin the top of the seventh inning. Leading off for Texas was slugger Jeff Burroughs, the man whom Hooten believed in his interview he had hit. "I knew him from Long Beach," Hooten said. "We'd played against each other in high school." Burroughs, who attended Long Beach's Woodrow Wilson High School, grounded out to the third baseman.

The next batter was Tom Grieve. Whether or not the sequence of events as recalled by Hooten applies to Burroughs or Grieve is irrelevant; what's important is that, according to Hooten, "I threw the first pitch and missed." Missed as in he failed to hit the batter. The instigation to throw at the Texas hitters had occurred the previous inning, when the Rangers' Jim Bibby hit the A's Gene Tenace. Now, recounted Hooten, "Reggie Jackson was out there [in right field] yelling, 'Hit him.' It was expected; they had hit one of our guys." Hence, Hooten summarily plunked Grieve.

It all seemed surreal, Hooten recalled. "I couldn't hardly [sic] feel my feet anyway."

Hooten made five more appearances before he was through. In all, over his first four games (including the debut) covering a total of 3⅔ innings, he allowed only a lone hit and no runs. In his fifth game, though, he allowed four hits and a run in 3⅓ innings, his longest outing, and in his final appearance, on May 6, versus Baltimore, gave up a two-run home run to Paul Blair. Two days later Dark sent Hooten to Tucson and called up Glenn Abbott. Hooten's brief major-league career was over.

Forty years later, Hooten looked back without bitterness on his singular opportunity. "I didn't use my head," he said of his approach on the mound with the A's. "I had developed an overhand curveball, one that went straight down. It was hard to control getting called for a strike. I also developed a slider—mixed fastballs and sliders." But, he emphasized, "I abandoned my changeup," his best pitch, "the one I had used in junior college."

In the end, Hooten reasoned, "I wasn't up there long enough to get comfortable; there just wasn't time to do that. They thought they needed to make a change. It wasn't like I didn't get any chances. I just didn't pitch well enough."

He never got close again.

Hooten hung on for a few more years. Following his demotion he was, understandably, "bummed out," and did not have a very good year (5.36 ERA and 1.670 WHIP); after the season the A's removed him from their 40-man roster. That winter and the next, at the urging of friends like Phil Garner and Dave Concepcion, Hooten played winter ball in Venezuela, a period he recalled as a "great experience," and in 1975, after attending the A's spring camp as a non-roster invitee, Hooten somewhat regained his footing when he returned to Tucson as a starter and made the All-Star team. That performance boded well for 1976.

It was not to be; 1976, a disastrous year, proved to be Hooten's final professional season. After once again attending the major-league camp, for whatever reason he began the year 0-6 as a starter, went to the bullpen, and finished 2-8 with a 5.60 ERA. In November he was selected in the expansion draft by the Toronto Blue Jays, but in March 1977 was released. At age 28, Hooten's baseball career was over.

In 2013 Hooten spoke candidly about both his final season and the intervening years. "I don't think there was one thing I can blame for what happened in '76," he said. "I did have some minor physical problems, but it was probably more a mental thing and lack of confidence. Although I didn't think so at the time, I'm sure my drinking also had something to do with it."

Indeed, Hooten's drinking has had a major impact on his life. "I'm sure [alcohol] had an effect on my ballplaying," he admitted. "I went into a tailspin when I finished playing. I was drinking enough. … I think it really affected my health; it didn't seem like it at the time, but it did." In 1973 he had wed Debra Ann Whitty, from Coos Bay. Their daughter was born in 1982. "Twenty seven and a half years ago," Hooten continued, "my first wife left to due to my drinking. I've been sober for the past 27½ years."

He's also been gainfully employed. When Hooten was released by the Blue Jays he wasn't sure what to do with his life, so he returned to Coos Bay, where he and Debra made their home, and started looking for jobs. He had already ruled out one other option: "I could have gone back to school, but I wasn't thinking good at the time." While on scholarship at Arizona University, Hooten had majored in architecture. "I don't know why I picked that major. It was a five-year program and I was already behind when I transferred. When I signed [with Oakland] I had only one class left to take—Design Sequence. But I never did." As a result, he never graduated; and yet, he continued, "I don't blame ballplaying for not finishing my degree."

Eventually, Hooten found "something I liked to do," and got into cabinetmaking, which led to the construction business. He became a licensed contractor in Coos Bay, and the sole proprietor of Leon Hooten Construction, General Contractor, specializing in single-family homes. Sadly, his second wife, Frances, whom Hooten married in 1988, died in 2008. In addition to his daughter from his first marriage, Frances had three daughters of her own, so Hooten has six or seven grandchildren, as well as some great-grandchildren from that marriage.

And do the people in Coos Bay know of the former major leaguer in their midst? Not really, Hooten sug-

gested. He doesn't get much name recognition. After all, "we're pretty isolated up here," although "it comes up sometimes in conversation."

Still, Hooten said he would never forget his baseball days. "I loved playing, that's why I signed. … It was a terrific experience and I wouldn't trade it. I had opportunities to get up there and stay."

"If I had just been a little smarter."

SOURCES

Personal:

The author expresses his sincerest appreciation to Leon Hooten for a phone interview conducted on October 3, 2013, and a follow-up email on October 22, 2013. Unless otherwise noted, all Hooten quotes are from this interview.

Leon Hooten player file at National Baseball Hall of Fame, Cooperstown, New York

Websites

Baseball-Reference.com

Retrosheet.org

longbeach.gov/park/recreation/sports/hof/baseball.asp

Newspapers

Long Beach Press Telegram

Colorado Springs Gazette

Arizona Republic

Tucson Daily Citizen

Fairbanks Daily News Miner

Scottsdale Daily Progress

Provo (Utah) *Daily Herald*

Oakland Tribune

NOTES

1   Over 26 seasons at Long Beach Community College, Hicks, who in 1988 was inducted into the American Baseball Coaches Association Hall of Fame, amassed a record of 514-257, and led the school to 13 Metropolitan Conference, eight Southern California, and three state titles.

2   *Tucson Daily Citizen*, May 16, 1970.

3   ibid

4   *Tucson Daily Citizen*, April 3, 1973.

5   *Oakland Tribune*, September 28, 1973.

Bill Parsons

By Rick Schabowski

William Raymond Parsons had a four-year career in the major leagues, compiling a 29-36 record with a 3.89 earned-run average. Among his achievements were being named the 1971 *Sporting News* American League Rookie Pitcher of the Year and being selected to the 1971 Topps Major League Rookie All-Star Team.

Parsons was born in Riverside, California, on August 17, 1948. His baseball career began at an early age. He competed in a number of leagues including Little League, Pony League, Colt League, and Connie Mack baseball. Twice he helped his team to a berth in the Colt League World Series, and in a losing effort in a 2-1 loss to Greensboro (North Carolina), had 13 strikeouts in a seven-inning game. While pitching in the Colt League he pitched a perfect game.

Parsons attended Riverside Polytechnic High School, where he played baseball and basketball. He was named to the All-Citrus Belt League in his senior year for baseball, was his basketball team's captain, and was named to a High School All-American basketball team. After graduation, he attended the University of Utah on a basketball scholarship. "I wasn't a high-school standout or anything like that," Parsons said. "I just liked basketball and baseball and when the scholarship offer came along, I decided to try to get an education first, but baseball always was in the back of my mind, and I attended Angels games in Anaheim as a kid. I really liked it. One day I decided to leave Utah and go back to junior college in Riverside."[1]

While attending Riverside City College, Parsons played both baseball and basketball. One summer he pitched for Ontario in the California Collegiate League. In nine games, he posted a 4-1 record, with a 3.10 ERA, striking out 71 and walking 38 in 61 innings. In the 1968 major-league draft, Parsons was selected by the expansion Seattle Pilots. Bobby Mattick and Lou Cohenour signed him to his first contract.

Parsons' first stop was with Newark (New York) of the New York-Penn League. He posted a 2-6 record with a 4.69 ERA, striking out 54, walking 41 in 48 innings of work. He split the 1969 season Billings in the Pioneer League, and Clinton in the Midwest League. With Clinton, he posted a 1.57 ERA, striking out 60 in 69 innings. He spent the offseason pitching in the Arizona Instructional League. On June 14, 1969, Parsons married Marcy Rae Rudd.

The 1970 season began with Parsons pitching for the Portland Beavers of the Pacific Coast League. In his first three starts he pitched two shutouts, but on May 5 his season came to an end when he was called to active duty for four months by his National Guard unit. After his discharge he pitched for Mayaguez, managed by Cal Ermer, in the Puerto Rican winter league. He attracted the attention of the Brewers

(successors to the short-lived Pilots) by winning four straight games, including a two-hit victory over Ponce.

Brewers general manager Marvin Milkes commented, "We've had nothing but good reports on him from Puerto Rico, and Cal Ermer said he's certain Parsons can make our club next year."[2] Manager Dave Bristol said, "Parsons will have every opportunity to make the club as a starter."[3] During spring training in 1970, Leo Durocher, then managing the Chicago Cubs, called Parsons a young man of "great skill and maturity for his age."[4]

Parsons made the 1971 Brewers roster, and his major-league debut took place at Milwaukee County Stadium on April 13, 1971, versus Vida Blue and the Oakland A's. Parsons pitched a complete game, scattering six hits, but lost, 2-0. He recorded his first major league victory on April 23 over the Washington Senators, striking out seven and pitching 7⅓ innings of shutout ball. He lost his next outing, but then won three in a row, pitching complete games in two of them, and lowering his ERA to 1.83.

Parsons had a a curve and a live fastball, but his best pitch was his change-up. "I've got confidence in it thus far," he said.[5] Parsons had a lot of confidence in himself commenting, "Pitching and winning in the majors is much more than I hoped for. I just wanted to come up and make a good showing in the first month. Now I have a good idea of what I can do. There certainly is a difference between the majors and Triple-A, but I figure if I can go through a tough lineup like Boston and California, I'm satisfied I can pitch well against anybody."[6]

One of Parsons' biggest supporters was Brewers pitching coach Wes Stock. "Bill has a lot of things going for him," Stock said. "He has confidence and he has poise. He can change speeds as good as anybody and is not afraid to throw the changeup in key situations. By doing that, he will make his fastball that much more effective, and he has a good fastball. You have to love the way he throws the ball with an easy motion. It's loose and will help keep him away from a sore

arm. We try to teach all our young pitchers to throw pitches with the same motion. And he does this well."[7]

A highlight for Parsons was a 4-1 victory over the Angels in Anaheim on May 14. Among the spectators were his parents, who were seeing him pitch professionally for the first time.

Parsons had some very frustrating losses during the 1971 season. He lost 1-0 five times, and lost four other one-run decisions. Four of his victories were shutouts. Starting 35 games, He wound up with a 13-17 record, with a 3.20 ERA. He finished second to Chris Chambliss of Cleveland in the Baseball Writers Association of American American League Rookie of the Year voting. Parsons called his selection as the 1971 AL Rookie Pitcher of the Year his greatest baseball thrill.

Parsons and new general manager Frank Lane clashed over salary before the 1972 season. Lane's stand was that the pitcher had to "establish himself as a consistent performer for more than one year."[8] After reaching a contract agreement, Parsons was the Brewers starting pitcher on Opening Day in Cleveland, posting a 5-1 victory, and for the home opener in Milwaukee, losing 8-2. By June 8 he had a 6-2 record, but then lost his next five decisions. He raised his record above .500 (8-7) with a victory over Minnesota on July 21, and finished the season on a strong note, posting his fourth straight victory on September 19, a complete game victory over the Yankees, to winds up 13-13 record with a 3.91 ERA.

After the Brewers traded Jim Lonborg to the Philadelphia Phillies, Parsons assumed the role of No. 1 starter for the 1973 season. He said the pressure of being No. 1 didn't faze him. "There was probably more pressure last year when I was coming off a good rookie season," he said. "I wanted to prove that my winning 13 games as a rookie was no fluke."[9]

A big concern for the Brewers and Parsons was a sore shoulder that limited him to 13 innings of work in spring training. Despite the shoulder issue, Parsons was the starting pitcher in the Brewers' home opener, and pitched 6⅔ hitless innings in a 2-0 victory over Baltimore. The rest of the season, however, was very difficult for Parsons. The sore shoulder restricted him to throwing batting practice and pitching out of the bullpen for a portion of the season. After he returned to the starting rotation, muscle spasms in his back caused Parsons problems. After a victory of Chicago on June 16, his record was only 3-4.

Parsons was frustrated with his progress, so much so that he contacted his former pitching coach, Wes Stock, who had been fired by the Brewers and was now with the A's. Parsons wasn't pleased with successor Bob Shaw's policy of "pitch-my-way-or-forget-it,"[10] and was happy the Brewers finally replaced Shaw with Al Widmar, who had worked with Parsons in the instructional league.

A memorable moment occurred on August 6 during an exhibition game against the Atlanta Braves in front of 33,337 fans at Milwaukee County Stadium; Parsons got to pitch to Henry Aaron. Parsons recalled, "When he came up in the sixth, I made up my mind I wasn't going to walk him again. I didn't want to walk him in the second, but I did and got booed. I said to myself that if it happened again, the fans would tar and feather me. So I figured with a three-run lead (5-2) why not throw him my best? If he hits it, he hits it, and that's what the fans were looking for anyway."[11] The fans got their wish as Aaron hit a home run and received another one of the half-dozen standing ovations the fans gave him during the game.

After finishing the 1973 season with a 3-6 record in 60 innings with a 6.79 ERA, Parsons sought to explore any avenues that might return him to his earlier success and pitched in the Venezuelan League for Caracas. Though Brewers general manager Jim Wilson's policy was not to permit his regulars to play winter ball, he allowed Parsons to do so "and see if he could find himself." Wilson also believed that "It might do him good getting away from everybody in our organization. He'd be in a completely different atmosphere."[12] Parsons posted a 6-2 record with Caracas, and afterward told Wilson, "My physical problems have been straightened out and I'm mentally much better prepared for the new season. I'm looking forward to it."[13]

However after spring training in 1974, the Brewers optioned Parsons to Sacramento of the Pacific Coast League. The displeased Parsons asked Brewers president Bud Selig to trade him. He lost his first game with Sacramento, yielding five earned runs in five innings, and was unhappy pitching in Sacramento's Hughes Stadium, with its 233-foot distance to left field (topped by a 40-foot-high net. "Our pitchers will be ready for the nut farm at the end of the year," he opined. "It's ridiculous. There is no way to describe it. By last count (May22) 172 homers have been hit there in 25 games. It's gotten so bad they don't even let fans into the stands until right before the game time."[14] In a victory by Parsons over Tacoma, Sacramento hit seven home runs in a 22-7 Solons victory. Parsons was also disenchanted with the Brewers organization. "I have no desire to go up to Milwaukee," he said. "It's not the town or the people. There are two or three people in the organization who don't provide any incentive. They've discouraged people."[15] Parsons and some of his teammates were also unhappy with an edict by Milwaukee that Sacramento players shave off their mustaches. Parsons reluctantly complied, saying, "I shaved mine only because (manager) Bob Lemon asked me to. If it was just between the Milwaukee club and myself I probably wouldn't have, but I like Lemon and didn't want to get him in trouble."[16]

Parsons' wish came true on June 24 when he was traded to the Oakland A's for Deron Johnson.

He was assigned to the A's PCL farm team in Tucson, then was called up by Oakland for the last month of the season. Reunited with pitching coach Wes Stock, he appeared in four games, pitching two innings, yielding one hit and no runs. His four-batter stint on September 28 against the White Sox (one hit, two walks) was his last major-league appearance.

After the season Parsons was sold to the St. Louis Cardinals. After 1975 spring training, he was sent to the Tulsa Oilers of the Texas League. In July he was traded to the White Sox with cash for Buddy Bradford. The White Sox assigned him to Denver for the rest of the season. In 1976, at the age of 26, he was out of baseball, moving to Phoenix, where he got involved in insurance and securities work. He attempted a comeback in 1978, joining the Seattle Mariners briefly for spring training. He was active as a consultant and doing marketing work for small companies, and as of 2014 lived in Las Vegas. Parsons and his wife, Marcy, had two daughters, Korey and Morganne, who have presented them with three grandchildren.

What had happened to a potentially great pitcher? Parsons told the *Milwaukee Journal*, "I just listened to too many people. What they wanted me to do wasn't what I needed to do. I was thinking about too many mechanical things and I didn't think about getting people out. In the state of mind I was in, I couldn't get my mother out. If you have confidence in yourself, you're going to make your pitches. It's as simple as that."[17]

NOTES

1 Larry Whiteside, "Rookie Parsons Pride of the Brewer Hill," *The Sporting News,* June 5, 1971.

2 Larry Whiteside, "Brewers Prime Parsons as Starter," *The Sporting News*, December 26, 1970.

3 Larry Whiteside, "Kids Add Kicker to Brewer Hill Plan," *The Sporting News,* March 20, 1971.

4 Larry Whiteside, "Slaton Gives Brewer Mound All-Right Label," *The Sporting News,* May 5, 1971

5 Larry Whiteside, "Rookie Parsons Pride of the Brewer Hill," *The Sporting News,* June 5, 1971.

6 Ibid.

7 Ibid.

8 Larry Whiteside, "Brewer Barrels," *The Sporting News,* February 19, 1972.

9 Larry Whiteside, "New Delivery in Parsons Message," *The Sporting News,* March 31, 1973.

10 Ibid.

11 Lou Chapman, "Aaron Touched by Milwaukee's Salute," *The Sporting News,* August 25, 1973.

12 Lou Chapman, "Brewer Suds," *The Sporting News,* September 8,1973.

13 Lou Chapman, "Brewers Seeking Solution to Parsons Mystery," *The Sporting News,* January 26, 1974.

14 Lou Chapman, "Parsons Seeks Trade Following a Look at Sacramento Stadium," *The Sporting News,* June 8, 1974.

15 Ibid.

16 "Solons Dislike Becoming Little Shavers for Brewers," *The Sporting News ,*July 6, 1974

17 Steve Berthiaume, "The Curious Case of Bill Parsons," *ESPN. com,* May 10, 2011

Gaylen Pitts

By Gregory H. Wolf

Baseball lifer Gaylen Pitts knows all about perseverance, patience, hard work, and fulfilling a dream. He toiled as a versatile infielder for ten years in the minor leagues and missed almost two full seasons serving his country during the Vietnam War before he got a chance on the big stage as a midseason temporary call-up to the Oakland A's in 1974 and as a September call-up the following season. He parlayed 44 at-bats in 28 big-league games and 13 years in the minors into a career spanning four decades as a respected manager, coach, scout, and talent evaluator, most notably in the St. Louis Cardinals organization.

Gaylen Richard Pitts was born on June 6, 1946, in Wichita, Kansas, the first of three children (all boys) born to Kansas natives Carl and Dessie (Duncan) Pitts. Carl worked as a produce manager at a grocery store, but yearned for more. In 1952 the family moved to Mountain Home, Arkansas, a picturesque small town in the Ozark Mountains, located near the Missouri border, where the family had regularly vacationed. They purchased a resort, Fisherman's Lodge, situated on Norfolk Lake, a local tourist attraction.

"As a kid I played catch with my father in the back yard," said Pitts of his introduction to baseball.[1] "And then I got involved in the town's Little League program and played through Babe Ruth and American Legion. I was always a shortstop in my youth and in high school." Gaylen was a natural athlete, gifted with speed, agility, and strength. At Mountain Home High School he starred as the quarterback of the football team and also played basketball. However, baseball was his passion since grade school, when he spent afternoons playing on local sandlots and learning about the St. Louis Cardinals through the voice of its legendary broadcaster, Harry Caray. "You couldn't help being a Cardinal fan growing up where I did in a small town in northern Arkansas," Pitts told the author. "We listened to all their games on the radio. It was Cardinal territory."

The right-handed Pitts distinguished himself as a strong-armed, sure-handed shortstop in high school for coach Don Riggs, who was also a bird-dog scout for the Cardinals. "Riggs was instrumental in my development as a player," Pitts said. He began attracting the attention of big-league scouts in his junior year thanks to glowing reports by Riggs. "Fred Hahn, the head scout of the Cardinals, who happened to live in Fayetteville in northern Arkansas, came over and started following me," Pitts said. Brooks Robinson's father (Brooks Sr.), a scout for the Houston Astros, followed me too. And there were also scouts from the Reds."

Pitts recalled that his parents were extremely supportive of his decision to pursue a career in baseball even though that meant declining a full scholarship to play football at Arkansas State University in Jonesboro and getting an education. Immediately after graduating from high school in 1964, Pitts had the opportunity he had been dreaming about. "Hahn took me to St. Louis to the old Busch Stadium-Sportsman's Park to work out on a Sunday afternoon with the Cardinals. I took BP and infield," he said. Following the teenager's impressive performance with big-league players in front of team brass, the Cardinals signed the 18-year-old Pitts at his parents' home. "I got an $8,000 bonus which I thought was a heck of a lot of money back then," Pitts said with a chuckle almost 50 years after that life-changing day. "The Cardinals also gave me an incentive bonus if I made Triple-A or Double-A."

Pitts began his professional baseball career as a shortstop with the Cardinals of the Sarasota Rookie League in 1964 (it was renamed the Florida Rookie League in 1965 and then renamed the Gulf Coast League in 1966). "It was a big transition," he said. "I came from a small town and a small high school, and I had never been away from home. I had to drive down to Sarasota where I didn't know anybody. But the Cardinals made me feel at home. I knew right away that I had to step up my game because everybody was so good." Pitts played in 56 of the team's 60 games, batting .227. He moved up to the Class A Cedar Rapids (Iowa) Cardinals of the Midwest League in 1965. He improved his batting average to .243 while playing in 98 of the team's 114 games.

From the outset of his professional career, Pitts was exposed to the "Cardinal Way" of playing baseball with a stress on fundamentals, situational hitting, and a cerebral approach to the game. "George Kissell was there overseeing all instruction," said Pitts. "You got taught the right way." Kissell, a renowned baseball instructor and Redbird legend, influenced practically every player who went through the Cardinals' system from the 1940s through the 1980s. "I had excellent coaching with the Cardinals and got started out on the right track. St. Louis had good minor-league managers who had played in their system." said Pitts. "My first manager was Fred Koenig and then I had Ron Plaza the next two years." Pitts said Kissell, Koenig, and Plaza were patient, yet demanding, and credited them for his eventual rise to the big leagues.

Pitts's third professional season was interrupted after he had played just 15 games for Cedar Rapids in 1966 when he was drafted into the Army. "I couldn't get into a Reserve unit even though I was going to school part time at Arkansas State in the offseason," he said. The Vietnam War affected minor-league and big-league rosters across the nation as players were drafted or had seasons interrupted to serve in the National Guard or Reserve. Pitts was initially stationed at

Fort Ord, California, where he trained as a radio operator. He was sent to South Vietnam in 1967 and was stationed in Qui Nhon on the central coast for 5½ months, seeing active combat as a specialist. He applied for a special early release through the Army's seasonal employment program and was discharged three months early in order to report to spring training in St. Petersburg in 1968. "The Army made me grow up," said Pitts candidly. "Even though I didn't want to go, I was glad I did because I didn't have to go into the reserves and miss time during the baseball season."

Pitts was reunited with Ron Plaza in 1968 with the St. Petersburg Cardinals in the Class A Florida State League after an almost two-year absence from competitive baseball. "It was a tough transition at first," he said, "but I was able to make adjustments rather soon." He was in excellent physical shape, but needed to hone his timing at the plate and in the field. After a month in Florida, Pitts was reassigned to the Modesto Reds in the Class A California League. Modesto was filled with young talent, including future big leaguers Jose Cruz, Willie Montanez, and Ted Simmons, but finished under .500. Pitts batted .259 and displayed the versatility that would later be his ticket to the big leagues, however briefly, by playing shortstop, third base, the outfield, second base, and first base.

Pitts progressed through the Cardinals' system, playing for the Double-A Arkansas Travelers of the Texas League in 1969 and the Tulsa Oilers of the Triple-A American Association in 1970. "Shortstop was my natural position, but I started to grow and get bigger. So I was moved to third base when I got to Double-A. I played a little second, too. They didn't think that I had the range to play shortstop anymore. I had a little power, so third base seemed like a good position." He clouted 11 home runs with Arkansas, followed by nine for manager Warren Spahn at Tulsa, ranking third on the team each season. The St. Louis Cardinals purchased his contract at the end of the 1969 campaign and added him to their 40-man roster.

In preparation for what turned out to be his first and only spring training with a big-league club, Pitts participated in the Florida Instructional League, where he worked closely with Kissell. Pitts laughed when the author asked him about his first impressions of the Cardinals players in camp in 1970. "Red (Schoendienst) was the manager. And we had all of those guys I followed as a kid. It was a little overwhelming. I lockered next to Dal Maxvill and we became close friends. He kind of took me under his wing and made me feel at home and relax." Pitts's stay with the Redbirds, coming off their worst season since 1959, was brief. "Back in those days you did not stay with the big-league club long, maybe about two weeks," he explained. "Teams wanted to set their roster a lot earlier than they do today."

Assigned to Tulsa, Pitts saw his tenure with the only organization he knew come to a conclusion in July 1971 when he was shipped to the Oakland A's for journeyman pitcher Dennis Higgins. "I went to Des Moines, Iowa, the A's Triple-A club in the American Association and played for Sherm Lollar. He was a real jewel to play for," said Pitts. Pitts played for the Iowa Oaks and Lollar again in 1972, clubbing 10 home runs, but batted just .220. He was moved back to shortstop to make room for hot prospect Phil Garner.

Pitts chuckled when asked to compare the A's and Cardinals' farm systems. "They were quite a bit different because of Charley (Charles O. Finley). He was the owner and ran things. You never knew what he was going to do," said Pitts. "Everyone had mustaches and long hair, but they let you play."

Beginning his ninth year in the minor leagues, the 27-year-old Pitts was at a crossroads in 1973. He was assigned to the Tucson Toros, the A's new affiliate in the American Association. With prospects Garner at third base and Manny Trillo at second base, Pitts was relegated to the role of supersub for the first time in his life. He played 43 games at short, 15 at second, seven at third, and even four in the outfield. Praised by manager Lollar for his "clutch hitting," Pitts batted a career-high .287 in 202 at-bats.[2]

After he started the 1974 season with Tucson, Pitts's long wait to debut in the major leagues finally came to an end. "The A's had three guys get hurt at the same time, (second baseman) Dick Green, shortstop Maxy (Dal Maxvill), and (third baseman) Bando. The A's needed an infielder who could play several infield positions," said Pitts of the confluence of injuries that prompted his call-up.

"We were playing Albuquerque in Tucson and Sherm Lollar called me in and told me I was going up. I caught an early flight the next morning to Oakland—they were playing an early-afternoon game. My debut was on Mother's Day. I got to the ballpark, but didn't expect to play. (Manager) Al Dark said, 'You're playing.' I didn't even have the chance to take BP. I got dressed, got acclimated to the signs, and was out there playing second base."

Batting ninth and playing second, Pitts struck out his first two at-bats, and then lined a single that drove in Ray Fosse in the A's 9-2 victory over the Minnesota Twins on May 12. Described by A's beat reporter Ron Bergman as a "refugee from the bush leagues," Pitts started the next day at third base, went 1-for-3 and scored two runs in the A's 11-2 win over the Kansas City Royals.[3] "Aging Rookie Gives A's an Even Break" read a national headline on May 14 after Pitts stroked three hits in four at-bats and drove in the only two runs in the second game of a doubleheader.[4] In the bottom of the tenth inning, he belted his second double of the game off starter Lindy McDaniel to drive in Ted Kubiak for a dramatic walk-off, game-ending hit, giving the A's an exciting 2-1 victory over the Royals. Pitts held his own during his six weeks on the A's roster, going 10-for-41 in 18 games, including eight starts at third base and three at second base. He also served as a defensive replacement at third, second, and once at first.

Sent back to Tucson in June, Pitts platooned at shortstop with Tommy Sandt and filled in at third and second. He batted .246 in 67 games. He acknowledged that not many minor leaguers with a .250 batting average persevere 11 seasons hoping for a shot in the big leagues. "Usually you don't stick around that long. But I was single and stuck it out. I was in Triple-A a long time. But it was worth it—I'll tell you that." Asked to describe the atmosphere and team cohesion on the 1974 A's, he said, "I felt comfortable with the A's. … Those guys were characters, but when it came time to play, they played. It was the best ballclub I was ever on. I was lucky to be there. They made you feel at home. We played hard, and played the game the right way. And we partied hard, too."

Despite his early season call-up in 1974, Pitts was not invited to the A's spring training in 1975. The jack-of-all trades played all four infield positions for Tucson and batted .268 in 135 games. He was called up in September when rosters expanded. He played in ten games, typically as a late-inning defensive replacement, but did not start. In his last official at-bat in the big leagues, Pitts doubled off Nelson Briles in the ninth inning, driving in Matt Alexander, and then scored on Jim Holt's home run in the A's 16-4 thrashing of the Royals on September 20.

Oakland began to groom Pitts for a future coaching or managerial position. He was known for his serious and studious approach to the game, and his success and longevity were products of his versatility and sheer desire to compete. "I was not playing every day anymore," he said of the 1976 season with Tucson. "I had the chance to sit back on the bench and digest everything. I wanted to get into coaching. I was like a player-coach for manager Harry Bright and threw

BP. When he was fired I took over the club for three days before Lee Stange came in." Pitts batted .261 in 106 games, and was still viewed as an ideal veteran role player, especially for teams like the Seattle Mariners or Toronto Blue Jays. "[Pitts] can play any position on the team [and] would be an asset to one of the expansion clubs," opined *The Sporting News*.[5]

Pitts was traded to the Chicago Cubs for outfielder Jim Tyrone on March 15, 1977, and was subsequently assigned to the Wichita Aeros of the American Association. "I asked for my release from the Cubs organization because I really wasn't playing anymore," said Pitts who batted just 12 times in the first six weeks of the season. "I knew Rene Lachemann, manager of the San Jose Missions, from my playing days. So I called him up and signed. I wound up playing every day." The oldest player on the roster, Pitts played in 92 games (mainly at third base and first base), batted .237, and served as an unofficial coach.

At the end of the season Pitts hung up his spikes for the last time as a player. "It was the right time to transition into coaching," said Pitts, whose big-league career consisted of 28 games in which he batted .250 (11-for-44). In his 13-year minor-league career he batted .248 in 1,249 games.

Weeks after retiring, Pitts began preparing for his first managerial position, with the Modesto A's, Oakland's affiliate in the Class A California League. "Back then you didn't have any coaches in the lower levels," said Pitts. "You were on an island by yourself and had to learn on the fly." After two losing seasons with weak rosters, he decided to take a year off. "The A's farm system wasn't run very well," said Pitts candidly. "[Farm director] Norm Koselke didn't have any baseball background [he was Mrs. Finley's cousin]. The whole system was in turmoil." The notoriously cheap Finley ran a remarkably understaffed front office without a scouting director.

Pitts returned to the Cardinals organization in 1981 when he was named manager of the Arkansas Travelers of the Double-A Texas League. "The Cardinals had a coaching philosophy," he said. "George Kissell, the field coordinator and guy who had been with the organization the longest, would take guys that had played in the organization and bring them in as coaches in the tail end of their career. Then they get a chance to manage in the Florida Instructional League. The coaches and managers all knew the Cardinals philosophy."

After two years with Arkansas, Pitts "stepped back" from managing to serve as Jim Fregosi's coach with Triple-A Louisville in 1983-1984. "I learned a lot from Fregosi in those two years," he said. "The time with him really shaped my managerial career going forward." Pitts skippered five different Cardinal farm teams over a six-year period (1985-1990), and guided the Travelers to the Texas League championship in 1989.

In 1991 Pitts made it back to the major leagues. "Dal Maxvill was the general manager of the Cardinals and we were friends," he said. "I didn't know manager Joe Torre, but Maxy told [Joe] that I'd be a good fit, so I was hired." Pitts served on Torre's staff for five years as a bench, third-base, and bullpen coach (1991 to 1995), during which time the Cardinals had three winning seasons in a period marked by labor unrest and a baseball strike. Walt Jocketty replaced Maxvill after the 1994 season and Torre was fired during the 1995 season. Pitts interviewed unsuccessfully for a position on manager Tony LaRussa's staff in 1996.

After serving as the Cardinals minor-league field coordinator for a year, Pitts resumed his managerial career in 1997. He piloted the Louisville Redbirds for one season, then followed with a five-year tenure as the skipper of the Memphis Redbirds of the Pacific Coast League (1998-2002). Affectionately called Chief by his players, Pitts was a hands-on teacher who stressed fundamentally sound ball like his mentors Kissell, Koenig, and Plaza. Given his experience as a minor leaguer, he could empathize with his players' frustrations, fears, and struggles. In 2000 he guided the Redbirds to the league championship. In anticipation of facing tough left-handers in the playoffs, Pitts encouraged Mike Jorgenson, the Cardinals farm director, to promote right-handed slugger Albert Pujols in his first year of professional ball from A-level to

Triple-A for the team's playoff run. Pujols played in three games in the last week of the season for Memphis, then batted .302 in 11 postseason games and hit the pennant-winning home run in the 13th inning against the Salt Lake City Buzz.[6]

"I was just worn out," said Pitts of his decision to resign after the 2002 season. "My hips were hurting and I thought I'd gradually get into something else, like scouting. It was probably a mistake. I should have returned to Triple-A Memphis." But the pull of baseball was too great to ignore. After interviewing for bench coach under manager Ned Yost of the Milwaukee Brewers, Pitts served as hitting coach for manager Cecil Cooper with the Indianapolis Indians, the Brewers' affiliate in Triple-A, in 2003. He was out of baseball the next two years in order to have both hips replaced.

Pitts made a successful return to managing in 2006 when he led the Class A Staten Island Yankees to the championship of the New York-Pennsylvania League. "The Yankees job intrigued me," said Pitts. "For one it was the Yankees. And secondly, I knew they had good players in their system and had some good drafts. And the pay was good." The Yankees wanted him to return in 2007, but the lure of returning to the Cardinals organization was too much. "GM Jocketty and I were friends and I knew the organization. It was like going home." Pitts piloted the Palm Beach Cardinals of the Class A Florida State League for two seasons. At the age of 62, Pitts retired from managing after the 2008 season. Over the course of 19 seasons, his teams posted a .511 winning percentage.

In 2009 Pitts was named assistant to player development for the Cardinals, and still held the position as of the end of 2013. "I go to all seven clubs during the season and to spring training," said Pitts, who still retained his youthful enthusiasm for the game. "I work with the players and the managers. A lot of them either played or coached for me. I'm another set of eyes on the players. I file reports on what I see. I report directly to GM John Mozeliak and Gary LaRocque, the farm director. I can work out of my home in Arkansas and travel by car to many of the teams."

As of 2013 Pitts resided in Mountain Home, Arkansas, with his wife, Julia (Ray) Pitts, a former schoolteacher originally from Denver. They met in 1984 when Pitts was coaching with Louisville, and married in 1985. They have one child, Travis.

"I was lucky," said the ever humble and modest Pitts about his 50-year career in baseball. "It doesn't always work out that way."

Acknowledgement:

The author expresses his gratitude to Gaylen Pitts, who was interviewed on October 22, 2013. Mr. Pitts also supplied additional information by email and read the final version of the biography to ensure its accuracy.

SOURCES

Baseball-Reference.com

Retrosheet.com

SABR.com

The Sporting News

NOTES

1   Author's Interview with Gaylen Pitts on October 22, 2013. All quotations are from this interview.

2   *The Sporting News*, September 1, 1973, 27.

3   *The Sporting News*, June 1, 1974, 15.

4   Press Dispatches, "Aging Rookie Gives A's an Even Break," *Milwaukee Journal*, May 14, 1974, 2.

5   *The Sporting News*, October 2, 1976, 31.

6   Dennis Abrams, *Albert Pujols* (New York: Infobase, 2008), 42.

Champ Summers

By Scott Ferkovich

Baseball history is filled with all variety of wonderful-sounding names. But has there ever been a more perfect name for a baseball player than Champ Summers? "With a name like that, you gotta be halfway decent anyway," Champ would say years later. "If my name had been George, nobody would have noticed me, but Champ?" Growing up, Summers had to constantly prove that he was as great and as tough as his name implied. "A kid would come up to me and say, 'What's your name?' I'd say, 'Champ.' He'd say, 'Champ?' And away we'd go. I got into more than a few fights because of my name." As evidence of his pugilistic past, Champ's left cheek was adorned with a large scar. "It happened a long time ago, when I used to roam the streets."[1]

It was his father, himself a boxing champion from his days in the US Navy, who gave Champ his nickname. "When I was born I was so ugly I looked like I'd been beaten around in the ring. They called me 'Champ.'" There was also a slightly different version of the tale. "Dad took one look at me when I was born and said, 'He looks like he just went ten rounds with Joe Louis.' It's a sad story, but true." His father always made it clear that he would be known as "Champ."[2]

Summers, who spent part of the 1974 season as a bench player with the Oakland Athletics, was born John Junior Summers, II on June 15, 1946, in Bremerton, Washington, the home of the Puget Sound Naval Shipyard.[3] A copy of Champ's birth certificate reveals his father's name as John Junior Summers, originally from Sparta, Illinois. The elder Summers listed his occupation as "self-employed photographer." His mother, Bette Irene Mace, claimed to be a housewife, born in Big Lake, Washington. A self-described hustler and scrapper, Champ spent a lot of his formative years hanging around pool halls. Despite having plenty of opportunities to get into trouble, he credited his strong home life with keeping him on the straight and narrow.

When he turned 16, however, Champ decided to get a tattoo of a Playboy Bunny etched on his right shoulder. He would live to regret the frivolous decision. "I hate that thing," he said in later years. "Now, it follows me wherever I go. It cost me $5 to have it put on, but it would cost me $5,000 to get rid of it."[4]

Eventually, the Summers family moved to Illinois. Champ graduated from Madison Senior High in 1965. He was a natural athlete, lettering in basketball, football, tennis, track, and cross-country. He was also a swimmer and a diver. Up to this point in his life, however, he had not yet played baseball seriously, claiming that while the opportunities were there, he simply had no interest in the game.

Upon graduating from high school, Champ enrolled at Nicholls State College in Louisiana. He played

basketball, but after what he called a misunderstanding with the coach, he dropped out after a year and a half. The "misunderstanding" actually involved Summers punching out a teammate. "I went to Vietnam for that," Summers said later. "They kicked me off the team. So I dropped out of school, and the Army grabbed me. It was the best thing that ever happened to me. Vietnam was tough. It made me a different person. I saw them put people in bags and decided they were going to know I had been there before they put me in one. I became more aggressive, more asser- tive. I came back home and got an education, some- thing I hadn't wanted before. If I hadn't punched that guy and gotten kicked out of school, I wouldn't have gone to war, and I might have settled for the kind of life my father had led." Summers said that his father had "worked on the railroad all his life. I had worked with him. I didn't want to do that."[5]

Summers spent 11½ months in Vietnam. The first six were spent as a paratrooper. The rest of his service time was on the beach, as a lifeguard. But while jumping out of planes, Champ witnessed firsthand the horrors of war, forcing him to grow up quickly. "I don't like to talk about it. Looking back now, it was probably a good thing for me, … It made me feel how insignificant I was."[6] He narrowly escaped with his life in one instance. While behind the wheel of a truck, he drove over a land mine. Fortunately, sandbags in the vehicle absorbed much of the shock. Summers suffered a concussion and a broken nose.

After the Army, Summers attended Southern Illinois University Edwardsville in 1970. He played on the basketball team for two seasons, averaging 18.8 points per game, including one game in which he scored 53. He was a talented enough player to earn a tryout with the Memphis Tams of the American Basketball Association. At some point, he was also offered a tryout with the Dallas Cowboys of the NFL. Champ had never played college football, however, and never followed up on the offer.

While at SIUE, Summers met his future wife, Barbara, a fellow student. After dating for about a year, they married in 1971.

During Champ's senior year he first began to play organized baseball. "I was playing a little slow-pitch softball and one day one of my friends said I should go out for the baseball team. Sounded like a good idea. … Why not?" At the time, he assumed that the skills needed for playing slow-pitch would translate over to baseball. "You run around in the outfield and catch the ball just the same, don't you?"[7] Summers approached the baseball coach, Roy Lee, and told him he wanted to try out for the team. Naturally, Lee expressed skepticism when Summers told him he hadn't played baseball of any kind since he was 13, and not in any organized fashion. Lee gave in against his better judgment, and Summers got in the cage and swung the bat. Coach Lee supposedly asked his new- found slugger where the hell he had been. Summers hit a pinch-hit homer his first time at bat in a game.

Champ's greatest thrill in college was ranking in the top ten in the NCAA in home runs (7) and RBIs in 1971. He was also voted SIUE's Athlete of the Year in 1971, hitting .340. Years later, former SIUE baseball coach Gary "Bo" Collins could still remember the day Summers came for his tryout, "riding down to the field on a Harley without a shirt on … his hat on backwards."[8]

Summers was not drafted by any major-league team upon graduation. But his baseball odyssey was not coming to a close. It was only beginning.

While playing at SIUE, Summers had been spotted by George Bradley, a scout for the Oakland A's. He liked what he saw in Champ, despite his relatively advanced age. A's owner Charlie Finley wasn't too excited about signing a player who was almost 25 and whose only baseball experience was 35 games in college. Bradley was a good salesman, however, and talked Finley into giving Summers a contract.

At first Summers himself wasn't sure he wanted to sign with Oakland, but his wife, Barbara, urged him to at least give it a try. If nothing else, he could say years later that he had played professional ball. On June 12, 1971, Summers signed for a reported $500 per month, no signing bonus, and reported to Class A

Coos Bay-North Bend in the Northwest League. In 65 games he hit .252, with three home runs and 34 RBIs. Champ hated the 15-hour bus rides, the lousy truck-stop food, and the dirty hotel rooms, but again, it was Barbara who encouraged him to give it at least one more year, knowing that it was something that he really wanted.

Summers played the following year at Burlington (Iowa) in the Class A Midwest League, finishing with 10 homers, 54 RBIs, and a .308 average in 97 games. That earned him a promotion to Triple-A Tucson for 1973, where he hit .333 in 94 games, but with only eight homers. He began the next season at Tucson again, but soon Oakland decided he had earned a promotion. Champ Summers finally appeared for the first time in a major-league contest on May 4, 1974, at the ripe age of 27. Against the Indians in Oakland, he was inserted as a defensive replacement in the top of the ninth, for none other than Reggie Jackson. In the bottom of the inning he got his first major-league at-bat, against Gaylord Perry, hitting into a line-drive double play to the first baseman. Thus, in his first game as a big leaguer, he replaced a Hall of Famer, and faced a Hall of Famer. His first hit came at the Oakland Coliseum on May 14, 1974. It was a pinch-hitting appearance in the ninth inning against the Kansas City Royals' Doug Bird, a groundball single to center.

By early June, Summers was back at Tucson. In 20 games at Oakland, he had only three hits in 24 at-bats, for a .125 average, with no homers and three RBIs. At Tucson he hit .263 with 10 homers and 59 RBIs in 94 games. That October, Oakland won its third straight World Series. Summers, though not on the team after June 10, received a Series share of $100 from the A's. (According to Champ, the check was actually $93 after taxes.)

That first season in Oakland, Summers lived with Reggie Jackson. Reggie, no stranger to self-promotion, taught Champ a thing or two. "I was autographing baseballs one day," he recalled, "and Reggie wanted to know why I was signing them John Summers. He asked if I had a nickname. I told him I had one, but I was afraid of what the other players would think if I used it. Reggie said, 'This is show business. If there were two Summers with the same ability, one named John, and the other name Champ, which do you think the fans would remember?'"[9]

In 1975 Summers started the season at Tucson once again. On April 29, after 17 games, he was informed that he could pack his bags for Chicago. Wrigley Field would be his new home. He had been traded to the Cubs.

Summers spent the rest of 1975 in the Windy City, mostly as a reserve outfielder and pinch-hitter. He hit .231 with one home run and 16 RBIs in 76 games. That home run, however, on August 23 at Wrigley Field, was his first in the majors, and a pinch-hit grand slam at that.

After the season Summers played for Culiacan in the Mexican Pacific League. He played every day, and made the All-Star team. Back in a Cubs uniform for 1976, he hit only .206, with three home runs in 83 games. The Cubs had labeled Champ as nothing more than a pinch-hitter. Perhaps the team felt that he was unable to hit left-handers, was too much of a defensive liability, or that he was simply too old. On February 16, 1977, he was traded to the Cincinnati Reds. He would become the team's primary pinch-hitter from the left side. The Big Red Machine, managed by Sparky Anderson, was coming off their second consecutive World Series championship. Summers knew that, barring injury, there was just no way he was going to break into such a great lineup. He understood his role on the team. He struggled for much of the year, finishing with a .171 average in 59 games, with three homers and six RBIs. By the end, he said, he was pressing so much, and so worried that the Reds were going to demote him, that he could hardly function. His highlight was an inside-the-park home run in June at Riverfront Stadium.[10] That year the Reds were bridesmaids to the Dodgers. Still, Summers earned a second-place booty of $2,011.35.

The following summer would prove to be a pivotal one in Champ's career, but it wouldn't be spent in Cincinnati. Just before Opening Day, the Reds optioned him to Triple-A Indianapolis. He had a monster season for the Indians, hitting 34 homers with 124 RBIs, while batting .368. "This season here," Summers said when it was all finished, "I'll never forget. It has probably turned my whole life around."[11] He won the American Association MVP award, as well as *The Sporting News* Minor League Player of the Year award.

Called up to the Reds in September, Summers wound up hitting .257 in 13 games with one home run, a titanic clout into the top-tiered red-level seats at Riverfront Stadium. After the season he joined the Reds on their tour of Japan, hitting .370 with five homers.

Champ was back on the Reds for 1979, but again it was tough for him to crack an outfield of Ken Griffey, George Foster, and Cesar Geronimo. He never got untracked, and after hitting only .200 with one homer in 27 games, he was dealt on May 25 to the Detroit Tigers. Tigers manager Les Moss had high hopes for his new acquisition. Moss, however, wouldn't see Champ very long in Detroit. On June 11, the skipper was unceremoniously let go. Taking his place was Champ's former manager at Cincinnati, Sparky Anderson, who had been fired by the Reds in November of 1978 after their disappointing second-place finish. The Tigers felt they simply couldn't pass up the opportunity to hire one of the most successful managers in the game. Platooning in left and right fields, Summers played 90 games for Detroit. His left-handed swing was tailor-made for Tiger Stadium's short right-field porch. He hit a career-high .313, with a .414 on-base percentage, while slugging .614. He banged out 20 home runs with 51 RBIs. He struck out only 33 times. Summers admitted at season's end that he hadn't been a very happy person until day one when he got to Detroit. He felt ready to shed his reputation as a platoon player. Sparky, however, saw Champ as a very good hitter, but a part-time one.

Summers was very popular in Detroit, especially with the fans in the right-field bleachers, which came to be known as Champ's Camp. He gained some national recognition in 1979 after a group of fans held up a banner during a *Game of the Week* telecast when the Tigers played in Milwaukee. The banner read "Champ Summers Fan Club, Berkeley, Calif." The fan club, which numbered about 30 people, organized a tour to follow their hero from city to city. The recognition Champ received in Detroit did not go unappreciated. "I love it here," he said. "I love the fans. Even when I do badly, they're on my side. Hey, I could be pumping gas today. I know how lucky I am to be here."[12]

The 1980 season saw Summers play primarily as the designated hitter against right-handed pitching, while making spot appearances in the outfield and at first base. Appearing in 120 games, he hit .297 with 17 homers and 60 RBIs. His slugging percentage was .504.

By 1981 Champ's playing time was being significantly reduced. That season the Tigers were in the middle of a race, narrowly losing out to Milwaukee for the second-half division title. (Because of the players' strike, the leagues played a split season.) It was a frustrating season for Summers, as he hit a mere three home runs with 21 RBIs in 64 games, while averaging .255.

On March 4, 1982, Champ was traded from the Tigers to the San Francisco Giants for third baseman Enos Cabell and cash. "(The Giants) must want me," he commented. "It was pretty obvious there was no place for me in Detroit." Giants manager Frank Robinson welcomed the trade: "It's good to have a guy like that on the bench because you know he has the capability of hitting it out of the park with one swing." In 70 games for San Francisco, Summers hit .248 with four homers and 19 RBIs. He particularly excelled as a pinch-hitter, with 10 hits in 31 at-bats, including two home runs and 11 RBIs. Off the field, it was a year of change for Champ, as he and Barbara went through a divorce.

The next season was a disastrous one. After being diagnosed with degenerative arthritis in his left shoulder, he went under the knife, effectively ending his year on June 26. He did manage to return to get four at-bats as a pinch-hitter in September, but went hitless. Playing in only 29 games all season, Summers hit a dismal .136, with no homers and only three RBIs. In December the Giants sent him to the San Diego

Padres for utilityman Joe Pittman and a player to be named later (career minor leaguer Tommy Francis).

The summer of 1984 was one of highs and lows for Champ. Reduced to strictly pinch-hitting duty, and now in his late 30s, he knew he was reaching the end of the line as a player. On August 12 he found himself involved in one of the most violent and ignominious days in baseball history. In a game between the Padres and the Atlanta Braves, several bench-clearing brawls broke out. In one, Champ made a mad dash on his own straight for the Braves bench, in order to get a piece of pitcher Pascual Perez, who had plunked Alan Wiggins earlier in the game. He was confronted at the dugout by a hulking Bob Horner (on the DL with a broken wrist at the time), who proceeded to throw Champ to the ground, assisted by two Atlanta fans who had jumped out of the stands. Several Braves players quickly swarmed onto the pile as Champ lay in the dirt. He also got a cup of beer thrown on him by one rowdy customer. Nineteen players and coaches were ejected, and five fans arrested.

The Padres finished at 92-70 to gain their first-ever division title. As for Champ, he saw action in only 47 games all year, and struggled to hit .185 with 12 RBIs. His only home run of the year, and the final one of his career and a grand slam, came on April 10 at San Diego's Jack Murphy Stadium. (Interestingly, Champ's first big-league homer, as well as his last, was a pinch-hit grand slam.)

Summers got only two pinch-hit at-bats in the National League Championship Series, without getting a safety. In the World Series, San Diego squared off against his former team, the Detroit Tigers, winners of 104 games that year. The Tigers ran over the Padres in five games. Summers had been looking forward to seeing some playing time against his old club, but Dick Williams chose to use Kurt Bevacqua as the DH against right-handed pitchers, even though Bevacqua hit from the right side.

After the first two games in San Diego, the Series moved to Tiger Stadium. Champ got a standing ovation from the packed house during the pregame introductions in Game Three. His only appearance in the Series, however, was as a pinch-hitter in Game Four. Facing off against former mate Jack Morris in the eighth inning, he struck out swinging. It was his final at-bat in a big-league uniform. But he received a National League Championship ring for 1984, along with a Series share of $130,000.

Summers wasn't offered a contract by any club after the season. Now 38 and out of baseball, he tried his hand as a salesman for a Mercedes dealership in Southern California, but didn't particularly like it. In December of that year, he met his future wife, Joy. They married exactly one year later, and settled down in La Jolla, where Champ enjoyed playing golf year round.

Still, Summers had the itch to get back into baseball. He grabbed the opportunity to be the hitting instructor for the Columbus Clippers, the Yankees' Triple-A affiliate, who were managed by Bucky Dent. In September of 1989, Yankees owner George Steinbrenner fired skipper Dallas Green, promoting Dent to the managerial post in the Bronx. Champ, too, was called up to the big club, as a hitting coach.

On June 18 1990, Dent was fired, along with several of his staff, Champ included. The Yankee coaching job would be his last gig in the major leagues.

In 2001 Summers signed on to manage the Gateway Grizzlies, who played in Sauget, Illinois, in the independent Frontier League. The Grizzlies finished with a record of 37-44. After the last out was made that summer, Champ hung up his baseball uniform for the last time. He and Joy retired to Ocala, Florida. Champ was diagnosed with kidney cancer in May of 2010. He fought the disease for nearly 2½ years, before dying on October 11, 2012.

"He loved playing in Detroit the most," Joy remembered. "He loved and adored Sparky. He loved the fans."

SOURCES

American Spectator

Belleville (Illinois) *New-Democrat*

Cincinnati Enquirer

Crain's Detroit Business

Detroit Free Press

Enid (Oklahoma) *News and Eagle*

Portsmouth (Ohio) *Daily Times*

St. Louis Post-Dispatch

San Francisco Examiner

San Francisco Examiner

The Sporting News

Baseball-reference.com

BND.com

In addition to the above sources, the author would especially like to thank Joy Summers for her wonderful storytelling during a telephone interview in January 2013.

NOTES

1 Jim Hawkins, "Boy of 31 Summers Warms Up as New Tiger," *The Sporting News*, July 21, 1979, 21.

2 Norm Sanders, "Former Metro-East Standout and Major League Outfielder Champ Summers Dies," *BND.com*, bnd.com/2012/10/11/2357039/former-metro-east-standout-and.html, accessed August 1, 2013.

3 During World War II, the citys population topped out at around 80,000. The war effort was at its peak, and workers flocked to the area to take advantage of the availability of shipbuilding jobs.

Bremertons history featured a few notable residents. Jazz legend Quincy Joness family moved to the city when he was 10. It is the birthplace of Bill Gates, Sr., the father of Microsoft founder Bill Gates. The latters grandfather ran a furniture store along with an ice-cream parlor in the downtown area. Scientology founder L. Ron Hubbard attended Union High School and began his writing career while living in Bremerton.

4 Jim Hawkins, "Boy of 31 Summers."

5 Phil Collier, "Tag For Summers: Man of Many Talents," *The Sporting News*, March 12, 1984, 42.

6 Greg Heberlein and Rick Hummel, "Are These Guys Just Average?", *The Sporting News*, May 31, 1980, 3.

7 Mike Myers, "Summers a Champ as Minors Best," *The Sporting News*, December 9, 1978, 30.

8 Aaron Goldstein, "Champ Summers, R.I.P.," *The American Spectator*, spectator.org/blog/2012/10/12/champ-summers-rip, accessed August 1, 2013.

9 Phil Collier, "Tag For Summers."

10 After nearly collapsing at the plate, he later admitted that, during his mad dash around the bases, he had nearly choked after swallowing his entire wad of tobacco, and was almost unable to make it to home.

11 Mike Myers, "Indy's Summers and DeFreites Offer Baseball's Top One-Two Power Punch," *The Sporting News*, September 2, 1978, 45.

12 Tom Gage, "Champ Knockout in Detroit," *The Sporting News*, May 24, 1980, 10.

Claudell Washington

by Eric Aron

"There is virtually nothing he can't do," said Willie Stargell.[1]

"He's the best player for his age I have ever seen or know," said Reggie Jackson.[2]

"He's going to be one hell of a player," said Gene Tenace.[3]

These were sentiments shared by many of the teammates, coaches, and scouts who saw such promise in a young kid from Berkeley, California, named Claudell Washington.

Washington, who would become a two-time All-Star and a World Series champion in 1974, came up quickly through the A's system and made an immediate impact. Beginning his professional career at the age of 17, he had a rare combination of speed and power.

After being called up by the A's in July of 1974, Washington did nothing but hit and was instrumental in the team's winning its third straight world championship. Showing tremendous poise at such a young age, the left-handed Washington hit an impressive .571 in that season's World Series.

Yet with all the lofty expectations, Washington did not become the superstar many projected he would be. He was often platooned and used as a fourth outfielder, and was criticized at times for his defense. He did have a lengthy 17-year major-league career, however, appearing in 1,912 games and hitting .278/.325/.420, with 164 home runs, 1,884 hits and 824 RBIs.

Washington does have his place in the history books, however. Among other accomplishments, he is one of only 14 players to hit three home runs in a single game for each league at least one time. He also holds the dubious distinction of being the batter struck out the most by Nolan Ryan in the Hall of Famer's 27-year career (39 K's in 90 at-bats).

Nicknamed Champ by his father and SuperWash by his teammates, Washington played for seven teams and was traded five times. Between 1974 and 1990, he played for the Oakland A's, Texas Rangers, Chicago White Sox, New York Mets, Atlanta Braves, California Angels, and the New York Yankees (twice). Although he had some pop, throughout his career he was mostly a line-drive hitter. Despite his home-run total, he never hit more than 17 in a season. Lifetime, he was a .278 hitter who hit over .300 only twice.

What Washington was really blessed with was speed. He stole at least 30 bases four times, including 40 in 1975. (As of 2014 his 312 thefts rank 153rd all-time). He reached the postseason three times, making appearances with the A's (1974 and 1975) and the Atlanta Braves (1982). He hit .333 in 39 playoff at-bats.

Claudell Washington was born on August 31, 1954, in Los Angeles. He was the oldest of four boys and two girls. His mother, Jenny, was an important figure in his life, as his parents were divorced after 25 years of marriage and he wasn't close to his father, Claudell Washington, Sr. His brother Donald played for three seasons in the Dodgers and A's organizations.

"I grew up in a good neighborhood," said Washington, an African-American raised in Berkeley. "Life was pretty easy. There were no gang fights or anything."[4]

Washington didn't play baseball until he was 11, when he began playing in numerous sandlot leagues, as well as Little League, Pony League, and Colt League. "I wasn't one of those guys who sat around and dreamed about being a professional baseball player," Washington said. He played baseball during summers "because my friends did it. I wanted to run with them … so I picked up a bat and a ball and did what they did. It was just one of those things where it came natural to me. I had good eye-hand coordination."[5] In 1965 he helped lead his team to victory in the Berkeley Little League championship game, hitting two grand slams, a double, and a triple. He also brought his team to the Little League World Series.

Still, Washington never played on the Berkeley High School team. "I didn't want to play baseball there because I had preferred basketball and track. I was a high jumper. … In junior high I'd been a pitcher and I started our team's first five games. Nobody cared whether I hurt my arm or not, so I quit the team. (He was 14 years old at the time.) I didn't want to go through that in high school."[6]

Washington graduated from Berkeley High in 1972, the year he was discovered by a police officer who did some scouting for the A's.

Washington was recommended to the officer, Jim Guinn, by the Berkeley High athletic department. "I sent him a form, he filled it out and he returned it," recalled Guinn. "He's a loner. Someone had to encourage him. I made a call and got him on the Berkeley Connie Mack team. I watched him for a month and worked out with him every day. During that month he batted about .600 and hit seven or eight home runs. If there had been any scouts around I would have signed him right away. But there weren't. I had no competition for him."[7]

Washington remembered it a little differently. "My manager (in the Connie Mack league), Jim McCray, had played minor-league baseball with Jim Guinn. … I think the Orioles, the Mets and the Pirates looked at me, but nothing ever came of it."[8]

In either case, Washington had been working as a janitor at a lawn-sprinkler factory when Guinn persuaded the A's director of minor-league operations John Claiborne, to sign him as a free agent. Washington's bonus was $3,000. "I put that money in the bank," he told the *New York Times* in October of 1974, "I don't care about home runs. I just want to be a .300 hitter, spend 10 or 15 years in the major leagues and make a lot of money."[9]

At his young age, Washington had developed broad, muscular shoulders. He weighed 190 pounds and was 6 feet ball. A Chicago sportswriter said, "Someone should tell him this isn't football. He can take off those shoulder pads."[10]

The A's assigned Washington to Coos Bay, Oregon, of the Northwest League, where he made $500 a month. There he met his mentor, manager Grover Resinger. "Grover Resinger helped me with my hitting, with my fielding, and with my baserunning. He kept my confidence up. … He taught me how to handle certain pitches. I couldn't hit the curve or slider, down and in, at first. He also taught me how to run the bases. I used to take wide turns.[11]

At Coos Bay, Washington hit .279 with 2 home runs and 15 RBIs in 33 games. He had nine stolen bases. Moving up the chain to Class A Burlington (Midwest League), Washington had a breakout year in 1973. He was named to the Midwest League and National Association All-Star Team. In 108 games he led the league in runs scored (92) and total bases (218). He was second in hitting (.322), RBIs (81), and stolen bases (38), and third in hits (144).

In 1974 Washington was promoted to Birmingham of the Double-A Southern League. He hit four home runs in the first three weeks of the season. The *The Sporting News* described two of them as "real tape-measure shots to rival those hit by Walter Dropo in the '50s and (Reggie) Jackson and (Dave) Duncan in later years."[12]

The A's needed a left-handed designated hitter and called up the 19-year-old Washington on July 1. At the time he was leading the Southern league in batting (.361), runs scored (64), total bases (168), doubles (23), and stolen bases (33).

"When I leave Birmingham," he told his teammates, "I'm never coming back. My goal was to make it up here by the time I was 21. … Now that I'm here (with the A's), I want to stay."[13]

Washington made his big-league debut against the Baltimore Orioles on July 5, 1974. Pinch-hitting for second baseman Ted Kubiak, he flied out to left. The game that really opened people's eyes to Washington came three days later. A sellout crowd of 47,582 was on hand at the Oakland Coliseum because Cleveland Indians pitcher Gaylord Perry, who was 15-1, was on the mound attempting to win his AL record-tying 16th consecutive victory. Serving as Oakland's DH and hitting second in the order, Washington was making his first major-league start. Perry struck him out in his first at-bat, but Washington got his first big-league hit, a triple, in the eighth inning.

Perry and A's starter Vida Blue were both going the distance in what would become a 10-inning game. With the Indians leading 3-2 in the bottom of the ninth, Gene Tenace drove in the tying run with a sacrifice fly. In the bottom of the 10th Washington drove in pinch-runner John Odom with a single for the winning run. He had played the role of spoiler, and despite striking out 13, Perry was tagged with his second loss of the season.

Impressed, *New York Times* sportswriter Leonard Koppett wrote, "Gaylord Perry's winning streak is over, and in the long run the player who ended it may become the better remembered of the two."[14] A's manager Alvin Dark said of Washington, "He has the kind of future you really get excited about."[15]

"He was very impressive even before the winning hit," said A's captain Sal Bando, "He was relaxed, waiting on pitches instead of lunging. He has strong wrists and forearms."[16]

"That's when I knew," said Washington, "that I'd be here for good."[17]

Washington told sportswriters he had never even heard of Perry before a televised game in Boston in late June. Asked if he was nervous, Washington replied, "I don't know anything about him. I wasn't nervous because I was concentrating too hard."[18]

Owner Charles Finley, in what he called a "retroactive pay raise," gave Washington a $500 bonus for the Perry game and another $2,000 for a 5-for-5 performance in Detroit on August 30.[19] For his part, Washington went 3-for-4 in a rematch against Perry in late July.

The team had to make some adjustments for Washington with his arrival, adjustments that Washington acknowledged may have stepped on some toes. "They moved Joe Rudi from left to first to make room for me. He didn't want to make the transition. I don't blame him. He was a Gold Glove out there. I understand that." Speaking about his relationship with A's superstar Reggie Jackson, Washington said, "Reggie might have acted better. I was stealing his thunder at the time, getting a lot of media attention that used to be his."[20]

In 73 games with the A's Washington batted .285 with six stolen bases in 14 attempts, five triples, and 19 RBI.

Washington always maintained a sense of humor and a "Joe Cool" attitude about his performance. Asked how excited he was playing in the World Series as a 20-year-old rookie, Washington said, "Not very. I get more excited watching pro basketball games on TV."[21]

In the 1974 postseason, despite losing Game One, the A's came back to win the best-of-five ALCS 3-1 over the Orioles. Washington hit .273 (3-for-11) in that series with a pinch-hit double in Game One, a 6-3 loss to the Orioles. The A's went on to claim their third straight world championship, defeating the Los Angeles Dodgers in five games. Washington appeared in every postseason game, including starts in Games Four and Five of the World Series. He was 4-for-7 (.571) with a .625 on-base percentage.

On Opening Day of 1975 Washington became the youngest player (20 years and 220 days old) to start on Opening Day for the A's. He played left field and batted eighth. For the season Washington led the team in batting average (.308) and stolen bases (40). He became the regular left fielder and because of his speed and tendency to hit line drives, manager Alvin Dark had him bating third. He played 114 games in left field. He hit his first major-league homer on April 16, off Kansas City Royals right-hander Nelson Briles in Kansas City.

Washington had an outstanding first half of the season (.315, 100 hits, and 32 steals) that he was picked to play in the All-Star Game. Asked if it was his biggest thrill of the year to be named to the AL squad, Claudell quipped, "No, Watching the movie' *Jaws* was. … Man, that scared me to death."[22]

Washington had a much more serious scare just a few days before the All-Star Game, when he experienced blackouts and dizzy spells. After a series of medical tests, he was cleared to play. In his first of two All-Star appearances, Washington went 1-for-1, with a single and a stolen base.

He finished the season second in steals (40), fifth in batting average (.308), and fourth in hits (182); He hit 10 homers and 7 triples, and drove in 77 runs.

As for the team itself, the A's were unable to bounce back from the offseason loss of Catfish Hunter, and were swept by the Boston Red Sox in the ALCS.

Before the start of the 1976 season, new A's manager Chuck Tanner moved Washington from left field to right field, a position he would play most of his career. Washington's defense was suspect, and he would carry the label as a below-average outfielder. He had, in fact, led the American league in outfield errors in 1976, with 11. Regardless of offensive production, the fourth outfielder/platoon stigma seemed to continue to plague him the rest of his career. Offensively, Washington was still productive. Despite a mediocre .257 batting average, his speed enabled him to steal 37 bases and leg out six triples.

The A's dynasty began to fall further apart with the advent of free agency. After Hunter became a free agent before the 1975 season, Reggie Jackson signed with the Orioles during the spring of '76. This was the beginning of the end, as most of the championship team began to become dismantled. During spring training of 1977, Washington himself left the A's in the first of five career trades. On March 26 he was dealt to the Texas Rangers for second baseman Rodney Scott, left-handed pitcher Jim Umbarger, and cash.

Although he got off to a hot a start with his new club (Washington was hitting .348 in late June), he was unhappy with what he felt was a lack of leadership and teaching of fundamentals. "Nobody was taking charge, not the manager … anybody. … Neither manager Frank Lucchesi nor any of his coaches had bothered to go over such things as cutoff plays."[23]

Washington also wasn't given any explanations regarding his playing time. "After Frank Lucchesi was fired as manager they brought in Billy Hunter. … I was hitting .366, playing every day. The Royals came to town for a doubleheader, with two lefties pitching. I had six hits and seven RBIs. That evening Hunter called me into his office and said Kurt Bevacqua would play against lefties. No explanation. No nothing."[24]

"That ticked me off," said Washington. "From then on I couldn't deal with it. And the tag followed me my whole career."*[25]

Washington played only one full season with Texas, finishing with a .284 batting average, 21 steals, 12 homers 68 RBIs, and 112 strikeouts. On May 16, 1978, the Rangers traded him to the Chicago White Sox with outfielder Rusty Torres for Bobby Bonds for Washington.

It was a troubled season for Washington. He reported to the White Sox 112 hours after the trade. (A traded player generally had 72 hours to join his new team.) Apparently he had been nursing a sore ankle, an injury he claimed he had sustained playing basketball during the offseason.

White Sox owner Bill Veeck was furious at the Rangers for dealing what he referred to as "damaged goods." The Rangers "told us that he would be ready to play the next day (after the trade). Obviously, that wasn't the case," Veeck complained.[26] Veeck went so far as to lobby the league for additional compensation. American League President Lee MacPhail upheld the trade, ruling that "There was no apparent fraud of deceit on the part of the Texas club."[27]

In Chicago Washington gained a reputation for lackadaisical play and loafing. "I never had anything against playing for Chicago," he said. "But I was depressed at being traded twice in a short time, so I didn't come here with a positive attitude."[28]

Washington played in only one game for an entire month after the trade, hitting the disabled list almost right away. He finished his first season with the White Sox playing in 86 games (he played 12 with the Rangers), hitting .264 with 6 home runs, and 31 RBIs. He again played poorly in the outfield, making eight errors.

The next year was no different. Washington made seven errors in right field. South Siders showed their displeasure in many ways. During a game at Comiskey Park, a banner in right field sarcastically read "Washington Slept Here." There were more serious incidents. "They (the fans) threw M-80s [firecrackers] at me in the outfield," he said.[29]

One of the few highlights of Washington's Chicago career came on July 14, 1979. In a game against the Tigers he launched home runs off pitchers Steve Baker, Milt Wilcox, and Dave Tobik. In the 12-4 White Sox victory, Washington went 3-for-5 with five RBIs and three runs scored

After two trying seasons in Chicago, the Sox traded Washington to the New York Mets on June 7, 1980, for career minor-league pitcher Jesse Anderson. The lowly Mets saw in Washington a much-needed left-handed power bat. His stay in New York was brief, but there was no lack of effort. "He plays hard and he seems to like the atmosphere around here," said Mets manager Joe Torre. "A guy who isn't happy wouldn't play as well as he has for us." Summarizing Washington's career, Torre said, "He's probably a guy who can play regularly but not in our situation where we use four outfielders."[30]

Washington had only one hit in his first 17 at-bats with the Mets, but broke out of his slump in a big way two weeks after joining the team. On June 22, in the Mets' 9-6 win at Dodger Stadium, he had another three-homer performance, hitting them off Dave Goltz (twice) and Charlie Hough. At the time he was one of only three players to hit three home runs in a game in both leagues (Johnny Mize and Babe Ruth were the other two). 11 others have accomplished the feat since for a total of 14.

Washington created a stir when he became a free agent after the 1980 season. Rejecting a contract extension offer from the Mets, he signed a five-year deal with the Atlanta Braves. The $3.5 million contract made Washington one of the highest paid players in baseball. Front-office executives throughout the game were unhappy with owner Ted Turner's new prize, fearful that the deal would affect the free-agent market, that other players who had generally underperformed might ask for similar money, if not higher.

"People talked about me being an ordinary outfielder because of the numbers in Chicago," said Washington. "But I hit 10 home runs and drove in 42 runs in 79 games in New York. I was ready and I was swinging the bat good. It was a good investment for Atlanta."[31]

In the end, Washington had some of his most productive seasons with the Braves. In 1981, he hit .291 to lead the team and picked up his defense, finishing third in fielding percentage among right fielders (.993). In 1982 Washington had one of his best all-around seasons, proving some of his detractors wrong and showing that he still had athleticism, durability, and talent. Washington played a career-high 150 games, hitting 16 home runs and a career-high 80 RBI. His running game picked up as well; his 33 steals were his most since the 1976 campaign with Oakland.

The 1982 Braves were a talented bunch with Bob Horner, Dale Murphy, and Chris Chambliss. The team won the National League West after a tight race with the Dodgers and Giants. But they lost three straight to St. Louis and were eliminated in the NLCS. Washington was 3-for-9 with a couple of walks in what turned out to be his last postseason games.

In his fourth season with the Braves, Washington hit career-high 17 home runs. He was once again selected as an All-Star. In a 3-1 NL win at Candlestick Park, he was 1-for-2 as a right-field replacement for Darryl Strawberry.

Despite the accomplishments on the field, it was off-the-field issues with substance abuse that put Washington into the headlines. He entered rehab in 1983 for use of cocaine and was arrested in 1985 for possession of marijuana. He was one of the players implicated in the Pittsburgh cocaine trials and was suspended for 60 days by Commissioner Peter Ueberroth. Like other players, however, Washington was able to avoid serving the suspension after donating a percentage of his salary to drug-treatment programs.

Instead of letting Washington leave the Braves as a free agent after the 1985 season, Ted Turner offered him a one-year deal. Washington initially turned down the offer until manager Chuck Tanner offered him a starting spot in right field and a leadoff spot in the order in 1986. "I don't care about what happened in the past," said Tanner. "What happened with anybody else doesn't mean anything to me."[32]

Apparently the Yankees agreed. On June 30 they acquired Washington and utility infielder Paul Zuvella in exchange for veteran outfielder Ken Griffey, Sr. and utilityman Andre Robertson. Between Atlanta and New York, Washington had rather unremarkable numbers: 94 games played, 11 home runs, 30 RBI, and 10 stolen bases. He re-signed with the Yankees after the season.

Washington's 2½ years in New York after the trade would have to be considered a success, with 1988 being his last great season. At the age of 33, he was able to stay healthy enough for 126 games, most of which were played in center field. He had an impressive .308/.342/.442 slash line and hit 11 homers, drove in 64 runs, and stole 15 bases. His off-the-field issues seemingly in the rear-view mirror, Washington also had the admiration of his teammates.

"Claudell's someone who has the respect of everybody. He's the one who gets us up when we're down," said Don Mattingly.[33] "He's done everything we asked," said manager Lou Piniella. "And he's been a force as far as chemistry and leadership on this club."[34]

The 1988 club managed to stay in the race most of the season, while Washington had some memorable moments. On April 20 in a road game against the Minnesota Twins, Washington hit the 10,000th home run in Yankees history, the most of any franchise. Near the end of the season he hit his only two career walk-off home runs in a span of three days. On September 9, in the second game of a crucial four-game series against the Detroit Tigers, Washington hit a solo shot in the bottom of the ninth off Walt Terrell. Two days later in the series finale, Washington hit a dramatic 18th-inning home run to complete a sweep and move the Yankees into sole possession of second place. His two-run homer off Tigers closer Willie Hernandez ended one of the longest games in Yankees history, an 18-inning marathon that last 6 hours and 1 minute.

During the offseason, Washington signed with the California Angels as a free agent. Angels GM Mike Port told the *Los Angeles Times* why the team made the decision to sign the free agent: "First, Claudell did hit .300 in the American League last year and he

played center field in (spacious) Yankee Stadium,"…
But we wanted him for his less tangible skills as well."[35]

Washington finished just one year of a three-year contract. He was traded a fifth and final time on April 29, 1990, back to the Yankees. The Angels sent Washington and reliever Rich Montelone to New York in exchange for outfielder Louis Polonia. Washington played just 33 games with the Yankees and retired after being released during the offseason.

By 2004, Washington was running a construction company in Oakland and was married to Denise Nolden, president of Contra Costa College in San Pablo, California. He was previously married to Cynthia Anita Callaway. The couple had three children, Camille Snowden, Claudell Washington III, and Crystal, who died in 2007. Except for A's alumni reunion events, he largely remained out of the spotlight.

NOTES

1 Gerry Fraley, "Puzzling Claudell Thinks Positive," *The Sporting News*, April 11, 1986.

2 Bruce Markusen, *A Baseball Dynasty: Charlie Finley's Swingin' A's* (Haworth, New Jersey: St. Johann Press, 2002) .309.

3 Leonard Koppett, "Rookie Who Beat Perry Touted," *New York Times*, July 10, 1974.

4 Ron Bergman, "A's Discover Mr. Kleen in Super Wash," *The Sporting News*, August 9, 1975.

5 Steve Kroner, "Second hit was a single highlight for Washington," *San Francisco Chronicle*, July 17, 2004.

6 Dave Anderson, "The Kid in Left Field for the A's," *Sports of the Times*, Hall of Fame file , October 18, 1974.

7 Bergman, "A's Discover."

8 Anderson.

9 Ibid.

10 Bergman, "A's Discover."

11 Ibid.

12 Wayne Martin, "Claudell Washington Blooming in A's New Crop at Birmingham," *The Sporting News*, June 29, 1974.

13 Ron Bergman, "Hot Swinger Claudell—Another Finley Find," *The Sporting News*, September 28, 1974.

14 Koppett.

15 Ibid.

16 Ibid

17 Anderson.

18 "Who's Gaylord? A 's Hero Didn't Know," *Akron Beacon Journal*, July 9, 1974.

19 Markusen.

20 Michael Kay, "Claudell takes center stage," *New York Post*, July 24, 1987.

21 Unidentified news clipping, November 8, 1974, from Washington's Hall of Fame player file.

22 Thomas Rogers, article from July 8, 1975 found in Washington's Hall of Fame file.

23 *The Sporting News*, June 11, 1977.

24 "Claudell Takes Center Stage: Road Warrior Finally Finds Home in Bronx," *New York Post*, July 14, 1987.

25 *Ibid. This may be a Washington quote but facts don't reflect his comments. Hunter came to the Rangers as manager in late June when Washington was hitting under .320. His quote seems to indicate or suggest having six hits and seven RBIs against the Royals in a doubleheader. Retrosheet does not show a doubleheader being played between Texas and Kansas City. Nor does the record show Bevacqua playing against the Royals for Texas in 1977.)

26 Joe Goddard, "White Sox Are Up In Arms Over Washington's Ankle," *The Sporting News*, June 10, 1978.

27 "A.L. Rejects Chisox Protest," unattributed July 8, 1978, article in Washington's Hall of Fame player file.

28 Richard Dozer, "ChisoxClaudell Joins Elite: 3 HR Salvo," *Chicago Tribune*, August 4, 1979.

29 Kay.

30 Jack Lang, *New York Daily News*, August 2, 1980.

31 Larry Whiteside, "He's Still Bouncing: Angel Claudell Washington Lands on His Feet Again," *Boston Globe*, May 26, 1989, 71.

32 "Puzzling Claudell Thinks Positive," unattributed April 11, 1986, article in Washington's Hall of Fame player file.

33 Kay.

34 Ibid.

35 John Weyler, "A Leading Man: Angels Signed Washington for More Than His Playing Ability," *Los Angeles Times*, March 14, 1989.

Herb Washington

By Rory Costello

Charles O. Finley indulged in many whims as owner of the A's—and hiring world-class sprinter Herb Washington was one of his most fanciful experiments. Washington's stint with Oakland (1974 and early 1975) was just part of Finley's longstanding infatuation with "designated runners." The track star was the second of six specialists whom the A's employed in this role from 1967 through 1978. Washington didn't have the longest tenure—Allan Lewis did—but he got by far the most press.

That status was often controversial. Washington came to Oakland without having played baseball since the summer between his sophomore and junior years in high school.[1] His presence on the roster raised even more eyebrows—and voices—among teammates than Allan Lewis had during his six partial seasons with the A's. The other specialists appeared on occasion in the field or at bat, but Washington never did either. What's more, the pure speed of "Hurricane Herb" did not translate into high base-stealing success—he swiped 31 in 48 attempts (65 percent).

As a result, his statistical value was slightly negative, and the team could well have benefited more from a more fully rounded reserve. Yet looking back, Washington contended, "If you ranked the players on that team [in 1974] from 1 to 25, I think my value was higher than the 25th player. If I was the 25th in terms of value, I'll take it."[2]

Nonetheless, Washington's baseball career was a unique and memorable oddity—no other baseball card besides his 1975 Topps entry has shown "Pinch Run." as a player's position. Much more significant, though, is how this bright and personable man went on to great success in business. Washington's company, H.L.W. Fast Track, Inc., became the largest African-American-owned McDonald's franchisee in the United States. He has given much back to his com-munity and schools. "Life's pretty good," he said contentedly in 2014.[3]

Herbert Lee Washington was born on November 16, 1951, in Belzoni, Mississippi. This is a small town in the Delta region on the Yazoo River; today the area is best known for catfish farming. Herb was the eldest of four children born to Willie B. Washington and his wife, Mary (née Haynes). He had a brother named Willie and two sisters, Georgia and Renea.

The Washington family moved to Flint, Michigan, when Herb was around one year old. His parents sought work in the auto plants. "Washington worked there too, for two summers, and learned the one thing he didn't want to do for a living."[4]

Herb grew up on the north side of Flint and attended Parkland Elementary School and Emerson Junior

High. He first realized that he had truly exceptional speed "probably when I was 11 years old, I was in fifth grade."[5]

After going to Northern High School in Flint for a year, he had to transfer to the city's Central High School because of an issue with school boundaries. He then began to compete in indoor track meets all over the country. In March 1968, in Milwaukee, the 16-year-old ran the 50-yard dash in 5.1 seconds. His time was tied with Charlie Greene, who won an Olympic gold medal in the 4x100 relay several months later, but Greene was declared the winner. Herb's track coach at Flint Central, Carl Krieger, said, "The pictures in the papers the next day proved Washington won."

Of greater interest, though, were Krieger's comments on Washington as a person. "Herb is good because he's intensely competitive. He has drive and concentration. Charlie Greene is noted for trying to unnerve his opponents and he tried it on Herb at Milwaukee. But it didn't work. Herb has superb legs and he trains hard. He's an intense listener and follows directions. There's not much more you can ask."[6]

Washington ran another 5.1 50 later in March—an unofficial world record.[7] After graduating from Flint Central, he attended Michigan State University in the state capital, Lansing. In 2004 he remembered, "My dad once told me that 'If Michigan State is dumb enough to offer you a scholarship, you better be smart enough to come home with a degree." Herb stressed the need to prepare student-athletes if they couldn't make it to the next level. "An injury can take your playing career away, but they can't take your education away."[8]

Washington earned a B.S. degree in education.[9] In addition, he met his wife-to-be, Gisele Gibbs, at MSU. Herb was still a bachelor while he was with Oakland; the couple got married on May 24, 1980. They had two children, a son named Terrell and a daughter named Arielle, who both also went to MSU.

As a freshman, Washington lost a race to another 1968 Olympian, John Carlos (best known for his Black Power salute on the medal stand in Mexico City). It was a big lesson, as Herb remembered in 2007. "I'd never been run down from behind. I'm in tears. And Carlos comes up to me and says, 'Schoolboy, you just stopped running.' I never forgot that."[10]

Washington played wide receiver for the Spartans football team as a sophomore and junior. Ahead of the 1969 season, he caught a long touchdown pass in the Green-White intrasquad game.[11] A report a couple of days later added that he had been making some fine catches in practice as a flanker.[12] However, he had just one reception—for 41 yards—in a regular-season game. He quit the heavily run-oriented team in October 1970 after appearing in just one game as a junior.[13]

Track remained Washington's main focus in college. In February 1970, at the Michigan State Relays, he beat John Carlos in a rematch.[14] The following month, the 18-year-old again tied his record of 5.1 seconds in the 50-yard dash—twice.[15] In February 1971, he tied the world record in the 60-yard dash, again at the Michigan State Relays.[16]

Though Washington had bypassed football as a senior, his extraordinary speed was still attractive to the National Football League. Especially after Olympic gold medalist Bob Hayes became a star with the Dallas Cowboys in the 1960s, many teams took a flyer on sprinters. On February 2, 1972, the Baltimore Colts selected Washington in the 13th round (out of 17) of the NFL draft. He was asked to report to a Colts orientation in early March, but informed the club that he was committed to competing in the Big Ten Conference meet.[17] Plus, Washington's big goal in 1972 was to make the US Olympic track team, and at that time amateur status was a much stricter requirement.

Just two days after being drafted, Washington set a new world indoor record of 5.0 seconds in the 50-yard dash, which also tied the outdoor mark.[18] A mere eight days later, he set the world indoor record in the 60-yard dash, once more at the Spartan Relays meet. His time of 5.8 seconds beat his own best of 5.9—a mark originally set in 1964 by none other than Bob Hayes.[19]

In late June and early July, the Olympic track trials took place in Eugene, Oregon. Many talented sprinters were competing, and Washington finished fifth in the finals in his event, the 100 meters.[20] In 1974, he admitted to being nervous. He added that at that time, he was better sprinting indoors than outdoors.[21]

The disappointment in Eugene meant that Washington was free to go to the Colts' pre-season training camp, which began on July 19. Newspapers reported that he mulled over Baltimore's offer but left immediately after reporting because he still had hopes of gaining a spot on the Olympic team (ostensibly as an alternate).[22] In 2014, however, Washington said, "We couldn't agree to a price—simple as that. What they were offering for a signing bonus was an insult. I made more than that under the table running track!"[23]

In February 1973 Washington equaled his own world indoor record in the 50-yard dash. It came in the same place as his mark from a year before, Toronto. He continued to compete in Amateur Athletic Union (AAU) events over the course of the year. Hasely Crawford, the 1976 Olympic gold medalist from Trinidad and Tobago, beat Herb in February—but for the rest of the year, Washington didn't lose a single sprint.[24]

That December, Oakland assigned pinch-runner Allan Lewis outright to Triple-A Tucson, and he never played again. Going into the 1974 season, however, Charlie Finley still wanted a pinch-runner on the A's roster. Alvin Dark (who had been named to replace Dick Williams as manager in February 1974) suggested Washington, whom he had seen win many televised races.

Washington had been working as a TV and radio broadcaster with WJIM in Lansing. Late that January, he said, "The big thing is the last letter in my station's call letters—M for money. If the bonus is big enough, I'll become a pro [in track]. I hope to break the world record in the 50 at Toronto. That should make me more salable."[25] At various points in 1974, press articles said Washington had been competing on the pro track

tour, but that was not so. The International Track Association (ITA), a professional circuit, was founded in 1973, but Washington did not join it until after the 1974 season.[26]

Despite his layoff, Herb was still interested in pro football. The brand-new World Football League was getting ready to play its first season, and in February 1974, Washington expressed a desire to try out for the Michigan franchise, the Detroit Wheels.[27] He also said that he was on the verge of signing with the Toronto franchise—but then Finley called.[28]

"When I got the message, I thought it was a joke," Washington recalled in 2007. "Then, I got paged. He said, 'Herbie, I want you to play baseball and be a pinch-runner.' I said, 'Mr. Finley, I'm going to need a no-cut contract. I know sometimes you just get rid of people.' He said, 'A no-cut contract? The only players who have those are Vida Blue, Catfish Hunter and Reggie Jackson! Are you telling me you're in the same league as those guys?' I said, 'No, but none of those guys can outrun me.'"[29]

Finley predicted, "I feel [Washington] will be personally responsible for winning ten games this year."[30] According to a January 1975 article, Alvin Dark counted nine games that Herb won for the A's by stealing a base that eventually led to the lead or winning run. A's captain Sal Bando, Washington's most outspoken critic, sniped, "Yeah, but how many games did he lose?"[31] In retrospect, Washington's calm but pointed comment was, "A captain is supposed to lead by example." As for Dark, he said, "I had a very positive personal experience with Alvin."[32]

The truth lay somewhere in between Dark's hyperbole and Bando's negativity. "Finley's Folly" came on to run in 92 games in 1974; a play-by-play study shows that many of his 29 runs scored came when his team was already comfortably ahead. His finest moment came on August 2; at Chicago, he scored the go-ahead run in the eighth inning after stealing second and coming home from there on a single. Vida Blue made the lead stand up.

Herb scored the winning run in two other games (on June 22 and July 3), but his speed was not a factor in either tally. In several other games, his runs scored were significant parts of victory, either helping the A's to come back, tie the game, go ahead, or gain needed insurance. The most notable of those came on July 8, at home against Cleveland. Gaylord Perry, who was riding a 15-game winning streak, took a 3-2 lead into the ninth inning. But with one out, Joe Rudi tripled, and the tying run came in because Washington entered and his speed enabled him to come home on a short sacrifice fly to left-center. "George Hendrick said he was going to throw me out, and he threw the ball into the backstop," Washington remembered with a laugh.[33] The A's then beat Perry in the tenth.

On the flip side, when Herb was caught stealing (16 out of 45 attempts), most of the time it didn't do any damage. There were three exceptions, when he got nailed while representing the tying run in pitchers' duels that the A's lost (on August 11, August 19, and September 25).

With his minimal baseball experience, Washington had to overcome several obstacles. The first was learning how to shift gears and turn on the basepaths, as opposed to blasting straightaway as he could do on the track. The second was learning how to slide. The third and most important was learning about the pitchers and catchers and how to pick his opportunities. "I have a world of reactions I've got to hone down to where they're instinctive," he told *Sports Illustrated* in June 1974.[34]

To start that process, the A's brought in one of the all-time greatest baserunners, Maury Wills. Looking back after the season ended, Washington said, "I only had six days in training camp with Maury. … It was a cram session and I didn't begin to relate to many of the things he talked about until July."[35] He didn't get the hang of feet-first sliding and stuck with going in headfirst.[36]

Washington did shag balls in the outfield during batting practice (upon the signing, Finley had talked about the possibility of giving him some action there).

He also got to take some swings in BP. Still, many stars—such as Reggie Jackson, Gene Tenace, and Texas Rangers pitcher Ferguson Jenkins—said in so many words that Washington wasn't a ballplayer, and that he was taking a roster spot that belonged to a pro who had paid his dues.[37]

Washington didn't get the cold shoulder from everyone, but eventually the grumbling prompted him to stand up for himself in a team meeting, showing the confidence and pride he had developed as a sprint champion. As a result, he could sit in the back of the team bus and give as good as he got in the repartee with Bando and Tenace.[38] "Gene Tenace was always good-natured about the riding," Washington recalled. "It was just what the 'rook' had to go through."[39] His teammates also gave Herb a glove and bat to dress up his locker.[40]

Having a good sense of humor helped Washington's situation a great deal. One of his favorite memories of his time with the A's featured an opposing catcher, Thurman Munson of the New York Yankees. Munson had a solid record of throwing out enemy base stealers: 38 percent lifetime, with very little fluctuation from year to year. Yet Washington was 3-for-3 against the Yankee captain-to-be, who also committed two throwing errors on those thefts. As Herb told the story in both 2002 and 2004, Munson told him before one game, "My grandmother could throw you out."

The next day during batting practice, Washington said, "Hey Thurman, there's a call for you in the clubhouse." After a suspicious Munson asked who it was, Herb responded, "It's your grandmother. They're going to bring her up."[41]

Though Washington was well liked as a person, Bill North—a first-rate base-stealer—turned out to be his best friend on the club. They got adjoining rooms on the road. As Herb told Leonard Koppett of the *New York Times*, "He was open with me. He told me he didn't like the job I was given to do, but that he liked me—and he's helped me as much as he can all along."[42] Vida Blue was also a comrade.

Washington pinch-ran twice in the AL Championship Series against Baltimore. Both times he was caught stealing, first by Elrod Hendricks in Game Two (the A's were up 2-0 but then added three more runs) and then by Andy Etchebarren in Game Three (the A's led 1-0 and that was how it ended).

The focal point of Washington's baseball career came in Game Two of the 1974 World Series at Dodger Stadium. Alas, it was a mistake. Dodgers starter Don Sutton took a 3-0 lead into the ninth inning, but he hit Bando with a pitch and gave up a double to Jackson. Iron man reliever Mike Marshall relieved Sutton, and Rudi then singled to cut the lead to one run. Rather than sacrifice, Dark left Rudi in while power-hitting Tenace was up, but after Tenace struck out, Washington came on.

Marshall was known for his pickoff move, which was self-developed, unorthodox—and highly effective. Vin Scully, calling the game for NBC, said, "Marshall, for a right-hander, is *very* quick in coming over to first base." Being the Dodgers broadcaster, Scully had seen it often.

The first pitch to Ángel Mangual, batting for Blue Moon Odom, was a strike. Marshall made one soft toss over to first. He then stepped off the rubber three times, feinted once, but didn't throw. In 1988, Charlie Finley said, "I remember telling the person I was with that Marshall was playing possum. ... Don't be surprised if he picks him off."[43] Sure enough, Marshall whipped a sudden throw over and caught Washington leaning the wrong way. Scully said, "He really set him up. ... He is hung out to dry." Steve Garvey applied the tag. By coincidence, both Garvey and Marshall were also MSU Spartans.

Washington pounded the ground and said, "Damn." Said Finley, "If I'd had a lever that would have dropped me out of the stadium, I'd have pulled it. I felt as if the whole world was looking at me and laughing."[44] With the wind out of Oakland's sails, Mangual then struck out on two more pitches, and the Dodgers got their only win of the Series. "I had never seen [Washington] on the basepaths until today," said Marshall. "I was his teacher. He was my student. I taught him child growth and development."[45] The pitcher wasn't drawing a condescending analogy—that was in fact their relationship while Washington was studying education at Michigan State.

Despite Washington's tenuous position among his teammates, none of them came down on him for the faux pas. Even Tenace, who had been critical of the roster choice early on, said, "He's a tremendous person, and he has done a tremendous job for us. I'll say this about him, he adjusted. ... You have to give him credit for that. I know I do. I really like the guy. He made up his mind it didn't matter to him what people thought, he was going to do his job, and he did." Dark also gave a supportive pat on the butt, and Jackson took the time to sit down next to Washington for a little pep talk on the bus ride from Dodger Stadium to the airport.[46]

Washington's confidence was not damaged; he said that the Dodgers would hear from him before it was over. It didn't quite work out that way, but he did at least get to appear in two more World Series games. He came on for Tenace in the eighth inning of Game Three, with the A's up 3-2 and seeking an insurance run, but he remained at first as the next two batters both made outs. Then in Game Four, after Jim Holt's pinch double capped Oakland's winning four-run rally in the sixth inning, Washington replaced Holt—but was immediately forced out at second.

After the A's polished off the Dodgers, Washington participated fully in the celebration. One wire-service photo showed him with upturned face as pitcher Darold Knowles sat atop the lockers and poured down champagne. He got a full Series share of $22,210, but later pointed out, "They didn't have a say. If you were there for the full season, it was automatic. I was one of the voters." He remembered some ribbing about what might have happened if he'd been there just part of the time.[47]

During the following offseason, Washington ran with the International Track Association. He found training for baseball easier than the regimen for track—but he also admitted, "You don't have to be fast to steal [bases]. There are two things more important than speed. One is knowledge of the pitcher and the other is the jump you get. Put them together and you compensate for the speed factor."[48]

In his second year, Washington was looking forward to developing and applying these skills further.[49] Near the end of spring training in 1975, however, the A's bought the contract of minor-league outfielder Don Hopkins from the Montreal Expos. Hopkins was another speedster from Michigan. In fact, he once ran the 100-yard dash against Washington in 1969 and finished second (his time was 9.5 seconds, 0.2 behind Washington).[50] Hopkins had stolen a lot of bases — 224 in 340 minor-league games from 1970 through 1974 — but hit just .249 with no homers and few extra bases. Still, he was a pro ballplayer — although Oakland released veteran outfielder Jesús Alou to make room for "Hoppy."

Charlie Finley proclaimed, "We're going to keep both [Hopkins and Washington]. These two pinch-runners are going to help us as our 24th and 25th players. … We used to pitch teams to death and now we're going to run and hit them to death." Dark toed the company line, though Bando shook his head in disbelief. Finley's sarcastic response was, "I don't know what the manager's committee will say. You know, the players on the team who think they run the club."[51]

"I questioned it," Washington said of the Hopkins deal. "Then I said maybe we can."[52] But then, on April 28, Oakland also acquired Matt Alexander in a minor-league deal with the Chicago Cubs. Alexander was another very speedy man who could play both the infield and the outfield, plus he wasn't a bad hitter. Reggie Jackson said, "We've got these two new guys — Alexander and Hopkins — and they can do other things, plus they run the bases better than Washington."[53]

"When they got Matt Alexander," said Washington, "there was no way. Not three runners."[54] Actually, the trio did play together briefly — all were used in extra-innings games on May 2 and 3. Herb made his 13th

and final appearance of 1975 on May 4. The next day he was released (Finley gave him the news in person). "I'd feel sorry for him if he were a player," said Sal Bando, with no malice intended.[55]

"We hate to give him up," said Finley, "but we have to because, for one thing, the pennant race is a lot tighter this year. We've got to have pinch-runners who can steal bases and also do some other things." The loss of Catfish Hunter to free agency was also a factor, according to Finley. Washington later explained, "He (Finley) said they might have to carry another pitcher. He didn't think I'd get the kind of experience I needed in the minors."[56]

"I'm not really upset about it," said Washington. "I would have been really disappointed and disillusioned if I didn't expect it. But I still didn't think it would be me when it came to the choice of the three, even though Alexander and Hopkins both can play other positions. I thought that because of what I did last year and how much I learned that I could be a greater asset this year." He added, "This isn't my biggest disappointment. That was when I didn't make the Olympics in 1972."[57]

Finley suggested the possibility that Washington could return late in the 1975 season or in 1976, and Herb believed him.[58] Meanwhile, he planned to get into the food business and to run in professional track events.[59] As it developed, however, Oakland used Hopkins in 82 games in 1975 and Alexander (who missed some time with a broken eye socket) in 63. There still simply wasn't room for Washington.

As late as February 1976, A's beat writer Ron Bergman reported that according to Finley, Washington had phoned a couple of times, but the owner said that Herb would not be with the A's that season.[60] According to Washington, though, "I knew it was over. Once I was gone, I was gone."[61]

Indeed, in October 1975 Oakland had acquired yet another man who would be used largely as a pinch-runner: Larry Lintz, a second baseman by trade. Lintz spent most of 1976 and '77 with the big club, along with Alexander. Hopkins made just three more big-league appearances, in September and October 1976. The A's kept Alexander (whom his teammates regarded as the most complete player of the lot) on the roster for all of 1976 and 1977, but released him at the end of March 1978. Lintz was cut right around the same time.

It's not entirely clear why Finley, in his capacity as general manager, became disenchanted with pinch-running specialists. He did use one more, though: Darrell Woodard, a second baseman who came up in the A's chain at the same time as the all-time king of stolen bases, Rickey Henderson. Woodard got into 33 games from August through October 1978, of which 22 were just as a pinch-runner.

Washington did rejoin the International Track Association in 1975 and came back once more in 1976, but the tour did not complete its final season. After that, he focused on his career with McDonald's, which had started when he got his first franchise in Detroit in the summer of 1975.[62] In 1980 Washington moved from Detroit to Rochester, New York, where he built up a chain of Golden Arches. In 1993, he said, "When I visited Rochester in 1980, I thought, it looks like there are a lot of burger eaters here."[63]

Washington's success in the area won him additional honor. In July 1990 the Board of Governors of the Federal Reserve System appointed him as a director of the Buffalo branch of the Federal Reserve Bank of New York.[64] In January 1992 he was named chairman of the Board of Directors of that institution.

Washington left Rochester in May 1998 to buy 19 McDonald's restaurants in the Youngstown, Ohio, area. He said, "It was about opportunity for really significant growth—nothing else. The city [Rochester] has been great. We've enjoyed it here. But the opportunity is such that when it comes, you have to be ready to seize it."[65]

H.L.W. Fast Track continued its robust growth. It was ranked at number 56 on the 2012 *Black Enterprise* "Top 100"—a list of the largest companies in America

owned by African-Americans.[66] As of early 2012, the company owned 25 McDonald's outlets in a territory spanning from Cleveland to western Pennsylvania. Total employment was about 1,500. Terrell Washington was working with his father as general manager.[67] His sister, Ari, also became an entrepreneur, starting her own boutique public-relations firm in 2010.

Washington also got involved with a different sport—ice hockey. In 2005 the Youngstown SteelHounds joined the Central Hockey League, and Herb was the club's owner. The SteelHounds played three seasons before the CHL terminated the franchise's membership in 2008 amid an ongoing financial dispute.

Michigan State University inducted Herb Washington into its Athletics Hall of Fame in 2000. In September 2010 Herb and his wife, Gisele, made a gift of $250,000 to their alma mater, establishing a scholarship for deserving MSU students who participate in men's varsity track and field. They also designated part of their gift to support the men's track program. Previously, in 2009, Washington had donated $20,000 to an effort to build a new track for Flint's Northwestern High School. He'd given up sprinting, but he still ran four miles about three times a week.[68]

Four decades after Washington ran the basepaths for Oakland, his name still cropped up frequently in baseball discussions. One prominent example came in September 2013, when the Cincinnati Reds called up Billy Hamilton for the first time. Hamilton, a man with blazing speed, had stolen 395 bases in five seasons in the minors, including an astonishing 155 in 2012. Among many articles that name-checked Washington, the *Wall Street Journal* ran one called "Billy Hamilton: The Reds' Designated Runner." Hamilton, however, came up through the minors as a true center fielder, and the Reds did not limit him solely to the specialty role. Cincinnati manager Dusty Baker said, "He's not going to be Herb Washington. ... He's going to be Herb Washington sometimes."[69] In a curious twist, Ari Washington became Hamilton's PR representative.

Herb never had to face a pro curveball, but looking back in 2002, he talked confidently about what might have been. "I felt like if I had spent the time in baseball that I did in track, I could have played. I just had not done the kind of training that was necessary to participate at that level."[70] Yet before that, he took a different tack. Recalling that Alvin Dark offered him a chance to pinch-hit after Oakland had clinched the division in 1974, Washington said, "Something suddenly dawned on me. … If I were to get an at-bat, I'd be just like every other major leaguer. So I turned Alvin down. If I hadn't, I'd have lost my significance."[71]

Reminiscing again in 2014, Washington said, "I was fortunate enough to be on a team with some really talented guys and some good guys. It made me grow up! You gotta depend on yourself as a sprinter, and that was reinforced on the A's."[72]

SOURCES

Grateful acknowledgment to Herb Washington for his memories (telephone interview, January 6, 2014).

Warren, Peter, "Designated Runner: Herb Washington," *Baseball Research Journal*, Society for American Baseball Research, Fall 2011.

Blau, Clifford, "Leg Men," *Baseball Research Journal*, Society for American Baseball Research, Summer 2009.

baseball-reference.com

retrosheet.org

msuspartans.com (Michigan State football statistics)

fpl.info/hallfame/99/washington99.shtml (Flint Public Library—Greater Flint Afro-American Hall of Fame)

msuba-det.org (Michigan State University Black Alumni website)

www.findagrave.com

NOTES

1 Telephone interview, Rory Costello with Herb Washington, January 6, 2014.

2 Telephone interview, Rory Costello with Herb Washington, January 6, 2014.

3 Telephone interview, Rory Costello with Herb Washington, January 6, 2014.

4 "Herb Washington: World-Record Sprinter & Business Success," MSUSpartans.com, February 19, 2007 (msuspartans.com/genrel/021907aac.html)

5 Telephone interview, Rory Costello with Herb Washington, January 6, 2014.

6 Bill Halls, "Washington, Wallace Duel Highlights State Track Meets," Associated Press, May 24, 1968.

7 "Schoolboy Sets World 50-Yard Mark," Associated Press, March 25, 1968. It was unofficial because the International Amateur Athletic Federation did not recognize indoor marks.

8 Joe Scalzo, "Former A's pinch runner pinch-hits for area coaches," *The Vindicator* (Youngstown, Ohio), March 16, 2004, C3.

9 Adrianna Mondore, "One of a Kind," National Baseball Hall of Fame and Museum website, February 11, 2013 (baseballhall.org/news/personality/one-kind)

10 "Herb Washington, World-Record Sprinter & Business Success", MSUSpartans.com, February 19, 2007 (msuspartans.com/genrel/021907aac.html)

11 "Mich. State Greens Rout Whites, 58-13," *Chicago Tribune*, September 14, 1969.

12 Bob Voges, "Good Test in Store for Spartans," Associated Press, September 16, 1969.

13 "MSU Sprinter Washington Quits Football," *Chicago Tribune*, October 21, 1970, C5. One of MSU's starting wide receivers, Gordon Bowdell, had a brief career in the NFL. However, the most successful pass catcher on that team turned out to be tight end Billy Joe DuPree, who played for the Dallas Cowboys from 1973 through 1983.

14 "Carlos Loses Dash at Midwest Meet," *New York Times*, February 14, 1970.

15 "Washington Buzzes 5.1, Ties Record," Associated Press, March 23, 1970.

16 Sandi Genis, "Washington ties sprint record," *The Michigan Daily* (Ann Arbor, Michigan), February 14, 1971, 9.

17 Bert Rosenthal, "Herb Washington, On Way to an Olympic Spot, Hopes to Do as Well with the Colts," Associated Press, February 19, 1972.

18 "Patty Johnson Breaks Record," Associated Press, February 6, 1972.

19 "Spartan Sets World Mark," Associated Press, February 14, 1972.

20 In Munich that August, Rey Robinson and Eddie Hart—the leading American candidates to win a gold medal in the 100-meter dash—were disqualified because the US sprint coach gave them the wrong time for their quarterfinal heat.

21 Kenny Moore, "Eff Ell Wyeing on the Bases," *Sports Illustrated*, June 10, 1974.

22 "Colts open pre-season camp in Tampa July 19," *Baltimore Sun*, July 6, 1972, D5. James H. Jackson, "Sprinter to decide on Colt offer," *Baltimore Sun*, July 9, 1972, B8. Cameron C. Snyder, "Thomas seeks Colt trades," *Baltimore Sun*, July 19, 1972, C1. Fred Girard, " 'Tampa Dew' Welcomes Colts," *St. Petersburg Times*, July 20, 1972, 1-C.

23 Telephone interview, Rory Costello with Herb Washington, January 6, 2014.

24 "Washington Keeps Sprint String Intact," Associated Press, January 29, 1974.

25 "Washington Keeps Sprint String Intact."

26 "I.T.A. Lists '75 Schedule of 17 Meets," *New York Times*, November 20, 1974. This article announced the signing of Washington. Wire service reports from January 12, 1975 also described Washington as "a new face" for the ITA.

27 "Sprint ace wants pro grid career," United Press International, February 23, 1974.

28 Ron Bergman, "Finley's Speed-to-Burn Plan Gives Athletics Sudden Chill," *The Sporting News*, April 6, 1974, 18.

29 "Herb Washington: World-Record Sprinter & Business Success."

30 "Finley Signs Washington as Pinch-Runner for A's," *The Sporting News*, March 30, 1974, 48.

31 "Herb Washington Waiting for Finley's Decision," Newspaper Enterprise Association, January 2, 1975.

32 Telephone interview, Rory Costello with Herb Washington, January 6, 2014.

33 Telephone interview, Rory Costello with Herb Washington, January 6, 2014.

34 Moore, "Eff Ell Wyeing on the Bases."

35 "From basepaths to the cinders," Associated Press, November 20, 1974.

36 "Herb Washington Plans More Thefts," Associated Press, March 18, 1975.

37 Eric Prewitt, "Herb Washington Has Lot to Learn," Associated Press, April 19, 1974.

38 "Herb Washington Waiting for Finley's Decision."

39 Telephone interview, Rory Costello with Herb Washington, January 6, 2014.

40 Eric Prewitt, "Herb Washington on Waivers," Associated Press, May 6, 1975.

41 Jorge L. Ortiz, "Where Are They Now? Herb Washington," *San Francisco Chronicle*, January 13, 2002. Scalzo, "Former A's pinch runner pinch-hits for area coaches."

42 Leonard Koppett, "The Herb Washington Experiment," *New York Times*, August 25, 1974.

43 Ross Newhan, "The World Series: Athletics vs. Dodgers," *Los Angeles Times*, October 14, 1988.

44 Ibid.

45 Ian MacDonald, "Marshall teaches Washington lesson," *Montreal Gazette*, October 15, 1974, 18.

46 Milton Richman, "Herb Washington says LA will hear from him," United Press International, October 15, 1974.

47 Telephone interview, Rory Costello with Herb Washington, January 6, 2014.

48 "From basepaths to the cinders."

49 "Herb Washington Plans More Thefts," Associated Press, March 18, 1975.

50 Ron Bergman, "Happy Charlie Does Jig Over Hippity-Hoppy," *The Sporting News*, April 19, 1975, 5.

51 Bergman, "Happy Charlie Does Jig Over Hippity-Hoppy."

52 "A's Cut Herb Washington; Roger Nelson Joins Club," United Press International, May 6, 1975.

53 Ron Bergman, "Loss of Catfish Hastened Herbie's Farewell," *The Sporting News*, May 24, 1975, 13.

54 "A's Cut Herb Washington; Roger Nelson Joins Club."

55 Eric Prewitt, "Herb Washington on Waivers," Associated Press, May 6, 1975

56 "Washington Eyes Return," Associated Press, June 13, 1975.

57 "A's Cut Herb Washington; Roger Nelson Joins Club." "Pinch Runner Washington Given Release by Champs," *Associated Press*, May 6, 1975.

58 "Washington Eyes Return."

59 Bergman, "Loss of Catfish Hastened Herbie's Farewell," *The Sporting News*, May 24, 1975, 16.

60 Ron Bergman, "Finley Buries All Rumors of A's Departure," *The Sporting News*, February 14, 1976.

61 Telephone interview, Rory Costello with Herb Washington, January 6, 2014.

62 Peter Gammons, "Pro Baseball," *Boston Globe*, June 15, 1975.

63 Franz Lidz, "Whatever Happened To...: Herb Washington," *Sports Illustrated*, July 19, 1993.

64 "Rochester Businessman Named Fed Bank Director," *Buffalo News*, July 21, 1990.

65 Mike F. Molaire, *African American Who's Who, Past & Present, Greater Rochester Area*, Rochester (New York: Norex Publications, 1998), 194.

66 "Black-owned businesses," *The Vindicator*, July 7, 2012.

67 George Nelson, "McDonald's Operator Plans Big Upgrades," *The Business Journal* (Youngstown, Ohio), February 3, 2012.

68 Telephone interview, Rory Costello with Herb Washington, January 6, 2014.

69 Owen Perkins, "Reds expect light September role for Hamilton," MLB.com, August 31, 2013.

70 Ortiz, "Where Are They Now? Herb Washington."

71 Lidz, "Whatever Happened To ... Herb Washington". According to the article, Nolan Ryan was the opposing pitcher, but the record shows that Frank Tanana and Chuck Dobson pitched the last two games for California.

72 Telephone interview, Rory Costello with Herb Washington, January 6, 2014.

Bobby Winkles

By Norm King

We've all had job evaluations, those nerve-racking meetings with the boss where he tells you how well, or poorly, you have done and what to work on to reach the next level. Bobby Winkles found out where he stood one day in 1958 from Walker Cooper, his manager with the Indianapolis Indians of the Triple-A American Association.

"There's just one thing that's keeping you out of the major leagues," said Cooper. "Ability."[1]

Not surprisingly, this rather blunt assessment soon brought the playing career of minor leaguer Bobby Winkles to a rather inglorious end. But it also led to a life in baseball that lasted more than 40 years and included stints as head coach of the powerful Arizona State University Sun Devils (1959-1971) and manager of the California Angels (1973-74), coach with the Oakland Athletics (1974-75), coach with the San Francisco Giants (1976-77), manager of the Athletics (parts of 1977 and 1978), coach and front-office executive with the Chicago White Sox (1979-85), and coach and executive with the Montreal Expos (1986-88).

Bobby Brooks Winkles was born on March 11, 1930, in Tuckerman, Arkansas, to Clifford and Devona (Brooks) Winkles. His family moved to Swifton, Arkansas, when Bobby was 9 years old and he went through school there while living on the family's 80-acre farm. While in school he had a seventh-grade teacher who had a significant impact on his baseball career—future Hall of Fame infielder and Swifton native George Kell. Kell taught Winkles the importance of concentration and practice, and even guided him on which position to play.

"George suggested that I become an infielder, and quickly second base became my favorite position," said Winkles.[2]

After graduating from Swifton High School, Winkles went on to Illinois Wesleyan University and graduated with a degree in philosophy in 1952. The White Sox signed him in 1951while he was still a student and thought enough of his potential to give him a $10,000 bonus. They sent him to their Colorado Springs affiliate in the Class A Western League. Winkles missed the entire 1953 season, spending the year in the US Army infantry. He married Ellie Hoeman that same year; they had two daughters, Kelly and Kristi.

It seems Winkles enjoyed playing in Colorado Springs because he kept returning there. He played 81 games there in 1954, plus another 52 games with the Memphis Chickasaws of the Southern Association. In 1955 he divided his time between the Sky Sox (108 games) and the Charleston Senators of the Triple-A American Association (44 games). He was back in Colorado Springs for 131 games in 1956, while also playing six games for the Tulsa Oilers of the Double-A Texas

League. Maybe Winkles got the hint about his future as a player before he heard Cooper's appraisal, because he wisely used some of his time in Colorado Springs to earn a master's degree in physical education from the University of Colorado.

Overall, Winkles played seven seasons in the minors, and while he batted a respectable .270, he hit only 12 home runs. His defense at shortstop wasn't exceptional, either. In 1957 he committed 42 errors at the position with Tulsa. He wasn't going to replace White Sox shortstop Luis Aparicio, a future Hall of Famer, with those numbers.

It's almost tempting to liken Winkles to Moses because it was at this point that he started performing miracles and leading the children of Arizona State University through the desert.

Soon after the 1958 season ended, Winkles received a telephone call from Clyde Smith, Arizona State's athletic director. After a conversation that lasted 20 minutes or so, Winkles was the school's new baseball coach. The interview didn't take long because Smith had already done his homework.

"There was an important factor that made us decide in favor of Bob Winkles," said Smith. "While he was taking his master's at Colorado, he coached an American Legion team, and I received a letter from a parent whose son played for him. He told of the guidance Bob had given his son in many areas, not just in how to play baseball. We thought he was the kind of coach we wanted. …"[3]

They also obviously wanted a coach who liked a challenge. Winkles took over a program that just two years before had been put on the budget chopping block by school administrators. They allocated the team so little money that it couldn't buy uniforms or equipment, nor could it offer any scholarships. The program survived because of Winkles' predecessor, Mel Erickson, and some spunky students.

"The players formed an 'unofficial' team, appeared in ragtag uniforms, wheedled equipment, playing fields and a schedule and made a good showing," wrote Frank Gianelli. "Press and public sentiment embarrassed A-State into action, and after a conflict of temperaments was settled with some new assignments, the Sun Devils got behind baseball."[4]

At a time when even a field was a dream, the 1959 Sun Devils baseball team would have been a success even if it won only one game. However, the team went 27-18 under Winkles' guidance, and gradually improved until it won the NCAA title for the first time in 1965 with a phenomenal 54-8 record. The Sun Devils won the championship again in 1967 and 1969. The '69 team won 56 games, which at the time was an NCAA record, with 11 losses.[5]

Winkles had a 524-173 won-lost record over his 13-year career at Arizona State, a .752 winning percentage. He sent a number of players on to the major leagues, including Gary Gentry, Sal Bando, Reggie Jackson, and the first-ever pick in the inaugural baseball amateur draft in 1965, Rick Monday.

Winkles remained the Arizona State baseball coach until after the 1971 season, when California Angels general manager Harry Dalton invited him to join the Angels under their new manager, Del Rice. Forsaking the job security he had coaching the Sun Devils, Winkles took the plunge into the major leagues. He also made it clear that the hiring of Rice influenced his decision to accept the offer. "I would not have worked for just any major-league manager," Winkles said. "I've known Del for 10 or 12 years and I have always respected him as a fine coach, manager, and a gentleman."[6]

The changes at the managerial and coaching levels resulted after the Angels went 76-86 in 1971. Hiring Winkles away from college baseball attracted considerable interest from the press, especially because he was not hired as a manager. The decision to go this route was simply a pragmatic one. As one sportswriter put it, "General manager Harry Dalton was seriously debating giving the (manager's) job to Bobby Winkles … (but) eventually concluded that the unprecedented leap from campus to majors would be too great a gamble."[7]

Hiring Rice, who had never managed in the majors before, was a gamble that didn't work out. Though his teams always finished above .500 in his four seasons managing in the Angels' minor-league system, Rice's one year as a major-league manager was unsuccessful. The 1972 Angels finished fifth in the American League West with a 75-80 record (a players strike delayed the start of the season and the team's first seven games were never made up), and team owner Gene Autry wasn't exactly singing at the result. Dalton fired Rice after the season and named Winkles the manager for 1973.

Winkles was not the first college coach to manage in the majors. In fact, two great major-league field bosses had prior experience coaching in the hallowed halls of academia. Hughie Jennings, who managed the Detroit Tigers from 1907 through 1920, had coached at St. Bonaventure University from 1894 through 1897. And no less a sage than the Old Perfessor himself, Casey Stengel, coached at the University of Mississippi in 1914 before going on to a Hall of Fame career managing in the big leagues.

Dalton wasn't the only person who thought that Winkles was the right man for the job. In his preseason prognostications for 1973, United Press International sports editor Milton Richman picked California to win the American League West title, and included Winkles' hiring in his reasoning. "I think their new manager, Bobby Winkles, has a way of getting the most out of the people who work for him," wrote Richman.[8]

Another reason for Richman's optimism was a pre-season trade that brought Frank Robinson to the Angels from the Los Angeles Dodgers, where he had had a mediocre season in 1972, with only 19 home runs, 59 RBIs, and a .251 batting average in 103 games. The Dodgers may have regretted the trade right from Opening Day, when Robinson hit the first pitch he saw as an Angel for a home run to help Winkles win his first game as a major-league manager, 2-1 over the Kansas City Royals. President Richard Nixon attended the game and told Winkles that he liked what he saw.

" 'He said he was glad to see the team run to and from their positions,' added Winkles, who makes his club hustle all the time when it's on the field."[9]

That hustle helped the team get off to a very good start, and the Angels were in first place as late as June 27 in a hotly contested division; on that date the fifth-place Minnesota Twins were only two games out. But a horrendous 10-19 record in July ended any chance the Angels had of winning the division, and they finished the season in fourth place in the division with a 79-83 record.

Unlike Rice, Winkles got a second shot and was retained for the 1974 season, which in hindsight might not have been the best move. Winkles and Robinson feuded from the beginning of the season, in part because Winkles had recommended that Robinson be traded. They even argued in the locker room and on the bench, and that may have contributed to the team's 30-44 record when Winkles was fired. What caused the feud depends on what newspaper article you read. An Associated Press piece in June said Winkles may have "resented the fact that some Angel players seem to have more respect for Robinson than Winkles."[10] After Winkles was fired on June 27, the *Baltimore Afro-American* had a different take on the situation: "Winkles admitted resentment of Frank's criticism of players on the team, asserting that Robbie was overstepping the bounds of an ordinary player, and hinting that his behavior was encroachment on his (the manager's) domain."[11]

The bickering would probably have been tolerated if the team had a better record, but the numbers didn't lie. Winkles was let go after the Angels lost, 5-0, at Oakland and was replaced by Dick Williams, who immediately named Robinson team captain.

Winkles barely had time to fill out his unemployment insurance forms when he was hired by the A's as third-base coach on July 9, reuniting him with former Sun Devils Sal Bando and Reggie Jackson. It's not normal for a team to hire a third-base coach in the middle of a season, especially when it is leading its division by 4½ games. But then, this was the A's under owner Charlie Finley, a club that was many things, but normal was not one of them. Not only did the players fight with each other and Finley, but Finley kept a circus atmosphere in the clubhouse with himself as ringmaster.

Before the 1974 season, Alvin Dark, who had replaced the departed Dick Williams as A's manager, had asked Finley for the right to hire his own coaches. Finley turned down the request, but suddenly changed his mind on July 8. With his newfound authority, Dark fired third-base coach Irv Noren and bullpen coach Vern Hoscheit the next day, and replaced them with Winkles and Bobby Hoffman.

The move wasn't popular with the players at the time, but they obviously adjusted because the A's went on to win their third consecutive World Series, in five games over the Los Angeles Dodgers. Winkles was voted a half-share of the winners' share of $22,219.09 per man by the A's players.

Winkles' joy at winning the World Series was tempered on January 26, 1975, when his daughter Kristi, 11 years old, died of a blocked vein in the brain. Despite the tragedy, Winkles continued coaching with the A's in 1975. The team won the West Division again with a 98-64 record, but lost the American League Championship Series in three straight games to the Red Sox.

Winkles didn't return to the A's for 1976. An article in *The Sporting News* said that he was going to operate the restaurant and lounge at the San Clemente Municipal Golf Course.[12] Winkles was a good golfer, and perhaps he was considering that job, but he instead remained in baseball, signing on as a coach just across the Bay with the Giants under manager Bill Rigney. He stayed with the Giants for all of 1976 and part of 1977 when an interesting offer came his way.

Jack McKeon was managing the Oakland A's when the 1977 season began. These were not the dynasty A's of the early 1970s. Bando, Rudi, Tenace, Jackson, Hunter, and the other members of those great teams were long gone. The team's leading hitter for the year

was a rookie, Mitchell Page, who batted .307. With a team of has-beens, yet-to-be's, and never-would-be's, McKeon had a 26-27 record after 53 games, six games out of first place. Nonetheless, after Oakland defeated Cleveland 3-2 on June 8, Finley kicked McKeon upstairs to an executive position, "(a)mid talk of weak team discipline and lack of organization…"[13] Winkles returned to Oakland to take over as manager.

The results were not good. The A's went 37-71 the rest of the season, good enough for last place in the American League West. They even finished a half-game behind the expansion Seattle Mariners. The losing, of course, spawned griping from unhappy players. Earl Williams, among others, said that the team's rookies weren't getting any coaching. "The coaching here is nonexistent," Williams said.[14]

Winkles must have been doing something right because the 1978 A's got off to a hot start. After splitting a doubleheader with the White Sox on May 21, the A's were 24-15 and had a two-game lead in the American League West. Then Winkles upped and quit and was replaced by McKeon. Winkles just couldn't take Finley's constant interference any longer.

"Bobby Winkles, withstanding pleas of his coaches not to quit as A's manager told them, 'I've had enough,'" wrote Dick Young in *The Sporting News*. "I hear that phone ringing in the middle of the night even when it's not ringing."[15]

It's a credit to Winkles' reputation that whenever he was out of work, it wasn't long before opportunity knocked on his door. After the 1978 season, it came via the White Sox. Owner Bill Veeck had hired Don Kessinger as player-manager, and he hired Winkles as a coach. Kessinger never really wanted the job, and wasn't terribly good at it, as he quit after 106 games with the team holding a 46-60 record. Tony LaRussa took his place, thus beginning his stellar managing career, with Winkles continuing as a coach into the 1981 season.

Besides being a year of the baseball strike, 1981 was also the year in which Jerry Reinsdorf bought the

White Sox from Veeck. In a meeting with general manager Roland Hemond, Reinsdorf said he wanted to build from within by teaching young players and not pay for free agents. Hemond knew they had a good teacher in Winkles and so the team named him director of player personnel. Winkles was responsible for nurturing young stars like Ron Kittle and Richard Dotson for the team that won the American League West in 1983 with a 99-63 record.

After several years in the front office, Winkles decided to get back onto the field in 1986, and moved north of the 49th Parallel to become batting coach with the Montreal Expos. His tutelage contributed to an un-expectedly good Expos team in 1987. That squad finished first in the National League in doubles (310) and third in batting average (.265), and third baseman Tim Wallach was second in the league in RBIs with 123. A team that many expected to finish last ended with a 91-71 record, four games out of first.

Winkles stayed in that post for two years, then became the Expos' first-base coach for 1988. Winkles hung up the spikes after that season, but kept involved in the game for several years as a part-time broadcaster for the Expos from 1989 through 1993. After that he retired to California.

Winkles received a number of honors in retirement. In 2001 the baseball field at Arizona State University was named after him. (The facility is called Winkles Field-Packard Stadium at Brock Ballpark.) In 2006 Winkles was one of the inaugural inductees into the College Baseball Hall of Fame.

In reflecting on his career, Winkles was happiest that he never had to look for a job; an offer always came to him.

"I never applied for a job in 43 years," said Winkles. "Somebody always came to me. And that's what I feel proud about."[16]

SOURCES

baseball-reference.com

books.google.ca/books

paperofrecord.hypernet.ca

beachwoodreporter.com/sports

google.com/newspapers

sportsillustrated.cnn.com/vault

web.collegebaseballhall.org

olemisssports.com

web.sbu.edu

NOTES

1   Roger Wallenstein, "Reminiscing With Bobby Winkles," *Beachwood Reporter*, February 26, 2013.

2   James Enright, "Banks Super-Salesman for Cactus Camp Sites," *The Sporting News*, March 29, 1969.

3   Jack Mann, "Red-Hot Baseball in the Valley of the Sun," *Sports Illustrated*, May 24, 1965.

4   Frank Gianelli, "Two Crowns Spotlight Arizona As Capital of College Baseball," *The Sporting News*, July 3, 1965.

5   It is difficult to determine the current NCAA record for victories because there is no consistency in the number of games teams play each season. For example, Wichita State won 68 of 84 games in 1989, but the 1990 champion Georgia Bulldogs won 52 of 71 games (source: ncaa.com/history/baseball/d1).

6   United Press International, "Angels Sign Arizona State Coach," *Palm Beach Post* (West Palm Beach, Florida), December 9, 1971.

7   Dick Young, "Young Ideas," *The Sporting News*, January 1, 1972.

8   Milton Richman, "California, Houston, St. Louis Named Possible Pennant Winners This Season," *Times Union* (Warsaw, Indiana), March 30, 1973.

9   United Press International, "Frank Robinson Makes President Nixon Happy," *Bend* (Oregon) *Bulletin*, April 7, 1973.

10 Associated Press, "Frank Robinson Might be Traded," *Meriden* (Connecticut) *Morning Record*, June 12, 1974.

11 Sam Lacy, "Dick Williams proves he's a politician too," *Baltimore Afro-American*, July 6, 1974.

12 *The Sporting News*, November 29, 1975.

13 Tom Weir, "Disciplinary Collapse Led to McKeon's Exit," *The Sporting News*, June 25, 1977.

14 Tom Weir, "Winkles Batted Down Criticism by Pop-Off A's," *The Sporting News*, October 15, 1977.

15 Young, "Young Ideas," June 10, 1978.

16 Wallenstein, "Reminiscing With Bobby Winkles."

1974 World Series:
"The Twilight Of The Gods"

By Curt Smith

Richard Nixon may have been the greatest baseball student to occupy the presidency. In 1936 Nixon, 23, saw his first big-league game. "I don't remember much about it," he said, "except that the date was July 4, the Washington Senators lost a doubleheader at Griffith Stadium, and a rookie named DiMaggio put one in the seats." In 1957 the now Vice President Nixon took part in an on-field tribute to the Senators' Roy Sievers. Overcome, Sievers broke down. In 1959 the VP spent time with Casey Stengel at an All-Star Game party in Pittsburgh. Stengel, a Democrat, was so wowed by Nixon's baseball knowledge that he left, saying, "That boy there may make me a Republican." In the mid-1960s, Nixon was approached to be both director of the Players Union and to succeed Ford Frick as commissioner, declining because, as he later said, "I had other plans"—winning the presidency in 1968. In 1969, 1970, and 1972, Nixon hosted an All-Star gala at the White House, threw out the first ball at the All-Star Game in Cincinnati, and outlined his all-time All-Star baseball team with son-in-law David Eisenhower, respectively. Sadly, on August 9, 1974, Nixon made history of a different sort, becoming, due to the Watergate scandal, the only man to resign the presidency of the United States.

For Nixon, 1974 bade adieu to his office. For the Oakland A's, 1974 bade faint adieu to an incredible baseball dynasty. Under Stengel, the 1949-53 New York Yankees had won five World Series in a row. The 1972-74 A's were the first team since then to win even three straight—a "three-peat," many said. In 1973-74, Nixon felt power ebbing. In 1974 a close student of the A's could see their dynasty ebbing. "We were still a great team," said longtime announcer Monte Moore, "but not quite as good as we'd been in the past." Let us revisit, to use the title of Wagner's opera *The Twilight of the Gods*—the last year the A's ruled baseball before free agency, among other things, ended Oakland's reign. At the time, it was riveting. Looking back, it is remarkable.

The A's faced 1974 with a new manager with an old past. In 1946-60, Alvin Dark hit .289, was a three-time All-Star, and helped the Braves and Giants win the pennant—1948 (Braves) and 1951 and 1954 (Giants). He was a clutch player, tooled in basics. Hired as 1961 Jints skipper, Dark took the 1962 team within a foot of winning the Series. Later he led the Indians before A's owner Charles O. Finley made him A's skipper for a second time, the first being 1967. His new hiring in 1974 revived a decade-old *Newsday* story by Stan Isaacs quoting Dark as saying black and Hispanic players were "not able to perform up to the white player when it comes to mental alertness." The quote might have been expected to harm Dark among A's players Reggie Jackson, Bert Campaneris, Billy North, Vida Blue, and Blue Moon Odom, among others. It didn't, partly because Dark and Willie Mays said he was misquoted.

By 1974's spring training, the crisis had faded. Mays, befriended by Dark as a solitary 1951 rookie, backed the new manager. Inexplicably, Finley on occasion shelved 1973 defensive star Dick Green in a mad campaign to rotate seven second baseman, solidify the A's up the middle, and add extra power. None worked. Green easily played the most games at second—100. Another Finley flight of fancy was "designated runner" Herb Washington, whose infamy crested in October. He had no baseball experience since high school, yet "Hurricane Herb" graced 92 games, never batting, scored 29 runs, stole 29 bases, but was thrown out 16 times. "Thus, the strange vagaries," said Moore, "of the Swinging A's."

A better first for the 1974 A's was another rookie who grew up a Giants fan in Half Moon Bay, California, near San Francisco, at 10 played the board game Strat-O-Matic, at 16 broadcast to himself at the Oakland-Alameda County Coliseum, and for 40 years and counting aired the A's, then Rangers, Red Sox, Orioles, and post-1996 Giants. Jon Miller has announced ESPN TV's or Radio's 1990-2011 *Sunday Night Baseball*, All-Star Game, LCS, Division Series, and World Series, winning two cable ACE Awards and the Hall of Fame's 2010 Ford C. Frick Award for broadcast excellence. If play dulls, he may mimic Vin Scully in English, Spanish, and Japanese.

Miller was 22 when Monte Moore hired him. In 1974 spring training he was nervous, wanting to impress. Ultimately Monte's *vitae* welded the 1972-74 Series, a 3,001-game iron streak, and 1962-1977, 1987, and 1989-92 A's, NBC's, and USA's *Game of the Week*. The Oklahoman brooked Finley's designated runner, mechanical rabbit, and orange baseball to call Hunter's perfect game, Billy Martin's Billy Ball, and later Bash Brothers Jose Canseco and Mark McGwire. Their common chord was Moore. In 1974 he was on the air as Jon critiqued his own play-by-play: "Not exciting enough, nothing's happening," Miller thought to himself. He didn't want to disappoint Monte.

Thus, the rookie began to practice sotto voce "Ground ball, *right at the shortstop! Unbelievable! He could have hit the ball anywhere! But what a miracle—he hit it right to him!*" Jon's play-by-play was exciting enough: It also sounded as if he should be committed. Moore looked at him, disbelieving, before turning off his mike: "What hell are you *doing?*" he asked. Between innings Miller expressed his fear: He was boring; nothing was happening. "That's ridiculous," Moore said. "We hired you because you're the best guy for the job. You sound great." Jon then exhaled.

By autumn 1974 Finley had owned the A's for 13 years "and had more broadcasters than managers—and he had more managers than any team," said Miller. Charlie had fired Harry Caray, Bob Elson, and Bob Woods—announcers who are in or should be in Cooperstown. Other teams had or would fire Hall of

Fame Voices like Mel Allen, Red Barber, Jack Buck, Bob Prince, Milo Hamilton, Ernie Harwell, and Curt Gowdy. That fall Finley inexplicably fired Miller. "Man, was I happy," Jon said, much later, tongue-in-cheek. "Are you kidding? To be associated with *those* guys?! My stock rose in the whole baseball industry."

Miller's big-league industry debut was April 4, 1974: a 7-2 rout of Texas in Arlington. For the A's, mediocrity crested on May 7, Baltimore winning, 9-3, to make Oakland 12-15. The A's then won five straight games, a skein repeated in late May and early June, to rise to 30-21. A six-game winning streak in July made the two-time champions' first-place AL West record 54-39. After July 31 the swinging and missing A's never won or lost more than three games in a row. If you erase July's 20-8 record, Oakland played only six games over .500. Worse, it was 25-28 in one-run decisions. "They weren't barn-burners," said Rangers voice Merle Harmon, whose 84-76 second-place team played .525 baseball, "but we weren't Murderers Row."

The A's won their fourth straight West Division title, but by only five games over Texas. Their 90-72 record was Oakland's worst since 1970. Catfish Hunter had a league-low 2.49 ERA, tied for victories at 25-7 and tied for second in shutouts with six, was third in winning percentage and fifth in innings pitched and fewest hits per game, and won the Cy Young Award. Ken Holtzman ranked third in walks a game. Rollie Fingers led the league game in games (76) and tied for fourth in saves (18). Vida Blue was 17-15 with a 3.25 ERA; Holtzman 19-17, 3.07; Rollie, 9-5, 2.65. The staff affirmed the Coliseum as a single, walk, steal, then sacrifice fly for a run park. On the one hand, the A's led the league in fewest home runs, hits and walks allowed, best earned-run average (2.95), and lowest rival on-base percentage and batting average. On the other, on July 19 they were no-hit by Cleveland's Dick Bosman. "We had maybe the best pitching of our three titles," said Hunter. They needed it, batting a second-lowest in the league .247, partly compensating with a league-high 164 stolen bases.

Billy North and Bert Campaneris placed first and fourth league-wide with 54 and 34 steals, respectively.

Reggie Jackson was again a one-man parade: second-best in home runs (29) and slugging average (.518), third in runs (90), and fifth in on-base percentage (.396). Joe Rudi led in doubles (39) and total bases (287) and was third in runs batted in (99) and fourth in slugging average (.484). Gene Tenace topped in walks (110) and was third in home runs (26). Sal Bando's 103 RBIs trailed only Texas's Jeff Burroughs' 118. Jeff was the AL MVP, followed by Rudi, Bando, and Jackson dividing the runner-up vote. Four A's regulars topped 20 dingers: Jackson, Tenace, Bando, and Rudi. Four hit at least .260: Rudi, Campaneris, Jackson, and North. By contrast, three others hit less than .212: Tenace, Dick Green, and catcher Ray Fosse. "Their defense was so good, especially Green's," said Moore, "that we needed—and had—the pitching to carry it."

Six A's—Bando, Campy, Fingers, Hunter, Jackson, and Rudi—made the league All-Star team. Yet in a sense, the '74 A's were a semi-deadball voyeur's dream. For one thing, they fought. Jackson and North wrestled in the Tiger Stadium clubhouse, Reggie hurting his shoulder. Fosse, trying to separate them, suffered a crushed disc in his neck, spending three months on the disabled list. For another, they played a high percentage of close, low-scoring games, drawing only 845,694, 22nd of 24 big-league teams. Oakland clinched the AL East in late September. The A's began their fourth straight LCS on October 5, losing to Baltimore, 6-3, at the Coliseum before 41, 609. Hunter's superb control was a double-edged sword: no walks, but home runs by Paul Blair, Brooks Robinson, and Bobby Grich. Next day 42,810 saw Holtzman counter, 5-0. Bando and Fosse hit homers, Sal after Grich dropped his foul pop. "That's how we are," Bando rhapsodized. "It's never wise to give us a second chance."

At Baltimore, Bando homered again as Vida Blue tossed a two-hit third-game jewel: A's win, 1-0. For a change, A's attendance dwarfed their rival's. Blue's complete game was witnessed by 32,060. Game Four at Memorial Stadium drew 28,136 to see O's starter Mike Cuellar go wild. In the fifth inning he walked four straight A's to allow a run. Cuellar left having

walked nine—with a no-hitter. In the seventh Bando walked and Reggie Jackson drove off the wall to score him. Two innings later a walk and two singles scored the O's first run: 2-1. Fingers then fanned Don Baylor to wave Oakland's third straight pennant. Their World Series opponent, Los Angeles, finished 102-60, had a National League-best 2.98 ERA, and scored an NL-highest 798 runs.

"I want my team to think baseball the way my wife shops," joked Dodgers manager Tom Lasorda. "Twenty-four hours a day." Bill Buckner and Steve Garvey batted .314 and .312, respectively, Garvey having 200 hits and 111 RBIs. Jimmy Wynn had 32 homers, walked 108 times, and knocked in 108 runs. Andy Messersmith and Don Sutton won 20 and 19 games, respectively, Sutton having a .679 win percentage. Davey Lopes stole 59 bases. Reliever Mike Marshall pitched in a nonpareil 106 games, had 21 saves, and was Most Valuable Player. The A's clubhouse needed therapy. The Dodgers reeked of happy talk. Lasorda preached harmony and Dodger Blue and his seafood diet. "I eat all the food I can see."

Fingers and Odom fought a day before the World Series opened. Five stitches closed a cut on Rollie's head. "The record is 15," he laughed, "held by many." In Game One, Jackson homered in the second inning at Dodger Stadium. In the fifth Ken Holtzman, not having batted all year, doubled and scored on a wild pitch and Campaneris's suicide bunt. In the bottom half, LA scored its first run on a single and errors by Campy and Jackson. The A's scored again in the eighth on a Campaneris single, North sacrifice, and Cey error on a Bando grounder: 3-1. Jackson then flied to center field. "[Bando] should come in and score," said NBC's Vin Scully, doing the Series with Moore and Curt Gowdy. "[Joe] Ferguson took it [from center fielder Wynn], with the better arm. Here comes the throw! They got him! Oh, what a play"—final: A's, 3-2.

Next afternoon a "cerulean blue sky," quoting Scully, hung like a canopy over Dodger Stadium. Amnesia momentarily hung over the A's: The world champions had forgotten how to hit. LA fronted, 1-0, on a walk and Bill Russell's and Steve Yeager's singles. In the sixth Ferguson pricked Blue for a two-run blast: 3-0, Dodgers. Oakland awoke in the ninth, Rudi singling Bando and Jackson home. Marshall relieved Sutton and struck out Tenace, whereupon Herb Washington pinch-ran for Rudi, Scully, Dodgers announcer since 1950, warned Washington on air that "he'd better be careful. Marshall has a terrific move, especially for a right-hander," at which point Mike picked Washington off first. Marshall then retired Angel Mangual to end the game. "The Dodgers with a one-run lead," said Curt. Scully: "Screwball!" "Gowdy: "That's it, getting him [Mangual!"] — Series tied.

Back at Oakland, the A's grabbed a 3-0 lead by the fourth on Ferguson's error, Rudi's single, and Campy's hit. LA countered with solo homers by Buckner and Willie Crawford — another 3-2 verdict, Hunter beating Al Downing. In Game Four, behind two games to one, the Dodgers led, 2-1, entering Oakland's sixth inning. The A's then coalesced three walks, a wild pitch, a sacrifice bunt, two singles, and a groundout into four runs, Fingers getting his second straight save. Ultimately, the owner of the most famous mustache in America appeared in every Series game but one, got a victory, added two saves, and was voted the fall classic's Most Valuable Player.

Trailing three games to one, the Dodgers sent forth Don Sutton against Blue in their win-or-go-home final. In the first two innings Oakland fronted, 2-0, on Bando's sacrifice fly and Fosse's homer. The Dodgers tied in the sixth on Wynn's sacrifice fly and Garvey's RBI single. Next inning Marshall stopped warming up to watch the Coliseum crowd hurl trash at left fielder Buckner. He continued watching while the trash was collected. "In a case like this," said Rudi, leading off, "you expect the pitcher to throw a fastball." Marshall did. Rudi swung, finding the left-field stands: The A's led, 3-2. Presently Jackson threw Buckner out at third base, trying to stretch a double, to begin the eighth inning "Von Joshua is up," said Gowdy with two out in the Dodgers ninth. "If the A's win, we'll go immediately to the Oakland A's locker room and the presentation. Here, it could be — he [Tenace] caught it — and the A's are world champions! Rollie

Fingers put 'em down one-two-three! The Oakland A's are the first team since the New York Yankees to win three world championships in a row!"

In 1933, the first year of Franklin Roosevelt's New Deal, a cartoon said of its agenda, "We have had our revolution, and we like it." A revolution now began in baseball. For nearly 100 years, a reserve clause had bound players in perpetuity to a club unless they were traded, sold, or released. Under Hunter's contract, Finley paid half of his $100,000 salary into a life-insurance fund — deferred compensation. In October 1974 Catfish charged that Finley had failed to honor it — thus canceling the entire pact, including the reserve clause. Panicked, Finley tried handing Hunter a $50,000 check. Hunter refused; Peter Seitz, a professional arbitrator from New York, ruled the contract void. "Come on, Cat! Get it all, man," yelped Reggie Jackson. Straightaway a bidding war commenced over baseball's first free agent.

"Three straight titles! Take that away!" Finley had bellowed. Seitz did, letting Hunter negotiate with any major-league team. On December 31, 1974, New Year's Eve, baseball's best pitcher signed with the Yankees — to quote Barry Maguire's 1965 famous song, forging Finley's, and thus the A's, "Eve of Destruction." Hunter's pact was worth $3.75 million, slightly more than triple the game's next highest-paid salary. The decision meant that after a certain time spent with a team, athletes could play an "option year" and then accept another offer. Economic capital claimed loyalty, affection for a team or area, even long-term common sense. Ultimately, mom and pop were overwhelmed by short-term greed.

In 1975 a big-league record four pitchers threw a combined regular-season no-hitter: Blue, Glen Abbott, Paul Lindblad, and Fingers. That year the A's dynasty officially ended, Boston sweeping Oakland in the League Championship Series, 7-1, 6-3, and 5-3. On October 17 Dark, only the third skipper to win both a National and American League pennant — the NL, 1962's Giants — was axed. More crucially, the Dodgers' Andy Messersmith and Expos' Dave McNally challenged the reserve clause's automatic-renewal proviso by playing a full year without contracts, then demanding freedom. The late 1975 landmark case was decided by a three-man arbitration board, Seitz casting the decisive vote to make Messersmith and McNally free agents.

"I am confident," Seitz said, "that the dislocation and damage to the reserve clause can be avoided or minimized through good-faith collective bargaining between the [two] partners"—the clubs and players. One by one, the A's left Oakland: in late 1975, Jackson for Baltimore; 1976, Bando for Milwaukee; 1977, Campy for Texas, Tenace and Fingers San Diego. Finley simply let them go. In 1976, he tried a peremptory strike, selling Rudi and Fingers to Boston for $2 million. "Anything to get money to be able to compete," Finley said. Commissioner Bowie Kuhn vetoed the deal as sure to make the A's *non*competitive. "He's trying to bankrupt me, drive me out of baseball," said Charlie, calling Kuhn "the village idiot." Eventually, Finley was forced to sell. Time and the rules had changed.

Baseball's next dynasty wore pinstripes and played in the House That Ruth Built. "I know they're the Yankees," said Jackson of the 1996-2001 Bronx Bombers, "but no one should ever forget what we did in 1972 through '4." Remembering them, prize Catfish pitching and Campy running and Reggie swinging—even now, a distant night, under a cloudless sky, with the moon jumping over the Bay.

Oakland forged baseball's greatest non-Yankees dynasty of the last three-quarters of a century. As a Red Sox fan since youth, I had watched the Olde Towne Team futilely engage the "three-peat" 1972-74 A's. It remained for Boston's 1975 postseason to put the final nail in the dynasty's coffin. I recall most of all knowing that when you defeated the Swinging A's, you beat the very, if not always the merry, best.

SOURCES

Virtually all material, including quotes, is derived from Curt Smith's books *Voices of The Game, Storied Stadiums, Voices of Summer, The Voice, Pull Up a Chair, A Talk in the Park,* and *Mercy! A Celebration of Fenway Park's Centennial Told Through Red Sox Radio and TV* (published, in order: Simon & Schuster 1992; Carroll & Graf 2001 and 2005, respectively; the Lyons Press, 2007: and Potomac Books 2009, 2010, and 2012, respectively.)

Books

Fimrite, Ron, *The World Series: A History of Baseball's Fall Classic* (New York: Time Inc. Home Entertainment, 1997).

Lowry, Philip, *Green Cathedrals: The Ultimate Celebration of All Major League Ballparks* (New York: Walker & Company, 2006).

Silverman, Matthew, *Swinging '73: Baseball's Wildest Season* (Guilford, Connecticut: The Lyons Press, 2013).

Thorn, John, Peter Palmer, and Michael Gershman, *Total Baseball: The Official Encyclopedia of Major League Baseball* (Kingston, New York: Total Sports Publishing, 2001).

Websites

Baseball-reference.com

Monte Moore

By Matt Bohn

During his two stints as a broadcaster for the Athletics, Monte Moore covered some of the best teams in their history, and some of the worst. Beginning his major-league broadcasting career in the final years of the A's time in Kansas City, he followed the team to the West Coast and broadcast six American League championship teams including the 1972-1974 world champions. Known for his work ethic, knowledge, and enthusiasm for the game, Moore was well respected by A's listeners. In 1974 columnist Bob Foster wrote of him, "It might be said that Monte is one of the better baseball play-by-play men in the business."[1] One Bay Area listener summed up Moore's appeal in 1977: "He is completely knowledgeable about his subject, he speaks clearly, has a good sense of humor and projects an image of a good, sound down-to-earth person; someone you'd like to know personally. Above all, though, is his professional ability as a sports announcer."[2]

Monte Lee Moore was born in 1930 to Travis and Gladys Moore in the small town of Hollis, Oklahoma. Growing up, there were few opportunities to hear baseball broadcasts. Moore's earliest memory of hearing a baseball broadcast was the 1947 World Series between the Yankees and the Dodgers. From that radio broadcast, Mel Allen became Moore's "instant hero."[3] Moore recalled in 1966, "This made me feel all the more that I wanted to be up there in a big-league broadcasting booth. I guess it was the first baseball broadcast I ever had heard because we didn't pick up much of anything out there in Oklahoma."[4] During his senior year of high school, Moore became ill with rheumatic fever and was confined to bed rest for three months. During his convalescence, he listened to sports broadcasts on the radio, including re-creations of baseball games by Gordon McClendon from Dallas station KLIF. Moore became more determined to become a sportscaster.

After graduating from high school, Moore enrolled at the University of Oklahoma to study radio broadcasting. He also hoped to make the Oklahoma basketball team. During his freshman year, Oklahoma basketball coach Bruce Drake (who would later serve as an assistant coach for the 1956 US Olympic basketball team) took Moore aside and made him an offer. "Monte, I know you want to be a sports broadcaster, we want to help you out all we can," Moore recalled Drake saying to him. "When you come to practice every day, bring a tape recorder with you and you go up in the upper level of the auditorium and while we're practicing basketball, you practice broadcasting what we're doing."[5] Recalling the incident in an interview with Visalia Oaks broadcaster Donny Baarns, Moore said with a laugh, "So he was kicking me off the team. I got even with him. In 1951 I married his daughter."[6] (Moore married Deonne Drake on December 13, 1951, and they had three children together.) Moore worked at the University of Oklahoma

radio station, KUVY, which reached only the university dorms. To promote KUVY's broadcasts of football games, basketball games, and other sporting events, he placed flyers in the cafeteria, residence halls, and other parts of the campus.

During the summer months, Moore played as a catcher with local fast-pitch softball teams. It was his catching ability that led to his first professional job. About a week before his college graduation in 1952, he was broadcasting a college baseball game from a table set up in the stands. Seated a few rows ahead of him was a man named Leo Morris who had pitched against Moore in softball tournaments and was aware of his playing ability. After the game Morris approached Moore and told him he was forming a softball team to play all summer and to go to the world championship in Clearwater, Florida. Morris, who had just taken a job as manager of a radio station in Duncan, Oklahoma, needed a catcher. Morris offered Moore a job with the radio station for the summer if he would agree to be the softball team catcher at night. At the end of this summer spent playing softball and working at the Duncan radio station, Moore reported to Fort Lee, Virginia, for a two-year stint in the Army.

Returning from military service, Moore learned that Leo Morris had moved to KSWO in Lawton, Oklahoma. Morris needed a sports director and hired Moore. At KSWO, Moore covered high-school football, basketball, and Cameron Junior College sporting events. He also did play-by-play for Sooner State League (Class D) baseball games. For road games, Moore provided re-creations from telegraph reports, a common practice at the time.

While Moore was broadcasting a high-school basketball tournament, a man from a radio station in Hutchinson, Kansas, was driving through Oklahoma and heard his play-by-play. The man stopped at the nearest gas station, called KSWO and offered Moore a job with radio station KWHK. Moore served as KWHK's news director and broadcast Big Eight basketball tournaments, and the East-West college basketball All Star Game. On weekends Moore an-

nounced games for the Wichita Vickers of the National Industrial Basketball League.

After two years in Hutchinson, Moore became the director of the Kansas University Sports Network, for which he covered all Jayhawker sports. Kansas University sports were carried over station KANU and a network of 24 other stations in Kansas and Missouri. Moore recalled, "Everybody in the Midwest heard Kansas games. If there was one big break for me, it was getting to do the Kansas games."[7] Wilt Chamberlain was the star Kansas University basketball player at the time. Moore hosted a radio show with Chamberlain (entitled *Flip'er With The Dipper*) in which they played music records.

After three years with the Kansas University network, Moore became sports director of Kansas City station WDAF in 1960. He broadcast Big Eight college basketball and football as well as games of the Kansas City Steers of the American Basketball League. Covering a press conference at the Muehlebach Hotel for WDAF, Moore found himself in an elevator with Kansas City Athletics owner Charlie Finley. Finley had heard Moore's basketball play-by-play and was impressed. Moore recalled, "Charlie looked at me and didn't ask me any questions about if I'd ever done a baseball game or anything. He said, 'Hey kid, how'd you like to do the A's games?' Just like that. And of course I was a little staggered but what I said was, 'That's always been my goal, to do major-league baseball.' He said, 'Well, we'll work it out.'"[8]

Moore went to Cleveland to broadcast the American Basketball League finals. On April 7, 1962, he got a call at his hotel from Finley, who told him he had worked it out so that Moore could broadcast the A's games over KCMO and still do football over WDAF. The season began just three days later and Moore, who worked very hard to prepare for each broadcast, hadn't even had an opportunity to cover the team during spring training.

Early during Moore's tenure as Voice of the A's, his enthusiasm for the team was evident. "I'm not down the middle, I'm definitely pro-Kansas City because I believe a broadcaster is more on the team than perhaps a newspaperman covering the club," he said in 1966. "As far as the players are concerned, I certainly point out their mistakes and say so when I think they are wrong. And I have found that the players don't want you to alibi for them. Still, I'm not there to knock. I'm there to boost as much as I can and try to tell as many inside things as I can about them."[9] In an interview with broadcaster Donny Baarns 50 years after joining the A's, Moore said, "I never said 'Come on Campy, get a hit.' I didn't use 'we' or anything like that. But I didn't mind people knowing I wanted the A's to win."[10]

Because of his enthusiasm, some writers accused Moore of being a shill for Finley. Moore told Baarns, "Finley never one time ever told me what to say on the air other than for promotional things. That's the only time." Moore recalled that Finley would also give him information about trades that were made before he would give them to the print media. "He used to call our radio booth and tell us about trades that were made even while the game was going on and want us to announce it. And the newspaper people hated it because they got scooped on the network, you know, and they blamed me for breaking stories. All I was doing was telling about the trades."[11] Though Moore respected Finley because he gave him his first major-league broadcasting opportunity, he would also concede that the A's owner could be difficult to work for and "one of the most vitriolic people that you could ever know."[12]

Moore's early years of covering the A's had few bright spots. "Those weren't exactly glory years in Kansas City," he said in 1993. "I went through a growth period with a lot of those guys."[13] The Athletics lost more than 100 games in both 1964 and 1965. After the team moved to Oakland in 1968, the winning record began to change. In 1969, the team improved to second place. Then came the three straight world championships from 1972 to 1974. In each of those championship years, Moore broadcast the World Series on NBC Radio with Curt Gowdy. Moore's World Series broadcasts were the "biggest thrill" of his broadcasting career.[14]

In 1974 Moore introduced the term "dinger" into the baseball lexicon. During a pregame radio interview with relief pitcher Darold Knowles, Moore was intrigued when Knowles mentioned that he had given up some dingers in an earlier game. Knowles explained to Moore that he had been referring to home runs as dingers in the A's bullpen. Inspired by this, Moore began using the term during the broadcasts and even obtained his own "dinger" as a sound effect. He explained, "It was a brass bell, kind of a smaller one, really. It was mounted and the equipment guy carried it for us. It was a little thing to put on the desk. And we'd even ring that bell on a road trip when one of our guys hit a home run."[15] The popularity of the dinger reached its height late in the 1974 season as the A's battled for their third straight division title. Moore announced on the air, "You know what, fans, we play the Kansas City Royals here next Monday night and we've got a doubleheader. Why don't we just have a dinger night at the ballpark? Everybody bring a dinger of some kind and let's ring those dingers." Moore "didn't ask the ballclub, didn't ask Finley, didn't ask anybody" for permission to plug this event.[16] He estimated that at least 20,000 fans of the nearly 50,000 in attendance on September 9, 1974, brought bells of various sizes. Oakland swept the doubleheader. Moore recalled that for years after that, whenever he encountered Royals manager Jack McKeon, McKeon would place his hands over his ears and say to him, "I never think of the A's without thinking of you and your blankety-blank dingers."[17]

By 1976 Moore had been the voice of the A's for 15 years, covered three world championship teams, and outlasted several broadcast partners (including Harry Caray, Bob Elson, and Al Helfer). After the '76 season, Moore went on a cruise to Mexico with ten A's players. Returning from the cruise, he found a bill from Blue Cross in his mail. Calling Finley's secretary to inquire about it, Moore was informed that he was no longer on the payroll as of October 31. Moore said, "When I phoned Charlie to ask about my status, he started yelling and cussing. 'Did you have a good time on the cruise with the players?' he asked. Then he screamed at me for fraternizing. He never said I was fired. He just hung up."[18] After the story of the apparent firing broke in December, Moore appeared on local TV and radio shows and many Oakland fans were upset on his behalf. One outraged A's fan refused to attend any more A's games because of the situation. By the end of the month, Finley had reversed the apparent firing and explained to the press that the situation was a misunderstanding.

In 1977 the *Hayward* (California) *Daily Review* conducted a poll about Bay Area sportscasters and Moore was rated the most popular. But Moore was ready for a change and his 16th season would be his last as the full-time radio Voice of the A's. "I was tired of all the traveling. My kids were getting to the age where they'd be competing in high-school sports and I wanted to watch them," he said.[19] In 1978 he bought Porterville, California, radio station KTIP. "I didn't want a big-city station; too much pressure on ratings. I liked the idea of what a small station could do for a small town," he said.[20] Under Moore's ownership, the station began broadcasting local high-school events like soccer, baseball, basketball, track, and water polo. Though no longer employed by the A's, Moore did the backup game for NBC's *Game of the Week* in 1978 and also broadcast Thursday night baseball games on the USA network from 1979 to 1983. Though Moore was regularly heard on national telecasts, he was deeply dedicated to bringing local sporting events to the Porterville community. On at least one occasion he changed his travel schedule so that he could announce a local high-school baseball game over KTIP and then work a nationally televised game the next day.

Moore returned to the A's broadcast booth in 1987 on an occasional basis, filling in for Bill King or Lon Simmons. The following year, he became the full-time television broadcaster, working 50 to 60 A's telecasts each season for KPIX and KICU. As he had in the 1970s, Moore covered three consecutive AL championship teams in Oakland. When KRON purchased the TV rights after the 1992 season, Moore was replaced with Dick Stockton. Stepping into the A's booth, Stockton paid tribute to his predecessor, saying, "Monte Moore was as fine a baseball broadcaster as

you could find in the country. He was a high-echelon guy."[21] Moore, who had no hard feelings about the replacement, would never again broadcast major-league baseball on a daily basis.

Moore sold KTIP in 1996 but stayed on to work as a consultant. In 2002 he began teaching a class on sportscasting at Porterville College. Mentoring aspiring sportscasters was not new to Moore. In 1974, at his recommendation, the A's hired a 21-year-old unknown broadcaster named Jon Miller to work with him. During his first game, Miller felt nervous and out of place. "But Monte seemed to sense that," Miller said shortly afterward. "He knew it was my first game and he went out of his way to help me. He's a very sensitive person and I appreciate what he did. I'll never forget it."[22] Moore mentored many other broadcasters, including USC announcer Pete Arbogast and sportscaster Gary Bender.

In retirement, Moore was able to spend more time with his family and his church. Moore's Christian faith guided his life. "As a lad I went to church twice on Sunday, Sunday school and prayer meetings on Wednesday," he said. "In addition to Christian parents, God gave me a wonderful Christian wife who is truly a helpmate in every way."[23] Looking back on his life and career, Moore said, "The Good Lord has looked after me."[24]

SOURCES

Busby, Bob, "On the Level," *Kansas City Times*, July 17, 1957.

Busby, Bob, "On the Level," *Kansas City Times*, February 18, 1960.

Curiel, Jonathan, "Giants, A's on the Air: New Faces, Voices, Stations," *San Francisco Chronicle*, April 2, 1993.

Curiel, Jonathan, "Stockton Offers High Praise for Moore," *San Francisco Chronicle*, February 9, 1993.

Draper, Dick, "CSM's Jon Miller; 'Coloring the A's,'" *San Mateo* (California) *Times*, April 18, 1974.

Foster, Bob, "A's Fire Their Sixth Announcer," *San Mateo Times*, November 23, 1973.

Foster, Bob, "Meet Monte Moore, Al Helfer of the A's," *San Mateo TV Times*, January 13, 1968.

Foster, Bob, "Oakland A's Still Without Radio-TV," *San Mateo Times*, February 8, 1974.

Gilmore, Tom, "Moore Rejoins A's Broadcast Team," *San Francisco Chronicle*, February 10, 1988.

Hostetter, George, "Gone From A's, Valley Gets Moore," *Fresno Bee*, February 16, 1993.

Hostetter, George, "With Monte Moore in Porterville, Even JV Teams Get Air Time," *Fresno Bee*, September 7, 1986.

Johnson, Lew, "Lew Johnson's Column; Notes and Quotes From Here and There," *Lawton* (Oklahoma) *Constitution*, August 2, 1957.

Larson, Lanny, "Porterville Radio Station Sold, Longtime Owner to Maintain Ties," *Fresno Bee*, January 31, 1997.

Levitt, Ed, "Accent on Sports." *Oakland Tribune*, December 8, 1976.

Lundquist, Carl, "Moore, Voice of A's, Warms Up Pitchers for a New Air Slant." *The Sporting News*, June 11, 1966.

Rose, Bill, "A's Monte Moore Happy in New Role," *Oakland Tribune*, February 14, 1970.

Stewart, Rick, "Miller at the Mike: He keeps WITS about him," *Boston Herald*, February 7, 1982.

Tibbetts, Jim, "Moore, Charley O. Reunite," *Leavenworth* (Kansas) *Times*, February 4, 1977.

Tonelli, Charles, "Monte Moore the Favorite; Fans Stick With Local Announcer." *Hayward* (California, *Daily Review*, October 5, 1977.

Tramel, Barry, "Cast of Characters—From Wilt to Bud to Joltin' Joe, Moore Has Called It All," *Oklahoma City Daily Oklahoman*, June 7, 1998.

United Press International, "Moore Will Man A's Microphone," *Omaha World Herald*, December 29, 1976.

Warner, Gary, "Rush Joins Moore on Air," *Kansas City Star*, April 11, 1965.

"'Dingers' Boost A's," *San Mateo* (California) *Times*, September 10, 1974.

"On K.U. Grid Hookup; University Station and 24 Others to Air Games," *Kansas City Times*, September 19, 1957.

"Veteran Sportscaster Lends Expertise to Local Students—Broadcaster Monte Moore to Teach Class at Porterville College," *Fresno Bee*, June 2, 2002.

"Witty Wilt Has Disc Jockey Show 'Flip'er With Dipper,'" *Salina* (Kansas) *Journal*, February 21, 1958.

Interview with Monte Moore by Donny Baarns on Donnycast.com, the official website of broadcaster Donny Baarns: donnycast.com/p/upcoming-broadcasts.html.

ACKNOWLEDGMENT

Thanks to Donny Baarns for permission to quote from his interview with Monte Moore.

NOTES

1 Bob Foster, "Oakland A's Still Without Radio-TV," *San Mateo Times*, February 8, 1974.

2 Charles Tonelli, "Monte Moore the Favorite; Fans Stick With Local Announcer," *Hayward* (California) *Daily Review*, October 5, 1977.

3 Interview with Monte Moore by Donny Baarns, on Donnycast. com, the official website of broadcaster Donny Baarns: donnycast.com/p/upcoming-broadcasts.html.

4 Carl Lundquist, "Moore, Voice of A's, Warms Up Pitchers for a New Air Slant" *The Sporting News*, June 11, 1966.

5 Baarns interview with Monte Moore.

6 Baarns interview with Monte Moore.

7 Barry Tramel, "Cast of Characters—From Wilt to Bud to Joltin' Joe, Moore Has Called It All," *Oklahoma City Daily Oklahoman*, June 7, 1998.

8 Baarns interview with Monte Moore.

9 Lundquist, "Moore, Vpice of A's."

10 Baarns interview with Monte Moore.

11 Baarns interview with Monte Moore.

12 Baarns interview with Monte Moore.

13 George Hostetter, "Gone From A's, Valley Gets Moore," *Fresno Bee*, February 16, 1993.

14 Baarns interview with Monte Moore.

15 Baarns interview with Monte Moore.

16 Baarns interview with Monte Moore.

17 Baarns interview with Monte Moore.

18 Ed Levitt, "Accent on Sports," *Oakland Tribune*, December 8, 1976.

19 Hostetter, "With Monte Moore in Porterville, Even JV Teams Get Air Time."

20 Hostetter, "With Monte Moore in Porterville, Even JV Teams Get Air Time."

21 Jonathan Curiel, "Stockton Offers High Praise for Moore" *San Francisco Chronicle*, February 9, 1993.

22 Dick Draper, "CSM's Jon Miller; 'Coloring the A's,'" *San Mateo* (California) *Times*, April 18, 1974.

23 Bill Rose, "A's Monte Moore Happy in New Role," *Oakland Tribune*, February 14, 1970.

24 Barry Tramel, "Cast of Characters."

Does The Way Lead To San Jose?

By Curt Smith

"I started at the bottom in this business," said actor Art Carney, Ed Norton in television's seminal *The Honeymooners*, "and worked my way right into the sewer." By contrast, the 1970s Athletics worked their way from baseball's top to its bottom. The 1972-74 A's won three World Series. The 1977 club made the American League West cellar. "What is it with the A's?" said Joe Rudi, who that year joined the Angels. "Connie Mack breaks 'em up [in the 1910s and '30s], now this." Oakland lost 108 games in 1979. Attendance plunged to 306,763, one game drawing 653. Oilman Marvin Davis attempted to move the A's to Denver, but the Oakland-Alameda County Coliseum Board blocked the sale. Stadium toilets and the scoreboard went on the fritz. They seemed a metaphor for the team.

In 1980 the Haas family of San Francisco bought the A's for $12.7 million, hoping that the franchise would regain its early-'70s sheen. A 1981 players strike caused the split season, each division having a first- and second-half titlist. The A's won the Western Division's first half, beat the second-half Royals, but lost to the Yankees in the League Championship Series. That year eight straight A's singled to start one game. "Crazy George" Henderson hatched the wave. In 1982 another Henderson, Rickey (no relation), stole 130 bases to break Lou Brock's mark of 118, "Billy [Martin] Ball" wowed an A's record single-season 1,735,489, and Raiders pro football president Al Davis took his team to Los Angeles. All of them helped A's caps and jerseys for the first time top Giants' merchandise in the Bay.

"I came over here [from San Francisco] in 1981," said A's announcer Lon Simmons. "The Raiders' leaving for LA changed everything, made the Coliseum a baseball place." Three billboards rose behind the bleachers. Left field's promoted events and future series; right's, line scores; Diamond Vision, highlights, crowd shots, and the highlight show *This Week in Baseball*. Cartoons showed the A's hitting other teams. Outside, the A's Swingers band dressed in green and gold. Inside, baseball's best high-tech stereo had people dancing in the aisles.

"With football gone, we can do anything we want," Tony La Russa said on being named A's manager in 1986. What La Russa wanted was to rebuild his team. The A's farm system bore Jose Canseco, Mark McGwire, and Walt Weiss—1986-87-88 Rookies of the Year. Dave Stewart won 20 games in four straight years. Pinch-runner Gene Nelson became the first AL pitcher to steal a base since Blue Moon Odom. In 1987 the Coliseum hosted its first All-Star Game: NL, 2-0, in 13 innings. Next year's firsts included 14 straight wins and 2 million in single-season attendance. Another late 1980s first was A's play-by-play on the field.

At the Coliseum, an empty space behind the backstop and runway led to each clubhouse. Spanish-speaking station KNTA put announcers in this space and a canopy above them to ward off foul balls. "Fans talk about feeling like you're on the field," said Hispanic radio voice Amaury Pi-Gonzalez. "We *were,* often sitting with pitchers who charted pitches." The mood was intimate, but vision bad: "liners over first and third got lost in the corner." The experiment ended because rival scouts thought A's broadcasters were stealing signs. They couldn't—couldn't *see* well enough! "On the other hand," said Ken Korach, A's post-1995 radio announcer, "their equipment never got wet."

The 1988 A's swept Boston in the LCS, showing how far rebuilding had come. "Another three-year pennant streak began [matching 1929-31 and 1972-74]," said veteran Oakland voice Monte Moore. Game One swung the Series, Dennis Eckersley yielding Kirk Gibson's ninth-inning thunderbolt redolent of *The Natural.* "That home run was good for baseball," said Eck, "but not for me." A year later Stewart, Mike Moore, and Storm Davis went 59-27, Oakland licked Toronto in the playoff, and the 1989 Series against San Francisco crushed fire (earthquake) and ice (A's sweep). In 1990 Oakland itself brooked a sweep by Cincinnati, despite La Russa's belief that "this may have been our best team." Jerome Holtzman, baseball's official historian, agreed: "Considering that they were defending champions, and how heavily they were favored, it's among the most stunning upsets since [Mays/Rhodes Giants versus Cleveland in] 1954." Loving history, La Russa could have skipped that chapter.

In 1990 Henderson was voted the franchise's eighth Most Valuable Player. On May 1, 1991, his 939th career steal topped Lou Brock's record. That night Nolan Ryan pitched no-hitter number seven. "The Express" accepted kudos with Gary Cooper modesty. As usual, Henderson acted like a braggart after his record swipe, telling the crowd, "Brock was a great basestealer, but today I'm the greatest of all time." The A's time was ending, though few knew so then. Oakland fell to fourth in 1991. In 1992, it won the West but lost the LCS to Toronto. "First to worst!" cried the '93 A's, placing seventh in a seven-team division. The Haas family sold the team to businessmen Steve Schott and Ken Kofmann. McGwire bashed 52 homers in 1995. Alas, his new Coliseum oozed sterility. "How bad is the makeover?" read the *Oakland Tribune.* "It makes the old Mausoleum look good."

You could not find a worse villain in any Western than Al Davis, garbed in black, plotting his Raiders' 1995 *return* to the Oakland that he had exploited as team president. Appallingly, he now pressured it to add *six outfield tiers* — aka "Mt. Davis," named for the Raiders boss — that blocked the Athletics' view of the East Bay Hills and ruined the park's baseball sensibility. "Since then, the A's have tried to leave," said their Voice, Amaury Pi-Gonzalez. "Why wouldn't they? Only a new park in the Bay Area will now save the A's. Thank you, Mr. Davis." To return, Davis demanded 22,000 new seats, including luxury boxes. The city caved: "They showed no loyalty to the A's," said Ken Korach. "They screwed 'em — anything to get football back." The hash turned surreal. Construction proceeded while the A's played their schedule. "Jackhammers were going off," said 1996-2002 manager Art Howe. "Outfielders couldn't hear how hard the ball was hit."

The facelift made Oakland open 1996 at Las Vegas's 9,353-seat Cashman Field. A 20-to-22-foot fence trimmed the outfield. Fifty-six billboards, including Caesar's Palace, broke a big-league record. Usherettes danced the polka between innings. Arriving home, Schott found that "We couldn't sell the extra seats, so we covered most of the upper deck," cutting 1991's 47,450 revised capacity to 35,067, the tarps a daily tickler of the seats' impracticality. The pre-Mt. Davis Coliseum hadn't been as tall as many other of the new postwar parks. The twofold effect was 1) The middle and upper decks, as Joe Mock of BaseballParks.com wrote, weren't overly steep; and 2) The unenclosed park showcased the scenery behind Oakland. Mt. Davis wrecked that view. Power alleys rose 18 feet to abut the bleachers. "To each side it's eight feet," said a writer. "It looks like an elephant in heat."

In 2000 Oakland bopped 239 homers, won the final-day AL West, and nearly beat the Yankees in the Division Series. Mt. Davis's sole consolation was a lesser wind, boosting offense, but at the price of warping a park. Since then, the team has sought might-ily to find a new home. Five times the 2000 A's were outdrawn the same day by their Triple-A affiliate, the Sacramento River Cats. "They'd worked so hard, climbed so far from the '70s," said Lon Simmons, "only to fall back into the hole."

In June 2000 the A's asked Commissioner Bud Selig for tentative assent to move to Silicon Valley. "If they receive it," wrote the *Contra Costra Times*, "they'll talk further with a group wanting to build a private stadium" in Santa Clara. The A's hoped to soon leave the Coliseum, only to still be marooned there a decade and a half later. New owner Lew Wolff tried to build a park in downtown Oakland or a high-tech park in nearby Fremont. Foiled, he turned to the South Bay market of San Jose. The Giants, selling out every game at downtown San Francisco's AT&T Park, claimed that *they* owned San Jose's territorial rights — a monopoly. Wolff said poppycock, or words to that effect.

In response, Selig formed a major-league committee in 2009 to rule on whether the A's could build an intimate baseball-only park in the San Jose market, 48 miles from Baghdad on the Bay. Unbelievably, five years later the committee had been unable to render even a tentative conclusion. "I just wish they'd reach a decision," said Wolff. "Can we build, or not?" The A's filed a lawsuit against baseball saying no club owned territorial rights. Meanwhile, the California state controller spurned San Jose's back-door attempt to sell the A's land belonging to the city's redevelopment agency, which was dissolved in 2011. In 2013 the club extended its lease on the Coliseum.

T.S. Eliot famously called April "the cruelest month." In a sense, each month has been cruel playing at what Selig curtly calls "a pit." In 2012, despite almost winning the pennant, the Athletics averaged 20,728 fans per game, 27th among 30 big-league teams. A year later, the still-swinging A's took the AL West despite drawing just 1.8 million, in the bottom-dwelling vicinity of the White Sox and Mariners.

"There is something wrong here," Wolff said of one line of empty seat after another, disinterest a greater threat than its won-loss record to the future of the franchise. Ironically, in the last decade the A's have lured a postseason cult — aka the "crazies" — to supplement their regular base, spur officials to take tarps off the upper deck, and convert the Coliseum into baseball's version of a madding crowd.

In 2013, for instance, the A's twice drew more than 48,000 in the Division Series against Detroit. "The trick is to bottle our postseason atmosphere for the regular season," Korach explained. "Drums beating, people standing, a celebration of the game. Rival players find it hard to think. Our players love every minute. It's the ultimate home-field advantage." The

A's need it before October, not simply in that month alone.

In 2013 an extra problem also surfaced, giving new connotation to the ancient term *baseball garbage*. Out of the blue, sewage from the Coliseum's plumbing system appeared in the team clubhouses, the Athletics dugout, and their coaches' dressing room. To the A's it must have seemed as if it weren't one crisis, it was another.

Crosby, Stills, and Nash sang, "Our house is a very, very, very fine house." If the Giants would merely cooperate, yielding what Wolff calls nonexistent territorial rights, a new A's house in San Jose would be very fine. It might even combine a Beaux Arts tower, a light tower in play, and a hill beyond the center-field wall — the best of the A's parks that came before in Philadelphia, Kansas City, and Oakland, respectively.

In December 2013, the *San Jose Mercury News* reported that a letter from Selig to the A's had surfaced in a federal court as part of San Jose's antitrust lawsuit against baseball. Belying Selig's neutrality, it told the A's that the team's bid for San Jose had been denied. What next? Relocation to Las Vegas? Wait until Selig left office in January 2015, then reapply? Wolff didn't say, not knowing. To those remembering, Shibe Park's splendor in the grass must seem a century and a continent away. To those hoping for a park worthy of the franchise, Diane Warwick's "Do You Know the Way to San Jose?" must seem as much a prayer as a song. Wherever the team finds a home, it is sure to make room to honor the Swinging A's of 1972-74.

SOURCES

Virtually all material, including quotes, is derived from Curt Smith's books *Voices of The Game, Storied Stadiums, Voices of Summer, The Voice, Pull Up a Chair, A Talk in the Park,* and *Mercy! A Celebration of Fenway Park's Centennial Told Through Red Sox Radio and TV* (published, in order: Simon & Schuster 1992; Carroll & Graf 2001 and 2005, respectively; the Lyons Press, 2007: and Potomac Books 2009, 2010, and 2012, respectively.)

Silverman, Matthew, *Swinging '73: Baseball's Wildest Season* (Guilford, Connecticut: The Lyons Press, 2013).

Contributors

MARC Z AARON is a Certified Public Accountant and Certified Valuation Analyst with a tax practice in Randolph, Vermont. He is also an adjunct professor of economics at Vermont Technical College, the Anglo American University in Prague, and the University of New York in Prague. A born and bred Yankees fan, Marc has four sons, coached Little League for six seasons, and, like Tony La Russa, retired after his team (sadly named Red Sox) won the league championship. Marc, a tournament tennis player, has been a ranked singles player by the New England United States Tennis Association (USTA) and has captained several USTA league teams.

MARK ARMOUR is the founder and director of SABR's Baseball Biography Project and the co-author (with Dan Levitt) of the book *In Pursuit of Pennants—Baseball Operations from Deadball to Moneyball* (Nebraska, 2015). He lives in Oregon with Jane, Maya, and Drew.

ERIC ARON has been a SABR member since 2002 and has contributed several bios for both the "team" book projects and BioProject website. In addition to his writing for SABR, he has contributed to other websites and magazines, including Throughthefencebaseball.com, NewEnglandFilm.com, and *Imagine* magazine. He lives in Brighton, Massachusetts and holds a master's degree in Public History & Museum Studies. He enjoys documentaries, playing hoops, and laughter Yoga.

THOMAS AYERS is a lifelong Blue Jays fan who was born and raised in Toronto. Thomas has earned degrees from the University of Toronto, the London School of Economics and Queen's University. Currently practicing labor and employment law, he has contributed several other biographies to the SABR Baseball Biography Project while enduring the Blue Jays' current playoff drought.

MATT BOHN is a native of Hemlock, Michigan, and has been a SABR member since 2003. His interests include the history of baseball broadcasting and the Detroit Tigers.

JOHN CIZIK grew up a Yankees fan in Wilton, Connecticut living next door to a Red Sox fan. Something must have rubbed off, because he married Jenny, a Sox fan, in 1990. A lawyer practicing in Litchfield, Connecticut, he has always had an interest in doing research on and collecting memorabilia of Connecticut-born players

ALAN COHEN is a retired insurance underwriter who has been a member of SABR since 2011. He has written over 20 biographies for the SABR BioProject, and done several game summaries for the SABR Games Project. A native of Long Island, he now resides in West Hartford, Connecticut with his wife Frances, two cats, and two dogs. He graduated from Franklin and Marshall College with a degree in history in 1968. During the baseball season, Alan serves as datacaster (stringer) for the New Britain Rock Cats of the Eastern League.

CLIFF CORN has lived in Oregon since 1956, when he arrived there immediately after graduating from high school in Kansas. Cliff taught high school mathematics for 31 years, retiring in 1991. An avid baseball fan since 1951, Cliff saw several A's games when the franchise was in Kansas City

RORY COSTELLO grew up as a Mets fan in Connecticut. The 1973 World Series was the first that he watched in depth, and it made a great impression on him, filling him with respect for the Oakland dynasty. He also enjoyed imitating Horacio Piña's distinctive delivery. Rory lives in Brooklyn, New York, with his wife Noriko and son Kai.

LORETTA DONOVAN started life in a family that followed the St. Louis Browns. When the team left St. Louis, it was not hard for her to embrace the Cardinal tradition. Loretta taught elementary school in the Hazelwood School District in suburban St. Louis for 30 years. She has been a member of SABR for about five years. She enjoys the insights she gets from the Bob Broeg Chapter monthly meetings. This is the only article that she has written for SABR.

GEOFFREY DUNN is an award-winning film-maker, journalist, and historian based in Santa Cruz, California. His films include *Calypso Dreams* and *Miss or Myth?* He is the author of six books including *Images of America: Sports of Santa Cruz County* and *The Lies of Sarah Palin*, which was on Amazon's best-seller list for more than a year. Dunn has had a life-long love affair with baseball. He was captain of his varsity baseball team, a semipro player, and served as assistant varsity baseball coach at Santa Cruz High School in the 1990s. He is a fan of both the San Francisco Giants and Oakland Athletics.

JEFF ENGLISH is a graduate of Florida State University and resides in Tallahassee, Florida, with his wife Allison and twin sons, Elliott and Oscar. He is a lifelong Cubs fan and serves as secretary of the North Florida/Buck O'Neil SABR chapter. He has contributed to multiple SABR projects.

GREG ERION is retired from the railroad industry and currently teaches history part-time at Skyline Community College. He has written several biographies for SABR's BioProject and is currently working on a book about the 1959 season. He and his wife Barbara live in South San Francisco, California.

SCOTT FERKOVICH is the leader of the SABR Ballpark Project. He is a contributing editor to the annual *Emerald Guide to Baseball*, and blogs about Detroit Tiger history for Detroit Athletic Co. He also writes for Seamheads.com, TheNationalPastimeMuseum.com, and *Spitball* magazine. Scott was the editor of the SABR book *Detroit the Unconquerable: The 1935 World Champion Tigers*.

A graduate of Columbia College in Chicago, he was a judge for the Casey Award in 2014.

JOSEPH GERARD has been a lifelong Pittsburgh Pirates fan. He grew up hating the Yankees despite being born and raised in Newark, New Jersey - his biggest regret in life is that he was only 2 years old in 1960. Because of Roberto Clemente, he developed an interest in Latin-American baseball history and has contributed biographies of five Latin players to the SABR BioProject. He lives in New York City with his wife Ann Marie and their two children, Henry and Sophie.

AUSTIN GISRIEL, of Williamsport, Maryland, has authored several works on baseball, including his latest, *Boots Poffenberger: Hurler, Hero, Hell-Raiser*. He serves on the Board of Directors of the New Market Rebels of the Valley Baseball League, and may be heard regularly as the baseball commentator on "Gordy's Sports World" on ESPN 1380 in Greencastle, Pennsylvania. Contact Austin through his website at www.austingisriel.com.

CHIP GREENE, a SABR member since 2006, has contributed to numerous SABR book projects. Additionally, he contributed sports biographies to the four-volume encyclopedia *American Sports: A History of Icons, Idols and Ideas*, published in 2013 by Greenwood. Chip edited *Mustaches and Mayhem: Charlie O's Three-Time Champions*, the SABR biography book project that chronicles the three-time champion Oakland Athletics. The grandson of former Brooklyn Dodgers pitcher Nelson Greene, Chip lives with his wife, Elaine, and daughters, Anna and Haley, in Waynesboro, Pennsylvania.

TOM HAWTHORN is a newspaper and magazine reporter who lives in Victoria, B.C., Canada. He is a frequent contributor to SABR publications.

JOHN HENSHELL is a freelance writer/editor/communications consultant. He has been promoting programs and producing publications for many years. John adds value to his employer's words through adept use of diction, syntax, context, and visual images. Much of his writing is about technology and how to use it. John lives in Beaverton, Oregon.

TIM HERLICH has been a member of the Society for American Baseball Research since 1996. In addition to Bill North, he has contributed biographies of Ray Washburn and Tom Cheney to the SABR BioProject. In August 2012, he appeared at the National Baseball Hall of Fame to commemorate the 50th Anniversary of Cheney's single-game strikeout record. Tim resides in Seattle, Washington. His favorite teams are the Seattle Mariners and Philadelphia Phillies.

PAUL HOFMANN is the Assistant Vice President for International Affairs at Fresno State in Central California. A native of Detroit, Michigan, Dr. Hofmann is a seasoned international traveler and frequent speaker at international education conferences. A lifelong Detroit sports fan and avid baseball card collector, his research interests include 19th century and pre-World War II Japanese baseball. Paul currently resides in Fresno, California, with his wife and two children.

JOANNE HULBERT, co-chair of the Boston Chapter and SABR's Baseball Arts Committee, spends long hours obsessively gathering baseball poetry when not at Fenway Park. A resident of Mudville, a village of Holliston, Massachusetts, she occasionally leaves her poetic pursuit to indulge in something completely different. She has found that there's always something poetic about the life of an obscure and often forgotten player who has a story just as important and valuable to baseball history as any hall of fame inductee.

MAXWELL KATES, as a young collector, received a baseball card of Andy McGaffigan and remarked, "I think that's the first time I've ever seen a Reds player with a moustache." Thus began the genesis of "The Bikers Beat the Boy Scouts," both as an article and as a lecture at SABR 44 in Houston. A chartered accountant who lives and works in midtown Toronto, he has attended games at 20 current ballparks, including Oakland - where he held the dubious distinction of running into Ray Fosse.

Jimmy Keenan has been a SABR member since 2001. His grandfather, Jimmy Lyston, and four other family members were all professional baseball players. A frequent contributor to SABR publications, Keenan is the author of *The Lystons: A Story of One Baltimore Family* and *Our National Pastime*. He is a 2010 inductee into the Oldtimers Baseball Association of Maryland's Hall of Fame and a 2012 inductee into Baltimore's Boys of Summer Hall of Fame.

NORM KING lives in Ottawa, Ontario and has been a SABR member since 2010. His interests focus on baseball history and writing player biographies. He focuses particularly on players and events in the history of the Montreal Expos. He has contributed to a number of SABR books including, *Thar's Joy in Braveland* and *Van Lingle Mungo: The Man, The Song, The Players*, as well as other publications. He is currently serving as editor for a book on the 50 greatest games in the history of the Expos. He still misses them dearly.

LEONTE LANDINO is a Venezuelan journalist who has a career with ESPN International as an award-winning baseball television producer and writer. He has covered MLB, MiLB, Caribbean Winter Baseball, and international baseball tournaments on a day-to-day basis since 1996 and has worked as a broadcaster and in the front office of the Tampa Bay Rays and the Zulia Eagles of the Venezuelan Winter League. Landino serves as Chair of SABR's Luis Castro - Latin America Chapter and has done substantial research on the history and business of the game in Latin America. In addition he continues his work of extension in baseball circles in academics, consulting and conferencing on a regular basis.

TED LEAVENGOOD is a SABR member and the author of three books, including *Ted Williams and the 1969 Senators*, and *Clark Griffith, the Old Fox of Washington Baseball*. He is Managing Editor and regular contributor to the historical baseball website, Seamheads.com and has been a frequent contributor elsewhere, including MASN Sports. Before retirement he worked as an urban planner for the U.S. Dept. of Housing and Urban Development, Fairfax County,

Virginia, and the City of Atlanta. He lives in Chevy Chase, Maryland, with his wife.

LEN LEVIN, a retired newspaper editor, has been the copy editor for most of SABR's "team" publications. He lives in Providence, Rhode Island, with his wife, a retired journalism professor, and roots for the Red Sox.

WYNN MONTGOMERY has been a SABR member since 1983 and was co-editor of (and contributor to) the 2010 Atlanta convention publication, *Baseball in the Peach State.* He has authored two articles that appeared in the *Baseball Research Journal.* One (Summer 2010) compares the careers of Georgia's two 1948 pitching phenoms; the other (Fall 2011) details the quickest nine-inning game in baseball history (31 minutes). His biography of Willard Nixon appears in *Red Sox Baseball in the Days of Ike and Elvis.* He continues to follow the Braves and stays in touch with SABR's Magnolia Chapter although he left Atlanta in 2011 and now lives in Colorado. His other baseball interests include the art and history of the game. He loves minor-league baseball and with two other SABRites makes an annual "B-4" road trip that feeds his passion for Baseball, Battlefields (mostly Civil War), Burial Grounds (historic cemeteries), and Barbeque.

BILL NOWLIN has been VP of SABR since 2004, which was quite a good year for Red Sox fans and has been explored in the oral history of that year's postseason, *Don't Let Us Win Tonight* (written with Allan Wood). A co-founder of Rounder Records, he's also authored or helped edit more than 50 baseball books (you could look them up!), a good number of which are free to all SABR members.

CHARLIE O'REILLY has been enjoying the national pastime ever since his father took him to his first game at Shea Stadium, shortly before his sixth birthday in 1967. He has watched the game in 48 states, the District of Columbia, Puerto Rico, and five Canadian provinces, documenting his visits on his website, charliesballparks.com. When he is not at the yard, he is doing personnel and safety work for a barge repair company in New Jersey, and he is also a volunteer

administrator with his local Little League program and district. He joined SABR in 1997.

ROYSE "CRASH" PARR is a retired attorney living in Tulsa, Oklahoma. His grandsons have played baseball at Jerry Adair Park in Sand Springs, Oklahoma. He and Jerry both have Cherokee ancestry.

NEAL POLONCARZ, a SABR member since 1997, was raised in the Philadelphia suburbs. His passion for baseball began when his family attended countless games at Veterans Stadium to watch the Philadelphia Phillies. In 1984, cupid slung an arrow through his heart (*or George Steinbrenner signed him for a zillion dollars*) when he attended his first Yankees game, at the Stadium. He hosted a sports-talk radio show at WVOX 1460-AM in New Rochelle, NY. An in-studio guest was devoted SABR member John Vorperian, an ardent Red Sox fan. Neal also interviewed Arnold Hano, author of *A Day In The Bleachers*; Andy Musser, a retired Philadelphia Phillies play-by-play announcer; and fellow SABR member, the late Ernie Harwell. Neal's essay is dedicated in the memory of former SABR member Ross Adell who recommended Neal write articles for SABR.

J.G. PRESTON is a freelance writer in Benicia, California and has extensive experience as a radio and television host, play-by-play broadcaster and media relations professional. He edited the Minnesota Twins' program and monthly magazine from 1988-90 and contributed to the Twins' program and yearbook for more than a decade after that. He also wrote the script for a video biography of Kirby Puckett that was narrated by Bob Costas. He writes about baseball history at http://prestonjg.wordpress.com.

RICHARD J. PUERZER is an associate professor and chairperson of the Department of Engineering at Hofstra University in Hempstead, New York. His previous research and writings on baseball have appeared in *Nine: A Journal of Baseball History and Culture, Black Ball, The National Pastime, The Cooperstown Symposium on Baseball and American Culture* proceedings, and *Spitball.* He was co-director of The 50th Anniversary of the New York Mets Conference, held at Hofstra University in April, 2012.

FRANCISCO "PACO" RODRIGUEZ LOZANO is a journalist based in Torreon, Mexico. He writes for *Vanguardia*.

RICK SCHABOWSKI is a retired machinist from Harley-Davidson and is currently an instructor at Wisconsin Regional Training Partnership in the Manufacturing Program, and is a certified Manufacturing Skills Standards Council instructor. He is President of the Ken Keltner Badger State Chapter of SABR, Treasurer of the Milwaukee Braves Historical Association, and a member of the Hoop Historians.

KEITH SCHERER is a criminal defense attorney. He has written for Baseball Prospectus, ESPN, The Hardball Times, and Bill James Online, and was a contributing author to books by Rob Neyer and Will Carroll. This is his first participation in the Baseball Biography project.

MATTHEW SILVERMAN is the author of several books on baseball, including *Swinging '73: Baseball's Wildest Season*, centering on the middle championship in the Oakland A's dynasty. He and Ken Samelson co-edited the SABR-backed effort, *The Miracle Has Landed: The Amazin' Story of How the 1969 Mets Shocked the World*. He previously worked as managing editor of *Total Baseball* and *The ESPN Baseball Encyclopedia*.

CURT SMITH, says Bob Costas, "stands up for the beauty of words." His 16 books include the classic *Voices of The Game*, *A Talk in the Park*, *Pull up a Chair: The Vin Scully Story*, *Our House*, and his most recent, *George H.W. Bush: Character at the Core*. Smith is a GateHouse Media columnist, Associated Press award-winning radio commentator, and senior lecturer of English at the University of Rochester. He also has hosted Smithsonian Institution, Sirius XM Radio, and National Baseball Hall of Fame and Museum series, written ESPN TV's *The Voices of The Game* documentary series, and written more speeches than anyone for former President George H.W. Bush. The

New York Times terms Smith's work "the high point of Bush familial eloquence."

ANDY STURGILL is a college administrator in suburban Philadelphia. He has contributed many articles to SABR's BioProject and its associated book projects. When he's not working or doing baseball research, he enjoys reading and visiting ballparks with his wife, Carrie.

CLAYTON TRUTOR is a PhD candidate in U.S. History at Boston College. His dissertation examines the history of professional sports franchise relocations. He has contributed biographies to several recent SABR team book projects.

DALE VOISS has been a member of SABR since 2009. He has written several player biographies in that time. He is a lifelong fan of the Milwaukee Brewers who currently lives in Madison, Wisconsin.

JOHN VORPERIAN, a SABR member since 2000, hosts and produces *Beyond the Game*, a sports themed cable television program seen in New York and www.wpcommunitymedia.org. A columnist for www.box-scorenews.com, Johnny V. has covered the current NASL's NY Cosmos and taught Sports Law and the Business of Sport courses at Concordia College and Manhattanville College. The American University alum hopes to see the A's adopt all-gold home uniforms and all-Kelly green road unis.

JOSEPH WANCHO lives in Westlake, Ohio, and is a lifelong Cleveland Indians fan. He has been a SABR member since 2005 and serves as Chair of the Minor League Research Committee. He edited a BioProject Book on the 1954 Cleveland Indians, *Pitching to the Pennant* (University of Nebraska Press, 2014).

SAUL WISNIA is the author of seven baseball books, including *Miracle at Fenway*, *Fenway Park: The Centennial*, and *For the Love of the Boston Red Sox*. He has coauthored, edited, or contributed essays to numerous others, including the SABR volumes *Spahn, Sain, and Teddy Ballgame*, *The 1967 Impossible Dream Red Sox*, and the upcoming book on the most memorable events at Boston's Braves Field. Wisnia is a former contributing writer for the *Washington Post* and feature writer for the *Boston Herald*, and has also written for *Sports Illustrated*, the *Boston Globe*, and *Red Sox Magazine*. A SABR member (Boston chapter) since 1990, he lives 5.8 miles from Fenway Park and shares his "Fenway Reflections" weekly at saulwisnia. blogspot.com.

A lifelong Pirates fan, **GREGORY H. WOLF** was born in Pittsburgh, but turned his back on the Smoky City and now resides in the Windy City area with his wife, Margaret, and daughter, Gabriela. A Professor of German and holder of the Dennis and Jean Bauman endowed chair of the Humanities at North Central College in Naperville, Illinois, he served as editor of the SABR book, *Thar's Joy in Braveland; The 1957 Milwaukee Braves* (April 2014). He is also editor of two additional SABR books, on the 1929 Chicago Cubs and the 1965 Minnesota Twins, to be published in 2015.

Join SABR today!

If you're interested in baseball — writing about it, reading about it, talking about it — there's a place for you in the Society for American Baseball Research.

SABR was formed in 1971 in Cooperstown, New York, with the mission of fostering the research and dissemination of the history and record of the game. Our members include everyone from academics to professional sportswriters to amateur historians and statisticians to students and casual fans who merely enjoy reading about baseball history and occasionally gathering with other members to talk baseball.

SABR members have a variety of interests, and this is reflected in the diversity of its research committees. There are more than two dozen groups devoted to the study of a specific area related to the game — from Baseball and the Arts to Statistical Analysis to the Deadball Era to Women in Baseball. In addition, many SABR members meet formally and informally in regional chapters throughout the year and hundreds come together for the annual national convention, the organization's premier event. These meetings often include panel discussions with former major league players and research presentations by members. Most of all, SABR members love talking baseball with like-minded friends. What unites them all is an interest in the game and joy in learning more about it.

Why join SABR? Here are some benefits of membership:

* Two issues (spring and fall) of the *Baseball Research Journal*, which includes articles on history, biography, statistics, personalities, book reviews, and other aspects of the game.
* One expanded e-book edition of *The National Pastime*, which focuses on baseball in the region where that year's SABR national convention is held (in 2015, it's Chicago)
* 8-10 new and classic e-books published each year by the SABR Digital Library, which are all free for members to download
* *This Week in SABR* newsletter in your e-mail every Friday, which highlights SABR members' research and latest news
* Regional chapter meetings, which can include guest speakers, presentations and trips to ballgames
* Online access to back issues of *The Sporting News* and other periodicals through Paper of Record
* Access to SABR's lending library and other research resources
* Online member directory to connect you with an international network of SABR baseball experts and fans
* Discounts on registration for our annual events, including SABR Analytics Conference & Jerry Malloy Negro League Conference
* Access to SABR-L, an e-mail discussion list of baseball questions & answers that many feel is worth the cost of membership itself
* The opportunity to be part of a passionate international community of baseball fans

SABR membership is on a "rolling" calendar system; that means your membership lasts 365 days no matter when you sign up!
Enjoy all the benefits of SABR membership by signing up today at SABR.org/join or by clipping out the form below and mailing it to SABR, Cronkite School at ASU, 555 N. Central Ave. #416, Phoenix, AZ 85004.

SABR MEMBERSHIP FORM

	Annual	3-year	Senior	3-yr Sr.	Under 30
U.S.:	☐ $65	☐ $175	☐ $45	☐ $129	☐ $45
Canada/Mexico:	☐ $75	☐ $205	☐ $55	☐ $159	☐ $55
Overseas:	☐ $84	☐ $232	☐ $64	☐ $186	☐ $55

Add a Family Member: $15 for each family member at same address (list on back)
Senior: 65 or older before 12/31/2015
All dues amounts in U.S. dollars or equivalent

Participate in Our Donor Program!
I'd like to desginate my gift to be used toward:
☐General Fund   ☐Endowment Fund   ☐Research Resources   ☐_____
☐ I want to maximize the impact of my gift; do not send any donor premiums
☐ I would like this gift to remain anonymous.
Note: Any donation not designated will be placed in the General Fund.
SABR is a 501 (c) (3) not-for-profit organization & donations are tax-deductible to the extent allowed by law.

Name _____

Address _____

City _____ ST_____ ZIP_____

Phone _____ Birthday _____

E-mail: _____
(Your e-mail address on file ensures you will receive the most recent SABR news.)

Dues $_____
Donation $_____
Amount Enclosed $_____

Do you work for a matching grant corporation? Call (602) 496-1460 for details.

If you wish to pay by credit card, please contact the SABR office at (602) 496-1460 or visit the SABR Store online at SABR.org/join. We accept Visa, Mastercard & Discover.

Do you wish to receive the *Baseball Research Journal* electronically?: ☐ Yes   ☐ No
Our e-books are available in PDF, Kindle, or EPUB (iBooks, iPad, Nook) formats.

Mail to: SABR, Cronkite School at ASU, 555 N. Central Ave. #416, Phoenix, AZ 85004

04/15

CPSIA information can be obtained
at www.ICGtesting.com
Printed in the USA
LVOW03s1703170716

496677LV00028B/312/P